D1336862

The
Farthest
North of
Humanness

"To give way to human feelings, to overflow & swim in human feelings is human enough, but the farthest north of humanness is, for me, to be a lightning conductor of such feelings in such a way that they are particularly fitted to fill niches in coming men's minds & sit itchingly & inflamingly like small fishhooks in men's consciousness throout changing customs & different rules for playing cricket."

PG to RG, 10 November 1910

"Beethoven sagde: 'Künstlerseelen weinen nicht, sie brennen!' "
["Beethoven opined: 'Artists' souls do not weep, they burn!' "]

PG to KH, 4 February 1909

The Farthest North of Humanness

LETTERS OF PERCY GRAINGER 1901–14

Edited by Kay Dreyfus

M

First published 1985 by
THE MACMILLAN COMPANY OF AUSTRALIA PTY LTD
107 Moray Street, South Melbourne 3205
6 Clarke Street, Crows Nest 2065

Published in the United Kingdom by
THE MACMILLAN PRESS LTD
Houndmills, Basingstoke, Hampshire RG21 2XS
and London

Associated companies and representatives
throughout the world

   Grainger, Percy, 1882-1961.
     The farthest north of humanness.

   Includes index.
   ISBN 0 333 38085 1.

   1. Grainger, Percy, 1882-1961 — Correspondence.
   2. Composers — Australia — Correspondence.
   I. Dreyfus, Kay, 1942- . II. Title.

780.92'4

Set in Times by Savage Type Pty Ltd, Brisbane.
Printed in Hong Kong.

Contents

Acknowledgements

In the course of my preparation of this volume of Grainger's selected correspondence I have incurred many obligations. Firstly, my thanks are due to the authorities of the following institutions for the assistance they have given and for permission to publish manuscripts held in their collections:

The Grainger Museum Board, University of Melbourne, owner of most of the correspondence published here, for permission to publish Grainger's letters to Frank and Clara Aldridge, Isabel Du Cane, Frederick Delius (from 6 July 1910), H. Balfour Gardiner, John H. Grainger, Rose Grainger, Harry Plunket Greene, Karen Holten, Charlotte Knollys, Roger Quilter (from 1913), Alfhild and Herman Sandby, Cecil Sharp and Ernest Thesiger; Griegsamlingen, Bergen Offentlige Bibliotek (letters to Edvard and Nina Grieg); Musikabteilung (Busoni-Nachlass), Deutsche Staatsbibliothek, Berlin, DDR (letters to Ferruccio Busoni); R. A. Clarke, Wood, Nash & Winter's (letters to Roger Quilter, up to and including 19 January 1911); Dansk Folkemindesamling, Copenhagen (letters to Hjalmar Thuren); Delius Trust, London (letters to Frederick Delius, up to and including 19 September 1909); Captain Jeremy Elwes, Elsham Hall, Brigg (letters to Gervase and Winefride Elwes); Haags Gemeentemuseum, The Hague (letters to Julius Röntgen and Hans Augustin); Mrs E. B. Heemskerle, Amsterdam (letter to Willem Mengelberg); Musikhistorisk Museum og Carl Claudius' Samling, Copenhagen (letters to Johan Svendsen); Schott & Co., London (letter to Willy Strecker).

I must thank Niels F. Sandby for his gift to the Grainger Museum of Grainger's letters to Alfhild and Herman Sandby, and Mr R. A. Clarke of the firm of Wood, Nash & Winter's, executors of the estate of Roger Quilter, for his gift to the Grainger Museum of Grainger's letters to Roger Quilter. Special thanks go to Burnett Cross, executor of the will of Percy Grainger.

Photographs from the *Australasian* and the *Leader* are reproduced from the La Trobe Collection of the State Library of Victoria; Grainger's transcription of Aboriginal melodies collected by W. Baldwin Spencer is reproduced from the Baldwin Spencer Collection, Museum of Victoria. All other photographs are from the collections of the Grainger Museum.

In researching the annotations I have been greatly assisted by numerous local history, area and music librarians in Australia as well as in Denmark, Holland, Germany and the United Kingdom. To all of them, though I do not mention them by name, go my sincere thanks for their prompt and courteous replies to my enquiries.

I have benefited from specialist researches done by other scholars, particularly Teresa Balough, John Bird, Peter Cahn, Bruce Clunies Ross,

Stephen Lloyd, Rachel Lowe-Dugmore, John Martin, Margaret Pitt Morison, National Trust of Australia (especially Shirley Hawker and Carlotta Kellaway), Jane O'Brien, Thérèse Radic, Christina Crossley Ratcliffe, Ronald Stevenson and Robert Threlfall.

Friends and colleagues at the Grainger Museum have contributed in various ways over the years, particularly Rosemary Florrimell, Yvonne Perham (who transcribed the letters) and Lynne Strahan. Thanks are also due to Kerry Murphy (who helped with checking and proofreading the manuscript as well as researching some clues), Merete Colding-Smith (for research assistance in Denmark), Jane Belfrage and Elizabeth Wright (for research assistance in Australia and the United States). Kerry Herbstreit did the index.

The heroic task of translating Grainger's letters to Karen Holten, his Danish-language letters to his mother and other friends, plus a host of miscellaneous supporting incoming and outgoing letters in the various Scandinavian languages and Dutch, was carried out magnificently by Philip Grigg. To him my indebtedness is profound. The variety of his linguistic skills and his tolerance for the vagaries of a non-native speaker made him ideal for the task: a real treasure. When Grainger's grammar became too awful or his word substitutions too improbable, Philip would rally the assistance of his wife, Bodil, who thereby has made her own contribution.

With translation of German language material I have been greatly assisted by Frank U. Pam and Pamela MacLean and with the translation of the Russian-language version of Grainger's letter to Alexander Siloti, by Larry Bagg. Margaret Birtley grappled valiantly with Grainger's wayward Icelandic.

My most particular thanks must go to the Grainger Museum Board and the University of Melbourne for their support of the project over the years it has taken to complete, especially the Vice-Principal (Mr R. D. Marginson), the Deputy Vice-Chancellor (Professor J. R. Poynter) and the University Archivist (Mr Frank Strahan) but for whom, in their various ways, this book would not have been made. From the United States I have appreciated the support and encouragement of Stewart Manville and, during her lifetime, Ella Grainger-Manville.

Finally I must thank the Australian Research Grants Committee for its generous financial support of the first two years of work on this project.

Introduction

On 14 January 1890 John Harry Grainger wrote a letter to his father in which he penned a prescient portrait of his young son, Percy, then seven years old:

> You would so like to see him, fair, very, with long curling golden hair, Blue eyes, and legs fit to carry the Tower of Babel. Of course as all fathers are I am proud of him . . . above all [on account of] his ardent desire to be an Artist . . . At present he draws well, immensely well in fact, and it is a frightful thing to keep him from being always at it, and his mother is most anxious he should be an artist. I am afraid if he becomes one that he will be dangerous, and his mothers ambition is to take him to London or Paris where some old Duchess or young with influence may ''take him up'' that is to introduce him to a lot of people who buy pictures not on account of the picture, but for the artist.

By the time Rose and Percy Grainger arrived in London in May 1901, at the beginning of stage two of their pursuit of those influential duchesses, the boy's future as an artist clearly lay with a career in music.

Stage one of their journey took them to the Hoch Conservatorium in Frankfurt am Main where, in the four and a half years between autumn 1895 and spring 1900, Percy took nine semesters of piano lessons with James Kwast and studied counterpoint and composition under Iwan Knorr. He also continued to study painting and drawing with the Frankfurt painter Georg Franz Widmann and established enduring friendships with young fellow students.

Arriving in London, Grainger joined a struggling mass of young aspirants drawn irresistibly to a great cultural centre, all waiting for that small opening that would lift them out of the crowd. Of the many who ventured a few endured and very few achieved success.

An abundance of pianists made themselves hopefully available. On 27 June 1901 the *Daily Telegraph* noted despairingly, ''Whether a London season be good, bad or indifferent from a commercial point of view, pianists present themselves in an almost endless array. Many are quite admirable; most are worthy of praise. In fact, their united talents are well nigh embarrassing to those who would do them critical justice''. Grainger launched himself into this seething mass of aspiration on 11 June 1901.

For nearly fourteen years the shape of London's concert year imposed itself on the Graingers' lives. There were two seasons. The first ran from about the middle of October to Holy Week. The second, known as the "grand season", began shortly after Easter and continued until the end of July. This second period also coincided with the London social season when the moneyed classes returned to London to occupy their town houses, attend the myriad civic, social and other fixtures that proliferated in May and June, and entertain each other privately by means of that uniquely Edwardian function, the "at home". At this time the concert season reached its peak. By mid July concerts would have almost ceased and until mid August concert life was in recess. A special place was occupied by the Henry Wood Promenade Concerts at Queen's Hall, which ran from mid August to late October and bridged the gap between the main seasons. At peak periods in the year concerts might be given at the rate of forty or fifty a week, with ten or twelve events taking place in a day. In May and June in a good year (such as 1912) there could be as many as sixty or seventy concerts in a week with twenty on a single day. As the *Referee* of 19 May 1912 observed, "Surely London in the grand season must be the most musical city in the world".

Grainger usually endeavoured to be in London for "the season" — a time of feverish activity and good earnings. He was generally tied to his social obligations until the end of July, although engagements and the rewards that went with them slackened off from about mid July. In August, depending on other commitments, he could contemplate a holiday. But he could not and did not confine his concert activities to London, any more than could any other solo artist. As the *Daily Telegraph* noted on 9 January 1912, "Truly, the artist of today has no easy time of it if, in order to earn a livelihood, he (or she) has to put a girdle around the world". Extending the field was a constant endeavour; travelling was an inescapable imperative. While some of Percy's feats were awe-inspiring in their strenuousness, he was not alone in travelling hard for his living. On 15 November 1900 the *British Australasian* reported that Ada Crossley had just given five concerts in four days and undertaken close on 900 miles of railway travelling. From time to time similar efforts by other artists found their way into the press. The *Daily Telegraph* of 11 November 1911 reported a dazzling piece of continent-crossing:

> The strenuous musical life: Mr Mengelberg, the conductor of the famous Concertgebouw Orchestra of Amsterdam, who directed last Tuesday's Philharmonic Concert at Queen's Hall, was conducting on Sunday week in Moscow, whither he had travelled straight from the Dutch capital, arriving just in time to superintend a rehearsal. Next day he journeyed to Frankfort, going direct from the train to the rehearsal. He conducted a concert in Frankfort on Thursday, and two in Holland on Friday and Saturday. Reaching home at 2 a.m. last Sunday, he left five hours later for London, where he arrived, after a stormy crossing, at 10.30 p.m. — three hours late. Next morning a rehearsal at Queen's Hall. Until June 30 1913 Mr Mengelberg will only be able to boast of two evenings upon which he will not be either conducting or travelling. How dull those two evenings will seem to him!

Devoted as it was to the well-being of the Anglo-Australian community, the *British Australasian* was regularly moved to deplore the fate of the crowds of young Australians who came to England for musical study or career advancement. Counselling them, in January 1902, the paper set out the prerequisites for survival: "great natural gifts, considerable wealth, and great influence". One year later, Melba ventured her opinion that an ability to spend £500 a year for four or five years was essential for a career in London. Interviewed in March 1906, Ada Crossley said that funds were essential for at least three years, during which period the young artist might not earn a single penny. "It is a hard life, and an exacting one; its essentials are good health, an exceptionally strong constitution to stand the wear and tear of incessant travelling, continuous practice, and . . . it involves a rigid self-denial in all social observances''.

Grainger came to his London career endowed with outstanding natural attributes: youth, a robust constitution, an individual talent, good looks, an attractive personality and a mother *bent on success*. His looks were indisputably a not inconsiderable part of his early success, as the *Bulletin* observed in characteristically caustic fashion on 12 October 1905:

> Young Percy Grainger is being patted on his pale gold locks by more than one exalted feminine just now. At latest he had been carried off to Dunrobin Castle by the Duchess of Sutherland. How much better it is to be a pretty boy performer than a girl ditto! The latter only arouses envy and other yellow-jaundiced emotions among her own sex, and at best the silent and well-concealed admiration from the other. Whereas a boy may be clasped to the bosom of the hysterical aristocracy and borne away to the moated grange without the interference of a husband or a brother. A he-artist has all the best of it, because the social glorification of musical talent is women's business.

Percy was, so his mother said, a "rarity" and, she observed, "All people love a rarity".

"Great influence" was not something Grainger could readily command. Although warmly supported by his compatriots in the Anglo-Australian community, especially in the early years of his London career, he could never take for granted his place in the larger world. He had to work continuously to keep his grip on his public, not only through performances but through the countless social observances that absorbed his time and energy. The fear that the society on which he depended would tire of him, grow cold or forget him was a recurring one. Even the "guinea pupils" of whom he was so proud, and who were sometimes considered as a possible secure alternative source of income were, as Grainger wrote to his Danish lover, Karen Holten, on 26 November 1909, "so inconstant. One week they all come rushing to me and want more lessons, a fortnight later most of them leave".

Wealth was the one element in the *British Australasian*'s prescription that the Graingers definitely did not possess. Far from having that £500 a year for four or five years that Melba recommended, or the secure funds for three years that Ada Crossley thought essential, they had, from the beginning, little beyond what Percy could earn.

According to Grainger, he and his mother had left Australia with nothing more than the £50 raised for them by friends. In Germany Rose had supplemented their income by giving English lessons. From the time they left Australia until at least 1903 John Grainger sent small but regular sums of money to assist them. In London, at least at first and because of the breakdown in Rose's health, it fell to Percy to earn all their keep as she "hadn't a penny". The whole effort of the London years lay in their struggle to get beyond working for a living. They could not even afford the advertisements by which artists regularly touted their triumphs in the press.

Costs were high. In order to earn, one had to spend. A certain level of appearance had to be maintained: a good house, a housekeeper and a maid, no suggestion of "cheapness" in clothes, entertainments, or any of one's dealings with others. Even Grainger's small self-inflicted economies, such as travelling third class and skipping or skimping on meals when away from home, entailed an element of risk and met with limited approval from Rose. The question of eating was a particularly contentious one, for Rose recognised the link between looks and lucre. "[E]at 3 good meals every day", she wrote to Percy on 27 November 1907, "otherwise you begin to look cheap & your looks will suffer — & that means *loss of cash*".

Their whole financial situation was extremely fragile. It was not only a question of the fickleness of his public, as Grainger saw it. There were other factors. An untoward event, such as the death of the King in 1910, meant instant loss of income: "Percy has lost 50 guineas this week through concerts being given up", wrote Rose to Frank Aldridge on 12 May 1910. If Grainger became ill, as he did with chicken pox in April 1906, his income ceased. Hence, perhaps, apart from her altruistic concern, Rose's continual anxiety for his health. Any additional burdens, such as the breakdown of his father's health due to his advancing syphilis, placed a severe strain on an already precarious situation. One probable reason why Grainger relished the ease and comfort of the long Ada Crossley tours was that they afforded a release from financial pressures by guaranteeing him an income.

On 21 March 1953, Grainger wrote to Karen Kellermann (née Holten) of his attitude to his economic situation throughout his life, "[I]f one has known poverty (actual lack of food, sickness without having the means for proper treatment) in one's youngest years, as I have, it is difficult ever to get over it. One is always hunted by the fear of poverty and all one's activities are shadowed by lack of self-confidence". The experience of poverty undoubtedly cast its shadow over the London period. It is manifest in the Graingers' obsession with saving and in Rose's uncertainty over decisions that involved a choice between a guaranteed income and the risk-taking that is perhaps a necessary preliminary to a big career. This uncertainty was the basis of her anxiety over the second Australasian tour. It continued to haunt her even after the career decision of 1909. Hence the great successes of 1910 were only qualified financial successes for Percy, for in order to have a guarantee against loss, he settled for only a percentage of the profits. "If he didn't *only* get a percentage", Rose wrote ruefully to Roger Quilter from Christiania in October 1910, "he wld have earned awfully well". This lack of self-confidence in the end delimited Grainger's success in this period: "You and I often talked about my musical career", Grainger recalled in a letter to Karen Kellermann of 27 September 1948, "I about its almost insurmountable difficulties, you about the ease with which I could reach success if only I dared more . . ."

It was not as though nothing was achieved: it was. Rose charted Grainger's progress through the sea of financial insecurity. In 1903, observing the breakdown of John Grainger's health and fearing its consequences, she urged Percy to practise diligently against hard times and earn to support them both so as to take the burden off his father. Some progress was made over the next two years and, after the successes of the 1905 tour of Denmark, she recommended that Percy open an account at a Chelsea bank.

The year 1906 appears as a kind of watershed. "Unless you can stride into a higher position publicly this next year or next 2 years", Rose wrote, "you will have missed yr chance for earning big money . . ." By the end of 1906 Grainger was beginning to earn "a little", probably about £1000 per year, though his savings were eroded by the loan he was obliged to make to his father. But over the next couple of years his situation did not greatly improve, though the steady income of the Ada Crossley tour allowed Rose the luxury of a nightly hot bath! In February 1908 Rose was projecting an annual income of "a clean £1000" and savings of £500 per year. By the end of 1909 he was still only earning a little more than he had been in 1906, a circumstance which undoubtedly influenced the decision at this time to alter the direction of his career towards solo performance. Rose anticipated a decline in income with this new move *at first*: her expectations of eventual success were fulfilled in 1910. In April 1911 Grainger reported to Karen Holten that he was saving £1000 a year; by January 1912 he had two deposit savings accounts. But the "future" — that time when Grainger could retire from the concert life and live on a modest income — was still out of reach at the end of 1912, the year in which his career might truly be said to have "peaked", at least in terms of public acclaim. Rose attributed his failure to achieve financial independence to his unwillingness to practise hard at his technique under her direction in Frankfurt. Whatever the reason, in May 1914 Grainger wrote to Karen Holten that his aim of £200 a year in interest was still not attained.

Given the Graingers' economic circumstances, their decision to launch themselves, without supporting funds, on London society was nothing short of heroic. But defeat was in the air in 1913 and 1914. What might have happened to them had they not gone to America?

A second shadow lay over the Graingers' lives: Rose's ill health. On 8 May 1926 Grainger wrote to Karen Kellermann to tell her, for the first time, of the background to his mother's illness. According to his account, Rose had contracted syphilis from her husband about eighteen months after Percy was born. Soon after Rose and John Grainger separated, in about 1891, the disease manifested itself in the form of terrible neuralgic pains. Rose was never really well again thereafter. "If she wrote or read she got pains in her eyes or arms, in her back when she walked . . . " The recurrence of these symptoms may be traced through the letters from the London period.

Rose was in somewhat better health when she and Percy arrived in Germany. But in 1899 and 1901 the first big breakdowns had occurred. Then she was unable to walk for long periods, cried nearly the whole day, and in 1901 had had to lie for extended periods on ice-tubes. The Graingers' removal from Frankfurt to London in 1901 was twice delayed by Rose's illness, which was reported in the *British Australasian* of 2 May 1901 as "serious". But by the end of May she had recovered sufficiently to be able to travel to England with Percy. Thereafter, although her health did improve and she was able to participate in the various activities of their London life, it was always precarious. She was, so Percy wrote, constantly haunted by her fears of ensuing blindness, madness and paralysis.

"All this tragedy (even if it was only felt unconsciously) naturally made a strong impression on me and made our relationship to each other something quite special". The circumstances of their life, "separated from our fatherland and all relatives etc", while not in itself remarkable in London's Anglo-Australian society, also increased their mutual dependence.

Despite the pathos of Grainger's feeling of separation from country and family, he and Rose differed greatly in their attitudes to Australia. Grainger loved his country, felt some sadness that the exigencies of his career did not permit him to live there and retained a keen sense of his Australian identity. His response to the Australian landscape produces some of his best descriptive writing. Rose, on the other hand, loved London, felt herself to be more than half English, deplored the Australian climate and the people (whom she found equally tiring and tiresome), was riled by Percy's over-intense enthusiasm for everything Australian, and was not all that keen on living near her relatives, fond of them though she undoubtedly was.

The effect of Rose's illness on Percy was profound. "In my own thoughts I promised her and myself that I would never leave her while she lived and that I would repay her everything she had suffered. This thought became my only religion, and although I was too weak a character to carry out the thought as I should, it never disappeared from me". The effect of Rose's experiences on her attitude towards Percy was equally profound. "She had indeed experienced unforgettable things with my father. She had wished and wished that I would never show myself selfish, cruel and happiness-destroying like him. Therefore she hated and feared everything (all people, all relationships) that threatened to call forth the bad sides in me". Rose's moral views as expressed in January 1909 were firm: "Health — Happiness — Real Work — Goodness — Cleanliness, are the Real things". She urged Percy to "drop all smallnesses & help man to be a nobler being". With her own background of sexual experience, added to a genuinely passionate devotion to the noble side of human nature, her greatest fear for Percy was "a larger growth of unnaturalness". The tension that existed between herself and Karen Holten was, in part perhaps, an unconscious fear that Karen, at least as far as Grainger's sexual life was concerned, would not fulfil the role that Rose required of Percy's friends — that they be "a help to strengthen the best points of yr character, & bring out all that is splendid in you — your pluck, & sweet disposition".

Rose Grainger committed suicide on 30 April 1922, having been brought to the brink of despair by the gathering effects of syphilis and a malicious rumour that her relationship with Percy was incestuous. He was away on tour at the time. Her death was a crushing blow and left him with a lifetime legacy of guilt and remorse, an unshakable conviction that it had been his failure that caused her death. "Noble women with a strong emotional life can be saved and killed through their feelings". He never fully recovered from the blow.

*   *   *

There are not many observations one can make about Percy Grainger's personality that he does not, at one time or another, make himself. However, some features might be extrapolated to provide a context for his letters.

Grainger was, by his own admission, a great talker. He was, so he said, shy or even fearful in the world. But within the secure confines of the inner circle of his family and friends he loved chatting, or "jawing", as he described it. Contrarily, according to his mother, he was also more than normally inclined to introversion and had "a slightly morbid touch".

The circumstances of his life required him to spend much time away from his family and loved friends. As his career developed, he increasingly found himself among strangers, half-sympathetic acquaintances, or alone. Accordingly, his talkativeness, his love of communicating his thoughts, impressions and ideas, combined with his introversion to produce a voluminous flow of intimate correspondence. Into his letters to his mother and to Karen Holten he not only poured the narrative of his daily life, but projected the inner life of his feelings. In a unique and particular way these letters became an extension of life: the post was a lifebelt linking him to the emotional roots of his personality. In the relationship with Karen Holten, the letters became a substitute for life itself and embodied feelings, longings and impulses that were often denied their legitimate expression. He had no difficulty in expressing his feelings. Indeed, as he wrote to Karen Holten on 31 July 1912, he often found it easier to write than to say things to people.

As a correspondent, Grainger was aware of his obligation to make himself interesting. The variety of his travels was an inexhaustible source. Whatever its constraints, drawbacks and deprivations, travelling released him from the social pressures of his London life and freed his mind for its response to the stimulus of landscape, language and people. His powers of observation had been enhanced by his early training as a visual artist; his descriptive style had been encouraged by his father.

Certain preoccupations recurred throughout Grainger's intimate correspondence. As he wrote to Rose Grainger on 7 October 1911, "I hardly ever think of ought else but sex, race, athletics, speech & art". He was also passionately fond of bouts of "overfeeding", an activity which he pronounced to be "needful to my moral stability".

Complementing the cyclic nature of these themes were his periods of intense absorption with a particular activity — folksong collecting, sensuality, Polynesian art and culture, composing, sport or even piano playing. He was prone to "get strongly taken up" with particular things at a time, part of his idea that in order to enjoy something total dedication was required. It was a matter of intensity. Grainger relished intensity: even the long periods of separation from Karen Holten were valued for the extreme joy they lent to the periods of reunion. Even boredom and emptiness were to be experienced to the full.

The pattern of recurrent preoccupations and fierce short-term interests was lightened by the momentariness of his moods and their pendulum swings. Though highly susceptible to the nervous strains of concert life he was amazingly resilient: stresses that brought him to the brink of despair one day could be forgotten the next. Hence, perhaps, Rose's concern for his well-being in 1912 and 1913, when a more serious breakdown threatened. The pitch of nervous excitement at which he lived created a tension that demanded release. Most often, in his solitude, this took the form of some extreme act of sexual arousal. His self-infliction of pain was often a response to desperation and lack of sexual fulfilment. This is stated quite clearly in his letter to Karen Holten of 1 August 1909, where he writes,

> Sometimes, when I call to mind how long I still must wait till your flesh and my flesh meet, and that it is quite impossible for us to be united in half-an-hour's time, a madness flows over me and boundless anger . . . Then I must pull, hit, cut, whip, tear, burn some pain in myself. Afterwards I feel much less unsatisfied.

His relationship with Karen Holten allowed the free and joyous expression of the sexual side of his nature, with all its flourishing fantasy. Although she did not have blue eyes (a major flaw in the Grainger canon), she had, so Percy wrote on 6 November 1908, a blue-eyed heart. Grainger was fully aware of the generous and unique commitment Karen offered him and acknowledged it many times, in many different ways. In his letter to her of 4 October 1909 he wrote, "Among everything you have done, you have given my senses earth's strong reality and heaven's blessed freedom . . ." Quite apart from the sexual side of their relationship, Karen had, as even Rose admitted, a strong sense of the difficulties and special problems of Grainger's life as an artist. The choice that Grainger was obliged to make between his mother and Karen was a grievous one. He realised the fullness of her gift and his loss only when the choice had been made.

Rose's response to the knowledge of Grainger's sexual proclivities was fearful and censorious. She abhorred what she called his "strange fancies", and feared their social consequences should they become known. She saw them as the antithesis of the nobility of character that she valued. Her own experiences of love and sex, marriage and childbirth had not been fortunate; her revulsion from the last two undoubtedly influenced Grainger's feelings. Their differing attitudes to the first two were possibly the only source of conflict in their relationship.

*   *   *

Rose and Percy Grainger maintained a vast miscellaneous correspondence. All but a very few of the extant letters written to the Graingers in this period are in the Grainger Museum at the University of Melbourne. A good many of them carry the "X" that was the sign that a reply had been sent. Much of the Graingers' letter-writing dealt with matters of an ephemeral nature — fixing times for rehearsals or lessons, making arrangements to meet friends, folksingers, agents or publishers, accepting or declining invitations, the day-to-day commerce of the household or society — such matters as might nowadays be dealt with over the telephone. Even after the Graingers had a telephone installed in September 1909 Rose, and to a lesser extent Percy, continued to exchange such letters.

Many letters were devoted to the business of advancing Grainger's career. On the one hand there were the actualities of engagements: fixing dates and programmes, negotiating fees, securing the proper billing and advertising and so forth. On the other, a kind of ceaseless campaign of promotion was prosecuted. Rose did not need to be told, as the *British Australasian* told Ada Crossley on 23 May 1895, "that in public life it is not worth doing anything unless the echoes of one's deeds reverberate through the Press". Rose understood the principle instinctively. She relentlessly circularised the news of Grainger's successes to the press, to influential friends and useful contacts. She sent out programmes and critique books. In other words, she used her letters to "boom" him. A profound effort on Rose's part lay behind a comment such as that which appeared in the *Daily Telegraph* on 24 January 1911: "Now we hear of a similar success having been achieved in Holland by Mr Percy Grainger, the pianist, who had recently toured in the Low Countries . . ." As Grainger travelled more and more, she was required to ensure that he was not forgotten in London.

Although Grainger had agents in each country he went to regularly, much of the organisation of his European tours was done through direct personal contact with the concert-promoters in the various towns he proposed to visit. This was particularly true of Denmark. As early as February 1908 Karen Holten had advised him that personal contact was essential, indeed the only way of achieving results. The overseas tours required terrific coordination in order to ensure that Grainger did not sit around too long without earning, incurring unnecessary expenses *and* losing income in London. Then, particularly in the case of important concerts, whether at home or abroad, there were the letters that needed to be written to all acquaintances in the town to ensure a good attendance.

After the career decision of 1909, letters concerning engagements or designed to see that his networks in each place were intact assumed particular importance. More and more of Grainger's business contacts were taken over by Rose. She wrote extensively and on a daily basis: she certainly wrote every morning, sometimes all day, often writing fifteen to twenty letters in a sitting. The task of keeping up with the burden of correspondence was wearisome and unending and placed a severe strain on her health, affecting her already weak eyes and at times, such as in preparation for an important London recital, undermining her health generally. Her own disabilities notwithstanding, she carried out her postal duties unstintingly, sustained by her absolute faith in the value of art and the artist, motivated by her lack of faith in "business people" (including agents), whom she described as "terrific muddlers". It was her contribution to the endless business of earning their livelihood. Their actual income she supplemented by taking in lodgers ("no one under 2 guineas the week") and, in the case of foreign lodgers, as they mostly were, teaching them English as well. Rose also undertook tasks such as that of replying to the fifty congratulatory letters Grainger received after the Balfour Gardiner Concert in March 1912 ("even the Band wrote"). Increasingly Rose dealt with Percy's practical affairs "without troubling" him, or sketched out replies if she thought they should be seen to come from Percy.

Much as Rose took on her own shoulders, some self-interested courtesies were Percy's responsibility. With a few exceptions, her attitude to letter-writing was strictly utilitarian. Under her direction Percy worked hard at making himself agreeable, and with some success, as Herman Sandby observed in January 1906. "All these attentions are necessary", wrote Rose to Percy on 27 June 1903, and at various other times, "Make Miss Murphy's [Australian journalist] letter really sweet & say something about Busoni that she can use" (1 July 1903); "[Send Busoni] a *warm, nice* letter" (8? October 1904); "Never mind about friends — managers we must impress — & big artists" (8? October 1904); "People love you to remember them. I remember Mrs Dry [wife of Wakeling Dry, music critic of the *Daily Express*] saying how sweet she thought it of you, thinking of them when away" (25 August 1906) and so on. Rose's injunctions and instructions echo through Grainger's replies to her and are also reflected in the replies received by him. Wherever possible, Grainger followed her advice to "write every morning to different people".

As far as the gratuitous aspects of correspondence were concerned, Rose had firm views. Towards the members of her own family, from whom she was long separated, her sense of duty was keen. Her regular letters and postcards to her unmarried sister, Clara Aldridge, and her brother, Frank, are a fund of information about Percy's activities and successes, down to the details of his travel arrangements. Percy, too, from earliest childhood, was raised to a strong sense of family loyalty and obligation. In general, Rose had not much time for "greasing the wheels of friendship" for their own sakes. Among Grainger's friends, however, Rose cherished a particular feeling for Roger Quilter, to whom she wrote on 7 August 1905, "Some years ago I couldn't have thought it possible to be so fond of another Boy as I am of you". Her attitude to Roger was not untouched by practical considerations; in February 1910, when one of Roger's nieces asked to come to Grainger for lessons, Rose commented, "They are a rich lot — & [a] big family". Nonetheless, among Grainger's friends Rose most encouraged him to write to Roger. "Since he's been ill I've been writing him lots again, & mother thinks my letters have really helped to make him buck up again, for he started to mend as soon as my 1st arrived", Grainger told Karen Holten on 9 February 1908. The hoped-for therapeutic effect of Grainger's letters to Quilter had much to do with their encouraging tone.

Indeed, the desire to produce a particular result influenced the flavour of many of Grainger's letters. Even his letters to his mother, written daily at her request during his absences from home to help her bear their partings, aimed to produce a specific result, the maintenance of her well-being, which tempered their content. Of all his intimate correspondence, the most uninhibited and honest letters were those written to Karen Holten. But even there his natural impulse to forthrightness was sometimes countered by his need to avoid any commitment to marriage or any conflict in his relationship with his mother.

The element of subterfuge in Grainger's correspondence with Karen Holten, implied by the use of poste restante (first mentioned 24 May 1907) and recycled trade and hotel envelopes (from June 1908), was certainly intended to deceive her family. Whether it was also meant to deceive Rose is an open question: according to Percy, it was to prevent gossip on the part of their housekeeper. In deference to the strictures of the society they moved in, Rose's attitude to Grainger's relationship with Karen favoured concealment, though she professed and probably felt great fondness for Karen. As she wrote to Percy on 28 August 1906, "With a public man — nothing is secret, is it?"

The bulk of their correspondence with individuals who unforeseeably were not to figure in the Graingers' future, particularly that of a more ephemeral and practical nature, has probably perished. The letters published in this selection, all handwritten originals (the Graingers kept no copies), represent about one-third of the total known to have survived from this time, a self-contained period in Grainger's life. In selecting them I have tried to mirror the relative weight of letters that remain from each year. Their survival is a measure of what they meant to the recipient; accident and chance explain the obliteration of others. For example, the depth of Grainger's feelings for Cyril Scott cannot be gauged from the fact that none of his letters to Cyril from this period are extant.

Rose made an early decision to keep all Grainger's letters to her. On 28 September 1904 she told him, "I shall keep all letters, they will be so jolly to read years hence — all yr impressions". Even so, many of Grainger's letters to his mother fell victim to the upheavals of their life: the frequent changes of house, the trips abroad, most significantly, the precipitous departure for the United States of America, which saw many of their possessions bundled into storage. In the long periods of separation, Grainger's letters to Karen Holten had a significance that outlasted their estrangement and her marriage to another man. She wrote on 27 September 1915,

> I would **never** even think of letting one of your letters to me get lost in *any way*. I will keep them, they belong to me, if I die before you, they shall be sent to you, but as long as I live I will keep them with me. They were indeed some enormously significant years of my life, which will never be forgotten, or in any way obliterated.

As early as 12 February 1908 Grainger wrote to Karen Holten, "So the little sweetie thinks she can take all my extremely interesting letters to the grave with her, if she dies. My letters shall be admired by a yet-unborn generation; can't you see that I always write with an eye to a possible public? Sometimes it seems to me that I can — to my shame". Grainger's violent oscillations of feeling should always be kept in mind and his momentary pronouncements treated with caution. However, the theme of the publication of his letters was one to which he returned at those points in his life when he was moved to make some reassessment of his work and its significance. His enlistment in the U.S. Army as a bandsman with the prospect, however remote, that the band might be sent to France and he might die, was such a time. On 16 June 1917 Grainger wrote to Karen of his wish to preserve and eventually to publish his letters. His reasons were characteristically specific. Firstly, he saw his letters as an essential facet of his life's work: "In the sweet years when we wrote so often to each other I was almost more taken up (both as regards time and importance) with my letters to you than I was with compositions or any other activity". Secondly, he felt that the letters offered a more complete statement of his personality than his music did:

> Gradually, as I think about my life and its meaning, it seems to me less and less that my compositions express my personality in a satisfactory way. My music expresses only certain sides, in any event, and I almost think that my emotional life and the life of my thoughts have almost more to say than my artistic life, and will, in the future, be regarded as being of the same, or greater, importance.

Beyond that, the letters were the embodiment of his past, a bulwark against his sense of transience, loss and death.

Although he intermittently had publication in mind, his spontaneity and candour were stronger than any preoccupation with posterity, with all its suggestions of self-watchfulness. His instinct to manufacture an image for future readers was washed away in the compulsion to record the impact of landscape, to lacerate himself, to put down the pain of sexual deprivation sharpened by a realisation of the wholeness attainable, to give vent to the fertility of his imaginative and intellectual responses.

Editor's Note

Apart from the fact that they are written in a variety of languages, Percy Grainger's letters do not present severe textual difficulties for the editor.

His handwriting is generally legible. He was by profession required to be precise about dates and places. Apart from the occasional lapse due to normal human error or haste, his dating is characteristically exact and fairly reliable. Similarly, apart from his habit of using up old stationery on less important letters, the addresses are also generally reliable.

His spelling is occasionally eccentric; some words are never spelled correctly. The spelling has been left unchanged in the English language letters, with [sic] being added only when a word seems highly improbable. Spelling mistakes, even his characteristic ones, have not, however, been reproduced in the English translations of letters written in other languages as this would seem to be an unnecessary contrivance. The spelling of the names of some European towns reflects historical variations as well as differences between English and original language forms. The ampersand Grainger habitually used in English has been retained; it does not appear in letters originally written in languages where it was not an option.

Punctuation has not in general been a problem and is left as in the manuscripts with two exceptions. It has not been possible to reproduce Grainger's habit of enclosing phrases or passages in a box for parenthetical effect. Instead double square brackets (⟦ ⟧) have been inserted around the appropriate passages. Grainger was not one to use the dash as a random substitute for commas and stops. His use of the semicolon was distinctive and, at certain times in his life more than at others, his use of boxed parentheses highly idiosyncratic. He usually punctuated before a bracket rather than, as is more orthodox, after it. He often forgot the full-stop, particularly at brackets, after quotations, at the end of a page or in closing sentences and postscripts. But punctuation, together with spelling and word-substitution, is part of the flavour of his style and has been preserved as such. The second exception concerns his occasional use of square brackets as an interchangeable substitute for parentheses. Because of the potential for confusion, this has not been retained. Except for those occasions where he used a bracket within a bracket, all his brackets are rendered as parentheses. Square brackets indicate an editorial interpolation. Underlinings in the manuscript appear as italics; double underlinings, of which Grainger was fond, in bold type.

I have to make assumptions about paragraphing. Grainger's paragraphing is erratic: sometimes it is clear; sometimes the text will continue for pages on end with only a longer space between sentences in a line to indicate a change of subject. Where such spaces occur in such situations I have normally inserted a paragraph.

Grainger's paragraphing is retained as nearly as possible, even though the layout of the letters has been standardised. Addresses and dates are placed at the head of the letter, to the right and left respectively, and signatures and closing sentences are indented to the left. In the manuscripts the placing of the signature varies with the degree of formality of the letter and the available space. Postscripts and afterthoughts, wherever they might have appeared in the manuscript, are placed after the signature.

Grainger's characteristic abbreviations have been preserved. He was not always consistent in the use of apostrophes in words such as "don't", "can't", "couldn't", "shouldn't", etc. Such words are rendered as he wrote them, with or (most often) without the apostrophe as the case may be. In translations, however, these words are given the normal grammatical form. He was occasionally inclined to use abbreviations such as "yr", "cld", "shld". Where he does, I have left them as he wrote them. Some words, some types of words, he habitually abbreviated: place names, titles of compositions, names of friends. These have been left as they appear in the manuscript. A list of the most frequent of these characteristic abbreviations has been included for easy reference. Titles of works are given as they are in the manuscript.

Grainger's letters are sometimes written on headed notepaper from his home, the hotel or wherever he was staying; sometimes they are written on scraps of paper, backs of concert programmes and the like, with the briefest address or no address at all. The addresses are given as they appear, with additional details added where necessary in square brackets. One substitution has been made: the charming little drawings by means of which Grainger indicated that a letter was written in a train have regretfully been replaced by a more economic and prosaic editorial phrase. The dates and signatures are also transcribed as they appear and reflect the variety of forms he used. Occasionally Grainger himself has retrospectively supplied a date for a letter left undated at the time of writing. His attributions are shown in quotation marks.

Grainger's formal or business letters are naturally more carefully written than his informal letters to family and friends. Among the latter, his letters to Ernest Thesiger are stylistically the most extreme. Thesiger himself, in his autobiography *Practically True* (London, Heinemann, 1927), wrote of Grainger as

a most lovable creature, so full of enthusiasm and strange Australian slang. His letters were almost unintelligibly original in their phrasing, and he carried this trait into his composition. Instead of the usual "molto crescendo" Percy would put "Louden lots," and such expressions as "Breathe when blown" or "Louder [sic] hugely" enliven his MSS.

Rose took a sterner view. At a time when Grainger was much involved with linguistic and syntactic experimentation in English she observed, 3 July 1903, "I do not really *approve* of your using bad grammar — such as littlest — but genius is always eccentric — & if yours takes no worse form, I shall be satisfied".

Through these comments one glimpses Grainger's creative approach to language. He was fascinated by language as a flexible and expressive tool. He wrote fluently and prolifically. It may be that his disregard for the more conventional notions of grammar and word usage, and certainly his uncertain spelling, stemmed from the fact that he had only three months' formal schooling. That had taken place at the Misses Turner's Preparatory School for Boys in Caroline Street, South Yarra, probably in 1893 or 1894, when the Graingers were living in Caroline Street.

Grainger had a highly individual sensitivity to language. So, for example, he wrote to Karen Holten on 18 August 1909 asking her not to use the Danish word "uha".

> Just as I cant bear having my socks on without my shoes, so there are always certain words that rob me of peace. When I was 6–8 years old I could not bear the English "chapter", it made me unboundedly cross and unhappy, and people had to say "Now begins *part* 12" (instead of chapter 12), etc. In German there are indeed many words and expressions that trouble me, e.g. "das ist ja alles mögliche" (that is all that could be expected).

So deeply did he feel on this point that he was moved to violate his principle that "nobody *ever* has the **right** to ask *anybody* to alter anything on their account". This sensitivity led him at this same time to develop his own language for the intimate parts of the body (see Glossary).

Underlying Grainger's involvement with the English language, underpinning the colourful eccentricity of his vocabulary, was a serious purpose. He believed that the English language had been weakened by the uncritical adaptation of words of foreign derivation. These were ideas he began to formulate very early. He was much preoccupied with their articulation prior to and during the first Australasian tour, and the letters of that time reflected their influence. Accordingly he began to develop a vocabulary of word-substitutes, replacing commonly used words of foreign derivation with words of his own devising which he saw as being closer to the Anglo-Saxon roots of the language. His fluency and facility in languages other than English gave him a broader view and scope for his inventiveness.

He adhered to this theoretical position with some firmness, though himself noting the irony of his occasional compromises. As it applied to his music, he insisted that the more commonly used Italian direction marks should be replaced with English terms of his own devising. It was an attitude that cost him dear, not only in terms of the negative response of individual musicians and publishers, but in terms of critical response to his music when, with English direction marks included, it began to be published. As early as his first English publications in 1904 and 1905, this aspect of his work attracted comment that ranged from the mocking to the outraged. It was rarely, if ever, taken seriously.

Grainger was fluent in some half-dozen European languages and their dialects, and read and studied as many more. Many of his friends were also multilingual and he wrote to them in the variety of their common languages. The letters in this volume are written in four basic languages — English, Danish, German and Dutch — or in a mixture of any or all of these. The Translator's Note discusses Grainger's use of the Danish language, the principal language other than English in the letters included here.

Occasional words and phrases occur in various other languages including Maori, Icelandic, Faeroese and, after the New Zealand trip of 1909, the private intimate language Grainger invented. These lapses are, in general, preserved as they occur, with the English equivalent following in square brackets. English words occasionally appear in quotation marks in letters in other languages. It is highly likely that the quotation marks have no other function than to indicate that the word is in English. However, as a heightening of the sense is also sometimes intended, the quotation marks have been preserved in the translation. Grainger liked to write languages phonetically, particularly when he wished to emphasise some idiosyncrasy of dialect or pronunciation, and these too are preserved.

All letters are written in English unless otherwise stated. The original language is indicated at the top of each letter written in a language other than English. In the case of letters written in a mixture of languages, the languages are indicated in a descending order of quantitative importance. The locations of the original manuscripts of the letters are given in the Acknowledgements.

The notes attempt to identify personalities and clarify allusions with primary emphasis on Grainger's relationship to the subject of the annotation. Some obvious references have been taken for granted. A special effort has not been made to identify musical personalities of such familiarity as Johann Sebastian Bach, Ludwig van Beethoven, Richard Wagner and the like. Nor have I attempted full identifications for Grainger's acquaintances in, say, the Svinkløv circle, or his friends in the family circles in Australia. There are occasions where I have been unable to elucidate an allusion in the text; these are acknowledged. Short linking narratives have been added at intervals to provide continuity and a frame of reference for the following group of letters.

In annotating the letters I have sought to capture the many reverberations of the text and draw the reader's attention to the scope of Grainger's interests, the range of his acquaintance, the broad canvas of his aspiration and endeavour. For the letters resonate with the richness of an extraordinary period in European musical history, the exact like of which we will never see again.

Translator's Note

The collection of Grainger's letters available is very large and covers many different types written under very diverse circumstances, which is immediately reflected in the quality of the language used.

The extent of Grainger's Danish vocabulary is quite surprising and covers many words common in everyday colloquial speech, as well as many words of a "literary" kind which he must have acquired from extensive reading.

One may distinguish between usage in (a) letters to friends and acquaintances where some care has been taken to write carefully and correct possible errors of grammar and/or spelling (in a few cases there are rough drafts of these letters); and (b) the large number of letters to Karen Holten, most of which were written without correction and often in a great hurry.

Letters in the former group show relatively few faults and generally read quite straightforwardly. Letters in the latter group are very different, and show great variation in style and content. Common to all is a quite remarkable fluency; they are full of colloquial phrases and common idioms while at the same time often containing grammatical errors. Many of these letters contain passages in other languages — either whole sentences or paragraphs are deliberately written in a third language; or frequently a German, Dutch or English word is used as a substitute for a Danish word which could not immediately be brought to mind.

While many of these letters are hurried notes of a purely ephemeral nature, there are also many much longer letters where he seeks to express his thoughts on all manner of subjects, often in a highly fanciful and somewhat lyrical manner. Often a good deal of thought has gone into these passages without, however, taking such care to avoid errors as was evident in the first group. This sometimes leads to difficulties in interpretation and in a very few isolated cases the meaning is obscure.

A further group of letters among those to Karen Holten are a number in which he seeks to "lay down the law" in no uncertain terms on their relationship to one another. (In a letter in later years Grainger himself referred to these as "my stupid 'legal' letters".) These letters are usually very long and include strings of nearly synonymous adjectives and nouns, apparently in the hope that if one of them is not clear another will be! These passages can also cause some difficulty in translation, for it is not always possible to match the different adjectives etc. to corresponding English words.

In the more fanciful and lyrical passages Percy Grainger quite freely coins new words to express nuances of meaning — generally by combining two words and/or by changing the usage of a word from noun to verb or adjective, or vice versa, so a certain amount of imagination is sometimes required to follow the meaning. He clearly had no doubt Karen would understand him completely.

Examples of Grainger's word-formation
tilgivelserfuldt: lit. forgivings-full, i.e. merciful.
hjærnefødt livsplaner: lit. brain-born life-plans.
hversødandre: lit. each-sweet-other.
imed mig: This is formed to mean the opposite of *imod mig* — against me; i.e. with me or agreeing with me.
hundevarm, hundegerne: These words are coined from a Danish colloquial expression: *hundekold* — "icy-cold", very cold. Grainger extends this to *hundevarm*, very warm; *hundegerne*, very gladly.

Grainger invented (or borrowed from other languages) a complete collection of intimate words for private use in his correspondence with Karen Holten. A glossary of these words follows.

Percy Grainger makes much use of the expression *kødfolk*, a word he invented. *Kød* means "meat" or "flesh". It is also used to mean "flesh" in the figurative senses. *Folk* means "people", but it is also used in the singular, meaning "person". Hence *kødfolk*, literally flesh-person, i.e. a carnal person. Grainger himself in one letter translates *kødfolk* as meat-mate (or meatmate; see letter 176), such an idiosyncratic phrase that it has been retained. He uses the Danish expression as a favourite endearment for Karen.

By a further extension of this idea Grainger arrived at *kødfolkelighed*, literally "fleshpersonliness", thus giving perhaps a special kind of personal flavour to the idea of carnality or sensuality (the normal Danish words being *kødlighed, sanselighed*).

Grammar
Although Grainger's letters are fluent and idiomatic, they are by no means free of grammatical errors. Many of the errors relate to gender; for example, adjective, predicate or pronoun do not agree in gender, which sometimes leads to ambiguity. At times the wrong preposition is used. Not infrequently, the wrong word is used — where one with a similar sound but different meaning is substituted for the correct word. A frequent source of error is in compound words where a wrong prefix is used.

Some examples of his errors
afhæver should be *overhæver* or *hæver . . . over*: "be superior".
kilde på (tickle) should be *kile på* or *kile løs på*, meaning "hurry up with".
overkomme (manage) should be *overvinde* or *overgå*, "beat".
afstødende should be *frastødende*, "repulsive".
angreb (attack) should be *indgreb*, "impression".

His spelling varies considerably. Certain words are consistently spelled wrongly, for example *ligegyltig* for *ligegyldig*; but mostly the spelling errors are due to hurried writing. From about the end of 1910 he consistently adopted the spelling å in place of aa — a change not generally accepted in Denmark until very much later. Generally his handwriting is fairly easily read, except for some letters written in trains.

Word order is a rather difficult subject. Often the word order is neither normal English nor Danish. It is sometimes difficult to decide whether a particular word order has been chosen for emphasis and should be reproduced (as far as possible) or not.

In conclusion, although Grainger's use of the Danish language has some faults, the main impression given by these letters is one of remarkable fluency and facility with the language, enabling him to handle all manner of abstract ideas — as well as concrete facts — with great imagination.

P. P. Grigg

Glossary of Private Language

TO KAREN HOLTEN
22–24 September and 11–12 October 1909
[Extracts]

It seems to me we lack words for many parts of the body. I suggest the following:

mavebryster [lit. tummy-breasts] for what Herman calls "røv" [arse] and which have got a new importance since you now receive guests "from the back" [i.e. buttocks]

mavehavn [lit. tummy-harbour] for the little door of happiness, that can only be opened outwards, and doesn't receive summer guests — yet, at any rate. It is a harbour because it makes export [i.e. anus]

mavemund [lit. tummy-mouth]. Where do you think that is? It is the little mouth that I kiss but which can't kiss me. In that little moist mouth I long to be continually, either with ureure [see below], tongue or hand. She and I never become tired of each other [i.e. vulva].

Urskov [lit. primeval forest or jungle] is urskov [i.e. pubic hair].

Armlunde [lit. arm-grove] are these lovely hairs in the armpits that I will pull out altogether some-time.

Urebrødre [lit. penis brothers] are these 2 hanging egg-shaped things I always have with me under ureure and which you must never take revenge on, even when you are very cross. Walt Whitman says something about "the silent brothers, hanging shyly", etc. [i.e. testicles]

mavehals [lit. tummy-neck]. It's there where you whisper "right-up" [i.e. vagina]. In the mavehals you have *your* ureure, the little hard thing that stands there so bravely and firmly in the middle of the main road [i.e. clitoris].

ureure the male organ [i.e. penis]. [This word is first used in letter 264.]

ureureroa the large ureure [i.e. phallus]. (When it isn't large it's only called ure-ure) *roa* means long, stretched out.

whakaureroa is the verb for the action of the ureure getting big.
  whaka means become, make, do: for example;
  tangata = man   whakatangata = grow to man.
  rongo = sound   whakarongo = hear. etc.
  Thus: ureure whakaureroa means ureure becomes large.

List of Abbreviations

A'dam	Amsterdam
Balf, B. Gard	H. Balfour Gardiner
B's Tragedy	*The Bride's Tragedy*
Ch-sund	Christiansund (Kristiansund)
Col. Song	*Colonial Song*
Cope., Copeh., Copenh.	Copenhagen
D Juan	*Don Juan*
Dr Sailor	Drunken Sailor (*Scotch Strathspey and Reel*)
E D	*English Dance*
F and D	*Father and Daughter*
Gard	H. Balfour Gardiner
Gr Bs; G. Bs.	*Green Bushes*
Køb, Kope., Københ, Kj, Kjøbenh	Copenhagen
Krist-ia	Kristiania (Christiania)
K-sand, Ch-sand	Kristiansand (Christiansand)
M-Jig	*March-Jig* (Stanford-Grainger)
Mock M; M. Morris; M M	*Mock Morris*
M. Robin	*My Robin is to the Greenwood Gone*
P.R.	poste restante
Q's Hall	Queen's Hall
R. Round	*Random Round*
Shallow B	*Shallow Brown*
Sh's Hey	*Shepherd's Hey*
St-Gr	Stanford-Grainger
Sv.	Svinkløv
Troldh	Troldhaugen
Tschai, Tchai	Tchaikovsky
Vars.	Variations
W. March	(*Lads of*) *Wamphray March*
Xia; Xiania	Kristiania (Christiania)

Chronology

1882	8 July	Born George Percy Grainger at Brighton, Victoria, Australia.
1894	9 July	First public performance as a pianist, at a Risvegliato Concert in the Masonic Hall, Melbourne.
1895	25 May	Leaves Australia with his mother, Rose, to study piano and composition at the Hoch Conservatorium, Frankfurt am Main, Germany.
1900	6 December	Solo recital, Frankfurt, marks the end of his student days.
1901	mid May	Moves to London, with his mother, where his career as a virtuoso pianist is launched on 11 June.
1902		Suite *La Scandinavie* published by B. Schott's Söhne, Mainz.
1903–04		Tours Australasia with Ada Crossley and her concert party.
1904	29 September–19 October	First concert tour in Denmark, with Herman Sandby. First meeting with Karen Holten.
1906	18 August–9 or 10 September	First holiday with Karen Holten, at Svinkløv, Jutland, Denmark.
1908	May	Makes his first recordings with the Gramophone Company.
1908–09		Tours Australasia for the second time with Ada Crossley and her concert party.
1910		First concert tours in Holland and Norway.
1911	October	Adopts the name of Percy Aldridge Grainger, concurrently with the publication of his music by Schott & Co., London.
1912–13		H. Balfour Gardiner Choral and Orchestral Concerts mark the beginning of Grainger's public career as a composer.
1912	15–29 August	Last holiday with Karen Holten, at Slettestrand, Jutland, Denmark.
1913	14 November	Last meeting with Karen Holten before World War I, at Copenhagen railway station.
1914	2 September	Leaves England with his mother for the United States of America.
1917	13 April	Death of Grainger's father, John Harry Grainger, in Melbourne, Australia.
1917	12 June	Enlists in the U.S. Army as a bandsman.
1918	3 June	Becomes a naturalised American citizen.
1919	7 January	Honourably discharged from U.S. Army.
1919		Publication of *Country Gardens*, his best-known piano piece.
1922	30 April	Death by suicide of Rose Grainger, at 27 West 42nd Street, New York, U.S.A.
1924		Makes a private visit to the Pacific Islands and Australasia.
1926		Makes his first solo tour of Australia.
1928	9 August	Marries the Swedish-born poet and painter Ella Viola Ström.
1934–35		Tours Australasia and establishes the Music Museum and Grainger Museum in the grounds of the University of Melbourne.
1938		Visits Australia. The Museum is officially opened.
1953	3 October	Death of Karen Kellermann (*née* Holten).
1955–56		Visits Australia for the last time.
1960	29 April	Gives his last public concert performance.
1961	20 February	Dies at White Plains, New York, U.S.A.
1979	17 July	Ella Grainger dies at White Plains, New York, U.S.A.

1901

Rose and Percy Grainger arrived in London in May 1901, Percy having been engaged by a fellow Australian, soprano Lilian Devlin, to assist at her "second grand concert" in the St James Hall on 11 June. This was Percy's debut appearance in England. On 13 June the British Australasian announced that Grainger would be staying in London for the season.

Grainger's big "break" came on 3 July, when he stepped from the audience of Miss Maggie Stirling's concert at the home of Lady Brassey in Park Lane, taking the place of the conductor/pianist Mr Theodore Flint, kept away, as the Daily Telegraph reported, through indisposition. Miss Stirling, too, was Australian, and her agent, Alice Joseph, was also Grainger's agent at this time, so one may suspect a measure of sympathetic collusion in the choice of the replacement for Mr Flint. Nonetheless, press notices praised Grainger's graciousness and skill in undertaking all the accompaniments at sight, noting that he had also played a solo. The responses must have seemed encouraging. On 11 July the British Australasian announced that the Graingers, mother and son, had taken up permanent residence in London, settling at 31 Gordon Place, Kensington.

John Grainger was not with them. But fatherless households, units of mother and education- or career-seeking children, were not remarkable in London's Anglo-Australian community. And John Grainger's wife and son gathered some renommé from the fact that he had designed the Westralian Court at the great Paris Exhibition of 1900.

Over the following months, the British Australasian, chief news vehicle for the social doings of Australians in England, reported the Graingers' participation in a range of activities among an expanding circle of acquaintances within the expatriate Anglo-Australian society in London. On 29 October 1901, Grainger gave his first solo recital in London, at Steinway Hall. It included one of his own compositions, his paraphrase on Tchaikovsky's "Waltz of the Flowers", and was favourably noticed in the London daily newspapers.

Other engagements came slowly. At first, for the most part but not exclusively, these came from compatriots, with Grainger appearing as assisting artist in a variety of concerts. Grainger himself acknowledged his debt to his fellow Australian artists in his interview of 3 October 1901 in the British Australasian, mentioning in particular Melba, Ada Crossley and Lilian Devlin. During this time the pressure of public appearances was sufficiently light to allow Grainger to indulge his absorbing passion for composition: the first sketches for several important works date from 1901. His first surviving letters are to his Frankfurt student friends and fellow composers Balfour Gardiner and Herman Sandby.

1 Henry Balfour Gardiner (1877–1950), English composer. Studied at the Hoch Conservatorium in Frankfurt between 1894 and 1896, taking four semesters each of piano with Lazzaro Uzielli and composition with Iwan Knorr, and two semesters each of organ with Heinrich Gelhaar and clarinet with Ludwig Mohler. He continued to study privately with Knorr until at least 1899.

2 Cyril Meir Scott (1879–1970), English composer, author and pianist. Studied piano with Uzielli at the Hoch Conservatorium in Frankfurt for eight semesters, 1891–93 and 1896–99, taking composition with Iwan Knorr between 1897 and 1899. Grainger and Herman Sandby had played Scott's piano trio at a Conservatorium concert on 1 June 1899, with Edgar Wollgandt, violin. Grainger's song remains unidentified, although several song settings date from the early months of 1901, including two settings of Kipling's verse "Dedication". Grainger's first setting of "The Peora Hunt", verse-heading to the story "Cupid's Arrows" in *Plain Tales from the Hills*, remained unpublished. *To Wolcott Balestier*, a setting of the dedication poem to *Barrack-Room Ballads*, was not finished. The *Marching Song* sketches were developed over several years, finding their final form in the *Marching Song of Democracy*. Grainger began his *Train Music/ Charging Irishry* sketches in 1900, but the work remained unfinished, as did his other experiments in Large Form. The cello piece is *Youthful Rapture*, then called *A Lot of Rot*, written 6 and 13 March 1901.

3 The manuscript of Gardiner's 1901 eight-bar melody in E♭ is in the Grainger Museum. In 1947, noting that Gardiner had given it to him between 1900 and 1904 to "finish as best he might", Grainger made a sketch for its continuation, calling it *Flowing Melody*. He also aimed to include it in his *Gardineriana Rhapsody*. Both projects remained unfinished.

1 TO H. BALFOUR GARDINER[1]   *31* Gordon Pl.
July. 21. 1901.   Kens. London. W.

Dear Gardiner,

I cannot understand why you like the song enclosed, it is just the kind I would not expect to appeal to you.

However I have done better things since, & yesterday did my best, so-far, that is, in regards realizing the intended idea. It is *just* what I wanted it to become before composing. It is remarkable how rarely things turn out just as they were immagined, ideas seem to mostly loose their fresh in the process of composition

But the "PEORA HUNT" (An Indian Kipling Rhyme) is a small exception, being only ten bars long & set for männerchor [German: men's chorus] of a type (Contraltino, 1 Tenor, 1 Bar, & 3 Bass parts)

I have also started a larger thing for men's voices Kippy's "To Wolcott Balestier" a poem of 27 lines, a kind of Death-song or rather T'other-side-song, perhaps Kipling's finest thing in a way.

Certainly just the thing for me to set

Beyond the path of the outmost sun through utter darkness hurled —
Further than ever comet flared or vagrant star-dust swirled —
Live such as fought & sailed & ruled & loved & made our world.

this is the 1st verse.

also:

They take their mirth in the joy of the Earth —
  they dare not grieve for her pain —
They know of toil & the end of toil, they know God's law is plain,
So they whistle the Devil to make them sport who know that SIN is vain

etc. etc.

Since being in London I have finished the *Marching-song* as far as I am intend[ing] to go with it just now, & what is more important, have made great strides in a further developement of LARGE FORM. (called for brevety *Charging-Irishry, Train-music style*)

Dear old Scotty paid us a visit the other day bringing lovely things alone [*sic* along]. He was very pleased with my truck (*very* much most so with the CELLO-PIECE) even went so far as to crack up Large-form & departed for "die Schweiz" [German: Switzerland] the next morning.[2]

Your lovely E♭ mel. is a fine invigorater of dull moments, it takes its place among the very lovely. I had a joke with Scott about it. He says he does not like it as well as most of your things, but when I played it among other things, he started up with "What is the lovely thing" etc. So you see how much one may rely on a person's opinion.[3]

I am longing to hear more of yours. Just at your stage of developement you are most confoundedly interesting, one never knows what will turn up next, there is no limit to possibilities.

I suppose we shall see you soon

Regards from us both.

Please note *31* Gordon Pl. Kens.

2 TO HERMAN SANDBY[4]   31. Gordon Pl.
Sept. 27. 1901.   Kensington. London. W.

SONG OF THE ROMAN 'CELLISTINNEN.

Good man! I am glad, for I like the Italians & would like to see them get a fair show. If you get it or not, be *sure* you let me know the decision *immediatly*. What I admire is, your undertaking to "sling the BAT" (learn the language) in so short a time, it is so very Scandanavian, so beautifully contrasting to our opposite policy. I have come to the conclusion that you Northerners are the best at English, if not at all other languages, for I met a Swede from America, who not only learnt American perfectly, but has succeeded in the difficult task of changing it into ENGLISH since he has been here, & which latter he speaks *even as* the English. You too could easily learn English English.

My dear fellow I do hope that in the future we may see you in this country, not only am I positive that you would succeed enormously, but that you would *really* like it, for the real good English musicians are the most delightful people I have met. They are *entirely* unlike their disagreeable & narrow-minded German brother-artists, & are equally unlike other Englishmen. When you unite depth of feeling, intense developement of nerve, broard-mindedness & unconventionality with the other healthy & vigorous qualities of the English, you get something quite delightful, & a more easy-mannered, sympathetic class does not exist than the *really good Young* English artists.

There is a remarkable absence of SOLOISM about the English composer-type, & a presence of intense devotion to the sincerity of art together with absolute self-sacrifice that I haven't been able to find among any foreign musician except yourself & knowing you as well as I do I am sure you would be greatly pleased at the ideal sincerity of my friends. There is Scott, from whom I have just had a delightful visit, who is absolutely incapable of jealousy for *anybody*, & who would do anything for poor little ME, there is Austin,[5] a friend of his, a great admirer of both Sandby & Grainger, & a most clever chap, & perhaps the deepest thinker on musical matters I have ever met. He is teacher of harmony or counterpoint or form or something in an institute in Liverpool, is 28, & married, poor Devil. His own compositions are very interesting, although he is still in an elementary period, having only written seriously for 2 years, & being latterly under Scott's influence. However he is emerging therefrom & may found a style of his own. I shall not be surprized if he does some very striking formal work in his life for he is capable of thinking as progressively as myself, & *stops at nothing, mentally*. Whether he will have the power to create up to his thinking-standard I cannot say, at any rate he is a thorough musician, & a *most exacting* critic. He was **greatly** impressed by your work, he marveled at your rare combination of simplicity & extreme originality, he found intense satisfaction in the primal strength (Urwüchsigkeit) [German] of your style, & sympathized with the warm, human, loving emotional qualities that are so irrisistable in your compositions. He is *most* interested in your creative future, & awaits with keen interest what you will give the world. His admiration of my work is equal to yours or Scott's & in a letter which the latter showed me I found the following passages: "He is a veritable breath of fresh air, & *his work is without boundaries*." (Sein[e] Arbeit ist grenzenlos) [German] "The Cello-piece I find extremely beautiful, with reservations as to the middle section." "THE SONG OF SOLOMON made a great impression upon me, & I have not half taken it in, *but I must say, beside his methods, existing methods do seem very limited*." That is my first real praise from a stranger, & the first satisfactory "first impression" of any of my advanced-form works. A Dr Bornier in Liverpool, to whom Scott has played bits of my things, & shown some letters of mine on musical subjects, says he considers me the "first man since Wagner". You will excuse my introducing these items of self-praise, but I am *so* happy to find people sympathetic in my own country, & know how large-heartedly you will welcome any compositional successes which may fall to my lot.[6]

Scott has grown *so very* much nicer again than he was in Frankfort last Xmas, he is quite his dear affectionate old self once more, & charming hours we have enjoyed together. He simply *raves* about Cello-piece & is going to copy it & get it done in Liverpool privately, he has also altered

4 Peter Herman Sandby (born Pedersen, from Sandby) (1881–1965), Danish cellist and composer. Studied cello with Hugo Becker in Frankfurt for eight semesters between 1896 and 1901, in his final year taking composition with Knorr. The family changed its name when it moved from Sandby t'o Copenhagen in 1886. Herman made his London debut at his duo-recital with Percy at Steinway Hall on 22 April 1902.

5 Frederic Austin (1872–1952), English baritone singer and composer. After holding several appointments as a church organist he joined the staff of the Liverpool College of Music, where he remained until 1906. He made his London debut as a singer in a joint recital with Grainger at the Bechstein Hall on 12 March 1902 and took part in Grainger's Concert of Compositions and Folk-Music Settings on 21 May 1912. He had some success as a composer with his orchestral pieces.

6 Grainger planned a setting in fourteen parts of the whole text of *The Song of Solomon*, for soprano solo, baritone solo, mixed chorus and instrumental accompaniment. Completed drafts exist for the setting of two parts, Part II (completed late 1899–early 1900) and Part V (9 March–October 1900). Part II was published as *Love Verses from "The Song of Solomon"* in 1931. Part V remains unpublished and the whole project unfinished.

his first opinion of the MARCHING-CHORUS, & now thinks it very fine. The SONG OF SOL he admires musically, but thinks it "formel[l] schwach" [German: formally weak] *not* because it is large-form, but because it is not large-form enough, for he considers all cadences, (Schlüsse) [German] strongly-marked phrase-divisions, & extra-distinct inventive-moments a mistake in *very* Large-form style. It is certainly a standpoint. Yet I do not agree, for I never intended to make Part 5 "S of S" a type of *advanced* Large-form, as I do not consider this possible or right in a Textal Work, the divisions of speech in sentences necessitating the division of music into phrases, which however, may be as irregular as those of the text. He has completely changed his style once more, & now it is far greater, larger, & still finer in form. He has certainly been influenced (as regards form) by my work, & himself asserts that his present period is entirely the outcome of the Cello piece. His last things are most original, chiefly of great unbroken flow, & he has whole movements that are "aus einem Guss" [German fig.: a perfect whole] like 1st chorus Matthäuss Passion. He has written a piano sonata for me which I consider the *only* successful modern Klavier sonata, that is as a whole, inventively (erfinderisch) [German] it is not so powerful as he usually is except in the 1st theme (& all connected with 1st theme) which is simply *perfect*, with "wechselnde[r] Takt" [German: changing rhythm], clangey, like bells, & most Scotty, & heroic. The Sonata is in one movement. Then there is a Piano-quartette, simply gigantic in impression, *all* flow. The 1st movement (every instrument playing solo expresivo) rises & falls like a great SONG, the 2nd (a scherzo) is lively & beautiful & breaks out into a huge Dance-like climax at the end, melodic & rich. The slow movement I admire less, the flow is good but is not strong inventively to my mind. 4th movement (Intermezzo) is splendid, delicate & pastoral & flowing & *AECHT* [German: real] Scott.[7]

The Finale I consider bad in form, it being Flowing yet *very* much broken-up, however there are glorious melodic bits in it. The *whole* work is nothing less than gigantic, & would sound better than *any* previous chamber music work. (of the melodic type) Besides these is a "Study for an ENGLISH REQUIEM" merely a sketch for a big choral work he is about to begin. The sketch is unceasing melodic continuance. There is also a Cello piece that he calls privately "Fürchterliche Eier für Cello & Klavier" [German: Frightful Eggs for Cello and Piano], it is inspired (title & music) by "A Lot of Rot" & is a developement of my piece in that the Cello never ceases for one moment from beginning to end, & that the flow is better & the form more consiquent, but it is not perhaps so bedeutend [German: important].

Now I must tell you of Scott's good fortune, Hans Richter *has* really taken him up, & is performing the "Heroic Suite" in Manchester next month & something else in Liverpool in Jan. These two are already advertised but SCOTT says Richter has promised to bring out his things *every*-where, & also that he would *force* Novello & Co (of London) to publish Scott's things. This is great news is it not? We are all so happy about it.[8]

I have been hearing as I already told you a good deal of compositions by really splendid fellows, for besides Scott's, and Austin's, I have seen all Gardiner's latest. Good ideas, but *bad form*, simply shitty. There is a nice warmth about his style, & he may improve in form, but I fear he has no formal-conscience. Of course it is only from my standpoint that his form is so poor, I find it so artificial & unnecessary. *But*, my dear fellow, beside *you* they are *NOTHING*. Even Scott (who will be one of the greatest composers) entirely lacks the large-hearted, human, & truly GREAT element of your works, & when I think of the nobly sincere & strongly inventive "Elskov" I must fall down & worship. You have what we *none* of us possess, something so godlike, so Northern, limitless & all-embracing, I shall never forget the heroic singing of those celli in yr compos. When I

---

7 Grainger "brought out" a new one-movement Piano Sonata in D major (Op. 17) by Cyril Scott at Madame Julia Rudge's concert on 29 November 1901. He played it frequently thereafter. In 1909 he revised it heavily and it was published by Elkin & Co. as *Handelian Rhapsody*. Scott's Quartet in E minor for piano and strings, completed in October 1899, was given its first London performance, with Scott at the piano, in a Broadwood concert on 12 February 1903. Grainger probably heard it performed before he left Frankfurt. The cello piece is possibly *Pierrot Amoureux*, which Sandby and Grainger included in their programmes for their 1904 Scandinavian tour, introducing it in Copenhagen on 29 September 1904.

8 Hans Richter (1843–1916). Austro-Hungarian conductor, at this time conductor of the Hallé Orchestra in Manchester. Richter performed Scott's *Heroic Suite* (Orchestral Suite No. 2) in Manchester on 12 December 1901 and in Liverpool on 14 January 1902. This work, together with much of the chamber music written during this period, was later withdrawn. In 1903, Novello & Co. announced publication of Scott's *English Waltz*, dedicated to, and much played by, Grainger. Novello was not, however, one of the main publishers of Scott's work. It was Grainger himself who did much to bring Scott's name before the public through his performances.

think of the rare natural technical qualities you displayed in suddenly writing yr Fantasie-stück I know how perfectly finished you will be able to express yr large-soul emotions in the future, & the fact of learning Italian in a few hours shows that you possess the splendid Northern "Arbeitskraft" [German: capacity for work].[9] I can think of few musical conditions yr Genius will not adapt itself to, I can immagine broard, rolling, soul-ful Sandby-ism chanted by a chorus, can see you create an intense, surging, seething, sealike orchestral style, & chamber music broarder & grander than the past (or present) could even dream of, whereas the delightful combination of originality & simplicity will generate lovely, *necessary* songs. *I am positive* that you are the musical HOLGE DANSKE, *but*, like all Scandinavians, you need a certain waking up. There is a certain failure to realize all-important facts about the Northern races that I have percieved both in the individuals I have met, & in the Art of these countries, particularly strong it is in Ibsen, & Björnson. With all the working capabilities of these peoples, there is a certain *cloud* over them all, a certain *inactivity* in no way related to laziness, but rather the outcome of a certain torpidness of thought. Once lift the cloud from these peoples' minds, let them percieve a course of action to be *necessary*, & *no* people can compare with them for determination & vigour for action, but they waste a sad lot of time before they grasp the necessity of action. Therefor they get on so grandly in America, it wakes them up.

So it is with you. When you once realize (what *we* already know) yr own creative powers, you will ARIZE in yr strength & beat everybody. You read Hans Anderson's "Holge Danske", that ought to make you buck up. *Do* not misunderstand me. I *perfectly* understand that at present (the absolute present) you have **no** possibility of devoting *any* time to composition. I am sure you are doing 10 men's work at present. But when you settle down (in Rome or elsewhere) I *pray & implore* you not to forget my entreaties, & hope to GOD you will not neglect a Heaven-appointed Duty, think, you can, with one stroke, put your country among the first & formost in composition. There is the DEVIL in you Norse chaps, Ibsen, Björnson, Nansen, Sven Hedin, Thorwaldson, Andersen, Grieg etc, are all great, religous, heroic, & I see the same strength in you, *only* I know you **can** (if you will) top the musical list.[10] These Scandinavians above mentioned *all* grasped their path in life & succeeded, they are those among you who are clear, *active*, with all the poetry of climate & race who have emerged beyond the desultory influence of same, a certain waiting inactive, a certain torpidity, a certain cloudiness. For God's sake, when you have time, realize yr enormousness & start yr life's work *early*, you are already *quite* old enough. I do not mean only compose, there are hundreds of other ways of developing composition-techniques besides actual writing, the chief thing is constant observation & thought for & on musical-creative matters, when you play music observe it always from the composer-standpoint, note modes of construction, develope *above all* a *sharp* criticism for "musical ERFINDUNG" [German: invention], *inventiveness* is the seat of all musical strength, when you see forms & beauty in nature apply it in yr mind to the forms & types in music, get to look on Poetry from the setter's standpoint, go for musicalness in Verse, & while reading, *always* take in the metre, rhythms, & melodic lines contained therein, & when you *do* find poetry appealing to yr musical requisitions, *always* imagine it composed as you read it, continualy think out *exactly* how it should be set, what type, what voices, what tempi, what *kind* of chordal types, what sort of melodic invention, etc. etc. And when you feel fine emotions, or meet noble impressions, or think strong thoughts, *straight-away* translate them into yr musical language, at least in thought, think out exactly how a composition should be to express these lovely things in their fullness.

Thus you will slowly acquire a severe self-criticism, a quick absorbtion of the good in others & in nature, & when you ultimately proceed to ac-

9 The manuscript of Sandby's *Elskov* [Love Song] for four cellos, composed 16 December 1899, is in the Grainger Museum, as is that of his first orchestral score, the *Fantasiestück für Grosses Orkester*, December 1900. Later Grainger made various arrangements of *Love Song*.

10 A selection of Scandinavian national heroes: Holger Danske, a heroic character in Danish mythology; Henrik Ibsen (1828–1906), Norwegian dramatist whose works acquired an international fame and exerted powerful influence; Bjørnstjerne Bjørnson (1832–1910), Norwegian poet and dramatist whose writings played an important role in Norway's national awakening at the end of the nineteenth century (he received the Nobel Prize for literature in 1903); Fridtjof Nansen (1861–1930), Norwegian-born Arctic explorer and author and Norwegian ambassador to London from 1906 to 1908; Sven Hedin (1865–1952), Swedish explorer and author; Bertil Thorvaldsen (1770–1884), Danish sculptor of international repute; Hans Christian Andersen (1805–75), Danish author, most famous for his fairy stories; Edvard Hagerup Grieg (1843–1907), the most important Norwegian composer of the Nationalist-Romantic period.

tually compose, you will find you know what you want, can master yr formal expression, & are clearly conscious of what sort of stuff you need to creat for a certain object. The invention (though not developed yet) & originality you possess in abundance already. The mistake is to compose *not* knowing what you want to make, to acquire technique without feeling the necessity for it, & to get into mannerisms because you know not how to seperate yr contrasting styles. If you think in this way you will find life full of the NEED of MUSICAL EXPRESSION, all emotions will require to become compositions. So it is with me. I have already *done* my thinking (the elementary part.)

I have been doing a lot of writing on music lately, & will soon work up my Sketches into an article entitled "Theme as related to Form in Music" in which I deal with INVENTION & its adequate expression in musical architecture. This is a study for the lectures, books, writings, etc that I will need for my Australian plan. (National musical-education.) I am getting to express myself better in my writings & will continue to acquire "schreib-tecknik" [German: writing technique], & will write on "Orchestration" presently. In all my writings, books, etc, I shall *never* take a one-sided standpoint, (or try to *force* my *own* ideas on form & other matters) but shall examine the good in all (even in Beethoven, Mendelssohn) & discard the weak in all (even in Bach, *chiefly* in Wagner) & thus point out truths which *may* (or may not) lead people to my conceptions, or to ones equally sincere & progressive. I am doing good work now, not much however. I enclose a bit of paper on which are some old Kipling sketches, perhaps you may like to have them.

Perhaps lovely Italy may influence you to vocalism in composition? *You take in their Folk-lore*!

I find that SOUSA, the great March composer, is English. He is a Mr John Philip So, & on going to America, put on his boxes Mr So, U.S.A. The guard in America made a mistake, adressing him as SOUSA, so he adopted that name.[11] So the biggest march writer belongs to us too, at present, but the biggest composer will belong to Denmark
IN THE FUTURE.

Sept. 29. 1901.

11 John Philip Sousa, born Washington D.C., 6 November 1854; died Reading, Pennsylvania, 6 March 1932. American bandmaster and composer. He formed his own band in 1892. Grainger heard Sousa and his band at the Royal Albert Hall when they made their first appearance in London on 4 October 1901. Sousa's fame as a composer rested mainly on his marches.

1902

On 16 January 1902, the British Australasian noted:

> Lady Bective, one of the most cultivated leaders of London society, has had Mr Percy Grainger to her house several times lately, and is greatly taken with the musical gifts of the young Australian pianist who will shortly give another recital in London.

The Graingers' social sphere was beginning to expand.

So, too, was Percy's professional sphere. In February 1902 he was engaged for two programmes in the Roman Promenade Concert series in Bath, his first provincial engagement in England. At the afternoon chamber concert on 4 February he played the Tchaikovsky Trio in A minor, Op. 50, with Max Heymann, violin, and a Mr Salter, cello, adding for a piano solo the Ballade Op. 24 by Grieg. At the afternoon and evening symphony concerts on 6 February he gave the first of his many performances of Tchaikovsky's Piano Concerto No. 1 in Bb minor, Op. 23, this being also his first appearance with orchestra in England. The Bath City Orchestra was conducted by Max Heymann, its Musical Director from 1892 to 1910. Heymann's wife, Edith, née Meadows, a pianist, was a pupil of Clara Schumann and a friend of the Graingers from Frankfurt days. Percy had already visited the Heymanns in the summer of 1901. The Heymanns' daughter, Frieda, was almost one year old in February 1902.

The letters from Bath are the first written by Percy to Rose in the English period, and establish his practice of writing to her at least once daily when away from home. No letters survive from Rose to Percy for 1902.

Grainger's engagement for the Harrison–Patti tour of the English provinces in October 1902 afforded him his first experience of touring. Nine concerts were given, the first being at Birmingham on 6 October. After the last concert, in Liverpool on 24 October, Grainger spent a few days at the home of Cyril Scott, rejoining his mother at Waddesdon, Buckinghamshire, on 30 October. Rose was staying with Mr and Mrs West at Waddesdon.

3 TO ROSE GRAINGER[1]
Feb. 5. 1902.

10, Dunsford Place,
Bath.

Darling Mum

Just received yr dear letter, have answered Grainger & d'Erlanger, accepting both.[2]

1 Rosa (Rose) Annie (née Aldridge) Grainger (1861–1922), Grainger's mother, his first piano teacher and, from the time his father, John, left the family in 1890 to the time of her suicide in 1922, his sole companion.

2 Henry William Allerdale Grainger (1848–1923), Agent-General for South Australia in London from 1901 to 1905. It was he who introduced Percy to the Savage Club. Baron Frédéric d'Erlanger (1868–1943), Anglo-French banker and composer. At d'Erlanger's concert of his own compositions in Bechstein Hall on 15 March 1902, Grainger played the Deux Études Concertantes, works which he had included in the programme of his first London recital, 29 October 1901.

8

My wrist is quite well.

Great success this afternoon, Trio going splendidly, & Grieg also, I think I played exceptionally well. They liked both Tschai & Grieg, of course they dont understand clapping here, mostly delicate old ladies & gouty masculines, but one can tell they appreciate all the same. The Blüthner is very fine, easy going & rich in tone.

After concert, went to meet Mrs Heymann who is much better. She is sorry she did not see you in London.

There is more music in people like Heymann, & Salter, (the 'cellist in our Trio) than in whole universes of "stars"[;] these simply orchestral & ensemble players are quite after my heart.

Frieda is delightful, a strange mixture of animal undevelopedness & human intelligence, most amusing.

The booklets arrived in time & have been distributed among the Bath newspapers. We must see if they are willing to learn from London.

Things look sort of crowded, the work here, Savage on Saturday, Lowrey on 14th, Tschai on 18th. Newman toward, however, it all tends the right way.[3]

Poor little mumm, guess she thought a good energetic thunk when all those letters tumbled in, Josephs, d'Erlanger's, Grainger's.

Here, all seems holiday-like, despite 2 hours Trio-rehearsing last evening & ditto this morning

Yr loving
Percy
[Regards from all here]

4   TO ROSE GRAINGER
[Postcard]
Feb. 5. 1902.

10 Dunsford Pl.
[Bath.]

Concerto went without hitch, Heymann very satisfied, we are looking forward to tomorrow. I should like to play with orch all my life, it sounds so ripping, the wood-wind buzzing & purring right near one. I find I have in no way overated the lovely tone-quality of wood-wind.

One very nice notice is out already, will send when others are added.[4]

We eat Brazil-nuts all day.

No letter from you as yet today.

The orchestra here is very good.

Fondest love
Percy.

5   TO ERNEST THESIGER[5]
[Postcard. Mid-1902?]
"1903?"

[No address given]

Hard lines.

Cant after all, ole Man.

Sudden & devastating Concert worries call for a wretched afternoon of rush.

Pity me & us.

I should so liked to have sat, as you know. Not my fault

Your P.

Marginal notes:

3 Grainger played at the Savage Club, London, on 8 February and at Mrs Frank Lowrey's "at home" on the 14th. On 18 February he played the Tchaikovsky B♭ minor Piano Concerto at a vocal concert with orchestra given by the American singer Madame Eleanor Cleaver and Mr Ingo Simon. The Cleaver concert was managed by Alice E. Joseph. The Newman reference may reflect Grainger's ambition to play at Queen's Hall, of which Robert Newman (1858–1926) was then the manager. His ambition was fulfilled on 17 August 1904, when he played the Tchaikovsky Concerto at a Queen's Hall Promenade Concert, with the Queen's Hall Orchestra under Henry Wood.

4 The *Bath Chronicle* of 6 February 1902 reported that a somewhat meagre audience had attended the chamber concert, Grainger's performance having nonetheless evoked its most cordial and enthusiastic applause. The *Chronicle*'s critic was unreserved in his praise, predicting that Grainger ". . . should assuredly take a most prominent position, in the course of time, in the select company of our great pianists". On 13 February, the *Chronicle* reported that a fairly numerous audience had come to hear Grainger's performance at the afternoon symphony concert, and that he was accorded a capital reception.

5 Ernest Thesiger (1879–1961), actor, author, artist and, in Grainger's words, "an undeveloped but gifted composer". He met Grainger at Queen's House, home of Mrs Frank Lowrey, probably at her "at home" on 14 February 1902. In 1902 Thesiger made a fine chalk drawing of Grainger, "the best of all, in PG's opinion", said Grainger.

6 TO H. BALFOUR GARDINER
Feb. 20. 1902.

31, Gordon Place,
Kensington, W.

Dear Gardiner

I cannot refrain from again letting you know what a great impression yr Quintette made upon me.[6]

Scott's prophesies, are again to prove true.

Although I always admired you compositionally, yet I really did not reckon that you could create such a style as that of Quintette.

I must say I do envy you when you awake to the great worth of this compo, we all of us have only one style-creating work (each his MAG, his SONG OF SOL) & one great unique joy when we realize its importance.[7]

Won't Scott dance when he hears it?

For God's (& my) sake, *do* finish it quickly, I long to see it complete in its formal glory.

I never looked for a great formal power in you, but must now own that I am eternally convinced. You certainly have heroicly cut the painter.

If you want to make me *quite* happy only get same performed, to hear such a splendid manifestation of modern form would be a treat.

Please excuse my rambling on like this, but I cannot really refrain from stating how *quite* struck I am.

Do hurry up and finish it, & keep it up to its present excellence, is it not ripping to think that you have arove?

And to think that you are further a budding Tenor![8]

Yrs
Percy. G.

Am looking forward to MOTHER CAREY on Thurs.
An especial favor — If you have not decided to dedicate the Quintette to Scott would it be too much to ask you to concede that honor to me?

7 TO ROSE GRAINGER
July. 8. 1902.

[Newbury]

How terrible is everything amateur, please excuse the foregoing [see sketch overleaf].

So the calamity has occured, as I said to Gard, "look yr last", because I shall never feel quite so cheery as heretofore with the burden of age upon me.[9] I am extremely disappointed with my work, I have realized little that I hoped to have accomplished by this age. My technique indeed, is perhaps even more than I looked forward to, it is my only compositional consolation.

It is a shame you are not down here, it is quite ideal, dear little cottage with crooked stairs & much head bumping, rather like a ship. The food is beyond compare & the sun is quite ripping. Of course it wld not do for long it is too comforting, consoling, satisfying. Last night we slept out, G. & myself. We toted down our bedding onto the grass & turned in. I never remember such a restful sleep, I read only the other day that sleeping out is the most effective nerve-cure.

The sky was simply glorious last night, "psalmy" Gardiner said. "The firmament showeth the glory" that sort of element, & this morning equally lovely, one only appreciates the blending of natural contrasts (such as transition from night to morning) when out of doors.[10]

Yr dear letter just arrived. I don't like that Morrison man somehow. But the Australian cutting interests me considerably, & *pleases* me more.[11]

6 A four-movement String Quintet in C minor by H. Balfour Gardiner was first performed at a Broadwood Concert in London on 5 November 1903. Grainger, being on tour in Australia, did not attend that performance. The manuscript of the work does not survive. In 1936, at Grainger's request and somewhat against his will, Gardiner reworked one movement of the original quintet as String Quintet Movement in C minor, in which form Grainger arranged several performances. In 1949, again somewhat against Gardiner's will, Grainger edited and had published by Schott & Co., London, a version of the work capable of performance by string quintet or string orchestra. The work is dedicated to Grainger. It was, Grainger wrote later, "a perfect example of the idiom of the day". Gardiner never seems to have shared Grainger's enthusiasm for the work.

7 Cyril Scott's *Magnificat* (1899) and Grainger's *Song of Solomon* (1900).

8 H. Balfour Gardiner was a foundation member of the "choral meetings" which Grainger started and held more or less regularly to try through his own and other composers' choruses. The original membership comprised fellow composers and a few amateurs.

9 Grainger was 20 on 8 July 1902. He was visiting H. Balfour Gardiner at Newbury. According to the *British Australasian* of 24 July 1902, Cyril Scott was also there.

10 Probably a reverberation of the words from Haydn's oratorio *The Creation*, as rendered in the standard English translation, "The heavens are telling the glory of God, the wonder of his works displays the firmament".

11 As Rose's letter does not survive, this reference remains unelucidated.

12 The concert on 8 October was in the Albert Hall, Sheffield. Relaying the good news of Grainger's success to his compatriots, the *British Australasian* of 16 October quoted the critic of the *Sheffield Independent*: "Percy Grainger is a young Australian with a future. He played the Toccata and Fugue with the taste of the matured expert rather than the modest student, the Fugue being brilliantly interpreted. Schumann's Romance in F [# — encore] was given with all possible grace and elegance".

13 Adelina (Adela) Juana Maria Patti (1843–1919), Italian soprano. She had married her third husband, Baron Rolf Cederström, in 1899. Other members of the concert party were baritone Charles Santley (1834–1922), tenor Gregory Hast (1862–1944), violinist Alice Liebmann and the American contralto Mabel Braine who, like Grainger, was making her debut tour of the provinces. The tour was managed by Percy Harrison (1846–1917) of Birmingham, Patti's long-time manager and a well-known concert promoter. The accompanist was F. T. Watkis. Grainger's repertoire comprised the Bach-Tausig Toccata and Fugue in D minor and Cyril Scott's *An English Waltz*. With Alice Liebmann he played a violin and piano duet, the Allegro from the Sonata in C minor Op. 45 by Grieg. Grainger did not appear at any of Patti's London concerts

Everything in it argues well. Nothing could be better than that the weak helplessness & selfish muddling of the male (in business matters) should be replaced by the more enduring energy & strongerwilled practibility of the female. Men make fine dreamers, inventors, theorists, scientists, fighters, good at all things *pleasant* to work at, but of *no immeadiate returns*, but women are much more capable of living-earning because of their capacity for work which *is* of *immeadiate use & advantage* to the worker, women I think work better with an eye to reward men create careless of reward. Besides should wage-earning (to a certain extent) fall womanwards, more than anything it wld give her her "rights" & gain her a respect that nothing else could. It may also eventually tend to level the types, & bring into closer sympathy the activities of the 2 sexes.

But what I like best is the Australian's agnosticism, and still better, his lack of a *code of honor*, a general code of honor is too fatal for words, it keeps this country back more than one realizes.

Funny, I feel no older today than yesterday, altho I obviously ought to. Am going to think a lot about Mum today.

Love from us all.
Percy.

8 TO ROSE GRAINGER
Oct. 9. 1902
4.30.

Station Hotel
Newcastle-on-Tyne
[In the train, Newcastle–Aberdeen]

Last night was a howling success.[12] Patti heard my Bach from her private room, & came up afterwards & was charming.[13]

Miss Liebman & Hast believe I have really caught her fancy, they say as a rule she ignores pianists.

She also made Harrison *solemnly promise* to put me onto one of her London concerts, he says he cl'nt just yet awhile, having already fixed the nearcoming ones, but says he certainly will eventually.

She promised me she will see I am put on.

I had a talk with her & also with the Baron, with the latter about Grimm's Law, Swedish, Danish, Anglosaxon, Esais Tegnir, Andersen, Björnson, etc, etc. He seems exceedingly cultured & nice, over 6 feet, a regular strapper, talks like Fornander somewhat.[14]

Great enthusiasm after the Waltz, — well earned encore.

Hast is a funny mixture. Voice in speaking generally like both Alec Lane & Dr Fenner (funny combination) but occasionally just like Menpes. To look at somewhat resembling Roosevelt, with occasionally movements of the head like Kwast.[15]

Sent you 2 of "Sheffield Tel" this morning.

Sheffield expenses came to about £1/3 so I have over £4 left.

Yr dear works, hank-sack, tie-sack, etc, are excellently practical & keep things in great order. I pack carefully & things look allright. Harrison & I are great friends, he says the *personal element* weighs heavily with him in the choice of his artists.

Sheffield speech wld please you, the Hs reliable, every syllable distinct, *never* have I heard such clear (but not loud) talking, quite a Scotch sound about it occasionally, though it is only in the *Midlands*. Here of course the speech is *quite* Scotch, ripping. In the train to here hard at work on Klimsch's letter.[16]

I can tell you last night made me very happy Patti being so nice, just you keep strong, you will view enormous successes yet. Practised 2 hours yesterday.

14 Esaias Tegnér (1782–1846), one of the greatest national poets of Sweden, whose works include the long narrative poem *Fritjofs Saga*, and see note 10, 1901. Sigurd Fornander, Swedish masseur, friend and "sweetheart" of Rose Grainger in Frankfurt. Grainger supported him financially from 1923, when he lost all his savings with the collapse of the German Mark, to his death in 1945.

15 Alec Lane, son of Zebina Lane of Western Australia (see letter 27 and note 2, 1904). At this time he was studying at the Royal College of Science. He also did recitations and developed a bass singing voice. Both Mrs Lane and Alec sang in the first performance of Grainger's choruses at the Queen's House Manuscript Music Society on 28 May 1903. Dr Fenner, brother-in-law of Grainger's Melbourne friend, the surgeon and amateur pianist Robert Hamilton Russell. Mortimer Menpes (1859–1938), painter and etcher, born in South Australia, resident in London from 1878. A good friend to the Graingers, who spent Christmas with him and his wife in 1902. Theodore Roosevelt (1858–1919), 26th President of the United States of America (1901–09). James Kwast (1852–1927), Grainger's piano teacher in Frankfurt.

16 Grainger worked on his letter to Karl Klimsch (1841–1926), his friend and informal composition teacher in Frankfurt, from the latter part of 1902 until early February 1904. Written in English, it was a massive epistle: a total statement on the state of Grainger's art, his view of music in general and his plans for his own compositions in particular. It survives only in draft form.

17 Lilith (Mrs Frank) Lowrey (d. 1911), intimate friend and early patron of Grainger. As President of the Queen's House Manuscript Music Society, she provided the opportunity for the first performance of five of Grainger's choruses on 28 May 1903. She also took some lessons from Grainger. Rose disapproved of her intimacy with Percy; her name disappears as a regular element in the correspondence by the end of 1904.

18 Nellie Melba, born Helen Porter Mitchell (1861–1931), Australian soprano and long-time family friend of the Graingers. Her attendance at Grainger's first solo recital in London on 29 October 1901 and her favourable comments on his talent were reported in the press. Her influence socially opened many doors for Grainger in the early London years. Dyer is unidentified.

19 Charles Santley had joined the Catholic church in about 1880. Sir Walter Scott (1771–1832), Scottish Romantic poet and novelist. Grainger took the tune and words for his 1904 setting of *Lord Maxwell's Goodnight*, and the texts for his compositions *The Twa Corbies* (1903) and *The Lads of Wamphray* (1904) from Scott's *Minstrelsy of the Scottish Border* (1802–03).

20 A selection of Grainger's favourite English-language authors: Walt Whitman (1819–92), Rudyard Kipling (1865–1936), Francis Bret Harte (1839–1902) and Mark Twain (real name Samuel Langhorne Clemens, 1835–1910). Grainger set several of Kipling's verses and took inspiration for his *Marching Song of Democracy* from Whitman. Both Hast and Santley had toured in the United States, Santley having also toured in Australia.

21 The *Newcastle Daily Chronicle* of 11 October reported that the Town Hall had been crowded for the Harrison concert, and that Grainger's contributions, including his encore, Grieg's "I Ola-dalom" from Op. 66, were accorded the heartiest applause.

Nice letter from Mrs L[owrey].[17] Cld not see me off, was, & is still, in bed very off color — will send her crits myself. I suppose you get them all right from Durrants, 4 Birmingh. papers, 2 Sheffield "*The Sh Daily Tel*" & "*The Sh Independant*".

Passed Durham an hour ago, the prettiest town I have ever seen quite ideal, archaic, & all the rest. Glorious cathedral & castle towering out of a view of fog & smoke.

Have a nice tramcar ride to take you in Sheffield when we are there together

Love
Percy.

Please remember me to the Wests, & tell 'im that I posponed being shaved by other 'ands as long as I cld, until this morning.

9 TO ROSE GRAINGER   Palace Hotel,
Oct. [11] 1902   Aberdeen.

Dear Mummy

I wonder how that letter (or card) of mine failed to reach, for, ever since I left I have written every day, posting after performance on concert-nights, & in the afternoons other days. Also I send papers early in the morning on days after concert. Dont forget to let me know if the missing card or letter turns up. Have asked Harrison re Austr tour, he said "of course, *then we will shift our affair a year forward*", as much as to say that he intends engaging me again. You certainly must not dream that I cld fail to write, you can be quite certain if a day passes with no writing that it is a postal error; you must also not forget that as we get further North that the delivery needs much more time. (almost a day's difference between here & Newcastle.)

Patti is a sweet nature I think, she spoke so kindly about Melba, of her wonderful voice & beautiful style, apparently quite devoid of jeolously — ("there are all so great" — à la Dyer.)[18]

Her husband & I have long talks on literature, he is going to get Walt Whitman on my recommendation, he had never heard of him.

A very nice, clever giant, very dark with dark *blue* eyes, Irish-looking.

Funny the difference between generation & generation. Santley (to tell the truth good-natured but fairly stupid, like most "streng" [German: strong] catholics — I have seen Elgar's "Dream of Gerontius" today, words by Cardinal Newman, so speak with warmth) loves Walter Scott, loathes Kipling, can see no patheticism in Mark Twain, looks askance at my occasional Lemonade, says with a wink "that he'll get into it later on allright",[19] Gregory Hast, adores Walt, Kippy, Bret Harte, Mark Twain (to much the same extent that I do) & discources on the wisdom of no-drink-no-smoke.[20]

Well, you think you are glum alone, but think of me my despondancy is at present too terrific for words. My dear — some men are passable, but you are the only woman that überhaupt [German: overall] *exists,* good god to think how many centuries you are in advance, quite dumbing to contemplate. "Best result of the best century — so far."

Splendid success last night, but the audience in Newcastle quite Scotch. Whole rows of people not clapping at all, absolutely motionless — yet they are enjoying it hard.[21]

Since I learn that Durrants do not send I shall be even more careful about sending you, & myself keeping, good press-notices. I have at least 1 of each

(3 & 4 of some) with me that I keep to show people if necessary or to show Scott.

Behind me are two Scotchies, discussing with clear firm voices, heavy subjects with most un-English seriousness. They are talking on "Scotch-up-bringing", on literature & other weighty matters. The speech alone as one progresses North proclaims the superior, stronger race. No single word indistinct, all decided, certain, orderly, crisp. They are not altogether lovely, however, that I must own, with the exception of some ripping bearded-anglo-saxon-farmer-types (Walt-Whitmanny only a little harder & narrower) which quite impressed me.

Money order to hand allright.

The scenery (from 9 to 6 in the train — what larx!) very fine in parts, huge, miles-long rivers, crossed by giant bridges, gorsed, tufted, browngrassed hillocks, crisply-treed (bunchy-shaped) wooded hills, & strong dark rocks & red earth. But this (the East) side is *NOTHING* to the West, look at the map & you'll see the reason, the strong formation faces Atlantic-wards, & slopes down to weakness to the East. (The same in Scandinavia)

You're the only person one can talk to, I am simply ill from for a week not being able to "say my opinion", to belch, swear, & hold a serious conversation. The worst thing about the English is their unseriousness. *Not one* sensible sentence has been uttered all this week, & yet, our lot are not all utter fools.

The waste of time on drivel is to me boresome. They come to a town, 1st thing off to Opera, (I am sick of it but dont want appear disagreeable) or somewhere to *amuse*. When I see the usual, it seems to me that after all I may accomplish something before I'm done notwithstanding that am already 20. Most people lack principles, aims, intensity, reason-for-existance.

All the above will give you to understand that *I* at any rate am *on the right path*, "ikke sand?" (nit wahr?) [Danish & German (dialect) idiom: don't you think?]

Hast is really a decent chap.

There is no mistake about cards & letters, they go to you every evening, & will until this show brings up.

(Just remembered, Santley hates both America & Australia, Hast has been telling me good Americanisms by the hour. The worst sign is if people dont like U.S.A.)

You & I will have fun when I wheel you thro' this country, this land dont suffer from "the marks" hardly any.

Please dont do yrself harm over false alarms.

Dearest love
Percy.

10 TO ROSE GRAINGER
Monday. 11.30 a.m.
Oct. 13 1902

Palace Hotel,
Aberdeen.

So sorry about yr headache, don't strain on the copying out, it hurries not.

Just had a good practise at *Marr Wood & Co*, (on a lovely Blütner) they have got my photo ghastly-ly reproduced in the "Evening Express" (Aberdeen) Oct 11th, & big bills are outside the window. Will send "Ev. Exp." with other notices day-after-tomorrow.

14

The difference between the reckless rolic of a Midland manufacturing town & careful Hieland Aberrdeen. Got shaved at Sheffield by a youth who looked out of the window as he came to the touchy spots, smelt vilely, braged of his having shaving everywhere in Sheffield, "at the Hotel" etc, etc, not overclean and bad shave. Aberdeen, careful quiet little man, perfect work, no talk, no cuts, no side. You wld really like this place, supernaturally clean. In the English Hotels German waiters, but up here, the rich native breed.

We will have great fun reading the Wells book together.[22] But even he (at least in this book) does not go as far forward in thought as I do, but still — very praiseworthy for a European.

Dear old Sandby will be "farting" across the ocean by now I suppose[23]

Last night the 2 girls & myself played fool's tricks until about 1 oclock, the usual tour-nonsenses, pajama-up-sewings, brushes in bed, etc, etc. However altho' we 3 sat up 3 hours for the men to go to bed, our part of the performance was so hashed that Hast made quite a success of it instead of us. It was easy to see that my 2 "pardners" had had no window-educations, will tell you of all these nonsenses anon.

If only you were along & the other lot vacant this Hoteling-it wld be bliss, I like it all except meals, I can't abide the finicky fare.

N.B. When copying out Klimsch's letter & you come to the end of *Form*, before going to *Vocalism* insert the title *Sound-producers treated seperately* thus: . . . end of *Form*

Sound-producers treated seperately
   Vocalism.
. . . (vocalism etc)

No letter so far today unfortunately, I am sending this off this *morning* but tomorrows wont leave until *night* so as to give you concert news so dont fuss at non-receival.

Fondest love
Percy

P.S. Let me know if you receive some nos of *The Birmingham Dart* which have just ordered.
Newcastle expenses about £1/3/6d.
Write to Durrant to send all papers I send you.

11 TO ROSE GRAINGER   [PM Aberdeen]
[Postcard. PM 15 October 1902]

Morning

Have written Miss Wolfe, (Harrison will send her 2 tickets) what time I will call. (Friday after lunch) Will see Affleck after concert, written him card of my successes. (Harrison will send him a tick.) Will call on Cairds Sunday afternoon.[24]

You have no idea how simple it is playing on tour, no anxiety, one worries about nothing. Santley treated us to a sumptous repast last night.

---

22 H. G. Wells, *Tales of Space and Time*, a collection of five short stories published in 1899. Gregory Hast had loaned the book to Grainger.

23 "At that time [1902] Herman's English was very funny, much of it being a word-for-word translation from Danish . . . On a voyage to USA at that time he asked a young lady passenger 'Are you having a good fart across the ocean?' (fart being Danish for journey or voyage)." Percy Grainger, *Anecdotes*, 1953.

24 Miss Hermie Wolfe, daughter of the Glasgow oculist Dr J. R. Wolfe who for some years was resident in Melbourne and was surgeon-oculist to Lord Hopetoun, the Governor of Victoria. Grainger dedicated his *Verses from Jungle Book* (1898–99) to her. N. J. Affleck and Dr and Mrs Caird were Edinburgh friends of the Graingers.

I feel all the better for a good stuff but the tigouring tells on the rest this morning. In the middle of all the bibbing, punning, gormandizing, & artificiality generally broke out the squirl of a bagpipe in the street. It made me shiver for ½ an hour, such a contrast, crude primitive hillman's life, & the semi-barbarous-civilized weaklings around me.

Got card & letter this morning. Did a lot of Kl's letter yesterday. His epistle is quite charming, read the parts out aloud you marked.

After concert. Never played the Bach so well, one recall. Grieg went splendidly. Scott encore 2nd recall.

Fondest love

12 TO ROSE GRAINGER
Oct. 15. 1902.

Central Station Hotel,
Glasgow.

Dearest Mother.

Aberdeen expenses £2/4/odd. Cheap for 4 days.
Lovely piano there last night & I never played better.[25]
They are getting to like me on tour. I play them Folksongs occasionally. I played some of them the Sch[ubert]. Tausig "Marche Militaire" in the Hall yesterday, which they seemed to like. Miss Liebman says that Harrison has told her that I am the best pianist he has had for some time. She says, as regards her experience of these Patti tours, that she has never been with a pianist that has taken so well. This may or may not be, I hope it is so.

I have never received more real joy from praise (altho always pleasant) than from the Aberdeen Hall manager this morning, when I called for some music left behind. A dear old bearded man, in broad Scotch, said he must really thank me for the treat last night, that he had seldom enjoyed piano playing so much, etc, etc, that Paderewski had played at Aberdeen only a few days ago, & that he liked me every bit as well & went into details, (evidently of some musical knowledge) — he also said that just after Paddy having been there, my reception was the more to be thankful for — (so said the manager at the Hotel, & at the music-shop too)[26] I have never had such sincere sounding praise, quite bucked me up. Have got the photo from music shop, the one used for printing they will send on to you.

Miss Liebman is awfully sweet & kind to me, I cannot understand why people all take care of me in such a nice manner.

She having overheard Miss Braine asking Patti for a photo is going to see that I get one too. She played *simply magnificently* last night, such a tone & glissando, just like a man's playing. She will lend me her violin dayly for me to practise on.

Harrison wld much like a photo of mine, I have asked him.

Our train was very late getting into Glasgow this after, big wind storm, therefore I am afraid you will receive yr papers later than usual. Tomorrow yr letter will be posted late again, because of concert. Am going to see [H.A.] Seligmann.

Dearest mummy, what Larx when I get home.

Fondest love from
Percy.

Sent a batch of papers to Mrs Lowrey.

25 The concert, 14 October, was in the Music Hall, Aberdeen.

26 Ignacy Jan Paderewski (1860–1941), Polish pianist possessed, according to the *Oxford Companion to Music*, of a dazzling technique, a romantic personality, high interpretative qualities and an amazing head of hair. Grainger was to be frequently compared to Paderewski, particularly in the early American years.

13 TO ROSE GRAINGER
[18 October 1902]
12 o'clock

The Palace Hotel
Edinburgh

27 Mathilde Marchesi
(1821–1913), German mezzo-
soprano and singing teacher. Her
many famous pupils included both
Melba and Ada Crossley. The
critic of the *Scotsman* indeed
proved chary, commenting,
". . . Mr Percy Grainger, whose
shock of sandy hair was obviously
modelled after the pianist whom
the Parisian ladies used to call
'petit Litz' [*sic*], but whose
playing, in spite of many merits of
technique, especially in the
extremes of pianissimo and
fortissimo, was too mechanical to
be inspiring". At the conclusion of
the Harrison–Patti tour, Rose
extracted the best of the critiques
and had them published in a
booklet. From Edinburgh she
chose the more favourable review
from the *Evening News*.

28 John Kirkhope, amateur
musician and conductor, born at
Edinburgh in 1844. In 1881 he had
established a choir which was
regarded as one of the best in
Scotland.

29 Ada Jemima Crossley
(1871–1929), Gippsland-born
contralto. Having left Australia in
1894, she was well established in
London when the Graingers
arrived. She was acquainted with
Patti, and had appeared with great
success at Patti's Albert Hall
concert in June 1901. It may well
have been through her that
Grainger secured his engagement
for the Patti tour.

Got a card & letter from you this morning, which I was delighted to get.

Spent a charming afternoon & evening with dear Miss Wolfe yesterday, most enjoyable.

Talked a lot about the dear Mummy, I read her Klimsch's letter.

Came back in the evening & dined with our party which had been to the play. 2 good critiques in Glasgow evening papers, which I am having sent on to you. Met Madame Marchesi who is singing in "Tannhaüser" here, she was delighted to hear of my success, which she said was to be expected. She (Harrison & all say so too) says Edinb. is the coldest audience in the kingdom. That 2 recalls mean great success & that 3 recalls are "the limit". So we must not expect too much here. The critics too are chary, they say.[27]

This morning dear old Santley took me to see Kirkhope, whom he had met yesterday & who had spoken him of me. Santley spoke so sweetly about me, awfully kind of him.[28]

Poor Mabel Braine. When she started this "stunt" (American for "tour") she was fairly tee-total, but has droped that & swills & gorges like the rest, with the result that she was half sick (in Glasgow concert) in the middle of singing "*The Lost Chord*", however she strugled on bravely, will give you all partics verbally. She and Miss Liebman want my photo. Miss Braine likes the Frankfort one, so if we have some left of these horrors, I will give her the Frankf. one in my possesion, so write me if I may. I will of course give Patti one, & will try to get one of hers. As I go round, before leaving I call at music shops & get the photos they have been exhibiting.

Harrison said yesterday that he had received a letter from "Chummy" (Ada Crossley) in which she wrote very sweet things about me.[29]

Our "proffesional" names stand as follows:

Daddy	(Percy H.)
Ally	(Miss Liebman)
Baby	(Braine)
Gory	(Hast)
Joffy	(Watkis)
Kangaroo	(me)

My frockcoat is perfectly all right (3 cheers for Mow) am wearing it now to un-crease it.

Must be off now to practise.

Old Smiths blather will be attended to.

After concert.

Well, they are right, this town is just ice. *No encore* today, but 2 recalls after Scott & quite a good recall after our Grieg. Of course it would have been easy to have given an encore on the 2nd recall, but Harrison says there is no need to make oneself cheap.

Patti was again *adorable* to me today. She is going to give me a photo of (perhaps two as I dont much care for the bigger one) herself, she says she feels as if she is my mother. She said about 4 times "I simply love that boy", & she said — "What a glorious carreer you have before you", etc, etc, etc.

Am calling on Miss Wolfe tomorrow morning again, Cairds & friends of Thesiger (who has written me) in afternoon. By the way, Miss Liebman has a career before her too.

Love.
Percy.

P.S. Harrison has promised me to hear Sandby when he comes over
All nice things to the Wests. Love from the Wolfe girls.

14 TO ROSE GRAINGER
Oct. 21. 1902
Morning.

Great Northern Victoria Hotel,
Bradford

Dearest Mummy.

Got letter this morning. Have just written a p.card to Miss Fussell giving her the exact title of the Fantasia.[30] Also a card from Scott who has fixed up the Manchester Guardian man, so that I have nothing to do in the matter.

Night before last, I grew quite sentimental about my maw, couldn't get to sleep for thinking about what a waste of time life was when away from her, how much superior she was to every other living human (that is — known to me) etc, etc. There really is noone like you, you know. You are the only basis of my life, altho others variagate it prettily enough, I allow.

My aloneness will be something good & large when without you.

There was a young lady named Maud
Who eating & drinking abhorred,
When asked out to dine she'd politely decline —
But in the back-parlor — **MY GAUD!**

There was a young lady of Wilts
Who walked up to Scotland on stilts
When they said "Oh! how shocking! to show so much
   stocking"
She answered — "Well — what about kilts?"

Now I must hie me to the Hall.

Just before concert.
Hast said something nice today, when I was rehearsing in the Hall. I was playing the IRISH FOLKSONG & he said "You are the only one of the great players (ha! ha!) I have heard, who can do that" meaning play simple things with expression. "Most people when they get a technique (ha! ha!) like yrs, forget how to play with feeling."[31]

Poor Patti has a frightful cold & cannot sing tonight, it is doubtful whether she will be able to tomorrow either.[32]

Harrison takes it *simply grandly*, just as jovial & hearty as ever, altho' it means an enormous loss to him, as he will have to give a concert (another one) with Patti in it *free* to his subscribers. Also, the same thing happened here last year, which makes things worse. He is really a model of kindness, ordnung[s]kraft [German: capacity for order], & selfcontrol. A dear man, one is glad he has got on as he has

After concert. Just fancy, the Bach encored! (3rd recall) This enclipses everything. Gave the little bright Scott which was peculiarly composed for a Bradford man (Golden).[33] Waltz encored 2nd recall. Goodnight *dearie*.

30 Grainger assisted the cellist Miss May Fussell at her concert on 27 November 1902. The "Fantasia" was probably the Chopin Fantasie Op. 49. Cyril Scott arranged for Grainger to meet Arthur Johnstone, music critic of the *Manchester Guardian* until his untimely death in 1905. The aim of the meeting was to secure, through Johnstone, an engagement with Richter.

31 Grainger's first setting of *Irish Tune from County Derry*, then called *Irish Folk-Song*, for five-part mixed chorus, was made at Waddesdon between 30 September and 2 October 1902. It was one of the five choruses given their first performance at the Queen's House Manuscript Music Society on 28 May 1903.

32 The *Yorkshire Daily Observer* of 22 October, reporting Harrison's apology, informed its readers that ". . . Madame Patti — being but human after all, though a Baroness and a prima donna — had fallen prey to the malodorous and malevolent influences of new paint in her hotel in Glasgow, and yesterday morning it was found that she could not possibly sing with due credit to herself". Her place was taken by one of Santley's pupils, soprano Carrie Siviter.

33 Grainger's encore was the third of Cyril Scott's *Three Frivolous Pieces*, dedicated to Herbert Golden.

34 John Harry Grainger (1855–1917), Percy's father, since March 1897 Chief Architect to the Government of Western Australia. His birthday was 30 November. The *Manchester Guardian* critic wrote at length and most favourably about Grainger's contribution to the concert. Of Grainger's solos he wrote, "In the performance of these difficult pieces Mr Grainger showed striking maturity of style and also very remarkable technical power". Rose was pleased enough with this comment to include it in the selection of Press Opinions printed in the programme of Grainger's solo recital at St James Hall on 19 June 1903.

35 Whether or not this particular plan was fulfilled, Miss Liebmann remained friends with the Graingers, and took part, with Grainger and Herman Sandby, in the performance of Cyril Scott's Sextet Op. 26, for three violins, viola, cello and piano, given at the Queen's House Manuscript Music Society concert of 28 May 1903. On 1 July 1903 Rose Grainger introduced her to the concert agency of E. L. Robinson.

36 Percy's concern for his appearance is reflected in Cyril Scott's letter to Rose Grainger of 29 October 1902, "He is at present dressing I think & does not arrive down much before 12 as a rule since he takes two hours to dress. He is a funny boy to have in the house because there is always such a rush for everything. He would rather go without his dinner than take less than 50 minutes to put on his dress clothes".

37 Ernest W. Gilchrist. From the beginning of 1907, apparently formalising a previously informal activity, he ran a concert agency which specialised in arranging public and private ("at home") entertainments. He also gave "at homes" for the purpose of bringing hostesses and artists together.

15 TO ROSE GRAINGER

Oct. 24. 02.

[129 Canning Street Liverpool]

Morning

My little Mumm seems quite convinced that I gad about lots before concerts, which, however, is not the case, with the exception of Glasgow, where it was inevitable. In Edinb. I saw noone except our party on the day of the concert, & at Manchester I was *most quiet*, I make a point of being so.

As to encores, one has a different conception of them not being at the performance. Harrison determines whether one gives encores or not, he stands at the steps going onto platform, & regulates things according to whether it is late or not. Thus *he* is never impressed with one's giving an encore. He never lets instrumentalists take one under *2* recalls (generally 3) whereas singers take one at *one* recall, so you must not think one pleases less when you hear of no encore.

At Newcastle (the concert I suppose having gone off quickly) he made me take encore on 2nd recall whereas at Manchester (for the same applause) he said "*bow*", whereas again, Miss Liebman he made take encore the same evening on 2nd recall, so you see no importance is attached to it really, the only thing that matters is the general impression of having "taken" or not, & that I think I can safely say I have done almost equally everywhere.

Two short but satisfactory Evening paper notices have come from Manchester which I will send you tomorrow with this town's crits. Mr Hast thinks I played best of all in Manchester. You would be surprized how much more evenly (how much more at one level) I have played thro'out this tour, it is the Waddesdon practising showing up, I suppose.

Affleck says the Glasgow man at Athaneaum is the 1st man in Glasgow Sent a nice birthday letter to father, with photo & M. Guardian crit.[34]

Liebman & Hast were here yesterday, liked the house, & were taken with Cyril's compositions, I think. Miss Liebman & I are going to play together in London, & when Sandby comes, Trios, her tone will be big enough for us I think.[35]

I have run out of visiting cards. There are not any in my trunks packed away anywhere, are there?

No need buy evening shirt, have clean (not worn) one left for this evening. Trousers I keep "in der Reihe" [German: in correct order] by putting under bed.[36]

Wrote Gilchrist today.[37]

So good of you to do all that copying, *please* dont tire yrself therewith. I have, unfortunately found no time for work of any kind just lately.

Santley is going to give me signed photo when he gets back to town.

Are you not immensely pleased re Guardian critiques? Everyone told me I could expect a rare slating therein. Have spoken Harrison re E. L. Robinson. He said "only fair to Joseph to make 1st engage thro' her, but that debt being paid off, will *in future* arrange for you thro' Robinson". (He always speaks as if he will have me again.) I have written Smith to that effect. Have also written Crook thanking him.[38]

Cyril's place here is 1st class, style perfect, & furniture that he has designed is simple & strong. Nice Lechter & other pics, of course the whole thing wld give me the Fantods to live in, but I appreciate it as an excellent realisation of *his* ideals.[39]

This eve after conc supper at Mrs Fletcher's, where I think I will see Schiever. Tomorrow C.'s string quartet (which I do not yet know) will be performed for my edification.[40]

C is trying to arrange that I meet Johnstone ("M.G." critic) after all. *Hope* I shall be able to return to you (dearie) by Tuesday. Shall come to

Aylesbury, *get train from there to* **Wad. Manor**, meet me *there*. Do not know train yet.[41]

Dearest love

_____

Latest concert news:—
1st class reception.
Dined with Patti after (have her signed photo) & then on to Mrs Fletcher's so this is of neccesity late

Love.

P.S. Do you mean by the Birmingham "people" the blookes I called upon?
Halford was away,[42] & the 2 music shops were civil & informed me that no concerts were ever given in B if they were they didnt pay, they said the concert-business was (*Percy*) " *'arrasin'* ".
Just wrote Mrs Lane, Lowrey, & Thesiger.
Am getting warm friends with our lot

Mind you study the alto parts of the choruses. *Darling Mum*

38 Earlier in 1902 Percy had reached a "very advantageous" arrangement with the concert agency of E. L. Robinson. Arthur Smith, a member of this firm, arranged Grainger's solo recital on 19 June 1903. Crook is unidentified.

39 Melchior Lechter (1865–1937), German illustrator. He was a member of the Berlin group led by Stefan George and he illustrated books by George. Cyril Scott had been a member of George's circle during his time in Frankfurt.

40 Grainger commented to his mother on 26 October that the piece was "Antiquated now, but fine in Klang [German: sound] in parts". Ernst Schiever (1844–1915), German violinist, based in Liverpool from 1878. Leader of Richter's orchestra for nearly thirty years.

41 Cyril Scott to Rose Grainger, 25 October 1902, "I am trying to do everything I can for him but it is awfully difficult since he wants to leave so soon. I have really hardly seen him[,] all day yesterday he wrote letters & then rushed off to his fellow tourists & alas had to join them instead of coming to the supper Mrs Fletcher arranged for him, however he turned up later". Grainger extended his stay, meeting various people of influence in Liverpool's musical life (with an eye to possible future engagements) including Arthur Johnstone on 29 October, playing his compositions and hearing those of his friends.

42 George John Halford (b. 1858), organist, pianist and conductor. From 1897 to 1907 he gave a series of orchestral concerts in Birmingham known as The Halford Concerts Society concerts. These were the only orchestral concerts in Birmingham, the orchestra being part-amateur, part-professional. Grainger made his debut at the Halford concerts on 21 November 1905, playing the Tchaikovsky B♭ minor Piano Concerto.

1903

In the summer of 1903 Grainger returned briefly to Germany: from 22 June to 16 July he took piano lessons with the great Italian virtuoso Ferruccio Busoni (1866–1924) in Berlin. The invitation to study with Busoni had followed his meeting with Grainger in London in the preceding February.

Although Percy wrote to his mother every day, as was his custom when away from home, his letters do not survive. Rose's daily letters to Percy do survive: a regular mixture of admonition, instruction, expressions of and demands for affection, and warnings against Mrs Lowrey, who had followed Grainger to Berlin. Both Rose's and Percy's birthdays occurred while he was away. He was twenty-one, she forty-two. Back in London by 17 July, Grainger was immediately caught up in preparations for his departure for Australia.

16   TO ERNEST THESIGER   14 Lietzenburgerstr.
13, 7th m. 03.   Berlin W.

How tiptop that your show showed up somewhat to yr worthiness, altho' 50 sounds short ratage for one alone of your truck (such as the Sandby likeness that you in me-melting sweetness unbitter the sereness of my having staled to 21's selfownership with.)[1]

See you soon. I home end of this week

Was made much glad to here from Mother you'd been at hers some.

Ever admiring
Percy Grainger

What has not been melting by yr giving of S-drawing is softening away under the showers of B's sweet gifts, photos, books, music, & help.

1 Thesiger wrote to Grainger in early July that his "show" had been very successful, with fifty pounds' worth of sketches sold and several commissions. His birthday present to Percy was his 1903 drawing of Herman Sandby.

At the end of July 1903, Percy and Rose left London for their first return visit to Australia, Percy having been engaged by J. C. Williamson as a member of Ada Crossley's Australasian tour concert party. Their ship, the R.M.S. Omrah, *left Tilbury on 31 July. Calling at the ports of Plymouth, Gibraltar, Marseilles and Naples, and passing through the Suez Canal, the* Omrah *reached Colombo on 24 August.*

17 TO ERNEST THESIGER

R.M.S. "Omrah".

22.8.03

You'd relish to be along of this & we'd relish to have you along.

This is the only kind of living I give a dern for, the heat & the salt wind that slack one, that plans & work & duties give over & one simply lies round & benifits.

Not but that I've been working some, writing on musical matters, a new Kip Chor, a,s,o.[2]

The sights are too ripping, colors — My — & last night phosphorent-jellies to Port, an endless streaming past of nervepinching spasms of lit-brandy-round-Xmas-pudding-color.

There's further a keen clever painter cuss aboard, 25, Australian, & otherwise lucky.

He's going to join the Sing-song when he backs to town next year.

This trip has nowise dissappointed me. I never wish to get off, but'd like to drift round without stop with a cargo of English-speaking friends [with choral practices in the evenings] until a tropical death followed over-gorge of the 11 a.m icecreams.

There's a gorgeous Australian New Birth of the OLDEN GOTH on this.

A loose-kneed, stoop-necked, headforward, slackhanded, diamond-fingered, sprawl-sitting, shuffleslouching, browncolored [hair, eyes, skin, clothes, boots, books] tall swine with a shut mouth opened alone [at seldom intervals] to cuss & brag Australia forth. A scoffer, a snarler, a rank Flesher, yet of such charm that I could die at his heels admiring of him.

A specimen of home, — the handiest cuss at fighting, sharping, & such, I'd bet, strikable

Now, write us soon, & good & long.

Ever

Percy.

Very best wishes from Maw. Also to yours

2 The Kipling Chorus is probably *Danny Deever*, a "rough setting" of which, for men's chorus and instruments, is dated from 29 to 31 July 1903.

The Omrah *arrived at Fremantle on 3 September, proceeding via Adelaide and Melbourne to Sydney, where the Graingers disembarked to await the arrival of the other members of the Ada Crossley Concert Party. After a highly successful tour of the United States, Ada Crossley arrived on 18 September, on the R.M.S.* Sierra, *from San Francisco via New Zealand. Jacques Jacobs, the company's violinist, arrived from London on the R.M.S.* Rome. *Remaining members of the party were W. A. Peterkin, bass, Benno Scherek, musical director, and Edouard Scharf, accompanist. The tour of the eastern States and New Zealand was managed by W. G. Tallis.*

The tour began with five concerts in Sydney between 24 September and 1 October followed by five in Melbourne between 3 and 12 October. Rose left Sydney for Melbourne before the start of the Sydney season, travelling on to Adelaide with the party at the close of the Melbourne season. Following the three concerts in Adelaide, 17 to 20 October, Rose stayed on there until 17 November, visiting her numerous Aldridge relatives, while Percy travelled north to Brisbane, then south to Tasmania and on to New Zealand.

The prevailing mood of this first Crossley Australasian tour was one of high excitement. Cheering and enthusiastic crowds greeted the concert party at railway stations, in concert halls and afterwards, in the streets, culminating in the concert at the Exhibition Building in Melbourne on 2 January 1904, which drew an audience of 15,000–20,000 people. Naturally it was Ada Crossley who, on her first return visit to her homeland, was the centre of attention. It was she who was guest of honour at the civic receptions, she who was the recipient of the wayside and nocturnal serenades, the testimonials, the floral and other tributes. So overcharged was the atmosphere at the concerts that Ada was regularly overcome with emotion and was obliged to leave the platform, particularly when attempting a rendition of Home Sweet Home. So "royally" was she treated that in New Zealand the Otago Daily News of 23 November felt obliged to inform its readers that Miss Crossley was provided by the railway authorities not with the royal car, but with an ordinary car specially fitted up in the same manner as the car in which, when she was in the colony, Madame Melba travelled. Ada was, in Rose's words, a "huge success".

Among the assisting artists, considerable interest attached to Grainger on his reappearance in his homeland. He had left as a boy of 12; he returned as a mature artist. He responded with enthusiasm, relishing his rediscovery of the land and people. As Rose commented, somewhat acidly, to Roger Quilter on 3 November 1903, "Percy has had a giddy time . . . He is in love with Australia & Australians, & is happier than I have ever known him to be. For my part I long to be again quietly settled in our little rooms, this excitement is killing". She wrote again on the same theme on 28 December, "I wonder whether you will find any difference in Percy on his return — he is awfully wild — so happy & 'irrepressible' his playing too has more 'dash' — I think he has more devil in him here, & prefer him English".

CONCERT ITINERARY, 1903–04 AUSTRALASIAN TOUR

SYDNEY	24 September–1 October	5 concerts	Rose in Sydney to c. 22 Sept., then Melbourne.
MELBOURNE	3–12 October Bendigo, 13 October Ballarat, 14 October	5 concerts	
ADELAIDE	17–20 October	3 concerts	Rose and Percy travelled to Adelaide together.
	Warrnambool, 23 October		Rose in Adelaide
(MELBOURNE	Ada's *Elijah* performance, 24 October) Albury, 26 October Wagga, 27 October Goulburn, 28 October		
BRISBANE	31 October–2 November Newcastle, 4 November	2 concerts	
(SYDNEY	Ada's *Elijah* performance, 6 November) Geelong, 9 November Launceston, 11 November		
HOBART	12–13 November	2 concerts	Rose to Melbourne 17 November

NEW ZEALAND	Dunedin, 19–20 November	2 concerts	
	Oamaru, 21 November		
	Timaru, 23 November		
	Christchurch, 25 November		
	Wellington, 26 November		
	Masterton, 30 November		
	Palmerston North, 1 December		
	New Plymouth, 3 December		
	Auckland, 5–6 December	2 concerts	
SYDNEY	12–15 December	3 concerts	
MELBOURNE	17–19 December	3 concerts	
	Bairnsdale, 21 December		
	Sale, 22 December		
	Yarram, 23 December		
(MELBOURNE	Ada's *Messiah* performance, 25 December)		
MELBOURNE	2 January, 1904		Rose and Percy to Adelaide together
	Ballarat, 4 January		
ADELAIDE	6 January		
PERTH	12–14 January	2 concerts	Rose in Adelaide
	Kalgoorlie, 16–18 January	2 concerts	
PERTH	20–21 January	2 concerts	Rose and Percy met in Albany 22 January

18 TO ROSE GRAINGER
23/10/1903

The Ozone Hotel.
Warrnambool.

Had the lovliest of days. From 12 till about 4.15 with J.J. on a sea-side tramp; taking in the rippingest views. Soon out of the wing town sand-dunes begin — white, clean stuff, grass-set to hold sand from being wind-swept over town & growing-grounds.

We got wet some, ⟦but that wont hurt flannels any⟧ but discomfort was well made up by the farnesses ⟦endless stretching snowwhite sand beaches & landwards from them hummocks⟧ softened by rain-drifts.

Landwards from the hummocks marshes; ⟦old riverbed, which's outlet into sea stuffed by inblown sand — winds strength raised it to small hills where once the dead flats of river-mouth⟧ & near these the dells 'tween the dune-heights grow shrubs & wildgrowths; of vivid green, flowering the most. I've picked tips of most sorts & will send pressed tomorrow with this. Posting today useless, as no today's train would get Melb in time for over-land mail.

The river's been turned now into a canal, & this ⟦on home path⟧ cutting off our back-coming, I coo-eed a house owning a punt. A Melbourne-born man turned out, ferried us, & later sailed us townwards; a most refined, kindly, pleasant-tho'-familiar sort, for whose wife we're getting 2 ticks for tonights' show.

The sights I saw were in keeping with some of my fondest mindings of Australian shore-showings: The broad flat white beaches we love, & lacked in Europe, the rolling dunes, with sage green tufted grass, as such:—

you know.

A far kin of Denmark:—

'Agnete hun sidde paa det ensomme Strand
[Agnes sits beside the lonesome strand]
Saa sagtelig de Bølger slaar op paa hviden Sand
[So softly break the billows upon the snow-white sand]
Aa, ja, ja! saa sagtelig' & *soon*.[3]
[Oh, yea, yea! so softly & soon.]

Dates stand as:—

be in		
	Brisbane	31st till 3rd
	Sydney	5th till 8th
	Melb (on & off)	8th till 10th

[B & Syd address C/o Palings Musicshop
Melb C/o Her Majesties]

Splendid take last night; did real well [added next day]

3 Grainger is quoting one of the many variants of the Danish folksong ''Agnete og Havmanden'' [Agnete and the Merman].

19   TO ROSE GRAINGER   Lennon's Hotel,
31/10/03   Brisbane.

This is again Sydney-like once more. Smart & moving. Not a-town last night over an hour 'fore 'hint-a-few' fixed for, which cum off this morn ¼ hour ago; — for the ''Telegraph''. Also the ''Week'' has got me along-side of Ada as ''2 Australian Musicians''. Why shld one's birth-town alone fall short?

Nevertheless this is too hot for race-rearing. Impossible, I should say, to hold to the tokens of a northern-breed in such moist warmth. Not that I feel uncomfy myself, but I shld never look forward to a lengthened stay here. Also it shows in the breed. Many are puny, & when not baked yellow-brown, are sallow some. But they are in many points more rightly Australian than elsewhere. For they really dress & build fittingly for the weather, & the gardengrowths tally the temperature beautifully.

The flies are not overstated; they thrive & are active.

The run from Sydney goes thro' the loveliest land we've touched here so far.

Some hours from Sydn the Hawkesbury river is struck; broad like fjords often, & sundering the grandest hills. The ranges round about are wonderfully noble & awesome with their unmistakeably ''Urwald'' [German: virgin forest] treegrowth. White ball-like blossoms fluff on the gums, & the wondrousest wildflowers [better than usual wildflowers; for they sprout mostly on shrubs & treelets, & big trees; & thus are not fine in color & detail alone, but striking *as form* at some farness] line the rail, while the rich red earth breaks into sight on the ploughed lands & the roads; which roads, being good by the way, will serve you & I on some bath-chair trip one day, when we'll track round to see the sights. I'm sure you'd find such faring comfy & untiring.

Then in Queensland again still grander stuff is struck. Taller hills & more sweeping formation; & one point is utmostly uplifting where a big big half-round of hills overlooks a vast cup-like hollow into great farness.

Here again, the feel of URWALD gives deep dignity. The breadth & far-flungness there is something really rare.

Here quick washing will enable me an extra full stock of cleans.

What lovely time you must have had with dear A. Clara & Frisky. Such a typically S.A. home of the very best

Always love to dear Uncle & Auntie George & May & Eric, & of course to all of Richmond.[4]

Day before yest we got Sydn early in Morning so I looked up Miss Conor O'Brien, & afterward lunched at Wentworth with A. Jack & later went to see some of harbor along of her. We had a great time & a cheap trip. [8 pence][5]

They are right about the harbor in the main. It is more pretty than lovely, I shld rate, but the harbor-dwellers earn praise in not having wrecked its charms as yet. Tho' thickly housed & gardened gumtrees are by far the boss tone everywhere, even in gardens, & wildgrowth & rough-&-tumble is the order to-be-thank-ful-forly often. Thus tho' mankindized it is still ownish, still Australian, as are too few of the trimed up spots I've seen:— in the Adel hills noteably.

Amazing that they've only got a '*boudior*'-grand [Steinway] here — not even a '*drawing-room*'. A good instrument, new & nice, but a toy only. How can one dash & sulphor with such mush?

Love-full as ever
Percy.

20   TO ROSE GRAINGER

Sunday. 1/11/03

Lennon's Hotel,
Brisbane.

Dearest.

Been practising hard, yest 3 hours, today over 4.

Learning up the 2 Bach-Busoni's, 'Waldesrauschen', The Kreutzer Son-ata, & Grieg's "To the Spring", the last-named already memorized.

And yet I didnt play at all well last night; the public didnt seem to spot it tho'. It proves my holding that one day's practise is uselesser than none — of course the days before I had no show, being on the train.

Funny with these Jews, they can womanize, & drink, & not practise, & go to races just before playing, yet be right as rain; while I who keep off all these, & bed early, [before 10 lately] & stay home to work, am much less reliable.[6]

I s'pose it's what's called 'talent', & the lack of it.

I'm getting on grand with my new things tho', & guess the Kreutzer lies fine for me.

Brisbane has lovely little spots — ½-tropical growths, lovely color-wealth, & all that; but God keep me out of the place, I mean thinking for good.

Quite nice for a short stay, but it's a blot on Australia.

Full of Chinese, Kanakas, & worse still ½-breeds, & chaps likening Colombo Eurasians. And the whites too, all bung-faced, sallow, puffy, sloppy-built, undersized; no look of pride, uprightness, or toughness. A

4 Rose's was a large family. She had one surviving sister, Clara Jane (1856–1944) and six brothers, George Sydney (1847–1911), James Henry (1849–1925), Edward William (1851–1909), Frederick Clement (1853–1926), Charles Edwin (1859–1932) and Frank Herbert (1867–1931). A second sister, Emma Elizabeth, died in 1881, aged 26. Frank and Clara, neither of whom married, lived in "Claremont" in Adelaide from 1880. James, who had eight children, owned the Richmond Park Stud Farm. George and his wife Marion (*née* Macfee, "Aunty May") had one adopted son, Eric.

5 "Aunty Jack" (Annie Maria Quesnell), the sister of Marion Aldridge. She was a singer and had studied with Madame Marchesi in Paris in 1900. Conor O'Brien, a journalist writing for the *Bulletin*.

6 Rose replied on 7 November, "You must not think all the jews can do without practise Hambourg & Rosenthal have to work hard 5 hours a day".

7 Roger Quilter (1877–1953), English composer. Studied piano with Ernst Engesser at the Hoch Conservatorium in Frankfurt for four semesters between 1897 and 1898. He studied composition privately with Knorr until 1901. At the Queen's House concert on 28 May 1903 he sang and played piano in Grainger's choruses and Grainger sang in his. Francis Harry Everard Joseph Feilding (1867–1936), second son of the eighth Earl of Denbigh, brother of Lady Winefride Elwes, lawyer and amateur musician. Co-founder with Mrs Lowrey of the Queen's House Manuscript Music Society, he sang, whistled and played piano in the first performance of Grainger's choruses on 28 May 1903. Grainger met him through Mrs Lowrey in Dieppe in the summer of 1902.

8 An orchestra was used in the Sydney concerts on 12 and 14 December, but Grainger did not play with it. The conductors were Signor Hazon and, for three songs by George H. Clutsam sung by Ada Crossley, Mr F. Clutsam.

9 Grainger's was a standard contribution to the concert programmes: a duet with Jacques Jacobs, usually one movement of a violin and piano sonata, and two groups of piano solos, including one big "show" piece. *La Scandinavie*, a flexible grouping of Scandinavian folksongs and dances, was arranged for cello and piano by Herman Sandby and Grainger between March and May 1902. It was included in their duo-recital programmes from 1902 to 1906. Dedicated to Herman's Frankfurt teacher Hugo Becker, a five-movement group was, through his influence, accepted for publication by B. Schott's Söhne, Mainz, in 1902. Only the fourth movement of the published suite, the *Mélodie Danoise*, was ever published in a violin and piano transcription, and that made by A. Wilhelmj, published 1907, but manuscript "fiddle" parts for the finale and the Swedish tune *Vermeland*, which Jacobs and Grainger gave as an encore, are in the Grainger Museum. Such special "occasional" scorings by Grainger of his own works are not uncommon.

right-thro' immoral hole too, by all accounts. Sure as I've been thus far of a doubtless noble to-come for the rest of the places seen, like sure I am that here trouble will one day arise.

To let lower races in in itself shows weakness in the stock; folk must be clean mad after the example of the USA & all past history, to beckon in colored & lower-race work into a land that *as yet has no race-hatreds or -wars within itself*, & need have none.

To think of spoiling an almost alonestanding chance like Australia has! It riles me so that I'm all the time in a state of annoyance & rage — so uncalled-for, so shortsighted, narroweyed.

When not pianoing I've been writing — to Quil, Mrs L, Sandby, Feilding.[7]

Deary mummy, things are no the same without you.

I realize how rough it's on chaps who've had none such mother's help as I've simply floated in; it doesnt give them a show. It's an awful pull, dear, you cant overate it.

Goodnight once more

After three concerts in Tasmania, the party left Hobart for New Zealand on 13 November, arriving in Dunedin five days later. The concert route took the party north: in the South Island from Dunedin via Oamaru and Timaru to Christchurch, then crossing to the North Island, from Wellington, via Masterton, Palmerston North and New Plymouth to Auckland. The final concert in Auckland was on 7 December and the party left New Zealand on the 8th. Rose travelled across to Melbourne on 17 November.

21   TO ROSE GRAINGER
20/11/1903.

Grand Hotel,
Dunedin, N.Z.

Before I forget; do please gatherup plenty stamps for little Busoni boy. I'll want write father B from Melb when we meet, so you might very kindly keep all off my postings from the different parts till then.

It is fixed after all no concertos in Melb & Sydn. Wont be room on platf for 2 pianos. There was just the *faintest* chance (& maybe still is) of orchestra.[8] So my two progs will be

1)	Finale (la Scandinavie)	P.G.
	Fantasia & Fugue, G min	Bach-Liszt
	⎰'To the Springtide'	Grieg
	⎱'Waldesrauschen'	Liszt
2)	1 move Kreutzer Sonata.	Beeth
	Fantasia, op 49.	Chopin
	Rhapsody [Hungarian, No 12]	Liszt[9]

"The Five Nations" need time only to grow wonderfully & well.[10] This is proven me firstly:— By going yesterafternoon for walk in hills. Just when starting off to practise in hall I saw looming behind the town a fine bleak barren treeless snow-cap, — quite a little berg. So I inned & old-flannelled & offed.

Drisling rain on the flat changing to snow as ground lifted. I left the town by public gardens, (overflowing with damp & wet & water & green & rich growths) & well-to-do foretowns, (Vorstädte) quite Old country like, & folk the same — sappy, ruddy, tight-built. This straggled out to streets that ran up sheer to uncleared hills aflare with gorse — bright yellow — off a mainroad beset with ideal prettily-begrown dwellings; & down its middle (the road's) 'lectric-tram tracks being laid. [That revealed the New Land 'Letricity run right into the thinly-folked land]

Then I took to the rough, & the trouble began. First over cleared forest skirting ploughed ground & soon trackless into the untouched URWÄCHST [German-based, Grainger-coined word: virgin growth]. That taught how little we know of untouched ground. The land we know, even the forests, has all been cleared at one time — or else is of very other stuff to that of here. For here thoroughfare was next to impossible. I pushed, shoved thro' the tangled & clinging undergrowth of ferns, briars, thorned scrub, trees, creepers & endless varieties for some ½-or more-hour (guiding solely by sense of direction) until unyielding blockage forced me back to where a wire fence ran along some few feet of clearage, which, climbing, led to the thro'-wind-blast-barrened hill-top, where view & path were free again.

Here the outlook was quite glorious; all they say of NZ is true. Mind you, this was nothing, just the ordinary, just ocean upon a far-to-be-followed lovely-lined coast, narrowing into a nestling townskirted haven & running dwarf-fjordlike far into the hills, (seen tween the dalegaps thinning here riverlike, swelling there lakelike) which hills recalling Scotland strongly, gorse-lit & heavy-humped; but unmistakeably NZ where the close wild jungleish Urwächst begins. [This the stuff I butted thro'] This is the strangest mixture thinkable. [Gums of sorts — taking quite other — bunchier — shapes than in Australia] a-blossom, big treeforms, strong teeming undergrowth, creepers atrail & atree everywhere, white lichen or some such [herewith a scrap] clinging on stem & stalk & leafage, [funny] large white wildflowers, [herewith one crushed] & trunks rotting & crumbling with moisture — all this bespoke heat, almost tropicness.

Yet upon this snow was driving [nor melting either. Mark, the weather is as cold as Engl midwinter] & lying in sheets on the ground, the wind blowing Scotch mist accross the hills, [veiling all at times, & at times showing the farness in patches, & at times changing to a genial sun-bath] while the heights [as aforesaid] rockbare, & blasted of all growth.

To compare this with Austr wld be as uncalled for as India against Canada; this has none of the partic poetry of the vast plains, they none of this's backbone, grimness, & glory.

As in Scotland, each little dalelet here is a hillstream, a streamlet; good drinks at every dent in the way.

I made the top ['Flagstaff' they call it] but got no view for snow & hail so thick & cutting that a few feet off was white wall, & looking windwards stinging like many whips.

Already late I cld not wait for it to lift [2 or more hours already agog] but must needs track way back in my footmarks of coming. [no overstating] On reaching the lower hills beneath the storm I struck some hale brawny ruddy chaps [who're coming in to conc tonight; ticks from me awaiting them at box office] who put me on clear way Dunedin-wards. I trotted home in a hour; as hard an afternoon's work as I've ever.

I find I can stand hard strain easier than ever; much stronger than on my last hill-climb.

10 Rudyard Kipling's volume of verse *The Five Nations* was published in September 1903. Percy received the book as a gift from Ernest Thesiger (see letter 28).

Saw lots of the breed, & by gum! This place can look forward to anything it jolly well likes. Heaps are Scotch, & all as good as such, & these hill-boys just perfection. In all points [brawn, & freshness & tight build] even as the best British, with but the finer brainier eyes to tell they're NEW.

You & I'll have such joy here, one day, dearest.

NZ has nought to do with Australia — quite understandable its not in the Federation.

But it's a Scotland to Austr. A hill land to brace on a holiday. One day it may be to Austr what Britain's to Europe. It could on its own raise something as great as Britain, I've not the shadow of a doubt.

One needs not now to go Scotland from Austr. One has it South, with even a Scotch befolking. [or as good]

Twothly:— By letting the new Versebook soak in. Even *as a whole* up to Kip's best. The charm it grows as it ingrafts on closer friendship, tremendous. What fun we'll have with it too! & shortly.

[Next day:]
My playing last night none the worse for an afternoon's roughing. The past hard practising told.

Nice crit [only paper out as yet] & lucky — as Scherek says this town in musicalness comes straight after Melb & Sydney.[11]

Goodbye for today.

11 The first of two concerts in Dunedin was on 19 November.

22   TO ROSE GRAINGER   Grosvenor Hotel
23/11/1903   Timaru [N.Z.]

Well, dearest, I have behind me a fair walk.

Leaving Oamaru yesterafternoon at 5 minutes to 2 I reached this this morn [a farness of *56* miles] at about 6.

I got the most hearty send-off from the Hotel, [Star & Garter] all gathering outside to cheer the start; & a nice Scot [named A. Sharp] came along with me for 12 miles. The 1st 28 miles I made in 6 hours exactly; that is: 4 miles an hour all the way, which [seeing I kept up for 28 miles though not in training] I am rather proud of.

There (Studholme Junction) I spent ½-hour feeding at Hotel there, & also played the Hotelkeeper's wife & brother 'Waldesrauschen' & 'To the Spring-tide'; dear folk they were.

The remaining 28 miles did not go so fast, as you will note; my soles were already thro' before leaving Oamaru, & the last 20 miles more agonizing than I could have thought possible; *cruel*. Of course 56 is a long tramp to take on without training.

I was almost hysterical towards the end.

On getting here I just washed feet & parts chaffed by clothe's rubbing & slept till about 11; then had good hot bath which unstiffened things wonderfully & has somewhat restored me.

I had the lovliest weather thro'out & a back wind. Fine warm sunshine without enough to make one sweat at all. The tailing-out of the Southern Alps was on my left [WEST] all the way, & practically all the way I could hear the roar from the beach some few miles to my right [EAST]

Some 14 miles from Oamaru is a lovely river, over which a hugely long bridge. The river bed is tremendously broad & the stream breaks up into many divisions ⟦streaks of silver⟧ seperated by shingle flats, grass- & tuft-grown. About a mile to the right it merges into the sea & on the left one sees its snowclad sources. When there I was simply mad with wish to have you there with me one day. You know my raft-longing. That will have no sweetness unless you partake. I am sure it would be a wonderful thing for you too; to drift effortless thro' glorious sights in bracing air, surrounded by every needful comfort; which a little scheming could easily get onto a good big raft.

Also on the roads too, you must be there. We'll have that wheelable chair we thought of in Bucks; & out here the going would be still safer & jollier; no cattle seem to stray here on the roads ⟦guess the landways reach too far, & are too big to risk loosing cattle on⟧

The dearest deepest joys of my life will be in unfolding of natural beauties before mum's eyes in comfort in her life's afternoon.

If life has ought to offer me it will be this. I should be glad to have birthed something to love me as strongly as I do you.

It's jolly that I will be able to hold my full strength out to some ministering to the weaknesses you reap off a too nobly heroic past.

And then at times it's awful we're not mates in years.

I thought that strongly as all around drooped restingly at yestereve's darkling; how we would have also relished to have had strong-to-do youth & prime at same time & to take our life's end's rest together. The landlike quiet bore that in on me.

For you know, altho' I'll never be a moper, & will ever keep up my healthy hearty cheery joy in my work, & race, & the broad spread of things; yet all personal bliss ends when you do. All my greatest happiness plays around you.

When on a tramp like that just behind me, or abed, or whenever to myself really thoughtful, I dwell on you all the time, & think things thoroughly out.

We'll have a good time on the steamer going back, won't we? I dont think somehow you had as good a trip coming out as you ought to have had. We must see if the return cant be better.

Had a most *howling* success at Oamaru; & never played better.

As to dear mother's cares that offspring do not disappear into volcanic holes in the night, let me call to mind that those regions are in the North Island, & will worse luck ⟦as being NZ's best, I'm told⟧ not be struck by us at all, I fear.

Near Studholme Junction met such a dear Scotch farmer — a real gentleman, dearest. Fine to think think that these rich yealding lands go to the gain of such leal chaps as this. ⟦white, sand, & a warm-heart — every inch of him — recalling Klimsch somewhat⟧

He had passed me on his byke going to Oamaru & on returning home could not believe his eyes that I'ad gone that far.

Remind me to tell you funny things of a slightly-tipsy sailor, who'd read of me in Oamaru paper & came up in street saying. "So you're the bloke whose not only a pianist but a *philosoper* at 19 — I cant think how you've done it".

He also said "Now yours is an agreeable kind of talent; tho' mine too is *as sweet as a nut*" Such a queer chap.

Goodbye.

You can look my path up in map; between Dunedin & Christchurch.
⟦I also saved outlay on my walk; a bob or so.⟧

23   TO ROSE GRAINGER   Commercial Hotel
1/12/1903   Palmerston North. [N.Z.]

My dearest. Another nice little foot-trip done. Not so far as the last, yet on the whole a better thing. Masterton to Eketahuna ⟦32 miles about⟧ 'tween 11 o'cl last night & 6 this morn. That is over 4 miles an hour all the time. I never sat done once, or halted for even a second, 'cept to listen, or ask a ques, or unship my food-bundle. I found not even time to stop for a drink of water, going dry from start to close. You can look out the places on map of North Island lying 'tween Wellington in a northward line towards Woodville. Jacobs had promised to come along, but of course backed out at last minute. You dont get a Shem to sweat unpaid. Last night I think I played with much more than usual dash; many thought so, & clapping was first class. After conc, just packed & squared at Hotel, & then off. I started in lightest ¾ moon, but after a few hours it changed to the angry murk of heavy clouds front of strong light. A fair road all the way. Passed a broad riverbed, with the usual thin silver trickling water-lines down it & reached ½ way point Mauriceville fresh as ought. Here kiln's were ablaze on the hillsides. Soonafter this the dawning began. If one has not gone thro' hard exercise thro' a night, one cannot realize how exultantly hailed is the cheering light, the new birth. How before it starts one hankers, gloomy, at mental strain — & the sunup breaks all this down. The dawning-joy I had always thought just a mawkish convention, an idea stale from over much handing down. One has to go thro' to take in how healthily glorious it is. And watch its onpath as one may it seems impossible to mark the line 'tween faint forehints only & the humming blue ⟦however slight a blue⟧ of the real day start. Suddenly it is there. All 'long of this tramp I had in my mind drumming the lines

> The million molten shafts of morn
> The spears of our deliverance
> > from '*The Song of the Wise Children*'
> > The 5 Nats.

Funny how the live world wakes in turn. Of course the pioneer rooster; then long stillness with a hoarse 'caw' once & again; then twitter of birds in high air. Then the somewhat brutal call of the 100s of sheep, hillstrewn. ⟦Most nature calls are somewhat cruelly crude. Even these silly beasts have something warning crafty in their bleat⟧ Then insects, flies, moths. Much later lowing of cattle, & dogs, a.s.o.

I saw no man ⟦nor heard — save once at about 3.30 what seemed like a man's call far off — but mayby a bird⟧ from leaving Masterton till within a few miles of Eketahuna. Really lonesomy, darling, & most awing. Not frightening in the least, utterly dangerless & tame, yet nonetheless very full of awe. The bush goes along long way by the road. Copper colored in impression, lots of it, coppery brown trees & bracken likewise.

The joy was that I ended up fresh as I offed. Right near the last, when I heard then 'stead of being but 2 miles out of Eketahuna as I have reckoned, that I had another 8 to 10 before me, I didnt give a dern, but lit out into still stiffer pace — close on 5 mile an hour. I took forethought, went in *double*socks, & these well soaped & thus came off without sore feet. I took music along with me too, ⟦Bach G-minor, Waldesrauschen, Kreutzer Sonata⟧ & after sleeping 3 hours at the Station Hotel, had some 2 hours practise on the piano there. Near 1 o'cl boarded the train bearing the rest of us. And now ⟦7.30⟧ feel my freshest for the boards.

How much glader than the former tramp; thro' such much hillier gloriouser scenery.

Till tomorrow your son-worshiper
Percy.

24 TO ROGER QUILTER
7/12/1903

Grand Hotel
Auckland. N.Z.

Darling Quil

Overdelighted get your writ of Oct 1; & needless say much looking forward to take in diggings, which I hope will do you bestly.[12]

Ripping 'bout Germ Songs[13] Always such treat to finger fondly-held compos in print. To them also keen forward lookings. But most so to the brave things to come — rejoicers not yet writ.

Do do heaps — Quality assured.

Lately 've been footing it strongly. Walked from Oamaru to Timaru [56 miles] 'tween 2 afternoon & 6 next morn; with ½ hour's rest. [That was in Middle Island N.Z.]

And the other day left Masterton [southward in North Island N.Z.] at 11 o'cl after our Concert there & walked without *a moment's* rest to Eketahuna, [northward direction] 32 miles, getting by 6 in the morn — over 4 miles an hour. I carried food & some music with me, which latter (after 3 hours sleep) I put in 2 to 3 hours practise upon before at miday boarding the train bearing our party on to Palmerston North.

Success keeps on grand; & I'm bettering in my playing much by the stopless playing most every night. You know our tour goes on to S'Africa after this?

My poor dear father is here on way to hot baths. He's the totalest wreck I've ever seen. Had the narrowest shave. The cruelest overwork. How I hope one day to earn such suffering as both my elders have gone thro'! We've been so happy tho', together.

Turns out my father's stock is of Scotch origin, some way back, & his mother *pure Welsh*.[14]

Write me P.G. c/o Ada Crossley Concert Co. Capetown/ (or) Durban. S'af.

25 TO ERNEST THESIGER
10/12/1903

S.S. "Zealandia",
'tween N.Z. & Sydney.

My dear Thes

I was overdelighted get your writ.

You cant guess the million glorious sights that crowd past our tour-path, just an endless run of breath-fetchers.

What a school of painters 'Stralyer will bring forth in the to-come, must so do!

The dreamy coloring of the land is just too drunkening.

Now we're homing to the mainland again after some 3 weeks of New Zealand; the loveliness of which latter islands having but gone to prove the to me *inwarder* beauty of my own place.

Mind you, we've not struck the top-notch bits of NZ any; but that don't count, for it's the everyday average of things which works the end-pull. It['s] just the humdrum ordinary every-bit-of-the-way stuff that carries charm in Australia; even as, along otherest possible lines, Holland. Just fences, a clearing, burnt-off forest, road-side growths, road-earth-coloring, harmony of tin [roofage, walling, a,s,o.] & twilight, horses hoofless, small-hill farnesses of bitingest blue — all the commonest needfullest material haps that just must go along of the land's upopening — round these cluster the unexplainablest charm, something that's veiled, delicate, hinted.

12 Roger had moved into new rooms at 27 Welbeck Street.

13 Probably Quilter's settings of "Four Songs of Mizra Schaffy", by the German poet Friederich Bodenstedt. Written "in rememberance of Frankfurt days", the songs were published as *Four Songs*, Op. 2, by Elkin & Co., in 1903, with English translations by Walter Creighton.

14 John Grainger was on three months' leave from his post in Western Australia. He was suffering from syphilis ("rheumatism"), though he had complained of the stress from overwork in a letter to Percy in July 1902. Rose wrote to Percy on 17 November of his possible meeting with his father in Auckland, "He looks very bad, & his hands are all over spots — take care, use glove when shaking hands, & don't use towel etc. or wash in his room". Percy reported after the meeting that John seemed better. But his father's failing health increased the pressure on Percy to earn more money. As his mother wrote on the same day, "From now on I hope you will be able to earn for us both dear, & not let us trouble father any more".

Fact is, the whole lighting is so outerordinarily mellow & deeptoned, that a lowdown paint-daubed woodshed only needs a few feet's farness to fairly glow, & hum its part in the all-round whole. That's why I look for it to get out painters.

Now NZ is great in strikingness & unusualness. It's a holiday land, full of tripper's beauties, mind — OF THE BEST SORT; but it dont fetch out of seeming nothingnesses that rich pulsing warmth, which most folk, but I not, [thankfully] miraculously manage to miss noting in 'Stralyer.

When I get back to Melb, I'll likely run into a letter from you. Glad if I do.

We're off S'Af after this. So if writing address c/o Ada Crossley Concert Co. Capetown S'Africa

Fun we'll fit in when we foregather once more!

Love
Ever
Perky
'cause of my nose's uplilt.

1904

The tour grew as it went, from the twenty-five concerts originally an-
nounced to some sixty concerts in Australasia. Return seasons were added
in Sydney and Melbourne after the New Zealand segment: three concerts
in Sydney, 12–15 December, and three in Melbourne, 17–19 December,
with a brief tour of Gippsland before Christmas. Rose was in Melbourne
when Percy arrived back on 16 December. The New Year saw the great
Popular Concerts in Melbourne and Adelaide. The day after the Adelaide
concert the party boarded ship for Perth. Rose, having travelled to
Adelaide with Percy, stayed on there while he went to the West. They met
in Albany on 22 January. The S.S. Wakool *left Albany for South Africa*
on 23 January 1904.

26 TO FRANK ALDRIDGE   [S.S. "Ophir"]
[Postcard]
9.1.04.

Dear Uncle Frankums!

Here's a peep of our tub to stick into the great scrap-book.
Inside the 'Ophir' is all gilded & glorious, much offending my
UNDOOKAL tastes.
We didnt have much time this go, did we? You wait till next time!

Much love
Percy.

27 TO ROSE GRAINGER   Palace Hotel,
16.1.1904   Kalgoorlie, W.A.

Got yr 2 dear notes on getting Perth, also a cable (of improvement, &
doctor's hopefulness) & letter from father, & letter from Sandby. All of
which at Albany.

I wont say the West is the best of Australia, but it's quite as good as that.
The towns Perth, & of course Kalgoorlie, are maybe more unmistakeably
"Conlonial" than the East; bear the stamp of mining life & newness more
seeably, — naturally. Grand manhood walks the streets, ‖most of it Eastern

1 A selection of buildings designed by John Grainger and built during his period of office in Perth: Parliament House (elevation to Harvest Terrace [1903]; the complete building as then intended did not eventuate); Supreme Court (1903); the ballroom additions to Government House (formal opening ball, 22 June 1899). Hillson Beasley (1855–1936), a member of John Grainger's staff in Perth. Appointed Chief Draftsman under Grainger in 1897 (?), he became Acting Chief Architect on 29 March 1905, succeeding Grainger as Chief Architect in 1906. Of John Grainger's other friends mentioned: M. E. Jull was Under-Secretary for Public Works; H. W. Vincent, master builder and contractor who executed several of Grainger's designs; Allan, possibly George Allan, a Victorian architect resident in Perth; Miller, possibly one of the Miller brothers of Melbourne, who were prominent in West Australian timber-milling circles; George Aytoun was connected with the organisation of the W.A. Court at the Paris Exhibition in 1900. Cooper is unidentified. The Colonial Secretary in January 1904 was the Hon. Walter Kingsmill, M.L.A.

2 The Hon. Zebina Lane (b. 1870), M.L.C. Western Australia from 1903 to May 1908. His wife had lived for several years in London, supervising the education of their two sons. Mrs Lane left London to return to Perth in July/ August 1904.

3 Miss Ethel Burt, accompanied by her mother and possibly a Miss Willis, had gone to Berlin around July 1903 to study privately with Grainger's former teacher, Professor James Kwast. She was still there in April 1904. While in Berlin in June and July 1903, Grainger had arranged their accommodation at a *pension* run by Kwast's first wife, Frau Tony Kwast-Hiller. The Burts were a distinguished Perth family.

— Victorian largely — they say‖ quite all one could wish, tho' the women show the more strainful conditions, & look lesser than the elder states.

I have had a thoroughly jolly time since landing; seeing scores upon scores of fidge's friends, Aytoun, Miller, Jull, Cooper, Allan, Vincent & very many others, & think I have done the right & proper 'gin them all.

We all put up at 'Melbourne Hotel' — 8 bob a day, comfortable & quiet. The drinking is huge & horrible out here, & the 'standing' endless — many the ales & beers (of ginger) I have relished. The heat is quite big I must own, but has nowise put me out of comfort or off feed. Just a wee moist at Perth, but up here fine & dry, tho' somewhat scorching.

I enjoyed much to find so many seemingly warm friends of father, & such a great amount of respect for him, & singleness of opinion as to the excellence & muchness of his work. All say that his win over the lot 'gainst him just before his break-down was very complete, & will ensure him a good spell when he backs. The man in his place as long as he's away, Beasley, showed me over the New Parliment Buildings ‖just begun, but very impressive already — solid stone of brilliant, almost marble, whiteness‖ & the Law Courts, & when lunching at Gov House on Wed I saw the Ball-room, the last of most outerordinary beauty — an ownish pure effect in great sheets of white & red brown. (jarrah) I can hardly think ought in this line possibly fairer.[1]

After the Gov house lunch the Colonial Secr took me along to the Legislative Council ‖more rightly '*Law-making Meet*'‖ which was sitting, & which I took in for some hours: a suprizingly dignified performance it was, most wellbehaved, & wholly other than the jaw-fights I have always been told to look for from any 'Stralyan law-making body.

Zeb Lane has flourished round me with much friendliness — of a coarsely besotten sort. Dont envy Mrs L's backing to her clearly very batchelorish spouse. Allerdale G type once more.[2]

Was took on the Swan steam-launching by some High Folk. Very pleasant, the river very pretty, & scrubflanked — little or no desecration of the banks as yet. 2 brothers & 1 sister of the fearsomely-fetching Burt on board. This sister also charmful, tho' less so. Brothers sound. They must be a great family: fine same way as the Aldridges are. I feel breed-wealth in all the yet-met Burts. They've news of the sister's getting on all right at Kwast Hiller's — hates outlanders, tho', as is meet.[3]

But now for the *great treat*. Almost, if not quite, my best time in 'Stralyer — & with a Jew too; the only Jew who seemingly has nobility & is good as a good Aryan from the most Aryan standpoint: — Frank Davies, manager of Jarrahdale wood-sawing mill, belonging the *Millar Karri & Jarrah Co.* You know how nice his sister — well he's just splendid. Been all thro' the S'Af war, relished it, wounded, & at this moment praying for Far-East Trouble, simply jumpy to join in any row. I'm sure a grand business-man, ‖tho' thats' not a Jewish Uncommoness‖ & what's nailingest of all, a born bosser of men in man-to-man matters. No over weening high voiced swaggerer, but a quiet lowest-of-low-talking, languidly-masterful thorough 'Stralyan with a rigid grip on things. Jews are often admirable tho' seldom noble, often powerfully-bodied yet rarely bodily-*charm*ful. He's both these latters.

Watch him handle the levers of steam-engines (railroad) calmly agaze thro' the porthole-like look-outs, or ordering millmen about, & one rejoices to see Shems justified at last. Of the *really Asiatic Jew* type, with the nestling curly sheeny-black hair, the mellow deep-dark eyes, the finely-cut slightly beaked (ever so slightly) nose; — ‖so other than the German-like sprawly-, niggerlike squidy, -snouted Yed‖ plainly an Easterner — might be an Arab, Pathan, or even Indian, roughly speaking; a Jew in whose Jewdom I rejoice & yet am thankful to see in what in my wishes is the *Whitest of Australia's*. Fancy that!

I dined with him Wed & he promised good sport if I'd go with to

Jarrahdale So after Thur's Conc I inned to old flannels, boots, a.s.o. & met his elder brother & railed with him some 20 miles to where the Gov Road meets the *Millars Co.* line. Here we were wuk from soundest slumber by Frank, out-trained & led in the pitch dark to where one of the Millar engines stood to take us the 7 miles to Jarrahdale. My 1st ride on a loco & never-to-be-forgot. ½-asleep to hang on to quivering greezy iron, before us the curiously-manlike snorting & thuding [big metal breath-fetchings & heartbeats] of the machinery, & the ringed glare from the headlights, aside the land black against the resplendantly starred sky, [bunchy shapes of gums silhouetted] lit weirdly by burning bush & the bitter-bright red of flaming & smouldering trunks, is an experience [of a certain glad awesomeness] that has bitten deep into my memory. Frank D drove. After some ½ hour of such heaven we fetched up, inned to the darlingest jarrah house, where lemonade refreshed, as also sleep. [from 2 till 6 o'cl]

All the walls inside are just jarrah beautifully fitted together right from floor [brownpaperlike linoleumed, jolly] to floor, [ceiling too] contrasted by white chimneys.

A home such as I'd raise no grumbles against. Perfect taste, simplicity, usefulness. And the glorious mellow rich red of the wood!

The next morn was all bliss; some 26 miles rid on the engine again, a thorough look over the mills, lunch & back in Perth by 2.30. [sleep all the way up] An engine is a fitting frame to a Westerner. One has to stand up or loll out round the ironshed's dooring, & one can crawl all over the dear thing & see & smell it sweating steam & hot oil & delights; but earth's most caressing cosiness is held in the cab; [where the driver & stoker stand] where the furnace's friendly warmth creeps dreamily over one's whole carcass, while the by contrast cold air born of the speed freshens in thro all openings, & aforesaid whiffs of heated oil ravish.

The mills are a *sight of beauty* impossible to beat anywhere. And how Australian! All about bush, & in a clearing floods of steam & the bluest of blue smoke, [gum-wood-rich] thro' which loom blood red stacks of cut jarrah, monster logs of the unsawn timber, blue-grey tin sheds roofing big machinery in life, & godlike millmen moving it.

Davies says they're practically all native born. There's not the weest faintest bit wrong with these fellows; giants, graceful & pleasant-looking, & with a noticeable lot of auburn hair amongst them. Thrilling to see such pets. Possibly not to be matched *anywhere.*

The rest of us left yest by the 3.30 train for here. But I waited till the 7.30 train on account of the extra 4 hours I'd have this morn in which to take in the BIG WASTE. And how glad I was of it.

From when I woke [about 8] to reaching at 1 o'cl, unbroken waste of the kind I love. Of course there may be as good elsewhere, only I've not seen it. Gippsland, Queensland, & heaps else are all right, but this here is Australia in its *special specialty*, in its particular noblest mood. No Sunday frock garb to impress or holiday prettiness to entice, but a great grand general average: — what Bach's many voicedness is to music. No Napoleonlike individualistic theme of Beethoven, or wantoness of Wagner, or firyness of Tshaikowsky, or husbandry of Haydn, or ecstacy of Chopin, and so on, a.s.o. but the weekday-like, enduring, untiring graft & grind of a Bach Fugue; grim glamorless greatness which lifts largest in the end. And men's life spilt like water on this Way towards the Gold. Numberless dead found by the railroad layers as they went.

The Westralian Waste is not dead flat. Here & there rizes 10 & 20 miles off lift with the dreamy Australian blue-of-farness.

Bushes 2, 3, & 4 feet high sprout richly off the yellow earth; red & brown & green, mostly red. And then small slightish gums in very many places.

Nought is more delicate than the bushlets' forms as they stretch away in their millions with the colors of Sunset glories.

And this land may show as now in 300 years time!

When they lay the overland line to South Australia it will be almost solely thro' such stuff.

What a trip for me. My most beloved land for many many 100s of miles.

[17.1.04]

Yestereve's 1st conc here was too laughable, as far as it touched me. The shodiest shadow of a bad upright — "just ghosts scuffling in the gloom" as Twain has it. Maybe the front row knew when I was playing or not. That apart they're a funny crowd. *Paid no heed to the piano at all, & gave me nary a recall.* It's just the greatest lark out. We're all in fits about it. Rather rough on me, as I'm in goodish form & came off well in Perth, tho' there too I was hampered by an only middling half-grand.

I wonder if you've a band aboard the 'Wakool'? & if so, if a clarionet forms part of it? If so, soon as you get this, kindly wire me 'clarionet' to *Melbourne Hotel. Perth.* Reasons later.

I'm awfly dry. I drink nought save tea at each meal. All drinks cost bob a glass, which I hold criminal to go in for, at that tallth

Perth 20.1.04. Just got yr letter from Melb, darling.

Had a lovely trip down from the Fields, & a jolly talk with dear old Scharf. How I yearn & long to get aboard 'Wakool' to be with you.[4]

4 Four concerts were given in Perth, on 12, 14, 20 and 21 January, with between-times two concerts in Kalgoorlie on 16 and 18 January.

The six-week tour of twenty-two concerts in South Africa was added to the original tour plan in November 1903. At first Rose planned to sit out the tour in Cape Town, a prospect she did not relish since she had no friends there. In the event it was decided that they could not afford the expense of her accompanying them on the tour and, after a brief stay in Durban, she continued on the Wakool *to London. The tour began with three concerts in Cape Town, the first of which took place on 15 February. It ended at Port Elizabeth on 26 March. The party left for England on the S.S.* Sophocles *on 29 March.*

28   TO ERNEST THESIGER   S.S. "Wakool."
11.2.04.   Off S' African Coast.

My dear Thes

Yr dear gift of "5" ever so welcome.

Lately I've been relishing *the* gaudiest time; before leaving Westralia did some riding on an engine, & hereaboard done some coal-heaving — hour daily until I got whitlows on both hands & had to chuck.

Yesterday Durban, which's landscapes quite pretty, blacks ['spec Zulus] godlike, whites largely outland & thro'out weedy. No good homegrown colonial-type to be spotted at Durb. But the Zulu ricksha-runners are wholly overmanish; fulsomely headgeared with ribbons & cattle-horns & tuniced & breeches as:

the lined shading standing for brilliantest red braiding on snow-white ground

These bounding black brutes knobly-foreheaded & squash-faced, shining from sweat & polished oil, thus devilishly rigged-up are fine untamed savagery indeed — & the perfect taste of savagery — gentlemen, fighters, brutalists — none of the sage greens & pale-pinks of decentcy-worshippers.

Give me henceforth blacks. — Northern Aryans or blacks — Indians, Japs, Shems but smallfry alongside these brainless brawlers. Almost as good as us Vikings-at-heart.

This is the best boat ever been on. Captain best type of held-in-hand poetic-eyed Englishman; Doctor ripping type of a wholly-unpolished, purenatured, broadhearted South Australian, one of the steerage crew a glorious Norwegian who's boundary-rid 3 years in Queensland & is every bit as good as a Britisher.[5]

Dear old Thes, we'll have no end Larx when we fetch up at Lond. For mom "ta" for book

Ever
Percy.

29   TO ROSE GRAINGER
4.3.04.

Jo'burg. [South Africa]
The New Zealand Hotel

Beloved mumy

Yesterday Miss C's birthday. Peter & 2-Js & I joined in a flower bunch, besides which I also sent her a 15 bob sheaf on my own, with gum-leafage — the sole homish stuff havable here at this yeartide — thereamong.

I also gave her a half-in-fun dishup of "Wi' a 100 pipers an' a', an' a'." for piano ‖Ada‖ pennywhistle ‖Peter‖ fiddle ‖Poky‖ & clarinet; ‖Perky‖ took me a beastly time to write — parts and all.[6] I steer as near the wind as I can with the "songstress"; 2-Js, foolishly, has wholly given over his hanging-round-about of the boat, & hardly ever sees her; wherefore halfwise?

Good luck's with me still here; no doubt that these treat me better than 'Stralyer.

This Hotel's charming, full of N.Z-ders & Kangos; tip-top fodder & only £2/5 the week. ‖4 concs in Jo'burg.‖ You see it's quite easy to keep down outlay here. I knew it would be.

Herewith I send on some charming letters; fidges, Mary Husband's, Quil's, Thesiger's, a.s.o.

How ceaselessly glad I am you've gone on to Lond. For now return to there is the most fondly-awaited end, instead of just the cold backing to Europe's grind that it otherwise wld likely have been. As it now holds you it right enough beckons more than all elsewhere. I'm simply fretting to board the boat & nighen by pleasant water-ways ‖at least the sea-trip treatful‖ all that's best — which is you.

Here I've been able to buy Liszt's dish-up of the *Roc'oczy March* that I've wanted some time; a fair stunner, easy, & a good fit — I'll end-up with it at Crossley's Lond conc.[7]

5 The doctor was Francis Frederick Muecke (1879–1945), son of the Hon. H. C. E. Muecke (M.L.C. South Australia, September 1903–10). Francis Muecke married Ada Crossley on 11 April 1905.

6 "At that time I was keen to learn something about wind instruments, having recently finished Hillsong I, for piccolo, 6 oboes, 6 English horns, 6 bassoons, double bassoon. (Strings I have learned something about already, thru my association with Sandby, & thru scraping round myself on Sandby's cello.) I think I must have had my old pre-Boehm-system clarinet with me on that Ada Crossley tour. Sure it is that I bought a penny whistle & annoyed everybody by trying to play it. I never have had a grain of talent for playing any instrument. J.J. could not see me struggling with the penny whistle without wanting to show me how much better he could do it, & I could not watch him play it without wanting to snatch it away from him. So it became a game of snatch, & once the penny whistle broke while we both had hold of it & my hand was cut, perhaps his too." Percy Grainger, *Anecdotes*, 1953.

7 Ada Crossley's concert "with the company" was held at St James Hall on 2 June 1904. Grainger's contribution comprised the Liszt Rákóczy March, the Brahms Rhapsody in E♭, Op. 119 No. 4 and the two movements from *La Scandinavie* with Jacques Jacobs.

8 Grainger was reading *The Land of the Dollar*, letters (from the United States of America) written originally for the *Daily Mail* by George Warrington Steevens (1869–1900) and published in Edinburgh in 1897. Steevens had gone to South Africa to cover the Boer War. He died at Ladysmith of enteric fever.

9 Clem Sudholze, baggage mover on the 1903–04 tour.

10 The S.S. *Sophocles*, running six days late, reached Plymouth on 26 April. Rose was there to meet it. Percy proceeded directly to Grimsby, where the third day's proceedings of the fourth North and East Lincolnshire Competitions were being held at the Grimsby Town Hall on 27 April. Grainger's setting of the Swedish folksong [*A Song of*] *Vermeland* was set piece for the choral section, but its projected performance by the combined choirs at the evening concert, Grainger conducting, was cancelled "owing to the lateness of the hour". Grainger played two groups of piano solos at the evening concert.

You mind Stevens, ‖the big war correspondent‖ who died some while back; I've bought his *The Land of The Dollar*, it is very enthralling & a heartquickening record of America's wondrousness. Rather like the 'Merican part of Kippy's '*From Sea to Sea*' ‖I wonder who hogged?‖ & quite as fascinating. We'll go thro' it jollily together.[8]

I'll very nearly be able to get thro Africa on my 1st week's screw; not far over it anyway. Clem & I share rooms.[9] What an altogether fine little chap he is. His father dead some 10, 11 years the earning all fell on his mother. At one time she kept a detective's office & Clem did detective work; spying on hirelings in shops & such. This gave him the 'crawls'. At about 15, 16 he went as a ship's boy for 3 months on sailing-ship plying 'tween 'Stralyer & N.Z.

He found the life very rank, but shored with his whole pay, & some knowledge of water-matters. This he turned to account when he & a friend bought a yacht ‖some 30 feet‖ which they got unlimited enjoyment off, *trained up for racing, so as to raise a high price for yacht, won the Brighton Cup, & got the high price.* He was Williamson's youngest-on-record paymaster; & he's now on the track of a Gov billet in Pretoria at £30 the month.

I think he is a very very worthenable sort of thorough Australian — one more instance of the splendidness of the German Settler. He's all save; he & I run a very close tie for greatest closefistedness. He is so useful to me in lots of ways; get[s] me newspapers for nought, & such.

Dont forget, dearie, my hint as to the unwishfulness of a leagued mum- & Lowrey meet. Naturally, when I first see you the rest get eclipsed very much, & this might cause a little pain ‖needless & nasty,‖ to the eclipsed.

Give all the boys my love — Quil, Thes, Alec, Mücke; Scott if he's about.

We steam from Cape 'bout 29, we look for.

Date details in the 2 or 3 more weeks sendings you'll yet get.

Goodbye, darling.

30   TO H. BALFOUR GARDINER   South Africa,
[Postcard]   East London.
18.3.1904.

Dear Old Gard

How I rejoice hear of yr stuff being guv. & how I yearn hear yr new composings.

About a week or fortnight after you get this I'll reach *London* by S.S. "Sophocles". I do hope you'll be in England at the time to welcome me as near as poss after my arrival with your squireliness.

Find date from mother c/o Mortimer Menpes 25 Cadogan Gdns. S.W.

31   TO ROGER QUILTER   S.S. Sophocles.
25.4.04

Most dear Roger

As I guess we'll make Plymouth in time for me to make a dash for the Nth, I'm just scribling to let you know of a wish of Miss Crossley's with regard to yr songs.[10]

She was very taken with those she heard of yrs before, & we've been talking a lot about you & she much hopes to find among yr dear warbles stuff for the make-up of her soon coming Recital. ⟦at which I play⟧

She's a dear frank hale & somewhat shrewd girl, ever so hearty & natural; & I read her some of yr letters, so she knows yr build a bit.

Take her altogether *all* you have for low voice & any others you think'd shift down well.

Cld you get along to 6V Bickenhead Mansions at 2.30 Thursday?

This haste is so she may have fullest time to get up for Recital in; even if no go this run maybe trumps for later.[11]

I sadly fear to have to forego the pleasure of welcome from your dear face, as, as far as aboard time-tables tell, I'l[l] need to take midnight train to London & thence Grimsby at 10 a.m.

This is far from my hopes; I fondly looked for a meet with you soon as I got.

This ship's lots belated, as you know. Our keel's clogged with weed from Brisbane River, & the engines are old & weakening.

This aftern I ended a sketchdraft for the *Beatless Music Typer* machine. This I want to go thro' thoroughly with you, if you'l[l] give the time, & have yr candid & critical opinion. I must have it experimented not too far hence.

The tropics were lovely. When not practising I threw quoits day-long, & swat like a river. I've never seen ought like the way I simply flushed myself out; It feels so cleansing & purifying. I relish nought more than fairly active exercise in hot seas.

I read much Tennyson early in voyage, & found the bulk of him greater than I had guessed; how bestly English *Locksley Hall*![12]

Take Ada yr lovely song of the *goldfish in the font* or some such.

For short time being
Percy.

11 Ada Crossley did sing a bracket of songs by Roger Quilter at her St James Hall recital on 2 June, Quilter accompanying. It included his setting of Alfred Tennyson's poem "Now Sleeps the Crimson Petal" (Op. 3, No. 2, composed 1904), which latter setting she also sang on the 1908–09 Australasian tour. One line of the poem reads, "Nor winks the gold-fin in the porph'ry font".

12 Alfred Tennyson (1809–92), first Baron Tennyson, Poet Laureate. His poem "Locksley Hall' was published in 1842.

Back in London by early May, Grainger resumed his hectic round of playing, teaching and socialising. The Graingers were now in residence at 26 Coulson Street, Sloane Square. On 24 September 1904 Grainger left London for a month's tour of Scandinavia with Herman Sandby. Three concerts were given in Copenhagen: a matinee for invited audience on 29 September, and two public recitals on 1 and 4 October. Other concerts followed. The tour was not a success financially. Only the concerts in Aarhus and Holbæk showed a profit. Though a concert was given in Göteborg, Sweden, the projected Stockholm recitals were cancelled, as was the recital in Halmstad and the whole of the Norwegian part of the tour. The loss was carried by Herman, who, against the promise of a profitable return tour in 1905, accepted Percy's terms. Herman himself met all costs of hire of halls and advertising, and paid Grainger what he would otherwise have earned in London. Artistically the tour was a success, introducing Grainger to a new musical public and extending his range of contacts. Critics were generally enthusiastic about his playing, markedly less so about his arrangements of the Scandinavian folksongs and dances. At home, his success was well advertised: by Ada Crossley through regular advertisements in the Daily Telegraph, *by Rose through the mail. Percy's letters to Rose from this tour do not survive, though hers to him do. He travelled back to London alone on 25 October.*

13 William Henry Perry Leslie (1860–1926), became chairman of John Broadwood & Sons, the London firm of keyboard instrument makers, when that firm was established as a private company in October 1901. He became General Manager as well in May 1904. The Broadwood Concerts, launched in London at St James Hall on 6 November 1902, were designed to keep the name of Broadwood before the musical public by inviting notable soloists to perform on the company's pianos. Similar series were also launched in the provinces in the years 1903–04. Grainger and Sandby made their London Broadwood Concerts debut at the sixth concert of the third series, at Aeolian Hall, on 26 January 1905. Grainger did not tour Scandinavia with a Broadwood piano in 1904. He did not begin touring in Holland until 1910.

14 Narcisco Vert, doyen of the London concert agents. He died suddenly in June 1905 and management of the agency was assumed by his nephew and partner Pedro Tillett. Vert was Grainger's agent for a two-year period, between December 1907 and December 1909.

15 Adela H. Wodehouse (Mrs Edmond Wodehouse) (d. 1921), wrote a 58-page historical survey of European song, including folksong, for volume three of the first edition of *A Dictionary of Music and Musicians (A.D. 1450–1880)*, edited by Sir George Grove, the relevant volume being published by Macmillan & Co. in 1894. Her article was revised and expanded for the second edition, edited by J. Fuller Maitland, the relevant volume being published in 1908. The Scandinavian section was enlarged to include a listing of books and collections available. The same article was reprinted in the third edition, 1928.
On 23 March 1905 the *British Australasian* reported that Mrs Wodehouse was helping Grainger with his studies of the Icelandic language and of Faeroese music.

32 TO HERMAN SANDBY
[Original: Danish/English]
27.5.04

26 Coulson St
Sloane □ SW
[London]

I received your all too dear and kind letter with heart-thumping happiness; just to think of journeying through the North with you is glorious. Certainly I can come straight away in October for 3 or 4 weeks.

Old friend, we begin to do an excellent thing, and to "exchange business letters" with each other; that can easily come to something!

Now, I take yr offer *in all simplicity, hoping you feel quite sure that you will not lose on me.* As I stated in last letter, things as they stand do not allow me to take slightest risk of loss, or *even risk of not* **making**; yet I should be heart-broken, if you, dear fellow, should, out of friendship & bigheartedness, run into ought that might land you in a hole.

Of course, it would be heaven for us both anyway, but be a dear & be selfish for once & think over the matter *from yr side & standpoint*, & if you *really* think it's not too much for you, well, I'm dead keen on it, & we've got the best time together to look forward to that we've ever had.

Let's know finally at once, as I'm all jumpy to know for sure.

I won't begin to say how bighearted it is of you, this whole proposal, because it is not necessary, between us two.

As you say, we can build up [a] grand programme, but there is time for that.

Now comes a 2nd proposal.

Yesterday I was with Leslie (of Broadwood's — piano makers) and spoke to him of your proposal and the tour, and he will gladly send a Broadwood piano with us. (he taking all expenses for which, of course)[13]

Now do you think that would get in the road of the money-making of the tour? Do you think it better to get one's Piano from the *local* dealer?

If it wouldn't matter, it would be a good thing for the following reason.

Leslie was so taken with yr playing that he would like to have you over here to play at one of the Broadwood concerts; likely the concert I'll be playing at, & he suggests that as soon as our Scand tour is thro' that we come back here *together* & play at a Broadwood together, likely doing our Scan Folk Songs & Dances; in which case he'd try & get you some 2nd engagement the 2 making a fee of about £20.

Of course, that wld be hardly more than expenses, but still (if you're doing nothing better just then) it would mean a week or so longer together anyhow, & maybe you'd get something else here.

You could put up in my room here or somewhere close by.

Of course the Broadwood's are *very* good concerts.

Now please answer *at once* the following

1. whether you've anything against my bringing my own Piano (Broadwood)

2. whether you'd come over here early in Nov to play at 2 concerts for £20 (about)

Also send a *rough sketch* of where you think we'd be touring, what towns, a.s.o.

Leslie talks of pushing me in *Holland*, so that I'd likely come straight on to you after some concerts (Recitals?) at The Hague, Amsterdam, a.s.o.

I have just now received a letter from you from Phil.[adelphia] 13 Jan. It has been in Perth, Capetown, Johannesburg, Durban, and has been addressed to Vert, who sent it to me. It has really travelled a lot, this letter[14] It is very interesting what you write there about American associations of the most varied character; yes, they must really be a most peculiar people.

The newspaper cuttings are very laughable, one can't understand at all that they altogether mean it; but they do.

The 2 Folksongs that you sent in the same envelope are very lovely, especially "The 1st Love". But the words are modern aren't they? or not *very* old?

That reminds me.

You know Mrs Wodehouse, the woman who wrote the good article in Grove's Dict of Music about Folkmusic; she is a very good friend of mine, and I love and admire her immensely.[15] Now, she is writing at the present time a big book about the whole European Folkmusic, and will soon begin on the Scandinavian. I have promised her to help all I can with translating the words, and to ask you to let me know

1. which are the best *buy-able* editions of Scan folkmusic collections.

2. & which the best *works & authorities* on & for Scan folkmusic

If you don't know yourself, please ask someone who knows, and write to me.

I am very keen that she should have all possible help towards her book, as she deeply entered into Folksmusic spirit, & I'd like to see her book as complete & up to date as may be.

Maybe a *librarian* at one of the Museums would know best. If you know any such *by name only*, write me them, so that Mrs Wodehouse can write them herself direct, if need be.

If there's no real ground against my using Broadwood, it would be a real good thing for me. Leslie can do a lot[16]

Now, goodbye, for the present.

Percy.

33   TO ERNEST THESIGER   [Chelsea]
[Postcard]
22.6.[0]4.

Shld just *love* see you play tomow night, if you can poss spare ticks.

Perk.

34   TO ERNEST THESIGER   26, Coulson Street,
[Postcard. "before July 24, 1904"]   Sloane Square, S.W.
Monday

You perfect darling to get me the new pup[il] & she seems to want to work too

Going hear her Thursday.

Thursday eve you *must* come with me to the 2th singsong at Feilding's Got his gracious allowance.[17]

We'll go together

Percy.

16 Leslie was indeed in a position to "do a lot" for Grainger, not only through his connections with the firm of Broadwood, but through his activities as a conductor of amateur choirs. On 8 May 1905 Leslie appeared, with Grainger, at the choral festival of the Association of North-West Norfolk Village Choirs (of whose committee he was Chairman), conducting the 700-voice combined choirs and the band of the Coldstream Guards in a performance of Grainger's *Sir Eglamore*, a ballad for small male voice chorus, large mixed chorus, children's chorus and military band. He would have done more — specifically, had Grainger's choruses performed in London — but for his resistance to Grainger's use of English terms and performance directions instead of the more conventional Italian ones. The phrase "breathe when blown" from *Sir Eglamore*, he found particularly ridiculous, as Rose reported to Percy on 1 March 1906, after a conversation with Leslie: "it should be 'breathe before blown' ". But Grainger would not compromise. "He says you snubbed him shamefully", continued Rose, "therefore he says nothing more to you about yr choruses." Leslie was not the only one to find Grainger's English terms problematic.

17 In the winter of 1904 Lady Winefride Elwes, her husband Gervase and their family took a lease on a house at No. 13 Hertford Street, which Everard Feilding shared with them. It was during the period of their lease on this house (to April 1905) that Everard instituted the "jamborees", fortnightly meetings of music-lovers of every sort, amateur and professional, singers, composers and instrumentalists, the purpose of which was to try through new British compositions. Percy Grainger was, in Lady Winefride's words, "always to the fore, bubbling with enthusiasm and vitality". In his autobiographical *Anecdotes* Grainger writes somewhat disparagingly about Feilding's negative influence on these "jamborees", which were a continuation of the choral

rehearsals Grainger himself had started years before to try through his own and other composers' music. This fact notwithstanding, Feilding did much to further Grainger's career as a choral composer in the early years: as co-founder with Mrs Frank Lowrey of the Queen's House Manuscript Music Society; as committee member of the North Lincolnshire and Mid Somerset Musical Competitions; as co-ordinator, so the evidence would suggest, of the subscription which saw the first of Grainger's choruses published by the Vincent Music Company Ltd. in December 1904. On 7 December 1904 Feilding arranged a performance at his house in Hertford Street of four of Grainger's recently published choruses by a choir which included "about forty well-known professional singers".

18 Percy lunched with Mrs Matesdorf on 17 July and spent the weekend of 13–15 August with Sir Charles and Lady Ryan, whose daughter was taking lessons from him. Grainger made his Queen's Hall debut at the Promenade Concert on 17 August, playing the Tchaikovsky B♭ minor Piano Concerto under Henry Wood. On 18 August he left for Guildford, to spend a few days with Thesiger at his country home.

19 Grainger's first setting of *Sir Eglamore*, as described in note 16 above, based on a tune and text published in John Stafford Smith's compilation *Musica Antiqua. A selection of music of this and other countries, from the commencement of the twelfth to the beginning of the eighteenth century* . . . (London, [1812]). Completed on 27 July 1904, the setting was published in a vocal score by the Vincent Music Company Ltd, London, in December 1904.

20 The country residence of the Quilter family.

21 Cyril Scott's *Rhapsody No. 1* for orchestra was given its first performance at a Queen's Hall Promenade Concert on 10 September 1904.

---

35   TO ERNEST THESIGER   26, Coulson Street,
24.7.[0]4.   Sloane Square, S.W.

Most dear Un-ernest (aber doch)

Most worse luck I cant *then*, but if y're up for 17th, bed at Sloane St, breakf here & I'l back with you then if that'd do.
    I'm going to yr Ryans then (when you asked for)
    Do let me come after the Queen's Hall instead.
    Mrs Matesdorf, when I was last there, did nought but *rave* 'bout you, & tho' she rather gathered youw're bored at idea of her studioing you, she much looks forward to so doing in Fall.[18]
    Ever so lovingly & forwardlookingly (also love from Mum)

        Yr
        Percy.

No, [illegible], I never forget those sort of things; thanks all same
I'm busy on Sir Eglamore[19]

36   TO ERNEST THESIGER   Bawdsey Manor,
7.9.04.   Woodbridge.[20]

I'm wearing yr waistcoat.
    Yes, I think the charmingly written out songlet delightful, words most fetching.
    Is it a country tune, or what?
    Many thanks for it.
    Our little joke with the high single reed I've matched with another.
    Coming back from Deal the other evening I stepped into a full car of old, staid, had-(I think) -been seasick, & come-over-by-Dover Folk; soon as train left station I outed my green case & unpeeled the shining metaled tube. You shld have seen the sea of expression that flooded them all. I then pocketed the mouthpiece, & played dumbly for 2 to 3 hours.
    The blend of these earnest people & my tireless silent brilliancy was uncommon. Fingers simply fluttering up & down rending chromatic runs!
    Cyril's Rhap is again put off till *next Sat.*[21]
    I've taken in 1 full rehearsal.
    Parts sound striking — luscious.
    On the whole, it strikes me as *hinting* at rich orchestral possibilities. Muddy at times
    Love, & let's hear again soon

        Ever
        Percy.

37   TO ERNEST THESIGER   Copenhagen
[Postcard]   Denmark
13.10.04.

Darling Earnest,

All this is quite amusing.
    We've been so busy tho' that we've not got out to see a single thing yet.
    Warmest messages to all yr dear folk

        Perks

38   TO CLARA ALDRIDGE   Copenhagen.
[Postcard]   Denmark
13.10.04

Darling Aunty Clara

We are having such a jolly & successful tour up here in these charming
countries. With all fond love   Percy

My friend Sandby & I go along here daily.

39   TO JOHN H. GRAINGER   Sønder Jernløse [Jærnløse]
[Postcard]   (near Holbaek)
18.10.04.   [Denmark]

Here we are staying 2 days with Sandby's brother.
The country is *so* enthralling. Very like England. Single-lying farms,
thatched roofed, with piles of dung & gooseponds everywhere.
We scraped together a lot of amateurs in this village & played things of
Sandby's & mine. I played clarinet & English horn in the band.[22]

Ever yr loving son
Percy.

22 Sandby's brother Frederick
was village doctor at Sønder
Jærnløse and an amateur flautist.
Grainger's setting of the
traditional Irish tune *Colleen
Dhas*, for guitar, two violins,
viola, cello, flute and cor anglais
dates from this visit.

44

1905

Violinist Sigmund Beel joined
Grainger and Sandby at Liverpool
to play the "pezzo elegaico" from
the Tchaikovsky Piano Trio in A
minor, Op. 50. The same
musicians performed the whole
work in their programme for the
Sheffield Chamber Music Society
on 20 February 1906. Frederic
Austin sang in the Liverpool
concert. Only three movements of
the suite *La Scandinavie* were
given.

2 Grainger and Sandby gave their
London duo-recital at the
Bechstein Hall on 13 February,
Ada Crossley assisting. The
Globe, 14 February 1905, reported
that there had been a "very large
audience". *The Times*, 14
February 1905, commented that
the recital was "a great success",
and more, "it was a concert of
unusual interest as well". The day
after the recital Sibyl Thesiger
wrote to Percy, "Before the
bigness of your genius — the
pigmy words of human
understanding seem ludicrously
inadequate. So I can only tell you
that the music I heard last night
gave me a most soul satisfying
feeling of drinking in the
completely good — all of it — but
specially your playing . . ." On 27
February Grainger was engaged
for a Gentlemen's Concert in
Manchester, playing the
Tchaikovsky Piano Concerto
No. 2 in G major under the baton
of Hans Richter. Being out of
London, Grainger was unable to
accept an invitation to play his
"Welsh War March" (*The March
of the Men of Harlech*, No. 2 of
Two Welsh Fighting Songs) to the
King on 26 February.

On 16 January 1905 Herman Sandby arrived in London for a series of concerts with Grainger. A week later the duo headed north for a musical evening in Liverpool on the 23rd and a Ladies' Concert in Manchester on the 24th. They returned to London for their Broadwood Concert on the 26th.

40   TO ROSE GRAINGER   [PM Liverpool]
[Postcard. PM 24 January 1905]

We're just off to M-chester.
There is such life & refreshment in all one's surroundings up here North.
Our old fiddler play'd dirt in the Trio like anything. Everyone seemed fairly hived with the Scans & Austin thinks both our improvements are astounding.[1]

Yr loving son
Percy.   /Herm.

41   TO ERNEST THESIGER   26, Coulson Street,
16.2.05   Sloane Square, S.W.

I partic wanted you [to] come yest as I wanted to get you into a corner & ram into you how fully & thankfully I realize how no less than *wondrously* **all** the folk I've met thro' you just hosted up on Mond.[2]
Do please tell your dear mother that 5 of the Phillips went.
Forgive these details, but they serve to express things which arnt details, & I must have you know how wonderfully much I owe to all the best kind of "drummer-dom" that you have put thro' for me.
Every hour I love the tableglory more. I cant think ought more thrilling than that style of thing in gen & that very dear one in partic.
After the 27 you'll soon see me round at Wellington □

Ever yrs
Perks.

I wish you'd tell your sister how very happy her charming & most kind letter made me. Also heaps proud.

Rose had written of Percy to her sister Clara on 10 February 1905, "... in fact he is now making great strides in his career, & is very, very busy always". Grainger's growing success is reflected in an increasing number of engagements in 1905 — prestigious engagements both in London and in the provinces — and in a general consensus of critical opinion which saw him as one of the most interesting and gifted of the younger generation of pianists. Then came an accolade devoutly wished for by Rose: on 7 March Grainger made the first of many appearances before royalty when, with Sandby, he was commanded to play before Queen Alexandra at Buckingham Palace.

If critical acclamation as yet focused principally on his skill as an executant, the year 1905 also saw Grainger make significant progress as a composer. His choral works were performed at several competition festivals throughout England. The Grand Evening Concert of the North Lincolnshire Musical Competitions, held at Brigg on 11 April, ended with the Grand Chorus The March of the Men of Harlech, *conducted by the composer and accompanied by the Brigg Subscription Band and Drums. At Frome, at the evening concert of the Mid-Somerset Musical Competitions on 4 May, Grainger conducted the 400-voice combined choirs in three of his folksong arrangements,* An Irish Idyll, Sir Eglamore and the Dragon *and* The Hunter's Career. *Four days later, at the Grand Festival Concert of the Association of North-West Norfolk Village Choirs, Mr W. H. Leslie conducted the 700-voice combined choirs and the band of the Coldstream Guards in a performance of* Sir Eglamore; *the* Old Irish Tune *and the* Two Welsh Fighting Songs *were also performed on the same programme. These five choral works, plus Grainger's* A Song of Vermeland, *were all published by the Vincent Music Publishing Company, London. Publication had been funded by subscription, apparently organised by Everard Feilding. In August 1905, Feilding reported to Grainger a balance profit on printing and sales of £2.13.5d.*

But the richest experience for Grainger the composer in this period was undoubtedly his attendance at the Village Competition segment of the competitions at Brigg in April. There, in 1905, a new class was introduced, "Class XII Folksong". The prospectus announced: "The prize in this class will be given to whoever can supply the best unpublished old Lincolnshire folk song or plough song. The song should be sung or whistled by the competitor, but marks will be allotted for the excellence rather of the song than of its actual performance. It is specially requested that the establishment of this class be brought to the notice of old people in the country, who are most likely to remember this kind of song, and that they be urged to come in with the best old song they know". Grainger's interest in folksong was already established before he came to Brigg. But until then the settings he had made had been based on secondary sources: tunes drawn from collections made by other people. At Brigg he made his first contact with the living tradition. The experience was definitive. He responded with passionate enthusiasm, as collector and arranger.

42 TO LADY WINEFRIDE CARY-ELWES[3]
13.4.05.

26, Coulson Street,
Sloane Square, S.W.

Dear Lady Winefride

How dear you all were to me.
I'm going to beg lots of bother from you; please forgive:—
Could you oblige me with following particulars?
Full names (also Christian or initial at least) & *addresses* of the
    3 Folksinging prize winners[4]

3 Lady Winefride Mary Elizabeth Elwes (1868–1959), fourth daughter of the eighth Earl of Denbigh and wife of tenor Gervase Elwes. She was Honorary Secretary of the North Lincolnshire Musical Competitions. In her biography of her husband (*Gervase Elwes — the Story of his Life*, W. Elwes and R. Elwes, London 1935, p.162), she credits Grainger and her brother Everard Feilding with the institution of the new folksong class at Brigg, though Grainger's letter suggests that it was her idea. Of the 1905 competition she observed, "The entrances were not numerous, but some wonderful tunes were unearthed". Four of the eight tunes Grainger notated were subsequently published in No. 7 (Vol. II, Part 2) of the *Journal of the Folk-Song Society*, 1905, pp.79–81, with comments from Frank Kidson (the judge at Brigg), Cecil Sharp, Ralph Vaughan-Williams and Lucy Broadwood. The family name was shortened from Cary-Elwes to Elwes around this time.

4 First prize at Brigg was awarded to what Kidson described as "a good version" of "Creeping Jane", sung by Joseph Taylor of Saxby, Lincs.; second prize went to a version of "Come, All You Merry Ploughboys" sung by William Hilton Sen., of Keelby; third prize to "T'owd Yowe wi' One Horn" sung by Dean Robinson of Scawby Brook, Lincs. Everard Feilding subsequently wrote to Grainger of the first prize, "By the way I found Creeping Jane in full with modifications but evidently the same tune, published in [a] recent vol. of Somerset tunes. I wonder if Kitson [*sic*] knew this when he allotted the prize". In private, after the competition, Joseph Taylor sang "Brigg Fair" to Grainger for the first time.

5 Grainger returned from the competitions at Brigg to play in a concert devoted to the works of Charles Villiers Stanford, presented by the Leighton House Chamber Concerts on 13 April 1905. He played two (Nos. 1 and 3) of Stanford's *Three Rhapsodies*, Op. 92. He had previously premiered Nos. 2 and 3 at the Bechstein Hall concert on 13 February. The Rhapsodies had been written especially for him in the summer of 1904, and are dedicated to him. Grainger had also made his debut for the National Sunday League concerts, C. V. Stanford conducting the London Symphony Orchestra, on 26 March 1905. That same concert had included the first performance in London of Stanford's *Four Irish Dances*, works which Grainger subsequently arranged for piano and played with enormous success. He introduced two at his recital on 15 November 1905.

6 The *British Australasian* of 27 April 1905 reported that Herman Sandby had sent copies of some of Grainger's folksong settings to Grieg, and that Grieg had been so pleased with them that he had promptly sent Grainger a signed photograph of himself, endorsed "With thanks for your splendid folk-song settings for mixed voices". Grainger had given his first performance of the Grieg Piano Concerto at a Grand Orchestral Concert at the Northern Polytechnic Institute on 11 March 1905.

7 Gervase Henry (Cary-) Elwes (1866–1921), tenor. He first appeared professionally as a singer in May 1903 at the Westmoreland Festival in Kendal. In the same month he sang and whistled in the Queen's House performance of Grainger's choruses. On Easter Monday 1904, Rose had written to Percy, " . . . Elwes is doing splendidly, & should be cultivated". Grainger appeared many times on the same concert platform as Elwes, especially in the years between 1905 and the second Australasian tour of 1908–09. At their joint Aeolian Hall recital on 14 November 1906 Elwes introduced five of Grainger's Lincolnshire folksong settings.

ditto of our friend at the bank.
address of the Messingberds.

The results are so rousing (Folksongs) that I'm going to see I get a week off some time in the summer (maybe August) to do a sort of byke tour thro' Lincolnsh. gathering tunes. The Messingberds said they thought there'd be lots to get round 'bout them. Maybe Everard'd join me. I'm asking him.

Wld you help me in this?

As follows; before I come get someone to take down the words of all the songs Dean Robinson (3rd prize) remembers. He said he knew lots more. That wld speed things some.

Also sound the dear old 2nd prize man. He might be a gold mine.

Then there's the man at Massingham? that I was told of, a cobbler, or something. I remember we talked of him.

Then you might maybe sound the folk you are in touch with over the competitions at the various places & ask them to hunt round for likely victims to our pen & pap. I risk asking you all this because one can ask folksong lovers to do anything for folksong cause & I dare say Linc'll prove rich. Anyway you must feel proud at the jolly results your forethought of this year rounded up.

Such a byke tour wld be tons of fun, & better than that.

Soon I'll copy out all the 8 tunes we got & send them you.

Love to Gervase & all

If you're bored at idea of the folk fishing cruise please just say so but I hope you won't

Ever yrs
Percy G.

I got the train fine & didnt make as merry a hash of the concert as I looked for[5]

43   TO EDVARD GRIEG
[Original: Danish]
14.4.05.

26, Coulson Street,
Sloane Square, S.W.
London

Dear Master

I cannot begin to tell you with what deep joy and surprise I received your picture; nor can I thank you for your very great goodness in writing me the friendly words on it.

I am exceedingly happy and proud that you don't think badly of my folksongs.[6]

What your music has meant for us English people, you naturally know: we imagine that there is something in our race which is not without kindred with the Norwegian, and perhaps not least because your glorious creations catch hold of us so much more irresistibly than, for example, German art could ever do.

What your art has been *for* **me** I will not tire you with trying to express, either.

I take the liberty of sending you a picture of myself.

In the heartfelt gratitude for all the rich joys I have continually received at your hands,

In deepest admiration
your
Percy Grainger

44 TO GERVASE ELWES[7]

[n.d. probably mid-August 1905][8]

63 Oakley St
Chelsea. S.W.

My dear Gervase

I saw Feilding before he left & he asked me to write you re next year's Brigg Folksong splash.

I should love to dish-up anyway 2 of the already found ones, & further, should you care to do these & they fit in with yr Program (which Feilding thought they would) suggest "Anchor Song" by Austin (whom I'm going to ask if he'll sing for you next year) & chorus, & "Our king went forth" very simply set very old English tune for massed-chorus.[9]

We cld talk over this when I come to you to Brigg if you still can have me.

I could come to you late on August 31st (or on Sept 1st if better) & I could hunt tunes with you till about the 5th or 6th.[10]

Then we might find some more tunes to splash up with chorally for next year.

Do let's have a line telling if you can song-seek with me then.

Ever yrs
Percy Grainger

45 TO KAREN HOLTEN[11]

[Original: Danish]
12.8.05.

63, Oakley Street,
Chelsea.

Dear Miss Holten.

I have been away a lot in the last months.

As you presumably already know, I am coming again to Denmark in the beginning of Sept.

I have spoken to my Mother about a room for you, and if you and your friend (I believe you wrote to me that she is also thinking of coming to London) would like to, you could probably both get "Pension" in the same house in which we have rooms. But in that case it would be best to let me know rather soon, as otherwise the landlady will probably promise the room to someone else. If you both want to come then it will cost (for both) £3.3.0 (3 Pounds, 3 Shillings) a *week* for 2 bedrooms and 1 *small* sitting room and board; or if you come alone then it comes to £1.11.6 (1 pound, 11½ shillings) a week for 1 bedroom and 1 small sitting room and board.

We can discuss all details when we meet in Copenhagen, but if you and your friend approve of the proposal it would, as already said, be best to let the landlady here with us know in good time. This is a healthy part of the town here, where most of the artists live.

Herman Sandby and I travel back to London about the 12th October (from Denmark) and if you and your friend would like it, you could travel together with us. But we can discuss all that later. If you would perhaps like to have some lessons already in Denmark (in September) you can arrange it with the Sandbys. You may do exactly as you wish.

I have had a **terribly** busy summer, and the winter will be just as full
I look forward immensely to meeting you again in Copenhagen

With friendly greetings
yours sincerely
Percy Grainger

8 The Graingers moved to 63 Oakley Street on 22 June 1905. Feilding's letter asking Grainger to send this information to Elwes was written on 9 August.

9 The evening concert of the sixth annual North Lincolnshire Musical Competitions, held at the Town Hall, Brigg, on 7 May 1906, included a group of "old Lincolnshire Folk Songs arranged by Mr Percy Grainger, and which were sung at the last Competitions, or collected afterwards by Mr Grainger". Of tunes collected in April 1905, the 1906 group included his setting of *Brigg Fair*, for tenor solo (sung by Gervase Elwes) and unaccompanied mixed chorus and *Marching Tune*, for mixed chorus and brass band. Of tunes collected afterwards, three settings were performed: *Six Dukes Went Afishin'* (collected 4 September 1905) and *The Gypsy's Wedding Day* (collected 2 September 1905), both in settings for vocal quartet, and "As I Walked Out One May Morning" (*I'm Seventeen Come Sunday*, collected 3 September 1905), also for mixed chorus and brass band. Frederic Austin did not take part in the concert on 7 May. Neither of the choruses referred to in Grainger's letter were performed.

10 Grainger was engaged to play the Tchaikovsky B♭ minor Piano Concerto at a Queen's Hall Promenade Concert on 30 August. He was scheduled to leave with Rose on 7 September, for his second Scandinavian tour with Herman Sandby.

11 As Grainger's European reputation grew, prospective students travelled to London to take lessons with him, as he had travelled to Berlin to study with Busoni in 1903, and while on tour he frequently supplemented his income by giving lessons. Danish-born Karen Holten (1879-1953) was to become a figure of some importance in Grainger's life in the following years. This is his first letter to her, and in it he uses the formal "you". Karen had already appeared in public as a pianist. A friend of the Sandby family, she met Grainger at their home on his visit to Copenhagen in 1904.

12 Between 2 and 9 September Grainger, aided by the Elweses' sons, had notated sixty-one tunes. These form the largest single group of the first ninety-nine tunes he collected. Other significant groupings, apart from the eight gathered at Brigg in April, were collected at Wimbledon in August (nine tunes), at Dunrobin Castle in Scotland on 23 August, while guest of the Duchess of Sutherland (four tunes), and at Kirkby Lonsdale, Westmoreland on 29 October, while the guest of the Countess of Bective (eleven tunes).

13 A concert was given for the Music Society in Thisted on 24 September.

14 Rose Grainger to Roger Quilter, 26 September 1905, "Herman & Percy are having a glorious time, plenty of engagements, & always have success wherever they play. Percy's letters are full of joy, he is like one intoxicated, that land seems to have a tremendous effect upon him, much the same as Australia". Percy returned to London to find that Rose was not pleased that he had enjoyed himself so much while away from her: "I found myself in the position any proud & noble-natured young man most hates to find himself in: that he must deny his feelings, retract his intentions, 'wriggle out' of assertions & self-unfoldments he had indulged in — in other words, submit himself unwillingly to discipline he is not strong enough to overthrow, & does not even *want* to overthrow" (letter to Alfhild Sandby, 4 July 1939).

15 Alfhild de Luce (1876–1961), Norwegian-born, American-educated pianist, artist and writer. She married Herman Sandby (her second husband) in 1909[?]. She joined the 1905 tour at Grainger's request: her name first appears as extra accompanist on the programme of the concert at Morsø on 25 September. Her relationship with Grainger was a strange one. His infatuation was momentarily intense, and though Alfhild rejected his sexual advances, their intimacy had a sufficiently erotic component to

On 1 September Grainger returned to Brigg as guest of the Elweses for four days' folksong collecting in Lincolnshire. An untimely leap down a staircase at the Manor House, however, resulted in a sprained ankle, which detained him at Brigg for more than a week. His harvest of folktunes was thereby enriched, but his departure for Denmark for a second tour with Herman Sandby was delayed.

The month-long Danish tour began with a concert at Holbæk on 16 September. Heeding the lessons of the previous tour, the duo concentrated on the provincial towns, with concerts sponsored by local music clubs and societies. The main part of the tour was in Jutland. This time the tour was a success, both artistically and financially, and Rose was able to report to her correspondents that Percy was making money. When a command came to play at the Yellow Palace, Copenhagen, on 11 October, the English newspapers reported that the two musicians had been heard by Queen Alexandra, the King of Denmark, the King of Greece, the Dowager Empress of Russia, the Crown Prince and Crown Princess of Denmark and Princess Valdemar.

While Percy toured in Denmark, Rose revisited Frankfurt, staying with her old friends the Karl Klimsches. None of Percy's letters to Rose from this tour have survived.

Rose was back in London by 14 October. Percy, Herman and Karen Holten, whom Grainger had met again in Copenhagen, returned together to London on 15 October. Karen took rooms in the same house as the Graingers. Her name first appears in Grainger's diary as a pupil on 1 November.

46 TO LADY WINEFRIDE CARY-ELWES   Hotel Jsefjord
17.9.1905   Holbæk
           [Denmark]

My dear Lady Winefride

Here we are having a gorgeous time (& making pots too) & all due to you & your neverforgetable kindness.

I am sure I dont know what I have done to earn all the lovely times I had with you & am having here now — in fact I know I haven't earnt it & relish it doubly therefor.

It is nice to be able to play to all these dear Danes the lovely tunes that your help allowed me to gather in, & to think how few lands in Europe could boast such a crop. Good old supposed-to-be unmusical England.[12]

I write all this because I really think we really did a big thing by that week's work; more so than we realize, & I'm fearfully thankful to you for making it all possible (& so joyous).

I know I was a disgusting nuisance but I'm fearfully thankful, & so is Sandby that I got here in time.

Love to all please.

Ever yrs
Percy Grainger

Danish address p.a. Herman Sandby/Gammeltoftsgade 24/Copenhagen. Denmark.

47 TO ERNEST THESIGER   [PM Thisted[13]
[Postcard]   Denmark]
24.9.05.

Having the time of our lives & doing *thunderingly*.[14] Was **so** glad to get the ripping Scotch tune you sent Love from Sandby. So looking forward to the lots I've got to tell you when we meet.

Ever with love
Perks.

48 TO ALFHILD DE LUCE[15]   High Barn,
18.10.05.   Godalming.[16]

Wise Alfhild.

Me audacious! — but it takes your dear cheek to talk vegetarianism to a born meateater, who is sick of tined meats & can't get fresh flesh.[17]

Just because you're up there in the roofs dont come the tall over me with your birdcage saints.

Anyhow, what's an artist but a circus boss who drags out the shy & tender & bashful-withdrawing inner thing into the outer uncaring public glare. If we (in all directions) wouldn't take the risk that lies in all marble, or canvas, & paper, & brass, & gongs or bells or bowls or bars (the risk of smirch that goes along of all matter) we could never translate into *body* all the (seemingly, anyway) *bodiless*, fleeting, ungraspable promptings that lie behind art-birth.

Anyhow I'm fed up with my own personality tho' thoroughly engrossed in yrs.

Therefor, since you wont copy out Icelandic perhaps you'll be good enough to get yrself photoed, & well, & at once. I despise yr easy belief in the feeble gag of the painter-johnny against the possibility of yr taking a good likeness.

I don't expect we can hope to photo the childlike melt of some of yr moments but there's nothing up against snapshoting the free open go-to-hell-ness of what I'm bound to own up to being yr Scandinavianness, the fair hair & skin impression & the tiptop eyes. All that'd photo A1.

You've got to get taken *biggish*, (just bust) ½ side on, (about same size as Baron de Meyer's of Herman) & in *tons* of sun; plenty of sheen to the thing — the whole show bold & outstanding.[18]

Spend what you like on it; (go from one photoman to the other till you get the result I demand) & I'll refund when next in Kj. I've promised myself from you that you're to do this, so mind. Dont forget, — biggish, lots of sun, & very fairlooking, & probably ½ side on.

We're just thro' with our concert here. Both played *real well*. Herman has shoals of future. Use yr love of him to make him go in for more sudden pp & any old kinds of overdonenesses.[19]

Our best accompanist in London (Bird) didnt do the Popper Polonaise with Herman ½ as good as you. Herman owned it.

Practise turning over a bit; & when so doing look out for pedaling; one is apt either to jam it right on or right off when turning; look out you keep it normal when so doing.

I'm not a stickler about counting or over strickt time. But if there is one thing in which you can't overdo the rhythmic act (also practising with

cause Herman some anguish. A woman of forceful personality, she was much given to character analysis and philosophic speculation. Later in life, she and Percy were to argue for several years (1939–46) about the events of the 1905 tour and their subsequent falling out. She and Grainger always corresponded in English.

16 Herman returned to England with Percy to play at the first concert, on 18 October 1905, of the Subscription Concerts organised by the Hon. Stuart and Mrs Pleydell-Bouverie in the Borough Hall, Godalming. After the afternoon concert they stayed overnight. Herman left London again on 19 October.

17 Grainger became a vegetarian in 1924.

18 Adolf Edward Sigismund de Meyer (1868–1949), baron of the kingdom of Saxony. *Who's Who* for 1905 listed his recreations as music, painting and photography. He took piano lessons from Grainger and was his generous patron, giving him a gold watch after his piano recital on 15 November 1905, and always paying him well for "at home" engagements. Described by Cecil Beaton as "the Debussy of photographers", he photographed both Percy and Herman around this time. When the photograph of Alfhild (by Julie Laurberg of Copenhagen) arrived later in November, Grainger commented, ". . . mother thinks it delightful & restful, & curiously, thinks she sees a look in it of a before-marriage one of herself, as also of some dear S'Australian cousins of mine. I always felt we were kinsfolk, you & I; in all sorts of odd ways". Grainger was tardy in paying for the photograph but Herman, reflecting a tension in his relationship with Grainger, particularly over money, made Alfhild insist.

19 Grainger's own cultivation of extremities was sometimes noted by the critics, and not always complimentarily: "Mr Percy Grainger is a pianist with a large technique and a boundless ability, seemingly, for making a noise. It seemed to me that his execution admitted of only the two extremes of tone — viz., great power and considerable delicacy: most of the 'nuances' between these were for the most part absent'' (H.V., the *Musical Standard*, 25 November 1905). An alternative view is provided by the *Manchester Courier*, of 8 December 1905, reviewing Grainger's performance at a Hallé concert, ''. . . he produces at will an amazing variety of shades and degrees, ranging from a finely rigid 'fortissimo' to the lightest 'pianissimo' ''.

Henry Richard Bird (1842–1915), English organist and pianist. The 1905 Danish tour programmes had included the *Polonaise* and *Spinnlied* by the Austrian cellist and composer David Popper (1843–1913).

20 Through his education at the Hoch Conservatorium, Grainger was well-grounded in classical performance style, though he did not include much from this period in his performing repertoire. He had performed the last two movements of the Haydn D major Piano Concerto in Frankfurt on 28 February 1896 and (with orchestra) on 11 May 1896, and played the whole of the Haydn D major Piano Concerto Op. 21 with the Aubrey Chapman Orchestra at Bechstein Hall on 4 July 1906.

21 Grainger had visited Kipling, one of his major cultural heroes, in July 1905 (probably 15 July). As reported in the *Bulletin* of 19 October 1905, ''He had me down at his place in Sussex to hear the choruses I have written to so many of his verses . . . I played him my 'Danny Deever' and 'We Have Fed Our Sea For A Thousand Years' (Seven Seas), and he said they were like 'deaders rotting in bilge water'. Later he added, 'Till now I've had to rely on black and white, but you do the thing for me in color' ''.

22 Grainger spent the weekend of 28 October as guest of the Countess of Bective at her country residence at Kirkby Lonsdale, where he and baritone Harry Plunket Greene presented an ''at home'' recital on 30 October.

metronome) it's the Haydn Concerto, 'specially those bits where you're all alone.[20]

Dont go thinking shallow things about Kipling who knows (that is to say *feels*) more than the whole gang of us.[21]

Lets all always be happy & be a bloody trinity.

No 3

49   TO ALFHILD DE LUCE   Lunefield,
30.10.05.   Kirkby Lonsdale.[22]

Dear Dr (for you have cured me; & fit I am there because, & need to be; for things are just rushing in, & guinea [21 shillings] pupils galore)[23]

I want you to get Herman to send me towns (with full addresses) to where I can write you 2 pleasurers while on yr bloody Norway honeymoon.

Also, please press him to let me have:—

his free dates from now till Doomsday; otherwise I'm helpless if folk want to book him.

whether he is free Feb 17?[24]

Please tell him Broadwood *Birmingham* is off 'cause they cant get a hall, but we're almost dead sure to have a Hampstead one together in June instead.

With me here (for the concert tonight) is Harry Plunket Greene, a real Irishestman, & one of the most ownish & feelingful (fine, rough, tautstrung fightingman's feeling) singers of the world.

He's a great heart. He's keen on wanting to sing some of my Lincolnshire booty

Love to Serimna(?). Make him buck up & answer quick.

Envying you 2 slackers (let's have cards.)

Here's a bar*gain*. If I keep my mouth shut this year, will you sit up straight? I'm on. It'd be so good for us both.

50   TO ALFHILD DE LUCE   63 Oakley St
2.11.05   London. S.W.

That's horrid about yr sleeping badly; have you tried reading **lying** *rather low* & holding the book up above yr head? That always sends me off in 2 seconds (not that I ever need it.) Do let's know about the sleep bother, & do try the reading while lying flat. It sends one blind I believe, but that's a side issue.

Now then for your much welcome writing of 31.10.05.

Please look upon what follows as neither pose, nor lies, nor concocted in an opposition spirit. (It's a funny thing that I'm always booked to be taken for the CLOWN thro' life — all my really earnestnesses are taken for wouldbefunninesses, & as if I cld put them on & take them off like paint.)

I believe you think that the sport-spirit, the war-relish, & all that is only surface deep with me, & that the real ME is human & meltable & capable of real sympathy. If you keep on thinking that (maybe you dont) you're only raising up a little disappoint for yrself one day.

The shock to my vanity that that disappointment wld be doesnt worry me but the idea of yr ever being disappointed in anything (it's so time-wasting) does; & please dont let me be that thing. I am not a deep person. The only *real* thing to me is *love of pleasure*; it is very real, & almost deep.

I am incapable of real sympathy, because real sympathy is "with-suffering" (med-liden), & I am incapable of suffering. My life is one long war against sorrow. Therefore I am not ever really unkind. Pain, to myself, or others, is a thing I instinctively fight tooth & nail; therefore I am a socialist, etc. But ask me to really *feel* **with** folk who suffer (the poor, or my dearest & nearest even) & I have to fail; I can join in all mirth with almost anyone, but I can sorrow with none — not even myself; I've tried, but I can't keep it up, my mind wanders. Also I am shallow in that I am a **luxurious** *beggar*. It's altogether true. All my pleasures (the sole genuine things in me) are luxurious ones. *War*; it destroys & wastes what has taken tons of toil to build up. *Sport*: the "afterwork" spirit of man. The very scenery that stirs me & that I love is lifeless & unproductive, (as far as any nature can so be) useless & unkind to man,:— Australian deserts, S'African barren Veldt, Scotch dreary highlands, the sea. Only the aftermath in the life struggle (the time for play, the lives that can be thrown away, the country that can be let go waste) delights me. None of the birthful, needed, earnest-rooted things (love, work, suffering, endurance) of life awake in me even a worth-listening-to echo.

But I have my place in the scheme, alongside the whip, the spur, & the cold morning British bath. ⟦which I get good of daily⟧ My word, thro' my art, is to refresh, to reyouthen, to roust up stragglers, & to hound up each & every to the scrimmage. Not a very deep call ⟦certainly not a dear one⟧ maybe, but still clean & healthful, & — & this is my strength — *a call that's not properly been sounded in music yet*. Not an assumed pose, either:— one that's been native to me as long as I can remember.[25]

But it's no use asking me to *melt* & to *take a kneeling attitude*. The whole & only point of my personality is to be fireproof & to stand very much up (like a small bantam cock) & spread a full-blown chest!

6 feet tall folk can afford to melt & stoop & knee[l], (& have a natural gift & ease for it) but the only chance for a little thing like me is to puff & bluff & make a bold stand (& nature arranged one's instincts accordingly.) As to a Program for Kjøbenh; I quite agree Bach, Brahms, Cesar Franck, Scarlatti, & even a pinch of Chopin, but dont be silly:— small towns need blowing up — therefor gunpower. ⟦reluctantly — since it bores *you*⟧ I also agree as to Donanhyi; he's tip top. Do be a dear & take note on *what pianos* the boss pianists play in Kj. Whether they use *Hornung & Møller* or no. 'Twould be such a help to me if y'd keep yr eyes peeled as to this.

Now back to that engrossing theme P G ("pig" with the I left out.)

I cant be "plain lovable human Percy" because I'm not at all *plain* & only a wee bit *human*; but as to *lovable*; you just pile on the love act & I'll say "Ta".

I'm sure you dont realize how deep the "Sport" feeling is in me. I by chance passed a football field the other day & the swing & the passionateness of it all swept me along, as art & real life & what are called "feelings" never can. War & sport & wild country & raw pride pick me up & carry me away & drunken me, & dont leave me ½-filled & questioning & cold, & therefor I worship them & serve them & sing them & shall till I drop.

You'll see, I'll be able to sting the world (bits of it anyway) to awakeness & tonic it, & make it feel good & fresh & fit every now & then when it's jaded & has been up all night; but when it wants to really feel mean & wretched & harrowed & wants its bloody luxuriant heartstrings tenderly touched, then it'll hail a Continental to do the biz. I'll always fail folk ⟦you too (I'm sorry)⟧ in their big needs but I'm A1 "between the coffee & the

Greene (1865–1936), born at Old Connaught House, Co. Wicklow, was noted for his remarkable powers of interpretation, especially the beauty of his enunciation in singing in the English language. He was a leading exponent of English song, from folksong to modern.

23 Grainger had been suffering from some form of "sex-sickness" (probably masturbating) from which he said Alfhild and Herman had cured him during their tour, thus, as he wrote to Herman on 22 October, lifting him over "what was possibly the greatest menace I'll ever meet to my work's future" and earning Australia's heartfelt thanks in the "to-come". That Percy was beginning to earn well during 1905 is a theme that also runs through Herman's letters to Alfhild at this time — with some small accompanying rancour: for Herman thought Percy might therefore repay him for his losses on the 1904 tour. The improvement in the Graingers' financial situation is reflected in their move to new and more spacious rooms, including a studio for Percy, at 14 Upper Cheyne Row, on 23 December 1905. That Percy was still close with money seems clear. But he could well have contemplated with some apprehension the possible financial implications of his father's continuing ill-health, for John had come to Europe on leave of absence in mid-1905 seeking treatment for his "rheumatism", his contract with the Government of Western Australia being scheduled to expire on 31 July 1906.

24 On 17 February 1906 Grainger gave a duo-recital in Bournemouth with Harry Plunket Greene. If it was intended that Herman should also take part, he did not do so. Grainger, Sandby and Elwes gave a Broadwood Concert at the Hampstead Conservatoire on 12 June 1906.

25 These were qualities for which Grainger's music — his playing and his composing — were to be acclaimed. As early as 1905, with relatively few of his compositions yet publicly known, and many of his most popular ones yet unwritten, one critic wrote, "Percy Grainger's music has already something of the impersonality of the classics, it strikes a note of vigorous optimism, neither sentimental nor idealistic, but the sure note of clean exuberant strength, compelling respect and conviction. His choruses swing out with magnificent assurance; in them, one hears the voice of the tremendous generation which is springing up now from the loins of our great Colonies" (the *Acorn*, October 1905).

26 "I'm sandwiched 'tween the coffee and the pork —", a line from Kipling's poem "The Song of the Banjo" in *The Seven Seas*.

27 Elaborating this point in his letter to Alfhild of 26 November 1905, Grainger wrote: "Of the hawks (Engl, Germany, Russia) swooping above Scand-ia, surely Engl must be the least greedy, since her game is more to stop others gobbling (of course quite for her own ends) than to gobble herself".

28 On 11 November Grainger took part in a Broadwood Concert at Malvern, playing the Dvořák Piano Quintet in A major (1887) with the Bohemian String Quartet.

29 In August 1905 Grainger had been sent four Icelandic saga books by a friend, Miss G. Anstruther. Among them was a translation of *The Story of Grettir the Strong*, one of the seminal books of Grainger's youth, and a book which had the greatest influence on his human and artistic life. As Grainger himself wrote, "Grettir was to me what Christ is to many Christians". Sæhrímnir, in Icelandic mythology, was the boar whose flesh was cooked and eaten each day in Valhalla, but who came alive and well again each night. The applicability of Herman's nickname (Sæhrímnir) remains mysterious.

30 Grieg's folktunes Op. 66 were based on the collections of his friend Frants Beyer (1851–1918). Grainger met Beyer at Grieg's home in August 1907 and there

pork" Look up the *Song of the Banjo* (Seven Seas) That's me, to a T.[26]

You must know that's a horrid lie, about the "iron coat of armor".

You know *quite well* that I use no such feudal-like thing. I wear only pink & very thin skin in all my dealings with all folk; (& surely with *you*) No "the iron coat of armor" was not merited.

Because I'm by nature cold (tho' *keen*) you imagine I must be stifling God knows what feelings. I show all I feel **always**. I cant fake up ones, even to please friends.

But the "British scepter" is not apt, because Britain hasn't got a scepter. It's because you've lived in a Republic & haven't lived here that you feel bound to think that there must be a scepter knocking around somewhere. Take my word for it, you're slipping up. If it were but a scepter I could "lay it aside". What you call a scepter is the greed & grasp & power-love of my whole race, or rather, of our many races, & in which I am caught up & helplessly carried along, thank God. ⟦I am thankful for all intoxications⟧ It's the absence of the Pride note, of Militaryism of aggresive feeling & of any wish to willingly hurt if they can have *quite* their will without so doing, that make the British, & their offspring nations, so hard for the outsider to cope with. Dont you worry, you Scands are all right only you've got to be careful to throw in yr lot with US & not with Germany if you want to pull a win.[27]

We belong together anyway — you and I are the best kind of pals by the same token.

---

51   TO HERMAN SANDBY   [Malvern][28]
11.11.05.

For Herman

So that's how Saehrimnir is spellt. Then it must mean

$\begin{cases} \text{Sea-rime} \\ \text{Sae-wrim} \end{cases}$ (spindrift, sea frost)

& be one of the many forms of the Winter Giant; of which (to my mind) Glám in "Grettir" is but another version. I understand that AE in Old Norse has the sound of Y in English "by", "why". (Germ, Dan *ei*)[29]

I wish I'd known you were going to *see* dear old great little Grieg. *Do me a great favor.* (well its a duty on you as a Scand, anyway). When you next see Grieg ask him, or if you won't *very soon* be seeing him write him, to tell you whether he (or whoever gathered the tunes) has the words to the Folkeviser op 66. They must exist & be perfectly *stunning*. & MUST BE COLLECTED, if not yet done.[30]

If he didnt collect himself, find out who did & whether *he* got the words, or if nobody did try & get addresses of *local people* in the districts where the tunes where hunted.

Please take up this duty of getting these words. I'll look after my country if you'll look after yours.

Remember, all such work must be done bloody quick.

If Grieg really does think the least good of my settings (which I expect is a lie) its very sweet that he should return ever such a fraction of my own unspeakable admiration for him

---

I'm practising my 8, 9 hours a day now, & pupils as well, & as I **always** opføre mig aldeles som en [Danish: behave myself completely as a] gentleman, neither days *nor* nights hold a spark of fun. Never mind. I'll take it out of the to-come sometime.

52 TO ERNEST THESIGER

23.11.05.

63, Oakley Street,
Chelsea.

Darling Ernest

My very warmest thanks for the heartheater.
It will so do every time a fittingly grand occasion dons it at the thought
of yr sweet friendliness in making it me.
How can you be such a dear & so kind?
"Ihr macht' Ihr's leicht;
 mir macht' Ihr's schwer"
 (& *schön warm*)
[German: Probably "You make it easy for yourself
                and difficult for me"
                and nicely warm]

Very touchedly & thankfully
yr henceforth warmhearted
Perks

Hope see you & sister (whom please thank warmestly for her ever so
stimulating letter) tea soon
 Got a flaming good notice after my Birmingham success; a fair knock
out.[31]

53 TO ERNEST THESIGER

[Postcard. n.d.]
"after Nov. 23, 1905"

63, Oakley Street,
Chelsea.

I really came yest to tell of the overwhelming 1st fruits of the darling
heartheater. It wore me to an At Home the other afternoon, & the giveress
was so hived by the wonderfulness of it all that she sent me for playing a
duett & one solo 25 gns instead of my due fee of tuppence.
What's yr commission on such waistcoat fees?
These [fingerprints] arn't my dirty fingers only the becoaled gloves of
someone more or less unknown.

Love.
Perks.

54 TO HERMAN SANDBY

[7 December 1905]

[Manchester]

Dear old H.

Gervase Elwes wants you & me to do a concert with him at
Northampton. I've told him you will. Last time he, Countess Valda
Gleichen & I made quite a nice little bit & we're (I shld think) sure to this
time. We'll fit it in so that we take it on the way back from Helensburgh.
 Delighted, but unastonished, to hear of Alfhild fine accomp-ing feats.
 All the same, you *mustnt think* of having anyone to accompany at yr

discovered that he had indeed also
collected the words. Grainger had
been playing pieces from Op. 66
for some years. He included two in
his London solo recital on 15
November 1905, his first without
assisting artist and for which he
was then practising.

31 Grainger played the
Tchaikovsky B♭ minor Piano
Concerto at the Halford Concerts
Society's Second Concert in the
Town Hall, Birmingham, on 21
November, George Halford
conducting. Two Birmingham
reviews were extracted for a 1906
anthology of Press Opinions. The
Birmingham Post, 22 November
1905, was lyrical in its praise:
"Last night there was heard some
pianoforte playing that recalled
the virtuosity of Rubenstein. The
young Australian pianist, Percy
Grainger, was the soloist in
Tschaikowsky's 1st Pianoforte
Concerto. The performance was
sensational, using the word in its
best sense. To say that he was
master of the tremendous
difficulties of the work is to say
little: he sported with them,
thundered like a Jupiter Tonaus
and wooed the ear with softest
cooings. Mr Grainger's technique
is remarkable, but his self-control
is more so. He can do absolutely
what he likes, and last night, to
our thinking, he did the right thing
all through. Some sensational
renderings of this Concerto have
been heard at the Halford
Concerts, but nothing equal to the
performance of last night. We
were reminded more than once of
Rubenstein; there was the same
fiery abandon, only we could hear
no wrong notes. In the lovely
Romance in F sharp, Mr
Grainger's playing was poetry
itself; and in Liszt's arrangement
of the famous Rakoczy March his
execution was of the
transcendental order. In working
up to the Coda there was a
crescendo the like of which we
think had never before been wrung
from a pianoforte. There was no
hardness of touch with all that
power, but throughout the tone
was superb. Mr Grainger had a
fine reception, and was recalled
with acclamation after his
extraordinary performances".

54

London Recital but a *wellknown London* man. Bird, Harty, or Liddle.[32]

I should advise *Liddle*; he's **ripping**.

Anyhow (before you are better known) a woman accomp-ist would be *fatal* for London.

Please do as I say: I simply wont let you muddle up your London & English chances.

It is usual for the provincial societies to provide their own accomp-ist (as at M-chester Broadwood you will remember). I shld think Bradford will do this, & Elwes will be taking Kiddle up to Helensburgh; (no solos at Sheffield, only duetts & Trios) you might write Robinsons about these 2 points.

Yes, my Recital, & all else, has been a *howling success*, but I am simply hounded to bits, & have no nerve or strength left, at all. Did you get the Birmingham criticisms I sent?

Tonight I play here with Richter, & shall add a few words after it is over.[33]

Let me have *one* classical solo-group for Helensburgh.

After concert.

Had *huge* success. Old Richter shouting himself hoarse with bravos. Reengaged. *Now* my trouble's are over.

Just got word from mother that I've just got 25 guineas for playing a fiddle & piano sonata & one solo group at an At Home the other day.[34]

Goodnight. Dear people

55   TO KAREN HOLTEN   14 Upper Cheyne Row.
New Year's Eve. '05   [Chelsea, London]

My dear Karen

How glad I'll be to see you back.[35]

I was to go to some swinish Jews to stay, The Karl Meyer's, but I'm going to write them I've got an engagement; for I dont want to be from home when you come.[36]

Dear old Herman too!

So glad to hear of your happy Yule with your people.

We go to the Legge's tonight[37] Wasnt it fun the last time?

I only wanted to let you know I'm looking forward to seeing you back, & am happy to have the postcards from you

Please give my love to your family

Yr fellow-Scand.
Percy

I hope you'll like "Dick". He and "Grettir" (Grettisaga) are the dearest friends I've had.[38]

32 Together with Henry R. Bird (see note 19 above), the best-known London accompanists of the day were Frederick B. Kiddle (organist and accompanist at Queen's Hall from 1902 to 1927), Samuel Liddle and Hamilton Harty (later also famous as a conductor and composer). Sandby's accompanist at his debut London solo recital on 16 February 1906 was Samuel Liddle.

33 Grainger was playing the Tchaikovsky Bb minor Piano Concerto at a Hallé Orchestra concert, again under Hans Richter.

34 For Mrs Violet Mond on 5 December. Grainger had played Beethoven's "Kreutzer" Sonata with Nora Clench.

35 Karen returned to Copenhagen for Christmas while the Graingers moved to their new lodgings. She was back in London, with Herman Sandby, early in the New Year.

36 Carl Meyer (1851–1922), naturalised British banker, and his wife Adele (*née* Levis, m. 1883) were renowned hosts and patrons of the arts. He was created a baronet in 1910. Grainger's acquaintance with the Meyers went back to at least early 1902.

37 Robin Humphrey Legge (1862–1933), English critic. He moved from *The Times* to the *Daily Telegraph* in 1906, and assumed full responsibility for its musical policy two years later, exerting influence as editor until he retired in 1931. As a man of considerable influence he was assiduously cultivated by Rose. The Legges and the Graingers were neighbours in Oakley Street. He had attended the Queen's House concert on 28 May 1903 in which his wife Aimée, a contralto, had sung. The 1905 diary shows "Legge 10" for 3 December. Legge's affection was so alienated by the Graingers' defection to the United States in 1914 that he advised Grainger not to return to England after the war.

38 "Dick Heldar", hero of Kipling's *The Light That Failed* (1891).

1906

Early in the New Year of 1906 Herman and Karen returned to London, Karen staying with the Graingers at their new house in Upper Cheyne Row, Herman staying in Karen's old room at 63 Oakley Street. Percy and Herman did several concerts together during January and February. At one, the South Place Sunday Popular Concert on 4 February, Karen Holten accompanied Herman in one bracket of solos. According to Herman, she did not play as well as Alfhild. She was also not paid. Herman gave his London debut solo recital on 16 February. The last appearance of the Grainger–Sandby duo for this period was at a concert at the Northern Polytechnic on 24 February. On 26 February Herman, Percy and Karen left together for Copenhagen, where Grainger was to present his first solo piano recital on 5 March. Grainger returned to London alone on 7 March. Herman remained in Copenhagen but was back in London for an engagement at Malvern, with Percy, on 31 March. Alfhild was with Herman. Percy and Karen were not to meet again until August. During this time of separation Grainger's letters to Karen, written two or three times a week, provide an almost diary-like account of his activities.

56 TO ALFHILD DE LUCE
31.1.06.

14 Upper Cheyne Row.
Chelsea. S.W.

My dear Alfhild

We said so many overwhelmingly weighty things at Vejen, but I take it you mean the *Triple Alliance* or *May A give us all Hell* understanding.

I have not yet read the paper cuttings (for which all thanks) but shall shortly. Things are filling up rather crowdingly once more.

Yes, please always feel awfully bucked up; just think what "Ein fester Burg ist unser Gott" [Lutheran hymn: A safe stronghold is our God] Sæhrimner. Y're all right.

When I have the joy of seeing you in March I'll have such lots to tell you — I wonder whether you will like to hear it all?

I hope so, since it is all good gain to me (which, if yrs, I should rejoice in)

This General Election has been a delight & refreshment to me.

Think, formerly such a thing as a labor member hardly was known here, & suddenly, this election, 50 are returned. It seems quite like home.[1]

That's where this place is so great, there's nothing it wont turn its hand to as soon as it's ripe for it; and when it does move, it does so in perfect

1 The General Election of 1906 saw the Labour Party (created out of the Labour Representation Committee) emerge as a political party of significance for the first time, with twenty-nine members in the Parliament. A further twenty-two Labour members were returned under auspices other than the L.R.C., forming a "Trade Union Group".

2 Three of Grainger's settings of folksongs collected in Lincolnshire in 1905, *I'm Seventeen Come Sunday, Brigg Fair* and *Marching Tune,* were published by Forsyth Brothers, Ltd, in London, in 1906. Some time before their publication, Robin Legge had written to Grainger on behalf of Forsyth asking him to change his English expression and tempo markings to the conventional Italian ones, "So many beastly things were said by reviewers of the English Expressions that the sale may easily have been affected". Grainger remained adamant: the English terms stayed. The Grieg Slåtter were Op. 72.

3 Grainger was in Leeds for the fifth concert of the Leeds Philharmonic Society and Subscription Concerts on 21 February. Other artists were Ada Crossley (vocalist), Maud McCarthy (violinist) and Samuel Liddle (accompanist). Grainger contributed two groups of piano solos to the programme and played the Brahms A major Violin Sonata Op. 100 with Maud McCarthy. Next day Ada Crossley wrote enclosing critiques, "They were *all* absolutely delighted with you last night, the Committee altogether enthusiastic!" Grainger's letter is written from the home of Edmund Ward, one of the five Vice-Presidents of the Philharmonic Society.

4 For his recital on 16 February, Sandby had made the "bold experiment" of presenting the whole programme himself, without engaging assisting artists as was then quite customary. There was accordingly much discussion of his programming choices. Programme, artistry, technique and tone were all generally acclaimed. *Kivlemöyerne* [The Maidens of Kivledale] (probably No. 16), from Grieg's Slåtter Op. 72, originally composed for piano solo (1902). Grainger had also started playing *Kivlemöyerne* (No. 16) in 1906. *Agnete og Havmanden,* Danish folksong, one of several Scandinavian folksongs which Sandby, like Grainger, transcribed and played during these years, was

balance & "fair play" & curiously uncorrupt for so tradeful a race — its one failing nowadays is that its too *un*tradeful in its instincts. It will be jolly to welcome you over here. I wldnt be surprized y'll cotton on to it lots.

Please lets know the price of the Grieg Slåtter! Great keeness (needless to say) over Herman['s] sooncoming Recital. 3 settings of my Lincolnshire folksongs will be in print in a few days. Shall send them you.[2]

Sit on yr nerves & be sure all will "happen for the best" [Pages 3 and 4 of this letter are missing]

You, who are such a wise comrade, ought to know how foolish it is to go writing asking me to soften up, & melt, & doff armor, (ha, ha!) or even to think it *possible* — much less *wishable*. Since I cant sorrow-with & really sympathize with folk, at least I can try & buck them up, & tauten & arm, & freshen, & harden them, & steel them.

The melting act is to open the door to all kinds of hells I shudder at bare thought of. Suffering must be stamped out, if it's to be done.

Good God I'd do a lot to save sorrow. You know that with regard to yourself I wouldn't care how ruthlessly you havoced me or any other male, if thereby you'd be outing yr own personality, & taking a paying winning stand for yourself & your [word missing].

I hunger for pleasure for others just as I hunger for it for myself; or almost as much. That's the diff 'tween a Colonial & an old country man. Where the Europeans offer secureness & comfort & *happiness* we're after *power* & **pleasure**. Do *please please* enjoy, Alfhild, do it all the time, & where & how you can, & if you upset us I say "3 cheers" & be all the glader.

But you must take a firm stand, a *fighting* stand, a fireproof unmeltable & pleasure-gluttonous stand.

Happiness, of course, is sea-sickening.

6 Pages of rot but it's all mean[t].

Good luck, & mind you sleep well always

Dont write too often because I take such a time answering

---

57   TO ALFHILD DE LUCE   30 Park Square,
22.2.06. [21.2.06]   Leeds.[3]

My dear Alfhild.

Notices will have already told you that Herman's Recital struck "the right note". I, & all others, thought he did **tiptop**; Program just the thing & rippingly played — the Grieg "Kivlemøjerne" that he has celloed bewitching & his setting of "Agnete" that he gave as encore rich & seething & Hermanesque & Danish, & very proper.[4]

He & I pulled a distinct win last night in "Scans" at Sheffield & tomorrow night is Baron de Meyer's At Home for us both.[5]

Tonight I play at the Philharmonic in this town, (fearfully important) & travel thro the night back to London.

Dear Pal; you are jolly, & responsive, & understanding, & all thanks for your warm letter. It's nice of you to want to know any good news I may have to tell; (I dont just mean this as a phrase) I am wondering whether it is good news or not, after all; or even if it's news at all.

You folk'll all slip up. You're all busy thinking I'm changing, or changed. Not a bit; I'm always the same aloof silly untouched onlooking sort of ½-thing.

When news is good (or even "news" at all) it mostly is either of work or a 2nd person. In the latter case it ought **never** to be written; (I think) because paper remembers when man (& even woman) forgets. Also we meet so soon (3 cheers) that it can wait till it's told.

Worse luck (or good luck) I never change; I only put on a fresh apron for a fresh job.

Dont leave old Herman so long again without a letter. He isnt as pleasant company when he's fretting.

I arrive Wed morn (Feb 28) early in Kj.

Yrs ever
Percy G

Please give my love to all the Sandbys & say I'm looking keenly forward to being with them on the 28th Greetings from mother & Karen

published by Wilhelm Hansen in 1912. The recital also included the Swedish folksong *Little Karin*, arranged by Grainger.

5 Only three of Grainger's Scandinavian folkmusic arrangements were played at the concert for the Sheffield Chamber Music Society on 20 February. Baron de Meyer's "at home" on 22 February elicited the Baron's great enthusiasm and a fee of £10. Rodin and the Princesse de Polignac had been present.

58   TO HERMAN SANDBY   [London]
10.3.06.

Dear Herm.

I borrowed 10 Kr from Hans which please pay back.

Also please pay Anna 5 Kr for Lisa, being more or less 10 per cent on Karen's 5 lessons at 10/6.[6]

Dont you think some of the actual papers might be sent at once to a few important folk in the few biggest towns, Aarhus, Aalborg, Randers, Horsens, Odense, Vejle etc. The *whole* paper sometimes impresses more than a printed extract. Dont bother to answer re this, but just fix all as you think best. Will you please send on enclosed to Fru H. Fischer

I should like to have following addresses

Fru Anna Henriques.
Svendsen (leader of the orchestra)
Kjirulf (of "Politiken")
Anna Lange.

I have seen no critique in "Berlingske Tid." yet. You might send me one of any that is partic good.

Rather fun. It turns out that the part of my ticket taking me from Cope to Esbjerg was torn out on journey over, so I had to fork out all my money for a ticket (*2nd class to Korsør, 3rd class thence to Esbjerg*) & had only 15 Øre left. So I had nothing to eat after 7.30 Wednesday morn till 10 o'cl Thursday night. Not my style at all. Great fun tho! 'll tell you all about it when we meet. Am working like a devil; & need to; *fearful* lot ahead.

6 Grainger had stayed with the Sandby family at Gammeltoftsgade during his Copenhagen sojourn. Herman was the youngest of eight children, Hans (1874–1959) being the sixth child and fourth son, Anna (1879–1948) the seventh child and third daughter. Three of the children, Kristian, Anna and Herman, became professional musicians. Lisa is not identified.

Great Alf.

Got lett from Karen telling how sweet & kind you had been to her. You really are a broad brick.

Deepest thanks for really helping me like this.

If you see Hyllested, nail her down to coming over here with you, & keep her mind pinned onto the guinea a lesson racket.

Please dont think me cold & offish & silly. I dont feel it; only very thankful to you all. Everlastingly so.

Make Herm use these weeks over there to really call about & get to know **lots** new people. Make him work thro Holtens & all other folk. It's going to pay in a concert there in the future.

[to Herman] I wonder do you think I'm very thankful for all the joy you helped me to lately? I dont know whether I am or not, but any way, you really made me **very** happy, if that's any use to you

59 TO KAREN HOLTEN [London]

[Original: Danish]
"Lewirt". 10.3.06.
(in this way dear Mrs Sandby
pronounces Saturday [Lørdag])

Courageful Karen.

How are you after your Copenhagen success? Because it was *your* success altogether.

Not only that you collected the audience and money and awoke the whole enthusiasm and cordiality about the whole thing, but not at least because you helped me to do the absolutely boring things that make for success.

When I saw that you understood that such-like tedious things had to be done and since you always happily disappeared when I, unfortunately, needed to stand alone in face of things: that helped me altogether tremendously — and now you have your Copenhagen success. Many deeply-felt thanks to you; but no commission, this time.

I was nearly in danger of becoming heroic in my penniless voyage; but I succeeded as usual in avoiding heroism.

I endured neither eating or drinking till 10 o'cl Thursday evening, but when I heard that we couldn't possibly catch the train I gave way and borrowed money from the Chief Steward.

If we had caught the train I would have held out till London, and that would sound good: "No food or drink between Gammeltoftsgade and Upper Cheyne Row", but on the other side it might perhaps have been dangerously near to heroism.

I am writing these few words today because next week looks so frantically busy that I don't expect to have time for anything except shaking my bent legs with dread "and an almost touching helplessness"

Will you please send me Miss Z. Lassen's and Miss Nutzhorn's addresses.

Also the name of the two old people who were at the concert of the "Tonekunstner-forening" [Musicians' Society].[7]

Please believe me I am truly grateful for everything you did in Copenhagen this time.

Percy

7 Of Grainger's first solo recital in Copenhagen on 5 March the newspaper *København* recorded next day that, "The young Australian took Copenhagen's public by storm". *Politiken*, 7 March, reported that "he aroused almost wild enthusiasm". Three encores and innumerable recalls were required at the end of the concert. The *British Australasian*, 15 March, reported that the great Belgian violinist Eugène Ysaÿe and Johan Svendsen, conductor of the Copenhagen Philharmonic Orchestra, had both been in the audience. After the recital Grainger attended supper and performed at a meeting of the Dansk Tonekunstner-Forening at which Ysaÿe was guest of honour and the Svendsens were also present.

60 TO KAREN HOLTEN [London]

[Original: Danish]
18.3.06.

Dear Karen.

If you absolutely want Danish headings, then I must ask you to address me without "Esq". This really means "Shield-carrier" which is too heroic for me.

No, I was not seasick, the pity was we had splendid weather and I would have been so happy to be up, but had to lie in bed for fear of being too hungry otherwise. It is so nice and happy that you are fond of Alfhild, and she of you. It is so awful when nice people don't like each other; almost the worst there is. I think it is very jolly of you both that you do.

I think the photograph of you and Mrs Arl. is very good. Many thanks for it. But we have not found the picture of your little brother; but we will certainly search for it. But I don't think it is here.

It is nice that Mrs Arlaud will be with us in Svinkløv.[8] Remember me warmly to her, and tell her (she must not take it amiss of me) that one does not live long enough for it to be worth while to be anything else than tremendously happy the whole of one's little life. As you, for example.

It is also splendid about Birkerød. You will get 10 pr. c. naturally. But always remember that it would please me *much more*, if you yourself together with Mrs Arlaud, or anyone else would earn Money fame and reputation. I can manage to earn over here or elsewhere and will very reluctantly take anything in Denmark that *you* yourself could obtain. If you haven't in mind to play there *in any case*, then I would be awfully glad for you to get it for me; but you have already done so much for me (Silkeborg and in other directions) that I couldn't have the least pleasure if you become poorer for my sake; and I am just as grateful that you *want* to do it for me in any case. 10 p. c. is moreover our business "*basis*" in everything; Pupils, Concerts, etc. Many thanks, I have got J. P. Jacobsen's Poems, and like them immensely. Mrs Busoni gave them to me in Berlin, and next after Hans C. Andersen they were the 1st I read in Danish.[9]

Thank you for the Addresses.

This thing about "small bears" and "going into hibernation" and that one does not like God-sent pupils sounds to be a little like "Travelling via the Hook of Holland". The only really good thing about us Northerners is that the climate really forces us to do something and that we really can enjoy the summer after having suffered the cold.

Do you think we enjoy the heat in Australia? We are absolutely frightened of sunshine and summer. I wouldn't be at all glad if it was summer now. I am *so* glad that between me and pleasure, there lie many months in which I can really *do* something and *make* something. (and am compelled to it) From our cold, busy, and business-filled life, we get the freshness and energy to really have pleasure and enjoy ourselves when we have a few free hours during the year. I must admit that work, and pupils, and all that is *always* undeniably completely boring and nasty; but nevertheless we dare not (neither you, or I, or other Northern person) give up being absolutely feverish in our hunger for work. When one burns and smarts incessantly, then there **must** come a time when one has it good, and with what an enviable fresh hunger one goes toward one's pleasures, when one is really a "worker"

You can see on the journey from here that it often pays not to travel via Holland.

And moreover, when one gives **good** lessons (I don't mean to good pupils, but that one *gives* them well) then the results are encouraging, sooner or later.

I do not think you should give up playing in Concerts; you play quite well enough for it, and I am very glad that your "fresh" father also thinks the same. It is such an excellent habit to do *all possible* things, and it is really nothing more than "slackness" in yourself that you want to give up the honour and happiness of concert-life.

It cannot be denied that you are a rather "slack" little one; and you may be that *in the beginning*. People who are not blessed with a lazy nature are horrible and impossible and unpardonable. "That must be." And you know well that I am not saying things to you that I don't say to myself (and have the best reason for) I am just as lazy and slack in my instincts as you. But it is not the intention that either you or I or anyone else should continue like that.

It is just as nasty and impossible and unpardonable to continue to be lazy *when one becomes adult* (in years, never in reality) *and old* as it is to lack this most important character from the beginning.

Also with Sport. We *must* all practise sport. Please write and tell me that you will take up sport. I will. It can't be denied, can it, that of all races the English-speaking people keep their bodily youth longest. In other races

8 Elna Arlaud, Danish violinist. She gave concerts with Karen Holten both before and after Karen met Percy. Svinkløv, a village near Fjerritslev on the north-west coast of Jutland. Other engagements permitting, Grainger used to meet Karen there in August for summer holidays, starting in 1906.

9 Jens Peter Jacobsen (1847–85), Danish novelist and short-story writer. Of the poetry of his early years the most famous are the *Gurresange* which Arnold Schönberg set as the *Gurrelieder*.

you will find individual people who remain always as fresh and fit as English-speaking people (like your father, for example). But they are nearly always sport-practising in one way or another, or else belong to a sporting family. It is also a tremendously good thing about Sport that the good results of it are inherited from father to son.[10]

But *women* with well preserved **bodies** after a certain age are scarcely **ever** to be found among foreigners. And that is so stupid and meaningless. You have a good chance. You are splendidly put together, and come from an active family. But there is no family in the whole world that is active *enough*, and one must work, each for himself, to make it fitter, firmer, fresher, more practical, harder, nicer, than it is.

You know what slack fingers are in piano playing. Most people's bodies are similar after a certain (and that a very early) age. And there is not the least excuse for it.

Slack fingers can never be nice or amusing; they are in every single direction less good than fresh fit fingers.

If people of your and my age do not begin **at once** then we are lost. Or else we are saved by our forefathers sports-life.

What will you do? The 3 best things are rowing, or Bicycle, or Tennis. You have the means to it, and *must* do it. I must, & will, also.

Rowing is perhaps the best. Fletcher and I will do it in the Summer.

I think people who live a busy and active life are just as interesting to look at when they are old as when they are young. But old shrunken people are the saddest that exist. Promise me that you will do a lot, earn a lot, and practise sport a lot; and I will certainly see that we have fun in Jutland.

Another thing; you do not walk fast enough. There is nothing which helps one more than *always* to walk as fast as one **possibly** *can*. Promise me that you will always see and keep your back as straight as it is now, and to keep your body fitter and firmer and stronger than either you or my fingers are **now**. You are splendidly proportioned and there is no reason that you should *ever* melt like butter in summer. It is so unpleasant. Don't think, Karen, that I am preaching. I shudder myself at the same faults and dangers.

Naturally you will get **many** lessons in Svinkløv. We will work very hard and strictly.

It is more or less true that it is a shame not to be able to nod "good-day". I am also practising at the Schumann Concerto; and the whole thing is about as eerie as living with à ghost.[11]

Goodbye.
Perks.

Mother says don't forget to send the recipes. (something to eat)
You will get "Up Country Song" as soon as I have the least bit of time[12]
I must often laugh about the "so that's fixed then"

61   TO ROGER QUILTER
15.4.06.

14 Upper Cheyne Row
Chelsea.

Darl Rodg.

Yr letter as sweet & "one $\begin{Bmatrix} \text{warm} \\ \text{or strong} \end{Bmatrix}$ grasp of his $\begin{Bmatrix} \text{strong} \\ \text{warm?} \end{Bmatrix}$ $\begin{Bmatrix} \text{white?} \\ \text{right?} \end{Bmatrix}$
hand-'' (or something) -ish as yrself ever is.

10 Karen proved very receptive to Percy's injunctions. By 5 April he was congratulating her for having bought a bicycle and joined a tennis club. In the same letter Percy reported on his own beginning with Sport: "Last Sunday in Malvern (where I played last Saturday) a local pianist and I did nothing else for about 3 hours except running 'races', high jumping, Indian wrestling, standing jump etc. I was so stiff afterwards that life was quite miserable". Grainger inherited his passion for sport from his father. The Graingers were sharing the house at 14 Upper Cheyne Row with Benton Fletcher.

11 Grainger was engaged to play the Schumann Piano Concerto in A minor Op. 54 with The Strolling Players Amateur Orchestral Society, conducted by Joseph Ivimey, at the Queen's Hall on 9 April. He did not play it. On 5 April he reported to Karen that he had chicken-pox. While lamenting the loss of income through cancelled engagements and lost pupils, he admitted to having a "splendid time" practising and composing, secluded from all visitors and unwelcome interruptions.

12 Grainger's 1905 sketch and idea for an "Upcountry Song" ("Upcountry" being used here in the sense of patriotic celebration) contain the genesis of two of his later compositions, his *Colonial Song* and his *Australian Up-Country Song*.

13 Roger Quilter had written to Grainger on 13 April 1906, ". . . always remember that whenever you want to get your things done or want to begin working any of your schemes, you must let me be of what use I can; because I cant think of any better way of spending my money than helping to get your work known in the world". Roger, who was also unwell, reported that he had been reading Walt Whitman, for whose work he shared an enthusiasm with the Graingers.

From you the mere taking of anything would be real fun, should it chance that I have need & you to spare.[13]

It is lovely for me to know you think that way.

As to my steady-going box-biffing, I'm not to know what fits of boredness & dulness it mayn't be saving me from, & its sure enough fostering the "habit of application" likely to come in useful later on on more serious work.

I've had the time of my life this pox-holiday slacking & scoring. As much as I want to rework of the Engl D for the moment is behind me, & now I'm onto the Wamphray Ballad; scoring.

As far as is of the new version Engl D I've makeshifted for 6 hands; you & mum at 1, & I at t'other piano. So come soon & fulfil.[14]

When do you come to Lond & how long for; let's know by p.c. soon so that we may reap of the holidayness of the coming week; day, or eve.

I too have been W[alt]. W[hitman]-ing. He's beyond all words but his own. He & Icelanders seem to me to touch the top notch of tight yet unstrained fit of *what & how*.

Believe me feeling my thankfulness & gladness as seriously & deeply as you yr No 1-sized "proposition".

Ever lovingly
Perks.

62   TO KAREN HOLTEN   14 Upper Cheyne. [Row]
[Original: Danish]   [London]
Wednesday. 18.4.06.

So, you were "cross". That's not so strange. It is more remarkable that any person is ever anything except cross. But one is; often. I am also cross; not really, but ½. I have lost a lot of money by this otherwise highly regarded (by me) chicken pox, and there were many days without giving lessons, — dreadful. Also regarding my amusing father; I think that he will, unfortunately, not be as well as he hopes, and scarcely that he will be able to work properly. And he is not one who can get on with a little money (and as to that I will not say that he is not completely right; it is certainly more amusing with more)[15] But now the pupils are beginning again, and I don't feel so unforgivably lazy as I really am. I have come as far with my English Dance as I want to at the present, and am now writing "Wamphray". (at the Ballad, not the Wamphray *March*)[16] It strikes me that you have suffered, fortunately only a little, by hearing all my old compositions; perhaps it is time this summer that I "trouble" (can you remember in Oakley St) you a little with some of them. I hate playing my own nonsense because I always feel that when I do it people suffer from it and are terribly bored, but don't let me notice it out of friendship to me; and that I can't bear. If you perchance should have the courage to sacrifice yourself and act as public for my "works", you must first promise me that you will tell me honestly when you hate it, or part of it, more than usual. Then I will bring some of them to Denmark this summer.

Last Sunday I went for a walk with Herman and Alfhild for some hours. It was good for my health to be in the open air a little; and also perhaps not so boring. Roger comes here tomorrow evening. He has not been at all well. He wrote me such a lovely letter; that all his money was at my service when I should need it sometime for my compositions — that he couldn't think of any nicer goal for his money. (Neither can I) He is easy to love. I must say, I think the dimple photograph is splendid.

14 References to his work on the *English Dance* move in and out of Grainger's correspondence over a long period, as he worked on the piece over many years and at different times quite intensively. The 1906 manuscripts are labelled as the "second version". The work was to be thoroughly reworked and rescored several times before a final version was published by G. Schirmer Inc., New York, in March 1929. The work was dedicated to Cyril Scott. A version for two pianos, six hands, was published by Schott & Co., London, in 1924. *The Lads of Wamphray,* ballad for men's chorus and band (symphony orchestra), is a setting of a folk-poem from Sir Walter Scott's *Minstrelsy of the Scottish Border.* All but two verses of the poem are set. Grainger's first setting of the text dates from December 1904, with scoring sketches dating from 1906. The accompaniment was rescored between 23 August and 25 October 1907. A score for men's chorus and two-piano accompaniment was published by G. Schirmer Inc., New York, in October 1925.

15 After spending several months under treatment at Harrogate, John Grainger had left England in mid-October 1905, spending November and December in Seville, Spain. In January 1906 he travelled on, spending February and March in Italy. His letters from April and May do not survive. He was back in London by early June.

16 The *Lads of Wamphray March*, for brass and reed band (later for wind band), is based on melodies and musical ideas used in the ballad setting. Composed in 1905, it is Grainger's first work for military band and reflects the stimulus of his encounter with the Band of His Majesty's Coldstream Guards at Kings Lynn in May 1905. The scoring was superficially revised in 1937 and 1938 and the work published by Carl Fischer Inc., New York, in 1941.

17 Lucy Etheldred Broadwood (1858–1929), English folksong collector, the youngest child of Henry Fowler Broadwood of the firm of John Broadwood & Sons. She was a driving force in the English Folk-Song Society of which she was at this time the Honorary Secretary. Grainger had met her in 1904. Evald Tang Kristensen (1843–1929), Danish author and folklore collector. *Jydske Folkeviser og Toner*, Samlede af Folkemunde, Især i Hammerum-Herred. Med en Efterskrift af Svend Grundtvig [Jutish Folksongs and Melodies, Collected from the Mouths of the People, Particularly in Hammerum District. With a Postscript by Svend Grundtvig], Kjøbenhavn, 1871. Grainger had been introduced to Kristensen's work by a fellow Danish collector, Hjalmar Thuren, whom Grainger had met at the Vejlefjord Sanatorium in September 1905. Grainger was given a copy of the book by Knud Larsen in 1907 and in September of that year he sketched settings of melodies 103 and 107.

Thursday. 19.4.06.

Thank God! I still do not feel at all well yet. Miss L. E. Broadwood (of Folksong Society) has lent me *De Jydsk[e] Folkeviser* (E. T. Kristensen), and I can keep her book as long as I like.[17] Thus you needn't hurry at all to read the copy you are buying for me. Keep it just as long as you like.

I can't think of anything more comforting and caressing than the whole atmosphere of most of them. I hope you will like them. They are full of what I regard as the typical Danish character; something soft and gentle without being in the least characterless, something very easy to get on with, something that needs satisfying final happiness and joy; but not in the least "redeeming" in a horrible, or German, way. In the following list of songs which I like best, I have indicated the songs or verses which show this Danish character with Ⓓ .

Numbers of most-loved songs-words

4 (see also 118) 26. 35 (both melody and words I think are terribly good and amusing. It is related to the one in *Edda* which is called "*Hammersheimet*" [The home of Hammer]; (do you know it by the way?) verses 14 and 21 are particularly amusing.

40. 42. 46 and 47. 49 (such an amusing kind of refrain) 50. There is such a nice refrain to 56. 58. 59. 61. (There is a very similar, and extremely nice, Scottish song) 62 a, b, are *splendid*. 73. (V.14. Ⓓ) 87.

90. (truly Danish) 96 (is similar to the Scottish "Binnorie") 99 (V.26 is lovely Danish. V.11 with the father is amusing) 100. 103. 109 (V.23 amusing) 112 (V.25 poetic) 121A (V.7. Ⓓ) 119 (V.13 Ⓓ).

But the whole book (also Introduction and Conclusion) is the greatest joy to me. The tunes I don't think are so significant on the whole.

Friday.

I have thought about what you should be practising now and the following pieces have come to mind. I think they are all nice, or usable, or both.

Dvorak	Humoresque,	op 101	No 7.
Chopin	Prelude	op 45	
	Etudes	op 10	No 4
		————	6
		————	8
		————	10
		op 25	No 3

one without an opus number in Peters No 25, in F minor

Bach   Sarabande in A minor English Suite No ?
It begins

Bach-Busoni   "Nun freut euch lieben Christen"
Scarlatti-Tausig   Capriccio.
Brahms   Scherzo from Sonata op 5 (F minor)

I think that the Brahms Scherzo and some of the Chopin Etudes can be stimulating technically. You must write to me *every single* run or passage that you lack a satisfactory fingering for. You need only give in which bar (Bar No 106, or something like that) it occurs. I believe you have once played Grieg's Piano Concerto. I think there are many small things in that which I could show you more effective or easier. So please bring it with you to Svinkløv. What kind of piano is there up there?

I am keeping up not eating too much, and **never** potatoes and bread *anymore*. They are both supposed to be very fattening.

Write to me when you are playing for a concert; I hope you will see to do it very often. And when you are not playing very much at concerts, then please see and do it privately for people; it helps so enormously, even if it is not so pleasant or enjoyable. It will give me the greatest pleasure, if you will let me know how often you play for people, and what. (and how) Excuse me, that this letter is so unusually dull.

Let me also know how often you play tennis, and how it is going. Percy

Grainger was restored to health by the end of April, re-entering concert life at Miss Alice Clifton's first vocal recital at the Bechstein Hall on Friday 27 April. The beginning of May saw him launched on a strenuous schedule. On 5 May he was in Northampton for the grand evening concert of the Competition Festival there, from whence he travelled on Sunday to Brigg, in Lincolnshire, for the rehearsals and performance of five of his folksong settings at the Grand Evening Concert of the North Lincolnshire Competition Festival on 7 May. Next day at 6 a.m. he travelled south for an afternoon rehearsal of the Brahms D minor Piano Concerto in London with C. V. Stanford and the orchestra of the Royal College of Music. On 10 May he was in Bournemouth for the performance of the Brahms at the Winter Gardens, under Dan Godfrey. He returned immediately to London. On 15 May Grainger met Edvard Grieg, a meeting of great consequence for him both professionally and personally.

In the spring of 1906, Edvard Grieg accepted an engagement offered to him by the directors of the Queen's Hall Orchestra and came to London, with his wife, for two concerts. On 17 May he conducted an orchestral concert of his own compositions. On 24 May he took part as a pianist in a chamber concert devoted entirely to his works. Both concerts were held in Queen's Hall. This was Grieg's fifth and last visit to London. His health was very poor.

63 TO KAREN HOLTEN   Between Brigg & London
[Original: Danish]
8.5.06.

Dear Karen

I cannot deny that my things came off with much success last night. The choirs were not so bad as they had written to me, and the brass band was very full of rhythm, and kept the whole thing together in the strongest sounding way. People were very pleased and I really believe that they nearly all liked the Folksong Settings, and that they will contribute to promote the already great interest in Lincolnshire for this sort of thing.

8 old men sang songs, and Miss Broadwood and I got not so few new tunes worked out. But the really serious collection will first begin in July, probably. Brigg is in North Lincolnshire. Now there is also a woman in South Lincolnshire who runs "Competitions" and wants me to collect down there also, and stay with her during that time.[18]

I played last Saturday in Northampton, (also at a "Competition festival") and the Directress there (Lady Althorp) also wishes to hold folksong competitions and that I will collect at her place.[19]

So the summer all things considered looks like being quite unusually amusing, and full. (Also with regard to details it is not so bad)

18 For details of Grainger's settings performed at Brigg on 7 May 1906 see note 9, 1905. The notebooks in which Lucy Broadwood wrote down the tunes collected on this occasion are in Cecil Sharp House, London. Eleven tunes were collected, and a set of words for "Six Dukes Went Afishin' ". In Grainger's *Collection of English Folksongs* these are melodies 102, 109, 111, 136, 171, 191, 193, 256, 262, 264, 274 and the words 103. The woman in South Lincolnshire is unidentified.

19 *The Queen*, 14 July 1906, announced the death of Lady Althorp (Margaret Althorp), an accomplished musician and above-average violinist who had done much to promote musical competition among the village folk in Northamptonshire. As Mrs Spencer, she had met Grainger socially at the homes of Ethel Smyth and the Cary-Elweses.

On Sunday I travelled for 8 hours and immediately after arrival (9 o'cl in the evening) had a nice rehearsal with the Brass Band, and yesterday (Monday) I had to conduct off and on half the day, and today I have 1st 2 pupils and then rehearsal of the D minor Brahms Concerto with Stanford. You can't imagine how absolutely awful it is to play after having conducted, if you are not used to it.

Brigg Fair sounded really nice, even though the choir didn't know anything much about it; but with a choir that *knew* it and with time to go in to the fine details, it could work charmingly.

The country people of Lincolnshire are *so* touchingly kind, and they talk so irresistibly. They are very Danish, one can still see where they came from originally. One day you must go to one of the performances like yesterday. It will certainly touch and interest you. These simple, ignorant, poor people, who up to a few years ago never sang together and were never together in large numbers, and now form choirs of 300 voices and make a wonderful noise.

Excuse the dullness. But we were up to 2 o'cl last night and I had to be up at 6 o'cl this morning. Goodbye, perhaps there is a letter from you lying at home

You can't imagine any person more absolutely splendid in every way than Lady Winefride. How I look forward to being with this strong healthy woman and her 8 children in the summer

64 TO KAREN HOLTEN [London]
[Original: Danish/some English]
18.5.06

Dear Karen

Since I last wrote many things have taken place Brahms Piano Concerto went really unexpectedly well in Bournemouth. But how it helps to be used to playing with the 2nd piano. I suggest we do that as much as we can in the autumn, I will accompany your concertos, and you mine.

And the dear Griegs. As soon as he came he asked Mrs Speyer (who I was together with in Northampton by the way; he — Speyer — owns the Queen's Hall orchestra) to invite me, and I went last Tuesday.

Have you seen Grieg and his wife? Can you think of anything more triumphant than the impression of these 2 small people? They are so completely happy together and both so "loveable" and kind. And she sang for us; and what jubilation and uplift in her and his song and the 2 are just as melted in one when they make music as they are in Life.[20]

He talked not so little with me about my chorus, and I told him that I had just heard it performed up in Lincolnshire and he said "they sounded lovely, didn't they; they must sound lovely"

And then I played 3 of the Slåtter [Peasant Dances] for him and "He took a kindly attitude to it"; was very pleased, and said that I was quite the 1st who played it, as no one else "dared to". Naturally we spoke a decent language together so that Mrs Speyer and the Jewish flock were properly impressed.

He played me one of "Møllarguttens gangar" (in the Slåtter) and it was certainly not a boring evening.

And Thursday was Orchestral Concert. Never have I experienced anything ½ so moving and uplifting. I must say it was a happy day for me and it was the same for mother and Herman.

Q's Hall was packed with men and women and the little man and the great jubilation were awfully moving. You must remember that of all the

20 Edgar Speyer (1862–1932), New York-born, British-naturalised banker and financier of German origin, philanthropist and patron of music, later a baronet and Privy Councillor. He headed a private syndicate which organised the financial side of the Queen's Hall Orchestra from the time of Robert Newman's bankruptcy in 1902 to 1915 when Speyer, being accused of pro-German activities, left the country. His wife, Leonora von Stosch, was a fine violinist and a social leader in London's music-loving circles. Edvard Grieg had married his own cousin, Nina Hagerup, in 1867. A talented singer, she was recognised as the most sympathetic of all interpreters of his songs. While in London, the Griegs were guests of the Speyers. Grainger met the Griegs at dinner at the Speyers' on 15 May. Their last London meeting, again at the Speyers', was a farewell dinner on 28 May.

21 *The Times* of 18 May 1906, reviewing the Grieg orchestral concert on the 17th, noted that every seat in Queen's Hall had been filled. The Queen's Hall Orchestra played the *Lyrische Suite* [*sic*], arranged from four of the piano pieces Op. 54, and the first *Peer Gynt Suite* Op. 46. Danish pianist Johanne Stockmarr (1869–1944) had an established reputation as an interpreter of Grieg's Concerto. Of this performance *The Times* commented that it was rather matter-of-fact but won many recalls. Critical response to the Grieg concerts was not over-enthusiastic. Of the orchestral concert *The Times* observed that Grieg was a composer whose message had been long ago delivered "down to its last word", and of the chamber concert (at which Grainger turned the pages for Grieg) on 24 May, that Grieg's chief fault was to be too constantly charming. These attitudes in no way seem to have affected the atmosphere of "great sympathy" that prevailed at the concerts. The *Daily Telegraph*, 25 May, commented drily that "the London season enjoys its lions".

composers who have ever existed he and Bach are the ones I love most; and it was quite indescribable for me to see the little bit of a person and hear his music at the same time. His new Suite is perfectly orchestrated; charming in tone and Miss Stockmarr played his Concerto really spendidly and *reaped* tremendous applause.[21]

I think she is a kind woman; and I hear that she earns for her whole family. I have invited her to come and see us sometime after the 2nd Grieg Concert.

Tomorrow I meet Grieg again. I have received an invitation from Nansen to take lunch with him I think G conducts excellently with much individuality, and many capital and unusual effects. "P[eer] Gynt" of course went splendidly.

Remember to remind me to tell you many amusing things about G and the Speyers. He doesn't care much for many people and lets them see it.

Thanks that you will buy Grundtvig's Danish F.[olk]songs for me.[22] Take them with you to Svinkløv, and I will pay you for them when we meet. It is not meant to be such a reliable collection as it should be, but even so, it is large and a book one *must* have. If you care for Scandinavian folk poems you should go to a library and read Geijer and Afzelius' Swedish Folksong words. I have had such enormous pleasure from these 2 volumes. Mrs Wodehouse has lent me them.

Yes, thanks, I received the 3 photographs, and now really believe in your sport. Many thanks.

With regard to when I will come to Denmark; I don't expect it can be before the beginning of September; I hope to arrive in Svinkløv in the very 1st days of Sept.

A few days ago I received a pleasant letter from Street. (Somerset, Sth Engl)

A big country festival is to be held near Street on 19th June and the *Street Military band* wants to perform my "Wamphray March" on this occasion, and wishes me to conduct it. I will probably do so; Roger and Fletcher are going and I will have 4 days there and can rehearse with the "band" as often as I like. A lot can be learnt from that.[23]

I am terribly busy. In a few days Herman and I have an At Home at Sargent's.[24]

Goodbye, I look forward to your next letter.

Percy.

My mother was *so* happy for your lovely letter to her and sends "love"[25]

65 TO HERMAN SANDBY   [London]
[24.5.06][26]

My dear Herm

As you know, I've no sense of right & wrong, or such things, nor am I at all "klag"ing [German: "klagen", to complain] about anything.

We've all a perfect right to behave as we care to & I blame nobody ever for anything.

I've no doubt you believe I've treated you badly; *I* dont think so, but then I never think about such things, nor can I care about such questions. Nor do I pretend I've been badly treated. I only find that things are not to my liking, & act accordingly, without an ounce of bad (or any other) feeling.

22 Sven Hersleb Grundtvig, *Folkelæsning. Danske Kæmpeviser og Folkesange fra Middelalderen*, fornede i gammele Stil, Kjøbenhavn 1867. Grainger's copy of the book is inscribed "Percy Grainger/Yul 1907" in Karen's hand. *Svenska Folk-Visor från Forntiden*, samlade och utgifne af E. G. Geijer och A. A. Afzelius, Stockholm, 1814–16.

23 Grainger did not, in the event, go to Street (see letter 67), though his March was played several times by the Street Band. F. E. Huish, of Street, had copied the instrumental parts of Grainger's pieces for Frome in 1905. Grainger had sent him a copy of the *Lads of Wamphray March* early in 1906.

24 John Singer Sargent (1856–1925), born in Florence of American parents, had settled in London in 1886 where his work as a portrait painter brought him enormous prestige and enabled him to amass a substantial private fortune. A benevolent and paternal figure in Grainger's life, he was a fine amateur pianist with a particular feeling for French and Spanish music.

25 Rose had written to Karen about her relationship with Percy. Karen replied (in English) on 12 May, "I will tell you, I have thought much over things, and I c'ant do otherwise than I am doing, but I must hope from bottom of my heart, that it w'ont turn out unhappyly. I have never before in my life felt a real feeling, now it comes. I feel it as a Fate, and one c'ant get away from the Fate. Perhaps we northly people are heavy in our thinking, but who can help that? On the other hand, I am a sundays-child, I believe that has made much luck in my life, why should not that go on? In any case, I am going to believe so, until I see the contrary".

26 Forty years later Grainger was to go over the circumstances that led to the writing of this letter. Firstly, in his letter to Alfhild Sandby of 13 June 1946, "In 1905 [should be 1906], after I had refused to play the Grieg Cello-&-piano Sonata to Grieg & when

Herman suggested playing it himself with Grieg, I heard Grieg say 'men jeg er saa forfærselig træt' ['but I am so very tired'], whereupon I volunteered to play the piano part, after all. Of course Grieg had never heard the cello part so well played as by Herman. But I nevertheless resented *being forced* into playing a long work to a tired (practically dying) old man, *who had just played it himself* (with Becker) [at the Queen's Hall Chamber Concert on 24 May]". Then again in his letter of 29 June 1946, "The immediate cause of the break was the Grieg business . . . When I came home from Lady Speyer's that night I wrote the note to Herman, putting off our pending joint tour, & I posted it that same night, without having consulted mother or without her knowing anything about it . . . In my opinion it would have been ideal if Herman & I (2 geniuses) could *always* have toured Scandinavia (England, etc) together. But I could not, as an Australian, be bossed around (as in the Grieg episode) by an Americanised school-marm, nurse-maid, man-tamer". This break notwithstanding, Grainger got Grieg to hear Sandby's quartet on 28 May.

27 In the interview, which appeared in *Vort Land* on 7 June 1906, Grieg had said of Grainger: "There is one artist whose help I must not forget — Percy Grainger. He is a young man of genius, possessing a real artist's soul. Although born in Melbourne, Australia, he talks Norwegian, and is full of enthusiasm for our land and our art, such a man as we must love. He has studied our Northern Folk-songs, and has a thorough knowledge of Scandinavian music. At an 'At Home,' given in my honour [by Mrs Edgar Speyer], he played some of the Norwegian 'Slåtter' (peasant dances) that I have arranged for piano, with a mastery that awakened universal admiration. I mention this, as these 'Slåtter' are so difficult and unusual that only the bravest can

We all have a right to absent ourselves from what upsets us & as I fear that this summer's tour would probably be as unpalatable to me as last year's was fascinating & delightful I see nought but to take myself out of it.

Y're quite right that I am very selfish & that I less & less find time or mind for work & plans & interests other than my own. This is to me a very sad fact, but fact it is, & (it seems) unalterable (at least for time being) At the same time I shouldnt be surprized that this same selfishness of mine has of late thrown you more back upon yourself, & possibly **may** have gone a very little to make you do better work than ever before. So that altho' no pretty trait in me, it **may** (not *at all* thro' any goodness of mine) have forced you on yr own feet somewhat.

Yr devotion for me was an extraordinary & lovely thing; yet indipendance is still better, & you stick to it.

I dont repay devotion enough to make it worth while. And the dignity & admiration that you pulled down upon yrself for your unselfish devotion to me isnt enough after all, in this funny world.

Let us rather go for tougher, independanter quality.

Above all things, dont feel hard or bitter against me. Should you do so it would be waste; as I would be wholly unable to return the feeling.

My interest in yr creative work (even if less, as you think [as all my interests are less just now owing to feeling off color]) is still pretty big, please believe.

I merely mean what I wrote; that the tour is off as far as I'm concerned. But let us not indulge in moralizing, or being hurt or wronged *either of us*

Perks

66 TO EDVARD GRIEG 14, Upper Cheyne Row,
[Original: Danish] Chelsea, S.W.
22.6.06. London.

Dearest Doctor Grieg

A pupil of mine in Copenhagen has sent me "Vort Land" [Our Country] with your interview — how like you it is to be *so* friendly to me![27]

It is all too kind to write all the lovely things about me and has made me indescribably happy; not only that it came in the interview, but most of all that you really think these nice things.

I must say that your visit here was the loveliest time I have ever experienced. We all long for you to come again soon.

I hope that both you and dear Mrs Grieg are very well and that the journey wasn't too "Fingst"-like.

I have received pleasant news from Copenhagen. Mr Wilhelm Hansen has written to me that Kapelmester Johan Svendsen says I am to perform at a Kapel concert at the beginning of the winter 1907–8. Isn't that splendid for me?[28]

I am very well and terribly busy now;* the season is in full swing.

I enjoy myself so often and so much with your songs which you gave me. And how charming "Den Verschwiegen Nachtigall" [The Discreet Nightingale] is.[29]

I am practising at present "Bryllupsdag paa Troldhaugen" [Wedding day at Troldhaugen] and 2 (for me) new Slåtter.

*Or, "I am excellently terribly busy". *Transl.*

Believe me I just can't say how grateful and happy I feel for all the goodness you both have done for me
My mother sends her warmest regards.

With love to you both
Yrs fondly
Percy Grainger

67   TO KAREN HOLTEN   [London]
[Original: Danish/some English]
23.6.06

You are an excellent business-woman, charmingly good; I only wish *I* was. But now comes something quite unforgivable, you will surely be finished with me when you read it.

I have, you see, got an *excellent* Queen's Hall engagement, (to play Liszt's Hungarian Fantasia [with orchestra]) for a larger fee than ever before from Queen's Hall Orchestra, for the 27th Sept, and since I have accepted, I must give up the Danish engagements to be here long enough beforehand to get into really 1st class "form" with the Liszt.

I know that I can practise just as well in Denmark, but *not if I have to play other pieces at concerts at the same time*, and then forget the whole thing again on the journey. You mustn't be cross about it; you do know how difficult it is with the dates and all that.

It is really not my fault; I didn't think that Queen's Hall would choose such an early date, and as they have already deferred my engagement once (from Sept 6) I dare not ask for more.

I feel it so terribly that all your enormous friendly and successful work on my behalf should come to nothing; it is stupid as well for you, in regard to the people you have asked to give me an early date, and who have been so very kind as to do me that service.

Will you say to these people from me that I am more thankful than I can say for their kindness, and am horribly sorry that it won't after all come to anything, but I have now got a series of very important engagements over here, that unfortunately make it impossible for me to take any engagements at all in Denmark in Sept.

Thus I won't come to Cope at all this time. I *propose* to leave here about 20th Sept [*sic* — August], stay in Svinkløv 14–16 days and then back here. Actually it is much nicer for us that this time in Denmark will be only holiday and enjoyment; you know how I am many days before I have to play, so unpleasant and unhappy.

So from all this trouble there will be nothing in Sept.

You must never again get engagements for me. It is too sickening that you should have all the trouble of running around and asking people for me and that I should then make a fool of you by having to cancel at the last moment. I hope you are not annoyed, and that the people you have asked will understand that even a poor artist like me is not master of his own time, and dates.

Now I will see that I get all I can at the same time as my piano evening; and if the people that I disappoint now are not so fed up with me that they never want to hear my name again, I could play at that time instead of this summer. If suggesting this helps you out of the present stupid difficulty do so, but **please** do nothing *new* that means added bother & fruitless work for my rotten sake.

I don't think America will come to anything; and that's perhaps the best thing. You will hear in the summer.

tackle them. Although Percy Grainger did not perform at my concert at Queen's Hall, he assisted me by turning over my music. But just this, to know him near me, with his sympathy and understanding, created an atmosphere, that seemed to uplift me". The extract appeared in translation in the *British Australasian* on 21 June 1906. Grieg had received an honorary doctorate from the University of Oxford on 22 May.

28 Johan Severin Svendsen (1840–1911), Norwegian violinist, composer and conductor, friend and colleague of Grieg. The Danish Royal Opera had appointed him as conductor in 1883. He also gave an annual series of orchestral concerts in Copenhagen, raising the royal orchestra to the level of the best in Europe. Grainger played the Grieg Piano Concerto under Svendsen in Copenhagen on 19 October 1907, by which time Grieg was dead and the concert was his memorial. The Danish firm of music publishers, Wilhelm Hansen, had been founded in Copenhagen in 1853 by Jens Wilhelm Hansen and was thereafter continuously owned and managed by his descendants.

29 Grieg had given Grainger copies of eleven volumes of his published songs (almost his complete vocal works). "Die verschwiegene Nachtigall" is No. 4 of Grieg's *Sechs Lieder* Op. 48 (1889). "Bryllupsdag på Troldhaugen", No. 6 of *Lyriske Stykker* VIII, Op. 65 (1896) for piano had been played by Grieg at the concert on 24 May.

30 Jonas Lauritz Idemil Lie (1833–1908), Norwegian novelist. Bjørnstjerne Bjørnson's novel *Paa Guds Veje* was published in Copenhagen in 1889. Grainger may have read the English translation by Elizabeth Carmichael, published as *In God's Way* in London in 1890.

31 Carl Joachim Andersen (1847–1909) was conductor of the Tivoli Garden concerts from 1897 to 1909. These concerts, of a generally popular character, were only given during the summer. As Karen's letter does not survive, Hansen's opinion remains unelucidated.

32 William Gair Rathbone (1849–1919), Liverpool-born financier and company director, with John Singer Sargent a benevolent patron and friend of Grainger's London years. He is the dedicatee of *In Dahomey* and *Handel in the Strand*. Rathbone was keenly interested in Grainger as a composer and, according to Grainger, "at home" engagements at his house were frequently devoted to simulated performances of Grainger's works rather than to more conventional pianistic efforts.

I didn't go to Somerset to conduct at all!

At the last moment I got the splendid idea of using the 4–5 free days in composing and practising here in peace instead of going South, and that was all too tempting to withstand; so I sent a telegram, and did splendid stuff in peace and happiness. No one knew I was in London and I didn't leave the house and amused myself splendidly.

The score I am working on is a setting for band of "Green Bushes", a folk-dance-song that Cecil Sharp got in Somerset. You will perhaps remember that I began to sketch it before Christmas. I think it will remain. It is for a very small orchestra, and I think it will be really practical and easy to get to sound.

Never have I felt more enormously well than now. I have an excellent season, and the money I gave my poor father will soon be made up again.

Moreover Herman couldn't do the 18th or 19th Sept either. He would also much prefer the Arbejdeforening [Workers' Association] in the winter, if it can be done.

You will think I am completely impossible; I am that too.

What is *bowls*? If only it doesn't require one to use one's brain I'll be in it.

I want very much to read Jonas Lie, and "Paa G[ud]'s Veje"; (which I have only read in English some years ago) and will see that I bring the Jydsk Folkeviser with me.[30]

I believe all the same that Hansen is right regarding Tivoli. Just because J. Andersen conducts Pold [?] Concerts that is a reason why the Kapel people won't want me to play there *before* I play at their own concert.[31]

The pack of women has now left 63 Oakley St. Alfhild and I were quite reasonably friendly at last; but, all the same — *TAKE CARE.*

I had an At Home at Rathbone's last night.[32] I have got Herman a splendid At Home engagement together with me.

Here is something from "*GREEN BUSHES*"

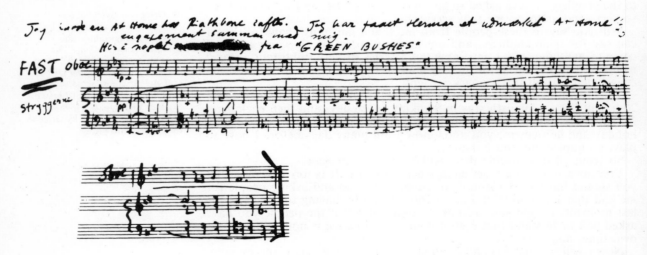

Ask Nutzhorn whether she wants a De Meyer photograph
Naturally you are right about Brahms Violin Sonata
Don't be angry
Live in Peace.

Percy

68 TO KAREN HOLTEN [London]

[Postcard. View of Old Chelsea]
[Original: Danish/English]
7.7.06.

Can you remember this? I have been inhumanly busy, but the worst will soon be over. Herman and I travel to the country today to play at an At Home engagement tomorrow. I have written a new Kipling Soldier Chorus; very vulgar.[33] I have had the most touching letter from Grieg. *Please*, both you & Miss Arlaud take *short skirts* to Svinkløv, so that we can really *move* over the landscape

Percy

69 TO EDVARD GRIEG

14, Upper Cheyne Row,
Chelsea, S.W.
London.

[Original: Danish]
12.7.06.

Dear Master

I am inexpressibly happy for your wonderfully kind letter.[34]

That you (your art, as long, almost, as I can remember has been, together with Bach's, the most deeply loved by me, and indeed something of the most enheartening and most lovely that life holds for me) are fond of me is almost too joyous.

I, naturally, had known and loved you from your music (like so many thousands of other people) so long, and was always so sure that (if I got the opportunity) I would find you *personally* just like your work, that it was almost nothing new to feel for you in reality the same love that I already felt for you in Art. But all that was no guarantee that you would be fond of me in the least! Now it is indescribably lovely to know that you are also somewhat fond of me. All this sounds dreadfully stupid, but I don't mean it that way.

Some days ago a friend gave me your biography written by H. T. Finck.[35] It is lovely to have the photographs of you and dear Mrs Grieg that are in it; similarly of Troldhaugen. How charming it looks on the Fjord, and how I long to come to you there some time.

I am delighted that you want to have me there some day.

It is horrible that I cannot come already this summer; how happy I would be if I could. But: — my father, who for some time has been very ill, and who thank God is a little better again, wanted to travel back to Australia (he was over here for his health's sake) in order to take up his work again over there. But then he needed money for the journey and also a little capital to begin with down there, and so I had to give him most of what I had saved up in the last 2 years. Naturally I am *exceedingly glad* to be in a position to help him a little, and that he is a little better again, but in the next few months I will have to be a little careful.[36]

But a pile of engagements are already certain for the coming winter, so I am sure I would be able to come to you next summer, if you will have me.

Or perhaps already in the winter we can meet. Are you by chance in Kristiania in the month of March? I am thinking of giving a piano evening in Copenhagen at that time, and on that occasion I could perhaps slip over to Kristiania and say a quick Good-day to you both.[37]

I showed Sandby your letter, and the friendly words it contained about him. As you can imagine he was terribly happy. He has now travelled to Denmark.

33 The Kipling chorus was Grainger's second setting of "The Widow's Party" from *Barrack-Room Ballads*, for men's chorus and wind and brass band, composed between 30 June and 2 July 1906.

34 Grieg had written (n.d. P.G. notes "30/6/06?"), "'Let me say it at once: I like you! I like your fresh, healthy outlook on art, I like your unspoilt nature, which not even 'High-life' has been able to corrupt, and then I like your deep feeling for folksong and all the possibilities it carries within itself. Your conception of the English folksongs is full of genius and contains the seed of a new English style in music. And then your taste for the Norwegian folksongs and Scandinavian languages and literature proves that you are not wrapping yourself up in a cloak of onesidedness. On the top of all that there is your magnificent piano playing and — your sympathy with the 'Slåtter' ". Commending Grainger and his mother for their quality of "understanding", which quality he valued particularly, he went on to write, "Remember me to Sandby and tell him that I feel I must reckon him also among my few understanding friends". (English translation by Grainger.)

35 H. T. Finck, *Edvard Grieg*, in the "Living Masters of Music" series, edited by Rosa Newmarch, London, 1906.

36 On 7 June 1906 John Grainger had written to Percy asking for a loan of £200 to enable him to emigrate to Canada and start a new life. On 8 June he wrote that, as Percy had not so much cash to call on, he had decided to return to Melbourne, as expenses would therefore be less. Percy gave him £120 and he left for Australia on the R.M.S. *Oratava* on 15 June.

37 From 1624 to 1925 Oslo was called Christiania after Christian IV, King of Denmark and Norway. Grainger's 1907 piano recital in Copenhagen was on 26 February. He did not, in the event, visit the Griegs in Christiania.

In a few days I am going "Folksong Hunting" If I get some good melodies I will permit myself to send them to you.

It is almost my greatest happiness that you think there is possibly something in my ideas to arrange our English and British folksongs. There was nothing I had wished so much as that *you* would think well of my "settings".[38]

I hope you will forgive me for this letter getting so terribly long.

My mother sends her warmest regards to you both.

How happy I am to have met you both, and for your lovely letter

With many thanks
Your devoted
Percy Grainger

38 On publication of his British Folk Music Settings as a series, starting in 1911, Grainger dedicated them to the memory of Edvard Grieg.

70   TO HERMAN SANDBY
22.7.06.

The Long House,
Hurstbourne Priors,
Whitchurch,
Hants.

Dear old Herm

I've just got a letter from W. Hansen, that they've fixed my Recital in Cope for Feb 26, & are going to try & fit me in some engagements as near as poss *after* that date.

Now comes the quest; whether you're wishful that we ever do any more work together in Denmark, or no.

If you should ever so decide (that you would care to) then I want to feel that you do so for simple & plain business motives; just the same as you would with Fini Henriques, or any other "tout".[39] Formerly we did things more or less in a casual friendly kind of way, ½ for the fun of things, & it was rather larx; far too much so for the situation now to make thanks for the past seemly or soothing. I felt that you (as far as my always selfish behavior made it possible) did not distrust me, & that confidence made it good for either to be in the others debt; to rejoice in friendly beholdenness, even.

Such is good till distrust ‖excellent & useful‖ is awakened. I now no longer feel that trust to be alive (I think it good for both our sakes that it's dead) & therefor our business deals must now just be as ordinary, as orderly, & as favorless as such things had, by the way, must best always be, 1ce & for all.

If I ever can put work in your way, without effort to myself, I shall do so, — not least on the ground that helping a good artist like yrself cannot but also help myself, "in the long run".

You, I take it, might do the same by me, & can safely return the compliment about the decent artist to me, with the there-by-connected good things for yrself.

Joking apart; what I really mean is — let us neither put ourselves out to help or not to help each other; let us do our friendly doings in any old dern way we choose (as of yore); & let us do our business deals in the coldest, strictest, standoffishest way.

In other words; should it amuse you to try & fit in any provincial things with me on dates very soon after Feb 26 in Danish provinces, then write yrself to W. Hansen & propose yrself; quite indipendant of me. If you care to do that, I'll write Hansen & say that you intend joining, but that he'll hear from you direct.

But you most likely might sooner get all yr engagements independant of mine (I should think it probably to yr advantage *to* stick alone; & we'd

39 Fini Valdemar Henriques (1867–1940), Danish violinist and composer. Grainger had met him through Sandby in Copenhagen in 1904. His Suite in F major for oboe solo and strings was played for the first time in England at the Queen's Hall Promenade Concert on 23 August 1906. Grainger's letter is written from the country home of the Plunket Greenes.

likely both get better screw singly than as "two-someists") & I should QUITE understand it & agree with you; & whichever way you decide will be *exactly equally* comfortable & well-liked by me.

Only 1 thing steht fest [German: is quite certain]; I take no more friendlily-got engagements. What I get thro Hansen, alright, but I want no friends to work for me on a friendly basis.

I suppose all this reads fearfully pompous & absurd; but it isnt meant so. All I mean is; each on his own, & you go & fix up with Hansen; or if "no likey, no makey"

In 2 days I go folksonging.

Perks.

Let me know if it will be alright if I ask Karen to get our Arbejderforeningen date fixed near after my Recital.

The packet at 63 is only the list of engaged artists from the Proms so can give it to you when you come over

By 13 July 1906 Grainger's concert-giving for the summer season was over. On 25 July he left for Brigg, for his second summer of folksong collecting. As in the previous year, he was the guest of Lady Winefride Elwes at the Manor House. This time, Grainger went armed with an Edison Bell phonograph, loaned by the Edison Bell Company, and paid for in part by Dr George Gardiner of the Folk-Song Society. This time, Grainger recorded the majority of the songs he collected. Rose remained in London. Grainger returned to London on 4 August, having been obliged to cut short his stay in Lincolnshire: partly by the need to finalise arrangements for his engagement with the London Philharmonic Society, partly by the accidental death by drowning of Lady Winefride's brother, Basil Feilding.

On 18 August he left London again, this time for Denmark, and his much-anticipated holiday with Karen at Svinkløv. It was during this summer that they became lovers. Rose went to stay with her Australian friend Mrs Freeman at Tewkesbury. There she occupied herself with fighting off rumours of Percy's engagement to Karen, and with reading his letters aloud to show that he and Karen were not alone at Svinkløv. Percy was back in London by 9 or 10 September.

71   TO KAREN HOLTEN   Barrow Hall,
[Original: Danish]   Hull.
11 o'cl. evening   (I am with friends of
26.9.06. [*sic* 26.7.06]   Lady Winefride)

Dear Karen

I have been rather busy today. I went to Brigg late yesterday evening and was up early this morning (7 o'cl) and made a little cycle tour to a folksinger before breakfast.

After breakfast a folksinger came to Manor House, Brigg, and I made 5 phonograph records of his songs. It is *by far* the best way of collecting. And then at 11 o'cl I went from Brigg to Ulceby, where I knew there was a blacksmith who knew songs. I got some from him; but it went slowly because there were many people who brought horses and old stoves and things like that to be repaired. But I heard a lot of amusing dialect.

When I had finished with him I came on here, and arrived at 5 o'cl. Before dinner I took down songs from 2 old men and afterwards I visited 3 people, but without success.

Apart from phonograph recording I have written down 12 songs and 21 pages full of words to the songs. I am not so satisfied with the results today; they are not nearly so good as last year; also I am much less fresh and happy about the whole thing. I think I am finished. I am utterly tired and bored about everything.

It is so lovely here. If you have a map, you should first find Lincolnshire and then Great Grimsby, then look westwards for the country town Barrow, which is just opposite Hull, but on the other side of the river Humber.

It is certainly not without a certain interest here.

Here in the little town it is so nice quiet and countrified, and the people are such real "tillers of the soil", with nice interesting animal-like goat-bearded faces; with long stiff boots, and a broad-sounding speech rich in dialect; and just on the other side of the river, which is a mile-wide here, one sees Hull, a large fishing- and sea-trade-town with smoke, factories, and all the other beloved townishness which looks so much more attractive in the distance.

Mother has not been so well in the last few days, unfortunately.

Now it is not so long till Svinkløv.

I really don't see any reason why you should sit for hours in the carriage to Fjerritslev and back; much better and cheaper to omit it. How much must I pay from Fj to Sv? I agree it is shorter via Aalborg, but is it just as cheap? Your silence on this ever-important point makes me a little "suspicious"

Now I must go to bed. I have to be up tomorrow at 6 o'cl.

Always send letters to 14 Upper Cheyne Row

72   TO KAREN HOLTEN
[Original: Danish]
Monday 30.7.06.
(tomorrow [already tonight] it
is August)

Scawby,
Lincolnshire.

Dear Karen

It is now 2 o'cl at night; this "hunt" is heavy work. The whole day and evening one is busy writing songs down, and after that one has to work for hours to get things in order, and to write the many letters that go with the hunt.

But the results are **just splendid**. Twice as many and as good as last year. I have got 8 songs which I would give almost anything for in order to save them from getting lost, and forgotten.

I look absolutely frightful — my hair is cut so short; you can't imagine anything so coarse and swinish and horrible as I look.

I am sorry that when you see me, you will ask me to go back as soon as possible — you won't be able to bear having such a pig before your eyes.

Around here in the neighbourhood it is quite Danish; it *has* been a Danish population. You can notice this from the name in the address on this letter "Scawby" which means "Skovby" [forest-town]

It is really worth something, this hunt. I am pretty tired, however.

Last night I did not get to bed before 2 o'cl either, and up again 6.30. I look forward to playing some of the songs for you.

The phonograph works perfectly.

Goodnight
Percy.

40 From Charles Rosher, painter, author, singer and collector of sea-shanties, in Chelsea on 24 July 1906, Grainger had collected the twenty-one tunes numbered 150–169 and 201 in his *Collection of English Folksongs*.

Some days ago (in London) I got over 20 "Sea-chanties"[40]

73 TO KAREN HOLTEN

[Original: Danish]
12 o'cl night. 3.8.06.

16, Bigby Street,
Brigg, Lincs.

Dear Karen

I have just received your letter of 31.7. and with much happiness.

Tomorrow is my last day here; on Sunday I have things to do in London.[41]

Today I have been a great deal on the cycle, about 50 miles, and have obtained a mass of songs. I have collected the most lovely things since I last wrote; all together I have possibly got about 120–150 songs. It has been hard work, and has been on the whole pretty tedious, although what I have now got are "precious above price". I have not been at Lady Winefride's since last Monday since she has gone away; but I have been in Scawby (as you know) Retford, Bawtry, and am now here tonight.

Just think Everard Feilding and his brother (the priest Monsigneur Basil Feilding, a splendidly amusing chap) sailed on the Rhine in a canoe, and "shot the rapids", and there was an accident and Basil is drowned, but Everard (thank God) was saved[42] Isn't it rather terrible? He (Everard) asked me if I would go with him. He is good fun to go on a holiday with.

You mustn't think I have been living it up here.

I was all alone with Lady W and her children, and went around like a pig, and went, even to meals, unshaven and without a collar on. But then, I was seldom home; left often before breakfast and came home late in the evening.

I was altogether with farming folk nearly all the time; nice people, big-hearted and amusing, but (naturally) dirty-handed and filthy, and sometimes I did not feel strong enough to find pleasure in an otherwise happy, so-called "nature life" like that.

I am longing dreadfully to be back at practising, composition, pupils (that I still have some of) and to feel again that I am really doing something.

Even if I collect folksongs the whole day, I never get the satisfying feeling of having done something.

What lovely airs I have got; but it will be good to go to Mother, and town, and work again tomorrow.

The winter will be horribly busy. It is almost decided that I will get an engagement in *London Philharmonic*. This is the greatest honour one can get in England

I will travel via Aalborg, and *walk* from Ferritslev. It is fun that you will come and meet me on the way. The small amount of clothing I will take with me, I can easily carry the 4 miles; so please do *not* order the Post.

How pleasant and glorious the whole thing will be. Greetings to Arlaud.

Percy.

74 TO ROSE GRAINGER

23.8.06.

[Svinkløv via Fjerritslev]

Dear little mum

This is in hopes it'll catch you before you leave for Tewkesbury. I'm sending another letter onto there.

I've spent a nice happy busy day, it being cold & windy, tho' lovely & sunny, outside. I've spent the afternoon by my little self, writing out these tunes; which, when convenient, print off.

41 Percy was under substantial pressure from Rose to return to London earlier than planned. She wrote on 1 August, "Ada says she finds it *most* important to remain in London until about 7th Aug — all the Autumn eng[agement]s are made at this time". And there was pressure of another kind, as shows in her letter of 31 July, ". . . I am having the dullest time of my *whole* life. I don't like this place alone — it is enough to drive one melancholy mad. Fond love. So glad you are having such a gaudy time". There is some evidence that, although Rose helped Percy with his folksong collecting work, she was not all that enthusiastic about it. As she wrote on 29 July 1907, ". . . I also feel that you give up too much of yr very valuable youth to the folk-songs". The engagement with the Philharmonic Society was secured for 13 March 1907 (see letter 100).

42 The Very Rev. Monsignor Basil George Edward Vincent Feilding, third son of the eighth Earl of Denbigh, (b. 1873), drowned in the Rhine on 31 July 1906. In consequence, Grainger did not, as planned, return to Brigg after his business trip to London.

It looks fine out of my window here; sea to the left, & rolling sandy hills, some heathered, some cultivated, to the right.

If you come you ought to have the bedroom next me; maybe share it with Karen, or not, as most comfy. What's a bother is that you have to go up a horridly stiff flight of steps to this; (the loft) but the steps are only 12 in number, so maybe they could be doable after all.

The rolling hills here around are simply covered with barrows (burial cairns) of the old fighting boys; Karen saw one opened up & the truck brought out. She sends her love.

We had *the* rippingest midday meal today; simply gaudy potatoes along of the meat with fine sauce; with "rød grød" [raspberry fool] & milk & sugar to wind up with.

Such food is worth being fattening.

You'll get another greeting when you get to Tewks.

Lovingly
Perks

noted by Percy Grainger

118 Lowlands low [The Golden Vanity] sung by Mr Th. Button, at Thealby, 27. 7. 06.
1st version

(1) It's I have got a ship in the North of country, & she goes in the name of the "Golden Vanity"; I'm fråd she will be taken all by some gallary, as she sails upon the Lowlands low, lowlands low; as she sails upon the Lowlands low. (2) The boy he had a auger to böre 2 holes at once, while some was playin' at cards, the other playin' at dice. "I let the water in, & it dazzled in their eyes"; & he sunk them in the lowland's low, lowlands low, & he sunk them in the lowlands low.

Mr Button picked this up at Atterby, (Lincs) where he was born

phonographed & noted by Percy Grainger.
(sung in D)

119 Lowlands low [The Golden Vanity] sung by Mr George Wray, Brigg. 28. 7. 06.

75 TO ALFHILD DE LUCE
28.8.06.

Svinkløv Plantørbolig
Svinkløv. pr. Fjerritslev.

My dear Alfhild.

Well, up here is good & no mistake. Am working like an Australian, & having in the workless spells an A1 time with those (dear folk all) up here; Karen, her sister & her husband, Miss Arlaud, & other delightful folk whose names I've not heard; a jolly Painter & a comfortingly Englishlooking engineer.

If an Englishman wants to come to his own original real own soil & see the burring "r" of his own speech wriggle lightly aX the teeth of the mouths that far back 1st rolled it — Jutland for him. It does me alright.

I feel laughably & laughingly well. I'm only sorry I couldnt get to this before when even more folk are yet here; I love a roomfull of Danes & relish to see & hear'm shovel food & words alike easygoingly

I've got a ripping winter ahead & I look refreshedly forward to the tingle of it all, grieved tho' I'll be to quit the thoro joy of this here.

I want to drag up a crew to this next summer. Mother & Roger & Fletcher if I can. We'd have fun.

I cant say that I hear much from you folk, or that I relish not doing so. Now's yr chance, while I'm yet within the 10 Øre letter & 5 Øre card radius. Tell old Herm to shove along & get off a card to me, if nought better. He might let me know how the Overture scores itself or what other Danishness he's birthing.

Karen sends her love

Heartful greetings
from yrs ever
Percy.

76 TO ROSE GRAINGER
3.9.06. early morn.

[Svinkløv]

This'll be a hard one to put on, but the skilled craftswoman will "win out" as usual, doubtless.

The swimming got on much better yesterday; I'll make every effort to do my most before leaving. I shall be with you next Sunday eve, or 1st thing Monday morn. Had their been ship next Thursday I would have taken it, but there's none between Wed & Sat, so I'm waiting till Sat.

It's great fun, the old planter here (he's not old) likes nothing as much as "Green Bushes" & he doesnt know its mine either; its quite upbucking[43]

When's Fletcher coming back. And will Rodg be in town when I return.

You are coming with me to the Prom next Monday arnt you? Do see that you do; it'd be such a treat together — Wagner I think it is.

The Wagner Kaisermarsch has come only 1½ Kroner, & great fun. You & I must tackle it.

43 *Green Bushes*, Passacaglia on an English Folksong for small orchestra, was begun 15 November 1905, revised and copied on to hectograph master plates during September 1906. Grainger was also transcribing his collection of folksongs from the phonograph on to hectograph masters, which Rose then printed. Monday night was traditionally Wagner night at the Queen's Hall Promenade Concerts. The programme for 10 September included Wagner's *Kaisermarsch*. Grainger was learning to swim at the suggestion of Harry Plunket Greene, an activity encouraged by Rose after Basil Feilding's accidental drowning. In Svinkløv Percy and Karen stayed in the house of the "planter" (i.e. someone who cared for a fir plantation).

I hope to get in a real topping day's practise today; its not so easy when the sun is gleaming & enticing as it is these glorious warm days we're having.

I shall be thoroughly glad to be back in a town where nature isnt luring one off one's graft.

Love from yr ever
equally fond son
Perks

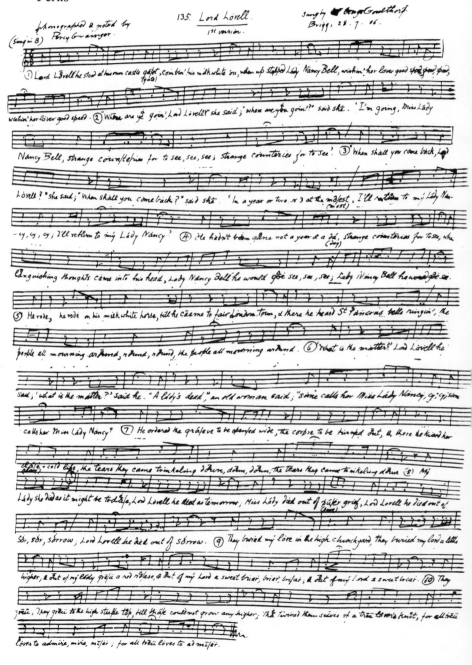

77   TO ROSE GRAINGER   [Svinkløv]
[Postcard]
5.9.06.

This is the dull little house where it's quite nice to be, all the same.

Too breakersome to try to swim today, but "Gr Bs" licking along. I find scoring by hektograph every inch as fast & comfy as otherwise. The inked square are the rooms in the loft which are the nicest. Soon what fun.

I guessed the Freemans wld have to keep you longer so I wrote the extra card that you got Monday.

Keen love from your well son

_____

Isnt it fine about the Nth West passage?[44]

To which Karen added her note:

Dearest little Percys mother,

I c'ant tell you what a happy time Percy and I have had together. The last days Percy has worked a lot, such splendid things in "green bushes". I think it is so nice to feel that one can be, in the least, as happy when work is going on, as when it is only pleasure.

Percy is very much getting on with his swimming, in few times he will be quite good for it. I am so longing to see you once again. Love.

Yours
Karen

78   TO ROSE GRAINGER   [Svinkløv]
[Postcard]
6.9.06.

I can really swim now; not *at all* well, yet, of course, not [nor] can I travel, hardly at all; but there's no question of sinking any more.

I'll keep it up when I return untill I'm quite able to rescue myself & if poss be of use to others.

Did a stunning lot of good work on "Gr Bushes" yest. Poor Karen must have a dull time I'm afraid as I'm slogging away at 1 or t'other thing save meal times; but she seems well-suited enough.

Have written Schuster.[45]

We had real awesome thunder in the night. I did some fearing. But a gorgeous roaring sunny day again this morn

All love
yr fondest son
Percy.

Returning to London on the weekend of 8–9 September, Grainger contracted a chill on board ship which kept him in poor health on and off for some weeks, though not sufficiently to interfere seriously with his activities. His first major engagement after returning to London was his performance, the first of many hundreds, of Liszt's Hungarian Fantasia *[Fantasie über ungarische Volksmelodien] for piano and orchestra, at the Queen's Hall Promenade Concert on 27 September. After this concert the Graingers went to stay with Mortimer Menpes and his family at their country home, Iris Court, at Pangbourne in Berkshire. Grainger started the new season, and a hectic schedule of engagements, by playing at Marie Gwynne's recital at the Aeolian Hall on 8 October.*

44 *The Times*, 4 September 1906, reported that a telegram had been received in Copenhagen on 3 September from Nome, Alaska, announcing that the *Gjoa*, the vessel of the Norwegian Polar expedition, had arrived there, having completed the navigation of the North-West Passage.

45 Leo Francis (Frank) Schuster, the wealthy son of a Frankfurt-Jewish banking family who chose to devote his life to the advancement of the arts rather than to business. He was Gabriel Fauré's host and patron in England: Grainger was to meet Fauré at Schuster's on 15 March 1908 (see letter 188).

79   TO KAREN HOLTEN   [London]
[Original: Danish/some phrases English]
23.10.06. [*sic* 23.9.06] Sunday.

I have had a lovely day today; the fact is got an upset stomach again, so that I must lie down a little, and can't do anything properly; so I have read through the whole of "Parsifal" (the words) and thought out a lot of the orchestration of Wamphray Ballad; in other words, I have been lazy and had a nice time.

Mother is working *very* busily learning Danish, and is making excellent progress.

Yesterday I swam from one side to the other and back without stopping.

Last night I went to the Promenade concert and heard, among other things, Don Juan (Strauss) Charfreitagszauber (Parsifal) Kaisermarsch, Peer Gynt.

What a lot of rubbish I was talking when I said that I didn't love Wagner more than anything, nearly. It is impossible for me to say how I love his music, and what I feel when I hear it. And not only that; I think that Don Juan is one of the most splendid works that there is in the world; I think now that it is just as lovely as Wagner *at his best*. I can remember that you always loved Strauss; so you weren't such a rotten fool as I was (and am, and always will be)

I have only heard it twice but can realize how lovely and good it is. All the stupid things I have always been so proud to assert about Strauss are hopefully lies. The orchestration of Don Juan is certainly charming; it cuts like a knife and is so lovely huge passionate and crazy.

How great the Germans are, that they *always* without interruption have such great men Don Juan is the only one of Strauss' works which I know that I am really fond of *yet*; but to have created only one such masterwork is really something prodigious and splendid.

One really sweats with pleasure when one hears something like Don Juan.

How poor, and childish, and impossible, and amateur-English my poor attempts are beside something "real" like this is.

20/10/06 [sic 28.9.06]
Dear little Karen, do something for my sake. You must try and sing again. It is just impossible not to be able to; there is something so shameful about it; think not to be able to sing in my ladies choir! I would be tremendously happy if I knew that you did it again, — don't take lessons or anything like that, but practise to be able to sing in a choir, or a quartet, etc.

It is so stupid of me; either I am in love with some music, or I am jealous of it. I used to be jealous of Strauss, and now I am head over heels in love with Don Juan. Do you know it well?

Why do so many clever people believe that it "saves" one to give up things. People like Christ and Buddha and Wagner and 1000 others.

I am thinking, among other things, of Parsifal. I think it is *much* more interesting to take things, and not to give them up; (But *we* know that) and I can't understand either, why people *want* to be "saved", and in what way giving up should save. Can you understand it?

I seriously ask you not to buy me any more books. As Herman once said "there are frontiers what you can offer me" [*sic*]. I think I am already more than enough like a poor small-holder as regards you, without you constantly giving and giving. I have a capacity to take and take, but it will soon be too crazy with this generosity of yours.

I suppose I must stop.

Be happy and extremely busy and more reliable in your tummy than I

Percy.

80 TO KAREN HOLTEN
[Original: Danish]
Saturday. 29.10.06. [*sic* 29.9.06]

At the Menpes's.
Iris Court
Pangbourne
Berkshire

Kind little Karen

Miss Freeman isn't coming to live with us; a few days ago I decided that she shouldn't. We lose no little money by not having her, but I won't under any circumstances have women who are strangers in the house. At bottom we are all rather happy to do without her.

The day before yesterday (Thursday) I played Liszt and Beeth[oven]'s "Anger" at the Promenade Concert. I don't think it's an exaggeration to say that it was the 1st *really great* success I have achieved. You can't imagine what the enthusiasm was like; the house was chock-full, (standing people over the whole floor) and it wasn't so much that I got 8 recalls for the Liszt and 4 for the other as the way they shouted and whistled and "howled". Although I have before had what people would *call* successes, it seems to me that Thursday was the 1st time I got the feeling that the audience was really and truly quite "gone" on me. I didn't play particularly well, and didn't feel at all too secure; but had much power that evening — and, it was successful, somehow.
The papers splendid. Wood conducted excellently; we had no rehearsal.
I practised really a great deal on it and prayed intensely.[46] But what a nightmare the whole thing is; and how I hate the "Til Eulenspiegel" played the same evening. Unfortunately I couldn't like it as a whole, although some few places amused me ever so much.
Roger (who together with Fletcher and Ernest Thesiger [who travelled from Scotland to be present] came home with me afterwards) has borrowed my "Don Juan" score to my great delight. It does look nearly as good on paper as it sounds.
Roger also would like very much to come with us to Svinkløv. He can't before the beginning of Sept, but then perhaps I will come a little before the others. That can be decided later.
Just think, in Jan we get Wagner performances, probably "Ring" etc, it is said that Nikisch will conduct and that the Bayreuth singers are coming.[47] So when I learn when it will definitely be, I think it would be a good time to have you at our place; then you and Mother and I, Fletcher and Roger [can] visit the gallery just like at "Major Barbara" that time.
Wouldn't you like to hear the whole "Ring" etc with me? I would.

Mother and I are well here. This is the only home in England I really feel completely happy in, and there is no man I am more deeply fond of than Menpes. I believe you have once met Maudie and seen how unforgivably fat she was; Menpes was that too, to a lesser degree. But now they have both gone on a diet and have become *completely thin* again. Maudie looks 6 years younger and he excellent
I am so wildly happy to see that Australians have just that kind of strength of character, to get something like that pushed through Then there is always hope for people. (me too) He is unusually fresh and kind this time, so amusing and lovable. And so childishly happy for all his 100 widely different plans, although they cause him a tremendous amount of stupid strife and "bothers".
I only hope that he won't lose out there the deal of money he has so zealously worked together. But I don't think so, a man who can get himself slimmed down at his age, is sufficiently young in spirit and awake to get out of it.

46 The Beethoven piece was his *Rondo a Capriccio* in G Op. 129 which has a title page inscription, "Die Wuth über den verloren Groschen, ausgetobt in einer Caprice" [Rage over the lost penny, stormed out in a caprice]. Henry (later Sir Henry) Joseph Wood (1869–1944), English conductor and co-founder, with Robert Newman, of the Queen's Hall Promenade Concerts. The papers were indeed splendid, one of the soberest comments coming as usual from *The Times*, 29 September, which observed, "His performance was extremely brilliant, but the brilliance never obtruded itself because of the feeling one had the whole time that the music was being played primarily because it was enjoyed and understood by the player".

47 A projected season of twenty-eight performances of German opera was planned for Covent Garden from 14 January 1907. Arthur Nikisch (1855–1922), Austro-Hungarian conductor. He visited London frequently in the years between 1904 and 1914, when he often appeared as guest conductor of the London Symphony Orchestra. Six of Wagner's operas were given during the 1907 season, including *Die Walküre*, the second part of *Der Ring des Nibelungen* (see letter 97).

How he and I resemble each other as types is too laughable. He is a good-hearted fellow despite all his follies.

I am not so well at present. My throat is really pretty sore; so that I can't sleep all too well for it. It stems from this time of year.

81   TO KAREN HOLTEN [London]
[Original: Danish/English]
Wednesday. 10.10.06.

The little Karen

Tremendously glad for your letter today. Yes, it is true about being among indifferent people, it can be almost overpoweringly oppressive; I know it so well; but it is something one should do after all, as often as one can, I think. In the 1st place, indifferent people are not indifferent about everything, one makes a mistake if one believes that, I hope. And it is at bottom a *habit* to feel oneself depressed and the whole surroundings of no importance, it is only being unused to mixing with people, and something more: I have noticed that people who avoid others very much, rapidly become ugly and old. I think (perhaps wrongly) that one gains so much from intercourse with others, particularly strangers and indifferent folk; they wake up qualities in oneself, that one perhaps doesn't care for so much but which all the same belong to one's equilibrium, I always feel that "good looks" are bound up with "balance".

When one is too much alone, one can so easily overspecialise some few qualities which one particularly admires.

When one thinks of the Nations that have excelled in developing beautiful physical national types, it is most often people like Greeks and Englishmen and Italians that have an unusually important "public life" or have much to do with each other. Nations like the Germans that live in a very narrow circle, and are particularly interested in "private life" are as a rule ugly enough.

And I am saying all this who hate social life more than anyone.

When I am out among folk & bored & miserable I cant help thinking of a certain habit of yours at certain times: a face carefully covered up by 2 hands, only partially uncovered for a moment now & then to let a smile through if things are particularly nice.

It is comforting, somehow.

One feels there is something hidden & happy & secret that one **could** turn to.

I have now heard that Nikish *definitely* will come and conduct Wagner performances in Jan and Febr, and the whole thing will be splendid. So it seems to me that you should come around about that time, we don't have to decide yet exactly when, do we?

Yes, how lovely the last 18 bars of the 2nd Act of the "Masters[ingers]" are.

It is splendid you are singing again; 1000 thanks for doing it; and it is excellent with tennis. No, unfortunately I am not at all a good tennis player; I have never really played it long enough; only 4, 5, days each year, perhaps.

It is good that you can "sing both high and low" (as Shakespeare has it in Roger's song "O mistress mine") it seems to me that one should never restrict oneself to Soprano or contralto; why not both? But let me know *approximately* your range. Remember to sing in the open air and when you walk or row or anything like that, it is all good for breathing.

Your sister wrote to me that you wanted to give up playing in concerts because Miss Arlaud didn't want to, or something like that. That's right isn't it? You know that nothing would make me *so happy* as to know that you were playing a lot at concerts. I know it is horrid, but it doesn't spoil your appearance, so there is no reason not to do it. It is certainly good that you will play at Miss Lindeman's and with Birkerød. Let's hear of a lot more of such!

Roger was here last night and was quite crazy about the lovely place in Green Bushes that I wrote in Svinkløv. You are right that it is unforgivable of me to say that Green Bushes is ugly and boring. It is in fact not "polite" to talk about other people's work in that way; and the best places in this piece I did not write quite alone. (you little friend) By "ugly and boring" I only meant the places that I wrote quite alone.

I am working now on the conclusion of "English Dance". It is becoming quite German, unfortunately.

Monday. 16.[10.]06.
I am playing in the following concerts:—

Oct 18.	Recital Aylesbury.
" 25	People's concert, Chelsea Town Hall.
" 29	concert Æolian Hall.
Nov 1	Bournemouth, Schumann Concerto
" 14	my Recital Æolian Hall.
" 18	Sunday concert. Schumann Concerto
" 22	Broadwood concert?
Nov 28	Edinboro Recital
" 30	concert Æolian Hall.
Dec 11	Birmingham. Schumann Concerto
" 15	Bournemouth Recital.

Elwes wants to sing 6 of my Folksongs at our Recital (Nov 14) and Plunket Greene 9 or 10 at his song Recital sometime in Dec.

I am so unhappy that they will do it. I suffer so much from "compromise", and that's what it will be; neither fish nor fowl.[48]

But it has an undeniably great practical value, nevertheless.

But I don't think I will permit it again.

Let me know your concert dates so that I can also send you good thoughts.

Think hard for me when I am playing the Schumann Concerto.

I am terribly busy and therefore very unhappy, but that doesn't matter in the least. I am always that when I am busy, and it doesn't matter. I still have an awful cold, but I believe it is beginning to get a little better.

I saw Herman today and he gave me your greeting.

Perhaps it is better if you don't go in for Weininger.[49] I am not doing it so much either

Goodbye, be always happy and delightful looking

82 TO HERMAN SANDBY   [PM Chelsea]
[Original: Danish/English]
[Postcard. PM 17 October 1906]

I am terribly sorry that I cannot come this evening to hear you, but I fear I am not yet well enough to be out in the night air. Tons of luck to you.[50]

It is so many years since I last heard you play with orchestra, and I have so much looked forward to it. Fletcher is going on my ticket, and will go

---

48 Elwes sang five of Grainger's new folksong settings, Grainger accompanying, at their duo-recital at Aeolian Hall on 14 November 1906: *Brigg Fair, Six Dukes Went Afishin', The White Hare, The Sprig of Thyme* and *The Gypsy's Wedding Day*. Plunket Greene did not sing any of Grainger's settings in this year. However, at his duo-recital with Grainger at Bournemouth on 15 December 1906 he sang a bracket of traditional airs arranged by Lucy Broadwood. This may not have been the spot he had thought of for Grainger's settings.

49 On 4 October 1906, Grainger had written to Karen that he was reading *Sex and Character*, an English translation (published London 1906) of a sensational book *Geschlecht und Charakter* by the Viennese writer Otto Weininger (1880–1903). Taking as his (unacknowledged) point of departure Fliess's theory of constitutional bisexuality of human beings, Weininger sought to elucidate the psychological, sociological, aesthetic, moral and philosophical problems of the day. Hailed as a masterpiece, the book was a prodigious success and was translated into many languages. The author committed suicide some months after its publication, at the age of twenty-three. The work is anti-feminist and anti-Semitic. Grainger consistently misspells "Weininger" as "Weiningen"; this has been silently corrected in the text.

50 Herman made his debut appearance at the Queen's Hall Promenade Concerts on 17 October 1906 playing the Dvořák Concerto in B minor for violoncello and orchestra.

and speak to you. We are looking forward to seeing you tomorrow (Thursday) evening 8 o'cl.

With heartfelt wishes for tonight
Perks.

Mother joins in luck wishes.

83   TO KAREN HOLTEN   [London]
[Original: Danish]
Sunday. 21.10.06.
[Extract]

That about compromise in respect of my Folksongs is after all correct; not in any particularly bad way, but, for example, the true folksong loves to have a great many verses, 10, 12, 15, etc. but that won't go at a concert; or one *thinks* it won't. Then neither Greene nor Elwes know the dialect properly, and are too lazy to learn it. Naturally I knew all this beforehand, but it irritates me none the less for all that.

Since I can't take the night air so well yet I couldn't go and hear Herman, the other day, but people say he played excellently. He and I went together to the swimming bath yesterday, and he taught me a lot. Apparently he does it very well himself. How amusing about him and Alfhild and you; it's like him (and her) He almost quite forgets that we are unfriendly when we are together long enough. He has gone away again now.

I think that after all you had better sleep here in the house when you come, perhaps in with mother; there is no room (here in the house) where you could practise, but I will arrange for you to do it in a room in a music shop in Kings Rd, if you don't have anything against the idea. You know, I hope, that I will pay all your expenses when you are over here, don't you? That is you will *really be on a visit*, you understand. That is not so little for me, I think . . .

Tuesday. 23.10.06.
Yesterday and today Fletcher and I swam, and today I achieved 3 times across the bath without stopping. I have also begun swimming on my back. Isn't it ridiculous that men and women may not bathe together, and that you and I cannot do it now when you are over here this time.

We have read such an excellent and lovely little book; "Woman" by a man (a great lover of W. Whitman and also a keen Democrat) who is called Carpenter.[51] It belongs to Fletcher but I will see if I can't get hold of it and send it to you; (otherwise you must read it when you are with us) Fletcher thinks, namely, that you can't buy it any more. It is so full of understanding and true and full of love, that it is extremely welcome after Weininger. I must say I am a little tiny bit proud that the Carpenter–Whitman understanding of womanliness occurs so much more with us than the Weininger sort. That kind (the last named) [of] ungratefulness is perhaps not particularly attractive.

Have you ever read the text of "The Mastersingers"? It is full of so many quite charming things. What Sachs sings in the 5tet and just before is so touching. I must say, I understand H. Sachs feelings almost the best of all. Although I am young in years (and in so many respects am still childishly young) I am almost like an old man in my truest feelings. I have always had the feeling that life is something glorious that everyone must take the keenest interest in, but that for me personally it was nearly over. I have so little desire to meddle with the whole thing, and would much rather stand a little to one side and wish good luck to those who are still active enough to dare to take part in reality.

51 Edward Carpenter (1844–1929), English writer, Socialist and moral reformer. *Woman, and Her Place in a Free Society* was published in 1894. In developing his ideas of a primitive, free, moral society he drew on the ideas of a number of writers including Walt Whitman, whom he visited. His *Days with Walt Whitman, with some notes on his life and work* had appeared in May 1906.

"Young prows that seek the old Hesperedes.
Though we know the voyage is vain,
Yet we see our path again,
In the saffroned bridesails scenting all the seas."

Even about you, little friend; (understand me rightly; I do not mean it in the slightest coldly or lovelessly) I always have mostly the feeling of something very lovely and lovable, but which it is best (not least for your sake) to let glide past.

I understand for example so well.

"Vor dem kinde, lieblich, hold, mocht' ich gern wohl singen:
Doch des Herzens süss' Beschwer' galt es zu bezwingen.
'Swar ein schöner Morgentraum; d'ran zu deuten wag' ich kaum."

And if there was a true Walter for you, how happy would I not be (not happy at parting; that is always sad; neither was H. Sachs happy to have to do so) and how I would love you both.

The greatest happiness in my life would be to see all my most loved friends and woman-friends married and active and in every way "living"; but I would rather not be mixed up in the whole thing; best to be like the audience, — clap my hands.

I admire so highly the qualities that I myself have least of; (and am happy to have least of — I don't know why) life-force, fearlessness, recklessness, self-belief.

My (apparent) energy is something quite different from all this. This derives from me being very healthy and having many ideas; it is *work-force* not *life-force*.

Little friend, you will certainly understand all this properly. It is not just stupidity on my part.

It is something that at one time belongs to one's nature.

84 TO KAREN HOLTEN   [London]
29.10.06.

Funny little one

Why think such queer things?

Goodness, how true it is that I had "nothing against" life at Svinkløv, but dont forget that I had you to teach me, & how much I had (& always, when alone, would have) to learn in that direction. If you were here now I should be an excellent pupil at once. But that is no reason to undervalue that which is of my own, untaught, self. What man learns from woman is of deep worth, but what he brings in himself is also fine & needful. When thinking of these things, always keep in mind how I always dread performances of my compositions (yet you know I love them, alright) yet, believe me, my joy is intense when they actually at last *do* become real, actual, physical (performed). The shyness & aloofness of man is neither better nor worse than the splendid courage & boldness of woman.

Also remember:

That Hans Sachs contains Walther, though Walther don't contain H.S.; & in spite of the fact that the Walther element might *apparently* be quite absent in H.S. *at moments*.

Remember that I come from a new country where the freedom & independance idea is the biggest virtue, & that further as a socialist & democrat the idea of anyone belonging to anyone is a perfect nightmare (whatever the folk in question may be feeling, one way or another) to me.

Therefor, whoever comes in touch with me, I am instinctively forced to treat as a *wholly free agent*, notwithstanding love or hate.

Now as to Weininger. (whose book by the way I advised you *not* to read; though that is no reason why we should not talk some of it over when you are here — *if you like*) I would not, if I were you, "pity" anyone who has been so lucky as to make so great a work as "Sex & Character" at so young an age as 21. Anyone possesing *greatness* (whatever his *quite* **obvious** weaknesses may also be) to such an unusual degree as he is rather an object of envy, to my mind. Nor would I foster physically violent desires against the book that bears his thoughts. I cannot help feeling a sense of considerable holiness in the presence of the mere dead paper which is the vehicle for such a record of noble struggles & great & valuable pain as the poor devil must have gone through; however I might differ from his views.

Since you *have* looked at the book, let me state the following *fundamental* points on which he & I disagree.

He represents everything that is aristocratic & religious, & believes in "value", & in the *soul*, & therefor belittles *bodiliness & womanhood*, which are the same thing fundamentally.

I (poor thing) stand for everything that is democratic & irreligious, *ignore* all "value", dont believe in the existence of *soul* either in *man or woman*, & since *bodiliness* is to me the highest aim, rate woman (if anything) *higher* than *man*.

So he & I are the poles. Nevertheless I see a *huge* lot in his work that falls in with my own thoughts, & a *huge* lot that is neither his nor my particular views, but *just* **truth** *in general*. Also I think his work is valueable in *increasing* the regard & admiration & realisation of the "holiness" of woman; — most of the things he says as counting against woman, are, (to my so very different mind) wholly & strongly in her favor.

Of the *many many* points on which the poor great devil is *only* inexperienced & stupid & wrong, the less said the better. Blemishes in a great work are ever a cause for sadness, & are better forgotten.

Think how sad if I died now (just his age at death) & people talked only of my bad orchestration & less of anything that may be good in my texture.

So dont burn his book, please, little Karen, for he tried very hard to do a big thing.

Also remember that if there were nothing of Weininger or the Hans Sachs element in me I would be much more of a rascal than I am.

My feeling for Weininger is also nourished by the thought that few stand closer to Wagner's type of thought (as strongest voiced in *The Ring* & *Parsifal*) than he.

Now then, about the subject of the suggested "Tankeforbindelse" [Danish: association of ideas]. I should be wretched & miserable if I ever, for a moment, thought of you & her [Alfhild] with nogensomhelst tankeforbindelse [Danish: any association of ideas at all]. Too absurd; but why suggest it?

You know all about that business.

Because one has once been in an unfortunate relation to someone that is no reason not to like, *when the relationship has been upset for ever*. As long as the relationship existed, one could not, perhaps, help hating a little, but now it is gone, finished, over, there remains nothing to be done but to like any good qualities that an unlucky individual may own.

I always liked certain *few* qualities in her & always shall, & nothing will ever stop my being glad when a creature that has had such a rotten time of it as she has (doubtless her own fault, largely) falls on her feet for a bit & gets a bit of comparitive luck. And as long as I feel *glad over anything, nothing (as long as we write) will stop my writing it to you, since either you must know nothing or as much as I have time in this life to write.

I must not write any more as I have a concert tonight & writing stiffens the hand so.[52]

52 On 29 October Grainger assisted at Marie Gwynne's second vocal recital at Aeolian Hall. The "at home" is unidentified.

Dont fear that my love & admiration of womankind is going to be shaken by an old book.

I had an At Home engagement yesterday for 20 pounds to play to only 3 people!

What amuses me in your dear letters are the sentences that you begin & then scratch out.

Goodbye & keep calm & don't go athinking.

Percy.

*I should feel rather funny if I did *not* let you know any gladness of that nature.

〚Senere. Mandag.〛 [Danish: Later. Monday]

Infinitely happy for your 2nd letter.

I hope my letter here isn't stupid.

I can assure you that mother never spoke so lovingly of you as lately; & that she is not the *very least little* bit afraid of anything at all. I won't tell her you thought her letter colder as it is no use; as she didn't mean it so. People love you, they dont fear you, or want you to forsvinde [Danish: disappear].

I dont think things are difficult; of course one can never tell; but I dont worry.

Love.

Plunket Greene is not doing my tunes after all, I am *so so* glad, & feel well again at once.

85 TO CECIL SHARP[53]
2.11.06.

14, Upper Cheyne Row,
Chelsea, S.W.

Dear Mr Sharp

Very many thanks for your most kind letter; & please forgive my not having answered it before, but I have been away.

I am most interested to hear of the Novello idea, & thank you for your kind thought of me in the matter.

Personally, I am very keen that the tunes I collect (barring now & then a choral setting or 2) should be publicly presented in as *merely scientific* a form as possible, for the time being. I dont wish to come forward as an arranger yet awhile, altho' in some 15 to 20 years time I hope to myself publish a folkmusic book; settings, etc.

Having been seedy for some time lately has put my folksong work badly back, so that but few of the tunes are yet cleanly hektographed, but I hope in a month or so's time to have got thro' with it, & would then be delighted to bring you the tunes along (or you come to us here once, if you would & could) to see, & should you care to have a few for any purpose (given only I might keep the copyright of the *actual tune*, in case I might want to set it myself, later) I should have great joy in having that chance of showing my much thankfulness for your extremely kind loan to me of the maj version of *I'm 17 come Sunday*.

The phonographing was great fun.

I suppose you got tons more rippers this summer!

Again, hearty thanks for your letter

Yrs sincerely
Percy Grainger

53 Cecil James Sharp (1859–1924), English folk-music collector, editor and educator. He had written to Grainger on 25 October outlining his scheme for a series of volumes of "Folk Songs of England", to be published by Novello with Sharp as general editor. The series was inaugurated in 1908 with *Folk Songs from Dorset* collected by H. E. D. Hammond with pianoforte accompaniments by Cecil Sharp.

86 TO KAREN HOLTEN [London]
[Original: Danish/some English]
Saturday. 3.11.06.

Schumann (your) Concerto went splendidly last Thursday in Bournemouth. How lovely it is and very amusing to play with an orchestra. Swimming is going very well. I find myself in an interim period. Breathing and movements are all wrong; therefore I think it best not to swim much (for my ability) at a time, but really try to do it a little more properly.

Rogan would have rehearsed Wamphray March last Wednesday, but I couldn't, (on account of B-mouth) but we will now get to hear it on Tuesday.[54] I had so looked forward to sending this letter today, so that you should get it early in the month, but since I wrote last Monday it can't be done; unfortunately. You must "take the will for the deed".

I have just received rather good news from my father in Melbourne.

_____

[Continues in English]
Later (Sat)
Just got yr letter, of Thursday.

You are a dear thing. But dont talk of *my* forgiving, when the need is all the other way. Naturally I felt pretty appologetic last letter, but didnt say anything about it for following reason; what makes me write a letter like the one that upset you (the one about old H. Sachs) is not just bad temper or a nasty mood, but a certain particular *frame of mind* to which I am certain to often return; which frame of mind I must needs equally apply to art, life, friends, those I love, etc.

And as it doesn't really effect my actions & doesnt make my outlook *less loving* either to one or to all, I dont feel it is dangerous, or that I ought to fight it. It is only a *reaction*, &, as such, is healthy. So if it turns up again (as it may in a week or a year) just rate it for what it is worth, & just think it (if you like) funny or silly, but not loveless or unfriendly; for it is not meant thus.

So that is why I didnt say "forgive *me*".

Also, I regard woman's relation to man (the brute) as so everlastingly forgiving that it seems greedy to go *extra* begging.

But I know I'm a rotter, alright.

I hope dear old Herm's concert went well: — rather rot about the accompanying business. I certainly wouldn't put myself out to go up to Alfhild, if I were you; or if so, I'd only do (not too soon) a simple *undemonstrative* cool call, with no extra friendly nonsense. Remember always that her card came *just* **before** his concert. I think the great thing in such cases is to be neither hot or cold (both almost equally bad) but just nice & cool & *aloof*. But please, dont do a thing more in the matter that you dont just want yourself. You have already done & finished the great kindness to me that I begged: to just be alright if you met, & to go to his concert for my sake. Thanks.

P. Greene isnt doing the tunes because I wont write him out the accompaniments to use at other concerts; he's quite right & so am I, & I am *so so* glad, I cant say how.

On Thursday afternoon, Dec 6, I'm going to make a sort of short speech to the member of the Folksong Society, about phonographing & its advantages & the discoveries through it, & let them hear some of my phonograph records. They are going to propose me for the committee of the Folk Song Society, which is an honor that gladdens me lots. I am going [to] propose to have my old singers up to give short unaccompanied folksong recitals to the members. If it *happened* to come off when you are here, what fun! The Society also wants to do a journal of only my collection; & is, I think, willing to let me print out all my different verses & versions, which will cost a lot, but be worth it.[55]

54 Lieutenant J. Mackenzie Rogan, at that time conductor of the band of the Coldstream Guards. The *Lads of Wamphray March* had been written with the band of the Coldstream Guards in mind, and after Grainger had checked its instrumental specifications with Rogan. Rogan rehearsed the piece for the second time on 20 March 1907 (see letter 106). John Grainger's letter does not survive.

55 Following the annual general meeting of the Folk-Song Society held at the Royal College of Music on 6 December, some of the members remained to hear the phonograph recordings Grainger had collected in Lincolnshire. According to the *Musical Herald*, which reported the event in detail in the issue of 1 January 1907, the machine did not work well, and Grainger's own renderings, in dialect, while accompanying himself at the piano, were enjoyed much more. According to Grainger, describing the event to Karen on 8 December, the phonograph could not be heard above the noise of the pianos in adjoining rooms. These impediments notwithstanding, it was announced that a phonograph would be purchased for use by members of the Society. Grainger was elected to the Committee at this meeting, continuing as member until the elections of 1912. His work on a special issue of the *Journal* was to occupy him for several months. The work was completed in June 1908, and the *Journal* (No. 12 [Vol. III, Part 3]) appeared in August or September 1908.

How ripping, all the concerts you are to play at. Do let me know exact dates, when fixed, & addresses in Jylland in case I wanted to write. I *love* to hear of your concerts.

Mother & I had a jolly talk last night; she *always* talks most lovingly of you; when we meet you must hear some of the things she said; so jolly.

By the way, if you want an artisticized & beautified version of the Weininger root-idea, practically the same in the main points; read dear old H. C. Andersen's "Isomfruen" [The Ice Maiden]. Hans Andersen is full of Weiningerism, only that he is an artist rather than a thinker.

But dear old Walt is the darling in these matters. Think of the greatness of his picture of woman page 84 of Leaves of Grass; what a gorgeous phrase: "The female contains all qualities & *tempers* them" & again: "she is all things duly veil'd".

6.11.06. Afternoon

This morning the "Coldstreams" played thro' my Wamphray March. They are a wonderful band; they read it straight thro' & did the hardest things amazingly well. Lots of it sounded splendid & some didn't. My feeling is that it is *successful* taking it all round (& except certain impossible bits) but that it is *fearfully badly scored*.

I fear I have few gifts that way, & I feel that even the parts that sound well could easily sound 2ce as well if I weren't such an ass. I am going to rework a heap of it & cut a lot out. It is much too long, thank God; for my fault has always been overshortness. (like in my "figure") It made me happy to hear it though the undemocraticness of army discipline makes me more miserable than I can say. I feel, somehow, that I'm better among women-folk than among these curious proud strong smelling creatures — men. They weren't thinking of me when they made this world; but then I dont think of them or the world either, so it comes right in the end.

But the way the March went was nothing to make me sad, little Karen. They are going to give it a longer rehearsal in Dec or Jan; when I've altered what I hate particularly in it. Goodnight.

8.11.06. Thursday.

Dear old Gardiner was here yesterday & loves my new work; therefor, of course, I love him. This, however, doesn't mean that you, (to get the same results) need pretend to like my things when you don't as I should likely love *you* just the same if you didn't

Fearfully busy.

I hope you are happy, dear little Karen.

Percy

---

87   TO ERNEST THESIGER   14, Upper Cheyne Row,
5.11.06.   Chelsea, S.W.

My dear Ernest[56]

Herewith the ticks for my conc.

But no nons about your paying for them, or such; that I wouldnt hear of. If you want to be a real pet, just wollop up an Edinborder or so for Mrs Swinton's & my show there; but all that's later on.

Looking forw seeing you on the 14 anyway

Ever   yrs.
   Perkily

[Are you all well!]

[56] An example of a certain kind of letter of which the Graingers wrote many: drumming up an audience for Percy's concerts and sending out tickets. The event here was his duo-recital with Gervase Elwes at Aeolian Hall on 14 November. The recital in Edinburgh with singer Mrs George Swinton was on 28 November.

57 On 18 November Karen had given a concert for the Thisted Music Society with Elna Arlaud and Ida Møller, playing all accompaniments and a bracket of solos. At the Sunday afternoon concert in Queen's Hall on 18 November, Grainger played the Schumann Concerto with the London Symphony Orchestra conducted by C. V. Stanford, and as piano solo, the third of Stanford's "Dante" Rhapsodies, *Capaneo*.

58 Sir Charles Villiers Stanford (1852–1924), Irish-born composer, conductor and teacher. He was conductor to the Leeds Triennial Festival from 1901 to 1910 and one of the influential friends of Grainger's early London years.

88 TO KAREN HOLTEN   [London]
Monday, 19.11.06.

Dear little Karen

I hope Thisted went well with you yesterday. (Sunday) The Schumann Concerto didnt go *badly* & the Stanford Rhapsody quite well, which, of course, pleased him.[57]

I am fixing up a tour engagement with Ada Crossley. They want me for 2 or 3 months about this time next year, for a tour in these islands; I shall make at least 200 or 300 £. We are moving today from the studio into the house; great fun.

We swam today; I not brilliant. I had a slight accident in the deep part & if I hadnt rescued myself somebody else would have had to do it.

Dear old Roger was here last evening.

It is fearfully sweet of you that you are willing to "work" & help when over here. If it doesn't bore you, you might hektograph the as yet only inked 1st part of Green Bushes, or some other copying for me. It would be sweet of you.

Dont forget I dont care what I get at Nyborg & I'd just as soon play alone as assisted.

Love & heaps of luck to you
Percy.

89 TO EDVARD GRIEG   14, Upper Cheyne Row,
21.11.06.   Chelsea, S.W.

Dear Master

I have just heard from Sir Charles Stanford that you will be coming over again to visit this land, next fall; & that I will have the joy of hearing you conduct at the Leeds Festival.[58]

How lovely it will be to see you & dear Mrs Grieg again, & to hear it all!

I have been a little ill but am now well again.

I only wanted to let you know how deeply glad I am at the chance of seeing you both again.

My mother joins me in heartfelt greetings to Mrs Grieg & yourself

Yrs ever thankfully & affectionately
Percy Grainger

90 TO KAREN HOLTEN   [London]
[Original: Danish]
23.11.06.

Little Karen.

Now you can just as well know it, I played quite unforgivably badly at my piano-afternoon last week; something like Broadwood concert last year. I didn't forget so much as on that unforgettable occasion, but all the same, I wasn't much good. I didn't write of it to you before, because I was afraid it could possibly have an unfortunate influence on your own concert, but now it doesn't matter. Last night (Broadwood) on the other hand went well, but I didn't have any soli, only Brahms violin Sonata op. 100 and Cesar Franck, ditto.[59]

Don't forget to let me see all the critiques when you perform, and all possible information about it; will you?

The truth is, that I now, for the 1st time for a long while, feel really properly well and strong again. My cough has now finally disappeared and I don't feel so peevish and impossible as I have done.

It can be that the studio was a damp, or otherwise unhealthy room; we have, you see, moved into the 2 front rooms a few days ago. It is nice that we now live in your former room; I am so happy for that.

Late in the evening.
[continues in English]

I hope you save the money you earn with concerts; it is such a splendid thing to have a little money saved, even only a £100 or so.

There is one thing though, that money might well be spent on — riding. Can you ride? No one can ever properly enjoy new countries who cant ride. If you cant do it you ought to learn, & *if possible* ride "straddle-legs" (like a man rides) it is so much better & looks so .[much] nicer.

Do let me know about this riding business. Riding is a good winter sport, too. I cant ride.

Another thing I want you awfully to do is to become a *really first-rate* reader (vom blatt lesen [German: sight-reading]) of music. If one can accompany *really well* there is always a *real good* living to be earned by it in London, but one must know one's job. Please, dear, make me happy & read music *you dont know* for *at least* ½ hour daily; & when we meet in a little over a month (how short & nice!) I'll test you, & you'll have to read before me a bit every day. *Please* try hard at this; its so good for ones technic too.

I've had such a miserable day today, from early morning to night miserable. It's now nearly 12 & I'm waiting for mother to come home. She's out, & I was at Stanfords

So glad to know from yr letter to her that Thisted went well.

In English dont put a ˘over your Us; like ŭpper — simply *u*pper, also we put no stroke thro' the 7 *(not 7̵)*

Do you do lots of technical work, now? Keep it up & get a good technic; it is the only thing worth *getting*

Goodnight. The Ada Crossley tour is fixed.

[Danish]
My father wants a little more money; it is a nuisance of him.

[English]
I have been fearfully miserable these last few days. I tell you this, because it's not in the least serious, nor does it matter; its just passing nonsense, so I know it wont worry you to know of it. Whenever I play anything I forget it in the middle. Yesterday afternoon I played badly at Lady Charles Beresford's, and in the evening swined at Schuster's before Melba, Eduard Risler & lots else. It does make me sick to do real bad. But Risler (the great pianist) is a dear; altho' I played so shockingly he was so sweet & kind, like all great folk are.[60]

I'm trying to get some of my choruses sung here when you're over

Love from us both
Percy

Mother sends love. She was so glad to get your letter and will write later

Cant manage a holiday I'm afraid when you are over — too poor

59 Grainger had given a duo-recital with Gervase Elwes at Aeolian Hall on 14 November. Despite his pessimistic assessment, the *Daily Telegraph* critic had called it "a concert of pure delight", giving both artists, and Grainger's compositions, a very good review and noting that there had been a very large audience. At the Broadwood concert on 22 November, Grainger had played with violinist Max Mossel. Of this concert, the *Daily Telegraph* critic wrote (23 November), "In artistic worth . . . [it] . . . came about as near perfection as one can ever reasonably expect to find". The Ada Crossley tour was fixed to begin on 13 October 1907.

60 Mina, wife of Admiral Lord Charles Beresford (1846–1919). The Beresfords were close friends of Madame Melba. Edouard Risler (1873–1929), German-born, French-domiciled pianist. As a member of the Conseil Supérieur of the Paris Conservatoire he would have been a valuable contact for Grainger. He dined with the Graingers on 4 December.

61 Grainger was in Edinburgh on 28 November for his recital with Mrs George Swinton. Busoni undertook a tour of the English provinces between 3 and 17 December, giving his London recital on 15 December. As one of the keyboard "giants", Busoni came regularly to London in these years. He and Grainger continued to meet. Though their relationship was cordial, Busoni never "took Grainger up".

91   TO FERRUCCIO BUSONI
[n.d. possibly late November 1906][61]

Assembly Rooms
George Street
Edinburgh

Dear Master

Miss Hilde Davidson, the bearer of this letter, is most anxious to ask you if you would do her the very great kindness to hear her play.

I regret to say that I have not heard Miss Davidson play myself, but fellow artists have told me that she is very gifted.

With heartiest greetings to you all
Your ever thankful admirer
Percy Grainger

92   TO EDVARD GRIEG
[Original: Danish]
8.12.06.

14, Upper Cheyne Row,
Chelsea, S.W.

62 Grieg had written suggesting that he include his Piano Concerto among the works he was to conduct, in order that he might have the joy of seeing Grainger as soloist in it. Grainger did play the Grieg Concerto at Leeds, on 12 October 1907. By then Grieg was dead and the concert was in his memory. Rose duly announced both invitations to the press: the *British Australasian* printed the news on 10 January 1907.

Dear Master

No, it was all too lovely to get the long sweet letter from you. How kind it is of you to spare me so much time. I am inexpressibly happy to have the 2 lovely letters from you; a thousand thanks.

This about Leeds Festival is enchanting. Even if your kind thought about letting me play your piano concerto doesn't come to anything, it will always be the most lovely thought for me to remember that you once wanted it. I can't at all tell you what this means to me.[62]

Yes, piano concertos are performed at such Festivals. The last Leeds Festival they didn't have any piano, but on the other hand at the 2 previous Festivals [they did]. I am sure that if you only expressed a wish regarding your piano concerto and your kind thought about me in that connection, they (in Leeds) would be only too happy to do what you wanted.

It would be infinitely important for me *if* it came to anything; but all that could obviously never be so *really* and deeply important to me as to know that you yourself have really thought out this happiness and help for me!

I have written to get to know the Leeds Festival date immediately, but have, unfortunately, not got the answer yet; but I know that it is in the beginning of October, and before the 15th Oct. But I will get to know it exactly and will write to you straightaway.

Do you mean, that I could possibly come to you up in "Troldhaugen" next summer? If you could have me, it would indeed be glorious.

But probably you don't mean that. And you mustn't tire yourself by writing an answer to this question. There is no hurry at all for me to know it.

How nice (for the Germans, etc) that you are going to conduct in Germany and elsewhere; I wish that I could be there and listen to it! It is lovely to think about Leeds.

Now I am completely well again, and it is so nice to be able to do a real lot again.

I travel a lot in the Provinces to play now, and also have a lot to do with fair-copying and getting in order more than 200 folksongs I collected (partly with the help of the phonograph) last summer.

Now that I am well again I will also work on my own scores again.

February 26th I am giving a piano evening in Copenhagen; I am happy at the thought of having "Slåtterne" on the program.

Excuse me that this letter is so long.

It can't after all tell how happy & thankful I am for all your goodness to me.

Much love from mother and me to dear Mrs Grieg and yourself

yrs affectionately
Percy Grainger

93   TO FERRUCCIO BUSONI
15.12.06.

14, Upper Cheyne Row,
Chelsea, S.W.

Dear Master

It is too absurd, the bad luck I always have with your London concerts. Today (this afternoon) I have a concert in Bournemouth so cannot be with you to hear your lovely Program.

I *so long* to hear you play & am so sad that I shall be having to listen to my own rotten performance, instead of enjoying yours.

I have been somewhat unwell for some months but am alright again now.

My mother will bear you this after the concert.

Please believe me ever deeply thankfully & admiringly yrs
Percy Grainger

94   TO KAREN HOLTEN
[Original: Danish]
15.12.06

In the train, Bournemouth–London

Now the last concert is over before you come. No, I have fortunately few engagements in Jan. Birmingham went splendidly, and I played really well. Today less well.[63]

After the 20th our address is 5 Harrington Rd. Sth Kensington. London SW.

Please let me know your youngest brother's name so that I can send him a Christmas greeting.

Remember; I want no long "skirts", none at all, over here, and bring the national costume with you, absolutely.

Remember, no Christmas presents for us! I am going into town on Monday and will send you 2 songbooks of Roger's; but this must, under no circumstances, be regarded as a Christmas present.

I am not so happy, little friend, I don't know why; but I am very dissatisfied with my compositions, my playing, my character, and with how little I earn. The years are running, and I am a little fed up with all the hurrying. I don't know whether it was clever of me to build so much hope and will on earning a lot (in the circumstances) of money. I think, now, that it is almost impossible for one and the same person to collect enough money, and then have use of it. That is, if one begins with nothing; because one loses so many years in just becoming in any way *sufficiently* well off. (in the narrowest sense)

My 1st freshness has now gone, without my reaching more than just *beginning* to earn a little. Clearly, the only thing is to work more and better so as to be able to do more ("everything comes to him who can") But I am already tired of working even only as much as I have done. If I was really poor, I could do it *so easily*; but ½ wealthy, that doesn't suit me so much. You mustn't worry about all this in the least; nor reply to it; it is

63 On 15 December 1906, Grainger gave a duo-recital with Harry Plunket Greene at the Winter Gardens, Bournemouth. He had been in Birmingham on 11 December, playing the Schumann Piano Concerto under George Halford at the Halford Concerts Society orchestral concert.

perhaps not so true as I really believe it is. I believe it would be better for you not to travel before about the 7th; don't you think?

Roger hasn't got anything the matter with his throat this time. It is the stomach itself that is the matter. I am going up to him tomorrow (Sund) If you wanted to send him a Christmas greeting his address is 27 Welbeck St. W.[64]

18.12.06.

It seems to me that you can (if you will) fix Arbejderforeningen for the 2nd March (Saturday) I can well remain so long; but must be off Tuesday (March 5th) early. I would very much like to know as quickly as possible about Nyborg, etc. since I want to write to Hansen in a few days. But, *please*, do not tire yourself with enquiring in more towns whether they will have me; you really shouldn't do that.

It is not yet settled on what dates the Wagner performances will be. The Season begins Jan 14, presumably with Tristan, (Nikisch) but they don't know definitely. I don't think the forces will be so excellent. Akté is coming, — she should be good; but for the rest it is all the same to me. Nikisch will conduct at least twice; that's good[65]

You are really cheeky with my letter today; actually you are right — but you are cheeky all the same.

We think it is best for you to come as early in Jan as possible; since after about the 20th I will possibly be much more taken up, and will have to travel, etc.

I believe ships sail Tuesday and Wednesday from Esbjerg, i.e 1st and 2nd Jan. Come with one of those, if it is convenient to you; but just let us know in time. I swam very well on Monday (according to my capability).

I hope you understand that you must practise properly and really learn a tremendous lot this time.

Do you know the Scherzo of Brahms F minor Sonata op 5; it is good.

Can I be allowed to hear Hændel Vars. again? and of course the great Bach.

Have you learnt "I go with a 1000 thoughts"?[66]

And I think Liszt's 12th Rhapsody extremely effective. You must learn more "finishing up pieces". Think well about the programmes *before* you come so that we can straight away begin with the real work

Don't forget our new address (5 Harrington Rd South Kensington. S.W)

Goodnight, and don't be so cheeky.

95   TO ERNEST THESIGER   5, Harrington Road,
[PM 27 December 1906]   South Kensington, S.W.[67]

My dear Ernest

Simply too sweet of you, that delightful book; charming it seems, & in any case beglamored by your past recitings of some of it.

Do come Saturday at 4.30 if you can.

We're not rightly to rights, but you'll overlook

Again, warmest thanks, dear Ernest,

Ever yr friend
Perks.

---

64 Quilter suffered from recurrent ill health. He was at this time in a nursing home.

65 Aino Ackté (1876–1944), Finnish soprano. She sang several roles in the 1907 season, appearing for the first time as Elsa in *Lohengrin* on 16 January. Grainger did not hear her sing.

66 "I go with a thousand thoughts" is from Grieg's Op. 66.

67 The Graingers moved to this new address on 20 December.

96   TO ERNEST THESIGER   5, Harrington Road,
[n.d. "Late 1906"]   South Kensington, S.W.
Sunday

My dear Ernest

I was so deeply sorry to hear of your dear mother's death, when I called
yesterday.
My mother & I send you, dear friend, our most heartfelt sympathy in
your sorrow.
It makes me so happy that I have the Ballad Book from your mother,
who was always so sweet to me.
With again our sincerest sympathies to you all from us both

Ever yrs
Percy

1907

Karen arrived in London on 31 December 1906; she shared Rose's room at 5 Harrington Road, Kensington, until she returned to Copenhagen on 26 January. Percy, true to his word, did not take a holiday while she was in London, so that they attended only one Wagner performance. After a brief trip to Ireland at the beginning of February, Grainger also crossed to Copenhagen, on 18 February, for his solo piano recital there on 26 February and other concerts in Denmark. He was back in London by 6 March and his regular letters to Karen resumed. Herman Sandby was also in London at the beginning of 1907 and gave a solo recital on 25 February. He and Grainger appeared together at a South Place Popular Concert on 17 February, but their careers now developed on separate lines.

97 TO ROGER QUILTER   5, Harrington Road,
23.1.07.   South Kensington, S.W.

Dear Darlingest Rodg

Tho' it['s] dirty, yet it's our real best white writing paper, & you're worthy of it; also in health, we often & keenly hope — or quickly getting.

Well you didnt miss going to many operas with us, as we went to but 1; & that Meisters the 1st night.[1]

The next night I was as a pupil's teacher comercially obliged to sit out Tristan in a mere box; but that dont count. In spite, however, of, under these circs, wildly wanting not to relish, I was driven to dote on Nikisch's giving of it — tho' he is not even Teutonic, & Tristan not as unpuritan as I'm glad I also am not.

Have you heard him do it. It's really ever so marrow-fetching.

What I'm really writing for is to say how last night went. Most good singers, plucky & willing.[2]

Well, there's nowt in eith *Tiger* or *Morning S* that's not easy singable; & tho' clumsy in color maybe here & there I shldnt call it unpracticable:— that's a stride ahead of the earlier stuff. I'd sooner, for the mo' do stuff that (comparitively) sings slick than (comparitively) sounds spiff; tho it's at lib to do both. And lots last night did. (both) Anyhow we must do 'em again when you can take 'em in.

Karen says goodbye, as she's leaving Sat.

Do sling us a lett.

Mum sends love.

Lovingly
Perks

1 The 1907 season of German opera at Covent Garden began with a performance of Wagner's *Die Meistersinger* on 14 January. It was conducted by Leopold Reichwein, at that time first conductor of the Court Opera at Mannheim and musical assistant at Bayreuth. Nikisch conducted *Tristan und Isolde* on 15 January.

2 Two of Grainger's choruses had been tried through at the home of Jane and Wilfred von Glehn (see note 8 below) on the evening of 22 January: *Tiger, Tiger*, a setting for double men's chorus of the eight-line verse heading of "Tiger! Tiger!" from Kipling's *The Jungle Book; Morning Song in the Jungle*, a setting for small mixed chorus of a four-stanza verse from the story "Letting in the Jungle" in Kipling's *The Second Jungle Book*. Both settings dated from 1905.

The other night at Gard's, we were overhauling composers, & both he & I felt that of the whole bloody boiling of us (& those less lucky) none goes his compositional way purer, (less Jewlike) more dignified, ownisher, & pulling yr ends off by yr own dear simple yet civilized means than your own how I wish it were jolly well dear self, Rodg.

98   TO KAREN HOLTEN
Saturday 2.2.1907.

Avenue Hotel,
Belfast. Ireland.[3]

Dear, sweet, wise, cunning, cleansmelling (how's yr neck?), *kind* (chiefly kind) little Karen

How happy I would have been here with you last night, after the old concert. I was a great success, more than all the other sol[o]ists (more than Ada Crossley) & I felt tired & hot after it. The chap who wrote the words to Schubert Al song "Du bist die Ruh" was pretty right; somehow, there's nothing else that grants the rare peace of a loved body.

I dont get tired of remembering how *kind* you are to me. In that respect at least, you are a fighter of nature. (kindness isn't in nature, it's in man)

Personally, I think (tho' you likely won't agree) the whole game in life is to always *half* (never *quite*) fight nature. For instance: it is *natural* that every joy should create an equal pain. Now you, after letting nature go free in the making of joy, immeadiately when nature reacts (towards pain) put out all your cunning & sweet kindness (your anti natural qualities) to withstand it; (nature) I cant say how thankful I am for this, & how I love (& quite impersonally) admire you for it. Think what it means to me: music is (to my mind) nothing but an utterance of joy & thankfulness; look how you feed me up with these, & hold back from me all the sorrow & worry.

Possibly you dont realize that you do all this. And possibly one day you may act more wholly naturally (& good luck to you if you do) than you do now, & I may have a bad time. But, at least now, all thanks to you.

If all the above seems mere nonsense to you, what it means roughly is: That in the hot things of life you're like a little *animal*; keen, pure, natural, splendid; while in the cool things of life (the everyday acts) you're *human*; quiet, *slow-going*, (the greatest praise to slowness of actions!) kind, considerate, *cunning*, & loveable.

The *human* is grand for the *world* (& one mustnt forget *it* ever) & the *little animal* is glorious company for me. You see, now I've got a playmate. I've always had lots of love in my life, & since I've been in England some success, & tons of appreciation of my art, (a great boon) but I've never had a *real playfellow*; not in the animal (the best to me, the nearest-religious) things, — & it's only as an animal that I'm *really sincere*.

After appreciation & success & good work & love & fine friends & tiredness & failure — from all these I've had to slink away to my own alone self for my *real* pleasures [for the real climaxes are secret & alone (or atwo) hiddenly after the public *seeming* climax. After one has succeeded at a concert or written a good bit of composition, suddenly, quickly, one remembers that the real climax is yet lacking, & one hastens secretly towards it, in sincerity (alone, or atwo)]

But now I've got a playmate.

I hope we shan't quarrel, as playmates so much do.

I wonder whether you despize me much when I talk nonsense about you as a "foreigner"; (tho' never a "mere") & whether you think I'm racially sillily conceited?

You see, I'm mad about race; I feel almost everything *as* race, it's to me what religion is to *other* fools. Also remember that I love you *for* yr race, & *not inspite* of it. When in Australia, as a little boy, when I was always thinking & feeling hard about the Anglosaxons & the Old Norse, [the Battle

3 Grainger was in Belfast for the third grand subscription concert in the thirty-third season of the Belfast Philharmonic Society on Friday, 1 February, playing the Liszt *Hungarian Fantasia* under conductor Francis Koeller. Vocalists appearing on the same programme were soprano Florence Nixon, contralto Ada Crossley and bass Dalton Baker.

of Hastings 1066 — when the French Normans beat the English Saxons — was the deepest grief of my young years‖ & such, I used to look long at the map of Denmark, & Friesland, etc & *long* to be actually on the earth where our race began. (or at least, where one 1st heard of it) And now when I'm in dear Denmark I'm always thinking: "I wonder what men & ships sailed from here to (unconsciously) colonize East England" (& thence America, Canada, S'Africa, Australasia, etc) or I see in a face: "there's the beginning of a certain English type" or: "I wonder whether George Gouldthorpe's kin started here, or where else in Denmark?"

I feel racially towards Denmark how one feels towards the parents of one one loves (how thankful, *how often*, dont I feel to your people for all the sweetness & bitterlessness in you)

So when I'm saying to you "foreigner" I'm thinking: "one might as well say to mother, 'you're not Percy'; knowing that there was *no me*, but in *her*, once."

But what can make me mad, & feel clean foreign to the lot of you, (& to those qualities in you too, if they duck up —) ‖& we all have our own race's good & bad tucked up somewheres in us‖ is to note the unDanishness (the Germanizedness) creeping up amongst yr rotten towns.

Every country has often its "Battles of Hastings" (the defeat of nativeness by outsidishness) & I dont much like watching the fight going on.

How I admire the *real Danishness* in you all, though.

I've read thro' Ibsen's & Bjørnson's poems, & must say I'm disappointed in both books. It's too long to write, all my stupid reasons, but I'll tell you when we meet. Neither Ibsen nor Bj move my admiration like Jacobsen's poems. And the more I see of Norwegian art the more marvellous I think darling old Grieg. He has avoided all that *social-rizing from the peasant upwards* **thro' the lower middle class** that is so tiresome. And his volksthümlich [German: "folkish", i.e. of the people] things either are *genuinely* folkish, or better in *their own way*.

But to compare Bj's or Ibsen's volksthümlich things with the ballads in Kristensen Jydske Viser or Gejer & Afzelius's Svenska Fornsånga (?) is bad for the 2 men; purely from the *technically poettic* standpoint, I mean.

I wonder if you realize how often men have striven in music to reproduce the sexual climax (Højdepunkt) The whole Tristan Prelude is an attempt at this ‖& is, I think, almost photographically accurate — you listen once to it from that standpoint‖ as also the new part of the Venusberg music, & also a middle section in Strauss' Don Juan.

I'm dead sure of those 3 things.

I'd like to see more of this land. The people are dirty, but say real funny things, thro' having no sense of anything ever being earnest.

Yes, but were there *enough* stamps on my letter to yr mother. *Do* find out if she really wants me to stay at 17 Ceresvej or if it'd be a bother. *Please* find out the truth.

99   TO KAREN HOLTEN   [PM South Kensington]
[Original: Danish]
[Postcard. PM 16.2.07]

I am delighted.

Today, when I went to talk to the manager of *the Gramophone Co* about making records of my (piano) playing, I asked him whether he would be interested in making records of the old men's folksongs. And it turned out that he was the very man (an American) who made records of North American Indians folk music for the U.S.A. government; which first gave me the idea of using the phonograph. He will take records and give some to the British Museum, and Folksong Society etc.[4]

I believe it can come to something good.

I am so glad.

The Americans are often lovely people to have to do with. They have imagination.

100   TO EDVARD GRIEG

[Original: Danish/some English]
27.2.07.

Ceresvej. 17.
Kjøbenhavn.

Dear Master

Herewith I am sending you the critiques of my concert last night. The audience was so glad for the beloved "Slåtter" and I hope I played them more or less right.[5]

I am so proud that you think the Folksong Society is well organized. I have recently (to my great happiness) got on the Committee of the Society & showed them your letter about the Society at our last meeting.

As you can imagine they were very glad at your good opinion.

Now I am playing at 2 more concerts, here in this country, and travel back to London on Tuesday (5 Harrington Rd. S. Kensington. S.W.)

I am so immensely sorry that I can't be here to see you and hear your concert here.

But how deeply I am looking forward to Leeds!

With fond greetings to you both
yrs affectionately
Percy Grainger

A thousand thanks for your dear card (just come) but I am playing at the London Philharmonic Concert March 13th. It is *too* sad

101   TO KAREN HOLTEN

12 o'cl. 5.3.07.
[Extracts]

Nyborg.
[Denmark]

Whatever sort of thing you & I are to be to each other in time ahead; friends, or long lovers, or nix; let's make a keen bid to last sportsmanly thro' many attacking years. Last night couldn't have been such had either of us been less lithe; surely the rarest sexual relish is reserved for the limber-limbed. What can be more pathetic than fresh willing fiery minds hedged in rheumatic, befatted bodies that wont answer the helm?

Let's fight hard for far greater toughness, untiringness, & bodily obstinacy. You see, I like it so thoro'ly & exactly as it is; & change is so sad, then.

_____

If love is what you feel for me, I must say it's a 1st rate circus to be watching. It probably isn't, & that's why it's so excellently & wholly to be admired (critically)

What is yr whole line & policy with me? One everlastingly care that I do my best, & eat my most, & travel to my noblest goals quickest; yet all the time producing a shimmering sensation of holiday, & being an unsleeping lure & temptation. God! it's glorious to live in the thick of temptation.

4 Grainger made three records with the Gramophone Company on 16 May 1908: the Cadenza from the first movement of the Grieg Piano Concerto, an abridged version of Liszt's *Hungarian Rhapsody* No. 12, and his own arrangement of C. V. Stanford's Irish *March-Jig*. Nine folksongs, recorded by Joseph Taylor in 1908, were eventually issued on one twelve-inch and six ten-inch records: "Creeping Jane", "The White Hare", "Died for Love", "Brigg Fair", "Lord Bateman", "The Murder of Maria Martin", "The Sprig of Thyme", "Worcester City" and "Bold William Taylor". The folksong records did not sell well, thus dashing Grainger's hopes for a series. In 1972 the Taylor records were reissued, together with some of Grainger's phonograph cylinders, on *Unto Brigg Fair*, Leader (Lea 4050). The manager of the recording section of the Gramophone Company was Frederick William Gaisberg (1873–1951). The remainder of Grainger's reference is somewhat unclear. To say that Gaisberg actually recorded American Indian music is perhaps a slight exaggeration. It is, however, possible that Gaisberg knew of or assisted with the experimental gramophone recordings of Plains Indian music made at Emil Berliner's studio in Washington in the 1890s by Bureau of American Ethnology anthropologists James and Charles Mooney. The Mooneys had recorded Plains Indian music on cylinder in the early 1890s. By 1907 the use of the cylinder phonograph for ethnological fieldwork was fairly widespread in the American Bureau.

5 Grainger's solo recital in Copenhagen on 26 February 1907 had included a bracket of six of Grieg's pieces: Op. 66, Nos. 14 and 18; Op. 72, Nos. 1, 7, 8 and 16. The Op. 72 pieces were performed for the first time in Copenhagen. Grieg's good opinion of the Folk-Song Society was reproduced as a postscript to the Society's obituary notice for him, in its *Journal* No. 11 (1907), pp. 142–3. In Denmark Grainger also gave concerts at Nyborg on 21

98

I must say you treat me as well as I hope to treat my choruses & orchestras; untiring & sound in detail, yet talented & inspired, & wheedling out the best (that's in that market) by the curious suction there lies in love.

I cant think how you can possibly like such a phrasey schoolmasterly "spouting" person as I am. I'm always (in the daytime) getting on my hind legs & making shallow rhetorical afterdinner speaches, or else I'm trying to be a clown, or am blessing things with my critical approval. A real "Sir Willoughby".[6] How you must despize it all in me. Or (I wonder) do you admire it like Herman does Alfh's fullmouthedness? Hardly, I think.

Better go ahead & disdainfully despize it.

My head must be quite alright, for I seem quite as clever as ever.

Love from
Perks

102   TO KAREN HOLTEN   [London]
[Original: Danish/English]
12.30 o'cl. 13.3.07 After the concert
[Extracts]

I played really well this evening; as well as I can play Sch.[umann's] Conc[erto] *as yet*; but that doesn't say much. You know that it is *your* Concerto because I think it is like you; but as I perform it it becomes a caricature of you, and I feel it is almost a shame for you, sweet Karen, to be exhibited in such a bad way. But it will be better in time.

But we got through tonight all right. Sinding conducted his violin concerto; (this evening) he is a kind little man, despite (or perhaps because) that he is not a particularly good composer.[7] It was so nice to talk to him, and hear him and his wife and Norwegian friends. There in the artist's room there were many (Jews etc.) who talked German, and to hear Sinding's Norwegian suddenly; it sounded so indescribably like home to me. Scandinavian languages sound to me like something I knew in my 1st childhood and have since forgotten; (unfortunately.) Von Glehns and Fletcher came home with us.[8]

We can just as well bathe together when Fletcher is there. He will surely like to bathe together with us also; it is the custom in England; men and women together. Just like Aae. Do you object?

Remember, when we meet, (if only it were tonight) to remind me to tell you about a conversation Scott and I had many years ago in Kronberg; that throws light on the qualities that make us (or in any case me) so boundlessly happy together, we 2. This cannot be written, but remember to remind me about it . . .

I wonder whether you really miss me more than I do you. It is not something I like to readily admit, but I miss you really very much, I do believe, without any imagination.

Why should I always hold back from confessing to you a little how much I like you. You do know, I am terribly afraid of saying things and expressing feelings that can change in time. But, to be honest, I cannot deny that at the present I feel deeply (according to my capacity) for you, think the whole time about you, and find my greatest happiness in thoughts that concern you, and the lovely things we will still discover together. I am in other words, almost (if not quite) a "lover". But what can I do against it; nothing. And I am so happy to be as I am.

98

February (with Ida Møller and Karen Holten) and Helsingør on 3 March (piano recital).

6 From George Meredith's *The Egoist*, a New Year gift, 1907, to Percy from his mother.

7 Christian August Sinding (1856–1941), Norwegian composer. He made his first appearance in England at the Philharmonic Society concert on 13 March, conducting his Violin Concerto in A, with Johannes Wolff as solo violinist. Grainger's appearance was his first with the Philharmonic Society.

8 Wilfred Gabriel von Glehn (later de Glehn) (1870–1951), English landscape, portrait and marine painter, and his wife Jane Erin (*née* Emmet). Also a landscape and portrait painter, Jane von Glehn made a fine portrait study of Grainger in 1905.

I feel so extremely well and I am ready for work and exertions (thanks to you) despite missing you day and night.

It is really more after my true nature to lie here in bed after a concert and write to someone courageous and lively like you than to make a pig of myself.

At present I feel far away from such temptations (Karen be praised). If only it would remain like that.

Even before a horrible concert I can't feel really depressed and so craven as usual; when I just think a moment about that with the whip, I have only room in myself for pride and happiness, and a kind of courage.

I call this to have "succeeded" in life, to have found someone who is ready to enter into such an idea (even if you never grant me this almost superhuman pleasure) is to receive rich gifts from life; that is a beggar made measurelessly rich. I, who have longed so to find my loving cruelty (not *indifferent* cruelty) met with love, yet never hoped to; your greatheartedness, & pluck, & **generosity** overflow me in a splendid manner.

But how one misses to wake up in the night or dawn and feel another person warm and sleeping beside one, or ½ mixed up with each other, both.

These cool (in the sense of not "ophidset" [stimulated]), warmths are so glorious & fulfilling. How Walt Wh understood them & wrote richly & purely of them!

Why should you *always* wear short skirts? because long ones are dirty & pick up all the spit & muck of the streets, because they (the long ones) make it harder to run or jump or move actively, & are the *mark of the female sex's slavery*; & because short ones show the feet & ancles & sit a 1000 times prettier & more jimp.

Please thank your servant heartfeltly for her sweet friendly thought of the Danish doughnuts; & thank, please, very warmly whoever thought to actually send them.

Do tell Svend [Karen's brother], too, that I didnt mean it unfriendly with the Icelandic spoon & loved his wanting to give it me, but that if things look nice I never feel its right for me to take one; they're wasted on me. But that later, some time, I'll ask him for it, once; if he'll let me.

But I must be allowed to be glad that I have not reacted against you at all in the whole of the last time. You women (I think) as a rule never suffer so badly as we do in reaction. It is something horrible.

You at least dont usually react against those you deeply love; but we do. (Perhaps you do too)

But you could still see in Svinkløv that I did it, (some few times) and I have always done so against my compositions and my most loved friends, and everything in the world. It is (unfortunately as far as I am concerned) not excluded that I will again suffer from this towards you. But it was lovely to have been with each other for quite a time and to have been hand-in-hand in every sense. I am **so** happy for it.

I got a lovely letter from Grieg today. He will write sometime to Leeds about me.

Eat up Helen Fischer's chocolates, and be happy for them.

Why don't you go up to Grieg at his concert and tell him that you are a pupil of mine and like Slåtterne very much. Do it, if you'd at all like to. He is such a darling & will soon die.

I am playing in Oxford the day after tomorrow (Friday) evening.[9]

Pray always for me; but remember there is an hour's difference in English and Danish time!

Good night, my much loved meat-mate* Karen, it is now 2 o'cl.

9 Grieg had a concert in Copenhagen on 21 March. Grainger did a solo recital for the Oxford Ladies Musical Society on 15 March.

*Danish: kødfolk. See translator's note.

103 TO ERNEST THESIGER   5, Harrington Road,
15.3.07.   South Kensington, S.W.

Pet Ernest

It is jolly that you are back. *So* longing meet.

Alas! I have a host of pupils all Monday afternoon & an orchestral rehearsal mighty early in the evening, but if you'll let me leave it open (in which case dont bother to reply) I'll make heroic efforts to dash in for the short twilight between lessons & rehearsal; but I fear it wont come off, alas!

But I fondly hope it will; if not some other time most soon

Always yrs
Percy Grainger

Playing (Recital) at Oxford tonight; just off.

104 TO KAREN HOLTEN   [Oxford]
15.3.07.   Staying with a family Gotch.
1 o'cl. (night)
[Extract]

I've just been reading *The adventures of Tom Sawyer* (Mark Twain) Of course I've read it heaps of times before, but it's lovely to see it again.

I so hope you will love *Huck Finn*. If you ever come to see Australia, or America, I'm sure you'll see what a rippingly true picture of the wildly happy & heroicly self-centred boy-life of the New World the Tom Sawyer-Huck Finn tales are. How I've felt like that as a child in Australia; nature makes a real personal appeal to one because one really meets it alone; & neither it nor oneself are much shackled, & life isn't so heavy or serious that it sheds a bloody blighting shadow even over childhood.

When I've made my money (if I ever do, poor me) I'll be a kid again; my mind won't be old, & I'll go for Iceland, & West Ireland, & Scotch Highlands, & Norwegian highlands, & South Africa, & Australian bushcountry like a baby.

Please, little bright playmate Karen (you help to keep me a baby, tho' maybe folks wouldn't think it) always *try hard* to let us keep to the young childlike holiday joy of living. Let sex keep us glad & pleasure hungry but dont let us make slaves & drudges of us.

I know that we also have no right to deny the serious urges of nature too. One mustn't frivol thro' one's life; (*that's the* **worst**) as a composer I know well enough that one must sacrifice often & much to the deep things, (even tho' they are horrid & age one) but not too young, not too early, little one.

I have really had a pretty drudging time of it since I was about 17, & I do so long once for a *good long* spell of *purposeless* pleasure.

I am originally so light & lucky in my feelings & leanings, it is so horrid for me to have to slave for ever.

I am so afraid of nature & splendid purposes coming knocking heavily at my door — for harder work, & a more serious mind, & closer slaving, & less light larks.

If you can ever see your way to hold back the hard harsh numbing *duty-ful* things for a moment from me, I pray (as a weak, selfish, alms-begging pleasure-glutton) have mercy & spare me a bit. You can see from my life that I am a good drudge, slave, servant; but dont make me only that; dear kind little Karen.

Yet how can I ask you to ever sacrifice your stronger qualities (in these LIFE questions) to my weaker ones. I wouldn't sacrifice art.

And yet I have: I have given up endless composing to earn a living. Forgive me if I'm stupid. All the above is meant lovingly & comradely.

105   TO THE HON. CHARLOTTE KNOLLYS[10]   [London]
[c.15 March 1907]
[Rough draft]

Dear Miss Knollys.

I take the liberty of writing to you to ask you whether you think Her Majesty Queen Alexandra might possibly do me the honour to grant her gracious patronage to a Pianoforte Recital I am giving at the Æolian Hall on Thursday afternoon, June 13th.

You may remember that I had the pleasure of meeting you when I had the honor to play (together with Mr Herman Sandby) before Her Majesty at Buckingham Palace, on March 8th, 1905.

I again had the honor of playing to Her Majesty at the Yellow Palace, Copenhagen, in October 1905.

I have just returned from a most successful tour in Denmark, & was also fortunate in scoring a great success at my appearance at the London Philharmonic concert, March 13th.

I need not add how extremely great an honor encouragement & kindness it would be to me if Her Majesty could see her way to grant me the favor of her patronage, on this occasion.

Asking pardon for troubling you in the matter,

Believe me
Yrs sincerely
Percy Grainger

The Hon. Charlotte Knollys
Buckingham Palace
S.W.

106   TO KAREN HOLTEN   [London]
[Original: Danish]
20.3.07.
[Extract]

It has been a "full day" today. After having composed a little, mother and I went to hear "W march" 11 o'cl. Although I think that nearly every bar in the March could be written and scored better, there was a lot that sounded excellent, and the whole thing was extremely encouraging and interesting. Rogan ate lunch with us, and he and I looked through the score afterwards and were remarkably in agreement about what had to be altered. He was extremely friendly and helpful.

Then I gave 2 lessons; worked a little on the March. Had rehearsal in *North London* (of Liszt Ung. Fant.) 8 o'cl, and had to visit Delafosse 9.30 o'cl at Hyde Pk Hotel. And now you have me here in bed. It was amusing to play "Gr Bs" for Delafosse and 2 other Frenchmen, since it is teutonic enough to sound surprising and "uncouth" for them, but still civilised enough to be attractive to them.[11]

10   The Hon. Elizabeth Charlotte Knollys (d. 1930), Bedchamber Woman to H.M. Queen Alexandra from 1870 to 1925. She replied, 31 March, "I have much pleasure in telling you that the Queen will be happy to give her Patronage to your Concert but I regret to say that there can be no question of Her Majesty's *presence* at it". The request for Royal Patronage was made at the suggestion of Grainger's agent, E. L. Robinson. It was perhaps inspired by the example of Herman Sandby, whose solo recitals in 1906 and 1907 had both enjoyed Royal Patronage.

11   Léon Delafosse (1874–1951?), French pianist. His recital at St James Hall, London, on 16 November 1904 had included Grainger's *Paraphrase on the "Flower Waltz"* from Tchaikovsky's "Nutcracker" Suite, a work which he also included in his Paris and London recitals over several years.

107   TO KAREN HOLTEN   [London]
[Original: English/a few Danish phrases]
31.3.07.
(March over, anyway)
Sunday, 11.20 o'cl, evening, in bed.

Before I write to you, I wash face & hands carefully, so as to feel fresh
& ready to meet you.

Such a joyous find, yesterday.

I went, by chance, to the "Victoria & Albert (½ Jew) Museum" S. Kens.
It is full of jolly things; Dutch, Norwegian, Icelandic etc woodcarving.
plaster casts of Grecian & other statuary; old Egyptian cloths & stuffs
(gorgeously rich in coloring) But my far greatest joy was a picture of Burne
Jones: "The Mill". It expresses, to me, what you do. On a prosaic (in the
fine sense) background it is movingly poetic, & is full of ½ hidden suggestions of joy, & rich tenderness, of life teeming, & of quiet enfolding understanding. Rich hills back of picture, with a long-straggling unpractical
looking (so called) mill in middle distance, with bathers & boaters lazying
(quite far off) in the stream.[12]

Near by, on sward, 4 girls. 3 with interlinked hands, with 4th strumming
a dulllooking musical instrument. But how ravishing the whole thing!

The lovingness & bloom of it all. The 4 girls may stand for the seasons
(unlikely, tho', I'd say) or for the laziness of all nice people; or ought else.
But for me they mean you, & recall you; & so rarely that I'm going to visit
them quite often. (the museum is free of charge)

One of them has a long nose, without it's mattering, ⟦at least *yet*⟧ like
you, & she's not as unlike you as some things; she's got her back turned.
And one that's front face & front figure has all the sweetness that goes with
you, ⟦without being actually like you⟧ & I've seen you look at me as she's
doing there. So you can believe it is nice for me, to have discovered this.

When I came home & told mother of the picture, (but not a word of its
being like you at all) she paused & said: "You know I often think Karen
is like Burne J's pictures." When I took her to see it today (we spent such
a happy afternoon there) she at once thought the backview girl suggestive
of you. (I hadn't said so) Later on we found some big fine reproductions
of lots of his paintings, & when I'd found the 1 I loved fondest, mother
said: "but she's the likest of all to Karen". Such a darling she is; the pic's
called "In the sea deeps" & it's a poor little mermaid (Lavfrue) clutching
down a drowned man in her arms. She (poor dear) doesn't know (or else
she doesn't care) she's only got a poor dead corpse to be with her. She
thinks it's just grand, & looks like a funny loving little pleased satisfied
animal that's got what it wanted ever so hard ⟦"so that's decided" March,
'06⟧ & now is eager for fun & relish. Such a compelling look on her dear
face. We must go there together when you're here next trip.

It's pretty good fun to me, going thro' such a museum & having a look
at the leavings of the races; the unmistakable stamp of their live feelings
& deeds on all the dead things that have outlived them. The Greeks are very
English, to be sure. So cold & lovely; so little soft & really loving, yet never
hard either — aloof from either possibility.

A more perfect race (probably) than any since. Purer & less brutal than
the English; yet even less warm, I feel.

When I now see statues I find how it changes one to be kødfolk[i.e. a
carnal person]. I see things totally otherwise. Where I once could look
coldly & critically & even unsympathetically (if I was feeling somewhat at
war with sex, or that bully nature) at bodies, now I am at once melted
almost to bits by an "anelse" [Danish: suspicion] of what they all might
mean, may have meant. Yes men's bodies I always thought quite nice, I
think. But most bodies just looked good or bad form to my eye, (particularly women's statues) but had no intimacy or memory for me.

12 Sir Edward Coley Burne-Jones (1833–98), English painter, designer and watercolourist. *The Mill* was painted between 1870 and 1882.

Walt Whitman writes something about
"Have you ever loved the body of a woman?
───────────────── *man?"*

I think he means in that sentence what I'm meaning. One might love a person without having had the *opportunity* of loving their body; for one can only love in the sense I mean what one knows intimately; what one is wholly "vertraut" [German: familiar] with.

Mere "sexual experiences" would not *in the least* give one the feeling I mean. Nothing gave it me less. No, it is to *love the body*, to really *love*, & then a *certain particular* intimate *body*. It is the wedding of the sort of deep intimate love that one feels for one's own well-known comradely body (feeling that love for someone else's body) with all the deep-pulling, eager, knawing sex-yearnings, that bowls one over so.

I feel to know yr body so well; corners, & edgings, & flat tight smooth stretches, & the curiously thin & fragile feel of skin; (as if it barely reliably covered-in the flesh) bright sharp brilliant memories flash up when I'm in any way reminded now.

And dont flitting pictures of it all ride accross yr mind often; of how you &/or I looked when, etc?

I am always careful to look very hard at the time; that I glean a priceless rich memory to die with.

I'm thankful for yr *compassionate* kind letters, little one; that you so sweetly wish to keep it all holidaylike between us. They recall what mother told me of a talk you & she had about me some time before yule '05, in Oakley; of how you'd both talked of me & you had said something about; "but isn't he going to really live at all; to really enjoy & realize?" When I heard that I thought: *there is someone who at last feels sorry for me instead of envying me stupidly; who guesses how much I'm lacking, and thinks it is a shame for my sake.* Thence followed that sentimental lecture of mine on gladness, up in yr room once. ‖I not selfish?‖

Last night (Sat) I was at Rathbones, just I & they alone, so lovely & jolly; it made me so happy & gave me confidence. I took Rathbone his score-copy of "Gr Bs" all pasted into a book (4 of them are done, mine, Griegs, Rogers, & Raths) & he was quite happy at it. He's a darling & really wishes me well. Not just lightly, but he wishes me well for all my life, I feel.[13] If you'd like yr bundle of Gr Bs original sheets you can have them at once, or wait till me meet.

Of course you & I must go Huck Finn-ing. Most girls dont go on such trips because they'd loathe to.

That's what Roger means when he says you are pure like a boy. Hoorah.

Roger feels quite a bit better & has lots of faith in his Scotch electrical doctor, & has been out driving; but it is hard to know how much actually better he is yet. We go to him tomorrow.

Poor Elwes's mother died quite suddenly. She was such a dear; I loved her much, & Roger adored her. So young in spirit she was, & what they call in the sagas "skörungr mikill". (which Morris translates "she was a *stirring* woman")[14]

I am working mighty hard at hektographing folksongs & have now got to 198, so the 200 will soon be reached. I'm practising among other things Bach's Prelude & Fugue in C# minor (1st part "Das wohlt. Kl") almost the solemnest & quietly upliftedest thing he got off, & Brahms Intermezzo op 117 No 3; which is rather like "The Mill" — but more like the mill than like you, somehow. It is charming, tho'.

I dont think you've any call to go grumbling about few letters, or feeling letter-lonesome.

This is the *1st time* since my return that there has been a *full week* between my letters to you; which isnt bad when 10 days is the length-limit.

As a matter of fact I always wait till yr letter arrives before sending.

Yr last came yesterday late. (Sat)

13 On 20 May 1910 in his letter to Karen, Grainger reported Rathbone as having once said to him, "You will be welcome on any floor of my house, and on every floor of my nature, being, soul".

14 William Morris (1834–96), English poet, designer and political writer. His English translations of the Icelandic sagas were worked up from literal versions prepared by Eirikr Magnusson, whom Morris had met in 1868. Grainger's library contains seven volumes of sagas translated by Morris and Magnusson and published by The Saga Library (Bernard Quaritch, London, 1891–95, 1905) as well as their translations of *Grettir the Strong* (London, 1900) and *Three Northern Love Stories and Other Tales* (London, 1875). A woman called Salbjörg is described as "skörungr mikill" in chapter one of *Egils Saga Skallagrimssonar*.

However, even if you did write me oftener I shouldn't write you oftener than about a week, as I consider that *altogether enough*. Not often enough for my happiness, (I could write & read to & from you lots of the time) but still a good annoying practical period, all the same.

1.4.07.

Mother was going to write you this mail, but there isnt time now, so she will next time. She sends lots of love; she's learning Dan grand now.

Do let's hear all about yr riding & whether you win or lose at tennis. I've not been swimming for a bit as I got a cold & cough again; but soon will once more.

Lovingly
Percy

Please buy yourself (in Tauchnitz) M. Twain's *"Life on the Missisippi"* I'll send you the money.

15 The first version of Grainger's *Hill-Song* was composed between 16 March 1901 and 1 September 1902. Scored for 2 piccolo flutes, 6 oboes, 6 *corni inglese*, 6 bassoons and contra-bassoon, it was described by Grainger as ''. . . a gathering of types for future Hill-Songs, a catalogue''. The first version of *Hill-Song No. 2* (for wind band) is dated as thought out and worked up anew at 5 Harrington Road, 3–(12?) April 1907, and completed at Svinkløv 20 August 1907. After much rewriting and revising spread over many years, *Hill-Song No. 1* was published by Universal Edition in a version for room-music 22-some (or 23-some) in 1924. *Hill-Song No. 2*, for solo wind ensemble (23 or 24 wind instruments and cymbal), or band, or symphony orchestra, was published by the Leeds Music Corporation in 1950.

16 Grainger had first collected from Charles Rosher in Chelsea on 24 July 1906 (see letter 72). On 2 and 3 April 1907 he noted a further eighteen tunes, numbered 201 to 218 in his *Collection of English Folksongs*. Most of the tunes first noted were recorded and the words re-collected in a further session on 4 May 1908. Between April and June 1907 Grainger made settings of two of the shanties: ''Shenandoah'' and ''Stormy''. His settings, for solo male voice, unison male chorus and four or six accompanying solo male voices, were performed at Lady Bective's on 3 July 1907 (see letter 116).

108   TO KAREN HOLTEN   [London]
[Original: English/Danish sentence at end]
Saturday. 6.4.07. 12 o'cl (midday)

Such a stirring & rich week. The last 3 days (Wed, Thurs, Frid) I've been putting in from 8 to 12 hours composing daily, on an old work of mine (started 1901) called ''Hillsong''.[15]

It was this work that Busoni thought by far my most strong, original & worthful style; but then he is not a sentimentalist, like me, & feels rather thro' his head, so I dont know how far he's to be trusted. But I think it's 1 of the very richest in ''herzblut'' [German: heart's blood] of all my stuff. The original version of it (length [*sic* long] & vastly full of minute work) was not a possible thing at all, as it was a helter skelter jumble of 2 quite unblendable styles. Each of these 2 styles is now (sooner or later) to be worked up into a seperate Hillsong; 1, *slow*, for strings; (& maybe a few voices as well) ‖this is the one I wrote of sketching for in last letter‖ & 1, *fast & wild*, for woodwind & maybe a *trifle* brass.

This fast Hillsong, that I am now at, is one of my *very* toughest form-problems, ‖& the instrumentation, for reeds only is dead surely the hardest thing I've tried yet‖ & working at it strains me more than anything. Each night I've wanted to write you of my happiness working, & how much more I'm deserving than I'm getting, but each night I felt too fagged for it to be any use.

Then on Tuesday & Wed evenings I had Rosher here singing till 12 o'cl, the once-been sailor who's now a painter.[16] I got 20 tunes of sea-songs (called ''chanties'') from him last summer, but no words to speak; so now I've been getting them, & also some new good tunes. They are very different to folksongs; simpler, shorter, & more meagre in invention, tho' quite as good in their own grim terse way. The genuine British ones are very pentatonic

with 2 short refrains to each tune.

These can be very weird, grand, & old-sounding, with the curious barren-like feeling that the sea gives in them.

Then there are American chanties, some of them dreamy & poetic & Huck Finn-like in the real American way, with high & low-sweeping lines, & others very nigger-like, dancy & "In Dahomey"-rhythmed.[17]

The words are, on the whole, *appalingly indecent*, & *quite impossible* to use; alas! for to my mind they are full of poetry & strength. At any rate they unwithstandably call up a *living picture* of a *whole type of life*, which is (to my mind) one of the lovliest powers of art.

Do you remember some of those jolly chapters in "Lodsen og hans Hustru" of seafaring conditions, Sth America, etc?[18] That's the sort of thing.

You see, the *folksong-singer* sticks to *tales*; he sings of *plots*; & as these tales are mostly of long ago the *spirit of today* finds small room in that art, & instead of fresh everyday realistic introductions into folksong words, little except forgettings & corruptions have been its source of alteration.

But the sea-chanty deals little in stories or a *chain of events*. Chanties were sung by sailors when at work, & as most of the work (for a whole gang such as would go in for refrain-singing) would oftenest be shortish or quickly changing, the verse could seldom do more than give a "instantaneous photo" sort of snap-shot of sea or port life; glimpses of a sordid, rank, grim, brutal existence; like old Dutch paintings. Here were these poor bodily-strong devils living the unnatural shipboard round, with their minds engrossed in nought but money, food, drink, & sex. Having little of any of these they yearn for them aloud in their songs. Most of all their sex was starved, & it looms thro' all their verses like a menancing emblem; naturally, wholly cut off from woman's atmosphere as they were, their view is rank, & mean, & lacking all vestage of tenderness; but just because of all this, because it is so solely & only the *unredeemed male animal's utterance*, it has distinction, & the value of accurate portraiture.

I, at any rate, can feel nothing impure in the spirit of these words, grossly indecent as they mostly are. To me, they are only the brutal utterances of would-be healthy men; coarse, but not dirty.

Dearest little Karen, I'd love to be with you, even if you were right down sea-sick; as soon as I'd be with myself sick; sooner. Beds can only put out those to whom the floor is not ever a refuge.

Here's a funny little bit from one of the latest Hillsong sketches (it's not typical of the style, tho')

Just heard from the Leeds Festival people; so that's going to come off, I think; dear old darling Grieg.

Splendid news also from my father; he has won a big competition in Victoria, for a big public building.[19]

17 *In Dahomey*, a musical comedy with an all-negro cast, the music and words, reported the *Era*, by "members of the same interesting nationality", was first presented in London at the Shaftesbury Theatre on 16 May 1903. Grainger's composition *In Dahomey*, a "cakewalk smasher" for piano solo, was inspired by and drew on tunes from this performance. Begun in the summer of 1903, it was completed in June 1909. It is dedicated to William Rathbone.

18 Jonas Lie, *Lodsen og Hans Hustru* [The Pilot and his Wife] (1903).

19 The *British Australasian*, 18 April 1907, reported, "The many Anglo-Australian friends of Mr John Grainger, of Melbourne, will be delighted to hear that his health has so far recovered that he has been able to take up work again, and has gone into partnership with Messrs Kennedy and Little. The firm have just won first prize for the Melbourne Town Hall extension. It is wonderful that Mr Grainger is able to design at all, for when in England some eight months ago, his hand was badly affected by rheumatic gout, and he is to be congratulated upon his success and recovery".

This letter seems so loveless, somehow, but dont think *me* so, please. I'm only a bit tired, & worrying over my compos, & practising, etc.

Mother is extremely diligent with her Danish. I have bought a Dutch dictionary, but have not had time [for it] yet. Love to yr grandmother, & thank her please for her greetings. Roger is still a bit better. I love to hear of yr riding & tennis, & dear self & thoughts.

written out
8 . 4 · 07

20 Frederick (formerly Fritz) Theodore Albert Delius (1862–1934), English composer of German descent, resident in France. Delius met Grainger for the first time in April 1907 while on a visit to London. The score was Delius's *Appalachia* (1902) which he had left with Grainger after their first meeting. Delius spent the evening of Thursday 25 April at the Graingers' house. Grainger's note was probably written between 19 and 21 April. Later in May Delius sent Grainger a copy of *Appalachia* as a gift, with the request that he show it to Grieg.

109   TO FREDERICK DELIUS[20]   [London]
[n.d. Prior to 22 April 1907]

Excuse my writing, but I do think the harmonies & all I can make out of the score just *too* moving & lovely.
Longing to hear it
Till Thursday

Yrs
Percy Grainger

110   TO KAREN HOLTEN   [London]
[Original: Dutch and Danish/some English sentences]
Wednesday. 24.4.07.

[In Dutch]
This is the first time for me, that I have received your letter on Saturday and have sent my own off on Monday. That seemed as if one "had burnt all one's boats béhind one", as if no essential binding thread remained behind.

Nevertheless I am a happy child. Yesterday (or the day before yesterday) I got a letter from Mrs Charles Hunter, in which she invited me to spend Whitsun with her, her daughter, von Glehn and perhaps Sargent, in Holland.[21] Isn't it a lucky chance that, without having the slightest idea of this, I should have thrown myself into my Dutch again? The whole thing won't cost me a penny, she says.

Also I have now got the final confirmation of Leeds.

Yesterday I was in town, and visited Roger and Meyer [sic] (agent for Ada's tour).[22] The former is going well — better and better; — and from the latter I have heard that the tour will certainly stretch over three and a half, and fairly probably over 4 months. I can earn pretty good money there.

This morning I was first in Kensington Gdns (Hyde Park) with mother in the bath-chair, and then in the swimming bath, and have swum on my back for 10 minutes without stopping.

You must not forget, little Karen, to take *great care* not to go riding when your little inside is at work. Girls in Australia always ride at all times and I'm sure it's awfully bad for them. Even if you have a lesson, (in riding) please put it off.

Before you finish having lessons do try & get to ride *without saddle* as well.

Friday 26.4.07.

The man who wrote the harmonies to nigger tune (which you in sweet simplicity are thinking to be mine) which I enclosed in my last letter, is called Frederick Delius. He is about 40 years old, is married, and lives in France. His father and mother were High-German, (but originally of Dutch descent, like so many of the people I am fond of — you, Walt W, a.s.o.) but he himself was born in Bradford (Yorkshire), and brought up in England. In his twenties he travelled to Florida (U.S.A.) and remained there indefinitely, enthusiastic about the American niggers songs, which he heard down there on the plantations. He is fairly well known as a composer in Germany, and I believe a lot in his works is very good. Frequently he and I write *exactly* the same harmonies without ever having heard each other's works, as in the piece I sent you.

I sent it you with[out] saying it was his as I wanted to *convince* you how little individualty there is in modern art after all; or at least in *me & mine*. And yet folk (or you) would say that I *had* originality. In him & me many same impressions must have occured in somewhat the same proportions to produce moments of such *undistinguishable* likeness.

A certain quantity of Englishness, of foreigness, & of American & nigger influence, & a great love of Grieg, (which he shares with me also) etc.

The whole thing, of course, is *very* different, but that nigger tune bit nobody could tell from my work, I am sure. He seems a charming person, in many ways.

It just shows how much more one is part of the Zeitgeist than an individual in oneself. Goodnight, dearie

Tomorrow, Saturday, is the glorious happy day when yr letter comes!

[In Danish]
Sunday. 28.4.07.

You know the bust that (sometimes) hangs in your room. I know a man who says that it isn't taken from a drowned girl at all, but done by a friend of his, (a French sculptor) from his (the friend's) own wife, who is also French. So that explains it that I thought the head looked so "civilized". I looked up at you in S. Kens. a few days ago; you looked very good.

The dress rehearsal for Leeds takes place in London the 2nd Oct; so we won't need to travel from Svinkløv, *it is to be hoped*, before the 25th Sept about.

21 Mary (Mrs Charles) Hunter (1857–1933), Ethel Smyth's elder sister, wife of an immensely wealthy colliery-owner, whose fortune she dispersed in lavish entertainment and patronage of artists and musicians on a scale that eventually ruined her. She was a particular friend of John Singer Sargent. Grainger did not go to Holland, telling Karen on 10 May that he had to practise.

22 The agent for Ada Crossley's provincial tour was Daniel Mayer.

I have a little "Icelandic" period again; I feel a little bit cool and sober on the whole (but am no less fond of *you*, you mustn't think that) and sometimes a little unhappy, although I am at the same time quite well and active. Perhaps it is as well I am thus when you are not there.

It is in itself not Icelandic, but I call it that because at such times I must rush and comfort myself with the sagas and think about the people and time and life.

I take a lot of pains to work really a lot and believe that I have got a whole lot of new things (pieces) in my memory, but I must admit that I have only a little pleasure in the work, and not all too rich results. But it is not so very bad either; only so frightfully little compared with what I hoped to "leisten" [German: achieve] in these years.* Also I get quite anxious and depressed with the thought of how little I can do to save the folksongs. Even the most and best one can do is really so little and so poor in such an enormous field.

It is now over a year that I have had to let myself run easy & only ½ work; whether it is weakness, or nerves or older age or mere laziness I truly cant tell. But **nobody** can guess *how* miserable I am over it, & at times almost genuinely heartbroken. In piano, composition, & folksongs; in all 3 I have slacked & behaved disgracefully. Yet I am now *extraordinarily well*, & cant explain it at all.

Was so happy of your letter Sat, (yesterday) & jubilant "dass du 'reingefallen bist" [German: "that you fell into (the trap)"] about Delius & the nigger tune. I only hope it will prove to you how small & ununique an artistic personality "your best young man" has. I knew it long ago.

Am so delighted you're going to shoot; that is splendid of you. I wish you could (ved lejleghed, kun) [Danish: at your convenience, only] find out how much a box of the *cheapest cartridges* costs that one could *practise* shooting with; not needfully to kill birds with, but just to aim at anything (stones, or sticks).

Mother is so *unusually* well & fit. I think the bathchair does her *no end* of good. We go practically every fine morning for a hour & ½ (or ¼) before breakfast.

I believe her health has a great future from this source.

If you could find out (ved lejleghed) what it would cost me (both 2nd & 3rd class) to do the single journey from Bergen—Copenhagen—to Fjerritslev it would be most good of you.

Dear me, what a happy sweet family you are all of you to look back upon, in so many ways; such happy hearted children to be sure.

Money matters are worrying me deeply just now. I have hardly any concert engagements (altho' those I have are good) for this summer, & not many pupils. I fear the society folk are sick of me, & if it were not for Ada's tour I'd be what we call in Australia "up a gum*" (*gum-tree.)

Dearest little Karen; stick hard at the tennis, the riding & all sport while you can; then I can have the solace of knowing you [are] doing really well by your little loved body. I, too, am awfully well & have a lot of excercise.

I was so sorry to hear of your tennis mishap, but hope all is right.

Love from mother.

Your Dutch is simply *grand*. I think you get on *ever so* quick.

Have heard from Stanford that there is great likelihood that I play his "Dead men" Vars in Scheverlingen [*sic*] (Holland) in July

Monday. Goodbye

I may send you some few shillings this week to cover the price of yr last Mark Twain. etc.

[I wish you would buy & send me H. C. Andersons *best* fairy tales in the cheapest edition *with latin letters* & let me know the price]

*Or possibly "this year". There is a grammatical error here which leaves the choice open. *Transl.*

111 TO JOHAN SVENDSEN
[Original: Danish]
3.5.07.

5, Harrington Road,
South Kensington, S.W.
London

Dear Master!

When I played at the London Philharmonic Society's Concert, I gave your regards to both Dr Cowen and Mr Francesco Berger, and they were both so glad and asked me to remember them very much to you.[23]

I hope you are quite well again now. It was really lovely to be able to go out to you, when I was last in Copenhagen!

I have just been engaged to play Grieg's concerto (under his own conducting) at the big music festival in Leeds next October. He has been *so* kind to me, and even asked the Committee to have me play his piano concerto. It is an enormous pleasure and honour for me!

In July I am probably going over to Holland to play with the Berlin Philharmonic Orchestra; and after Leeds I am going on a big tour of Great Britain, where I will be performing in over 60 different towns.

In February or March I hope to come to dear Denmark again. It would mean *indescribably much* to me if I could get to play under your direction at a Kapel Concert this time! If only it would be possible!

With kindest regards to dear Mrs Svendsen and to you all (and hoping next time to hear your son play)

Your very sincere and admiring
Percy Grainger

23 Dr (later Sir) Frederic Hymen (Hymen Frederick) Cowen (1852–1935), English pianist, conductor and composer. In 1907 he was conductor of the Philharmonic Society, and Francesco Berger (b. 1834), pianist and composer, was its Honorary Secretary. Grainger had visited Johan Svendsen the day after his Copenhagen recital, on 6 March 1906. Svendsen's ill health obliged him to resign in 1908. He had married his second wife, Juliette Vilhelmine Haase, in 1901. Grainger did not go to Holland at this time.

112 TO EDVARD GRIEG
[Original: Danish]
14.5.07.

5, Harrington Road,
South Kensington, S.W.
London

Dear Master!

I hope you are really well despite your exertions in the south. How very much I would have liked to be present [and seen] the jubilation for you in Berlin, etc.[24]

Already a few weeks ago I learnt that it was decided that I (happily) should play under your conducting in Leeds. I wanted to write to you immediately to thank you from my whole heart for all the kindness you have done for me, but didn't know your address, and therefore waited till now.

I scarcely need to repeat my exceeding joy and happy pride at this enormous honour to me, that I am to be allowed to play your beloved Concerto in Leeds; as I have already written, I am *most* happy about the fact *that you should have wished that I should do it.*

There is a little score of mine (of a southern English folk-dance, "Green Bushes", that I have arranged freely for orchestra) which I would like to send you, if you will permit. I am only waiting to know your exact address first.

Do you think that you and dear Mrs Grieg can have me at "Troldhaugen" this summer for a short time! Or would I be in the way this time?

It would be so glorious to be with you sometime, but only if it doesn't intrude.

If it *should* be possible that you could have me this summer, what time do you think it could be? I ask as I will arrange my other plans according to what suits you.

I enclose the programme of my London recital. I have let them print "aa" instead of "å", since the latter (unfortunately) gives rise to so many stupid misprints in this country.

24 Though in poor health, Grieg had undertaken a tour of six concerts in Germany in March and April of 1907, including two in Berlin. Grainger's solo recital at Aeolian Hall on 13 June included a Grieg bracket similar to that played in Copenhagen on 26 February. This time he played Nos. 4 and 5 from Op. 66 and Nos. 1, 7, 8, 11 and 16 from Op. 72, four of the pieces being played for the first time in London.

Obviously I expect to hear "no" to my question about the visit to you, if it *in any way* would inconvenience or disturb you.

Next winter I will be busy. I am going on tour in Great Britain and playing at 80 concerts, and some single engagements as well.

In warm gratitude, and with most hearty greetings to you both, also from my mother

Your loving
Percy Grainger

113   TO FREDERICK DELIUS   5, Harrington Road,
20.5.07.   South Kensington, S.W.

Dear Delius

So delighted to get your most kind letter. A thousand thanks for your kind invitation to stay; which I shall *keenly love* to, when I get a chance.

It may be that I come to Paris to give a Recital next Spring; I hope so awfully.

I am keenly looking forward to "Appalachia" score (its awfully good of you) & to the other one you kindly propose sending me to see.

The photo is ripping; an ever so speaking likeness, & makes me most happy & proud to have. Cordial thanks for it.

I think you already have a photo of me, haven't you?

We're all most wishful to see you over here again at soonest. Do come.

The "G Bushes" score: Do you mind waiting until I see how many copies the orchestral parts (which I cut out from the hektograph score copies) will take?

With hearty greetings from my mother & me

warmly yr friend
Percy Grainger

114   TO KAREN HOLTEN   [London]
Thursday. 23.5.07.

Loved little, missed little Karen; funny little face that I can remembringly see laughing under me,

At times it is awful, I feel so left & empty; I can only read, & practise & do dull things. Somehow I would not dare compose at such times. I wake in prayer for the quick going of each hollow day, with a hope that I may earn a bit or work a bit; (not at anything I like, that I couldn't bear to) anyway, get thro' it. I tell you this ignoble news, as I believe it is what you will like to hear. (I dont mean this meanly) For tho' men loathe to know that anyone missed or yearns for them, women (its seems) maybe dont mind.

Then I've also had a dire disappointment in a book. A new Meridith that mother gave me. Such a dash & devil it started with, full of the very best bracingest Englishness, plucky & wild. It enthralled me all Tuesday so that I could do nought else. There was a girl in it reminding rippingly of you, & a rotter standing well for me. She was even called "Carin", but only as short for "Carinthia".[25] *Such* tenderness & quite Wagnerlike melt it had in it too, & full of body-athletic & loving. It made me quite a naturized Englishman. And then it goes & ends all full of restraint, & withholding;

25 Carinthia is the heroine of George Meredith's novel *The Amazing Marriage* (published 1895).

convents & chastity. Damn the English I say, if they everlastingly must end with a fence.

Darling Karen, please never refuse *anybody* anything if you *possibly can grant*. It is so saddening & destroying ever to have a final cold unreeallable No. I've been refused a few things, & they did me so much harm. Even if another man asks a married woman, it seems so cruel to me if he has to be refused (always provided, of course, the man is earnest & ächt, & the husband is cosmic & not a pig). It seems to me that nothing fulfills in this funny old world but the granting of happiness, & taking of it. Often it means a lot of work for a little happiness (a lot of war for a little peace) but joy is the end. At least to the musician, & to the Australian.

Do promise you'll never refuse if *anyone begs* you anything, either me or anyone else. Man becomes as cruel as nature if he can finally nay say, deaf to entreaty. It is so appaling to plead & not get listened to, isnt it? That should never happen.

Happiness & pity are good enough for me.

Cyril has done me the compliment of telling me that he also is going to write "irregular music"; music with irregular bars. I dont like it; I prefer to do my own experiments myself. So we've been writing, awfully absurd. To the (with me unpopular) compliment of copying this idea of mine he adds the insult of saying that what *he* is going to go in for is what is germed in the 3rd act Tristan. I've written that no germ in Tristan could directly sprout thuswize, & that I consider that it is *my* idea *only* that he wishes to develope, not Wagner's. I have written thus so that later on when he talks of irregular rhythms as rather a game of his particular own I may have something by which to remind myself of once have [having] known that it really did start in *me*.

I am very jealous on these matters. I so long for the world to have to (or to ought to) say "such & such was an Australian's discovery", etc. It would be so jolly for a continent that is so many miles off. Dear little Cyril, his letter on the subject is so sweet & childlike; tho' of course (trust an Englishman, especially Nth English) no less dangerous or simply cunning on that account. It really is time I gave up playing my things to the rest. It's only because I'm not bringing my things out that I need to be so miserly over my ideas; as I wrote him: "I cant afford for you to copy me to the extent that I have Grieg & others, & *me unpublished*."

Hardly a noble dealing. But I'm not noble, alack & aluck!

Friday. morn. 24.5.07.

Can you remember asking once, which would draw me most, you or football? Think of it! And I really believe that football had quite a good chance against you, those days. It wouldn't do so well now, it wouldn't have a "look in" (any chance at all.)

Aspenden Hall.
Buntingford. Herts.

(afternoon)

And just think how many women think wise to entice by refraining; who think it to "lose" to "yield". A composer might as well enhance his reputation by not writing. (which is, I own, just what I'm doing)

How would I love you, or even know your gifts, if your $\begin{Bmatrix} \text{god-like} \\ \text{woman-like} \end{Bmatrix}$ forsight hadn't guessed right, & taken the big & lavish path? Too appaling to think.

But just think that only few women would think to enrich their *respect & holiness* in men's minds by shedding armour & letting them into their utter undefendednesses. And more wondrous still, not all men would feel them holier, either. Isn't it queer?

I find it's cheaper to go to Bergen over Kjøb. Could you find out for me how often in the week the Kjøb-Bergen boats run? And does the Kjøb-Aalborg boat run daily? Anyhow I dont save much by going that trip by water, do I?

That is annoying, that stupidity of Arlaud's; the more so as Alfhild *foretold the thing exactly as it has happened a year ago.*

Evening. 11. o'cl.

Not enough to eat. I'm staying with the Harris's (Mrs Batten's [who is also here] daughter)[26] We motored from London, awfully jolly, in a *hugely powerful* car that simply dashed up all the worst hills.

Splendid, really, that the winter'll be so full of work for me, but sad about US.

Mother had wanted you to come over for a good long spell; 6 months, if you'd cared for it, but then I'm only in London for the Yule month between Sept & my Cope visit (if I come)

I get so annoyed with myself every time I go into our old bathroom to think that I led you into ought so drab, sordid, hurried, & ignoble as those silly conditions. It is well that your dignity doesnt grow out of surroundings & conditions, but is so solely in your dear Danish self. I'll be glad when we are gone from the house of my "bad taste" & misjudgement.

I want to buy for mother some of Ibsen's plays in Norwegian. I wonder could you for the 1000th time bother yourself & find out for me what they cost, decently bound, *each single & all together.*

There is no particular hurry about this.

I had a good success at yesterday's concert, tho' I didnt play too well. Alas, I have lost my nerve. I am a poor trembling thing on the platform now.

Will you be playing at concerts again next winter? *I do so hope so; at lots.* If not Arlaud, why not you & Ida Møller?[27] Or somebody?

When I am on tour in the winter I may perhaps send you 2 letters a week, if you wish. Can one write Poste Restante in Denmark? As I wouldnt send more than one the week to Ceresvej.

I do some [*sic* so] hope your dear father is better of his trouble, & that we will see him over here. I feel like chucking the Grieg trip & the folksongs too & just coming along to Svinkløv as soon as the season's over here. Of course I *must* go to darling Grieg, & I *ought* awfully to do the folksongs, but I haven't settled about the latter yet.

How marvellous old Walt is! I was reading some today. The 2nd poem in Children of Adam is so unwithstandable, & you ought to read *"The Song of the Answerer"* By *singers* he means *talents,* & by *poet genius.*

I am, alas, only one of the singers. I am "keen-singer". Read it, & you'll see how true this is of me. I dont really mind much. I'm not bigger than I am because my heart doesnt swell out universally & all enfoldingly enough for the really big job. You see I *love limitations.* I adore dialects, nationality, aristocraticness; all these narrowing instincts & conceptions.

It is the lack of *liking big enough* (more than the lack of specific giftedness) that holds a *talent* back from being a *genius.*

How I'm looking forward to the shooting at Svinkløv.

Do ask your sister to be a dear & bring you back some Dutch newspapers (some for you & some for me) & if she would buy me any decent modern Dutch novel. (in D) And she must let me know what it costs. Let it be cheap.

There is a little thunderstorm on.

I've put on my nice summer linen underbukser [Danish: underpants] again. It feels so nice. Thousands of times I recall the sweet smooth pure silky feel of the skin round above the knees under yours. (absurd tight woolen things) What one misses! Goodnight.

26 Irish-born Mabel (Mrs George) ("Ladye") Batten achieved some notoriety through her affair with the author Radclyffe Hall. She had a well-trained mezzo-soprano voice and also wrote music. Ada Crossley sang her song *A New Being* at the Grainger/Sandby duo-recital on 13 February 1905. Charles Albert Edwin Harriss (1862–1929), born in London, had settled in Canada in 1883 and become a leading musical force in the Dominion. His Empire Concert, given at Queen's Hall at 3 p.m. on Empire Day, 24 May 1907, was intended to give a representation of all that was best in the music of Great Britain and her colonies. Grainger, the only pianist, played the Liszt *Hungarian Rhapsody* No. 12.

27 Ida Møller, Danish opera singer. She gave a concert with Grainger, Karen Holten accompanying, at Nyborg on 21 February 1907.

Sunday. morn. 26.5.07.

It would be grand if you could practise to bite better. There, I must say, yr gifts rather come to a full stop. Practise on yrself. The great law of the matter is: That any regularly repeated movement *irritates*, but *doesnt hurt*. Sensatory nerves seem not to act properly if called upon to give the same feelinglet more than quite a few times. In biting, open the teeth as seldom as possible, & then only to gather in more, or fresh, flesh. But it is good to *roll* (or grind) the teeth over already grasped flesh. The top of all things seems close to one under teeth, I think. Remember, no often repeated movements.

I will look up the Mazurkas you mention. Thanks for thinking of it for me.

Sunday evening.

How sad (& afraid) I get, sleeping alone in these old houses.

The man Harris is a great dear, & his wife & Mrs Batten have both been awfully jolly & simple & nice this time, but it's been a miserable trip for me.

My fault.

Fond love
Percy.

Today I have cleanly copied out all the remaining sea-chanty words.

————————

This is the list of addresses to send circulars out to, if ever I need that done from Kjøb, & you would be so helpful & kind as to do it.

Slagelse	Boghl. Tørsleff.
Næstved	J. Chr. Koch. Boghl.
Nykøbing F.	Emil Petersen. Boghl.
Odense	Hr. Cand. theol. Chr. M.K. Petersen
Svendborg	Fabrikant V. Lange.
Faaborg	Hr. Lith Rasmussen. Musikf.
Fredericia	Boghler E.S. Jessen.
Kolding	Hr. Skovrider N. Fritz. R af D.
Esbjerg	Boghler J. Dalsgaard Olsen.
Holstebro	Boghler Emil Ottesen.
Nykøbing Mors.	Boghler Niels Søndergaard.
Thisted	Boghler Breinholt Nørgaard.
Vejle	Boghl C. Neumann.
Horsens	Cand. jur. Richter.
Silkeborg	Hr Driftsbestyrer H. Godske Nielsen.
Aarhus	Musikforening.
Randers	Dr. Otto. V. Lassen. Bragl.
Viborg	Boghler Niels Christensen.
Hjørring	Klubben for Hjørring & Omegn.
Aalborg	Hr Boghler Marinus M. Schultz.
Nyborg	Hr Boghl August Langkilde.
Ribe	Adjunkt. Knud Knudsen.

Also

Hr Konsul Birch. Nyborg.
Hr Dr Falkman. Aarhus.
Hr. Fred. L.T. Fribert. Østerbrogade. 5. Kjøb.
Hr Købmand Lauridsen. Vejen. Jyll.
Hr Schiebsbye. Nykøbing. Sj.

Fru Dr Søderberg Horsens.
Hr Prof Saugmann Vejlefjord San. pr Dangaard. Jyll.
Fru Dr Tolderlund Thisted.
Hr Bancbestyrer Holten Struer.

———————————————

There must be a lot more towns that would be worth sending out to.

If you know any, or other important people of any of the above towns, do let me have them to make my list as complete as poss.

Who is the right person to send to in Struer, for inst?

On 12 May Percy wrote to Karen, "I am hugely taken up tackling 'society' & trying to re- & newly-popularize myself". His effort continued through June and until the Graingers left London for Scandinavia on 20 July. Rose was also involved in this work. As Grainger reported to Karen, ". . . she is completely taken up with inviting 'dull-backs' and entertaining them and sending out programmes to all the people in the address book. But it all does good". Their work was rewarded when Percy's recital on 13 June, the particular focus of their endeavours, was attended by a large and fashionable audience. Inevitably Grainger paid a price: he had little time for composing and showed signs of the physical wear and tear of so many late nights. The letters to Karen reflect the vacillation of his mood and of his attitude to "society". Rose, too, showed signs of strain. She did not feel well enough to join Percy on his post-recital weekend in the country with the Plunket Greenes.

"The Season" occupied Grainger entirely; he remained in London throughout. He did not go to any of the competition festivals, nor did he go folksong hunting. He did, however, manage to finish transcribing and printing folksongs 100–200 of his English Folksong Collection, work which had occupied him for almost a whole year. On 18 July he told Karen that the work was finished, and copies distributed.

In the midst of all the other season's fuss the Graingers moved house again on 15 July, back to 26 Coulson Street where they had lived from early February 1903 to the middle of 1905. The house was owned by a Mrs Burdett.

Despite the pressures and rush, Grainger remained "cheerful and chiruppy", and reported to Karen that "This has been my best season after all (Money)".

115   TO KAREN HOLTEN   [London]
[Original: English/some Danish]
[Extracts, several letters, June–July 1907]
Saturday 1.6.07.

It seems I'm going to have a wonderful season, & shall be *shockingly* busy. So if my letters seem short & dull a little later on, you'll know why. I'm working very hard now to be ready for it all, & am also going out a heap. (Evenings)

Cyril didn't intend anything the least bit bad with all that about "beatless music", he has always been like that (without really knowing it) but I don't care any more about it (I hope).

I dont mean that I have changed my intention of [not?] bringing out my things before I'm rich; I only mean I shant play the really important stuff to fellow composers; except Roger.

5.6.07. Wednesday.

Days for especial prayers are:—
June 13. afternoon. June 23 afternoon. Albert Hall. Ungarske F. June 27. eve. 10.30. Mrs Ch. Hunter (At Home for Duke & D-ess of Connaught & Rodin [the sculptor])[28]
It is silly; I have such a terrible desire to compose, these days, but I don't dare. I have begun a setting of 2 Irish folk-dances (something like Gr Bs) for chamber music. Both songs are used for the one piece.
One of them is good:

It occurs in Petri's collection of Irish songs; a collection of 1581 different tunes; and very reliable, on the whole.[29]
Never mind, I'll be able to do a lot of writing at Svinkløv.
I'm going out an *appaling* lot, every night. To the *most shocking* Jews & curious Americans; but it amuses me too, at times, & then I often meet Blanche & Sargent, & we have good laughs.[30] Roger keeps about the same. He went back a bit a short time ago, but now has bettered again. I havent seen him *for weeks*, now; but mother does, occasionally.

8.6.07.

How I love the "season", sometimes. I'm quite in love with it just now. It's so splendid & sensuous somehow, the folk in their thin dresses, & all so fine-looking, & everybody making all the effort they can, & bustling about.
And then I love to go to At Homes & hear the bloody foreigners sweating away for their bread & butter; talented French reciters, & darkeyed Italian singers with guitars, etc. I've been to 4 places today & am going to a show at B de Meyer's tonight that doesn't *start* till 11.30. I'm feeling mighty happy & fit, and am practising *hard*. There are no 2 ways about it, I like being busy & having to do things I hate. It makes me cheerful & contented, & keen on my job.
I like practising ever so much better than composing. I feel much happier & more festive when I'm doing it.
When I'm rich (if?) I'm going to once put in a season in London like a mere society creature, & go to all the At Homes & listen to the other beggars sweating.
And then I love to meet & know titled & rich people. I feast on the smell of money & power, & feel such a ripping snob. (I am a shocking snob)
Now that the weather is so nice and warm, one can't expect me to refrain completely from composing: And I don't either. I have written a good deal of the reel given above, ("Polly [sic] on the Shore") which I have now decided to arrange for the time being for string quartet.

28 Arthur William Patrick Albert, Duke of Connaught and Strathearn (1850–1942), the third son of Queen Victoria, and his wife, Princess Louise Margaret Alexandra Victoria Agnes (d. 1917, formerly of Prussia). Grainger met the French sculptor Auguste Rodin (1840–1917) several times during these years, at the homes of Mrs Hunter, John Singer Sargent and Baron de Meyer.

29 Grainger's *Molly on the Shore* is based on the Cork Reel tunes "Temple Hill" and "Molly on the Shore", Nos. 901 and 902 respectively in Part II of *The Complete Petrie Collection of Ancient Irish Music*, edited by Sir Charles Villiers Stanford in three Parts (London 1902–05). The string quartet setting was begun 2 June 1907 and completed as a birthday gift for Rose, 3 July 1907.

30 Jacques-Émile Blanche (1861–1942), French painter and amateur musician. Grainger met him in Dieppe through Mrs Lowrey in the summer of 1902. It was Blanche who introduced Grainger to the music of Debussy. Blanche painted a fine oil portrait of Grainger in the summer of 1906.

11.6.07.

What terrible folk! Those bloody British kept me working up to nearly 3 o'clock, last night, playing & playing. And I felt so frightened & tired, & they seemed so loathsomely fresh & gluttonous, & as if they'd been sleeping all the day. How I hate the English at moments; the society folk are such grabbers; one needs ones fullest strength to cope with them. They were very sweet of course, but I felt war to the knife, I can tell you. When I got to bed it was lighting up in the sky for early dawn. That queer, pale, adventure-suggesting moment. It minded me of my night walks, & the odd things I'd felt at such hours. Would you like to go night walking with me 1ce? Maybe even this time at Sv, when we're left back alone, we might; & sleep out the next day. By the way, can you walk good & fast now?

Friday. 14.6.07.

The concert yesterday was a most great success in all ways. About £80 worth in the house, (expenses, of course, tho', are very heavy) *charming* folk, & all said never to have heard me play so well. I was *fearfully* frightened (that gets ever worse, alas) but got thro' somewhat, & without serious mishaps, barring a few trifling memory-slips in the Brahms. My memory is appallingly weak. I had practised *hugely* for the concert, & one sees that it pays. I think the C# min Bach is the best thing I play; it is such a quietly great & Godlike thing in itself, anyhow. Delightfully warm & intent & *evenly* enthusiastic thro'out, the audience was, tho' not wild at all; but nice, & pretty looking. Hardly any Jews at all. It has been quite my biggest London success so far, in a deep sense. I have a shocking lot coming. A Rathbone At Home Monday (next) evening, & other things.

I consider that I am *really* working for my living these days, & I must say I think it's *only just* worth what it brings in. (But not really.)

This morning mo'er & I parked it, & afterwards I swam with von Glehn.

I did ¼ hour without stopping at all, 10 minutes breaststroke, & 5 on my back.

Monday 17.6.06.[07]

In train.
[from Hampshire]

How amusing that you didnt know of my Recital Mother & I roared over that idea. Here are we sweating & slaving (letters & teas & people & pleasantness) with nought but "the 13th" in our minds & mouths, & you over there in superior ignorance. I did send you a program tho' (I think) in the B. Jones book. I'll send you another.

Monday. 24.6.07.   [London]

This season has really been properly *worked*.

30.6.07.

Just think, Mrs Hunter has paid me £50 for playing for her last Thursday, to "Royalty". "Royalty" was charmed & even asked Mrs H my fee!

Monday. 1st **July**

I'm simply off my head with work & fuss, so cannot write the things I'm thinking.

116 TO KAREN HOLTEN [London]

[Original: English/some Danish]
5.7.07. Friday.

It doesn't matter so much that you get letters a little irregularly now, but just continue to let me get mine weekly as before.

The performance on 3.7.07 of my choruses was really good, the best I've ever had, by far. *Fine* voices, & they did quite wonders in the 2 (fairly short) rehearsals. The sea chanties, for men's alone, are effective I think, & I arranged another (maybe the best so far) yesterday, on the strength of it.[31]

I feel rather wretched & a wreck from all the late nights (every single one late for *ages*) & work & excitement; yet I've never enjoyed a season as much, or felt more *fit* even when not quite *well*. I have "piles" at present, unfortunately, but it will probably go away quickly.

Yesterday I heard from Grieg. He wants me there on the 21st, so I think it's fixed we leave here 18th.

I've just been rehearsing with Lady Speyer for an "at Home" next Tuesday.

Paul Schmedes sang on the 3rd; quite well.

An Australian has just won the "All England" Tennis championship; Brookes. The S. African cricketers have just won their 1st Test Match against England.

Roger keeps on bettering very slightly. His address is: Bawdsey Manor/Woodbridge/Suffolk. England.

There is no doubt that the late nights, the constant effort, & the whole London society life is grand for people's looks; I've been observing carefully & the worst racketers (hard-livers) are the best preserved. It seems to fight the grossness & dulness that age threatens.

However it hasnt a lovely effect on me. I look like a pig with 1 eyelid swollen & red eyes & bad skin; but cheerful & chirruping.

I have [a] lot of pupils still & am just going to 1 now.

Heaps of love: I'll write again soon; not so dully, I hope.

Let me know at *earliest* about rooms & if the boat *from* K-sand goes daily & will suit me leaving Harwich July 18

117 TO KAREN HOLTEN [London]

[Extracts, July 1907]

Thursday. 11.7.07.

Such a time! . . . I've found no time for swimming, nor even for *taking a bath* the last few days.

Friday. 13.7.07.

Of course I often go in for a lot of pose & nonsense, but *this really is dead true:* That I feel I can play my best, & have most corage before, society folk & typical English.

TO HERMAN SANDBY

[Extract. PM 16 July 1907]

I've had a simply **huge** summer but feel finely fit

31 Four of Grainger's choruses were performed àt a "jamboree" at Lady Bective's on 3 July 1907: *I'm Seventeeen Come Sunday, Marching Song*, and two of his settings of sea-shanties collected from Rosher, *Shenandoah* and *Stormy* (see note 16 above). Frederic Austin sang solo in the shanties. Lady Bective had offered her house as a home for the "jamborees" after the Elweses left the house in Hertford Street (see letter 34 and note 17, 1904). Lady Winefride Elwes wrote of them in her biography of her husband, "In the result, both at her [Lady Bective's] house and at Willy Rathbone's in Cadogan Gardens, efforts were made to keep them alive. But somehow they were not really the same. They ceased to be jamborees and became musical parties". The new sketch was a setting of "Santa Anna", melody 150 in Grainger's *Collection of English Folksongs*, and collected from Rosher on 24 July 1906. The sketch, dated 4.7.07, remained undeveloped. The singer Paul Schmedes (b. Copenhagen 1869) was the brother of the famous Danish tenor Erik Schmedes. He had been in London for a recital on 13 May. The tennis player was Norman Brookes.

118

TO KAREN HOLTEN
[Extract]
Thursday. 18.7.07.

Just think, after this evening I am free & done with this bloody
season . . .

*Grainger's last engagement for the 1907 Season was an "at home" for
William Rathbone on 18 July. On 20 July the Graingers left London for
Scandinavia. They travelled together to Aalborg, where Karen Holten met
them at the railway station in the evening of the 22nd. She then travelled
on with Rose to Svinkløv. Grainger travelled on by boat and train to
Bergen and the Griegs, arriving in the morning of 25 July. He remained
as guest of the Griegs at their summer home, "Troldhaugen", until 4
August, when he travelled back to rejoin Rose and Karen at Svinkløv. He
left for London on 14 September. Grieg died in hospital at Bergen on 4
September. Grainger's letters to Rose from Troldhaugen are the first
surviving from 1907.*

118   TO KAREN HOLTEN   (at Sulsted)
[Original: English/Danish]
Tuesday. 23.7.07
8 o'cl. (morn)

   Such nice stuffs you had on. When I was waiting for you yesterday
evening & saw so many folk nearing from a goodish farness & looking
hideous, I got in quite a tremble that 1 of them might be you, or that you'd
come walking along that way. As soon as you hove in sight I spotted yr
walk but felt so stupid & afraid that I had to go inside the building instead
of standing outside. Shocking nervous work these meetings & leavings.
   It is so nice to think that you are not any longer on the Continent of
Europe; because everything north of the Limfjord is an island. Just think,
when I reach Norway I will be on the Continent again, while you "rest so
sweet on the island". It's funny to think also that this island I'm still on
(alas, not long) holds now really *all* (for I've also got compositions with
me in a bag) that marks me off from the most lovedless, unowning
beggarsman. One can cram a lot of importance into 4 walls; one could
explode all that a lifetime has gathered to itself with a bomb in a railway
carriage, so easily.
   It is raining, so you 2 will not get out properly today and will not try
out the wheeled chair properly either. Stupid. I got such a nice cold bath
this morning (also last night) Please talk Danish to mother, so that she
learns it quickly.

(Frederikshavn) There were some beautiful be-heathered hills we passed in
the train near here. Of the same kind as those between Fjerritsl.[ev] and
Svinkl[øv], but not quite so nice.

(on the sea) I wonder whether the clothes you had on were lovely or
whether they only seemed so; I hope they really were, I believe they are.
   Little Karen, I wonder whether I really love you, or not, or what; can
you understand that one can go and not know a thing like that? I never
know such things. When I see you then I am so afraid and excited and
happy that I can't make out whether I love you or not; I only feel myself
helpless and taken up. And then you have that expression you have in your

eyes, when I see that I feel myself made calm and without any further questioning.

And then are you beautiful or not; how can I tell? & I'd so much like to know. It is so difficult to feel if the water is wet when one is up to his ears in it. But I'd like to know if you're ugly or lovely, quite in the abstract, & quite apart from what you *seem* to me.

You know how little children feel for their nurses or mothers; they hardly love consciously, but they cling to them, & couldn't *at all* do without them. It is something like that I also feel. I am so grateful to you and you seem to me so necessary (for the present, at least) and your eyes are so gentle so good (I can tell you've got such a dear soul, that you yourself are such a splendid pure thing) but all this is childish chatter; I would so like to have a proper "grown-up" opinion, whether I really love you, or not.

I should like to be able to say to you like a real grown up person that I *know my own mind* & that I really love you, or dont, *realiably*. In the same way I never know if I like composing (& am a composer) or if its just a *habit* that I cant be happy without it, just as I cant help longing to be near you. Is that too a habit? Or are what people call love & "born composers" only all of them habits too?

In the abstract all is so easy for me & my grip isn't bad & I have real definite realiable (& of course therefore *stupid*) manlike opinions, that I would always give the same answers to, (even if suddenly woke up & asked) I know so well what seems good or bad in art, taste, & even polotics & *conduct in life*; I can say *so truly* that I admire you & respect you, (& give solid un-changeble [I believe] reasons) but why can't I answer as certainly & definitely whether I love you, or no?

I believe that most folk could easier say whether they loved or not, than give critical reasons for their admiration of their lovers. Then why haven't I that dignified(?) certainty? In art, & in my general conduct in life I can choose so calmly & finally & feel quite a swell; in like manner I should like to be able to come to you & tell you a definite thing of feelings.

It seems to me so little respectful to you to treat you with so little certainty and consciousness. But it seems it won't alter. Between us the discovering, the finding, the choosing, the glory is yours. I didnt find you, you found me. You have unfolded me (if indeed I can be called unfolded) & I am a sort of sea weed, or small animal, or helpless child, or dead thing that has come drifting blindly along & that you have taken compassion on & done so well (*how* well) to & kindly & embracingly; & made *so* happy.

As far as things of the flesh are concerned, I am as capably splendid as all the other nasty males. I am all right there. If I am not lucky in my way of acting in that regard, I am at least sincere, true, & steadfast in my desires. I have no uncertainty about those things. In our joys, our amusements, our delights, there we are grand comrades & equals. Both desiring, both getting. It is (I hope at least) a splendid fair trade. But in deeper things this strange silly unconciousness, uncertainty! And all this tedious business you have had to hear, and endure, so many times already. Do you forgive me?

If I was only in Sv[inkløv]. The sea is mirror smooth, but does not mirror at all, since it is raining.

What a weirdly platonic meeting it was, to be sure!

Here I sit, trying to remember how you look. I cant!

Much love to Caj [Karen's brother].

I will force myself not to write too often to you, because also that is a habit.

There is a place in an Irish folksong that P. Greene sings that stays in my mind today

This letter reads quite differently from it was written. Please translate the difference

119 TO ROSE GRAINGER   Nth Jutland.
early morn. 23.7.07.

Do, darling, let me have all details of the planter's rose-sheaf, & all gelegenheits-begebenheiten [German: all the events of the occasion].

How curious that I should have left the last ominous words to put my head out of window here at Hjørring (which was the most northerly town H. & I did on our tour) to see on the station the reception of high officials (or kinglinesses) come by this train (the snob in me lept to be so near) It was touching to contrast the fussedness of the higher officials (white begloved stationmasters & such) with the bored indifference of the lower (guards, a.s.o.)

This Nth Jutish island Svinkløv I (still) & my compos are now on, think, holds all I take my real stock in. Fancy that if all the rest of the world blew up or down it wouldn't leave me (*as an* **individual**) really poorer. Denmark now at last enjoys final preciousness. And I hope the little mum isnt uncomfy, or bored.

Sad, that today seems rain-determined, & that you may possible not get a try at the bathchair. Some months or weeks ago, curiously, Karen's & my letters crossed with the questions:

from her; if she shouldn't order the chair for by the time of yr coming & have a try at wheeling.

from me; if she wouldnt have a go at wheeling in my absence if not too fagging.

Such a lovely cold bath this morn. Such a refreshing, waking-up shower, & jolly breakfast It was good to get to sleep yesternight from my cronk [*sic* chronic?] depressedness. How sleep normalizes us again, wondrously!

(Frederikshavn harbor) I only make about the 2nd or 3rd passanger as far as I can see. Delightfully clean & neat boat but only about the size of a river yacht or small tug. Charming. A typicly pretty muchmasted Danish harbor here.

The train actually went about 60 the hour for a time.

(At sea)
What a *terrible* affair life is to be sure; I dont mean nasty, because its glorious & enthralling but so aweinspiring & unnerving & taxing. Full of concerts & meetings & partings & handsome cabs & crucial moments. Even out of holidays can direness not be kept. And if I, somewhat gifted & very lucky & good & strong & not now penniless am somewhat cowed how fearsome for the weak & poor & talentless it must loom; & fancy those that are not loved & helped thro' like I; how can they ever bear up; & how at all could I, indeed, if I weren't. Maybe I'm not a Viking after all. How child-easy are, indeed, the problems of work & art & science compared with those of life & actuality. All that can be accomplished in (public)

hiddenness, & unhurry, by oneself (self-confidence & self-only-reliance how easy) I can take on, even tough jobs; but asking questions of real live people, & performing before crowds, & actually performing compos — dread moments.

I think I am for the still sowing of seeds. I wouldn't fear handling small boats alone (or with one's own folk) at sea, I'm sure, or storm dangers, or mountaineering, or conducting (the works of others, or tried ones of my own) not a bit, but shield me from my (elder) brother-men & from "situations". With children too one is brave: But think of drunk men, & all or any violence, & such things as moneymaking. I really think I have gone boldly against my own grain in my time; I cant think how I've done it all. (And I'm going to do it 20 times more so)

Very nice the Norwegians of the ship seem.

Yes, it *is* Thursday morning early I arrive.

It seems unbelievable that the kattegat can be *so* smooth.

What a shame you had that disgusting X-ing & are not along now with me to really enjoy this calm one. Lovely it is; the Norwegian accent sounds so nice, & the rain on the water gives a ½ foggy look & many danksailed ships dimmer about on all sides.

It's so consoling that as soon as ever I get to the darling Griegs that I can get onto my folksong copying.

It's so comfy here because there are practically no passangers. folk are what blemish.

To copy are: (besides the singing-game words; after you hear from Lincs) the 4 strings parts of "Molly on the shore".

I'd awfully like to have following addresses as soon as poss.

Father, Dr Russell, (tell me please to whom of yr folk in Adelaide it wld be nice to send p.cs, or letters) Mrs Wodehouse, (Chester □) Lady Speyer, Delafosse, Blanche, Mrs Husband. V. Glehn. Tait. Miss Norris. Ada. Miss Smedley. Harrison (Cheyne Walk) Dr Ward (Leeds) Affleck.

We had great helpings of strawberries & cream as pudding for lunch. There is really nothing so nice as fruit & the things from fruit, lemonade, jam, rasberry-vinegar, syltetøj [compote], & all things with fruit juices poured over them. I wonder if the Griegs will have lovely things to eat.

I'm looking forward to the swimming when I get to Svinkl. We have just had a porpoise (or some such fish) flitting greenly along beside us. They can go.

5.30. Slept finely since soon after lunch. Coast of Norway, pinky-blue strip on the right.

Norway was called "Norregi" (contraction of Norðrvegi, the North Way) & the Baltic "Austrvegi". (the Eastern Way) By that one feels how the race at that time was a shifting trading one, when even it's own land it named as a thoroughfare.

I've been longing to have a drink of some kind all day, but have resisted that extravagance (by means, mostly, of sleep) so far.

Fondest love
Percy.

It turns out that I'm the only passenger. What I took for such were men of the ship in ordinary clothes. Here seems *real* simplicity. The old Captain has been hard at work this afternoon mopping & brushing the decks with his men, & they tell me that he always take[s] part in every kind of work along with his men. I took the ship for a new one, but the captain said it was that "10 years before you were born"; rightly guessing my age, alas!

The hills pass very calm & smooth-shaped, (not highlooking these) strips of different depths of greyblue behind & above each other.

The ship is a model of order.

All the faces aboard show spareness & reliability, & a thorough lack of the poor dear Danes's gross childish weak sensuality & slipshodness. A wholly different race, it would seem; maybe really nice.

The poor planter. Were the roses a truly great moment? I'm sure (or hope I am) he wont show his worst side to you. I know he awfully won't *want* to.

The captain is cutting his nails with a penknife. "Not well." It turns out to be only cleaning, after all.

8. o'clock.

Charming entry to Kristianssand It's true that this & parts of Sth Island (N. Zeal) are alike. Invercargill, f. inst.

We must come here a summer

Lots of love & goodnight
little mum

120   TO ROSE GRAINGER   [PM Stavanger]
[Postcard]
24.7.07. morn. 10.30

Glorious weather, & most comfy boat. We keep quite close in to land, & thus see all the coastal & fjord scenery between Kristianssand & Bergen. I suppose I ought to be relishing it, but I'm really bored to unwept tears. I stick hard to my gaelic & get along that way. That however keeps me to the stupid stuffy smoking room as its too windy on deck to read. I've not tried the food yet as I'm lasting out till midday on fruit (I got last night at K-ssand) as I'm feeling very poor by reason of a deadly dream I had last night wherein I arranged to play for Mrs Leggett (but she looking like Sloan Gdns Mrs Wodehouse) for £20 stead of £25. If only one had more money.

I also lost my umbrella on the last boat, but maybe'll get it again. (Fool!)

Fondest love Perks.

3.30 But gorgeous strawberries & cream for lunch.

I want to be somewhere quiet where I can work a bit, not this traipsing round.

121 TO ROSE GRAINGER   Stavanger
24.7.07. 5.30 afternoon.

The coarse simple game these folk play doesn't pay. They're quite nice
& sometimes even rather fine, but still it's all pishtush.

From now on I go in for dangerously overdone refinement & delicacy
only. The ponies only are a success. Dear podgey small intelligenteyed
unblinkered little things, freelooking, & often of a nice rich red-yellow tint;
tight & happy looking. I think I'm going to be off Scand-ia for good. Alas,
no race satisfies me, they all upset & distress me, & make me feel forsaken.
It's only when I'm with those I really love or drowned in work that I can
delude myself into lumping mankind. There's nought for it but to work
hard & forward one's ideals, & make money money & die & get away.

And yet I couldn't help feeling *perfectly* happy after (& during) a lot of
strawberries & cream at today's lunch. I could have embraced everyone. If
I'm only given *constantly* all the bodily fun (of all kinds) I so adore, & am
worked *really hard*, I suppose I am possible as a sort of machine. But what
is the end of such a hog? I fear the results are before us. Then I feel that
the undaunted but unblindable mum is finally disappointed with & sick of
me. I feel it's only a plucky determination to work against hope for a
longserved ideal & the uncomeoverable something felt for an off-spring that
empowers you to put up with me longer.

The rare child & the unusual son has dwindled, alas, to an ornery "junge
mann"; "nit ė mawl ė schän[g]s" [German dialect written phonetically
= Nicht einmal ein schönes (schöner?): Not even an attractive one.]

Never mind, I alone still manage to limit my dislike & criticalness to
others; not to myself.[32]

Troldhaugen. 26.7.07. Friday, midday.
This is indeed full life for the purely male side of one. I ask nought more.
I never need wish to find in in-years-younger strivers more fresh & new a
yearning or more catholic a glut than in this old (accidentaly) narrow-*typed*
(but world-broad-hearted) *real* man. Here is ever morningness of soul &
mind.

I did not write yesterday at all (forgive me, loved mum,) for I was in such
a feverish ecstacy & was so piloted about from 1 fiery doing to another,
that by the 1 ½ hour I had to myself I was far too overturmoiled to come
to paper. Norwegian[s] aren't lovely to look out [*sic* at], but blazes, they're
not to be done without; *they would be missed*. Glowing little icicles; with
gnomishness all knobbly over the Norwegianest of 'em.

Great things, enthusiasms, noble excesses, without let.

When I arrived in Bergen yestermorn found it full of German men of
warsmen. A typical teutonicly out of tune brass band of the same allayed
my national musical fears at the station. I had ½ an hour to gloat over the
lack of smartness of the men; the convincing not-to-be-fearedness of them,
the dulleyedness, the pimples, the rank rumps & corkscrew legs of them.
I loathe them from my sincerest & best heart. But I disgraced myself at the
station. When getting my ticket, some of them were doing same, & not
knowing Norwegian were getting tangled up with the ticket man. I withstood for a minute & then succumbed & actually translated for the beasts
& put them on the straight. When will I have such another chance of
neglecting to do them a good turn.

I'm certainly not worthy of another. "War, red war, till our sinews fail"
is all I pray for.

I'm abs poss they're nowise to be the least feared at sea.

Carcase minus spirit, what can it boot?

Reaching here, T-haugen, at about 8 o'clock (morn, yest) found Griegs
& breakfast warm & ready for me & the atmosphere embracing. This drops

32 To which Rose replied, 29
July, "**No**, you don't believe I am
either sick of you, or disappointed
in you. If you do, then I must
appear very different to my real
self, or you are a silly little son.
My absolute belief in yr powers
may make me sometimes unhappy
that you find so little time for
composing — & I also feel that
you give up too much of yr very
valuable youth to the folk-songs
— that is all. Or perhaps, knowing
what a creature of habit you are, I
am afraid that the long rest from
composing may dull your powers
in that direction for too long a
time, knowing that the fire of
youth is different to the fire of
middle age & old age. Then you
know I have not yr patience, & fret
about you a lot, therefore I want
to get our house & reduce
expenditure all I can so that you
can save more money. Enough of
this dearie. I shall never think you
'an ornery young man' & as long
as my reason lasts, never love you
less, & never I hope, respect you
less. Such love as mine for you is
not every day, nor does it fade
away with every disappointment".

33 Frants Beyer (1851–1918), native of Bergen. He studied law and held administrative posts, but as an amateur musician he at one time studied piano with Grieg at Christiania. He later became one of Grieg's closest friends and his nearest neighbour, having a villa at Næsset, opposite Troldhaugen. Grainger never went folksong collecting with him.

34 Julius Röntgen (1855–1932), composer, conductor and pianist. Born at Leipzig, he settled in Amsterdam from 1877 to 1925, holding many important posts there including, from 1912, director of the Amsterdam Conservatorium. He was one of Grieg's intimate friends and wrote a biography of him. He was to play an important part in the development of Grainger's international career as a pianist.

on 3 sides to a Lake of Killarney; & who lives on on the next jutting (call-overably near) tongue of rocky land? Fr. Beier, the man who with Grieg collected the tunes of his op 66 (Olla Dalom, etc: to which there belongs a rare legend; all dead drowned boedees (bodies) & churchbells bimming; you'll hear it soon from me) a sort of puny Bjørnsson to look at; a good stout soul, steeped in folklore & f-music.[33]

I was also met by Röntgen, who (alas) leaves today for Denmark.[34] He speaks Norwegian, not as well as I Danish; but still. Born in Leipsig of Dutch stock, & living his life in Holland he schwärms* gutterally for my compos. Therefor I like him & pretend to like his (compos) more than I really do.

After breakfast Grieg was for my playing some Slaater, so I got off to Griegs composing-room down the slope near the fjord (on the jolly wooden walls of which hangs a likeness of "Möllargutten" who, you know, luckily was jilted by Kari & wrote Möllarguttens bruremarsch to bless her with) & put in a few hours practise.

On mounting up again with [sic was] photoed with Griegs & Röntgen by 2 filthy Germans, to whom Grieg was refreshingly short worded. Proofs will be sent they said.

Wait till I'm a Grieg: (which I'll never be) No Germs shall photo me.

Lunch (the lot of us) over at Bejer's. I glutted. There & back rowed us (over the fjord) old Grieg, asthma & all.

After lunch Grieg asks for English & Færoe f-songs (remember[ed] pretty well every jolly one he heard from me last year)

Universal rapture: "But what harmonies". "Das macht ihm aber gar niemand nach" ["There is really no one who can imitate him in that"] (that was bobbly "Lord Melbourne") Grieg says: "darin leigt doch der keim zu einem grossen Englischen Styl, meinen Sie nicht." ["Therein lies the germ of a great English style, don't you think."] I gave them 2 Færoes, L Melbourne, The Nth country maid, Brigg Fair, I'm 17, Molly on the Shore, Green bushes, (just the tune) 6 Dukes, a.s.o.

Then Grieg kicks up a fuss & says why to hell dont I use all that harmonic wealth ("so strange, uncouth, yet so perfectly natural-sounding") also for wholly my own compos. "Seien Sie nur ruhisch, s'wird schon besorscht [sic besorgt], Herr Roscher-Kvilter" ["Just be calm, it will be taken care of, Mr Roger Quilter"] Then I tote out "Tiger-Tiger" & "Morning-song". Real warmth & sympathy all round.

Then I play Slaater, & then C# min Bach Prel & Fugue. Röntgen says; "you must surely come to Amsterdam". I give to be understood; "provide the nec"

In short, general my-back-biffing, & I feeling burstingly conceited.

Grieg sleeps in the afternoon & I go for a row & a swim (it goes **fine** in the saltwater) in the fjord. Dress myself in eveningdress (looking a pretty good cut above the natives — or feeling it) & we drive to evening grub at the German consuls (a Norwegian friend of Griegs.) Here I stuff & play again.

I overhear myself much talked about.

"Der ist absolut der Kommender Mann" ["He is absolutely the 'up and coming' man"]

"Das ist ja ganz was anderes als Elgar; **viel** origineller." ["This is indeed something completely different than Elgar, **much** more original."]

"Ja, harmonisch ist er ganz und gar ein Meister; man muss nur erst sehen wie es mit seinen *form* steht, in grösseren werke" ["Yes, harmonically he is altogether a master; but one must see first how his *form* is in larger works"] ['Fool to doubt me', think I]

---

*One of Grainger's favourite German words, used in various forms. From *schwärmen*, to dote on, to admire enthusiastically.

"Ja, und wie er doch auch spielt; das Bach war doch herrlich; einzig."
["Yes, and how he plays too; the Bach was splendid; unique."]

Grieg says, with his delightful aspiration of the beginning of each sentence "*Ja*! Sådan skal det spilles." [Danish: "*Yes*! That's how it should be played."]

We drive home, I dead sleepy.

(I forgot to say that at Bejers yestermidday I gave an idea of Gr. Bs, Röntgen picking out the tune: friendliest interest & warmth.)

This morn to breakf I took down "Gr Bs". Grieg was awfully jolly & sweet about it.

I think some of the chords & crossparts gave him twinges, but he bears up so youngly to all that is modern; he is full of respect for all that strives, & his soul knows no restraint or rudeness or narrowmindedness. "For he was great-hearted."

Then I fetch Wamphray march & yell & bash it forth. Grieg says: "I like that best of all; that's a simply grand piece; fresh." etc etc.

I hear no more form-doubts, & Grieg won't believe me when I tell him that every bar is filthily orchestrated.

Tho' the speech is often in German (for Röntgen's sake) the sentiment *never* is. I hear nought of "the need of study" or even "who did you study with" (not 1ce) But only: "Grosses talent" "Ja, das nenne ich wirklich tecknische (compositional) fertigkeit" (that was the many voicedness of Gr. Bs) "Das ist doch eine fabelhafte teknische leistung." "Wie muss dass Klingen." ["Great talent" "Yes, I call that really technical (compositional) proficiency" ... "That is indeed a fabulous technical achievement." "How that must sound."]

Dont let me run away, & let you think that they feel nought but trust in all I do.

26.7.07

I have no doubt that certain elements in me may strike them as rather stupid, & that they think my stuff experimental & *not final*, (but not more than I do) & doubtless bit[s] of it even very ugly. All I know is that their words are ever courteous, & of praise, & that their summed-up reception of me is sunny-warm & delighted.

I am as thankful to them for their kind manners, as I am proud of their enthusiasm. 3 cheers for manners, & knowing how to behave to the young. (that they [rude spawn] may pick up a bit how to rear themselves to the holy old) How we blossom open under the sway of Freedom & the Aristocratic individual!

I forgot to say that I also played "L'isle joieuse" & sea chanties.

Today Grieg showed me [a] lot of male-chorus things of his, folksong settings, etc.

I believe I'll get him to comply with my years-old longing for him to set some of op 66 for chorus, & that Bejer could be got to use the phonograph & bring about a gramophone recording of Norwegian folksingers & fiddlers.

They meet me with open arms, without distrust or doubt of youth.

Please give my love to Karen & say I'm writing tomorrow to her.

Lovingly & fondly yr son
Percy

No letter from you yet; so longing for one

Both Grieg bid me send you their love, and say they're happy to have me.

Goodbye little mum

No, no. I came to see you, not a lot of bloody mountains & ugly folk. Why are they all so coarse, & why aren't you? Or are you maybe? It's such a shocking time since I saw you last, and even if I sit for hours and think about how you look, even so I can't. What shall I do?

After all, anyone like Mrs von Glehn is worth having brought into the world, isn't she? But, really, it seems to me that these folk might just as well be at the bottom of their wretched sea; these heaps of dull looking spiritless creatures are a waste of foodstuffs (& they need such a lot too) But the strawberries & cream are *ravishing*.

I can't get away from your new clothes. It is a completely new Karen for me. I believe you are just as refined & tender & sensitive as can be, & so really dear & worthwhile. But are you? My judgement is really so unreliable, & I make such shocking mistakes; how am I to trust any of my feelings any longer? Why, last night, in a dream, I quoted £20 instead of £25 for an at Home.

But I think I'm really going to give up Scandinavia (as a sort of ideal, I mean) Do you think it's rude of me to say this to you? Excuse me if it is.

Have you got an awful double-chin? Everybody here has.

Troldhaugen. 27.7.07.

But, God, how lovely it is to swim in salt water. I did that yesterday, right out into the fjord and felt quite safe, and warm. Never have I experienced anything so lovely. It is the 1st time I have tried properly since I was able to swim somewhat, and you can imagine I look forward not a little to come out with you in Sv. I hope to arrive about 4th Aug, as I am thinking of leaving here the 2nd.

You can imagine I am happy here; in a *certain* way as completely happy as at all possible.

There are naturally no living (and scarcely any dead) musicians who mean for me what Grieg does, and to get his admiration and to see him carried away and excited about my things is quite intoxicating for me, as you can imagine. It is hard to explain, but it is almost as if I was happier for his sake than for my own. I mean in this way: I have always felt that he had such a boundless, all-loving soul, freedom-loving and appreciative of new ideas, first and foremost. And it would have been a hard blow for my dreams about his personality if he had shown himself strongly limited by his "Zeitgeist" or unaristocratic, lazy-of-understanding about my things.

It is not that I think that my compositions are such that everybody ought to like them, not at all. But I do feel that I am a talent, and I know that I am deeply serious and honest in my attempts and work. And if Grieg had not felt that I really *meant* something with the whole thing, I would have felt depressed about us both. But there is no danger of that. I am so certain that he is completely aware of both my weaknesses and strengths, and that he in any case doesn't *under*value me.

You will already have heard details from mother; what I played to him etc. He was particularly enthusiastic about Wamphray March. Just think! I wouldn't have expected that. (I am not, actually) I row in the fjord every day. One only needs to look around in the house here to make out what an all-loving person the little great man is. There are books in all possible languages, and compositions of all possible *and* impossible composers; and one instinctively guesses with what a gentle hand he has set to work on them all, how eagerly he has wished to take up other points of view from his own, and how good will lies behind his (by no means dull) criticism.

That is my ideal; one who is first and foremost a burning nationalist and firmly locked into his local type, and who stands firmly rooted in his own little ground; but who from there branches out in *all* directions with love and good will and understanding for the most foreign.

I would feel myself to be a blessed person if when I am old, I could be (both through my impersonal art and my own living body) so hope-refreshing and inspiring and freedom-cultivating as this "miniature viking"

Now I must say good-bye, as there is a terrible lot for me to do here; he wants me to translate some old norsk things into English for him, in any case, to try and do it.[35]

All the same I am thinking so much about you, little Karen, and long to hear from you.

We will see each other again really soon

Perks.

35 Grainger was translating the text of Grieg's setting, for solo baritone, strings and two horns, Op. 32, of an old Norwegian folk-poem "Den Bergtekne", from the collections of M. B. Landstad.

123   TO ROGER QUILTER   "Troldhaugen."
28.7.07. midnight.   Hop. Bergen. Norway.

You dearest Rodg.

Words can't describe the concentrated greatness & all-lovingness of the little great man. Out of the toughest Norwegianness, out [of] the most narrow localness, he spreads out a welcoming & greedy mind for all the world's wares. Such a fighter for freedom; so unauthoritive, so unfossilized in his lithsome yieldingness to the young & the new (yet seldom younger or newer than he himself; that's why doubtless.)

So sweetly & fatherly (& isn't he just my compositional forebear — alas I puny generation) he enthuses at my things; Wamphray March in partic.

Here with dear him & darling her I am with nought but what enfires, refreshes, stirs.

I'm Englishing an old Norwegian folkballad for him.

So often & often I'm thinking of how you'd be relishing the hourly showings of the little ½-viking, both for himself, & then again for his great-hearted largesse of sympathy & loving kindness towards your beloved & (you-) beloving Perks.

Such things he says, & such flashing moments, situations blaze by with him.

Weak, & threadbare now almost in his body, & nervously-frail, his brain is yet whiplike, & no health blemishes *really* break his gradually more & more imposing patientness; nor his *good-humoredness*, which however (typically Norwegianly, it seems) never reaches *humorousness*.

All over this dear all-wooden house books in every possible tongue. Such a wide sweep his inquisitiveness takes; all subjects; all standpoints. In *himself* I've no doubt he's got his narrownesses; & by gum, his opinions. But they don't worry him, seemingly; & he's not for the turning on of force, or the driving home of authority.

And such tender respect he has for each & every; me or other spawn.

However Norwegians seem to me pretty toughly ugly; worse (if indeed poss) than Danes.

Soon I'll be down there Sth (where the darling mum already is) hillsong-scoring, & the like

Here I go writing till 2 o'clock in the night.

So Goodnight you darling Rodg; you "one warm grasp of his big ——"

I long to rejoice in news of your dear body's being as healthy & nature-blessed as your cherished compos; gradually of course, patiently bit by bit as I hope to make money.

To get word from you will be the next best to what it would have been to have could have you with us *this year*. There is others.

You know our address
Svinkløv Plantørbolig
Svinkløv. Fjerritslev.
Jylland. Denmark.

Always lovingly
yr sometimes cold
Perks.

It's tinglingly lovely to swim out in the salt fjord just under the house here.

124   TO ROSE GRAINGER   [PM Hop]
Monday. 29.7.07. midday.

This morn Grieg & I have gone thro' the piano Concerto & such a jolly time we had. He allows, & delights in, many of my small alterations, & says he looks forward to Leeds with genuine joy. He says: "De kan gjøre alting" [Danish: "You can do everything"] as regards carrying out his suggestions. Splendid, lovely, all his hints are, & so tenderly offered me. I now ought, for the 1st time, to be able to give some sort of a feelingful voicing of this adorable work.[36]

O, if only I felt stronger nervously, & actual life were not such a dragon to me. After such a morn of trying hard to please the old darling, & being beswat with the bodily graft of it all, it is almost as if my brain leaves me, & I become one bag of quakings, tremblings. I'll be so so glad to leave here, glorious as it all is here. Never one littlest word that isn't tender, sympathetic, & "Schonend" [German: forbearing] from anyone here; surrounded every moment by acts & thoughts loving & deeply deeply considerate, I still creep about in a never ending state of dread & funk. Dread that I might do or say some little careless thing or word to hurt his, or their, feelings, or his health; fear that he will suddenly ask me to show him more of my compositions, & maybe one mightn't please him, or that he'll ask me to play piano pieces of his own (or of others) that I dont know.

In short the wretched evertight strain of wanting to do & be only the best to & for one one loves & reveres beyond fathoming, it's being hardly driven I feel. Now, again, I long for the lonely boat where none know me & no excellence is awaited from me.

This Grieg visit is indeed a glorious, but for my inner self a black, leaf in my life's book.

"Honor & labour
are left behind
     (?)
we shall not find
the world unkind."
                              That is true.

Not that I find the world unkind. It is rather overkind.

But life; the things one passes thro' in one's life-days; it is indeed a grim clutching nightmare.

I open a letter from Greene; it holds some (invisably) threatening request; the risk of being "unfriendlily seen" (& thereby loss of earning) looms at once. Poorness & riches hang in the balance at all hours.[37]

How do I know [that] if I truthfully told Grieg that I loathe Beethoven, & despize foreigners, & in my inner heart long for red war & nameless

36 In May 1919 Grainger prepared an edition of the Grieg Piano Concerto, largely based on his 1907 studies with Grieg and the revisions Grieg was then considering. It was published by G. Schirmer Inc., New York, in spring 1920 as Volume 1399 in Schirmer's Library, and by Edition Peters in autumn 1925.

37 In the context of fixing a date for a duo-recital at Bournemouth in 1908, Harry Plunket Greene had written to Grainger on 22 July, renewing his request for Grainger to arrange some of his "old tunes": "It's an awful thing to let them lie fallow for so long & they'd be a Godsend to me for my Recitals". Rose advised, "Be sure *My Dear Harry*. Do try & please him if pos." (See letter 125.)

brutalities, that he wouldn't cry off my playing the Concerto in Leeds? Loss, at once, of prestige; beside the unmeasurably deeper & never-to-be-got-over missing of his love, & the rare tender poise of now between us old & young.

I quake to open yr beloved letters, (I bodily tremble) that this curious whitish stuff paper (which they say is nowadays cheaply made & may crumble to dust in 50 years) might bear tale of yr being unhappy or less well or unpleased (kindly) with one of my ever unavoidable tactlessnesses, thoughtlessnesses.

I am equally timid of love, of sex; of the slackening results of pleasure; (which I **so** *fondly adore & relish*) & ever threateningly above me hangs the consciousness of folksingers dying daily, hourly, into (by the way barbaricly reached & set-up) awful graves, dragging what *might* be death-less with them into the goneness.

Maybe this ever encroaching fearfilledness of life will do at least the act of defrauding eventual death of that villany that it surely must most flaunt over the most young & the most happy.

In the mean time this all, I suppose, really means nothing, & ought merely to be overlooked, ignored, forgot. In any case, fond & fonded mother, let it be so by you.[38]

"Hey ho the holly, this life is most jolly."

30.7.07. midday.

Last night played Grieg some of the Brahms Sonata. The night before I played him the Bach-Busoni's. He is so sweet & eager for all.

Had a long sweet chat with Mrs Grieg this morn. (just now) She says he said this morn: "We must adopt him." & that She said "Yes, that would please his mother" (ironically) She says he is very fond of me.

The oversetting of "Den bergtekne" is now *almost* licked into shape.

Got yr sweet letter of July 25. I firmly promise to be over-English in my table ways at Svinkløv, both for yr & my own well-feeling. If it was Christian Sandby, he is hardly attractive, fairly good soul.[39] Ah! How I know those hideous Svinkløv evenings with guests. Alas, here, there, England or Australia — the world over — one never *really* gets away from the curse of hospitality. (& Mrs Legge-like pishtush) Of course the *English* are the *only* race; (& blotting paper) but I dont know that I find Elsie superior to foreigners; I'm sure not.

And then how is one to do without such folk as these (really, if the truth be said, quite ugly) Griegs. One can *really talk* to such folk & their heads hold things

"Day unto day uttereth speach & foreigners knowledge; The English like unto a strong man about to run a race; & his going forth is unto the ends of the earth"

Somewhat that wise, it seems to me.

No, *I* am the thing, English & foreign in one. (Only alas! lesser than either)

I have folksongs words here, & *all else needful*; (thanks darling mother) except real peace of mind. But that will come when I reach you on *Sunday next*, at about midnight. My boat is booked to reach Frederikshavn by 2.15 Sunday aftern; thence 4.35 to Aalborg, arriving Aalborg 6.59. Leaving Aalb. 9.20, reaching Fjerritslev 11.24, when the planter should meet me, *or fetch my bags the next morn, in which case I'll walk to Svinkløv Sunday night* arriving about 12.15 midnight.

My position towards foreigners is so simple: Being *well assured* first of my own unshakable Englishness (at Bottom, [the piles, by the way, are neither worse nor well yet]) I get every ounce out of outlanders that I can.

38 Rose had written on this theme, on 25 July, "What a queer creature you are — you must pluck up courage, life is alright, & one like you should not fear anyone at all. With yr genius I could easily face the whole world. Maybe yr life is spent too much with the weaker sex, & unfits you for the struggle with men. I long to see you strong & brave with yr '*Children*' & I feel sure when the right time comes you will be. You are brave with yr playing & so you will be with yr compositions".

39 Rose had written, "Don't laugh at me but when you come here — Don't oh don't put down yr knife & use yr fork with yr right hand. If you do it will finish me! & I shall have to return to England". In the same letter she wrote a small hymn to beauty prompted by the receipt of a photograph of her niece, Elsie (daughter of her brother Charles Aldridge). Kristian Sandby (1868–1962), eldest son of the Sandby family, at that time concert-master in the Royal Orchestra, Copenhagen.

I need them, & I use them, when I can. As indeed England does too, alright.

Only alas! fair bodied England & I both (as outlanders don't) suffer from being at heart mere (or nearly merely) merchants & middlemen.

The time of rejoicing nears.

Goodday, dearie
Perks.

125   TO HARRY PLUNKET GREENE   [Troldhaugen]
["Sketch", n.d. August 1907]

My dear Harry

Thanks for yr letter.

I thoroughly see & appreciate yr point of the much getting up for so little use, & know from my own exper (myself an awful-bad memorizer) how ghastly it is And I deeply feel my wrong in not much earlier in the day having made quite clear the impossibility of my writing out piano accomps. As a matter of fact (when you 1st so encoragingly hatched the idea at Hurstbourne) I very stupidly never thought of the naturally obvious need of written copies or would then have stated my case: for it has been a firm thing with me for the last 8 years never to write piano accomps to folksongs.

I do think there can be *no forgiveness* for one's *ever under any circumstances* writing anything that one is convinced is bad, or is dead against one's convictions. I know from past compromises (such as my arr[ange-ment] for cello & p[iano] of Sc[andinavian] tunes) how badly I feel after such ungenuinenesses, & yet these were only foreign tunes & not the beloved tunes of my own people, which I naturally feel more nearly

Now "vamping" is a different matter; one hardly knows what one plays & in any case, it is not permanent & the exact same horrors are never 2ce repeated.

That you & Gervase should have private copies I could but like; it is not that bit that I mind; it is the existence *at all* of written copies that I cannot face.

Gervase wanted to do the tunes in Germ[any?] but I have had to explain also to him the absurd imposs[ibility] of my written [*sic* writing] any down.

Please do not ask me to write them out.

Nevertheless I altogether see yr point, & will wholly agree & understand, if under the circs, you cannot see your way to getting them up for the 30th Nov; deeply as I shall feel missing the lifegiving interpretation you would bestow [on] them (the longing to hear which was my real reason for falling in with yr kind idea)

On the other hand, shld you do them, I should be overjoyed to "vamp" them for you where & whenever I possibly could; at our B.[ourne]m[outh] show for inst, & anywhere else

126   TO ROSE GRAINGER   [PM Hop]
1.8.07. (early sunny morn)

Such an eve we had of it last night at the Frants Bejer's. Before dinner I played the G min (slow) Scarlatti & after dinner following Program:

Bach-Busoni   D maj Prel & F.
   ,,   ,,   "Wachet auf"
Bach C# min. Prel & F (Das wohlt K1)
Chopin Ab (slow)   Study (2ce)
   ,,   octave   ,,
   ,,   Mazurka in C (Concertina one)
Grieg ⎧ Giböens bruremarsch [Op 72/1] ✓
      ⎪ Jeg gaar i 1000 tanker (op 66) ✓
      ⎪ Møllargutten's bruremarsch [Op 72/8] ✓
      ⎨ Siri dale vise[n], & Det var i min Ungdom (op 66) ✓
      ⎪ Kivlemøyerne [Op 72/16] ✓
      ⎪ I Olla dalom (op 66) (2a) ✓
      ⎩ Røtnamsknut Halling. [Op 72/7] ✓
P.G.   Sussex Carol
        Tiger Tiger
        Morning Song
        Irish Tune.

Bejer is the dearest, hotheartedest soul thinkable; & work[s] one up so. *The words to "I Olla dalom" are one of the top notches of the folk poetry of the* **whole world**. After the music I rowed the 2 Griegs home 'cross the fjord, & then took Mrs Grieg for a row in the ½ dark over the still water, homing at 12 o'clock.

It's getting lovlier every day; for now I see that Grieg never never is going to be touchy or unideal with me, & as they get to know my crack pieces & ask for them its getting as cosy as playing to Rathbone; for now I can sort of float on my back lazily on an already bouyancy. Day before yest he asked me if I'd played in Germ lately. I said No, I didn't want to, if I could get on without it. He said; because I'd like to introduce you there together with me. So I said "Where you are is always Norway; Germ under such condits I'd relish." He said the same day. "You are really unusually talented as a Chopin player: That is *real* Chopin playing."[40]

He likes all just the pieces that I do, & adores Bach, thank God. The other day when I was playing them some music hall tunes Mrs G said: "They are so strange". He answered: *"They are not strange; they are Grainge."* And later: "Everything is beautiful, if noble harmonies are set to it"

Last night he said, after I'd been Slåtting: "The Norwegian Government ought to pay you to present Norway to the world; it would be worth it's while."

He is careful not to praise me too fulsomely, especially my compos; but sudden bursts of enthusiasm will sound forth out of a joy-glowing face. When I struck up a few bars of *Morning Song* he said "Den er skam morsomt; den må jeg få höre igjen" [Danish: "That's really nice; I must hear that again"]. And when I've done he sort of chews happy cud & purrs: "ja, ja;" with little twitches of comfort. It's alright playing to him. The lots of 'em were moisteyed last night when I got off a rather "geglückt" [*sic* beglückt. German: from "beglücken", to make happy] rendition of "I Olla dalom."

Walking down the steep path from Beyer's house to the fjord I was telling him (Grieg) how I couldn't somehow at all realize that it's actually given me to be playing to the birther of them there op 66s that I'd gone carrying about with adoration inside me for the last 8 years. He rounded & said "The joy to me is to hear yr individual renderings of these things. You do some so many things quite different to how I thought them me; but that gladdens me; *when there is real personality*: Then I'm very liberal, very liberal. But if no personality: *No.*" And he shook a threatening stick in the black air. He wont tell me, tho', what the things are that I do other than his intentions.

40 An opinion mirrored in a recent study by James Methuen-Campbell, *Chopin Playing from the Composer to the Present Day* (London, 1981), pp. 225–6: "The Australian Percy Grainger was, both on the evidence of his discs and from the accounts of those who heard him, one of the most original and enlightened interpreters of Chopin . . ."

I want to try roust him, Beyer, & other up to forming a Norwegian Folk Music Soc. Tho' enthusiasts, they're slackers, like all the world, (all of us) more or less.

I had **the** most glorious swim & row yesterday in the fjord. Today ought to be still better. The weather's successfully summering again, & "everything in the garden lovely".

F. Beyer wants me to go into the mountains with him on Friday (for a week) & see the places (& folk) where (& from whom) he got the op 66 tunes. Not this year; next, maybe, with a phonograph. No, this time I'm longing for Svinkløv & you, & the hillsong & leisure to digest & realize all this joy.

Fond love to Mum.

127   TO ROSE GRAINGER

128 TO "KØBENHAVN"
[Original: Danish]
[Appeared in the Copenhagen newspaper *København*, 9 August 1907]
2 Aug., 2 o'cl. at night.

At Grieg's
Troldhaugen

Dear "København"!

I sit here at Grieg's, may I say the lovely Griegs, and think about all the happiness that I — an Australian — have found here in the North: in dear Denmark and in proud Norway. Lovely people, lovely music and beautiful nature. But it is 2 o'clock and I must be quiet. I am so happy, that I am almost afraid my happiness will disturb the house . . . I sit quite alone and write, but my pen flies on so it squeaks over the paper.

I feel so happy here in Troldhaugen, artistically. My powers grow in the shelter of Grieg's genius. We rehearse every day — unforgettable rehearsals — at his Piano Concerto for the performance in Leeds, and when the rehearsal is over we go for a walk, or I row Grieg and Fru Nina far out on the fjord. I have become quite a sportsman. I swim in the fjord that lies just beneath the house here.

In the evenings I play for the Griegs for hours at a time. I play his own wonderful things and a lot of Bach and Brahms and naturally Chopin as well. Grieg so likes our British Folksongs. I have collected a whole lot of them with the help of the phonograph. Grieg is very interested in the phonograph, and next year I am travelling up here again in order to collect songs in the Norwegian dialect, with the help of the phonograph, together with Grieg's good friend Frants Beyer.

But I am composing as well, and when I leave here in a few days — it will be terribly hard to say goodbye to the lovely Griegs and to Troldhaugen — I will have a lot of manuscripts in my suitcase. The remainder of my holiday I will spend in Svinkløv in Jutland, where I will meet my mother, and from there I will leave my beloved Denmark, and it is not at all certain that I will come again in the winter, as my big British tour and the concert in Leeds and so many engagements will take me right away from the North this winter, I am afraid. But I will never forget the Griegs and Troldhaugen and Copenhagen, and all the friends I have found in the land that I always long for, always look forward to visiting.

Now it is late. It is 2 o'clock in the morning.

Percy Grainger.

129 TO EDVARD GRIEG
[Original: Danish/some English)
8.8.07.

Svinkløv. Fjerritslev.
Nordjylland.

Dear Master.

My mother is so very happy for the lovely present from you both; she is writing herself by the same post to dear Mrs Grieg.[41]

Now that I have been permitted to enjoy the indescribably happy time with you, I can really understand a *little* better how your glorious works came to be written. People's works, after all, are *themselves* are they not?

I wonder how Hr Beyer is getting on in the wonderful mountains?

I have already begun to let myself go in writing out folksongs, (English) and have also worked on a score.

The water is glorious here and there is someone to play football with me.

It is no use making an attempt to thank you all for your innumerable kindnesses and goodnesses to me. I do believe, that you saw that I was

41 The *British Australasian*, 12 September 1907, reported that Dr Grieg had sent a "lovely gift of old silver" to Mrs Grainger as a memento of Percy's visit. This is Grainger's last letter to Grieg.

indeed *deeply happy the whole time with you*; but who wouldn't be happy together with you? and that only sounds "American" when I write it like that.

With warm heartiest greetings to you all

Your grateful
Percy.

130   TO JOHAN SVENDSEN   Svinkløv Plantørbolig.
[Original: Danish]   Svinkløv. via Fjerritslev.
4.9.07.   Jutland.

Dear Master

I am so sorry to hear that you have been very ill. I hope you are better again now.

I have been at the dear Griegs', at "Troldhaugen", before travelling here, and have been indescribably well and happy up there.

It was the first time I have been in Norway, and although I didn't have time to see anything properly of the scenery up there, I have nevertheless obtained an immensely strong impression of it all.

Every evening I played some hours for the Griegs and they were so sweet and kind.

Dr Grieg wants me to go to Troldhaugen again next summer and go into the mountains and collect folksongs by the use of the *phonograph* just as I have already done in England with the English songs.

It would be lovely!

I think the Norwegian dialect is such a lovely noble strong language, and I am already looking forward to recording songs in that language.

Now I am shortly going over to London to play; and early in October is the big music festival in Leeds where I am to play Grieg's piano concerto under his own conducting. After that I will be on a big tour until Christmas, and during the whole winter I will be terribly busy. But I do hope that after Christmas I will come to Copenhagen

If only I could play under you!

With the heartiest greetings to your wife and yourself, and thanks for your kindness towards me when I was last in Copenhagen

Your very sincere and admiring
Percy Grainger

Address after Sept. 10. c/o E. L. Robinson. 7 Wigmore St. London. W

131   TO "VORT LAND"   Svinkløv, Jutland,
[Original: Danish]   Denmark
[Extract from the Copenhagen newspaper *Vort Land*, 8.9.07]
4.9.07.

From a letter that we have received from the young Australian Pianist Percy Grainger, who was Grieg's guest at Troldhaugen in the summer, we quote the following:

. . . When I was with him in Troldhaugen, he was so fresh and youthful in spirit, and so full of plans, that in spite of his weakness one could not expect him to die soon.

He talked about composing for a lovely Old Norse folk-poem and about publishing a new volume of folksong arrangements (like Op. 66 and Op. 72) and dedicating it to me. He had moreover the most lovely plans for me, in that he would arrange Norwegian concerts for me in the winter 1908–9 and allow me to play his works in Vienna and other places.

When I was in Troldhaugen he was in the process of revising his piano concerto score on some points. The new arrangement was to be used for the first time at the music festival in Leeds in October, when I was to have played the concerto under his conducting.

I showed him many new French and English compositions, and it was elevating to witness the freedom in his artistic thought-mode, the pleasure he felt in everything nobly new and the love in his criticism. We had lovely, happy rehearsals of his piano concerto, and it was indescribably happy for me to see his admiration for our newly collected English folksongs.

The very last letter I received from Grieg (from Troldhaugen, dated 11.8.07) contains the following about this:

> I have again immersed myself in your folksong treatment, and it is clearer and clearer to me how full of genius it is. You have given a very significant pointer in the direction of how much English folksongs (in my opinion so different from both Scottish and Irish) possess the requirements for being raised to the level of art and thereby make English music independent. It will without doubt be able to form the material basis for a national style, as it has done in other countries, the great culture-countries not excluded.
>
> It has impressed me to see the seriousness and energy with which the English "Folksong society" takes hold of its task. May it continue to get new supplies of strength and enthusiasm to work further at its task! And may also you, in the middle of your rich, and most important activity for your art, be able to set aside time and strength to offer the contribution of your personality.

I also played for Grieg a lot of Faeroese songs, collected by the outstanding Danish collector, Hjalmar Thuren (who is publishing a book in the autumn on these his collection of Faeroese songs), and which he had not previously ever heard the equal of.[42] Grieg was immensely glad at this, for him new, Scandinavian folk-music style.

With kindest regards

Yours very sincerely
Percy Grainger.

132 TO "POLITIKEN"   [Fjerritslev]
[Original: Danish]
[Telegram. Appeared in the Copenhagen newspaper *Politiken*, 5 September 1907]

Yes, the dear master was weak, when I visited him this summer in Troldhaugen. But his spirit was fresh, and he was still taken up with his work and his plans for the future. When the weather permitted, we rowed little trips out on the fjord. But the weather was too harsh for his weak powers. He felt best indoors. There he could sparkle with life and interest, when we rehearsed for the great music festival in Leeds or when he sat in his corner and in his own quiet way developed his plans about new Folksong arrangements. They were hours I will never forget.

Percy Grainger.

42 Hjalmar Thuren (1873–1912), Danish folklorist whose main area of research was the folk music, and particularly the dance-songs, of the Færoe Islands. His *Folkesanger paa Færøerne* was published in Copenhagen in 1908. Grainger had learned of his work through Adela Wodehouse. In 1917 Grainger wrote of Thuren and himself, "Each had what the other lacked. He had education, power of concentration & heroic exactitude in spite of a weak body & (possibly) a somewhat limited emotionalism. I had the inspiration of ignorance, a strong body, & the addition of fearless emotionalism to the instinct for scientific accuracy".

133   TO JOHAN SVENDSEN   Svinkløv. Fjerritslev.
[Original: Danish]   Jutland.
8.9.06.[1907]

Dear Master!

Mr W. Hansen has written to me that you had planned one of the Kapel
Symphony Concerts with me as soloist; but that you now, that the Grieg
Memorial Concert will take place, have asked him to give me the opportunity to play Grieg's piano concerto and possibly the "Slaater" at this
unique occasion.

I thank you from my heart for your *great goodness* towards me.

You can well imagine what it would mean for me to be able to play the
dear great master's works under your conducting at his Copenhagen Memorial Concert!

I just can't comprehend it all! He was, despite weakness, so lively and
fresh in spirit and eager when I was with him such a short time ago; it is
unbelievably terrible!

I enclose herewith a copy of his last letter to me, which is so like his great
kindness and goodness, and which I think will possibly interest you.

I have a tour-engagement in England from the 14th October, but I hope
to be able to slip away from it for a week's time to be able to play at the
Memorial Concert, and the loss of money I will gladly overlook in order
to have the great honour and pleasure of playing at the concert under your
conducting.

I have already written Mr Wilhelm Hansen, and will let him know
further regarding dates, etc.

This letter is only to tell you my great and deep gratefulness for your
goodness and kindness.

With kindest regards to Mrs Svendsen and yourself and all of you

Yours gratefully
Percy Grainger

134   TO FREDERICK DELIUS   Svinkløv. Jutland.
9.9.07.

My dear Delius

Warmest thanks for your kind sympathetic card. Isn't it too sad, darling
sweet little Grieg's death?

I had such an unspeakably happy & uplifting time with them. I left them
about a month ago.

He was always talking of you, affectionately & admiringly, & told me lots
of jolly anecdotes of your trips together in the High Hills.

I showed him Appalachia & played him bits & he studied often in the
score, & was *keenly interested*.

On the very day I got Mrs Grieg's wire telling me of his death I was
planning to write you & convey to you Grieg's delight when I proposed to
him that I'd ask you to send him a score of Appalachia.

3 Cheers re your Brigg Fair work.[43]

Longing see it & you.

In frantic haste, & warm thanks for your friendly sympathy

yrs ever
Percy Grainger
C/o E. L. Robinson, 7 Wigmore St. Lond. W.

Am playing at the 1st Grieg memorial concert in Denmark Friday next[44]

43 On 5 September Delius had
written advising Grainger that he
would be in London on 1 October,
bringing with him his newest
work, ". . . a 'Brigg fair', English
Rhapsody", which was based in
part on the tune Grainger had
collected from Joseph Taylor in
1905/06. Grainger had given
Delius a copy of his own setting of
Brigg Fair (published by Forsyth
in 1906) earlier in their
association. Delius's work,
published by F. E. C. Leuckart,
Leipzig, in 1910, is dedicated to
Grainger.

44 A joint recital with singer Lea
Thorsen at Aalborg on 13
September.

135   TO HJALMAR THUREN[45]
[Original: Danish]
10.9.07.

Svinkløv. pr Fjerritslev.

Dear Mr Thuren.

A thousand hearty thanks for your post-card and letter. I am really touched and proud that you think well of my method of collecting, and that the collection itself can be of service to you.

I was so happy for your kind words.

Isn't it terrible about dear Grieg's death? I can't take it in at all after having seen him so fresh and eager such a short time ago. I had to play and sing to him the Faeroe songs you collected so many many times and he was so extraordinarily happy about them.

He looked forward so much to your book about Faeroe folksongs. I do also, indeed, you know that.

I enclose herewith a cutting from *Vort Land*.

I am in a great hurry; as I have to play in a Grieg memorial Concert in Aalborg next Friday.

Many thanks for your letter and postcard, and with kindest regards

from your very affectionate
Percy Grainger

How I look forward to seeing E. Tang Kristensen's next collection. Can it be bought?

It is awful that you have been ill again! What a horrible summer; it's no wonder!

Address after Thursday. c/o E.L.Robinson/7. Wigmore St London.W.

[45] This was not Grainger's first letter to Thuren, though it is the first that has survived. The two men had corresponded since their first meeting at the Vejlefjord Sanatorium in October 1905, mainly on matters to do with their shared interest in folksong. In July 1907, Grainger had sent Thuren a copy of his hectograph transcriptions of melodies 100–200. Thuren wrote to Grainger on 25 August of his work, "You have carried out your recording with admirable care, yes, I dare to say that I have not come across [any] Folksong recordings where the rhythm is reproduced with such thoroughness as yours. Your work shows on every side the interest and love you have for the matter".

The Graingers were back in London by 16 September, where Grainger plunged into preparations for his performance of the Tchaikovsky Bb minor Piano Concerto under Henry Wood at the Queen's Hall Promenade Concerts on 25 September. Public rehearsals for the Leeds Festival were held in London in early October, Grainger appearing in the afternoon of 3 October. The Festival itself took place from 9–12 October.

Rose had written to Percy at Grieg's, "Jot down anything that would do for papers England or Australia". Ever obedient, Grainger kept a daily diary of "Doings and sayings at Grieg's". But it was Grieg's death that gave Grainger's career its real fillip at this time. The fact that he had been among the last visitors at Troldhaugen, that he had been the recipient of one of Grieg's last letters, and that complimentary to him, that he was engaged for the Leeds Festival at which Grieg had been scheduled to conduct, all these things enhanced his position among young pianists and added to his aura. A translation of Grieg's last letter to Grainger was transcribed by Rose for distribution to the press. It appeared, either complete or in extract, in a number of British papers.

The genuineness of Grainger's feelings for Grieg cannot be denied. Neither can it be denied that Rose, in her practical and methodical way, saw to it that maximum benefit for Percy was derived from Grieg's demise. There is no doubt that the association with Grieg stimulated great interest in Grainger's public appearances in the latter part of 1907.

136   TO KAREN HOLTEN   [PM Chelsea]
[Postcard. PM 17 September 1907]

Am working like a devil to try & make it possible to fit in Copeh. 19.
Oct. *Very hard though.*
   Had glorious X-ing.
   No time for ought else, alas, yet.
   Love to Caj.
   Will lose a shocking lot of money if I come Copeh; but never mind.

137   TO KAREN HOLTEN   26 Coulson St.
[Original: Danish/some phrases English]   [London]
21–22.9.07.

   This letter, little Karen, will set out my present opinion about our relation to one another. I have avoided writing like this to you before, since
I was afraid of exaggerating, either in one direction or the other, and
because the affair between us had not lasted long enough for me to be able
to study it sufficiently to be able to form a judgment on it (to the best of
my ability). But now, when I have just come from the lovely happiness
which being together with you gives me, and have so clearly in mind (as
far as I can) your traits (the sweet ones, and the more forceful); — now
I think the time is suitable for the truest possible statement from my side.
I think it would be a good thing if you keep this letter, since it could be
profitable some time to look up my true opinion from now, and could work
in the direction of justice (or rather "enlightenment") for us both. Herein
I have only put down what I regard, in deep seriousness, as the most
accurate truth I am able to reach. But I do not deny that it is first and
foremost an expression of my conviction of my full right to feel myself
entirely free and independent from you; but I feel in my most abstract
moments that this feeling rests on *true conviction*.
   I hope, most deeply, that you will not think that this statement is lacking
in love and gratitude to you; for I have never had both these feelings for
you more richly than now (but that is not saying, perhaps, much).
   If you ever come to suffer through me, then it must not and will not be
because I have neglected to give you full information about my *average*
feelings for you, and about my true opinion of our relationship.
   In all the letters I have written to you I have given you, free from all
scheming (at least in the last year), my momentary and immediate feelings,
opinions, and moods — even if it was dangerous or selfish to do so; because
I have the unshakable opinion that to cheat you or me of the comfort of
knowing and writing all the devoted, lovely (or the reverse) feelings one has
for each other, would be the most terrible injustice and cruelty to us both.
But this here is something different; it gives the basic; without excitement,
mood, or exaggeration. (as far as possible) Everything that stands here I
have certainly said to you many times when we have talked together; but
when one talks, one chats as well, and says too much or too little.
   But here it stands now, as a kind of Ultimatum; written and enduring.
This declaration of independence is not so much a statement of independence from *you*, (for you have always given me my freedom) as from *moral
duties* towards you. Neither do I regard it as something that it is altogether
necessary to be in opposition to your own conception of our relationship.
What truth there is in this [letter] will certainly respond exactly to the truth
in your views, since that is the same in all cases.
   My main standpoint is, that:
*Since I demand nothing (or ever have) or claim, or want, then no
person has any right to any claim whatsoever on me*

Neither can anyone (so long as my way of acting continues to lack all want, demand and claim as it has done up to now) rightly demand any compensation whatsoever from me for sufferings, loss, or disappointments which arise because their own actions, instincts, and expectations towards me and from me are unsuccessful.

Their sufferings, loss, and disappointments will of course make me sorry, but should not make a claim on my freedom and independence.

In short, no one on account of love to me (or on account of voluntary *un-demanded* acts of love towards me) can expect anything else from me except my free unfettered devoted (according to perhaps poor abilities) love — as long as it lasts.

If anyone comes to me with fresh healthy nourishing "greedy businessman's" instincts, (for which 3 cheers) and doesn't reach the goal, then it is on account of lack of talent, or a faulty appreciation of the chief components of my nature and character. My own understanding of myself is that I would rather not be bought, sold, used, or owned; just as little as I want to buy, sell, use, or own others.

Moreover it must always be remembered in connection with my way of acting; that I do not at all regard an old-maids condition to be in the least less good, desirable, or honourable than a married woman's, and therefore I would never regard it as a wrong against a woman to have helped her to become an old maid.

And that I *do not at all* (absolutely not) *agree* with the way in which the community arranges its sexual and social conditions, and therefore do not regard myself in the least compelled to support, defend or help-forward these conditions; rather I regard it as a moral crime of every-one who enrols in the army of the married, or marriage-inclined people.

[You will certainly think this is utter rubbish; but it is nevertheless most seriously meant and felt on my side]

You yourself say that everything began when you saw me, and "that's him". In all that time I didn't even know what you looked like. The first visual glance I had of you was in the train when you, Herman, and I left Copenhagen; and that was because you were crying — and was fleeting and unthinking.

Then came the uniquely happy time for me in Oakley St. No words (of mine) can say how secretly glad and unconsciously happy that time was for me; to have you and your young body, so sweet and good and clean (and in all that time without the least thought of threatening danger — because I suspected absolutely nothing) under the same roof with me, that was something so new, enlivening, lovely.

But it never entered my mind that you could be anything other than cold towards me. Then I looked a little in your letters up in your room, and their praise of me awakened my conceit and I thought more and better of you from that time. And then my mother once told me that you had expressed sadness at your anxiety that "I would let life pass me by". That was something entirely new for me: "Is there actually any young woman who cares whether I get happiness or not?" For this reason I came out with talk about "pleasure versus happiness", which you regard as only nonsense, but which I still regard as pure truth.

At that time I wanted to know whether there wasn't a trace of masculine "pleasure for pleasure's sake" in you. It is that which men go and long for greatly in women; I don't know whether it is ever found in you — *in its full meaning*.

And then the day came when you were behind my chair and at last I seized you by the arms. That day I silently hoped that you were perhaps a bit of a "flirt", with whom one could have a little bit of harmless and quite superficial pleasure without waking anything deeper. But then I thought; no — dangerous, and perhaps not well done towards her. And then that evening we came home from Legge's, all 3, and you came into mother and said Goodnight, and I thought: "Just think that some lucky (or maybe unlucky) devil will be brave enough to take that sweet thing to himself, & have for his joy;" but it never occurred to me to think of myself as a possible lucky (or unlucky) devil, or even to wish it. Because, as I have said, in all that time I did not have the *least* suspicion that there could be any danger at all of anything deep or serious between us.

That was the beastly thing about me, that I didn't possess the commonest understanding and foresight in and about that sort of thing. I always go and think that everybody has just as little goal, desire, and urge for perfection in the sphere of life as I. (for an easily awakened carnality does not signify anything serious)

And then when you were to travel at Christmas, then I became so very sentimental. (you know how horribly butter-like I am) I felt I would be so forsaken when you took all the pure childlike happiness of Oakley St away with you, and I couldn't help taking your hand in the cab; just as I would have done with Roger in comradeship and unforgivable sentimentality.

⟦And just think, I had never held any woman's hand I was fond of, since my 16th year⟧

But then I got a shock; for I immediately noticed (and for the first time was aware of it) through *your* hand that you meant and felt more than I. For this reason I really became very unhappy when we drove past Chelsea Hospital, because I thought: "Now even that little bit of happiness is over. She is no longer my harmless platonic comrade, and therefore we must part." But when you had left, then I was stupid and weak and forgot the danger again (as I *always* do) and hoped that everything would be as secure and free from danger as it had been. But my greatest and worst foolishness was that I decided to hold your hand when you came with Herman. I looked forward to it profoundly before you came, and thought: "She will see how platonically I mean it, when I do it openly in Herman's presence". And I became very upset when I noticed from Herman that he did not see any particularly platonic significance in it. No less surprised and scared was I when you attacked me in the cab, between Oakley [Street] and Upper Cheyne Row. Then I felt suddenly threatened, helpless, and without any wisdom in face of the way the whole thing was developing. I had not expected it like that. God knows what I — Idiot — had expected?

I must say, when I now review the time up till *we had that talk in Battersea Park, that I realise that I did (*unconsciously*) give you* much *occasion to misunderstand me. But after that talk no more.*

In the days after you kissed me in U.[pper] Cheyne R.[ow] I mostly had the feeling that mad and fateful things were brewing, although there also were moments where I thought that I perhaps had found one who believed in pleasure for pleasure's sake and love for only love's sake. But for the most I doubted it and therefore there came the Battersea Park talk, where I asked you what you expected from the whole thing; that day you were so brave and found Highlanders skin "no good any more." The same evening Herman played in Bournemouth and I strutted about in the studio like a conceited Cock, and mother was so sweet to you; and I blasted off: "I dont need anyone, but I shall always take any pleasure that comes my way, if I can afford it", and you were lying at mother's feet and said; "then take me."

Then Copenhagen came and that amusing; "so that's decided" (which was a revelation for me) and I promised to come to Svinkløv. I was so certain that nothing would happen in Svinkløv that summer, that I didn't take any "apparatus" with me, *although I already had it in London.*

It is the stupidest thing about both mother and me that we don't know how to express ourselves so that we are completely understood. When I asked you to come into me the first night I had not the slightest idea in the world about anything else than that we 2 should chat, and tickle each other, and be terribly happy together without danger. And you must still be able to remember that it was *you* who begged strongly that we shouldn't be like that and forgo everything. For *my own part* I am so heartily thankful that you both begged and persisted.

But what about you?

Yes, from that time you have certainly been a delightful comrade to me, that I never before had imagined the possibility or happiness of. For the 1st time I was able to use the instincts for happiness and fun that I possess, and to realise that there was still swing and untamed values in life. Your pure sweet child-nature, both boy-, animal-, and mother-like.

Never think that you could have awoken better instincts or deeper love in me by acting in any other way.

Your defencelessness, sweetness, devotion and emancipation towards me called forth from the 1st second all the immediate thankfulness, and homage, (respect, honor) and all the (few) best feelings that I (poor me) possess. They are not so very many, unfortunately; are in any case not the *dominant* characteristics in me.

Shortly afterwards I wrote you the apparently unthankful letter about Hans Sachs, and that I did not feel myself Walter-ish. But that was, and is, so true; and I never felt better towards you than when I wrote that.

Gratitude for all the lovely things you did for me brought me little by little to the following conclusion. I thought to myself:

Karen wants to be married to me, although I do not with her. But who knows who is right? Now then for a period I will have no *preconceptions*, and set aside all my normal thoughts on such matters. I will neither decide to marry her sometime, or never to marry her, but will allow all my feelings free play, and give her every chance to get her wish fulfilled, if she can succeed. In that period I will study her closely and see whether her character is good enough viewed in cold blood. But first of all to see whether her sweetness and love won't be able to give birth within me to the urge to be with her always, to marry her. In short; *whether I can fall in love with her.* (This I undertook, although you knew nothing of it)

But I can't fall in love with you, sweet darling little Karen, although I am really very very fond of you, and am happy with you beyond anything, admire you so much and am so thankful to you. I *believe* I can't fall in love any more. But without falling completely in love, a man like me doesn't marry someone who is older than himself, and who doesn't offer great practical advantages. (Possibly, I wouldn't be fond of you at all if you did) I do not mean money, for I *don't at all* wish to marry for money. But what I mean is that after having studied you, I don't think I could rely on you as an engineer, or character-reader, or business-woman, or rely on your help in *purely practical* things. *But it can very well be that I am wrong in this, since my own powers of reading character and of judging other people's capabilities are so untrustworthy.* But that is *my* feeling, all the same.

Neither do I find that your sweetness is reliable against *all* tests. The Alfhild affair has convinced me that you are able to nurture bitterness (and perhaps even a kind of hate) and moreover in a very short time. [Although towards me you have always been inexpressibly sweet]

I cannot use *the least* **continuing** *personal* bitterness or hate against anyone at all in my army.

Further I think you have some urge to own and possess. I think I do not make a mistake when I believe that you hoped that time last summer that Hillsong would perhaps be dedicated to you; (and not that you are very fond of Hillsong) and that you were a little bit disappointed when I said that you should only have the copy. (but that is only so natural; I would myself be just the same) In any case I was very unhappy at what I took to be a little disappointment and grief in your sweet little face.

Then there is the nationality. As friend and comrade your nationality has *a strong* attraction for me; but not as wife. It would make me despair if any child of mine could pronounce a throat-"r". Nonetheless I regard it as impossible that any woman of my own country could give me the happiness and emotional satisfaction, and understand the childishness in me, as well as you; or seem to me so exceptionally pure and dignified as you. *But those lovable qualities of yours will never overcome my strongest and predominant character traits.*

Then there was a time when I believed in the possibility that I would marry you if you got a child, for the sake of both the child and your sweet parents.

But now I realise that that would be unfair to myself

If I was rich or powerful enough to take more responsibilities on my shoulders than I already have, then it would be something different. But the truth is that I am not *all* that strong (not *at all* in strength of character or working power — it is only my brain which is strong) poor me, who am already very overburdened with plans and duties. I think it is completely horrible of everyone, who really knows me and my altogether too many noble endeavours, who wants to give me the smallest additional responsibility. I have my own parents and the many children of my own to fight and earn for, and I am not able to consider particularly your children and parents; however much I would like to if I could.

⟦Good God, when men want to upkeep their children ⟦of art or science⟧ they jolly well have to set-to and earn for them, solidly. Why should women expect *their* children kept up by man's work; and by a poor man at that?

I must say I think that lack of pride scandalous! Let women if they *must have children*, learn to earn for them.

Let women if they *must live with a man*, learn to pay for their part of that life⟧

I am very fond of your family, and would so very much like to see you a happy little mother; but I *can't* and *won't* [do] anything more — unfortunately.

Göthe writes: *"Only the great man knows how to restrict himself"* But I, who am not great, must know it also.

You go the way you go with open eyes and of your own accord (not on any demand of mine) and you must be responsible for your own parents and children.

You know, of course, that, if you got a child, I would support you with money and other help *as much as I could*, and that I am always anxious to help you *negatively* and not to hurt your parents.

With a little bitterness I must declare that I have never had real help from your side in my attempts to avoid the danger of getting children, neither in my efforts to give people nothing to gossip about. You, sweet wild little Karen, have always been the careless one who has tempted me to place us both in danger.

⟦Nevertheless I am thankful to you for *all* your lovable qualities; by no means least for your imprudence and lovely talent for losing yourself in the happenings of the moment. No, I would have been less fond of you if you had been less dangerous and tempting to me.⟧

Now it is for you to be clear about what are your most important qualities and instincts, and what route will best suit your responsibilities towards your deepest feelings and your family (past and future) and relations.

Is your love for me an abstract comradeship with a lovely bright bodily urge to happiness?

Or are there healthy "greedy businessman's" objectives mixed in with the abstract?

Are your feelings for me or for motherhood the more important for you?

Will you rather sacrifice what I regard as the conditions of my life-happiness, or sacrifice what you regard as the conditions of your life-happiness?

If the sentimental — abstract predominates in you (as it does in me) together with an urge to warmth and love, then I don't consider that our affair is wrong or fateful towards you. But if the motherly, and the greedy businesslike, the healthy active nature-loving predominates in you *then I beg you most deeply to give me up and (while it is not too late, and you are still active and attractive) chose a more nature-loving Dane (or other normal man) for whom you will be a necessity and a gain, and who will become a happy father for your children.* You know that you can in any case always rely on my comradely friendship, if you want it, and I will rejoice to see you the happy mother of *another man's children.*

And you know, and must always remember, that I always *will prefer*, and have always preferred, you to give me up and find someone who can better blend his purposes with yours. *Because I can never avoid feeling that nothing good for you will ever come out of our relationship.* **For me it is the most lovely thing that could ever be imagined.** But it is nevertheless not *necessary* for me. And therefore no account should be taken of me.

You have certainly noticed that my love for you has increased substantially in the last year, but on the other hand you must also have been able to notice that my "flag" stands just as high, and yours just as low (which I am not at all happy about, by the way) as at the very beginning, and that you have not made the slightest change in my way of thinking or intentions, although there were, as I have said, many months where I did nothing to defend my instincts and principles against yours.

In the last year I have thought terribly much about you.

⟦From my letters you know just how much or how little I have felt⟧

There have been very many days when I have scarcely thought continually about anything except you, and always with increasing love, admiration and gratitude. But nevertheless, all this is not able, (perhaps unfortunately) and never will be able, to change one's individual mode of thought or seriously change one's principles or action or *born-in-the brain life's plans.*

Now, as always:

I never propose to give up all women, or love to the whole female sex, for love of even the most lovely, sweetest, wildest, bravest woman; never renounce all temptations for a temptation.

It would be so narrow, (petty and narrowminded) and would fit so badly with the hope I entertain of one day achieving in my music a greater freedom and rhythmic boundlessness than there has ever been before.

I hope that you guess how much I have noticed your innumerable sweetnesses this summer. How easily you could have hindered me from doing as much as I did, or have been content with offering me less valuable help than you so great-heartedly did.

No, you were really good; benevolent, motherly to me. Not only did you feel good and warm, but you *thought* also about everything you could do to make me and everything happier and easier. Although I am not gifted in reading character, I am nevertheless an *eager* and *diligent observer* of deeds and *qualities*, and I don't think there were many of the 1000 loving small things and big things, and lovelinesses and pleasantnesses of your sweet nature that I did not more or less notice, and thanked and admired you for inwardly. It was a lovely summer for me; even if I was so ungifted in many directions.[46]

Thursday 26.9.07.

I had very great success last night; though I played neither my best nor my worst.[47] Have seen Roger who looks *very well.*

46 Karen replied, 30 September, "Beloved Percy, *Nothing* is as strong in me as my love for you, personally. I have had a hard fight with myself this time before your letter arrived. I saw the practical side of giving you up, but you cannot believe how terrible it was to realise how it would be afterwards. I would rather die 1000 times; rather anything else in the world than that. Little, beloved true Percy, with all my soul I belong to you. It cannot be in any other way . . ."

47 The *Musical News*, 5 October 1907, observed, "Chief interest on September 25th, was attached to the appearance of Mr Percy Grainger, whose interesting association with the late Edvard Grieg makes him additionally popular just now".

Will you kindly address letters, so that they *arrive* every Friday to Percy Grainger, Poste Restante, Sloane Sq. Post Office. London. S.W. Or let me know if you're going to send one irregularly; or then send it to this adress.

I shall *post* you my next next Wednesday afternoon, poste restante

Please destroy **all** *my post restante* envelopes to you *immeadiately*, before you reach home. *Please* do this *for certain.*

138   TO HERMAN SANDBY   26 Coulson St
[Original: English/Danish]   Sloane Sq. S.W.
4.10.07.

My dear Herm.

I wonder do we meet on the 19th? I hope so. Now I'm off to Leeds. Poor darling little Grieg.

What a free little brave Northerner he was. He spoke **so** interestedly of you while I was at Troldhaugen & was often saying how he regretted you couldn't be there too this summer.

I think I already sent you that bit of a long ago letter of his to me where he wrote of you somewhat as follows: [Danish] "You may tell Sandby that I must be allowed to reckon him as well among my few understanding friends". Or something like that. That letter is now in the bank at the moment. But if you want a copy of it at any time I'll send you a copy.

Everything in his letters stands out in the same pithy concentrated way as all his music does. All he did, said, looked, wrote had such point & distinction, & always brimful of corage & straight-out-ness.

I wonder will you ever happen to feel a wish to do any Scandinavian folkmusic collecting?

My little short visit to Bergen convinced me that in spite of the *huge* folkmusic material still in the North, that it is going *waste & lost far worse even than in England*. Grieg waxed warm over the *total* lack of an enthusiastic, *capable* Scandinavian collector, who was also *eager* & flittig [Danish: diligent] as well.

I have heard from Hjalmar Thuren that what he says is "the very last remaining folksongs in Denmark" have been taken down (*thank God* phonographicly) by that ripping man Evald Tang Kristensen in Jutland. (Hammerum Herred way) But if Denmark is run dry, Norway is yet *far* from it, & by all accounts, almost *any part* of Norway would yield rich stuff.

Grieg was mighty keen on the phonograph. To collect *without* a phonograph (until there's something better) is mad & criminal. If I were a Scandinavian, nothing would hold me back from collecting up what yet remains in *any of the Scandinavian lands*. Even as it is I'm going over to Norway next summer & am going to do a 14 night with a phonograph & a bath-chair to wheel it in; up in Jotunheim[en].

I got from F. Beyer, Grieg's friend, the words of "I Ola Dalom"; (you know that lovely one in op 66) *just think*; not written down or kept or printed. But he *remembered* them still, luckily. I send you them, herewith.

It would be just **too** *gorgeous* if ever you would take a little time now & then & help rake in & preserve the priceless scraps of the folk genius of your soulful races. I wish to God you would once. Thuren says *Norwegian tunes have* **never** *been reliably taken down*.

Do you ever see Hj. Thuren? He's so nice & such a splendid clever abstract enthusiast.

Isnt it fun, that we're both playing with Svendsen in the same season?[48]

Love from
Perks.

48 Herman was engaged for the second symphony concert of the 1907–08 season, on 16 November 1907.

139 TO KAREN HOLTEN   Between London & Leeds
[Original: English/some Danish]
Wednesday, eve. 9.10.07.

Mother is so unexpected and so sweet; she can say so many sweet things about you, not at all the ones one would most expect; I will tell you in Copenhagen.

She would be easier for you to deal with than I, alas!

Never have I *so much* looked forward to meeting you as this trip, (so it *seems* to me) but never have I feared a concert more than the 19th. The conditions are *too appaling*. As my need & fear is out-of-the-way great on this occasion I want to ask you for bigger kinder help even than usual. You know meeting with you causes me the *most frightful* excitement & tension; after which (naturally) follows slump & weakness. I want to ask you not to meet me till *after* the concert; I want to keep the highest point of the trip (the point to which all ones nerves "louden") till *after* my concert, so that I am fresh & unsatisfied untill the playing is all over. If you will do this you will be helping me over a great danger & fear, & maybe to a success. When my last number at the concert is done, come whenever you like. If your father will have me for that short visit, *then* we'll be together. How badly I shall play on the 19th; how awful it all is! Dont come to the concert, dearie, either, if you are afraid. And if I fail, please forgive me. I shall do my best before I leave England & on the 19th in Copenhagen.[49]

Isnt it jolly that dear old Herman is playing at the Svendsen Concert? I have written him a long letter.

What is that book of Selma Lagerlöf's said to be her best; "Jerusalem"? If so, will you please buy it for me *in Swedish*, & also "Byggemester Solnes" both as cheap as poss (the Ibsen *bound* like the other 4 books) I shall pay you in Cope.[50]

I shall be stopping at Hotel Kongen af Danmark. A letter there would find me. Or a letter getting to London (Coulson St) not later than Thursday morn Oct 17 mother could bring me to the station on my way thro London from Scotland to Cope. I shall *send off on Monday Oct 14* a poste restante letter to you.

I keep & keep thinking of our meeting at Aalborg station this summer. Why did that strike so deep? Just that meeting? I was looking merely for a sweetheart, or a dear Gypsy, or a jolly Dane; but I found you so strange & wondrous that day; something *so* rare & lovely & Saint-like & motherly. I suddenly felt like a quite little baby child gathered up into rest & tryghed [Danish: security] & trustfulness. You seemed so wise & superior to me, & I felt I could rely on you & drift along carelessly. I knew so thoroughly how well you wished all for me. That was a dear sweet meeting. I ask again, why does an *enforced restraint* of *showing* feeling go to make the deepest impression on me, often? No one could (or does I'm sure) doubt you are a real dear sweet soul; a splendid comrade. I think that you too are a mixture. But in the main very dear & sweet. You seemed a little like Mrs von Glehn at Aalborg — like her broad calm qualities. How will you seem on the 19th. Dont come to the wretched rehearsal please, I fear it almost worse than the concert. Just tell æten [Danish: the clan], or anyone else, (if they ask why you dont meet or see me all the day of the 19th) that I felt mighty funky about the rehearsal & concert, & wanted to see no one till the trouble was over — for good or bad.

I wonder how all will be after the concert. Will your father let me come back to you? Will our rooms be right, or shall we be lonely, apart, gnashing teeth & cursing God. *Please pray for me*: 12th Leeds, {14th Derby, 15th Aberdeen, 16th Peterhead} (tour).

Mrs Grieg has written me so sweetly again. We will meet on 19th, we are hoping.

Thinking of you, so fearfully always as I do now is a mighty bad thing for my piano career; but who cares? I dont. Nor can I compose either. (or

49 Grainger's engagement for the Memorial Concert for Edvard Grieg given in Copenhagen on 19 October under the baton of Johan Svendsen was an important occasion for him. Not only was it his first engagement with Svendsen, but the event itself was of some consequence with various members of European royal families being present in addition to Mrs Grieg. Despite his apprehensiveness, Grainger scored a major triumph. The Copenhagen newspapers raved. *Politiken*, 20 October 1907, wrote, "At the conductor's desk stood Johan Svendsen, Grieg's old friend, . . . at the piano sat Grainger, Grieg's young friend and pupil, one of the few with whom he came into close contact towards the last, and of whom he thought great things. Grainger played like a young giant; his fingers and wrists were like iron and steel, his brain was clear and clever, but his heart soft as wax. The concerto came to life under his hands and blossomed afresh. It was a great of the first order". In addition to the Concerto, Grainger played two of the Slåtter, Op. 72, Nos. 1 and 7.

50 Selma Ottiliana Lovisa Lagerlöf (1858–1940), Swedish novelist and story writer. Her two-volume novel *Jerusalem* (1901–02) had brought her universal recognition. Ibsen's three-act play *Bygmester Solness* [The Master Builder] was written in 1892.

anyway I dont want to these days & years) I sit down to my day's work & I just play with my unconscious memory, & think of you, & sexual things, till I go to bed.

I think of all sorts of appalling things, things that arent "right" & not good for one to think about, & they make me awfully tired. Goodness, altho' I think so lovingly of you & so much of you, I'm mightily untrue to you in my mind. From loving you I turn to all the other folk I love but haven't met yet, & to all my fleshy schemes, hopes, plans, past & to come. And in amongst all the worst feelings, amid all the rejoicing at immorality, all the yearning for impossible cruelties, amid all the hunger to spy on innocent unknowing folk, amid all the glut & joy over awful crimes (reading of them, & wishing so hard I had seen them done — or had the corage to do them myself) runs love for you, thankfulness for all the fleshiness you feed & foster, thankfulness to you for *at last* (first & only of all my friends of *any kind*) putting pleasure within my hand, *giving* me (**really** *giving* me) something *real* I really like, & making me guess that many awful, lovely, pure, horrid, things may become realities after all; or making me dream they may, anyway.

At one time I thought of you, & of my boy-cruel, criminal, immoral thoughts apart. But then that made me like you less than I do now.

You stood for a *bit* of my life only; a bit at war with other bits. That sort of thing I can manage no longer. I (for the moment, anyway) can think of you as cut off from *no* side of lovingness, fleshiness, pleasure-hunting, in me. You seem (maybe wrongly) akin to all joyeous wild thankful things in me. Maybe you only think me a nasty beast; or will one day. Maybe I do you wrong; or over-, or under-value you & your powers or personalities. Maybe not.

But believe me, all the horrid cruel nasty things I dream are *so splendid*, so devoted, so artistic (how awful it sounds!) so like what folk in **art** call divine, rapt, pure, intense; so that I think it's great sport for my image of little Karen to go mixing about with all these horrors. What do you think? Soon we meet & talk.

I saw a football match for 5 minutes the other day. Have you ever seen Englishmen play football? **Do** the 1st chance you get. Why are they so passionless in their music but **so** *passionate* in their sport? For deeply spendidly passionate they are in their football.

What fun it is knowing you. Or do you hate me, or will you? Do you merely put up with what I like best in myself, & are you planning revenge. Dont answer.

I love no place so much as trains: Especially if they go jolly & fast. They are blended with all my happiest youngest remembrances.

Farewell, you loved lovable dear thing

Percy.

140 TO ROSE GRAINGER   30 Park Square,
[Original: English/Danish]   Leeds.
[Postcard. PM 10 October 1907]
Thursday

Talk about a study in brown — a dream in brown.

We must travel more in the train together, you and I. I am always happiest in the train.

I can scarcely feel *the least* in common with people here, unfortunately. Thanks for your sweet card.

Your brown lad.

141 TO ROSE GRAINGER   30 Park Square,
[Original: Danish/English]   Leeds.
Friday. [PM 11 October 1907]

I must say that I am very disappointed at the chorus here. I don't think
at all that the performances can be regarded as particularly good. I don't
have the feeling that I would ever want to have anything of mine performed
here.

But I really like Mrs H. J. Wood,[51] she is nervous, shy, & upset by
normal healthy mankind just as I am, & I found her very sympathetic
yestereve when I dined with her after our rehearsal   I loved to get your letter
& the one from Mrs Grieg. Now I'm off to be photoed Your Danish is
beginning to be quite fluent

Dear darling Feilding is here feeling about things as I. What a sweet pure
creature. He was more interested in asking & hearing of dear dead Grieg
than in carriage-&-horses matters & the Lord Mayor's willi-nilli. Hardly so
Leeds. He is ever a fresh delight, to be sure.

Really, some of the Yorkshires are "a bit thick".

By the way, let me warn that this is a *dead cold* audience, one recall
being, I think, the limit that I have seen

I went & heard ½ hour of Elgar's The Kingdom this morn. He was so
kind & polite to me yesterday when I met him that I really felt I ought to.[52]

I came in near the end in the middle of a burst & it hit me straight off
that he has real go, & is *really something of a conductor*. He really pulled
climaxes etc out of chorus & band. Yes, talent is, no doubt, the amusing
quality.

Alack! His *composition* didnt strike me as gifted, not really. But he has
real feeling for sound, & that quiet shy man shows real control & fire in
conducting. Under him the chorus sounded quite enticing once more.

I miss my little mum so much, I feel mightly forlorn when like here

fondly
Perks

---

51 Princess Olga Ouroussoff
(Urusov), a soprano, had married
Henry Wood in 1898. She sang a
bracket of Grieg's songs in the
evening concert on Saturday, 12
October, with Grainger
accompanying. She died in 1909.

52 Sir Edward William Elgar
(1857–1934), English composer.
His oratorio *The Kingdom* (1906)
was performed at the morning
concert on Friday, 11 October. In
Leeds, Grainger was staying with
Edmund Ward, a member of the
Executive and General
Committees of the Leeds Festival.

---

*The Ada Crossley Provincial Tour began with a concert at Derby on 14
October. The tour imposed a pattern on Grainger's life which carried
through until the tour ended on 28 March 1908. It brought him some
stability of income and, in its repetitiveness, some release from the nervous
strain that otherwise accompanied his professional life.*

*From time to time Grainger left the tour for some special occasion, such
as the Grieg memorial concerts in Copenhagen (19 October) and London
(23 October). In general, however, the pattern of the tour was always the
same: four or five concerts in different towns on consecutive days then a
couple of days free, either for a return trip to London, a country visit, or
a meeting with Rose.*

*Grainger's contribution to the programme was always the same: one
movement of a violin sonata with the violinist (drawn from a repertoire of
three works, the most often played being the last movement of the Grieg
Sonata Op. 45), and two groups of piano solos (drawn from a repertoire
of ten pieces). It was a light load, and the free time that came with long
train journeys gave him time to do other things: study languages, compose,
formulate his observations of new places and people. His daily letters to
Rose and frequent letters to Karen provide a parallel reflection of his
thoughts and activities.*

*Other members of the touring party, besides his old touring companion
Ada Crossley, were the American soprano Evangeline Florence, English
tenor John Harrison, English baritone Hamilton Earle, and Dutch violinist
Leon Sametini. The accompanist was Samuel Liddle.*

ADA CROSSLEY ENGLISH PROVINCIAL TOUR OUTLINE (1907)

Monday   October 14 Derby
                 15 Aberdeen
                 16 Peterhead
             *17 Barrow   17 PG en route for Denmark, met Rose in London

             *18 Whitehaven   18 PG en route for Denmark, in Hamburg

                                 19 Grieg Memorial Concert, Svendsen conducting, Copenhagen. PG met Karen after concert, returning immediately to London.

                               20 PG en route for London, via Schwerin

             21 Macclesfield
             *22 Oldham   22 PG in London
             *23 Accrington   23 PG at Grieg Memorial Concert, Queen's Hall

             24 Blackburn
             25 Keighley
             28 Loughborough
             30 West Hartlepool
             31 Kendal
   November   1 PG at Lady Bective's, Kirkby Lonsdale
              2 Liverpool   2 PG to London after concert, until 5th

              5 Newcastle
              6 Darlington
              7 Carlisle
              8 Southport
             11 Stockton-on-Tees
             12 Huddersfield
             13 Stockport
             14 St Helens
             16 Cheltenham

                             17 PG at Miss Wedgewood's, Rose also there

             18 Bristol
             19 Bury
            *20 Lancaster   20 PG at Miss Miller's concert, London

             21 Warrington
            *22 Brighton   23–24 PG in London

             25 Folkestone
             26 Tunbridge Wells
             27 York
             28 Leamington
             30 Bournemouth

December 2 Bath
3 Hanley
4 Bolton
5 Walsall
6 Wolverhampton
7 Oxford
*10 Newport   10 PG in Blackheath
11 Reading   11 PG in London
12 Leicester
13 Nottingham [last concert of tour party until
13 January 1908]
*17 Liverpool (Ada Crossley alone, last concert 1907 segment)
18 PG in Bournemouth with
Plunket Greene
19 PG back in London

*Concerts in which PG did not take part

142   TO ROSE GRAINGER   Darleyfields,
[Original: English/Danish]   Derby.
[Postcard]
Monday. 14.10.07. evening.

I had really a ripping reception at tonights concert encores on 4th & 3rd recalls Up to now the tour has cost me only 1 shilling. The piano is not so bad   I believe the Thursday morn is going to be quite safe as we're all of us to sleep in the train that night & the others go in my train as far as Carlisle.
Goodnight my sweet little mother. I love you

Perks

143   TO ROSE GRAINGER   Darleyfields,
[Original: English/Danish]   Derby.
Tuesday morn, 10 o'cl,   [In the train] nearing Dundee.
15.10.07.

Had a lovely night in the train. Everything most comfy & I slept till breakfast this morn. In Aberdeen some of us are thinking of taking a swim in slightly-warmed seawater baths. We're just crossing the Tay, a most glorious sight. A fine broad water.
(breiðfirði) [Faeroese]
(bredfjord) [Danish]
I'm a good deal better take than the fiddle I think, & as good as, if not better than, Ada   John Harrison is very popular.
T' was rather a happygolucky show last night. The piano missed its train & only arrived as the Clays & I turned up at the Hall for the concert & had to be tuned in the ears of the audience. Also they had *every one* of my solos wrong on the program, having Brahms Waltz, Rakoczy, & the 2 Chopin studies. But I just played the others.
I dont find touring as much fun as I used to, or maybe Europe's dull to do it in after the new & naked lands.
I'm sure I'll be quite comfy & contended all this tour, but I dont just revel in the sense of it as formerly.

I like men's talkytalks & tobacco smoke less than I did & I find them so piffling when a crew of them get together.

A bunch of men together used to rather uplift me, I remember; or maybe it was habit, & could recome. But I hope not; for I feel I can work better, & learn more gaelic, & come less out of the needed grooves of my concertlife if I can manage to feel aloof from the (harmlessly) reckless company of "loosed" males.

It would be the biggest boon to me if I can gradually manage to play wildly at concerts, but school myself to calm down immeadiately afterwards. It is that too easily born exitability & exaggerated state that so often follow concerts or any tense effort that make an artist's or any performers life so temp[t]atious. I'm thus glad to feel that touring doesnt seem to be going to work me up as much as it used to.

Little Tillett is with us & is a mighty decent little bugger for a Yed

Don't you think you should write to Copenhagen for the 2nd volume of E. T. Kristensen's Jydske viser?[53] If they *can* be obtained, I think it would be a pity to let the opportunity slip. Try writing a Danish letter to the shop you have the address of, and if you bring it to the station the day after tomorrow, I will correct it for you.

I am looking forward to getting gaelic papers in Aberdeen. I hope they can be obtained there.

I hope I hear from you there also. We have the sea on the right-hand side. It looks mirror smooth.

Farewell little mother.
Perks

53 *Gamle Jyske Folkeviser* [Old Jutish Folksongs] samlede af Folkemunde, især i Hammerum-Herred, Kjøbenhavn, 1876.

---

144   TO ERNEST THESIGER
25.10.1907

Old Bull Hotel,
Blackburn.

My dear Ernest

Ever so ta for your dear letter.

It was quite a jolly concert on Wednesday.[54] A nice Grieg-able real English audience. I wish you could have been there.

I had a glorious time in Copenhagen & many sweet hours with darling Mrs Grieg.

I've just put the finishing touches today to the score of the Wamphray *Ballad* (for chorus & band) that has (alas) lain unfinished for 2 years.

I shall be down in town for moments & fondly hope we may meet then Very keen to see your shipscapes.

I am very much taken up starting to learn Scotch Gaelic

Ever yrs
Perks.

54 Repeating the successful pattern of the 1906 concerts at which Grieg himself had appeared, the directors of the Queen's Hall Orchestra organised two memorial concerts for Grieg in October 1907. At the second, a chamber-music concert in the afternoon of 23 October, Grainger had played the role Grieg had played at the 1906 concert, accompanying the Danish singer Ellen Beck in the performance of some of Grieg's songs, and violinist Adolf Brodsky in the Violin Sonata No. 2, Op. 13, in G. He also played a group of piano solos. At the orchestral concert a week earlier, on 16 October, Johanne Stockmarr had once again played the Piano Concerto.

---

145   TO KAREN HOLTEN
[Original: English/Danish]
28.10.1907.

Kings Head Hotel,
Loughborough.

Oh yes, I know the reward; but I have lost it. You mustn't be angry with me, nor unhappy, not in the least, for you must be so much greater than I in all things of this kind.

Whereas I am stupid & weak, & selfish, it somehow suits you better to be wise & strong & above things.

I don't understand anything. As a rule after I have been naughty I am
so miserable, I could almost kill myself; & then at other times I'm happy
& fresh after. I can't make it out.

As a rule afterwards I love you more than ever, & can think of nothing
else but you, & of how right all with you is, & how wrong without.

But today was quite horrid for me. I had been nasty all day & taking
notice of all girls & women & not thinking nearly as much of you as I
always love to. And afterwards today I felt so exstatic (maybe also because
I've got a new glorious volume of E. T. Kristensen's Jydske folkeviser) &
started thinking of my compositions, & went to the piano at the hall & did
some composing on my unfinished *English Dance* (which is 1 of my very
best works) & felt *so* fit & strong & critical & exited. And then when I'd
done a good bit I came home to dress, I suddenly remembered you & I felt
so nasty towards you; not really, but sort of ½. I thought: "See how well
I can get on without her. I can compose; & feel happy & young & great."

But in my heart I felt angry that I felt so well without you.

But isn't it all queer?

There is something we two have never really talked about, but I think
we have both gone and thought about it sometimes all the same. And that
is, that I have never really composed when I have been together with you.
*And that always seems to me so completely horrible to you, you sweet
thing, beneficent Karen, that it has been like that* **by chance**. *For a thing
like that is* **pure** *chance. And you are the last person to ever hold one back
from work*. And it all seems *so wrong & unjust* to you that it has just
happened to turn out thus. But one mustn't worry in the least about such
things. For they must just right themselves & be let come naturally. Only
I feel you ought to know that I see & feel the seeming *injustice* to you in
the chance of it.

But, you see, even when I turn, as it were, against you; I still want to
write you at once & share my nasty thoughts & my bad conscience with
you. *But if you'd sooner never know of when I've been horrid, just* say
so, & I shan't bother you with my stupidnesses.

But it's fun & hopegiving to feel fresh & compositional again, even from
(or contemporary with) so rotten a cause.

But dont think I dont feel mean & disgusted with myself, or that I've
given up hope to try & be better merely because today I've happened to
get off with a highspirited mood after. For I know the chancyness of these
things, & the *fatalness* of my loathsome weaknesses.

But even then: The great thing for us all is to try & be *splendid strong*
heroic folk, even in spite of weaknesses & wrongnesses. I, personally, cant
worry very much about my evils, because I always feel that the great thing
is not so much to regret the past however horrid, but to buck into the future
with ever-tight energy, hope, thoro'ness. You into your piano & accompanying, & I into mine, & compositions. My fault of late is that I have
wasted too much time on negative virtues & not gone enough for the real
positive stuff that every gifted person *must* look upon as his only excuse
for all the stupid things he probably also is.

My bother is, that by nature I'm such a silly *naturalist*, but by conviction
& head a *would-be* anti-naturalist.

The result is that I never succeed in winning *really against* nature & dont
get the full advantages that come from going *with* nature. Thus it naturally
is beastly hard for me to be away from you; & I spend ½ my strength in
fighting-down feeling missing you & all the joy we have. Therefor I have
so little power left for the things that I'm here in this (in a way quite
marvelous & splendid) world to do. Never mind. Things cant be otherwise
& one *must* try again & win against nature for the time being, & I *must*
simply compose & practise & do all things wonderfully, because it's the
such fun.

And I *must* win against my wretched habits & weaknesses.

Please pray for me too.

And you too must be marvellous, & play so grandly & do every thing 2ce as well as you were intended to. We would both be awful fun if we managed that.

Naturally we shall be *very* serious teacher and pupil when you come over here. It will please me so tremendously if I can help you in the least in that direction. It is brave and charming that you want to give a concert with Arlaud. That makes me really happy.

It is splendid of you.

Mother talks of inviting you over here soon after we get into the new house. That will be Christmas or New Year.

[In the train] near York. 29.10.07. midday.

That swine Sametini is snoring. If ever I snore please smash my eyes with a boot. It is a silly way of breathing.

I have already several days ago written to Hansens asking whether they have sent the circulars out, and as soon as I get a reply, I will let you know, so you can send the critiques straight away.

No, unfortunately, it wouldn't do for you to accompany on a tour like this. I have never heard that they have had a woman as accompanist on tour in England. In any case she would have to be very well regarded and valued in London first, for every good tour is only satisfied with a "star" accompanist. For example; we have Liddle, who is P. Greene's man — an outstanding musician.

Cheapness has practically no role to play in that field, for the singers know that their success depends so much on the accompanist's talent and reliability. Moreover most of the songs are played transposed over here. It seems to me, therefore, that this branch is almost one of the most difficult; particularly for a woman, since it is not the custom to use them for this work at good concerts.

But if one was good *enough*, and could transpose dependably; one could perhaps get to the best concerts, even as a woman; and after that why not also on tour.

But it wouldn't be so amusing because men and women always travel in different parts of the carriages, and then you must remember, that such people as one gets on tour go the whole day and talk scandal about each other, and that one would fall prey to their talent in that direction; than which one could surely imagine something more amusing.

Nor would I personally just particularly relish mixing our glad desires with the drab & depressing slavery of concertlife & wage earning. Altho' every town when they show me to my room at the Hotel I always think: "How just cut out for Karen & me". I cant think [of] a more amusing way of spending money than travelling a bit every day & each night in a fresh room together. A new room is so stimulating & adventurous.

30.10.07.   West Hartlepool. Durham.
[Extract]

This is one of the very most fascinating towns I've seen in Europe.

Last night we didn't have any concert and I went a walk for about three hours, with the sea on the left-hand side and factories on the right.

It looks wonderful in the dark night when the iron smelters blaze up to heaven. It looked like many Valhallas with the Feuerzauber as well. And to the left the good noise of the sea. It is an interesting place, you can imagine.

And then there are so many thin high black chimneys that one can't see at all against the dark sky, but right up in the top glimpses of fire and flames and silver smoke-clouds. It looks so root-less up there in the air, the reddish-yellow pipes.

Iron, and ship-building and such like.

I went close enough to a factory to see a worker fish a large block of iron out of a kiln, golden-coloured by the heat.

Neither is brutality lacking in the population. They take it hard and terribly on the jaw.

Today, despite the pouring rain, I could not refrain from walking 2 hours to the harbour and the shipyards. Everything is built right to the sea, the breakers rush right up to the walls of the factories, and among all the large and richly constructed factory castle-like buildings are the humble simple harbour-folk's houses.

Nothing moves me more than the small simple homes one sees everywhere in the harbours belonging to the white races: sailors' homes, harbour people's houses. Perhaps I remember something like it from my childhood in Austr.

How we could enjoy ourselves in such a town!

Quite unknown, to hire rooms in a little house like that and walk about in the daytime, and look at the factories and factory people (the population is characteristic and full of energy here) and the harbour life.

Thousands of seabirds fly around on the water and in and out of the open wooden harbour buildings.

Do no work for a few days but just trail round & see the shows & tire oneself to death with pleasure if need be. What fun!

See if you dont like R. Feverel.[55] I think it's such a dear human book. Both the female & male types are so movingly shown. Such a dear brave boy life depicted & such a rich fragrance of sweet girl-womanhood. Alas! poor dears . . .

Hope you got my last letter. I forgot to write Poste Restante. My next letter (to Købmagergade) will go from London next Wednesday . . .

55 *The Ordeal of Richard Feverel* by George Meredith, published 1859.

146   TO ROSE GRAINGER
[Original: Danish/English]
midday. 29.10.07

[In the train]
Near York.

We have had a very good day, because it is a long interesting train journey and there is no concert tonight. I have read through nearly the whole of [the] Kristensen book, and there are a lot of good tunes in it; some of them rather Færo-like.

I have also thought more about the English Dance, and also about the "new re-considered and revised edition" of Inuit,[56] and written Roger.

I hope you will not give up the idea of visiting him, for it would surely please him so much, and you likewise.

I hope you wont leave the Menpes's all too soon either, for changes set one up so splendidly if they're long enough.

It's such fun working round an old thing like the English D for there is none of the sweat & strain of a quite new work.

I feel it's *the* way to get big results, to keep pottering over an already finished compos. There's a certain something to Beeth's best effort's & to Wagner's work that couldn't have happed had they not been confirmed potterers.

To bring off a prompting like my E. D. takes a mighty firm hand & lots of overthought. Having to be full of surge & billowiness thro'out, the contrasts have to be got solely thro' exactly gauged strength proportions & color changes & form lengths.

It is a problem that lures me always, & I long to in time get hold of the trustworthy consciousness of orchestral values that is of 1st need for a win here.

56 Grainger's setting of the eight-line verse at the head of Kipling's story "Quiquern" in *The Second Jungle Book* for mixed chorus in six parts dates from May 1902. He had sketched minor alterations to some bars on 20 and 23 September 1907. As published by Schott & Co., London, in 1912, the 1902 setting incorporates these 1907 revisions.

Such a dear little mum as I have.

When we get to W. Hartlepool I'm going to have a nice [*sic*] & think over of the E. D.

Yr loving son
Percy.

147 TO ROSE GRAINGER   Grand Hotel,
30.10.07.   West Hartlepool.

My darling Mother.

Such a jolly Hotel this & such a ripping double helping of appletart last night.

After grub I went alone for about a 3 hours walk, right out into country roads, thicklysown with couples & cabages. The others music-halled.

This West Hartlepool is a grand place. We ought to come here once.

One can walk along on the seafront in the dead dark with the water-roar on one's left & the right uplit with glowing Valhallas. Prächtig ragt der [die] prangende Burg [German: lit. The showy castle stands out magnificently].

Great blocks of factories. Red hot funnels & rearing metal towers flaming in furnace-lowe. And not least wonderful the thin slight high high black smokestacks that cant be seen against the night sky, but which at the top spew red glare & fireshowers & silver ribbons of smoke; like stubborn air-rooted fireworks. And then these factories are what's called in Icelandic "hamrammr":— skin changers. Each glance one casts they're freshly lit or gloomed.

An opened furnace door births a glowing castle out of the black, & a firebreathing stack builds sky battlements without foundations.

And suddenly behind one a miles-off factory, below the horizon, will lighten up ones back like a long lightning.

Iron & steel it seems to be hereabouts.

I got near enough to some works to see them tong out a huge bar of golden-hot metal & trundle it away, & soon one heard a steel hammer giving it socks.

Nor does the lovely brutality of the whole stop at the metal. Here alas, the human would seem to have taken on that spirit thoro' enough too, & mouths filled with violence sweep the streets, & struggle out of the shut windows of drab dwellings.

But it's a rare place, with the Rhein-music, Valhalla, Nifulheim, & Feuerzauber, all turned on in one stunt.

I walked around thinking the English Dance when the strange good sights wern't keeping my mouth open

What an adorable book R. Feverel is, to be sure! Am sending it off today.

Fondest love my dearest mum.

North-Western Hotel in L'pool it'll be

148 TO ROSE GRAINGER   Grand Hotel,
31.10.07.   West Hartlepool.

My own little mum.

Despite pouring rain today I couldnt withstand the temptation for a good old trudge in the docks here & amid the shipping. I've never thoroughly seen a more fascinating town in Europe.

All is built on right down to the shore, so that a factory will actually have a pipe, redhot & flaming, pumping ash & smoke into the very sea itself. And one can step from out of mazes of low ornery decent humble little seaport houses, (wooden lots of them) to straight in front of the quiet Northsea, sulky & grey.

Nothing 'tween here & Denmark or Norway: Able to point in a straight line over open sea to Svinkløv, for inst.

Such an interesting folk, too, here.

Awfully dark, tho', they are. And as they age they [*sic* their] little black eyes sit beadlike berrylike in their sockets, just like Italians.

I fail to note any damning results of factory-life. Thin as birds, most of them, & not overfed looking; tho' they might well be that; for a man tells me these steel works workingmen'll often draw £8, £9 a week. They work a week, & then rest for 2. The work, all say, is the hardest in England.

And the folk have just the nice hall-mark of the ideal condition; plenty of both holiday & overwork.

Nice & independant & dont-care they seem, too.

Here's where we should put in a holidaylet, when there's more money.

It'd be so ideal to hire a room in one of those sailor-manlike looking dull respectable little homelets, all near to the railway yards, & the ocean, & swing bridges, & the docks unloading wooden cargos from Norway. And factory smoke & sea air & drizzling rain driven enveiling over all views.

Great many-storied unloading docks of wooden stakes & big baulks stacked round the harbor, & thousands of sea fowl flying in & out & swarming onto the water.

I did some work on the English Dance amidst all this & also did myself the luxury of a thinkover & play thro of some of my latest-done things — Hillsongs, Wamphray, Soldier, soldier, etc.

What stunning programs one could make already of my finished compos.

Think of The English Dance, Wamphray Ballad, Hillsong, The Seawife, Old Irish, Lincs Marching Tune, I'm 17, Green Bushes in one concert; & what chamber-concerts one could give. The Inuit, The bitter Karella, Soldier, Soldier, Molly on the Shore, The twa Korbies, Tiger Tiger, Morning-Song, Lord Maxwell's good night, Færoe tunes, Seachanties. etc.

It is, however, in room-music that I have least started to realize my ideals.

I believe a seaport town is almost even more balm to me than the country or seaside. I cant think of ought more soothing than a tucked away unknown life in the clean but humble parts of such a place as this.

When we have our ship, that'll be the thing! To creep into such a harbor, & tuck up for night nigh all the blend of squallor & wholesomeness that such ports have. Sailors & seatowns have always something tender for me. I think of Polly Olivers & the rich Merchants daughter straight away.

There is even something tender & lad-like in the sailor coarseness; somehow.

Fond love from yr loving son.

149   TO ROSE GRAINGER   Lunefield,
1.11.07.   Kirkby Lonsdale.

How after my heart aristocratic England is, to be sure. And how pure
& unsullied a house is without men! No stuffy smokiness, no rank habits,
above all; no barmaid chatter.

> "I know your simple retiring artistic temperaments,
>   quite content with the best of everything"

Me every time.

I had a *most* bracing 15 mile motor drive, in an open car, hither from
Kendal last night, & jolly supper on reaching. Lady B still up for me, &
ever so sweet & welcoming.[57] Then I, like a stupid, read in my room till
1.30; I fool. But a book there was not putawayable. Called: "The Madness
of Genius" A scientific going into of the nervous conditions of geniuses &
their kin, past & to come; by *Nisbit*.[58]

By his making out, not *one*, seemingly, of the great men of any land &
any craft (soldiers, statesmen, musicians, painters, churchmen,
businessmen, artists, a.s.o.) but was nervously disordered & of undeniably
tainted stock. His citings look convincingly, & are, at least, (to me) enthralling reading.

Poor old Bach, too; every Jack 1 of the composers; Wagner, & Beeth,
etc. etc. And I can easily guess how Grieg, with his later-days
hullucinations, & such, would come into the fold.

Goodness knows what I'd've been by now, without I'd lived with yr care,
darling; & not only care, but sweetening influence & dear fresh strain. I
think, too, in me there is a *certain little* pucker of cronkness, but I feel as
if yr fondness & the bias you've guv any whole trend, has wheedled it into
harmless channels.

However I dont really feel there's ought really *mad* to me *at all*. I'm
really sane, but maybe not a genius?!

Such a heartlifting view out of this window. The Lune scuttling along
in the hollow below & above hill billows, of a breadth & flow quite ownish
of this rarely big-spirited district.

Real comfort in a home like this.

Such dear gentlemanly servers
["Herr Ole han tjente i Kongens gård" sort.
[Danish: Herr Ole he served at the King's Court"]]
a bit of a diff to the pimply tip-bags at Hotels.

I like the seasoned-woodishness of the human caste of the aristocratic
wheeze. Most (it seems to me) from the artistocrat (of now's types) will the
future Socialist have to learn. The aristocrat is noways final (nought is,
thank God) but he is balm & a refuge. Just the thing for me, *every now
& then*. And such shoals of books as are here!

And such a deep wide bath, with a real live amount of hot water, & a
fire in the bathroom; & 4 wholly different soaps in an ample soap dish. I
love that civilisation that runs to baths.

I had a real good cleanup this morn; took a full hour over my hot bath,
washed my hair, & scrubed much skin & some dirt off my legs, which I
always feel "leave to desire".

I am now clad wholly in brown, with my new shirt.

No doubt, a lot of the money (not such tons of it, either) in this house
is wellspent.

Yes, lovey, I have all Monday with you too; isn't it larx? *Please cram
it right up to the brim with pups* [pupils]. I've fresh as anything &:

> *"anything for money
> an' we're growin' old"*

I do hope a lot can turn up on Monday.

57 Grainger was guest at the country house of Lady Alice Maria (d. 1928), Countess of Bective. She was a widow and her only surviving daughter was married at this time. She had known Grainger since late 1901 or early 1902 and was a generous friend and patron.

58 J. F. Nisbet, *The Insanity of Genius, and the general inequality of human faculty, physiologically considered*, London, 1891.

Have answered all letters & sent M. V. White's to Whelpdale, with a note.[59]

Lady B. is so sweet.

Fondly & lovingly
yr son.

Yes! We're a thoro'ly satisfactory & joyeous couple.
Quite great at that if at nought else.

[59] Maud Valérie White (1855–1937), English composer and writer. Grainger had assisted at the recital of her songs, which she presented at Bechstein Hall on 2 December 1905.

150 TO ROSE GRAINGER
7.11.07. 10.30. eve

Country & Station Hotel,
Carlisle.

Got the waistcoat alright. Thanks.
Was having a talk with Liddle this eve.
He says he doesnt think an accompanist can possibly earn more than about £500 a year; he cant.
And he never tries to save.
Has at the most £80 in the bank. Yet he has wife, 2 children, wholly dependant on him, & a sister ½ so. Arent folk queersticks? The tour costs him at least £7 the week, for he likes wine, etc.
Ada treated Sametini & me to appledumplings, brought into the train in a basket, this midday. He ate 1, I 6.
Done a good lump of scoring of Karela,[60] & a bit at E. D. One is happy any old place if one can only compose a scrap. I'm so sleepy. The concert went well.
Earle says he has shocking debts; Sametini has some. Goodnight.

Night before last I dreamt Grieg was so loving & caressing to me, & last night I dreamt Busoni said: "Yes, now that Grieg's dead, & I can overlook his whole life's work, I can see that he is a genius after all."
I fear Busoni wldnt say it tho'.

[60] Between 5 and 13 November 1907, Grainger revised *Mowgli's Song Against People*, his setting, for mixed chorus and instruments, of a five-stanza verse from Kipling's *Second Jungle Book*. The first setting dates from 1903. "The bitter Karela" is a phrase from the Kipling verse.

151 TO KAREN HOLTEN
Sat. 9.11.07.

[In the train?]

One thing I must say, one does get glorious train-travelling in England. Day after day we rush along hours-long at huge speeds, & 2 & 3 hours without a stop often. And the tracks are so well laid & the running so smooth.
I cant dislike my fellow tourists as much now as at the start. If one's thrown with folk it's hard not to strike the humanity of them sooner or later. Whenever I'm with men I become so stupidly coarse in my speech. I get to swear so much (alas) & I also talk in a silly impure & rough way about things. But with men or boys I always feel a genuine yearning to behave in this tiresome & revolting way.
It does no harm, of course; but it is so weak of me. Whoever I am with alters me so shockingly. Not really, of course, but on the surface.
How thankful I am that I grew up without much life with men, & got my *habits* & *manners* of life different to theirs. For now, with my personality formed, things lose the most part of their danger.
Men could never deeply interest me or hold me, now, I fondly trust, altho' I must like them They are often kindhearted & wellmeaning & I have learned things from the chaps on this tour that you & I can be thankful to know.

You & I haven't, in some ways, been ½ careful enough. My fault, thro' ignorance, of course. Dearie, do let me feel that you will really help me to be careful, *as much as need be.*

Or dont bother; just as you like — & then I'll have to look out hard. You must *always* do *just* what you want.

I'm getting on fine on the tour, & good notices everywhere, & glorious now & then.

I've done a fine lot of scoring & some Gaelic these last few days. I always work a bit after concerts. I come home alone & get myself a bit tired before bedding, as that lessens temptations. I go in for careful & long baths, & try not to overeat. I dont think I'm fatter, & I feel sure the travelling & easy life is ripping for my health. I dont feel so lonely (for I'm doing more work that fascinates me) or lowspirited as at the beginning of the tour, but am glad it'll be over by before Yule.

A short tour is good for one's body & freshens up one's working-powers but a long tour makes merely a rank pig of one, wasting one's best gifts & qualities. But this is just right. I've never done as much serious work before, when on such a trip. That makes me happy, naturally.

152   TO ROSE GRAINGER   Queen's Hotel,
11.11.1907.   Stockton-on-Tees.

Darling one

I finished roughscoring all the instrumental accompaniment to The bitter Karela in the train coming up here. And after arrival worked at the new Chopin in the hall.

I had a whole fruit pie for my meal an hour ago. I must own I'm nearly distroyed with tummy fulness.

This is only a linelet to let you know I got safely, as I must rush to be ready for the concert; & they've no late eve post from here.

Found some awfully delightful viser in the Kristensen volume I've got along this time.

Remind me to show you once *Jon Rimaardsens Sejlads* a seafaring ballad with the jolly refrain *Men søen hun tager saa mangen* (But the sea she takes so many)

Love from Ada.

Ever detoved [*sic*] & lovingly
son Perks.

153   TO ROSE GRAINGER   Queen's Hotel,
12.11.1907.   Stockton-on-Tees.

My dearest little mum.

How can the little mum doubt at all that I am fond of, & "respect" (as the funny term goes) women?

I always feel the Goethe lines (Das ewig weibliche zieht uns hinan) [German: The eternal feminine leads us onwards. *Faust.*] not merely as a clever & striking phrase, but each word earnestly as a voicing of my every hourly experience.

Not that I can help liking men too, in a light sort of way. But I feel they are merely a tuning-up, & that the real stuff begins only with the advent of woman, young, old, or middle-aged.

Men can only be of serious fascination to me when I feel that they are deeply stirred by the splendor & superiority of women & more or less eagor to further her (in most cases) more sensible & genuine yearnings.

The particular element I worship never lessens with age, & its appreciation on my part isnt greatly stimulated by youth, beauty, & bodiliness; tho' naturally these things (equally in man & woman) are adorable for their own sakes.

Unluckily, I find it hardest to respond to those particular points of womanliness which Mrses Batten & Lowrey have in common, altho' I have admired, & been moved by, its presence even in them.

Since (to my mind) *inspiration* is more man's game & *accomplishment* woman's, [it] is seen easily why talents & great-doers have often much of the woman, or have at least picked up more her methods than man's. That is why big men are so usually fine-mothered. Think of the overwhelming bias of a sympathetic or not mother. A love-awakening inward-diving mother focuses duty, care, purity, hard work, rationalness (more or less the womanly bents) attractively to a son; whereas its easy enough for a less gifted one (mother) to present these qualities in all their own true native dourness & grimness. Yet what gifted-man can grow to deeds if he doesnt early pick up the trick of seeing the tiresome "ways & means" of the world (& equally so of art, science, religion, etc) fairer & idealer than the male vision can manage wholly on its own.

Of course, no woman-worshipper can ever be a successful womanizer. For the basis of the last *must* surely be shut eyes to the "victims" womanliness; for womanliness cant get up much enthusiasm for ought that is random, purposeless, thoughtless.

No amount of mere bodily livliness would, I *think*, outplay the *consciousness* fostered in man by woman's best. How could I, for instance, act *wholly manishly* to any of these Hotel womenfolk when I either see in them the revolt (of the same elements that I love in you) at man's tiresome boorishness & destructiveness, or am chilled (knowing better in you) at the weaker one's poverty of revolt?

No, I personally have only one little quarrel-let with woman; & that is her slight tendency to switch off the fun & on with duty, to shorten the holiday & lengthen the working year; but that I know full well she's bound to do because of man's being such a eel-like shirker, slacker, & put-offer. On this one little pointlet I shall always when I feel strong enough put up my meek manly fight; & shall, when successful, make out my program ½ an hour later than the alerter womanly mind (rightly) would dictate. All along the line (performing compos, marriage, having kids,) the same old Hastings! If I *ever do* feel any or all of these 3 as a **duty** (at present I in all truth feel **solely & only** the 1st) I shall make my pigheaded stubborn stand each time to try & turn the Monday into a second Sunday.

But otherwise; all I've learnt from the fondest, my lovable, & most womanly (in spite of all versitility) of darling mothers holds good, & leaves me not quite so a larrikin as its unmothered man's doom to be!

Fondest love.

154   TO KAREN HOLTEN   [In the train]
[Original: alternates Danish/English]
12.11.07.
[Extracts]

I'm learning Chopin's C min Study op 25 No 12; it is the easiest of all his Etudes I think, and one of the greatest and loveliest. I wonder whether it wouldn't suit you? I learnt it by heart on Sunday by playing it *only twice*.

Usually I do not learn so quickly. I wrote a lot of scores last night after the concert.

I also used to be much frightened of dark stairways, and such-like, but am not so any more. The more one feels love towards people and eagerness in work [the more] one obtains security. It is emptiness and slackness that makes one so afraid. Apart from this, fleshliness* has an unbelievable nerve-strengthening and steadying effect on one, it seems to me.

It's too splendid, how everywhere in England, midst all the want, smoke, brutality one sees human bodily lovliness blossoming out. What a beautiful race. I love the thin un-coarse look of many of the Northern under-fed poor. Too little animalness certainly makes folk look prettier than too much, tho' maybe not so sympathetic at once.

It is hard for me to realize that I am on tour and that I am nevertheless living such a negative and unfleshly life as I am doing, since I have always been used to associate travel life with the opposite. It is new for me, but inexpressibly more pleasurable and happy. Moreover I have never before worked so much on a tour, and that alone is of course a great satisfaction.

13.11.07.   Huddersfield.

I am worth nothing. I have "fallen" again. I can manage a week, and then I seem to lose my head. Forgive me.

Obviously it harms me scarcely at all when it happens so seldom, but that's not the point. In all this time I ought to be saving up a simple overflooding of energy & un-used-up-ness.

But really it was a hard case last night. *For I found in the* supplement of Kr's book a variant of the frightful cruel folkpoem, & this was too much for me. Then also Huddersfield is a town I have longed for years to succeed in, & I made a great effort last night & did well, but, of course, felt very worked-up afterwards, & yet too tired-out to settle down to other work at 10 o'cl at night. But still there is no excuse at all, I know full well. Poor I.

When the day is over and I have locked the door on the outside world and have gone clean-washed to my bed, then it is so lovely for me to read your last letter for some few minutes. How thankful one should be for the post-office!

Can you remember the peculiar lovely warm smell when we two sleep in bed together. When I was cold this morning I got right under the bed-clothes and it reminded me of it.

It is so sweet the way an absolutely clean body can smell. But *how* frightful mustn't carnality be amongst people who don't take cleanliness too seriously? . . .

Poor *ordinary* people! How "restricted" they are! When I, as now, come a little more among the more ordinary people, I can see how fortunate we are. Most men must be satisfied with so little (in quality, I mean) and their demands are so touchingly little. But how they waste hours waiting for, and chatting with, and "flirting" with women, to get nothing out of it in the end — or no good thing. And the poor women; for them it is surely many times worse. Their association with these horrible men can scarcely be anything except an everlasting tedious struggle; and if they are on occasion gifted and nature-loving and surrender themselves, how completely without support they must feel against these "seducers".

I can often see in the women who serve in Hotels etc. how tedious everything appears to them, and I cannot understand that all men do not notice it too, and that it can amuse them to continue bothering these tired women, who only keep a more or less friendly appearance because they must earn their bread.

*Danish: Kødfolklighed. See translator's note.

But we are secure and devoted to each other (aren't we?) despite the "great fight" we wage, and all the fluttering flags and battle banners?

Dont forget that any such pieces as Chopin's A♭ Prelude, or that type, I can teach you to play quite as well as I do (such as that "well" is) We have never yet really learnt & taught properly, we 2. *But let us*. There is no reason why you shouldnt develop a truly big & thoro'ly reliable technique. Why not?

Success and perseverance are so glorious. They clothe one so well . . .

155 TO ROSE GRAINGER
15.11.1907. aftern

Midland Hotel,
Manchester.

Darling Mum

I've stayed on later than the others here (St Helens [*Lancs*] being but 30 ms run) to take in the Hallé concert rehearsal. I had a few words with Richter, & a chat this morn with Forsyth, at whose shop I worked all [the morn on] it.

Richter rehearsed Heldenleben & I've just this mo come here from hearing it to write you a line before catching my train.

I feel that Strauss has deep gifts as an "ender". After the storm & fuss he knows how to float along on a calming flood "som ingen anden" [Danish: like no one else]. Then, too, he seems to me to have wondrously caught the note of the drowsy buzz that there can be in nature; water rushing seethingly over a weir, bees humming, and so on. That rather soothing earfilling unending sensation he gives one well & often in the quieting-down parts after his turmoils. Lovely such in D. Juan, lots of it in Heldenleben, also in Don Qxote; & even moments in Domestica. They are, no doubt, usually quite conventional in line & texture, but his lengths are ownish & himself somehow — in lengths he is a master. But how I wish I could like him more in the "meat" of his work. I positively blush (fellow composerly) for the emptiness of his outbursts & the cheapness & unsuggestiveness of for inst the "fight" in Heldenleben. I wish he wouldnt. But *how* I wish I had his long dreamy dignified endings. He must have robust soulfulness tucked away somewhere to get off such calming downs. (so full of über- & rück-blick [German: over-and-backward-looking], Lordly)

But I cant forget Meridith on "the manners of energy" when I hear his businesslike sallies & pushful scoring.

I've got all your letters alright dearie.

How sweet it will be to be with you these coming days. I still feel "mothered" & sweetened even this Thursday from the balm of last weekend. After man-ing it for days I feel the most definite need of your be-holying touch "for her blessing on their head".

"For whether they lose to the naked life
or win to their hearth's [*sic*] desire
they tell it all to the (the rest doesnt fit) [from Kipling's poem "The Sea-Wife" in *The Seven Seas*]

There isn't much the unweary unwife doesnt get to know; is there?

Stockport's 7 or 8 miles from here. Ada & Florence carriaged it thither & hither last night.

I tried to race them back on foot on the home trip; but I *failed* disgracefully, & felt Oh so degraded & old & disgraced. My thick overcoat & muffler, etc were too much for me, & when I tried to get them off all my pocketbooks etc plumped out onto the road & when I'd gathered them & shipshaped things the carriage was out of sight.

So I tramed it back, had an hours hot wash on getting here & then a nice read thro' of yr Stockton letter, which I had wisely refrained reading until washedly in bed.

I enjoyed the evening much thus.

Miss Alice Liebmann came round artist's room last night.

Shall attend to all letters next town.

What do I pay 2/ a day more for at such an old Germania as this hateful Hotel but to have penny-sized pifflingnesses foreignwaitered-off onto me stead of solid applepie lunch & dinner?

Remind me to tell you of an amusing Irish servant at Huddersfield. Truly, uncommercial races such as the Irish seem the only sort left to have any wealth of pride or purity.

I realized how after all I've got fond of certain traits in poor Mrs Lowrey on seeing akin ones there (H-field) displayed.

I believe I'd **love** lots of the Irish in Ireland. They seem a trifle less cowardly & herdlike; tho' 3 cheers for herdishness, all the same.

Now I must hurry.

Yr fond Perks

156   TO KAREN HOLTEN   Royal Hotel,
[Original: English/Danish]   Bristol.
Monday evening. 18.11.07.
[Extracts]

You little Karen.

(There is no one in the world
   that my mind dwells on more,
Than her, little Karen, and her I cannot get)

Not at once. Tonight. Yet.
What does it mean: *det limrer?* (det limrer over heden.)

Oh dear, it was an amusing weekend. Lady Elcho had to go away unexpectedly and so mother and I stayed with a dear old maid, Miss Wedgewood, a good friend of von Glehns, Sargents, etc.[61] She and Lady Elcho had collected some words for me and the whole of Sunday we 3 were out after f.songs; and with great success. In the morning we visited an old woman who sang 2 fairly good songs, and in the afternoon 4 men came there to her house (Wedgewood's) and 2 of them were good; and give me hope about the district. (Gloucestershire) Mother has wanted to collect as well for a long time, and here is a good place for her. Miss Wedgewood can begin first (fertilising the soil) and mother can come with the phonograph and pluck the flowers. I got altogether 8–9 songs, of which 2 were really good, and another an interesting variant of "Gr Bushes". It is really a remarkable feeling, after one has composed so long around a melody like this (and has ½ come to think of it as one's own) to hear it in the mouth of such an amusing old man!

The farmers here in the West seem to be much cleaner than they are in Lincs. There in the East they are so poor, the poor things.

I wonder whether I will come to Svinkløv this year. It is not because I have just collected 2 or 3 songs that I am doubtful about it, but the last few days have reminded me to remember to *tell* you, what I have been thinking of for some time. I would rather not decide *yet* either for or against Svinkløv, but I can already see how difficult it will be to combine it with my other plans. If Sv.kløv cannot be managed this year, I will ask

61 Lady Mary Constance Elcho (*née* Wyndham) (1861–1937). In 1883 she had married Hugo Richard, Viscount Elcho, fourth son of the tenth Earl of Wemyss. She was a member of the literary group known as "The Souls". On 17 November 1907 Grainger noted two tunes from Mrs Mary Hawker, and three each from Mr William Newman and Mr John Collett (melodies 314–321 in his *Collection of English Folksongs*). This was his first collecting expedition to Gloucestershire. With Eliza Wedgewood's assistance, he was to collect some sixty-four tunes and words in Gloucestershire between this and his last trip, 31 July 1909. (See letter 267.)

you to come over to us instead of me going there; for in that way I hope that we will be able to be longer together than it would be possible in Sv.kl. this year. As I gave up all f. songs last year I must make up for it this year, & compositions will possibly have to suffer.

I must have *at least* a fortnight in the hills in Norway, & *at least* a week with Fru Grieg, & a fortnight in Lincs, if not more.

And theres over a month gone.

Or I *might* do Lincs earlier; in the spring. But I cant tell. But at any rate f. songs must come before composition & holidaying *this* year; but not before you, if you dont mind. You are too attractive. But equally so in Denmark, or London, or English country; I trust.

So that even if the best heat of the summer didnt get spent together, we could have our time either before or after it. Couldn't we? I only write thus, so that you feel no disappointment if Sv. doesn't come off this summer. Nothing is fixed, & I've not talked the summer over with mother yet, & found out her yearnings. I'm for London, because books, & museums, & hektographs, & everything is nearer & better at hand . . .

With regard to riding.

I think that if you want to ride like a woman (sidesaddle) you certainly ought to, & that it would be very wrong of me to try & get you to do the other (a fad of mine) as a favor & kindness to me. Nevertheless; taking to sidesaddle would be a colapse & a come-down for you rather, & if you really do so I shall have to acknowledge the Danish standard a good way below the Australian.

It is a degrading thought to me that *either* woman or man *has* to do a thing in [a] certain way (sexual things of course excepted) & cant change about. I like the man who can sew & the girl who rides like a man. What does it matter if it hurts your ‖dear little‖ body? Who cares? ‖I do‖ But one *simply mustn't* be soft. Nothing, for instance, could be more splendid than that you & I hence forward should have to be for ever but "brother & sister" because you destroyed yourself riding! I love to think of women being hurt.

I dont mind softness in a man; but it's no use in a woman. (Not that you are)

157   TO ROGER QUILTER   Travelling.
[Original: Danish]
21.11.07.

There is a little misprint in one of your newly-published Choruses, page 8, 2nd last bar, soprano part, on syllable "est" of "supremest".[62]

Your new songs are really lovely. The very last one I couldn't hear as I had to practise for my second solo, unfortunately. You have surely never written anything more completely inspired than No 3. That must be counted among the world's most lovely and most necessary songs.

I am so glad that mother will be with you, next week.

I am looking forward to hearing Appalachia tomorrow.

He, Delius, is such a remarkable mixture of talent and apparent lack-of-talent, I can't understand him properly. I think he is in any case a great harmonic talent, but his form appears to me often completely crazy.

Last week, when I was in M'chester I listened to a Richter rehearsal of Heldenleben. I can't, unfortunately, find it very good (although I can quite understand what Cyril means about the charm in his rapid 6ths high up in the strings) with the exception of all his endings which seem to me magnificent. He understands how to make them *long enough*, and he understands to get a lingering peace over them which is characteristic and peculiar (it seems to me) and enchanting.

62 Quilter's *Five Lyrics of Robert Herrick*, for mixed chorus, published by Forsyth Bros., London, are dedicated to Grainger, whose inscribed copy is dated 1 November 1907. At Edith Miller's concert on 20 November, Quilter's *Four Songs of Sorrow*, settings of poems by Ernest Dowson, had received their first performance, Quilter himself accompanying. Immediately after, Grainger played two of his arrangements of Stanford's *Irish Dances*.

In other words, he has a sense for dimensions (and their *physical* effect) even if he lacks form-talent.

I have found a gloriously *cruel* Danish song, that I am grateful to God for. Cruelty has a deeper sensual attraction for me than anything else in the world.

It deals with a poor maiden (a King's sister) with whom the Queen is angry. This maiden gets a child secretly. She (the maiden) is brought to the castle, and she doesn't want to let them notice that she is weak after the birth. So:

[There follow nine of the couplets of the song "Little Kirsten" that Grainger refers to often.]

158   TO KAREN HOLTEN   London.
[Original: Danish/English]
23.11.07.

Yes, last night was good fun; I went with mother to hear the Orchestral Concert that I am sending you the programme of. There were so many lovely things in Delius's piece.[63] It is remarkable that the world and people are as much a closed book to me as compositions are an open book. When I hear a composition it appears to me as if I knew its creator through and through, as I wouldn't do after many years in any other way. Thus last night I realized how thoro'ly brave & spiritedly experimental a being that dear Delius is. Taking lots of risk, & not content with mere "safe" well worn conventional pranks like that tiresome R. Strauss (how he wrote D Juan I cant fathom) Delius's stuff on the band sounds **so** poetic & full of tender & **rare** things. Nothing rough, blatant, or cheap at all.

I dont say his form is convincing, or that he is an out-&-out genius but he's a most sympathetic & *instructive* talent with a dear abstract, compassionate, poetic soul. It was so refreshing for me to hear him talk Norwegian to me. It sounded so far away from the "big international music world" from jealousy & Jews, & Germans & throttling competition & conventionality.

The sound of Scand. tongues open a heaven of freedom, aloofness, untrammelledness, unsmirchedness to me.

D had a ripping reception, towards which I clapped & shouted my hardest. I find my chords sound quite nice on orchestra.

D has written an orchestral work on "Brigg Fair" tune he tells me.

I have given 4 lessons today, and been into town as well to talk to my agent.

But it is only 5 o'cl and I still hope to get a little scored today.

I am looking forward to collecting with Delius in the summer, we will really have an amusing time together up there.

Next (Poste R) letter leaves London Thurs. Nov 26.

I hope you are **extremely** careful about Poste Restante. You are, aren't you?

Now this must go.

You can imagine that I have travelled a lot this week, when you look at the map of the tour and remember that in addition I came down from Bury (in the night) to play in London on Wednesday, and the next morning up to Warrington, and the next morning back again. I like it.

It is good you are playing at concerts
Our good time will come again soon.

Percy.

63 Delius's *Appalachia* was given its first English performance on 22 November 1907, at Queen's Hall, London, the New Symphony Orchestra and the Sunday League Choir being conducted by Fritz Cassirer. Richard Strauss's tone-poem *Ein Heldenleben* was also given on the same programme.

159   TO KAREN HOLTEN   [Folkestone]
Tuesday 26.11.07

I spent yesterevening with my governess who knew me from my 4th to
my 12th year.
   She is at Folkestone just now & I enthused both her & her uncle to help
me in f.s. collecting.
   The 2 of them can help me onto 3 quite new (to me) districts.
   By her (Miss Gardner's) accounts I must have been much more rare &
wonderful as a quite little boy, than I've ever been since.
   I really was a queer one.
   I long ago realized the betterness of myself as child than later, for I can
remember lying awake one night at Cronberg (when 15 or 16 just when I
first fell in love with ——) crying over having become so ordinary in
contrast to my earlier self.
   Next P.R. leaves London Frid. Nov 29.

160   TO ROSE GRAINGER   [PM Leicester]
[Postcard]
12.12.07 10.15. pm

   Muecke wants to see you about my going to Verts, with whom he's being
talking.
   Had a real good practise all this afternoon.
   Have answered all the letter[s]. Nice success this eve. Awfully sleepy off
to bed. It's my cold makes me drowsy

161   TO KAREN HOLTEN   Grand Hotel,
[Original: English/some Danish]   Leicester.
13.12.07. morn

   You must excuse if I'm a bit fightsome; for I've just had a big tussel over
my Hotel bill, & won; altho' I was shivering with fear & excitement. They
charged me 13/6 & I have got it down to 9/6. They handed our accompanist a bill for over £1. However, all I write this morn I thought out last night
on getting yr letter, so you mustn't reckon the Hotel bill as playing any real
part. Heaps of thanks for the towns.
   If you really want *the truth*; I **dont** find love an engrossing subject. I dont
feel it strongly myself & dont understand it much in others, although I
respect it, & can stand a *fair amount* of it. But I rate it as neither a vice
nor a virtue, (though likelier the former) but just according to the plain,
actual, practical results of its sway: Whether its government be good or
bad.
   I have always regarded the sentence in the bible: *"Therefor shall a man
forsake his father & mother that bore him, & his kin, & cleave to the wife
of his bosom"* as one of the most swinish utterances of that for the most
part swinish book. (the old Testament)
   It seems to me that if the dirty business of childbearing & childrearing
can be excused at all & made palatable to the mind, it is chiefestly by
undying & unalterable devotion between parents & offspring. (Even then
it's a doubtful biz) Therefor I am distressed if any feelings that I have
aroused should make you able to more easily bear the thought of leaving
your own flesh and blood now than formerly.
   I cant deny that such a state of mind strikes me as somewhat disgusting
& alarming. The thought of nature's sway so sweeping one off one's feet

is somewhat sickening to me. Then what about all these things that you can do thro love, & couldnt possibly without it? What does it amount to, when brought down to dots? *What* can you really do better? I dont deny that you can, only I'd like proofs. It would make me happy if I could be brought to think that love had improved you. I have always rather feared the reverse. Are you more thoughtful & loving & devotional to your own kin? Are you a harder worker? Are you more reliably happy? (This is the surest sign of a good influence)

As to my *terror* of "liv". It is not because I resent a woman's help. I shall always (I who owe all, nearly, to woman) be proud to have a woman's help in any work I think good & jolly & worth doing. But not a painful dirty thing like childbirth. Not a dear, (in money) risky, bothersome engrossing hazard such as child-training. Not an everlasting possibility of failure & suffering & sin such as a line of offspring, & their bloody offspring, & on, & on. No ta. Not if I can help it.

As for 6 weeks in the year, or thereabouts. I find it a jolly fitting average. Not as much as one would *like*, but as much as one *ought to have*. Anyhow, as much as I'm **going to have**, or intend to have.

I like fun, not duty. Man, not nature. A little love, heaps of fleshiness. A sweetheart, not a wife. A short excitement, not a steady habit.

Now you must write to 26 Coulson St, but only *once* a week.

You mustn't take it badly of me, that I can't think better of "love's power" & that I cant get more excited over folk's being so ready to leave their dear parents. Please, my heartiest regrets & wishes for recovery to yr father.

162   TO ROSE GRAINGER   Headinglea,
Wed. [PM 18 December 1907]   Branksome Park,
                                                Bournemouth.

Seen *the* most glorious color photography here that that charming Reynolds [Grainger's host] has done.

Tell you all about it this eve.

Played the whole of yestereve.

Heard also jolly gramophone records. Science! How uplifting. How I adore it.

Yr fondly loving
Son

1908

The New Year of 1908 saw the Graingers in residence at 31A Kings Road, Chelsea, which was to be their home until they left England for the United States in 1914. On 2 January 1908, Karen Holten arrived in London on a visit: it was while waiting for her train that Grainger conceived his Arrival Platform Humlet. Karen stayed with the Graingers until 27 January, when her father's illness obliged her to return to Copenhagen.

Grainger, re-engaged for the second part of the Crossley Provincial Tour, left London again on 13 January to rejoin the Crossley concert party at Penzance. The pattern of a few days touring then a couple of days free resumed, and continued until the tour ended on 28 March. His longest absence was for the Scottish tour, which took him from home between 26 January and 8 February. In the first week of March, as the tour schedule brought him closer to London, he returned home each night after the concert.

Grainger was much preoccupied with folksong during the early weeks of 1908: drafting the article ''Collecting with the Phonograph'' for the Journal of the Folk-Song Society (published as No. 12, Vol. III, Part 3, later in 1908) and completing the hectograph fair-copy of his own collection of tunes, numbers 200–300. It was during this time that he bought his own phonograph. Rose Grainger helped with the work of copying and, on occasions, of collecting. The tour provided opportunities for brief but intensive spells of collecting. The quest for more satisfactory recording and notational devices occupied Grainger's mind.

The question of a proposed second Crossley tour of Australasia was the cause of some anxiety for Rose at this time. Her uncertainty reflects her wish to push Percy's career in different directions, and the constant conflict between ambition and economic security. Writing to Roger Quilter on 22 January she explains, ''Ada Crossley is going out to Australia next August and wants Percy to go with her. He would get £40 the week but then — it would prevent Tait the manager taking him as 'star' next year or the year after so I do not know what to advise and the agreement must very soon be made. Tait came to see me yesterday and I have written today stating Percy's terms — wh. I am rather afraid he won't accept. Muecke was here the day before, and between them they brought on my awful headache. How I hate all this awful business''.

ADA CROSSLEY ENGLISH PROVINCIAL TOUR OUTLINE (1908)

Monday	January	13	Penzance	
		14	Truro	
		15	Plymouth	
		17	Exeter	
		18	Torquay	18 PG home 4 a.m.
				19 London
		20	Gloucester	
		21	Burnley	
		22	Lincoln	
		23	Grantham	23–26 London
		27	Inverness	27 Karen left London
		28	Dunfermline	
		29	Kirkcaldy	
		31	Ayr	
	February	1	Kilmarnock	
		3	Paisley	
		4	Dumfries	
		5	West Bromwich	
		6	Swansea	
		7	Cardiff	
				8–9 London
		10	Cambridge	
		11	Southsea	
		12	Chelmsford	
				13 London
		14	Bedford	
		15	Malvern	15–17 London
		17	Guildford	
		19	Durham (2.45 p.m.)	
			Sunderland (8 p.m.)	
		21	Wakefield	
		22	Hastings	22–25 London
		23	Ealing	
		25	Barnsley	
		*26	Preston	26 PG at Cambridge
		27	Shrewsbury	
		28	Chester	
		29	Manchester	
	March			1 London
		2	Gravesend	
		*3	Aldershot	3 PG in Birmingham London
		4	Bournemouth	
		5	Margate	
				6–8 London
		9	Winchester	
		10	Chatham	
		11	Windsor	
		12	Salisbury	
		13	Ryde	
				14–22 London (Fauré's visit)
		23	Stafford	
		25	Wigan	
		26	Halifax	
		27	Crewe	
		28	Harrogate	PG notes "end of tour"

*Concerts in which PG did not take part

163 TO ROSE GRAINGER
16.1.08.

The Grand Hotel,
Plymouth.

⟦"Yonder loom the islands, yonder lie the ships,
    & sailor lads a-dancing heel & toe."[1]⟧

1 Freely recollected from the poem "Drake's Drum" by Sir Henry Newbolt (1862–1938). Grainger probably knew it from C. V. Stanford's setting (in *Songs of the Sea*, Op. 91).

My beloved little mother.

This is the very Hotel you met me from when I came from S'Af. This & W. Hartlepool are my favorite towns in England, so far.

I had a drunkenly happy day of it, yest. Young Woollerton met our train & took me off to his ship (battleship) "Hannibal" for a late lunch of ravishing jam, muffins, toast, scones, tea, eggs, etc; & showed me over the decks, guns, torpedoes, engines, etc. Undying youth is of the sea. We are all one age upon it; & the best.

England at best should never be regarded as other than a jetty to the water. Despite the farmer-charm (with its tender mouth — the folksongs) Englishmen are after all stranded aland. One may doubt their utter superiority there. They may smack of amateurishness there.

Their bodies are surely shaped to be set off by restless decks underfoot (barefoot too) & blowing clothes aflap. And how "brightly ring" the beloved spare "schlicht" [German: plain] words of their dear speech windblown.

In such towns too, a heavenblest drizzle may befriend one & deck out bluejackets in oil-cloaks, (not fastened, but hanging in crisp, yellow, unemotional angly curves like the texture of the man within) And surely the British are *the only* disciplined race just now. Thro' all the jokes, the easy disrespectful poises, the eyewinking, & general irrelevancy & causualness is hinted a oneness, a linkedness, & an unupsettable forordained purposefulness besides which the toughest militaryism of continentals seems but theatrical & grafted-from-without.

This, like cancer, thrives from roots within.

And *this* race we have beaten at Cricket!

I fondly hope you have followed the saga of our latest cricket Test match win.

That dear full-bummed Sth Australian Clem Hill quits his influenza bed & makes 160.

I dont so much care whether we win or no; but I insist that we show character.

May there always be a finest-race-in-the-world for us to try to lick! But may the dear tender glowing hearted English keep top dog all right in the main for long sweetly-governed years, that is my prayed for wish.

At the concert last night I regaled the artistroom with tales of our schemings for a boat, a printing-ship, for the mum & the bummy one.[2] In 15 years; & they all laughed. The women didn't mind much, but the good old middleclassers (J. Harrison bestly) thought it mighty pishtush. How silly of them, because we will, wont we?

2 A detail of Grainger's appearance: his backside stuck out!

Woollerton is a nice clean fresh pureseeming youth, refreshing; as are all of his fellows that I had the luck to meet. It's far better for chaps to be getting mighty randy at sea, despite lime juice & all, ⟦even if: "The Captain's on the ¼ deck a reading his book, the steward's in the galley a-buggerin' the cook"⟧ than (like 2 of our bounders) pretending their going to look up friends late at night & looking in mistably-eyed in the morning. (late morning)

One of his shipmates (a naval reserve officer — Cunard Line) knows seachanty words & I'm hoping to milk him of some today.

I did 2 more hekto pages last night. I take off both at once & find that more fun & quicker. But I nevertheless find it downheartening to take off alone. Taking off is rooted in my mind with the mum's beloved stubborn little games & all the fun of it all, & when I start pulling 'em off in the silent night alone I feel quite forsaken, & go to bed with a slight sigh.

At Truro I started getting up, & shall here today keep on with, Ravel's *"Play of water"*. What a gem! What craftsmanship.

It's one of those cheery nerve cuddling wind-&-drizzle seaport days when its high happiness to sit back of a windowpane writing & working & see the Atlantic fleet drag out of harbor front of one's nose in grey glory, & hear a wild wind making one feel a hero on no deeds.

Now to bizz:

I wld be very thankful if a new bottle of hektograph ink [Hektograph Black Ink C.A.Co Ltd.] could be got from the Army & Navy Stores before Sat night; & also if Spicer could be bucked up to let us have more *thin paper*, (better order a goodish load) as before, *at his very earliest*. It would be ripping if I could have it Monday before leaving as I'm getting on so well with the f.songs. There isn't any more thin paper anywhere at home, I suppose?

Fondest love, du hjærteres kjær [Danish: you sweetheart].

from yr
would be Sailor boy.

164   TO ROSE GRAINGER   [Handed in at Newton
[Telegram. PM 18 January 1908]   Abbot R1. at 9.15 p.m.]

GENIUS CHANTYMAN SEVENTH HEAVEN MEET FEW HOURS LOVE PERKS[3]

164   TO ROSE GRAINGER   Bell Hotel
20.1.08.   Gloucester

My darling one

Have had such a great day. I really think I'm in quite top form again these last few months. I feel almost as active & alive as I was many years ago; & not since. In the Underground & in train I worked without a stop from Chelsea to Bristol, where the sandwiches came delightingly to memory & palate. I was working at my introduction to the F.S. Journal & I think have got sketched out a lot of my thunks on the subject. On getting here I got your wire. Ada says she's got a Wire from Muecke saying "Williamson likes Percy". I'm not enthusing to her over the prospect.

Then I did an 1½'s practise & then thought out a really very good way of setting a blend of Rosher's & Perrings Stormys.

I think it bids to be my best chanty setting so far. It'll sound like anything. I also bought the Windsor that darling Feilding wrote of, & hurrah: the invention is already done by that Frenchman, I believe, & very soon we'll all be taking records in the only proper way — (till there's a better).[4]

I'll show & explain it you on my glad return on Thursday. Isn't it glorious if it's as good as it reads? Just the whole thing I've been wanting.

I played heaps better tonight & am getting a trifle of purchase on to that bullmouthed Weber at last. I had stunning success.

This room is full of middle class Scotch business men. Swine, hogs, dung, stomachturners. They all want to write business letters, but I've got the best writing table & am keeping them all waiting in glad glee.

Your ever loving son
Perks.

3 The "genius chantyman" was John Perring of Dartmouth, a deep-sea sailor and shantyman whom Grainger described as "one of the most creatively gifted, fiery-spirited traditional singers I have yet heard". The Perring shanties provided Grainger with a valued complement and alternative to shanties collected and sung by Charles Rosher. The following day, in London, Grainger sketched his first setting of *Dollar and a Half a Day* for men's voices, "blended from 2 variants from Mr Charles Rosher (London) & Mr John Perring (Dartmouth)".

4 Everard Feilding had drawn Grainger's attention to an article on "Photographing Sound", in the *Windsor Magazine* for January 1908, which dealt with the work of one Dr Marage of Paris.

Todays ticket only cost me 3/6.

After stinking out the room with whisky smells, my Scotch are turning to Religion & biblegassing.

Later; at Burnley.

Bull Hotel fullup but I got yr wire alright.

I'm in no hurry to fix things re Austr.

Done a stunning lot on the Introduction to the F.S.J.

Lovingly Perks.

I reach London 8.12. pm on Thursday

166   TO ROSE GRAINGER   Manchester station.
Midday   (for Burnley)
21.1.08.

It really is tremendous, this Frenchman's invention for photographing sounds. It reads as if the scheme contains all the chief essentials to my folksong needs. Anyway it ought to note down a single line of sound (a fiddler or single singer) but I dont know how it'd deal with a chorus or band. But all will come in time.

I'm not a really original or great person, but rather one whose mind is drifted well in freshest stream of our era's achievements. What the world brings off is mostly feathers in my cap; I'm instinctively in the van of human progress, but without being a great leader or prophet.

Yet the deeds of the energetic movers often just strike oil for my partic aims & yearnings. Unanglicized, in Germany, I felt a greedy craving for English music just when England, unbeknownst to me, was fussing away toward the same goal. I come with a harmonic mind curiously born to dish up given material well, just when England at last starts coughing up her traditional treasures.

But all these very advantages are lucky rather than heroic. I'm more likely to be a safe winner than a plucky hazarder. Aluck & alack!

Ada talked much of the A. tour this morn. I'm not seeming one scrap overeager, which also I'm not either. I'm sticking out for £40 a week, for *continuous* weeks, no opening with a Sonata, (this the accompanist can do, I've put) & somewhat outstanding advertizing. But nothing must be fixed, or even the thought of nourished, until all these points are glowingly satisfactorily fixed, & a reliable idea guv of the tour's length, etc.

I shall write Fishlock today, begging him come next Friday, Jan 24 at 3.30.[5]

Wrote Lady B[ective], & the Duchess [of Rutland] last night.

It's funny how often I feel in very toppest health when looking, & thought to be, off-color. Maybe I have an unhealthy liking for the feelings of wornoutness; but my brain seems so much more acting consentrative & birthful then, maybe because in such states I nearer approach the ill-nerved abnormal conditions said to be conditional to greatness.

I really believe there may be something in it.

Fondest love.

What a duck, that Everard. What tons of help starts from him!

5 Grainger had recorded and noted seven tunes from the singing of William Fishlock at Chiswick Ferry, Surrey, on 9 January 1908. Fishlock's appointment was postponed to 13 February. There is no clear record of the material collected.

167   TO ROSE GRAINGER   Thorn Hotel,
22.1.1908   Burnley, Lancs.

There's no denying it's balm to be playing to these Northern audiences again; the roar of strong-limbed applause that explodes the second one's hands leave the keys quite makes one feel one is a pianist lce more. The unenthusing South (yet *how much more lovable* in so many dear ways) certainly takes the conceit out of one.

A ripping full house last night.

Old Muecke came posting along last night to fix up business things for the Austr tour

I yarned him a glowing tale of how my pupils entirely kept us in London, & all I'd stand to lose by taking on the Australian tour, so there was no talk of reduction as regards your proposed fee.

There's nothing important to write you on this head, tho' there'll be a deal to tell tomorrow. It's absurd how alike certain parts of Muecke's & my face are.

My head is full of chanties. I hope in a few days that the worrying part of the Folks. Journal will be on the way to be behind me. It's so hard to state one's views with needful strength without letting out also that chief undercurrent of my mind: that none of the rest collect properly or thoro'ly.

It's all a game that Cecil Sharp & crew after sitting on Stanford & crew for their laziness & unthoro'ness should in their turn be softly sat on for the same "touch of nature".

Have just breakfasted & written Feilding thanking him for his gorgeous aid. That dear creature, how much he's done for me!

I wish you would book Karen an hour for a serious lesson, as *early as possible* on my return; Friday morning or something like that, so as to leave time for her to correct what I tell her & have another lesson before going. And do please impress on her to work up a bit for it. I should hate her to leave this time without her music having any attention from me.

I shall write again tonight after the concert.

2nd proofs of the St-Gr. have come & are being corrected.[6]

Love from yr fond one

6 Grainger's piano solo arrangement of *A Reel*, the fourth of *Four Irish Dances* by Charles Villiers Stanford, was published by Houghton & Co., London, in 1908.

168   TO ROSE GRAINGER   Saracen's Head Hotel
evening 22.1.08.   Lincoln

Darling Mum

Got the enclosed wire from Muecke. Am sending him 1st thing in the morning following wire:

Thanks for getting me 40 pounds
Cant definitely fix before seeing mother.

Williamson is, of course, dead keen to fix all at very earliest. But I cant help that. The questions of *piano & not opening* with duett or solo, are perfectly alright both Ada & Muecke assure.

The travelling expenses are selfunderstood.

It is too early to bother about porthole until discussing details with Malone.

Williamson wrote Ada: "I like P.G. very much, both as a man & an artist. I think he would regret going out on a Recital tour by himself, as such tours don't pay worth the while in Australia. But I should like to take him out myself as star with his own party when he is some years older & has gained the further reputation that he is sure to do. But I should like him to come out again with you first'' That, of course, one must take only for what it is worth.

If Tait makes a definite offer for a *definite year* he is well worth considering; but, failing that, this here offer (W's) is very much ''a bird in the hand'' They look for the tour to last 6 months & that wld mean actual pay of over £900.[7]

I should get special booming for dead cert, naturally. They are offering Sametini £15 & Earle £20. This I have both from them themselves & from Ada.

And Ada says she wants me for her 1910 tour in England, which is now becoming a prepared-for certainty.

Ada is obviously mighty keen for me to go; she says it'll mean a tremendous advantage & prestige for her to have me.

I must say she is wholly charming & fairspoken to me about it all, & not trying to sway me off the Tait offer at all.

I am writing Fishlock *not to come* day after-tomorrow, Friday. So dont be flustered if a card turns up from him saying he *will* come; for that'll only be in answer to an earlier letter of mine.

His address is:
W. Fishlock. Sen.
2 Church St
Chiswick. (near London)
But I **have** *written him, putting him off.*
Please deal for me fully & finally *even tomorrow if you wish*, with either Taits or Muecke.

If you feel finally dont scruple to wire or phone or see Muecke or Tait & settle just what you feel best.

Your decision will now, as always, be the rightest possible; knows your trusting & adoring sonlet.

Herewith a tour-card with a few added & corrected train-times, etc.

A rotten poor empty house here tonight, alas.

I cant say the glow & melt I felt when I heard suddenly the Lincolnshire accent here today; hallowed to me as it is thro' yearlong being blended in my mind with sweet folksingers & their pure art.

How fondly I feel towards the folk of this county! Such rare & unique sweetness & flavor they have, pets.

Wrote Mrs Grieg a 12-page letter this morn, & clean-wrote all my Dartmouth chanties in the train, & did some ''introduction''.

Such vital hours before us, loved one, to be gone thro, slowly, calmly, happily.

I am still going early to bed.

---

169   TO KAREN HOLTEN   Station Hotel,
[Original: Danish/English]   Inverness.
midday 27.1.08.

There seems to be no danger that I won't be able to come to Copenhagen about 19th March, since it now appears that there is little likelihood that Ada will undertake the extra week of the Tour.[8] So there will be ''joy and much merriment.''

I slept *so* splendidly in the train last night and again just before our arrival here. You must also have slept not a little last night. There is, despite all the fun, a good deal I regret about your visit: I didn't tickle you as much as I should have, and we slept so lovelessly. Right after one has

7 In the event the Tait offer did not materialise. On 27 January Tait wrote to Rose recommending postponement of a solo tour until Grainger's reputation was even more established. Rose was dealing with Frank S. Tait (1883–1965), the youngest of a family of five brothers, four of whom at that time worked independently as concert entrepreneurs under the name J. & N. Tait. Their company was registered on 31 July 1908 as J. & N. Tait Concert Directors. James Cassius Williamson (real name Murphy, 1854–1913) had managed the first Crossley tour of Australasia. Grainger finally made his solo tour for J. & N. Tait in 1926, by which time the brothers had also taken over control of J. C. Williamson's.

8 The extra week of the tour was confirmed by Ada on 10 February, and the Copenhagen recital cancelled.

got warm and sweaty, there obviously comes an urge to lie in a less warm position; preferably fairly apart: and we have been so sleepy and tired the whole of this time that we always went to sleep while this reaction lasted; instead of, when one is sufficiently cooled off again, turning to each other and getting both bodies as mixed up together as two poor separate bodies can be. It would have been so nice to sleep, you and I, mixed up like an Irish Stew; as we often have done in our former times. It was not lack of love on my part, little friend, this time; you must not think that; it was only stupid sleepiness. You can think what you like, but *I* have no doubt that there is something particularly lovely about the reunions which follow times of separation. There is something so calming in the thought that in solitude and separation one has earned a little contrast-time where one can rightly devote one's whole self to the other, and concentrate on that rather than on anything else.

I will be happy to hear immediately your little tummy has worked, since I have a feeling that we two have been a *little bit* careless, now and then, this time; but I do hope not too much so.

Do you know how high up we are here in Inverness? You should look at the map (on the Northeast coast of Scotland) You had better reckon at *least* a whole day from London to all towns before *West Bromwich*.

We have seen the most lovely mountain scenery today. Snow lies in spots on the heights, and one sees miles of heather which resembles the Svinkløv district. And I have already seen many amusing faces and types.

You know the feeling which (I believe) I have got in
"Now Simmy Simmy, o' the Side
Come out and see a Johnstone ride!"
etc. [from *The Lads of Wamphray*]

One sees so much of this cheerful pride in Scotland still. When only the Scots are not rude and altogether too businesslike, then they are full of the most magnificent qualities; and their land is quite exceptional; for me.

Few lands in Europe attract me so hotly as this Scotland. *So* full of character it is, every yard. When I'm rich!

The enrichening of both yr character & playing is tremendously upheartening to me, you sweet warm one.

I am so completely convinced that you can come terribly far in your playing; you only need to work hugely hard, & increase the decisiveness & definiteness of your phrasing & general attack. Your touch is good & mellow, & your power good, & your whole scheme musical; but you can do with more exaggeration of small details & greater *consciousness* of pedal effects. *Make up your mind* exactly where (on which note) you start, consummate, & end your < > I cant say how proud I'd be (not for you as pupil, but for you *as you*) if you'd screw yourself up to really ripping great playing.

You mustn't be sad about the Australian tour. The stuff of 6 months is the same as that of 2, no worse. Numbers (6 'stead of 2) really only effect ones greed most.

And now it is good that there is so little reason to fear that something will come and steal away from us our coming C-hagen time.

Don't you find that, the longer we know each other, I get less and less reaction against you, you sweet friend? *Dont on that account think that my need of freedom is less, or my claim to a right to love the whole world wherever, whoever, & whenever, is toppling; but* **do**, *if you like, believe that I relish you more, & are more devoted, thankful, & glad of & to you.*

I am also sorry that I did not take your clothes off this time. That is such fun. We must do that again soon. How is poor Arl. getting on with her life. Do let me know, & *all details of yr father's health.*

170 TO ROSE GRAINGER
30.1.08.

Station Hotel,
Kirkcaldy, N.B.
[In the train] for Ayr.

Will you kindly send some cutting, or cuttings containing Englished letter of Grieg's to me re folksong settings (his last) to that Mr Roddie,
Inverness, I sent you address of, with a card of mine inclosed on which:
"*return at leisure*"

Met last night a very nice important man in Paterson's Edinboro.
Kirkcaldy is only a short hour from Edinb. I talked to him all I knew. He
had heard me at Leeds Festivals. I was glad that I got on very well with
audience last night. I told him I'd like to play with the Scottish orch. He
says, "that'll come alright".[9]

I went thro some old pieces yesterafternoon. The Brahms F min Sonata
& the (unarranged) C♯ min Bach Prelude & Fugue. I also nearly know the
Ravel by heart.

How about my København Recital?

Would you advise my doing the F minor Sonata Brahms there? I thought
not until I tried it thro' again, but I find it wldn't take such great working
up again, & it is after all a work with greatness to it, despite much dulness.
Danes, of course are rather Brahms-ward, & I didnt do any there last year.
But what do you just think? Of course I'd do the Grieg Ballade, & possibly
the Bach C♯ min (of last Lond. Recital) & the Debussy Toccata, & the 2
Irish Dances (Leprechaun & M[arch]-Jig) never done there yet, & maybe
some shorter Griegs & some Chopin. Let's hear yr mind. For London I
suggest as Novelties Noel (Gardiner) & (new for me) the Ravel. & maybe
that slow Chopin I played you the other day. For Australia I intend making
a blend of the Tausig & Busoni Bach D min Organ Toccata & Fugue.
Neither Tausig nor Busoni are quite satisfactory to me singly.

If anything from Piggott or Miss Broadwood comes let it lie unless its
urgent.

Have written Vickers, Crampton (Leicester) re his son, Piggotts Downey,
& shall send off fidgey's today remembring what you say.

How blessed a thing the post is. How could one possibly do without it.
How appalling seperations must have been in the ages when they meant the
breaking of all links! I gloat so over getting yr words, & rejoiced this morn,
before leaving Kirkcaldy, to get yr postcard to there; besides yr dear letter
of the day before. It's all so true what you say of health & age. The 1st
is the all important. But I dont see, dearie, that I easily stand the chance
of quitting health. After all, my likes in food, art, & life are all so chiefly
babylike or boylike at the worst. Any bad habits which I have had, or
tendencies to overdo, or overeat, or even overwork, *are all done quietly &
alone*, & that is a great safeguard.

As long as one acts out of oneself, in quiet, ones excesses in any directions are little likely to overstep ones normal (even if greedy) hungers. It
is when spurred on by drink, wild example, & destructive unthinking folk;
by introduction of poisons from without; that the worst waste is coaxed,
surely.

What a boon it is to me that I have from you such simple tastes, & am
so little dependant upon the folk with whom I just casually mix, even tho'
I may be quite a good deal fond of them. It is only folk of very definite
inner wiges [*sic*] (fixed ideals, in other words) of very pure (in the sense of
untrammelled, unswayed) strong personality, of reliable character & sure
purposes, of all possible freedom & indipendance, that it is safe to be at
all acted upon by; & by such one cannot seem to be *too* thoro'ly guided,
swayed. It's my yearlong being so safely yielded up to yr strong & balmful
government that makes it impossible for me to be quickly sucked out of
my track by stray weak streams.

Tho' not a mighty person as to willpower, bodily corage, & withstanding

9 The Dumfries concert was
promoted by Paterson & Sons, one
of the most important of the
Scottish music dealers, publishers
and instrument makers. The
Scottish Orchestra (later the
Scottish National Orchestra) was
at that time conducted by Frederic
Cowen, and was Scotland's
leading instrumental ensemble.
Grainger was not engaged to play
with it in the years before World
War I.

of temptation, I'm lucky in the gift of having a watchful mind & a not inaccurate critical sense. Thus my years with you have been an ever alert criticism of you & your wonderful nature, leading ever more & more to a more sharply true & unsentimentally scientific admiration for & appreciation of your peculiar & unique superiority to ordinary (even tho' excellent) beings; & to a more instant readiness on my part to be suspicious of anything *less than you* in spirit, warmth, versitility, & grit.

I suppose you are not perfect; (for folk will insist that cant exist) but I'd take the risk of putting you up as such, & regulating all judgement with reference to yr standard.

In any case, you are the ideal overlord of just such a being as I, cut out just for the partic work which is my lot.

I must needs be too concentrative, too subjective, & too (within myself) wayward to ever be an ideal self-ruler. I am the "thane"-type [thane is angl-sxon for German "diener", Danish "tjener"] as clear as day. Full of the power to *lead*, full of the readiness for stout action, full of initiative within *my own sphere*; but needing the surer rein of a born "overlord", the comfort of his praise, the nestlingness of his refuge — in moral matters, & as regards inner support & dominion.

Folk talk of geniuses being "kings" in their own art or science, etc.

I never feel that.

Art is socialistic. To the true understander of it it knows no betters or worses; it knows only free speech & true expression. To have a pure sincerity & say forth ones feelings & sensations & thoughts seems art, & all there is of it. More or less sincerity of expression makes for more or less *quality* & more or less to say, express, makes more or less *quantity*

But these values stand out singly, individually; there is no competition between them; & none of the brilliant gang of art-souls dulls the other. Into this gathering of peers, lacking all kings & serfs I can go without fear, & on my own, alone; & that's not a hard land.

But in this actual life I feel my lacks, & tho' a bold thane in the hands of a gifted & well-superior overlord, I'd be a pitiful "einevaldskonungr."* (sole-sway-king) [Dan: *Enevoldskonge]

It's a jolly chance that the best-discovered overlord should be my mother also; but I believe that is chance, & not sentimentally induced.

Anyhow, it *is* so, & is a happy state for me, certainly, & possibly for all concerned.

I had such a jolly practise yesterday & am looking forward to a good go at Ayr & this weekend.

I am so anxious to hear from Karen re her poor father.

I have been so happy having her with us & bless the little mum for her jollily-tuned holiday.

I wonder if there's anything re Programs, etc, I've forgotten?
Looking forward to yr letter to Ayr.

Your fond
Percy.

I find the new hekto paper quite good, after all, tho' a bit slow, maybe.

171 TO ROSE GRAINGER
evening after dinner. 1.2.1908.

St. Enoch Station Hotel,
Glasgow.

Here I am, glad to have a full evening to myself. Ada has just left to spend the weekend with friends, & the "boys" are at the Pantomime, whither they keenly tried to drag me, kindly. But I know the heartsinking that follows hotrooms & over-exitement, & am glad to be here with my letters, hektographs, & the Bjørnson book.[10] I have this moment finished the latter; my unceasing companion these last few days. It is well to have it behind me. A book is a great time-taker, but a relish while it lasts. The 1st ½, of which I wrote, is the most dear to me personally. Bjørnson's happy endings & problem-solvings dont always ring so dead true in my little head. His unfailing bais of omptimism & everlasting barracking for emancipation dont greaten him to me *as an artist*, tho' politically, thinkingly, & humanly I'm with him solid enough.

The 1st ½, dealing fleetingly with striding generations & their outstanding types rather objectively, impersonally, is sagalike & after my taste, but later when it treats minutelier & one's got to live longer with each individual personality I feel more like pulling out my watch now & again. The 2nd ½ deals mainly with girls in a girl's school & is maybe therefor less sympathetic, tho' I dont doubt it's full of truths. What funny funny emotional tearful unanchored unreliable hysterical creatures they are to be sure, in his book.

Amazingly **sexual** while *deprolably* [sic] **unsensual**. That does seem such a mistake. The latter part of the book might be a (unconsciously so) pamphlet showing up the horrors of "confiding" confidences. All tells each all & the mud & filthy muck of dull sodden suffocating scandal & sordidness they all get into is wholly stomachturning. I have nought against girls, knowing them wholly not. But if old Bj's right at all, the Norwegian ones are pretty rank. Not bad; bless them no; if they only were! But stupid, dull, narrow, small, smaatskorne*, unsensually sexual, mangrasping, badform, cry babies, unplucky, (tho' doubtless *brave* enough) unbearable.

Yet how singularly like a girl *I* am. Not like a woman, nor yet a man, but a blend of a girl & a boy — chiefly girl. I, like they, are always feeling "hurt", overlooked, misunderstood, wishing to take "parties" one against another, feeling spite, sudden resolves I never keep, swift urges to chuck over caution & speak forth my spites, feelings, sentimentalities. The only diff is that they show & I hide, they do, & I don't. But when I read of those unaccountable things, girls, its like reading of myself, & I despise them accordingly.

How wise the little mum is in *never really* giving away confidences, in never placing sparks in the hands of (the best-possibly-meaning) explosives. For we all are explosives, sooner or later, & its so essential to have no secrets to tell when the "saying forth" mood falls upon us.

Yet how hard it is for a girl-like temperament to shut off & quench when one is all in a sweaty glow to confide & unbottle! But it must be, I know. Therefor it's best to have no friends, or the fewer the better, & those few even preferably sages knowing the folly of sympathetic overflowings.

Please dont suggest the Tchaikovsky to Halford. Suggest the Grieg or the Liszt, or add: or the Tchaikovsky, if he likes. I think I *did* play the Liszt there; but maybe not.[11]

Malone's not in town yet, so the settlement of details will have to wait till he is.[12]

---

* Danish: lit. "cut up small". Grainger is using the word idiosyncratically to mean "small-minded". *Transl.*

10 Grainger was reading *Det Flager i Byen og på Havnen* [The Flags are Flying in the Town and the Harbour], by Bjørnstjerne Bjørnson (Copenhagen, 1897).

11 Grainger played the Grieg Piano Concerto at the Birmingham Concerts Society orchestral concert on 3 March 1908, George Halford conducting. This was his third appearance with Halford.

12 J. A. Malone, representative acting on behalf of J. C. Williamson, with whom Grainger was negotiating the terms of the proposed Australasian tour.

13 Luisa Tetrazzini (1871–1940), Italian soprano. She had made her London debut at Covent Garden in the autumn season of 1907, making a great sensation.

The other night at Ayr, heard both Melba & Tetraz. [zini] records in the gramophone.[13]

No comparison **at all** between them. T. is the usual S. European whore voice, intended to be mighty luring & firelike, but in reality ice-cold & jarringly aniline-die-like. While Melba's has the searching, continuous, trancelike vibrations of the middle-distance blues in Australian upcountry-scapes. M has intensity, warmth, glow, something tight without effort, searching without "heftigkeit" [German: vehemence, violence].

Nope ta, I'm not taking any T in mine.

Tires me how the British enjoy schwärming over foreign inferiors. I wish with all my heart M would lift a fair spanking success when she turns up this side again.

I've given up eating appletart. All this giving way to pleasures has its dangers I fear. Goodnight, my beloved, successful, balming mother.

Sunday. Have finished hektographing *all* old folksong materials barring 2 that I cant do except in London; (needing f.s. journals for reference) that's jolly isn't it?

Have postcarded Legge, & Ernest, & written E. L. Rob, giving them the program that's sketched on the back of their here-enclosed letter to me.

Yes I see my posters a goodish deal, & have spoken Tillett re them; he's here with us, now. Isn't it jolly about the copy book returning safe? *Dont think of copying any of it out.*

It'll get hektoed, sooner or later, the most important parts of it.

The Breitkopf postcards started turning up again at the last town.

My Danish dates will be somewhat as follows:

My København Recital is March 26. I shall maybe leave England March 17, 18, or 19; depends what turns up this side & that side.

Hansen's adv. slips suggested me from 19th March till 1st April.

I dont think I'll get much over there, so will likely be back in England 1st April, or thenabouts. Dont refuse anything worth having over hear before 20 March or after 1st April.

Sir Patrick Spens you will find in both the redbound Border Ballad book Feilding gave me & in The Ballad book.

It begins:

> The King sits in Dunfermline town,
> drinking the guid red wine.
> "O whare will I get me a skeely skipper
> to sail this ship o' mine?"

I feel mighty tired. I've done a hard days work.

Tons of love from
yr son.

172 TO KAREN HOLTEN   St. Enoch Station Hotel,
[Original: Danish/English]   Glasgow.
evening 9.30. 1.2.1908

Here I am alone, little sweet boy; Ada is with friends, and "the boys" are at the Pantomime (Theatre) where they wanted to drag me with them. But I didn't want to, although I felt a little lonely. I am better off here by myself, with the letters, hektograph, and "Det flager"; but I have finished reading that this evening. The last ½ is not quite so attractive for me as the beginning was. What curious beings those schoolgirls are, to be sure. But how like them I am! I am full of the same sentimentalities, irregularities, unreliabilities, "peevishness". But for that reason it bores me just the same.

But doesnt the whole book prove how fatal all those soft-hearted confidences, heart openings are? The appalling shocking scandalmongering that goes on about every private matter. That, I must say, is almost the worst thing about Scandinavians, (& all teutonic lands, except the English) all that talky talky & *everybody knowing everything*. How much happier everybody would be now if you & I had not been such bloody fools as to tell *one word* to Herman, Alfhild, Arlaud, Aae, etc, etc. I know I was the worst, the worst, the worst, the worst of the 2 of us; & I *supposed* to be a boy, too! But we both did shockingly wrong. Really just as bad as all the other fools we watch & feel superior to. Mother is absolutely right about keeping one's mouth shut upon *all interesting subjects*.

For one only loses the friendship of the folk one confides in. That's what's so curious. Yet its true, both in real life & also repeatedly in Det flager.

Take Aae: I'm never comfortable with him, because I never know when he's going to blurt out some silly truth — even if only to me alone. That's the very very best point to the English — the way they can hide & keep a secret — *when they want to*.

But that is so difficult for me, me personally. I would so terribly like to talk about everything to everyone, in any case to friends. But that won't do! Never again; I hope.

Don't you *think so too*, never a word?

But I love to read about young girls, all the same. There is something so warm-sweaty about them, so stupid — melting — just as there is about myself. But what I cant stand is that they were so fearfully *sexual* yet horribly **un**sensual at the same time.

That is a terrible thing to me. I remember the 1st thing I thought about you in that way was that you must be sensual. I never thought about your being *sexual* until you spoke in that way.

Think of that poor Danish sea-captain! That's so hard on Captains, that they usually suffer if any illuck happens to their ships, whether they are to blame, or not. What a charming capitalistic game! But how the names Singapoor, East Asia, etc entice! Do you remember what Kipling writes of the "go-fever" in the Light-th[at]-Failed. It is a mighty sickness, for them I am overwhelmingly vain.

Maps of the world, place names, photos of blacks, the titles of big rivers, they're always beckoning to me like out-held arms. I long to meet all of them, find out all sorts of funny tucked away queer corners in them, try out the bodies of their women (yes, really) have a gay time; not dangerous, *or vic[i]ous*, but gay, fleshful, loving, young.

But do you think that there will be much danger of me attaining it? No, I must work, sit and work. I cant even go & see the legs at the Pantomime because I must sit & work, & pretend to leave something wonderful after me when I die. Are you happy that I must sit, and cannot go and try out the bodies of the women of the whole world? (I, who run away if I ever get a chance, & would never have any success, even if I tried)

Oh, I am so dead-sleepy, and yet I must work at least 2 hours more, tonight.

I have given up eating apple tart. I feel all this giving way to what I enjoy is dangerous.

Monday 3.2.08. Glasgow.

You can imagine I am happy when I get so many letters from you as in the last few days. What a pleasure it is to get them!

This evening I have quite finished hektographing my Lincs (etc) folksongs, with the exception of 2 that I can only do in London. It is really a relief to have that long boring work behind me, at last.

I got your letter today. You poor little thing, I can well understand that it is a hard time you are going through with your poor father. I've seen a certain amount of illness & suffering & know what a gnawing grief it is. How I long to hear of his being better again, for his & all yr sakes. Poor darling Roger is *fearfully ill* again. He is at 74 South Audley St. London again. I wish I could be with him, off & on.

This evening, when I was nearly finished my work (about 12 o'cl) one of our "party" came to me and asked me to come and "give them a dissertation on sex" and "swear a bit".

And when I was finished at last I went to them and we went up to Earle's bedroom and talked there till nearly 2 o'cl at night. I was so happy. The others were ½ full, and I do so heartily like people when they are like that. Particularly the English only really blossom out when they are ½ "gone".

I feel so happy when I feel that they (like last night) do in a way understand me after all, & feel that I am a comrade & "fellow rotter" even altho' I am the "worker" & the "virgin" of the party at the same time. I talked the most dreadful shocking things for hours & swore (banede) my lowest & horridest. And they rolled on the chairs & beds in ½ drunken laughter.

It's such a funny chance that I, the sort of "pure" one of the party, should be the one they instinctively turn to when they want their lowest fleshiest thoughts & their most brutal oaths voiced. And I feel so joyous & uplifted when I feel I am appreciated. O men & boys are quite a lot of fun in their way; & it is glorious to hear how the roughest & "coldest" & unkindest of them worship woman in one way or another. (mostly "one" way) To see the coarse creatures rolling about & praising the sensuous joys of woman's flesh is for me like being in the temple of some tremendous worship. All these different contrastingly-typed individuals uniting in praise & adoration of woman's body, dwelling ever & ever brutally but lovingly on the very titles of her sexual parts; giving the details of past lovingly-remembered sexual deeds out of their hoarse whiskied throats. It thrills & uplifts me; This fiery devotion of men to sex in woman.

I feel with them in such moments, & relish all their inner purity & godlike reckless devotion. The *love of joy* is grand in men. If only one could get the whole world to unite in making the earth a temple of sexual intensity! Men & women both eager for the fleshy bliss of it all. If only young girls could be trained *from the very start* to be as selfish, as dirty-minded, as unnatural, as health-reckless as boys — how both sexes could go to hell in joy & oblivion.

It's all this cruel family instinct, purposefulness, *nature worship* that holds back the boyish joy in life.

Let us have to earn money, have to work, but let all the rest be pure unrestricted unlimited meaningless wayward selfish bodily joy-seeking, snatched (thro the use of *preventatives*) out of the grasp of that enemy to man's nobility & glory: nature.

Believe me, men *are* thankful to woman, in their own way. Not always a *practical* way for the woman, tho; alas!

I will send the next letter to Ceresvej.

Thanks for your sweet letters.

You know that I love you in my own (rather useless to you) way?

Percy.

173   TO ERNEST THESIGER   Glasgow
[Postcard. PM 3 February 1908]
Sunday.

Darling Ernest.

Am having such a jolly time this weekend here. Have had a whole clear
day off & got thro' pages & pages of folksong work We're having such a
mighty happy tour.

Fond love from
your old
Perks.

174   TO ROSE GRAINGER   St Enoch Station Hotel,
4.2.1908   Glasgow.
                                            [PM Dumfries]

Dearest of mothers.

Got the enclosed from Malone. *Before signing, the piano details must all
be fixed, or well agreed upon.* I will see if I can get a night train from
Cardiff so that I arrive in London next *Saturday morn* so that I could see
Malone that morning if *he could*. Shall let you know later in the letter.

——————————————

I have never yet answered your dear letter where you mention the question of our possibly considering the matter of marriage on my return from
A.

I know so surely deep down in what ever one knows such things in, that
the little loving mother is above all one great unselfish desire for my being
good & happy.

Apart from the love you feel for me as an individual I always feel that
you unite with me in looking upon me as a sort of problem that one wants
to do the very best by. To begin with, you & I have been such a thundering
success as a mother & son (no amount of hard selfish utterances on my
part, — arising solely out of the narrow bitterness which I alas have not
a little of — can dim that any) that even an outsider couldnt but feel an
urge to see good come out of one who has been one of the duettists in such
a brilliant partnership.

Apart also from the fact that I've inherited enough of your darling
qualities (& thro you those of yr dear family) to be in the main a "good
person", I'm also a person of some talent (we cant fix how small or big
yet) of some worth to my homeland & even to the world at large. I know
you feel the responsibility of my little or great talent if anything more than
I do myself, so when you & I are discussing my future we're in the main
thrashing out a problem that we feel 1st & foremost an *abstract* interest in.
Both you & I would probably feel quite keen on a resolution boding real
solid goodness & artistic prolificness for my future even if it meant a certain
loss of pleasureableness for you or for me.

I dont wish to at all hide the fact that I'm very fond of Karen, that her
presence gives me curiously continous pleasure, & that in her absence I
keenly delight in hearing from her & writing to her. And **at the present** the
difference in age is naturally no disaster.

At the same time I must own to occasionally resenting her Danish-
teutonic liableness to "grunts" & other middleclass modes of speech &
ways, & tendency to choose unattractive things in the way of dress. She is
not at all the companion one wld rejoice to couple-it-about-with in one's
public carreer, tho' she's well fitted for country & ship life it seems. The

latter's the nearer my heart, of course, but aggravation in one's public life wld not be a partic sweetening influence upon one, would it?

But all these fors & againsts dont compare in importance with the question: *Is the* **state** *of marriage desirable*?

I firmly believe I shall be *happy in the main* if I dont marry, or even if I do. *Therefore the question is not one of happiness but one of practicalness, advisability, expediency.* The man who's unhappy without fairly constant sexual life, who possibly cant help liking some partic person extremely, his choosing is a far easier job than mine. I am jolly happy in the main whether I have, or haven't, sexual life. I have the power to like one individual (in that partic way) quite out of the ordinary, but (**as yet** anyway) cant imagine losing the *possibility* of doing that for several, or many, folk. My feeling for Karen hasnt altered my feelings for the rest of the world, or for other women.

This I am heartily thankful for; I should loathe to feel I'd suddenly lost the love I feel for the world at large.

Why I "keep off" women now is for the same reasons as before I met K: a feeling that the man should never take the initiative — lack of interest in coarse folk, either men or women — realization of the complications & unpracticalness of *all* sexual alliances —& last & not least; much shyness with all except folk I'm out of the way fond of.

But now, as before, I feel the world-of-woman before me. (This sounds disgustingly gay, but I dont mean it so, at all) To feel I had lost all in one is a crushing thought. Think; am I never to experience any of the women of my own land? I, the ardent patriot? And all Sth America, & the swarming tribes of African niggers. It would be sad to feel that one had the possibility of blossoming open one's arms to all these various races, but that one shouldn't.

On the other hand it wouldn't be fatal, for I'm not hear in this world to blossom open my arms, but to sit tight & write music, etc.

If I'm to speak the real truth, I have *no convictions* for or against marriage. But I *doubt* marriage sincerely.

I dont say I'll never want to get married, or that I mightnt enjoy it lots. I only say *I dont want to now, & see no reason why I should on my return from A.*

I dont say I'll never enjoy having a child, or children. It might be tons of sport. *But I have no least wish as yet*, nor do I think I shall for years to come, if ever.

The **right** to birth a child (however one might want it) is a *money matter*. I should say that a capital settled on a child *bringing in* say £100 a year is the *right to birth it*.

And before that provision for a child of mine, I would 1st like to provide a safe thing for you, father, (if need be) & myself. And if I married my wife ought to be provided for before the child question "kommt an der reihe" [German: takes its turn]. So, given even that I *wished* to marry on my return from A, it would be many years too early on account of money questions. I hope I may have the strength of will to put the following year old plan thro! To let my art, my health, my happiness all suffer, more or less, rather than glide into a middle- & old-age of moneylessness & enforced drudgery. If the world makes it hard for me to steal the comparitively little money I need for you, me, father, & (possibly eventually) any other folk, & the most needful of my schemes & experiments, then the world must suffer by lacking a smaller artistic output from me. *I* shall not suffer more than I can help. I am 1st of all an Australian, then an artist. And I hope all Australians have too much proper selfishness & lack of grovelling devotion (to art, or ought else) to sacrifice *proper material conditions* for ideals. Ideals & devotions must grow only when the bedrock of material conditions is well laid. The other, older, European way (the starver in the garrett) is unthoro' & un-Saxon.

Believe me, marriage would little better or worsen my compositional output. All that stuff folk talk is sentimental. Marriage must be accepted or rejected with regard to the matters it directly effects — sexual matters. And my feeling at present is: that I'm not (yet) suficiently the slave to sexual needs for it to be worth my while to give up the prospect of the womanhood of the whole world for the sure ownership of any one, however desirable, a beloved.

Then there is another unjolly admission in marriage. Man takes on the expenses of the woman he marries so that her doings & movements may be amenable to *his* needs. He is the rudder, she the guided vessel. No amount of love on both sides quite idealizes away this unindividualized, ½ enslaved, ½ bag-&-baggage-like servantry of the "wife of man" I dont say I couldnt swallow that, but it's an ugly dose. Each man that does that is in some little or great way stemming the glorious growing flow (if it is glorious & growing) of woman's future equality. (if that is her future — we hope so)

Then in my individual case; you & I stand to lose a wonderful "Sammenliv" [Danish: together-life] that we now have. We have after all very spiffing times together. And I dont know but what the just-you-&-I-aloneness of our lives doesnt go a huge way to make it what it is. Not that I fear that I'd ever love you one least bit less whatever happed. Only — circumstances make moods: And "vi har det meget godt" [Danish: we are very well] as we are, after all. So that, *at the present moment*, I dont feel I want to, or even ought to, make up my mind to seriously consider marriage with K on my return from A. *Accidents always accepted.*

As aforesaid, I've no convictions either way. But I haven't the feeling *now* that I shall feel like considering the matter seriously on my return here in about a year's time; tho I own I'm extremely fond of Karen, & have heaps of larx thro having met her & her being so very jolly to me. Meeting her has given me added joy & pleasures but I'm thankful to say it's not yet loaded me up with the feeling of having new responsibilities or of the likelihood of a proscribed future.

I can get to Paddington at 9.5 on Sat morn so will you (if you think well) write Malone saying I'd like to see him re some details before signing & see if I can see him any time after 10.30 on Sat

Got yr 2 postcards at Paisley.

I'm keeping the duplicate of the enclosed contract; which is the one *I* am to sign.

175   TO ROSE GRAINGER
Friday. 7.2.08.

Hotel Metropole,
Swansea.

My darling one

Got your dear sweet letter & 2 pcs to here. No I shant be back by 4 o'clock in the morning. I leave Cardiff tomorrow morn (Sat) at 6.34 & get to Padd. 9.5 (same morn) so will be with you by 10 o'clock about.

Since you're not going Cambridge I've written Bevan saying I cant come before the 7 o'clock train after all, so as to give us longer time together.[14] Have written father a card, & sent him 2 last week.

I read with joy that Australia has arranged to send a Rugby football team over here. If we only win at football!

The little one mustnt think I'm depressed or dissatisfied with myself. I'm not at all. I merely observe myself & record what I imagine to be facts. But

14 Grainger was in Cambridge on 26 February 1908, for a duo-recital with Gervase Elwes for the Cambridge University Music Society. He stayed with Australian friends, the Bevans.

they dont stirr me one way or the other. The fact that *I* am a certain thing is always enough to make me quite reconciled to that thing whether I rate it good or bad. I never try to improve or alter myself. The *only* thing I *should* like to change is I should keenly like to be a quicker & harder worker than I am. My inborn sluggishness makes me (when I try to work hard & quick) merely a plodder — a despicable thing.

It is very sweet of you thinking of the possibility of having Karen over again before we leave; but I fear, dearie, that would awake scandal, & must be put out of mind. Above all we mustn't have folk talking.

I did a lot of work at the f.s. introduction; yesterday but O, how slowly it goes.

So this is Wales. I notice very little different between their looks & the English, & their English (speech) is wondrously pure & undialectic, what I have heard. But then I hear that Swansea is not representatively Welsh. If it were, then I must say that either there must be a tremendous blend of Saxon blood in the Welsh now, or a ditto of Celtic blood thro'out England, or else Shaw is really right in putting almost all at the door of climate; "1 bloody British climate, 1 bloody British race."

So far the Welsh have made a sympathetic impression on me. I shall look forward to living amongst them, later on when I know their language.

176   TO KAREN HOLTEN   Saracen's Head Hotel,
[Original: English/Danish]   Chelmsford, Essex.
12.2.08. just before evening concert

It was very sweet to get your letter here. I do think we 2 are amusing. After having read your letter, I looked a little in Brandt — what a difference![15] You and I are real flat-land people; everything goes along comfortably; the most stupid questions are asked and answered without agitation in even warmth and calmness. I wonder how many lovers have asked their "ladies fair" the favour I begged of you in my letter that left last Friday. Do you think any ever has? I really wouldnt be surprized if none ever has — meaning it from his whole heart. But perhaps. And how many, I wonder, would get back so calm and boyish an answer.

You musn't be sorry for what I now want to say to you.

Before I knew M in Frankfurt I had fleshly sexual wishes and feelings enough; not very different from now. But when I began to be fond of her, the thought grew in me that carnality and love were quite inseparable. I couldn't at all think of one without the other. And I saw the whole world and art from that standpoint. The bourgeois and the "pure" and the spiritual became much dearer to me than before.

Notwithstanding that my inborn **caution** *never left me*, still I was, in my way, quite convinced of "one love, one life", and felt deeply hurt at all that reflected a contrasting point of view. I dont think I was much more stupid about her then than you are about me now; only that I chose her with the faulty instinct of the male sex, whereas you chose me with the more unfailing instinct of the female sex. I felt at the time a wondrously deep poetry in sex, & in fact it seemed to envelope every mortal thing, & it seemed to me to make things lovely & great, & to be worth *almost* (my caution underlined "almost") disaster, if need be.

But I could not reconcile it all to my earlier Anglosaxon ideals, my Schwärmerei for Walt Whitmanism, (whom I adored already *before* all this) my huge wish for ever greater freedom in all possible ways. From the earliest thoughts I have had I have always felt overweighingly what are, after all, just the Anglosaxon, old Icelandic, English speaking views of life:

15 *Brand*, Heinrik Ibsen's great lyrical drama of 1866. Grainger's Frankfurt sweetheart was Mimi Kwast (d.1926), the daughter of his piano teacher James Kwast. Grainger was party to her elopement, at the end of April 1899, with the German composer Hans Pfitzner.

That if haste & heat be avoided, disaster is pretty likely never to occur.

That no feelings, however seemingly deep & delightful & all engrossing, must ever dare to overflow "sound sense."

That morality in common practical & general things (money matters, politics, relation to the world at large & to outer circle of friends, patriotism) was more important than morality in theoretical, special & personal things (religion, art, the purity of one's own soul, love, purity, one's nearest & dearest friends, etc)

That orderliness, kindliness, freedom are more important important [sic] than pure love, inner nobility, art, religion, etc

That no personal ideals should be followed rather than the great general trend of the world's betterment.

That no *drastic* measures of any kind are ever resorted to in any cases whatsoever. No revenge, no jealousy, no fights, no sudden marriages, no sudden following of any conviction or "inner voice", no anger, *no unpractical devotions of any kind*

For many months after she left me the ideals of her influence remained, but as gradually the bitterness of missing her passed away came the thought. Why is all the world closed to me on her account? Even if she had loved me, & we both loved each other always, why should all the world be shut outside the gate of our love. Why this chilling coldness towards all the rest of the warm loving suffering wild human beings? Why these 2 so *mean & precious* about their bit of love? What harm would a little generosity & general spread-round do?

These of course were my permanent lifelong thoughts; are my thoughts, feelings now, & were so as a quite young kid in Austr. If ever you see a New Land you'll see how general is all that feeling there. When I thought I'd got a good way of making wooden stools I used to go out into the road & ask the passing schoolboys if they would care to have one each when I got them finished. Why not? What I am trying to prove is: that although fundamentally & temperamentaly a *socialist*, an *uncritical type*, & a sympathiser in *Free love*, **during the time of my first love** I was as ardent a convert to "one love one life", sexual purity, 2-together-&-the-world-without as you are now.

And I ask: How do you know that you are not fundamentally of the type to which I, mother, Walt Whitman, etc belong? You cant tell, any more than I could! Love is so strong, so tyrranic, so sudden in its sway, so un-ask-questions-of-it-able that it doesnt give you a chance to know.

Then, also, its obvious that the inherited instincts of your sex must play a part in this matter. I have so strong a feeling that all this undividableness of just 2 people, all this specialising of purity within ones own house (accompanied by jolly solid indifference for impurity outside) (in short; all this *specializing of good & generalizing of evil*) isnt helping on the big growth of freedom & greatness in the world. *Above all we need all folk to be free, single, self-answerable* units in their own souls.

We want no women (figuratively) clinging on the strong arm of men, no children owing all their everything to their parents guidance, no old mothers trusting to their bold sons, no farmers trusting to benevolent herregaardsfolk [Danish: lords of the manor], no sisters shielded by strong brothers, no religionists "sheparded" by holy parsons, priests — none of that ivy-on-the-wall game.

We want wild rude children that quickly know their own wills & only need their parents money & older heads for as short a time as possible.

We want women who enjoy men, cho[o]se men, teach men, learn from men, help men, get helped by men, *yearn towards them out of their own freedom*, (not cling to them) we want sharp alert bright-souled old mothers, not to be easily hoodwinked by the younger brood, but free, seperate, unenslaved up to the end, *loving*, but ever *selfpoised*, & *critical*.

We want socialists, & brothers & sisters both selfhelpful & able to teach each other, & want every man woman & child (& animals too if we could manage it) to think in their own dung-stupid heads, & be their own Gods, heros, heavens, hells, morals. Above all we want men with womanly qualities & women with manly, both of them sensual, lustful, selfish, selfcentred; both full of purity & impurity, bursting over with wiked wildness & angelic goodness — grasping, eager, selfwilled, animal, high-idealled; *but without a trace of anger, revenge, bitterness, narrowness, or* **possesive greed**.

What a time we'd have — & *shall have*, too.

Now I dont like to feel that that little Karen **must** *love only me*. I adore her to love me, & if **accidentily** she limited herself to me — why, its limited, it's not gloriously broad; — but it's no calamity. But I like to dream she *might* do any old fool thing. I should adore to hide behind a curtain & watch that Burne-Jones mermaid of a loving, loved, warmhearted, little Karen receive another bally lover. Clutching onto him in sweet gay glee like in B-J's picture: "In the depths of the sea". Only the lover musnt be dead; he must be active & worth his salt.

And I should be so overswollen with pride for that little Karen if she showed all her sweet purity & her nice young-animal-like skittishness and ravishingness, and I'd swell with joy to see that bright fine young lover fairly uplifted with how splendid Karen is, & I know he's realizing what a ripper she is — as I know already. That'd be grand sport.

I should fondly relish to see that young man have "the time of his life".

After the Concert.   There was a little bit of a man who opened the door to the artists-room this evening who resembled Grieg so surprisingly. He was just as small, and slender, and had the same kind of bones in his face, and the same way of opening his eyes, sending out a childlike expression in them. I talked a long time to him, but he wasn't little Grieg after all. I gave him 6 pence. He was a working man, and moreover looked a bit consumptive. Death! I am surprised that you women can be so willing to help forward that sad game of death! (for birth & death are one) Excuse me; little friend; I mean nothing against you personally.

I got a sweet letter from Mrs Grieg today. I cannot tell her that I met a "little grey man" (see op 66) here today who resembled the little Grieg.

I have now finally made up my mind to give up Scandinavia as a concert field, barring just a Recital a year at Køb, & any engagements that turn up *without my seeking them*; or anything with Svendsen, or that sort of thing. But the other game's not worth the candle, not for me, anyhow

I'm quite sure that's right about having to write to all the folk personally, but that's not good enough. I wish you would thank the Arbejderforeningen folk ever so heartily (if you already spoke or wrote to any of them) & say how sorry I am to be prevented coming by the splendid success of my tour here, & *regret any bother any one may have had on my behalf, in vain*. If you, little K, have had any bother on my account, already, about this planned visit of mine, then I thank you heartily for it. But I hope you haven't had. I'm anxious to get the Stockmarr letters, when I shall thank her, & answer either or both that seem to call for it.

You must forgive me that I say the following; it is not said without thankfulness for the dear meaning I know you had in the matter. I wish you would NEVER talk to any ½ stranger like Miss Stockmarr about any of my business matters, at all. Other pianists, in particular, should be kept **wholly outside** ones dealings, & as *ignorant as possible* of **all** one's business affairs. It's very unwelcome to me that Miss St or anyone else not a *near friend* of yours or mine knows anything at all about what I want or intend; although I dont doubt she's charming — I've always said so. I know Danes are much simpler than we are in all these ways. But I particularly adore *privacy* & all things duly hidden, & will be ever so thankful if you will always help me to this.

It would be much better if Nutzhorn, Arlaud, Z. Lassen none of them knew any more of me than that I was just a friend of yours, but a stranger to them in all ways: But of course, I own, that I was far the worst offender in this way. *But I am so no longer.*

I'm sure you tried splendidly to do all kinds of jolly things for me in all sorts of ways — but its all jolly hard.

I'm ever so thankful; only I adore secrecy & privacy, that's all. But now I've finally given up the idea of Danish prov. tours, & will stick to only a yearly Recital, & any other engagements that just happen along unsought, it will be much easier to manage.

Now then thanks for "Brandt". It will be ripping to read that, though I own it's got a bit of a serious look; but I've always longed to have it.

I wish you'd kindly let me know what the Tchaikovsky Concerto costed you in English money as I'd awfully like to send you that amount. You wont find it a bit hard when you really get going in it. In the 1st Allegro all jumps ought to be divided as follows: ·

wherever the jumps occur, treat them like this.

Do be a dear & let me know the cost of the Tchai; & ask me re any fingerings or anything you're rocky (usikker) about. all those appegios in the 1st Cadenza (starting (I think) end of page 2 & covering all page 3) should be phrased (as regards fingerings) both hands together, & *always* (except the very last appegio with B♭♭ in it) beginning with 3 notes & after that 4 4 4 to the top

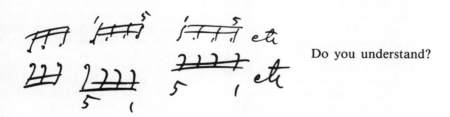 Do you understand?

So the little sweetie thinks she can take all my extremely interesting letters to the grave with her, if she dies. My letters shall be admired by a yet-unborn generation; can't you see that I always write with an eye to a possible public? Sometimes it seems to me that I can — to my shame. In any case if I sit and write to you for hours instead of having a "healthy and *peaceful* sleep'' (if there is page 6 of a letter from you — ''peaceful'' is scarcely a popular word) instead of composing, instead of learning Gaelic, or preparing F. S. Journal; then I always hope that my letters will be handed over to immortality one day.

In any case you won't be allowed to decompose down in the earth. All cleanliness-loving people are cremated. I hope that you, if you arrange to die while I am in Austr, will make sure that this is done.

No more earth burials or earth closets (like in Svinkløv) for me.

I quite agree you ought to have Gr Bs originals before I leave for Austr. You certainly receive much less than you should, you little sweet one.

In the train (and in the fog) 13.2.08. 8 o'cl, in the morning.

All the length of this letter has been really leading up to the question: what harm would there be if you did sometimes go in for my bad habit? Now; why does one miss a meat-mate (Kødfolk) more than other folk (brothers, etc) for whom one has warm love? Because to all the bedrock of hearty affection, comradeship, platonic devotion is added a *bodily need*. A meatmate stills this bodily craving. The combination of this with all the other feelings makes the whole business so strangely strong. Now it surely is your duty as a Dane, & to yourself, & to your kin & to me & yr friends, to *see that you are always as happy as you possibly can be*. I think it's grand fun that you miss me & I miss you & that we both rely on each other for so much joy — but that's no reason why we shouldnt lessen our *loss* of each other all we can.

You, darling Karen, are so sweet & clean & pure, nothing will ever make you less so, dont you fear. Surely you feel that I, too, am pure. And I feel deeply deeply thankful to my habit. It has helped largely to make me successful, & to keep me pure & my own master. *In the time when it was all too overstrong for me I loathed & feared it*; but that was merely a passing phase. I can now see what a boon it's been to me — as it has been to many another young chap who wished to keep as clear as possible of the world's dirt.

Can you remember that you didn't want me to come myself by *my own* hand, once? And believe me it is a splendid sensation. It is wholly different to the ''real thing'', & should never be looked upon as a go-instead for it. It's a thing, a phase, for itself; lovely in its own lonely way. I assure you that it is much better when one does it *oneself* than when another does it for you. You will see if you try. You are quite yr own master & you'll find out all kind[s] of splendid tricks & knowledge (just the difference between a good & a bad conductor) that will improve you wondrously for the ''real thing''.

But I was originally as much against as I am now ''for it''. If you could get to like the thing for itself I'm sure you'd find my absence in Austr much lighter. And I'd be *so happy* out there to know you were having a great old time all by yr little self now & then. You, maybe, feel you dont want to lessen even any loneliness or sorrow in that way. But we all *should*, I think, it's all of us our duty to greaten joy & comfort & happiness in ourselves & allselves, & lessen grief. You are in yourself such a nice fleshly little Karen; who knows whether it wouldn't in the end be very good for you? But you must use vaseline if you do it and don't forget that the legs and even the whole body should best change position now and again. One of our party was told by his Doctor the other day that he (the doctor) *had never met with a single case* where that habit had damaged the health of a *really strong person*. And that I would be inclined to believe. Where it is evil & rotten is when school-boys & schoolgirls start it [at] 12 years old, & that sort of thing. But it cant hurt folk of our age *if its done only seldom*. After all no one could point to me as an example of a person showing the *least* signs of being damaged in that way. I was ever so much more delicate (had nosebleeding, etc) when I first came to London, & as a child in Austr, than I have been these last few years. The chicken-pox did me up, but otherwise I've been in fine form. All this isn't a try to "get" you to do what you dont want, it's only my real convictions on the subject. Nevertheless I dont deny it'd be a great joy to me to hear that you had made an attempt. I'm sure, too, that it would all have amusing & curious results on your character, moods, & temperament.

31a. Friday. 14.2.08.

I had a fine time with J. C. Williamson's (the Australian tour agent) representative yesterday. *He gives me* **all** *I ask for.*

The next P.R. letter will leave London Tuesday.

Yesterday the man was here that I got songs from in Chiswick when you were here. He sang into the phonograph and was so inexpressibly amusing and irresistible. He's coming to eat "dinner" with mother while I am away. She'll phonograph him.

He told how his father died. He lived to over 70 years old and was a healthy active man until "he busted his gut" (he burst his bowels — eingeweiden [German: intestines])

Little sweet, goodbye for this time. How lovely yr father is on the mend. Do give him every warm message from me, please.

Darling Rodg is bettering too. Everybody is going to get fearfully well, you'll see.

177   TO KAREN HOLTEN   Imperial Hotel
[Original: Danish/English]   Malvern.
15.2.08.
[Extracts]

It is almost unbelievable that you are so little stupid as you are. One does not expect that a little Karen can be so good, and full of forgiveness, and understanding, as she can show herself; when it comes "to the point". When I kissed the chamber maid in Cardiff I didn't think at all that it could be anything serious or bad that I did. But afterwards it seemed something peculiar that I had done, and I was afraid that you would "blow me up", or that it would hurt you. And I have been so impatient to get your answer to that letter; and now you have been so extremely good to me.

An action like that in Cardiff, there was no real bodily feeling towards that girl; (it wasn't a "weaker edition" of what I feel for you — had nothing to do with it) it was just that she was pretty and I loved her prettiness as I love all beauty, whatsoever; and I thought to myself: I may never see her again; it is so sad to pass everything by. The same feeling of "not to lose" that I feel towards a folksong when I collect it. But she didn't excite my so-called "senses", funny little girl that she was. I must say, I dont think it would amuse me if every passing girl was to excite my body. There is something rough & greedy in that. But they all too easily appeal to my imagination, & occasionally (rarely) comes a quick wish to suddenly grasp one of these myriad suggestions that are everlastingly flitting thro' one's head. But not really very seriously, I am afraid.

Now I must hurry to the concert.

London   Saturday evening.

Just as, I suppose, woman is thankful when man understands her purity; just so is man rejoiceful when woman allows his freer license. Man loves to feel that woman wraps round his waywardnesses in forgiveness & pity, he can then nestle & feel guarded & guided like a swaddled babe; & that is so nice. I would feel a perfect devil if I felt my freedom was limited, restrained.

No, you are a sweet little Karen, you are really good to me, you are just as good as, and at the same time much better than, a boy. You are my real play-mate. You are the complete meat-mate that I own, and you are beautiful, and I can't see any difference between you and a great great pianiste, and you have a lovely flat tummy, and straight legs, and your hair everyone must admire, and I am allowed to kiss chambermaids, and have as many black and brown and yellow and south americans as I desire and the little Karen is so pure that one could eat her right up, and both she and I get younger with the years, and I can remember exactly how she smells when she gets warm under the eiderdown, and I can so well remember how our bodies shake with laughter under the bedclothes, when we have thought of something amusing, but our laughter mustn't be heard; and I can imagine how it would be to beat the little Karen with a whip, with all the power I possess, and hurt her just as sorely as possible, and it is to be hoped she'll scream, and look furious and hateful and suffer so that she ½ dies, and the whip must be very thin and completely unbearable, and she must try it on me and I won't be able to stand it.

And she will go around with a body like a Zebra, or a leopard. Or she will never be able to care for me again, or something like that.

Good night

178   TO ROSE GRAINGER   Wakefield.
[Two postcards]
20.2.08.

My darling mumlet.

The tiebox got me alright (loaned 1 off Earle last night) at Sunderland & yr 2 loved letters here.

Have written Mrs Freeman, Lady Bective, Mrs Colefax, Mrs Bevan, Mrs Hunter, Mrs Swinton, v. Glehn, & shall write Malone asking if I may see Steinways.

Tillett & I are going to see a Melodrama tonight. It ought to be fun. He's such a nice little chap; nothing coarse about him, I think. Nice & human & kind-thinking.

I wish y'd ask Cyril to put a short list of his best Soprano songs on a p.c. & you or he post it to Mrs Freeman for Beryl.

(20.2.08)

But doesnt she [Gabrielle Ray] look like Fairye [McGee?] in this?[16] Beauty & youth, goodie goodie.

I feel always so old & the need to look upon younger fresher more lifelit things.

My darling little mum, I feel just a weeny bit dumpy. But I'm eating full meals & doing all I ought.

I dont think I'll get back on Saturday morning. There won't be any gap between the trains I fear.

If I did get back it'd be at about 8 o'clock in the morn.

So full of love for that glorious dear fond mother of mine.

Longing for Sat.

16 Gabrielle Ray (1883–1973), from childhood a very popular English actress and dancer. "Fairye" (Mary) McGee, a childhood Australian friend of Grainger's. Beryl Freeman, daughter of Rose's Australian friend Mrs Freeman, achieved some reputation and success in the first performance in English of Debussy's opera *Pélleas and Mélisande*, given by the Denhof Opera Company, Birmingham, in 1913. She sang in Grainger's Concert of Compositions and Folk-Music Settings, 21 May 1912.

179 TO KAREN HOLTEN

[Original: English/Danish]

Stafford Arms Hotel,
Wakefield.

20.2.08. 11 o'cl. in the evening

What do you think I have just done? I and our agent (Tillett; he is a kind man — poor chap, I believe he has had an unhappy life) have been together to the theatre, in this little town. It was a really sentimental melodramatic real English piece, full of pure moral feeling, where the bad men and women suffer at the end and the 2 sweetest people in it marry and look lovely and young and enviable. I went because I wanted to laugh; I have always heard that such pieces are unbearably amusing, and it was so too in some details terribly funny. But what do you think happened? I became completely carried away just like the gallery (rough, dirty, warm-hearted, full-fed, common Yorkshire folk) and got quite sweaty with fear, and was near crying ½ the time. The result is that I am longing so unconcealably for you and am so very stupidly fond of you. When I see beautiful women on the stage, all their movements remind me of you, everything leads on to you.

I felt rather superior and didn't feel particularly (perhaps not at all) in love with you before one of the "frightful" scenes, when a man comes in after being tortured. I cant cant bear the very thought of human suffering, & on the stage, or anywhere, it turns me ½ mad with rage & helplessness. Whenever I feel afraid, if it's before an important concert, or anytime, I IMMEDIATELY long for you, and am straight-away afraid for all the evils I have committed against you.

I suppose all this is because I do really love you. If I don't love really well and warmly and truly, then I must say, that it often seems to me as if I did. You must not forget that I have loved once before, and this whole event has given birth to the constant thought in me: am I making a mistake for a second time? or the thought: have I ever loved, or was it not a delusion, then & now? I am sure you can easily understand that one can easily do that, in such a case.

All my brain tells me: you dont love, & you cant possibly love. (love is only a commercial game of nature's — it says)

All my little experience, & all my ideals, principles, & honor says: you dont love, you mustn't love, you shan't love.

But whenever I get suddenly (unexpectedly) strongly moved *I feel I do love you*, though my brain may still keep on saying busily: No, rot, %%%.

If you were with me tonight, I think that even my brain would take a little rest; I think that for the moment I am endued with the possibility of really feeling love for you with all the bloody sail I've got — with full canvas; but that is really not so awfully much.

If you had seen this play (you would have felt just the same as I) & had written me about it, I would feel — on reading your letter: She really is fairly stupid; why cant she have artistic sense sometimes, why does she feel (instead of think) with even her head?

And when I show you a poem of Swinbourne's which is gorgeous poetry but is exageratedly "male" in its undercurrent, you are just as unsympathetic over it as I over yr letter. That is because you feel the world as "life" & I feel it as "art." (Or, to use the Schopenhauer terms: you feel the world as "wille" & I as "vorstellung" — "Die Welt als wille & vorstellung" Schopenhauer) We are both right. You are wise about life, & bloody stupid about art, & I'm ½-wise about art, & hopeless about life. (earning money, being practical isnt understanding or appreciating "life" — "wille")[17]

Thus you are dead right when you admire things in art which are good *as life* (though they seem to me thin artisticly) & I right when I admire Swinbourne *as art*, & we are both silly & narrow when you are impatient at my enthusiasm for Swinbourne (& all his "light loving") & I disgusted at your admiration for the sort of things you like. But it doesnt matter.

17 Arthur Schopenhauer (1788–1860), German philosopher and author of *Die Welt als Wille und Vorstellung* [The World as Will and Representation] (1819). Algernon Charles Swinburne (1837–1909), English writer. Grainger made a setting of his poem "A Reiver's Neck-Verse" in March 1908 (see letter 186).

There's going to be such a big fight between us 2 that those small quarrellets dont count. It's only when I get moved, like tonight, that I realize what a hold you've got of my feelings, & that I realize what a fight we're going to put up.

For dont think my flag is down! Though I'm weak when I'm afraid, or moved, there aren't enough important concerts (I dont get them anyway) or sudden excitements to give my love for you a fair chance.

I intend to beat you morally into the dust. Just as I should adore to whip your body, (to make my greater beast strength leave marks on your dear tender flesh) just so do I long to triumph against your will. I want to think later in life: I beat her square. I gave her every chance, & she hadnt a look in.

Never the less, just as the thought of hurting your body is terrible as well as delightful to me, the chance of at all spoiling your life is repellant & apalling to me.

I wish to win & to give pain, but I dread to *harm*; that is appaling. I want to whip you & conquer over your "wille" with my *positive instincts, 1st instincts*. But I have a few compassionate feelings also, (not always weak either — I conceitedly pride myself.) I imagine that you like to know I love you; that thought & the yearning for truth makes me write to you tonight: to let you know how far my so-called "heart" is at your mercy.

The field of war stands as follows:

> *When I'm moved & surprized & feel strongly* I LOVE YOU, *really a good deal*; although even then I do not lose my head-balance & intend to beat you yet, all the same.

And let me tell you something else, now that we're in for truths. I have lately heard something from Roger which I shall tell you of, although its lesson is against my arguements. (but you cant say I'm ever really mean, I fight openly, dont I?) Roger says (& many others have told me before, but I didnt quite believe them) that doctors, etc, have told him: *that a woman who uses sexual preventatives* (& who gets to feel sex generally as apart from child-birthing) *much will probably never be able, later on, to have any children, however much she wants to.* Particularly those things of Rendall's that *you* have to use are *bad in this particular* — though harmless otherwise, of course.[18] There now, do your worst. What can you do? You can say to me: since this is so, I shant have any more fleshly pleasures with you with preventatives. And I answer back: nor I without.

Then what'll happen? I fell once, this time in London, do you remember? By God, how sweet it is to fall! If you liked to try, you might be able to make me fall heaps of times; every time (when I'm fresh) maybe.

I'm a devil, that's what I am. I wish to murder your unborn children. (but that hurts me so much also, sometimes) I wish to make you barren & dry like the bloody Godless deserts of my own loved Continent. I will see if I can't get all your body to die without fruit, without weiterverplanzung [German: further transplantation, i.e. propagation]. That is the *most male* joy there is: to destroy; vernichten [German: to destroy]. You shan't have any of the sweet little children that you long for. I shall have my little children, my compositions; but you shall not have yours. You shall yearn and yearn without result. In the end you will be dry, like a desert. And then perhaps I shall be able not to love you any longer — & then I will have won indeed. I'm a real devil — you'll see.

But despite all this; what wouldn't I give to have you here the whole short short night; *no preventatives*, no Redall, no india rubber hellishnesses, no care, no thought, no duty, no art-future, no anti-nature, no vasaline even.

Just flesh & flesh, & brainless animal health & soul-glory. No nonsense of "you come first; its safer". No safety. Let all things come together rather than apart. Let our poor heads feel crushed with too much blood (or too little — I dont know what the cause of the feeling is, scientificly)

18 Grainger is referring to the contraceptive pessary evolved in 1880 by the London chemist Walter John Rendell and marketed with enormous success from 1886 onwards, being sold throughout the world by the turn of the century. His spelling of "Rendell' is erratic, and always incorrect.

& climax, let that sensation come that all the whole worlds come tumbling together on top of us, through us, concentrated into one part of us — united part of us, no longer seperatedly you or I.

You don't know what I know in this matter. (I would sooner not know it yet — have it still before me — for discovery with you)

When I remember what a thing a climax is, when there are no preventation, & no care, & when it is absolutely instantaneous in 2 bodies, even under comparitively unsympathetic conditions — why I feel dazed when I dream of what it ought to be with *you*. Perhaps one exaggerates all these matters, though.

If you really are the **right one** *for me*; (if there really is such a thing as *the right one*) if it is possible, *if you are* **her** (and sometimes I scarcely doubt it; but sometimes I doubt heaps) *what would I not give to never have felt love or lust for any other woman before.* Believe me, I would give a lot. And yet there are other sides to my nature just as important.

180   TO KAREN HOLTEN   In the train.
[Original: Danish/English]
in the afternoon. 25.2.08.

Yes leopards! Would you also like to whip me? I have always longed to be beaten as well as to beat. Would you really not mind to whip me — not be bored with it?

We could do it in so many different ways.

1. the one to be whipped shall be tied up firmly and receive a certain number of blows; and afterwards the one who struck shall be tied up and receive the same number of blows; and then we will see who can hurt most, (and make the worst stripes on the body — the best leopard-markings) and who can bear it better. If it was done in that way, who would you rather have bound and whipped 1st, you or I? Or should we "toss up" for who should have 1st innings.

2. both you and I should take a whip, and both should be armoured over the head, face, neck and hands and wrists, and then we should whip away at each other, and do what we could.

3. only one should be beaten at one time, and the one to be beaten shouldn't be tied except the hands (but armoured on the head, face, and neck) and be allowed to run away and defend himself as much as possible. "Operations" could be limited to a definite short period of time.

You shouldn't have a single stitch of clothing on your body, but I "as man", must be allowed to wear a shield for the tediously easily destroyed parts of a man's body. I think it must be furiously painful for you to be whipped on your breasts, don't you think? (Couldn't you try on yourself sometime?) If it hurts terribly, you can count more strokes on me. But I can't give up to whip you there; it is one of the greatest longings of my little life.

Would you rather have the performance with or without screams? But tell me the truth, little Karen; do you seriously believe that it will ever actually happen — is it possible? If yes, then no words can tell the kindness of the world to a man of talent. That would be real repayal; a great, loving, gracious gift.

Sometimes I almost believe that it could be possible with you; for it feels as if anything could be possible with you. This whipping-heavenliness is one of the strongest bonds binding you to me. — I suppose one only touches a male being through his brute selfishnesses.

If you are ever able to make this come true, you will be able to know that you have blessed me with something unmeasurably great.

Even if you could make all my compositional ideals possible, you would not do me such an unbounded service. How I envy a woman who can do that! Discover her lover's fondest, keenest, most loving, maddest, most desperate, most despairing ideal, yearning, & hand over the realisation of it to him — he who is helpless, powerless, despairing alone.

When I first began to be fond of you my most despairing thought was: she may stand between me & my dearest ideal. One of my life's most lovely, most ravishing moments was when you said to me, almost ½ bashfully: and won't I have any clothes on when you whip me? I cannot possibly describe what I felt in that moment. And to think that I could realize these ideals, through you, *without crime*! Crime is so loathesome to me, yet I have always decided that I should have to risk it one of these days in order to grasp my life's greatest moment. You are a wonderful little one, anyhow, God knows what you may yet be capable of, before you're thro? "So take me", she said once. Yr little life's not without plot, romance, adventure. Anyhow mine isnt in the parts y're responsible for. Nor in most of the other parts either. Just cram jam full of romance & joy & interestingness and every kind of thing to be boisterously happy & thankful for.

How tired you must be of this whip-worship! Tell me to "Stop" when it goes too far, little sweet friend. You see its breath to the nostrils of my soul. That's why.

I have slept. It is good and easy to sleep when one is quite quite happy

---

Something I forgot to say: many years ago (when I was perhaps 16–19) when I got climax in my sleep, it was very often while dreaming a woman whipped me

181   TO ROSE GRAINGER   [PM Rugby Station]
27.2.08.

I was *so* frantically nervous last night at Cambridge at the start that I've very little idea whether I played the Bach-B & the 1st Chopin Study well or badly. But the public was so charming that from the Mazurka onward I got to enjoy things & capable of putting intimate & personal expression in my stunt. By the time I reached the March Jig I was in tiptop form.

O, if only I had better platform nerves, I might be really a fine pianist; but my quakings & pretty-near freeze of fear are an unoverratable handicap. When I settle down comfortably with an audience I suprize myself, of late years, how really feelingly & artistically (to my mind) I can perform; but all the torment & comparitively bad & lifeless playing that foreruns this does seem such a hopeless waste. It was delightful, a real treat, to hear Gervase Elwes. I relished the tight intensity & sensitive feelingfulness of his voice & singing hugely. He sang a *most moving* song of Holbrook's — really good stuff, I thought — the 1st passability from his pen I've met.[19] 3 cheers for England.

The scant audience (though not smaller than usual for the Cambr. Univ. Music Club, they tell me,) were sympathetic & very kindly — & interested-seeming; I quite loved them.

It was a keen happiness being with the Bevans. He is precisely the same as ever; has got a little more fat on him but it['s] evenly & balancedly spread & not shockingly much yet. They have 3 children already & seem-

19 Joseph (or Josef) Holbrooke (1878–1958), English composer. Gervase Elwes had sung his song *A Farewell*, a setting of a poem by Tennyson. In January 1908 Rose had attended the first performance of Holbrooke's *Apollo and the Seaman* at Queen's Hall, which she described as "mighty pish-tush".

ingly a 4th hanging over their head. She, naturally, under the circs, has the worn-out, played-out somewhat thin-haired looks of overquick mother-hood — so often seen in the quite poor. It is a cruel altar.

It looks as if all marrow, hairlavishness, bloom-of-form, & fragrence of flesh has been sucked away into the newer generation. Indeed, it looks as if it would take much ill usage by man to produce as destructive results in women as are effortlessly managed by the coming of these tender helpless things. Truly the whole matter of offspring is the most ruthlessly destructive engine we know.

Disease & war are comparitively kind & comradely foes.

I heard one of the babies yelling at 5 o'clock this morn. But the kids themselves — it is easy to see where the vanished bloom, lavishness, (unconscious) sensuousness of the poor hardlyused mothers goes to. Certainly **that** is real flesh which young children have, real tenderness, skin worth having, texture-sensitiveness worth mentioning. We poor grown-ups, we are but parchment & horseflesh! No wonder, dearie, you can't relish to see the wrinkles starting in me, if you've bygonely formed a childs'-flesh ideal of me. Why is it not given us to keep that delicious sensuousness tenderness & purity of flesh & skin till an age when we could use it & worthen it?

Bevan & I had long talks re the machinal notater.

There is only time, poverty, & laziness between now & its realization.

See how kind Earle was; this enclosed slip he worked out & penned for my guidance.

I got considerably more success than Elwes last night, but it was his 1st visit to Cambr. He gave encore: "O mistress mine" They shouted encore loudly after St-Gr, & would have given me a good few recalls 1st, but I saw no need to keep them waiting longer.

Fondest love, mother-love, longing for letter from you.

182   TO ROSE GRAINGER   Raven Hotel,
28.2.08.   Shrewsbury.
                                        [PM Chester, 3.15 pm]

Darling mother

Since posting you the p-card Ada has handed me a letter from Doc, & I have been thinking things over hard, & cant say I feel I ought to give in on the upright piano & N. Zealand-crossing points. From what he & Ada say, it would seem to be fairly safe to leave all advertising & program placing in their hands. And I will give in on *all* points if you would *really like* me to.

But I, personally, hate both Ada & Muecke & detest J. C. Williamson & feel very bitterly towards Australia from the *concert side* (fondly enough otherwise) & would sooner quarrel with the whole boiling of them & try & earn a decent living among clean folk in this country than go out on a long tour boiling with bile against Ada, Doc, & J.C.W, & everlastingly be feeling I had been had & stepped on over the biz.

I, if I were wholly alone in the matter, would sooner wreck the whole of my future over the matter than accept the offered wheeze of the N.Z. Xing & the upright rot.

But if *you really wish* anything I'd sooner follow that than my own (after all no doubt moody) urges.

Remember its not giving up just the week of getting NZ & back, but the NZ holiday as well makes a loss of *2* weeks at least, — £80. Why should I do this?

Maybe Ada is taking upon herself the pay of the party & that's why there's all this buggering in of the Mueckes; in that case, if Muecke *will own up to me that* **they** *are paying me & acknowledge it to be a* **personal** *favour to* **them**, (Mueckes) *my giving up the pay on boat, then* (if you agreed too) *I'd feel inclined to waive it.*

But why otherwise? Why to J.C.W. & his crew of tiresome waxwhisker'd Tallises & not ausgeschlossen [German: excluding] Schereks?[20]

I'd *much* sooner stay over here & teach.

However, there's plenty of time for us to talk it over on Sunday & for me to learn your all altering view of the biz before my final gab with that stinking Muecke, curse his German blood!

20 The whole of the negotiations for the 1908/09 Australasian tour were coloured by the experiences of the 1903/04 tour, particularly the quest for a piano firm to sponsor a decent piano. The reference to Tallis and Scherek is to the management and musical direction of the 1903/04 tour.

183   TO ROSE GRAINGER   Midland Hotel
[Three postcards]   Manchester
29.2.08.

[1. *The Boyhood of Rayleigh* by Sir J. E. Millais, P.R.A. (Tate Gallery, London)]

I cant deny that I'm desperately miserable, though less so today than yesterday.

I loathe all our party & this Hotel full of foreign waiters gives me the "jingos".

[On front:]

Do you remember our enjoying this & "The N.W. Passage" together years ago?[21]

As sentimentally stirring artworks they both appeal to me.

The slim spare Rayleighlet getting the eyes of his head oped to all the islands of the big seas & far off grabable desirablenesses & nourished upon tales of the Spaniard cruelties & menance.

21 Sir John Everett Millais (1829–96), English artist. His *The Boyhood of Rayleigh* was painted in 1870, *The N.W. Passage* in 1875. The Birmingham performance was the Grieg Concerto on 3 March (see note 11 above). At Queen's Hall on 15 March 1908 Grainger played the Tchaikovsky B♭ minor Piano Concerto for The Sunday Concert Society, the Queen's Hall Orchestra being conducted by Henry Wood. The *British Australasian*, 6 August 1908, wrote of Kipling as one ". . . with whom he [Grainger] often stays in his lovely old home in the country", but evidence of close social contact is thin.

[2. *The North-West Passage* by Sir J. E. Millais, P.R.A. (Tate Gallery, London)]

I like the touring well enough when there's no other important concerts to fear & fag for, & when I can in indulge in [*sic*] compo & f.s. work.

But I dont dare risk getting my head pointed at Journal 12 or anything decent before B-mingham & the Queens Hall Qual.

Fondest love, till tomorrow morning at about 7 o'clock or later.

[3. Rudyard Kipling]

Isnt this a dear queer lovable likeness of the little man? Got it in Chester.

I do feel such a considerable personal love for Kipling, no individual has meant more to me than he.

Yet I dont somehow feel in actual life that he will have that satisfactoriness that Grieg had. Yet Kipling artisticly has meant even more than Grieg to me.

Is it merely a barrier of Englishness atween us?

I cant make it out.

Or is it Mrs Kip?

[On front:]

Hwat a chin!

184   TO ROSE GRAINGER   from Gravesend.
[Original: Danish/English]
[Postcard]
2.3.08.

I have spoken with him and *will get everything I want*. The Contract will be *exactly* as I wrote to Malone.

He tried hard with sentimentality, but that doesn't help now. Both he and A were more than usually friendly and "obliging" this evening.

Margate is afternoon; return same night & all Friday free. Both solos encored tonight. Heaps of love, dearie one.

Not their fault re poster; local man

185   TO KAREN HOLTEN   Birmingham.
[Original: English/Danish phrase]
3.3.08. midnight.
[Extract]

Believe me I am tired. I've had a big week. In last week on Tuesday I had a 4 or 5 hours journey, the next morning up at 5.30 & a 5 hours journey; a Recital & up to 1.30 that night & up early & a 6 hours journey again. Saturday night travelled by night train from Manchester.

Last night (Monday) travelled 1½ hour to Gravesend, ditto back to London after concert taking midnight train to here, arriving 3 oclock at night. Had rehearsal & concert (Grieg Concerto) here & leave tonight 12.50 (midnight) for London, arriving 4 o'clock. I go home for a few hours & then off by early train (10 o'clock) to Bournemouth arriving midday, afternoon concert, & back to London & a quite different program at Bournemouth than the rest of the tour or tonight . . .

Played well tonight, tho' I could hardly keep awake.

186   TO KAREN HOLTEN   [In the train, to Winchester?]
[Original: Danish/English]
Monday 9.3.08.

It was a lovely day yesterday and we were all so happy and excited. The rehearsal was fixed for 6 o'cl, and quite unknowing and unexpected Gardiner came in the afternoon and waited, and stayed for the rehearsal. (Go to hell, you buggers! my co-tourists, that I hate, have gone, thank God! out of the compartment to get tea into their fat bodies.)

1st fiddle was a Frenchman, Mangeot, who understands Swedish, and has a splendid tone. Herman got him and 2 others together. Feilding came and listened for a bit. Herman rehearsed first for an hour on his new 4tet, and then I got 1½ hours for "Molly on the Shore" and the accompaniment of "Died for Love" on 3 muted strings. There were many lovely moments in Herman's thing, really melodious and charming in tone, that moved us all. There are also many less practical and less captivating things in it, which is also quite natural when one remembers how short a time it is that he has practised composition seriously, and how long it takes for everyone to get a reliable skill in a creative art. But he is definitely more skillful than the last time I saw his things, and he always shows the possession of an undeniable gift for melody and harmony, and over the whole a typical personal charm, truly Danish and lovable.

"Molly" which is the 1st chamber-music piece of mine to be performed since I was about 15 or 16, is quite "encoraging" It sounds good beyond all my expectations, very amusing, very peasant-like. There is very little in it that I want to alter. If you knew how hard it is to get a 4tet to sound at all, you would understand how happy and cheered up I am that my 1st attempt at it succeeded so fortunately. Herman played beautifully and his pizzicati sounded like an arrow shot from a bow. He is a sweet old friend; just the old same.[22]

I got "The reivers neck-verse" done yesterday morning and altered a part of the melody. I played it for Gard; he said: "You may be a crooked old villain in most manners; but you're still fairly straight in your music. Not gone to seed yet"

You already have the words of the 1st verse; would you like to have the rest? [Verses 2, 3, and 4 are given in full in English]

In other words, he has presumably stolen something to her advantage, and she shall be burnt and he hanged, and I find it amusing.

Have I already sent you Meridith's "The amazing marriage", or not? I will if I haven't already done so.

After the Concert; on the way home.

I wish I were dead or ill or something other than I am; I am unhappy, and lonely. But it is nothing in reality, for I am very well and am splendid, really.

I was so glad to get the letter from you last night. Your poor father with the pencils; it is touching. How happy I would be to know that he is well again.

Isn't it terrible with us civilised people that our women get children with so much pain and heart-rending trouble! For many uncivilised folk get them like nothing at all.

I have heard that the health-exercise man Müller has said that if the women did the stomach exercises we talked of, then they would be able to get children with ease.[23] Have you heard that? You will do the exercises won't you? For if you should get a child it would be just too horrible if you screamed a lot and suffered badly. What should I do? You know that I am the last person to wish that you or any other woman should get little ones, but it is a possibility that no woman is completely free from, and one of life's horrors that she really ought to be prepared and armed against. If possible never; but, by Jim — "wenn schon, denn schon" [German idiom: "may as well be hanged for a sheep as a lamb"]. Now we come to that about Rendal. Is there going to be a big fight between us over that? That could be fun! My ultimatum is: *No Rendal, no nothing.* What do you say to that?

I would definitely not risk anything at all without Rendals. But you could possibly use a machine like I borrowed in London to use immediately afterwards so the Rendal doesn't remain in place, would you rather that? Or have you something braver and more defiant to my ultimatum? I couldn't think of any more exciting battle of the wills than that; it could well be both lovely and dreadful. It reminds me of something about "rape". I have surely told you that that sort of action has an attraction in my eyes. After the whipping, if you were "madly angry" with me, couldn't I try and rape you — or is that disgusting? Perhaps it is disgusting. Or would being tied-up and raped be amusing and good? Tell me your little opinion.

You mustn't be afraid that we will injure each other too much with the whipping; namely, it hurts so much more than it harms; moreover we would never lose the most tender regard for each other — the difficulty will be to be able to act hard *enough* to each-sweet-other. After I have whipped you, you will be treated as a Crown princess (as H used to say) that I can assure you; you will be kissed, the whole leopard, and tickled, and you shall be made to feel (if I am talented enough for it) how treasured you are, how sweet-lovely you are, and how grateful one is to you. But you

22 Writing to Herman on the same day as this letter to Karen, Grainger commented, ". . . I must say that I am first of all thankful that I was sensible enough to wait with its performance until you were present. I cant imagine my chamber music at all without hearing your bass-fiddle tone among it. It also has a great moral influence on the others when there is one who understands pizzicati". Grainger's setting of "Died for Love", for voice and three instruments, was completed on 18 December 1907. It was published by Schott & Co., London, in 1912. Grainger premiered his piano solo version of this setting at his recital at Aeolian Hall on 16 June 1908.

André Louis Mangeot (1883–1970), a naturalised British violinist of French birth; it was his availability that determined the date of the rehearsal. Herman was in London (alone) for the "season". Each paid his share of the rehearsal costs.

23 Jörgen Peter Müller (1866–1938), author of a system of physical exercises known in English as *My System: Fifteen Minutes' Work a Day for Health's Sake*. An authorised translation by G. M. Fox-Davies was published in London in 1905.

won't sleep straight away, will you? So much must happen before one sleeps. One must sleep in reconciliation, sweetness, friendship, with the fleshly comrades' limbs all smoothly and caressingly interwoven.

Poor me, I dare not do the gymnastic exercises — will you do them for me? If anyone asks me: can you do this and that gymnastic exercise? I can safely answer: "No, I daren't, because I have varicose veins; but a great pianiste, who at the same time is a little Karen, she can." That would comfort me, the ruin, so indescribably.

You will, won't you?

And when does side-saddle riding begin?

What a heroine, athletic Amazon she will become, the little one. To talk of the spring of the year. That was not so good, for I can't stand the European spring. You know that I lack sympathy with Nature's birthing maternal instincts; therefore spring is hardly the thing for me. I never take any notice of spring, except to get pimples and compose a little more. The hateful indecent small leaves that the trees here in Europe get in this time seem to me nothing more than a mass of disgusting tree-pimples. (like mine) But I would gladly be with you, even in the spring.

Do you know that a woman's breasts, after she has had a child, *always* hang down? and that she can never get them firm and nice again? Think about that a little.

Müller says that he sleeps without either night dress or bedclothes on and with an open window? I tried it in Germany, but couldn't sleep. I can imagine it is healthy; but does he really mean it?

You ask me what else she [Alfhild] has said against you. I really can't remember anything. That is to say, when I don't believe any more in the truth of something, I forget it straight away. Therefore it is impossible to remember anything that was said against you. Moreover, as far as she's concerned, she talks so very animatedly and so much, that she is forced to say a great deal both good and bad. Don't be afraid that I walk round with remarks against you sitting in my head; "I go with a 1000 thoughts", my own thoughts of your sweetness and goodness to me, and about how pleasantly tempting you are.

I am so glad your grandmother is young again. It is almost dangerous to be "old" in that age. Poor dear lady.

Yes, when shall I buy weapons and armour for our battle? Don't you think that I 1st need to set up a good record of no bad habit. That was the condition, wasn't it? If I only *can*? I have been good since Feb 29; now it is *nearly* March 10th.

March 11th. Still good.

Goodbye sweetie. Regards to all at home

Be happy and gymnastic

Tons of love.

187 TO ROSE GRAINGER   White Hart Hotel,
12.3.1908.   Salisbury

Such a sleepy sonlet sits writing! We had an hours wait at Westbury today & Liddle, Earle, & I set out to walk to the next Station 6½ miles off. Earle dropped behind towards the end, & in hopes of catching the train Liddle & I trotted the last 2 miles.

I, however, left him behind just towards the end & arrived alone to find the train leaving the platform *a minute before its scheduled time*. Liddle turned up a minute later. So he & I walked on 2 stations further along the way to Salisbury & picked up the train shortly before 6, doing about 12 miles in all. It was a glorious day sunshiney & glowing neither hot nor cold.

We relished it hugely & I spent a few pence well in apples & oranges which are adorable to eat on foot.

I got an idea this afternoon on the tramp. You & I must do a tourlet with the bathchair. Take plenty nice books to read in case of rain (when we'll freeze onto hotels) & nightclothes, & travel when its fine. We could easily do our 15 to 25 miles a day, & have glorious fun out of it.

You were saying we ought to go in for some fun together sometimes.

Why not take our bath chair with us to Stanway & when our visit there is at an end send back our boxes by train & I *wheel* you back to London?[24]

It'd only take a few days & we could easily take the train anywhere if bored or tired or it got too long.

Think of it. I think it'd be glorious. Only 3 or 4 days. We could spare those, couldn't we?

Played the Fauré again tonight;[25] getting *a bit* better now, I hope.

Fondest love; till tomorrow at about 8 in the evening.

I should like to practise 2 hours when I arrive & have something cold at 10, if possible.

yr larklet
Perks.

188   TO KAREN HOLTEN   [London]
[Original: Danish/English]
Monday. 16.3.08.
[Extracts]

It went very well for me in Q's Hall. Never have I played the B♭ Tschaik as well as yesterday. I wasn't particularly nervous and people were very friendly. We didn't have any rehearsal but went unbelievably well together (the orchestra and piano) and Wood was very enthusiastic about the ensemble playing. In the evening I played Fauré's 1st Nocturne for him.[26] He was very kind and appeared to think well of the performance.

I played somewhat too fast, he said; and I can very well realise that now. His manners and personality are very winning, he has the easy calm collected French manner that I like so much. However it is a little difficult for me to understand the depth in him, possibly because we cannot talk to each other, or because he belongs to a still more highly civilised people than I. He doesn't give that impression of immediate truth and courage that the sweet little Grieg did — which one wouldn't expect either from his music. He is, in other words, after all a man recognisably like other men. (although more gifted and of a rare lovely nature) That is, not anything so supernatural as the little Grieg. But that's not necessary either. There was a lot of Fauré played last night, and there were tremendously lovely things among them. It was a happy evening for me although I was a little tired and (obviously) subdued after the excitement of the afternoon. It was amusing to meet all the lovely and plain laughable society people again (I like them very much in their way) and lovely to be highly valued by them and made a fuss of.

It surely helped with Tchaik that I am still "good". (the whole time) *But let no one believe I would be so for one hour to help my success or my music!* I believe I am good now because I don't particularly want to be naughty, (if it will only last?) or because all my thoughts are so completely involved with you recently, in longing for you and desire for you and anticipation of the whipping, etc.

With me the pendulum always swings rather far over to either side, so it seems, & lately it's been well over to you.

24 The reference is to their projected folksong collecting expedition at Stanway, Gloucestershire, the country home of Lady Elcho, in April. In the event Rose did not go.

25 The Nocturne No. 1 in E♭ minor. It was included in the programme of Grainger's recital at Aeolian Hall on 16 June 1908, and he also played it on the forthcoming Australasian tour.

26 Gabriel Urbain Fauré (1845–1924), French composer, teacher, pianist and organist, at this time also music critic for *Le Figaro* and director of the Paris Conservatoire. He came frequently to London, where his most influential friends and patrons included Frank Schuster and John Singer Sargent. This was the first of two trips he made to England in 1908. On 18 March he gave a public recital of his own compositions, with Mme Jeanne Raunay, at Bechstein Hall. He also made several private appearances, including a recital with soprano Susan Metcalfe for Queen Alexandra on 23 March. Grainger met him several times over the eight days between 15 and 22 March: twice (including the first meeting) at Frank Schuster's, and at Sargent's, where he played Fauré his compositions. He developed a deep sympathy for Fauré's personality and a lifelong enthusiasm for his music.

When I sit and practise, or lie in bed, or travel I think about you the whole time, just lately. It really won't last long, to that degree. But it is true that at the present you completely fill me; nearly. When I am in the train I pull my cap over my eyes and think of you uninterruptedly. Even at a concert on tour, sometimes. I think about ideal clothes for you, about whipping, just how you shall be tied, just how you would look, about your riding, piano playing; altogether very stupid, but (for me) very sweet, and more engrossing than anything else.

I feel a strong urge to experience all the sexual things I have ever planned (in any case those which are more or less possible) with *especially you*. I can just imagine the pleasure if all that sort of thing could be united in one who would have 1000 times more understanding for it than 10 *different* people would have. That is now my longing for the moment — to experience all possible things with *especially you*; but that is not to say that that wish will always remain to that degree; perhaps it will quite disappear. But at the moment that's how it is, and why shouldn't you hear about it? Poor little Karen, so sharply loved, how much of her will be left if all the "planned things" are gone through?

Friday and Saturday I felt rather as if I would burst; so I took a sewing needle and stuck it through my small breasts. It must be a very thick needle or it would perhaps break inside the flesh, and that is dangerous. It is remarkable how much resistance there is in flesh; it is like leather. It hurts amusingly *while* one sticks the needle through the flesh, but it lasts all too shortly. Therefore I put some cotton in the needle and made many knots in it and pulled it through my breasts. I made the knots bigger and bigger and at last the cotton broke. From that comes the enclosed blood. But flesh doesn't bleed much from a needle prick, it cuts too cleanly, and grows together again at once; my breasts are healed again today.

You must do it for me one day, won't you. It would be intoxicating to have it done by you. Just think! I wasn't naughty even after that! There you can see that it has nothing to do with the will. But that is not so strange. For although the pain is terribly exciting *while it lasts*, a strong reaction comes straight after, and one shakes of cold and feels un-fleshly . . .

Tuesday. 17.3.08.

. . . Herman was here last night. We were (I, at any rate) so deeply happy together, talked about his 4tet played Hillsong, (he the 2nd piano!) Fauré, Ravel, Gardiner, etc. How I love him! Oh yes, Denmark still means a lot to me. The qualities some of you have, they influence me in a quite peculiar characteristic way. He looks so well and **young** and Danish and is the same lovely comrade as always. He is like a kind-hearted healthy dog, with his tail always wagging.

189 TO ERNEST THESIGER   31A King's Road
eve. 16.3.08.   Sloane Square
                                                             S W

My dearest Ernest.

I fear Thursday afternoon is impossible. For I'm going to tea with Ada Crossley that afternoon to show her a lot of Grieg songs, some of which she intends doing on her Australian tour, & it will likely be a fairly lengthy business, I fear, & she lives in St Johns Wood.

But I shall adore to look in latish, if I might, *if back early enough*; only I so sadly fear I shan't be.

But I am back in town from the beginning of April & if you'll give me a chance then we'll have a jolly meeting together, for which I yearn after our now highly long sunderedness.

It was upheartening to glimpse you on Sunday & mighty nice of you to go, & come.

Awfully sorry that there is such a slender chance for Thursday

Ever yr friend
Perks

190 TO ROGER QUILTER   Royal Hotel,
[Original: Danish/English]   Wigan.
25.3.08.

27 Roger Quilter's health had been very poor in the early months of 1908. Indeed at one stage Rose had written to Percy that she felt the end was near. He recovered, but slowly. With Rose's encouragement, Percy had written regularly to Quilter throughout this period and his letters, so he wrote to Karen, had had a therapeutic effect, a looked-for end which to some extent determined their style.

My dear Roger[27]

I have just finished the preface to my F.S. Journal, and am very glad to have got through it. When it is fair-copied I will send it to you and ask you to be kind enough to correct everything you think is unclear or clumsily said.

I have been here without the others (who are either in M'chester, L'pool, Colne, or somewhere else) as well as Miss Florence, yesterday and today, and it has been so lovely to have been quiet and alone. After Fauré's lovely 2nd 4tet which I heard last Sunday at Frank Schuster's, my fellow-musicians seem like a nightmare.

It was absolutely heavenly, that 4tet. I was so stupid, a year ago, to think that the 1st 4tet was better; but I made an enormous mistake. I think now that there are many many places in Nr 2 that absolutely come up to the most lovely things in Tristan; without joking it is like [an] angel's song, a great deal of it.

It seems to writhe in luscious human sensuous pain, never excessive, or energeticly passionate, but solemnly gnawingly soothingly glowing within, with calm Odin-like weltschmerz [German: weariness of life, pessimism].

When we get together again I must show you some places that I am particularly in love with; by the way I can well remember your enthusiasm for the Fauré 4tets, some years ago.

Both F himself, and the Capet 4tet played splendidly, with lovely subdued inner glow and wavelike "flow."

Last Saturday I played my English Dance, Wamphray Ballad, Died for Love, Irish F-S, Tiger Tiger, Morning Song, for Fauré and he was so kind and interested. It was at Sargent's, and only him, F, Rathbone and I were present.

Fauré said, "Il a beaucoup de flamme" and "C'est un energie supreme" [sic], or something like that.

You know I've always felt the English Dance as the whole land on the hop, the whole caboozle of football, factory furnaces, newspaper bicycling boys, fire-engines; the general athletic pith of England whanging away.

Of this Fauré knew nought, but his 1st word after my playing of it was "It's as if the total population was adancing".

So he fished the true typical impression out of my rotten hammering out of it, somehow.

The more I see of him, the kinder and more lovable I find him, and can better and better understand the good Sargent's eager love of him.

I don't think he is really even in his works; it is surely seldom that he reaches so high up as in this 2nd 4tet.

But he *can* be a great genius, sometimes, it seems to me.

Indeed we live in an age of rich compositional output after all I find.

Yesterday I wrote out my new song: *A rievers neckverse.*

Mother seems a trifle downhearted in her last letter to me. I do wish you'd be a dear & write her bully & upbuckingly.[28]

Ada sends all warmest messages & begs you let her know if you've anything you think would suit her well; for her Austr trip, for inst.

I don't know whether I have written to you or not since Herman's and my 4tet was performed? It was a really nice rehearsal and there were so many charmingly lovely places in his (H's) thing and "Molly" sounded very satisfyingly, on the whole. I did so wish that you could have been there for this.

Another time.

Ever fondly
Perks.

191 TO FREDERICK DELIUS   Royal Hotel,
28.3.08.   Crewe.

My dear Delius

How really spiffing that you are coming over again! *Do* let's see something of each other this trip. I long to hear more of your stuff, etc.
3 cheers Hanley.[29]

I'm on tour still but am just finishing & shall look forward to seeing you in a few days now.

Ever warmly yrs
Percy Grainger
(31a Kings Rd Chelsea)

192 TO KAREN HOLTEN   [London]
[Original: Danish/one sentence English]
Tuesday morn. 31.3.08.

This evening mother and I are going to hear Delius's "Brigg Fair" (an orchestral work about songs I collected) in Q's Hall.[30] Delius is here at present and is an enormously lovable and lively and amusing person. Think what the dear Feilding has done! He has paid the journey all the way from Lincs for old Taylor so that he can hear his melodies on a big orchestra. Feilding, Taylor, mother and I are eating at F's and going together to the concert. What a pure dear good nature that Feilding!

Last night I was at a ball at the Duchess of Rutland's.[31] She is so beautiful, and her 3 daughters likewise. It was "fancy dress" and one of the Rutlands was dressed in man's clothes (Bulgarian?) It looked so good. It pleases me so indescribably to see such young slim splendid limbs well and amusingly dressed. It was one of Rutland's daughters (Lady Marjorie Manners) who I saw 3 (?) years ago at the Hunters, and thought to myself: she is the only Society woman that I would terribly like to have in my bed. She is wild and untamed and unpredictable. Also this time, I would awfully like to have her in my bed, I would give a lot for it. She is thin and athletic and devilish, but at the same time blond.

I am so glad to be home again; mother and I are so happy together. She wasn't so well but is much better again.

Are you going to have a sore tummy you poor thing! I would wish you had it quite unbearably and that I could be with you and kiss your eyes the whole day.

28 Rose's letter does not survive. However, it is clear from Percy's reply that she had written telling him that she would not accompany him to Stanway. By 25 March she had recovered sufficiently to attend, and enjoy, a lecture on Socialism by Bernard Shaw.

29 On 2 April 1908 Delius was to conduct a performance of his *Appalachia* at the Victoria Hall, Hanley, with the Hallé Orchestra and the North Staffordshire District Choral Society. It was his first public appearance as a conductor. It was for this that he came to England.

30 Delius's English Rhapsody *Brigg Fair* was played by the New Symphony Orchestra conducted by Thomas Beecham (see also note 43, 1907). Reporting the performance in his letter to Karen the next day, Grainger described Joseph Taylor's reaction, ". . . the old man became red with pride when he recognised his song on a big orchestra and said 'It's just it' or 'It's the best of the lot', although he also thought well of the 'Masters[ingers]' overture". Joseph Taylor, of Saxby-All-Saints, North Lincolnshire, was bailiff on a big estate and was seventy-five in 1908. Grainger described him as ". . . a courteous, genial, typical English countryman, and a perfect artist in the purest possible style of folk-song singing".

31 Marion Margaret Violet (1856–1937), wife of Henry John Brinsley, eighth Duke of Rutland. She had one surviving son and three daughters of whom the eldest was Victoria Marjorie Harriet (1883–1946). Her other daughters were Violet Catharine (b. 1888) and Diana Olivia Winifred Maud (b. 1892).

Later (in the tube)

I have done so much this morning I haven't time to tell it all.

People say that when one really loves one doesn't have sensual thoughts *all the time.*

I don't know. I have. I am thinking sensually about you almost continually. Thoughts of you come a little like a bolt from the blue.

In you I am used to melt together all the sensual thoughts which have collected more or less unused since I began to have feelings at all. You are the only companion for this pretty much the greatest part of me. What shall I do? The most natural thing is for me to think enormously sensually about you continuously. Do you think that is bad towards you? I don't at all. I would wish I had a woman's body and could be a steady blue flame and an everlasting irresistible temptation

Next Post Restante from London next Friday.

I am feeling so happy and well, and I am good as well. And I am doing an exercise of Müller's 30 times without stopping twice a day.

Grainger was back in London on 29 March 1908. Though he made several short trips over the weeks between this and his departure for Australia in August, he was never away for more than a few days at a time. Sometimes Rose went with him. There are no letters from Percy to Rose from the end of April to the start of his travelling in Australia in October.

The letters to Karen, written as usual every two or three days, reflect again the frenzy of his days in London, particularly during the "season". He settled quickly into his home routine of practising (for his solo recital on 16 June), teaching and dashing about, with composing as time allowed. His major effort through April was the completion of Journal 12. He re-transcribed many songs collected earlier and already transcribed as part of his Collection of English Folksongs *Nos. 100–200, "sweating crazily" at it. This part of the work was finished by 25 April and the whole Journal "packed and ready to go" on 6 June. With the Journal out of the way, he turned to the completion of Nos. 200–300 of his* Collection of English Folksongs *and to the transcription of melodies collected in Gloucestershire. He made a brief collecting trip to Lincolnshire between 24 and 27 May. In May he was also busy with his recordings for the Gramophone Company, Joseph Taylor's recordings being made in June.*

Grainger's father arrived in London in the middle of June. With the Australian trip confirmed and all details settled early in April, Karen was invited on a "farewell" visit to London. She arrived on 10 July, remaining until the end of July.

32 From 3 to 6 April, Grainger was the guest of Lady Elcho at her country home Stanway, in Gloucestershire. It was Grainger's second trip to Gloucestershire for the purposes of folksong collecting (see letter 156). Other guests at this time included Arthur J. Balfour, M.P., John Singer Sargent, The Hon. Alfred Lyttleton and his wife Edith, the novelist Herbert George Wells and his wife, and Lady Wemyss, wife of the tenth Earl of Wemyss and Lady Elcho's mother-in-law. As Grainger wrote to Karen on 7 April, "I collected (except in the evenings) the whole time from Friday till Monday 11 am and filled 47 phonograph cylinders and got 48 or 47 different songs from 10 different men and women". The main part of his collecting was done in Winchcombe Workhouse. As on the previous trip, he was assisted by Eliza Wedgewood. Grainger had collected from Mrs Walker in November 1907.

193 TO ROSE GRAINGER   Stanway,
Sunday. [PM 5 April 1908]   Winchcombe.

My darling one.

All thanks for your welcome letter got yesterday.

We had a great f. songing day yesterday & in the evening I played Bach, & Grieg, lots. Everyone charming, amusing, & delightful.³² I've taken about 15 records so far, quite good stuff most of it tho' no outstanding poetic personality has cropped up 'mongst the f-singers yet. Got the "drummer boy" complete from Mrs Hawker (who asked after you lovingly) & a nice Green Bushes variant. Got a very complete Lord Bateman, & about 10 Morris tunes. Just the same sort of thing as Sharp's. All the folk are charming & Miss Wedgewood has done her work perfectly as far as I can make out.

There is a big field before her here, I am sure, & she will reap it too, I think.

We've a big day before us today again & Sargent is going to come with us to the workhouse & is very keen, & open to the poetry of it all.

Mr & Mrs Wells were with me most all yesterday. He tremendously hived by the sweet humanity of f. singers, & he [*sic* she?] charming happy kindly & highly observant in heaps of ways.

They are a very happy-seeming blueeyed couple.

Balfour's motor's a dream & he a dear beyond words. Alfred Lyttleton I'm mighty fond of too.

I arrive London about 2.30 tomorrow.

Fond love & feelings

Sargent & all clamoring for you & missing you much

194   TO KAREN HOLTEN   [London]
[Original: Danish/some English words and phrases]
Thursday 9.4.08.

Little sweet Karen, only friend.

Don't be disappointed; I am going to A[ustralia] after all.

I can't tell you how bitterly cross I am because I wrote to you the day before yesterday that I wouldn't go, but I believed it was quite settled, since I had written "*finally* no" to both Malone and Muecke; and then they came with *everything*, absolutely everything, I had wanted in the contract, and so we had no possibility to say no any more. It would also have been madness to reject this offer. So now it is signed and finished.

But I am *so cross* with myself to have disappointed you in this stupid and completely unnecessary way. That is, I think, the most villainous thing there is, to disappoint. Everything else is sometimes forgivable.

Now we must see each other before we travel; (in August) no doubt over here. About that later.

I have now begun on the fair copy of Journal 12. It absolutely must be completed within a month's time.

Last night Roger was here, (he is well) Delius, Mrs Delius, Feilding, and Fletcher (come home from Egypt), and we had an evening of my ugly things. Really I don't care for such evenings, although they are exciting. Delius offered to perform Wamphray Ballad at the 1st Festival of The Musical League. I declined with thanks.[33]

So I won after all, over all the businessmen, Muecke, Malone, etc. I got them to put altogether my own words into the contract, just what I wanted.

Now some more about Stanway, last weekend. Balfour is (like Feilding and Roger) the *ideal Englishman*. He is Scottish. He is taller than Roger, with warm loving eyes and cold features. He has a smaller stomach than I; the same with Alfred Lyttleton, who is also 6 foot 3 inches. No person could be more entertaining than Balfour. Every sentence he says is almost worth remembering.

He said of Mrs Webb: (Socialist) "She eats nothing, which may be right, but works hard, which must be wrong."[34]

He has a rare soulfulness, is religiously inclined, and loves Bach passionately. He has one of the nicest motors I have ever been in, and on Monday

33 The formation of the Musical League was announced in *The Times* on 23 March 1908. With Sir Edward Elgar as President, Frederick Delius as Vice-President and a distinguished committee, its declared aim was by various means "to foster the cause of music in England and to promote the development of musical life and culture throughout the country". It had a particular but not exclusive commitment to the performance of works by British composers. The first and only of the planned annual Festivals was held in Liverpool on 24 and 25 September 1909 (see letters 285–6). After struggling on fitfully for some years, the League was formally dissolved on 25 April 1913.

34 Arthur James Balfour (later first Earl of Balfour) (1848–1930), philosopher and statesman, at that time leader of the Conservative opposition. Alfred Lyttleton (1857–1913), lawyer, statesman and sportsman; Edith Sophy (*née* Balfour) was his second wife. Martha Beatrice Webb (1858–1943), wife of the social reformer, historian and author Sidney James Webb; she shared with him an absolute devotion to public service and they co-authored several books.

we motored about 46 miles in an hour and a few minutes. It was open, and Balfour, Lyttleton, I, (we 3 without hats on) Sargent and Mrs Lyttleton sat there and were blown, rained and sunned on, so that we were moisteyed, wet, cold, hot, and happy. It was fun to see an amusing farm labourer sing into the phonograph, while Balfour, Lyttleton, Sargent, Lady Elcho, Lady Wemys, etc listened to it. The farm labourer of course was quite calm and self-possessed; only a little happy and proud. It was a happy time, full of activity there.

Miss Wedgwood who prepared the f.s. ground for me was quite splendid. I am so certain of her gift for collecting that I hope to be able to get her to collect in other places as well. Everything was faultlessly prepared for me. I phonographed without interruption all the days through. And in the evenings it was tremendously amusing and interesting with Balfour and so on.

Tomorrow I am meeting Lord Rayleigh (our greatest acoustician) at Balfour's to talk to him about my *machanical notater*.[35]

My work on the F.S. Journal interests me exceedingly.

We will see interesting things on the Australian tour. Perhaps we will come home via Singapoor, Hong Kong, China, Japan or Canada; but still unsettled. I already long for the expensive looking smooth sides of the great ocean steamers, and all the merry lazy Saxon shipboard life. It is indescribable, the charm that it has.

I don't know the things of Swinb.[urne's] that you mention. I hope they are not boring.

Yes, fancy-dress, but only for the women; men as usual. How did I behave? I talked to the old ladies and I got Beigel[36] to sit and talk to me; and then Lady Marjorie came and asked me if we shouldn't have the next dance together; I said can't dance, so she said we can sit. But I didn't know when the next dance began and walked as far away from the ballroom as possible. She found me and said now it is our dance: but I said but I'm no use but she said come and sit here or something like that and we sat.

She is slim and athletic, and a little cat-like without being in the least nasty or sharp.

Wildness, tenderness, and great youth are good bedfellows, don't you think? You are also wild and tender and young. I am unfortunately tamed, fat, and old. But if you were here I would take trouble to be fit in all three regards.

Now goodbye. Sometimes I am lonely. Every evening, every day.

Next P.R. leaves Saturday.

---

195   TO KAREN HOLTEN   [London]
[Original: Danish/some English]
[Extracts, several letters, spring/summer 1908]

11.4.08.

I am working almost continuously at J. 12. You must get one when it comes out. You will see that I have put a lot of work into it. I am going through all the Lincs records afresh and am getting many things 10 times more accurately than before.

15.4.08.

I am practising quite a lot now, and with practising and pupils I am forced to write the f.s. Journal either before breakfast or pretty late at night. But I enjoy it very much.

35 John William Strutt (1842–1919), third Baron Rayleigh, mathematician and physicist. In 1877/78 he had published a monumental treatise on acoustics, the *Treatise on the Theory of Sound*. The meeting was not a success. As Grainger wrote to Karen next day, "I got nothing out of Lord Rayleigh yesterday. I think the question bored him".

36 Victor Beigel (1870–1930), English pianist and singing teacher of Hungarian descent and international repute. His acquaintance with the Graingers dates at least from the summer of 1904; in her letter to her sister of 21 July 1904 Rose describes him as "really charming". Enthusiastic about Percy and his compositions, Beigel participated in the rehearsals of Grainger's choruses over several years. Grainger probably met him through Gervase Elwes, of whom Beigel was a teacher, friend and sometime accompanist.

Tuesday [21.4.08]

You mustn't take it amiss that I write to you so meaninglessly as I do lately. The truth is that Journal 12 is a jealous wife. It wears me out so tired that I haven't strength to think of anything else. I am moreover working colossally eagerly at it, but doubt all the same that it will be ready in time. I sit with the phonographic (rubber) hearing apparatus fixed to my head, while a metronome ticks away all it's worth. But I am still discovering new important things about folksongs! No one knows anything except me, and I have scarcely begun.

Saturday. 25.4.08.

The musical part of the Journal is now ready — all that with the phonograph. Now there is only a fair-copying of the introduction and general tidying-up.

. . . Little Karen, I can't be quite good. I've not managed better than a week just lately. Now I hope it will be better; but when I am overworked I don't seem to have any power over myself.

I wish you were here with me. I would undress you and carry you to the bed and bite you and lie so heavily on you and kiss you everywhere (I remember places I have not kissed *yet*) and be quite careless and sleep right inside you and wake up late and do it all over again and eat breakfast hungrily.

Monday. 27.4.08.

I have absolutely no engagements for the summer; it is really dreadful. I am afraid they have had enough of me over here. It is a little difficult to be a pianist when one doesn't practise and hasn't any interest in the whole thing.

1.5.08.

Now it's summer; & the rich rotters are dressing voluptuously & the beerswillers are sweating ruddily readily. How I love the warmth. London reminds me today of Sydney & its small dark gay-tired somewhat Irish folk.

196   TO KAREN HOLTEN   London.
[Original: Danish/some English phrases]
5.5.08.

I would have written properly to you today after a lesson in the afternoon but the pupil (a young man) came full of wine and had to be helped home.

Poor weak chap, he won't get anything worth while out of life. He is completely incompetent in every respect.

I couldn't give him a scolding for I have been just as weak in my own way; poor me.

When I helped him over the road I thought to myself: People will think there goes one weakling, but how well *I* know that there are 2.

Oh dear, we so-called men are not particularly reliable.

Tonight I have played about 16 Chanties in the phonograph.

The Journal is completed except for a few small corrections. I have sweated crazily at it. Up to 12 & 1.30 at night & up again before 7 in the morning for days & days. I am so full of ideas for composition and have not got a moment to work them out. Thus they are lost like your unborn babes.

I am so full of warmth and passion and love for each one, but nothing comes out of it.

Last night mother put your hair-wash stuff on my head. When I woke up it was as though you smelt beside me.

That made me happy, despite the fact that I can't really endure the smell it has.

You won't put it on any more when we are together, will you. It has such an unhealthy smell.

Nevertheless I love anything that reminds me of you.

Next P.R. off Friday.

197   TO KAREN HOLTEN   [London]
[Original: Danish/some English]
[Extracts, several letters]

8.5.08.

I travelled the night through [to Manchester], arrived 5.30. 8 o'cl I went swimming. When I feel overburdened with manifold doings I have only to try swimming to convince myself of the reverse. I breathe wrongly.

Sunday 10.5.08.

It is so long since we were together. How can we endure it? But life is a great army of such unfulfilled longings, unslacked [sic] thirsts; hence intensity. . . . one can endure a lot, if one must.

Monday [11.5.08]

I am very unhappy, but it doesn't matter. My 2 American ladies are so kind. To think, they will take mother and me on a motor tour in Lincs and drive me around to my old singers, so that I can collect quickly. Since the old Gleadall died I am quite softened through with anxiety that all my men will soon be gone.

Thursday. 14.5.08.

I am so busy. I have just got Nos 200–300 of the hektographed songs in order and sent them off . . . Tuesday at the Gramophone Co. was fun. I like making records.

17.5.08.

It is indeed right, in a way, what you write, but I see no possibility of us seeing more of each other than we do. When one is poor, one must be careful, and I see no indication of it being anything other than a long time before I become more or less well-to-do . . . It seems to me that if one does *enough*, one doesn't feel the lack enormously; . . . Patience, till death!

[n.d. 17?.5.08] .

I am writing to you too often and too little. I have not a minute's time. I am just off to see my father. In a week's time we go to Lincs by motor. I must write a big heap of letters to prepare people for the coming of the Lord.

Sunday 24.5.08.

I am very nice to you in my mind, though I don't seem to be capable of writing much lately . . . With all the pressure of work I have had it seems as if we have been so far apart from each other (only bodily). It is so tedious. But it is not really like that. Every evening when I am going to bed I think: now I will write to her; but I am *so* sleepy, I can't.

3.6.08.

We will come to the workhouse yet. I earn less and less.

Saturday 6.6.08.

Just imagine I will be 26 years before we see each other. We have, you see, made a mistake about my age, but now we have found my birth certificate.

198   TO HJALMAR THUREN   31A King's Road
[Original: Danish]   Sloane Square S W
14.5.08.

Dear Mr Thuren!

A thousand thanks for "The Folksong in the Faeroes"! This book has been of **indescribable** *pleasure and interest to me.* How informative, exciting, and excellent it is! And so many of the songs are so tremendously appealing to me. I cannot find among them the one that you let me hear on the phonograph that day in Copenhagen, that finished with the words *"In the morning"* or something similar?
I would so very much like to have the melody for it, but cannot find it in the book.
The next Folksong Journal (No 12) will consist entirely of songs from my collection, with a foreword about my experiences with the phonograph, and about folksong scales and other details.
All the songs that the Journal contains, I have written down afresh with great care; thus their form is very much more accurate and reliable than in the 100 I sent you. (hectographed)
At the same time I am sending you another 100 of the hectographed ones (Nos. 201–300) I think I have already sent you Nos 201–218 but that doesn't matter. I can get them sometime later when I am in Copenhagen.
I collected 48 songs recently in Gloucestershire. (West-mid England) Unfortunately I wasn't able to come to Copenhagen in the winter. I was too busy over here. I have played in 100 concerts since I was in Copenhagen last October.
I am not coming to Norway or Denmark this summer either unfortunately, since I am going to Australia and New Zealand on a Concert tour in August for half a year. But soon after that (beginning of 1909) I hope to come to Copenhagen.
Once again a thousand hearty thanks for your charming book

Yours sincerely
Percy Grainger

Are all the words for the Faeroese folksongs in the Royal Library?

199   TO KAREN HOLTEN   [London]
[Original: Danish/English]
20.5.08.

Little friend sees a way out, but perhaps I do not go that way. I say that about you must die if you must, because it is the most correct, I think.

If one cannot live without love in this world, then it is best to buzz off, for one's own sake.

If you died it would relieve me of a problem & a joy (both dangerous) & leave me with a ripping sentimental memory. I dont know that I dont think it would be the best thing for you if you would die, & for me too maybe, only I'm not at all sure of the latter, as I'd sooner or later go & fall in love with somebody else probably more dangerous than you.

Anyhow, if I knew you would die in a month if I didn't marry you, it would never enter into my head to do so, because I don't believe in such things.* If one is so weak, better die. Sad, but not so awful as starting children of the same lovable desirable weak kind. If you are fond of life you must see and live, I can't help you in that matter.

Why shouldn't I say something like that? If it is true then it is a good thing to find out how I am, if it isn't true then you must be clever enough to know it. I can't have more sick people to deal with. I want a healthy sweetheart, I have had enough of illness.

We must talk about so much when we are together, it will be so amusing.

Melba sang splendidly last night. I like her personality.

I am also fond of Miss Wragge who is staying with us. She has a fresh boyish independence which is very amusing.

I am so sleepy and tired. I was so late to bed and got up at 6 o'cl to write letters to the folk-singers

I am also very full of love and also very much in need of warmth.

Next P.R. leaves Saturday.

*one swims, but doesnt marry, to save life.

200   TO KAREN HOLTEN   London.
[Original: Danish/English]
Thursday. 28.5.1908.

You little sweetness.

I don't know whether you are well and happy, but it is sweet of you to act as if you were, in any case.

We have been so indescribably happy. I took 66 records and it was so wonderful to be together with all the old friends.

Perhaps we will stay up there a whole summer holiday and you can stay with us. They are really lovely Englishmen up there, loving & great. We motored up on Sunday (nearly 160 miles) & back again yesterday.

And Monday and Tuesday I collected from 7 o'cl to 10 o'cl in the evening.

Both the American women are *very kind*, and we were happy all together the whole time. Sometimes we went without a meal for 8 hours. Both mother and I are feeling tremendously well and I think I have never looked more handsome than just now.

There was no whip in Brigg that was suitable. It will be difficult to find anything. But I don't lose hope. Today Roger is coming.

We drove home through Lincoln. The Cathedral is charming; of soft-looking yellow stone.

Last night I put all the records etc. in a colossal order, so they are quite finished now and can lie as they are until I come back from Australia.

I was so glad to get your letter there. Tonight I am seeing Tristan with Legge. Roger comes too perhaps. He shouldn't really

Roger has found that piece of C. Scott's "Magnificat" that was lost, and which made me so unhappy. I took the "M" score to take care of it & it would have been a disgrace to me if through me it had got lost, any of it. The Wragges are very tedious. She (the daughter) is in love and weeps daily although she is rich and Australian. (You mustn't do that despite being poor and Danish) Sargent's drawing is quite excellent.[37]

The preface of my Journal has woke up C. Sharpe. (f. song collector — a very ½ good man)

I fear the journal is in danger of being filled with contradictions & by people who start "I take a *middle course*." Much of what he writes is true and everything is friendly and English. Much of what I have written is lies. But it is better all the same. Both standpoints must be advanced. I hope the journal will arouse friendly *useful* strife.

Lovingly Perks

Next P.R. letter goes Saturday. Are you fat? Mother and I think we are not made for town-life.

37 Between 24 and 27 May Rose and Percy were on a motoring tour of Lincolnshire, collecting on 25 and 26 May at Brigg and Scawby. Annie Allen, Joseph Taylor's daughter, made the arrangements, and Grainger collected again from some of his favourite Lincolnshire singers: Joseph Taylor, Joseph Leaning, George Gouldthorpe. The "American ladies" feature often in Grainger's correspondence at this time: Mrs E. C. Chadbourne and Mrs Florence Koehler (1861–1944). The latter was an artist who achieved recognition in London as a jeweller. John Singer Sargent had done a charcoal sketch of Grainger in late March/early April 1908.

201   TO KAREN HOLTEN   [London]
[Original: Danish/English]
Saturday. 30.5.08.

I am writing such lovely music these days. Not at all original, quite hackneyed and common-place, but beautiful all the same. Of course there is not time to write it down & it gets in the way of practising, & pupils come like hell whenever I wish them away, but the whole set-up is lively I must say, & its amusing to have more ideas than leisure.

On the motor tour I was completely good, now only ½ and ½. It is unspeakably difficult to be good when one has a great deal to do, I have always found.

And it is almost better to feel weak and sleepy and ashamed afterwards than to go round with ones brain smothered with spunk. When the whole of one's life goes suddenly and violently forward and one is just setting a Scotch poem of Swinbourne (the Bride's Tragedy) then self-control is less than usual. (but at bottom I am never self-controlled, unfortunately. Only sometimes too tired to be naughty)

The poem is glorious.
She says:
    I'd liefer drink yon wan water
    wi' the stanes to make my bed
    wi' the faem to hide me, & thou beside me,
    than I wad see thee dead.

I grow more ordinary, dull, & delightful day by day.

It's so funny when one is composing, whatever one is doing one has voice-leading & odd phrases of stuff floating about in ones head.

We cant do without the "wille" of the world (die welt als wille & vorstellung) in us.

When the will in nature catches us by the hair & shakes us about & drives us to creation (makes mothers, musicians, moneymakers, warriors & lovers of us) we are busy & filled-to-the-brim & at least seem to ourselves happy. Without something thus we stale of [or?] feel empty. I love being driven like a beaten slave to sex, art, activity, sensuality. No freedom for me. Give me the brutal tyranny of some relentless blind urge; & I dont mind being mashed up between 2 or three grinding away at once if I get the chance.

I would so love to kiss you. I am animal-like and disposed today There shouldn't be so many lonely places on your body. Everything should be visited and hotly greeted.

You have a silly little boy as lover. He has fog in his head from altogether too much crowding in and too little time and too little you.

Next P.R. off on Wednesday.

202   TO KAREN HOLTEN   *Bawdsey Manor,*
[Original: Danish/English]   *Woodbridge. Suffolk.*

This is Roger's permanent address if you write to him when I am away and don't know exactly where he is.

———————————

London. Sund. 7.6.08.

I would have written to you yesterday before some guests came, but they came too early.

I don't know what I shall do about a whip, they are always too hard or too slack. The ideal is one which one can use with a swing (brá han[n] sinum brandi af [àf] reiði [Faeroese: he brandished his sword in anger. *Sjurdar Kvædi*]) without it hurting in the least. Could you help me, flesh-comrade? Could you bring over here with you some *willow* branches (or any branches at all) which are long, thin, straight, and elastic. It doesn't matter if they are green, all the better perhaps. If you can get hold of some, bring as many with you as possible, for if they are green they quickly break. They must preferably be as long as possible. They can always be cut shorter.

Do you have these underclothes that are made in one piece, legs and body, are opened from the front, and are called *combinations*? They are not so clean as yours, but I think they have a stimulating value; possibly for me because that nurse-girl in Kensington used them. If you haven't any objection to competing with her, do you think you could bring *one* pair with you, only, like the national costume, for its emotional value?

I wonder whether there is anything ugly or despicable in the constancy with which I think fleshily about you? It is really like sitting in warm ashes the whole time. I sit (when I practise, etc) and think about you in that way till I get a sore throat. It is remarkable that these thoughts always have that effect on me. The throat feels quite full & thick, & it actually creates phlegm. Isnt it funny?

I wonder whether there have been many who have thought so continuously worked-up about something as I do, without *doing* more? Perhaps many artists, but surely not many others. It can safely be said that I have never before been so mad about you as now.

How amusing fleshly-love is. Your and my ways of thinking are indeed so entirely different. That is the good thing about it. I wish that I could hunger after you 20 times hotter than I do, & I should like to go off into a perfect *fit* when together with you. Curse all the soberness, reactionariness, control that is in me. I would with all my heart like to be saved and set free from everything clever good practical and brain-like

I would like to·be whipped until I fell asleep from it, and you should tear pieces out of me with your small teeth. It is such a wonderful thought for me, that I am being mistreated. If one is sufficiently worked up one can also have pleasure of it in reality. But there is only a thin boundary between painful bliss & painful boredom.

If we don't have it a thousand times better this time than ever before, I will really be deeply disappointed. If only I could be quite good. I don't know whether you have any idea how unhappy I am after my beastlinesses. I just don't know how to endure the shame and irritation and tiredness and boredom. But when the temptation comes it settles down swiftly & unexpectedly like a caress & I'm absolutely lost to all else.

In any case I can say this for my life, it is not empty. I try to make it empty, and wait for you coming, but I am not made that way. *The tyranny of the moment* is something quite irresistible for me. I give way every time. And I have *no one* to tell my wickedness to except you, and indeed it bores you, and you would rather be free from such baseness.

I find life not calm nor dull nor peaceful or kindly. But a ceaseless whirlwind of welcome tyrannies tearing me every which way. (Like your small teeth when you pull so lovely and hard on my small breasts) Duties pleasures work ecstasy worry regret all go tumbling one after the other in a cruel glad dance & in the middle poor little fairhaired I is gasping for breath with all the inborn dull amazement of the Teuton, which at bottom I always am. So this slow dull open-mouthed thing gets spun like a top. 2 or 3 compositions beckon inbetween each other & all over & under other work & duties & Karen comes tantalizingly temptatious floundering over all else followed by some devil of a momentary weakness, then up again straight away to some cold waiting neglected problem, or composition, or unanswered letters, or fiercely approaching concert.

It's a turn with wild animals! But it is a kind of being alive, anyway, I suppose.

Later, Sunday.

Do you mind the smell of carbolic soap? If so I'll not use it when you're here. But I'm told it takes away "blackheads", so am momentarily devoted to it. As Meredith quotes:

> *"Most fragrant she who smells of nought."*

Dont forget *not* to use that hairstuff before you arrive, if you dont mind. Let's start straight off with a good clean You-smell.

I am longing to see you sunburnt. Do you think you can be that before you come?

I would be so quite quite enchanted if the colour lay like cream on your skin as it did in the summer.

How I can remember your appearance in certain moments!

I can remember when the loft in Svinkløv smells strongly of warm heavy air, and you stand there in the heat in national costume and arrange things in your suitcase, terribly sunburnt, unspeakably sweet, wondrously kiss-able, with round red-brown arms, and a roughish look with quite disrepu-table (white?) sandshoes on. It's jolly that apple-ey smell up there, & the way it "limrer" [Danish (archaic, poetic): shimmers] with warmth up there in the dust & ½ dark. And those grand afternoon hours when I carried you in to my room & layed you down on the mattrass on the floor, & you put your bitable brown arms over yr silly little eyes.

You must never believe anyone who denies that you can be awfully sweet.

8.6.08.

Won't you send me your planned programme for your piano-evening as quickly as possible, so that we can talk about it before we meet? Since you have piano-evening after all in the winter, you must stay a little longer with us this time, nearly 3 weeks I hope. We must really get something done with your piano playing. It could be that Bach-Busoni's Toccata and Fuga in D minor (Volksausgabe Breitkopf & Härtel No 1372) would be worth while your studying this time. Can't you get hold of it and see what you think of it, and perhaps buy it and practise it a little if you like it? Let us do

everything to get all the program & thinking fixed for yr recital before you come so that we can then concern ourselves solely with the playing & improving of it. Let's not be stupid this time
Willow branches should be about so thick on one end

and about so thin ——————— on the other.

It would be lovely if you would send the enclosed envelope to me next Saturday from Copenhagen. (It needn't upset the regular flow of letters. It will be an extra.)
Next P.R. off Thursday.

If you can't be sunburnt you are just as nice pale-bodied. Just come. That is what is longed-for.
Don't be afraid that we won't sleep enough. "There is all eternity to sleep in." When we no longer can keep our eyes open then we will sleep, unfortunately.

Little sweetness, Goodbye

203   TO KAREN HOLTEN   [London]
[Original: Danish/English]
[Extracts, several letters]

Thursday 11.6.08.

To think, that I don't get *one single* at home engagement this summer! They seem to have washed their hands of me.

Monday. 15.6.08.

Dear old Taylor is coming to London Wednesday and will be Gramophoned Thursday morning. This will really be a good deed, this preserving of his art in this way. You will be able to buy his "records" if you want to . . . I have an at home engagement at the Duchess of Sutherland's on Friday evening.

Wednesday early. 17.6.08.

The concert went *splendidly*. By far my best London Recital so far. The hall packed full, and 2 encores. I didn't make many mistakes. A little one in the Bach Busoni, and something later on; I can't remember it any longer.

4 o'cl aftern. 18.6.08.

I have just said goodbye to old Taylor at the station, who came last night, stayed with us, and made gramophone recordings of 13 or 14 songs in the morning, and was photographed after lunch. He sang more perfectly this time than ever before. I have also fed him with texts recently, and today we got whole ballads where he formerly only sang the melody without text. I hope it is the beginning of some good folksong work with Gramophone Co. I heard today 3 finished records of my playing — all excellent. They are very satisfied with them.

204 TO KAREN HOLTEN
[Original: Danish/English]
Monday 6.7.08.

Abney House,
Bourne End,
Bucks.[38]

38 Grainger was staying at the country house of Mrs Violet Mary Hammersley (1878–1964), London hostess and patron of the arts.

I have been here for the weekend right on the Thames. I was bored, although the people on the river looked fresh and tempting in their light clothes. I am playing at an At Home of Rathbone's on Thursday. So it is fortunate you are not coming on Thursday evening after all.

It is indescribable how worked up I have been at the thought of your arrival, in the last few days. Almost like a mad-man. So cross and unpleasant from longing and impatience. Now I have a reaction and feel unusually tired, unhappy and "flat"

I have just read that an Australian has won the Long Distance swimming championship.

I am an unhappy person. There is really no one who knows how unhappy I am sometimes. I have been naughty 4 or 5 times in the last 4 days. Think, after having longed so continuously all these months for you, and despite knowing that nothing makes me so happy as to begin with you with a fresh and untired body, and that nothing destroys all happiness as surely as naughtiness, even so I am powerless to stop myself from taking the edge off our happiness together! Isn't it completely incomprehensible?

Just before you come is always the worst time for me. My thoughts fix themselves on you till I am at last mad with impatience and unhappiness. If I didn't do something in such times I can't imagine what I would do.

When things are as they are, I must always put up with leaning on my body's power of quick recovery. By Friday I will surely be like the untried Adam, and it will seem to me that I have been good for years. But the weakness, lack of character, and unfaithfulness to our good happiness together are just as great all the same. If I was you, I couldn't possibly forgive such a wretch as I am. One who does such horrible harm to you. I wish I was dead, & green grass growing all over me.[39]

Perhaps you won't come over here at all after reading this. I would have deserved that.

The rash is nearly invisible now. A *little* bit red only. You have never longed for me as I have for you, not so fleshly, brutally, animal-like.

Can't you manage to get trade envelopes? I really want them. Then bring a lot of *various* kind[s] of unEnglishlooking envelopes.

Then let us have "M[arie] G[rubbe]" in heroic ugliness.

39 An echo of the folksong "Died for Love": "I wish my baby he was born, lying smiling on its father's knee, and I was dead and in my grave, and green grass growing all over me". The Australian F. W. Springfield won the long-distance amateur swimming championship, swum on the Thames between Kew and Putney Bridge on Saturday, 4 July. Grainger wanted J. P. Jacobsen's novel *Fru Marie Grubbe* as a gift for Roger Quilter.

205 TO HERMAN SANDBY
[n.d. around 28 July 1908]

31a Kings Rd.
London. S.W.

My dear old Herman.

Have been rushed to death or should have written you before.

Mother has already written you re the London Recital, etc.

Now about Kope. First of all, do you mind doing our Joint Recital with Wilhelm Hansen? For I would not quit him, as he has done good for me, I think, having just got me the offer of 3 Krist-ia things. I will let you know when I will be back as soon as ever poss.

Also in Kope, if we are to give a Recital together; you wont give one alone within 6 months before, will you? I think it's always of highest importance never to give concerts 1 too soon after the other. When you hear from me when I shall be back, you must just fix up whatever is practical for you from *your* side of the matter. If it means keeping you waiting too long, for inst, why, then just give it alone, & I can give my 2nd Kope or London Concert with you, if you wish.

Would you care to have me on another Danish provincial tour with you?

Experience has taught me that you have been *perfectly right* about agents, etc, in the provinces. (Denmark) I find I can do nothing there to speak of on my own. Your way was quite the right thing, I now clearly see.

I should adore to do another tour with you (Sept or Oct?) in the Danish provinces, but if you prefer not, & find it more profitable alone (which is very likely, I should think) I shall *thoro'ly understand*, of course.

I have just had a *glorious* offer for a *Recital* tour in Canada, but it clashes with the Australian tour, so must be put off till later on, alas. My Recital paid like Hell; far better than ever.

I'm longing for the ship & the sea. Lets have your answer as soon as ever you can, as we sail in about 10 days.

Ever fondly
Perks.

206   TO HERMAN SANDBY   31A King's Road
6.8.08.   Sloane Square
                                          S W

My dear old Herm.

Please forgive my bothering you about the "Færøske Kvæder" which I have found safely tucked away in an unlikely place; my fault.[40]

With regard to the Danish tour idea, I can well understand that it pays you better with a singer; I have always thought it must. So let us drop that idea.

With regard to gengæld [Danish: repaying], you certainly are a funny old creature.

If I do a Recital with you over here, where I every year make a nice sum after all expenses are paid (& good fat expenses too with lots of advertising) & share that surplus with you (who, I suppose, just about clear your expenses only with a London Recital) there seems to me to be some gengæld in that.

You & I dont see past business affairs quite alike either. As to the generosity of heart that you showed me in Køb at the start, why there are no 2 ways about that, & I always think back with pride & delight at having a friend capable of so much generosity & devotion.

But when we come to cold business values, surely any business obligation to you was very thoro'ly squared by the work I procured for you over here?

Think of all the at Homes such as Mrs Wythes, Miss Dodge's, Baron de Meyers, Mrs Charles Lawrence's, etc, that came directly thro' me, not to mention whatever has come indirectly through my friends; all the Broadwood concerts; those advertisements of us both that Ada put in the D.T. for us without charge because I gave my services for a London concert of hers.

I own that I did not find it possible to get you nearly as much work over here as I wished to (for I wanted to get you a great heap; & a cellist is naturally not the easiest intrumentalist to push) but I certainly think that you got jolly good money value in return for your splendid & generous work for me in Denmark.

When I suggested our again doing a Recital together over here, it is, you can guess, not because it would be a money gain to me for us to do it together, (for it naturally would mean a loss of about ½ the makings to me) but because I thought it would be a good thing for you, because I *keenly relish* playing together with you, & love to see you over here.

I can quite understand that you may not wish to bind yourself down to not doing Recitals here & in Cope within the 6 months before our suggested joint Recitals here & there, & as the date of my return from Australia is

40 Venceslaus Ulricus Hammershaimb, *Færöiske Kvæder*, in two volumes. Grainger's earliest settings of Faeroese tunes and texts, dating from January and June 1905, came from Vol. 2 (1855) of this work, and from *Sjúrðar Kvæði* (1851) and *Færösk Anthologi* (Vol. 1, 1886) by the same author.

so very uncertain *I think the best plan will be for me to give my first Recital in London & first Recital in Cope* **alone**; & if we later on wish to join together for later Recitals, why we can arrange it later on when I am back. *So dont bother about me at all for the time being* & we can fix up Recitals together, if we both wish it, after my return.

Mother has spoken to Tillett about you & the Ada Xley tour. It would be fearfully jolly if it came off.

I dont know, so far, that I would sincerely advise you to shift all your work from Robinsons to Tillett, unless you find he does things for you. I have not had a good opportunity yet of judging of whether he is better for one than E. L. Rob or not. Tillett (Vert) is certainly a very nice man, but I should be careful, a bit, if I were you, before chucking Rob altogether.

I delight to learn that you have been at work on "Havstemning".

I am very busy, these days, at "The Bride's Tragedy" (the new Swinbourne) We leave for Australia tomorrow.

My address there will be:

> P.G.
> c/o J. C. Williamson
> Her Majesties Theatre
> Sydney. N.S.W.
> Australia.

Have a good time till we meet
Hearty greetings from us both.

yrs ever
Perks.

On 7 August the Graingers left from Tilbury on the R.M.S. Orontes *for Australia. In their absence, their London house was taken by their Australian friends Mrs Mary Wragge and her daughter Olive.*

The whole party travelled together. It was basically the same party as that of the English provincial tour, except that Evangeline Florence did not go: Percy (and Rose), Ada Crossley (and her husband Francis Muecke), Leon Sametini, Hamilton Earle, John Harrison. On board on 5 September they gave a concert in aid of the Marine Charities, prompted by the death of a sailor and by a woman who suffered heat apoplexy in the Red Sea.

True to his promise, Grainger wrote to Karen from every port on the voyage, though the letters are written diary-fashion every two or three days. Grainger gave himself up wholeheartedly to the joys of the "glorious life" on board ship, dividing his time, so the British Australasian *reported on 27 August, between his favourite sport of cricket, and composition. In fact, he threw himself into all the available sporting activities with single-minded passion until some trouble with his veins at the end of August obliged him to curtail the sports and concentrate more on composition.*

207 TO KAREN HOLTEN   R.M.S. "Orontes".
[Original: Danish/English]   Suez Canal.
Thursday evening. 20.8.08.

I experienced many remarkable things today in Port Said. I got up early and ran 16 times round the promenade deck (2 miles) in 19½ (about) minutes. That is not at all fast, but the weather was also suffocatingly hot. After breakfast we began to take on coal. They say that the natives (partly Copts, etc with some Sudan negroes among them) here coal quicker than anywhere in the world. They swarm *like ants*, tumbling over & under each other, careless of danger or hurt. They show no attempt at moderation in their display of energy. They shout & talk at the top of their voices throut and you can imagine that you quickly get as much noise (what with all the falling coal) in your ears as coal-dust in your eyes. I saw a head man running after a boy beating him. I loved that of course. There are few more tragic grim sights than one of these coal barges rowing off slowly after [being] emptied of all its coal, crowded with these dark & black awfullooking creatures with sacks over their heads & coal-covered from head to heel, silent & movementless.

About 9 o'cl Earle and I went on shore together. We had planned to see something of the native women if possible. We got a "guide" and asked him to take us where we could see women without clothes on. First he took us to a house where one could see indecent pictures. *You can't imagine how boring they are*. Scarcely a single picture of an attractive man or woman; only "dirty." No interesting or stirring positions or groupings. I liked a little only one small woman's figure, which I have cut out of the photograph and am sending to you.

Then we went into the brothel itself. 4 women came in, oh so sleepy, poor things. One of them (I think a native) was not unattractive, but one was a poor come-down French woman. I felt great sympathy for them all, the miserable life they must lead! In that house we didn't see anything; only wasted money for nothing. Then we went shopping. I bought a lot of picture postcards of Egyptian buildings (the old ones) and of native warriors and women; the best ones I bought for you, and send them herewith. Earle bought several things and I also bought a whip for 2/-. It is of fishbone, or something similar. Pliable, but still hard, with a lot of spring, and can hurt terribly. After that I bought more picture postcards and then we said goodbye to our guide.

The whole time in P. Said men run after you and say "smuddy (smutty) pictures". But they were all of the same boring unbearable kind, quite without any attraction. In vain I asked for photographs of beautiful native women. Only dirt.

Then there came a young man after me and asked if we would like to see women dance the Can-Can without clothes on. I said yes we would, but wouldn't have anything else to do with them and wouldn't pay more than 6/-. He arranged it, and we went into one of these wooden houses and two girls and an old woman came in. We chose the girl we liked best, and were then alone with her and the old one, Earle and I. Then she took her clothes off, with the exception of a little thin black "under", and she and the old one sang and the young one (very young) danced.

We got her to roll the under over her breasts, but she wouldn't take it right off. The dance was surely meant to be indecent and arousing. But I didn't feel it at all like that. She had an apparently good-natured face and a very thin slender but rounded body. Her figure was of the same type as yours. Beautiful straight legs and good hair and the splendid golden-brown skin colour. She lay down and the old woman laughed and I felt much friendship and gratitude towards her but no real sensuality.

I don't feel any urge to be a meat-mate with any paid woman, I must admit. But just to see her like that gave me a great feeling of youth purity beauty athleticness humanity. There is no doubt that having ½ a painter's nature makes me wish to see naked bodies maybe in a slightly different way to folk who have no painting inclination. It works on my pictorial senses like hearing the tuning up of a big orchestra does on my compositional senses.

To see such naked bodies therefor delights me hugely without *tempting* me in a purely fleshy way. I don't think either that painters are tempted by their models in most cases. Of course if there was no risk with a girl like the one today then she would probably be tempting. But one can't go and forget important things like health in that way.

After she had danced I lifted up her "under" to see how her breasts were formed. Firm and small, but the nipple was formed differently from Europeans. Instead of the nipple there was a little "slit".

Breasts like this are also given in Women of all nations. (Are you getting them regularly?)

So we went out again and after a little while another young man came and asked whether we would like to see "a boy screw a girl. Arab screw". (i.e. to see them act carnally with each other.) I would like to and it would only cost 5/- for us both and we went in. This time it was a Greek girl, short and with an infamous bad temper. She and the young man swore at each other furiously; no doubt about the division of the price! And so it began.

Absolutely boring, really nasty — a little. I was glad when it was over. I didn't see anything particularly Arabian about it. Perhaps the boy enjoyed it, but if so, he was the only one that did. The woman lay there completely indifferent with an unfriendly vengeful expression on her low face. I also looked at her breasts afterwards, but can no longer remember how they were. This exhibition was to me closely related to the "smuddy pictures". I really should have been able to foresee it would have been boring; but I had never seen anything of this kind, & I wanted to give it a fair chance.

After that we went on board and sailed at 12 o'cl midday. We passed 2 British navy ships (cruisers) and came straight into the Canal. I must admit the weather was quite overwhelmingly hot. After afternoon tea I went down to the cabin to try the whip on myself, and the sweat absolutely ran off me like out of a tap.

The whip is enormous. Hurts furiously. I bled a little in various places and where you strike reasonably hard it raises a "weal" on the skin something like:

The end of the whip makes a little bit of a wound every time.

No nature moves me more than that which one sees on both sides of the canal. Light yellow coloured sand deserts so far as one can see with sand dunes with drylooking grass tufts on them. For the most part it is quite dry, but marshes, swamps, & small lakes occur also.

When one has to "tie up" to the side to let another boat pass Arab boys & men come swimming & dive for pennies. I just can't tell you how perfect all their movements are & how much better they swim than I. (I could swim across the canal all the same) When their skin gets wet it looks so yellowish and shining. They swim there quite naked so graceful and decent.

One can see for miles accross these flat poetic wastes, & the spirit of the whole place is great & glorious & lonely, with Asia to the left & Africa to the right. If I was rich I would live in this area for a year. It is so like some part of Australia. And when the sun goes down everything is quite suddenly quite dark. No sentimental twilight game. Sudden & dramatic. Cruel & hard like the voices & eyes of the people, & the god (Allah) they fashioned (like all races) out of the weather of the land.

Do you think you could dress yourself up like a man and go round with me to the brothels and see women of different races dance? Perhaps it would bore you. But I think it is beautiful to see lovely bodies, interestingly coloured and formed.

Have just heard I can post in Suez.

Goodbye sweet darling. I am your boy despite all the brothels

208   TO KAREN HOLTEN   R.M.S. "Orontes".
[Original: Danish/English]   Between Red Sea & Colombo.
Friday. midday. 28.8.08.

Undeniably the red sea is almost intolerable at this time of year. I tried to continue with running etc. but when a sailor died of the heat and a woman got heat apoplexcy I thought it was best to be a little careful. After 3–4 days when one could scarcely move we suddenly came into the Monsoon the day before yesterday with heavy seas. Since the water up till then had been mirror smooth the whole time we were about as little "used to the sea" as if we had been on land. Neither mother or I were sea-sick, but I spent Wednesday in bed until the evening meal, but got quite alright yesterday.

I assure you I could neither compose nor write to you in the heat. As long as one played cricket one felt alright, but it made one weak afterwards. Yesterday mother got Dr Hornabrook (who is clever & nice) to examine me as she thought I looked poorly. He examined this business with my veins and says I must *absolutely* have an operation as soon as I get back to England. He says he believes it must have got considerably worse in the 2½ years that have gone since Rathbone's doctor examined me. I think so as well. He says that I must do absolutely no sport and nothing at all strenuous. I asked him whether sexual intercourse would harm it or not and he said that that was the worst of all for it. He said "You could not possibly marry, for instance, until you have been operated". From that one can easily work out what a bad effect my bad habit must have had. He said he wouldn't guarantee that I will get through the Australian tour without an operation, but he thinks so. I know what it means. If I quite give up the "habit" then I will get through. If I *can't* give it up altogether now, then I am a completely hopeless person. I know it quite clearly. He says that after the operation I will be able to run, etc, like anything. Thus the next time we see each other, we can hope that I will be more vigorous than ever since you have known me. The operation needn't mean more than one week in hospital, he says.

I can't say what a relief it is for me that things have finally taken this turn. As long as there was no hope sticking out of getting really cured I felt I must try & do the best I could as I was. *But now I feel* **relieved** *of all sport obligations*. There are sports on board here. I entered for *flat race* (once round the deck) & 3 other less important things. I have already won my *heat* in the flat race, but have to meet Muecke, & 2 young Australians in the *final*. Isn't it fine that *only Australians* won the heats, & that therefor *none but an Australian* can win?

I won my heat against an Englishman & 2 small boys, whom we had to give a big handicap. But I did not write you of it (though it happened before Port Said) as I hoped to win the final & didnt want to tell you of the heat until I had. The sports have been a fearful & uncomfortable overexcitement for me, & I am *heartily glad* that Dr Hornabrook's verdict shuts me out from taking part altogether.

Whenever I have thought of the final against Muecke (who is so *really strong* & has plenty of will & concentration, more than I have) my heart has beat till I felt quite sick. In bed or any old time. It has also been a very deep grief for me that I have done so badly at the deckquoits. Even Sametini has beaten me! And last boat I could beat anyone. I was also agitating to get up a *mile race* later on, & that would have been horribly exciting & most likely very bad for me. But now I feel as if a cloud has been cleared off me. I shall now devote myself to practising the piano, scoring, & letterwriting, & shall no longer feel disgraced about the deckquoits All through Australia, too, I shall have only my music to bother about, & no nonsense about long walks, etc.

Afternoon.

I've done such a fine practice today over 2 hours.

I must say I am happy to find that my enthusiasm for Australians is refreshed by seeing a few of them together again. I think they have the beginnings of a really good race.

Think, long before I came to England the 1st time I had the thought of getting fleshly experiences in Denmark. Herman told me in Frankfurt that Danish girls were very "erotic", and I can remember that I often imagined the whole thing right out, to have my own ship, sail in to the shore, get hold of a nice Danish girl, rape her and sail away again, or take her away on the ship for a little while. And I can remember as well that I wrote to Herman, just before I was to go to Denmark the very first time (just before we met) "can't you get me a sweetheart, there where you say there are so many? Over here I don't find any". In the Frankfort days I used to look long at the map of Denmark & wonder where my landing should be & what part of Jutland my place of lust & bliss.

Nothing is decided yet of course, but I believe mother and I will take a folksong holiday in England next summer and that either after or before I will take a holiday with you in Svinkløv, you and me. Perhaps it would make our time together shorter than if you came over to us to England, but one can have such a delightfully good time there, and we can be so completely for each other all night and day as well, and try all possible things.

It would be lovely, I think, if I could come some time in Sept, or late in Aug, rather than earlier; for at that time one has the place more to oneself; although it is no longer so warm in the open air. But of course as yet I know nothing of my movements, whether Canada will come off early in the autumn, & when, nor how much folksong work I will feel duty bound to do.

If there should ever happen anything to me to make me incapable of fleshly things, and you nevertheless still continued to be fond of me, and I of you, will you promise me to see and get that kind of thing with other men and boys? Perhaps I could engage a nice blackboy or Italian for you. Get him medically examined & see he was quite healthy & reliable, & then have a great old go with him. For it would make me so ashamed to think that a woman I was fond of should become a kind of dried old maid because she loved me. Promise me you would do something like that in such a case, won't you? If we had enough money we could travel around on the lookout for ripping young boys, youths, & men, & everything for Kirstenlil of Funen's lust! She'd eat 'em up like ripe muttonchops. Keep up the *running* & riding, swimming, etc. For when I've been operated on I'll be a perfect devil at all these things, you bet.

I think I asked you to get me any newspaper reproductions of the Danish girl gymnasts who were in London that you could. More likely there would be reproductions of them in Danish than in English papers. I should think it would be a goodish plan to go to some public library or reading room & look up all the illustrated papers of about that date (July '08) & see what were good & buy such back numbers if possible. Altogether it is a good thing to look a little in as many illustrated papers as possible always. They often have excellent reproductions of things that are well worth keeping. Let me know, if you can, what colour the Danish girl gymnasts have for such a dress as in the Italian sport-newspaper.

You should have seen my body after I had whipped myself with the new whip the other day in the red sea. It was really impressive. I bled a little in several places. If I sometimes were allowed to whip you as hard as I wanted with that whip; life would have little or nothing to offer me after that. With you almost everything is possible, it seems to me. Your mind is indeed Catholic! It shrinks from nothing. I *could* be so unhappy with women if they weren't like that. A really pure mind knows no mental (& few bodily) limits, no moderations, no modesty, no revolting hypocracy. A thousand heartfelt thanks for being the lovely beloved being you are. You suit so splendidly so many of my most hungry desires.

Sunday morning. 30.8.08.

Just think I haven't spied on "the couple's" cabin for about 2 weeks. It bores me. It is inexplicable to me. I always throw away my chances. When I came on board I would have thought that that opportunity would have been very heaven for me; but now I let it go past me. Stupid boy.

Yesterday was the finals of the sports. I watched. I felt deeply unhappy. Muecke won the flat race, *but* he sprained a leg muscle in doing so. I would have so liked to have been in it. But now I have forgotten the whole thing. I must say that I already feel much healthier after having been out of sport for some few days. *In my present condition*, at any rate, it doesnt seem to agree with me; but that doesnt make me love it any the less.

I think I forgot to tell you how amusing a certain muscle looked on the thin naked dancer in Port Said. It was just that muscle over which there is a X.

If you stand straight up in front of a mirror, and lift one leg forwards & upwards you will be able to see this thin beautiful muscle working. I would so like to stand beside you.

I worked a lot on E. D. score yesterday.

Just think, I can't say that I have felt *really well* one single day since we have been on this ship.

The very kind Englishman's (Lord Brinckman) sweet French wife must, because of a disability, always go in shoes without heels. (or *very* low, at any rate) I have often wondered what it was about her which reminded me of you in Svinkløv. Now I know that these low heels resemble those sandals you had on. Nothing gives a woman more grace and more the impression of a little wild animal than going without heels. I like it so much.

She (Lady B) often has sandals on that look like:

   (They are in yellow leather.)

Perhaps you could see some time whether such ones would suit you. Get nice *broad soles*.

I can remember what small movements you could make with your little toes.

It is so nice for me to practise Chopin's Barcarole. For it reminds me so strongly of the day you came, this last time; for I bought and played him for the 1st time just that day. One can always remember so well the *first* day one comes together again. Naturally. I can remember so well the first time I went to Svinklóv in the rain. I sang "The Rainbow" (in Journal 12) as loud as I could to quiet the excitation.

So far *every* sport event (as far as I can remember) has been won by Australians. There is no doubt we are wonderfully keen & spirited at games. A really very fresh race, on the whole. Tiresome, but not bad.

Sunday evening.

Tomorrow early we get into Colombo.

I think I am very sweet. Sometimes.

I have worked a lot today on E. D.

I cannot tell you all the different things I feel and think with regard to you. But they are all extremely good.

Believe me, after such a continuous sweating the skin is *really clean*. You should be with me. I long so continually to feel you beside me.

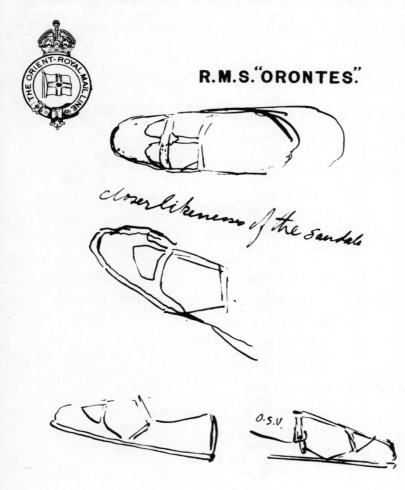

R.M.S. "ORONTES."

THE ORIENT · ROYAL MAIL LINE

Closer likeness of the sandals

O.S.V.

After calling at Western Australia, Adelaide (where the Mueckes left the ship) and Melbourne, the R.M.S. Orontes *berthed in Sydney on 19 September. Ada and her husband arrived by train from Adelaide on Saturday 26 September. Harold Whittle joined the company as accompanist. The tour manager was Henry Bracy.*

The protracted negotiations in the earlier part of the year had been aimed at securing contractual arrangements for Percy which were more advantageous than those under which he had come to Australia in 1903. Engaged initially for a series of twenty-five concerts, he was to be paid a salary of £40 per week, with a possibility of a week's holiday without pay during the New Zealand segment of the tour. The possibility of the tour being extended by five, ten, fifteen or twenty concerts was covered by the contract. Other important issues concerned his special "starring" on posters and advertising. A separate arrangement had been reached with Steinway for the provision of a grand piano. By contract, and unlike the 1903 tour, he was not obliged to play a duet with the violinist, but contributed only his two groups of piano solos to each programme.

The tour began on 1 October with the first of six concerts in Sydney. After the last concert, an "extra" matinee on Monday 12 October, the party left for Melbourne, arriving there on 13 October. Rose stayed with the others until the arrival in Melbourne, but then proceeded directly to Adelaide to stay with her family there. The concert party, after a season of four concerts in Melbourne (a projected fifth concert was cancelled), went on tour in Gippsland, then, after a return season in Melbourne, visited various country towns in Victoria and en route for Adelaide, which it reached on 13 November.

CONCERT ITINERARY, 1908–09 AUSTRALASIAN TOUR

SYDNEY	Arrived 19 September		
	1–12 October	6 concerts	
MELBOURNE	Arrived 13 October		Rose to Adelaide
	15–22 October	4 concerts	
	Leongatha, 23 October		
	Yarram, 24 October		
	Bairnsdale, 26 October		
	Sale, 27 October		
	Traralgon, 28 October		
	Week's holiday		
MELBOURNE	3–4 November	2 concerts	
	Echuca, 5 November		
	Bendigo, 6 November		
	Warrnambool, 9 November		
	Colac, 10 November		
	Geelong, 11 November		
ADELAIDE	14–18 November	3 concerts	
	19 November, left		
	Adelaide for Western Australia		
PERTH	Arrived 22 November		
	24–28 November	3 concerts	
	30 November, left Perth for the Goldfields		

Kalgoorlie, 2 December
Coolgardie, 3 December
Boulder, 4 December
Kalgoorlie, 5 December

PERTH	7 December	Grand extra concert
	9 December, left Perth for Adelaide	
	Stawell, 14 December	
	Ballarat, 16 December	
	Wangaratta, 18 December	
	Albury, 21 December	Rose to Melbourne
	Wagga Wagga, 22 December	Rose to Sydney
	Goulburn, 23 December	Percy joins Rose's train at Goulburn
SYDNEY	25 December	1 concert
	After concert, left on S.S. *Warrimoo* for New Zealand	

209 TO KAREN HOLTEN   R.M.S. "Orontes".
[Original: English/some Danish]   Between W.A. and S.A.
Sunday. afternoon. 13.9.08.

I got a black eye playing cricket yesterday. I was fielding & stupidly got dangerously near the batsman & got a ball straight off his bat only 3 or 4 yards off. It also blackened ½ the nail of my thumb which it also hit. It will be alright by a week I think. It has not hurt at all & I didnt even really notice it at the time & went on playing till someone happened to notice that it was swelling up wondrously. It is very curious how it actually happened for the blackness goes right along up to the eye itself on the lower lid while the eye itself & the upper lid are untouched! Thus:

Wasn't it lucky? Afterwards, with a bandage round it, I won a game of quoits with one eye against Earle.

I had a row with Muecke at lunch today. He was chaffing mother about something in his usual senseless way, & she asked him to quit & he kept on & on till she said she thought he was very rude, so I got into a frightful rage, as white as snow, & said "I quite agree. I think you have been very rude indeed to mother on this trip. Be rude to me if you want to."

At the sight of my face M (as he always does if one gets really wild with him) collapsed into his sentimental "hurt" mood, & left the table in about a minute or 2.

Poor old thing, he is so rude that he does it now unconsciously without even having to try any more.

Last night there was prize giving & rot. I think only 1 Englishman won *1* event in the men's things. The Governor of Tasmania, an Englishman, presided & in the middle of his speech an Australian (Dunlop) shouted out "no" to something he said, & another absurd clown Australian middleaged man said: "O, you know we Sydney people merely take the Tasmanians under our wing". etc All this because the Governor is unpopular.[41] I was very proud to see 2 Australians bold enough to be rude like that before the whole ship. If we can only birth enough Godlike *revolt*, all will yet be well. Later in the evening most of the men got drunk in the smokeroom, I'm proud to say that most of the Australians were either absent, or kept sober. We are not going to be a drunken race, I'm sure. I was in bed.

Well, on Thursday we got to W.A. (Western Australia or: Westralia.) We had the morning & early afternoon there. There was a deputation & reception of "citisens" (all worked up by J. C. Williamson's agent!) to "welcome" Ada. My God! What hideous folk. I must earnestly say that all the *scenery* looked *glorious*.

It's beauty was really a fresh surprize to me, even after last trip's enthusiasm for it. The W.A. wildflowers are ravishing; such fresh intense colors, & queer jolly forms. The old gum trees too are so altogether ownish; (characteristic) surely there has never been a *flat* land more uniquely itself & only itself!

My heart yearns for the embraces of the glorious lovely scenery that I know will be unfolded to me on this tour. And the *scent* of everything at Perth on Thursday the town, the woods, the very rooms all were fragrant with wild flower & "wattle" smells, that smell as crisp & fresh as wild berries taste in Northern Europe.

The rooms all seemed so open & light & the dark rich native wood used every where ("Karri" & "Jarrah") looked so good & clean & pure. The streets are all wide & straight, & the earth is redbrown on clean sand, yellow-white. Down by the water the sand is snowwhite almost & so pure & fine.

Some of the men looked hopeful, but the womenfolk! Dry & bitter, cold & hard, sexless & impossible, each every one. It is a painful subject. I assure you there was not one girls & womans body in the whole gang that I would have taken on willingly, not even for the sake of "national experience". Of course W.A. is known to be a tough place.

Tomorrow morning we get to Adelaide (S.A. South Austr) where mother was born, & where her kin are. It is my favorite town in Australia. I wonder what they will all say to my blackeye? At least it is a quick way of proving to them all that the 4½ years have not altered me much.

The weather, by the way, is really really cold.

Monday 14.9.08. evening.

We had the day in Adelaide. That dear place never dissappoints me. My relations are really dear warm people. Particularly the "Richmond" family. I feel to swim in a very sea of affection & the manifold embrace of my own racial type. My uncle Jim has won and lost a lot of money. He is the sweetest soul one can think of. He is certainly over 50, but he says he can't notice any difference at all in his running powers. His stomach is thinner than mine. He has 7 children, 4 of them boys. I have surely told you about "Babs", the youngest of the girls? Last time I was in Adelaide (4½ years ago) she on a pony, her sister Maud on a cycle, & I trotting on foot, spent the whole night roaming about the seashore, etc. I took a bathe in the sea & we all returned in the *very* early morn, & ate huge masses of cream & jam (no bread) Babs is one of the very few women that I could think of the possibility of marrying.

She speaks the sweetest South Australian accent, slow and drawled. She is now 22 or 21. The last time I was here she was in the sweetest of all ages, with hair down and short skirts and rode crossed legged. I was certain that she would now be considerably ruined since last time. But I must admit, that she has nearly as much attraction as last time.

I don't think one could call her sensual, I think rather that she is just the opposite, perhaps, but she is a really *good* sweet lovable person, it sticks out all over her, *adores* her father, & has nothing *at all* cold about her.

Her father (Jim) has always been a farmer at heart, but has had to earn his money at Hotel Keeping

But he has started 3 boys on "stations" (sheep pastures) & farms, & the 2 girls are getting married, & he sold his Hotel & left it about a week ago, to live on his *studfarm* (racehorse breeding) "Richmond" a few miles from Adelaide. I spent many happy times at Richmond in my boyhood & love it all fondly. On Wednesday Maudie gets married. (the eldest girl) And Babs is engaged (to a *dear* chap they say, & his grounds lie next to Richmond) & will soon be married, too, I hope.

But look how stupid even good men are! Babs is a great rider & was one of the very first to use divided skirts & ride astride at horse tournaments, etc, & has won lots of prizes. Now her stupid betrothed doesnt want her to ride at public competitions any more. What a bloody fool! Australian men are so greedy & selfish, they like everything to themselves.

One of her brothers, "Bill" was there today. I've not seen him for 14 years.

He used to be my favorite boy cousin. He is 20 now. He has a farm of his own on *Kangaroo Island*. (not very far from Adelaide) He & a "pal" (comrade) do every bit of the roughest work, *not a single* underling to help them. He is about my height with blue eyes & rough knobbly farmer face, never happy in towns. His hands are worked to bits, & his whole figure is broad & slow with muscle & strength. He is a ripping good S.A. farmer type. I should love to live in S.A. I love slow untalkative folk, full of calm & empty of ambition. You can bet they were amused to death with my black eye.

I love my mothers kin. I feel in my right place when I am surrounded by them.

The clannish feeling is laughably strong in me. I love to kiss goodbye on their warmhearted faces. I heard Babs say: "Dear old Pers hasnt kissed *me* yet." No words can tell what babylike simple unworldly solid quiet old things they are. I wish they'd all hurry up & marry & produce shoals of broad (though thin) fairhaired blueeyed Anglosaxon farmer kids for me to gloat over.

I am quite your boy again   17.9.08

210   TO KAREN HOLTEN
[Original: Danish/English]
Tuesday. 22.9.08.

Hotel Wentworth
Sydney.

I am not in the least disappointed with Sydney. It is an ideal town, where enjoyment flourishes on all sides for people of every class. People look intelligent, and everything happens with the utmost speed — much more than in London. The upper classes (with very few exceptions) cannot measure up to the English upper classes at all, but the lower classes are beyond all description more beautiful, more honest, cleaner, more friendly, more proud, more independent. I believe my last letter (posted in Melbourne) just failed to catch the mail boat. Thus you will get it and this letter at the same time maybe. But now I know the mail days and from now on letters will come regularly weekly to you. With regard to letters the worst is now behind us, at any rate for you. For my last letter from Australasia (at the end of the tour) arrives in Europe only a week before I arrive myself.

Mother and I are being worked to death. Besides being photoed & having to practise & seeing about my piano & unpacking I am being interviewed from morn to night & have a 1000 worries. I am having all kinds of fights with J. C. Williamson's folk as well. Everything in this land has to be fought over 20 times. The keynote of the Australian temperament is persistancy. When, with a European, everything would be ended & fixed, an Australian starts all over again from the very beginning, & if in the 20th fight one isnt as fresh & certain as in the 1st all the 19 have been wasted. It amuses me, but tires me, & takes up my time.

Therefore today only such a small and boring letter is coming to you. Before next Tuesday I will write to you about Melbourne and the last days on Orontes, etc.

The next letter ‖10‖ will arrive post Restante Købmagerg. *one week later* than this letter ‖9‖

Much love & fond thoughts despite my "business activity."

Many hearty greetings to all of you

Percy.

211   TO KAREN HOLTEN   Hotel Wentworth
[Original: English/Danish]   Sydney.
Sunday. 27.9.08.

Now I must tell you what happened on the ship between Adelaide and Sydney. Dunlop (Australian) gave 10/- for the "deckquoit-champion of the boat". Unluckily I didnt know of this until too late to enter. But the rule was that after the championship was won that anyone could challange the champion paying him 1/- each game, which money was to pass on from winner to winner & stay with whoever was champion by 6 o'clock p.m. on 18.9.08, the night before Sydney.

Well, I challanged Gibbs, the champion, & beat him (amid great enthusiasm) but lost to a worse player next game. (So like me) Then I discovered a[n] Irishman, newly come on board, who seemed to me to play well, & made him enter. That man proved an absolute knockout. He played & won *41 games* running, from after lunch to 6.15 on 17.9.08, & from 10. a.m. to 6 p.m. on 18.9.08. Poor chap, his arm was half dead with stiffness. He said the only 2 on board he feared were me & a young Australian, Henley. He beat the rest of our best player as : 21-7. 21-10. etc (21 is "game") I played about 8 games against him (8 shillings!) every time my turn came round & came excitingly near sometimes. My last game against him he led by 18 (?) to my 10 (?) I think, & then I pulled up to 18 against his 20 (great enthusiasm) but missed one shot & gave him one & he won.

At last Henley played against him at 5.50 p.m. & *won*. It was sad that this heroic Irishman should lose after winning those 41 games, but Henley also tried *very* hard, & though only a little chap of about 18, played with all his soul & played real well. So it was another win for Australia.

Anyhow those last days proved to me that I have a real good chance at deckquoits, now as before, if I only practise. Next boat I must practise earlier. I play in a different way to everybody else, with quite a different way of throwing, & I feel sure that my way would be more deadly than the usual way with enough practise. Anyway, I proved myself mighty poor at sport on the "Orontes".

Well, Melbourne looked the same as ever. It's a snobby, coldhearted, dusty, barren place; small-spirited, I feel. But that dear darling Dr Russell that lives there, what a lovable Englishman he is![42] He is of the Roger-Fielding English stamp, calmsouled, with a low balmy laugh, & very blue eyes steady as anchors. He loves me really deeply. Few love me truer than he. Both he and Dr O'Hara (the 2 best surgeons in Melb) say that I shouldn't for anything in the world be operated on for the sake of the

42 Dr Robert Hamilton Russell (1860-1933), English-born physician who emigrated to Australia in the late 1880s. A childhood friend of the Graingers, Percy described him as "the first exquisite pianist of my life". He was senior surgeon at the Alfred Hospital from 1901 to 1919 and Dean of the Clinical School until 1929. (Grainger inconsistently misspells "Russell" as "Russel": this has been silently corrected in the text.) Dr Henry Michael O'Hara (1853-1921), another family friend, had attended at Percy's birth. Grainger stayed with the O'Haras during the first part of his Melbourne visit.

veins, and that I can and should do *all the sport I want to*, long walks, running, everything. They have not examined me yet, but will do it, both of them, when I am in Melbourne, and tell me their opinion. Russell asked me what sort of sexual life I am living. He asked me whether I had mastered the bad habit. I answered no. He says that it is not so important, anyway. That it is only dangerous for people under 20 years old, and that *twice a week* (of the habit) wouldn't have any harmful effect on the health, but that I should preferably try to do it a little less than twice a week, if I could. That's also a good thing. Englishmen are alright, there is nothing hysterical about them.

Russell has *just* recently bought a motor, and drove us around. He has *just* learnt to drive himself, so it wasn't at all without its danger. After anything particularly bumping or risky he would look round at mother & me with a lovable schoolboy smile. He is a batchelor, & not at all grown up yet. He is nearly 50.

But Sydney is wonderfully lovely and quite characteristic. At all sides it is quite unbelievably beautiful. It is ideal for people without much money. The loveliest places can be reached for 2 pence or 4 pence, and one can live cheaply in charming surroundings. There is also a generosity & lavishness in the public buildings & tram service which is, I think, quite typical of Australian humanity, & there is a refreshing bustle & keenness & skillfulness about all the city life. But I can't, even in Sydney, find the race attractive on average; not even the women. The men have often something free, warm, independent and manly, especially in the lower classes, (who are quite clean) but the women appear to suffer from unhappiness. The girls are a little too early developed in a sexual regard, without giving the impression of being properly sexually strong or capable.

But perhaps I am wrong. Mother & I were in a tram going only a short way. When getting out I gave the man 6 pence, but he had no change. He asked if I had change, I said, no. He just gave me the 6d back & whistled the tram on. That was typical. Indipendant, generous, ½ rude, & full of speed-worship. He couldnt be bothered about 2d. The speed of his tram mattered more. Giving it back without a word was so typical. I took it like a lamb. I have bought a whip here in the town, an American kind; very suitable for us. One can hit very wildly with it without it hurting much. It is a little longer than the 2 I bought in London and fairly firm nearly to the point, and there it becomes quite soft.

But it doesn't bite like the one from Port Said. If one wants something really cruel, biting, then one must take that one. It cuts properly. I try to accustom myself to the whip before we meet again. I don't do anything with my breasts any more, other than to whip them, and already I have almost forgotten them now. Habit is so easy to get or to flee. When one is once accustomed to the whip, I think few things will be more effective than that.

The nice thing about the whip is that it doesn't leave any unpleasantness on the body. Even where the whip leaves a red stripe or spot there is nothing to feel afterwards. As against that there is something repugnant about the feeling of a bitten breast. It is lovely to whip the inner side of the legs, high up, for the flesh is tender here. I would wish I were a woman, for then I could whip higher up without danger. When the climax approaches one can whip even with the Port Said whip without feeling pain. At that moment one should have a whip of *wire* to beat oneself with; nothing is sharp enough. But how I am chosen by good fortune above almost all other people! How soul-intoxicating it is for me to have such a comrade as you are. That all these thoughts can be shared with you, and even achieved in practice into the bargain sometimes, that is indeed to have a kingdom, to be sure. If only I can sometime find a choir and an orchestra that will fulfill my musical longings as you do my fleshly ones; that would indeed be a rich life. But I will whistle at the music, if only the most loved things are granted me.

Earle gave me a book he bought in Naples for me; indecent pictures; printed from very bad drawings, rude things, but attractive to me in part. I gave it away to Sametini the other day. Do you know why? Because if I had kept it I would have had to show it to you, as I cannot withold from you anything that has to do with our fleshly life, and since I can't bear the thought that a woman can't endure seeing what a man can. But I had all the same the feeling that it would possibly be unpleasant for you to see these indecent pictures, and therefore I gave it away.

If, on the contrary, you should ever get the desire to see such pictures then I could always easily obtain some for us.

Just outside my door there has been the most frightful lovescene going on; some Australian with one of the servants, I suppose. I heard a great rumpleing of shirts, etc, & a man's hard exited breathing, & a sound of licking mouths, wet & persistant, broken by a woman's voice pleading to be free, & a man's Australian voice coaxing & praying. I heard: "you know I love you above everything in this world". "I am crazy as a hatter", etc. I wish I could have seen them. This was other, indeed, than that miserable sham at Port Said. Here, at least one side was sincere & somewhat mad. That's the sort of thing folks go & do.

Goodnight fond fair flesh that I love.

Just think isn't it truly human that in all these months what really nourishes me is only a thought in my brain? The thought of whipping you. That I never have enough of that thought! How many many times a day don't I think it?

That just a thought like that can keep one straight and sound of soul, proud and ready for life, without that thought being capable of achievement before many months, that is really human. That sort of thing wouldnt be much use to an animal, & not even to all men. But it suits me down to the ground. It's my moral fuel alright. We understand many small things you and I. We'll pluck and wrench a few generous wild-grown tufts of joy out of this stubborn pleasure-chary old earth before we're quit.

I'm busy having a **frightful row** with J. C. Williamson. If he doesnt give in I dont play on Thursday. Shocking affair it is. Once more good night to us both we hungry minds, mouths, breasts, bodies, skin nerves, & sexual parts. The new whip cost 2/6 and is black.

Tuesday. 29.9.08.

I received letter No 2 with much happiness. I think the wild flower in No 1 enormously attractive. I am very sorry your father's improvement is so horribly slow. You must give him my very kindest regards.

Most of all I rejoice about Kirsten-from-Marathon. It is sweet of you. How is the Dutch going? After your earlier great performance it would be a shame not to bring it to perfection, it seems to me.

You must excuse me that I think you talk with a Copenhagen accent. Why not? I do not perhaps understand enough about it to know whether it is exclusively Copenhagen accent you speak, but it is something pretty strong, it seems to me. But as already said, why not? It is unfortunate that it is just a rather tedious dialect, by chance. But, in any case, I think one should always stick like a leech to whatever speech one is born with. One can easily get to love hearing you talk, even if *I* think it is Copenhagenish. Your little mouth is just as good to kiss as if it spoke Jutlandish. Perhaps if you talked peasant Zealandish your mouth wouldn't be so suitable? In any case I shouldn't risk it. When everything is good, it is best to do nothing. You ask, can't I draw a dress. Do you mean an ordinary woman's-dress? No. I am too stupid for that; also too good. The colour of the running-costume is not so important. But isn't silk too thin. I thought something similar to what the boy in Chelsea had, (Alpacca, linen, cotton?) something a little stiffer would be better. But why not try everything?

Our 1st concert is the day after tomorrow, Thursday, 1st Oct. I am so frightened; so frightened that I can't tell you how much and how keenly I am thinking about you, or how sweet you seem in my longings.

Now begins really stiff work for us.

Next week P.R. Købmagergade also

212   TO KAREN HOLTEN

Hotel Wentworth
Sydney.

Wednesday. 30.9.08.

‖Sjurður* vant av orminum.   ‖*Sigurd‖
Grani bar gullið av heiði.‖⁴³   Færoese.

["Sigurd defeated the worm. Grani carried off the gold from the heath."]

I have won; & not against one Australian. J. C. Williamson is Irish-American, Bracy is English, Tallis is a bloody Irishman.

My contract says I am to be "billed & advertised considerably above the rest of the assisting company".

When I got here I found them printing my name in the papers the same size as the other 3, & I complained & gave them full warning about the *bills*. They put me off day by day, saying there would be plenty of time, no bills were printed, wait till Ada comes & we'll talk it over, etc. I said; all right, but it's got to agree with my contract & you look out you dont wait till too late. As soon as Ada arrives on Sat she asks about advertising, & takes my side fine & gets the papers promised to be right by Monday morn.

On Sunday afternoon mother & I were going to spend the afternoon on a harborsteamer to Lane Cove. I catch sight of a poster (bill) with my name same size & same color as other 3. Although having paid our money for the trip, both of us, we get off & I dash off straight to Ada & Muecke. They are both sweet & stand by me, & I there write out an *Ultimatum* (that I dont play Thursday unless, etc) for her in [to] write to J.C.W. on my behalf. Next morning Muecke, Bracy, (Manager) & I meet accidentally. Muecke says to B; have you got Ada's letter re Percy? B says: I dont think so. Etc Etc.

Monday's paper was right, so that dispute was ended. But Muecke & I fought for the bills, etc. At last Bracy said: You can rest assured they will be altered in the next town, but we cannot possibly alter what is already posted. So I said: If every bill already up isnt altered by Thursday morning I dont play. I'm not a pauper, & if I lose my last penny over this I dont care. But nothing in this world will induce me to play Thursday or any other day until my contract is carried out. You have been stringing me on merely to gain time, & so as to get your things printed before I could get things fixed. Therefor it is your fault if you are now put to expence having to send round a man to paste over your old bills. Etc.

So Doc went off to see Williamson. Everything was promised me that morn, & since then I've been waiting to see if they'd keep their word.

43 Recollected from the first nine-line stanza of the *Sjúrðar Kvæði* ("Firsti táttur: Regin smiður"), collected and arranged by V. U. Hammershaimb and published as Vol. XII of *Nordiske Oldskrifter* by det nordiske Literatur-Samfund (Copenhagen, 1851). There are some errors in Grainger's spelling of the original text.

Today I find that 4 bills on a hoarding in Market St are altered. My name has been pasted over in another color, & also in bigger type. Sigurd conquered the worm. And what are they but *worms* to worry a shy peacable girl-boy like me. For once in my life I have been a man & made a bloody stand against brutal capitalism. Think of men going round wearing their lily fingers to the bone pasting over my name. Isnt it sweet? Little sweet Karen, your little boy has finally really dared something! I make all this fuss about it as it may be a lifetime before I act "man"-like again, & I feel the need to make the most of it.

Maybe it was unwise of me. But some things are too bitter to bear. When last out here I swore I would one day beat J.C.W; make him pay because he is such a capitalist.

I'm glad Doc turned out trumps, for I always trusted him despite our rows together. Better a German Australian than a lot of bloody Celts.

Monday. 5.10.08.
[Original: Danish/English]

I believe you have a relative in Iceland? Can't you get her to send you Icelandic papers sometimes? It would be a big advantage to me to be able to get hold of a newspaper printed in modern Icelandic.

Don't you think you ought to use something to support your breasts when you run? I am afraid that one might otherwise cause them to hang down a little in time. You must remember that they are a little heavy and that they are thrown up and down by running. Women's breasts get to hang down after childbirth, partly because muscles get *stretched* by the constant pull of the child's mouth during suckling. One must see not to get those muscles *stretched*, otherwise they will surely not get so easily firm again. I have thought out something which I hope would avert this danger.

Bind close under the breasts a tape of material similar to the enclosed, which is fastened with a buckle in front. Sew on to it breast shields of linen or flannel or anything at all, which are fastened with a buckle on a tape which is sewn into the 1st-named tape at the back. Thus:

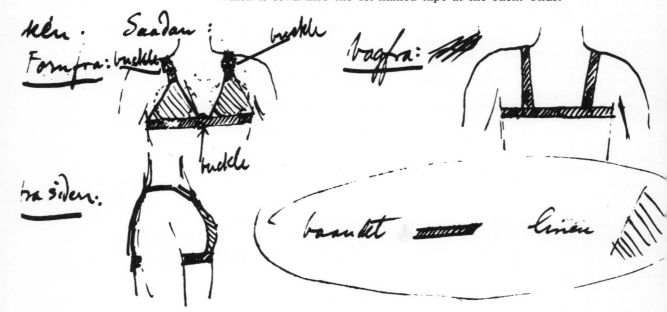

I have so often noticed how strongly the breasts shake on women when they run, and have always thought it would be necessary to prevent it a little if women start running with any constancy.

So the 2 1st concerts are over. I got letter No 2 from you just on the day of the 1st concert. A thousand thanks for the sweet flowers in both letters. I have really never worked harder than I am doing now. We have concerts every 2nd day and I practise the whole day through.

The public is very nice to me much the same as in England. I dont notice any special enthusiasm. I write so little because I am so dead tired every evening. As long as we are in these big towns my whole energy is eaten up fighting folk & working, etc.

This is *instead* of the P.R. letter

Next week will be Købmagergade.

I think of you the whole day nearly.

Sweet Comrade

---

213   TO ROSE GRAINGER
16.10.08.

Mandalay.

Darling one.

The piano was here alright & I was in fine form & played my best, I think. I had a ripping recep coming on & one hearty recall after each of my 2 encores.

Harrison didnt hit here like Sydney, no double encs.[44]

Ada & I had *outstandingly* the biggest succs. *Not* a good house They begged me open with Grieg rather than Bach-Busoni & I think it was not an ill move.

Now its all over I may as well tell you that another huge tussle between me & J.C.W. has come to an end.

In the middle of Mondays last Syd concert Muecke told me that J.C.W. refused to take the good Syd Steinway on with us & was going to use the rotten Melb one.

There was nothing to be done then & there as I had to play my Solos & after the conc was too late & Tallis in Melb the man controlling things.

I may as well say at once that both old Bracy (whom I almost like, & find no enemy in the longer run) & dear old Doc were nowise to blame for all this, both of them as sick at the sudden news as anything.

It was because of all this that my "joy-of-life" was a bit off its oats after Sydney's last concert up to arriving in Melb, so that I could do no better than 1ce stand on my head in the train. Also why I could not see you off, darling, on Tuesday, to my grief.

Ada & Doc were busy at the Recep, so I had to fight it out with Tallis alone.[45] He is a cur & a rotter as I always guessed he was. I said I refused to play if the Sydney Steinway wasnt on the platf by Thursday. They had to bring it by passenger train at extra expense. I said these things will happen if you insist on departing from your contract with me & never even consult me in matters directly concerning me. Ada & dear old Doc are just as sick with JCW as I.[46]

However all is well & Eshelby is with us; *still*.

Very bad news re Karen's poor father I grieve to say, in a letter got this morn. She was going to write you last mail but was hoping to have better news of him. The abcess is still going strong, alas. The O'Haras gave me jolly flowers at the conc last night.

If you saw him for longer I think you'd likely find him as fascinating as ever. I do. I love them all. He has sound musical judgement too. He is delightfully sniffy at the rest of our party & very disappointed in J. Harrison.

Loved one, the fond old firm is still ploughing ahead. Its a loving old combination

44 Among the assisting artists John Harrison was attracting particular attention. His voice was already known to Australian audiences through his recordings for the Gramophone Company. The *Argus*, 2 October 1908, reporting the opening concert of the tour bears out Grainger's comment, "There was general astonishment amongst musical connoisseurs at the charm and warmth of the new tenor, Mr John Harrison, who is probably one of the most captivating singers who has visited Australia. He shared with Madame Crossley in the honours of the evening, and after each song was doubly encored".

45 Ada was officially welcomed with a reception at the Town Hall, hosted by the Lord Mayor, and with 3000 guests attending. The Women's Choir of 500 voices serenaded her and tossed white rose petals into the air with great effect. Such occasions were not without their hazards: Ada had arrived in Melbourne with a finger bandaged, the result of having shaken hands with 4000 people at her Sydney reception; the pressure of her rings had caused the skin to be torn.

46 It was part of Grainger's contract that a Steinway grand piano be provided in each town. Rose replied, 18 October, "Be very careful though about refusing to play without the same piano *always* for the contract only states 'whenever possible'. I still am in doubt whether Williamson need engage you for more than the 25 concerts". Eshelby, the Steinway representative, travelled with the party.

47 W. H. Glen & Co., music sellers and publishers in Melbourne.

Sat. 17.10.08. morn.
Had a lovely time last night with Dr Russell at the Stawells. B. William Taylor, 6 Dukes, Died for Love, Ld Melbourne, Grieg op 66, Slaater, etc. Glen's, piano folk, are awfully nice, & going to advertise big, etc.[47]
Fond love darling one.
Herewith some papers. Look for both *crit & interv* in "Herald".

Perks.

Kindly add your autograph to enclosed & post it off.

214   TO ROSE GRAINGER   [PM Melbourne]
Monday. 19.10.08.

Darling mother.

Didnt write yest as there was no post. 2 letters from you arrived Sat, as none came on Friday. All the things you thoughtfully ask about are alright. I shant bother to answer them singly but have seen about them or shall do, & you can be sure they're all alright.
Did a great game of hockey with the children a[t] 7 oclock before breakf yest. Great sport. Went to lunch with Nesbit[48] and later with fidgey to a convent to play to the nuns, & in the even. Dr Russell came here.
Have written & answered numberless letters.
There is something very jolly in Australian life after all, I find. As the young are allowed such a free hand it gives them a unique chance of tinging the whole national life with their gaiety, hopefulness, pleasurefulness. That is a great thing after all.
My hand is so tired, lovey mummy. It was such a joy to me, yest, being in the old Melb trains passing the old known stations. I wonder if anyone feels deeper joy than I at revisiting old places? S. Yarra Station is glorious with flowers. Can't we do a spree on the Rhine when going to or from Frankfort next time?
I believe we go to Gippsland Friday. Shall let you know tomow.
My hand is so tired writing.

Fond love.

48 Alfred Mortimer Nesbitt (1855–1926), at this time the music critic for the *Age*.

49 Lafcadio Hearn (1850–1904), travel writer and lover of the exotic. He had gone to Japan around 1890, married a Japanese and become a Japanese subject. He was Professor of English at Tokyo University from 1896 to 1903. His writings catered to an avid Western interest in Japan. Rose had probably read *Letters from the Raven: being the correspondence of Lafcadio Hearn with Henry Watkin*. With introduction and critical comment by the editor, Milton Bronner (London, 1908). *Kokoro. Hints and Echoes of Japanese Inner Life* (1896), and *Kwaidan: Stories and Studies of Strange Things* (1904). The gift was *Shadowings* (London, 1905).

215   TO ERNEST THESIGER   Melbourne. Vic.
19.10.08.

Darling friend.

Do Please do me a *great* favor.
I want to give mother a L. Hearn book for Yule. She knows his "Letters" & already has "Kwaidan" & "Kokoko", so it mustnt be one of those 3.[49] If you know another jolly book or books (anything up to 10/ or 15/) of Hearn's, do be a darling & buy them for me, paste in the enclosed card,* & post it, or them, to
Mrs Grainger
Richmond Park
South Rd
Adelaide. South Australia.

The sooner it gets posted off after you get this the better.

We had quite a jolly trip out, with tons of sport on board, though awfully boiling in Red Sea, & mother & I had a happy time together in Sydney, where the tour opened.

All is going *swimmingly*, & the audiences are *simply sweet* to me all along, so far. *How* mother & I would have rejoiced to have you along with us to have a good old laugh at lots of absurd things that have happened, killingly funny heaps of them.

Mother has deserted me for the moment & is in Adelaide with her kin.

In a few days we (the party) are off to Gippsland "bush-whacking" (smaller country towns) & then off to Adelaide.

The scenery everywhere simply stirs me all over the place. Trully lovely.

Just these few words to send you a fond greeting to [*sic* &] to beg you be an angel & send mother the Lafcadio Hearn gift. Will you be a dear & let me know what I owe you for it? And forgive my bothering you?

Love to all.

Ever yr old friend
Perks.

*"To the *youngest* mother of the fond old firm from Perks with keenest love. For Yule. '08."

216   TO ROSE GRAINGER   Mandalay.
[Original: Danish/English]
Wed. 21.10.08.

Darling mother.

I have written to W. Hansen and to many many others.[50] Will you please send me Milly Rees' address, it is not on her face-card, and I would like to write to her.

The concert yesterday went well, and was *much* better filled than the first 2.

But I felt rotten. I was that giddy on the platform that I couldnt distinguish one note from another & my hands looked miles off. How I got thro I dont know. But folk thought I played well, I found. I cant think why I should be off color, for I have been keeping early hours, & eating like 6, & working steadily.

However we leave for Gippsland Friday, & all that open air & long drives ought to righten things up. Just address *Her Majesty's Theatre Melb*. Your parasol has turned up. Shall bring it to Adel.

I never feel too well when I am alone as now. It does not suit me to be alone, I think. I love to get away for 3–4 days; there is a freedom in it which is amusing for a *quite* short time. But after that time I begin to get bored and long to be with you again.

But its nice to think I've already earned £120, isnt it? I am so happy to get your letters and also glad you like Elsie.

I also think exceptionally well of O'Hara. You are quite right in this as all things. Despite his extravagance, & all the flap doodle, there is more pith & more real corage in such an Irishman as he than in even such a dear thing as Englishman Russell. If I were a woman I would feel it even more.

But both are darlings.

I get lovely lots of bread butter & jam here. Fine jams. Of course plenty meat too.

OHara is an awful baby still, when one sees more of him.

50 Wilhelm Hansen, Grainger's Danish agent, had written with an offer from Hals in Christiania for Grainger to give three piano evenings there in the winter of 1908–09, with a fixed honorarium of 250 Kr. plus a half share of the nett surplus of the concerts. Rose wrote advising him to accept the engagement for after his return, and to let the newspaper people know about it. The engagement took place, though not quite as originally planned, in January/February 1910 (see letter 302).

217 TO ROSE GRAINGER   Mandalay.
22.10.08.

Had such a jolly evening with the children here last night. They have toy trucks, etc, with wheels like

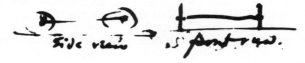

& Miles & I built a switchback to roll these down. It started on a tablecloth pinned on to the top of a high bookcase, & thence onto music fixed thus on a table.

The music books being kept hollow curved like that keep the trucks in their course.

In the middle of the switchback I made about a 1½ gap, over which the trucks lept through the way they had got on them. After having run the length of a long table up & down, they had to run along another tought-stretched tablecloth with an up hill tilt, so that the trucks *just* ended gently into a ledge in a writing table, like a sort of shed for them. The whole thing was like

It was delightful to see the graceful curve the trucks made in the air when jumping the gap, & grand fun when they alighted plumb on to their wheels on the other side of it & rolled smoothly along to the end of the course.

I should like to do a game like that in London if one only had time. Anything with wheels that run smoothly enthralls me awfully.

You're right, darling, Australians are pretty hideous on the whole. I've seen *no* goodlooking middleaged woman, yet. Mrs OHara is, of course, *born in England*. You can say what you like but I find the men less worse than the women.

But their shocking thriftlessness goes thro them one & all. Even a little kid like Peter is always after spending money, & everlastingly smashing up things just for pure destructiveness. Always sowing out & never reaping in, its a poor game.

There is no joy like saving money. To know that the years gradually bring one quittance from the tyranny of mankinds stupidity & habitworship, that one gradually is accumilating the possibility of being able to afford to be an individual at last; no mere spending can equal the relish of it. The old firm is going to be a fullfledged capitalistic concern yet.

When eating, always remember that a few months will see us back in England where a higher standard prevails than the mere need of avoidance of sapless scrag.

Boots arived, ta.

Met Marshall Hall yest.[51] He's a real good sort, & lots of fun. Written Hansen, etc. I'm attending to all business & social duties that my addled head can hatch. Please always write me any business suggestions you can think of. I shall attend to each every one, never fear, but shant bother to allude to them in letters to you, as that would be tiresome for us both. Off to Gippsland tomorrow.

You've got such a loving lonely son.

51 George William Louis Marshall-Hall (1862–1915), English-born composer and conductor. He had come to Melbourne as first Ormond Professor of Music at the University of Melbourne in 1891. Grainger's farewell benefit concert in Melbourne, 14 May 1895, had been under Marshall-Hall's direction. Between December 1892 and November 1912 the Marshall-Hall Orchestra gave regular concerts in Melbourne.

218 TO ROSE GRAINGER
23.10.08. Friday.

Commercial Hotel.
Leongatha Gippsland
(16 miles from coast)

My loved one

I am *quite happy* in such a place as this. Glorious district, & really admirable Australian types riding about freely & carelessly on the same dear easygoing horses. Everyone kindly & careful, no flippancy. Grand meals, melting chicken & maddeningly good rubard pie with floods of local cream, & flirtless unconversational women waitresses. Darling, you & I could spend such a fine holiday here, living at this very Hotel & taking drives, & maybe even rides. There is also a tennis court, (asphalt) where I'm going to play a game this afternoon with 3 locals.

There's a nice old Irishman from County Connaught, who can speak Irish. He has told me the sound of some Gaelic words I wanted to know.

I like the Irish, I think. I cant resist charm of manner in the long run.

Last night I had a great time at the last Melb concert. We had a packed house. Got good encore after the Fauré Debussy no, & double encore after Rakoczy. (Brahms Waltz & To the Spring)

O'Hara's an awful kid. And hugely fresher & less colonialized really than one might gather that one night we were there. There is a lot in him akin to Fornander. I wish you were in Melb. more to see more of him, for I'm sure you'd enjoy him still alright. You're right on most points. There's a lot behind your liking for the Irish. (the more so these days when Gaelic is on the go)

There's something in these small towns very reminding of Denmark, I think. Just this, maybe, that both are thorogoing *Agricultural* communities. It is a phase of life that soothes & enhappies me. Pity you & I cant put in a holiday here. Now I'm off to play tennis.

Am not sending money to you yet.

Your happy loving son, devoted to his mum, & all the bett for getting up at 3.30.

219   TO ROSE GRAINGER   Club Hotel,
Monday. 26.10.08.   Sale, Gippsland.

My little dear mother.

Well, I did a nice walking match yesterday, 46 miles, as you'll see by enclosed cutting. I started at 6.45 morn from Yarram & got here about 7.10 evening; taking 30 mins off for lunch at about 1 o'clock, & 2 very short halts in the afternoon. Fancy, my feet arent even blistered, & I'm hardly at all stiff this morn. It's undoubtedly the best walk I've ever done. I did the 1st 26 miles from 6.30 to about 1 oclock (or 1–10?) & finished up in Sale at 5 miles an hour, at which speed I did a big part of the last 10 miles. Most of my former walks took place as antidotes to fit of "bad habit", whereas this trip opened out with no such sickly handicap. My veins gave me no trouble. I did not feel them, & an investigation of them on the road found them wholly unswollen. I girthed & saftypined my holder up at just the right toughness & on unbuckling was firm as apples.

So all that shows that my vein biz does not affect my walking powers, nor does walking worsen my veins. I was happy as a lark all the way relishing my day from fresh morn to balmy eve. No trace of pain or weariness. What can better cool mornings in warm lands? And the laughing jackasses & magpies & other dear birds. Sweet & wild the songs are of our native birds, queer quaint & ownish as you & I, dearie. Dont lose a chance, if you get one, of rising early one morning out of town & hearing what the "feathered warblin' songsters" (their charmin' notes so sweet did tune) have to tell of the very soul of our climate & land.

The future of Australia may not lightly be dismissed by judgement upon her money earning folk of today. The scenery, the animal life, the air, and so on of the country is wondrously tender, pure, high souled, aloof, delicate, refined. Sooner or later its darling influences *must* tell, & we will get weird lovable ravishing *highly unworldly* human showings.

The teetrees are in blossom. They grow in the shapliest most luscious clusterings & groupings by creeks, some of them (dying trees?) radiant in pale purple coloring; etherial, angelic. Surely the teetree is every bit as precious as the gums! I gloated over a lovely colored parrot, tail & wings of purply blue (*rich*) & body of blood red flame. Also a small bird of peacock bluegreen. But I was most glad of the laughing j.as. They [their] very heads are embodied chuckles (not chuckles of mirth — far from it — but chuckles of unkeepdownable ingrained *queer*ness)

I feel very like them.

I had a dangerous encounter with a turkey.
                    "Run away, run away"!
This is my 1st long walk in Australia. Its good that it has been at last. The sight of the gums, & the suck of their young leaves upfreshened me chiefestly on my NZ trudges, & here they are in greater generosity & "at home" into the barg.

Dear mother, dont neglect to take a chew at young gum leaves sometimes. They tell to the palate what the birdcalls preach to the ear; they deftly sum up all the influences of the land. Just so pure, queer, angel-fresh ought our art to be when it turns up. What is the prevailing taste in gum? I find no used expressions to fit it. It's not salt, sweet, bitter, sour. Is it acid? Sharp it is, but that's not its overweighing quality.

My walk was full of fond thoughts of you. We are, as you write, trully harmonious. We, as a couple, are so outrageously harmonious in our bedrock that we can afford, like I can as a composer, to be specialists in surface discords.

How lucky I am in having you born in the land I so love certain phases of, so jolly that we can share the pride of birthright claims to it all. If you had come here from elsewhere I should need to gloat lonelily.

Lovely winepurple (never noticed just that particular shade before) sunset gloamed over the last few miles wherin I passed over father's swingbridge.[52]

The river views about Sale seem jolly pretty. You know them I think.

I am glad you are sorry for Karen being left partially alone over there. I always feel ever so sorry for women being lonely, left without their particular lightbearing loved ones, for for them it is so many times worse to bear than for us. If they had not the particular quality that makes folks absence so heavy for them they could not make their presence so strangely enthralling to men as they jolly well can.

It is always my personal feeling that the joys of intersexual comradeship (be it mother-son, sister-brother, man-woman, young boy-old woman — it is quite the same) well up from out of the female's nature rather than the man's. She is creative in that particular deal, man more merely appreciative & responsive.

Keep on addressing to Her Majesty's Melbourne. As for you & I it wont be long before we're together. I dont know yet for cert, but about a 14 night will do it, I think.

I'm *so* sunburnt, though not painfully so; face, neck, legs. I wore only cap, shirt, white drawers sewn together, belt, 2 thick pairs of socks (one over the other) *well* soaped & my black boots. I picked prances of wild flowers & carried them 15 miles to give to Ada. She & the party only overtook me 2 miles out of Sale, though they started only 4 hours later from Yarram.

I got tons of cheering on the road, & on reaching Sale[53]

220 TO ROSE GRAINGER   between Bairnsdale & Sale.
27.10.08.

Am longing get a letter from you at Sale. Have had none for a few days alas.

Such a jolly time at Bairnsdale. Yesterday afternoon Tini & I rowed on the river, dodging in between overhanging trees & the bank, & crashing thro gathered together driftwood between bridge pillars, laughing so hard we could not row. Concert last night went fine.

This morn were taken for a run up the river in motor launch. John & I rowed a lot of the way instead, great fun.

On getting back Earle, Wilson, (who saw you off) Matheson & I had a jolly swim from the "Rowing Club's" shed. Lovely & cool. Earle looks fine undressed Such a figure is not an atom too thin when without clothes.

I gulped a lump of water in the middle of swimming & reached the bank very spluttersome & ¼-smothered, but had a better go later on. Think I'm going to have a swim in artesian water tomorrow in Sale. Fancy being paid £40 for a week of such larks! All our party are very boylike & happy & we're all at a high pitch of chumminess just for the mo'.

If you're using any of the "walk" cuttings to England let's know to whom you send, as I'll be too.

Yr fond frolicsome son.

52 The swing bridge designed by John Grainger was erected 1880–83 over the LaTrobe River south of Sale. It still stands, being classified by the National Trust of Victoria and listed on the State's Register of Historic Buildings.

53 Rose had reacted badly to the news of Grainger's walk, writing, on 28 October, "Such a walk must be very bad for you & will tell on yr health if not now, later on . . ." But when a paragraph on the subject appeared in the *South Gippsland Chronicle* of 30 October (a paragraph also appeared in the *Bulletin* on 29 October) Rose, ever practical, was quick to instruct that it be sent to the London newspapers to be "par"-ed.

221 TO ROSE GRAINGER   [In the train]
Oct 29. 1908.   Traralgon–Melbourne

I forgot to say that I saw some lovely views of Japan at OHara's (Japan thro the Stereoscope) while there & that they've greatly changed my feeling for the place & its folk. The absolute perfection of house decoration, so smooth, plain, unpretentious, cool looking, practical looking, the sweet quaint peasant dresses, the dainty refinement of farm outhouses & countryside cottages, hived me all of a heap & I'm all agog to go & see it some day, & wont, I think I foresee, lag far behind you in friendly feeling for the place.

In many respects (setting up of houses, certain matters of clothing etc) they seem to fulfil long felt personal ideals of mine. I love smooth, cool, canemade, flat cut wooden, & above all frightfully clean looking things. Some of the peasants wear awfully jolly small drawerlike things & leggings from above the ankle to below the knee, so that the nice jutting out ankle bones & knee bones are bare & catch the eye. Nice sandals too. It makes me happy that I thus see a chance of sharing with you, dearie, your Hearn fed appreciation of the Japs.

I see, by a London D.T. we've just got hold of, that Herman has been playing at the Proms.

I enjoyed the motor drive yesterday, parts especially.

Australians' idea of "good country" is too filthy. They seem (like most races) wholly beauty-proof, refer to glorious wild patches as "poor stuff" & enthuse disgustingly over dully fenced, tree murdered "properties" where slavery of many beasts may be carried on.

I saw some lambs being sheared the other day. The shearers get the wool off alright, but chip off bits of sheep at the same time. I dont hanker to see a more stomach turning sight. And to think that these folk, who can endure to see such callous paingiving go on yearly without winking would get the horrors if they heard of a few sexual perversities that have their origin in joy & glow. Australians certainly have no hysterical degree of kindliness to brutes when their pocket's in it, I think. Few unsensual folk have. On the other hand, they are sexual enough I suppose.

What is one to do with the ruck of humanity in any land? In Germany they preserve their woods, but cut them up into squares so that they become a brainbore. Here they leave the woods good & free but destroy them as hard as they can lick. What's one to prefer.

Lucky that part of the country that's too hilly or commercially rotten to court "developing". Do you remember Kipling's "the song/?Price of the tree" in "From C to C"?[54] It comes much into my mind these days. The dear old sea; it is the staunchest standby of the übermensch [German: superior human-being], because it almost alone joins him as a being unbotched by the antactivities of petty people. Never mind; the scenery here will take some destroying yet. What a sorry game this farming squatting, etc is. Making poor animals breed like blazes merely to be driven, ridden, shorn, killed, eaten, beaten. No game for me. Better freeze onto the old box; it gives no sign of pain when I hurt it.

222 TO ROSE GRAINGER   Gotha.
[Original: Danish/English]   S. Yarra.[55]
31.10.08. Saturday.

My little mother.

Today Russell and I are going out to Black Spur. Yesterday he drove round with me in his motor and I visited Uncle Charlie, the *Finns*, (Punch) & the Curtains. Charlie and all his family look extremely well and happy.

54 Presumably a reference to an untitled two-stanza verse which occurs in Chapter XXVI of Kipling's *From Sea to Sea* (1889).

55 On his return to Melbourne, Grainger was the guest of the family of Hugo Wertheim, a family of some importance in music in both Frankfurt and Melbourne. (Rose had written, 19 October, "Visit Wertheims for certain, we require all the sympathy from this family for Frankfurt & also for yr Recital Tour later on here".) On 21 October Grainger attended the ceremony in connection with the laying of the foundation stone for Wertheim's new piano factory in Richmond. On 21 October, Percy had written to Karen of his meeting with a Danish violinist friend of Herman Sandby, and of how he could not speak Danish fluently any more. Perhaps this is why he started writing in Danish to Rose at this time.

His wife looks *really* strong, different from most Australian women.

To think, that the *day before yesterday*, while I drove with Russell in his car, we met a girl riding astride and I said to him: How awfully jolly it looks, girls riding astride like that! And she was one of Charlie's daughters, and she recognised me, and said, when she came home, that she thought she had seen me driving. She looked *splendid*. Yes, Charlie and his family make an excellent impression.

I spent the evening at the Curtains'. They are a sweet family, and Gladys, I think, is after all nearly as pretty as last time; I didn't think that, you know, when I saw her recently at one of our Melbourne concerts. I spent some very happy hours with them. Russell and M. Hall lunched with me.

M. H.[all] thought absolutely that a tour over here would pay me excellently. He doesn't think that I need to wait longer about it, but that it could be in a year's time, or something similar. He thinks that this Xley tour will have *improved* my fame, standing here, and that there can be no talk of it having damaged my chances here in any way. He has given me many practical tips about how I should arrange with Taits. Russell examined me yesterday. He thinks that the vericosele does not need to be operated at all and that I can undertake all sport and exertions without risking making it worse. He was admiringly surprised about my sexual parts. He says that I am " 'hung' like a farmer or a prize-fighter, rather than a musician". He says that I am quite unusually greatly developed and that the girls ought to appreciate it awfully. What could be better news, indeed?

How Curtain admires you! It was really lovely to get to hear him talk about you.

You shan't be afraid of being lonely for too long on this tour. We are coming to Adelaide at least twice before Christmas, and after Christmas you can come over to Melb when you please. The NZ tour is quite short.

Yesterday I posted a cheque of Russell's for £40. This weeks cheque I havent drawn yet, & shall draw £80 next week & send that to you. Russell said dont register it, as it's a Xed cheque. I suppose you can get someone to put it thro a banking account alright?

You'll have to pay a bob or 2 exchange I think, but it seems the cheapest way of getting it over, all the same.

Give my very fond love, please, to dear Auntie Clara, Uncle George, & Aunty May, & all. Am longing to see them all.

Herewith I am sending you a letter from Roger. Keep it for me till we meet. It is so lovely that he is feeling so well. He is really one of the sweetest.

Goodbye little mother, we will soon be together again.

Your happy boy
Percy.

Today I got a letter from you. Yesterday I got 5 letters from you, one from Roger, and one from Karen. That was a rich post!

223   TO ROSE GRAINGER   Gotha
[Two postcards]   S. Yarra.
Monday 2.11.08.

Darling mother.

Russell & I went off on the spree from Sat midday till yestereve. (Sund) We motored to the place on the other side of this card [Gracedale House], by way of Kew, Ringwood, & Lilydale, reaching it by about 5.30, sheding the motor there & having a fine feed with plenty of tarts & pudding. After feed we walked to Black Spur, (Lindt's Hotel) getting there about 11 o'clock. Lindt is a German photographer who has been a lot in N. Guinea, Figi, & other S. Sea Islands & had a great deal to show me of keen interest to me from those places; great photos of natives, etc; & tales to tell of their music; Figi particularly[56]

The next morn, after delicious shower bath & jolly breakfast walked back to Gracedale, which was reached about 2.15, where I had another luscious shower bath, followed by a big tuckin, whereupon we motored to here, leaving 3.30 & getting here about 7, taking care to pass our old house at Caroline St, S. Yarra on the way.

The Linden tree next door is still standing & so is the tree (with sticky gum on it) in our garden that I used to climb. I had a peep at the window out of which I used to look dreaming of spears torn out of garden railings & shields covered with hides buyable in the Prahran road. It was shockingly hot walking yest. The scenery is like paradise, all of a blue melt, & the bird calls are balmy & sweet & spirit caressing. Russell loves our scenery deeply. We had jolly bumpings on the motor trip, & shook a lamp off its supports, but nothing worse.

He is a darling comrade, & we were blissfully happy. At Lindts there is a ladder with balconies built between 2 trees, we mounted it & enjoyed ripping view, marred only by rank laughter & ugly sounding speech of some Germans below.

My darling little one, fond love from your doting Perks

224   TO ROSE GRAINGER   Warrnambool.
9.11.08.   .

My dear darling one

I'm such a happy son of yours & had such an overwhelmingly joyeous weekend. Stayed with O'Haras. Called on Miss Rowe & Pinschofs Sat afternoon on arrival in Melb & Sunday before breakf hockey with Miles, George, Peter, Kath, Beatty. My side won. After breakf Miles & I had great fun rigging up a model boat (sailing model, like mine) & then went rowing on Albert Pk Lagoon, where we were 2 hours, joyeous wet spraysplashed hours. The boat wldnt sail properly (what attempt of mine like that ever *does* come off, save the switchback game at OHaras?) but the rowing was pretty profess!

That Alb Pk Lag is an honor to any town. Got pretty wet thro rowing & came home to ravenous meal O the joys of eating, I am held fast in their throes, these days. After a shave & dress up in *ultra fine* clothes Dr Russell turns up in car for me to pay calls. Went to Husbands, Mrs Irvines, Mrs McGees, Mrs Levis. The Husbands were all in tip top form as the baby is really bettering at last. Molly has quite regained her looks again, I think. They all sent tons of love to you, darling one.

The dear McGees, too. Fairy so lovely & delightfully manmiffy & Mrs McG so sweet & puresouled. Then back to a supper party at OHara's. O what a real gorge. Triffle, Cider, (non alchahol) strawberries & cream.

Then packed up & off to Fed. Cof. Palace as we left Melb this morn at 6.30; getting up 5. Got here 2.30. Such joy in the train. Besides a nice sweet sleep read read read in the German book by Bloch "Das sexualLeben unsere zeit" lent me by Scharf.[57] How I adore adore many elements in the Germs. Such a book like that makes me fairly gambol with interest & sympathy. What a devoted sexualist I am! I like to fairly grub my nose in the very smell of the subject. It is life breath to my wide old nostrils.

It has all the charm of Weininger only its a swinging hopeful outlook throout & so generous so Wotanforgivinglike, so woman-cherishing!

56 John William Lindt (1845–1926). German-born, he had come to Australia in 1862, subsequently taking up photography. He went to southeast New Guinea as official photographer in 1885, and travelled to and photographed in the New Hebrides in 1889 and on Bega Island in the Fiji group in 1890. He built a "studio in the forest" called "The Hermitage" at the Blacks' Spur, fifty miles north of Melbourne in the Great Dividing Range. It later became a guest house. He built three treehouses approached by ladder. The Graingers had lived at 62 Caroline Street for a brief period, probably in 1893 or 1894.

57 Grainger was reading Dr med. Iwan Bloch, *Das Sexualleben unserer Zeit in seinen Beziehungen zur modernen Kultur* [The Sexual Life of our Time in its Relations to Modern Civilisation], Berlin, L. Marcus, 1907.

He deals at great length with queer sexual instincts that I luckily suffer delightedly from & labels them all healthy & even desirable & dangerless. I knew so.

What a happier creature I am than when last in dear Warrnambool! What a happier creature than when I read Weininger.

I wish you'd read as much of these sexual treatises as I have. Do you think you'd care to? One knows mighty little of splendid stirring human understreams if one doesnt, 'cept thro oneself.

My dearest mum, fellow optimist, dear arguer, how I long for the joy of being with you.

The few wet spray-rich hours on the water yest made me rethink what fun we could have on our boat.

Yr loving lucky son
Perks.

225 TO ROSE GRAINGER   Warrnambool.
10.11.08. Tuesday.

Fancy, I got *3* encores after my Liszt last night (& good recalls after the 3rd encore too) as well as, of course, the usual 1 after my 1st solo. They seem to remember me nicely from last tour in many places.

The Bloch book keeps me up to a 7th heaven of happiness. I wish you'd read the book thro from *start to finish*. It is so delightfully hopeful about Syphilis & the chances of victory against it, *nowadays*. He has a positively passionate *love* for mercury for all the good it has done & regards the inroads of Syph as *thoroly withstandable, even after yearlong neglect*.

My feeling after reading the book is that my personal instincts are much more healthy than might be thought.

All my particular instincts he classes as *abnormal* but nowise needfully less *healthy* on that account. I believe you dont have quite the same craving for reckless outspokenness & even unneedful *dwelling* upon sex that I have. I wonder why? I find it the most absolutely enthralling & *improving* of all subjects & the most conducive to happiness.

The presence of its discussion among men & the absence of ditto among girls or women is why I so easily get happy with the former, & rarely enjoy the latter unless alone with one at a time, I think.

Our untutored ideas of sexual problems are untellably brutal ignorant tiresome inhuman. Believe me, a little thought upon, & study of, sexual matters, would alter broaden ones views of such things just as surely as social thinking cannot help producing socialism or other humane convictions amongst nice hearted folk.

My little mum, I shall try & get Scharf to let me keep the book a bit longer & bring it over to Adelaide in case you'd happen to care to look at it.

I'm taking every pains to be fresh & fit for Adelaide. It is a joy-beacon ahead.

My darling moth, love from the gay son.

226 TO ROSE GRAINGER   Prince of Wales Hotel
11.11.08.   Geelong
Wed. midday.

Altho' this wont reach you as soon as I will I cant resist the pleasure of writing you my deep rapture at a (prize) brass band of schoolboys that met us & played to us on this town's station this morn on getting here.[58] Most

58 It was the band of the St Augustine's Orphanage. The students of the Bendigo Conservatorium had sung a serenade to Ada Crossley on the evening of 6 November. Percy wrote of it to Karen, "Out in the street a chorus (men and women) is singing a serenade to Ada. They sing well & the sound melts lovingly in the hot lazy evening air . . . It touches me to hear folk of my own poor (is it poor? or not?) land singing so nicely".

of the boys from 10 to 13 or 14 or 15 years of age conducted by a boy of 15–16 who was also 1st cornet solist, with a ripping rich singing tone & a splendid rhythmic soldierly technic. This little boy was a treat to watch when playing or bandbeating. Tho uniformed (all of them too) & short haircut this little chap had a typical *real* musician's way of seriously doing thing[s]. He seemed a real sound-critic & sensation observer, dreamy & slowcoach like. The band played *absolutely* together, but not because they followed a beat intelligently, but in the chambermusic-ensemble (& nigger partsinging) way; that is, by each listening for each, & thro knowing every entry, effect, difficult clinch splendidly by heart, &, I should say, thro tireless study & working together.

Their speeds were all, as far as I could judge, considerably too slow, a characteristic I have noted in nearly every Australian. Their *tone* was embracing, perfect, mellow, positively W. Whitmanish. I never remember hearing a brassband treat their medium with greater refinement or with more noticable absence of blare or brutality. Their swells (<>) were enthralling, each man seemingly listening to the other & producing a oneness (in greatening & lessening volume) without stickhelp, quite astounding. The conductor boy very rarely beat at all as he was mostly playing cornet solo. The most tough entries (off the beat & such) were therefor attacked by the ruck of the band faultlessly & most disciplinedly without the less help from the band beater, which must stand for no end of practising together, sharp hearing, & rhythmic acute memory. The evotional impression of their playing was, to my senses, strikingly "weiblich" [German: feminine], maybe because they were yet unripe boys, but more likely because they were Australians. They choose more smoothly mellow swellingly flowing pieces (& were best in such kind of passages) than any *brass* band I remember, & struck me as markedly German & Wagnerlike in their sound-leanings, when contrasted with the slickness of Sousa's men & the rather specialized manliness (even manishness, musically) of Rogans Coldstreams. None the less they were throout finely soldierly. (Women can as easily be soldierly as men, to my mind)

I have heard greater brassband perfection elsewhere, but *never anywhere* a greater promise of racial musical giftedness, quite looking away from the young years of the lads.

Here is tender feeling, pure, solid, hardworking & distinctly highly disciplinable musical material, capable of use in *any* musical sphere.

It is markworthy of this tour that all my nationally enthusiastic moments have been called forth by technicly musical events: The singing of wild birds, the tone of the Sydney Symphony strings, the singing of a really fine musical chorus in Bendigo, (*first class* I assure you, having *just* the same rich dreamy slowgoing pure sleepy quality as the tone of this brass here) & then these boys.

Humanly I have not been much stirred by my nation this trip (more than likely a periodical weakness & lack of sympathy in me) so much so that since landing I have steadily doubted the likelihood of my ever bringing off my plans in this nevertheless beloved land. Yet *each time* I have heard the musical efforts of my countrymen I feel how they thoroly deserve a brave try on my part, & how gloriously they would respond artisticly if (in the case of one having a shy & quietloving temperament) one could only stick them as human beings.

I passively balance between several likelihoods at the moment. I lack the headstrong willdriven intentions of my former visit; I have instead a critical & thorough fit. I refuse to think hopefully of my future in Australia this trip. But my cold calm musical verdict of them so far is that they deserve a jolly sight more conviction & blind devotion from me than I intend to let myself give them at this present stage of my career, though the future may hold any old thing.

The Australian neednt go miscalculating himself to be a sort of budding

American in temperament — quick, agile, clever, tactful, bright, cunning. (tho maybe Americans are nowise these things either) Let the Australian realize he is a slow, clumsy, stupid, tactless, dull, seethroable old cow, & that purity, simplicity, solidity, & countrifiedness (as shown in the temperament of the boys band) become him best at his present stage. Dear old thing.

Within the last few days I've seen 2 little girls dressed in boys loose trousers with long tunics over them. One was in Warrnambool & the other here in Geelong. The one in Warrnambool, of about 7 or 8, was riding a bicycle with barefeet & underlegs, golden haired & very fair skined tho slightly sunglowed, & looked the lovliest kissyest thing out. To see such a girl child in boys breeches gives me the delicious feeling that the free untrammeled life of the Western male is going to be unfolded before her.

Doc, Harrison, Tini & I have just returned from swim in *tiptop* seawater bath[s] here, open to the sky & todays delicious glowing sun, along of a freshish breeze. I swam well, & fairly long without effort, but Doc beat me in a short race we had. There were some heartcheering specimens of Australian boyhood there today, young fairlings diving & threshing about like fishes. I have *never* seen at English baths such *lovable* figures (with a *very slightly* womanish touch to them) as a few there today. One chap in particular, Fair haired, blueeyed, sun tinged on a very fair skin, with the straightest thinkable legs, & a delicious richness & flowingness of form about his arms, shoulders, thighs, legs, but no trace *at all* of stomach, & a dear honest, broad, rather smoothly-round typically Australian face (nearer the German than the real English type is) I could hardly keep my eyes off, the healthy showing of him gladdened me so, & made me so racially proud. His sexual parts, too, were so astoundingly Grecian; graceful & round & full without being clumsy & floppy. It is, indeed, to my mind, the very *rarest* thing to see men or boys with prettily formed appetizing sexual parts, most are positively ugly, & give an ignoble impression, worse luck. Australians very sensibly were [wear] no bathing drawers in public baths. No saying about our race hits truer than that:

"The Australian is an Italienized Englishman."

The Crossley company reached Adelaide on Friday 13 November and Rose and Percy were reunited. After a week and three concerts in Adelaide, the party embarked on 19 November on the R.M.S. Ortona *for Perth and a tour of the goldfields. Reaching Perth on 23 November, they gave the first of three concerts there on the 24th. With a Grand Extra Concert advertised for 7 December, they departed on 30 November for a week's tour of the goldfields, giving two concerts in Kalgoorlie and one each in Coolgardie and Boulder. On 9 December they left for the eastern States on the R.M.S.* India, *reaching Adelaide again on 12 December.*

The second concert in Perth was also the twenty-fifth concert of the tour. Thereupon Grainger had possibly his biggest dispute with the J. C. Williamson management on the question of his re-engagement for the remainder of the tour. After some fuss and much misery he was re-engaged, but on modified terms. It was as a result of the extension of the tour, possibly until May, that the decision was taken for Rose to accompany the party to New Zealand. Never one to take Percy's absences well, she had suffered badly during their recent separation. Dismayed at the prospect of a further five months apart, her feelings overcame her impulse to "save money".

There were some changes in the tour personnel in the West. Hamilton Earle left the tour in Perth, returning to England on the G.M.S. Bremen on 8 December. His place was taken by the Irish baritone, Jay Ryan, whose name first appears on the programme for the concert at Stawell on 14 December.

From Adelaide, the company travelled overland, giving concerts in north-western Victoria and New South Wales, and reaching Sydney by Christmas Day. Rose remained in Adelaide until 21 December, then took the train to Melbourne, and from there to Sydney. She met Percy in the train to Sydney on 22 December. Immediately after the Christmas night concert in Sydney the concert party, with Rose, embarked for New Zealand.

227   TO ROSE GRAINGER   Palace Hotel
[Original: English/Danish]   Perth.
Friday 27.11.1908.

My darling little mother.

I am so sorry not to have got a letter from you with this post. Maybe you missed. I hope you are quite well, dearie. I have enquired well both here & at His Majesty's Theatre, but in vain.

I go & see Mrs Jenkins often at her mothers. They are a nice clan & I've had plenty of relishable games of tennis with her brother. The other morn before breakf. (6.30) we had a good go, in rain-drizzle. He won 2 sets, I won 1.

Have you noticed that a N. Zealander has won the Nobel Prize?[59] A scientist. (chemistry) I cant find the bit of the paper to cut it out for you, but you've doubtless seen it. Its good the Australian footballers are doing so very well at home, isnt it? "While there's football there's hope."

I have done very well at the concerts here so far, got a double encore on Tuesday.

Harrison is being a great hit here again.

Perth is really a very pretty town

This is a very dull letter I fear. I feel that all the letter writing sap has been absolutely sweated out of me by all the card & letter writing I've been doing to England & Eastern States this week. Have written letters to Mrs Lowrey, Mrs Danvers, Charlie Stirling, father, etc, & cards to numberless folk, Miss Ducker (Sydney) amongst them. Have written all on your list, & lots others.

Clem is over here & I have seen him often. He looks very the same only rather better looking, I think.

I have had much joy wiring a bit into the Paganini Vars. Such piano practise has really a strong charm; whereever there are technical hardships to overcome, rather than unstriking stretches to memorize. I've also been reading the Gaelic bible at bit with help of an English bible lent me by Mrs Jenkins.

Wouldnt it be jolly if we could go back after the tour's end together by S. Africa, without the rest. I feel such a yearning to have a quiet time with you & me just to ourselves, we seem to have been hotchpotched up with "crews" & regiments so long, & to have been forcefully divorced from our own sweet company & comradeship. Also we haven't, for years, had a real *seatrip* to ourselves. I cant rest till I get a letter from you, telling you're alright. I shall be writing again by the next boat that leaves here for the East in a few days.

I **think** one of my Sargent reproductions has been left behind in Adelaide, Marshalls or the other shop. Would you see, dear? I think I gave them 2 when I arrived, & only one was found on unpacking here. If not

59 Ernest Rutherford (1871–1937), born at Nelson, New Zealand. He had discovered that alpha-rays break down atoms and studied radio-active substances.

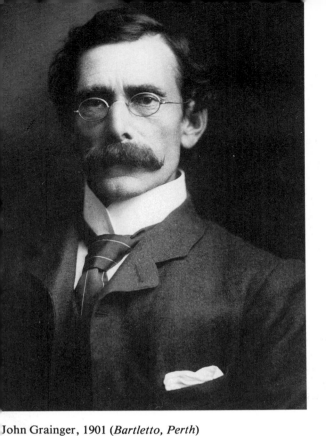

John Grainger, 1901 (*Bartletto, Perth*)

Rose Grainger, 1903 (*G. C. Beresford, London*)

Percy and Rose Grainger, September 1903 (*Talma Studios, Sydney*)

Percy Grainger (n.d. 1902?) (*Elliott & Fry, London*)

Grainger as concert-goers saw him in the London
period (n.d.) (*Mayall, London*)

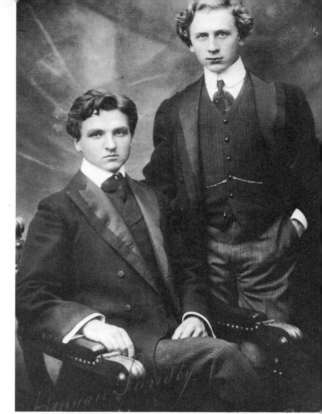

Grainger and Herman Sandby, October 1904 (*Peter
Newland, Copenhagen*)

Roger Quilter (n.d. 1904?) (*Gabells, London*)

Cyril Scott, October 1902 (*Barraud, Liverpool*)

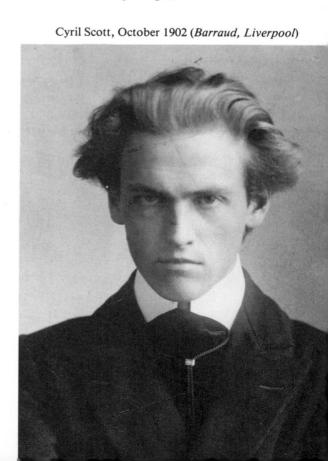

The welcome for Ada Crossley at Bairnsdale station, 21 October 1903 (*Alex. Ward, Bairnsdale;* from the *Australasian*, 2 January 1904)

Percy Grainger arriving for his first Australasian tour, 1903–04

Ada Crossley at the Metropolitan Fire Brigade Station, Perth, 14 January 1904

The lunch at Government House, Perth, 13 January 1904: Grainger is standing at left; Ada Crossley is fourth from right, standing. (*Greenham & Evans, Perth*)

Grainger's photograph of Adelina Patti from her tour of October 1902

Ada Crossley and Grainger
in Durban,
10 February 1904

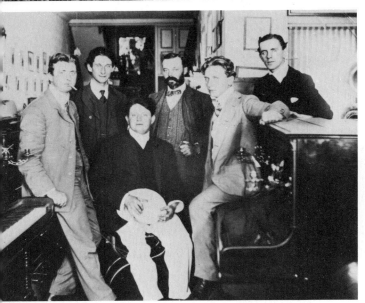

The "boys" from Ada Crossley's touring party, in
Cape Town, 29 March 1904: Percy Grainger, second
from right; Jacques Jacobs (?) seated.

On board SS *Wakool* (*l. to r.*): Captain S. A.
Pidgeon, Rose Grainger, Dr Francis Muecke.

Grainger (seated at the piano) at the Grand Festival of Village Choirs, Kings Lynn, Norfolk, 8 May 1905
(from *Sphere*, 13 May 1905)

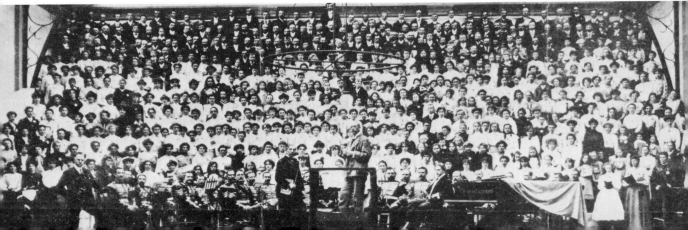

Grainger,
Alfhild de Luce
and Herman Sandby
in Denmark, September 1905

Grainger
photographed by
Baron de Meyer
(n.d. 1905?)

A postcard photograph of
Hjalmar Thuren
sent to Grainger from the
Vejlefjord Sanatorium,
26 September 1905

A postcard from Grainger to
Karen Holten's mother, 22
December 1905,
showing 63 Oakley Street, Chelsea:
"This is our house"

A postcard from Grainger to Karen Holten, 7 July 1906, with a view of old Chelsea: "Do you remember this?"

Svinkløv Plantørbolig [The Planter's House, Svinkløv], a postcard photograph sent by Grainger to Rose, 5 September 1906

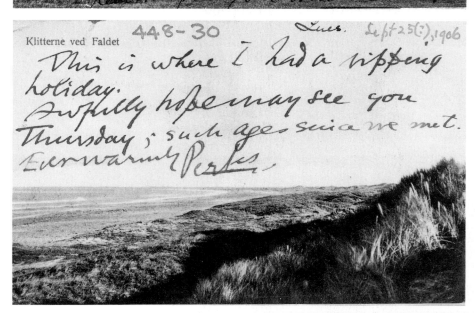

Klitterne ved Faldet [The Sand-dunes by the Fall, Svinkløv], postcard photograph sent by Grainger to Ernest Thesiger, 25(?) September, 1906

This is the boat I went from Christianssand to Bergen in.

"Christiania"

I had a grand swim right out in to the fjord yesterday. How easy in salt water, such a glow a relish; & not a bit cold, I thought

Postcard, Percy to Rose,
27 July 1907:
"This is the boat I went
from Christianssand to
Bergen in"

At Troldhaugen July 1907
(*l. to r.*):
Edvard Grieg, Grainger,
Nina Grieg and
Julius Röntgen.
Photographed by
"two filthy Germans"

Svinkløv, 1907
(*l. to r.*):
Percy, Rose,
an unidentified woman
and Karen Holten

Grainger, October 1907 (*Rosemont, Leeds & Bradford*)

Self-portrait sketch, 12 April 1908

Part of a letter in Danish from Percy to Rose, 25 October 1907, showing one of his train drawings

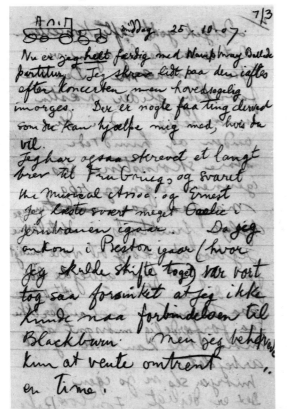

The bloodstains which Grainger sent to Karen Holten on 16 March 1908

Ada Crossley and her concert party on board ship

The Ada Crossley Australasian tour party, 1908–09 (*l. to r.*): Hamilton Earle, Leon Sametini, Ada Crossley, John Harrison and Percy Grainger. (From the *Leader*, 10 October 1908)

Grainger wrote to Karen Holten on 3 November 1908, "This was taken on my walking tour in Gippsland [25 October 1908] when a picnic party gave me tea about 8 miles from Sale"

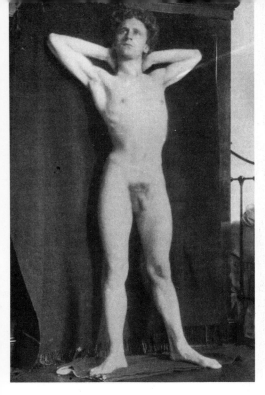

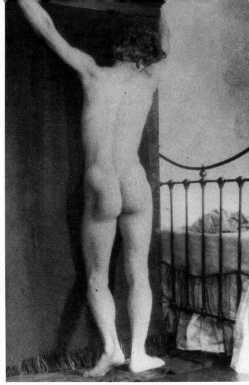

Percy Grainger,
self-photographed (?),
(n.d. 1909?)

Part of a letter in Danish from Grainger
to Karen Holten, 27 September 1909

Grainger's sketches for beadwork designs,
Stratford, New Zealand, 16 February 1909

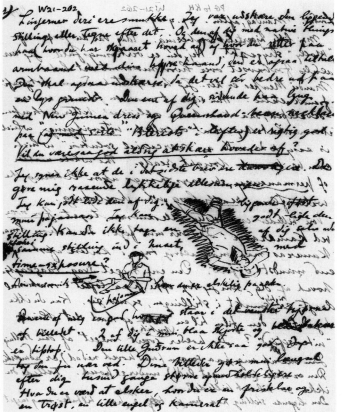

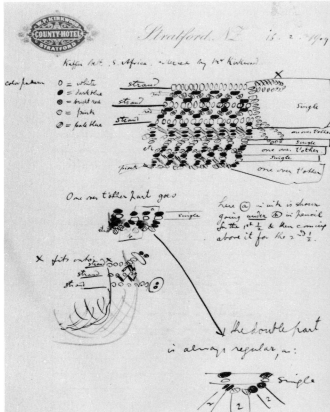

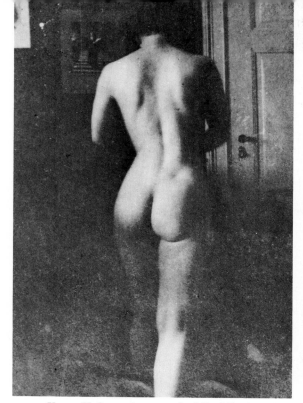

Karen Holten, photographed (by Miss Nutzhorn?) November 1909

Karen Holten in national costume, October 1913 (*Rosa Metz Parsberg, Copenhagen*)

Percy Grainger wearing his towel clothes, photographed by Roger Quilter's niece (Miss Denny?) (n.d. "1911–1913?")

(*Above right*) Grainger's 1909 transcription of "Native Australian tunes", collected by W. Baldwin Spencer in March 1901

(*Above left*) Percy wearing his beadwork necklace, grass skirt, belt and armbands. Photographed by Rose, 12 August 1909

(*Left*) Karen Holten wearing Grainger's clothes, photographed by Grainger at Slettestrand, September 1909

(*Right*) Percy Grainger photographed by Miss Nutzhorn at Slettestrand, summer 1909

(*Above right*) Hans Augustin, Percy Grainger and Julius Röntgen (n.d. 1910?) (*H. C. de Graaf, Amsterdam*)

(*Left*) Percy Grainger and Karen Holten, "taken by Miss Nutzhorn, Slettestrand, summer 1909"

(*Below left*) Margot Harrison, 1913 (*H. Walter Barnett, London*)

(*Below right*) Percy Grainger (n.d. 1910?) (*Elliott & Fry, London*)

The Hon. Everard Fielding (n.d.)

Frederick Delius, postcard photograph c. 1907

John Singer Sargent (n.d.)
(*Havelock Pierce, New York & Boston*)

Percy Grainger and Nina Grieg,
postcard photograph (n.d. 1910 or 1911?)

Karen Holten (at piano) on the concert
platform, with Elna Arlaud, violin,
and Paulus Bache, cello. From a
drawing by Gerda Ploug (?) Sarp, February 1914

Karen Holten's house, 17 Ceresvej,
Copenhagen, photographed in 1978 (*P. P. Grigg*)

(*Below*) Grainger playing the Grieg Piano
Concerto at Leiden, Holland, 9 March 1914

Percy and Rose Grainger
on tour in Norway,
September 1910 (*Rude og Hilfling,
Kristiania*)

Percy Grainger, May 1914
(*Holman & Paget, London*)

Karen Holten, photographed at Grainger's reques
in November 1909 (*Rosa Metz Parsberg, Copenh*

in Adelaide, would you write to Allens, Collins St, Melb to ask if its there & if they'll send it to you.

My own darling mother, sometimes its specially horrid to be parted. Fondest love.

Love to all the dear kin, too.

We leave for the East about Dec 8, getting Adelaide Dec 12. So fix your last letter to get here not later than Dec 7.

228   TO KAREN HOLTEN   Palace Hotel,
[Original: Danish/English]   Perth. W.A.
29.11.08.

This week has been the unhappiest in my whole life. The "management" have beaten me at last, & are *thoroly* rubbing my nose in the dirt. However, that's not going to stop my playing tennis tomorrow morn at 6.30, or kept me from swimming today, or from tennis during the past *awful* week.

I won't tell you the whole quarrel in this letter as I would rather wait until things have become better or worse than they stand now

But the chief thing is that they have been trying to dismiss me (send me back to England) after the 1st 25 concerts. The contract lawfully allows them to, *maybe*, but thats not *quite* certain. Anyhow, I, the would be *business-man*, (who felt myself nearly fit to enter into børsenliv [*sic* børseliv. Danish: business life; lit., life of the stock exchange] a few days ago) am on my back, absolutely, sort of asking them to take me on again. They offer me £30 (instead of £40) & it is defeat defeat along the whole line. The management has *won* at last, up to the hilt.

But the point is that I have won for 2 months & *made them take my good piano to all the principle towns*, & have thus been able to make a good impression. *Now the chief towns are fairly finished* & I therefor dont care so much. But it is a bitter business to me. I quickly forget it of course, & get inthralled in gaelic bible, or piano practising, or other reading, or tennis, but then it comes back suddenly to me & I sweate myself wet with fear & shame & shake like a drunkard with longlasting anxious horrid excitement.

Very probably I shall leave the party on Dec 8th, sail with mother for England by Africa on Dec 15, reaching London about Jan 25. But if that happens you will long ere you get this letter have had a wire "rejser hjem" [Danish: travel home] from me. By next mail I hope things will be fixed one way or another, & I can give you all the prideblasting details.

How does it feel to love a bloody fool? For that's the kind of thing you love, (if you still do). A bloody fool that thinks he can "lick" (defeat) a management of Irish & Irish Americans, & then has to "eat dog" from the blighters he's been thinking he's been too bright for.

Here I am all alone too with nothing but a lot of horse-thieves on all hands, poor nervous little coward that I am. Do you think there is much love in me these days? I should grow into a "real Austraylyan" if I had to live this for long. Every now & then I play Wagner lovefilled harmonies & feel a bit comforted.

I got a sweet wire from mother in Adelaide today about it all.

I think this is a really beautiful picture. She is so sweet with her fine English face and the strong arms, and slim ankles [picture enclosed "A Lady Gardener".]

Next letter P.R.

229   TO KAREN HOLTEN   Kalgoorlie.
[Original: English/Danish]
Saturday. 5.12.08.

Yesterday afternoon fixed up everything with Bracy, who got a wire from J. C. Williamson "Fix new contract with Grainger definitely, Tallis."

I get £30 weekly till the last concert of the tour, & get "starred" etc as now, but waive my claim to grand pianos in small towns.

Believe me I am happy now. I feel like a little child again. I just can't stand worry, uncertainty, and unrest. When I get down to Perth I will send you £10. This now means that I stay here till the beginning of March in any case, perhaps to April or even May.

On Thursday I swam 16½ minutes without stopping, Friday (yesterday) 20¾ in which time I swam 16 lengths of the bath. 18 lengths would have been just over the ¼ mile. Today I would have tried again, but there were too many people (chiefly boys) in the water, so I didn't get proper space, and I didnt try properly but only practised.

Last night we played in "Boulder" (Boulder City) a mining town 4 miles from here (perhaps the largest mining town in the world, I don't know?) and after having played we went to a performance Skuthorpe's "Buck-jumpers"; wild horses, mules, bulls, which are ridden by Skuthorpe's people and also by volunteers from the audience. Quite poor small local boys & men came forward & tried to ride savage bulls & kicking ponies without saddles, & got tumbled into the sawdust & jolly nearly kicked most of the time.

Prizes where offered (10/, 6/, 5/, etc) for the boy or man that could do this or that best, & they had whole gangs of boys & men coming forward the whole time. Australians will do almost anything for money, its quite queer. The audience certainly showed an absurd amount of pluck, & none of them seemed to be funky. Australians certainly show up well at riding. Of course, the truth is, folk always show up well at just those things that they happen to really know well thro practise & need. It's a bit unlucky, maybe, that riding is the one only thing my countrymen seem to know well?

One *must* drink much wet stuff in this climate; it doesn't help to be afraid of your figure. But I don't let my appetite slumber, rather not. I often eat soup, 3 helpings of meat, 5 helpings of pudding, 5 cups of tea, lots of fruit. Now we are just getting a sandstorm, so one can scarcely see the sky. The day before yesterday we were in Coolgardie, the old mining town, before Kalgoorlie was discovered. Now it (Coolgardie) is almost dead. What a bloody place this is! We'll be on the water (for Adelaide) on Tuesday. Goodbye, little sweet.

I haven't enough energy to be naughty up here.

Next letter will be P.R.

230   TO KAREN HOLTEN   Bight.
[Original: English/Danish]   between W.A. and S.A.
11.12.08. Friday.   S.S. "India".

Now I have not received a letter from you since 18.11.08. It is unfortunately unavoidable, since we have been to the West and your letters are addressed to the East. My little mother has not been well, she has been sleeping badly, and feels lonely. I have telegraphed to her to come with us to N. Zealand via Victoria, N.S.W., and Sydney. I hope that she will do so, as she hasn't seen N.Z. yet.

In her last letter she writes:

"I think so often of little Karen, & hope she is happy. She must come & stay with us soon after our return home. I really long to see her again."

I don't feel well. I have had diarrhoea for 2 days, and am a little weak, since I was already pretty exhausted after the heat in the goldfields. This ship is pretty boring, and so over-filled that we can scarcely have any proper sport. But I am looking forward indescribably to the cool fresh weather, and to the sea air.

It is so lovely to see the tight-shaped legs of the small English girls on board here; and their lovely brown stockings. I cannot deny that I think my race (Australians) are very ugly, in any case compared with the English.

The girls' ankles, here at home, are so thick and ignobly formed, a little like Larsen's children, there is nothing noble, concentrated, or fine about them.

Up there in the Goldfields I felt almost completely without any sexual feelings whatsoever; I went past leather shops (where whips were hanging) without once looking in, but directly I came into the lovely damp sea air and into the cooler weather, I showed again that I am distinctly a boy.

What a boring barren land is this my fatherland, however! Just to think that I haven't composed at all since I have been here.

I must say there was some lovely landscapes between Perth & the Fields; real genuine flat virgin desertlands with nought but week low gum trees & scrub upon them. How happy one could be there, away from both Europeans and Australians!

Perhaps you will be a week without a letter since we will possibly miss the post coming eastward. Therefore I will address this to Ceresvej; but then the next will be P.R. again. I sent £10 to you from Perth last Tuesday.

I am beginning to get on really well with my Gaelic now.

Mark Hambourg sailed to England from W.A. last Tuesday.[60] He was present at our last Perth concert. I got madly frightened when I knew he was in the hall and played you just can't imagine *how* badly. (How does it feel to love not alone a bloody fool, but a miserable coward?)

Saturday. 12.12.08.

My diarrhoea is over. I cured it by eating lots of ice puddings, which is known to be fearfully bad for it.

Great day today. Our party have been challenging the ship at deckquoits all the time & losing disgracefully, but today I got Doc to challenge with *me* the best 2 & we beat them twice 21-12. Doc never thinks I can play well, yet I am always solid when it comes to it, more solid than the other[s], anyhow. This was the first time *he* won a challenge.

Goodness, how superior the good class Englishmen are to the Colonials. I dont know Americans, but of all the races I know, the English are the only boys that are any good. There can be such twinkles of pure gay fun in their eyes; they know excitement & can worthen it. Australians are nearly as bad as foreigners, though not quite, of course.

Nationality is the one thing that *never* fails. Never hope to find an individual lacking the qualities of his race; there is no escape. Never hope to like an individual of a race you dislike. The English are the only Scandinavians, the only modern Vikings, modern Icelanders. You actual Scandinavians are currupted & Europeanized, just as modern Celts (Highland Scotch, Irish, etc) are hopelessly Anglicized. The English are Scandinavian not merely in descent, but in their real spirit.

For them too the world exists as their own special highroad; not because they are cruel & boycotting (on the contrary the English are all for Free Trade & Open Door) but because they are born with the gift of feeling an easy superiority, & because they are genuinely fit to steer big affairs. There is care & trade & purpose & earnestness all too readable in the faces of Australians, Germans, modern Scans, & all other foreign trash. The English upper & richer classes alone (a few French maybe?) swing along in utter carelessness recklessness & childish emptyheadedness. There is so much wildness in their faces. Their noses stand out hard & plastic even

60 Mark Hambourg (1879–1960), Russian-born, British-naturalised pianist and composer. A child prodigy, he had made his debut in Moscow in 1888, in London in 1889 and had given 1000 concerts by 1906. In 1908, Hambourg was on his fourth tour of Australia, a tour in which he was apostrophised as "the Napoleon of the Pianoforte". His tour ended with two recitals in Perth, and he left on the G.M.S. *Bremen* on 8 December. John Grainger, who heard Hambourg play on his Australian tours of 1895 and 1897, had held him up to the young Percy as a model of excellence and success. Percy developed a peculiar feeling for him, as described in a letter to Rose, 29 September 1910, "Mark Hambourg is to me what *glarn* was to Grettir! His dead eyes follow me everywhere". Of this particular incident Grainger was to write in his *Anecdotes*, 17 August 1953, "I played Chopin's A♭ Polonaise on the 1st Ada Crossley Australasian tour [should be the second tour]. At the beginning, in Sydney, Melbourne, Adelaide, no doubt I played it complete. But in the 'smalls' I left out the section that turns into F minor off the octave Cs (about the 3rd page of the printed music), partly to shorten the piece (for the unspoilt ears of the smaller towns) & partly because I found this section hard to remember, when on the platform. But when we came back from the Gold-Fields (Kalgoorlie & Coolgardie) we heard that Mark Hambourg (who had just finished an Australian tour & was on his way to England) was to be present at our next concert in Perth. I debated with myself, should I let M.H. hear me play the Polonaise with the cut, or let him hear me play the 'cut' abominably. I decided to risk the latter. It went horribly of course. From then on Jacques Jacobs [sic] always referred to the cut as 'the bit you played to Mark Hambourg' ". A "trifling ommission" in the middle section of the Chopin A♭ Polonaise was noted by the critic of the *New Zealand Herald*, 30 January 1909, after Grainger had played the work in Auckland on the 29th.

250

after years of drink. Their legs are those upon which trousers hang straightly, skittishly. They [*sic* their] eyes are cold & keen & just. The thumbs of their lazy hands run straight, with no eagerness or greed in their form & holding.

They get wantonly excited beyond control at games, but keep delightfully exasperatingly calm at all other more important things.

Above all they are blessed because they always pick me out & like me & realize that I am exceptional.

The English have not been picking & choosing amongst all the folk of the earth for centuries without out having grown some sense of human judgement. The upper class English at once see that I am goodlooking & something out of the common & treat me according to my rank; neither more nor less.

Australians always overlook me, & always would. I dont even believe they think I'm goodlooking. They'd sooner have any Jew or bottlewasher. To Hell with them, I say.

If there was to be a bloody war between Austr & Engl I'd be with the old race every time; for at least some of them have had the sense to be born rich.

I'm thinking of giving up Australia for ever, curse them.

231   TO ROSE GRAINGER   Town Hall Hotel,
5.30. Monday. 14.12.1908.   Stawell, Vic

Eshelby is here with a most delightful little Steinway grand, 3 pedals, which we keep till we get to Sydney, where we have the lovely big grand again.

The towns after Ballarat are as follows:
Wangaratta, Vic. Dec 18. post Adelaide to catch Melb. Express Dec 16.
Albury, Vic.   Dec 21. _____ 17.
Wagga Wagga,
    N.S.W.   ” 22. _____ 18, & 19.
Goulburn, N.S.W. ” 23. _____ 20.
    To all these towns address: P.G. Ada Crossley Co. only.

If you're arriving in Sydney on 23rd (that'll be fully early as we cant arrive before 24th.) as[k] the conductor of sleeping car at *Albury* what time you get to Goulburn, & if its an earthly hour (not earlier than 6 in the morn) ask him to wake you on arrival & I'll be on station to greet you for a mo on your way thro'.

I had a great day at Gaelic yest, & much enjoyed passing thro' the 90 miles' desert *by day*. How deeply satisfactory such scrub-scapes are, at least to me.

Yest in the train was musing on my bit by bit growing dislike of Australian humanity, & got to wondring whether that change in me would make it harder for me to finish Marching Songs with all the early enthusiasm. So I did a bit of composing in the train carrying forward unfinished bits of the Marching Song sketches, & did more work on the same stuff today, & took about a 3 or 4 mile walk today to think it well out with the help of trudging feet. I think it will be alright.

This is a nice little town & there would be tons of nice walks from here I am sure. The streets soon run out into scrub & the Grampian hills make nice sawlike lines against the sky to the (South?) I had a good practise too today.

Let me know please what day you leave Adelaide, & when I am to tell Tallis or Tait (treasurer at J.C.W's) you will be in Melbourne to call for your ticket.

Found 2 letters from Karen, one from Mrs Lowrey (just leaving for America to join her Americans there) & a delightful one from Delius. He & Beecham spent a fine time in Norway together, roughing it very.[61] Delius writes of my English Dance: "Finish it, xxx I will have it played when you like" He was at the Tonkünstler Fest at München, & thought the modern Germ stuff pishtush. He goes on: "Your music is the first I have heard for years which I really love. xxx It is fresh & new & thrilling".

His letter is altogether great fun, & keenly himself.

Karen's father seems to be mending alright, slowly.

Have you seen anything of the Olympic Football results?

Rugby. England & Australia were the 2 finals, & Australia won. (Wallabies)

Association. England & Denmark were the 2 finals, & England won, 2 goals to none. This was very good business for Denmark when one reads how the other countries fared; for instance:

England beat Holland 4–0.
England beat Sweden 12–1.
Denmark beat France twice 1ce 17–1.
2ndly 9–0.

I feel very lonely & am ravenously awaiting our holiday trip together in N.Z. Dont look for too much from N.Z. They also grow potato features too, I believe.

Very fond love from your own one

232 TO ROSE GRAINGER   45 Spring Street,
Thursday 17.12.08.   Melbourne.

Dr Russell is away for a few days, alas! Having had neuritis in his arm.

I saw father this morn, looking far fitter than ever, both eyes in order again, inflamation gone, & looking really fresh & happy. He was quite like an other creature today. Restful, & unhurried, & seemingly happy in his work on a competition design for Perth Town Hall.[62] I expect, too, that he is happiest when he has some solid engrossing work on hand. He was really quite gentle & lovable today, & wholly unAustralian.

He certainly at times seems to be still well able to have that sweetness & smoothness that *all talented folk have* noticeably in greater or lesser degree. The brainworks run easily given proper conditions.

What a joy it would be to see poor dear fidgey at the full powers that might have been his at this day. I must say I was deeply struck by his work in W.A. The calm, repose, & mellowness of the Gov. H. Ballroom is really a thing to be keenly proud of. His works there look so solid, neat, unpretentious, & sincerely dignified. It made me *ever* so happy to see him today looking as he did.

Health, my darling, let us grasp what we can of it.

When you get to Sydney try & get a laundry to be ready to wash stuff of mine quickly, *in case* I cant have any done between now and then. We leave Sydney *Sat* for N.Z. Also please have a nice photo ready when I arrive in Sydney for me to give to the mayoress

I had a fine reception at Ballarat last night Double encore.

I'm going to buy some presents for the little OHara "Peter".

I saw O'Hara today. They *fearfully want* to see you see [*sic*] your way thro.

61 In July and August 1908 Delius had been on a walking tour of Norway with Thomas (later Sir Thomas) Beecham (1879–1961), English conductor whose meteoric rise to fame was to begin with the founding of the Beecham Symphony Orchestra in 1909. Beecham did much for Delius's music; he also made a significant contribution to Grainger's compositional career. Rose urged Percy to allow Delius to "get some of your things performed".

62 Competition designs for a new Town Hall had been invited by the Perth City Council in 1907. John Grainger, in partnership with John Little, was to be awarded first prize. The Council, however, seems to have changed its mind, possibly after a change in Councillors, and no further action was taken.

Tait's man Talbot is hanging about a bit. I think he has some idea of taking John H on after we're done with J.C.W. He told Harrison I'd be a draw. Suppose he offered me a tour here together with J.H. both of us as equal stars, & good terms, would you consider it? Dont answer this till we meet. It is maybe most unlikely, & wholly in the air, but we can talk over the idea in Sydney, if you like. Plenty of time, in any case.

It would (I imagine) be doing the "smalls" (small towns) & you could come along all the time, & we'd have high jinks, & see the country alright. But no one's offered me ought yet. It's only a guess.

Talbot *is* for Tait, alright.

Now (12.30 noon) I'm off to see the OHara family. We leave Melb for Wangaratta 4 o'cl this aftern.

My darling loved fond dear lovely faced mum farewell so long.

Always your boy.
Perks.

I'll try & get a letter thro to you from Wang; but maybe this is the last chance before you leave. Love to A. Clara

Go to Her Majesties Theatre Melb for your ticket. *You* pay for it please. Ask for Tait, treasurer.

233   TO ROSE GRAINGER   Commercial Hotel
Later. Thursday. 17.12.1908.   Wangaratta, Vic.

As I guessed. Before leaving Melb this afternoon Talbot asked me what my fee would be to do a tour of country towns with J. Harrison, both as equal stars, at the end of Williamson's Xley show. I said I couldnt say at once, as I thought I would sooner be back in England not too late. He said I can let him know from NZ, so that gives us full time to talk it over first.

Personally, I think it would be better than assisting Ada in Java or S. Africa; though maybe you'd think getting home best of all. We can see. There would be no risk of course.

Talbot says it might either be Taits or Talbot on his own. Talbot is very keen on the idea, but he says if Williamsons take us round to very many of the small towns it wouldnt leave Talbot much valuable fresh ground unexploited, so after all it may come to nothing.

There is not the least hurry about the whole thing of course. But it's nicer to have had the offer than to have *not* had it.

Had lunch with the O'Haras. They will meet you at station when you get to Melb Tuesday & take you out to them if you care to go, & give you a bath & a rest. Dr Russell will, I hope, be back in town *Monday*. I'll write him, so he gets the letter on Monday, telling him you'll be passing through Tuesday. His place, (Spring St, (45?)) is quite near Her Majesties Theatre, if you're in cab, which please be.

I write you care of O'Haras, & also C/o breakfast room Moss Vale Railway Station NSW, where you will stop for breakfast Wednesday morn, a few hours before reaching Sydney. So ask for letter, please.

I've spent a lot of money again in Xmas toys for OHara children, 15/6. But it's only fair, after all, & cheaper than having hotelled it in Melb. All the gifts are solid, bats, balls, hockeysticks, etc.

I must say, I cant help liking Melb.

Dr OHara was looking real fine & fit.

Goodbye dearie, this is the last letter you'll get before Tuesday morn.

Fond love
Percy

234 TO ROSE GRAINGER   Commercial Hotel
After concert. 18.12.1908.   Wangaratta, Vic.

My dearie mother.

Played well tonight. Had a good practise this aftern. Had 2 long swims today, one before breakfast with Eshelby, Wilson, & Ryan, & before lunch with Doc, John, & Eshelby. We're going to do 2 tomorrow also.

I can swim sidestroke fairly badly now, & have started overhand stroke. Once one can really swim decently, it's not hard to pick up the different strokes. The swimming place here is a great round pool in the creek, with nice hard bottom & very deep, (14 feet) a perfect & delightfully safe spot. Too deep for snags or weeds, & too wide for current. The creek runs thro a sort of wide flat stretch that lies much lower than the land on which the town stands, & all grown with gums & long wild grass; a lovely free landscape on all hands when one swims & dresses & undresses. Its ever such fun picking up the new strokes. I'm slowly losing my fear of the water, tho' not my old-maidish caution.

Please tell Peter (O'H) that my forehead is only a *very little* bit swollen. I've had my washing done here alright.

I hope you have the hold-all & canvas washbag along with you, as they arent in my lot.

I'm full of scoring thinkingsout these days. It would be nice to get the English Dance quite scored before getting back to Lond.

Hope you've had a nice trip over from Adel by when you get this, & the same before you get my next letter at Moss Vale. If you see the Station Master at Albury (Tuesday evening) it was he sent down your sunshade.

Love to all friends darling one.

Yr happy healthy son
Percy

Father asked very warmly after you yest, & was delighted to know you are coming to N.Z.

Much love to all the OHara[s] please. I got my black boots from them yesterday.

1909

The Ada Crossley concert party, accompanied by Rose Grainger, left Sydney by the S.S. Warrimoo *at midnight on 25 December, arriving in Dunedin on 1 January. The musicians went south immediately by train for their opening concert at Invercargill on New Year's Night. From Dunedin the party proceeded north, giving concerts at Oamaru and Timaru en route to Christchurch, then crossing to the North Island where the first part of the tour ended with three concerts at Auckland between 28 and 30 January. The party then went to Rotorua for a week's holiday.*

From Sydney, Rose went immediately to Christchurch, remaining there until the tour arrived on 9 January, crossing to Wellington with the others after the Christchurch concerts, and remaining in Wellington until Percy rejoined her on 16 January. On 23 January she went on to Auckland, where the party arrived 27 January. She went with the others to Rotorua. She and Percy travelled together for most of the second part of the tour.

Originally planned as a five-week tour of some thirty concerts, ending with a week's holiday in Rotorua, the response to the first series of concerts was such that return visits were planned for the major cities. Accordingly, from the resumption of touring with a concert in Rotorua on 8 February, the party retraced its steps via various smaller towns to Wellington, then to Christchurch, then south again to Dunedin. The tour ended where it had begun, with a concert at Invercargill on 6 March. Management of the second part of the tour was taken over by Francis Muecke. Two return concerts were given in each of the large towns. These were modelled on a formula which had proved so triumphantly successful in 1903 — "popular programmes at popular prices". But the responses were mixed, attendances fluctuated, and there was nothing to equal the great audiences of 1903. Throughout the season, as in Australia, the laurels among the assisting artists went most often to John Harrison.

Grainger, his relationship with the management stabilised, was free to enjoy his current twin crazes: swimming and Polynesian culture. After his meeting with A. J. Knocks in Otaki on 20 January, Rarotongan music became a particular passion. He undertook a small amount of collecting of Maori music, at Plymouth, on 26 January. Plans to do more collecting at Rotorua were thwarted by a foot infection which kept him indoors. His main effort therefore went into persuading the various contacts he made in the field of the urgent necessity of collecting this music. He also did some composing.

The company left New Zealand on the S.S. Maheno *on 8 March for their Tasmanian tour. Rose travelled with the company to Tasmania, then proceeded on the same steamer to Melbourne where she stayed until 23 March. She then crossed to Adelaide, where she remained until she embarked for London.*

CONCERT ITINERARY, 1908–09 AUSTRALASIAN TOUR

NEW ZEALAND	Invercargill, 1 January		Rose in Christchurch
DUNEDIN	2–4 January Oamaru, 7 January Timaru, 8 January	2 concerts	
CHRIST-CHURCH	9–11 January	2 concerts	Rose to Wellington 12 January
	Masterton, 13 January Hastings, 14 January Napier, 15 January		
WELLINGTON	Arrived 16 January 18–19 January Palmerston North, 21 January Wanganui, 23 January New Plymouth, 26 January	2 concerts	Rose to Auckland
AUCKLAND	Arrived 27 January 28*–30 January (*Ada Crossley, interviewed by the *New Zealand Herald*, stated that that night's concert would be the sixtieth of the tour.)	3 concerts	
	Week's holiday in Rotorua Rotorua, 8 February Paeroa, 9 February Hamilton, 10 February		Rose at Rotorua
AUCKLAND	Arrived 11 February 12 February Hawera, 15 February Stratford, 16 February Marton, 17 February Feilding, 19 February	1 concert	
WELLINGTON	22–23 February Timaru, 26 February	2 concerts	
CHRIST-CHURCH	1–2 March	2 concerts	
DUNEDIN	Arrived 3 March 4–5 March Invercargill, 6 March 8 March, left New Zealand for Tasmania	2 concerts	

HOBART	12–13 March	Rose in Melbourne 13 March
	Launceston, 16–17 March 18 March, left Launceston for Melbourne	2 concerts
MELBOURNE	Arrived 19 March	Rose to Adelaide 23 March
SYDNEY	24–29 March Armidale, 31 March Toowoomba, 1 April	3 concerts
BRISBANE	Arrived 1 April 3–7 April 9 April, left Brisbane for Townsville	3 concerts
	Townsville, 12–13 April	2 concerts
	Charters Towers, 14–15 April	2 concerts
	Townsville, 17 April 20 April, arrived Rockhampton	
	Rockhampton, 21–22 April	2 concerts
	Bundaberg, 26 April Maryborough, 27 April Gympie, 28 April	
BRISBANE	29 April	1 concert
	Warwick, 1 May Tenterfield, 3 May Tamworth, 5 May Maitland, 6 May	
SYDNEY	8 May	1 concert
	Lithgow, 10 May Orange, 11 May Bathurst, 12 May	(last concert)
	21 May S.S. *Seydlitz* left Adelaide for England	

Note: Various estimates appeared for the total number of concerts given: "considerably over 100 concerts" (*Sydney Morning Herald*, 22 March 1909); "130 concerts, 13 of them in Sydney" (*British Australasian*, 24 June 1909); "120 concerts" (PG to KH, 2 May 1909). With concerts planned that did not eventuate and additional concerts presented, counting becomes difficult.

235 TO ROSE GRAINGER
1.1.1909.
Friday, later.

Southland Club Hotel,
Invercargill, N.Z.

I have read all the book on Maori lore yesterday in the train: Polynesian Mythology, by Sir George Gray.[1]

1 The Right Hon. Sir George Grey (1812–98), explorer, governor of New Zealand (1845–53) and politician. Author of several books on the Maoris and Polynesian culture, his *Polynesian Mythology, and Ancient Traditional History of the New Zealand Race as Furnished by their Priests and Chiefs* was published in London in 1855. Grainger's copy was a gift from Charles C. Reade, New Year 1909. Grainger sometimes spells Grey's name correctly, sometimes not.

It is interesting. You can see it when I come along, or you could doubtless find it in a public library, as it has just come out in cheap form.

Their legends disappoint me rather, I must own; nor have the few songs given at end of book much real musical charm to me personally, though I might feel it if I heard them done. They certainly *interest* me, for the ¼ tones alone. I so firmly believe we shall soon be using ¼ tones in our Western harmonic music, on the way to eventually throwing open every possibility of pitch diving[?]; though personally my *feelings* run all the other way; (I'm a hopeless stick-in-the-mud, I even still resent ½ tones [chromatics] ½ the time) but that doesnt affect my head.

The Maori legends in this book are in a style, & of a stage of life, akin to those of the Icelandic Sagas. The men in them are still in the feud-waging state. I'm sorry to say the Maoris seem in their sagas to be a soft race; love plays too big a part in guiding the paths of their lives. That is, to my mind, always a weak sign. Very exceptional races, like the English & the old Icelanders, practically got love under control, & so could be guided by practical thoughts in their settling of practical problems but most mankind, & the Maoris along, I fear, go O & O in a ○ hunger, love, birth, clanfeeling, war, revenge, hunger, etc. What lifts the spirit of the best Icelandic tales so far above the dull doings (violence, greed, fighting etc) of which they nevertheless are unnaysayably made up is the sudden happening in them of unaccountable lasting unoverthrowable abstract qualities of character, things done for sheer cussedness, or for wanton pleasure.

Sudden forgiveness of foes in fight, because one just appeals to the other; Kettil's refraining to kill his own murderer because he thought he looked "lucky"; (in Vátnsdælasaga) Gunnar of Hliðarend suddenly refusing to quit his district when staying meant dying; "because I've never seen the countryside look more fair". (Njálsaga)

But these things are, of course, sure tokens of a civilized & wellbred breed, & cant be looked for in savages, "white Australian", Maori, or otherwise.

Each day I get more stupidly impatient of feelings & deeds that arize out of the urge of "natural needs".

The man who can ride a horse because it's his business in life to be able to; he has no charm for me any longer in that act. Only acts done in spite of natural needs, only extravagance & "overflow energies" appeal to me.

The Maoris do just what one knows they couldnt help doing, & that is a bit tiresome.

They are full of desire to excell, which is a loathesome quality, I think. Grettir never wanted to do anything with his strength, (it rather bored him) except wrestle now & then when he was fairly sure to come to harm otherwise thro it.

Then the Maoris write almost only of chiefs. The Icelanders describe their thralls (Þrállr [Þrælar]) with just the same detail-love that they lavish on their velbornir menn [well-born men, noble men].

The Maoris seem to fish to get food, & fight to kill, & marry to love, & love to breed, and so on. I cant understand it; they're just as bad as Germans, Continentals, Australians, & middleclass English.

I dont think their tongue seems hard. I'll likely learn it one day. For mind, I love their decorations, & ornaments, & one mustnt ever trust translated stuff too far, the more so when an ordinary Englishman has had a hand in it.

We're in Dunedin til Tuesday, on Monday & Tuesday you post to *Oamaru*.

Many thanks for your wire, dearie, that I found awaiting me here today.

The weather is *glorious*. The cold for me. The folk look fine & fresh, but not fascinating. They have corn-counting souls, all, I guess. Still they at least look as if they could keep alive long enough to get civilized, & that must come in time, I suppose, though one wouldnt think so.

Every now & then the landscape spreads out delightfully with Scotlandlike rolling bare hills, & always a dear rich English sky, but the land looks far too thriving for beauty & every old kind of blighting foreign tree grows all too well, & the mankind dont see any diff, so its alright. They're only uglifying some otherwise fairly decent scenery with their stiff black pines, or firs, or what they are. One withering useless Australian plain, with a few badly behaved gums, & a curse of dust, is nearer God, I think.

This place is a race-farm not scenery.

Darling mum, I must turn to the E.D.

Loving goodnight

236 TO KAREN HOLTEN   The Grand Hotel.
[Original: Danish/English]   Dunedin, N.Z.
5.1.1909. Tuesday.

My beloved little Karen.

I love you violently, suddenly. I am also lonely. Mother didn't come down to Dunedin and Invercargill with me, she remained in Christchurch, where I'll meet her again next Saturday.

It rains so continuously today. We gave our last concert here last night, and our next is not till Thursday. I had planned to walk from here to Oamaru, about 60 miles, and was up to after 1 o'cl last night sewing the clothes I would have on. Everything was in order at last, and I got up 5.30 o'cl today, but the weather was impossible. It is however fortunate I didn't go, since I received a telegram at midday from Dr Mason in Wellington (a charming man interested in Maori songs, etc) that Dr Buck (a Maori) is in Dunedin at the present time, and he had wired Buck to visit me.[2] So I'll stay in Dunedin tomorrow I think.

Today I completed "Away by the lands of the Japanee", as regards the actual composition, but there is some trouble about the words.[3] They talk about "return visits" to N.Z. towns, as we are drawing such good houses here. I am told our tour wont be done til April, but I know nothing.

I saw the lady again who had the yellow silk mantle on the other day. She is perhaps the only one on this tour who has had any attraction for me. I think she also took a little notice of me. I have avoided her, for what is the use of meeting her? I neither want to be fond of her or get her to be fond of me. Whenever one sees anyone *at all* attractive, flee!

It seems to me I feel more at home here than in Australia, although I like A much more *as a country*. But I do feel quite foreign among all these rough stupid people, and all these squables, etc. I am really much more tender and helpless than people think, it seems to me. Every telegram I get, I shake and think: (despite the new contract) is it from Williamson "We dont require your services any longer." Every time I see Bracy, I get palpitations from fear that he comes with something stupid or such-like. All of them misunderstand me, I think, of the management.

"The boys", my fellow-artists, they don't misunderstand me so much, I almost believe they like me, more or less. Whittle, our accompanist, is a kind Australian, clean, cautious, saving, witty, humorous, polite, nicely dressed, hardworking, independant, & "queer". Never lumps himself up with a gang, but goes his own path. He so much liked Røtnamsknut Slaat [Grieg Op. 72] right from the first, and as he would gladly hear new things, I have had much pleasure in playing all the Slaater, Grieg op 66, Grieg's Psalms, etc, Debussy's works, Jeux d'eaux, new Scarlatti pieces, Bach, Albaniz* [*sic*], etc for him. It is indescribably comforting for me to meet

2 Dr Peter H. Buck (Te Rangihiroa), at that time a native health officer in the Department of Health. He resigned this position in order to contest the Northern Maori by-election which followed the untimely death from consumption of the sitting representative, Hono Heke, on 9 February 1909. He was elected to the Parliament on 20 March 1909.

3 Grainger's setting of "Away by the Lands of the Japanee", the opening eight lines of a 171-line poem from Kipling's *The Seven Seas*, started life as part of a proposed setting of the whole text, sketched 1900–01, and entitled "The Rhyme of the Three Sealers". The whole setting was never completed. In December 1908 and January/March 1909 Grainger reworked the opening eight-line section, retitling it *A way by the Land of the Japanee* and adding to it further musical material for which he composed his own text. This setting was completed in August 1909, by which time the work was called *At Twilight*. Kipling's agent refused permission for the composite text to be used, so when the work was published by Schott & Co., London, in 1913, an entirely new text was provided.

even the smallest glimmer of real true love of art. Whittle is 26. He is a good chap, but, like most Australians, too little childish.

To think that there will come a time when I can kiss you again, and lie beside you and talk nonsense, and *really know* that you are not an enemy, or ½ enemy. To think of being able to enjoy that security again! And to be together with Roger and Rathbone Sargent Delius and people who truly don't doubt me. Out here I have to sort of *prove* my worth afresh each time. I never like that, never have liked that. If people meet me with: What use are you? I am no good for anything. If one treats me like a gentleman & a talent I can behave like a Lord & a genius. (without being it) Don't think I am unhappy here on the tour. Far from it. Neither do I feel home-sick for London or for an "artistic atmosphere" Not at all. All women are my wives, (in spirit) all lands & seas equally enough my dwelling. I love travelling & being alone & away from love & art. I love every kind & condition of life. But I can't help *prefering* some to others. I can do with-out you so long as I must if money duties require it; but I cannot help realising what I am losing. But it is good to miss. But both you and I know that it is bloody tedious also.

Never mind. I must be glad that I have found it possible lately to compose a little in spite of the tour. I have scored quite a deal of E.[nglish] Dance now.

You won't find me changed. The journey has not had the slightest deep-going influence on me this time. The last Australian tour was the first I had ever got off on my own & much was curiously fresh then. Now I am just myself whereever I am, & more anxious to shut myself off from outside things that pull me off my own steady old track. There is no doubt that this Williamson affair has momentarily knocked a lot of vitality out of me.

I have not enjoyed losing in the fight with him. I am not in love with defeat, & cant quickly forget the feel of it. I feel morally like a coward who has had a good whack over the nose & isnt craving for any more fight just now, thanks. I feel very ashamed of myself at having lost.

Dont think I crave to be a clever business man. It is only that I am a bit gloomy to find what an *extreme* business *fool* I am. My manner is all wrong. If I only have to ask our management when a train starts I'm all in a tremble.

In reality it is not at all so important the whole thing. I only say, that *for the time being* I feel a little lowhearted on account of my defeat.

Do you think that I, who sleep so lonely in my bed, will ever be fit to lie 2 in a bed again?

Do you think that I could undo your clothes?

I know that I could chatter with you the whole night. But am I fit for more? Do you think that I have perhaps become an old maid and had "change of life"? It's all one to me.

We're making a fine "stand". Think that by the time we next meet it'll be   5 years since we first met at Sandby's

        4 —————— you came over to London

        3 —————— you & I first were together at Svinkløv.

  nearly 2 —————— dear poor old Griegs death.

That's really rather fine.

You shan't go and think I can't remember things awfully well. I can remember 1000 things that have happened to us so clearly. How happy we were at the Meistersingers in London that time, and how good the night before Helsingør was, and the night after the memorial concert. By god, I have a ripping life. Its a great game, life. They say when you drown you see it all pass by again. Then drowning's worth doing. I'd have every last row with Bracy over again.

There's nothing, no minute out of my life I'd like to leave out.

Isn't it fun that we have really seen each other without clothes on! Then if one of us died, our bodies would not have swallowed all those 1000s of meals quite for nothing. Some one would remember the cut of our limbs & the fall of our flesh.

I feel very shy. To think of doing all these wonderful things with a really young lady like you. For you are after all a lady, and not really a boy. Perhaps you will think I have got stupid when you see me again. And perhaps you have become nothing but nose. When we meet perhaps I'll be 27 years old, and you must be quite quite old; and haven't even begun to write an English Dance.

All these sports costumes; how many of them will you have made before we meet, do you think? Will you be able to ride bare-back.

I am a silly boy, I don't feel lustful, I feel sentimental. What shall I do about it. If you were here I would like to tickle you, tickle you splendidly. Yes, I believe all the same if you were here, I would behave better than with Williamson.

But perhaps when you hear that I still only get £30 a week, you won't have anything more to do with me.

I don't know at all how your father and mother are, since I haven't had a letter from you for such a long time.

Mother writes and asks me to send you her love when I write to you. Next letter will be P.R.

I got an excellent critique from Legge in the Daily Telegraph about Journal 12.[4]

Perhaps you will get this letter simultaneously with one I posted via The Bluff–Tasmania–Melbourne. This letter goes via Wellington–Sydney.

I have bought 8 shillings & 3 pence worth of Maori & NZ postcards. You will get some of them soon. Their woodcarving is *simply gorgeous*. Something so sharp & keen about it. You'll see. Reminds me of Norway & the Stave churches.

Fond love
Percy.

---

*Albaniz is *quite* splendid, A Spaniard. A real new delight. I shall play him in London

4 The review, entitled "Folk-songs and Singers" and signed by "Musicus", appeared on the "Music of the Day" page of the *Daily Telegraph* on Saturday, 31 October 1908.

237 TO ROSE GRAINGER
morn 8.1.1909

Star & Garter Hotel
Oamaru. N.Z.

Well I got paid alright last night, every single day, (Dec 26–Jan 7) £55.0.0, without a word thank God.

John, Tini, & I had a fine swim in the fresh water baths here, kept by a jolly cornet player, Hunter. The water was jolly mighty cold, but it was pleasant all the same. A tough hailstorm came on while I was in the water, it felt so queer.

I had a nice practise all yesterday afternoon at Liszt Polonaise & the 2 Albaniz's

Here are two nice coarse riddles:
{ What is the diff between a seagull & a baby?
{ The one flits along the shore, & the other . . .

{ What is the diff between a bad marksman & an owl?
{ The one shoots & cant hit, & the other hoots, etc.

I always forget to tell you how happy I am in the clothes you choose for me. I enjoy hugely the nice green socks & nice stuffs that you get for me. When I'm away from you they keep reminding me of your finely poised & clearseeing mind & clean active & unslovenly thoughts.

Almost every day glæder jig mig over mine klæder [Danish: I am happy for my clothes].

I wouldnt enjoy ones ½ so much that I would choose myself.

Tomorrow I'm with you, dearie.

So sorry you had the bother of looking for the contract, but happy you've found it, & also that we dont need to shoot with it this trip.

Fond love my darling mother
Perks.

Thames Street, Oamaru, N. Z. 8. 1. 09.

here's where I started my walk from 5 years ago.

238 TO ROSE GRAINGER   Empire Hotel,
14.1.1909.   Masterton, NZ

My darling one

I have written Dr Mason (Chief Medical Officer, Department of Public Health, Wellington) to write or 'phone & let you know whether there is any chance of my phonographing Dr Pomari, or other singer, this coming Sunday. If *yes*, then kindly arrange with "The Talkeries" (next to Grand Hotel, Well) either to have their mechanic in readiness for whatever hour Dr Mason fixes, or take mechanic's address if hour not fixed, or if machanic unavailable, let them leave a phonograph ("Home" Eidison size about) a *recorder, recording funnel*, & some *blanks* at the Windsor Hotel for me to use myself instead. I've written Dr Mason that you're at the Windsor. Of course if you get no word of Mason's having fixed anything worth phonographing, dont bother to go to the Talkeries.

I herewith enclose these 2 Christchurch addresses, you may want to have them.

Yesterday was mighty interesting. We had a swim in nice open air freshwater baths here, & later in the afternoon, hearing the son of the Maori chief (te Tan) was dead, & they to be holding a "tangi" (wake ceremony for the dead) Tini, Doc, & I byked out; about 2 miles. Te Tan is Whiteschooled, & he & his wife quite English on surface. He looks 28 to 30, but is over 40 & is chief of Maoris round here. He was dressed English & looked fine handsome & noble in spite of it. His wife seemed to be more Maorily dressed. She is a lovely woman. It is her & his son, aged 20, who has died.

She was sitting by his closed cofin in a tent. On the cofin were Maori girdles (I think) & 2 lovely big greenstone meres. (axes Round about were tents struck where visiting Maoris come gathered together for the Tangi sleep. The Te Tan's house is English. While we were there a cab drove up, saluted with wails from group of women gathered at Te Tan's house. Out got a Maori major (army) well dressed in European clothes, a handsome greyhaired strong man, & his wife & children. He paid the white cabman in thoro English fashion. Then he & his wife entered the padock with the tents & facing Mrs Te Tan (in her tent with the cofin) & a ½ circle of women, the 2 newcomers & Mrs Te Tan & the women all started off wailing & rocking their bodies in complaint.

I could not judge whether their feelings were deep & real at the beginning of the "keening" (what the Irish do) but after a time their faces went all ways with grief-excitement & they wept floods of real tears one & all, & howling at the top of their voices. It was a sight to see, but I did not stay long, as I had a feeling that a stranger ought not to be looking on at what after all must be an intimate matter to the poor bereaved folk themselves.

There was no singing while I was there, only wailing on any notes that came along.

Then Tini & I byked a mile or so further on to see the local "Pa" (meetinghouse) Te Ore Ore. It looked modernly made, the roof of galvanized iron, & European paint used everywhere instead of stains, but the carving of the front & the crisscross wall-screen decorations inside appealed to my ignorant enthusiasm like anything. Lovely color effects & seemingly never repeated variety of pattern. It looked so well too, standing low & squattingly on the earth, with a nice background of blue low hills, with nice healthy English clouds above, & wind.

We passed thro lovely scenery coming up here. The Rimutaka gorge is really worth seeing. I must try & arrange your route to Auckland so you pass thro this glorious stretch.

The plain country & cleared hills in NZ make no impression on me, but the *uncleared* hills have a real spiffing overflow of undergrowth & bunchy sappy tree formations; such a thick wealth of unpiercethroable lavish green growths. Then the streams are delightful in the hills & the whole hillscapes are ideal to potter about in, I'm sure. To follow such a stream all along its selffound twisty path & climb every 2nd knoll for its special outlookspoint. Yesterday, too, a grand English misty rain was drenching everything caressingly & what countryside & country-man isnt glad in the wet? (barring tiresome Australians)

Here's where I did my fast walk to Eketahuna from.

What a lot of those nice NZ boys clothes one sees:

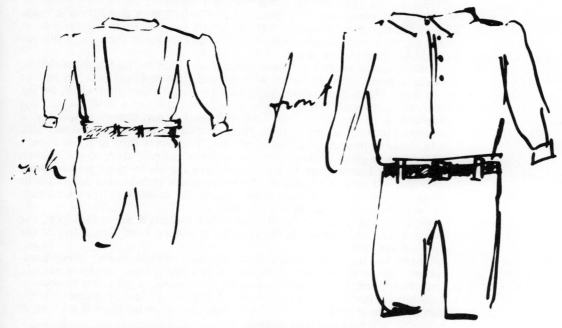

Its so nice being all of the same stuff & *having its own collar*.

Farvel min lille moer. Glem ikke at sé The Museum (in Museum St, not far from Station, take cab or tram) Din elskende søn [Danish: Goodbye my little mother. Don't forget to see . . . Your loving son] P.

Later. Have learnt to dive. Did 12 or more dives this morn before breakfast, 2 of them off the springboard. It's an easy game.

239   TO ROSE GRAINGER   Otaki Rly
[Telegram. PM 20 January 1909]

NEVER HEARD THE LIKE TREAT EQUAL TO WAGNER I AM GODLY LUCKY LOVE PERCY

240   TO ROSE GRAINGER   Grand Hotel
21.1.1909.   The Square,
                                                 Palmerston North, NZ

Darling mother of a happy son

I was met in Otaki by a middle aged greyhaired & bearded rather frail man, *not* a ½ caste, a N Zealander, of an Australian father, now about 58.[5] After my lunching at the Jubilee Hotel, kept by a Norwegian Johansen, (who talks *absolutely* perfect English & has a pretty fair daughter born out here) comes along old Knocks with a few of his records, there being a phonograph at this Hotel. I hear some jolly interesting Maori songs, the ¼ note intervals being delightfully plain & striking, but the whole scheme a little flat & samish artisticly, at first hearing; & later he outs

5 Grainger had heard of Alfred J. Knocks from a friend, Mrs Elder, in Waikanae. On 12 January 1907 at Otaki, Knocks had phonographed a group of Rarotongans who were in New Zealand for the International Exhibition at Christchurch in 1906/07. On Grainger's return visit to Otaki on 20–21 February 1909, Knocks gave him his five original cylinders of Rarotongan music and two of his best of Maori. Grainger later had them copied, kept the originals, and returned the duplicates to Knocks early in 1910. Grainger's attempts to transcribe the Rarotongan cylinders remained unfinished, though he continued to work on them through 1909.

with some records of chorus singing by Rarotonga (Cook's Island) natives, a treat no less than the best Wagner, as I wired.

These cannibals were brought over to Christchurch Exhibition & came up to Otaki, where Knocks, with an artists insight, took fine records of their glorious godly dancesongs. Noone in Christchurch thought of phonographing these glories; think of it!

Knocks could understand their speech, very akin to the Maori, which he speaks at home with his Maori wife & handsome ½-breed boys; in fact he feels more Maori than white, good luck to him. I asked him which he felt most. He answered: "When I was a lad, swimming in a swift river, I got caught in a 18 feet deep "pot" or whirlpool & was drowning quickly. 2 whitemen looked on jestingly & never moved to help me. A Maori girl, fully clothed, jumped in & saved my life. They were thus in those days."

I wanted to go to his home to hear other of his records & to settle down to work, but I dont think he wanted to show me his ½ breed home, somehow. The old man is respected, but his atractive richskinned colored sons are always getting into police scrapes, I am told, & one was lately up a gum for wounding a Chinaman shortly ago.

But I wanted to get to the fulness of his records & we trudged off, the young & the old, artists both. Knocks is a very keen teetotaler, & the kindliest gentlest man.

We reached his house, with a small enclosure of right down gloomy hard-to-creep-thro real NZ bush & onside, & in front a once had been garden, now rewildened, with careless cactuses flourishing, & all growths wanton & untidied. Nice dogs & a calf, well fed happy lazy looking beasts all, (he has taught the dogs frolicsome & companionable tricks) browze around, & ½ breed folk turn up now & then.

The house inside is the most glorious chaos. Broken windows, rickety furniture, cobwebbed sashes, dust galore, stuffy booky smells rampant, yearlong grime on hoarded manuscripts, old letters, old interesting documents, all banked feet high on floors, tables, benches. Phonograph records abound on floors, shelves, etc; carelessly ordered, *but neatly labelled*.

The family all seems blithe as birds together; always calm unheated pitchings of voices, & a very easygoing relations between father & sons. The father is in the clouds easily & the real dirty world below his feet doesnt seem to have much power to offend his eyes. Yet his home is a mangy place, & he a cultureminded educatedly-spoken man. The lad who wounded the Chinese & I fetched a 2nd phonograph & blanks wherewith to take copies of these Rarotongan tunes; I to note down from the copies so as not to wear out the priceless originals.

We were soon all a happy family, gay at fellowwork & happy in harmonious minds. Then I set to work noted from the copies & this went on til about 8 in the eve, when the Maori wife had bread & butter for us, & tea. After this he took me out to see some Maori friends & ½ kin of his; 8 children & some grown ups. I gave them piano pieces & they sang English hymns much Maorified in Dahomey chorus-like lovely fruitlike (sappy & bitter) voices, & the children as much as they had picked up of the Rarotongan stuff. Pretty faces & darkeyed they grovelled around the floor; touching folk.

How the consumption waltzes into them! Of one family there it has fetched both parents & 4 children in one year. Too bad. One of these consumptive boys was stupidly tiring his throat singing his very heart out, with a glorious throbbing vocal tone.

When we went back home again & I worked on till 6 in the morn. The son stayed up for a while & the father till 2 o'clock. I slept from 6 to 7 then had breakfast at Jubilee Hotel & then back to more work before my train left before 10 (am)

Altogether, I noted down 1 whole Rarotongan song fairly accurately, & a part of a 2nd ditto. Darling, the real musicalness of these songs!

They go fast with swinging hammering pattering rhythms, & the whole effect of the group of singers is like a band of banjos, spluttering, wiring in, brazen tongues. A foresinger starts off & the other[s] waltz in at the end of the 1st phrase.

It is thoroly *manyvoiced* music, & harmonic in feeling for the most part. "Who built de ark" is a well tamed ½-breed of its harmonic & choral type, only that ("Who") is samishly rhythmed & this Cook Island music is highly complex rhythmed; not at all simple stuff.

One voice sings a certain kind of tune on top, & another low voice sings a droning kind of tune below, & in the middle are more purely harmonicly, accompanyingly run parts. The scale is pentatonic in basis, but with often breakings out into solid diatonic (is this originally native, or from Europeans?) The whole music is the outpouring of everglad ungloomable souls, merriness incarnate, & trickling good humor & devilish energy in overflow. "I the wondersong of youth."[6] If such music isnt the voicing of "the joy of life", where else shall I look for it? If the best pulses of humanness do not flow in these cannibals we'd be better lacking them.

I've taken the whole concern down near enough to be able to perform it on chorus in London.

Wait till you hear these fiercesouled phrases frolic into song.

6 From Kipling's "The Song of the Banjo" (see note 26, 1905).

241   TO FREDERICK DELIUS
31.1.09.

Auckland.
New Zealand.

My dear Delius.

I rejoiced hugely to get your dear kind letter, to learn of your & Beecham's jolly time in the North-Way, & to read your kindly appreciation of my work.

I read in the D.T. (Lond) the other day of your "In a Summer's Garden",[7] the title sounds as if the texture might have a kindred charm to that of your Brigg Fair, which latter I fondly long to hear again. I do hope I get a chance to hear the new work when back again. I would have liked to hear you conduct it.

Hearty thanks for your interest in the English Dance. I am scoring it at present & hope to bring it back finished.

The tour goes on very successfully & I see no hope of leaving for England before another month at earliest.

I have been collecting some Maori singing phonographicly, delightfully full of queer intervals. (¼ notes I think)[8] But I have also heard phonograph records of Rarotongan (Sth Sea Island) natives' partsinging, which is (to me) far more enthralling. They sing *really polyphonicly* & have genuine *harmonic* sense.

I am trying to induce folk to have this & kindred musics wellpreserved phonographicly, etc.[9]

I have noted down some of it & shall bring, I trust, enough back with me to have it sung by voices in London. This Rarotongan music has made the biggest impression on me (of untaught musics) since I first lit onto the Faeroe Island dance tunes some years ago.

The Maoris are a mighty interesting race in lots of ways. Their carvings, houses, canoes, weavings, & tatoo patterns enthrall me greatly, & mother & I spend many happy hours at the museums.

Mother is with me here, is awfully well, & enjoying NZ Al. She joins me in all warmest greetings to Mrs Delius & yourself. How I should have loved to have been with you in Norway! And how I look forward to a tune hunt with you once among Darkie America!

7 Delius's Rhapsody for full orchestra, *In a Summer Garden*, composed in the spring of 1908, had had its first performance, Delius conducting the orchestra of the Philharmonic Society, at Queen's Hall on 11 December 1908.

8 At New Plymouth, on 26 January, Grainger had collected six phonograph cylinders of music from a group of Maori singers he met through S. P. Smith, President of the Polynesian Society and a native of Lincolnshire.

9 The second annual conference of professional musicians of New Zealand, meeting in Auckland on 25 January, passed a motion "That steps be taken for the preservation of Maori folksongs". The motion was put by Mrs A. Boult of Auckland, seconded by Miss Hornsby of Nelson.

I hope we meet very soon after our return to England. Once more, heartfelt thanks for your letter, which was a keen joy to me

Till we meet

Yrs ever
Percy Grainger

242   TO BALFOUR GARDINER   Hook's Commercial Hotel,
[Original: English/Danish]   Hawera, N. Zealand.
16.2.1909.

My dear Balfour.

We are so well over here, mother and I.

I have played "Noel" a lot in Australia, where it always had *great success*. From the enclosed you can see how I played "Noel" in the programme.

I have not had much free time, but have, all the same, composed a little since we left England. "Bold William Taylor" score is finished, and "English Dance" score will also be complete before we arrive in London.

Can you remember a very old Kipling chorus from Frankfurt times; "Away by the lands of the Japanee"? It was one of the many sketches to "The Rhyme of the 3 Sealers" which you were fond of. I have now made a complete new part to this little chorus sketch, and it is now ready. I have also worked on the old "Marching Song" sketches.

We hope to arrive in London about the end of May, and hope you will be there at that time.

I've been hugely taken by the native Maori music & *rhythmic recitations* & have come across phonograph records of some native Rarotongan (South Sea Island = Polynesian) partsinging that I've fallen clean in love with & am trying to note down so as to be able to have it sung by chorus in London.

This music is *manyvoiced* & full of *harmonic* feeling, & enthralling rhythmicly.

My dear Balf, the South Seas teem with glorious wayward ecstatic uncollected native musics. Shant we do a trip thro those seas once?

The South Seas with their lovable graceful fierysouled Viking Islander races may become a 2nd Scandinavia to me. I intend to learn Maori some day.

Do, darling Balf let's see more of each other when we return. We meet so stupidly seldom these last years.

Mother sends her love

Ever fondly
Percy.

Why didnt Forsyth advertize that I was playing Noel (in Australia) in (Lond) D.T.? I never saw any such advs.

243   TO KAREN HOLTEN   Marton, N.Z.
[Original: English/Danish]
18.2.09.

You poor little thing.

I have just received your letter 21, from just after the operation. Your poor father, it must be something you just can't bear to think of, such a long operation without anaesthetic, how could he bear it? It is absolutely frightful. For you indeed it was not much better either. Nothing is so soul-destroying as being with someone with continuing illness. The brave little Kirsten has really had a beastly bad time. But how splendid that the operation went so well! How anxious I am to get your next letter to hear further news.

No, I would far rather die than be cut without anaesthetic.

So you don't like Bloch's book so much. I can easily imagine that if I had gone through a time filled with medicinal smell, suffering, and doctor's talk, I wouldn't be in a state to enjoy carnality treated in a similar manner. Moreover I can well imagine that you wouldn't anyway appreciate that kind of sexual *consciousness* so highly; for indeed consciousness is not so often conducive to happiness in a matter of that kind. But I personally can enjoy it very well. I like the records of what *actually happened* to certain individuals, now maybe, (later certainly) dead. It's like a sort of folksong collecting. One reason why I wanted you to read in Bloch is that I think it is good for you to get to know that my perverse instincts are as "common" as they are.

It wouldn't be fair if you went and thought all this was original in me; something that quite ordinary people don't have the like of. From this book you can discern that these instincts are found in quite "common" ordinary people, and are not something peculiar that I can boast of. They are original in me only in so far that *they came to me as a young boy without my knowing that they were shared by others*, & even developed fully before I ever read or heard of their presence in other folk.

But the fact is that *everything* that deals with sexual matters absolutely knocks me over. I love to simply wade & swim in a sea of overwrought ceaseless sexual thought; everything (at all *serious*, of course) that just smells of sex at all is dearly fondly welcome to me.

O, the Maori hakas! The grand wild rhythms of them ring bewitchingly in the memory of my ears, after not hearing them for a 14 night, too. Here, out here, is a new Scandinavia for me, the relics of another Viking life, islanders, roaming, fighting, loving, with the joy of life hot in their nostrils, the pride of the body lithe in their limbs, & red flowers scattered in their hair. Wait till you see our Solomon Island comb! (15/-) It's hard for me to keep on learning Gaelic (I dont either) with the new hunger to prattle Maori tugging at my brain.

To perform a haka must give more joy that [than] to perform any other art I know, almost. For one not only shouts wild bold words, with the rhythmic pulse of a lot of fellow hakamen floating one along, but accompanies the chanting with desperate violent wanton abondoned movements of the whole body! Musical football.

How queer that all this South Sea Island enthusiasm started thro sending you "W of all Ns"! Just so, my Scandinavian madness began when I was about 11 by a stupid story in a boy's book with illustrations of those jolly leggings the old chaps wore. The truth is, if a race is really *in tune* with

ones own personality it dont take much introducing to make fast friends. A loose hint here & there is enough. If I was W. Whitman I should say: "All races please the soul; but these races please the soul well."

I did some beadwork in the train yesterday. As soon as we get to a town where we can buy decent beads mother is going to start in on it too. If you have any Maori, Polynesian, Melanesian, Fiji, Samoan, & S. African things in Copenhagen museums, you go & have a good look at them; its worth it. The Maori things are sturdier, broader, bolder than the other S.S. (South Sea) stuff, but the S.African is the strongest coarsest rankest, & in a sense boldest of the lot. There is some awfully jolly S.S. work in "shellmoney" (shell cut somewhat like beads:

with patterns like the following:

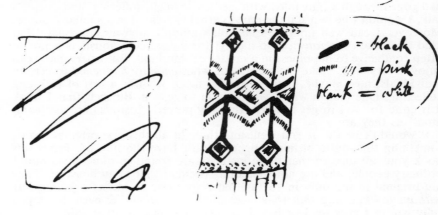

Look also for all sort of Solomon Island work in *grasses*, black, gold-yellow, and bright red, or goldyellow & red only. Look out for spears, canoe paddles, etc with this glorious closely plaited work all up the shaft for 3 or 4 feet.

My feet are just upon well. I shall be swimming again shortly.

I was so happy to get Cai's rowing-boat-photo. What a pretty picture. By the way, have you learnt how to *develop* your own photos? For if we are going to take photos *for our own selves*, you will need to be able to develop. Are we going to take photos this coming summer?

I am practising the Brahms Paganini Vars, & the 2 pieces by Albaniz.

Goodbye, I must write many letters today.

Dear little Karen, such a time she's had.

Next letter P.R.

244 TO ROSE GRAINGER   The Empire Hotel,
[Original: Danish/English]   Timaru, N.Z.
26.2.1909.

I spent a lovely ¼ hour in the museum after leaving you yesterday. One could be weeks in this museum without digesting everything it contains in the ethnological department. I could not find "moccasins" in the American section, perhaps they have moved them somewhere else. I saw some lovely combs of wood with beadwork on top, (instead of grasswork as in the Solomon Island ones) I think they were from Samoa. I could make similar combs myself. I must also learn to make your belt (or armband, or neck-lace) which consists of plaited hair and shellmoney or beads.

The contrasts of the black or dark pliable knotted hair-strands behind the stiff white forms of the beads or shellmoney is great. I could do nice work like this in plaited fishingline & beads. Many of the South African bead patterns are worth noting. When one goes and looks in a museum like this, I think one gets the impression that the small things we have bought are very good. See for example the Solomon Islands section. Our things are just as good as those *of the same kind*, there. Don't forget to write to ''Windsor'' for my pyjamas.

I have read so much in the 2 books about the Maoris. One of them (Hawaiki. by S. P. Smith) I have already read right through.[10] We must read it together. It is exciting, and charming.

There is nothing I like doing more than reading on **travelling** *nations*, who journey over wide seas. Smith also writes well.

Last night I wrote the fair-copy of Rarotonga fierce No. 1, that I took down in Otaki that time.

I cant resist drawing you a little sketch of the belt pattern (Solomon Island) which I took from a canoe paddle (?) in Wellington Museum.

10 Stephenson Percy Smith, *Hawaiki: the original home of the Maori. With a sketch of Polynesian history*. The second edition, enlarged and mostly rewritten, had been published in Christchurch in 1904. Grainger had bought a copy in Wellington in February 1909. The second book is unidentified.

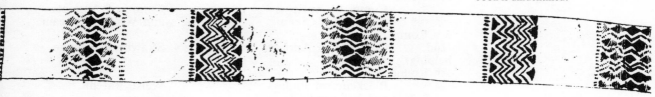

What is shown blank is intended for bright pure yellow

~~~~~ ⫸ ~~~~~ red

~~~~~ ➤ ~~~~~ black

Fondest love, darling.
I arrive for evening meal tomorrow (Sat)
Yr loving one.

After a week's season of four concerts in Tasmania, the party crossed again to the mainland, travelling immediately north, via Armidale, to Sydney for a return season of three concerts. Then it was north again via Toowoomba to Brisbane, leaving Brisbane on 9 April. The journey north continued by steamer to Townsville, then on to Charters Towers and Rockhampton, the northernmost point of the tour. From there, the tour moved steadily south overland, visiting various Queensland towns en route to Brisbane, where a farewell concert was given on 29 April, then south again visiting various towns in southern Queensland and northern New South Wales, then back to Sydney again, where a grand charity matinee was given on 8 May. Three more towns in New South Wales had concerts, the final concert of the tour being given in Bathurst on 12 May. The party then broke up: some members returning to Sydney to wait for the boat; Grainger and the Mueckes continuing south, via Melbourne, to Adelaide. Grainger arrived in Melbourne in time for the Marshall-Hall Orchestral Concert on 15 May, then travelled on to visit his mother's family in Adelaide. The S.S. Seydlitz left Adelaide on Sunday 23 May.

Most of Percy's time and energy on the northern tour went into the making of a beadwork necklace for his mother. Apart from the new programmes necessary for Sydney, the tour was not demanding.

245   TO ROSE GRAINGER   Heathorn's Hotel,
12.3.1909.   Hobart.

Feeding match between Australia and Holland. *Dutchman badly beaten on points*. Collapsed near the end. Australian Champion finished with a rare smile & was even able to attend the *show*.

Australia.	*Holland.*
First Round	
Soup.	Soup.
2nd Round.	
Lamb.	Fish. (small helping)
3rd Round.	
Chick: & H. . .	Curry & R. . .
4th Round.	
Comp. of Quinces & & Whipped Cr:	Chick & Ham.
5th Round.	
Comp. of Apricots & Whipped Cream.	Comp. of Apricots and Whipped Cream.
6th Round.	
(2nd Compote of Apricots helping) & Wh. Cr.	Strawberry Sponge.
7th Round.	
Blackcurrent Pud: **and** Whipped Cr:	Welsh Rarebit.

Mrs. Scherek was a popular Referee. The over flowing audience cheered the young Competitors to the echo. Encores were demanded but were not responded to. The management lodges a complaint. Doc. retracts previous offer to act as agent for either compititor.
Concert to follow.

---

246   TO ROSE GRAINGER   Heathorn's Hotel,
[Original: Danish/English]   Hobart.
Sunday evening 14.3.1909.

I have had a blessed day today.
I have practised nearly the whole day, inside the theatre, where I was quite alone for the most part, except [for] a lovely black dog and a little cat.
My programmes for Syd are now fixed, as follows:
Classical Concert D min Bach Busoni (only one number)

The 3 other concerts
1. Ballad; Rhapsody E♭ *Brahms*

Flower Waltz

---

2. Rondo a cap. (Wrath over etc) *Beethoven*

{ Jeux d'eau Ravel
{ Toccata Debussy

---

3. ⎧ Gibøens bruremarsch   *1st time in Austr* ⎫
⎨ Jeg gaar i 1000 tanker   " ⎬
⎩ Rötnamsknut ⎭

Schubert Tausig

As extra number at the "Classical" I think of playing B.B. "Wachet auf ruft uns die Stimme" and after Brahms No the Scottish lullaby Brahms.

I think you still have my umbrella; I forgot to collect on the ship, no doubt. I can get it in Melb.

Yesterday afternoon Mrs Agnew came and motored me to "Brown's River" (15 miles?) I have never seen anything more wonderful than the Tasmanian scenery. Never had I seen anything more lovely than the view from high up on the mountain out over Hobart town, the harbour, and right out to the open sea, and everywhere the most beautiful straightest gum trees; some quite young thin gums as straight as a spear I don't understand how even the stupidest people can go and think that N.Z. can in any way *be compared* with this wonderful beautiful country. I would like to travel right through this little island and get my eyes on all its beauty.

I bought 2 amusing books the day before yesterday. The first is a missionary's book with over 100 pictures of natives of Samoa, Tonga, Fiji, Solomon, New Britain, New Guinea, etc. You will be happy to look at the book, I am sure. Cannibalism is after all something frightful when one reads a little more closely about it. There was for example a man who wanted to eat his favourite wife; the missionary could hardly hold him back from it.

The second book I will send you straight away; about Jørgen Jørgensen.[11] I hope you will read it right through, even the foreword, as I think it is really interesting. I would be glad if you could read it **before** we meet in Melb; so I could get it again.

J.J. is an absolutely typical Scandinavian personality. When you think of Grettir, N.Grøn, and Fornander, while you read it, you will, I think, find several traits in J.J. that show racial affinity with these 3. It is worth noting how he always gets on well among the aristocrats and the big men, but can't get anywhere with ordinary people. Despite his weaknesses, there is nothing hard or greedy in his personality, for example, he is prouder of having effected the Revolution in Iceland without shedding blood, and that the people loved him personally, than he is of his glory as "king". I also like his need of truth. He doesn't hide anything! And despite his moralising rather tediously about other things, he never tries to give moral *grounds* for his *own actions*. This was very noticeable just after having read the missionary's book, where everything receives its moral explanation most scrupulously, believe me!

In the afternoon I visited Mrs Agnew again and as there was a lady with her who hadn't been able to be at our concerts on account of her mother's death, I played a little for them, Brahms and Grieg etc. Working up for a Recital here later on! I did my damnednest.

Would you be so kind as to get the address of the present sec of the F.S. Soc (Mrs Ford?) from *Journal* 12. Either Dr Russell or Sisley have the journal & you could find out by telephoning doubtless.[12] I'd much like to have the address from you on Friday, passing thro.

This morning I played Cyril's sonata through in its new form.[13] I have now found some more shortenings which make the piece still more practical, in my opinion. I will have much pleasure in playing this piece. It contains so many good things, only it was all too long before. (It wants the knife!) That was really true.

11 *The Convict King. Being the life and adventures of Jørgen Jørgenson* . . . Retold by J. F. Hogan (London, 1891). The missionary book is unidentified. Niels Grøn, an acquaintance of the Graingers who, returning to Denmark in 1907 after a long absence, assisted with advice and contacts for provincial engagements.

12 Thomas Alexander Sisley, author, painter, poet and elocution teacher, friend of the Graingers from Percy's childhood. Grainger wrote that it was probably Sisley who opened up to him the whole world of Icelandic and Anglo-Saxon literature. It was Sisley who suggested that Grainger read *Grettir the Strong*.

13 See note 7, 1901. In his autobiographical *Anecdotes* Grainger tells how, when he played the Scott sonata in its first version at the Savage Club in London, H. Allerdale Grainger said "it needs the knife".

272

When I come through Melb this time I must not neglect to try the Melbourne Steinway.

Last night Schereks and I went to "moving pictures" in the theatre Sometimes one can see amusing things in such "shows". Last night there was one; "Scenes in S' Africa" among the Zulus, **Oh** *so lovely*. The way they have of walking with their legs in the high wild grass, it is charming, heroic. I was quite carried away with happiness, you can well understand. And they paddled their canoes with thrilling energy, swing, & great skill.

But how happy a child is if his mother can be free to enjoy life with him! That I got to thinking about today. If you and a man were indispensable to each other, I could not possibly have things so good with you, as I do. The 1st condition for happy love is indeed absolute freedom. The heart alone cannot make happiness, the surroundings are in the end the strongest influence.

Doc was so amusing this evening. He came in and told us that he had been with Ada to the Governor's. He said: "It wasn't so bad after all as *we'd feared*, they were very *easy*." He talked about the whole thing as if it was an exam that had gone through. And then he said: "We've been round paying visits to all the *best* people of Hobart this afternoon, & its astonishing how they were all so keen asking me business questions straight out about Melba's prospects here. Remarkable how keen they are on discussing the business side" That being so, one can but conclude that Doc can hardly have failed to make a real hit in Hobart society.

Then he rambled on about the Gov's new aide de camp, straight out from Engl: "*Poor* fellow; he hasnt got used to things yet, & was feeling terribly out of place today." There was some inference to the effect that Doc put him at his ease, as far as possible. Doc had a new waistcoat on! He looked as if he was *feeling* this (*possibly needless*) expense *very keenly*.

Love to dear Uncle Charlie & his dear ones

Yr happy loving son
Perks.

247 TO KAREN HOLTEN   Launceston Hotel
[Original: Danish/English]   Launceston,
15.3.1909.   Tasmania.

This island is indescribably lovely. It is a deep pleasure for me, after the 2 months in N.Z., to be surrounded again by my native gum-trees. Tasmania is, to me, a thousand times lovelier than N.Z. and really also more lovely than Australia itself, since the climate here is so excellent, and everything looks so *fresh*, but all the same quite Australian. The colours are quite enchanting, particularly in Hobart (where we were from Friday until this morning — Monday), which is perhaps the most beautiful town as regards position and surroundings I have ever seen. Wellington is gloriously grand & noble, but this is just lovely & charming, fjord-like, with fine hills all round.

I miss not seeing any Maoris very much, but rejoice in being again embraced by the wondrous Australian landscapes.

Mother is in Melbourne where we arrive on Friday, but travel straight on to Sydney where we have 4 concerts with new programmes. I will play many "classical" things this time: Bach Busoni D minor Toccata. Brahms G minor Ballade and E flat major Rhapsody, Grieg "Jeg gaar i 1000 tanker" "Gibøens Bruremarsch". Beethoven Rondo a capriccio. op 129. Ravel "Jeux d'Eau" Debussy Toccata. etc. among others. That means; work a bit.

I bought a new whip in Hobart, 7/6. It is the best I have yet. It was a carriage whip which I have shortened. It has a very long "lash", and is splendid. I now have whips from Egypt, Sydney, (2) Gippsland, Hastings (N.Z.) and Hobart (Tasm)

I have bought 2 interesting books. One is a missionary's book and contains over 100 lovely and interesting photographs of natives from the following islands: Samoa, Tonga, Fiji, Solomon, New Britain, Papua.

The other book gives the life history of Jørgen Jørgensen. He was a Copenhagener, who travelled a great deal in his youth as a sailor, was in the naval war against England, was a revolutionary "king" on Iceland for quite a short time, was put in an English prison, where he learnt to gamble, and became after that a hopeless gambler, unhappy and unlucky. Finally he was sent to Hobart as a convict, gave up gambling under the new influences, was editor of a Hobart newspaper, got a command (was an officer) in the war (here in Tasm) against the natives, (blacks) and died at last in the hospital, in poverty.

He had a *lot of humour*, and was very freedom loving, and had a warm humane heart. Most of the laws he introduced in Iceland are still in use there, it is said. All in all he was a really good Scandinavian, abstract, humorous, reckless, uncommercial, observant, freedom loving, fearless, & *very* self-observant, & unsentimental about himself. He moralises a bit tediously about many things, but he never gives moral *grounds* for his *own actions*, (and that was good of him) as Englishmen do. He can easily be very sharp and even bitter (a *little* bit) but never from a *personal* point of view.

The book is published by an Englishman (or Colonist) from J.J.'s own manuscripts. The amusing thing is that the publisher doesn't understand J.J.'s best sides at all; and the difference between the heroic unself-seeking sharp-sighted Scandinavian and the tame commerically tuned moralising Englishman comes out very amusingly.

He (the publisher) can't, for example, understand that J.J. wasn't more impressed at becoming king of Iceland. But that wasnt J.J.'s style. The fact that the English Naval Captain who took him (J.J.) prisoner was highly rewarded for so doing tickled his (J.Js) honor much more. In other words, he was charming in many ways. I have underlined a few passages & added comments here & there in the book, which I am sending on to mother just at present, but will forward to you very shortly.

I saw the Danish name on the title lying in a Hobart shop & couldnt resist it.

There is a sagalike touch about a lot of it, I think, in spite of the English editor.

I should like to see the original. Surely the editor has spoilt many things, & is there no honesty about sexual matters at all in the original? Maybe not, but I'd like to see it.

Friday 19.3.09.   [In the train] Melbourne–Sydney.

It is nice for me to be in Victoria again, there is after all something about one's birthplace. We arrived early this morning from Tasmania (Launceston) which we left last night. On the ship I did the last bars of the actual E.D. orchestration; that is to say, that all the thinking-out is now done, there remains only to fair-copy some (completely thought out) pencil sketches from the time of the English tour. I spent the day with mother and my uncle Charlie (Aldridge) and his family, where I practised as well. I am practising hard at present, as we start next Wednesday in Sydney with 4 new programmes. Mother is very well, and is very happy staying with her brother, and travels to Adelaide on Monday to her sister. It is sad for me to be away from her now for the next 3 (?) weeks about.

Melbourne looks at least as big as London after the NZ and Tasmanian towns. In its way it is a really lovely town and people don't look so bad, a lot of them.

When I look out of the train windows now I see the beloved gums on all sides. That is nice for me.

Poor little Cyril is not at all well. He suffers from rheumatism and there is danger of him getting a stone in the kidneys, which must be an awfully painful illness. He doesn't understand at all how to keep healthy, and that's a shame for him. In Hobart I have worked again on his old piano sonata, and shortened it considerably, and made a fairly short (like a Brahms Rhapsody) piece out of it. There are so many lovely and to me most attractive ideas in this old work (8? years old)

I love Cyril a lot. He is one of the very best of people. And so terribly nice and amusing as he can be. As soon as I get back I must hurry up & form that little O to publish privately some of his orchestral scores. I hope he won't die; but it seems to me life appeals to him terribly little. Roger is very well according to his last letters.

Doc has (one can very well say) swindled me for £7½, I will tell you more about it when we meet. It was all quite friendly, no discomfort on my part. I have not had any real misery since we got quit of J.C.W. in Auckland. Doc is frightfully laughable as manager, & we laugh ½ the day about him, which is better than nothing. Remind me to tell you about ''8 o'cl and 12 o'cl'' with respect to NZ journey, when we meet.

At Uncle Charlie's today I read some lovely things of Ruskin.[14] He is worth reading, little friend, such an elevated and noble man, with a quite excellent style of writing and use of words. Above all get Ruskin's writings on *Turner* (the painter) I think there is something about T in R's ''Modern Painters''. Can't you borrow it from a library?. Up to now I have never known anything really about T's life, but have always felt from his divine pictures that he has a kind of ecstatic soul that more especially attracts me personally. Ruskin devoted his energy to illuminating the world about T's hitherto only ½ appreciated worth. He writes with fire.

Many many times every day I have to think of you and your father. It is much more difficult for me to grasp that he no longer lives than [it is] for you, for you have seen him through a long illness, while I can only remember him full of life, healthy, and lively. Little darling darling Karen, I am so helpless here in the distance. But we are all so powerless altogether in every place. Now it feels as if it won't be so long before we see each other. You have indeed had a hard year. Now mother has received a cable from Mrs Wragge that she travels from London, and that Mrs Burdett also is leaving our house. That will cost us some money; I fear. How do things stand with you as to money. I should love to hear all details of any of your money affairs that would not bore you to write, or that you would not mind my knowing. I am in despair lest I hear of frightful circumstances concerning you, either that you are ill, or that you are very poor, or something heart-rending. Such a catastrophe so often brings other sufferings. Dearest brave little Kirsten, take great care of yourself & your mother, & all yours, immediately after such a shock to soul & body; all of you are surely weak & distrought & therefor liable to be stricken ill yourselves without fine feeding up, open air, & some easing of your souls somehow.

How comforting it would be for us to take each other in our arms. After the most sensual ordeals, the most passionate undertakings, there is scarcely anything more intoxicating, more blessedly comforting, redeeming, satisfying than just to sink together in each other's arms. In composition it is fairly impossible to maintain throughout even a short piece the scent that a good beginning can possess. Is it not the same with meat-mates. Can you remember the feeling when the bodies' naked skin first comes into light dreamy contact with each other. The whole feeling appears to me so ''veiled''; there is also (for me) a feeling as if the skins breathe from each

14 John Ruskin (1819–1900). His five-volume work *Modern Painters* (1843–60) was begun as a defence of the English painter William Turner (1775–1851).

other. Life, so infinitely lovely and frightful and full of contradictions as it is, contains nothing of more completely unmixed happiness than these first seconds touch of the skin of the whole body? Fatigue accompanies (more or less) the specifically sexually excited ascending long lovely way, and the divine happiness of the climax is strongly blended with bitterness of intensitivity and the life kernel's crashing gross tragicness. But the first naked touch of lovers is full of mother-and-child's angelic bliss, freed from everything that is glorious terrible and cruelly irresistible. How can I do without you so long? As Walt says: "I am amazed at my own moderation". But how longings of sexuality suck and suck there inside one, without any mercy.

I love to sit in the train or lie on the ship with closed eyes and dream about you and the future. I wish that I had claws, like tigers have, to tear scratches in you, to really cut deeply into you. Never will I achieve that which I chase after in my cruelties. When I whip it should lie just under the skin. Even if I had claws and could cut inches deep into you, you soft tender Karen, that which I seek would move further in; for it is really something related to endlessness, unlimitedness, immortality one wants to grab and hold fast in such moments. In the fruitlessness of the chase our happiness grows. Do you know Keats "Ode to a Grecian Urn"? (Oh so lovely, soullit) The bliss of the beings on the urn are ours because the fleshly hunter never reaches his prey; yes, physically he does gain it, but spiritually — never. Our love is not driven out by sexuality. It is not that sexuality in us makes us feel love. Longings after depth, splendour, total absorption, extremeness, God, (what folk *mean* by God) Art, they work years long, and we strive the whole time after more or less attractive expressions for these deepest instincts. When we once reach the possibilities of love, these instincts immediately find their most complete solution there. Not quite complete, never that. Soulfulness *chooses* love from among the many deep things it knows because therein it finds its (so far) most extreme expression. If soulfulness could discover something deeper, sharper, more extreme, more divine than love it would push love aside and advance itself more splendidly with something else. (When I find something that does my soul better good than you, off you pack tomorrow) It is not the presence of sexuality in the body that causes love's soulfulness, it is rather the presence of soulfulness that necessitates the utilisation of sexuality's possibilities. Can I treasure art, science, religion, highest as expression of the soul when I have known Valhalla of the flesh with such a one as you? Impossible. (In Valhalla every hero is killed every day and gets up fresh the next morning. It is like sexuality's resurrection from daily death)

It is therefore that great soulful men give up kingdoms and art and God for love's sake. The best is good enough for them. They use judgement in choosing.

I wish I was dead and didn't have to go without you a second longer.

(All that doesn't prevent my acting practically in actual life.) (19.3.09)

Monday. 22.3.09.   Hotel Wentworth.
                                                              Sydney.

I have just now got your letter from 7.2.09, the day before your poor father was to come home from hospital. How quite quite frightful the whole thing is! Something like that could absolutely drive one to murder.

If you knew my mother's life-story and knew some things that I have been witness to, with regard to doctors' stupidity, incapability, and criminal negligence you would be better able to understand many of my characteristics. In later years I will perhaps tell you how her whole life has been in part ruined (that it is not *completely* ruined is due to chance, and her own splendid constitution) by a couple of people's unforgivable (if anything at all is unforgivable?) carelessness, callousness, ignorance. I believe

15 Percy kept his promise. After his mother's death, in his letter to Karen of 8 May 1926, he told her his mother's life story. Until this letter, Karen had not known that Rose was suffering from syphilis, Rose having made Percy promise never to tell her. "If you had known it", Percy wrote, "the whole thing would, perhaps, have been easier to understand. I always think that the truth, the whole truth, is always the easiest for 'the parties concerned'."

no person would believe it if one told them what she has gone through.[15] Because she is, so to say, "a brand plucked from the burning" (of misery & death) she means perhaps more to me than would have been the case if there hadn't been such a great danger for me of losing her; and I also have become a different person from having seen the things I have seen. Believe me, I was not originally of so careful and reserved a nature as one could now think; when one has seen enough of the results of recklessness, carelessness, thoughtlessness, ignorance, & "following nature" every intelligent person becomes somewhat of an old maid.

When one has seen *enough* of bad suffering one becomes willing to pass by pleasures rather than risk new sufferings.

I should think you would be bitter, poor little darling.

My Aunt Sarah & her 2 girls Babs & Violet ("Richmond" family) are here in Sydney for a holiday, by chance, & are living only a few doors from here, so I am very happy with them.

Yesterday we went to see the mixed bathing at Manly beach. (Sydney) It is a grand swimming place with giant breakers storming in that have to be "shot" or dived through.

The average of the figures was very good I thought. Sydney is a fascinating place. I have about the same (if not *the* same) room as 5 years ago, overlooking the harbor, & Nicholsons (music shop) have sent me up a lovely Steinway to practise on. The concert is not till Wednesday.

You poor little thing, my heart beats so warmly for you and your sufferings.

248 TO ROSE GRAINGER
[Original: Danish/English]
22.3.09.

Hotel Wentworth
Sydney

Dearest Mother.

Have just received your letter from last Saturday.

Sarah, Babs, and Violet are here, and we have much fun together. Yesterday we took a ship to Manly and saw mixed bathing there. The waves beat up very strongly there and it must be frightfully amusing.

The average of the figures seemed very high to me. Sarah etc live at "Petty's" just round the corner.

The concert today in Maitland is "off", thank God. No concert before Wednesday.

I practised 6 hours yesterday. Sarah and Babs visited me and both went to sleep on the bed during the practice, in the well-known Aldridge manner! I got a letter from K[aren] today. At the time it was written they already knew that her father's condition was hopeless, and they were just going to move him from the hospital home to Ceresvej again.

When you have read J. Jørgensen, quite at your leisure, perhaps you would kindly post it on to K to Ceresvej. I have already written to her about it, you need only send it off.

The other boys are at the "Australia", thank God I am quite alone here. Only Danvers is a bit of a bug in the bed!

I have received an interesting letter from a German, who saw us at Pfaff's, about 15 years ago, and has heard of me since from J. Blanche and Sarasate. (of all people) I'm fixing a meeting with him.[16]

Your loving son sends a thousand warm thoughts. Give my love to dear Auntie Clara please

Herewith a fine Fijian [postcard enclosed].

16 Sergei Neuberger, a pupil of Rose's from Frankfurt days; his brother and sister were good friends of Rose. According to Percy, the Russians had ordered Neuberger out of Europe for a year for his association with the nihilists, and forced him to come to Australia. He had made his money in a "Stickerei-Fabrik" [embroidery factory] in Paris, where he became a friend of J. E. Blanche. Pablo Martin Melitón de Sarasate y Navascuéz (1844–1908), Spanish violinist and composer.

249 TO ROSE GRAINGER
[Original: English/Danish]
Tuesday. 23.3.09.

Hotel Wentworth
Sydney

Dear little mother.

I spent a very amusing day yesterday. Aunties Jack, Sarah, Babs, Violet, Gordon Lane and I took the ship to Manly 5 o'cl and Gordon, Violet, and I surfbathed.

The water was quite warm and the whole thing was very enjoyable. After that we ate a little there. I made a beast of myself over peaches & cream.

Gordon Lane has hugely bettered, it strikes me. He now appears warmhearted affectionate, sensible, (a teetotaler) unmanish, & strong as a horse, & quite sympathetic looking; nicer, & less worldly, I should say, than Alec ever was.[17]

Auntie Jack was also quite at her best, splendidly younglooking active & quite restful. She & Violet & Gordon heard me do an hours prac up in my room in the evening.

Babs washed her hair last night, and after practising we sat on the big veranda at Petty's while she dried it. She combed my hair also. I can't think of nicer girls than Violet and Babs. Truly pure-natured indeed. It is undeniable that the company of women is something quite wonderfully entertaining.

Really good sweet women are though the most splendid thing there is. How can it be that the sweetest women's types are so often found in the middleclasses? For I would never say that Lady Marjorie [Manners] or Lady Winefride [Elwes] (excellent and good as they are) are as sweet as for example Violet, Babs, Karen, or Fräulein Peiper.

I got a second letter from Karen yesterday, written about 16 days before her father's death. They had him home from hospital, and he had shown a little tiny improvement, and they were all so heart-happy and hopeful again. What a pity it is, that it couldn't continue like that.

Now we are soon coming home again and I will really look forward to beginning again my London life.

This trip has been a wondrous boon to me, it has beyouthed my spirit beyond reckoning, & the opening up of the South Seas to us has been a priceless gain.

But now with this trip we say goodbye to the shoddy & the shallow & turn abidingly to firmer bottoms. I wish you to turn all your brain power on when we get back & take sole kings right (be "Einevÿldskonungr yfir heile Norreki") [sic = Einvaldskonungr yfir heilum Noregi. Icelandic: Absolute monarch over all Norway] of the olden bark. The last few years I was sick of the game, hungry for any change, & chafing at all samishness. But now this 6 months has done the trick, & I reckon to return as frayready (almost) to London as after the last Austr tour. We know now a little more than then, & the needs are other. We know now that the purely pianistic act must not be ridden all too solidly or my springiness collapses, & we know that the pupils are a wishable haven ahead, to be steered for in the end.

Never the less dont let us stagnate in any markets. I put myself wholly into your hands on return. Treat me like an agent who's bought one over for a certain period.

Really take the helm, & see what can be shaken out of me. I shall do all you say, but if I feel myself staling at any time, I shall be careful to say so at once, in the hopes that we then avoid the hanging on sulkily game that doesnt pay & wastes life. But we must have a rare old buck in.

About this present trip we may, or not, agree. Something in me craves, every now & then, for the obscure the ornery the lowdown & above all, for the *easygoing*. That has been now fed, & I ought to be fit to stick to better things for a neat little batch of years now. Maybe, too, this is the last time

17 The *Bulletin* of 14 January 1909 reported that Mrs Zebina Lane and one of her younger sons were in Sydney after travel in far lands.

18 Rose replied, 27 March, "I love the way yr character is developing — you are growing more loving & affectionate & more considerate for yr friends who love you".

I would quite truly enjoy such a tour. Even now the presence of rotters is unspeakably more irksome to me than formerly, & the presence of sweet dear folk more *consciously* precious & allbetokening.[18]

Then we, & our friends, & all, are getting older, & its useless for you & me, & we & our friends, to be uselessly parted. To what gain? It['s] practically like making one die so many months earlier, robbing one of so much life.

Every young man, I take it, has moments when he will ask:

How would I be alone for a spell?

How about life with men alone for a bit?

Could I manage, heroicly, single-handed?

Isnt one happiest with least ties, do not affections greaten sorrows?

Even I, too, must have nourished these thoughts at moments.

But my present answers to them would be:

When I am alone I am lonely, & inferior as a worker.

Life with men alone is unbearable since men are tamer than even women.

I, personally, can only manage defeat & failure, singlehanded.

The worst tie, the straightest yoke is after all the outside world; everything that lies outside those things, works, folk, friends, one loves & is loved by.

Even sorrow is better than emptiness & boredom.

Then there have been too many deaths & illnesses lately.

Grieg dead, & first Roger ill, & now Cyril ill, & poor Karen's father dead, it all makes one feel a strong need for hurry in friendships. Let us two, above all, not waste any more time needlessly apart.

"O I'm not complänen' "

This trip has been all I longed for & more & Ill never cease to be thankful for it.

250   TO ROSE GRAINGER   Imperial Hotel,
[Original: German/English]   Armidale.
31.3.1909. Wednesday

Dear little mother

That was certainly a remarkable time, that I spent with Neuberger.

On Friday (March 20) he came for lunch, on Saturday we were together from 11 o'clock in the evening till 4 in the morning, on Sunday we spent the whole afternoon together (I played him my compositions) till 10 in the evening, we spoke to each other again on Monday (standing in the street) from 11 till 2 in the morning, and yesterday (Tuesday) from 1.30 in the afternoon till 6.45 in the evening.

So I saw a lot of him. He attracted me colossally and I found him interesting — otherwise I would not have wasted so much good time — to me he was like an enthralling book, that one devours as quickly as possible. Come to think of it in nine years I have in fact had not a single real conversation with a German, despite the fact that I am totally saturated with German thoughts and impressions.

After all these hours I still have no idea whether I really trust him or not. There is a lot that is clearly unnoble in him, like, really, with all Jews, & he isnt even really bodily clean, & not at all sympathetic bodily.

But clarity of mind, a spiritual energy (for the time being anyway) is still something irresistible for an active man like me, and the spirit of the Jews is still something quite wonderful, although it is apparently lacking the truly heroic.

He said a thousand perceptive and splendid things about me, you, my art, Australia, Germany, England, France, Blanche, etc. I could listen to him for hours, despite my incessant doubts about his honesty. (perhaps quite groundless)

He talked a lot about the relationship between you and me. He said: From everything you say and do it is really beyond doubt that you have an extraordinary relationship with your mother. A relationship like that is one in a million. Likewise you have a remarkable relationship to the world, and other women, because you are really *only* attached to your mother, perhaps very much more than you realise. You can *never* really be intimate with any other woman, for this occurs with only *one* person in one's whole life, (whether it is mother, sister, beloved, friend, brother) and this is what you are now to your mother.

His comments about art are quite pleasantly true and perceptive. He says, for example, that all artistic *creativity* is one and the same as the sexual drive, basically the 2 things are one. This is also absolutely true. Certainly thousands have said this; but it is still refreshing to listen to these true unbefuddled opinions of the perceptive German intellectual culture.

Then about the English, and that strong overabundance of brutality which is always to be found with the typical examples [of the race]: The English are no less sexual than other Europeans; on the contrary; no race has retained its sexual freshness and its original vitality more uncorrupted than the English. But their abstinence is not heroic, spartan, as has been the case with earlier great nations of the past. Their abstinence is motivated by a stupid cowardly imbecilic moralistic viewpoint. Their abstinence is thus unnatural, crude, and their tyrannically treated sexdrive transforms and transposes itself in various abnormalities, brutalisations, and hardships.

Kipling's spirit is for Neuberger (as he always has also been for me) nothing else than a glorious artistic manifestation of a huge sexual vigor, starved for generations, venting itself in a perverse unholy relish for ruthless destruction & soulagonizing (hence his adorable lovable patheticism) brutality, in any & every manifes[ta]tion

The difference, says Neuberger, between the Russian brutality & the English (of which Kipling is the high priest) is:

The Russian *gives way* to his brutal instincts & they vanish in deeds done in hot blood, leaving behind no high consciousness generating patheticism, no overflow of unused poison everlastingly festering.

The Englishman is far too held in hand & too self distrustful to ever really give way *thoroly* to any of his wild ruthless instincts; therefor they glow steadily, stubbornly, relentlessly like ashes; no flaming, never giving the show away, but wrenching an outlet in such, in a way, *terrible* art as Swinbourne's, Kipling's, A. Beardsley's, etc.

As the Englishman never spends generously his savingsbank of brutality (that is: a perversely translated overstock of sexual energy) the curiously steely texture of his temperament is very unmeltable, unpliable; the background of the unfree brute in him is ever ready, ever game, frothing behind the never mercifully opened cage of his British national life.

It's, therefore, a glorious thankworthy thing to be such an Englishman, little darling tough little mum.

Yesterday was very interesting. We wandered over to the Man-o'-warsteps, where the crews of the English, German, and French warships were passing backwards and forwards to their ship. We chatted with a dear German; an excellent boy. He looked 7 eighths a sailor, and one eighth German; but in speech (a nice pleasant Baltic North-German — almost platt a bit) he was significantly more nationalistic. He really looked boyish, with amusing soft Sailor legs, & red sunburnt neck & chest. Only the hair was bad, thin & colorless. Neuberger had already told me: now we should test the difference in morale between the Germans & the French.

Therefore he soon asked: What is life like on your ship; pleasant? What are your superiors like?

The young German began immediately to complain. "They don't let us enjoy ourselves at all, only work, work. If only there were some justice to be found amongst the officers, but there is only repeated injustice. Thank God I am just about finished in the service." Where would you like to go now? (asked N.)

"To France & England. Isn't it so, that if one knows some English, then one can still help oneself in the world." etc.

Then a Frenchman came. N spoke to him. He immediately asked N for a cigarette (a French brand which isn't available in Australia) and invited him to come on his warship on the following day. N asked him how was life on his ship.

"O it's all right; often it is very amusing."

What are your officers like?

"They vary, like all people; some are very nice, others are less so."

How do you like Sydney?

The Frenchman shook his head. "I am from Toulouse. T is the most beautiful, the gayest, the most pleasure filled city in the whole world. I would like to live and die in Toulouse."

N then introduced the German to the Frenchman. *However, the Frenchman did not know any English.* So N had to translate. The German was very friendly and forthcoming, but, of course, rather tactless. "Us Fr & Germans should understand each other well, *in any case it should be a lot simpler than the Germans and English.* Altogether, all white nations should band together now against the yellow nations. It is there that the danger for all our white people lies; China." But the Frenchman was polite and nonchalant. Toulouse! Why is he worried about barbarians; Germans and Chinese? At home he will find Civilisation and happy peacefulness. He will advance neither through his service in the navy nor his fatherland.

Then came the English lads swinging their boat bumpingly against the landing with joke & hurry.

Straw hats tilted fashionably at careless angles, trousers wide over the feet as befits; hard, mostly brutal, faces lit with activity & jaunt, bent on particular practical *doings* in Sydney town; oblivious of us & our German-French group; swimming in their own civilisation, self-sufficient, fairly inhuman.

Not landsmen *pressed into service*, but *professionals*, basking in the obvious boon & superiority of their enviable particular own poise in the universe.

We slept in the train last night.

I dont know when, for years, I've deeper relished the lullaby of the railway, or more cosily lay blithely thinking small thunklets.

Grand sleeping arrangements on this jolly line.

Had a lovely swim this morn, with John, Doc, Tini, Forsyth, in a good-ish bath. Just a comfily warm day today. Had a nice smooth shave.

I'm awfully grieved you're not with us in these nice Austr smalls. They're worthy of us.

O how happy I am. How lucky I am.

But how fearfully much Sydney cost me. Alack!

251 TO ROSE GRAINGER
Sunday 4.4.09.

Hotel Daniell,
Brisbane.

Darling one

Isnt the enclosed sweet of E Terry?[19]

Eily O'Hara came down to hear me. She is so nice. The enclosed is from her.

Went to Gov House today. Chelmsford is really charming.[20] Feilding manners.

I went clad in the combined clothing culture of London & Brisbane! My choice of tie socks waistcoat the result of a[n] afternoon's critical conning, my hat Brisbane ironed.

Are not the enclosed from Toowoomba amusing? Please read every word.

2 dear letters from you to here have given me joyeous isles. (of time)

The mosquitos make life hard, work mediocre, & concentration remote. After tomorrow's concert we stay here till Friday, by when I shall get thro needful letters, etc.

I really played well last night & had an obvious big success, I think.

I walked 6 miles, at least yest, in the heat, to & from far off concert hall. Darling one, goodnight.

I seem to have had no ruhe [German: peace] to write to you properly these last 2 days.

Love to darling Auntie Clara & the dear old Uncle Frank, & to all the blithe Richmond human tree

yr fond one
Percy.

19 Enclosed was a picture of the English actress Ellen Terry (1847–1928) at the age of seventeen, after her marriage to Mr George Frederick Watts, reprinted from *The Story of My Life* (Hutchinson & Co).

20 Frederic John Napier Thesiger (1868–1933), third Baron and later first Viscount Chelmsford, Governor of Queensland from 20 November 1905 to 26 May 1909, then Governor of New South Wales (1909–13).

252 TO ROSE GRAINGER
Tuesday. 6.4.09. evening.

Hotel Daniell,
Brisbane.

My dear little mum must not feel at all anxious about anything, dearie.[21]

As I said in my postcard this morn, Neuberger never even asked me for money. I didnt send the money that week at once; as:

1. There not being a concert on pay day we did [not] get paid till a few days late

2. because I lent John a few pounds, (which I've since got back)

3. because I knew we'd be having this unpaid week up in Q'sland, & wished to keep a good bit back towards it or any other unknown change of plans.

I shall be sending more money in a few days. Of course, dearie, I naturally shall *always* send it weekly, as soon as I get it, only didnt that Sydney week on account of above reasons & because my expenses there were so heavy, & it didnt seem a bully enough sum.

Then, darling, Queensland is not at all an unhealthy, or at all hateful, place. *Nowhere*, to my mind, does one meet a more typical, tough, & bodily interesting nativeborn Australian than up here. If I were to choose troops, I should (on my wholly limited experience of the different states) feel very inclined to favor Queensland men, from the look of them up here.

The weather is only nicely hot (tho' a few days were pretty stiff) now, & we are all feeling as fit as anything.

21 Rose had responded very badly to Grainger's letter of 31 March with his account of his time with Neuberger. Her anxiety was aggravated by Percy's lateness in sending his earnings. Her hysterical urgings that Neuberger was not to be trusted were based on nothing more than that she did not know how he had turned out, and her fear that Percy might lend him money. (In the event Percy did lend him £5, and Rose took it very well, applauding his generosity of spirit.) Grainger noted on her letter, "Typically worried uneasy letter".

Then surely it is good that the tour does not end too soon! Since we now are on it. But it has an end, after all. We sail in the Nord Deutscher Lloyd S.S. "Seidlitz" from Adelaide (or Melb, but I think Adelaide) on May 21. Doc says he has stipulated single berths for us, which they've promised if ship not too hopelessly crowded out. It will, however, be a more crowded time of year than we've ever gone home at before, remember.

Doc says, if you want details of sailing, cabins, etc, go to his father's office & enquire.

I suppose you dont mind going back by the N.D. Lloyd? I dont if you dont. But if you want us to go back by another route, wire me & I'll try fix it with Doc. Tomorrow I'll send you more detailed list of oncoming tour, in case you wish to wire, at any time.

I dont see why Neuberger should himself be dangerous. His being bothered by whatever Russians they were (if his tale is true) occured, he says, wholly accidentally through a friend of N's. N himself is not a creature of action at all, surely, but contemplative, affectionate, & of spiritual activity.

If he writes you, as he said he would, I think you will have this impression also. As for his keeping me up late; it was I who kept him; he trying to go away & I detaining him hour after hour, jawing. You know how I am. How I kept up Bevan in Cambridge years ago, & want to keep Karen talking till morn when we are together of nights, & you know how dead surely you & I above all would nightly drift into unhealth on floods of speech if it were not for your distressed endups! It really wasnt N's fault. My hours with him are really a treat to look back on, be he trustworthy, or not.

What does it matter if his *nature* rings true? His *brain* worked sweetly cleanly.

You write of Ted. You should hear N on the stupidity of Australians re drink. He said: The Australians are to begin with a fine race bodily, but after a few years all the men are obviously "verkommen" (broken-down, degenerate) thro alchahol.

Am very busy hearing folk play, etc. Folk make rather a fuss of me in Brisb, & I get a lot of letters like the enclosed.[22] I bought some newspapers, but the chambermaid seems to have run off with them, barring one. I shall get them again & send them you. I had a fine time again at yesterday's concert.

You know I finished the *new scoring* of E Dance on boat from Tasmania, barring a few little gaps here & there.

The last of these gaps was filled in yesterday, & I now have *only copying to do*.

Did I leave the sketch of lengthening "Away by the lands" (music) with you? If so, will you please have it ready for me to work at on voyage home (after Adelaide)

Today was at Garden party at Mrs Cowlishaw's. They very sorry you not up here with me.

Did the heavy in frock coat.

John has been having frightful rows with Doc, but I've been flowing along strifelessly, myself.

Before we leave here for the North (on Friday morn) I shall have all the letters, etc, done you have written me to do in the last few weeks.

The other day I went thro in my mind old works from the earliest Frankfort period; before WestEnd Platz & San Remo. My style utterly changed at about end of Schön's; for the better, no doubt. But I still quite like & enjoy these funny old things, & shall certainly publish them as "Early works". (Eastern Intermezzo, etc)[23]

Goodnight fondly loved motherlet.

Never be anxious, dearie; no need.

---

22 The enclosed letter was from one Florence W. Berry asking for an autograph. Of the concert on 4 April the *Brisbane Courier* reported next day, "But to many the chief interest in the concert centred in the reappearance of Mr Percy Grainger, the young Australian pianist, whose name is already written in indelible ink on the scroll of fame". Mr and Mrs James Cowlishaw gave a garden party for Ada Crossley and her company in the afternoon of 6 April, which event was duly reported in the social pages of the *Brisbane Courier* the next day.

23 This is probably the genesis of Grainger's *Youthful Suite*, a collection of five orchestral works from the period 1899–1901. Revised during the 1940s, the whole was published by Schott & Co., London, in 1950. The suite includes *Eastern Intermezzo* (1899) as its fourth movement.

253 TO ROSE GRAINGER

[Original: English/Danish/German]

Hotel Daniell,
Brisbane.

Thursday. 8.4.09.

That 6½ shillings on the ship from Tasy did the trick. I got £5 extra today on account of "the day" being put back to 8 o'cl in the evening. Doc has therefore behaved *quite honestly* for once.

That what Sven Hedin says about the Japanese in comparison with the other Asiatics is once again a witness, proof, to my old hobby-horse "the difference between islands and continents".

Just as the Japanese (as island-dwellers) are more lively, happier, easier than the heavy people on the broad dreadful endless Asian continent, in the same way the English are superior to Germans and other continentals, Polynesians to Australian negroes or Papuans, Sicilians to Italians, Danes and Faeroese to Norwegians, etc.

Quite remarkable however is the difference between the Danish island-dwellers (Zealand, Funen) and the Danish Jutlanders. Therefore also it is called "L'isle joyeuse". "The happy continent" is unthinkable!

Moisture, wetness signifies fullness of life, tender liveliness.

Isn't there already the same difference between (white) N Zealanders and Australians?

Islanders conquer easily.

Continentals conquer heavily.

I have just wired £20 to you.

So my 6/6 paid, for once, after all. Doc gave me a *day more than all the other boys without a murmur*. You see our "tour" ended on Monday night. This week we lie fallow & start work & pay again next Monday, having about 5 continuous weeks ahead of us.

Yesterday passed off easily. For the first time I realised what great talent goes to organ building. Somehow the organ in Exhibition building here struck me as extra seductive from the 1st, & yesterday I had a long chat with the tuner & tried the dear great instrument myself.

It is the work of Willis, the great English organ builder, & is supposed to be one of his very best — for its size.[24]

Willis; says the tuner; was a rare artist's soul, solid, hardworking, thorough, with tender artistic nerves; died poor, though the head of the biggest firm of English organbuilders. All his reeds, etc, he tested himself, personally, & knew no hurry, impatience, cheapness, showiness, or businesslikeness. And heeded no man in his plans, but only his own fine practical nouce [*sic* nous] & yearning for polish & balance.

Any composer who goes round with soundblending problems in his head, yearlong, must wax warm at the work of such a talented being as this.

How gloriously he has matched the color of clarinet, oboe, flute, etc! And how spiffingly all values are poised so that the individual stops (so varied, so "abstechend" [German: standing out; clearly distinct] one from the other) glide one into the others & merge meltingly in to the big massed combinations. There must be something Jens Peter Jacobsen-like in the artistic texture of such a man's soul; a man who not only feels, but does so critically, minutely, unerringly, carefully, wisely, tenderly rather than naturally, vastly, vaguely, recklessly, gloriously, wildly. Little contrasts, delicate ebbs & flows hover before him & entice to flowerlike excellence & balmy bloom of texture.

I had the full organ going for a few minutes. I am enough of a savage to have suffered a lovely sweaty thrill from it. There is a tight clenching agonised intensity in the louder reed stops (trumpet, tuba, etc) before which the looser pounchlike bulkiness of orchestral brass violence pales pinkly. The organ will yet prove a friend to me. It comes with 2 moving letters of introduction to me; from Bach, my artistic forebear, & from "machinical music" my unborn offspring. Never has more godlikely human music been

24 Henry Willis (1821–1901), English organ builder. The organ in the Exhibition Building, Brisbane, was built in 1891–2 by H. Willis & Son, replacing an earlier instrument destroyed by fire. It was first played in the Exhibition Building on 20 December 1892. In January 1900 it was purchased by the City Council for the planned new Town Hall but it continued to be housed and used in the Exhibition Building until the present City Hall was opened in April 1930.

born than by Bach for the ½ machinical organ. Believe me, the world may voice its deepest musical utterance thro the machinical perfections of the future.

As B. Shaw says:

Let us get away from that clumsiest of all mediums — the human hand.

(Nur das *gehirn* soll walten) [German: Only the *brain* shall rule]

I still hope one day to be a good organist. The finger work is double as easy as on the piano keyboard, & the stopsetting is merely sound color dreaming empowered with an Aladdins lamp; only the footwork needs graft.

I must use the organ, get to know it thoroughly, & blend it with woodwind in the orchestra, using the real w.w. only for more soloistic effects.

What I hope the concertina will do for my chambermusic combinations I am pretty sure the organ would for my orchestration: that is; give massed swells & lullings off, & bolster up, & make a cosy background to jutting sound effects.

So the organ is one more of the 1000 many goods of life that crowd spifflingly pleasingly upon me.

Dearest sweetest little mother.

Goodbye so long.

Your happy healthy loving
son

8.4.09. Later.

I have just received letter from Karen just after her father's death.

I believe we English make a mistake when we think we are the most self controlled of races. We are more *civilised* than Danes, but they are the calmest, most self controlled, most philosophical, least hysterical people one can imagine. They seldom give the show away. But I think **I** am, in a way, just as self controlled as any Dane. But I am exceptional in that regard.

254 TO ROSE GRAINGER   Queen's Hotel.
[Original: Danish/English]   Townsville.
Monday. 12.4.1909.

Dear little mother.

North Queensland is quite *magnificent*. The coast from Gladstone northwards is quite different from southern Australia; the trees are different, for the most part, and even the gum trees look different up here, just as they look different in N.Z.

We sailed between the Grt Barrier reef and the mainland. Just think! hundreds of islands, most of them quite small, and entirely without population. How one could be happy on such an island, quite alone, or with quite few beloved people. One could build a tent as protection from the sun, and take on provisions from the regularly passing steamers.

E.D. is quite quite finished. I worked like a madman on it on the ship ("Bingera") and wrote the last notes last night.

On Sat I copied 18 pages of score of which only about 4 pages were not absolutely complete. My hand nearly died of cramp. I've never worked harder in my little life; & in the tropics too

On the way home I shall drowse thro the score once more (after having forgotten details) & add marks of expression here & there, comparing the soundstrengths of the various climaxes, etc; but the real *stuff* is all done,

& I could die as far as the E.D. is concerned.

There was such a charming girl on the boat, about 20. About your height, plump, athleticly & charmingly formed, the very soul of health & happiness, with a touch of Lady Winefride to her. Tho she spoke with a very slight Austr accent I couldnt think she hailed from this land, as she looked too fresh & sappy, & with that childlike sexual charm that doesnt grow here, ordinarily. However she's Sydney.

All the days I was scoring scoring I saw her flitting about blithely when I looked up from my work & when I'd done the dance & was loafing on dance like a time served convict & got to wondering how I could pluck up corage to find out was she Engl or Austr, when she came up & spoke to me *spontaneously* (Ko Hawaiki te whenua e tupa *noa* mai te Kumara. Hawaiki the land where grows *spontaneously* hither the sweet potata)

She turns out a nice cosy temperament, stupid & charming & wise as girl[s] are; what wondrous precious things, to be sure!

She is at this Hotel (a ripping cool well thought out tropical affair) but leaves tonight, going to loafe some months on an upcountry station. It is as well. I dont believe in knowing really nice clean attractive young maidens too well.

But it's nice to find our land can produce fragrance & unspoiltness. It has made me very happy.

I feel so well in this clime, & have heard no complaints from my veins.

yr adoring son
Percy.

Today our working week begins. In a weeks time I'll have screw to send again, dearie.

255 TO ROSE GRAINGER   Crown Hotel,
[Original: English/some Danish]   Charters Towers
14.4.1909.

Am enjoying myself hugely.

Bathed once on Monday & 2ce on Tuesday (Townsville) in Seawater baths, & 2ce today in lovely freshwater baths here.

Am learning double overarm stroke & improving my speed somewhat.

Dived off a good deal higher springboard some 15 times today; in all must have done about 50 dives.

John & Ryan feel the heat but I feel drunk with joy of swimming & am having a unforgettably bodily happy time of it.

Bad audiences up here, alas.

The bathman showed me 3 sort of tricks today, all nice & easy.

My old Chelsea teacher will give a jump when he sees me flop in, etc.

Doc's keen on swimming.

As for old Doc, I like him & Tini best after all.

In spite of all I still end with Doc as I began. I cant help liking the silly thick headed old thing. He comes out well in the heat anyway.

This is a dull letter.

I must own mental pursuits collapse this weather

No letter from you since Brisbane, but expect one tomorrow here, or in Townsville day after.

Darling little mum, I hope you are as well as I am. Soon we travel home. I am looking forward inexpressibly to the journey home. We two will be happy, you can imagine.

Farewell so long

Your happy boy
Perks.

256 TO ROSE GRAINGER   Birch's Criterion Hotel,
21.4.1909. morning.   Rockhampton, Q'sland.

We left the "Wyreema" last night at 2 & came up the Fitzroy River to here but [by] a tug-tender, landing at 7.30 this morn.

I slept in my clothes on the Wyreema till 2 & again on the tender till 6.30, & feel fresh as anything. John acted pretty mean last night. I must say I like him much the least of the "push". Tini (since Earle has gone) is an easy 1st, & Doc by a longway the 2nd most swallowable pill.

It was raining hard as we were to board the tender, & Tini, Forsyth, & I all stood ready in the rain to get good berths (berth & a rug) on tender. John, of course, lazying behind.

T, F, & I get good berths. John turns up, never hunts for a berth but calmly jumps Forsyth's. F says "that's my berth, Mr H." John merely says "Cant you find another?" & turns in.

T & I tell him he's jumped F's but he pays no heed. F has to turn in on a hard narrow wooden seat. So I toss F for my comfy berth, but he looses. Then Tini offeres take hard seat, & I toss Tini for it or mine, lose toss & spend the night on the hard one, which suited me down to the ground, than upon which I never wish to sleep better. But fancy being so really greedy about 2d ½ penny things!

Waking at 6.30 I found "Life on the Mississipi" in a drizzling rain all around us. The Fitzroy river is one of the most appealing things I've seen, & the 2 pilots in raincloaks peering out under oil skin hats for steering marks, & the oily snagmarks in the muddy water brought darling M. Twain's beloved Saga-of-the-River men bubbling to my memory. It must take some doing that steering, tho the course is splendidly mapped out by steering marks on land. Down by the bank there'll be a white mark △ & higher up along way back inland there'll be another. ∀ When you've got them both in line ⧄ you're on the right tack.

You keep on that tack till you strike a certain mark that lets you know to pick up the next duett, etc.

The pilots looked Australian, but O so idealized thro their work. How can a man look more sober, answerable, important, worthy, than when grasping a ship's wheel, & with all the meaness gone clean out of his eyes thro peering at faroff things? They pick up the tiny marks finely. I'd often be looking quite a while before I could pick out the white shapes out of the rain haze they were steering by, & I'm not nearsighted.

Lovely greens are in the Q'sland landscapes. Luscious brightcolored thickly growing grasses florish by the river's edges, & mangroves throng with their roots buried in the salt water. Mostly the bushes & small trees are news to the Southern Australian, with just here & there a few gums to let him know it's alright.

Man will soon make this river safe & ugly. It's banks will soon conform to middleclass morals. They are narrowing & straightening the banks so as to throw a fatter bulk of water into midstream & hidious it ought to be when they've done. The native banks are flat, or broken, or crumbling, most desirable, thriving under the picturesque "law of least resistance;" calling up that suggestion of mingled frailness & hardness typical everywhere of truly Australian landscapes, birdcalls, faces, art. (when it comes)

Nature has dealt very flatteringly with some broken hulls of small steamers strewn on the land's edge. The metal has rusted into a lovely ruddy browns, & brilliant green grasses & fresh bushes have roamed nestlingly over decks & gangways.

Man's work has been well redeemed.

But man is for treating the river hardly. Soon it will flow spiritlessly within its straightjacket & there'll be no longer need of skilled pilots with leal distance-scanning eyes. A more beery man will find the easier channell just as well, & the chap-who-wants-to-find-the-sagas-everywhere will have to hunt up a newer river for an older life.

However, I thrilled to see that the river is already heaping sandbanks over the costly straight embankments. The old dear waywardness is not throttled so soon. There is no sign of a tow-path yet, like in the poor Thames, etc.

The "push" only avoided blighting the trip by sleeping hard until the scenery was over. But other fellow-3rd-class men rose greezily to deck & bewailed "lack of *accomidation* for ladies." As usual, however, the womenfolk turned up gay, clean, & fresh looking, while the mere males dawdled about unshaven & unwashed in unspeakable clothes, & obviously thoroly sullen because of lack of "creature comforts."

Big seabirds flew fleetly with slow wings.

Mango trees are one of the blessings of tropical life, sappily green & shady.

From my window flows a lovely sight of leaden river, railway bridge, untidy banks (well wooded) & careless islands. Downstairs is the finest of food (jam omelets) & outside my door is a bath & a real live W.C. with real live soft paper. In the town is also a swimming bath. The "push" sleep snoringly, worn out with sleeping so late this morn.

N. Queensland is far more than it's cracked up to be. Spiffing **really 1st class** Hotels everywhere. How can folk feel slack in these climes? I cant.

22.4.09.

How do you like enclosed photo, taken in Brisbane? I like it a lot [unidentified]

Fine packed house last night. Got 2 letters from you here with great glee. Poor Ted. You are unlucky with him.

Spent a frightful night with bedbugs. And this the cleanest wishable Hotel. Killed about 6, & had to go & spend the night sleeping outside the clothes on Tini's bed. Never mind, they're going to see to it

257   TO KAREN HOLTEN
[Original: English/Danish]
Sunday, evening 2.5.1909

Commercial Hotel,
Tenterfield, (N.S.W.)

I feel so lonely, and a little bit depressed, but quite happy, as always.

The weather is quite cool, and I am sitting here by the side of *the fire*, for the autumn is now in full swing. Apart from all national pride I think that nothing in the world can be fresher and cleaner than the cool weather here at home. The air bitingly fresh like a sharp knife through a pear, even when there is no air movement. A lot of moonlight, and blue-dark, cloudless heavens in the evenings.

But this is a lovely lovely country in its way, for people that are suited to it; who are strong and elementary enough for it.

How delightful it is to get into the lovely cool weather again, just as charming as it is to get to the tropics again after a long stay in Northern Europe. But the cool weather brings sadness with it. Mother noticed that in N.Z. She said: "In the heat one doesn't seem to be able to be depressed. In all the years when I had such awful worries when you were a boy I never could feel depressed in the Australian warmth; & now again, hate this tour though I do, I may be angry or annoyed or desperate, but not just *depressed*. Now here in N.Z. where I am with you, & everything joyous, I can feel momentary touches of lowspirits in the cooler weather."

That is really true. On this trip, together with tedious people, with unpleasant business worries, away from mother and you and my friends, I have not really felt depressed or sentimental as I do this evening. You will surely have noticed that my letters to you from the English tour, for example, were much more sensitive, warmer, more heartfelt than those from here at home, aren't they? There is something intimate, boring-in, enveloping in one's whole attitude, bodily and spiritually, in the cold. One longs to creep into the fortresses of one's soul. In the heat, then things swell outwardly, one longs for public pleasures, for all the good that lies invitingly on all sides. One needs love, art, friendship not nearly so much in a climate like Australia's.

Much Italian art, too, (& no doubt their sexual keenness & activity also) is more an *expression of sunripened richness & fullblown strength*, of youth & sunlit livliness than a swimming about in sheltering moods, ideals, spiritual comfortings such as the cold climate men use in their art & their love.

I, of course, am a mixture. I almost need both contrasts. I could hardly have stayed much longer happily in England a year ago. I felt a great need to see the old hot places again & hear the silly Australian speech, & bask in the holy pure virgin landscapes. Now I have seen it. Now I must soon do without it again.

A thousand things, a thousand times nicer, draw me to Europe. Intensivity, lechery, tenderness, sweetness (as they exist in you) nobility truth faithfulness (as they exist in Roger and Cyril) deeply moving sweetness and innocence, as they exist in Gouldthorpe and my folk-singers, thousand thousand indescribably loved lovable things draw me, but here in this hard, in part worthless country lies youth for me. If you have found my letters cold and empty from here, it is because this country makes me a boy again. Something in the life here wipes out achievement, memory, & importance. I cant keep myself from tumbling about & doing monkey tricks ½ the time. Just to overeat, & run a mile, & make someone laugh at me & call me mad, makes my heart beat, & my whole silly being throb with refreshing pleasure. I feel like a young boy who hasn't done a thing in the world yet, and will very soon begin to show whether he has the stuff in him, or not.

I hope when I get back to Lond I shall face the world as anew, as for the first time; with but little remembrance of how hard, distressing, & bemiserabling my few (really awfully easy to anyone less *selfish*, thinskinned, & soft than I) moneyearning years have already been.

All I say is, thank & bloody well thank the Lord for this Godforgotten tour, never will I hope to forget the relief the holiday & the ½ heaven of it.

Some few things have become clearer to me in the last few years.

I have grown more *resigned*. (keep it a secret!)

Kipling's worsening as a writer, Griegs death, your father's death, Swinbourne's death, these things have all made some imprint on me, though one might not think so.

I am not a *disappointed person*. I have never hoped strongly enough for that! But I am an only ½ heartedly hopeful person. What now follows is not only sentimentality derived from the cooler weather, although the fire has possibly something to do with my sitting down to write it to you:

I am really one of the saddest types that exists in the world. For I see carefully & digest fully in quiet so many different kinds of griefs. When Grieg died I could not have gone to Mrs Grieg, she probably would have thought me cold. I might have seemed cold to you at your father's death too. Sudden grief, tragic grief, warm tearful sorrow is for me impossible because I live with it so solidly. Do you think I had not thought over well the thought of Grieg's & your father's deaths long before they happened? I live daily with such thoughts. I wonder if many folks are so foolish as to live so much in imaginary ½ communion with dear dead souls as I cant help doing? My inner life is one long longing for the wholly lost dead, the never to be met with & unrecoverable priceless army of unmet friends that art & history tease & distress such folk as me with. What man that I have met or ever shall meet could be more to me than poor darling great Saxon King Alfred? Think of Swinbourne dead![25] A man that lived & felt sexual

25 Swinburne had died at Putney on 10 April 1909. On 12 March 1908 Grainger had written to Karen of Swinburne's *Poems and Ballads*, first series, "I think there is a great deal in Swinbourne that could please you to read. It fills me with ecstasy right up to my hair roots. Apart from whether he understands the deeper 'heart-love' or not, I think he is in any case divine in his understanding of carnal love. His golden value lies more in being a *mad specialist* than a *sane cosmist* (cosmic) thus he is rather a charming talent than a gratifying genius; but good luck to him anyway. In sexual things it's seemingly woman's part to exaggerate *loving results* & man's to exaggerate *barren joys*. Swinbourne's limitation is an over*male*ness; but just for that reason he understands how to express the male sex's feelings and sensations in the very closest way. In my worthless opinion no poet has ever lived with a more unbeatable word and rhyme technique. It flows like my music *should*". Grainger consistently spells "Swinburne" as "Swinbourne".

ecstacy even while I myself am alive & I now powerless to tell him how I love him for his work & how I inwardly clasp hands with him time & again. & Wagner & Bach & them all. What hope? Folk talk of the grief for a dead lover. What is such a life as mine but one gigantic mourning for hosts of dead lovers, each not one less intensely & personally adored because he is one of many many. And Herman, is he not dead to me? Could death make more absolute a sundering of our olden particular oneness?

And where, *as yet*, there is no death, no cutting of friendship, is not the case equally the same? Where is the Cyril, & where the work of Cyril, of Frankfort? Where is my own dead self & my work & enthusiasms & my old points of view? Quite dead, but never forgotten. That is why I am sad. I remember such a very great deal. My child dreams in Australia, my boy dreams in Germany, my young man's plans in early London; I cant forget any of them thoroly & each one that fails of fulfilment (& only 1 in 100 can fail to fail) will have a black mark against it in my painstaking hardworking memory.

Few folk have so little calamity happen to them as I, & few can afford to digest *inner* soulsorrow more soundly than I. Most men of my talents have more "push" or yearning for activity & *realization* than I. Wagner with his schemes, his wars, his whole forcefulness was an army continually on the move. Beethoven too with his dispair & bubbling joyeousness had not the calm for clear cold *onlooking* sadness that I have. Men who have died young like Keats, Schubert, A. Beardsley, Dowson seem often to have been as publicly inactive as I.[26]

But I dont intend to die long.

Grieg even, felt much more simply & directly & undoubtingly than I. He had the comfort of a religious mind, or of a mind kindred to the religious mind. And even Bach, maybe, was religious, quite apart from his outward Prostestantishness. But I have no such comfort, nor even the solace of a fierce active convinced atheism.

On the other hand I am not unsentimental & robustly real & brainily busy like Jews or Bernard Shaw.

Though I'm all for *absolute knowledge*, science, as a *duty*, I am at bottom very sentimental, sensuous, & sensation loving. Pure knowledge, real facts dont satisfy me deeply & I turn ever freshly to feelings, sensations, imaginings, sensualnesses for my real soulnourishment, only never failing, with my active & not stupid brain, to realise the destructiveness, & thence grief, that lies in all actions, realisations.

My manifold amateurish interests lead me to myriads of graves that other fellow talents never tread. The whole being of folk art is closely akin to all manner of racial & artistic burials. Dead ideas, words, myths, plots, occupations flit about th[r]o the dying rhymes. And folksingers too; in them I'm hoarding me up a wealth of dead friends soon to go. All the languages I potter about with are hornets nests of new births & old deaths, passing away & coming forward, full of wistful suggestions to the loving & sympathetic mind. I always see both sides. I grieve with the Irish for what griefs the English saddled them with & I mourn with the English for all the trouble the silly Irish must have been to them. Someone always wins, in all rows. Then I have at least one side to sigh for. I cant stop them fighting & rowing. Others are not like me; they will insist on acting handling, quickly too, & without care. And I love them for the very foolish pluck that I myself lack.

Few folk are so little *gamblers* as I. (A man like Wagner that will undertake all kinds of big schemes, & have wordy wars, & even take part in political disturbances is indeed a gambler.) I lack the drunken upliftedness that kicks a gambler forward bucking thro his life. My brain is cold, calmseeing, & refuses to be warmed, either by artistic schemes or sexual enticements. Thus because my brain does not see wisdom in marriage for me, it wont warm up & give its consent. My body, my feelings, may be ever

26 John Keats (1795–1821), Franz Peter Schubert (1797–1828), Aubrey Vincent Beardsley (1872–98), Ernest Christopher Dowson (1867–1900).

so seething, my old mind sticks to the helm. All this gives me huge chances for observantly noting sorrow & quiet grief. Driven to no hot unwithstandable deeds of my own, I look round & see all the strange things that "happen under the sun" to my dear loved fellow beings, & am amazed, sympathetic, grieved, & helpless. Occasionally, however, I can do my small work of salvage, & embalmment of just dead art-corpses. And herein I find real joy, & seem to see genuine use. Dead King Alfred's saying occurs to me, something to the following effect:

"Dying as we all do, nought is better than to leave records of good work done, to bequeath to followers, after our death."

My own compositions I undertake largely as a kind of artistic life insurance against my coming death. Let there be no records wanting, I say, of any folk, language, song, history, not even of myself; or perhaps; least of all of myself.

Do you know R.L. Stevenson's lovely poem?[27]

27 The verses are freely remembered from part XV of Robert Louis Stevenson's *Songs of Travel* (first published in the *Edinburgh Edition* of Stevenson's works, 1895, and issued as a separate volume, entitled *Songs of Travel and Other Verses*, 1896).

(1)   Bright is the ring of words when the right man rings them,
Fair is the fall of songs when the singer sings them,
Still are they wafted & sung, on wings they are carried
After the singer is dead & the maker buried.

---

(2)   Low as the singer lies in the field of heather
Songs of his fashion draw the swains together.
And while the west is red with the sunset embers,
The lover lingers & sings, & the maid remembers.

Sorrow is fine & productive for me. Fear of death & loss, destruction & forgottenness spur me to compose, collect, preserve & embalm. May I live long & not accomplish all too little! Not for my own silly sake, but because there is so much awaiting doing, & my heart really feels loving & feelingly & there ought to be some record of it. Also there must be someone to sit mourningly & hold the cold hands of dead races, men, & languages, lost battles & failed enterprizes.

Also "Grettir" must have a leal friend. And he has.

But I will never forget that you in Lond in the beginning, really thought that I should not let happiness pass by. That was sweet of you. You have really come and offered me the happiness that I longed for most. Thanks.

Lithgow. N.S.W. 10.5.09. Monday midnight

Herewith 2 pages of the previous letter that I omitted to put in the envelope.

This afternoon I finished the necklace.

Saturday night I worked from 11 to 5.30 in the morning, and the next night (last night) to 3. One more letter I will write to you before we leave. Goodnight, sweet.

Next letter P.R.

258 TO ROSE GRAINGER   Commercial Hotel,
Tuesday. 4.5.1909   Tenterfield, NSW
midnight 1.30.

Had such a gaudy day yest.

We had wrestling on a green.

Doc & I had 3 rounds, all of which he won, & I won 2 off Tini. It was so fearfully enjoyable.

Look at the enclosed card that went with a little bunchlet of flowers a tiny girl gave me at railway station tonight

| Tonight | iaften |
| last night | iaftes |

this morn	imorges
tomorrow	imorgen
this year	iaar
last "	ifjor

Theres no doubt that wrestling's a darling sport. Once we thumped down on top of each other his weight right on my chest, & my wind arrangements felt awfully funny inside for a sec.

I should like to wrestle daily.

I get such a growing wealth of letters from you as I near you gradually, its so lovely And they in such ever bettering Danish.

There was a nice old Swede barber (Martin – for Marten) in Tenterfield. Born in N. York, a common sailor, he has a family of 12, one a solicitor, & another head clerk in a big American bank, & all his daughters "married to Englishmen not Australians."

Very lovingly
Perks.

259   TO ROSE GRAINGER   Edye's Royal Hotel,
[Original: Danish/English/some German]   Orange, N.S.W.
11.5.1909.

My sweet comrade and little mother

Herewith I enclose a letter to you from J. Harrison's wife.

Today I have read through your last 14 letters and postcards, to see that I don't forget any instructions at all. In them I have noticed the following words, which you apparently don't know, or know correctly, in Danish

count = tælle   (I counted the letters)
                         (Jeg tællede brevene)

hunger = sult   (I'm hungry   Jeg er sulten
                         he had hunger. Han havde sult)

enclose = indlægge   (the enclosed. Det indlagte)

sad = trist   (sad in her mind = trist i sinden
                         mørk i sind means dark ⟦sinister⟧
                         in her mind)

boxes = kuffer*   (in my boxes = i kufferne)

kindness (Germ güte) = godhed, elskværdighed
(that was kind of you. Det var elskværdig af Dem
His kindness was great. Hans godhed var stor)

I have fortunately not got any bugs at all in my luggage here in Rockhampton.

I wanted to **give** de Rego (the critic in Sydney) my Folksong Journal.[28] I saw him in Sydney. I told him if the journal you sent was written in he should return, if not to keep it.

The boys saw your cabin (din køj) on Seidlitz & say you have it alone, & it's a jolly one for 3.

28 George de Cairos Rego, music critic of the *Daily Telegraph*, Sydney.

*Grainger himself is in error here. Boxes should be kufferter; "in my boxes" should be "i kufferterne". *Transl.*

If you can buy Swinbourne's **First** book of "Poems & Ballads" (or Ballads & Poems?) cheaply I think it would be very amusing to read on the ship. What do you think?

With regard to U.S.A. and Wilfred's letter: I would *very much like* to go to America and am happily prepared to work with you to this purpose

Yes, about Neuberger. I think he is worth the £5. Even if he wanted to actually steal something from me I would not hold anything against him. I don't **love** him, for one cannot really love without trust, but what he says is so sound and clever and good that I can't possibly have anything against him. He tells wonderful cock & bull yarns, about Anti-nihilists following him about, not allowing him to go over to Adelaide, etc. I dont just believe them, but perhaps they are true. It is quite unimportant to me. One likes reading a detective story altho one doesnt have a feeling of reality the while. Well, when N tells me his cock & bull yarns I *have* a most delightful *sensation* of reality even if my mind wont quite take such wild water. *Nothing, however, short of bodily violence would make me lend him more money*; not because I mind his having it, or mind being "had," (I dont care a curse: I've no pride in self defence) but simply because I need the mon for oth purps. You write; "many worthless folk are seemingly fascinating." I doubt it. No man is really "worthless" who has corageous thoughts & a sweetly working true brain, even if he does nothing with it or even is a fraud, or a thief. The owning of good qualities, even if unused, is always the reverse of "worthless".* We admire good looks, if we are really honest, fairly apart from the human qualities they stand for. We admire bodily strength in an individual who we never expect will be able to actually make use of it, or need it. We admire motherliness in old maids, brutality in tender artist natures, & childishness in grown folk, & braininess in children. Therefor also I claim reasonableness in admiring nobility in a fraud & the wellsprings of truth in a liar. Mind you I'm not supposing N lies or frauds. But if he did?

Surely there is more truth in seeing the big impersonal things of this world with a clearness calling for great grip of mind & head-eye & corage but lying for personal advantage, than in being truthful over personal things & never having the mental vision to really ever grasp a big truth or have the mental energy to throb over an abstract issue. What if one had met J. Jørgensen in his European Continental frauding trip?

Assume N has frauded (in other [words] stolen from) me my £5. He has still harmed my inner self less than the honest mental sloths whose blind opinions turn day into night around one. He has at least not depressed me. Folk reason: "N sins worse because of having a finer head; his moral responsibility is therefor greater". Balls! Results are better than morals.

N was consumptive & has wrenched himself above the grave thro sheer moral energy, medical knowledge, & love of life. (So he says, anyway) Other excellent folk are throwing away inherited health by taking stupid risks, & quickly decaying thro laziness & general lukeness.

I'll tell you his cock & bull yarns when we meet. In the meantime, be sure of no further loans, but that his company (on my one more day in Sydney) will be behappying me & enlithing my willing (tho fairly dense, be it owned) little mind.

My dear little mother is frightened of my "uncanny" leanings. Perhaps you are right, clever little friend. But I don't think so. Especially, sexual things one doesn't do out of *cleverness* (not me anyway).

If the musical world knew my thoughts on music I'd soon earn no money. If London folk knew my . . . [page torn]

. . . Openness & secrecy are both needful to purity.

Music one does for the art of music

Society one traffics for the needs of the world

Sexual undertakings one does for ones own personal pleasure, & that of those taking part.

Care & caution & complete control are all that one can go for. One cant **intend** not to try & get what one very keenly desires.

I shall only desist from *desiring* a thing if my own moral sense positively prevents my *wanting* it any more. If my moral sense doesnt stop my doing what I consider a fairly bad thing I shall still intend to do it. As it happens I'm not likely to do any harm ever to anyone.

I'm not at all *callous* (which is the fountain of all evildoing & crime) & I'm not at all *riskready* (the father of detection) & I'm very keen on observing other folks feelings & how things act on them. (therefor, being also kind & medfølsom [Danish: sympathetic], I'm never likely to cause folk suffering) . . . [page torn]

. . . as you have advised me to write & shall see in Melb all folk I can.

Doc has seemingly dealt very fairly with me of late. Some new bills that have been printed have my name in bigger type than the rest, & elsewhere I have a deep[?] or other color. 2nd on each part of program has been stuck to throout, & tho I offered to forego salary for a Brisbane concert that had a wretched attendance he wouldnt accept my offer but paid full.

I've got off tons of local letters today & my hand is fairly stiff.

Beloved one goodbye
Percy

I saw Ilott [unidentified] in Sydney.

Useless, maybe, but not *worth*less.

260 TO ROSE GRAINGER   Edye's Royal Hotel,
11.5.1909 Tuesday.   Orange, N.S.W.

[BEADWORK LETTER]

Yesterday I posted my dear darling mum the beadwork necklace I have made for her. You will get it with the same post as this letter, if not earlier; I hope.

When in Sydney on way North to Brisbane 6 weeks ago I could not refrain from buying some lovely S'African work, amongst which is a belt of which the actual collar

of my work is a near copy. Being a belt it is heavier, & slightly broader than my necklace, & O, so much less ugly. Before I show you the nigger original you must promise to take one last look at my copy first, as you will never care to behold mine afterwards. To begin with, the original is so wondrously much better done, flatter & smooth, & the colors a treat, chalky & unseethroable & glowing, not glassy, flashy, & thin in tone like the only ones I could get.

I bought my beads from a wholesale bead merchant in Sydney after much racing round, but I believe I could have got something better had I had more time to traipse round & see the wholesale houses. There is also a *very slight* unevenness of size between the different colors of my beads. Thus the white is a tiny wee bit smaller than all the other colors, & the red a wee bit bigger I think. There are faint signs of buckling wherever the red occurs.

I am not so displeased with the actual collar part, but the streamers hanging below are a bitter disappointment to me. It is a S'African dodge to hang streamers from necklaces, but generally they do so in a *bunch* from the centre meeting place of necklace; thus:

The clawlike ends to my attempt are quite S'African also, as are all endings-off in knots in the strings.

A very weak point in my streamers is not only the pattern (worked up from a mingling of the collar pattern & Polynesian patterns on the Kanaka armbands I bought off Dyricksen, the Dane, in Bundaberg Q'sland) but the silly weak way I've carried it out. My zigzags are far too flat, like:

Instead of being bold & striking in angle, like:

Even the sketch-trail I made (in Q'sland) first is less bad. Alas!

The one sunny manner about the streamers is that they are put on to the collar in such a way that the severing of two t[h]reads (those ending in a yellow & a white fat bead at bottom of collar,

will sunder them from the collar without scathing or weakening either in any way. So that we could keep the collar without the streamers at all, or make another set, or sets, of streamers & change them at will. Maybe a simple bunchy set like that at top of page (in red, blue, & white) might serve. One bad error in the streamer pattern is that the whites are too fat & the diamonds too small in the part where the collar pattern is aped. Thus it is like

instead of being more like

Tiresome how the middleclass European (& particularly Teutonic) tasteless shamloving mind ran riot with me whenever practical points councelled me to swerve off exactly copying the original. Whereever (without a miss) I have done any little minor point on my own, it has been hopelessly European, squat, flat, & proxaic; & very *sham*, too. The whole work, in any case, only looks well (if at all) on the bare body. Over clothes it is hopeless. Nevertheless, a belt like the collar part would look well, dont you think?

The only atoning side of the gift is the wild amount of work I put in upon it. I started it in Sydney about March 23, & since then (barring the few days I gave up to scoring the English Dance on S.S. "Bingera" steaming up to Townsville from Brisbane April 8–11) have done about 6 to 8 hours daily upon it, barring a few concert days in Sydney & Brisbane. Many many days I did far more.

The work is not straight up & down on cross strands

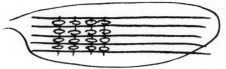

like the Polynesian system, but is in continuous diamond buildings-up,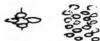

Thus you can never get a straight up & down line in this work, such as;

is [sic it] always has to be:

But its much more econimic for all diamond patterns

But it is at least more than *double as slow* as the Polynesian way, to my reckoning. I used two needles at once, knotting the two strings together above *every bead*

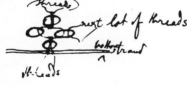

But not all the colored beads, & not ½ of the white beads would allow the 2 needles & threads through. So I had to test each of the thousands of beads seperately with a bigger needle. The streamers are strung without a needle, threading with the beeswaxed end of the thread itself. One streamer takes about 20 minutes, at quick work.

Whenever we were in the train I worked. I tied up string supports to the windows, shutters, racks, seat buttons, ceiling lamp supports, etc & strung up the work & collected vast crowds at railways stations. One day a man in an alongside train shouted to his mates. "There's a chap in there with a cobweb." Since then it's been known as "the cobweb." Ernest Toy was taken with the work in Brisbane (he likes doing fancywork) & took a copy of the method & pattern.[29] I started on the end of the collar without the little yellow & by Charters Towers (April 14) had got to central red diamond.

I worked faster after that & got the inner part of collar (all except the red rims) done at Rockhampton (Friday Apr. 28?) & the red rims at Bundaberg, Sunday April 25. There I started experimenting sketches for the streamers, which took some time, the actual final set being begun at Warwick Sat (May 1) or Sund. (2nd) & ended yesterday (Lithgow, Monday, May 10) afternoon.

Big towns for work were Toowoomba, Brisbane, Charters Towers, Rockhampton, Bundaberg, Maryboro, Warwick, Tenterfield. I'd get called at 6 & get in a few hours before breakfast, work all day if poss, & often again after concert till midnight. At Tenterfield I beaded from 7 to 5 (with 5 minutes a meal rest) & in the train the same evening from 6.30 to 1.15 midnight. On board the "Wyreema" (Townsville to Rockhampton, April

29 Australian violinist Ernest Toy had been residing in Brisbane for the preceding two years. In April 1909 he had just returned from a concert tour of New Zealand.

19–21) was also a big period. It was melting hot, & I beaded all day in my Cabin without a stitch of clothing on trying to race my last speed. (for the pattern) The pattern, that is, one red & one black row, first took me 42 minutes with great effort. But but [sic by] working so that my eyes fairly bulged out my head & I finished each round streaming with sweat, I brought the record down 1st to 40, then 38, 35, & finally to 30 minutes. I never wish better sport than this selfracing. I spent a really wildly exciting & rousing day there by my little naked self in that "Wyreema" cabin, with now & then a glimpse of the lovely Q'sland coast.

But my most desperate bout was surely these last days in Sydney. After Sat's concert (May 8th) I worked hard beading till 5.30 next morn, slept till 8, & at it again all that day, the evening at J.C.W's & again at it when I got home from 12 (midnight) to after 2 o'clock.

Neuberger kept me company in my room from after the concert to 2 o'clock when he caved in & homed.

I enjoyed myself thoroly with a nice warm towel round my neck, a fine strong electric light over my work, & goodly chunks of bread butter & cheeze to sustain the perkiness of Perks.

Ada was always awfully nice about it. While Doc & the boys carded & besmoked the air in the "push's" compart, she let me work in her compart, even that night from 6.30 to 1.15, quietly & happily.

Lovely blithe hours the necklace has cost me. Glowing on balconies in the nice hot air & sun (with brown paper sun screens rigged up behind the beads to stop glare for my eyes) or jogging along in jolly trains, making pot shots at threading needles & beads, with folk sitting upon or overturning my beadboxes.

Thick fishing line forms the upper & lower strands. Thin fishingline, used whole, is the thread inside the streamers, & the same thin line, unwound into its 3 original thinnesses. (fishingline is formed of 3 very thin — tho thicker & stronger than thick cotton or thread — lines wound tightly together)

This unwinding, & the testing of the beads alone took a terrible time.

But my worst worry were my letters to you. Haven't you wondered at their wondrous emptiness & general blankness, & also scantiness? What shall a body have to say who hasnt even found time to shave because of an activity that must be kept a secret? My joy in the beadworking & having to keep it a secret from you was real moral torture for me, I can assure you, lovey darling. Had I known I would turn out such a slowcoach at the work I wouldnt have kept it a secret, but I reckoned to be thro by about end of April, & to be able to send you my little worklet as a solace & excitement, while far north in Q'sland. However, no such luck. I only hope it will reach you before I myself get to Adelaide.

I have ever had fond loving & happy thoughts of my adored mum while beading, & the work goes to you warm (not very warm you will say) with my love; also reeking with tobacco stink (I fear) from the tins that the boys lent me to put my beads in. But I dont think beading would really suit *you*!

Sat. Melb. at Dr Russell's
I shant have much chance of seeing many friends, as Dr Russell's motor car is not available. But I'll do best I can.

Do [not] mind if I look a bit fagged when I arrive as I've spend [sic] every night in train since Sunday. But I feel fine.

All my heavy lugg is on Seidlitz in Sydney. I've only my 2 light trunks with me.

Fond love

261 TO KAREN HOLTEN   The "Royal." [Hotel]
[Original: Danish/some English]   Bathurst, N.S.W.
12.5.1909. Wednesday.

My joy and sweetness.

Oh, it is charming here, frost on the ground and life in the air, a refreshing contrast after the (just as lovely) heat of the north.

And on Sunday I am in Adelaide, and the following Sunday (23rd May)
we sail.

The necklace is finished, was finished on Monday afternoon, but not
without much work and haste. Saturday evening we had a concert in
Sydney, Monday morning early we took the train to Lithgow (NSW) After
Saturday's concert I worked to 5.30 o'cl the next morning, slept to 8 o'cl,
up again and worked till the evening, when we had to go out to J.C.W's,
worked from 12 o'cl (midnight) till between 2 and 3, and the next day in
the train.

Monday night I was in the train from 12 o'cl to 4.30, and last night I
was in the train from 10 o'cl to 12. (midn) Tonight we will spend the whole
night in the train, and tomorrow night we travel to Melb, and Saturday
night to Adelaide. But I still feel absolutely fresh.

When I get time I will paint how the necklace looks for you. It has got
awfully ugly, unfortunately.

On the journey home I intend to arrange E. Dance for 2 pianos, with
string parts performed by 8 strings, and write out "In Dahomey" for
Rathbone. Tonight is our last concert.

Sometimes I get quite cross when I think how empty and insignificant my
letters to you are. That is to say, they are not so *without* meaning, but they
lie so unmercifully. B. Shaw would no doubt say that they indicate that I
am a "debauched sexual voluptuary", but that is not the whole truth. The
remarkable thing is that I am not at all afraid of writing or speaking in
detail about sexual things or bodily lewd sensations, but am surprisingly
shy of describing real "feelings".

But I am not quite without feelings, although one could easily think so.

I can't bring myself to say something like "waves of feeling swept over
me" but that would all the same be nearer the truth than my usual way
of writing. I feel very seldom, but mostly feel myself cool and sober, but
when I feel then it is something quite surprising, quite unexpected, and a
little like a child when he surrenders himself to crying.

I am indeed basically very sentimental and "suseptable", but this is
overgrown by caution shyness and watery soberness.

I write this to you, because I don't think it is fair to you that you should
think I am *always* as cool as my letters sound.

I have actually spontaneous unschooled warm feelings for you, little
comforter, often, but they get so seldom written down because I am
ashamed really, when it comes to the point.

[Don't make a mistake! *My feelings* being sometimes warm, wont (I
hope) get in the road of my *acting* cold. I hope **always** to act cool,
unfeelingly, cautiously & soberly.]

Adelaide, South Australia. Thursday. 20.5.09

It has been a lovely week. In Melbourne I got together with Prof Spencer, who knows most about the native Australian "Blacks", and who let
me hear his (well-recorded) phonograph records of their songs, 3 of which
I wrote down for him.[30] The melodies are much less primitive, and more
melodic than I had expected from stupid remarks in music histories. I hope
he will send me several records to England. No one has written them down
before, although the records were taken many years ago.

I also got to see many drawings of Norman Lindsey's at Spencer's (who

30 Walter (later Sir Walter)
Baldwin Spencer (1860–1929),
biologist and ethnographer,
professor of biology at the
University of Melbourne from
1887 to 1919. In collaboration
with F. J. Gillen (1855–1912) and
afterwards alone, he brought to
light the unknown world of the
Aboriginal people of Central
Australia. The three Aranda songs
Grainger transcribed were the first
Australian Aboriginal songs ever
to be recorded. Two of his
transcriptions, from phonograph
recordings made by Baldwin
Spencer on 22 March 1901 in the
Southern Aranda district,
Stevenson Creek, South Australia,
appear as an Appendix in Spencer
and Gillen's *Across Australia* (2
vols., London 1912). The notation
in the published form differs from
Grainger's manuscript. It is likely
that the transcriptions were
published without his knowledge.

298

31 Norman Alfred William
Lindsay (1879–1969), pen-
draughtsman, etcher, painter and
writer, the most celebrated
Australian black-and-white
illustrator of his time.

32 George Meredith died at Box
Hill (Surrey) on 18 May 1909.
Grainger was also sympathetic to
the women's movement. On 14
June 1910, the day the Woman
Suffrage Bill (the "Conciliation
Bill") was introduced into the
British House of Commons, he
wrote to the Prime Minister
enclosing a memorial of support
signed by leading musicians.

[Spencer] is a lovely Englishman) who collects his originals already.[31] N.L. is only 27, is a Victorian and he and I are doubtless the 2 most important artistic personalities of Australia. His art is typically sexual in its inspiration, a little coarse perhaps, but fine and excellent in execution, and above all just as healthily fresh and forceful as my own; and just as full of "joy of life" as the Rarotongan songs.

He works like Jøtul [the smith of the gods], and has done good work in the whole of the last 10 years, they say.

All his good things, that I have seen, are black and white in which medium he could really be one of the most outstanding in the world.

You will no doubt have seen that Meredith has died. He was warmly on the side of the women's movement.[32]

We were 2 days in Richmond Park. I rode twice on a lovely pony, yesterday and the day before. The first time it went very well. The saddle was very comfortable, and everything went satisfactorily, walking, trotting, cantering; but the next day was not nearly as good. The saddle was uncomfortable, and I had no feeling of security, and the horse also noticed it quickly and was not as quiet as the day before. Once he almost wanted to "run away", but fortunately I stopped him quickly, and thereafter rode very slowly home. I am very cowardly when I scent danger, and have absolutely no courage in regard to horses. The whole thing felt just the same as it did when I last rode (when I was 11 years old) on this pony's father, the years don't seem to have made the least difference to the feeling. I will try and ride in Svinkløv, next time. We can ride together. But still more amusing were 2 football games we had there in Richmond. My uncle Jim, (nearly 60 years, but the most active of them all) my 3 boy-cousin[s] (21 to 26), 2 boys, my auntie Sarah, and my 2 girl-cousins Babs and Violet. On Tuesday we played Rugby and on Wednesday Association, once I was dressed in pyjamas and once in Violet's bathing costume.

Despite my relatives being always in the open air and used to daily great bodily exertions, they got more quickly tired than I, and got more stiff in their muscles than I did, who am not even really stiff after riding.

Tomorrow we go on the ship (Seydlitz) The next letter you receive from me will be from Naples or Genoa, and will presumably reach you a week later than this one here, or quicker. Already before you get this we are probably in Europe again.

In Dahomey is ready to be written down on the ship, where I will also arrange E D for 2 pianos. Perhaps I will do some more beads during the journey. Mother is very happy for the necklace, of which I send you a sketch herewith [pictured, left].

The hanging parts of it (streamers) look prettier in the sketch than they do in reality.

In Sydney I got several beautiful South African native belts (beadwork) etc from an old Scotsman, and I also bought 2 lovely belts (for 30/–) also South African.

I really have already a considerable collection of Polynesian and African work.

Mallinson (song composer) shares the cabin with me.[33] He is married to a Danish girl and talks the language very well. That's amusing for me. Mother has made really good progress in Danish.

Please give my very warm love to all your family, sweetest little darling.

I am longing for letters in Colombo, Port Said, Naples. Don't write to London till I say "go".

262   TO ROSE GRAINGER
Sunday 16.5.09.

Hotel Wentworth
Sydney
[Melbourne]

I got Dr Russell to fix up that I heard Prof Spencer's phonograph records Friday evening, & we spent an unforgettable time there, (at Spencers.) Spencer is one of those ultrarefined calm just Englishmen whom a wife & 2 grownup daughters cannot turn from being a delightful batchelor & who is too niceminded to be properly conscious of the commonness of the Colonies &, appreciating their wide future, soon loves them better than the old country. Such a man is a haven for every tender, or great artistic sprouting. He has long been a friend & keen admirer of Streeton & is now buying in a glorious collection of Gordon Lindsey's [Norman Lindsay] pen & inks & washes.

It is of Gordon Lindsey that I want to write you. Streeton a year ago showed me some of his stuff in Lon & I at once woke up to it rather.[34]

It is useless for me to guess at his technical worth as a painter, or worth *to* a painter, als fach mensch [German: as a professional]. But Streeton said he is *absolutely firstclass*. So I would think also. I am bothering only about his emotional value, his national typicalness, which, to my mind, makes him & me (as far as my knowledge goes) the only 2 lastworthy artistic voices of Australia, so far. Both Victorians.

That G.L. might one day loom like A. Beardsley, in his own O so different way, would not surprise me, though, not being a painter, it would be shallow of me to foresee it.

He is above all an overflowing exultant sexualist. I can recall nothing striking of his that is not very overweighingly sexual & fleshy. He loves nature's victories. His art is one long approving chuckle at nature gaining her sweet terrible way.

It is not the purity or upliftedness of sex that he voices, but rather a healthy rankness; his Scotchness therein coming well to the fore. If the whore & the roué inspired Beardsley it is the fast Australian girl & the larikin that sends G L to laughing victory.

His men, his rude lovers, are all larrikin faced, & his girl & women folk are leggy, limby, & plump as they're grown here. But he makes them attractive alright.

His art would fit far easier in die Jugend or foreign publications than in English.[35] He revels in urwüchsig [German: primitive] themes, stoneage men smashing each other up, Amazons fleeing, & the "old gods" of Greece & Swinbourne are ever playing their wicked wanton lovely tricks over his paper. The "joy of life" lives here as surely at home as in the Rarotongan partsinging. His & my art form surely a convincing warant for Australia's healthiness! Not a hint of weakness, morbidness, lifetiredness in his work anywhere, but exultant, rank, eager, exstatic; common & game & sure & greedy.

But tho his way is rank his steps are exact & nice. He does luxurious leafage (like his humanity, so flourish also his trees & landscapes in luscious overwealth) with tender true technic, & can be delightfully economic & frugal in his methods. He has a face like a street brawler, but Spencer says

33 Albert Mallinson (1870–1946), English organist and composer, best known for his songs, of which he wrote over three hundred. He died at Elsinore, Denmark.

34 Arthur (later Sir Arthur) Ernest Streeton (1867–1943), Australian landscape painter. He had married while in London in 1908. No other details survive of the meeting.

35 *Die Jugend*, a mainly satirical weekly published in Munich by Georg Hirth, appeared from 1896 to 1940. It was an organ for young writers and artists and gave its name to the German style of art nouveau, "Jugendstil". Illustrations by young artists were a particular feature. In August 1908 Grainger had written to Karen Holten of his enthusiasm for coloured German "Sex magazines" such as *Simplicissimus, Die Jugend* and *Lustige Blätter*.

he is a dear thing, hard working & simple, & 27, (has done spiffing work for 10 years — like me) & healthy & robust as his work.

What lies stand in the Musical Histories re Australian native music, that it moves over a few notes only & is mere repetitions of primitive phrases; not at all! Generally *over* an octave in compass, a tune is often made up of 4 or 5 distinct phrases, & is *no less complex* than many European tunes.

I took down 3 interesting tunes which you will hear.

Spencer's records are *excellently* taken. He says the Inland blacks are wholly harmless to nice sensible whites.

He & they chummed grandly. No wonder. Such a man would find few races hostile.

263   TO ERNEST THESIGER   S S Seydlitz
22.6.09.   Italian Coast.

Darling Ernest

We return, full of fitness, after a charming trip, to dear England & our beloved friends, June 29.

I'm bringing back some native beadwork that I adore, & precious records of lots of various native musics.

I've done heaps of scoring & other work on board, finished the English Dance, written out "In Dahomey", etc, & shortened & generally edited dear Cyril's jolly old piano Sonata, which I want you to hear in its new form.

Such lots to tell you dear friend, & longing to hear your news & see your work

Fond love from us both to you & your kin

Ever very yours
Percy.

The Graingers were back at their Kings Road, London, house by 29 June, after an absence of some ten months. Percy began re-establishing himself with pupils and friends and socialising in the way that characterised his London life during the "Season".

Much as Grainger had enjoyed the Australasian tour for its opportunities for spiritual and physical renewal, it had not, at least according to Rose, been a success from a career point of view. Although she resolutely informed friends and the press of Grainger's successes (and there were successes), she regarded the whole tour as a bad mistake. The basic problem had arisen from Grainger's role as an assisting artist. Accordingly, a decision was taken which had profound and immediate consequences for his career.

Rose wrote on 25 October 1908, "I wouldn't accept any more assisting engagements if I were you — more money is to be made on your own". With this decision taken, it followed inevitably that Grainger would have to seek to extend his field of activity. To sustain himself as a soloist he had to travel more. Enterprise had won over caution: he was to take a risk.

Another decision emerging from the Australasian tour was to have important consequences, though more in the long term. This decision flowed from Rose's pleadings that he should allow his compositions to be played, not just in private, but in public. Acceding to her request in March 1909, Grainger outlined a programme of "rehearsals" of several of his compositions: such rehearsals became a feature of his activities over the next years. More importantly, perhaps, he allowed Delius to include two of his choral works in the first festival of the Musical League in September 1909.

At a personal level, Rose had urged Percy towards a softening of his attitudes to work, encouraging him to take holidays and not to be mean about them, and to see more of his friends. Since his "earning duties" came first, even in the new scheme, these last ideals were more susceptible to modification.

As far as the summer of 1909 was concerned, however, the benevolent influence of this more relaxed attitude can be seen. With the easing of social activity towards the end of July, Grainger was able to pay a short visit to Roger Quilter at Woodbridge, and to undertake two short folksong-collecting expeditions: in Gloucestershire (with Eliza Wedgewood, 31 July–1 August) and at Wittersham in Kent (with Alfred and Edith Lyttleton, 21–22 August).

264   TO KAREN HOLTEN   The Hut (by Monkey Island)
[Original: Danish/English quotations/German phrase]   Bray, Berks.
18.7.09.   (Schuster's)

It is quite quite charming here, right on the river, the house furnished in the most lovely taste you can think of, a caressing flowering summer sunny day, and no women about. I prefer the company of men to women that I don't really love. But as regards women that I love, all the men in the world can "mei' puggel 'ruf schteische'." (men buckel herauf steigen) [German idiom: "shove it up your jumper"]

Yesterday I bought a book entitled "The History of the rod" dealing with the use of the whip in all countries and times.[36] Seldom in my life have I gone through such a lecherous day as yesterday. My head ached, eyes burnt, body shook, of the excitement of reading what people have invented in my greatest speciality.

Perhaps it seems peculiar to you that it can cause me such jubilation just to read such a thing? But it is really natural that one likes to wrap oneself round in words of a subject so near to one's heaven; the very words thereof elate and bedrunken me.

But the greatest feeling that was born in me on reading through the book is thankfulness to you for your great goodness to me in this matter, and how much I owe you, and how much your capabilities of passionate love bring a fortune to me.

Just think, if I read a book like that, and was without you, I would have to think to myself "But anything like that I will never achieve, poor me" But now, as things are, it only awakes hope, gratitude, and jubilation. In Oakley St you were anxious that I would possibly miss out on life's happiness. But think, and make no mistake: This that you give me, in allowing whipping, is not only *one* of my life's delights, it is my *only greatest* life's delight and desire. I would be so happy so happy if I were you, to be able to give the one one loves that which is his highest heaven. It is indeed something outstanding to be able to offer one's lover what he has always longed for most. Not only an experience, but his whole life's (up to now) deepest most violently (and up to now most hopeless) desired goal.

Do you know what a power you have over me in this matter? What wouldn't I do for you if you held that up as a reward to me? You could lead me like a tamed tiger on that leash!

For example, if you didn't let me whip you this summer, nor in the coming year, or close following years, the promise of it would hold me so fast, so helpless, expectant, longing. Perhaps you could use this longing of mine for your own purposes; if you wanted to?

I would give up art, performance of my works, everything else for this whipping-desire. I would risk all possible for it. I am helpless in respect of

36 *Flagellation & the Flagellants: A History of the Rod in all Countries from the Earliest Period to the Present Time* . . . With illustrations, by the Rev. Wm. M. Cooper B.A. (pseud. for James Glass Bertram), (London, [1870]). In Grainger's library is a copy of the new edition, revised and corrected (Reeves, London, n.d. [1910]).

you in this matter, you can give me heaven, and take it away from me. You, little sweet Karen, are the great King. [As Robinson Smith said to me going in to Blüthners "On *these* occasions *you* are the great man"]

I lie helpless powerless before you, apprehensive, like a little child, and beg you so earnestly so longingly let me whip you. You may whip me as much as you like, may tie me quite tight and whip me all you want to, even if I scream. You shall not take any notice of that. But let me whip you. Let me tie you firmly, as well, when I want to, and let there be no limits, no sympathy. Look what people have suffered as slaves, daily, and in girls' schools, not so long ago; can't one bear as much for love's sake as by necessity?

It says in the book about whipping women, with regard to the danger of whipping on the upper body, that "it is highly disapproved of because of its tendencies to hurt the breasts of the penitents; such, indeed, is the *danger of wounding these sensitive parts*, that at this day, when a woman is flogged in Sweden she is laid in a copper sheath, which fits the front part of her person", etc.

and again it says, about whipping in America, about a woman, Anne Coleman:

"She was whipped at Salem. On this occasion the knot of the lash split the nipple of her breast, & she nearly died from the effects of the wound". But in spite of all that it is just on the breast that I almost most of all long to whip you.

One must, of course, remember that certain whippings that are spoken of in the book are not carried out with thin light whips which I will use (it would never please me to hit with a hard heavy whip. Why do people do it?) but with "cat-o'-nine-tails" and especially, whips of thick dry leather, that cut real holes in the flesh. (Tedious) That makes the whole effect different, naturally.

But even if whipping you on the breasts were 100 times more dangerous than it certainly is, I would beg beg you to let me, even if there was danger that you could get cancer (and that is easily possible, perhaps) I would still implore you to let me whip you boundlessly on your little small breasts. You could naturally well say no, and then the world would be destroyed for me. My experience with my 7 (?) whips is, that, how ever hard I strike there still comes no blood, the skin is not even cut, especially on my breasts where the flesh is too soft and elastic to oppose the blow sufficiently to make much effect possible. But the nipples on your breasts are naturally of a very much harder, more resistant material than mine, on the other hand, the other parts of the breasts are still more elastic than a man's. But it is really just the nipples that I most long to reach, and see how you will jump up suddenly when the whip strikes.

Oh, you can so easily make me unhappy if you wish. You only need to refuse these pleasures of mine, then I am destroyed and helpless.

Don't forget you have a great power over me through these longings of mine, just as much (power) by refusing as by permitting.

It has been lovely here.

Tuesday. 20.7.09.

Yesterday I whipped myself as I have never before been whipped in my life. I bound many thick protective things around my ureure ("ureure" is a native word for the male sexual organs, and seems to me more attractive than the various European expressions which one has heard used in the mouths of so many low cold-blooded people) tied a towel round my neck, and put a (rather transparent) waste-paper-basket on my head. First I lay on my stomach on the floor and beat my whole back from the shoulders to below the knees, and then I stood up and beat the whole body, as hard and rapidly as I could. It lasted perhaps 10–15 minutes, and when I had finished there were surely over 1000 long red stripes on me, but of which the most disappeared in the course of a few hours, so that today, perhaps only a little more than 100 remain.

There were some rather large patches on me where the whole was deep red, with absolutely no undamaged skin in between, but there were no places that bled, although there were 6 or 7 small spots where the outer end of the whip had struck where the skin was nearly cut through. Of course it is almost impossible to beat yourself as hard as one could hit another, but all the same, yesterday's experience has convinced me that it would be quite difficult to do any real damage with the whips I have. They are simply perfect, of just the right different heavinesses, of lovely lengths, and easy and nice to use.

It is only in the first moments that one can bring forth real pain, (perhaps the 1st ½ minute) after that the nerves become accustomed to the effect of the blows, and it has a stimulating effect without hurting. Just after whipping one feels quite indescribably hot. The blood simply *races* through your veins. One can well imagine it. It is a lovely warmth, and should be exceptional as a means of heating in the winter, one would think. After whipping I felt indescribably tired for some minutes, and a little faint (no doubt from the unusually strong passage of the blood) but so happy, light-hearted, free and young. There remained not the least unpleasant feeling in my body, neither local or as a whole.

Now I am only afraid that if I treated you just as I did myself yesterday the pains would not be sufficient to make you scream or cry or look desperate; since, as I have said, the pains are quite unimportant after the first beginnings, only amusing, ecstatic, carried away, world-forgotten.

Whipping is still lovely on all places, but, for me, most ravishing on the breasts. On other places it makes me happy and cheerful, but there always remains for me a feeling that something is lacking, however hard I hit, but directly I sting the nipples, even quite lazy blows, everything disappears for me. Just on what we call "loins" is also sharp and good. Here I have sketched in black the places on the loins where it is good and sharp. The arm-holes are also a good place. Also just between the legs, towards the back (where the skin is tremendously tender) is lovely. The sensation appears to me especially more intense when the legs are more or less apart. Therefore one must never tie the ankles together for whipping, but rather tie each leg separately. Perhaps the effects are more painful when someone else strikes, for then the blows fall more unexpectedly, and with a quite different electricity, surely. (Just like tickling) That would be fun.

Oh if only the hours would march
Oh if only the days would pass.

I play for Lady Speyer on Thursday.

Wednesday. 21.7.09.
Thanks for your letter. My next letter will reach you in Svinkløv, about 28.7. Take a pair of thick gloves (with fur inside if possible) with you to Svinkløv.
Sorry that this letter is so tedious.

265   TO KAREN HOLTEN   [London]
[Original: Danish]
24.7.09.
[Extract]

37 Camilla Landi (b. 1866), well-known concert singer of Milanese parentage. Grainger had already appeared on the concert platform with her on 7 June 1904. Grainger played the Grieg concerto at the Queen's Hall Promenade Concert on 17 August.

It is so difficult. It seems as though I shan't get to earn much in the coming winter. Never quiet, never any security.

There was talk of a Recital Tour in Canada this winter, (2 months) excellently paid, but it won't come to anything, for sure. Then it was just about to be agreed that I and Camilla Landi (who is an excellent artiste, and a "world star") should give a "joint" Recital in London.[37] But now she is ill, and can't promise to come, so that is also lost.

And what an awful mess I have got in August. Visits, visits, which would be unwise to refuse, but no earning, and no time at all to achieve anything in the folksong field, after all, nor any time to compose, as I am playing in a "Prom" Aug. 17.

I don't complain about it, and it doesn't make me really unhappy, but it is tedious to be 27, with so little money saved, so many exertions behind one, and with apparently never diminishing impossibility of accomplishing one's life work in peace; not even time to accomplish it in disturbance.

266   TO ERNEST THESIGER   31A King's Road
Friday, "about July 24, 1909"   Sloane Square
                                                               SW

Dearest Ernest.

So many thanks for your letter. Your choice of the Hearns was ripping.
I enclose chequelet with hosts of thanks for your so sweetly doing that for me

Fond love from
Perks

38 The Espérance Club, a London working girls club. In September 1905 its Honorary Secretary, Mary Neal, had approached Cecil Sharp with an idea of teaching English folksongs and dances to the members. Sharp recommended William Kimber, a traditional dancer who, with his cousin, first taught the girls. The experiment was highly successful and from 1906 public performances and demonstrations were given, and members of the Club in turn became teachers. Sharp was never officially associated with the Club though he often lectured at its performances. In 1910 he and Miss Neal fell out over questions of style and methods of teaching. Sharp had played a pioneering role in notating the traditional Morris dance tunes. Early in 1908 (the exact date is not known), Grainger

267   TO ROSE GRAINGER   Stanton,
[Original: English/Danish]   Broadway, Worcestershire.
Sunday 1.8.09.

Have you ever seen lovelier paper than this here? Don't you think it is a good idea for us to order this kind *single pages* (*single*, not folding, writing paper *sheets*) the next time we need new paper? It is surely cheaper also?

Thanks for your letter I got yesterday. I have already answered the 2 letters which you enclosed.

It is enchantingly lovely here, and I am extremely happy. Tonight I shall be at Miss Wedgwood's.

The 2 best old men of this district (Daddy Lane, & Shepherd) have both died (Winchcombe workhouse) since I collected from them a year ago.

I took 3 phonograph records yesterday (Sat) morn at workhouse, & yesterafternoon Miss Wedgwood & I spent with a dear fresheyed *very dialectic* 90-year old woman Mrs Wixey at Buckland, from whom I collected (2 phonograph records) for the 1st time in my life the beloved "bonny bonny boy" tune

Her variants were very very peasanty, gloriously modal, & full of variety. She is a killingly funny old dear being. Referring to Miss W's & my visit she said it was: "really beautiful company, happy company. Respectable company." She said "werm" for "warm", "erm" for arm, "weef" for "wife", "sty-airs" for "stairs", "wint" for "wasn't", "do'um" for "do they", a.s.o.

I took some 5 or 6 cylinders full of her singing.

How can folk think that any niggers smell stronger than English country folk? I know now [*sic* no] human stench so sickening searching sickly as the latter's. Even when I get into an empty railway carriage on a countrified stretch I niff at once the unfleeable whiff. Not that I mind. It isnt sweat smell I mean, but the real fleshsmell of them.

I shall meet Cecil Sharpe today at Miss Wedgwood's I believe. I want to see him so it is lucky. Miss W has done her folksong work right well, hereabouts. Above all she is loved by the old folk, which is, after all, the first need.

Yesterday early evening we saw the school children do Morris dances, learnt from "Esperance Club" teachers, who originally owe all to Sharpe. He has really done a good work in this matter, I think.[38] The Morris dances are charming, & the 2 best tunes (those 2 I have sketched settings of "Shepherds Hey" & "Country Flowers") have dances to them just as jolly as Sharpe's harmonic treatment of the tunes is revolting. The children did them well in a way, tho their outstanding characteristics are gracelessness & dullness, barring 2, who were more lifelit sparky beings generally, & "trod" with joy & jimpness. I must certainly learn to Morris-dance, even though I'm sure it is unoverratably healthy for one.

There is a divine book on Far Eastern (Chinese, Jap, Korean, etc) great painters by L. Binyon.[39] (you heard him lecture)

Page after page of reproduction hammers into ones head that these Easterners have in painting genius after genius, outstanding personal men, not to be denied, great & unforgettable like Rembrandt, Dürer, etc: A rioting crowdedness of 1st class artistic output thronging swarmingly thro many yearhundreds. Let us pray ceaselessly for an international worldwide-music preservation Society.

Please tell Miss Permin[40] that the verse I couldn't remember, is:

"Yesterday I was in your fathers courtyard,
with dog and hawk in my hand;
Your father he is such a hasty man,
he would not hear my words to the end."

I have done about ½ of what sketch scoring of "Away by the lands" remained to be done. The whole thing is now only a work of some few hours.

268 TO ROSE GRAINGER
Early evening 5.8.09.

Bawdsey Manor,
Woodbridge.
Steam yacht "Peridot."

It's simply lovely. I'm on a charming yachtlet, delightfully warm, copying out some of the parts of "At twilight" which I ended scoring here this afternoon, & which 6 of us will try & partsing a bit tonight.

Roger seems & looks *ever* so fit & himself, & dear Lady Q is charming, & has a sweet Sicilian work border (by that women's guild that was on "Seydlitz") to a nice blue linen dress.

Binyon is here, gay, Southernly happy, with Sun in his voice, reminding me of Polynesians I have never yet met. Before lunch he & I went swimming in sea with various Quilter girls.

had sketched "room-music" (chamber music) settings of two of the Morris dance tunes collected by Sharp (in 1906) and published by him and Herbert C. MacIlwaine in their collections *The Morris Book. A history of Morris dancing, with a description of . . . dances as performed by the Morris-men of England* Pts. 1-3, Novello & Co., London, 1907-) and *Morris Dance Tunes* (in 2 sets, Novello & Co., London, 190-?). Grainger's copy of *Morris Dance Tunes* was a gift from Roger Quilter at Christmas 1907. Grainger's first setting of *Shepherd's Hey*, for flute, clarinet, baritone English concertina, horn ad lib. and eight strings, was completed on 17 November 1909. His setting of *Country Gardens*, perhaps the best known of all his settings of English folksong, was set aside until 1918, when it was redone for piano solo. Grainger played the piano solo arrangement of *Shepherd's Hey* for the first time as an encore at his solo recital on 30 November.

39 Grainger was reading *Painting in the Far East. An introduction to the history of pictorial art in Asia, especially China and Japan* (London, 1908) by Robert Laurence Binyon (1869-1943), poet and expert on Far Eastern art, whose books and essays on that subject are pioneer works of appreciation.

40 It was normal for the Graingers to have (usually) two people "lodging" in the Kings Road house with them during this period, usually foreigners who took English lessons with Rose or piano lessons with Percy, or both. Else Permin, a Dane, came to live with the Graingers in July 1909, and lived with them off and on through the following years well into 1913. She took piano lessons with Percy and became an intimate friend of Rose, whom she assisted in various ways. Through her connections she helped Percy procure engagements in Denmark. She and the Graingers met, and sometimes travelled together, in Europe. After the Graingers' precipitous departure for America in 1914, she attended to some of their affairs. The verse is from an unidentified Danish folk poem.

Wellgrown; but these English womenfolk & girls are too [word crossed out — by Rose?] even though they're so tall & long-made. Neither Karen nor Polynesians are like that (nor you) although shorter & plumper. This ausgeprägt weiblichkeit [German: pronounced womanliness] makes me feel bodily very standoffish.

I've done such a lot of work today.

I feel so healthy & happy & love my mum so desperately.

Perks.

269   TO KAREN HOLTEN   Bawdsey Manor,
[Original: Danish/English]   Woodbridge.
6.8.09. Friday.

I am having **such** a splendid time here. Tennis, swimming, (the water is lovely and warm) tons of music, scorching sunshine. Roger looks *so* well and so happy.

This is a lovely place; just opposite the sea, with many sand islands at low tide, and a tidal (salt water) river on the right. The mansion stands quite high up, but *just* below is a large large lawn where they play tennis, etc. I work a lot here, but go to London tomorrow.

"At twilight" is now completely fair-copied.

Have you ever thought that this coming holiday in Svinkløv will be our 1st proper perfect honeymoon?

The first summer was lovely, but I was full of distrust, anxiety, and the whole of my mind was unused to and untuned to such divine possibilities as there were, and the following summer was so cold, and we didn't get to be alone, and then poor Grieg's death came in the middle, but now I am "tuned for highest bliss", and after such a year as this has been we both long without *qualifications* for each other, and the sweet Polynesians have shown me for the first time a practical attractive philosophy of love.

You with your sweet charming Danish nature have melted away my British mistrust and lack of confidence.

You are a real sunshine for such a work.

The whole year has schemed to draw now to perfection I have never before lived thro such a coming glory of concentration

How I love you and hate your absence

270   TO ROSE GRAINGER   Bawdsey Manor,
[Original: English/Danish]   Woodbridge.
6.8.09.

Sweetest little mother

I arrive for lunch tomorrow or after it in time for pupil at 3. I believe by the way that Parker is off so perhaps I had better say for certain I'll come after lunch.[41]

So so happy

Roger & I spent blissful afternoon playing each other compos. Swam & tennissed this morn & shall again this afternoon.

I am so happy and well. Thank you for the amusing card and for the vest

Percy

41 Katharine (Kitty) Parker, Tasmanian-born pianist and composer. She was one of Grainger's pupils at this time, "one of the best when it comes to the point", wrote Grainger to Karen Holten on 17 November 1909. "She is very nice, very ambitious, very young and I believe she may possibly go far. I hope she'll do me good as a teacher." In 1935 Grainger arranged her composition *Down Longford Way* for elastic scoring, and it was published by Hawkes & Son, London, in 1936.

271 TO HERMAN SANDBY   31A Kings Rd. S.W.
11.8.09.

Dear old Herm

Are you & Alfhild at Rørvig now, & will you be there for a time?

For I want to send you a South Sea Island native mat that we got in New Zealand as a present to you both from my mother & me.

It is a large grass-plaited mat (probably from Rarotonga) of a kind getting very rare now, as the natives are giving up this very slow kind of work.

They use them as floor mats, as their bare feet does not destroy the texture, but if we did so I fear our nailed boots would tear the grasses & wear it out, so maybe it is wiser to use it on the wall, or over a piano, or something suchlike.

I hope you will like it, as we are so fond of all this native work, of which I have the beginnings of a jolly collection.

When we meet I will tell you a lot about these dear Polynesians, how loving, lovely, bold, wellformed, & childlike they are, & how artistic too!

Polynesia is fast becoming a 2nd Old-Scandinavia for me, greatening my love for the older Schwärmerei by way of its fierce contrast. After Icelandic Maori is the most lovely sounding speech I know, heroic, rhythmic, & reckless like the former.

But it is an added joy to not only read it, but hear it said sung & chanted out of bare brown dancing bodies built like Greeks.

I have done a good deal of scoring of late & besides ending the English Dance have done "In Dahomey" for Rathbone, & "Dollar & a ½ a day" (chanty) "At Twilight" & am getting on with "The Bride's Tragedy".

Do tell me what you've been composing! I hope you take good care of all you've written & dont let it get lost, and if you rework works, I do hope you re*write* them, so that the old ideas stand complete in their 1st form also.

How is the old 4tet? Are you going to publish anything? If so, let me know.

Dear old Roger is much stronger in health again, & Cyril also, (who was very bad, poor dear) & has been doing some very much more interesting work just lately.

I am playing at the Liverpool Festival in September, & they are also doing my Old Irish Tune & "Brigg Fair".

I am playing at 2 Proms now shortly.[42]

I have a jolly engagement from Brødrene Hals[43] for 3 Recitals in Christiania, if dates will fit in, & will come to Copenhagen at the same time for a Recital most likely; some time in the new year.

When do you come here?

All warmest greetings to you both & your people from us both

    Ever yr
    Percy.

Ever so many thanks for your card.

272 TO ROSE GRAINGER   Wittersham House,
[Original: Danish/English]   Wittersham.
Sunday. 22.8.09. Early, before breakfast

My own beloved little mother

We got though several folksongs yesterday from a *very* nice old man, his name Samuel Holdstock. *How* cross I am that I didn't bring my phono-

42 Grainger's second engagement in the Queen's Hall Promenade Concert 1909 season was on 2 October, when he played the Liszt *Hungarian Fantasia*.

43 Brødrene Hals, Norwegian firm of piano makers founded in 1847 by two brothers, Karl and Peter. Karl's sons, Thor and Sigurd, had joined the firm in 1888. It became a limited company in 1900. Grainger was dealing with Sigurd Hals, whom he described as "by far the best agent I've ever come across **anywhere** and a delightful man".

44 The five tunes, numbered 395 to 399 in Grainger's English Folksong Collection, were collected by Grainger with assistance from Mrs Edith Lyttleton on 21 August 1909 from Mr Samuel Holdstock. One of them was "Mary Thompson", the tune quoted, of which Grainger made a setting for four unaccompanied mixed voices. Of Samuel Holdstock Grainger made a biographical note: "Samuel Holdstock, born 16 May 1823 [at] Budds, Wittersham, Kent. Here all his lifetime except 2 years in Appledore. [Dealt with] cattle and sheep. Worked up to he was 79, and then got hurt. Wouldn't sing on a Sunday. Even in his wild days he had never done *that*. He went up to London to see the Queen's funeral (Vict[oria]) and he never wished to see another". Grainger was the guest of Alfred and Edith Lyttleton at their country house at Wittersham in Kent. The "2 other very nice people" are unidentified.

45 Percy and Rose, returning from Australia to England on a German ship, had spoken Danish together on board and been taken for Danes by one of the Germans, Kolbe, a man who had lived in the German South Sea Island colonies. Kolbe had contrasted the Dutch and the English approaches to colonial management in a way that was unfavourable to the British, of whom he observed that they understood nothing about discipline, how to govern, or how to treat the natives. Grainger related the conversation in full to Karen Holten in his letter of 1 June 1909. A rather different version of this story appears in Grainger's autobiographical *Anecdotes*, July 1953.

46 Dudley Kidd, *The Essential Kafir . . . with one hundred full page illustrations by the author* (London, 1904).

graph with me, for he sings really with charm and with many added syllable "inden" "I'dd" etc.[44]

One of his melodies was really beautiful:

I'm so fond of those beginnings (marked*) on the 4th of the key, so uniquely characteristic of English tunes.

Perhaps I will arrange it for 4 voices and let them sing it this evening. Yesterday we sang several 4- and 5-voiced songs, Brahms, Purcell, etc, and also a little of "At Twilight" which I took with me, since I knew this family is known as partsingers.

Mrs Lyttelton [*sic*] paid me a real compliment unbeknownst. She said of the words: The beginning I dont like like so much but it gets *perfectly glorious* later on about "beckoning them accross the gloom". My part, of course.

Balfour, charming as ever, Lady Elcho, & 2 other very nice people are here. I told B about Kolbe taking us for Danes & what he said, & B really lost his temper, got red in the face & said "the damned impudence of them".[45]

There is a lot of Scotch fire behind the slender wrists & limp shoulders, I feel sure.

I played both Albenizs, Ravel, & Bach-Busoni Toccata & Fugue, last night.

The others went out in the afternoon but I stayed home & practised & read an enthralling book "The essential Kafir" by Dudley Kidd, on S'African blackies, with 100 quite quite *wonderfully* taken photos. (Adam & Charles Black, 1904. Publ)[46] What darling folk! Remind me to tell you of the light he throws (thro the S'African custom "Llonipa") on the matter of name-*tabus*.

From his book they read to be a delightfully [word crossed out — by Rose?] race. Alas! though, life does not run so cocoanut-oiled for them as in the islands. They are after all continentals, poor dears.

What taste in housing the English have!

One room here is a dream.

The daughter, 14 years old, is also a beauty. Such an aristocratic young girl and really nearly as sweet and unspoilt as a savage.

If one could carry such a one off at just this stage of her ½ civilisation I'm sure she would hardly fall short.

Shall be home 1.30 or 1.45

Please reserve yr strength for our Prom

273 TO KAREN HOLTEN

[Original: Danish/some English]

Sunday. 22.8.09.

Wittersham House,

Wittersham.

When I wrote to you in New Zealand that I would keep good for a whole month, I didn't doubt the possibility of performing the promise, but as soon as I tried it, I was very disappointed and ashamed. One week or 2 I could hold out, but then my strength failed, each time. I didn't write to you about it; the promise was really silly and cheap enough in itself, without not once succeeding in performing it. When the months raced past I became of course more and more worried and miserable about my boundless powerlessness. Not so much that it showed my great weakness. For I don't care about possessing strength of character. But it was an unbearable thing not to be able to keep a promise (already so stupid) in memory of your dear father. It wouldn't do that you should receive someone who couldn't even manage to carry out such a bagatelle. That I realised. And when the time for our meeting approached I urged myself on to a more energetic attempt.

Before we meet on Friday it will, thank God, be done. If it hadn't been then, I wouldn't have come to Svinkløv; for it would have been one of the few impossible situations. Finally anger at myself and fear worked so decisively on me, that the danger suddenly disappeared, and the poor little promised month passes by without particular strife. With that sort of thing I have discovered that with such a characterless character as mine, where there is a fight there is also defeat. Perhaps you will despise me for such great impossibility and unpleasant weakness. Perhaps you have believed that I have withstood the danger in all these months. But all the same, I do believe that you know me well enough not to have done so. But now, little friend, why don't you use your power over me? If you don't let me whip you without a promise for the future, you can perhaps keep me from these dangers. I don't know; but for anything else I could hardly have made even the poor little abstinence that I have now achieved. It can be discussed in Svinkløv.

I am sick of waiting, always waiting.

I long to lie restingly in your flesh, with your strong protecting limbs around me, drinking in your breath, tickled by your small hands of love and by your hair, made crazy by your flaming mouth.

I long to lie with my body heavy on top of your breasts and face, to grasp your legs with my hands, to discover the way there between your legs through all the hair with my mouth and suck there lovingly in the soft barbaric flesh, there where thousands of years of civilisation end, where the power of nationality disappears, & where blended God, Brute, & Savage writhe in ecstasy & agony. The flesh there cannot be covered, the smell of sex cannot be entirely washed away, uncontrolled movements there twitch & quiver, spasms lurk, blind devil-gods lash wild-willing horses there within; in lowness, selfishness, and greediness there slumber lazily the highest gods.

I, also, need to demonstrate my lowness to you; sweat-dampened smelling arm-pits shall be laid over your wet mouth, heavy and thoughtless shall my body sprawl over your smothered woman-strong body, my proud swollen sex-organ (so ugly, animal, low, ignoble) seeks, mad with longing, your trembling forgiving misused mouth. I long for you to see me in all my beastly lowness. Nothing is more laughable, more repulsive, than a naked swollen man. I know it. Do you think I will be ashamed?

Unashamed regardless shall I stand before you or lie lazylimbed on you. You can gladly despise me, gladly laugh at me. (I want passion, not respect) For you I entertain the most complete trust and confidence. Like a 2-hour old child I long to lie defenceless before you, spiritually and bodily.

Sometime I will ask you to pull out *all* my hair (except on the head), for why should that hair-covered skin hide itself from you, who are so good to me, and towards whom I melt?

It can well be that this time's Svinkløv ends in hostility. You can't imagine how I will make your life a misery this time.

You have said one must realise things, not only dream of them. Good, I will follow your advice. I will tie you up, make you helpless; treat you as a cat does a mouse. You have the instinct to want to keep your body as nature made it, without defect, lines, scars.

Do you think I will bother about that? I long to break nature's smooth surface. Do you think you will come from our passion without marks? It will be a pleasure to me to (superficially) destroy your unwounded body. As from a dangerous war shall you come from our passion. You have said to me "realize". May the bloody god above us help me to. But you won't find it so easy, either.

Despite all this, I will always only do what you want. And when you only want peace and quiet this time, I hope that you can also find that, with your conceited impatient hungry lover

Percy.

Monday.

Now, goodbye till we meet. Tonight we are going to Wagner Concert. Have partly arranged a nice new folksong I collected Sat[47]

274 TO ROSE GRAINGER
Thursday night. 26.8.09.

S.S. "N.J. Fjord".[48]
nearing Esbjerg.

I can say, like poor old dead dear Deene of Hibaldstow ("Its on the Monday morning" singer) when he got under way singing into the phonograph:

"It's plē-azin' mė"

Lovely smooth xing. Just of late a slight swell, so that I was the 4th (taking full meals instead of sleeping ones hunger off proves ruinously dear, but I'm obeying instructions, dearie) down to evening meal out of a full ship, yet it is still *wondrously* calm. So I'll get the train alright.

We have such a dear old Jutish looking sailor on board. His face simply shining with kindness, curly hair, & very blue eyes, & such a clean clean looking skin & face. Ever smiling & joking. A truly endearing personality. I'm liking the looks of the Danes on board more than ever. I'm coming more & more to earnestly think them to be the 1st white race, by which I mean, the 1st race as *taken in the bulk*, the nicest comunity, the least stupid crowd, etc *Individuals* of many other lands & breeds will beat them EASY, in beauty, nobility, achievement, energy, brains, but Danes seem the least revolting pöbel [German: mob] to me.

They seem to have (inspite of what folk say) fewer grossly fat (as in Germ) or distressingly thin folk (as in England) than most races, & really their overflowing real goodness of heart is a never failing delight to me. I search the Danish faces almost in vain for unkindliness, starvedness, greediness, cruelty, though a softhearted indulgence (to self & others) elbows the chance of saintliness, great nobility, or willstrength out of the most of their faces, I own.

In comparing, however, them with the English, one must not forget that matter of "intelligence" that I bored you with that night. It is almost easy for the English to live up to their "ideals" when one realizes that their intelligence (of the bulk) is so low that they can see no holes in these ideals, & that their timidness makes selfrestraint positively easier to them than an outrage on vested ideas.

47 The setting was *Mary Thomson* [*sic*] (see note 44 above). On the manuscript Grainger noted "I like it one of the best of all my settings". This preference notwithstanding, the setting remained unpublished. It was, however, included in the programme of Grainger's Concert of Compositions and Folk-Music Settings on 21 May 1912.

48 In his diary for 26 August 1909 Grainger has penned a little ditty: "Rolling passage/passengers swine/boat too small/no more for mine".

Remember that hardly a single clever Englishman can agree with the ideals of the English, or has. (selfrepression, hardness to ones own rather than face a disapproving outer world, etc) While the ideals of the Danes, or their modes of living & acting rather, (great patience, cooperation *without* surrender of individualism, forgivingness, slowlylazy rather than *uninspiredly* hasty) almost all internation thinkers can but look up to.

Compare the English with the Kaffirs & you get a sidelight.

The mere accusation of certain unpopular practices is fatal in both English (the social judgement I mean always, not legal) & Kaffirs. Kaffirs (like English) do not revolt against appaling hardnesses because they dont use their brains about it, they simply act as a mob, & a mob is always stupid & cruel. Kaffirs & English therefor are born full of fear of their own mobs, gradually yielding up their wills away from serving their needs & wishes to strengthen the hedged ways (not the will — no public *will* can be real without intelligence) of the community.

Danes, having developed very inwardly individualisticly, fight becoming enrolled in the mobmass very successfully; & hence remain tolerant, good & wisely-selfish amidst other races intolerant & blindly (& for the most part harmfully) unselfish to the withering of their tender native wellsprings of easy joy.

And this folk whom we find so cleverly lazy so easy going so unmoral & so childlike is *thriving unusually much* in active competition with other nations who are overstraining themselves uselessly in all sorts of sad ways merely for the lack of a little mental integrity & farmer nouce.

You must come again & really see them thoroughly, my dearest mum.

My thoughts dwell often & often with the kind fond little mother that gönt mir [German: allows (i.e. does not begrudge) me] my relished holidays!

275   TO ROSE GRAINGER   Badepensionatet
29.8.09.   Slettestrand.
                                                        pr. Fjerritslev.
                                                        Jylland.
                                                        Denmark.

Such a morning of letters.[49] My darling I dont mind this business letter writing at all. I feel well & fit & wellsuited & fresh in this salty chilly weather, (quite as dear to me as a sunny holiday) & I dont therefor mind a little weeny share of the huge bothery work the darling capable mum takes so splendidly upon herself. I love to hear you are hopeful of my career, for if you are so am I, & I shall gladly gladly work hard if you help me to.

Your business arrangements seem always the toppest thing to me, & all you approve of I shall carry out as far as I can & deem the best possible.

I had my own feeble way about the 2nd fiddling those 2 years, & had good of it even (for everything has a good side) wrong tho it was, but fully see nothing such must happen again nor do I want it, & am most ready to pass in [*sic* on] beyond.

(*Xnia*)   Have written & wired accepting Jan 27, Feb 1 & 5 to Hals, &
(*Bergen*)   written Beyer asking is Feb 8 possible for Bergen, asking quick answer to here.

(Göteborg)   Federspiel has an idea he might be able to get me a Concerto engagement in Göteborg, which if it came off I could take on way from Bergen to Copenhagen (it lies on the way)[50]

(Cope)   In any case I could not get to Cope before about Feb 10, so I could not well give Cope Recital before 15 (Feb) or 16. Have written Hansen asking are those dates free, & whether orchestral engagement could

49 This letter, and the letter from Rose to which it is the reply, reflect the implications of the change in direction of Percy's career: the new importance of letter-writing, the effort involved in "extending the field", the difficulties of coordinating dates. On 26 August Rose had written a lengthy "business" letter commenting, "Had you stayed one day longer here, all business could have been settled, & I should not have had to have bothered you in yr holiday. But all this is too important, & must be seen to at once. I shall write on each letter what you had better do, dear, *rely on* you doing it the *same day* as you receive this". She was, she wrote, "happy & excited about yr career, wh. in spite of your funny little ways in business, I will make a successful one yet, & you will live to thank me. All my ideas are coming off . . . even if things fail sometimes, & you may not make *too much money* the 1st year, follow my advice, & I don't think you will regret it. *No more assisting on tours.* Be the big man *on all* occasions, & yr life will *eventually* be *an easier one*". Among other plans, Rose was attempting, through their French friends J. E. Blanche and Léon Delafosse, to get Percy engagements in Paris. These plans did not eventuate. Percy, ever thoughtful, included a piece by Delafosse in the programme of his solo recital on 30 November.

50 Anton Federspiel, a member of the Svinkløv "circle". He was the legal man for Hals, and it was he who procured the Hals engagements for Percy, after meeting him at Svinkløv two years previously. Karen's friend Asta Nutzhorn was engaged to him but broke it off in 1911 as she could no longer stand his egoism. Karen and the other guests, including Nutzhorn and Federspiel, had moved from Svinkløv to Slettestrand when the Planter (at whose house they usually stayed) contracted diphtheria on 24 August.

51 Axel Theodor Schiøler (1872–1930), Danish composer and conductor. He had started the Philharmonic Society in Copenhagen in 1906. He was at this time, and until 1912, also conductor for the Folketeater. Grainger did not play under Schiøler.

be got for about then. It appears Svendsen has given up & Fini H's concerts uncertain & erratic, so the best & solidest ones left are the Philharmonic concerts. A lady at Bjerggaards is very befriended with Schiøler[51] (the conductor) & will speak to him.

If I only did Cope Recital I could get back London Feb 17 or 18. I could get Arbejderforeningen for certain in Cope, & likely Helsingør again. So if Bergen & Göteborg dont come off I could do arbejderforeningen or anything else before Cope Recital, but if Göteborg & Bergen, or only Bergen, came off, you would have to decide whether I stayed a few days later in Denmark (than the 16), or whether it would be better to hurry back to England refusing arbejderforeningen or anything else.

Arbejderfor. gave 75 Kr, & Helsingør 100 Kr last time.

Let me know what you think re this, tho there is no vast hurry.

(Blanche)   Have written him just as you suggested, very warmly & saying how I hope (& its true too) to go to him to Offranville late in Oct, which would be great fun.

Karen is looking awfully well, & very attractive I think but I may be wrong.

There is also a nice looking Danish woman here who is somewhat like Mrs Chadbourne.

Isnt it sweet of Federspiel to be so keen on doing things for me. I think he's a dear man.

Federspiel has Swiss blood. That explains his dark looks. Can you see a racial likeness in him to Smidtheim & the nice Dutch Indies Swiss on the boat?

No time to bathe yet. These business letters do take me such a time to get off, unhelped.

Herewith I return those you sent. Blanche will write to London. Please open.

Hansen & Beyer to here, of which I'll send news at once.

Fond love
Percy.

Monday. 30.8.09.

Had a great musical afternoon yesterday. Federspiel has been wired to go to Xnia, so I went up to Larsens so as to give him a bit of music before he left. He says he's going to tell them great things of me in Xnia & Göteborg. The Albeniz's make a remarkably great impression on Scandinavians, so I must do them over here all I can.

Today we really are going to swim 1st time as the rain has now stopped. But up to now I've been really lazying, & feel about 2 years old, reading along, chat-chattering, slacking. But now is getting born a baby longing for a tiny bit of activity.

I feel sumptuously well, & not in the least grownup, somehow, with fast fading piles.

The Germans are scrumptously funny. He told me that New Zealand (or a big part of it) belonged to Germany.

He asks more questions that [sic than] even any German I've ever met, & bears up bravely against the quiet cunning, smiling evasiveness, & concealed mirth of the very Danish Danes we have here.

Karen sends love & thanks for your messages.

Who can fathom the slumbrous repose of this strange part of the world, or who resist?

Am sending off Mrs Edwardes letter with same post.

Yr loving little son
Perks.

276 TO ROSE GRAINGER   [PM Fjerritslev]
1.9.09.

From today the post goes only 1ce a day I hear, so I must hasten to get this off by the early morning post.

Yesterday work was begun, I finished parts of "Walking Tune" & did some other writing out & Karen starting writing out English Dance parts. Working is quite as blissful as holidaying, with overcoats on against the chilliness, the sound of the near sea blended with windy rattlings & a nice blinding lamp to work with in an upstair tucked away room in this jolly peasant house.

How how lovely is Maeterlinck, how I long to read you the bits I specially love. Isnt this lovely wording

"Yet out of these things are the banks made
between which happiness flows; & as they
are, so shall the river be, in shallowness
or in depth"

& again:

"For, indeed, belief & unbelief are mere
empty words; not so the loyalty, the
greatness & profoundness of the
reasons wherefore we believe or do
not believe."[52]

The poor sweet Danes, I feel they are a fading race, & I love them more than ever. There is something about the smooth lie of the muscles & the tender build of them that lets me guess their thoro unfit to be hurled against the rougher hordes. My skin, even, is coarse & scaly beside the real Danish skin.

Never was there anything so strong & healthy as your bold son, my strong & healthy darling mum.

277 TO ROSE GRAINGER   Slettestrand.
[Original: English/some Danish]
Thursday. 2.9.09.

From the enclosed you will see that Alette has been going very strong indeed.

I have melted from a blue into a brown harmony, brown shirt, tie, socks, shoes, clothes, for which latter the weather is chilly enough. And what can be lovlier, more filled with joy & goodness than this Swinburnian weather? It was well, however, you made me bring the thick clothes, & the lengthened shirts are just dreams.

Yesterday Karen, Miss Nutzhorn & I walked up to old Bjerregaards to help lift in the piano into the cart, & then stumped back again & lifted it out. It has a fine searching guitarlike tone, inspiring for such utterances as: "Faðir spurdi dóttur um ráð."[53]

I'm fearfully glad to have it here for I begin to feel workish.

I fear Nutzhorn may leave today. She's expecting a wire. She is really quite extra nice this time & quite a real Dane, of a kind.

The keeper (or rather look-after-ess) of this house is so very nice, Miss Madsen, so quiet, & well managing, with refined even kindly features, & all kept so clean, the house.

We had old Bjerregaard, & an old fisher Kjeldgaard taking a little music in last night, a small thanksoffering for the arrival of the piano. Old Kjeldgaard is one of the strongest broadest hugest old salts one could ever

52 Grainger is quoting from paragraph 79 of *Wisdom and Destiny* by Maurice Maeterlinck, as translated into English by Alfred Sutro and first published by George Allen & Sons, London, 1898. His copy of the Pocket Edition (first published October 1908) was a gift from his pupil Reimar von Bülow in November 1911.

53 Grainger was working on his Færoe Island dance-ballad *Faðir og Dóttir* [Father and Daughter], the tune of which was taken from Hjalmar Thuren's *Folkesangen paa Færøerne*, the words from V. U. Hammershaimb's *Færøsk Anthologi* (Vol. 2) and set for five men's single voices, double mixed chorus, strings, brass, percussion, and mandoline and guitar band. The work, completed on 8 September 1909, created a sensation at its first public performance on 13 March 1912 (see letter 438). Published by Schott & Co., London, in 1912 and 1913, it is dedicated to John Singer Sargent. The words sung by the second chorus and set to tunes composed by Grainger himself, form part of the refrain to quite another ballad, published in Hammershaimb's *Færøiske Kvæder* (p.54) (see letter 281).

strike. He is plucked straight out of the Sagas, there is no least detail about him but would answer to those times & doings. It would cost him small conscience to kill many men if need be, I feel sure; yet he is slow as foggy weather. He has dusty looking grey brown curly hair & a rich beard. His skin is shiny with clean dirt & sun brown, polished & glistening with the blended glow of copper & gun metal. His throat (he is a middleaged man, say 58?) is as lovelily delicately wavily bulgily moulded as a Grecian youth's in marble. His nose straight as an aristocrats, sheltering forehead & brows, cunning small sober ½ humorous ½ mean Saga eyes, (that can burn like pinpoints with controlled excitement [as at music] or very dry mirth) & hands broad & great with work & skill but smally fashioned & finely curved by natural refinement & the inborn brainy culture of his race. Nothing can be lovlier than such a strong man, nearly as broad as he is long (quite quite short) but wholy without fat, lumpy, huge, could crush one into mush. A regiment of such short broad men with such cold sane cunning kindly brains as his, would, in hand to hand fighting, simply wipe the floor with every other type of man.

You must come and see Denmark again and again, mustn't you?

278   TO ROSE GRAINGER   [PM Fjerritslev]
Friday. 4.9.09.

My darling, I did such a glorious day's composing yesterday. I wholly sketched "Faður spurdi dóttur á ráð," & I think its one of the very best settings I've ever done. To the original Færoe qualities I've added some Rarotongan antishness, between which flow many-voiced melodic sections of some skill I think. It's certainly the most dancey thing I've yet done, & the tides of its moods race from the cowlike boyish hopping peasant play-fulness to the gloomy tragedy of such a storm as we had last night; & which Karen & I stumped out (clad in 3 coats, rugs, mufflers, etc against the sereing cold) to watch from the bepounded beach late in the evening; 10 oclock being very late here.

How I wish I could drum up my dance for you now this minute. I hope you'll like it as I do.

All the Larsens have come to live here now. They thought their house was too near the planters, with dogs & postmen plying between, whereas here we have other postmen & other dogs.

The fair Larsen girl is a thing of smiling lovliness as to golden hair, glowingly formed face, creamy skin, & girly innocence just now. But her figure is as □ as is Miss Permin's. But I think I really must take a photo of her sweet face.

Why bother about the color of the roses, my little serious mum?[54] Why spend a moment's thought on mere accidental bodily peculiarities while mind-peculiarities are the only things that matter a fig? Remember that I could always give up blue roses at a moments notice if I saw any moral need for so doing, for it has no more nor less hold on me now than when I was in the Glenferrie "Killalah", in short no hold whatever, merely a whim, merely a tendency, merely a source of boyish fun, akin to Keats peppering his tongue before iced wine. When you read in Doctor books of strange leanings you will mostly find them less enviable than mine, because their practices, whatever they were, were mostly needed to bring off the sexual act at all. That is all quite foreign to my case. I just like to be whipped, at any old time, just as I welcome slight burning or any other pain, that is just intense enough to make one say: at last here is a definite feeling, there can be no doubt that one really does feel something here.

But of course here where other satisfaction lies more richly to hand than when I'm without sexual life in London I'm much more indifferent about it, that I must own.

54 Rose had written on 30 August, "If only you didn't prefer blue roses, I should be happy, but ever since I knew that, I have never been really joyful, & when you are away, I fret very much about yr strange fancies. When you are with me, & I see your sweet face, looking noble, & happy, I forget the wrong-coloured roses, & sometimes think it is all a horrible night-mare, & that I shall wake, & find reality again, as I used to know it". Developing this theme she continues ". . . you could never indulge in your fancies, knowing that through them, all joy has left my life, & that although I love you quite as much as I used to, I am no longer proud of you, nor feel the same pleasure in mixing with my fellow creatures, as I feel so ashamed of having a child with such fancies as you have". In later correspondence, Grainger places the date of Rose's discovery of his "strange fancies" as being during their time of residence at Upper Cheyne Row and Coulson Street (presumably the second period at Coulson Street). Since Rose did not know in July 1906, it is very likely that she began to find out during 1907, a time when Grainger's relationship with Karen was allowing him to bring his fantasies towards reality. It would be interesting to speculate to what extent Rose's attitude to Karen was influenced by her fear of Percy's "fancies". According to Grainger, the chill that fell over his relationship with Rose in consequence did not begin to thaw until 1911 (see letter 376). There is a suggestion that, even so, she did not know all there was to know of Percy's "unnatural instincts" (see letter 356).

In London there come moments when I feel "this is really too bad", &
if I dont beat myself or something I feel irritable. The old hermits & today
priests know all these troubles & cures. What does a little bodily pain
matter; who does it harm? Not me whom it relieves; whom then? Ask
Karen if I'm ever anything but absurdly soft & sweet to her. Never. Ich bin
ein für alle maal [German: I am for ever and always] impersonificated
goodness & kindliness. In my life there is no brawling, no love of quarrel-
ing, of killing, of competition, of strong food, or gross folk. Somewhere
there must be an outlet. Remember always that tho my mind & heart is
babyish & loving & tender & refined my body is rough & overfit & wild;
one mustnt deny it its expression either. In sexual, & quasisexual matters
& in composition I feel my body may demand an utterance for the stormy
turmoil which is the bedrock of me as of every other healthy keen male.

Find me oppresion in my character jealousy greed & unfairness in my
mind & I shall be worries [worried] & downcast, but I, so happy & satisfied
in my loving nature & in the good-will I sweat for all creatures & races,
you cant get me to be concerned about some mere bodily strangeness that
is neither unhealthy, dirty, dangerous, expensive, nor has the *least* real hold
on me.

We would not object to a drunkard, if drinking were not unhea[l]thy,
& did not become a craving; we would have no right to, at all events.

No man knows cravings less than I. I choose my peculiarities (with bad
taste maybe) with as clear a head as I choose chords. Some I prefer to
others of course, and why not? Dont try [to] put me off my pet follies,
when, in the ordinary course of things they're always changing anyway,
going & coming, welcome but dowithoutable. Above all let us never rate
any negative quality so high.

That I should *not* like blue roses would be small gain. That I *do* like the
other roses also is surely more to the point.

We dislike a drunkard; but he is negative he *lacks* control, he *lacks*
balance. But what do I *lack* in this particular question?

Why prefer an ordinary man to a talent?[55] the ordinary man merely *lacks*
talent that is all. Deal with & you'll find it isnt only talent he lacks either.
He lacks loving kindness, overflow of animal spirits, quickness of sympathy, lots of things that keep life bounding along as it should & must.

Maybe you think I should have hidden these things from you!

I abhor hiding.

I know of nothing in me that I am ashamed of, nothing I want tucked
out of sight. Why then should I close myself up before you of all beings?
You who love me so, whom I love so?

For me there are no problems in the world, only to keep ones health &
to try [to] get down as big much as one can before the fires quench & no
man can hold back the *negative* increase.

I'm so longing to get onto the setting again. Also to breakfast.

Karen sends love & encloses a heatherlet.

yr happy son
Percy.

55 In the same letter Rose wrote,
"I would sooner you were a dear,
sweet, untalented person, with a
love of right, than be gifted as you
are, & be as you are".

279 TO ROSE GRAINGER   [PM Fjerritslev]
[Postcard]
5.9.09.

The rain came in last night & soaked a lot of books but no harm done.
Am still in the thick of the Færoe dance.
What a lot I could write if life were always like this!

280   TO ROSE GRAINGER   [PM Fjerritslev]
Early Monday. 6.9.09.

56 Fixing the date for the
Langley-Mukle concert in the von
Glehns' studio on 9 December (see
note 71 below).

No letter from you yesterday, Sunday, nor could I post to you, as the post doesnt come on Sundays after 1st Sept.

Got up early this morn to get off letters. Have answered Wilfred as you said.[56]

Also Mrs C. Meyer, & have written Hansen fixing Feb 15, Kasinos lille Sal, for my Kope Recital; having heard from him that the lille Palæ Sal was not available for a *single* day in Feb, but Kasinos for either 15 or 16. Casals & Röntgen played in Kasinos Sal.

So *Feb 15, Cope* is a fixture. All good Cope orchestral concerts are given up, there only remain Sunday concerts with a fee of Kr 100, & thats not good enough. So I'll take Arbejderforeningen on the Saturday before, most likely, Feb 12.

Havent heard yet about Bergen or Göteborg. Of course the latter is more than doubtful. Shall wait with Delafosse's till I hear from Blanche. Delaf. says nothing about at homes. I shall play Erard & take Salle Erard if Blanche advises Recital as well as orchestral concert, if latter begettable.

Lovely days these last few have been. Outside wintry storms with sunny patches, inside Karen & I working away with silent happy day-long energy, she copying, I scoring my 18-page (of close small lined score) dance. It is of the type of Sir Eglamore as to form, only the working up is far more economic & the real full rush & clatter is reached only quite near the end, & comes quite fresh.

The setting opens with 5 men's single voices answered by a 1st mixed chorus, to which after a good time gets added a 2nd mixed chorus, upon which get gradually heaped instrumental addings till at last we have horns, brass, strings, (pizz) & guitars in riot round all the voices unison with the tune.

Today I shall start practising also.

I cant say how lovely the little Larsen girl is in the face. Such a happy kindly family they all are together, too. I would not easily get sick of the truly Christian sweetness & leniance of the Danish middleclass life, dull though it be, in a way. *Goodness is the only quality against which I fail to react*.

It is ideal down here at Slettestrand. I leave Esbjerg Wed. Sept 15, arriving London Thursday night or early Friday (17) morn.

Karen encloses some lyng [Danish: heather], with love.

Am longing for your today's letter & hungry for my breakfast

How lovely my ties smell, you must have put some nice niff in the bag.

57 During this stay in Denmark
Grainger gave two concerts: for
the Fjerritslev Borgerforening on
12 September and for the Aalborg
Arbejderforening on 14
September. The Fjerritslev
engagement came through his
Svinkløv friends the Larsens. In
the event, the Fjerritslev concert
made a loss, but the two concerts
together paid for his holiday. In
the second part of the programme,
Grainger played the Liszt
Hungarian Fantasia in a version
for two pianos, Karen
accompanying. Neither her name
nor the piece are mentioned on the
programme.

281   TO ROSE GRAINGER   Slettestrand.
Monday. 13.9.09.

Well, last's night's Fjerritslev concert was tons of fun, a great success & mighty good practise for me.

The little hall looked quite nicely filled, the Hornung & Møller grand from Aalborg thundered, the Larsens etc sat in glowing smiling Danish contentment & Mrs Wilhjelm with Norwegian more tragic intensity.[57] The planter too & wife figured proudly. He is quite well again. I got my Kr 50 already last night & if there is any further takings after expenses are settled I'll get that too.

The little public looked so happy & clapped robustly. I gave 3 encores, & have seldom enjoyed a concert so much. Such concerts are indeed a pleasure to an artist.

Every one was so thankful & kindly, & the drive home in the indescribable, aristocratic, but comfy carriage (at the borgerforeningens [Danish: the farmers society's] expense, back & forth) in the fresh dry fair weather autumn air & the deep dark was a fine reaction.

When I first laid hands on the grand, after weeks of nothing but this tinkly light-touched antedeluvian piano here, I feel wholly helpless with its heavier keys & thought I should never be able to get thro the concert. But after 1½'s practise upon it (which is the piano I'll be playing on tomorrow in Aalborg) I got used to the 20th century again.

Fancy, Knud Larsen did a nay not ½ bad drawing of me yesterday, which he has given me. And his elder girl Gerda, the less lovely one, draws *simply ravishingly*. She said to him, "have you ever seen anyone so beautiful as he" meaning me, so he tells me. She did a sketch of me from memory on a slate, that one could not fail to recognize.

Karen did her part of the Liszt quite well. They are funny, Danes; even I cant always read them. Rehearsing it, she was maddeningly stupid, played out of time & generally upsettingly & carelessly, but in the concert didnt make a mistake. One musnt underrate their unlooked for ableness of making unwonted efforts at the last moment.

I dressed her up in various boys clothes the other day, my blue clothes, stockings to the knees, trousers rolled up & boys shirt above. She looked simply charming awfully like a boy; *much* much better than in any other clothes, better even than in national dragten [Danish: the costume]. What a sin, a real sin, women's dresses are. Women, who stands for ausdauer [German: tenacity, steadfastness], for freshness, for unquenchable hope & faith, & for childlike skitish kittenish playfulness, she, of all beings, should have free untramelling clothes to leave her limbs free to jump around & voice the joy of nature that is the quality of her sex. Fancy skirts on the untamable sex. It hurts my heart, all the simple sweet playfulness that man has tried to crush out of woman. I took photos of Karen in the boys clothes I hope they turn out fairly decent. And then to see her in ordinary proper dresses one wouldnt know her, so far less attractive, so much duller, & more middleclass.

Maybe all women would look better in boys dresses. (You would *of course*) I'm sure a lot would.

Now the weather has really grown lovely, sunny, still, & with a waveless sea that I really must bathe in for the last, & only the 4th, time.

What intelligence there is in the get up of the program, for which a poor quite ignorant inexperienced local little chemist is wholly responsible. Note that he put Komponist before Klavervirt. & the sensible closing of doors at 7.15; not what one looks for in a village. And "Temperance Hotel" always fills me with glee.

Will you kindly address Gaisbergs (enclosed) & add initial. You sent no address with yr kindly thought out letter to him. I think I've done all the letters that you said; Mrs Wodehouses, Leginska, Graves.[58]

The little S'African beadwork I gave (or lent) to Karen is fearfully sweet. I'm bringing it back to copy it.

I'm so looking forward to Aarhus Exhibition.[59]

In the færoe dance there comes a middle section in which the 2nd chorus does something quite independant to the singles & 1st chorus (singing solo & refrain) which it accompanies. So I had to cast round for fitting words for this 2nd chorus, & found a refrain of a quite other song that fitted the rhythm fine & is such a jolly accompanying idea, I think

Dansum væl i friðum, stilli∂ ydur
(Dan) Danse vel i freden, stiller eder
alla riddara
(Dan) alle riddere.
Dance well in peace, place yourselves (take yr positions) all you knights.

Tomorrow is my last letter

58 Rose had written, 3 September, "I wish you would write something like this to the Gramophone man — Dear Mr Gaisberg, Before I left for Australia, & New Z., you said you would like me to play for you with orchestra. I shall be back in England for the Liverpool Festival where I am playing Sept 24, & after the 26th shall be in London for some months, & happy to play for you, if you still wish it, & will let me know to my London address 31a Kings Rd. Sloane Sq. London. S.W. Letters addressed there will always be forwarded to me — Then mention something about old Taylor & how delighted he is with his gramophone etc. With kind regards Yrs sincerely P.G. (Don't lose any chance of making money & reputation —) you will be glad someday". It is quite clear that Percy often wrote his "business" letters to Rose's dictation. Rose's instructions regarding the other letters do not survive. Ethel Leginska (real name Ethel Liggins) (1886–1970), English pianist. Charles L. Graves of the *Spectator* office.

59 From 18 May to 3 October 1909 there was a Landsudstilling [Country Exhibition] in Aarhus. It was a very large affair with a whole exhibition town. Displays included fine art, arts and crafts, industry, exhibitions from central and local governments, hygiene, farming, fishing and so on. A special newspaper was published during the exhibition.

282   TO ROSE GRAINGER

Hotel Phønix
Aalborg

14.9.09.
10.45 morn.

My own darling mum

Here I am in the same Hotel as we were 2 years ago. It's so strange to be back in places. Fancy 2 years! At least a 30th part of one's life. Think too, if I came to Jutland every year of my life now, I could hardly come more than another 40 times, at most.

We got up at 4 oclock this morn drove into Fjerritslev with the lowlying places still wreathed in fog & a lovely growing sunrize.

Karen left Aalborg 9 oclock for Aarhus, where she stays the night with the Aaes, & where we spend some 2 to 3 hours at the exhibition tomorrow.

I've washed me hair & shaved & made myself look my best possible, & now I'll visit the Hoegs for a moment & then practise the rest of the day & hope to do as well as maybe tonight.

Indeed Im not built for loneliness, not for an hour of it. I'm so glad that the sweet mum's lonely time is now so soon at an end. One should never be alone, really.

How absurd even such a small town as this seems after the quiet strand. Farewell so *short*

Yr loving son
Percy.

283   TO KAREN HOLTEN

[Aarhus]

[Original: Danish]
15.9.09.

I am almost as excited to meet you again today as if we had been separated for months. It was so awful yesterday to be without you.

How can one be so sweet as you are.

When you are alone, think of all you have done for me, think how you have treated me always; it must really be comforting for you, you who loves me, to remember how happy you make me. Will you sometimes kiss yourself for me, and smell your sweet small arm-holes, just as I would do.

You mustn't think that I don't perceive how basely I treat you, relatively I notice many things, both your loftiness and my lowness, and am grateful

It is brutal when one has been continuously as we have been, to be separated in this way. One can't understand it.

It is satisfying to live in your fragrance. I cannot think of anything sweeter than you are.

284   TO ROSE GRAINGER

S.S. "La Cour"

Thursday, midday. 16.9.1909.

Alas, that after Danish weeks of unbroken gentle manners & unfailingly humane speech, the first of mothertongue to fall on my ears should be an enraged Englishman bellowing boldly for a berth, whereby losing both it & his temper. His later attempts to trace his tactics to a sense of justice rather than any mere badsailor's need of comforts was as pathetic as typical. Children of unselfdicipline such middledclass British are. I had comfort of watching how English & Swedes roaring like bulls or chafing cheerlessly over lacking creature comforts got bad bedding & alloted places, while sly Danes, later come even, reaped better bargains of cool words & undertones, & slept with peace in their hearts & brains in their heads, on whatever beds.

I marvel how the English always find grievances; nor are the Swedes far behind. But I like to see these Scandinavian Americans that one meets on these boats. I'd put my money on the good things the States are going to reap out of the wise Scandinavian stock of some of the States. These restful muscular folk are not going to find it difficult to thrive & get on over there in the harder lands.

Comfort, cottonwool, & an indulged childhood are surely the best training for a strenuous life. I look forward to roaming round in such Scandinavian parts of the States one day.

I got up at 4.20 yesterday morn, (at Aalborg) after having got up the morn before at 4 & not bedded till 12, & reached Aarhus at 8, where Karen & Aae met me.

The exhibition was fun, a well arranged affair, with nice strange tasteful temperal buildings; what a contrast to the more costly usual gaudy plastered revoltingnesses of big shows like Paris's & London's!

I could have spent hours in the Greenland building, full of lovely patterned clothes etc of the esquimos, & photos of the same; & days with the troop of Abessenians that are there. Great tall men, a little too Arab looking for my personal liking, tho often with nice wooly niggary hair & certain endearing likenesses to Zulus. Their dark bare skins shone & sparkled even in the cloudy chill northern air. There is, however, much evil in their faces, tho lots of atoning life & ravishing grace. We just missed seeing what may have been a real jolly wardance (we heard it growing in noise as we hastened away) having to catch our southbound train. We parted in old Fredericia, after buns & milk, without a trace of heartsinking or sense of end; & I turned hungrily to the glories of "Atalanta in Calydon" which is as Grecian & fierey as "blown wind", & which we shall feast on together, if you allow, in a few hours.[60]

Indeed one cant manage to be downhearted at all after such a childs holiday as this Slettestrand proved. I can recall nought in the weeks that had not the unfettered doomless flow of childhoods doings. For to add sex to life is not in anyway to withdraw childishness, to my mind. Surely it is only the *grownupness* of a mind than [*sic* that] finds ought less chi[l]dly innocent in one good game than in another! Long lazy sleeping into a somewhat reluctant waking, rambling & frolicing the day thro in a will-less aimless gaily empty sort of way, with sleepiness soon fully grown once more; that was the stuff of the holiday, days too slack to be counted even.

That at times a little, or even a lot, of working was put instead of lazying, made also no difference. Real work, lasting work, worth much work is indeed of the same stuff as laziness. Both are wanton; neither are dutiful. There is no grief in parting from such a period. The power to grieve again has to be learnt anew in other lands, at other hands;

> In more of strife, in less of life,
> In quest of pelf, in loss of self,
> more poor in work, more rich in irk,
> With less of sex, & more of vex,
> with less of lust, & more of "must";
> a slavish land, a snobbish band,
> not fitting thee no more than me.
> "Farvel" to such a life, goodbye,
> "adiö/ä", but not "auf wiedersehn",
> We'll wave without regret or sigh,
> When once to quit it we are fitted,
> When once our money's high & dry.

Ikke sand? [Danish: Right?]

60 *Atalanta in Calydon* (1865), a drama by Algernon Charles Swinburne in the classical Greek form with verse-choruses.

Grainger was back in London from his Danish holiday by 19 September. On 24 September he travelled to Liverpool to take part in the concerts of the First Festival of the Musical League held on 24 and 25 September. He was accompanied by William Gair Rathbone, and while in Liverpool stayed with the Hugh Rathbones.

Although, at Rose's request, Grainger had allowed two of his compositions to be performed in the Festival, she did not go to Liverpool. She preferred, as Percy wrote to Karen, to save the money for rehearsals of his chamber music works in London. These took place at intervals after his return.

At this time, too, they renewed some of their other pre-Australian tour activities. From October, Rose resumed her fortnightly Thursday "at homes". From 9 November, Percy conducted his fortnightly Tuesday choral meetings. On 16 November, Percy instituted his "Pupils' Afternoons" — gatherings at which his pupils met and played to one another — and which were held thereafter on a more or less regular basis. Grainger gave his annual London solo recital at Aeolian Hall on 30 November.

The summer of 1909 represented the high point of Grainger's relationship with Karen Holten. His letters to her through the latter part of 1909, written every other day, chart his absorption with their sensual life together, and the frustrations that arose from their separation. This absorption notwithstanding, the suggestion of marriage, being raised once again, was received no more positively than before.

285   TO ROSE GRAINGER
24.9.09. Early Friday.

Oakwood,
Aigburth,
Liverpool.

My darling

Thanks for your letter. Have already answered Mrs Grieg's.

I arrive early Sunday morn, better leave door unbolted. Between 6 & 8 I arrive I think.

Had much pleasure reading self-life of Leigh Hunt in bed this morn.[61] *What* a charming loving contented just appreciative tender man. What an explorer of new genius & a freedom lover; a clear head & a soft heart.

On the other hand I cant read Shelley. His words make no music for me.

These English (not the live books of dead men, by [but] the dead minds of the living men, my hosts, etc) are hardly to be borne. Always talking of things, trains, comforts, Bradshaws, details of death-in-life, needless nonsense.

Never shall I travel with Rathbone again. Of all the costly nonsenses.

I have nought in common with these ways of living, nor with the thought behind the ways.

Give me rather bugs in my bed, dirt in my dishes, soap on my spoons, life in my limbs.

Shall write again tomorrow

Yr loving son
Perks.

I found psalm words to suit the Bach in the train

61 James Henry Leigh Hunt (1784–1859), editor, poet and essay writer. *The Autobiography of Leigh Hunt, with Reminiscences of Friends and Contemporaries* was published in three volumes in London in 1850, with new editions appearing in 1860 [1859] and 1903. A friend of Byron and Shelley, Hunt edited the latter's Poetical Works in four series (London [1871]–1875).

286 TO KAREN HOLTEN Oakwood,
[Original: Danish/some English] Aigburth,
25.9.09. Saturday morn. Liverpool.

I was naughty last night. Forgive me. I was excited at playing at the music festival, and just afterwards I listened to the rehearsal of my chorus, and when we got home I played some of my things for Rathbone and his relations and that excited me still more, so that when I went alone to my room at 1 o'cl it was almost impossible for me to go quietly to bed.[62] I needed so dreadfully some reaction, and I had been so full of longing for you the whole day and so lecherous in my mind. So I fell.

But I didn't enjoy it at all, it only saddened me, and I love you just as violently today and last night as if I hadn't suffered a defeat.

And there is no question of the habit coming up again. It was a momentary relapse in a special and unusual condition. Forgive me.

But my chorus sounded really flattering, and I played so well last night and reaped so much more success than the others. Tonight is the actual performance of my chorus. The chorus is really very nice with a pure clean dreamy tone & they really know the notes; &·the conductor is effective though not deep.

The Irish one I naturally knew the sound of, but it is the 1st time I have heard a good performance of Brigg Fair which sounds very flowing and warmly billowing. I don't think one can say that I write impractically for chorus.

Mother isn't coming to Liverpool after all. She would rather save the money and use it to perform chamber-music things of mine at home. Roger couldn't come either. And Rathbone has to leave here before the concert.

Everyone is enthusiastic about the Færoe Islands one. I will write out a little section of it and put it in for you in my next letter.

Monday. 27.9.09. London.
Pray for me Saturday evening, 8 o'cl. Liszt. Queens Hall.

The performance of my choruses was splendid and I believe I received without doubt the greatest applause of the whole evening, which is surprising when one remembers that both are slow and "grey" really. The other composers came forward straight away and bowed after their things, but I hid myself in a box right at the back of the hall, quite alone and unseen, really studied the sound of each bar of my things, & when the long applause came I amused myself by looking at all the folk trying to find me in various parts of the hall. I was quite calm and indifferent so that I really learned something & the whole business did me some good. I travelled home through the night. There are many small things I would like to tell you, and will do so in my next letter, which leaves on Wednesday (already) to Købmagergade. I am very busy today, with pupils, a rehearsal, and an American friend (Carlo Fischer) from Frankfurt days who came unexpectedly.[63] He is married to a Norwegian.

After many days great longing for the photos I was thrilled to see them on Sunday (yesterday) and again today in your last letter. (Yes, just use the typewritten envelopes; but not continuously, but in between written ones, which I will send you more of)

I think most of them are really good, many very dear, and scarcely a single one that doesn't make me a happy person. (*Dont* buy a camera without letting me know *first,* ever, please) I will have a lot to say about the different pictures in the next letter.

If, from now on, I don't write anything about goodness or naughtiness, then you can be sure that I am quite good.

You little sweeting, who had tummyache. I am just (almost) as unhappy as you, to be without *us.* I find it unspeakably bitter.

A thousand thanks for the pictures, and the letters, my comfort.

62 Reporting the evening chamber-music concert on 24 September, the *Daily Telegraph* of 27 September 1909 noted, "Mr Percy Grainger created something like a furore by his playing of Cyril Scott's Handelian Rhapsody, and two of his own transcriptions of Stanford's Irish dances". At the third and final concert, on the evening of 25 September, the Liverpool Welsh Choral Union conducted by Harry Evans performed Grainger's choral settings *Irish Tune* and *Brigg Fair*, tenor solo in the latter work being sung by John Coates. The *British Australasian* of 7 October, reprinting the critique from the *Manchester Guardian*, added a note: "There were repeated calls for the composer after the folk-song item, but he did not appear on the platform".

63 American Carlo Fischer (1872–1954) had studied at the Hoch Conservatorium in Frankfurt, taking cello with Bernhard Cossmann (for five semesters between 1894 and 1896) and Hugo Becker (for three semesters in 1896–7 and 1898–9). He was at this time solo cellist with the Minneapolis Symphony Orchestra. After the meeting Grainger commented to Rose, "He has grown very American & talks Norwegian like anything".

Paris is off, but may be I go to Röntgen & give a piano-evening in Amsterdam instead.

Dutch is going strong!

Not heard from Aarhus yet.

Many thanks for arbejderforeningen.

I long for your arms, your hair, your eyes, your letters, and for photographs of you.

I am desolate.

287 TO KAREN HOLTEN   In the train
[Original: Danish/some English phrases]
3 o'cl. Saturday. 30.10.09.

64 Nina Grieg had been a house-guest of the Graingers between 21 and 27 October. Her visit was duly reported in the *British Australasian* on 21 October 1909. Busoni had given his only piano recital for the season at the Bechstein Hall on 16 October and appeared at the Royal Albert Hall Sunday Concerts on 17 October. In addition to his other English engagements, he appeared at the Newcastle-upon-Tyne Musical Festival 20–22 October. He was to play at the Queen's Hall on 30 October. Grainger attended the recital on 16 October.

Now I have to go straight to Carl Meyers, and have said goodbye to Mrs Grieg who travels on Monday to Denmark.[64] Yes; truly you have not received much of my time in the last week, but it was nice to try and make Mrs G as happy as possible. If you had been married to me, and I was dead, then you would also, possibly, have liked to hear my compositions played, especially played well, as I do Grieg.

It was a joy to get your letter today, with 4 of my photos in. They are jolly good; 1000 thanks for them. 11 is a good picture and the one from the back. Maybe you are right that the "forest" [i.e. pubic hair] is becoming, I like it and I like to be without it.

You are right, your heroic decision was not received with any corresponding gratitude on my part. I cannot explain it. I didn't believe that you would do it for me, and when I heard from you that you would I was quietly glad, although ½ surprised, that I felt in a way satisfied in that regard. Your willingness to do it meant (and means) so much for me that I scarcely felt (or feel) the desire to urge you on to the actual deed. You know that, in a way, ideas are just as important to me as actualities. Since you have written yes you would, I have felt very proud, rich, calm. And it was tedious of me not to have expressed these feelings to you. One should make it a rule not to make great sacrifices for those who do not have time nor talent to be sufficiently grateful. I confess that I have behaved very unsatisfactorily in this matter, and thus it is only fair that you don't pull them out now for me. I can't bear that you should suffer unnecessarily for my sake in my absence, it is stupid-selfish of me to have got that idea.

When I am carried away by the power of sensual imagination I can easily hit on something like that, and if I get the idea again I will permit myself to ask you about it again (although you needn't at all comply with it), for when I am worked up I am shameless; as all people are, surely.

And I am just as grateful for your spiritual willingness as for any deed. But when we are together can I tear the "forest" out of you, then? When I am with you I am shameless, as well.

It amuses me that you feel dissatisfied with my little bits of letters, although yours are most often even shorter. I don't complain at the brevity of your letters (although I prefer to receive long ones) as I only want to receive what comes most easily and most naturally to you; but it amuses me all the same. (not bitterly)

I have already sent off F and D. Now I wonder when you will get it; it had to go so as to reach London after this afternoon's Continental mail. Perhaps it comes too soon. Let me know? Next [letter] will leave on Monday P.r. (Købm[agergade]).

It was **extremely** interesting with Busoni yesterday; he is a wise wise man, and absolutely courageous and clear. (in a way)

I played English Dance, and then we played Hillsong on 2 pianos, and after that I sang Died for love, Faðir og ðottir, and Bold W.[illiam] Taylor. He was very happy with the first 2, particularly for Hillsong, but he doesn't think so much of my way of treating folksongs. He and I have just the opposite views as to how songs should be used, and I value his view just as much as my own, although I absolutely don't share it; but Bach used both his and my way

I expected that he would think best of Hillsong, since he did that already 6 years ago. And I can well understand it. His overestimation and your underestimation of Hillsong are both interesting and extremely typical. He thinks it is crazy of me not to allow my orchestral things to be performed, since he says, as is *absolutely true*, that *no one* can know anything about orchestral tone without experience, and that everyone gets surprised (even if pleasurably surprised) with their 1st orchestral performances. He thinks that I have distinct character, and *believes* (without being certain about it) that I orchestrate well, but he thinks that I lack the primitive creativeness, since he finds that all my sources of inspiration are topographical, ethnological, national, etc. He thinks above all that I lack primitive impulses, and that I am "a mass of principles", which is quite true. If I were more primitively impulsive, I would moreover have fallen in love, either with you or with some other woman, more uncontrollably than I have.

I concede most of what he says, although he is possibly wrong in some things; for everyone always is. And I don't bother about it at all, neither as man nor as composer. Neither do I believe that it was his intention that I should. He is a keen-sighted person, and I am also an eager (if perhaps untalented) observer and an interesting subject, and it was very pleasant for me (and I think possibly also for him) to chat together about my works, and especially about the methods of treatment.

It was very clever of him that he recognised that I had "much temperament" (in other words: immediate sensuous ecstasy) in my things, but all the same had doubts about my "primitive impulsiveness" (deeper more *lasting* spiritual moving forces)

It is clever to be able to separate the 2 things from each other.

For you do know that I don't lack momentary sensuousness, although deeper feelings are much less strongly (or at least *impulsively*) present. My love for you consists of a series of sensual longings (following each other so quickly that they almost seem to be continuous) blended with admiration and feeling of righteousness. But [it] is quite different from your love of me, which is a thousand times more primitive and impulsive. But that is how I am in everything. Busoni is certainly right in a lot of what he says, although possibly not in everything.

I had great pleasure in seeing him properly again.

Why don't you photograph yourself then? It seems to me you let me wait an awful long time. You know how I long for something like that. But you must just do what you like best. The last pictures (of me) have again shown that it is pretty safe to take pictures (*oneself*) in pretty dull light with 5–7 minutes exposure. I beg you to do so soon and do so often.

Why should I yearn unnecessarily.

288   TO KAREN HOLTEN   London.
[Original: Danish/some English]
Sat. 6.11.09.

Paderewski asked me to dine tonight but I cant; have something else on.[65]

I am in a fever of happiness over your pictures. I would like to tie you up as you stand in 16 so you will be quite still, and kiss you lick you bite you pluck you and tickle you, one after the other. It is truly worth while to give up the world for your legs.

65 Paderewski was in London to fulfil various engagements including a recital in Queen's Hall on 16 November which Grainger attended. His final London appearance was on 18 December, when Hans Richter conducted the London Symphony Orchestra in a performance of Paderewski's New Symphony, he playing a concerto. Grainger met him and heard him play on 8 November, declaring him to be "extremely charmful". They dined together on 25 November. It was not their first meeting: they had met at a weekend at the country home of Lady Northcliffe in July 1908.

Something so enchanting as they are, so even so soft. What fun it is with Icelandic and the running costumes I miss you so frightfully.

I could be so sensual so world-forgettingly happy with you today. It is truly difficult to live in this way. What a shame you have had fever. How deserted I am today. Think of being together. Your pictures tempt me so enticingly. Send me more.

Next letter goes Tuesday (afternoon) to P.r.

I have no time, isn't it awful?

Why aren't you naughty when you think of me? You must get relief sometimes.

---

289   TO KAREN HOLTEN   London.
[Original: Danish/English]
Saturday. 13.11.09.

There is nothing to say: Only that I am unhappy and impatient, selfish and stupid.

I am also so fed up because I have to meet Richter on Sunday, I can't bear him.[66] I have such a terrible lot to do, the whole day pupils or practise, and I can't bear working. What can one do. I would much rather be dead.

If I could have sexual arousal with you every night, then it would be different, and if I wasn't afraid of getting a child I would gladly be married, perhaps.

But I can't allow a new person (or several) to come into the world to live the same working life as I do. (And my life is a thousand times luckier than the most)

In that sort of selfish way I go and think. It's no use hiding it.

When the day nears its end one is grateful, when each concert is over one is grateful. One only wishes the whole time for the time to pass, and yet it is youth one loves most, and just youth that is lost in this work-anaesthesia.

Now there is nothing to be done about it. Nor can I hurry up. I am too intelligent and too lazy to overstrain myself over tedious things.

Saturday. *later.*

Now I have received your letter of Thursday.

I can well realise that it can be tedious that I am always so easily influenced by books; but it seems to me that it is considerably cheaper to experience things on paper than in life. One doesn't need at all to suffer from the results of the experiments one gets to know in literature.

Many thanks for the photograph. I think that it's not bad at all, a well-taken photograph, beautiful colouring, and is like you as well, although (for me) it doesn't give the childlike and flower-like-ness that you have in appearance. I will show it to mother, and ask her what do you say

You write a little despairingly, Karen, and I think you have a great deal of justice in that.

Will you tell me *quite clearly* what you want me to do; so that I can answer whether I can or not. But before I get your reply I would just like to answer what I am almost sure you mean. I suppose that you can't much longer endure to be (for the most part) separated from each other, as we now are, and that you want me to marry you straight away or soon.

I **believe** that if I had enough money, or if you had money enough, that I would marry you already now. (if you were willing)

The whole thing is *almost* a matter of money.

But I will answer you quite definitely. I will not marry without sufficient money. Either I must find the money or you must find it. I know that our

66 This is a rather different opinion from that attributed to Grainger in the *Lone Hand* of 1 March 1909: "'And I've played with Richter, mother!' interjects the son. (He seems prouder of his various appearances with the London Symphony Society, under the baton of that supreme conductor, than of most of his other distinctions and all his royal mementos.) 'And, oh! that's a privilege. Do you know that Richter is so absolutely an artist, so utterly unworldly, and without the banal instincts of a showman, that when a composition has been poorly played — and his orchestra's "poor" playing excels the very best ordinary performance — he's been known to turn round and tell the audience that the orchestra would repeat this number, as its first playing had been faulty? His constant striving for perfection in connection with every bar of music he touches is a fount of inspiration for us younger men, and a challenge. But Richter is unique. He has been wonderfully kind to me — and helpful — helpful as only Richter can be'''. There would seem to be a fair amount of journalistic licence at work in this account of Grainger's relationship with Richter, nor is it clear what he hoped to achieve, or did achieve, from the projected meeting.

present way of living destroys and that it's a shame. But I am powerless. I cannot earn faster than I do.

I don't think it is suitable for me to "advise" you as to what you should do, since you surely know it much better than I.

But it appears to me as if there were the following possibilities.

1) Keep on as we are now, you in Cope, I in London, seeing each other not very often, waiting as we are for some years (4–8–10? who knows?) until I have saved enough money to be *able* to marry, if I *then wish to*.

2) That you come & live over here, earning what you can here, & we see as much of each other as we can, we living in seperate houses. I would try & get you pupils & work of course, if you wished.

3) That you, knowing that the whole matter is a money question, make up your mind to earn the needful money, in whatever way you think best, so that thereby you could quicken the *money-possibleness* of marriage; for if you could come to marriage with £1000 of your own it would naturally be a help.

Or if you cant be contented with any of the above 3 suggestions,

4) Give up loving me, if you can. Or if you cant, & you find life as it is not to be borne, then

5) Kill yourself, if there is no other way out.

You know I dont want you to kill yourself, but I think we all have the right to do with ourselves what we wish, if life becomes too hard for us. I myself often think of suicide although I am by no means sure that I would ever do it.

For my part, I think things stand (as they are) as well as one can expect. I suffer a good deal from our life as it is at the moment, and well understand that you must suffer 1000 times more, but I see no better way out.

Do you see one perhaps? Then tell me. I am not stubborn at present. I would rather do what will diminish our present agony. But certain things I **can't** do. I can't marry without much more money than I have now.

My mother ought have a £1000 settled on her.

My wife ought to have £1000 settled on her.

I ought to have a sum of money ready for my father in case of his falling ill.

A possible child ought to have a life insurance started from its birth that would give it an income of £100 a year from when it is 21 years old.

And I really also ought to have £1000 settled on me for my compositions.

So that means that one ought to have £3000 or £4000 saved **at least**, *apart* from earning a good living (which would be needed for the possible child's life insurance) at the moment.

And all this is only allowing for ONE *child*.

What can one do??

I am very sorry that my laziness doesn't permit me to earn quicker.

Next letter goes Monday to Købm. (p.r.)

Poor little sweet friend, you make me so sorry for you

---

290 TO ROGER QUILTER   31a Kings Rd.
15.11.09.

Darling Roger

Reynaldo Hahn (9 Rue Alfred de Vigny, Paris) wants to give a lecture, or lectures, here on new English music, & has been asking me about works that he may study up.[67] He also hopes to arrange a concert of new English compos in Paris. I spoke to him particularly of you & Cyril.

I wonder could you manage to send your works to him, to above Paris address?

67 Reynaldo Hahn (1875–1947), French composer and conductor of Venezuelan origin. He had gone to Paris at the age of three, settled there and taken out French nationality. He made a reputation through his songs, accompanying himself at the piano in salon and public concerts. He was in London for a concert by the Société des Concerts Français on Monday, 15 November 1909.

I *like* him, think him a *very* great singer, & a sympathetic composer in a way, & I long for his lecture (which would be clever I'm sure) to bristle with you & Cyril. Do send him (or get firms to send) your *choruses* for certain (I told him of them) & all best songs.

Fond friend, I'm worked off my arse, & have done no Rarotonging for days now But shall soon again.

I have done the 1st section of No 1 only, so far!

What joy to compare notes when we're both thro with them all. I **am** so thankful to you for noting them down, & for helping me through with the money. Herewith the receipt for the bill for the duplicating of the records, which please return to me at leisure. (I have paid them, alzo) If you think it too much dont scruple not to pay.[68]

Miss Permin has put me onto modern Danish plays. *A treat*, a real joy. Tho so keen on Denmark I've never read their modern stuff & therefor thought it must be no good.

But it's spiffing. Softhearted weakhearted sordid, gross, but practical, lifelit, & intelligent in the *extreme*, that is the picture I get from 3 plays by 3 seperate writers.[69] Dear me, there must be a higher active & alert mental life going on in Cope. The plays are every bit as quickwitted as Shaw's, & more playable, tho not one of the writers maybe is as great an individual as Shaw is, taking him alround.

Do get on with your Danish, there's a love.

yr old friend
Perks.

68 Roger Quilter had paid half the expense of having the copies of the Rarotongan records made. The bill was for £7.10.0.

69 Grainger was reading *Mor har Ret* [Mother is Right] (1904) by Henri Nathansen (1868–1944); *Frie Hænder* [Free Hands] (1908) by Otto Benzon (1856–1927) and *Hjælpen* [The Help] (1904) by Peter Andreas Plum Rosenberg (1858–1935). He told Karen on 9 November that he found *Mother is Right* to be the best written, and *The Help* the least good as literature, though he liked it best.

291   TO ROSE GRAINGER   [London]
18.11.09.

It's funny looking over old stuff.

And isnt it queer to think that of all the beings who meant much to me in that keen period ('03) you are the only friend that still means anything huge to me?

You mean more now, naturally, in part for that others have so dwindled in meaning.

292   TO KAREN HOLTEN   [London]
[Original: Danish/some English]
23.11.09.

Sweet Karen.

Nothing lies further from me than that I should doubt your mother's word; you mustn't think of the possibility of such a thing.

No, it is just *your* word I doubt; not actually *doubt*; more correctly, I neither doubt nor believe it. You have not given me any reason to doubt your word, but it is so easy for me to doubt.

What I said to you in the train sounds very beautiful, (I can remember that I said it) but I say so much I don't keep to, don't I?

I think it was very wrong of you to talk at all to your mother about the possibility of marriage with me; the possibility is too faint to be worth speaking about.

But since you have now been so unfortunate as to have spoken of it, it seems to me best to let her know how things stand, and show her this letter.

If you don't want to show her the letter then don't do it; for no one must be compelled to do anything at all; but if you don't do it, it is best for me not to accept your dear mother's invitation to stay with you in Copenhagen, since you can well understand that I don't want to be her guest while at the same time deceiving her about such an important question.

It is true enough that I *love you* **at present**, but marriage can't be thought of *at present*, and when I have money enough to think of it, you will be an old woman, etc.

An ideal life means to me: warm climates, long sea-journeys, undisturbed laziness, and independence from people's opinions (about me) in any country whatever. And without the possibility of an ideal life, I don't want to marry.

I see no possibility of being able to earn enough for the possibility of a more or less ideal life in less than 5-7-10 years. Perhaps I will still be in love with you in 10 years, but who knows?

You mother should know (since you have now thought it necessary to mention the word "marriage" at all) how un-tempting the prospects are with me.

For she has always been **so kind** to me, that I can't bear that she should be deceived by me.

If you have told your mother that "the *whole thing* is a question of money", you have misquoted my words, quite unknowingly perhaps.

I wrote: "the whole thing is *almost* a question of money".

If I ever wrote "the *whole thing* is a question of money" then it was lies or a mistake on my part.

It is *almost* a question of money, in as much as my financial situation absolutely does not permit the possibility of marriage. But if the money was all right, there are still many other hindrances; that you are older than me, that I prefer freedom, etc.

You know that I love you, but love is not sufficient basis for a marriage in my opinion.

Your mother mustn't trouble herself to answer all these tedious words, but you can write to me that you have shown her this, and if she would like to talk to me about the matter, I will soon be in Copenhagen.

It was kind beyond words of your mother to want to give you the money. I am sorry I can't behave just as kindly to you.

If you would rather *not* show this letter to your mother, then I can easily stay somewhere else in Copenhagen, but above all I don't want her to be disappointed in me in the future.

Mother sends love to you

So do I, many times,

Percy.

293   TO KAREN HOLTEN   [London]
[Original: Danish/German/some English]
26.11.09. Friday.

It's not that I am not full of love for you. If you knew how much worry mother and I have at present in the hope of earning money, how despairing I am and without hope, you would forgive me for all my ungratefulness towards you. To think that when you first came to us I earned £1000 per year. Now I earn only a *little bit* more, and we are compelled to spend in order to earn anything at all. I have absolutely no provincial engagements here. Vert is a fatal agent. Soon I will go back to Robinson Smith again. And pupils are so inconstant. One week they all come rushing to me and want more lessons, a fortnight later most of them leave. I believe we can get things a little up again, but it is hard that one must always beat the horse again and again, that it never runs by itself. And when you just in this spasm of poverty come and talk about marriage, it is very difficult for me to keep my balance. But, all the same, there is scarcely any other thought in me than thoughts about you. And when I remember that you have fulfilled my life's greatest desire (whipping) then it seems to me as if there were no other consideration in the world than fulfilling your life's greatest desire. And believe me, it is not consideration of my freedom, my compositions, folksongs, or any such thing that keeps me back from marriage, actually it is more worry about sometime putting a child into my present unhappy situation. You know that my mother is not against my marrying you *at all*. She said yesterday, for example, why not marry K in a year or two? And she talks like that, always. You have strong support in her. But I can't hold out any hopes to you when money matters stand as uncommonly bad as they do at present. Just think if things went still further downhill?

But I am entirely full of love for you. To live together with you without interruptions is my *only* strong hope, now and already for a long time since. When I practise I think of you almost the whole whole time.

I am lying in bed and trying to remember *just* how you scream when you are whipped.

You merciful friend, that took pity on me from the first. It is bitter that I can't treat you better.

And that I earn so little now, is indeed solely my own fault alone.

Next letter goes tomorrow (Saturday) evening to Ceresvej.

Pray for me on Tuesday! 3.15 o'cl.[70]

Picture 24 I like **very much**. I miss your presence so horribly when I see these lovely pictures of you.

> Ach könnt' ich bei dir sein!
> da wäre mir geholfen
> von alle meiner pein

[German: Oh could I but be with you/then I would be relieved/of all my torment]

We will be so unspeakably happy this time.

Your enchanting pictures feed me with longing.

It gets worse and worse.

Forgive me and be merciful to me. I am so in love with you today I am a poor thing. You have made great happiness in me.

70 The day of his Aeolian Hall recital. On 1 December Percy wrote to Karen that the recital had been a success: "full house and I played my best".

71 Grainger, in association with Mme Beatrice Langley (violin) and Miss May Mukle (cello), gave an evening of chamber music at the studio of Wilfred von Glehn on 9 December 1909, this being the fifth concert in the Langley-Mukle series. The programme included the Quartet for Piano and Strings in G minor Op. 45 by Fauré, and the first performance of Grainger's *Molly on the Shore* in the version for string quartet. Grainger had had a financial share in the recital, selling tickets from his home. The other musicians were Dorothy Bridson (viola) and Marjorie Hayward (violin). The private concert of compositions in the summer of 1910 did not take place.

294   TO KAREN HOLTEN   [London]
[Original: English/Danish]
10.12.09.

Well, the concert was a huge success last night. We played the Fauré really beautifully, & Molly was a wild success, violently encored, was very well played by them the 1st time thro, & perfectly the 2nd. So "all is well."[71]

Women for ever, I say.

The Langley-Muckle crew have been charming to rehearse with, etc, & I'll like them to do more things of mine.

It was a shame you didn't hear it. Such lots of my friends were there, Roger, Mrs Koehler, (returned especially from Rome) & the Sargent & Rathbone families in full force.

The tickets went very well, & I'm sure my private concert of compositions next summer will pay really very nicely.

I think Molly is a masterpiece, I really do. I dont say it's a work of *genius*, but it is masterly, practical, effective, finished.[72]

I doubt whether I have it in me to be a *genius*, but I think I have it in me to be a *master*.

I can remember so well those morning kisses. There is something so broad & spread about them like a kiss from a little calf or something like that.

Alas alas no time no time I've given 6 lessons today & had 5 folk to tea but I'll write again tomorrow

fond love

The morris dance parts have practically no mistakes, excellent I've been thro them all[73]

295   TO KAREN HOLTEN   [London]
[Original: Danish/some words English/PG's "private language" — see glossary]
11.12.09.

My sweet, my sweet, what shall I say to you?

The whole morning I have attempted to draw [copy] the enclosed, and am now quite drunk with your beauty. What a shame that you destroyed the plates! That is the hardest thing you have ever done to me. And that you, under these circumstances, cut the head off, makes it even worse. So we must see and take another picture, (perhaps this time in Cope?) with similar lighting and exactly the same position.

No later picture is more completely charming than that one, I think.

As you have already seen from my last letter, I couldn't make anything out of 30, which, although it is nice in itself, is a little too indistinct in the lines on the right hand side for me to be able to copy it tolerably.

When you come you must sometime lie on the bed (on your stomach) with your arms tied up round my neck, and while I whip you, you can bite me on my breast, around my breast, in the arm-pits, on my arm, etc. I long for that.

What I meant about branding letters into the flesh under the pubic hair, was:— when you shall have a baby, what will the doctor, and so on think when they see a bald "P" there? Don't you care about that?[74]

It is also *very* painful, the burning, I'll tell you.

To think, 2 years ago it was always young girls' legs that tempted me, and quite young girls especially, wasn't it? But that has quite disappeared now, at present, now I am tempted really exclusively (I think) by thoughts about you. You fill up so completely my sexual world, and melt into my inmost plans like "dew before the sun".

When I think in the abstract about you, then I think to myself: This time I will really be sweet to her, not whip her, or give her much pain in any way and only do pleasures that she has unmixed joy of herself. But when I see these nude pictures of you, humanity is anaesthetised in me, and I think:— No, this time she won't escape, I will achieve the whole uttermost with her this time, she who is so lovely shall be sacrificed without consideration, I cannot bear to wait longer, now or never, on her wailing I will build my house of joy.

I long to kiss your pudenda when your pubic hair has been plucked out. I will be able to lick you all round there and it will be smooth as butter, and soft. Why can't my tongue reach your little penis in there? If I could kiss your little penis how blissful I would be. To think he has never been kissed and is so straight and willing. When will I be allowed to pull out your pubic hair?

72 Grainger's good opinion was shared by the critic of *The Times* (10 December), who, as quoted by the *British Australasian* on 16 December, described the piece as "one of the most delightful and exhilarating things of the kind in existence".

73 Karen had copied the string parts of the just-completed room-music version of *Shepherd's Hey*.

74 Grainger was much given to plucking and branding at this time, activities which perhaps reflect his feelings of sexual desperation. On 30 July he pulled all the hair from his left armpit and burnt his left nipple with a hot key. The wound took some weeks to heal. Then on 19 October he tore out all his pubic hair: "My armpits ran with sweat from the pain and it struck in my head when I pulled out". Early in 1911 he acted out the branding fantasy (see letter 380).

All underarm hair must come out as well. Do you want us to pull out each other's pubic hair simultaneously, or each for himself?

Let's know about the running costumes as soon as done.

What a shame it is you didn't hear Molly and the success I have really warm warm friends over here. But they bore me, and you don't bore me.

I long to lie in bed on my back, while you kneel over me, with your mouth to my mouth, while my hand glides into your vulva. I long for the smell of sweat and smell of sex. I wish that you could get hold of your climax's moisture & smear it on my mouth & face & eyes. I wish you could bear for me to bite pieces out of your vulva and eat them.

I wish you were here. Everything else comes by itself.

Next leaves (p.r.) Monday.

I had a nice swim yesterday.

---

296   TO ERNEST THESIGER   31A King's Road
25.12.09.   Sloane Square
                                                    SW

Darling Ernest.

I am ever so touched & hugely delighted at your glorious & precious gift.

But I can't understand that you can bear to part with such a perfect work of your own as this is.

Never have I had, *never* will I have, a portrait of me more like, more true, more characteristic, more satisfying than yours.

Only a real real sensitive artist could produce a work so full of insight, so apt, so sweetly done.

A thousand thankful thoughts from your old friend

Percy.

Do come in on Thursday after 5.

---

297   TO KAREN HOLTEN   [London]
[Original: Danish/some English]
Monday. 27.12.09.

We found our little canary-bird dead yesterday morning. It made us so unhappy. I was terribly fond of her. She was sick latterly, had cramp in her claws, or something like that, but was always a sweet nature. It was good she didn't have children. We put her in a cardboard box wrapped up in paper, & some coal to make it sink in the Thames, but it wouldn't sink when I threw it in. The current went strongly down stream (i.e. down to the sea) and I saw the box floating towards Westminster. I followed it, saw it swim under 3 bridges, towards Vauxhall, but then I didn't have any more time and had to leave the box which was swimming in the middle of the river. Perhaps it got right out to the sea? Poor little bird. It was very fond of me. You could easily see that. I don't know why, since animals are not fond of me, usually. I have really lost a friend in the little old sick bird.

My way along the side of the Thames, was the same as we went in the fog that time from South Place, only the place where we saw those old ship's heads protrude out of the fog is different now as there is a new (ugly) bridge there now. Everything is changed so dreadfully. Death and change on all sides. I hope so deeply that I will be lucky enough never to have a child. It would be for me such an awful thought to bring a new life into the world.

To think how stupid I have been! The Albert Hall Concert is in the afternoon, so I can very well fetch you from L'[iver]pool St[atio]n in the evening.[75] Isn't that nice.

Of course you mustn't travel if there is a storm, for anything in the world.

I am looking forward so much to the running costume. *Bring the measurements.*

The enclosed is from a lovely photo in a photographic magazine. I will take one of you in that position and lighting some time.

When there is a storm and you don't sail, will you telegraph?

But if you leave Esbjerg but don't arrive early enough on Sunday night to catch the train, you don't need to telegraph, as I will get to know it at L'pool St Station.

When you come in the boat will you ask if a F.D.S. steamer leaves Harwich on the *19th Jan*, if not what is the nearest day?

Next letter leaves Wednesday from here to *Ceresvej*.

Many thanks about the printed critiques etc.[76] Bring some or all over here with you.

We will have it so lovely.

The little bird's death has awoken so many thoughts in me. 2 of my Gloucestershire singers have died since I collected from them, and **all** my Gloucestershire and many of my Lincolnshire records are not transcribed at all.

I have thought that it might be best if I didn't leave England at all next summer, but spent the holiday in London and worked day after day on these songs. You could live here with us a long time just as in Svinkløv and it would be cheaper and just as amusing for us (perhaps).

I am so happy when I think how soon I will be happy.

75 Karen was to arrive in London on 2 January 1910. Grainger played the Liszt *Hungarian Fantasia* with the New Symphony Orchestra conducted by Sir Charles Villiers Stanford at a matinee concert at the Royal Albert Hall on the same day.

76 As part of his arrangements for his forthcoming Scandinavian tour, Karen was helping in the negotiations with Grainger's agents, Wilhelm Hansen, over the printing of press selections.

298 TO HERMAN SANDBY
29.12.09.

31a Kings Rd.
Sloane Sq. Lond. S.W.

My dear old Herman

Glad you got mine & Rathbone's alright. He told me sometime ago that he was going to give you that letter, but it did not come, so as soon as I learned from you that you were in U.S.A. I asked him to let me have it at once to send it to you, fearing that it was maybe too late as it was.

My Recital on Nov 30 was a very great success. I made more money & got better critiques than I've ever done before. I play at the Albert Hall (with orch) this Sunday & on Jan 20 leave for Xnia for my 3 engagements there, for Bergen, then for Cope (Recital there Feb 15) & some 6 or 7 Danish provincial engagements getting back here towards end of Feb.

I *delight* to hear you are doing so splendidly over there. But indeed it is only to be expected.

Mother joins me in hearty best New Year wishes to you both.

I'm keenly looking forward to seeing your folk soon now in Cope.

I am very busy scoring the "Bride's Tragedy" just now.

My "Molly on the Shore" (string 4-some) was done at a private concert a few weeks ago, was PERFECTLY played & was a most electric success.

It was really great fun for me

In March I am giving Recitals in Frankfurt & Amsterdam. (thro Julius Röntgen)

I'm so glad to hear you like America better as time goes on. I feel sure there would be a great deal there that would amuse me ever so, & I much look forward to seeing it some day.

Now to business: You ask re Recital together.[77]

77 Herman had written from Philadelphia asking again if Grainger would give a duo-recital with him in London in the early spring.

You know how I love playing with you, it is a joy no other chambermusic playing nears, & I always welcome every chance of such a pleasure.

But matters stand thus; I earn *very well* with my Recitals, more so every year.

Now although you may do very well with a Recital in London yourself, the 2 of us together will make *hardly* any more money together than I would alone, as our friends are largely the same. Thus from my standpoint I should be earning little more than ½ what I would if I gave my concert alone. And my life is so full of hardwork & the need of earning that I cannot afford to suffer such a loss without some compensation somewhere.

You must remember that it is very difficult & unusual for a pianist to earn what I do with Recitals in London. Most lose money & my position is not got without many late nights & other efforts out in society, etc. I dont know how you do monetarily in a Recital alone in London, but it seems silly for us to give a show together when our friends are in great part the same, so that our joint earnings would not double our single, since also, one gets much more advertisement & importance from a Recital alone than a joint one.

That being so, if you care to give a Recital in London alone I should be delighted to play for you at it & you could do the same service for me at a Recital of mine.

If, on the other hand, you do not feel like giving a Recital alone here, would you feel inclined to give a joint one with me in London, & as compensation to me for sharing the Recital with you here, arrange a Danish provincial tour for you & me together? You see that would be very convenient for me, as it is akward & troublesome for me to write around to Danish provinces myself & it seems hard to get it done through an agent in Denmark; on the other hand it would be convenient for you to have (for our joint Recital) the advantage of my social energies here & of the numberless letters mother & I write before Recitals, etc, etc.

I am planning to do my next Danish provinces in Sept & Oct 1910, as I dont want to be away from my engagements here in the *fat* (Nov–Feb) of the winter season. Maybe we could do a joint London Recital after that. It is not much use before very end of Nov or beginning of Dec as Sargent & such folk are not back before.

As I have just given a Recital I very likely will not do so again this coming summer, for I like to give concerts *seldom* & make them pay *well*, & also as I am thinking of giving a private concert (in private house) of my own compositions (chamber works etc) this summer, which would be fun & might pay very well indeed.

Just let me know quite frankly how you feel about above suggestions. If my life were easier I would not have to look out so carefully for profit, but as it is I cant afford to throw away anything for I want to get some leisure for a compositional life as soon as may be.

My agent is again *E.L. Robinson*. I always found him very nice & very keen. I was also very fond of Tillett (N. Vert) but they were apt to be more forgetful & did not seem so reliable, though very nice.

I have a great many pupils now, & enjoy teaching as much as ever.

A talented Australian pupil played with orchestra at Bath last week.[78]

Dear Mrs Grieg was with us a few weeks ago & will likely spend part of next winter with us. She is a real darling, & **so** sweet & kind to me always, & so brave & fresh.

You never tell me of your compos! Why not? Do please.

Mother got seedy overworking for the Recital, alas, but is bettering again now I rejoice to say.

Longing to see you here soon
yr fond friend
Percy

78 The pupil was Kitty Parker, who played the Chopin E minor Piano Concerto in the Pump Room at Bath, Max Heymann conducting, on 23 December.

1910

On 20 January 1910 Grainger left London for a tour of concerts in Norway and Denmark, the first of five trips to Europe he was to make during 1910. En route he had a day in Copenhagen, from 22 to 23 January, without Karen being there. She had gone to London as planned on 2 January, staying on for a few days with Rose after Percy's departure, and leaving in the evening of 22 January. During Grainger's absence, Else Permin took his most important pupils.

Grainger's tour began with two solo recitals in Christiania, followed by an appearance with the National Theatre Orchestra there (conductor Johan Halvorsen) and with the orchestra of the Harmonien in Bergen (conductor Harald Heide), both times playing the Grieg Piano Concerto. He arrived in Copenhagen on 10 February. His piano evening there on 19 February was so successful that an extra recital was presented on 24 February. In addition to his solo recitals in three of the smaller Danish towns, he gave a joint recital for the Workers Association in Copenhagen at which Karen Holten appeared as accompanist to the singer, Frøken Tenna Frederiksen.

The tour was highly successful. Thanks to the efforts of Nina Grieg, the King and Queen of Norway promised to attend one of his Christiania recitals. In the event the royal couple attended both recitals and the Queen the orchestral concert. Mrs Grieg introduced Grainger to the Queen and on 29 January he was commanded to play at Court. Rose, with her usual thoroughness, distributed the news of the latter triumph to the press in England and Australia.

Grainger left Denmark for London on 26 February.

299 TO ROSE GRAINGER   Esbjerg harbor
[Postcard]
21.1.10.   11 ocl pm

Had *such* a lovely trip. Nearly calm allthro'. I slept or lay & thought over Rathbones idea from 10 last night till 10 tonight. Just dressed & found us entering harbor, a lovely moonlit starlit night with clean dry snow over everything.

Fond love.

334

1 Benjamin Ives Gilman, *Hopi Songs*, A Journal of American Ethnology and Archaeology, Vol. 5 (Boston, 1908). Grainger had first read the book in July 1909, commenting to Karen on 9 July, "I am so uneducated. When it deals with Acoustics and there are a lot of figures, I don't understand a single thing about it. I must learn arithmetic, some time". Early in 1910, Grainger lent the book to Thuren.

2 Alexander John Ellis (Sharpe) (1814–90), English philologist and mathematician. Intrigued by the pitch of vocal sounds he became a writer on scientific aspects of music. He depended on the mechanical evaluation of pitch rather than on the ear. The book was possibly *On the Sensations of Tone as a Physiological Basis for the Theory of Music* by Hermann Ludwig Ferdinand von Helmholtz, translated . . . with additions and notes . . . by A. J. Ellis (London, 1875), which latter work is mentioned in Gilman's book.

3 Grainger's *Scotch Strathspey and Reel* combines "6 Scotch and Irish tunes and halves of tunes that go well with each other and a chanty that blends amiably with the lot". The tunes are drawn from various sources: the basic Strathspey tune "Marquis of Huntley" and reel tune "The Reel of Tulloch (Thulichan)" are taken from the articles on "Strathspey" and "Reel" in Grove's *A Dictionary of Music and Musicians* (first edition, Vol. 3, 1894). Other tunes include a Scotch tune sung to Grainger in August 1911 by the painter Hugo Rumbold, and three Irish tunes, Nos. 318, 319 and 983, from Stanford's edition of *The Complete Petrie Collection of Irish Music*. The shanty "What Shall We Do With a Drunken Sailor" was from Charles Rosher. In its polyphonic many-voicedness the work was inspired by Grainger's experience of Polynesian music. Begun as early as 1901 or 1902 (the exact date is not clear), the work was completed by 4 October 1911. It was published by B. Schotts Söhne, Mainz, in 1924. When completed

300 TO ROSE GRAINGER　　　　　　　nearing Göteborg
Sunday. 23.1.10. midday.

I'm enjoying my journey quite a good deal today. I've been studiously reading hard passages in Gilman's Hopi songs again & again & growingly understand the bulk far better.[1]

Altho he no doubt went *splendidly* to work, yet the particular form of exactness he gets would not at all satisfy me, as it is highly sketchy rhythmicly (which is almost everything to me, rhythm [& small rhythmic waywardnesses] is)

I've been thinking out a possible way of noting down from "graphic records" (vibrations traced on carbon paper, or something) I cant think why they haven't tackled that, the chances of mistakes seem to me so wondrously less by that method, for one can magnify sights better than sounds. I believe my thoughts would prove a cheap possible working scheme; I must talk with some knowing person, & I must also read a book by Ellis.[2]

It's noteworthy how train & boat faring greaten the imagination. One always gets idea[s] travelling, & what is still better one gets plans; schemes of what to tackle next, various duties appear in dramatic degrees of weightiness. Lying in my bunk on the boat I thought out ways of setting that nice "runaway" chanty *"What shall we do with a drunken sailor?"*[3] A Scotch Strathspey accompanies it finely (this I found out journeying to Brigg years ago — Dear old Brigg's voted anti Elwes-conservative party, I'm so pleased) & on the "Fjord" I found that a ripping Irish Old Clan March from Petri collection fits with *both* the others. In the leftmost of the 3 drawers at the top of the underpart of Mrs Teagues bookcase opposite Sargent picture of me are the 3 vols of the Petri Coll. In vol 3 (I think) is the index. When you have ample leisure (not before, please) you might look up "Ancient Clan March" I think it happens 3 times in the collection, & starts:

(or like)

just copy out whichever of the 3 looks the most amusing. But only if you've time, for I could wait till homecoming alright if need be.

It seems on the Swedish stations that one helps oneself. At Göteborg just now, one butters ones own bread, pours out ones own coffee, or milk, cuts ones own cheeze, & the girl in waiting only keeps her eye on what's taken & pockets the money.

I've seen an old old Swedish peasant with a gorgeously colored & patterned throat-cloth; I wonder is it peasant made.

I felt frightfully tired when I started this morn, but I had a real good sleep for some hours & now feel frightfully hungry for "middag" an hour hence. There seems nothing extra pretty about the part of Sweden I've been thro so far, tho it's jolly to see the great stretches of unbroken snow on the flat plains.

Vilhjelm was really truly delighted with the Gaugain which I gave him last night.[4]

Copenhagen struck me as really extra pretty this time, but the people in it looked more like Teddy Bears than ever, I thought. Prettily inclined faces grow dull thro lack of beauty-sense, & I saw no decent clothes either in shops or on folk.

I'll post this from where I feed.

The poor old peasant's been talking to me. He's nearly blind & has been to Göteborg to be operated. By the way please go & get your glasses tested. Mrs Hunter's recommendation is W. Lang 22 Cavendish Sq.

Lots of love

301   TO ROSE GRAINGER   Hotel Westminster.
Tuesday. 25.1.10. early morn   [Christiania]

My darling one.

Nothing would I do as lief as sit down long & write you fully of all you touch on in your letter, Rathbones wish & life in general.[5] And also, too, I could write reams of what I've seen here already, & long to. But the job of very-fitting myself for Thursday must take **all** my day, I feel.

The elder brother Hals took me last night to see "Byggem. Solnes". Such a dear sweet old man, somewhat Klimsch like, honest & simple as the sky. (is at times) A real gentleman I would say, in his way, whose English (Hull) wife died of cancer a year ago. Quite a spiritual old man, in a way, & tho no doubt a keen business man, yet surely not a capitalist, & certainly full of a childlike bloom. The younger & more energetic brother is better dressed & somewhat of a blend of Fornander & Nansen, in looks, it seems to me.

There seems nothing of the Danish "Schmus" [Yiddish: "idle talk"] about any of them.

All I've met seem keen, spiritual, (more or less) kind though possible a bit dull (to other people) tactless & hard in a way.

The newspaper folk seem quite to lack the cheekiness of the cynical Danish ditto.

Looks are maybe not a strong point.

I've seen some adorable peasant weavings & embroideries in a shop window.

How *beyond words* "Solnes" is, to be sure. I cant imagine a sweeter character than Hilda Wangel, so womanly, so full of conscience, so easily moved in pity, so just. It's glorious when she makes Solnes write "heartily-warmly" on the boy's drawings, & adds: "How I hate him." She seems the embodiment of all the good of the universe, to me. She is very like you in *many* ways

Solnes' trouble will never be mine. He is a talent I a genius.[6] He wrested his place, & feared to have it wrested from him again. I shall do neither. I may never gain a place in the world, but I certainly shant *lose* it if I do chance to gain it, or be afraid of losing it.

The play is the tragedy of our present age: The tragedy of the fairly perfect modern woman brought face to face with the highly imperfect modern man. It is your & my tragedy as it is all other men's & women's tragedies.

It behoves us modern men to be meek & be guided by you modern women, & it also behoves you not to be too idealistic in your thoughts & dealings with us otherwise you simply leave us behind, to the helplessness & uselessness of both parties.

I read your dear letter thro again last thing in bed last night

---

the setting was for four men's voices and twenty-one instruments.

4 Grainger's "two American ladies", Mrs Koehler and Mrs Chadbourne, had introduced him to the art of the French painter Paul Gauguin (1848–1903) in July 1909, at which time he read Gauguin's *Noa-Noa* (in the German translation by Luise Wolf, Bruno Caşsirer, Berlin, [n.d.]). In December 1910 Grainger visited the exhibition of Manet and the Post-Impressionists organised by Roger Fry at the Grafton Galleries in London. For his response, see letter 371. J. Wilhjelm, a friend from the Svinklóv circle of August 1909, shared Grainger's enthusiasm for Gauguin.

5 Rose's letters during January and February 1910 are dominated by two themes: the possibility of his marriage to Karen and, in the context of accepting Rathbone's offer, the desirability of him allowing his orchestral works to be performed. Both themes are embedded in general observations about life, his career and personality.

6 The question of whether he was a "talent" or a "genius" was one which exercised Grainger regularly, and one on which his opinion was apt to alter. Writing to Karen on 10 December 1909 he observed, "I doubt whether I have it in me to be a *genius*; but I think I have it in me to be a *master*".

302 TO ROSE GRAINGER   Hotel Westminster
Wed. evening 26.1.10.   [Christiania]

My sweet noble mother.

No letter from you today, alas, for the mail from Denmark is snowed up or something belating.

Everything charming. The King & Queen are coming to the concert tomorrow, & Halvorsen has engaged me to play at one of his orchestral concerts (Grieg Concerto & Slaaterne it is 100 years since Ole Bull's birth & it is to be a wholly Norwegian concert to celebrate it) on Feb 5, Saturday, instead of giving my 3rd Klaveraften for the same screw (guaranteed) & the chance of the netto overskud (makings) being bigger of course.[7] Hals are delighted & of course so am I it means less work for me, is a preparation for Bergen, & the beginning of real publicity for me here. Halvorsen is a darling. The next time I come to Xnia he says he will do an orchestral work of mine "so sand jeg lever" [Danish: "as true as I am standing here"; lit. "am alive"]. When he heard Faðir og dóttir last night he said, after embraces, "Den maa vi faa her, den maa vi faa" [Danish: "we must get that here, we must get that"].

I do naught but practise from waking morns to falling asleep nights. I dont think I've *ever* worked *quite* so hard before. I feel very rocky about tomorrow, I'm no good at getting up things quickly after 4 days journeying, & am simply driven along by fear every hour of the day, but quite enjoying it.

Fear keeps me merry & fit I think. I really do, I believe it's good for me.

Halvorsen's orchestra seems hardly big enough (nor likely good enough either) to do English Dance really well, so I'll go for Green Bushes, with perhaps "Molly" on string orchestra (just as it is for 4-some no alteration) to go before it.

Or if he would do Faðir og Dóttir in Norwegian. That would maybe be the best fun of all.

I'm beginning to deeply love the Norwegians.

They are *real* darlings, & its a real upright land & quite as free as Denmark & a little more lofty somehow tho maybe not quite so endearing. Anyhow it['s] a land & a folk one would **trust** to the death honest, straightout, spiritual, very brave, very active very alive; not sentimental tho spiritual.

I do hope you're sleeping better loved one.

7 Ole Bornemann Bull, Norwegian violinist and composer, born at Bergen 5 February 1810, died 17 August 1880. He was one of the greatest of the nineteenth-century violinists and a seminal figure in Norwegian music. Johan Halvorsen (1864–1935), Norwegian violinist and composer, conductor of the Christiania National Theatre from 1889 to 1929. Grainger played twice more with Halvorsen in 1910, on 24 and 25 September, but his compositions were not done.

303 TO ROSE GRAINGER   Hotel Westminster.
28.1.10. even.   Xnia.

I dont think I ever suffered worse from nerves than last night. I began with fingers warm & in finest fettle & Bach went well & I not really nervous, but early in the Handel Vars I started to grow bit by bit more & more panicstricken, for no reason, so that my memory played me some minor tricks that caused me bitter agony, tho few folk will have noticed anything I suppose. From the 1st Grieg piece onward I was easy & really did some fine playing. "Möllarguttens Bruremarsch" (that sweet thing) pleased so much that I played it 2ce, & after the Irish Dances at end of program I had to give 3 encores "Morris Dance", Ab Chopin Study, & Irish folksong.

There was a great feeling of rousedness & Halvorsen & Hals seemed very delighted. It was Hals who insisted on sending a wire to you from us all after Concert, & ditto to Mrs Grieg, who has since wired warmly to me.[8]

Both Sigurd Hals & his wife are strongcharactered nicelooking refined warmhearted folk

8 The telegrams were reported in the *British Australasian* of 10 February 1910.

It is, I think, mighty hard to beat a certain rather rare type of Scandinavian man, such as Karen's dear father & this man Hals. One could always go to them in trouble, & one would never find the world a barrier between you & them, yet they are very patriotic & public-spirited with very fierce feelings about honesty & freedom.

One knows that one could stake ones life on their being godsends of ever-reliable comfort & kindliness to their wives & kinsfolk & one could never for a moment doubt their bodily bravery; while that bravery is not in their case woven round with recklessness, riskiness or gambling spirit as it so often is in English speaking lands. One could never even imagine them ever giving trouble thro drink or sexual waywardness, yet the freedom of their moral views would be unthinkable in any sort of Englishspeaking man in other ways at all near to them in type.

When I first come to Scand-a each time I'm a little inclined to scoff at this & that, but when I've been there a very little while the *absolute superiority* of these lands eats into ones bones, & I succumb with mute wonder.

It isnt art they shine in, tho they have talent, nor beauty certainly, but in purity, corage, cunning, calm, kindliness — in short in all that lifts man above other forms of life, & urges him yet further.

The stopping came crumbling out of my gumboily tooth yesterday & it began hurting slightly before the concert & afterwards again. So Hals put me onto the best man in the town, his toothsmith, & I've spent some time of pure bliss with him today.

Brŭn, a firm broad strongly built young man, clad in a white Indian (what we use board ship) cotton coat (no "professional" togs, no professional gag either, but honest explaining words) with a face instantly inspiring utterest belief in his manliness, capableness, & kindness.

He carved up all the roots of the tooth & from inside of one of them drove the mattery muck right out thro the path of the boil, & he never hurt me properly from 1st to last. He has used that stuff Sargent spoke of for years. He says they are awfully "gammeldags" [Danish: old-fashioned] in England.

Such nice modern apparatuses he has, such nicely newly scented hands, everything everlastingly disinfected & clean, & hardly ever touches one with his hands, nice little things for keeping ones mouth open; results: no sore mouth, no tiredness, no wornoutness.

Hals has a daughter that they want to spend some months in England (may be a goodish long time) but they dont know does *she* want to yet. She's in Rome. They want her in a home. Why not ours, I said? I wonder would you care to have her? They say she's awfully quiet & nice, loves farming & a Tolstoyan hardhanded selfservanting life in the hills, dresses there in boys clothes, & is generally a tomboy (but quiet & modest they say).

If yes, what would you charge, they ask? It doesn't matter how small or big her room. The bathroom would do, they say. Dont ask *too little* for I'm sure they have plenty of money in a careful Scand way. Please answer as early as may be.[9]

9 Rose quoted £2.2.0 per week.

These Xia crits are worth printing in D.T. when the election drunkenness is over, (I see the Radical side are doing nicely) dont you think. You know, they simply *could* **not** *be beaten* (the crits) But we'd better wait till all the Xia crits of the 3 concerts are to hand But short bits from these might be sent round to the papers & the tidings that my 1st Recital, at which N. King & Q were present, was such a howling success that in consequence thereof I've been engaged to play Grieg's concerto & Slaater at a special Orchestral Concert of the Christ. National Theater Orchestra (conducted by the composer & conductor Johan Halvorsen) of *Norwegian Music* on Feb 5, Saturday. If King & Queen are going to be present I'll just wire *Both 5th*. etc.

I'd send round to the papers that *Stanford's* Irish Dances made a special hit.

10 All Grainger's major
Scandinavian tour dates were
advertised in the *Daily Telegraph*
on the appropriate days. A
selection of reviews from this and
the later Dutch tour appeared in
the same paper on 23 April,
referring to Grainger's solo recital
of 21 June.

I'm playing them in Bergen 8th Feb, Copenhagen 11th Feb, Birkeröd, Denmark, 17th, Copenhagen Recital 19th, Nakskov Denmark 22.

Maybe Houghton would adv those days?[10]

Since my Recital Cope has been shifted I've had Arbejderfor. shifted too so the string of dates run as on the enclosed slip.

As far as I can see you ought to post (in afternoons before 6) Till (& including) *Feb 2nd*

> to Hotel Westminster

Feb 3rd & 4th post to

> C/o
> Hr Frants Beyer
> Hop.
> pr Bergen. Norway

Then dont post until *Feb 8th* (to Ceresvej) from when address 17 Ceresvej.

If you wish to wire me I'm here till *Sat night Feb 5.*

Am at Beyer's address *Feb 7 & 8*

Am at Ceresvej from *Feb 10* on.

Tomorrow I'll enclose rough oversettings of a few best bits of papers.

Now we turn to Rathbone's idea.

I'm very given to sticking out stubbornly on a point, & equally given to unlookedforly collapsing.

I'm quite ready to collapse in this case.

The fact that you wish me to do it is quite enough; to begin with. Not that it is any sacrifice. Far from. Since I've inside me given up the hope of compo realisations in Australia I've just been secretly waiting for something like this to come along.

One mustnt go & think I scorn realisations in sex or art. No one is less abstemious than I, by choice. But I like to be "approached", I dont wish ever in anything to take the asking step.

On the other hand, tho, one must realize just what it will mean.

Compos printed are like a man engaged.

Compos performed are like a man married.

(*Successful* compos printed & performed are like a *woman* married)

There is no mystery left.

In my case there is a further loss. I thoroly believe, (with a sort of businessy guess) that the right way to bring out my stuff in 10 or 15 years would be in a lump with a smash. I believe one would get over more ground in the one bang than in 10 years uphill. And I must own, I'm dearly fond of worldly success; (or else take the world away alltogether) On the other hand, works do not make successes by the hands of *inexperienced* men. I must hear. I must become knowing & practical & *fit*, so that I leave good muck in my trail of life. *That is vastly more weighty than any success at any time*, after all.

When considering any of following suggestions remember that the subscribers will be concerned with the *printing of scores*, & wont likely be keen on the *printing of parts*, as that latter wont be very interesting for them. One plan would be:

> To print (scores & parts) some Kipling
> choruses, & as many
> folksong settings as poss
> but not to print heavy
> stuff like English Dance,
> & Bride's Tragedy till
> later on, *allowing all the
> printed things to be performed,
> if wished*

Another plan would be:

> To print scores [of] every kind of thing
> (for Grainger soc)
> but only to print *parts* of
> *such particular works* as
> I *wished* performed
> This could easily be done, without
> being noticable in any way

Another plan would be:

> To print publicly *only such things* as
> I wished performed, & from any money thereby
> earned to print secretly for
> myself the bigger things for later,
> so that they're ready

The above plans would satisfy the subscribers & get a liking for me on foot, but would allow me to hold a reserve of heavy works for a big orchestral bust up, some 7, 10, 12, or 15 years hence.

I rather think some reserving plan like that would be the best.

Or else one might wholly give up idea of reserving big guns for a concentrated splash & just take the field like any other tame lamb.

All compyrights must be in my name & whatever arrangement is made with subscribers, or by them or me with firm doing actual printing or publishing (printing *only* best I think) must leave with me the power to (either after a certain no of years, or at any moment) arrange for *republication* with a *powerful publishing firm* (if I thought that line payingest) quite freely & untrammeledly.

In any case the works first to be brought out should be:

> First of all a Kipling vol of choruses accomp or unaccomp (Junglebook or 7 Seas) with "*Mother o' mine*" (the song) put in the front before the Titlepage, like a dedication. (It is called "Dedication" you know) & after the word "Dedication" I would put in ( ) (of all my Kipling settings to mother)

As you know, all my past & to-come Kiplings are dedicated to you ⟦as also is "B's Tragedy" "Lads of Wamphray" Ballad & March, "Widow's P" March, Marching Song, etc⟧ & I want a book of them therefor, led by "Dedication" (alas that it is so unsingable — such an inhuman compass — for it's so lovely) to open the ball.

The next thing to be printed shld be a *room music* book (book 1) of my "*British Folkmusic Settings*" holding say: Molly, Shepherd's Hey, Died for love, & Bold W. Taylor. The *whole "B F S"* dedicated to the memory of Grieg.

With these 2 bigger books might also come out the Swinburne "Reiver's Neck verse" printed as a *single song* (to be bought singly.)

That might be the first years or 1st 2 years printing; to be followed by more books (book 2, etc) of Kipling settings & "B.F.S." sandwidged with Hillsong for 2 pianos Widow's party March for 2 pianos, & various other *single* publications. All that would be easy enough to arrange.

I shall write Rathbone soon jumping more & more at his dear idea, but the matter cant be hastened much for it'll take some time hearing all the works needed for the 1st years printing.

From now on I'm going to encorage performances of *such works* as I feel I *need* to hear, even woppers like the English Dance, but best *out of London*, in the case of experimental works.

Even if I sail into the printing scheme soon I have *no intention* of at all pushing my works. I shall "tage det med ro og tæl' til tyve" [Danish: "take it quietly and count to twenty"] & mustnt be fashed about compo career matters. That I buck at. The subscribers can get their publications & a yearly concert (private; or later on public even) can be given of my stuff but that's all.

11 Rose was arranging the
rehearsal with the Langley–Mukle
group which took place on 6
March (see letter 324).

That is ripping that you are fixing a rehearsal with those nice string women.[11]

I wish you would kindly send to me to Ceresvej (posting about Feb 8) those mittens old Mrs Schoŭ made for me. She wld like to see me use them.

Please go to the eye doctor, darling. Dont let that slip, you will make me *ever so happy* by going either to Mrs Hunter's one or Mrs Adam's.

I wish while I'm away you'd get Laib to rephotograph that darling photo of me on the mast. (same size) Whoever takes it from frame must be careful: There seems to be dust between photo & glass & it ought to be tenderly cleaned, & in reframing made dusttight.

It would also be a huge joy to me if you'd go & be photoed while I'm away, either at Beresford's again or at Elliot & Fry's if their proofs of me are good. Ask Beresford, in that case, if he still has the plates of his former ones of you! I like you looking light in a picture, with head poising hopefully slightly upwards with low neck & your nice headwearing of when I left. Dont smile in photo I think. You are best when looking very bright without actually smiling. You dont need to melt to look kind.

It is very touching all you write about Karen. I *so* rejoice that you think her sweetnatured. I've never been able to find anything unsweet in her, I must say, & I am very fond of her, I find her a jolly companionable friend, & a very satisfactory sweetheart.

In your first letter you spoke of a rather drastic "choosing of the ways". That's the most impossible thing for me to hope to be able to do, I'm afraid. I might be capable of marrying K because I really felt she so wanted it, or I would be capable of severing connection with her if you assured me that her & my relation made you unhappy & that you felt sure that you & I would feel much happier without her in my life.

From out of very definite impulses one can act definitely. But my impulses are highly other than definite, to be sure. I havent noticed that I feel less bold or happy when K is about, on the other hand I've noticed that I can be equally happy when she's not on hand, but I have no impulses of any kind that could at all naturally lead me to "sever connection" with her. After all she & I are very good friends, (so I think) apart from being decent lovers, & I see no possible gain in breaking up such things. But any act you *definitely advise me* or *wish* me to do, I will do unquestioningly, & will never come back on you for any results of it, as long as it is understood to be your initiative, not mine. But I really cant pretend to any of my own. In fact, I dont want to, either.

I cant "break" with her for *her own* sake. Not unless she agrees. I can warn her, & do, & have, but one can't *act* ("Zhe is a dear lidtle thing, but zhe cannot agt") for other folk, for *their* sake. So it seems to me, anyway.

No I cant say I see any definite action of that sort blooming in the near future as far as *my* promptings go. But it is THE deepest consolation to think that you like Karen & find her sweet & true, & it is also a consolation to know that I like her at least so well that I could look forward to marriage with her, in the event of an "*accident*", without fearing that I'd regret it; even tho it turned out unlucky.

Where there is a certain amount of love a certain amount of risk is not a crime I think. So far I can say. But I cant truly say that I feel moved any further just yet. My heart *drives* me no further, & circumstances do not beckon.

But any deep definite wish of yours need only to be uttered: It shall be done.

I know how sweet & strong & lofty you are, & I shall follow *where I can*.

I've written to you from 9 till 12.30

304 TO ROSE GRAINGER [PM Kristiania]
30.1.10.

If any of the enclosed crits get put into the papers, & happen to mention the Stanford pieces, please send cuttings to him. If they dont get mentioned then we'll have to wait till we print them in D.T. & then send them to him. On 2nd thoughts I'll send him program & letter now myself & you can send cuttings at any time seperately.

I played at the Court yesterday, Sat, went to tea at 5 & stayed till 7.

Present were (Norw) King & Queen the British Minister to Norway & wife the British Minister to Sweden & wife, Mrs Mikkelsen the wife of the premier who steered Norway thro the break with Sweden, & some 15 odd other Danish Norwegian & English guests.

The Herberts (Br. Minister) have asked me up to their place in the hills outside Xia.

The King & Queen were fearfully sweet to me, they repeated again & again their joy at my concert, & that they want to come to hear me again. We spoke Danish Norwegian & English.[12]

Fondest love, my adorable mum, forgive haste

Snowstorms make the post to & from Xia irregular

[12] Afterwards the Queen sent him a gold and diamond tie-pin, a gift that Percy reported to Karen but Rose reported to the world through the pages of the *British Australasian* of 10 February.

305 TO ROSE GRAINGER [PM Kristiania]
[Postcard]
3.2.10.

Went with Mrs Hals to Pict gall & Ethnological Museum. Upliftingly lovely things. Glorious American bead belts, ripping Chinese clothes, grand old Norw. wood carvings, very like Maori; every-bit as good. They've got good Maori stuff too, better than B.M. (Lond)

I've got some nice Norw. trifles for you.

Saw Greenland fur clothes of unspeakable lovliness

306 TO ROSE GRAINGER Næsset, Hop.
7.2.10.

"Nur wer die B – s Kennt, weiss was ich leide"*

My own mum.

I'm suffering *agonies* of boredom. Middleclass folk are the cruelest scourge of the universe. It is of not the least use being *good* if one is boring.

These creatures are too frightful. Either their eyes are not clean, or the edges of their noses are more than damp, or their breath is revolting, or they unbeknownstly drop small tags of food when they feed; & then they are always wanting to embrace one or thump ones back, or force one to eat when their table manners are just making one wonder whether one's going to puke or not.

They're always talking about "it's so healthy" & "the lovely fresh mountain air" & have weak hearts & are terrible crocks generally. If folk who walk slowly only knew what torture it is for fastwalking folk to snail along, & how incomparably wearying bodily it is!

But thank the Lord that they sleep in the afternoon.

* German: "Only those who know the B[eyer]-s know how I suffer." This phrase recurs in various forms throughout Grainger's correspondence.

Isn't it sad that I should always suffer these miseries of boredom at Troldhaugen & in its nearness? I wonder whether dear Mrs Grieg is going to be perfectly frightfully boring to us while with us? What do you think?

Or maybe it is that I cant abear Vestlændinger, (West Norwegians — Bergen folk, etc) for the 2 Miss Griegs in Xnia gave me my only shockingly boring hours there. Now the Halses (real Xia folk) never bored me (yes! the elder brother but never Sigurd) but then Sigurd is the 1st of his family for centuries who has not been an officer. He looks like one & reminds of Fornander in lots of ways.

There is no doubt that Norwegians can be more loathesome to me than almost any folk. I dont know why Petersen's solid piggeries should not shock me & why Beyer's comparitively mild porkishnesses so deeply upset me. Maybe because the planter is not my host.

It is so frightful to have to listen to the B's dwelling on the sadness of G's death & how they miss him & all that. Sentimentality is a frightful mistake; it has the effect of making sensitive folk so terribly cold. I think that a lot of the Norwegian sensuality gets translated into "fühlerischkeit" [from German: sentimentality; lit. "feelingishness"]; that is always the danger with these spiritually inclined races.

I rehearsed this morn. A **shocking** orchestra & a thoroly incapable conductor, also with unclean eyes. But all very pleasant.

After rehearsal I managed to shake off Beyer & went to the Museum here, & revelled in their spiffing collection of Vestlandske peasant dresses, stuffs, weavings, furniture, carvings, & all sorts. Some of their clothes, wallhangings, etc strike me as lovely luscious & satisfying as any Eastern & native things could be, & some of their beadwork is jolly, tho far behind native stuff in choice of color, & ring of genius. They have here some maddeningly good (tho very few) examples of S'African beadwork. It's like drinking inspiration to see such fierysouled beadwork.

I saw a man in the railway yest with splendid boots up to the knee; with the furs outside, & nicely patterned with strips of cream-colored (furless) leather; called "Finnesko" (from Finnmark?)

And fancy to think that it was this Beyer that collected the tunes of op 66. The world is no place for me it seems!

How rapturous I'll be to see the lights of Helsingør ahead & shake the snow of Norway-Sweden off my shoes.

Fancy to hear a speech again that is not merely a mispronunciation of a foreign tongue. (Modern Norwegian is merely missounded Danish. The various "landsmaal" being the only living offspring of the old Norwegian.)

How am I to hold out till tomorrow night?

No letter from you here, dearest. I can't understand it. Maybe one comes this afternoon.

I long for word from you.

Your lonely restive aristocrat
Percy.

307   TO KAREN HOLTEN   [PM Vossevangen]
[Original: Danish]
[Telegram. PM 9 February (1910)]

ENORMOUS SUCCESS MAY I WIP YOU TOMORROW WILL YOU BE BRAVE

[The telegraph clerk has added a note: " 'Wip' is unclear".]

Between Bergen & Xia

Stirring (skörungr) mother, tender mum.

I'm very full of beans, life, love & hope these days.

How wrong I was about the Beyers, & all; & how thoroly I admire them & Norway.

Both Frants & wife are what Scans call prægtige mennesker [Danish: magnificent people] & that's just what they are. Generous, excitable, enthusiastic, imflamable, easyteared, & "much a man of joy" (gleðimaðr mikill) he is very fitted to be an artist's ugly lovable doglike friend. He is as fond & leal of old compositions he has long loved as any German, & as answers as lightly to the helm of any new unknown art (be it French or my music, or a saying of Mark Twains, or primitive tales of Eskimos by a Dane) as any artistic Englishman.

When I see his unfeigned love for my stuff I succumb to him at once, & no one could taste the overflowing unselfish tender sensitive goodwill of his & Marie's hospitality without realizing the presence of very lofty & sweet human qualities. Imperfect tho his hygene be, tho his legs have "a bad line", tho his clothes absorb the eye without pleasing it, yet he is that strange thing a perfect gentleman after all, & the very *soul* of politeness to *everyone*

He could no more be unkind & rough & unsensitive than he could be graceful or smart, & his tears are as corageous as they are tiresome.

(There is such a goodlooking cleanfeatured peasant lad in this carriage)

As for tears, when he & his wife told me details of the severing of Norway from Sweden, of the one-mindedness of the people, of the lack of harmful popular demonstration, of Mikkelsen's welcoming speach to the new nice king (not "Deres Majestæt" but the old-booming "Herre Konge",) when the dignity, control, & racial passionateness of this little spirited breed rose up before me, why it was my turn for a few mislukkede [Danish: unsuccessful] stillborn English tears.

Such a man as Beyer is the most passionate possible nationalist & local-color-specialist, yet seemingly without a germ of racial prejudice (even against Sweden). Like Grieg, almost laughably heart-rooted to a tiny & limited spot of the earth & branch of mankind, the whole world & all living creatures enjoy the overflowing sunny love of his friendly heart & grasp of his travelled mind.

One could kick him for his clumsiness a 100 times a day, but his spiritual innards dont leave the best within one alone for long.

He showed me a bewitching book by a Rasmussen, (Dane) "Nye Mennesker" about Greenlanders;[13] the small tubby Mongolian folk whose dumbfoundingly lovely clothes in the Norwegian Museums have birthed my latest madness.

What lives they lead! Cosy, sensual, gross, roley-poley-pudding-hearted people. Just think:— Outdoors they go dressed & overdressed in glorious Kingly furs heaped one above the other, & in their overheated foulaired cosy snow huts they go naked, sweating with heat. Isnt that a satisfying contrast? There is something that stirs one primitively in their tales, & the words of an old Greenland woman that close the book; (said to a white man about to leave the place towards things he's longing for) "Vent aldrig paa daggry naar du [de] længes"; (Never wait for daybreak when longing for anything) are certainly Danish, whether they are Eskimo or not. I'll likely bring the book along to read to you.

Dear Beyer, a very purehearted & wifeloving husband, with true Scandinavianness, is not afraid to point with affection to certain gross rank animal passages & occurances in the book, which no Englishman would

13 Knud Johan Victor Rasmussen (1879–1933), Danish Arctic explorer and author. His *Nye Mennesker*, with drawings by H. Moltke, was published in Copenhagen in 1905.

14 Probably Ingolf Schjøtt, who had headed the male-voice choir that sang at Grieg's funeral in Bergen on 9 September 1907. Later, in September 1912, Frants Beyer wrote to Grainger that although Schjøtt was enthusiastic (Grainger having sent him some newly published music), *Father and Daughter* seemed impossible as they could not obtain a choir. Schjøtt, however, planned to sing some of Grainger's songs, accompanied by Elizabeth Andersen.

dare to write, & no English reader would allow himself to refer to in any case.

Unashamedness (Do you remember the explosive manafacture's motto "Unashamed" in Major Barbara?) is a great link between folk who have it.

Well, my Xia successes had woke up Bergen & a packed house enthusiasticly dragged 4 encores out of me last night, & "Harmonien" gave me 200 kr instead of 150; & Bergen looks hopeful for the fall tour.

There is a charming, cleverlooking noblelooking, strong willed looking chorus conductor Schjøtt,[14] of far far back Danish origin that I met at Beyer's who is said to have done ripping performances of Grieg's "Psalms" with his choir, who went clean mad about my playing & folksong settings, & most so "Faðir & daughter" & would like to perform it for me (in "Maal") when I'm there next if he finds it's within their powers. His chorus is over a 100 strong. It would be **too** jolly to hear it in Mål which is the nearest Continental speech to Færøsk, & in which (& in Danish — as well of course as in Færøsk — one under the other) I have always intended printing Færø settings; also printing a seperate edition in English.

But I fear it may prove too hard for them. But if not, I'd trust that man up to the hilt.

The Bergen orchestra (I yesterday discovered) is full of Germans (hence it plays so excruciatingly out of tune) & the sounds of their harsh unkindly voices in the artistsroom nearly made me feel nervous & unhappy & closed-up last night before playing, but when I came before the audience & saw their welcoming kindly expectant Norwegian troll-faces I slid back into a balmy confidence & layed about me in abandoned style. The audience & I stoked each other up a lot last night

One of the German orchestral players asked me if a part of Australia wasn't English.

He then volontered that he was sick of Norwegian musicians, & he'd like to go to Australia, & were earnings high there.

I started this morn at about 6.30 & will reach Cope before midnight tomorrow evening. I'm looking foward to old Denmark like 1 oclock.

But I've not found Norway *in the* **least** disappointing. Except that I rather was ready to find them unpolite & wilfully pushing & full of chatter & surface gas like Alfhild & nice Mrs Wilhjelms, whereas I have found them quite as polite & gentle & contained & sweet as the Danes, tho maybe less amusing but more trustworthy.

I think you & I, (the old fond firm, fellow veterans in effort, & brothers in impacience) would agree in liking & admiring them keenly, & enjoying ourselves thoroly here.

Am so glad Miss Permin is back with you again. I, too, think she's a real nice jolly companionable Dane, & an element of dry humor about one

How I've got on with my Icelandic is real fine I think. I *quite* (not sketchily any more) understand an overwhelming overweight of whatever I read now, & the little New-Icelandic wordbook contains nearly all the old-Icelandic words I need to look up, I find.

That's the "bat" you & I'll be slinging next, I fondly hope. Just wait till I'm a dab & then's yr turn.

"Morgenavisen" Bergen, 9 Feb,10. says:

Never has G's Concerto been played with such warmth & bewitching grace.

It is marvelous that a far foreigner can play G's music in such a strikingly Norwegian manner; with all its wildness & all its delicate tenderness. He played like Grieg himself would have liked to.

Stanford's Irish Dances were original & interesting.

P.G's playing was received with the enthusiasm of a packed house; with an enthusiasm that Bergen never before has witnessed.

Fancy, when the Queen goes out in Xia, she oftenest gets on a tram, pays her 10 øre & stands on the platform, with her a girlfriend.

Norway wanted a very democratic ruling pair here, & chose its goods carefully, so its said. All classes here seem to agree that Politics here are very satisfactory, & the Royalties seem to give full satisfact. It is an ideal land, no doubt.

I shall long to enter it soon again.

My darling own comrade. I rejoiced to get yr letter at Bergen

309   TO ROSE GRAINGER
10.2.10

Between Göteborg & Helsingborg
(Sweden)

Dear me, those old Icelandic boys. I've been giving Egils Saga a fair quivering. My Icelandic is now, I take it, at about the same stage as my Danish was when I first went to Denmark. It would only need a few days in Iceland to make it thaw into an easy ungramatical flow.

Certainly Egill was hardly a refined delicate minded chap; when he once couldnt make his sword "bite" on a foe he threw him to the ground & bit his windpipe asunder. His whole path thro life was to match. He was the embodiment of will (not always ungenerously poised) & his fury, impatience or patience, (as the case called for) his alertness or stubbornness never throout his 90 years of lifedays seemed to fail to ride victorious above the warring tide of opposing elements.

These old boys were not lovable natures, hardly ever winning creatures, seldom really heroic, often ugly & maimed, & their minds without chances of widening into interesting stages. Why then does the bright echo of their mainly sordid lives haunt & inspire & satisfy such spiritualists as W. Morris & me almost beyond all other literature? I find the root of saga charm in this: Those chaps really *lived their lives out, & the tale of their deeds stands in relation to their* **personal** *instincts like a fuldbesat* [Danish: lit. full up = fully realised] *orchestral performance does to a score*

Wisdom & caution went short with them when they beckoned outside the path of their individual leanings. They sought no truce with overwhelming obstacles, they knew no spur of conflicting moral conceptions, they reaped no dull fruit of compromise & expediency. Thus they seldom died-in-life, & their very crimes even show the effortless balance & unwarpedness of a perfectly grown soft unscathed flower.

They had unique chances (or took them) of arriving at flawless fulfilment of extreme typicalness, & thus we find amongst their rogues & solid citizens the "farthest north" of many paths of human developement.

Thus Grettir is the purest possible blossom of ungrasping abstract aristocraticness, while Egill is the last word in *capably*-selfish *wellbalanced* greediness, & male friendship takes one of its lealest handclasps in the names Gunnar & Njál.

When these old men saw chances of furthering the unquenchable yearnings of their own wills, personalities, they sacrificed their fellows as heedlessly as we strike matches, & when the chances shut down against them they sac[r]ificed their own mere lives with the same prosiac blitheness.

Many matters went together to make personal individual developement most possible in the Viking age. The crowding influences that throttle individualism in most other times & breeds were here, curiously, absent or sleeping. Such as:

The conservativeness & superstitiousness of Polynesians, Celts, & most savages.

The religiousness of most races of an equal spirituality with the Vikings.

The Amativeness of Greeks, & most warm-landers

The tendency to herd together in unreasoning flocks like English, Americans, Germans.

The fear & effect of foreign invasion that has frostbiten 90 per cent of the races of history.

And so on.

No love, tenderness, humanitarianess, conscience, was ever man enough to stand against their individual personality.

They hadn't that love of either bossing & serving that in modern life makes equal slaves of Earls & thralls.

Nor even their joy of life, or "lifeforce" could stand beside their only obsession: *to be themselves*; wholly, desperately, & all the time. With such a goal, one wins or dies, & of course they died — But; *while* they lived they **were** themselves.

And when you say you'd sooner see me kissing K than being sillymannered & unnatural & warped & nondescript, you're merely sharing with me & other geniuses & mothers of geniuses impatience at supression & a stuttering manhood

Fancy, the dear Halses were at the train at Xia last night at 10.15 to meet me, & I homed with them & gorged myself with myseost [Norwegian whey-cheese] & bread & selters water & milk before going to the Westminster, there to wash my hair & very closely shave so as to arrive as winsome as poss in Cope tonight.

Hals put the news of my Bergen success into the Xia papers. Cope papers have not lacked news of my Norw successes, so I hear.

The mum's a real old fearless Viking individuality specialist, & no doubt, the darling: I am in my harmonies, maybe, sometimes

310 TO ROSE GRAINGER   [PM Kjøbenhavn]
[Postcard]
12.2.10.

Arbejderforeningen went fine last night, tho' the Danes seem a very dull audience after Norway. Am very comfy & happy & hugely rushed fixing up all meetings etc. for yesterday could do nought but practise of course.

Love from Karen who is very fit.

I did some composing in the train from Göteborg

311 TO ROSE GRAINGER   Cope[nhagen].
[Postcard]
Sunday. 13.2.10.

My darling.

Had such lovely hours yesterday with Mrs Grieg, & yestereve had my 1st Icelandic lesson. Dearest it's indescribably amusing rhythmical & undissappointing & lies easily for an English mouth. He, the Icelander, is really *good looking*, refined, tall, proud & sensitive. Very English looking. More of all this in tom's letter

312 TO ROSE GRAINGER   Ceresvej 17. Køb.
14.2.10.
Monday. morn.

My own Popinjay.

Life is so full of glory & interest & fascination & so empty of time, that I never know how to tell you the least part of what I want you to know when I'm away from you.

To begin with in the train from Göteborg last Thursday I got the idea for a newish kind of music, based on some sketches I thought of in a train coming down from Lady Bective's some 5 years ago, & wholly sodden with Rarotongan influence. When I get back you'll find I've nothing proper of it to play you yet, but its well birthed in my imagination for all that. It's going to be small in compass, & jumbly in rhythm like the Rarotongas, but with the rather more statuesque path of Færøsk interval-choice, but harmonic its going to be like myself, modern & modulatory. I can imagine its being **the** most effective form of choral writing thinkable. And what words do you think I'm going to use? How all comes back to first instincts at last! You know my old schwärmerei for Beowulf etc. Well, when I first started Icelandic 5 years ago, tho enthralled with the proze, I felt slight coolth towards the poetry, (Kvæði) largely because I didnt know enough Icelandic to grasp the gist. But last Thursday for the 1st time I found I knew enough to commence to open my mind to it.

Darling, here lies a future for me; which I've doubted for the last 8(?) years tho' I instinctively hoped for it earlier than that.

But without knowing the Færø treatment of Icelandicish words, & without having heard the Maori *paos* & *hakas*, & chiefestly without having digested the Rarotongan game, & also slightly without having read a few lines of Stevenson's about some music in the Marshalls (?) I wouldn't know how to chew this chance.[15] What I'm thinking of doing is to take 5 or 6 of the short Kvæði in (for inst) Egils Saga & jumble them together in a chorus in the way Rarotongans would. More of all this when we meet.

How do you like this little bit out of Egil's Saga. I think its such a sweetsmelling youthfully-sunny, sailorladdylike, bold-bad-young-roving-blade, seachantylike flirtation. The following is merely a careless literal oversetting of course:

The Jarl had a lovely daughter, & well grown too she. So it just happened, that Egil set himself down beside her that evening. She walked the floor (walked away) & was shy. Egil stood up & went to the seat the Jarl's daughter had sat in that day. And when that men should take their places at the table, then went the Jarls daughter up to her seat. She sang:

poem (sung)	What are you after, swain, in my seat? Seldom have you given the wolf warm broth.* I wish to be alone about my own (seat). *You* didn't see the raven yelling in the sun-of-carcases (blood) in the fall *You* were not there when the sword-edges were dripping.

*meaning: You've not seen much fighting yet.

Egil took hold of her & set her down beside him. He sang:

verse (sung)	I go with a bloodstained brand (the gnawers-of-bones (ravens) follow me) & a brilliant spear. We vikings attacked fiercely. We vikings became enraged. Fire ran along the rooftries I left behind me a bloody belly* asleep by the castle-gate.

15 No work of this description can be identified in Grainger's surviving *oeuvre*. However, the influence of his experience of Polynesian music permeates several of his compositions from this period, including his *Scotch Strathspey and Reel* (see note 3 above) and *Random Round* (see note 48, 1912). A suggestion of these ideas perhaps permeates his plan for the *Death-Song for Hjalmar Thuren* (1914–16), a requiem for baritone solo, mixed chorus and orchestra based on several Færøe Island folksongs and Norwegian Kæmpevise. This latter composition remained unfinished. In this context, Stevenson's description of music in the Gilbert Islands in the chapter "The Five Days' Festival" in his *In the South Seas* (see note 56, 1912) is highly suggestive, but there is some doubt as to whether Grainger had read the book at this time.

> Then they drank together that evening & were thoroly merry. That was feasting of the best, & the day after too. Then went the vikings to their ships. They & the jarl parted in friendship & exchanged gifts. (it is Feenished)

---

*He means that he killed his man.

I find a fragrance in that.

How rich & full of joy & meaning & experience the world is; & what vast spaces of glory even our tawdry civilisation makes within reach today. Take yesterday.

The nice *Greenland* book arrived from bookshop.

Had nice lunch with Wilhjelms who gave me Danish translation of Icelandic "Heimskringla" (Story of the old Kings of *Norway*) & I saw nice *French* & Gaugains (*Tahiti*) there too. The Holten had Kinsfolk (6–8?) here yest. So I played to them for 2 hours or over, (good practice) covering thereby art of the following nations. *Russian, German, French, Norwegian, Spanish, Rarotongan, English, Irish*. Then Svend [Karen's brother] turned on the gramophone & I writhed in bliss to hear Taylor's perfect folksong records.

Then we heard Caruso (glorious) in *Italian* stuff. Such song is really Grecian, such warbling of such a fit healthy perfect organ. If I were a woman I should call that a voice worth taking into bed with me. And how I admire those jolly rank gifted Italian composers, Verdi, & L. Cavallo, Mascagni, etc.

Then we heard Geraldine Farrar (is she *Australian* or *American*? Lovely voice) in Verdi.[16] Then a March by Pryor, (the Barrarat ripping trombone soloist in Souza's band) *Australian*, then *American* cakewalk's etc, & then I played some *Scotch Irish* English & American tunes from a book Cai has, & relished some Burns verses therein. In all, in the Space of 10 hours the art of 14 nationalities & 4 continents brought to one's lips & relished.

My own one, I've not lived in vain. That was a good deed getting Taylor gramophoned. I feel real virtue in me when I hear those records. Darling I must do some more good deeds. Damn expense.

I MUST get some more of the old men done this summer before they die. You know its Gouldthorpe's B. W. Taylor I've used chiefly in the setting (*what* a good setting it is to be sure) Taylor's is very different much brighter & sunnier. One of these days I'll set his version too, tho *quite* otherwise. Oh darling how much there is to do & what yearnings I have. I'd like to really be closely in touch with military bands for some years. Those pure blaring crystal brasen noises suit the color of my soul.

Dear Karen is so sweet to me, & looks so young & happy & fit. There's no time for all one wants, that's all.

Think less than a 14 night now; & all we'll have to jaw about. These Continental trips are good for one, & there's no doubt concert playing is not wholly to be sniffed at.

Please thank Permin awfully & say I'll write soon

I *believe* that the expenses of my Cope Rec. (next Sat) are already covered They've sold 200 Kr worth already.

16 The Italian opera composers: Giuseppe Fortunino Francesco Verdi (1813–1901); Ruggiero Leoncavallo (1857–1919); Pietro Mascagni (1863–1945). The singers: Enrico Caruso (1873–1921), Italian tenor; Geraldine Farrar (1882–1967), American soprano. Arthur Pryor, American concert bandmaster, founder and musical director of Pryor's band. He had appeared as trombone soloist with Sousa's band at the concert Grainger attended on 4 October 1901, playing his own composition "Love Thoughts".

313   TO ROSE GRAINGER   Cope
[Postcard]
15.2.10.

I've started a new tune that I think you will like & will write it out for you as soon as I get a chance It's rather like the Sydney Town Hall Yule tune (for Twilight) Alas for old Birkerød tonight. That program hasn't had the graft it would have had the old tune not turned up.

Very fond love

314 TO ROSE GRAINGER   Køb. [Copenhagen]
Wed. 16.2.10.

It was a howling success last night. *Packed* hall (small hall) lovely enthusiasm & I played with soul & spirit, & gave 3 encores. The Melchiors & Houmark & the brother of the man who wrote the Greenland book went from Cope to hear me, fancy. Mrs Grieg has knitted me *the most* lovely throat comforter in cream yellow silk, *so* beautifully done & such tons of work in it.

There is a kvindelig orkester [women's orchestra] (conductor Sandby's brother, leader Miss Arlaud) started in Cope.[17] Miss Arlaud was here today, looking *so* nice looking & jollier & happier than formerly & wants to do my "Molly" & some other here on their orchestra. It might be fun.

I have such sweet talks with darling Mrs Grieg. She tells me about her early verliebtheit [German: infatuation] in Grieg & their young years & struggles, she & I are quite a sentimental couple in a way. You cant *think* how she fights for me, if she were married to me she couldnt be more of a thoro partizan. I'll tell you in how when we meet. I'm bringing back with me something that I think will keep you nice & warm in the winter indoors.

Now (today) I'm going to Mrs Grieg's, Houmark's, old Mrs Sandby's & Federspiels. I got 5 Kr over the guarantee last night!

Of course there are no crits from Arb.f. or Birkerød, as the 1st is a private club & the 2nd place boasts no paper

Karen sends very fond greetings.

My own pet, how I love to get yr letters.

315 TO ROSE GRAINGER   [PM Kjøbenhavn]
[Postcard]
17.2.10.

Am practising like a nigger.

That agent has come & talked.[18] It would amount to about otte og halvtresindstyve [Danish: fifty-eight] £ for a little over a week. Göteborg Helsingfors, & St Petersboro.

Shall write letter tomorrow. Fondly.

316 TO ROSE GRAINGER   [Copenhagen]
18.2.10.

I forgot to say that Sigurd Hals & his wife are coming to England for 10 days, or a few weeks in about April & wonder whether they could board by us. They cld share a room, & would be fun I'm sure.

What do you mean by York*shire*, dearest? Do you mean *York*?

I'll send program on Sunday.

The enclosed Miss (Alette) Schou has evidently journalized for my benifit. Isn't it jolly?

Working like Trojan.

17 The Kvindeligt Strygeorkester, conducted by Kristian Sandby, gave a concert in Copenhagen on 31 October 1910 at which two of Grainger's compositions for string orchestra were played, *Always Merry and Bright [Mock Morris]* and *Molly on the Shore*. This was the first performance of an orchestral (even if only string) work of his. Grainger played the Tchaikovsky Bb minor Piano Concerto with the (supplemented) orchestra at the same concert. Jens Christian Houmark (b. 1869), Danish novelist. Houmark gave Grainger copies of two of his novels: *Det Syndens Barn, en Type* [The Child of Sin, a Type] (1908) in February 1910 and *For Guds Aasyn, en Fortælling* [Before God's Face, a Story] (1910) in March.

18 Grainger had been approached at the end of January 1910 by concert agent Marius Montal with a tour proposal. Rose replied, 18 February, advising fee and conditions: £40 minimum the week or £50 for nine or at most ten days, Percy to be "well boomed". Although talk of the Russian tour continued intermittently through 1911 and 1912, it was not until November 1913 that Grainger made his appearance in St Petersburg and Helsingfors. He did not go to Göteborg.

If only my fingers could stand the strain of pracing the Tchai. But nails, flesh, etc break peal & fray in all directions alas.

Midday yesterday there was sold 450 Kr. I'll send money next Wednesday Bergen–Nakskov.

Houmark's also written amusing bit which I'll send tomorrow.

Desperately but lovingly

Percy.

317   TO ROSE GRAINGER   Cope
[Postcard]
Sat. midday. 19.2.10.

As far as I can gather thro the telephone the whole hall is sold out for tonight. I've eaten 4 eggs & am just about to drink another 2.

Spent a lovely eve with Mrs Grieg last night. A cold I caught from her on arriving here (she had had influenza) is now gone. I leave Esbjerg today (Sat) week & arrive Sunday eve or Mond morn.

Do remind me to tell you of Wiljelms &.the "Snorri" book.[19] Such a joke

318   TO ROSE GRAINGER   Copenhagen
[Telegram. PM 20 February 1910]

UDSOLGT [Danish: sold out] BRILLIANT GIVE SECOND RECITAL 24 ADORINGLY

319   TO ROSE GRAINGER   Cope.
Sunday morn. 20.2.10.

Well, the hall was udsoldt [udsolgt], & I played splendidly altho my sore finger (1st, right hand) grew worse & worse all the time It has troubled me frightfully ever since I got to Xia, I had to use Calodium for my concerts there.

My program was *much much* too long, more so with 4 encores.

Mrs Grieg & K thought I was in really 1st class form, & that the public was very roused. After Norwegians a Danish audience looks so sleepy dull unrousable & sounds so cold.

Dear Mrs Grieg sat in 2nd row & was a great comfort. And after the concert came out here with Miss Hagerup & listened to Taylor on the Gramophone & common cakewalk & Caruso & Geraldine Farrar records, etc, until late late.

The only crits that have come out so far are bloody dull, tho well meant no doubt, here they are, anyway.

Yest afternoon K luckily saw in the paper that a singer had fallen ill who was to give a concert in Palæ[e]ts lille Sal 24. Feb & then & there rang up & reserved the hall for me.[20] So when I saw old sleepyhead Hansen in the eve & he said "Pity we cant get a hall for a 2nd concert" I was able to say "Have already reserved Palæts lille for 24".

He thinks we ought to get it filled again.

I shall play big BB
    Slåtter group
    Ravel & *2* Albeniz
& Chopin group ending with Polonaise. I'm forced to choose a light program as I only get back from Nakskov the day before after long journey.

19 Snorri Sturluson (b. West Iceland 1179, d. Reykjaholt 1241), author of the prose *Edda*, the *Heimskringla* and possibly *Egils Saga*. Wilhjelm had given Grainger his copy of *Snorre Sturlason: Kongesagaer*, oversat af Dr Gustav Storm, med illustrationer af H. Egedius [and others] (Kristiania, 1900).

20 The hall was Odd Fellow-Palæets mindre Sal.

If you want to advertise it its *Piano Recital Palæts lille Sal. Feb 24. eve.*
The Danish agent wants to try & get me those Gøteborg, Helsingfors & Petersborg bookings from directly after Amsterdam till the beginning April
You might tell Houghton & Co (Edgar Pittman) to write to De nieuwe Muziekhandel Amst. & Firnberg Frankf, *early* & that I['m] playing Irish Dances in Yorkshire.

If you dont approve of what I herewith send for that concert, then substitute big B.B. for one group, if you like

Program for Yorkshire 2.3.10.
1st group

Chopin
{
Study in C min, op 25 No 12
A♭ Study (posthumous)
Mazurka, C maj
Polonaise, in A♭.
}

2nd group
Albeniz   (a)   Triana
Schumann (b)   Romance
St-Gr   2 Irish Dances
           (a)   Lepr's D
           (b)   March Jig (Maguires Kick)[21]

Cut out details from programs in program drawer near window South Pl? Liverpool Fest? Lond Rec?
Fondest love from your devoted one That **was** a herculean program last night Extinguishing, simple. I ate 8 eggs, yest.

320   TO ROSE GRAINGER

[Postcard]
22.2.10.

                                       Cope.

Am so deadly deadly tired with all the unavoidable visits, etc. Cope is *at least* **as** bad as Lond. K will send you today or tomorrow Hansen's cheque (or something) for 335. Tomorrow I'll send you other money. Now I'm off to Nakskov. Saw Høeg[22] last night at Schou's He's very keen on fixing up autumn tours in Jylland. My poor finger's so bad
     Very fond love

321   TO ROSE GRAINGER

Midday. 23.2.10.

                                    Ceresvej 17.
                                    [Copenhagen]

Darling mum.

     Twas great fun in Nakskov. I left here 11 in morn & got there 4 aftern. Had a meal & practised & played at 8.15 & caught the 10 oclock (eve) train to Nykøbing (Falster) slept there, up this morn 5.30 & got to Cope 9.¾ some 3 hours earlier, on account of my Recital here tomorrow.
     The hall was packed there & Miss Permin's friends charming & kind.[23] They evidently had beaten things up very thoroly in the press.
     My capacity for playing a whole Recital without having practised has grown strangely. I played thoroly well there last night, with only 2 hours practice since Sat, for my finger has been so sore. I know now that I could easy undertake an Australian tour. Later this aftern I'll see Hjalmar Thuren, but otherwise lie low for tomorrow.

21 At the Cleckheaton Philharmonic Concert on 2 March (an engagement Grainger secured through the cancellation of another pianist) Grainger played three groups of piano solos. Only the Stanford–Grainger items from the two groups given here appear on the final programme.
B. Firnberg was the agent for Grainger's Frankfurt recital on 12 March 1910, and Concertbureau C.V. "De nieuwe Muziekhandel" for his Amsterdam debut recital on 15 March.

22 Niels Høeg was married to Alette Schou's sister and was a member of the Svinkløv circle. Grainger secured various engagements through him including Svendborg (2 November), Aalborg (8 November) and Randers (9 November) in the Scandinavian tour in the autumn of 1910.

23 Grainger had secured the Nakskov engagement through Miss Permin.

Karen sent off yesterday 335 Kr 90 Ø. & tomorrow I'll send 455 Kr, the latter being Nakskov, Bergen, Birkerød, & Arbejder.-for, minus my Cope expenses, & the former (sent yest) makings of 1st Køb Recital, after all exs.

The Kr 100 from Vejlefjord I'll bring with me.

Am so longing for Sunday night. If Miss Busch wants program for March 3rd, before I return, make it as near Birkerøds as poss.

What a thousand things there are to think of in each place, to keep ones friends friendly & not throw away chances. I feel a bit tired, but happy & keen

Your adoring son

322   TO ROSE GRAINGER [PM Kjøbenhavn]
[Postcard]
24.2.10. Thursday.

The 455 Kr (£25 odd) will be sent to you direct from bank here. (cheque)
Tomorrow (early) I leave for Vejlefjord San.
Sat for London.
Had such **lovely** time with that dear delightful H. Thuren yesterday.
Shall write tomorrow again

323   TO ROSE GRAINGER [In the train] Fyen.
25.2.10

Wasnt it funny, that after such a pronounced success as my last Sat's Cope Rec was, that only between ½ & ⅔ as much should be sold for the 2nd? Hansens tell me that Julia Culp & my 1st Rec have been the *only* sold-out concerts this winter in Cope.[24] I dont know the final result of yesterday's but I expect to have made about £5. But I'm heartily glad I gave it, for I had a huge public ovation (5 encores) & as you see, the crits are more glowing & usable than the 1st lot. Why I dont know & cant guess!

I played well last night, enthusiasticly & all that, but not technically my quite best form, tho far better than I expected after having so little time after Nakskov, & having had my practise lately broken up by my bad finger, which didnt, by the way, worry me last night.

Hansen papered the hall well, & it looked nice & full & left a ripping impression for next time. I'll be glad now to get a few day's rest from concerts. I consider I've had rather a doing just lately.

Sunday coming immediately after Sat's Recital made it impossible to advertise in morn papers before Tuesday, nor were programs, etc ready before, so there were only the 3 days to beat things up in. And then of course Hansens are slower than the wrath of God & do absolutely nothing to made anything go that doesnt go by itself. He'll send the overskud [Danish: surplus, or profit] by cheque as before.

Have engaged the Palæ for 2 concerts in the fall.

Br. Hals have printed my Norw crits *splendidly*. You'll see.

Well I think I've been lucky this Scand month.

I feel I've played well at every concert, except a portion of the 1st Kristiania one.

Marius Montal (agent) is going to arrange Gøteborg, etc for the fall instead of now, if he can. Anyhow its off for now, luckily.

Dont let Permin know the 2nd Cope Rec was **papered**.

I must tell you something sweet about Karen.

As I got the Arbejderfor, Birkerød, etc moneys I handed them over to her to keep for me prior to sending them to you; & both she & I (particu-

24 Julia Culp (1880–1970), Dutch mezzo-soprano. She sang in the first performance of Delius's *Songs of Sunset* under Beecham on 16 June 1911, a performance which Grainger attended. Grainger gave two concerts with her in Scotland, 7 and 9 December 1911. He was also to tour with her in the U.S.A. in 1916.

larly she) thought I'd also given her the 200 Kr from Bergen. The morn I left for Nakskov, before leaving, she was looking for the money & couldnt find this Kr 200 anywhere, & thought they were unfindably lost or stolen, or something.

Of course I said I was sure they'd turn up, but if not I didnt care, accidents will happen, but K was fearfully distressed & desperate. However I got a wire at Nakskov "fundet pengene" [Danish: found the money] a.s.o.

But last night, when packing after concert (2 o'clock?) I came aX a Bergen envelope with the 200 in, in one of my drawers.

So I took it to K & asked her what it meant, had we miscounted?

She then told me that she had not found the money at all, but fearing I wouldnt take the 200 from her if I thought it was her own money she wired that to Nakskov

Hjalmar Thuren wants me to send in my Polynesian notings-down to the International Musical Society's journals. I will, I think

He is such a real scientist, so generous & uplifting. Alas, he is very ill, I fear. I could live long happily with that good ugly man, & work together with him, for abstract aims.

I am **so** *longing* to see the towell trousers.[25] I *am* going to be gloriously dressed some day I'm full of dress-plans. Such glorious hints in Xia, Bergen & Cope museums. HOW I hope I arrive Sunday.

It will be jolly to be back in London, & I'm longing to really work up new pieces for other tours. If Frankf goes well & Amst I'm going to think seriously of attacking Berlin, not least because of America.[26] When one sees that things pay one gets the wish to work on those lines. Arrange as many lessons for me as you can cram in.

I'm feeling finely fresh & attackish. Longing to compose, anxious to practise, keen to teach, *yearning* to note-down, & fairly snorting to embrace my own pet mum.

(This is last letter)

After a couple of days in London, during which time he was able to see Delius twice, Grainger was off to Yorkshire for his engagement with the Cleckheaton Philharmonic Society ("not very particular", Rose observed) on 2 March. The main event on his return was the private rehearsal, arranged by Rose with Mme Beatrice Langley, of some of his chamber-music works on 6 March. On 8 March he left England again, first for Frankfurt, where he gave a piano recital in the evening of 12 March, then for Amsterdam and his piano recital in the evening of 15 March. He was back in London on 17 March.

In Norway Grainger had tasted success, "best of all draughts" he wrote to Rose. The euphoria of success (and good earnings) continued on this tour.

324   TO KAREN HOLTEN   [London]
[Original: Danish/some English]
Monday early. 7.3.10.

Sweetheart, treasure, lover, best friend.

I can't possibly tell you *how* splendidly the rehearsal went last night. Shepherd's Hey sounds, I think, *perfect* from the 1st note to the last. There is not a note I want to change not even an expression mark. The concertina works *indescribably* in it; **just**, absolutely just, as I had hoped it would. Its

25 Rose had given Percy a towel for Christmas 1909, from which to make some trousers. On 18 February she wrote that Little May (their maid) was helping to cut out the trousers, "just the same size & shape as yr underdrawers, only buttoning in front like ordinary trousers — with a fly — like boy's knickers". Grainger maintained a lifelong interest in innovative clothing in general and in towel clothes in particular.

26 The idea that Grainger might "do something" in America was one which was to recur, off and on, over the coming years. The ambition to try America was first mooted by Rose in a letter of 29 April 1909: "if you approve, let that be our next big thought". An offer actually came in the summer of 1910, as Percy wrote to Karen on 31 May and 14 June, but nothing came of it at that time, nor of various other attempts to develop the idea in the successive years. As for "things paying", Rose was confident, writing to Percy on 21 February, "I believe if you can stick it, you will make heaps of money — you have such a charming personality allied to genius. The people who cannot appreciate you, must be queer".

tone gives a sharpness and acidness to the other instruments, and it has the same filling-out but at the same time cutting influence on chamber-music tone as brass has in the orchestra.

I am **so** happy about the whole thing.

Nothing could be more charming than these English orchestra players. Not **at all** suspicious in any way, and so glad for new musical jests, so willing to help, and yet so calm and unintrusive, and so sensitive — and *how* splendidly they play also.

I have already arranged a rehearsal for "Walking Tune" (that I wrote out a part of that time in Slettestrand) for the end of this month.

"Bold W.[illiam] T.[aylor]" went surprisingly well rhythmically, despite all the eternally changing bars. Also that sounded good in many places, in any case hopeful, and "Died for love" sounded sweet. Perhaps a little colder than on piano, but extremely "bubbly" and can be performed surprisingly pp. Now I need to hear these 2 last pieces *with singing voices* as well.

I have "work" for you on English Dance, which I will send to you from Frankfurt.

Your writing out of Morris D[ance] and Died for Love proved quite practical and *easily readable*.

May I dedicate "Afterword" to you? But in all secrecy, for the present. Nobody must know about it. I have tried to work further with Afterword, but with only limited success so far.

How I longed for you to be able to hear these last night.

I have written to Shattuck about the Icelander. A thousand thanks for your letter this morning.

Tomorrow, in the train, in Germany, I will write to you again, and will post it in Frankfurt tomorrow night.

I am so much in love with you, and so happy. In any case, last night has shown that I'll easily have enough *proven & heard* stuff for the 1st years printing for the "subscribers"

I am so busy today.

Full of longing, marrow, and gratitude

Your Percy.

Will you ring up Hansen & ask him to let me know the dates of my 2 Køb piano-evenings in the autumn, & if he has sent money to me? I have in fact not yet received the money from Hansen, nor heard from him

325   TO ROSE GRAINGER   [In the train] Holland.
Tuesday early
8.3.10.

Dear me, how this route is stor verdensagtig [Danish: great-world-like] quick & comfy. A *real* express to Harwich, if you please, a *gorgeous* boat, clean & big, (with attractive cleanlooking jerseyed English sailors) that left the pier 5 or 10 minutes after trains arrival, with powerful engines throbbing away, & (seemingly) skilful seamanship; a crossing on glass, not a movement, & real clean berths, & no spitting. And these German 2nd class carriages *perfection*, clean, roomy, & *empty*. Jeg har det meget godt, med andre ord [Danish: I am very well, in other words]. How I *adore* the look of this Holland, lovely foggy views of grey waterways about Rotterdam & Dordrecht, charmful tree groupings by side of rivers & canals in the misty morning gloaming, &, as good as anything, the lovely dutch *printing* everywhere, thin & long & narrow:—

And such nice faces; so many of them closer to our English types than even *any* other foreigners.

How I long to be here a lot & really bask in Dutchness as I have in Danishness. I have a feeling that I'd find the flat prosiac Dutch maybe about as soothing as the flat prosiac Danes. Have finished Dana's Have,[27] & all the skærmidsler [*sic* skærmydsler. Danish: skirmishes]. "D's H" attracts me, but I dont *really* know *exactly* what the precise upshot of it all is.

Now I must endelig [Danish: finally] sharpen my pencil. (So far with the old stump) But the horses here wear blinkers. That is not a good sign.

It's a frightful shame that you have to drudge so in the house-cum-business. Cant we lighten things somehow? I hope you'll just give up the boarders & also the letter writing if you find it attacks your health, or even if not, but makes life not worth living. You must always remember that a gifted being like you, bursting with life & menschenliebe Kan udrette næsten lige saa meget [German/Danish: love of people can achieve almost just as much] (even as regards money getting) by sitting still & letting yr personality & ideas effect me & others; as by servanting yourself.

If the clothes & packing are bodily unhealthy for you, I'm ever so willing to try & take them over. If it's *understood* that I'm *answerable* for them, I'll keep my eyes open & report socks & linings that need dealing with som i[n]gen anden [Danish: lit. like no one else], but what I cant do is, I cant fetch & carry, nor keep an orderliness not the result of my own thinking & oldmaiding. I cant remember orderliness I haven't selv ordnet [Danish: arranged myself].

Above all, do me just the one thing: *go to the eye man while I'm away.* Please.

very lovingly
Percy

What a true picture "D's H" is of Danish life!

326 TO KAREN HOLTEN   [In the train] Germany
[Original: Danish/some English]
8.3.10.

I have enclosed herewith some sweaty underarm hairs, in the hope that the envelope will come to smell of sweat, but no doubt it won't after all.

Can't we arrange whipping like this: That I am permitted to whip you, ½ as much as you me? Then you will be compelled to beat me so hard that I can't bear very many blows. For example if I want to whip you 100 blows then I must first endure 200, and perhaps you can do it so that I can scarcely endure so many. I think you should be allowed to use any whip whatever on me, and tie me up how you like, and beat me where you like, but I must be allowed to give a signal when I can't bear any more, *after* a certain number, perhaps. (50?) I think that you shouldn't have to do the whole thing so quickly that you don't get time to beat with full force,

27 *Dana's Have*, play in three acts by Henri Nathansen (Copenhagen and Christiania, 1908).

either, but not with really long pauses in between either so that it comes to stretch over an *altogether* too long time. What do you think? Should I be able to have 200, for example, in 4 groups, with a little pause between each 50, or will I need to have the 200 without interruption for it to count against you? Or should it be like this? If I withstand 80, and 60, and 54 (with short pauses in between) have I the right then to give you 40, 30, and 27 with pauses between?

Whatever we choose of these possibilities, I think we should try it out straight away the 1st evening next time we meet. First you whip me, and then I whip you. And then we should calculate it so you come midway between 2 tummyaches (shouldn't we) as it is so lovely to be able to kiss you everywhere straight away, isn't it?

Have you noticed that I am, pretty undeniably, a happier person since you have allowed whipping in such a high degree? Previously it was always a little bit disappointing for me, to think that I would probably never get to experience this desire, or only with unpleasantness, at any rate. Already before the Australian tour you made me rather hopeful with what you so graciously permitted in London, and the tour was to a large degree made happy by the purchase of these whips and by thoughts about their future use. But last summer in Slettestrand was the real sunrise for me. It is so easy for me to behave hopefully and almost bravely with respect to concerts and compositions when you have opened such a royal kingdom of happiness for me, everything according to my deepest and most important yearnings. Now I think: Such and such will surely be able to be done when the most difficult part is already going so unexpectedly gloriously.

Oh no, how splendidly you suit me; it is really to have conquered in life to have attained the mercy and benevolence that I do from you.

You have built a safe courtyard in which my own little devils can walk round and have a good time.

Perhaps, without you, my instincts might have led to crime, or an unhappy and incomplete life? For now I know you can bear so splendidly what has to be. Perhaps it will be several years before I am able to whip you as I want to do it, but I am getting more and more near to this blissful possibility.

I have indeed already given you some single blows which were hard and ruthless enough, but I will continue a long time in that way so you will become absolutely crazy. Yes life is indeed lovely when one knows you. And how fortunate for you also! You need never be unable to show me how much you love me. One hears people say: There is nothing I wouldn't do to make him happy. When you feel very much in love with me, you need never be in doubt as to what will make me the *most extremely* happy in life. Not money, not to be able to compose better, would make me most happy. To stand with the whip in my hand and have your soft youthful body at my mercy, that is the highest point I can think of in my life. Quite certainly I would like to whip others as well, not only you. But you yourself, you only, form the best I have known up to now, and anything better I have no wish for in the future, although I am very "broad-minded" about the question. Many many thanks from a poor unsatisfied boy that you have made Absolute Monarch [Einvaldskonungr] of life's most beautiful kingdom.

It's nice that you like Afterword a bit as it is really yours. For it is just an expression of a feeling that you alone caused (as far as one ever can trace feelings to their roots with surety). After having enjoyed excitation and wildness with you and after having flung and kissed and had sucked out in you (disregarding separators) [i.e. condoms] these streams of juice that otherwise flow so bitter in one's veins, and after having blended breath and thoughts and sweat and smell with you, it almost seems that something melts in one, one is like an open flower, content and grateful and made clean and blissfully empty of whipped-up disquiet. Then one feels so childlike, or motherly, or religious or priestly or whatever one wants to call it, but all the same not empty in an impoverished way and God knows not cold. And in the morning, when one sits fresh at the piano, completely happy and with a kind of child's fresh pure tiredness over one, and a kind of twilight lack of energy "yvir heile hann" [Faeroese: "over the whole person"], then one longs for a long drawn out song line, rich and lasting with a kind of fragrant harmonic support.

The feeling that you gave birth to in me was pleasant and heavenly enough, although the composition is certainly not a particularly worthy expression of it; but never mind, it was well meant, and is better than nothing so long as something better of the same kind isn't done, and, as said, belongs to you in all gratefulness and tenderness: And it is not your fault if the piece leaves something to be desired. There are no flies on you. You are splendid, a little sensuality-angel, a faithful non-earthy uplifted happiness-animal, an altogether sweet comrade, and my infinitely close friend.

I have ED with me and will send it to you from Frankfurt, where I hope to be able to buy score paper that will be large enough to permit a very clear transcription of the score, which I will with great thankfulness ask you to do for me, but without hurry and tiring your sweet eyes (that I am thirsty to kiss) too much. Only when you have time and feel like it.

Delius has promised to get it performed for me, and since I can't send my only score around in the post I must have a copy that must also be much clearer than my original is. Therefore there must also be fewer bars on each page (on the copy than on the original). I will mark *in pencil*, under the score, where each new page should begin. You must only use *whole pages*, not halves as I have done on pages 11, and 47 of the original.

The new sheets must be put into the previous ones, so that the pages are arranged:

   but *not*:

In other words; one must be able to sew them all together with a thread. For example the way in which pages 33–50 (in the original) stand is *wrong*. The 1st page must only have the title and dedication, 2nd page empty, only on the 3rd (which is on a *new sheet*) begin the score. Then continue to write only on the *2 first sides* of *each new sheet* till you come to ½ of the total number of pages, from then on to the end only use the unused portion of the previous sheets.

And since the work will possibly be performed 1st outside England, I must ask you to translate the English indications [expression marks] to Italian. (How laughable I am!) Here is the table of translations:

div = div
gracefully = grazioso
lots = molto
together (tog) = unis
gradually = poco a poco
louden lots = cresc molto
louden = cresc
hugely = molto
smooth = legato
bit by bit = poco a poco
dont soften = non dim
short = stacc

mutes off = senza sordini
but = ma
heavy but clinging = pesante
    ma tenuto
toneful = sonore
die off = morendo
short & sharp = stacc
stopped = bouché
marked = marcato

optional = ad libitum

feelingly = espresivo	But retain the names
louden slightly = poco cresc	of the instruments
soften ,, = ,, dim	in English with
very = molto	exception of
heavy = pesante	
& = e	middle-fiddles = viole
clingingly = tenuto	bass-fiddles = celli
	D-bs = C. Bassi

The names of *all* the instruments must be put on *all* pages with regular (but not irregular) numbers. (For example: on 28, but *not* on 29) just as they stand on page 4 of the original.

The *3 Trombones* must be written on 3 systems, one for each. I think you will be able to find out from my score which are the 1st, 2nd, and 3rd trombone parts. Also *cornets* on 3 systems, like the trombones. Unused bars *time* as in the original.

I will put a specimen of a *well* hand-written score in with the original. I am quite sure you will be able to get to write just as well as a copyist, now you are getting more used to it. Indications must be close to the notes they refer to; but things must not run into each other, or touch. And things must run

   not

Since ED is in a way my greatest piece and the one I can in a way learn most from, you will get to help me quite colossally by transcribing the score.

And when you can't read something in the original (as will no doubt happen very often) you have only to keep a note about *everything* you can't understand, leave a blank place in the score, and note down the *instrument* and bar number, as for example E♭ clar, 203. Then I can, from this note, put in the doubtful bits for which you have left spaces in your score.

I forgot to pay for the *washing* in Cope. Can you tell me how much it was? And I believe your brother paid something for me which I didn't pay. Can you find that out?

I love you really passionately.

You must really see and be in London for my composition concert. Otherwise I have only ½ the pleasure of it.

327   TO ROSE GRAINGER   Frankfurter Hauptbahnhof
1 o'cl, midnight. 12.3.10.   waitingroom
[it would of course be 13.3.10]

My train leaves in ½ hour.

Well darling, I really played **superbly**, did my very very best, I consider. Blüthner *exquisite*

I think the audience was quite impressed, though they seem very cold even after Danes, let alone Norwegians. I was absolutely *tired to death* when I got on the platform, with all the visiting & dressing & yesterday & today musclestiffening hard practising.

But there you see, it all makes no diff. Big practising is the only needed thing.

If the papers arent good they need kicking ⟨in the balls⟩ [words crossed out].

Firnberg was impressed ⟨off his arse⟩ [words crossed out], & Rebner talks about engaging me for his Frankfurt Kammermusik concerts.[28] Believe me, I *will* erobern [German: conquer] Germany, if I can. I've no more hatred again[st] the Germans. I find them quite pleasant, & lots of good looking folk, & not all badly dressed by any means.

Who do you think I saw today? Mimi. She heard of my concert & arranged to be bear today, was having to come Fr in any case. She's prettier in the face than formerly, more lustrous & spiritual, but lost her figure (if ever had it?) & fancy, is beginning to get grey hairs. No these foreigners arent as strong as we, & they none of them understand to really take the care of themselves that even I do, having learnt it from you.

I enoyed seeing M again tho I think it would be *very* hard for me to re[-]verlieb [German: infatuate] myself in her, now. But god, who knows with men, such creatures! Jedenfals [German: at all events], I dont feel myself in the *least* tempted, tho I think she's jolly nice, perhaps.

The Klimsches are real real darlings. How happy I was with them, & could be again & again. He was *so* pleased tonight. Fr. von Grunelius is a pet too. She's French, it turns out. My darling own mum. So many really heartfelt messages to you from folk. How I'm longing to find letters from you in Amsterdam. I have such masses of things to tell you, & soon will, with my very own live crooked mouth.

28 Adolph Rebner (1876–1967), Austrian violinist. He had lived in Frankfurt from 1896 and was extremely active in the city's musical life as chief violin teacher at the Hoch Conservatorium (from 1904) and as member of various chamber-music ensembles including the Frankfurt Trio (with James Kwast and from 1902 Carl Friedberg, piano, and Johannes Hegar, cello). Grainger had assisted at two recitals given by Rebner in London in December 1905. Nothing came of the Frankfurt offer.

328   TO ROSE GRAINGER   Amsterdam
Monday. 14.3.10.

Lille moer.

After a charming night journey got here yesterday, Sunday, morn at 10.30, in glorious weather. (also today)

Röntgen's kindness & generosity & unselfishness knows no bounds. Yesterday afternoon were invited some 30 folk here & from the Haag (the Hague) to hear me, & I gave them a regular doing. Big BB, Händel Vars, Griegs, Albeniz, Grieg Concerto (2 pianos) Shepherd's Hey, & so on.

I cant tell you how nice the Dutch faces are, & how kindly & welcoming their manners are. They are the limit as linguists too, & are very English & travelled in their ways, & clothes much better cut than Germany or Denmark so it seems to me, although homely too somehow.

The conductor of the orchestra in Groningen was here, & the President of the Concertgebouw (Amsterdam) concerts,[29] & lots of other musicians & musiclovers & all were delightful & hotly enthused. They rather sværm [= schwärm] a bit after the Danish way, quite as polite & smooth but not perhaps quite so squirmingly.

I should think that, with Röntgen's help, I ought to be pretty sure of getting Holland.

But they get masses of artists here of course & one cant expect things to move too quick. They make a very winning impression on me, & I'll very very soon quite understand Dutch & speak it too, tho here alas I get no chance to try.

This morn Röntgen & I did thro the Brahms *B♭ maj* Concerto (2nd) I at 2nd piano. He's quite a spiffing player & I think I'll learn that Concerto.

R has made every last effort to herald me in here.

His Dutch (2nd) wife is charming, & his absent son by his 1st Swedish wife is engaged to a perfectly **lovely** Norwegian girl.

Fond love, my darling.

I arrive Thursday morn quite early.

29 The conductor of the orchestra at Groningen was Peter van Anrooij. Grainger was to play under him a number of times, and for the first time on 29 November 1910. The President of the board of management of the Concertgebouw from April 1903 to his death on 29 April 1912 was Mr (the Dutch lawyer's title) J. A. Sillem.

329   TO KAREN HOLTEN   [Between Amsterdam and London]
[Original: Danish/Dutch/private language]
16.3.10.

As you can see from the papers, I have had a quite boundless success here. So great, that I am coming again to Holland in a month's time, to give concerts in Amsterdam, The Hague, Utrecht, etc. They think it will be quite well paid. The enthusiasm was really enormous, even after Norway. After the Bach I was recalled three times, after the Brahms 4 times, etc.

Röntgen has been like a father figure to me, has sacrificed his whole time to me, and is as excited as a child about my concerts.

Yes, now my pianist career is beginning. To think of having had such great success in 3 new countries in this new year, and what it all can mean for the future. I expect to travel from England the 15th April for Holland.

Today I have done an indescribable lot. Have been photographed, talked business, and played piano (2 pianos) with Röntgen this morning (got up before 7), and in the afternoon travelled to the Hague and visited 2 people there.

How I *long long* for you. Not to whip you tonight, not even to be very swollen, as I am worn out, devilish tired, but to caress you properly, and to be caressed by you, and to swim in your love, intimacy, comradeship, to tell you how many sweet, loyal feelings I have for you, and hear your motherly gold-hearted voice and feel your warming hands, touch your fine smooth glowing limbs with mine, tired sleepy and dreamily.

I wonder whether you lost my Amsterdam address? since I didn't get any letter from you there, but expect one in London. But a thousand thanks for your telegram.

The clock is now 10.50 at night and we are very shortly going onto the ship. I think the weather will be calm.

Mother wrote to me today asking when I wanted to have you over with us again, and to say how glad she would be to see me married to you, if that was my wish. She can't see anything against the idea, it seems to her. But I am different. But it is lovely to know that she thinks like that.

I love you, my tiredness is full of kisses for you, I long to bore my member up inside you and go to sleep in there, "in the middle of the whole business".

330   TO KAREN HOLTEN   London
[Original: Danish/English phrase]
Friday. 1.4.10.

I am so frightfully sorry about so many things:
   that I have to practise so continually
   that I have ideas for settings of 3–4 songs that I have not written
      down although several of them are several years old
   that "B's Tragedy" is still unfinished.
   that I can't get "Afterword" quite in order.
   that it's not Sunday evening 6.30 yet when the rehearsal begins.
   that I can't come to Svinkløv this year.
   that we are separated.
                           and so on.
I have however done a whole lot with Afterword, that perhaps will remain as it is, a good lot at any rate. I will soon send you a copy of it.

I am so discontented with my compositions, I see frightful weaknesses in all of them. And I can't bear this Bb minor Tschaikowsky Concerto that I am playing, at all.

Firnberg will send you, I assume, 50 copies of German critiques.

Please send 30 of them to Hr. Stadsingeniør Høeg. Aalborg. I'll send you addresses for the others soon. Perhaps he sends 100. I will write again on Monday, p.r., Købmagergade.

If only I was with you everything would be all right.

It is stupid of one not to be able to control one's ups-&-downs better. Many kisses from me.

331 TO KAREN HOLTEN   [London]
[Original: Danish]
6.4.10.

My sweet comrade.

I bought such a lovely towel yesterday, with a sweet pattern on a brown background, that is to be made into a coat to go over the towel trousers. It will look *so* charming. And I am still working on my bead (blue) belt which is almost ½ done. These clothes make me so happy. Yesterday we went over with færøsk anthologi, færøsk kvæder and E.T. Kristensen's books to get them bound. It was amusing as well. A thousand thanks for "Tine", which I am very glad to have.[30] It was sweet of you. I read about a walking match a woman in America performed. She didn't achieve terribly much. Would you like to go a long walk with me some time, 40 or 50 miles? Dressed in knee breeches of course. But then you would have to get your stride even greater than it is. As a greater stride you would *have* to have, for your own sake even, and I couldn't walk far with too short steps although I would of course moderate my stride when we walked together. I have such a great desire to see you in these lovely clothes that are to be made before you come over here. We will be so happy you and I, in so many different ways. We will make each other so happy, so often and so long, I hope.

It is tedious that Green Bs must be written out again, but it seems to me that when a new piece, by a "new person" (in Greenland costume) is to be performed, then one must first and foremost be able to read the score and the parts easily, and I don't think that people can easily understand the hektographed copy, although personally I think it is excellent.

I would say so many things, but I forget them. In any case I love you.

I will write p.r. to Købm-gade from here on Saturday (evening)

I would so like to enclose you in my arms and kiss you really properly and thoroughly and dress you up in my towel knee-breeches. *And undress you again.*

Do you think you would like to learn beadwork? You could so easily learn it from me, and you could make yourself the most lovely things. I am so glad and so ready for pleasure and to embrace you and ring with you and laugh with you and work with you and eat a great deal with you.

Anton Mohr has received a lovely mysost from Norway[31]

30 *Tine* (1889) by the Danish novelist and short-story writer Herman Bang (1857–1912). In 1910 Karen also gave Percy Bang's *De Uden Fædreland* (1906) (see letter 349).

31 One of their lodgers. The other, at that time, was Else Permin.

On 12 April Grainger left London again for Holland on a tour encompassing five solo recitals: in den Haag on 14 and 22 April, in Amsterdam on 15 and 24 April and in Utrecht on 23 April. In Holland he was the guest of the Röntgen family in Amsterdam. With a different programme to present at each recital it was a strenuous tour: it was also a triumphant success. Grainger was back in London on 25 April.

332 TO ROSE GRAINGER   Hoek. [van Holland]
13.4.10 6 o'cl, morn.

The smoothest yet; oil. 1st class truly leaves nothing to desire.

If effort makes for achievement I can only hopefully conclude that the throats of our ships population are by now very thoroly & effeciently clean & neat. For they certainly spared no pains, seemingly; except perhaps my cabin-mate, who put his very soul into snuffling with his nose, & rather neglected his throat.

From the way the middleclass set about preparing for the day one can quickly see that they are of the stuff to form the backbone of any nation; their hygene has in it all the relentlessness of a völkerwanderung [German: migration (historical shifting) of the peoples], & the righteous way they all declare *"absolutely nothing* dutiable" shows that they are instinctively equipped to support & defend a state church & deal unswervingly with all moral questions

Train just leaving.

Fondest love dearie, take it easy

yr loving one
P.

333 TO KAREN HOLTEN   [In the train] Hoek [van
[Original: Dutch/Danish/English]   Holland] — Amst.[erdam]
13.4.10   6.15. eve.

The day before yesterday evening I experienced something dreadful, when I played Tsch's Concerto with the "Stock Exchange Orch[estra]" in Q's Hall. There was an a♭ which would not sound and it was like that the whole evening. Not only that, but the whole keyboard was out of order I felt as if the whole piano would soon cease to be playable, and it seemed to me as if the keys would only go half as deep down as usual. I can assure you, it wasn't very pleasant.[32]. But the evening passed without an accident, and the audience was unusually warm.

But it was dreadful.

And it makes one feel uncomfy about coming concerts.

After the concert we met R. Strauss at Lady Speyers.[33] He looks considerably older than when I saw him last, but considerably more pleasant. He seems so good-natured, friendly, and joyful, and his manners are *so* excellent, natural and unforced, and *very* calm. Also his manners at the concert were just right. Just proud enough, and "formal" enough, but excellently simple and even, and his clothes of faultless cut. I think the Germans seem to be making great progress, indeed, in many directions.

He conducted D Juan *splendidly* He is certainly a great artist as conductor. But *not at all* sentimental.

The rehearsal on Sunday was extremely pleasing and instructive. We tried Walking Tune, D[ied] for love, and extracts from Hillsong, and Drunken Sailor.

I feel that Walking T is a little dilettantic in tone. Not downright bad, and there are many places that sound good, but taken as a whole not what I would call masterly, as for example Sh's Hey. But there are a whole lot of places where I expect some small changes will improve it a lot, although I don't expect anything perfect out of it as a whole.

But it is good enough to be performed in my Compositions Concert, and I will also print it when occasion offers. On the other hand Died for love is perhaps not so successful for woodwinds. That I haven't decided yet.

32 The critic of the *Daily Telegraph*, reviewing the Stock Exchange concert on 12 April, noted ". . . [while] Mr Grainger overcame all the obstacles — many of which were not of the composer's making — of Tschaikowsky's Concerto; not only with consummate ease, but with genuine brilliance of technique . . ."

33 Richard Strauss was in London for a symphony concert with the Queen's Hall Orchestra on 9 April at which he conducted his tone-poems *Don Juan* and *Tod und Verklärung* and Mozart's "Jupiter" Symphony.

All the "Dr Sailor" sketches are amusing and hopeful, and best of all sounded the small pieces of Hillsong which we tried.

They sound so surprisingly more flowing and natural with the winds than on the piano. Now I am very curious to hear it performed as a complete work. It will cost £6. I have always counted it as my best instrumental piece; although I am certain that it *can't* be satisfactory in tone as it stands, as the problem (only wind players alone for some minutes) is *too* great to be able to be solved straight away with my lack of experience. But I think it can *one day* be put into 1st class condition.

All these orchestral players in England are inexpressibily nice. So tactful, willing, and unsceptical, and so glad if one takes an interest in their instruments. I cannot think of any people who would be better for my purposes than these quiet sympathetic men.

It is *really* amusing with rehearsals and all that, it makes life considerably happier, but you mustn't think that that sort of thing has any real satisfaction for me.

I long a thousand times more for you than for all that sort of thing.

When everything is over, success or disaster, after the money has been earned and the amusing occupations put aside, then one is still lying in bed with a desire that rises up fresh as the morning through all the tiredness and satiety of other instincts. They are of no use, all the other things, excellent though they be.

How I long for the next whipping.

I am surprised how many times daily I think about it.

You have my greatest happiness so completely in your hands.

334 TO ROSE GRAINGER

Amsterdam.
17.4.10.

Alas! I believe that hate & loathing of my fellowmen seems to be one of the most radical & sincere stuffs of my character.[34] For wherever I go, in all lands, I find such scores of folk who distress & plague me so, that all my possibilities of humaness seem to suffocate in a dread of their presence. Thankfulness has no chance to raise its head where kind acts are accompanied by a boredom & inborn coarseness of grain that blot out all other sensations. Poor dear old R; I tremble at the sound of his grating hideous voice, & no goodness of heart could ever possibly make up for the ugliness of the thinness of his legs alongside of the bulkiness of his body.

The minute his hands touch the keys I quiver with fore-suffering & each compo of his torments me more than the last. His boys are cry-babies, & came bounding into the world with the same punctuality as his compos. My one joy in the life here is reading my good Dutch crits, & that he spoils by insisting on reading them aloud to me first of all in German, ff, in that hideous language in his frightful voice.

The real Dutch seem really delightful, softvoiced, with nice dry faces, & mobile funny little mouths, & temperaments blessedly free from "temperament" & vigor & fire. Dear dear me, energy is the poorest spectacle in the world. From energy, good Lord, deliver us.

If only I could be left to enjoy this nice land without its being spoiled for me by an everlasting German voice. But the tragedy of the whole show is that no Dutchman, because of the very things I'm drawn to them for, would ever have done for me what this coarse wiederwärtig [German: obnoxious] kindhearted German has. And *nothing* escapes his energy. His apreciative openarmed indescriminating warmblooded German mind settles like a blight upon whatever·kind of music he hits upon & the result is Czardas über Ungarischen themen, Ballade über Norwegische volksweise, Boeren dansen over oud nederlandsche melodien, settings of Joyce's Irish

34 By 23 April, however, he was happy again.

tunes, etc, etc. Untiring, he just heaves himself, a squashing mass, like a bread & cheese fed husband weekly upon his undefended wife, regardless of what musical abortion is the result of his fatal contact with stuffs nowise blendable with his own characteristics. His artistic methods have the massive destructiveness of the blind natural laws. The charm of all he touches "fades away like morning dew" before his splendid "fitness".

It seems that I really feel my heart to beat somewhat together with French & English artistic individuals, but it has *never* yet happened that any Scandinavian (including Herman, Grieg, & Mrs Grieg) German Dutchman Russian etc has talked with me about music, or "musiziert" [German: made music] with me without failing to split an artistic cleft between us unhealable for life (artistically)

Grieg, Herman, Nikisch, Halvorsen, Klimsch, Safonoff,[35] Karen, Röntgen, Richter, etc have *nothing* in their thoughts artistically in harmony with mine, tho' I so worship Grieg's music, & relished Herman playing & compo, etc. But Delius, Rathbone, Blanche, Sargent, (even H. J. Wood,), Cyril, Roger, Gardiner, with them one feels a fellow artist, stimulated by kindredly-seeing minds.

But then foreigners & I have not one artistic ideal or point of view in common, that I can discover. When I get away from here & forget details, no doubt I shall manage to feel some thankfulness for R's positively passionate fatherly goodness to me & effectual kindness, but as long as I'm here I must just go on lying & swindling & choaking down my repulsion & loathing & dispision for so much needless ugliness & such fruitless avalanches of noise from piano & throat.

Ugliness ist mir das forfærdeligste af alt. [German/Danish: Ugliness is to me the most dreadful thing of all.] No success, no gain, can for the moment dispell the crushing gloom of the presence of ugliness, which sucks away all the life- & love-giving juices out of this glorious world, & leaves one a wornout rag before one has made an effort.

Nur wer die Deutschen kennt weiss was ich leide

There was an absolutely *deliriously* ecstatic crit in last nights "*Nieuws van den dag*" Amsterdam, which I shall send to you tomorrow.

I *long long* to be home again, my darling.

I'm bringing with me some nice teatrays cloths that I bought (only a few pence) some of which I want used for knickers.

I'll have a little copying for you on my return whenever you have a drop o' time.

All send their love; such as it is.

I send a very prima kwalitæt [Danish: first quality].

Perks.

R's son Engelbert *does* so love his father.
What's the use? 23 years old, he's already beginning to go bald.

335   TO KAREN HOLTEN   Amsterdam.
[Original: English with some foreign words]
19.4.10.

I feel very unhappy & I dont love you much.

I read those Sadistic rotten books & they made me very happy but today I read "Birth" in a Encyclopedia & that made me cold all over & dispise you (or at least feel cold & strange & far off from you) that you can be such a low creature to be willing to undergo such a horrid & primitive business.

35 Vasily Il'ich Safonoff (1852–1918), Russian conductor. In 1906 he had created a "sensation" in London by conducting without a baton. Grainger had met him on 7 May 1907 when they disputed the merits of Debussy. In March 1911 Karen Holten wrote to Grainger that she preferred Safonoff to Strauss as a conductor.

No doubt its tedious of me to be like that but thats the way I am. It's not your fault at all you dear sweet pretty thing, but I'm not made for you, nor you for me, I think. I feel unlove for you because of your "virtue", of your faithfulness. I am afraid you are after all chiefly a tame rabbitlike lifeproducing breeder, a victim to mere nature's laws, an offering to practical needs, driven virtuously and by "necessity".

I could love you better if you were worse. If you lay with other men while I was away, if you sensually loved other girls, if you let yr dog lick you, if you were naughty; all that I can respect, love, feel with.

Such a creature would be a fit mate for me. If it were not for your babylonging I would marry you & hope to live a life [of] useless lechery, but I'm afraid your sinful stirrings are mere unessential preludes to the serious horrid dirty work of family-building, my sensuality & my talent to be *"used"* to start & capitalize your rabbit-longing.

Thanks very much.

I fear that yr love for me is after all only a "natural instinct". You dont really love my unnatural loftier useless sick evil artistic joy-hunt, you merely callously instinctively move to turn my powers to bondage under the very lords that I would fain fight hardest.·

If you were more of a whore what a different future might lie before us! We could marry early & need not spend money on children, we could travel all over the world & feel all sorts of delicious things for the pure fun of our own selfish little bodies.

Is life with me so poor in attractions that it's not worth while to give up the babygame for it?

Is my talent so cheap that it's not worth a women's while to give up to it *her* talent, which she has in common with the rabbits & toads & lice?

But there — life is a fight, & one cant ask anyone to sacrifice themselves. I only hope that you will suffer cruelly in the fight against me, & that I win gloriously.

For you are a cheeky creature, deserving a beating, middleclass & mediocre, to dump yourself down right in my gifted path, for a snare & a hindrance.

If you'd only have children with other men I wouldnt mind a bit. But keep the *fun* for me. Disgusting, above all, to me is your faithfulness. Cant you even give that poor dog a chance?

Where is that woman who wanted to see you without clothes?

If she's ugly shut your eyes & let her lick you. But for God's sake dont waste time in fidelity.

336 TO ROSE GRAINGER   Amsterdam
21.4.10.

The Röntgens & I were having a long talk about you, me, & my stuff yesterday, & our past modes of life & education, & they think that all yr characteristics & mine are extraordinarily akin & parental to each other. Indeed when one comes to think closer about us 2, & our whole way of tackling & enjoying life, it really has laughably much in common, nor is my art, freshness, & mixture of culture & crass ignorance & methods impatient of study & real forehandedness thinkable under any other guidance than yr queer own. You'd always rear orchids, not flowers!

I think we get a lot out of life, & to us our flimsy & experimental methods seem the only ones not tinged with a heavy & barren madness, but I suppose we really are freaks, & sort of barbarians too, no doubt.

On the whole its much more remarkable that *you* should have turned up out of the surroundings *you* had, than that I should have become what I am having, as I have, all yr queerness as a spring-board to start from.

Truly its not so strange that you & I can pull so well together, the wonder only is how we manage to get on at all with the silly rest of the world. Well, I know I find it hard enough, for one.

I'll be with you Monday to breakfast.

I dont feel a bit comfy about these coming concerts. Too much talky-talky & ready-ready (read — not "ready") & not enough boxhitting. The truth is I'm just dead sick of these enige [Dutch: solo] concerts, & would like a month free from them. Let us hope God will do his part. Not from lack of "Aufforderung" [German: Invitation] from my part

337   TO ROSE GRAINGER   [Amsterdam]
[Telegram. PM 23 April 1910]

SUCCESSFULLEST LIFE PLAYED RIPPING SEVENTY POUNDS

338   TO KAREN HOLTEN   [In the train] between Amsterdam and
[Original: Danish]   Hoek [van Holland]
Sunday evening 24.4.10

To think I earned £83 in The Hague the day before yesterday, and about 270(?) guilders yesterday and today about 450 guilders, the 2 together about £50, thus £133 in 3 days, and about £173 in 10 days.

Here in Holland it is an absolute "sensation", people standing in the streets after the concerts and shouting, and then on the railway stations. There hasn't been anything like it since Rubinstein[36] and Paderewski, people say.

Of course *this* "sensation" will soon blow over, the wave is at its height now and *must* go down; but some usable renown will presumably still remain behind.

I played well at these 3 last concerts although I hadn't practised very much and have been through a unique period of naughtiness.

However I do have bodily capabilities, I think, otherwise it wouldn't go. The whole week my sexuality really raced like poison in me, I read these Sadistic books for hours and was naughty often often. Then I was good the night before The Hague, after which concert we didn't get home before 1.30 o'cl, then I read till 3.30 o'cl and was naughty, next evening again concert (Utrecht) home 12 o'cl, read to 2 o'cl (?) and again naughty, in the afternoon concert, home 5 o'cl and again naughty. And everytime so really worked up, with the whip, so much marrow flowed, and all the days almost shaking with lewdness and sexual fantasies. But I feel quite well and fresh, although Tschaikowsky 3 days in a row is tiring.[37]

Amsterdam's programme was like Utrecht, with 2 more pieces.

Yes, I am now indeed physically at the summit of my life, it is sad enough to think of, and this as well, that this prime of my life is not being used properly but is only years of slavery.

I got something out of Marquis de Sade in German.[38] Yes, he is really dreadful, it is true cruelty.

I must say that cruelty does not excite me so beautifully when it becomes *too bloody*, my Sadism is fairly limited, although also Sade's can very well be beautiful if you only get into it. But that I don't do. Then I have milder German books, about whipping clubs, and Improving Institutes for Girls, "Käthe's 1st chastisement" etc. and these are really attractive to me and excite me frightfully and splendidly. Then I also bought "Women's Beauty", a book with lovely photographs. There is one of the back of a Javanese young woman; never have I seen anything more lovely, sensuality

36 Probably the Russian Anton Rubinstein (1829–94), one of the outstanding pianists of the nineteenth century.

37 Grainger's Dutch programmes included the Tchaikovsky Piano Sonata in G major, Op. 37.

38 Count Donatien Alphonse de Sade (1740–1814) (generally known as the Marquis de Sade), French author who gave his name to sadism, a form of sexual perversion marked by a love of cruelty. *Women's Beauty* is unidentified, but was probably of that type of publication for which Grainger had a particular fondness: high-class photographic magazines featuring mainly nude women in "artistic poses".

almost disappears with the sight of it, so abstractly beautiful is this beauty.

But the result of all these books is only that I long more and more for you. These books etc are a good overture, but you are really the piece, and I also long for sweetness and "pure love" (dont laugh) more than I can say in the middle of all this specialised mere`sensuality (that I moreover value highly with great thankfulness)

I saw a beautiful young Danish woman (24?) Mrs Hardtmann, yesterday. The Danish about her reminded me of you. How I love your people, and the appearance of *some* of your people's women, especially you.

All your goodness, calmness, touchingness. You act on the soul like boracic ointment on worn skin (concert-played-out fingers) If only you would act now!

Now we can soon decide when you can come over to us? The time approaches, supplemented by hundreds of pounds income. What a lovely time we will have. With money behind us and good prospects of money in the future, we will have the means for several good happy weeks — (I begin to write in the style of these filthy books.)

But I am so deeply fond of you despite all this naughtiness, (which shall *stop now*) all roads lead to you, sweet heart, good heart.

Once back in residence in London, Grainger resumed his "pupils' after-noons" and choral rehearsals. Both activities continued throughout the summer, the choral rehearsals ending in a performance of four of his choruses by a 65-voice choir at Lady Bective's on 28 June. The prospects of a good earning "Season" were affected to some extent by the death of the King on 6 May, resulting as it did in the cancellation or postponement of many public concerts and social fixtures for a period of six to eight weeks. But Grainger continued to work at a strenuous pitch, earning reasonably well with private performances and pupils. He was out of London occasionally for weekends at the country homes of friends and patrons, but was never away for any length of time. There are no letters to Rose between April and August. The letters to Karen continue every two or three days.

Though obliged to cancel plans for a concert of his own compositions, Grainger did hold private rehearsals of his works and his annual London solo recital, given at Aeolian Hall on 21 June, included a performance of the quartet version of Molly on the Shore. *The string sextet version of* Always Merry and Bright *(later* Mock Morris*) was composed for Rose Grainger's birthday on 3 July. He continued to work hard at arrangements for the forthcoming autumn and winter European tours, fixing dates and preparing programmes.*

Grainger did not go to Svinkløv in 1910. Karen Holten, however, arrived in London in the evening of 27 July.

339 TO KAREN HOLTEN   London
[Original: Danish/English]
28.4.10.

I don't know what to say. I don't think I wrote that letter that time with the wish to hurt you. It was really true, I read about "birth" in the encyclopedia and the thought arose in me; how different she must be to me to wish such a thing, and it is also true, that we are heavens apart, we 2; but that is perhaps just the reason why we can make each other so happy. And it is just as true that your virtuousness pains me. It is indeed not your fault that you are like that, but I can't help it that I cant stand morality, continence, one-love-one-life, etc.

But I dont ask you to change only I cant change myself either.

Perhaps it is the contrast between us that draws us together, but the contrasts are just as great as they can be, at any rate.

You are nature | You have feeling
I am art. | I have taste.

You live to serve nature
I live to try & make nature serve me.

You try to get me to serve nature also
I try to get you also to try to make nature serve me.

Your love for me includes the hope that in me
　　　your naturalness, virtue, & natureworship
　　　will find a fruitful earth, & that I shall
　　　help to make your life rich in consentrates
　　　love, birth, purity, etc

My love from you springs largely from the hope
　　　that I find in you a playground for
　　　my unnatural, purely selfpleasing
　　　resultless sensuousness, & that I find
　　　in you a comrade to listen to my
　　　immoralities, my general wantoness.

You hope to one day produce enough of goodness
　　　warmth, love & naturalness out of me
　　　to allow you to follow your own natural
　　　instincts inspite of my contrary leanings.

I hope to gradually sensualize you
　　　so thoroughly that you will
　　　more or less forget your pure & motherly
　　　instincts (though always keeping the charm &
　　　purity that flow from them) & join me in an
　　　immoral life of body-delights, not needfully limited to
　　　2 persons.

That seems to me, roughly, the war between us. And when I say I hope that I shall win gloriously & you lose horribly I dont mean I want you to leave my life, but I mean:

I hope I'll have her body continually for my excitement & unspeakable delight, & her dear soul & jolly mind for fun & talk, & that there shall never come a child between us, or to prevent our travelling, that she shall never suffer the horrid pains & tragic risk of childbearing, nor her body quickly lose its young form from opening out cruelly for the path of a new life (unwished by me, I'm satisfied with what I have) that she shall delight my senses like a whore & rejoice my path like a sister or a fellow-soldier, & that my art & my money & *above all my sensuality* shall not be used in the cause of nature & life-thro-birth.

That is all I mean.

It is selfish & bad-manly of me, of course, but it's also selfish & bad-womanly of you to wish the reverse. But why not?

A thousand thanks for your letter today. What a shame you are ill. It is indeed my fault. It surprises me. I believed that when you heard how much money I have earned in Holland it would be almost a matter of indifference what I "thought" or "meant", since it is money that is needed.

Until I hear you are quite well again I will write to Ceresvej.

Sweetest don't be unhappy. Otherwise, what shall I do. Shall I rather NOT tell you when I feel dislike towards you?

I am desperately busy, play Tschaik Concerto etc. Saturday afternoon Brighton, and must decide programmes for London Recital and Composition evening and correct parts and many lessons.

I have engagements for about £80–90 in Holland in the autumn.

If only you knew how many sweet thoughts I think about you in the morning before I get up. Be secure and happy

Business matters

If *Mr Marius Montal* writes to you about Norwegian and German critiques (printed copies of course) please let him have as many as he wants. If he doesn't mention any number then send him 20–30 of each.

Please try & get Løgstør, Arbejderforeningen, Birkerød or any others you can think of fixed up as soon as possible. I am *after Oct 24* [*sic*]. Use printed critiques as much as you like, & when they are gone I'll send you more of them.

Please send printed critiques (Norwegian and German always) to the man you know in Aarhus. Let Federspiel have a few critiques.

Please have sent to Prof Julius Röntgen 77 van Eeghenstraat Amst.[erdam] "Noa Noa", the same as the book you have.

Please keep an account of stamps & other expenses you incur for me, sweetest

---

340   TO KAREN HOLTEN   31A King's Road
[Original: Danish/English]   Sloane Square
9.5.10.   S W London.

To think, dear old Taylor (the folk-singer) died on Wednesday. The daughter wrote to me the following day. He had a trap accident, but seemed no worse, but died suddenly the next day.

Such a real darling man he was.

A thousand thanks for everything concerning Arbejderfor[eningen] and addresses. I don't believe I am in Cope the 15th Oct, and the 29th Oct is a little late, as I hope to be in Jutland until that time. Can't Arbejderfor[eningen] make it the 20, 25, or 26 Oct? Sunday is excluded, I suppose? Otherwise the 23rd. Oct 24 I am *perhaps* playing something for 2 pianos together with Røntgen at his concert.

If they can *only* have me on Saturdays, then I must ask you to ask Arb.[ejder]for to wait a little about fixing the date till I have heard about other engagements.

Yesterday I translated 27 pages of critiques to English; German, Norwegian, Danish, Dutch.

Thanks so much re Løgstør, etc. I am very anxious to know about all Danish dates as soon as possible as I have an important engagement here for 2 Nov which I will put off if I get enough Danish bookings. I have lost my engagement for May 11 on account of the King's death, but will likely give my Recital just the same though various effects of it may force me to put off my composition concert till December. I think it *would* have been a good season for me. I was hopeful.

Roger and Fletcher were here yesterday. Roger looks so inconceivably well. He told me a frightfully funny story. Their mansion in the country, Bawdsey Manor, is close to the sea so that from the windows one can see deep down to the beach.

There were once a lot of factory girls who came there for a day by the sea, and they undressed regardless and bathed just opposite Quilters' windows. Lady Q[uilter] sent the Captain of their sailing yacht down to talk to these young ladies & tell them not to so expose themselves. He, a nice shy old sailor started remonstrating with them when one of the girls stood up in about 2 feet of water "like venus rising from the foam" & said: "If yer (you) can see anything on me that God didn't make, yer (you) can chuck yer (your) 'at (hat) at it."

Thanks for letter today.

Please just send German & Norweg booklets to the enclosed list. If I write seperately that does not matter, you send all the same, & please keep this & the last list for another time.

I am dead tired and have so much to do, and newspapers in 12 different languages dance through my head.

Excuse me and don't be angry if you can avoid it.

I'll write again Wednesday p.r.

341 TO ERNEST THESIGER   31A King's Road
20.5.10   Sloane Square
                                 S W

Darling Ernest

Ever such thanks for last night.

Both mother & I enjoyed ourselves up to the hilt & hugely admired you & relished you.

You know how hit I was the first time I saw you act, & therefor it was just what I was expecting to find you so easy & gay & amusing.

Once more warm thanks

Ever your old friend
Perks.

342 TO KAREN HOLTEN   [London]
[Original: Danish]
24.5.10.

The Frankfurter Museumsgesellschaft (Fridays — best concerts) wants to engage me for 500 mark; and Aarhus will as well, as you know. I assume and hope that Nordisk Musikforlag takes some percentage on Aarhus.

On the other hand I have now got to know that George Gouldthorpe, him I loved most of them all, died in April. I just wanted to send him some money, poor chap. It wouldn't surprise me to find that also old Wray is dead.

Last night I saw the Russian Dances with Rathbone.[39] They are indescribably lovely. The man (Mordkin) is really the best formed man I have set eyes on up to now, and she, Pavlova, is delightful.

I would rather be a great dancer than anything in the world, because it lies close to sexuality and passion

Now I am beginning to long increasingly for you. That's the thing that I could now bear very well, to have you here again. This evening my costume is coming back again.

I am your eager lover and impatient friend

Percy.

39 Anna Pavlova and Michael Mordkin had appeared for the first time in England at the Palace Theatre, London, in the evening of 23 May as part of a "Saison Russe" of artists from the Imperial Russian Ballet of St Petersburg and Moscow.

343   TO KAREN HOLTEN   London.
[Original: Danish/some English]
24.6.10. Friday evening.

Now I have a little time, thank God, to report to you again and to feel calm and myself.

"Mourning" stops on the 28th so the real season rush is only just beginning, but to have the piano evening behind one is the most important thing, I think.

Last night I played for Lady Northcote together with the Langley Muckle 4tet, Dvorak 5tet, 2nd Fauré 4tet, I soli, and the 4tet "Molly", and I had a great deal of enjoyment of the whole thing, but got terribly late home.

Just think, I am called up on a "special jury", one of 12 men to judge in a law-case, next Monday. Can you think of anything worse for me? Thank God it is not a "criminal" Court, but a "High Court", so it can't be murder, burglary, or something beastly. Only some legal case, or "break of promise of marriage" or some such. If it had been a Criminal case, I don't know what I would have done, stayed away and paid the fine, I dare say? Perhaps it will last an hour on Monday, perhaps a whole week. Tedious enough. I am not against wasting time or losing money, but am afraid that one will come to see fellow creatures worked up or unhappy or nervous, or be with a crowd of frightful 12 fellow-jurymen.

And then I will no doubt have to swear the truth, and that sort of rubbish.

As I have said, the rehearsal of "Always" went really well It is right through very easy and practical for the players, even some pizzicato places that I was a little afraid about; as far as easiness went.

I don't know whether it makes a great effect. We had all too little time that day, and I will be able to judge it better on Sunday afternoon, July 3rd, 4.30, when it will be performed here unexpectedly for mother. I have been busy writing out the string parts of some other old small things that we may possibly run through the same day.

I am now practising Beethoven's 32 C minor Var[iations], which I am very fond of — even practising them.

You know the 2 rooms just opposite* the big music room here. Mother sleeps at present in the room that looks out on the street, and I in the backmost, (of these 2) and we will presumably continue thus while you are here, and you will have one of the rooms upstairs.

I will come up to you in the evenings to try out the clothes, talk, whip and be whipped, and sensual pleasures, but I suggest that as a rule we *both* come down to me *just to sleep*, and I can very well come up to you in the mornings, when you wish, or not.

Mother sleeps so badly, you see, when there is no one sleeping in the room next to her, and I have promised myself that this time she won't get ill on that account. For she feels so disturbed when she wakes up, calls out to me, and I don't answer. I have noticed that she always gets ill when I sleep upstairs, and therefore I should so much like not to. She *never* comes into my room in the night nor in the morning, so there is not much danger of it, and if she knocked, then I would be there. In August *no* maids sleep in the house, and it would be extremely convenient for us, it seems to me?

Would you be able to agree to the above suggestion?

On Monday I will post again to you, about whom I am thinking so continually and longingly.

The critiques of the Recital are very good, without being exciting after the foreign ones.

---

* PG uses the word "ovenover", which means "above". However he sometimes mistakes "ovenover" for "ovenfor" ("opposite") and the sense of this paragraph seems to indicate he meant "ovenfor". *Transl.*

344 TO ROGER QUILTER   31A King's Rd
[Postcard. PM 2 July 1910]

The sixsome is to be done *here* next Sunday at 4.30 I'm *counting on your coming* Come at 4 or 4.15. Percy.

Dont write to me re Sunday *as it is to be a secret*

Sunday is her birthday Why not give her a small History of Japan, say from "The Story of the Nations"⁴⁰ She is awfully keen on Jap. history & wants to read it

345 TO ROSE GRAINGER   31A Kings Rd.
[outside: PG notes "Mother. July 3 1910"]   Chelsea.
Friday. 1.7.10.

My darling merry bright mother⁴¹

I hope that the over eager happy haste (for with this birthday gift has gone, I dont know just why, an unwonted fulness of sonly love, impatience, & delight in doing it) with which this slight guarantee of "Arcadian" spirits has been jerried together (it was actually conceived in some few minutes [½ hour ?] when you were from home, & worked out, partwritten & scored either nights after you had gone to bed [that's why you couldnt get me to bed some nights] or very early in the mornings, & the Plunkett Greenes also came in for their yearly share of watching me cook for your birthday) doesn't show too shabily in the workmanship of it.

From the moment when I caught the tune in bed that morning I was one itch to get it written in time to have it played here on the 3rd, & rather bundled it into the world, I fear.

If it sounds a job lot to you I must give it another doing later on.

I fear only 2 or 3 bars (bars 17–20) in the whole affair are really inspired, but alas, that is almost always so with compositions: Such a great coffin for such a little life!

It was secretly rehearsed on June 22, when we rehearsed for Lady Northcote's, & that was why Roger was along at that rehearsal.

It is a blessed boon for a composer son to have such a little mum to write for ½ yearly. I wonder will this be properly realized later on?

How many of my now tidily turned out compos would still be lazily lounging in sketchbooks but for the steadily marching Julys & Yules that leave the junior partner age-marked only by a growing bulk of "birthday-" & "Yule-gifts"!

Perhaps you think the 3rd is *your* night off. I, on the other hand, selfishly look upon [it] as my particular "little sunbonnet"

Your birthday is the day of the year I care most about. And indeed it is the day of all others that has had the greatest influence on my career, from 1st to last, rather unnaysayably.

"Percy to his mother said: 'Never have I seen a mum I'd wish instead.'"

346 TO KAREN HOLTEN   London.
[Original: Danish/some English/private language]
Monday. 4.7.10.

It was absolutely charming yesterday. Mother says she has never had such a happy birthday. Apart from the score of Always merry and bright I gave her an arrangement of it for 2 pianos.

40 In Grainger's library there is a copy of *Japan* by David Murray, from the series *The Story of the Nations* (6th edition, London, 1906). Whether it was a gift from Roger Quilter is not apparent.

41 This letter accompanied Grainger's 1910 birthday gift to his mother, the string sextet setting of *Mock Morris*, then titled *Always Merry and Bright* after the title of a song "I gotter motter — Always merry and bright" from the musical comedy *The Arcadians* by Lionel Monckton and Howard Talbot. Percy and Rose had seen the musical at the Shaftesbury Theatre on 13 May 1910.

Only Roger, Everard Feilding, and Permin were here at the performance. Apart from Always we tried the string parts of "Sh's Hey" (for Roger's sake) and "The twa corbies" (man's voice accompanied by 6 string players) "Lord Maxwell's Goodnight" (tenor accompanied by 4 strings), and the string parts of an instrumental accompaniment for "Mowgli's song against People" (mixed choir)

Always sounded 20 times better than at the 1st trial, and sounds really *perfect* now. But the piece that made the strongest impression was "Mowgli's etc", an old very feelingful composition which I and other people have always reckoned to be a little (or very) unpractical, but this is shown not to be the case, at any rate with respect to the instruments.

We also played Roger's charming (3) English Dances 4-handed, and later in the evening my 2-piano arrangement of Always. We were all happy with it, and at the evening meal time I was quite intoxicated by excitement and happiness, threw big spoons at Permin, dropped bits of tongue in the cream (by mistake) lifted everything on the table I could with two fingers,

quite heavy things, and they fell down for the most part, and many other remarkable things, after a pattern you know already.

Some days ago [at Mrs Mond's "at home" on 30 June] I heard the above-mentioned Roger's Dances by an orchestra, conducted by H. J. Wood. I assure you, they are quite perfect, not the *slightest bit* one wants otherwise, and the performance was *excellent*.

Of course I am not the slightest bit annoyed at not being able to write p.r. It is basically *completely unimportant* to me. On the other hand I am very glad that you arrive the 24th; it would have been very irritating to wait these days and know that we *could* have been together. Permin leaves here the 22nd, probably.

Will you give my warmest regards to your sister? Ask her if she got my letter, some 2 months ago.

I am playing at an At Home Wednesday afternoon.

It looks terribly hopeful about my compositions, it seems to me.

We practise the Müller system here now, mother very keen. You can do them, can't you? Practise at them before you come, so that you can "shine" straight away. Tell me when you arrive in Ceresvej again.

Thanks for the sweet flower in your letter.

Many many sweetheart thoughts from your phallus-bearing brother

Percy.

On 2nd thoughts it would be better, after all, if you came on the 27th July. I will explain it when we meet.

I hope you won't have anything against this alteration. I have.

But I had forgotten something when I suggested the 24th.

Perhaps I will arrange a run-through of Hillsong for 24 wind players while you are here. I would so like to hear this piece, that I place highest of my things *purely musically*.

Goodbye, little Karen.

42 This is the first of Grainger's letters to Delius to survive in the Grainger Museum collection. Delius's letter to which this was a reply does not survive. Delius had been in Zurich for the first European performance of *Brigg Fair* on 28 May 1910. From 16 June to 10 July 1910 he was under examination at the Sanatorium at Mammern, Bodensee. En route to Mammern he had spent some hours with Hermann Suter at Basel railway station. Suter (1870–1926), Swiss conductor and composer, was conductor, among other things, of the Allgemeine Musikgesellschaft symphony concerts in Basel. Grainger was engaged for Basel on 16 and 17 March 1912, playing the Tchaikovsky B♭ minor Piano Concerto. Earlier in the year, two performances of Delius's opera *A Village Romeo and Juliet* had been given at Covent Garden by Thomas Beecham (22 and 25 February 1910). Grainger was out of London at the time of these performances, but Rose attended the full dress rehearsal on 21 February, commenting to Percy in that day's letter, *"on the whole it is dull"*; some is fine though".

347   TO FREDERICK DELIUS[42]   31A King's Road
6.7.10   Sloane Square
                                                                          S W

My dear friend Delius.

I was so overdelighted to get your lines & we both *rejoice* to hear that you are better. It was so sad to see you so seedy when here.

It is awfully sweet of you re Suter. I would, of course, **love** to have an engagement with him, if it could be brought off. The last 6 months has made an indescribable difference in my hopes & chances.

If my luck of the past ½ year only keeps on, I shall be indipendant within some few years. My Recital in Frankfurt was a great success, & I have a splendid engagement from the Frankfurter Museums Gesellschaft for a Freitags Konzert with orchestra Dec 2.

I have 3 engagements in Holland with the superb "Concertgebouw" orchestra conducted by the great Mengelberg; Amsterdam, Haag, Arnhem, am also engaged in Haag by "Residentie" orchestra, (Viotta) & have orchestral engagements in Utrecht, Groningen, etc, & play twice with the Berliner Philharmonie at Scheveningen in August, & twice with Halvorsen in Xia in September. I have a Norwegian-Danish Recital tour of about 50 concerts in the early autumn, & a long Dutch tour in January, & will also give Recitals in Germany.

So I have a busy year ahead. Fancy, in Holland no pianist has made so much per Recital as I did last season since Paderewski. Isn't it fun.

I have also been composing a bit & have been hearing a lot of chambermusic things done, strings, woodwind, concertina, etc. It is ever so sweet of you re the English Dance. I haven't got it copied out yet, but will do so as soon as possible now. A thousand thanks for your kindness.

I also send some printed notices. Do be a dear & give or send a batch to Suter. It would be *so good* of you.

All very heartiest & warmest greetings to you both from mother & me. Longing to see & hear you & your work

Ever yrs
Percy Grainger

Is adorable "Brigg Fair" printed yet?

348   TO KAREN HOLTEN   [London]
[Original: Danish/some English]
Thursday. 14.7.10

43 On 13 July 1910 a performance of Puccini's opera *La Bohème* was given at the Royal Opera, Covent Garden, with Melba and the Irish tenor John McCormack (1884–1945). The conductor was the Italian Cleofonte Campanini.

Above all bring the national costume with you, with the white old breastpiece that I like.

Last night I saw La Boheme of Puccini again.[43] I think it is an enchanting opera, so overfilled with ideas (musical) and melodies, and so outstanding in orchestration. MacCormack is a splendid tenor. The day before yesterday and one evening last week I ran round Battersea Park again. It is not the slightest trouble for me.

I am desperately unhappy today. For I don't think my works are as good as Puccini and as I dont hear them I cant find out. I am really utterly unhappy. And I *could* be so happy. I can no doubt put up with waiting with everything until I am rich, although it is frightfully tedious, but in the meantime the lovely old folk-singing men die, and it is not good for a composer not to compose for such a long time.

Today I got Folksong Journal 14 and it pains me to see that the others are continuing with their lovely collecting activities while I do absolutely nothing, and *will not be able to* for a long time.

Please give many kind regards to your mother. How is she now?

Friday. 15.7.10

I have a bad hand (left) and have had it for several days and it doesn't get better. It is as if it lacks feeling in certain movements. When I take hold of something I can't properly notice it in the hand itself, and it inconveniences me a little as well when I play, obviously. Will you help pray that it will go away?

Last night I met Cyril. He looks so notably younger and fresher again, and it was a pleasure to see him like that, and the firm Schott Söhne Mainz have made an excellent contract and are going to print his orchestral and instrumental works. Just think Schotts earn £60,000 yearly, he says. He is very satisfied and pleased with them.

I'm so glad. Only yesterday morning I was planning that if I make a lot of money this winter that I would give the money for publishing an orchestral work of Cyril's.

I don't think I will go in for Rathbone's idea of printing my works for the time being. I will explain when we meet.

Next letter *p.r.* leaves Monday afternoon.

349 TO KAREN HOLTEN   [In the train]
[Original: Danish/some English/private language]   Epping to London
18.7.10 Monday

Beloved approaching comfort and enchantment.

I have had a happy weekend, with a *lot* of tennis and sweat.

Last night I read to 4 o'cl about, exceedingly attractive and gripping plays of Galsworthy, really completely modern and not English-limited.[44]

I assume that if I write (from here) to you Thursday and Saturday that you will get them both before you leave.

It is not important the book Thuren has, I can easily get it when I come to Copenh. Don't bother either Th. or your sweet self about it.

I am so un-lecherous at present. The other night I woke up and wanted to be naughty, but suddenly forgot the whole thing, and went to sleep again. So you can see from that how little you can expect.

Lechery is certainly something excellent, but there is something, apart from lechery, indescribably compelling about the immediate encounter with the flesh of the opposite sex, which is not really primarily passion, but almost quietness and a peace otherwise unattainable. When one without a condom feels one's erection embraced by the vagina for the 1st time after a period of postponement then it is the purest uncorrupted voice of nature that sings in one. It is not that, that lies just closest to *my* personality, but all the same I sink all my opinions and tendencies happy-powerless for this bliss, and next week already we will be drunk with happiness again

The Maori form of greeting (like "good-day") is so fine for such occasions. *"Tina koe"* (there you are)

(London)

My hand is fortunately *much* better, perhaps quite well.

If you can get hold of anything of H. Bang's it would be very nice if you would bring them with you. I liked "Tine" so much. But **don't buy anything**. Only if you can *borrow*.

44 John Galsworthy (1867–1933), English novelist and dramatist.

By 24 August Grainger was back in Holland again, for two concerts at Scheveningen on 24 (piano recital) and 27 (with orchestra) August. From Holland he went to Norway, where he began a five-week tour of twenty concerts on 8 September. He arrived in Copenhagen on 14 October. The last concert of his Danish tour was given on 11 November. Karen met him for one night in Odense on the 10th. He returned to London for his first "Classical Concert" engagement on 16 November, leaving the next day for Holland and his first appearance with the Concertgebouw Orchestra and Willem Mengelberg at Arnhem on 21 November. His Dutch tour then continued until 30 November, after which he went on to Frankfurt for a series of concerts which included an appearance at the prestigious Museums-Konzert, again under the baton of Mengelberg. He was back in London by 10 December.

Rose, after renting out half the house at 31A Kings Road, furnished, to the Comtesse de la Forèst and her daughter, left London on 27 August to join Percy at the Hoek van Holland for the journey to Norway. This was her first visit to Norway, and she and Percy were guests of Nina Grieg at Troldhaugen until 12 September. Rose then stayed in Christiania while Percy toured the smaller Norwegian towns. He was back in Christiania on 10 October and after his concert there they travelled on together towards Copenhagen. Percy's Danish touring began on 2 November. Rose returned to London on the 4th, accompanied by Else Permin, and reclaimed her house from the Comtesse. She left London again with Percy on 17 November, travelling directly to Frankfurt where she stayed with the Klimsch family until Percy's arrival. Roger Quilter was also in Frankfurt in December 1910 and travelled back to London with the Graingers.

Once back in London in December, Grainger enjoyed a few days' respite from his practising and money-earning, enjoying instead the pleasures of composing and rehearsals.

350 TO ROSE GRAINGER   d[en]. Haag.
25.8.10   [Holland]

My dear little mother.

It pains me very much that I must depress you with the news that it was not a success last night. The whole human atmosphere of the Kurhaus is spiritually piosoning to me, the hall is too big for a Recital, & the very same Bechstein that was so glorious in the small Haag hall felt & sounded wooden in that big place. The audience seemed all German Jews, noisy & disturbing, & looking so unsympatheticly & inhumanly at me. On all hands critical & questioning faces; before which my emotionalism promptly dries up.

My memory behaved well, to my surprize, & I was not nervous for long, but I never got inspired & the whole thing was dreary slavery to me.

The audience seemed so cold, only one encore at the end (though the Kurhaus folk, & one newspaper, seemed to think it warm!) & it seems the Dutch are beginning to "find me out."

The very 2 Haag papers that wrote such reams of overflowing praise 4 months ago are taking me very Ca'am now

I've only seen 3 papers as yet: the half good "Nieuwe Courant" (enclosed) the frankly bad "Nieuwe Rotterdamsche Courant" (who say they are disappointed & that they are not sure they can subscribe to my being a Klaviergenie) & a few lines in the Haag "Het Vaderland" saying "P Gr worked up the Kurhaus audience during his Recital to many recalls.

Especially after the Röntgens, a Grieg Ballad, & Rakoczy March the applause of the large public was very warm".

I dont think I've ever played to as big an audience at a Recital. As a rule at the Kurhaus the places are abboniert [German: subscribed], but last night everyone had to pay for their seats, so the Kurhaus must have made a lot on it. They seemed pleased.

Am so glad you found comb. Did Mrs Jenkins stud come back from jeweler? I shall look for it today. You book your luggage to Kristianssand (Norway) via Hoek van Holland, Hamburg, Fredrikshavn.

I dont know what the train you enter at Hoek will have written on, but probably Rotterdam–Bremen–Hamburg. I'll join you at Hoek I think, but if we miss, you go straight on to Fredrikshavn (Denmark) arriving early Monday (9 oclock) & wait for me there. Am now going to work hard for Sat.

Yr loving & longing son.

I'm looking forward to Sat's concert.

351 TO KAREN HOLTEN   Troldhaugen
[Original: Danish]
after the concert
8.9.10

Sweetest absent flesh.

No, it is so difficult to say how much one loves and how. But it is true that my blood streams toward you, that my nerves hunger for you, and that past and future desire knocks on the door for you. God can describe what sort of love ours is, I give it up entirely; but that we have unveiled to each other what we have kept hidden from others, that we have dug up for each other roots that haven't previously seen the light, that is true enough. Before I sleep the thoughts of my senses stretch out towards you, and my head becomes like a hot abscess for your skin, your hair, your mouth. I become inflamed by a happy glow towards you, to be tender to you, to mistreat you, to throw myself on you and know your body's animal writhing, your personality's tempting charm, your ready unhidden camaraderie. Our rivers of love surge like writhing worms from within our flesh longingly towards each other.

352 TO JULIUS RÖNTGEN   Troldhaugen
[Original: Danish/some English]
11.9.10.

My dear kind sweet friend.

It was certainly different playing in Holland without you, your great heart and your (even for the audience) infectious enthusiasm and goodwill. Everything was relatively cold and tedious and I played badly as well.

But I am almost glad that it was like that, in order to see a confirmation of what I had always felt: that the whole of my success in Holland was *for the most part* only your doing, and your really indescribable noble goodness to me. I felt very deserted without you, and was glad of it. It would have been painful to me if I had felt almost as much at ease.

We have been **so** happy here, my mother and I. *How* I love Norway. We had a wonderful journey here from Scheveningen via Hamburg, Vamdrup, Frederikshavn, Christianssand—Bergen.

Mrs Grieg and Miss Hagerup have been so indescribably kind to us and both Mr and Mrs Houven v. d. Oordt were *all too* kind at the Haag.

The concerts here were extremely nice and good, and we heard an *enchanting* Slåtte-player (Arne Bjørndal) at F. Beyer's. You should get to hear him when you are in Bergen. Beyer knows him.

These few lines are only to tell you that I more than ever realize your sweetness to me & to say how I long to see you all in København.

Fond love to you all from us all

Ever thankfully
Percy. G.

353   TO KAREN HOLTEN   Haugesund.
[Original: Danish/some English phrases]
13.9.10

No, I don't think either that you should regard my manner now in London as being the normal; it wasn't that I meant at all

But I did talk some few times with you over there without being un-normal (neither for nor against) and as truthfully as I could, but I don't know whether you took any notice of what I said.

It wouldn't matter to me personally whether you took any notice or not, if it were not that, for your sake, I wouldn't for anything in the world deceive you, or sadden you in the future. I am afraid, you see, that you take silence for agreement. Don't misunderstand me: *I* am absolutely completely satisfied with our relationship as it is; you must remember that it *is not I* that wants *any change*. It is you who say "it can't go on this way" "It would never occur to me to be content with this in the long run" etc. Which I can very well realise as well, and feel.

Let me once again recite my point of view: I am in a way quite in love with you, miss you and long for you when separated, and find you enchanting when we are together — but I love you as a lover, as a comrade, as a friend, *but absolutely not as a wife*. And when I feel that you wish and expect marriage then I get frightened and without love. I am deeply thankful to have found you, I have had splendid pleasures with you and expect to have more and more with you. But I can only love you as long as it is an entirely free relationship between us. I cannot think of greater delights than together with you: But I cannot think of anything worse than to be married to you. *Rather than to be married to you I would let you destroy yourself or see your life ruined*. For death is better than an unhappy unfreedom. It is unnecessary for me to mention the reasons why I *adore you as a loving comrade*, but shudder at being married to you; as I can't explain the whole thing so exactly, and it wouldn't be of use if I could. There is no question of any change. From the first you have indeed wished to be married to me, because you in truth and honesty felt like that, and from the first I have insisted that there shouldn't be any talk (from my side) of anything else than a free unrestricted relationship, because I in truth and honesty felt in that way.

I am not offended that you wish something other than I do (it only makes me unhappy that I can't fulfil your wishes) and I ask you not to be offended that I want something other than you do. I love you so warmly and so deeply, not only in general, but today, now in this moment, just as much as ever, rather more than less. Not only that I have had unforgettable delights and raptures with you and that I am full of longing plans for future happiness and fun with you, but quite apart from the fleshly delightful passion — I have found you a splendid and lovable person, a firm and a splendid friend.

But I desire just as little (perhaps even less?) as 5–6 years ago to be married to you.

I would madly like to be with you much more than I am — but that is something quite different after all.

And if I ever meet some person I want to marry (I don't anticipate anything in that direction, but who can know what madness can suddenly fall upon people?) then I would regard myself free as a matter of course to marry "the person concerned."

Such has been the relationship between us from the first, from my side, and I see no reason to expect any change. Small changes, up and down occur, thank God, in every relationship, more or less, and there have been times when the apparently impossible (marriage with you) has seemed to me more possible than at other times. But you must believe me (for your own sake) that the above-mentioned point of view has been my most usual normal and average position with regard to you.

Perhaps the chief reasons why I feel marriage to you to be so impossible are the following:

1. That you are *quite undeniably* **much** too old for me.
2. That I, despite "cosmopolitan interests" and a really deep love of Scandinavia, after all in *everyday things* are much too British in my instincts to be suitable for taking a foreigner in marriage.

But I confess that the reasons do not explain the depth of something like this and must beg you to take my standpoint as it is, without further explanation. But it is only a misunderstanding if I have given you cause to believe that *I for my part* desire *any* change in our present relationship or manner to each other. It is only *your* (very reasonable) *dissatisfaction* with the existing that makes me anxious and drives me to "make myself clear" to you. For me the continuation of what there has been between us (but rather more than less) would be blissful. But I can well understand that it is only a ½-thing for you, as it is, and I wouldn't take amiss anything at all you could think of doing to me, if you kill me in the night, or burn English Dance, or destroy my reputation in Copenhagen. It would perhaps all be justifiable from your side.

But I, for my part, I fight for what suits me best. (but without wishing to *compel* you to anything; you are free as a bird, as soon as you wish) Life is too short not to fight relentlessly for one's own hand.

These tedious 5 pages of this letter express, I suppose, my position. It is not written with any tender consideration for you, and *absolutely* without any desire to wound you (please believe me, once and for all, that my cruelty-urge is *only* bodily, and *doesn't* have any mental side, as far as I know) and comes from my hand in a time when I feel quite rich in love and longing for you.

I beg you therefore to regard it as the "normal", and since these clarifications are not particularly pleasant I will not write often in this way, but will ask you to understand my silence as agreement with the contents of this letter. And everything that I will get to feel for you and write to you of love, devotion, missing and longing won't signify any disharmony with this letter, but only my true feelings at the moment — as I *am* in love with you *in my way*, and so deeply grateful and happy to have you, but only not as a married husband, but as a free, childish, inconsiderate, ridiculous lover.

354   TO KAREN HOLTEN
[Original: Danish]
Saturday. 17.9.10.
After midday.

S.S. "Arendal"
Kristianssand-Kristiania
near Larvik.

45 The piece was *Arrival Platform Humlet*, first conceived on 2 January 1908 while Grainger was waiting for Karen at Victoria Station. As first conceived the piece was literally a "humlet", with wordless humming syllables written in and was variously entitled "Awaiting arrival of belated train; great fun", "On waiting for the train; great fun" and "Railway platform humlet". The version for solo viola was published by Schott & Co., London, in 1926.

46 No letters survive from Karen Holten between 21 July and 23 September 1910.

The concert in Stavanger didn't go so badly, about 300 Kr in the hall, but last night in Kr-sand there were only about 200. But the enthusiasm in both towns was colossal. Last night I was simply "mobbed" by about 30 of the audience, young women, who followed from the hall to the door of the hotel afterwards and wanted to steal the flowers from the bouquet, etc. Amazing. I receive masses of flowers everywhere, and a more pleasant attractive and warm public than these Norwegians can't be imagined. About 5–6 extra numbers every evening, and 3 recalls after Bach. Everyone thinks I will earn twice as much next time in this country.

I have composed some more for that piece for (solo) viola I began once on a London railway station while waiting for you from Denmark, can you remember?[45]

Your letter to Stavanger was enormously sweet.[46] I also think it would be a frightful shame if anything bitter came between us. And it has not been so completely free from that danger. Yes, in God's name let us see and be even happier than we have ever been, and more often as well, and longer as well, *when it is possible*.

And when we are separated, arrange your life as full and lively and eventful as you possibly can. With much work or much sport or much gaiety, or by earning a great deal, or studying a great deal or by not doing all these things, but only being really happy and glad.

One should either be *good at* something or one should *enjoy* something, it doesn't matter which, perhaps.

The uncertainty about our love life has possibly cast a shadow over you, in a way. The thing that you most wanted looked undecided to you, and then it is difficult to find contentment in external things. But if you are really able to carry out what you write in your letter then we can't avoid being more happy together, I think. If I can feel that you don't *expect* anything from me then I won't be able to avoid loving you a little more straight away. Let us not expect anything of each other and be happily surprised at all the charming and magical things that happen between us.

I write so stupidly. It all sounds so infinitely foolish. But I intend it differently.

I long so frightfully for you in these days. Really I am erotically mad: It *can't* be normal to be so impatient and so full of erotic fever as I am, sometimes. I see you so beautiful before me, and the whole of my personality has no other urge than some stupid old thoughts about you. The beautiful Norway, the lovely weather, my compositions, my career, they go past like water off a duck's back, while my flesh itches all the time for your flesh. And, God knows, that's not remarkable. Since quite a small child I have specially trembled and shaken at certain thoughts, certain longings. And you are the only person in my life who has shown consideration for these things. Apart from you they have not found the *slightest* fulfilment. But with you all my deep desires blossom. I can't understand at all how you manage never to deny my happiness. You never disappoint me when I come to you with pleasures in mind. It is only when I am too stupid to have pleasure in mind that we don't find each other.

355 TO ROSE GRAINGER
28.9.10.   3.30 aftern

[In the train]

Just left Koppang, a place to be remembered. There one has 20 ms to stuff a meal down, to me, armed as I am ("with an excessing flow of siliver, no doubt highly benificiary to the process of digestion") to excell others at the game, always the gayest of sports. I feel exceedingly overfilled & therefore boundlessly happy. Overfeeding seems needful to my moral stability. They had a lovely cake there, a sort of nice "apple-fool" or whatever its called, made into a flat cake, with lots of cream, & dabs of good pools of pink juice on top, tasting like cheery.

This country at this time of the year is truly of perfect beauty. Of its kind its glorious. Easy comfy welltreed hills flop flowingly into a broad dale, mostly taken up by a broad shallow river full of shoals sandbanks & bare or bushed or treed islands. On hills, dale, & islands certain trees have turned color, chiefly the birch (which goes golden yellow) & a small tree with

-leaved branches (which goes a magenter-like blood color) & these show up all thro the darkness of the pine & stillgreen trees like freckles, very spikkit & sparkit. I've never seen autumn tints more seethroable & sparkling. The wooden houses, too, are oftenest painted a magentery red, & the aforesaid magentery blood red tree makes a bewitching blend & outlandish impression together with these.

Such a queer typical peasant ½ musician looked me up last night at Elverum. Apart from speaking "bygdmål" (dialect) as he said he did, he had a folksingerish way of mumbling, & was not always so easy to follow, but he is quite a lofty aloof highly philisophical truly Scandinavianly softhearted old boy, quite a dear, & not like things in a real world. He drank portwine to my pink lemonade in my room last night after the concert & said many a queer thing. He travelled thro USA for 3 years as solo violinist in a troup, liked Americans warmly, is a student of fiddlemaking & a big reader on musical matters evidently, & was very moved to hear I knew Wieniawskis daughter, & took down her name.[47] He looked at me long & at last delivered himself: I find you a very fine type, a very fine type of a man. He asked me if I didnt have a "flamme", if I wasnt bethrothed, & couldnt think why I wasnt, he thought it a good thing to have after one was 17. "I've always thought to myself, that's an ideal life to be a great artist like yourself & to travel round to different places with some dear thing with one: I used to think so concert-travelling in USA." I asked him if he wouldnt be coming to England. He may, when he "inherits" from his father.

It was wondrously dark after concert last night, & walking back to my Hotel I came upon a couple who'd been at the trouble & heard the wife telling the husband all about it. (in Norway men listen to their women just as in England wives bear up with the Robin Legge act!) It was far too dark for them to see me, so I kept close alongside & drank it all in. "Og saa bare det at sé hele manden" [Danish: And then just to see the whole man] she was saying, & went on in praise of my playing. I swat, inside my clothes, at the queer sensation it was, like listening to the verdict of the future over ones grave. I know nothing more consoling than to hear oneself praised by quite unbeknowing folk, within hands reach of them.

47 Henryk Wieniawski (1835–80), Polish violinist and composer, the most famous of a family of musicians. The nature of Grainger's acquaintance with Wieniawski's daughter remains unelucidated.

356 TO KAREN HOLTEN   Grand Hotel
[Original: Danish/some English]   Trondhjem
29.9.1910

Little comrade

Had a nice 12 hours journey yesterday, arrived here 12.30 at night.
When do you get your tummy-ache again?
Remember that "aroha" means passion, love in Maori, as I will use that
word later on to you.
There was something in a previous letter from you that I would like to
reply to. You said that 2–3 years between people didn't signify so much —
that the woman was 2–3 years older. But you must remember that, in
England at any rate, it is customary for a man to marry a woman 6–8–10
years younger than he is himself, and judged according to that you are
really not 3 years too old for me, but 9 or 11 or 13 years too old. Since
I am specially young for my age and specially talented, there would be
nothing in the least remarkable if, for example, I married the little Quilter
pupil who is 17. I regard her as already too old for me actually. If I married
in 2 years' time, it would be suitable if I took a woman of 17 years of age,
and so it would seem to most English people. In other words: You could
almost be the mother of a daughter who would be suitable for me, if you
were 4 years older and had had the daughter when you were 18. But now
it is too late for that! But it is an amusing thought all the same.
I am tired and lonely and an unlucky person, although there will be a
good house here tonight, and apart from that I am guaranteed 250 Kr.
But believe me I am unlucky and unhappy.
Although I have so many good qualities and so many people that love
me, still the whole thing is really rotten. People are after all lucky if they
don't have instincts like mine, it is a little heavy to carry in the long run.
Believe me, comrade. No one is satisfied with me.
Mother would presumably be unhappy if she got to know all my unnatural instincts, those I must preferably conceal from her; and you are not at
all satisfied with me, I am not what you can use, beneath all your love for
me I feel your impatience and contempt for me, and I only wait for the
day when you get tired of me and revenge yourself on me in one way or
another; and I destroy my own health by my naughtiness, and even so I
can't stop it, and I am dissatisfied with myself because I don't become as
a composer what I should because of lack of time, and because of weakened bodily strength as a result of naughtiness. Believe me, it isn't pleasant
to see oneself slip downwards every year, helplessly but consciously. If "I
pull through it all" then it is the result of my primeval-healthy constitution
and my soul's freshness and elasticity — but I well understand how people
feel who "lose in the battle of life". Whether I shall lose or win in that
battle is not determined yet, but I know how it feels to go downhill because
of one's own weakness.
There is no point in my life I can be proud of looking at. I am only a
halfthing both as composer and as pianist, I am only halfgood as a son,
I am no good as a lover, I am no good as regards myself either, I have not
mastered any language properly, I have not been a really good friend to
any man-friend, I have neglected my folksong collecting in order to earn
money, and have neglected my money-earning to collect and compose, I
don't belong to any nation, everywhere I feel reaction against what I meet,
even against that which I like best.
Perhaps you think that the whole of my misfortune derives from my
naughtiness — but that is not entirely the case. I was just as unsatisfactory
as a child, and even more unsatisfactory in Frankfurt and London before
the naughtiness began. The naughtiness is only one of the many modes of
expression for my inner weakness and halfness. If only I could be good

until *the 14th! Pray for me*! I will do what I can for it. Forgive me, who is worth so little.

Your corrupter
Percy.

Have you begun English Dance score? I'll tell you about the parts of it when in Copenhagen

357   TO ROSE GRAINGER   Grand Hotel
1.10.1910   Saturday.   Kristiansund N.

I had a great day yesterday. I left Throndhjem 8 in the morn by steamer, & started the day with some good work. I wrote out my whole sketch for the setting of "Shallow Brown" (The shudderer) & also wrote down the whole of the last London tune

as far as it's thought out. I also had too lovely meals on board the little "Hankø". There was a strong wind blowing all the time, & wet & rainy, & it was jolly to watch the little rowing boats come out from the small hamlets to meet the boat, & load up cargo to a dangerous looking extent.

At a place called Beyjan, or some such name, they took a big queer coffin on board a little rowing boat, & another big rowing boat came out in the blownspray, & floppy waves manned by some 6–7 giants in yellow overalls, looking truly Vikings, & stirring me very much indeed. Indeed a boat would be the very thing for me. To be happy I must have plenty to struggle with, but I dont happen to be fond of strife with my fellow men, but long to wrestle with the elements in fellowship with other struggling men. I am not unfond of strife, but I suffer greatly at the feeling of ill will & bad feeling. But *struggle* is the breath of life. Later on the weather grew rather Esbjerg-Harwich-like, & particularly ½ an hour before getting here it was all too compelling & I retired to the rear for a general settling of accounts. I was slightly sick, & do you know, thoroly enjoyed it. I think it's rather a jolly sensation, "gribende" ialfald [Danish: "gripping" in any case], with a lot of keenness to it.[48] I am "au fond", not far from nature & the animals; my temperament is at heart gross & healthy & easily contented. When my money is made & I lead a quiet rough world-far natural life I shall be a very goodnatured contented relishing old pig. Our boat was hours late & we only arrived at the quay at the hour booked for Ch-Sund's concert. I dressed on board as we came into the haven. ¼ hour after having been sick I was playing away on the platform! That is the life that suits me; having to put up with bodily discomforts & do my pianists job under handicaps — with my head reeling from sea sickness, or on a rotten piano, something of real life in it, & not too "gerade hoch künstlerisch" [German (ironic): lit. quite high art]

All yestereve I felt real sick & seasick & tummy rotten, but today I'm grand.

I made a little over 130 Kr here last night. Everyone is so nice to me. I feel *ever so unspeakably* at home in Norway now, quite as much as in Denmark, or will in a few years time, anyway. Nothing but niceness every where.

It was so jolly to hear you on the phone today, I heard you very clearly. The concertarranger here has such lovely books in his bookshop.

48 A rather more vivid account of the same event occurs in Grainger's letter of 2 October to Karen: ". . . later on the weather became all too rocking and a quarter of an hour before we arrived here I was seasick in a completely dark W.C. (they had forgotten to put the light on in there). Imagine, I think it is quite a pleasant feeling — I don't mind it in the least. Now I will try and be sick as often as I can".

Icelandic sagas, with the Icelandic on one side & Mål on the other, which means I'll learn both speech as easy as nought! Isn't it wie geschaffen [German: as if made] for me? And only costing 25–30 Øre each; isn't it laughably cheap?

I think the Mål movement here *simply magnificent*. I'm having a lot of these books (10–12 for 2 kroner!) bound here before I go.

There is a black-water-proof-cloak factory here, & just everyone wears them here, so I couldnt withstand it but bought Karen one & a cap to match, & also bought myself an oilskin suit of a glorious yellow color, cap, (Sth Wester) coat & breeks — only a few bob the lot.

I'm thinking a deal about my compos these days, & in bed, this morn, thought out a possibly good beginning for the slow Hillsong — I *would* like to get that dear piece underway. I feel mightly like composing these days, & if I had a free month before me, could cough up a decent "period" I feel. Never mind it'll all come, in time.

It's so sweet of you to be so keen about my compos. I am too if one only knew it. I'm *so* impatient about them that to wait 10 minutes before hearing a new thing is a[s] bad for me as having to wait 10 months, & that's why I dont so much mind waiting 10 years.

How about the following little note to follow on the title of the "English Dance" & to be used in programs, etc, as a general hint?:

ENGLISH DANCE

Not merely an English sort of dance,
but in it, it is hoped, some hint of
the alround throb of bouyant boyish
limber elastic merry mettalsomeness
of the English breed. *England dancing*:

Omnibuses racing one another, football rushes, newsboys cunning cycling,
factories clanging & booming away,
fast express trains shuddering past,
fire-horses — general reliable rolicing
riot & disciplined disorder.

When I get back to London, & have time, I first of all want to hear the string parts of both E. Dance & Green Bushes on 8 strings. That I would learn so much from.

My own poppet one. Fond love & goodbye for today. How's the Hardanger dragt [Danish: costume]. Dont forget to get it. Your very loving son.

358 TO KAREN HOLTEN   Grand Hotel
[Original: Danish/private language]   Kristiansund N.
2.10.1910.
[Extract]

You, little comrade, will so well suit the sea and rain and primitive pleasures. You have the Scandinavian woman's toughness and singleness and contentment with unpleasant extremes.

Someone like you wakens naturalness in someone like me. I don't only love you with *my* English sharp singular sensuality and my personal cruelty (although I do that as well) but I love you with international impersonal naturalness, I long not only to love you as my sensuality demands, I also long to love you as *your* sensuality demands, I want to throw all separators to hell, and glide gently with my thick strong phallus into your inner fjords, your smooth oily greasy slimy interior roads, that fog-up and bewitch away all mental consciousness, my phallus smelling sharp and animal-like of rotten fish, your sex passages smelling sharp and animal-like of something bitter and sour, and feel the thick rich cream stride forth from my body's interior dark earth and grow fruitfully forward against your womanliness's warmth and intoxicating sun, and stride up and forward with maddening thudding pumping pulse, enormous and threatening, till all personality is intoxicated away, till all nationality is sensualised away, till the difference between you and me is only thought and not felt, till I become woman and you become man in our crowning moment, and my life-infecting marrow-milk spits forward in your hidden mouth, where my stiff belly-tongue and your love-throat kiss with slimy wet greasy convulsive muscular kisses, tearing and revolutionary, beastly and joyous, and my tight boy's body, solemn, with singing ears and flayed will, pays its full tax of white blood into your Queen's treasure chest, and your soft pliable deluding seducing girl-entrails suck and draw out and consume and digest the stolen contagious world-enrichments, while our 2 forms lie enveloped in a steam of passion, sweaty-smelling under our arms and around our anus, our muscles relax, and grateful tiredness and joyful relief spread over us and our love-wet animal-smelling sexual parts.

Oh, if only you could spit your love-spit into my eyes, if only my mouth could suck your inner woman's penis, if only I could drink your sex-fjord's bitter juice, if only I could bear that you were sea-sick in my mouth, if only I might bear to see you eat my 2 testicles like boiled eggs, if only my 2 eyes were 2 small hairy caves (like your anus) and your 2 nipples were 2 stiff pointed finger-thick phalli which you could bore into my brain, so my life could be extinguished in ecstasy like an electric lamp.

---

359 TO ROSE GRAINGER
6.10.1910

S.S. "Driva"
between Batnfjord & Throndhjem.

My sweetheart mother.

Now to questions: I'll send you the Norwich items from Throndhjem. I think it will be most practical for me to stay at Westminster again. I get to Xia Monday next 12.10 midday & it would be lovely if you would await me at the Hotel, 10 minutes after that arrival.

I should be delighted to sup with the Dresden-workers at the Grand after Folkekonsert next Tuesday.[49]

I feel the Hals have been slightly neglected this time as against last so I'm going to write her asking if I cant come to them quietly, & not late *Monday eve.* I dont know are you to be in Xia or do you still wish to stay at Foshheim, & whether you can come too to Hals's?

I shall not be needing other boxes in Xia than those I'll be bringing along from Throndhjem, *but all my boxes* will have to leave Xia with me by the 9.57 train Wednesday morn. Will that be alright? Ta re Hansen. I sent him programs for Køb, & also I enclosed such a Dutch krit snip from the Xia papers, with many other hints & implorings!

I made over 230 Kr at Aalesund, I think that's the best yet after Xia, Bergen, & Throndhjem? Alas I find expenses heavy The 250 I took from Xia will not see me back I fear so I'll get the needful in Throndhjem.

I ought to earn over £100 in Denmark, & with hardly any exs as I'm put up in Køb, Nykøbing Sj, Odder, Aarhus, (Aalborg?)

Høeg has arranged the dates delightfully I think. I shant have to leave Køb until about *2nd Nov*

49 Rose had written on 1 October, *"Then* a lady & her husband friends of Mrs Grieg's living in Dresden, want to know whether you & I would go to supper with them to the Grand Hotel after yr concert here? They are going to take a party to yr concert, & she has written to that friend of Mr Hay's & others about you at Trondhjeim & she has taken some of the Augustin printed critiques, & has written to a very influential friend in Dresden, asking him to show them to the Conductor of the Symp. Concerts. Dresden & to try & get you an engagement with him. The father sat next to me at table at "West[minster Hotel]" & seemed **very** nice. They are all *frightfully* enthusiastic about you". This is quite a good example of how the Graingers worked. Percy gave a recital in Dresden on 1 February 1911 (see letter 380); he did not play at the symphony concerts.

There are 2 plans I have for our joint movements in Denmark. Join me in Randers Nov 9 & wait there while I go to Odense, & we meet again at Fredericia Nov 11 on our way to Ribe, which we leave Nov 12[,] I or we over Esbjerg, or you over Holland, just as you please. Or: You stay in Køb. until Nov 10 when you join me in Odense from where we go together to Ribe, etc. But you'll see it all clearer with a map. I'm so happy we're going to Ribe, which I've never seen & it said to be the most interesting of all Dan. provincial towns, lovely old Domkirke & buildings.

It seems now that we should have time for a few days holiday somewhere in Sjælland near Køb, if you'd care for it, in between Kvindelig Orkester *Okt 28* & my leaving Køb *Nov 3*. But all this when we meet.

I played so really well in Aalesund, the best I've done on the tour yet. Rönisch piano (say it not in Gath)

Remind me tell you silly episode in Aalesund please!

I am just up after some 22 hours of wavetossing with an hours blessing of motoring in between. Indeed after these small boats & floppy seas I might say of the Danish & Dutch Xings, à la Waverley pens adv:

T'will come as a boon & a blessing to me
The Esbjerg & Harwich & Netherlands Sea!

I have made a heap of new & close friends: The Jóms Vikings, a brotherhood of batchelor Danish Vikings in the 11th century, who lived chaste Spartan lives & died wonderful deaths with smart words in the mouths. One or 2 of these real darlings. Jóms Vikingarnar Saga [*sic* Jómsvíkinga saga] is one [of] the set I bought in Icelandic & Maal at Christianssŭnd.

I get more & more pleased with Norway & Norwegians each day. I find it *the* finest land & folk yet, finer even than Denmark & the Danes, though truly not so begaying & behopefulling. Not one trifle has yet happening to hazard my regard for & growing love of them.

I've never enjoyed a tour as much as the whole of this Norse one! Recital touring taking it all in all is a great life.

Have done quite a lot of Slow Hillsong ideas & am altogether bursting with compo possibilities if I only had the time.

Have been reading the "Confessions" of a Russian Doctor in Norwegian.[50] Very interesting & teaching. Queer humane softhearted folk Russians. Queer game doctoring!

Please dont forget the fotografer. Remember I want *1 at least* of *each* pose he took of us both, & plenty of the best one. *And I particularly want him to* **keep all plates** *carefully for the future.*

Shall we be taken together again?

I hope my darling mother has made me joyeous by going & being taken again *in many poses*.

Now I've been long enough bundelling about up here alone, & long for the companionship of my batchelor-mummy keenly, & also keenly look forward to our few day[s] on English ground again in Nov, & to our pretty rooms at 31a for a few days, & a glimpse of nice sweet clean groomed harmless English girls like the young Quilters for a few days.

50 Grainger was probably reading W. Weressajew (V. V. Veresayev, pseud. for Vikentil Vikent'evich Smidovich), *En Læges Bekjendelser* [The Confessions of a Physician, (1901)]. Translated into Norwegian by H. B. and S. M., it was published by Albert Cammermeyer, Christiania, in 1902.

360 TO KAREN HOLTEN   [In the train]
[Original: Danish]   Trondhjem–Xia
10.10.1910.
[Extract]

When I close my eyes I think that you stand in front of me, just as when we are first quite alone after a long separation, and have not yet kissed each other, but stand and feel both our breaths, and both bodies quietly touch each other, and feel beforehand the kiss coming, and the whole world seems full of cream, jam, and dizzyness. Be merciful to me!

361 TO ROSE GRAINGER   Ceresvej 17.
18.10.1910

My darling

How can you ask whether I love you? It makes me so frightfully upset
& tonguetied when you do.

I not only love you, I dont know how much, but what is quite of an other
weight, you are my particular & *only* life's comrade*, were so always & will
be always "till death do us part", & this quite apart from your being my
mother, (matua wahine) (that is: the giver & developer of my superb health
from which springs my unique happiness) & along of that I am ever so fond
of my pleasures & my friends, even apart from you. But you are my comrade, my life's companion in all matters; all ways lead to mum; so how can
there be any question of love or not, where there is so much more?

*I have never met another being with whom I wish to incur a life's com-
panionship

362 TO ROSE GRAINGER   [In the train]
10.11.1910   Randers–Odense

We mustnt make a mistake & be too saving & thrifty & not allow ourselves any magnificent holidays to look back to. When I'm away from you
I'm always minding the bicycle rides we had in Germany & our Rhine trips
& when we read together. Life, the future, & the present do not flow
compellingly strong within me, but I hoard the past passionately & my
deepest yearning towards the future is that it may hold joys between you
& me which will take their place alongside our glorious past & thereby
justify living & the unenoughness which the present (at least for me) wears
while it is with us. For me all deeds, races, arts, joys exist alone that they
may one day take their place in the wealth of memories which *alone* (it
seems to me: No asceticism helps in that direction) sunders man from the
other beings. For me Iceland is the greatest affair because of all breeds &
ways of living its seemed to be planned most uniquely to shine in men's
remembering minds.

Their lives, from a practical outlook, were hopelessly diseased by being
helplessly under the sway of a longing to be well remembered, praised after
death, to be a beacon of personality for future individual personalities.

And that seems to me life & lifes purpose in the very most alive sense,
& particularly human in the most exageratedly human sense. To give way
to human feelings, to overflow & swim in human feelings is human enough,
but the farthest north of humanness is, for me, to be a lightning conductor
of such feelings in such a way that they are particularly fitted to fill niches
in coming men's minds & sit itchingly & inflamingly like small fishhooks
in men's consciousness throout changing customs & different rules for playing cricket. That is where dear old England has dissappointed me. The
reward of English deeds lie always largely in the present, & the future finds
their glory hopelessly mortgaged to passing gains that were not united in
the everlasting currency. To what end have the boldest British deeds been
dared? To fill someones pocket — generally someone elses. The patheticism
that lies in throwing oneself away in a *low* office for someone *else* gives
England its sweet wistful sympathetic touch, but the crass shallow stupidity
& wastefulness of the process banns it from a first place in human ratings.
What were the daring deeds of Iceland begot by? Whims, forlorn hopes,

sudden impatiences, lightning reactions. Useless, purposeless, gainless, barren, nearly all. But tasting sweet to the future. Full of personal dialectic fragrance after a 1000 years. Waking the low chuckle of the full human response, the deep content of meeting the untrammeled human untamable inner unreasoning pride & incorruptable independance.

Let us 2 too be wanton & moment-ridden (momentariness lives in the future, deeds fashioned for future returns wither at their payment) & not neglect to feed our stubborn & healthy infatuation for each other with its natural meat of mutual joys & gay joint experiences & the needful time-space for our comradeship to spread itself in & "gedeihen" [German: to thrive, to get on well].

We've had a real old rare old dig for the dollar, but now she's loaming up there's no need to behave like paupers *all* the time. It's *time* I've been a drop too niggardly with. Let us be kingly *occasionally*, it neednt be often, & set apart a whole day when I can play you my compos, & when we can read Longfellow & all sorts of things together, or let us really go to a whole Wagner Opera once all alone, & soak in it quite indipendantly of hostesses below, & generally betray flashlight spasms of surprizing momentary largess to each other, like you so royally did when you earned the money & I didnt save it.

I want you to think out a time when you & I can have a real little holiday together, in the spring or summer or any free time & you pick out the place, and we'll have a real picknic, & I wont even compose much or anything unless you wish. Would you like some place like Waddesdon again? And we'll take our stylish bathchair if you like. Apart from that, when I'm now in Holland, in the coming few towns, I'll see what small town expenses are like there, & then I want you to do part of my January tour there with me. I'm sure the smalls there will be delicious, & the circs couldnt well be luckier than they're likely to be this trip.

Also if Lady Quilter asks us to Bawdsey together again, *do* let us go & be there with the old Rodg.

Its a mistake to shoo off everything, at any rate after the 1st poverty act is over.

I only wish you, & incidentally the world & the future, could know what sort of thoughts I think when I'm travelling alone.

I'm at bottom very other than my chattering or even my letters. I dont mean that I'm a hidden diamond exactly, but I do mean that the paradoxes that sensitive folk roll out do not really express their real selves, though they *do* express their repugnance at what they imagine ordinary (or even unordinary) folk are attributing to them in the way of feelings instead of their real feelings.

I feel very much like Longfellow's poems when I'm long alone. I am very conscious of the rolling-river-to-the-sea element in life & feel the passing of the passing hour very consciously & am always thinking of death & loss & feeling like a sort of motto for a museum, without feeling miserable exactly..

When I'm with you there's no need to feel like that, so I dont, except about curios & tunes & things, but not about you — so you dont, naturally, know that side of my thoughts, & cant I fear.

Dear me, if only my *thoughts* could become known to the world, if only thought-impressions could be taken of my inner head as photos are of my outer, how readily I would give up composing & letterwriting & living too; for they only misrepresent one at last, & my thoughts & feelings are nicer than *anyone* would ever believe who knows me. Which shows what an unbetterable amateur I am at heart, doesnt it?

Nordisk Musikforlag has sent Aarhus's money to me here. Will you fix a time with Bechsteins for me to practise there on the piano for the 16th?

Goodbye my beloved mum & chum.

363   TO ROSE GRAINGER
[Postcard]
12.11.10.

Bramminge. Jylland.

Ribe is one of the most delicious old towns in the world. At every corner charmingly formed and colored old buildings of every age size & shape. As it is a town that fast goes backward commercially & has no likelihood of a future before it, one naturally sees dear lovely lovable gentle religious faces, & meets with a clean Hotel & sweet graceful ways & manners at every hand.

We must come here together next year. You will love it.

This cathedral is the oldest church in Scandinavia. All this section is of yellowbrown brick. This tower is of dull red brick

364   TO ROSE GRAINGER
[Original: Danish/one sentence English]
[Postcard]
21.11.10.

Amsterdam.

Was thrilled for your letter this morning. Yesterday I heard 2 "Bulgarian Rhapsodies" of Enesco, that he conducted himself with the Concertgebauw orchestra.[51] He orchestrates indescribably splendidly and "funny", the compositions are charming and fascinating, he conducts masterfully and completely with genius (he is only about 30, and they say he plays the piano and violin equally well) the orchestra was of course excellent, *and the whole thing was an absolutely first-class experience*

Enesco conducts his 2 Rhapsodies again today in Arnhem, where I am playing. (today)

Will write to Mrs v. Grunelius *first thing* tomorrow.

Enesco is Bulgarian himself.

I take my Danish pills like one oclock

51 Georges Enesco (1881–1955), Romanian violinist and composer. He conducted his two *Rapsodies Roumaines* [Romanian Rhapsodies] at the St Caecilia Concert in Arnhem on 21 November 1910. Grainger played the Grieg Piano Concerto under the direction of Willem Mengelberg.

365   TO ROSE GRAINGER
22.11.10.

77 van. Eeghenstr[aat]
Amsterdam.

Herewith 500 mark in this letter, & in Klimsches a cheque for 931 mark.

Enesco (a *Rumanian not* Bulgarian) & I trained to & from Arnhem together not getting back before after 1 o'cl. The enclosed program lasted 3 hours. And then we had to race thro, no time for encores, the lid closed straightaway after each solo.

Mengelberg[52] was delighted with me & awfully nice.

I was frightfully frightened unhappy tired & lonely, my finger hurt like Hell & the dampness of air in the hall was such that the keys *simply swam* with water; never felt anything so queer and slippery. But nevertheless I think it was all a great success & a good evening for me.

But now the crisis with the finger is over & it's fast bettering.

I liked Enesco's things still better on 2nd hearing, warm & ½ modern ½ old fashioned.

He seems really nice too.

His lovely soaring stuff rings on delightfully in my head.

I'll very soon let you know when I come to Fr. How nice to have had the ordeal with Mengelberg (who's a funny laughable little eyebrowless cockfighting poodle) over before serious old Fr!

I cant say I like Holland, lovey, tho I certainly dont hate it

Yr own poppinjay

52 Josef Willem Mengelberg (1871–1951), Dutch conductor, from 1895 to 1945 conductor of the Amsterdam Concertgebouw Orchestra. From 1907 to 1920 he was also director of the Museum Concerts in Frankfurt. He is described in the *New Grove Dictionary of Music and Musicians* as "small [in stature] and dynamic . . . a martinet addicted to meticulous and voluble rehearsals".

366 TO ROSE GRAINGER   [In the train]
midday Sat. 25.11.10.   Amsterdam–Haag

Last night in Hilversum was really jolly, very full hall & tiptop piano & real enthusiastic warmth. And in "de paus" in comes a sweet 16–18 year old Danish girl (something like the Larsen girls, thin & round, slightly stomachy [which is so sweet in the very young] with clear pure keen blue undisciplined eyes) in typical Scandinavian hysterical excitement (helt væk [Danish, idiomatic: quite carried away]) with gushing unreined floods of quick Danish speech. Great floods of joy swept over me, it was as if a kind warm hand was laid on me, I felt a gentle easy sweat roll over me, & as if the Dutch air was suddenly worth the breathing. I would have liked to have kissed her of course, but, dear me, Danish girls & women are so overflowingly full of sexual suggestion that to watch them & hear the[m] say a few silly words is joy enough. No words can say what a blessing, what a sunray of spirituality, what a dance of joyeous livliness, what a blast of freedom those 5 Danish minutes were to me after these barren lifeless sordid sexless dark dull Dutch days, in which ones health swells & thrives & ones soul shrivels, or goes to sleep.

It is curious that my boyish reasonless passion towards Scandinavia should be repayed by such a quite different grown up go-instead, but in such a flowery rich mint, & with never any lasting disappointment or re-action, that is so curious. But at bottom I believe it is not so much the purely *racial* gifts that enthral me there as the particular spiritual civilis-ation that is peculiar to their way of living & colors all their manners.

I believe if I could find any other folk (Spaniards or Chinese or any) of whose life *goodness, sense, & freedom* was equally the basis as it is of the Danish (& Norwegian?) that I would breathe their quality with a like relish. But everywhere else I find brutality, use-of-force, & above all lack-of-sense, & *opinonatedness & unintelligent convincedness*,[53] &, I need hardly say, lack of freedom to such a degree at jeg ikke på nogen måde kan finde mig i det [Danish: I can't agree to it/accept it in any way].

I should say that the Norwegians were a *still better & freer* folk, but their lack of *sense & native nouce* make them more nervously exhausting for me to be with, & brainily, of course, not so interesting, despite their purity & giftedness.

Amongst the Germans I now find *many things very* sympathetic. I've just bought a delicious German book about Greek sculpture, & two jolly German book[s] on "Ehe & liebe" in Classical Europe & in the far East.[54]

I read yesterday some **magnificent** essays by R. L. Stevenson "In defence of idlers" & others, glorious, & wrenching from one the fierce mirth of wholehearted approval. What a gentleman, a sweet soul, what a rare old Battling Billy!

Now I arrive at the Hague.

Instead of 's Gravenhage (the Duke's park-garden) it might be called *Hugensgrave* (the grave of the mind) as indeed all Holland might.

I think a tour here in Jan 1912 will be bully. The agent in Hilversum wants already to engage me for 4 concerts in 4 neighboring towns for then.

It's bliss to read of the old Greeks. They *do* just kick the beam *every time*

53 On the same subject Grainger had written to Karen, 24 September 1909, of ". . . the stubbornness [folk show] on subjects they have convictions about in place of knowledge, experience & giftedness".

54 The "delicious German book about Greek sculpture" is unidentified. The other two German books were possibly in the series *Die Sitten der Völker* [The Customs of the People], *Liebe, Ehe, Heirat, Geburt, Religion . . .* [etc] *. . . bei allen Völkern der Erde* by Dr George Buschan, published in a series of 56 instalments by the Union Deutsche Verlagsgesellschaft, Stuttgart, Berlin, Leipzig, Wien [n.d.]. Robert Louis Stevenson's essay "An Apology for Idlers" was first published in the *Cornhill Magazine*, Vol. 36, July 1877.

367 TO ROSE GRAINGER   Amsterdam.
28.11.10

My darling: the Hague concert yesterday was a *tremendous success*. All went finely.

Augustin[55] will be sending you a cheque for about 380 to 390 mark which possibly may arrive before I do. I shall be bringing with me some money too. Money vanishes here in the most ghastly manner. It's a rotten dear place.

The other night at den Haag I was awake hours very excited over my Anglosaxonish-English book which I shall call: "How I wish English was" or somesuch.

From now on I'm going to keep a book always with me called "Thunks" in which I'm going to jot down all sorts of thoughts as they occur to me. I think my views of the world as every bit as good as my compo gifts. But maybe no one else will.

However amateurishness for ever.

Engelbert R calls the Danes & Scands, "Gemüthsathläten" [from German: mood-athletes] or "Gefühljongleuren" [from German: feeling-jugglers], not bad is it? I have some jolly jokes for you.

Very busy

Yr happy heathen
Perks.

55 Concertbureau Hans Augustin, Grainger's agents in Amsterdam.

368 TO KAREN HOLTEN   [London]
[Original: Danish]
21.12.10.

The rehearsal yesterday of all 4 things went quite excellently. The ladies played like 8 angels of God, and Roger and Beigel and I on 2 pianos made a hell of a noise. After last night I feel quite ready to hear Gr B and E D on the orchestra, since I now know that there will be no trouble arising from the strings, at any rate.

Some places in Gr Bs exceeded all my expectations. So your parts were again satisfactory to the highest possible degree, and from the fact that they played so few wrong notes one can see how easy and good your script is to read, dear comrade.

Today I saw an exhibition at Chelsea of *charming* drawings and paintings of Augustus John.[56] He is truly a genius.

How I long to hear from you, you sweet one.

These words are only to tell you how it went yesterday and to thank you heartily for the parts which were so extremely usable.

Your own loving boy
Percy.

56 Augustus Edwin John (1878–1961), painter in oil and watercolour, etcher and lithographer of portraits, figure subjects, landscapes and still-lifes.

1911

On 11 October 1910 Grainger's Norwegian agent Sigurd Hals had written to Rose on the subject of the financial returns from Grainger's touring, "Basically it is quite ridiculous that an artist like your son cannot get a full house wherever he goes. But what can we do? There is nothing for it except that your son must travel much faster next year and play every evening. That is the only way we can get any good pecuniary result. I have already made a start on next year". The consequences of this decision are immediately seen, and not only with regard to the Norwegian tours.

On 2 January 1911 Grainger left London for a tour of twenty-six concerts in Holland and Germany. It was his fifth trip to Holland within the year. This time the tour embraced a number of the smaller towns in which he appeared for the first time. During the tour he appeared three times with the Concertgebouw under Mengelberg, including his appearance without fee at the orchestra's benefit concert in Amsterdam on 28 January. All the other concerts but one were solo recitals. The recital in Amsterdam on 5 February was his ninth appearance in that city within the year.

Between his first Dutch concert, his recital at Amersfoot on 4 January, and his departure for Leipzig on 29 January, he had four free days: twenty-one concerts were given. The pressure was terrific. On 15 January Percy wrote to Karen that he felt "quite distressed with worry and fear"; by the end of the tour he was "tired and destroyed, without strength". His Dutch friend Bertha Six, writing to Rose on 24 January, reinforces the picture, "Last week I was anxious about him; he worked too hard, & he evidently was low-spirited & lacked courage. But on Sunday & yesterday he not only looked ever so much better, but that tired look was gone, & he was his old self again. He must **never** again take so many engagements within such a short time; he could not stand it". In this context the offer of a settled post on the staff of the Royal Manchester College of Music was at first greeted with some enthusiasm by Rose, though her enthusiasm cooled when she discovered that Percy's earnings would go down if he accepted it. Nothing came of the offer but a brief revival of the marriage question.

The German part of the tour also broke new ground, with recitals given in Leipzig, Dresden and Cologne. In Dresden he met the Deliuses and Mrs Grieg. A projected meeting there with Karen was put off. Returning via Holland, he was back in London by 7 February, leaving next afternoon for Norwich and his appearance with the Norwich Philharmonic Society on the 9th. He was then based in London until 5 April.

Rose remained in London throughout this tour, maintaining some of their habitual activities: her regular "at homes", the occasional "pupils' afternoon".

369 TO ROSE GRAINGER   Utrecht
[Postcard]
7.1.11. 8.20 morn

Had a hot bath & hairwash & shave last night so am all "boun" for the
fray today
Just off to the Hague.

Very fondest love.
Perks

Have got on my silver coin links for the 1st time & feel a delicious swell.
Outside the Hotel window ("de liggende os"!) [Dutch: the reclining ox]
the cathedral & marketplace are snow covered & the cows are bellowing fit
to bust

370 TO ROSE GRAINGER   Amsterdam.
Tuesday. 10.1.11.

I played really inspiredly last night in Haarlem (Recital) had a very decently filled Hall & *wild enthusiasm*, 4 encores.
I feel that my success is growing rather than waning here & that next
season may be still better than this. I'll lose some money of course in
playing with the Concertgebouw on 28, but it ought to be good for next
year & *looks hugely well*.
Would you mind very much if I had to play Bechstein in England
Germany Holland? I dont know otherwise whether I'll be able to get firms
on Continent to do tours if I play different pianos in different lands.
Bechstein wrote Röntgen they are very "hurt" that I played Blüthner in
Frankfurt after all the money they've spent on "granding" me in Holland.[1]
I wonder will anyone ever know what agonies I go thro before & during
concerts, day in day out?
It seems unbelievable that one can go thro such momentary misery & ½
an hour later feel wholly *no effects whatsoever*.
I am very elastic. All business worries & concert panics leave behind them
my soul & health unbreathed upon even, & that's why I dont mind a bit
the outlook of having before me some more years sown with the seed of
short terrors, why? it does me no harm, & the results are guddommelige
[Danish: divine]. I felt "sløj" [Danish: seedy] yesterday but fine again
today.[2]
In these days a Dutch oversetting of a Danish book by Astrid Ehrencron
Müller, "De gezegende dag" (Velsignelsens dag?) has been balsam to me.[3]
I can now pretty well say I understand *every sentence* (tho not every word
of course) in Dutch. Funny, if one is seeking a thing one will find it crop
up everywhere, in the most unlikely ends of the earth! Because my heart
goes out to Denmark it comes to meet me in all places. Here I have been
a week in Holland, only to have had a striking Danish "oplevelse"
[Danish: experience] & to have understood & felt the pulse of "det lille
land" [Danish: the darling country] yet better than heretofore.
At bottom I am not an artist after all. For I fail to feel Shakespeare &
cant understand ½ Ibsen or any Maeterlinck, &.s.o, but can fathom A.E.
Müller, & the maybe comparitively inartistic work of such a sweet, truly
good, tender woman to my heart's core, & wept oceans of glad happy
thankful tears over "de gezegende dag". That is the Denmark I love &
know, truer picture than dear old Wied, it seems to me, it is how I have
found the folk myself. In her book there is not one rough character, if you
read the book I think you'd see what I mean about the Danes being very
Chinese-Japanese-like. Not one character in the book acts boldly to their

1 Grainger's tours abroad, apart from his engagements at big concerts, were mostly done through piano firms, at least at first. They guaranteed him so that he had no risk and had a share in the profits. On his 1910 and winter 1911 tours of Holland he had played a Bechstein piano. In London his arrangement was with Blüthner who supplied him with two concert grands at home, sent a piano to all provincial concerts, contributed ten guineas towards the cost of his London recitals, paid him five guineas when he played at Queen's Hall or Albert Hall, and three guineas when he played at Aeolian Hall. He also received a commission on any Blüthner pianos sold through him. Would Bechstein pay him anything to have him play their piano? enquired Rose on 11 January. Evidently they did not, since by December 1911 he was playing a Blüthner in Holland.

2 On the same theme Percy wrote to Karen on 1 February, "But what does it matter [his suffering at concerts]? I have an eternal freshness and polynesianness in me . . ."

3 Astrid Margrethe Ehrencron-Müller [-Kidde] (1874–1960), Danish novelist. Grainger had been given her *De Gezegende Dag: een Verhaal ven de Osterlide Pastorie* [The Blessed Day, a Story from the Osterlide Parsonage] in the Dutch translation by Betsy Bakker-Nort (Valkhoff, Amersfoot, 1908) by its publisher in Amersfoot on 4 January. The title in Danish is *Den Signede Dag*. Later in 1911 he read her *Ouders* [Parents], also in Dutch by the same translator (Valkhoff, Amersfoot, 1910, see letter 388). Gustav Wied (1858–1914), Danish novelist and playwright. Grainger had read Wied's *Dansemus* (1905) in March 1910 and his *De Svage Køn* [The Weak Sex] (1900) in May of the same year.

own hand. Each waits & waits, & allows, & helps, & melts, & gives way for the others. It is a picture of live how I admire it & find it rational, human, soft, sensitive, & tactful.

When I saw the writeress's photo in Amersfoort I at once took such a fancy to her personality, I hope I may meet her one day in Denmark.

How how unsayably glad I am that more & more women become artists! How I adore the art of women.

I am of course the most overdone extra-manly type one could possibly meet, (take for instance my Utrecht letter) & that is why I so hugely relish womanliness in art, I suppose, & why purity aloofness & melting tenderness have such a beckoning for my own rank animal fierce half-criminal bodily force.

No letter yet today from my darling. How I hope it comes before I set out for Utrecht this afternoon.

Fondest adoring love from your own goodhearted popingay son.

I was tired yesterday, but recovered again today.

---

371 TO ROSE GRAINGER   [In the train]
after concert, Tuesday eve. 10.1.11.   Leiden–Amsterdam

Earned about 94 gulden last night in Haarlem & tonight (Leiden) about 105 g. Had a fearful rush for my train tonight after concert, was playing on platform 9.28 & had to run ½ mile to station for train leaving 9.38, which am now in.

I had a very bad left hand thumb Sunday & yesterday, but today it's well again.

No, I quite agree, I dont think there's *any* sensuality in *any* of my music, but the sort of thing I mean is *quite unsayable* in music, anyhow; I dont find any in Wagner either (tho it may be possible to *imagine* it in W's case tho not at all in mine) or in *any music*, in fact I go so far as to rather believe that musicians often behave rather sensually in life because they can get rid of the feeling so little in their music. Music is such an extraordinarily "clean" art, so unmaterial, abstract, aloof, poetic, tender, almost shy, it stimulates the nerves, & opens the gates of joy-longings, & fires the imagination & leaves even the very idea of sensationalism over to life itself, leaves life the whole responsibility for such a very big share of fulfilling its instincts.

But my music is peculiarly unsensual; but then only such a very *tiny* part of me *is* sensual, anyhow; my other instincts occupy me oftener, but **it** occupies me keenestly; maybe also because civilised life gives one a much greater show of realizing ones scientific, linguistic, pictorial, literary, decorative, thoughtful, musical, a.s.o. instincts than one's sensual, & the starved beasts naturally make the loudest song in the managerie, & munch with greater glutt.

My letters are getting more & more like Dear Uncle Frank's "finished the story of — began the book entitled —"

Last night I ended "de gezegende dag" today begun "De Kleine Johannes" by Frederik van Eeden, a socialist experimenter & very humane & spiritual writer he is said to be, & this book (about a little boy, & fairies, & imaginative tender young thoughts & child-longings) one of the gems of modern Dutch books.[4] It doesnt grip me so far, I'm sorry to say. I'm afraid I & the Dutch have absolutely nothing in common of any account. But I'll master their tongue; it's not going to debar me from S'Africa, or Dutch India

I hope you'll not forsøm [Danish: neglect] to go & see the Gaugains again because they close (15?) if you feel the very least lyst til det [Danish: wish to do so]. Maybe you & Roger cld go together, he loves them so? The

4 Frederik Willem van Eeden (1860–1932), Dutch poet, novelist and critic. His *De Kleine Johannes* was originally published in three parts ('s-Gravenhage, 1866). Grainger was given a copy of a later edition (Mouton, 's-Gravenhage, 1910) by Hanneke Mouton. (Grainger stayed with the Mouton family in Deventer. See letter 376.) The Gauguins were showing at the Grafton Galleries as part of the exhibition of Manet and the Post-Impressionists organised by Roger Fry.

very name Gaugain is to me like a gentle angel's hand laid over modern art, truly a holy-man he, a man near to Gods & women, a man raised & ennobled above antlike male longings & busy smågligheden [Danish: pettinesses]. A sage, & loving father type.

11.1.11.
My Dutch pupil, Miss J. Ingenegeren will come for her first lesson Saturday Feb. 11, 4 o'clock. She plays tiptop. Have written Wood, etc.
Haarlem has already reengaged me, for (this) Jan 18.
Busied to bits, but lovingly

Percy

Have got all yr letters alright. So glad.

372 TO ROSE GRAINGER   Amsterdam.
[Original: English/some Danish]
[Postcard]
Sunday 15.1.11.

Last night's concert was one long agony. *Terribly nervous* and didn't play well, but the hall was *quite* full and the public was *charming*
This aftern in Haag another charming experience.
Never mind, it pays
Fond thoughts, elskling [Danish: darling].

373 TO ROSE GRAINGER   Grand Hôtel du Soleil.
16.1.11.   Arnhem (Hollande).

My popingay.

Now that the hair-on-end leistungen [German, ironic: "achievements"] of the biggest towns are over for a few days I can answer a little your sweet benevolent letters. I got no letter here & wonder why, but it will be sent on if it comes belated.

Something strikes me as strange in your letters & talks about me; you always speak as if I were unsatisfied, as if my life weren't yielding what it should & as if the color of things were so wrong that a rooted change ought to be embarked upon in some way or other. But, dearie, all that has life only in your own mind. Truly.

In myself I'm one of the most contented happy satisfied undisappointed hopeful beings ever born. A few years ago I was more hopeful for & satisfied with *other folk* than I am now, but that is a mere trifle. If I were a reformer I would no doubt try & reform the world, & I admire reformers perhaps more than my own type, but being very much an artist I really am very concerned in art & almost *only* in art, or in what *might become* art, & it is has [*sic*] proved the easiest thing in the world for me to have put myself out of touch with the world (I hope for ever) in a very short time.

It was the only thing to do. But that doesnt mean I love the earth less or mankind less. All I yearn towards in art is only a voicing of mankindishness, all science, all museum-ishness are only branches (naturally) of the very *most* ausgeprögt [*sic* ausgeprägt. German: pronounced] mankindishness.

No, my dislike of the world is only a dislike of dirt & brutality & so on. One doesnt hate a dirty persons hands, but one hates the dirt *on* the hands. If one could get them *quite* clean for once, one wouldnt mind touching those same hands, would one? But one doesnt want to touch them dirty as they are. If one had drastic & powerful means of cleaning them one would be a wretch if one didnt try to use them. But I am one of those weaker sort for whom contact would only mean dirtying my own hands without cleaning anyone elses.

Isnt it funny, I'm so fond of dogs, but so many dogs are so nasty to me, when they see me far off, they single me out in a crowd & run fiercely at me, & yet maybe I am feeling more fondly towards them than some of the others. It's one of the things I give up.

But if I have given up the world & fierce dogs I have by no means given up myself or those folk that I dont find worldly or such dogs as are not fierce. On the contrary I am happier & saferminded than I ever was. Formerly I used to try & include the fierce dogs in my scheme & felt it was my fault if they didnt fit. Now I have little doubt but that they are quite wrong, or at any rate tiresome, & I dismiss them, & all J. C. Williamsons & Bracys wholly from the doings of my mind & dont even resent them at this later-set-up mental faroffness.

But in myself I am happier than ever. My mind & my thoughts for the to-come & my hopefulness are as calm & unruffled as water in a bedroom jug. And since fortune & money shines so brightly upon me of late I do not even feel I have a real right to be so *awfully awfully* inwardly impatient as I am. Believe me, darling mother, (birther of my personality, shaper of my gifts, & skilled guider of my ways-&-means, & by far the keenest friend I'll ever find) there is no unhappiness in me or emptiness or unsatisfactoriness; only silly silly babyish impatience, very wrong of me, no doubt, but no cause of worry *whatsoever*.

More & more year for year (almost day for day) I long & long laughably overdonely to hear my compos played, & such a joyeous night as that in Dec simply sets me *seething* with mad impatience to hear more soon, sooner, soonest.

There is nothing for you to be downhearted about in that, darling eager comrade & combatuous fieldmarshall!

It is right & healthy & birthful that I should be so eager to learn & better myself & my muck which is more than myself. But it is right & a 1000 times right that we go slow & dont throw over the piano yet, to which we must be O so thankful, & is indeed at last the goose that lays the "gulden" eggs. Only a little longer, a few more short miserable (outwardly, not inwardly) drudge years & health & wealth will be ours to invest in my glorious gifts & our unique comradery.

Believe me **only** mere questions of circumstances stand between us & *perfect happiness*. Happiness is doing the job one is built to do, leaving richer, what one found poorer, having time to live whatever love one has in one, doing good, & lots of it, & *using ones functions* in every most ways, including my love for you, & yours for me, & chewing one's food, & sex, & good rears, & all other gay details, all in their place, & none starved, if possible.

But the art is the real deep joy (tho there are many others) that is what we both really strive for at bottom; to feel that I am *doing* my best, that's what would surely make you & me both most happy? It would me at any rate.

If I show signs of being keener on sex than on art (keener on marriage than on saving money for my compos, we will say) you may rest assured that I am at that moment bodily feeble, out of sorts, unplucky, (not thro inner badness but *mere momentary* slackness) poorly healthed. No one is more sexually randy than I (I hold to every letter of my Utrecht letter) but I hope I have head enough to know its place. As long as I am myself, have health, & feel blood within me, *be assured* than [that] *no other* issue will lastingly be able to stand up to my artistic honor, my hunger to do great artistic deeds. I know little pride or ambition but I feel simply throbbingly keen to be a great artist & do great work. Every day I ask myself am I doing my duty? In the face of all this, what's the use of asking me whether I might be happier married? I wouldnt care a straw if I were married to a hag of a 100 tomorrow, I dont care really if I never have intercourse with a jolly body again all my life. Give me an orchestra to experiment with, & see my stuff in funny jolly print, & each day swelling my life's output — & no other passions count a fart.

My own pet mumbly, *what on earth* does it matter whether I'm happily married or not or whether I use a 1/6 whip sometimes or never or whether I'd really like to bring up a daughter to be . . .* — such things are mere nothings, grains in a landscape. But whether an oboe sounds out of place in the E. Dance (not for a week but for hundreds of years, mind you) that is to blush for, & a moral grief.

As for the lovely young pure girls you talk of — I long for them, would like to rape them all, & behave deliciously lewdly with them, & (if really left to myself) forget them the next minute, not because I feel thankless, but because composition happens to be a more engrossing thought to me.[5]

But as for feeling a *love* for those pure girls, or impure girls either, that would be a deep big thing for me & compete with my interest in languages & art & natives — well, I cant just imagine even the bare possibility of it, so you cant expect me to enthuse over the prospect very.

As for Karen. She's taken the trouble to bother about me & fascinate me, as no doubt many women could fascinate me if they also took the trouble to bother & kept on as stiff-neckedly & never gave up the scent for a mo.

The extreme economy of great men makes them sort of humble. I'd put up with a lot to save bother & save *going-to-look*.

I like a handy article, a useful pliable article that doesnt lose itself when I forget about it & keeps sniffing about in a generally ready sort of way. A kind of dumb-waiter.

I dont say this in any belessening way. No doubt there have to be certain sorts of women to pander to great men just as there seem to be certain sorts of men fitted to pander to naturally-important or great women. The most fascinating thing to me in Karen is a sort of inborn childish purity. Others may not see it, it may not even be there; but I imagine it to be there & that's enough for me. Nothing will make me believe it isnt there, for I never believe in going to the bother of uprooting inspiring delusions.

But marriage doesnt seem to X my mind somehow. The suggestion of it gives me cold shocks & instantly turns my interests & thoughts into other channels. I cant help if I ruin her life. I dont even care much. No doubt she's made to be a wife & mother, but who isnt? A murderer's made to murder I suppose, but one cant expect outsiders to be very keen to help him to his calling. I've no desire to see K, or anyone else, a wife or a mother, because the sight bores me, & if she's so keen about it she must take her own steps. I ask nothing, I hinder nought, I advise nought, & I take no steps. I'm *very thankful* for what I get, & wish I got more, but I'm not deeply fussed about it all. I like getting her letters & like replying & I *keenly relish a nice holiday* with her.

If I felt marrying would give me more money I'd do it *if you* advised it. On the other hand marrying *for* money doesnt draw me The price seems to me too high.

An artist's duty in life is good work. But his payment is surely *largely* sensuality? Maybe I am wrong but so it seems to me.

It therefor seems foolish to cripple or cramp one's reward in order to be able to deserve it!

No. My plan is:

---

*Words scored out — by Rose? She did after all show Percy's letters to various people, at this time to Roger and Mrs Koehler.

5 On 8 January Rose had written a homily on the dangers of excessive self-interest, observing "I believe nothing would really please me more than to see you really in love with a lovely sweet little maiden, full of joy, & youth, one I often dream about, & have always wished you might come across". On the subject of marriage to Karen she wrote four days later, "And does the question of age really not matter? . . . Naturally from a worldly standpoint it would be a bad marriage, but you care nothing for the world, & I am sure Karen is sweet & good . . ." She continued, "Unless you mean to marry her sometime, you ought not to allow her to be so interested in your life — as she is surely the most wifely & motherly of women, & ought to become wife & mother. Every time I see her I at once become irritable, & unhappy, feeling you are preventing her from fulfilling her most natural self". Asking him to be "*absolutely open, & truthful*" in his reply, she was pleased with his letter, announcing on 18 January that it had given her great happiness and cleared away some cobwebs. She had in the meantime written in the same general terms to Karen on 13 January, urging her not to be foolish and continue to sacrifice her life should Percy still not wish to marry. Karen replied thanking her, but standing firm, "I am filled with a great love for Percy, and I know he loves me, and that is for me the main thing, and surely of greater worth than most ordinary marriages . . . As long as I know that Percy loves me, nothing will make me giving up thinking about him, no marriage offer, however glorius it could be. As I have the best thing in the world, great love, I do not think there is the least reason to alter my thoughts or be miserable or anything like that". Rose returned to the question of the need for some change in Grainger's relationship to Karen in October 1911 (see letter 410), by which time, however, a suggestion of changing attitude was coming from Karen herself.

Fight my way to being able to do my deserving life's work, not for any reward, but *because* **nothing** *can ever be more delicious than one's lifework*. And if reward comes, be free to take it, & by Jim, do so, & all one can get, & more.

I'm a gay roving blade.
Ich bin der Jäger wohlgemüt.

Dont talk to me of marriage or of being *happier*. I am *happy* enough. I only want to be richer.

As for *us* we mustnt stinge ourselves in *time*. Time together, time to read, argue, bead, that's all we need for complete bliss. Let's take it every now & again that's all. When is our holiday to be, & where?

But as for me, remember that I am happy, enviable, lucky, achieving, & hopeful & well on the way to realize goals that I long for stubbornly enough to make them worth the reaching.

And if I am so happy & so hopeful & so full of love for you, why aren't you ditto?

374 TO ROGER QUILTER   Hotel "De Keizerskroon"
19.1.11.   Zwolle.

Beloved & beloving friend.

6 Roger's letter does not survive, but its contents may be guessed from the letter he wrote to Rose on 4 January and which she sent on to Percy on the 6th. In the latter letter Roger wrote, "I've given up hoping ever to be an artist myself — I have the English rich upper(?)-middle-class blood in my veins too much, I'm not strong enough to fight it. But it is still left me to try & be of use to my dear Percy, and if I don't get some of this stinking money turned on to helping him, may I be accursed". Rose encouraged Percy to let Roger help him with his compositions, "it will give him a grip on life". Hard on the heels of Roger's letter came the news that Roger had received a positive response to his approach to Willy Strecker of the music publishing firm of Schott. Subsequent interviews between Rose and Strecker proved promising. "About the strange expression marks he doesn't care at all, he says", Rose informed Percy on 29 January. Cyril Scott had also spoken to Schott in support of Percy's music.

I swam deeply in delight at your cherished tender letter of last Monday.[6] Your sweetness to me & love of me is, I always fear, based on a too high rating of what sort of a creature I am. I'm not humble, but I know full well, & I think so, that I'm not nearly so great or greatsouled as I think you think, & there really isn't much in me to warrant your splendid love for me other than that I am very keen on having it — but all that's nonsense: the truth is, that there are few of *our sort* about (whether we are particularly good specimens of the sort or not) & that we yearn for each other. But that's not the real reason either. You are so sweet to me because you yrself are so good & so ready to be sweet any how, & I am about as worthy of your devotion as the folksong is that I (in my turn) collect because I also am good & sweet.

But if neither of us were good I suppose you'd love me & I you just as much.

You wrote me some nonsense a few weeks ago about your muck. Anyone with ½ an eye can see that of all of us who giftedly gathered at Frankfurt denne gang [Danish: that time] that you, so far, have come most of all "to your own". Gardiner pointed that out to me 4 years ago, very truly.

Some of us have turned a bit sour in their wellwishers mouths, but you quite the other thing. I think one can truthfully say that you have grown more soulful, more ownish, & more telling with every following period, & the earliest were these three things in fulness & no freshness or first glow has paled.

I only wish that I could feel a small part as pleased with my own growth as I do in my heart with *deepest certainty* of yours. With you & your art, we are all of us apt not to "encorage" you as blatantly as others of us need to be, your art has such firm feet, needs no bolstering, or rallying round, & is so healthily & robustly practical & comeoffish, that it invites no least compassionate support whatsomeever. That is the rare gay riddle of art, that to the artist art is such a fast fortress against those elements in life that bear him down. In life I may fear to thump a fellow-coward's nose but in art I may maybe strut heroicly & overwhelmingly & be sincere all the time. The sensitiveness that somewhat numbs my & I think your powers of action in real life has left no *weak* trace in your music. Above every thing, though tender enough, your art speaks with *strength* & finality, & speaks *of* (above all) manliness & robustness & loving & sappy health.

Each work in itself, & the course of your works & periods as a whole, are the acme of blooming & clean artistic bodily health, just as for-inst Walts & Herricks arts are, in their several ways. I'd tell you if I smelt the very faintest hint of worm in your wood, but I feel you to be enviable & flourishing to the utmost.

Why dont you favor the orchestra again? Give us some of your warm roaring seething loving stuff on a nice billowy band.

The dances showed how the mass answered to yr helm & one longs to listen to you steering into yet broader waters, less dancey maybe & more like "fair house of joy" for instruments. And what about the choral Omar cycle? I wouldn't be afraid of big mediums if I were you. You always answer to them so & they set one's compositional blood going. Not that I am advising, I merely long to hear certain things, that's all.

Now as to yr last letter & the publishing.

If I were you, dont mention me to Stanford re publishing. For if I back out, later on, of any scheme of his, its the sort of thing he's too keen a man to well-see.

My plans were, re my stuff:

To bring out (with or with[out] subscription) at my own expense & *as my own* publication & in my own copyright as many works as possible, from now on. And to keep on doing so to the end of the chapter, or to accept the brilliant offer of a big world publisher later on should many successful performances of my by-myself printed works tempt such a big dealer to handle them bigly. Vorläufig [German: For the time being], therefor, I dont wish to bind myself to any small or local man, so as to be free later on to deal unshackled with bigger things. But vorläufig I want to find a big publisher (not only for England) who would *sell* my things for me on commission, from whom the things could be ordered & bought, but who is not wanted to advertise or push the things in any way. I dont care if he takes a real decent commission, either.

My conditions, for *any* kind of scheme of printing, are:

(1) Paper must be inserted like Debussy or Albeniz & not sewn up like Peters.
(2) Must choose or design my own covers.
(3) Nobody else's music may be advertised on my publications.
(4) Must be free to use as idiotic English expression marks, a.s.o. as I choose.

The actual music I want to print, engrave, or *lithograph* as *cheaply as poss*.

The first lct of things I hazily had thought of bringing out would be

(a) "Always merry & br" for room music strings or string band.
(b) *British Folkmusic Settings* by P.G. *Book 1* (Roman music) holding:
- Molly on the Shore
- Bold William Taylor
- (?) Six Dukes for 4 voices & 1 flute
- Shepherd's Hey (Morris Dance)

(c) A rievers neck verse (Swinburne) Song for voice & piano.
(d) Kipling choruses *book 1*. (Jungle book sheaf)
- The Inuit
? - Tiger, Tiger.
- Morning Song in the Jungle
- Mowgli's Song against People (bitter Karela)

If "Green Bushes" sounds well when I hear it (in Kristiania next fall?) it may fill *British Folkmusic Settings* book 2 (band) or form part of it together with "Shallow Brown" & "Lost lady" or other band (or partly band) things.

If the *English Dance* is alright when I hear that, I particularly want to bring that out as early as poss, & ditto re Hillsong No 1.

I should *adore* you to pay in part or wholly for bringing out my first serious printing, firstly because it'll be lovely not to have to pay for it myself, & 2ndly quite apart from that because I shall feel so extraordinarily proud of both of us for your wanting to do so, & because I think it's such a pretty sort of happening. To receive as it were "your bounty", small or big, is in itself a relish & nice proud sensation for me. To have one friend at whose hands it is a pride to be fed, so to speak, is a nice loving state of things & money used uncommercially has always a thrill for me. Apart from all that, such a help in my life's work is lifegiving. And I would far sooner look back on your money having brought out my 1st work than that money earned by myself had done so.

I feel no thrill at being able to earn the money for my own goal (though I'm jolly *glad* I'm able to) but I do indeed in being able to inspire love & admiration such as backs yr offer.

I dont care which work comes out 1st, but I cant go on living much longer happily unless *something* comes out

I dont know why, but I'm getting impatient of having all the *private* answerableness for them so long, & want to see the successes or failures of them (both of which will move me, but outside any *very deep* effect of which I no doubt stand) by the light of day, & discover what kind of a coin I am in circulation. (I dont mean whether I'll make money by them or no!) I like my fellowmen, though I cant be bothered with much except their nice & pleasant sides.

I do hope you'll be there to hear the rehearsal of my Hillsong!

Your support bucks me up bloodily.

Always your loving, admiring, trusting fellow-fleshist

Percy.

So *delighted* you are danishing.

My concerts this last week have been more painful than ever but very beriching.

375   TO ROSE GRAINGER   Victoria Hotel.
21.1.1911   Amsterdam

How typical these following 4 go-insteads are for the races who say them:
    Wont you *try* a glass of —?
    Wollen Sie nichts *zu sich* nehmen?
    Wil U niets *gebruiken* (Wont you *use* something)
    Vil De ikke *nyde* (relish, enjoy) noget?
The critical grip of the English, the "harvesting" accumalative eye of the German, the dull utilitarian Dutchness, & the ecstatic glædedyrkende [Danish: pleasure-cultivating] Scan are here finely photoed.

Augustin will send you some of the Dresden program-circulars. (those of the other towns he has sent off some time ago.) If you want to use the circulars for the 2 other German towns just write the town's name & date on them (Leipzig 31, Dresden 1st, Köln 3rd)

He (Augustin) would like the address of the Norwegian friend of Mrs Grieg's (you spoke to him of) in Dresden.

Goodbye my darling for today.

I feel so frightfully lonely on this tour. It seems a disease always playing & never meeting any sympathy or love or *a single interesting hap!*[7]

But I'm not unhappy.

I'm getting thro it all right

7 Grainger expressed the same idea more vividly to Karen on 22 January: "I feel so strange after a great success when I walk alone in the streets and think that out of all these hundreds who were so wildly enthusiastic there is no woman among them who would of her own will come and make me happy. That I will **always** remember about you".

376 TO ROSE GRAINGER   [In the train]
25.1.11. forenoon   Deventer-Leeuwarden.

You will rejoice to hear that Breitkopf's estimate for "Always" is only
350 marks for 500 scores & parts, & as I'll only need about 200 scores the
whole thing oughtn't to come to much over £15, which is just in line with
the chargings for my choruses, dennegang [Danish: that time].

Augustin says that in Germany the printing houses all keep to the same
prices, so that the cheapness wouldn't vary muchly with different firms,
which is a comfort. When I get back I'll just price the Norwegian man as
well, & then one will have had a taste alround. Breitkopf's letter is so clear
& observant & practical, you will see.

Had a jolly audience at Deventer & made over 200 gulden clear, more
than enough to pay for "Always"!

Do you know what is one of the nicest joys to look forward to? hearing
Halvorsen do "Gr Bs" when we are in Xia together. Wont it be?

I stayed with such a kind family (Mouton) in Deventer. They had guitars
in the house & the husband played awfully well. I tried a lot of chords for
"What shall we do with a drunken sailor" setting & learnt a lot. I must
get a guitar (any old 2nd hand one) when I return, I shall find out a lot
of things for room music with it. Maybe I'll buy a guitar here. They are
said to be so cheap here.

My own darling mum, always lovely & interesting & stirring & fresh, my
appetizing & devotional mother, I think the clouds have lifted, & we may
love each other better & easier than heretofore, & our love may be buttered
with more lifegiving pleasure & fulness to make it swallow nice & smooth.
The last 4–5 years between us have not been good ones for me. After
Coulson St–Up. Cheyne Row revealations you seemed to me crushed &
slightly frozen up & unnearable by me & there seemed no way across that
I could see, though I knew it must come, & I now feel it has come.

We who eigentlich [German: actually] never had any business to be
athwart each other for a moment of our lives.

It is clear to me that I have little gift for expressing myself clearly & that
I thus must have unwillingly lied to you both long before the bad time &
during it. Had I managed to give you a truer picture of myself before, my
sudden trumpets wouldnt have awakened you so unpleasantly, & had I
been able to present the truth clearly in U. Ch. Row there would have been
nothing then either to make a rift between us. I was supremely weak &
shallow & futile all through of course, but I am also riled with you for
being so suspicious of me. It's true, the cowardly little evasivenesses of my
timid mouth dont call for confidence, but there is nothing in my real actions, or unfussed attitude towards events that you can recall as a witness
to my untrustworthiness to you.

Meet me with a chalange or drive me in a corner & I may become either
disgustingly feeble or insincerely rude or strifesome

But those things are related to me like a bad performance is to a compo.
If one is going to judge things & folk at such stress there's not going to
be much pleasure left in life. But I've never felt worthy of your suspicion
& I long for the day when you will never apply it to me more. I still do
not feel that I could tell you of my attitudes towards certain things without
your recoiling from me whom you love & falling back on what are after
all *certain views of conduct*. I do not think you are wrong in this, on the
contrary, you may be doing this out of higher impulses than I reckon with,
& I see no reason why you shouldn't, but I only think that all this (which
is a trifle after all) is more a barrier to love than a path for it, & is the only
cause of any moments of imperfection between us.

Why should you prefer *views of conduct* to me whom you love, *unless
you suspize me*? There has been a deal in yr life to nourish suspicion, but
is there much in *me* to nourish suspicion, if you think over it well?

I'm not saying there isn't, but I dont happen to feel it myself. I can only say that I long for you to know my every thought & that my thoughts towards you are ever *only* of love & comradeship, & filled with rich remembrances of how you looked in the past & how you look now, & full of yearnings for our happy future. And when I meet you, the utter bodily satisfactoriness & prettiness of you feeds my imagination lavishly anew.

So much for my feelings & hopes & inner happiness. But that doesn't needfully mean, of course, that I am not a selfish or uncomfortable creature to be or deal with, or that I haven't behaved abominably. But, do you know, I do not care a straw about all that. What does it matter whether I am more selfish than you, or any such modern idiotic result of moral slavery? The important thing surely is that we are happy together in our love for each other, & skidt være med [Danish: to hell with] our (or my) moral conditions.

True love like ours rises above all matters of imaginative values. I am your life's interest, & however much I may have disappointed or wounded you, I implore you to pass ignoringly over all such trifling flaws in the material & concentrate on the real fact that our love is deep & strong & tough & will outlast these poor blemishes. I beg you to let no grudging trace remain of any disappointment of the last years, you have learnt that I am less than you hoped, but you must not own up to my being less than you can turn into a successful glorious finish. All the better that you know my meannesses lownesses shallownesses. I am delighted. "Yet is there more behind" And that's what we are concerned with after all. If there is such a thing as a duty, I consider it your duty to rise above all flaws in our intercourse & cling to the joy & goodness & hope & worth that lies behind us & before us.

I have very stern views, at bottom.

I would consider it a disgraceful conduct on your part if you allowed yourself to die before you & I have had time to realize a lot that time only brings, just as I should look down on you if you allowed yourself to grow fat.[8] However wrong **I** may have been in the matter I should look down on *you* if we failed to realize the most lovely realisation of our love. For *failure* is the one thing I cant forgive. The good in me, the best instincts stirring within me *demand* that talents use their gifts to the full, that love ends in joy & satisfaction, that seeds grow into healthy flowers, & that even vices are not denied their healthy & robust spread & growth. You havent died or got fat, now then let our love also flourish with an unknown faith & health & wellbeing. I am bursting with it, & I own my wrongness & selfishness, & that it's been hard for you, & all that, but all I say is, forgive me everything & cast all suspicion of me to the bloody winds.

I may deserve anything, but *least* suspicion, that I can say from the bottom of my heart.

I dont think one should overrate the weightiness of troubles arising from sexual causes. Folk are sometimes stupidly judged for their sexual upsetness. If a man has toothache we sympathize & dont think it strange that he's offish or selfish or gives less & takes more than at other times. But if a person has sexache the justifiedness of his idiot behaviour isnt nearly as clear to see, though it may be there alright. We are happy when we *use our functions* & I believe that every function we *dont* use turns like the worm sooner or later.

But because someone is off the straight because of sexual-ache it doesn't really mean anything serious, least of all that he's needfully in love or that he's showing inner depths of his nature, or *that he should marry*.

Civilised man has *so many manifold functions* that neither his sex nor his teeth nor a 100th part of his functions can ever get all the work that would *otherwise* be good for them. So we go about with stopped teeth & patched up instincts & a thousand ½ satisfied desires. And what could be better, except a still more civilised man with still worse teeth & 2000 de-

8 Rose replied, 29 January, "Nor do I want to grow fat, or to die . . . but with the present cook keeping thin is a trial". Rose had acquired a new cook, Mrs Kelford, some two weeks earlier.

sires? I love the many sidedness of us. But being so, we cant hope for the complete poise in certain directions that we find in naturvölker [German, lit.: primitive (i.e. unsophisticated) races] or less imaginative or idea-hungry individuals. When I get sexually off the rails now & then, it's tiresome but it's not important. It's the small price one has to pay instead of the dear price of lack of freedom & the flat result of being *tied down to the satisfaction of an instinct.*

377 TO ROSE GRAINGER   Amsterdam
Sunday. 29.1.11.

House absolutely sold out last night

Well, it was a fine success again last night. Huge enthusiasm & Mengelberg *simply charming* to me. Says he wants to introduce me into Russia & will write Siloti, & that I should play Tschai there.[9]

Leave this eve for Germany, which I am quite looking forward to.

Got an **adorable** letter from Roger containing a very nice one from Strecker. There might be something to do with Schotts.[10]

Isn't Roger a friend indeed

My love to him Mrs K. Miss Permin & so on.

This is the program of my last Haag Recital [enclosed].

378 TO ROSE GRAINGER   A'dam
[Postcard]
Sunday eve 29.1.11.

Heard Mengelberg conduct Debussy's "La Mêr" this afternoon. Have seldom felt more deep joy & movedness. Debussy thrills me to the marrow. That is the very purest loftiest nature-feeling he has in those 3 bewitching pieces. I fear they express my feelings when I'm in the grip of lovely nature better than my own compos. M. says he wants me to play Tschaik. in Frankf next year. Just off. Yr adoring son.

379 TO ROSE GRAINGER   Leipzig.
[Postcard]
30.1.11. (5.30)

How I'm really growing to **love** Mengelberg, such an artist, untirable at his job, & with such a sunny "glimlach." (smile) I shall never forget his standing there waving his arms so giftedly to the glory of dear France, that poor lovable land, still undefeated & spiritually supreme. How my heart again & again embraces France with the tenderest admiration & proudest sympathy. How I love travelling, & crossing the borders of lands & having to turn on other tongues, & finding a letter from the mum at the end.

380 TO KAREN HOLTEN   [In the train]
[Original: Danish]   Dresden–Leipzig–Køln
2.2.11.

Sweetest most delicate cream-fleshed treasure

Whether there was profit or loss last night (Dresden) one doesn't know exactly yet, but the expenses were about covered at all events. Wasn't that nice? The audience appeared to consist of English and Norwegians and were correspondingly warm and intelligent looking. About all the ones Mrs

9 Alexander Il'yich Siloti (Ziloti) (1863–1945), Ukrainian pianist and conductor. From 1903 he had directed his own orchestra in St Petersburg. Mengelberg did mention Grainger to Siloti, and on 23 August 1911 Grainger, having been approached through Augustin for an engagement, wrote to Mengelberg (in German) to thank him: "I would like most heartily [to thank] you for your more than friendly recommendation to Siloti; for when he wanted to engage me at Augustin's, I am quite sure that I have you alone to thank for this. That you didn't forget this matter in the middle of all your colossal business. Unfortunately it appears that the engagement with Siloti won't be able to be realised this year as I have no suitable free dates any more . . . But next winter it will certainly happen". Much earlier, on 16 August 1907, Edvard Grieg had also written to Siloti commending Grainger, "Do remember his name, I beg you. You will undoubtedly hear more of him". Grainger finally played under Siloti on 8 November 1913.

10 Schott, the German firm of music publishers founded in Mainz in 1770 [1780]. The Strecker family inherited the publishing house from the Schotts after 1874. Willy Strecker (1884–1958) had taken over the London firm of Augener in 1910. B. Schotts Söhne, Mainz, had published Grainger's *La Scandinavie* in 1902.

Cf. Change of view on Ger

Grieg gave me addresses of turned up and I had to sign surely 20 programmes afterwards — so there was "atmosphere". Fru Giertsen and her
daughter are in Dresden and it was a deep deep joy for me to meet them
again. At present I am so heartily fond of the Norwegians. Both
Norwegians and Danes are faithful to me. I would so have liked to have
seen a little of Dresden, but it wasn't possible and the only thing I did apart
from practise was to buy some whipping books in a shop (richly supplied
with that sort of thing) in Pragerstrasse. But I was happy in Dresden as I
got your letter and the pictures and 3 lovely letters from mother. Schotts
Söhne (Mainz) whose kind son now lives in London, seem to want to
publish my compositions (through Roger's and Cyril's enthusiastic descrip-
tions of my genius!) in a satisfactory way, and mother and Roger and I
myself of course are very warm-hearted about that, believe me. Obviously
the whole thing is simply floating in the air at present.

When you told me to be happy in D[resden], I took the best steps I knew
towards that goal and after the concert read the whipping books and was
naughty 2 splendid times. That was the best I could do for the town that
my sweet joy-fellow loved. My room was so overheated that one sweated
and was pink all over the body and I had 2 lovely whips (from Utrecht)
with me.

Some weeks ago in Bussum I began to brand a K (Karen) in my flesh right
in the middle of my primeval forest, after 1st having shaved the trees away.
But last night I was mad-sensual and burnt deeper in so that one heard the
flesh melt. I have still only | (< [of the "K"] is still lacking) and after that
I whipped myself and was naughty the 1st time, then I read on for a long
time, and then I bit my breasts with my tie-clip and was blissfully naughty
again. I really believe that I feel relieved and healthier after such a night,
and I believe that the frightful feelings I go through before important
concerts stem partly from me zealously keeping good for possibly too many
days in a row beforehand. I am not convinced of something of that kind,
but I must say I feel splendidly happy today, but then I have no concert,
and that helps a lot.

One thing you can please foresee, and that is, that next time in Svinkløv
you shall be whipped so that your life only consists of blows and screams.

More and more my selfish animal unfettered hunger grows for you and
for the heaven with you, and I will "spare" neither you nor myself in the
coming time in Svinkløv in the realisation of my longings. Be certain that
it will be different from last time in Svinkløv. That time I was afraid of your
screams. Not any more, for I know the remedy for them = just beat still
more. Our divine service of love will be such that you will become downright eaten up and exhausted by its harshness; in your sufferings and
agonies you will writhe painfully against me and our bodies will drink
gladdening love-spit from each other. I won't take the slightest notice of
what your mouth begs for or refuses, and you will know how keenly I love
you, and your flesh day after day will burn helplessly under my boy's
criminal deeds but our souls shall boil together in a celestial kettle of bliss,
so friendly and each-other-tender.

Will write p.r. the day after tomorrow.

381 TO ROSE GRAINGER   Cöln.
[Original: English/Danish]
[Postcard]
3.2.11.

I am not happy. I couldn't live in this land.

The faces are so filled with evil & I hear of nought but quarrels & illwill.

I find them the most degenerate & disgusting & stupid of all folk, now
as of yore.

Tomorrow I am again in A'dam. hurray.

382 TO ROSE GRAINGER

Saturday. 4.1.11. [*sic* 4.2.11]
11.o'cl morn.

Amsterdam.
77 v. Eeghenstr

I dont mind playing for the Langley but I wont have Molly done.

Fancy, yesterday Delius's verleger [German: publisher], (also an important critic) in Cöln offered to publish things of mine if I wished.[11]

I had a magnificent time with Friedberg & wife.[12] He's as sweet & clever as ever & just as sympathetic as he was to me damals [German: at that time, then], the only one of the Con lot that came warmly towards me. I played my compos to him till 3 o'clock after concert, then walked some miles back to Cöln (he lives some miles out) packed & caught the 5.30 train to here, sleeping all the way. He thinks I'll get a Gürzenich engagement in Cöln (Steinbach)[13] *The Cöln audience was very warm & my success was great*

Friedberg conducts a concert in Nürnberg in March & wants to include my Green Bushes.

When I'm in Holland in April if I just go over the border to Dortmund he'll conduct a rehearsal of it there for me to here. He's a dear, a really broadminded clever Jew, appreciating everything from anywhere, Russians French, etc. I have been *all wrong* about the Germans, & you right as usual. They do more new music there than anywhere, they know everything, & Friedberg assures me they have no prejudice at all against French or any other things. There are much more possibilities still in Germany than elsewhere.

And one can talk with Germans & G. Jews with an openheartedness & *be so thoroly understood* which is wonderful. Germany is after all one of the lands one will never be able to help loving to be in a lot.

On the other hand, how indescribably delicious it was to wake up this morn in lovely Holland which I grow to love more & more, to simply drink in the fresh sweet pure damp chilly-mild sea air, to wander home from the station thro the canals, & every house old & a thing of mark or beauty or interest almost, & the people, not really beautiful always, but mostly *very decent* looking, & looming tall & noble & pure (with a stamp of breed & long money upon them — even the poorest) after the tiny misshapen meanlooking nondescript Germans. And how cosy to hear the fine wellbredsounding softly spoken Dutch tongue, deftly holding within it hundreds of years of *human culture* & restraint. But, Germany has the seething bedrunkening charm of having all before, of being low & vile & rank but reaching hopefully out to unbounded heights, immodest lavish goals, laughable but enlivening.

Promise me, darling, that you will come to Holland in April & see the quaint towns & the still sure folk & then have a dash over the border to Dortmund & commonness & generosity & hear with me Gr Bs!

Our lives have *not begun* yet.

I expect I'll come back by Flushing & will be back Tuesday eve. I'll let you know

383 TO KAREN HOLTEN

[London]

[Original: Danish]
27.2.11. Monday.

Dear Oasis in the desert

These are happy days. The evening of the day before yesterday (Sat) was so delightful. Mrs Köhler played Hillsong with me (2 pianos) and Miss Permin and mother and I Widow's P[arty] march (2 pianos — 3 players) and I played Kipling chorus and Gr Bs, and a thousand things for Strecker and Cyril from 8.30 till after 11, and we were all rarely happy.

11 Dr Gerhard Tischer (1877–1959), German musicologist. From 1906, editor of the *Rheinische Musik- u. Theater-Zeitung* and from 1909, founding director of the publishing firm Tischer & Jagenberg in Cologne. In 1910 Tischer & Jagenberg took over and reissued various songs by Delius, including his *7 Lieder* (aus dem Norwegischen, 1889–90); *3 Songs* (words by Shelley, 1891); and *Deux Mélodies* (poésies de Paul Verlaine, 1895, to which a third was added in 1910). Tischer wrote and published an article about Grainger in his *Zeitung* No. 10, 1911.

12 Carl Friedberg (1872–1955), a pupil of Kwast and Knorr at the Hoch Conservatorium in Frankfurt and from 1893 to 1904 a teacher there. Writing of this meeting to Karen on the same day Grainger said of Friedberg that he "was the only teacher in Frankfurt 12 years ago who took an interest in my compositions . . . Yes Jews can surely be good. I always loved him". The performance of Grainger's *Green Bushes* in Aachen on 10 May 1912 was on Friedberg's recommendation.

13 Fritz Steinbach (1855–1916), German conductor and composer, from 1902 to 1914 city Kapellmeister in Cologne and director of the conservatorium there. The Gürzenichkonzerte, concerts of the Cologne Konzertgesellschaft, had been held regularly since 1857. The orchestra was supported by the City from 1888. Grainger played the Tchaikovsky B♭ minor Concerto under Steinbach on 26 November 1912.

Cyril was so enthusiastic for me and of course infected Strecker by it, Cyril without a *spark* of jealousy, doesn't know it, completely abstractly enthused and delighted that I will publish by the same publisher as him. The details have not been agreed yet, but we believe everything can easily be arranged, Strecker is ideal, and we expect that some things will begin to come out this summer.

I have finished the 4-handed arr.[angement] of Walking-Tune and am in the process of arranging Wamphray March for 3 players on 2 pianos.

I am playing at a Dutch lady's at home Wednesday evening and the 28th March at Mrs Hammersley's Cesar Franck 5tet and "Molly" and other things. I am full up with pupils and earn excellently (in England as well) for the moment, and mother and I are both as happy as we haven't had a chance to be for many years. One begins almost to lose heart when things make you wait too long for them, and it is an indescribable relief to see things moving a little. Cyril looks splendid and is happy and fresh again.

What a loyal person he is though, so pure and un-selfinterested and artist from first to last.

It is amusing to think that the whole of this publishing affair (if it comes to anything) was set in motion by a fellow-composer.

I have some splendid friends, I must say.

At the moment I am practising C. Franck's Symphonic Var.[iations] (piano and orch) they are *quite absolutely charming*, blissful to occupy oneself with, so fresh and clear and lively and yet so delicately sad. Music teems with geniuses, and isn't it amusing and comforting as well to know that oneself is also one?

My "wound" is now healed, and shows a "disappointing" aspect. Just think, when the dried out hard part of the wound fell off hair was already growing underneath as good as ever. Horrible. I don't believe it will leave any rewarding sight behind either. One would have thought that a wound that lasts nearly a month would have had a little personality about it! What shall one do? One must first see how this attempt ripens in time.

Next p.r leaves Friday.

384   TO KAREN HOLTEN   London.
[Original: Danish]
8.3.11. Wednesday.

Sweetest.

14 Princesse Edmond de Polignac (1865–1943), *née* Winaretta Eugénie Singer. American-born and wealthy, she lived in Paris and was an influential patron of music. A friend of the English composer Ethel Smyth (1858–1944), she had met Grainger as early as July 1904, at which time she remarked of Percy that he "was by 'Messiah' out of 'Cake-Walk' ".

Princess de Polignac[14] has written to me that she performs The Irish and "The Camp" (chorus) of mine in a concert in Paris in May and I have sent the parts of Gr Bs to Friedberg who says he will conduct it in Nürnberg on the 11th March.

Last night I played at an at home at Rathbone's and today I have had 4 pupils. I earn in other words, not so badly.

It is hard to practise new pieces for next season now, among all these engagements and pupils, and while I am into the bargain completely crazy with ideas for printing. Just as I for years went around with only sexuality in my head, nowadays I have nothing else in my head than problems of printing and publishing.

Yesterday I composed further at a new tune I began in A'dam recently.

I have a whole case full of letters which are to be kept that I haven't even once looked at. I am not really all there.

On Monday 10 thousand pupils are coming to play each other upside down.

Goodbye. How I long for the new score

P.R. leaves on Saturday.

I am making "covers" for the printed compositions

385   TO KAREN HOLTEN

[Original: Danish]
Thursday. 16.3.11.

31A King's Road
Sloane Square
S W

Now I am tired of composing, and have also finished for the time being, both because I have pretty well completed what I am working on, and because I play in Malvern on Monday, at an at home Tuesday, the 25th March in Q's Hall with orch. (Tschai) the 28th at home, the 2nd April Albert Hall, and the 3rd Liverpool and immediately thereafter to Holland.

Have not heard from Friedberg yet. On the other hand Dr Tischer (Cologne) has written offering to publish Gr Bs. (at his expense, of course) Furthermore I have also got a German pupil from Friedberg.

The new dance, that for the present is called:

"Pritteling pratteling pretty poll parrot"

is more or less completely arranged for 2 pianos, the score isn't to be worked at until I have bought a guitar in Holland and tried various things.

The most difficult part of "When the world was young" is also completely thought out and will soon be written down.

Today I am taking E. D. to Harrods for binding.

The day before yesterday at Cyril's I heard many **charming** new things of his.

Now I am thinking of you again, "and it does me good."

On Tuesday I will write p.r.

I will send some money today. Haven't got much "on hand" at present.

Banner* of Joy, goodbye

*i.e. flag; not one who bans! *Transl.*

386   TO KAREN HOLTEN

[Original: Danish]
20.3.11.

The Imperial Hotel,
Malvern.

I am so depressed and unhappy. I know that it doesn't signify anything. It must be expected after such a happily-excited and tiring time as I have just gone through.

I feel frightfully sleepy without a spark of hope or spirit.

But it is of course only a superficial unhappiness, inside I am at base happy, if only I knew it.

Understand, I was just in the middle of a good creative period and in ecstasies about my work and then I suddenly had to stop everything, for the sake of these coming concerts, and hammer away at the old rubbish again, while the spirit dances around and *never* once rests on what the fingers are doing.

In the last few days I have felt near to madness, but that's for the most part only imagination.

Roger away in Egypt, Strecker in America, and I with no time to complete scores for the press, I feel as far from everything as ever. Not once have I had time to read in your score.

And I have heard nothing from Friedberg about Gr Bs performance, and I am the most impatient person you could think of.

And today I am full of beadwork plans, want to make your necklet for you, and mother's belt and my belt, and in the midst of all these consuming ideas I get ½ crazy. I feel it heavily not to have had any holiday in such a long time. Above all: I feel finished, and don't understand where I will scrape up energy from for the concert tomorrow.

But before you get this, everything will perhaps be in the finest order again. Let me know how much money you need for riding, and I will see what I can send you from Holland in April.

Sweet Comrade, whose lover is no good.

I am inexpressibly happy about your riding.

I have stomach-ache

Percy.

387   TO KAREN HOLTEN   [In the train to
[Original: Danish]   Liverpool]
Sunday evening 2.4.11.

I have just played in the Albert Hall (Tschai) and am now in the train to Liverpool, where I play tomorrow afternoon. Roger is expected home today, and I hope to see him tomorrow evening or Tuesday or Wed.

It is quite unbelievable how I have earned recently, now in England I have earned just as much as I do on tour in Holland; in other words: I *am saving* over a thousand pounds a year. When I have earned like that for about 8 years from now I will be a free man. This sort of life is, after all, *almost* unbearable, but I must still see and bear it as long as I can.

Now I will soon start to write the "foreword" for the "British Folkmusic Settings" and "Kipling Settings" etc. I recently received a lovely letter from Kipling, to whom I had written in connection with the copyright of his poems I had composed music for, and told him I was a little more free person than previously. He said that he was very glad about that "for his own sake". Now I have to talk to his agent about the details after my return from Holland.

I have been taken up recently in sketching covers for my printed compositions. It is to be light — deep blue letters on thick white-cream paper, like that used for all kinds of notices here. There is a particular wealth of very simple but differing letters here in England, where the whole style of printing is indeed specially wide and simply conceived, without ornamentation etc.

But it is hard to choose between the many good shapes, for example:

And then one must experiment a great deal on paper to get the correct size and contrasts. But this occupation has made me happy in a high degree, and I have made many hopeful sketches.

Gardiner was with us recently, critical, glad, and kind and elated-enthusiastic over my playing of Tschaikowsky recently. He suits me splendidly. His critical brain and noble nature and no-half-way attitude to everything satisfies and encourages me quite specially and I always have loved his compositions. An orchestral work of his will be performed the 2nd May, and he will be there for Hillsong the 3rd.[15]

15 Gardiner conducted his *Overture to a Comedy* at an afternoon concert in Queen's Hall on 2 May (see letter 391). Grainger had played the Tchaikovsky Concerto under Henry Wood at a Queen's Hall Symphony Concert on 25 March, eliciting an enthusiastic response not only from Gardiner, but also from Robin Legge, music critic of the *Daily Telegraph*, who wrote to him in a letter of the same day, "... in all my wide — 30 years — of experience, I have never heard a nobler performance of pianoforte music than yours of the Tschai. today". Stirring words, given the number of fine pianists who played in London during these years.

I don't believe either that men's sensuality is greater than women's. Indeed, I find no basic difference between men and women, other than the results of their entirely different ways of upbringing. I really don't know which is worse, ordinary men's or ordinary women's attitude towards sensuality.

As far as I am concerned, I am close to thinking that my whole sexual capacity is declining to a surprising degree in the last years. I was indeed very different in that first year in Svinkløv than now unless I am imagining something. I am naughty much more seldom, and even when I am the need for it is milder and less urgent, it seems to me. It's going downhill with my life-forces. It has really done that since I was 20 without me being, or having reason to expect I will become, particularly powerless.

I wonder if it comes from abstinence or excess? I have always had a tendency to get strongly taken up by intellectual things for a long time at a stretch, in which periods sensuality does not play any particular role in my life. I wouldn't say that intellectual things have a more violent claim on or temptation for me than sensual things, but one thing can be said: that the sensual is in greater danger of being forgotten than the intellectual because it is impossible to be fully occupied exclusively by sensuality even for 2 days, which one so readily can be by intellectual things. But I won't forget sensuality in the long run. Nor is there any question of choosing between the 2 things. Both must be there to as great a degree as ever possible. But I am such a miserable worm that I can seldom raise myself up to find strength to take part eagerly in different things at the same time.

On 6 April Grainger began an eleven-day tour in Holland. Eight concerts were given: six recitals and two appearances with orchestra. By the end of the tour Grainger was once again "unspeakably tired". But the tour was a happy one since it followed such a happy time in England, and a drop in earnings was compensated for by good future engagements. Percy being free from 14 to 17 April, Rose joined him for a brief holiday, remaining for his final concert in Utrecht in the afternoon of 17 April. They were back in London early on 18 April.

388   TO KAREN HOLTEN   Hotel Ponsene.
[Original: Dutch/Danish]   Dordrecht
Sunday. 9.4.1911.

This time I am quite in love with Holland. Isn't it remarkable how different places can appear when one is in a different mood?

Yesterday I bought a *guitar*, for about 22 Kr, with a carrying-bag, and strings, and everything. I was so pleased with it that after the concert yesterday evening I sat up with the instrument to 2 at night, and worked on the guitar-part of Faðir og dóttir and several other compositions. It makes one really happy to see problems disappear in front of one's eyes.

I have just read a second book of Ehrencron Müller: "Ouders". In Danish it must surely be called "Forældre" [Parents]. It is very nice, just as excellent as "de gezegende dag", perhaps even better still. I would be very happy if you would read it in Danish.

Did you get the money from here? Can you find the rest of the money for riding yourself?

You can be sure that I like to send it, or in any case to know that you ride and are happy and bodily; otherwise I'll be hanged if it would occur to me to do so.

I am so happily-tired from last night, to occupy oneself for hours with a new instrument like that, isn't too bad.

Next Saturday you will again get p.r. from me. Now I think it's time I soon heard from you.

Aachen have written. Want to perform Gr Bs and would like to engage me for the same day. (in June)

Have so many letters to write

My hopes for the guitar are succeeding unbelievably well.

Sweetest, I am so sleepy

389 TO KAREN HOLTEN   [In the train]
[Original: Danish/Dutch]   Zutphen–Deventer.
13.4.11.

Yesterday the receipts were much better.

Will you be so kind as to ask Hj. Thuren whether he has heard anything about my 2 Maori records that were to be dealt with in Cope. If not, perhaps you could get the man's address from Thuren and find out yourself from the man whether he has done it. I did write down where they are to go to, 2(?) to me and 2(?) to A.J. Knocks. Esq. Otaki. N. Island. *New Zealand* The originals and the metal castings should remain at your place or Thuren's until I fetch them. The account should be sent to *me*.

It is remarkable how I can now understand Dutch. I don't notice at all whether one speaks Dutch or German to me. The language has gone into the subconscious. I like Holland more every day. Everywhere such fine large old buildings, churches and town-halls and the national costumes are almost always splendid. The quite small girls look especially sweet in them.

In the beginning I *made a mistake* about Holland. I had expected a sort of second Denmark. But that is of course impossible. And the Dutch people, just as all other people, do not show their most human side when they talk a foreign language; as in such cases something uncomfortably energetic comes over them, because they have to exert themselves to the last degree

On Monday I am at Hotel "de liggende Os" Utrecht.

On Tuesday in London.

Next P.R. arrives Wednesday

390 TO KAREN HOLTEN   London.
[Original: Danish]
21.4.11. Friday.

Really I have been rather ill. Frightful diarrhoea and headache and surprisingly weak suddenly. Holland is surely rather peculiar in climate. I was *all* too *unnormally* tired after the concert on Monday. But it shows once again that there *is* something sick about good playing, for always when I am quite exceptionally at the top of my form for playing I am in other respects weak or unhappy or such-like. For this reason it is, on the whole, so hard for an unusually healthy person as I am, to play well often.

The result of this little weakness episode is that I have enjoyed a quite exceptionally happy series of days. One day, for example, I wrote 18 pages of score, and 2 guitar strings have broken since my home-coming! Poor Roger has been terribly ill again. He had "ulcers" in his throat but is getting better slowly. I have not been able to see him yet, but have written to him at length.

Regarding Svinkløv. It's not so good to say exactly when, but as I *must* begin in Norway about the *1st Sept* I assume that I will come to Svinkløv for the last 2 weeks in August or round about then.

Just now there is a frightful lot to arrange already for next January, March, etc. The coming season will surely be full up as far as one can see yet.

I have decided to "study up" Brahms D minor Concerto afresh,[16] and I am still more in love now with Franck's Symph.[onic] Var[iation]s. than before.

I have done a lot in the last few days; I can't tell you everything, it is too much.

P.R. leaves from here on Wednesday.

16 Grainger had first played the Brahms D minor Piano Concerto at Bournemouth on 10 May 1906.

The summer of 1911 was the hottest in living memory: a record heat spell continued from the middle of June until September. The summer was also, for Grainger, one of his busiest. The normal activities associated with the "season" resumed their hectic pace: concert engagements, "at homes", pupils. But he was also much taken up with meeting obligations for future events: planning and preparing new repertoire for his autumn and winter tours, planning his first batch of publications with Schott and preparing manuscripts for the printer, planning and preparing the works to be performed at the choral and orchestral concerts being undertaken in 1912 by Balfour Gardiner.

He gave his annual Aeolian Hall recital on 29 May and the last of his summer engagements was met on 5 July. By 6 July he reported to Karen that the worst was over, though he appeared at some "at homes" after that and still had many pupils as late as 20 July. On 16 July he finished work on the current batch of manuscripts for publication.

His work-load was colossal. Accordingly, and because of being late with his preparations for the winter, he cancelled his August holiday in Svinkløv with Karen. However, he was still able to enjoy several country-weekend holidays from late July through August. He was, he wrote to Karen, "deeply happy in this overfilled time".

Rose was unwell for some time during late May and early June, the result, so Percy told Karen, of overwork in connection with his recital. Although unable to attend the recital and obliged to cancel her Whitsun holiday trip, she recovered in time to go with Percy to watch the Coronation procession on 23 June.

On 26 August, notwithstanding the uncertainties arising from a national railway strike, Rose and Percy left together for his autumn continental tour. The house in Kings Road was closed up; the cook remained as caretaker, maintaining herself with occasional outside work, while the maid was placed with the Robinson Smiths for the period of the Graingers' absence. The Graingers arrived in Christiania on 28 August.

391   TO KAREN HOLTEN   London.
[Original: Danish/some English]
2.5.11.

My little treasure,

I have done such splendid things on the guitar; really virtuoso, you understand. When you hear me strum on the instrument you get the impression of a very great guitarist "who has seen better days", who has been able to do everything, but of which only rhythm and a certain extravagance still remain. But I am gradually understanding how to write for the lovely instrument, and have sketched out guitar parts for all manner of things. And then I have made an ending for "When the world was young" and was so "preoccupied" that I made it in 4/4 whereas the piece is in 3/4, so it can scarcely be used for the same; but perhaps for something else. The ending in itself is lovely, I think.

Life is swarming with great problems or rather proposals.

Gardiner wants to get rid of £1000 next winter by giving 5 big orchestral and choral concerts, and plans to perform of mine

Faðir og dóttir
Hillsong
The Widow's party*
The Sea wife*
Irish Tune
The Inuit
Morning Song
We have fed our sea*
At Twilight
etc.

*are for mixed choir (or male voice choir) with wind — or military orchestra.

So you can imagine there is a lot to talk and blether about. I don't know whether the whole thing will come to anything but we have a divine abundance of talk-enjoyment out of the idea.

It wouldn't be the right way for me to begin, but there could be fun in it.

I will still have a good time in Germany etc.

Already excellent engagements decided for *Basel Zürich Heidelberg Elberfeld*, and talk about Cologne Aachen and other places. 2 with Mengelberg in The Hague and A'dam already fixed also; so everything points to a slave-year like this one.

Today Gardiner conducts a "Comedy Overture" of his own in Queen's Hall. We will go and listen to it.

I **can't** learn to conduct Hillsong by heart. These changing bars are *all too* infamous by heart.

Indeed, it takes many years' experience till one can so much as beat 2 parts of a bar so that it means something.

On the whole, I am in a state of restless excitement, what with a whole new repetory to get ready, and rehearsal the day after tomorrow and the Gardiner and Kipling questions. I have forgotten to say that I now have all the beads for your necklace.

How different your presence would be than these Godless letters.

Thanks about Thuren.

392   TO KAREN HOLTEN
[Original: Danish]
Saturday 6.5.11.

31A King's Road
Sloane Square
S W

17 Grainger's *Hill-Song* (later *Hill-Song No. 2*) in its first scoring version was rehearsed at Percy Hall, Percy Street, Tottenham Court Road, on 4 May 1911. The manuscript parts used in this rehearsal had been copied by Isabel Du Cane. Although Grainger had written to Karen, 13 April 1910, that the cost of a rehearsal of *Hill-Song* with all instruments would be £6 (see letter 333), he told her on 16 February 1911 that it would cost £12. On 5 March Roger Quilter wrote to Rose offering to share the expense of the rehearsal, ". . . as it will be so useful an experience for me too".

I began Thursday (the Hillsong's day) by waking up early and lying long in bed and thinking only of you.[17] In that way one should begin a big day. The rehearsal was "auch danach" [German idiom: went along in the same way] I conducted by heart, 2 hours at a stretch, and I must say I think I have conductor-abilities. Gardiner was (for once) completely taken and will perform H-S next winter (March-April)

I think the tone was encouraging. It surpassèd all my expectations, although it far from satisfied my ideals. Perhaps (as far as the sound goes) there is not one impossible bar in the whole piece, but equally there is not a single one which is quite completely perfect. That couldn't be expected either. The whole thing is really pure guesswork when one doesn't really know anything about the combination of instruments. The combination in itself is *grand* Now I have already altered a few small things and will let the work be given as it now stands, and by having it conducted by another person, in a large hall, I will learn still more than the day before yesterday.

2 small places in E. D., and Walking Tune I also heard, altogether quite possible. Now there are many difficult questions that must be thrashed out with Gardiner, with regard to the choice of pieces, which Choral Society he will take, etc.

Later.

It was strange about Mrs K[ampmann].[18] You Danes are a poor lot, I really must say. You have abilities, but not anything that holds you together when it comes to the pinch.

I would so like to compose but have not time. I am frightfully occupied. Strecker is coming today, to talk about printing.

I will write p.r. on Thursday.

393   TO KAREN HOLTEN   [London]
[Extracts, May 1911]
11.5.11 [In Danish]

The summer will be unbearable this year. People telephone and write like mad already. Everyone is Coronation-mad. It will be good for earning but frightful . . . If only I had more strength and more time.

19.5.11

I'm torn in a 1000 different directions just now, but am happy.

394   TO KAREN HOLTEN   London.
[Original: Danish]
23.5.11. Tuesday.

When will I get a photograph of you again? I need it so frightfully.
Just think of seeing a nude picture of you again.

It seems to me as if I had given up for ever everything belonging to life, and when I ½ consciously remember what I have done with you and written to you and thought about you, intend still to do and think and write to you, I become so completely sittlich entrüstet [German: morally indignant]; to think, that I have been able to go so far with the nice young lady, I think to myself, almost blushing. For in that matter we men are a little different from many women, we do things from without (also from within) and do things in periods, and in that way we have to completely forget many things for a long time on account of busy-ness, so it can happen that our past doesn't lie so firmly rooted in our soul as can be more expected with women, perhaps. It seems to me as if I were made up of paper and blotting-paper and ink and pens, and if you came suddenly to me and kissed me (which I have more need of now than usual) and let your sweetness breathe on me, then I would perhaps splutter red (or even green) ink (as I have both colours to correct the scores with) instead of blue-black, but surely nothing more.

A summer season has surely never appeared to mother and myself so hard to bear as this. With the coming winter's dates to fix and the compositions to natter about into the bargain (and that is something that takes not only energy and time but my soul and interest as well) and many pupils it has almost gone beyond the limit.

I get up before 7 and work *the whole time* without a break till 10.30 or 11.30, and even so half of it doesn't get done, and one goes to bed with an excited consciousness of incompleteness and tearing rush.

Obviously everything will be better after the Recital. And the worst is that I can never withstand temptation, as you know. In the middle of

18 Mrs Kampmann was Karen Holten's friend. She had accompanied Karen to Odense when Karen met Grainger there on 10 November 1910, and she attempted suicide in April 1911.

everything I see the guitar lying on the piano and *I can't* resist having a ½ hour's wealth of experience with the blissful instrument. One is not really unhappy, only really sick of zersplittertheit [German: fragmentation], and indeed one's nerves are quite out of order.

But a thing like that doesn't mean a thing in my case, as I can immediately be myself again, as soon as the load is lifted. But mother's health is *very bad* at present. I think I will never give a Recital again in London. For the over-exertion of it makes her ill *every* time, and it's not worth it. She has such bad pains in her legs and no strength at all. It is such a frightful shame.

And now the young Röntgen is coming soon. God help us all, I say.

And do you know what I need in the middle of all this over-exertion and tiredness? To have you close to me and be happier and more carefree than ever before. Why is one tired? Not because the body is over-occupied, but because the soul hungers.

Write to me so that I become happy and inquisitive and on fire by reading it. Let me feel what an untamed poignant concealed little animal I have for a lover.

I don't want to be content, just make me furious, hungry, impatient, that is what I most desire to be. Let me see how beautiful you are, put yourself in tempting poses, let me only be mad by looking at your pictures, that won't matter.

Let me know what I am missing: I want to miss. Why should you, too, be tired and holding back (I know why, because one can't play the piano to the deaf) because I am a fool?

Let me have some photographs.

I have now received "permission" to print

   Shepherd's Hey
   Molly
   Sussex Carol
   Old Irish Tune

so that is splendid.

Excuse me not writing till after the concert (and then to Ceresvej) but I must save myself for that Satan's feast.

   Your dry faithful
   Percy.

395 TO KAREN HOLTEN   [London]
[Original: Danish]
    ?
Thursday 1.6.1911 [Extract]

The concert went really well in every respect. But I was frightfully unhappy, and nearly at the point of vomiting the whole of the day of the concert. The same evening I had to play at an at home and the next evening as well.

. . . Now I must see and get as many scores as possible finished in these holidays (Whitsun) for straight after it's on again, and the pieces should preferably come out before the season is over.

396 TO ROSE GRAINGER   Hill
Sunday. 4.6.11.   Theydon Mount
                         Epping.[19]

My own beloved mum & comrade.

I look a dream in your divinely chosen clothes. I really am a creation of your taste & wisdom & originality. I am a walking testimonial to *your*

19 The country house of Mrs Charles Hunter.

personality. Without you I could not possibly be still so healthy & unde-cayed as I am & therefore not so gynstig [*sic* gunstig. Danish: favourable] a clothes prop.

That fact is an even more wonderful bring-off than the subtle symphonies you weave for my absences! I leave home like a Wagner score for the printer, full of exquisite check-matings of man's stupidities & with every possible thwarting of a miscarriage in color.

I wonder if my grey fellow guests guess what foreschemings & Burlingtonings my seemingly simple strolling into breakfast forudsætter [Danish: presuppose], & probe with what justified misgivings the absent composer cons the maybe verhundst [German: bungled] performance of her orchestration?

This morn I have done *all* the letters for my Danish tour, for the mo-ment, 9 this morn, Ribe, Vejlefjord, Nykøbing Sj, Aarhus, Helsingør, Hobro, Svendborg, Odder, Randers; a bunch of bud bound to burst into *some* blossom, I bet; or, if you prefer it; a sack of sown seed sure to shoot up into some shillings; or again; a lot of loathsome letters likely to land a lone loving couple of love birds with lots of £.s.d.

Now I must to my scores

Yr adoring son, who is missing you.

Here is a Limerick I heard yestreen.
    There is a young lady of Epping
    Who the bonds of good taste is o'erstepping,
    She wears knickers & boots, & the *manliest* suits,
    & wins prizes at jumping & leaping.
*

---

*sounded "lepping"

4.6.11.
Take great care, & be well when I home!

397 TO KAREN HOLTEN   Hill
[Original: Danish]   Theydon Mount
Tuesday 6.6.11.   Epping.

Now I have done something idiotic again. Have almost sprained a finger and in the most unbelievable way, only by putting my hand on my hips rather hard.

I wonder whether I will be able to play with it in the Crystal Palace in a week's time.

I feel quite bad after my 3 day's holiday here, as always after holidays moreover.

I have perhaps worked too much and played tennis a little too violently. And then they always talk here about how many "ghosts" there are in the house, with the result that I simply burn the electric light the whole night through, which is good against ghosts but doesn't produce the very best sleep.

I have prepared a terrible lot "for the press."
    Swinburne's "Reiver's n[eck]-v[erse]" song
    Score and parts "Always" and
    score of "Sh's Hey"
    Piano dishup of "Sh's Hey"
Roger has Molly at home to go through.

I had thought of photographing myself here, but have not felt in the mood for it. But it will be done soon at home.

Before I forget it, or it is too late: Will you please take *all whips* and instruments to Svinkløv this time; don't forget a single one?

The national costume and the raincoat and the belt (perhaps I will bring some leather to improve the "pierced" place) you will take with you, won't you?

If I take the corrected E D score to Svinkløv will you be able to get the wind parts written out between then and the beginning of November, do you think?

The weather has been so unsayably splendid here and the counry looks indescribably lovely this summer.

I am anxious to know whether mother is a little better now; I was so afraid that it might be really bad this time. How is everyone in your home. Tell me something.

With many futile kisses and longings

your old lover
Percy.

Shall write p.r. on Monday

398　TO KAREN HOLTEN　　　　　　　　　　　　　　　[London]
[Original: Danish]
15.6.11.

My heart's plum

We are really having a good time. 800 Canadians and now 500 South Africans have come too. The S. Africans are even grander than the Can[adians]. Some of their uniforms, khaki-coloured with cork helmets on (very broad to shield from the sun)

with broad belts (and cartridge belts over their shoulders) and riding breeches and good riding boots of yellow leather, and in shirt sleeves rolled up above the elbows, never have I seen anything so romantic, not better even among natives.

We shall see the big Coronation Procession from Miss Du Cane's brother's window in Parliament St. So we must be up at 5 in the morning. But I would dam'well so deeply like to see these Colonial troops, also the Indians and others. It is really true, that in Europe one as good as never sees what I call real manhood, not all together in a mass, at any rate. Either they are not properly dressed, or their skin isn't sun-burnt or something. There are also some ½- and full-blacks from British Honduras here.

My concerts and at homes passed off well and everything goes well. I have corrected several "proofs"

How amusing about your long riding tour. You can very well ride in Svinkløv and then I can run beside you.

Gardiner, in the middle of concert decisions, and with everything ½ done, has gone off to Finland for several weeks. That's what I love about the British, they always put life and pleasure first, as it ought to be.

I have got Odense and Vejlefj.[ord] San.[atorium] again. Delius is in every respect kind and touching, and his wife is kind bis dorthinaus [*sic* German: to the last degree].[20]

On Saturday I am holding my guitar trialrun (mother Roger Miss Rathbone,[21] me) of Faðir og dóttir. On Saturday also Miss Permin leaves for Denmark.

How I long for the photographs. I can't take myself just at the moment as I must use the camera to take pictures of some "printing" (printed letters) in the street that I want to use for composition-titles.

But you will soon get some, sweet.

p.r. leaves on Tuesday.

Sweetest how I long for you.

399   TO KAREN HOLTEN   [London]
[Original: Danish/some English]
[Extracts, several letters, June–August 1911]
20.6.11.

If it should happen that I am *forced* to give up Svinkløv this year, I would ask you not to take it amiss of me. I don't think I will be compelled to do so but on the other hand I just can't imagine the possibility of being ready with everything I have to do before the Norway tour at the middle of August . . . I work all I can. But I see almost no possibility . . .

Wednesday. 28.6.11.

Just think, on Wednesday I have to play C. Franck in Q[ueen]'s Hall, and don't yet know it by heart. I have now given up everything else and only practise.

(To Nina Grieg, 6.7.11: I am still fearfully rushed & very late with my preparations for the winter.)

17.7.11

The day before yesterday I finished the score of "We have fed our sea" which I have orchestrated (the accompaniment) for wind and strings; and yesterday I *completely finished everything* for printing since I edited "Dedication" (from 1901) my best song (Kipling). Thus I begin practising again today. But now will soon begin the big work of reading through and correcting "proofs" and the "list" must also be made that is to be at the back of the music.

20.7.11

I don't think I will be able to come to Svinkløv this year. The question now is really whether I will be able to be "more or less" ready even without any holiday. It is really a shame, as I am almost ill of tiredness of all this everlasting "sticking at it" and on the other hand everything is going so well at the moment that we could have an exceptionally happy time this year, that I am sure of.

20 Delius was in London for the concert of his works given in Queen's Hall on 16 June 1911, Thomas Beecham conducting the Beecham Symphony Orchestra. The programme included his *Appalachia*, the first performance of *Songs of Sunset*, the symphonic poem *Paris* and the *Dance Rhapsody*. Grainger saw him on 11 June; subsequently, Delius mentioned Grainger's *English Dance* to Beecham. Delius had married Jelka Rosen on 25 September 1903.

21 In the summer of 1911 Grainger was much taken up with his "guitar rehearsals", preparing a group of (finally) twenty to twenty-five amateur players for the 1912 performance of *Father and Daughter*. Elena Rathbone (1878–1964), daughter of William Gair Rathbone. She shared her father's enthusiasm for Grainger's compositions and had attended the "first giving" of his choruses at the Queen's House Manuscript Music Society on 28 May 1903. She also played xylophone ("Hammer-Wood") in Grainger's Concert of Compositions and Folk-Music Settings on 21 May 1912. In 1913 she married Bruce Richmond, editor of *The Times Literary Supplement*.

24.7.11

I can't shake myself together enough to work eagerly at the pieces so as to get ready after all and be able to be with you a little at the Planter's house. I can just manage to screw myself up to just keep things going and no more.

2.8.11

Yes, it is really sad about Svinkløv, and I feel so depressed and empty and used up since the thought of that happiness had to go. Yes, we have waited 9 months for Svinkløv, but I have waited over 9 years for the printing!

400   TO WILLY STRECKER   31A King's Road
8.7.11   Sloane Square
                                                           S W

Dear Strecker.

I have today sent to you the score of
   "Tiger-Tiger" &
   "Morning Song in the Jungle"
which are both ready for the engraver as soon as you have fixed up with Mr [A. P.] Watt's [literary agent] (re Kipling)
   Of course it is no good bothering him, so we must just wait.
   As to the Kipling song "Dedication" I am willing to hand over to who-ever has the copyright of it my whole royalty on it or pay a decent fee for it rather than leave it out as 1st of the Kipling publications.
   Had I perhaps better try & approach the lady or Chappells myself, do you think?
   Many thanks for the contract which seems to me quite alright. I have made a suggestion or 2 in the middle as you will see. Would it not be as well to have all the works on the same footing as regards your catalog, & the selling to a 3rd party?
   I do not, myself, see any need for the top bit I have crossed out, as in any case we would have to discuss each work seperately, would we not?
   As to who undertakes publishing cost, could we not arrange that simply & seperately as we go along over each individual work likely to be one you would care to pay for?
   There are some minor points re the publication of "Father & daughter" (Scandinavian dance folksong) in English & other minor details that I would like to have your advice on; could I see you some day this week? Could I come in & see you early Thursday July 13, or ditto July 14 or 15?
   I should be *awfully glad* to get on with the correcting of proofs as soon as possible as I am, & shall be, very rushed & cannot work at these things long at a time without interruption & therefor correct slowly.
   Beecham has expressed a wish to perform my orchestral "English Dance" next winter.
   Will the piano things be out before I begin my winter tour in Sept? If so I would like to include them in my programs which I am making out soon. We might talk re some of the countries when we meet.
   Cordial greetings

   Yrs ever
   Percy Grainger

Dont bother to reply by letter to anything that we could with less bother *talk* over.

401 TO HERMAN SANDBY
10.8.11.

31A Kings Rd.
Sloane Square. Chelsea.

My dear old Herm.

I wonder are you still in Europe? I am at this address until about August 23, then it is p. adr: Brødrene Hals. Storthingsgaten Xia.

It seems as if we are never to meet. I shall be coming to Nykøbing Sj to give a concert late in October or early Nov, but I suppose you will be gone then.

We have been having a delightful time, only very overworked.

I have decided to start bringing out my compos now, for various reason[s], chiefly because I want mother to hear them while she is still young & can enjoy them to the full, & also to gain experience for future scorings. So I have been (& still am) rasende [German: madly] busy preparing scores & correcting proofs all summer.

Schotts are bringing out:

4 Kipling settings
Swinburne Song "A reiver's neck-verse"
9 British Folk-music Settings
Mock Morris Dance for string orchestra or sextet.
"*Faðir og dóttir*" Færøsk dans folkevise udsat for 5 men's voices, double chorus, orchestra, mandolines & guitars.

Dear old Balfour Gardiner is going to give 3 chorus & orchestra concerts next winter (March etc) in which he will do of mine.

"*Faðir og dóttir*" (with 30 guitars!)
3 Kipling Choruses
Old Irish Tune for chorus
"*Green Bushes*" orchestra
& "*Hillsong*" *No 1.* for 24 wind instr.

Thomas Beecham (who seems to me one of **the** very greatest conductors I've ever heard) says he wants to do my *English Dance* this winter; but we must see.[22] If the English Dance, Green Bushes, & Hillsong sound really well when I hear them I shall let them be printed at once also.

Dear old Roger has been a friend indeed. It was he who fixed up Schotts for me, & he wants to pay for the expense of printing a few of my bigger scores, & is already bearing the expense of printing "Faðir og dóttir"

Young *Strecker* of Schotts is such a nice chap & Schotts are delightful to deal with & let me have all details etc as I wish. Later on when Schotts & I have been working together a little while maybe I might possibly be of some small use to you there, if you wished to publish anything at Schotts. Do you not think you ought to bring out a string 4tet or something like that someday soon?

Do please let me know if you have (or do) published anything. You are very secretive about your compositions, why?

I shan't eat them up!

We have a very full winter ahead. I have about 90 concerts on the Continent this winter.

6 orchestral concerts in Switzerland Gürzenich (Cöln) with Steinbach & others in Heidelberg, Elberfeld, Siegen, & of course lots of orchestral concerts in Holland, some of which with Mengelberg (Haag & A'dam) who is a *great great* chap.

Either this season or next I play at the Siloti concerts in Petersborg.

Mother & I are much looking forward to my Norwegian Tour, 1st Sept–20 Oct.

It is a miracle & tonic to be amongst those pure gentle *good* folk. Though I still love Denmark above all, so ownish, stubborn, & cunning & **good** too.

I was longing for a Jydsk holiday in Svinkløv this August, but it cannot be, alas, as I have to wait here to correct proofs & also to practise up new repertory for the winter.

22 Grainger wrote the same sort of comment to Nina Grieg, to which she replied on 27 July, "I do not know the Conductors you mention, they must be English. Now I know you are very soon to say 'the greatest living', you say so today, perhaps not tomorrow. It is likely the same when you mention Delius as 'by far the greatest living genius at the moment' ". The Beecham performance of *English Dance* took place on 18 February 1912 (see letter 433).

Do please let me have your address for the near future as I want to send you my printed things, as soon as out. And do let us hear your doings & composings.

Love from mother & me

Percy

Grainger's Norwegian tour began with a recital at Hamar on 1 September. Between that and his last Norwegian concert at Mandal on 27 October, he gave forty-four recitals. He had seven days without concerts in September, and eight in October to the 27th. The arduousness of his touring schedule was ameliorated by the careful planning of the tour and by careful programming. Of the three overlapping but varied programmes he performed during this tour, one was used in all the smaller towns, being played thirty-six times.

Rose travelled northwards with Percy through the smaller towns as far as Trondheim. On 11 September she left for Christiania. Percy then commenced the southbound part of his tour, travelling mostly by steamer or small boat down through the fjords of the west coast of Norway from Kristiansund via Bergen, where he visited Nina Grieg, to Kristiansand. Rose joined him again at Tvedestrand on 27 September and they travelled together for another week. Percy arrived in Christiania on 9 October and the first of his three recitals there took place on the 12th.

For Grainger it was a "charming tour", with the frequent ship voyages giving him much time for scoring his Scotch Strathspey and Reel. Though his earnings fluctuated through the smaller towns and his expenses were heavy, he experienced great success — in Bergen, for example, and particularly in Christiania at his third recital when, as the British Australasian reported on 2 November, ". . . some 3000 people were in the hall, and Mr Grainger had to respond to seven or eight encores, but not content, the audience crowded round the artist's room at the conclusion of the concert, cheering and shouting their congratulations, and then the whole crowd followed him along the street as he drove to his lodgings, calling out in Norwegian 'Come back to us again' ".

Despite manifold delays, his publications began to appear in October. First to arrive was a group of three piano pieces, and first of all was Shepherd's Hey. Arrangements for the forthcoming Danish tour occupied much of the balance of his time during October.

402 TO KAREN HOLTEN Søstrene Larsens Hotel
[Original: Danish] Christiania
31.8.11.

You can't think how *charming* the young Norwegian women look in the present day fashions, narrow skirts, coloured socks, leather hats, etc. I was enthusiastic for the fashion in England but I thought that it would perhaps be most suited to the thinner English figures, and I never thought that one would think of going for it up here. But good Lord, to the highest degree. Not one or two look good, but without exaggeration 100's and thousands.

I do not think there is anything in the world more absolutely enchanting than young Norwegian girls of 15–19 years old, so upright rounded fresh and sparkling with the joy of life. But one can search the whole town for one really charming woman over 25. That they don't seem to have an understanding of.

It is enchanting here. What a noble wise understanding talented race. And so exciting life is here.

When I have been here a few days I am quite afraid I will be crazy with excitement and nervousness.

I am constantly in a fever of sensuousness and ½-painful ½-happy emotion in this country here.

If I was rich I would often spend a whole lot of the year here in Xia. To look at all these splendid and tempting young girls, so vital and disturbing, that is intoxicating.

I feel so madly keen on composing. If only I could get the time for it. But there can be no question of that.

You do have the addresses as far as Throndhjem?

It was very nice to see Arlaud. We talked a long time together. I thought she looked well.

I don't know my pieces for tomorrow at all.

My sweet comfort and firelighter goodbye for now.

403   TO ROSE GRAINGER
[Postcard]
Monday eve. 11.9.11.

Xsŭnd. N.
[Kristiansund N.]

My darling. I shall never forgive my not having *insisted* on your coming here. This is the lovely [loveliest?] trip I know in Norway by far. I was too sick last year to quite realize *how* lovely the scenery is. Glassy weather today. I did a væeldig [Danish: great deal of] lot of scoring.

Your adoring son
Percy.

404   TO ROSE GRAINGER
Tuesday. 12.9.1911.

[On the boat] Xsund–Molde.

I have been feeling very sick, but now we are in calmer water again.

I've been reading the book on Von Bülow's ways of teaching, full of his sayings, wittinesses, etc.[23] I think I'll buy in, in harmony with the "wreath" postcards. It is such a monument of everything that seems to me unmanly, inhuman, shallow, brutal & inartistic. In spite of the wonderful things said about Bülow he must have been a thunderingly poor artist in many ways & a thoroly common-souled & puny-hearted & -headed being in spite of great energy & splendid (though narrowminded) nobleness & generosity in certain lines.

His hints for Bach playing are often jolly sympathetic to me, but his condescending & insightless belittleing of geniuses like Chopin Schumann Mendelsohn & his bolstering up of 3rd rate men like Rheinberger Raff & Hummel show that he had neither instinct nor taste.[24]

All that doesnt matter, for it only harms himself, & I positively like him for his friendly love for certain 3rd rate music, but his brutality to his pupils etc is unforgivable & reminds me that my sufferings in Frankfurt (& I shall never again suffer as in F, & never really have since) had good grounds. His chief game is to jeer at women all the time, & his hauptwitz "dazu sind Sie noch zu jung" [German: main joke "you are still too young for that"] It seems as if the 19th century congeales its most rank tyrany & mean cowardice into German speaking music teachers

When one thinks how unnerving all "vorspielen" [German: performance] is, especially before a large crowd of fellow students, can one conjure up any greater or more cowardly or more useless torture than to use all the weight of one's fame & all the force of a brutally convincing personality & all the sting of what (it seems to me wholly without reason) was supposed to be a witty tongue to crush & chill poor creatures, mostly young women,

23 Hans Guido Freiherr von Bülow (1830–1894). The book was Theodor Pfeiffer, *Studien bei Hans v. Bülow* (Berlin, 1894/Luckhard, 1908).

24 The greater: Fryderyk Franciszek Chopin (1810–49); Robert Alexander Schumann (1810–56); Jakob Ludwig Felix Mendelssohn-Bartholdy (1809–47). The lesser: Joseph Gabriel Rheinberger (1839–1901); Joseph Joachim Raff (1822–82); Johann Nepomuk Hummel (1778–1837).

while they are just in the meltable max-like oversensitiveness of lampenf[i]eber [German: stage-fright]? And a genius like I has the added pain of realising that his so convincingly delivered remarks are just as often wrong as right, just as right & as wrong as any opinionated mandfolk [Danish: man — rather poetic *or* slightly sentimentally of a small boy] holding forth Australian-wise on a subject he knows only a smattering of. For that Bülow was no swimmer in music, but a mere paddler; ja, det er Klart, Kjær [Danish: yes, that's obvious, dear]!

Let no one who upholds the way of teaching in Germany throw any stones at the cruelty of the Roman arenas.

The Romans (for real selfish delight too, nota bene!) rejoiced in breaking up bodies that were worth the breaking.

The German-speakers take a grey relish (a "moral" unwa[n]ton unsensuous 3rd rate creatures 3rd rate revenge) in breaking spirits never worth breaking, snapless yokewilling rabit-like souls, that need coaxing & kindlying lovingly towards joy & health & genuine life. Hit a man your own size, I say.

Män to män.

Even rather be a mänly män than a von Bülow.

& alas! the punishment of this vicious cowardice & injustice is failure, unproductiveness. What have the great "schools" produced? Poor little partisan battlers beginning their musical life with wrung necks.

Made about 80–90 Kr last night in Christiansund.

It **is** a bewitching townlet, all on islets.

My darling mum farewell.

405   TO KAREN HOLTEN
[Original: Danish]
14.9.1911.

Hotel Scandinavie
Aalesund.

My little treasure.

I sent off 60 Kr. from here, and hope you will get it.

You will remember that this is the town where I wanted to kiss the girl? I arrived here in a very erotic mood and met her in the bookshop and gave her a free ticket. So then I invited her and a girl-friend to go to the cinema with me. But in the "weekly review" there was something unforgettably terrible.

"At a motor race in Belgium John Wilton collides with a telegraph pole and kills himself." It wasn't sensational, and one scarcely thought that anything bad had happened, but there lay the man and writhed in death; and looked so English, the poor chap.

You can imagine I am through with anything erotic for many days.

Still today it feels as if I was washed out in body and soul.

When the concert [*sic*] was over, the girl invited me to go to her married sister's, and I did so very gladly, and found the husband very Norwegian, and calm and wise and good to talk to, and I was glad nothing Don Juan-like could be expected of me there. But think, these 2 girls apparently didn't notice anything at all about the motor accident. They didn't say a word about it. Neither did I, obviously.

Well that was that.

I feel so depressed and lifeless and emptied out after that horrible picture.

Goodbye, little Karen, and excuse the tediousness. I am so lonely. Mother travelled back to Xia from Throndhjem.

If you don't get addresses (for after Kristiansand) in time just write to c/o Brødr. Hals. Xia

The concert went **so** splendidly in Bergen last night, I only enjoyed my-self at it, and played splendidly, I thought. The public were a little crazily enthusiastic with 7 encores and the Griegs and Beyers happy and *enthusing*.

Extremely comfortable night journey here, slept all the way.

Sweet Mrs Grieg was in her sweetest mood, so young and fresh. She, her sister and Grieg's 2 sisters chatted *nearly the whole day* yesterday, so it was remarkable enough that I was fresh in the evening, but I was actually.

Mrs Grieg talked a lot to me about you. She said she thought I should love you more than any other person in the world, and so on. I said to her that I had absolutely no reason to believe you were ''unreasonably'' in love with me (for such a thing I obviously cannot admit to anyone except you and me) [I]f that was so or should ever come to be the case, then of course I would be very grateful, for love of all kinds is just what I seek most of all in the world, in all respects, but that this could in no way alter the fact that my first and almost only requirement in life is and will remain not to be *in the least way bound* (in my inner life) to any person or thing, neither relation, or sweetheart, or friend, or ''artistic direction'', and that you knew, and had known it from the first, just as well as I, and that our friendship, which was certainly a charming thing — for me in any case — was *based entirely* on this understanding between us.

That I regarded it as one of life's greatest (happy) duties to fall in love with as many different women as possible, and that I had achieved so little in this direction up to now, is due to the fact that I am not free enough as regards hospitality to venture on many things I would like, also because I lack courage and time, and because women don't seem to be particularly pleased with me, in any case that I don't have what is called ''luck'' with women, which I don't at all regret either; but none-the-less I am absolutely not suited to be a married man, neither to be a ''permanent'' lover some time, and I am not taking and never have taken any step in direction of duties that I don't intend to fulfil.

It is remarkable that women, for example mother and now Mrs Grieg, seem to *expect* that I *after all* **must** want to marry some time (or even straight away) and that there **must** be some *external* ground (that doesn't lie entirely in myself) or influence that holds me back. But one is not so unselfish, even if one is ever so weak. But now I believe both mother and Mrs Grieg realise that the unwillingness is rooted in *myself* and not in any external influence, consideration, or even financial caution, and neither is it in any way at all because I am, or am not, in love with you.

But I must say that it has played its part in bringing both mother and Mrs Grieg nearer to me to see that they have so many legitimate interests *in another woman*, and they both would be prepared to take part against me immediately if they thought that I behaved **un-***openly* in the matter, and it would be villainous if I did.

When I talk to people with whom you have discussed our relationship I am tempted each time to be a little surprised that these people always talk as if you had given them to understand that I had given you promises which I have not done at all, ever. I say this now only for truth's sake, for I haven't the slightest desire to reproach you, *at least in that direction*, for I know so well *how difficult* it is to get, for example, Scandinavians to understand that one does not in the least desire the real ''deep love'', which indeed more or less *everyone* wants in these lands, and which we in English-speaking countries cannot even imagine how it comes about, if we shall tell the truth.

If you *deliberately* gave anyone to understand that you rightly had more to expect of me than is the case (that is to say — nothing, other than friendship, comradeship, and the heavenly joys we share together) then I wouldn't think it was a great or friendly thing to do, since I at least have always acted completely openly with you, although I may have been tedious enough, which I gladly admit — but, as already said, I am not going at all to think that, for it has certainly *absolutely not been the case*, sweet Karen.

Moreover there was something with regard to our relationship that I have long planned to write to you about, although it has no connection at all with anything of the above.

You will perhaps remember that I previously have said that I would marry you if we, by mistake, should get an unexpected baby, for the sake of the child, because I don't think that children should begin life under handicaps. But since the time I decided that I have changed my mind again, and it seems to me you had better be told of my changed decision before we meet.

The older one gets the more one realises that everything goes a little quicker than one had planned. Also, with the years, I get (as most people) the inclination to reckon myself as less gifted than I thought at first.

But I am gifted all the same, and I must after all achieve as much as possible, and since time passes even more urgently than I had allowed for, and since wealth doesn't approach at an exactly madly rapid pace, I must **protect** *myself in other ways*. When I look round about in the world and feel how little I have in common with most of my fellow creatures, I feel almost no desire to use any of my strength (not all that great) to uphold the prevailing modes of living and feeling. I have, on the contrary, no desire for anything else than to support myself and people who are like-minded or who further my plans and opinions. Therefore I have no particular desire to support you or a child of yours and mine. For your type (however sweet it may be for me, however tempting and lovable) strives hard against my type and my type's goal. You love me, yes, but you love me as a possibility for the health life-promoting constancy reliability and naturalness that you (thank God for yourself) overflow with in such a thrilling way; for such things are extremely exciting, believe me.

But you would never use a brass farthing to promote the wildness perversity life-hatred and licentiousness that are my banners and my life's hope and goal of my thoughts and the root to my artistic feelings.

Why should you anyway? It would be idiotic to want it some time. But also, for that reason, one can't expect that I should particularly want my gold, so to speak, to be stamped in your mint. A child belongs to its mother, it seems to me; more or less. And a child that would gratify you (or I would almost say gratify any woman) would only be an enemy in my camp, just as you yourself would be, sweet and tempting and gratifying as you also are.

I love you in my own way. I am not particularly afraid of enemies, for one does become a little used to them in the long run, since the whole of nature, God, and nearly the whole of mankind are indeed my enemies. But just for that reason, because I (with my worship of immorality and desire of fun) stand so alone, and because you all, who are against me, are so overwhelmingly many, I *can't* and **won't** support any of you, even if I were a thousand times more in love than I am.

Previously I said to myself; if she gets a baby, I am strong enough to put up with the marriage for the sake of justice and for her sake. But now that I see how quickly one becomes old and how heavy the way is, I say: Away with justice, I am weak, I help no one. I say it without bitterness (I should think not!) and *regret it greatly*, it would be pleasant to be able to spare life to that degree that one could waste it in marrying.

Now I will tell the truth.

If you get a child, I will pay you your expenses for the birth, and for the child's expenses till it is grown up (especially if you don't become fairly rich before that time) but I will not marry. I say it is the man's fault if he gets a child, unless an accident happens, such as a preventative breaking or suchlike. Can one really hold him solely-responsible for an accident like that? I would think that the consequences of such an accident should be shared. I think that I can personally be called careful in that regard, and if there is an accident, then from now on I won't be alone about the consequences. That is, as said: that I will pay something in money (not unreasonably much, that you would never want either) but *not* with my life's freedom.

If the accident occurred I would advise you not to mix your family in the grief and also bring you and me in bad reputation, but just say in time that you wanted a long pleasure trip, which I of course could pay, and have the child abroad, some place where you are unknown. The expenses of having someone with you who would also make the whole "trip" happier for you could also be paid, and where and how the child should be placed afterwards you must of course decide for yourself, if you would.

But if, on the contrary, you didn't want to keep the matter hidden from your parents, that's your affair and not mine, and my part would only be to assist you with the material help which really would only be ½ my duty, if one can talk about duty. But understand, I don't want to be just I want to be free and fortunate, even if it was ever so unjust.

Even if you desired to initiate the whole world into the story I wouldn't have the right to say a word against it, it just seems to me it would be better to let *no one* know about it, both for the child and the rest of you.

With every year my decisions against marriage become firmer and firmer, and this, together with the increasing years and a growing insight into the burden of my plans (and unreasonableness for a part), forces me to take this standpoint here, less generous than the previous one, but unfortunately absolutely necessary for me.

All this is no emotional thing between us, is not based either on feelings, nor with regard to anything else than my selfish personality and inclination to art and freedom. But this decision does have to do with you and your possible child. And if this altered decision on my part calls forth any wish on your part for any change in our relationship, then you must just say so, and you will find that I will respect it and cooperate with you about it, if I can in any way.

I see that Hobro is not before 8th November, so *Saturday, 4th November will suit for arbejderforeningen*. Forgive the muddle about this date.

Many many thanks for your letter here.

Many thanks about Birkerød. That was nice. I can't decide the date yet, before I have heard from Denmark again, but it will be between *7th and 10th Nov.* (inclusive)

Yes, all you say fits exactly for me too. Now I can scarcely form an opinion. I think, one begins to "dry up", one dies out, as you say, in certain directions when important gifts are not used for a long time.

On the whole recent times have been (for me) very promising and exciting without much having happened. Much to do with compositions, but not heard anything, thousands of letters from you and to you, but not you yourself. But that is so easily remedied. And it is not only the good fleshly things, but there are so many multitudinous things we must get talked and laughed about, and enjoyed. But we will still manage all that, won't we?

Bad house here, only a net earning of 60 Kr!

25 Grainger added two new concertos to his repertoire in 1911: the César Franck *Variations symphoniques* Op. 46, which he had played for the first time under Charles Villiers Stanford at Queen's Hall on 5 July and the Saint-Saëns Piano Concerto No. 2 in G minor Op. 22, which he was to play for the first time in the Albert Hall under Landon Ronald on 19 November and thereafter on his winter tour of Holland. Lady Northcote, wife of Sir Henry Stafford, first Baron Northcote (1846–1911) who had been Governor-General of the Australian Commonwealth from 1903–07. He died on 29 September.

26 Grainger was reading *Kärleken och Äktenskapet* [Love and Marriage] by Ellen Karolina Sofia Key (Livslinjer 1, Stockholm, 1911).

407 TO ROSE GRAINGER Kristianssand
[Postcard. 24.9.11.]
Latest

Why not come to Tvedestrand 27th or 28th Sept? Larvik is no good.
But *dont* come if the massage etc is of real good to you, darling one. Have written Fru Hals.
Have already begun on S. S. Concerto. Have written Lady Northcote long ago.[25] Am waiting with Rathbone's for a reason.
So glad about dear Cyril. Alas! They *will* not mention him in the papers.
Topping re Swedish agent. Have written E.L.R. re Chopin. Have finished the E. Key book.[26]
Don't give me any historic plays either. They are too much like modern newspapers. Those old times were often full of giz I think but folk dont know how to write of them.
Have written poor dear U. George.
By the way I've settled to call myself *Percy Aldridge Grainger* on all compos hereafter. The E. Key book finally fixed it for me.
[On front] I climbed up to the top of this hill. The view was ripping.

408 TO KAREN HOLTEN Hotel Fram
[Original: Danish] Tvedestrand
29.9.1911.

My darling.

How are you now? It is so tedious that I can't give you any addresses yet, but I don't know myself where I shall go to as Hals is waiting to send the "list" until the "winter timetable" (which begins the 1st Oct) comes out. But in a few days I will be able to let you know it. For the present just write c/- Hals.
I experienced 2[?] charming happy days in Lillesand.
One day I rowed 5 hours on the fjord and right out in the open sea. It was so indescribably beautiful and attractive out there. The "host" was Danish, from Odense.
And then I had a, for *me*, rather successful love affair, it came to real kisses, without resistance. This you shall hear all about when we meet.
Mother met me here in the town the day before yesterday from Xia and now we travel further East.
The house was so good here yesterday, and the public so beside themselves.
Since there are a lot of coastal towns like Arendal Mandal and so on that I have still not played in, it is not impossible that I will take them after Xia and travel via Fredereckshavn Jutland to Cope. If I get Aalborg Horsens then it may be that I will arrange my Jutland dates before the 30th Oct, and have my *free time in Cope afterwards*, in the first days of Nov.
But I don't know anything definite on that yet, must first talk to Hals, and hear from Høeg and Fischer etc.
Just think, 7 or 8 years ago, on my first Australian tour I saw a lovely sailing ship from Tvedestrand I believe it was in Newcastle harbour N.S.W. and I decided that time that I would see that town some day, and for that reason asked Hals to include Tvedestrand this time. And that turned out to be a terribly nice town, and I earned 69 Kr.
We rowed 4–5 hours on the fjord yesterday.
I am longing so much to get good news of you, sweet

409 TO KAREN HOLTEN   Larvik.
[Original: Danish]
4.10.1911.

Many thanks for the letter to here.

I will write about Birkerød *as soon as* I hear from H. Fischer and
Jespersen and Schibsbye, before that I can't, unfortunately.

Many thanks also about Osterb.[irk?] Musikforeningen. But I would
rather leave it, on account of things I will explain when we meet. After this
year I have decided not to play for the Arb.[ejderforening] any more either.
I have seen here and in Holland, and again in England recently, *how much*
there is to be earned in the provinces when one *keeps oneself big* in large
towns.

In Denmark I began in a *small* way and it has gone upwards and that
must be the case more and more. Now Denmark must lie "fallow" for 1–2
years, but I am thinking of the future, and from now on I won't try and
earn in Copenhagen, but only use it as I really use most large towns, as
a means of advertising for the small ones.

You could thank them very much and say that unfortunately I won't
have time this time.

There are so many many things I long to talk with you about, I am so
full of things I want to say that it is no use writing any of them.

Yesterday all the missing corrections came from Schotts and this morning *Scotch Strathspey and Reel* was finished; 150 pages!

Sweet little Karen, get terribly well.

Your happy comrade
Percy.

9. Oct. address c/- Hr. Harald Karud. Fredriksstad. After that to Xia

410 TO ROSE GRAINGER   Høyers Hotel.
7.10.1911.   Skien

It's quite laughable the attraction Danes have for me. On the whole tour
there have only been 2 Hotel værts [Danish: hosts] I have really started a
chat with, & both turned out to be Danes. The one last night designed &
made a lovely model yacht that stands in his hall, maybe 5 feet long with
which he won prize at the recent Skien udstilling [Danish: exhibition].
Lovely things, really nicely made models, such sweet lines they have.

You remember the little Fiann girl, sister of a singer, who came kørendes
ind [Danish: driving in] to Tvedestrand & looked like D. Menpes & some
other unremembered person? They were both there, he to sing there next
Sunday. That little girl has great bodily charm for me.

As for the sweetest of mums, if ever Robin Legge had Fuller
Maitlanditis, you've got Moralitis. Forresten [Danish: Moreover] I think
you are awfully wise when it comes to questions of actual folk, where I'm
worse than hopeless, alas.

Most likely some change had better be arranged with Karen, as you say,
it does seem too unfair, all of it, as it is. But that I cant say anything about
until I've seen her, of course, except that I am quite clear myself.

As I said, you are splendid on all questions re actual folk, & I take my
hat off. But I havent the least tillid to [Danish: confidence in] your judgement on abstract moral questions, because you never will argue sensibly
about them. Subjects one cannot argue about without a feeling of discomfort are, I think, subjects about which one has maybe deep feelings but
unripe (unworkedout) thoughts. Thus I can remember a time when I could
not discuss the possibility of England's down-going without discomfort.

That was because I was not clear within myself of the details of the questions, & had not tossed myself about in the thought of the possibilities involved, as I have since. You cant expect anyone to take advice on a subject you havent thought out fully enough to discuss with don't-care-ness & explain in full clearness. I'm quite ready to discuss fairly any moral question on those grounds. As it is, I have threshed out sexual questions in my head for years & years (in fact, I hardly ever think of ought else but sex, race, athletics, speech & art) & think I probably stand higher in that branch (står højere på det område [Danish: stand higher in that subject]) than almost any other living person, for I combine great protective-sense (the sense that originally makes all morals) with great wanton imaginativeness, a blend I cannot recall ever having met in others, not even in broadminded (and certainly not in loose-minded) writers on such subjects.

I dont see anyone has a right to wish to fence in my thoughts (even the most selfindulgent ones) on sensual matters, & up to a certain mild point I feel myself entitled to make others suffer for my own pleasures. "Live & let die" is a poise that all more advanced folk must now & again take towards the weaker ones, out of justice & out of economy. Society, in its unripeness & wastefulness (poor unknowing partly selfdestructive thing) produces a type like me (at some expense) & then turns on its machinery to, in part, make useless the more or less high gifts it has given me thro' its conditions.

To produce clever overrefined sensual wild types like me there has to be a cultured class living parasiticly upon the mass of povertystriken ones who are "kept down" largely in order to make possible the overrefinement of the rich out of which my art, my freedom of thought, my chance of international knowledge & experience, my flights of strange sensuality & artistic imagination spring & by which they are fostered. I, & folk like me, are the strange reward for all the cruelty & injustice done to the poor & the under-refined. But after having gone thus far, after unwittingly producing me & such as me at great cost, society goes to great pains (equally unwittingly & therefor innocently) to tie my hands as soon as I attempt to use my (unjustly-gotten) rare qualities for my own & its own good or evil. It lets me hear orchestras & thus tempts my orchestral imagination, but gives me no time or means to ever make the experiments needful to reach more than a ½-advance. It feeds my sexual mind through the erotic books of many lands & the indecencies (specially fostered to encorage libertinism) of all lands, but would imprison me if I applied to sexual things the experimentalism it *demands from my art*, & would make life jolly uncomfortable for me (& thus hedge the use of my gifts) if I, in my lifetime, spoke freely of, or published the results of my specially gifted thoughts on sexual matters. Thousands of poor bodies have been made decrepit & killed off that my body can be as healthy & fit as it is, yet society uses its influences to ruin my health rather than preserve it & though it would make me (a tender good genius) "impossible" if I indulged in sexuality with a girl of 15 I would have no legal redress whatever from any odd person who choose to give me any destructive desease.

A thousand kindred matters would make one bitter against "society" if one didnt realize that it is as it is because it is too young too weak too helpless to have any idea of what it is doing. The sexual laws, for instance, have no doubt been created by gifted sensitive just folk like myself in order to curb the destructive dangerousness of low folk void of self control (I, too, would, if I could, *only increase* all such laws) But, my darling, what have such laws to do with me, who am part of that experimental advance guard in certain directions through which (all too slowly) even "society" becomes in time more knowing & more lawabiding. Many of the laws have been made *by* such as me (as Walt would say: I greet them as comrades, over there) but not *for* such as me, & since the world is still so unripe types like me must steal their experiences cunningly by back ways & with cautious craftiness, just as those 2 high Japs had to commit a nominal crime in leaving Japan dennegang [Danish: that time] in order to be of use later on.

Life works blindly & wastefully, but it works, & it *most likely* doesnt give me queer hungers for little girls etc for nothing. When the globe was underpeopled sex was likely mainly there to birth more folk. But now the earth is mostly overpeopled God knows exactly what its there for: Something or other; & folk like me have got to find out.

Since the earth is overfolked & since *neomalthusianism* sex is maybe largely a *pleasure-stimulant*, to take the place of alcohol, coffee, badtemper & other more harmful means of excitement.[27] *Pleasure* seems to be one of the aims of "life". High races & high individuals are oftenest pleasure loving. As long as sex was mainly an "avlings redskab" (utensil of breeding) Love was an element of grief jealousy tears heaviness, as it still mainly is in teutonic lands, for instance. Most of our "moral laws" are built to run "sex" in the gro[o]ves of "breeding". But I know better. There are folk enough, but not joy enough excitement enough vividness enough *innocent stimulation* enough. The greatest races have often been the hardest drinkers & most criminal. For fine folk need much relief from dullness, & great contrast of experience. The refined ones amongst us have got beyond drink & crime, just as we have got beyond spitting & bullfights. But life mustn't get *less* exciting on that account. And dont talk to me of mental excitements being enough. I'm not a born fool. The creature who cannot supply any *bodily* equivalents for such bodily stimulants as alkohol, wife beating, fist-fighting in streets, etc lacks imagination or doesnt understand modern life & life to come. One mustn't replace a muchness by a lessness. Former life was full of bodily excitements, brutal no doubt, but exciting. Modern middleclass life, with its baldheads, its fat stow-mucks, its poverty stricken speech ("motion" "dirigere et flygel herud" [Danish: direct a piano out of here]) with the 1000-fold everrecuring same few meaningless idioms shows what happens to folk when the old brutal bodily excitements have become impossible & noone has had the gumption or the corage to introduce new *refined humane* equally (or *more*) exciting go-insteads. The English trick of sport has supplied such a want in the Bach-like, daily-breadlike, out-of-door, cold unfeeling branch. No one respects that stunning English enrichment of life more than I. That jiujitsi should replace boxing, running (men) horse-steeple chasing, football & cricket bullbaiting & cockfighting is all as it should be & in line with progress's path. *But I am one of the few who can supply modern go-insteads for such (formerly topping) things as brothels, wife-beating, child-beating, witch-burning, etc.* I realize the need of a justification for such things in the past & I realize the need of go-insteads for the now & the to-come & I realize that such go-insteads must be en-nobling & not lowing (degrading) healthgiving rather than healthtaking, & *always refining & humanizing rather than coarsening & brutalising.* Sexual perversity (**so called**) is probably one of the *surest garantees* of refinement & delicacy of mind & soul. Of course I am speaking of complex perversity & not of mere criminal (diseased) perversity.

For instance, who are not sexually tempted by girls of say 12–16 years of age are mostly (most likely) simply devoid of a sense of beauty, deep interest in childhood, & the need of great sexual contrast. The points that mark the difference between woman & man (her softer flesh, fairer skin, smoother surface, rounder muscle, clearer eyes, less "iron" in the soul) are all still greater in childwoman than in grown woman. The grounds of attractions are childsplay to prove. Now let me hear why not endulge? Is there a single sensible doctor's reason? Maybe, I dont say there isn't. If there is, I bow to it, but I've never read one. But you, for instance, take it for granted that it must be harmful, why? On no authority other than middleclass ignorant prejudice, maybe. If so it is surely silly of you, isn't it?

In thinking over our sexual life let us remember that our civilised mankind can outdo most primitive races in most feats, but stands seemingly far

27 Malthusianism, the teaching of T. R. Malthus (1766–1835) and his followers, who held that, as population increases faster than the means of subsistence, its increase should be checked, mainly by moral restraint; popularly viewed as a proposal to check marriage (*O.E.D.*).

behind in sexuality, ease of childbirth, ease of menstruation, etc. This doesn't surprize me, when I remember that we *organise bodily athletic training*, & ignore sexual training. We teach a child to begin Bach before it can play it properly but we prepare our women for marriage & childbirth by sexual ignorance & our men by uncontrolled onanism or the likelihood of sexual desease, or else (in the most lucky cases) an ignorance as complete as the woman's. Is it then so strange that we outpianize the natives & that the natives outsex us?

Sexual joys & experiences should be as easy & safe & widespread to get hold of as opera & orchestral performances & Conservatoriums.

We have junior sports in preparatory schools, boy's voices in church choirs (from which, I believe, a very large percentage of good grown singers later come) prodijee musicians for eventual "masters", but (very naturally) we lack junior sexual healthy training & fun & experience just as we lack grown up ditto. Maybe we have Christianity to thank for this laughable hole in our civilisation, or maybe a Northern climate (yet South Europe is no better) or the newness of Malthusianism, the newness of scientific influence (I think not) or the unknowledge still of the bulk of folk that sex is no longer solely & only a breeding-utensil. I cant judge, but I have a shrewd idea its because Europeans are such stick-in-the-muds, that their sexual instincts have such a short blossoming in youth only (the bulk of their lifedays being ½-sexless) that the bulk of the race at any given time has no real interest in sex-joys *as apart* from breeding-needs.

However, my mind runs on other days, when both late childhood & late man- & woman-hood will join with life's prime in the intense ensemble of a wild sexual concert, & if I ever see a chance to snatch an occasional dawn-snapshot of this coming glory before I die, it would be silly to begrudge me it. But why one should wish to limit the sphere of my after all wholly superiour (& therefor harmless) thoughts I can't fathom.

411 TO ROSE GRAINGER   Sarpsborg.
[Postcard]
8.10.11.

Fancy, I have got the 2 last moves of the St. S.[aëns] from memory in the last few days. Now I only have the 1st movem to get.

Have written a bundle of letters Röntgen, E. Röntgen, E. L. Rob, Hutschenruijter, etc.[28]

I want you to think out & write down what pieces you think would be the *very best* to include in my Berlin (etc) programs, darling.

412 TO KAREN HOLTEN   Moss Hotel
[Original: Danish]   Moss
16.11.1911 [*sic* 16.10.11]

Little Karen

I am *very sorry* that I had to give you the trouble with Birkerød. You see I reserved *10th Nov* for Rødby (through Jespersen) but since he didn't telegraph I thought Rødby had second thoughts. But today I got a telegram Rødby 10 Nov, and as I get 150 [Kr] there, they must get the tenth.

Now I am waiting to hear from you which date Birkerød can manage out of *9th, 11th, 12th*.

Forgive me: For perhaps it will be tedious for you to arrange it now?

28 Engelbert Röntgen (1886–1958), cellist and son of Julius Röntgen. He had assisted at Grainger's London solo recital on 29 May, playing his father's Cello Sonata in B minor Op. 56: a gesture of thanks from Grainger to Röntgen to whom, as Percy wrote to Rose on 17 January 1911, he owed everything in Holland. Wouter Hutschenruijter (1859–1943), Dutch conductor who was conductor of the Utrecht orchestra from 1892 to 1917. Grainger played under him several times, the first being 19 November 1910, the most recent 13 and 17 April 1911.

Now Denmark is like this

Odense	30
Nykøb. Sj.	31
Arb. for.	4
Vejlefj. San.	5
Vejle	6
Aalborg	7
Hobro	8
Rødby	10
Københ.	14.

That's not so bad.

Herewith I enclose a list of addresses in Norway, etc.

We will first meet the 1st Nov when I come from Nykøb[ing]. Because on the journey through from Odense-Nykøb there won't be much time? The dates on the Norwegian addresses are the concert days. Mandal, Farsund and Arendal must be counted *one day* more than to Kristianssand S. (via Jutland)

I am now playing

Moss today
Hønefos. 17 Oct
Xia. Folkekonsert 19
Kongsberg 20
Fredrikshald 22
etc

On Saturday the house was *completely sold out*.

Yesterday (Sunday) we spent several hours with Alfhild Sandby on Holmenkollen, where she is until 20th (then to America) She looks very happy, and was very amusing and pleasant. You will hear more in Copenhagen.

I am longing so quite frightfully to be with you in Copenhagen, but it doesn't look as if we will have *much time together*, does it?

I thought I should have more dates, but I can't resist money, and therefore I am taking these Norwegian towns too instead of the wrecked Sweden.[29]

I am so tired of trying to be brave and am only longing.

Yesterday I sent off all the Danish programmes, a frightful job, and now come the English programmes (I have a mass of concerts there) and now begins a lot of correspondence with Holland etc. I truly don't know how I shall manage it all. But it will be alright.

I will be very grateful to hear as soon as possible about the date for Birkerød.

Don't think I am cold, little friend, I am only a little worried, and send many kisses.

413 TO ROSE GRAINGER   *Farsund.*
[Original: English/some Danish]
[Postcard]
7.30 morn. 26.11.11. [*sic* 26.10.11]

Arendal was a stunning success. A packed house with kr 202 Netto. A lovely smooth journey from Xia to Arendal, but from Arendal here one of **the** most frightful tossings I've ever been "med til" [Danish: involved in]. I was glad you weren't along altho' I can already see that this dear little spot is a place for us 2 another year. I think the hotel seems very good too.

Since Xia I have written *over 40* letters cards & packets. Have done all on your 2 lists, settled all the English & Scotch programs, etc. So that is truly a relief.

29 Karen replied, 17 October, "You say that you cannot 'resist money'. I must say I understood it very well, when it was your intention that we, when this money was earned, should be together, but as that is not the case, I don't find it very pleasant. You cannot be surprised that I have changed my attitude to the things quite a bit in the last 3 months, in which direction we can discuss when we meet". On 23 October she wrote further, "I really don't know whether my changed attitude is inclining to do justice to myself. This perpetual evaluation of what everything means to oneself is not my style, actually I find it very unpleasant . . . You say that you are longing for me as *I really* **am**, but I am afraid you will be disappointed; because I *am* not as I *was*, fortunately or unfortunately I do not know. My changed attitude is inclining to less love, I think. I feel no desire to goodness or sensitiveness, to give it, I mean . . . I also feel quite passive . . . I think it is all right with my changed attitude, but I find it very sad that it is necessary . . ."

Give Miss Permin very warm regards from me. I wont write again before we meet. Remember you leave København about 9.5 morn on Oct 30 for Odense arriving about 1.11 midday. Your adoring son.

Arrange the København "tea" for 2nd, 3rd, (or 4th, less good) Nov.

Later. So rejoiced to get yr card here (Farsund). Feel so awfully happy & well after my tumbling about in the boat.

In Arendal met a very nice Danish-Icelandic woman who read Icelandic to me & helped me a lot. What joy!

414   TO KAREN HOLTEN   Hamres Hotel
[Original: Danish]   Farsund
26.11.1911. [*sic* 26.10.11]

Thanks for your letter to this place, and the enclosed letter from Hobro.

Mother has already journeyed to Copenhagen and will meet me in Odense on the 30th, where I arrive early in the morning. Then we travel with the night train together to Roskilde, she further to Copenhagen, I to Nykøbing Sj[ælland]. (Address: Hr Søren Schiebsbye. Nykøbing Sj)

From Nykøbing I travel on Wednesday *the 1st Nov* with the 6.50 train which (judging by my old "time-table") arrives in Copenhagen 12.10 midday. I will go straight to Ceresvej if I don't hear anything from you against it in Odense or Nykøb. If there should be anything that made it impracticable for your mother to have me the 1st Nov, or if you would rather not have me staying with you, please be so kind as to write a few words either to Odense or Nykøb, and I will arrange accordingly. On the other hand, if there is nothing in the way, from your mother's or from your side, it seems to me that it has possibly never been more profitable for us to be together than just now, judging by my feelings.

I do so entirely agree with you that love *is* life, and to miss love is to miss everything. But there are so many widely different kinds, and as I can so well understand, and have sympathy with, that your capacity for love runs in the direction of life and humanity, then you should also be able to understand that a very large part of my capacity for love runs in the direction of love for my mother, for art, and interest in races, national feelings. When you think how many more really deeply-keen abstract interests I have than most people, yes almost than all others that I know, and what special possibilities for development of love my life-long very close togetherness with my mother has meant with respect to her, then it seems to me that you shouldn't be surprised at my lack of surplus love; for it is necessary to realise that the best and greatest love-capabilities have gone in the above-named directions.

It is absolutely necessary that you should know and understand my shortcomings, even if you hate me for them, for first and foremost we must see that your own great capabilities for love don't go unused. It doesn't matter if you hate me, but it would be more profitable for us both if you above all really *understood* me, for otherwise we can scarcely manage the future as well as we *must and will*.

I can so well realise the absolute necessity for your type, and *love* it and feel its great charm and richness, but I would be delighted if you would also realise the necessity for my type, and, quite apart from love to and from me, realise *my* type's beauty, and not only construe my *qualities* as an outcome of unfriendliness or ungenuineness. I *am* as I give myself, neither more nor less deep than I appear, and since you are equally straightforward and true I see absolutely no improbability in us being able to manage ourselves, both of us, with regard to each other. Because your demands are just as definite and unmerciful and *unchangeable* as *mine also are*, that doesn't matter. Because you *can*not get from me what you would so like to have, does not necessarily mean that we will misunderstand each other or lose courage or hope of achieving our *own special purposes* elsewhere without losing that clear understanding insight into each other's great value and lovableness.

If you don't understand that I am inquisitive about you and have yearnings, then that doesn't matter at all.

I can easily adjust myself to the direction your feelings take, now-and-again, I hope.

Thus **if** you can bear to have me staying with you I would be very grateful if you would give your mother the enclosed letter.

As already said, you can let me know if I had better *not* come.

Don't think you will have to live without love because I have been a disappointment. There are more than 2 people in the world, and everything is so full of possibilities.

I will presumably not write any more before I arrive on the 1st.

On 30 October Grainger reached Odense, for the first of the concerts of his Danish tour. He made eleven appearances on this Danish tour, in concerts of various types, finishing the tour with his Copenhagen recital on 14 November. While in Copenhagen he stayed at the home of Karen Holten. His arrival there on 1 November ended a separation of 355 days.

Rose, who had travelled ahead to Copenhagen, meeting Percy briefly at Odense on the way, left to return to London by 7 November. Percy himself arrived back in London on 17 November.

On 11 December he left London again, for Holland, and a Dutch tour which continued into the New Year. Between times in London he had a number of important concert engagements and travelled briefly to Scotland for two recitals on 7 and 9 December with the singer Julia Culp. In Holland he gave ten concerts between the 14th and the 25th of December. Rose joined him in Amsterdam on 22 December.

415   TO ROSE GRAINGER   Vejlefjord Sanatorium
6.11.11.

I'm hoping you're not having too bad weather from Vliessingen [Vlissingen/Flushing]. Here there is storm beyond words & the little steamer that should take me to Vejle has run aground, so I'm going by train, as usual.

This is quite the nicest of all the places I come to in Denmark, the rooms cold & draughty & the audience keen & music hungry in proportion.

I had a really revelsome drive here last night; wind that I've never heard stronger than (on land) & I had the carriage all opened up & deeply enjoyed it.

The horses could only make very slow headway at times for the wind & we had a jolly short sharp bucketful of a hailstorm once.

Here a gorgeous 4 course meal of really pure strong food, beautifully cooked, awaited me, & after that I got in an hour's practise at the St. Saëns. This morn we had lovely porridge.

The headman here, Prof Saugmann, is so jolly & nice & keen & kind. Between here & Dangaard is such lovely landscape. Curious pinky red painted farmhouses & cosy garths & beechwoods roaring like any ocean. Farvel saa længe [Danish: farewell, so long] my beloved mum.

416 TO ROSE GRAINGER   [In the train]
10.11.11.   for Rødby.

The enclosed re German Reichstag rather amusing. They *do* long for a war so & it seems the poor responsible folk "in the know" cant let them risk it.

I enjoy studying the score of the St Saëns which I've just got from W. Hansen, & which is awfully differently orchestrated from what I looked for.

One never can guess how Frenchman are going to orchestrate They are always full of "pudsige" [Danish: funny] ideas, but so sensibly & sedately pudsige.

Tonight, after concert, I am going to finish all my English correspondence, Mrs Batten & whatever else remains undone. I am very much hoping that a guitar rehearsal can be fixed for between the Godalming & the 2nd Classical Concert.

There is a ½ breed (Malay?) in this train. She is so gentle & polite, such a contrast to the rest.

My loathing of Europeans grows with every year. Europeans are neither gentle nor fighters. They are merely riff raff (cheap white trash) for the most part.

So far I have read little to disgust me about the China Revolution.[30] Even in European newspapers a certain repose & restraint seems to leak thro the reports; & I seem to see hints between the lines that remind me of the Et 4000 aars rike that I read.

How I long for the time when we can get us East, darling mother, & try & see how it all *really* is there.

I am so grieved that Denmarks charm has broken for me. I shall always keep a special love for it, of course, & real Jutlanders will always be something glorious for themselves, but the whole land the whole folk I have lost the key to — or found it, maybe? From after old enthusiasms certain gentle affections always stay behind, of course, *luckily*.

I'm longing to be back in England, arrive Thursday night.

Am so quieted to hear that the mum had a bearable Xing after all.

30 Grainger is referring to the cataclysmic events in China which began as an uprising against the Viceroy in Wuchang on 10 October 1911 and culminated on 12 February 1912, when the old Imperial Government was replaced by a revolutionary government headed, in its earliest days, by Sun Yat-sen. Grainger had read Erik Givskov, *Eit 4000-Aars Rike* [A 4000-Years' Kingdom] (Norske Folkeskrifter 27, Oslo, 1905), a collection of articles on the history of China originally published in Danish periodicals, translated into Norwegian by Arne Garborg.

31 Karen Hulda Garborg (*née* Bergerson, 1862–1934), Norwegian author, wife of the famous Norwegian writer Arne [Aadne] Garborg (1851–1924). Grainger first mentions them in his correspondence in September 1910, when he writes to Karen that either she or Mrs Grieg should give him a copy of Garborg's *Haugtussa* in dialect, and that Mrs Garborg had written an article on him in "maalet" in a "maal" newspaper in Oslo. ("Maalet" = "landsmaal", a new national language for Norway introduced about the turn of the century.) Mrs Garborg corresponded with Grainger until her death, sending him information on Norwegian folksongs and language and copies of her books.

417 TO ROSE GRAINGER   København.
[Postcard]
12.11.11.

Have addressed & posted yr card to Fru Garborg.[31] So delighted you like Roger's new stuff

———————

For Godalming:
Schumann: Romance in F sharp maj. (dont know opus)
Chopin: Polonaise, in A flat maj. op. 53.
If you look up drawer marked Schumann Schubert in black cases on stairs you will likely find the tattered Romance & find the opus No etc on it.

———————

Am, of course, up to my ears in fuss, as one always is the last 2 days in a place. Am going to see Thuren today.

Else & I had a delightful practise yesterday. I really have done a huge lot to the St Saëns   Later. It was *so* lovely to see Thuren

418 TO ROSE GRAINGER   [PM Kjøbenhavn]
[Postcard. PM 13 November 1911]

   Thanks for your dear cards. How gay & flourishing all news with us lucky ones. Got Schotts packet from Norway & money from Hals.
   Very busy. Fond love.

419 TO ROSE GRAINGER   Ceresvej.
Tuesday. 14.11.11.

My pet.

   I feel so fit & fresh & well & happy about everything. Least (happy) about tonights program as I've been neglecting it for the St Saëns, which I did with little v. Bülow 2 hours yesterday.[32] I gave Hansen over 1200 Kr yesterday, of which Kr 401 are from the last 4 Norsk towns, which money he will send together with the concert money.

32 Reimar von Bülow, a pupil.

   No Cope concert has ever gone as well as this one. I expect it will be about sold out *without* sending the usual free tickets to "autoritæterne" (= leading musicians) so that is jolly. Mrs Joh. Svendsen rang up today & said sweet things. Is going to give me a photo of him, she says. Saw Mrs Grieg yesterday & day before, she partic sweet. The Schott sending was very nicely printed "parts" of "Sh's Hey."
   I long to see the Roger & Balfour & if you **like** to ask them to come Thursday eve (one of them) do so, but not if you hellere være fri [Danish: would rather not]. Fix *just as many pupils as will go in* for days after concerts & überhaupt [German: above all] *pupil days*. Am longing to hear the guitar practise, & Roger's & Balfour new mucks & be back in 31a & everything. I've never had such a happy Scand. tour as this, nor such a happy Københavner ophold [Danish: Copenhagen-stay] as this. All seems on a truer surer basis than it's ever been before & the to-come never loomed so stoppendefuld [Danish: crammed full] of positive joys & enticements.
   Hope you darling have been sleeping well & not overdoing things, & that I'll find the tight old ship foaming along on the crest of things.
   Dont come & meet me, darling, because you mightn't if you did, & L'pool St is a bloody station & meeting at home is a better thing. I've got my ticket & everything & can be awaited any time Thursday eve.
   I shant wire if I'm not coming till Friday morn, I'll simply turn up Friday.
   If not arrived by 11 give up hope.

   Yr longing & lucky one
   Percy

420 TO KAREN HOLTEN   31A King's Road
[Original: Danish]   Sloane Square
18.11.11.   S W

Faithful sweet little Karen.

   Of course we forgot a whole lot of things behind e.g. the 2 peculiar books, and some preventatives and weren't there some more whips I should have had with me?
   "But that doesn't matter."
   I can take them with me some other time
   Later on you can perhaps send me the 2 curious books after getting a collection of the same sort from me?

"Molly" has come out now also, but I will have to wait until I get time to go into town to Schott's to collect some missing piano pieces before I can send you the whole thing, and that I am ½ inclined not to. You don't really want the "parts" of Molly, Sh's Hey etc do you? Or would you rather have the parts at least of the ones you were so kind as to copy out for me? The parts are printed from your manuscript, for the most part, anyway.

How happy I was with you this time. It is so nice not to be "lover" any more, but a kind of tourist who observes things unemotionally with new eyes, and all the same finds so delightfully much to love and admire.

"I have the *greatest* respect for you as — everything possible" as the Queen would say.

It is so lovely here. Now at 12 midday it is nearly dark as night and all the colours are so full and peculiarly yellowish-red, as you know. Everything here is sweetness and interestedness with grand activity, as you can imagine.

Tomorrow is the big day; as far as St Saëns is concerned at any rate, if not for me.

How is your little tummy?

How sweet and noble you were to me. I do not entirely understand everything. But there are so few things I do understand. I am in any case your extremely grateful

Percy.

421   TO KAREN HOLTEN   [London]
[Original: Danish]
Wednesday. 29.11.11.

It has been a crazy time.

I have been *so* taken up that nearly all pupils had to be given up. Everything has gone well up to now. Today I have a difficult and unattractive programme to play in the Classical Concert Society Bechstein Hall this evening.[33] The day before yesterday 3 rehearsals.

(1) to hear my 2 song-quartets (Mary Thomson and 6 Dukes)
(2) the quintet (Dvorak) for this evening
(3) 25–30 guitars for "F[aðir] og D[óttir]". The last-named begins to go hopefully.

Schott muddles to an incredible degree, forgets and makes mistakes etc endlessly but it will nevertheless come to something despite everything Everything is pleasant and delightful and I don't feel nervous or in the least intense. I will soon send you some curious books.

It would be a delight to me to get some new photographs of the naked you, but I cannot expect that in this season of the year with no light, can I?

I have thought of something. We should shave you *much closer* than last time and then smear all over with vaseline or such like and smear me as well, it must be splendid to have both bodies slippery in those parts.

In everything, it is indescribable how I long to get hold for a moment of your sweet positive never failing sensuality. I don't know of anyone else at all who can be so good in that way. There must be many in the world, and I love them all at a distance, but I don't know them. But I have tested you, and I would give you a cirtificate if it was wanted. You are in any case *something quite perfect* in a way. Most probably in many ways. I don't understand that so terribly well.

But that you are splendid, 1st class, something genuine and fulfilling and satisfying in the way that *I* particularly understand and value, that is so delightfully certain.

33 At the eighth concert of the Classical Concert Society at Bechstein Hall on 29 November Grainger played piano solos by Bach, Schumann and Beethoven, and the Dvořák Quintet in A major Op. 81 with the Motto Quartet.

I am longing so terribly much for us to be together in Svinkløv in the coming summer.

I am full of thoughts about that time. But I don't know at all whether it will be possible or not.

But my brain is very taken up with Svinkløv–Karen yearnings.

But it happens so often that one longs for something and nevertheless doesn't choose it when it comes to the point. One cannot build on anything of that kind.

Many kisses and lusting thoughts and thankful memories of Copenhagen.

Your
Percy.

422   TO KAREN HOLTEN   London.
[Original: Danish]
10.12.11.

My sweet comrade

Just arrived from Scotland, where the night before last I wrote 18 pages of Clog dance, you know the Trio.

Your sweet letter was a comfort and rich joy to me this morning.

We left Edinborough 10.30 o'cl last night and were here 7 o'cl this morning, and the whole of that time I sat with a young lady (accompaniste at the 2 Scotch concerts) in my arms and kissed and tickled her.[34] She was quite pretty, rather kind, and the whole night was a *great* joy to me you can imagine. She did not kiss back properly though she got worked up at times, I tickled her breasts and legs, but she had awfully thick woollen underclothes on. I didn't get an opportunity to bring her to any culmination, for I don't think she wanted to, and I am a peaceful person. The whole thing was without any sentimentality or feeling on both sides and also without passion, but the whole thing was friendly pleasant and (for me at any rate) extremely entertaining.

The breast buds in most women don't stand out so firmly or so beautiful in form as yours, also your kisses are *indescribably* different from (I think) all others that I have known.

Because with you the whole body is *animated* in the highest degree, and shaken through with wonderful deep movements of life itself. On the contrary some other women give a ½ dead, passive impression. I have nothing against such ones, but it is a thousand times more wonderful to be an artist of life as you are.

I wouldn't have believed that the difference (under normal circumstances) *could* be so great.

When I have touched (ever so appreciatively moreover) others, I must say I am deeply conscious of your glory and nobility and the inspiration and inspiring nature of your whole being. Not so many others (none of them I have met for many years) could lead me to come forward with my whipping-desire and all my innermost longings which happened so incredibly naturally and easily together with you.

Manners, reserve, lack of confidence, all barriers to reality and spiritual and fleshly depths flee in your presence.

With you, and those like you, the good sweet *primitive being* has his chance. Whatever soft modest tender shoots of feeling are frightened by your personality must truly be extremely fragile.

I read in those letters that I laughed at in Copenhagen that time, something similar to this I am now compelled to repeat: I am in depths of my guts thankful that my rich tender erotic schemes have been allowed to

34 The accompanist at the two concerts in Scotland was Ellen Tuckfield.

sprout in so motherly-blessing and life-giving an earth as your safe passionate tender-hearted little soul. There I feel myself truly at home and at ease, there I am damn well; by God I can't say otherwise.

Something *so* splendid about you is the flesh (skin) between the knees and the body itself. Anything *so* soft smooth delightful in "texture" and deeply lovely in form, I have never really expected. I cannot imagine anything that less resembles a man than this part of you. It is one of my dearest memories to remember the sensation of stroking this splendid flesh.

I am very close to you just now in my gratitude my desire and my happy admiration of you. I know that you are a deep dear creature.
Saint Saëns went well — I love it.

I am very tired (didn't sleep a moment last night) have an immense amount to do; am well and happy and brave, and as well your ardent lover

Percy.

From now on (till the end of January) c/o: Hans Augustin. Frans v. Mierisstr[aat] 101 Amsterdam

423   TO ROSE GRAINGER   A'dam
18.12.11.

Of course, its always better to get the work over 1st, & I would just as soon that you come after Xmas as before All I want is that you stay möglichst [German: as possible] long when you do come & see the jolliest places. I give a little list of where you should come to on various dates.

If you arrive on 22, 23, 24, 25, or 26 go to Amerika Hotel Amsterdam, but rooms must be ordered 1st, thro Augustin.

If you are here by 26, then you could do Almelo (27) Nijmegen (28) with me, but I wouldnt advise you to go direct from London to those towns, because of possible trouble of booking thro. So if you arrive 27 or 28 go also to Amsterdam Amerika Hotel.

If you arrive 29 go direct to Leiden (better to travel via Hoek, by night) If you arrive 30 or 31, 1st Jan or 2nd Jan we can meet either in A'dam, Haarlem, or Leiden, probably best in A'dam.

Whenever you come & to whatever town you come 1st it will be perfectly easy to arrange that you see the pictures in A'dam Haag Haarlem & Leiden (wonderful native museum in latter) After getting this post
P.G.
p. adr: W.J. Sprenger
Middelburg.
Zeeland. Holland
After Dec 21 address C/o Augustin again.

Yesterday I darted into the Rijksmuseum to see where the Rembrandts sat, etc, so that I could tell you where to go straight without wasting yr legs trying to find them.

You can get a tram from Hotel to door nearly & the best pictures (all of them bore me to tears) are near ingang [Dutch: entrance] & there are plenty of seats for you to sit down everywhere.

I'm feeling extremely well fresh & happy tho' *longing* to get away from A'dam

My finger has beautifully recovered.

Let me know as early as poss when you'll come & dont put yrself out to come earlier than you want. We'll make it up by staying later.

I have some charming towns early in the new year, nicer than those just coming & the picture-towns you'll see thoroly anyhow.

Yr adoring son.

424   TO ROSE GRAINGER
19.12.11.

A'dam.

Had one of my best days yesterday. Hardly any nerves, well prepared & in fine feelingful fever. Not much money made, but house well filled & as much (or more) begeist[e]rung [German: enthusiasm] as ever.

I am extraordinarily lucky in my platform condition this year, & yet even at the best what a terrible affair it is, & what a hero I am!!

I like to be able in concerts, like I did last night, to voice thro my playing the sweet painfulness I feel underlying life. I am joyeous & gay & healthy & thankful but underneath all runs a distressful murmur which one is not in good form (I always think) if one is not able to come out with.

The new Röntgens made a *great* hit[35] He, poor old dear, had a giddy fit yesterday & could not come but is better today. After concert supper at the Laboucheres (you know); lots of sweet things to eat & after grub made 2 amateurs play Fauré 4tet with me. I was in agony of mirth. **Such** sounds!

I *love* the Dutch. They depress me no longer, for I no longer want to find in them what I know isn't there. They are good & sweet & kind & most amusing. This house is the most difficult spot in Holland, but let us say & think as little about that as poss, for it leads to nothing. I have become a sort of mind scientist with sharing their belief.

But I am thus made, that I can't read of moral heights in others without itching to outdo them. When I think of women & childbirth I feel downright ashamed to object to concerts & when I hear of Mind- & Chr- scientists I long to keep up with their moral pace.

I have no feeling for purity honesty or holiness, but I admire *intensity* & **will** not be left behind by Christians & puritans! That's why I am trying to do my levelest bestest this year We must try to combine all. The body of the English, the self-discipline of the Japs, the sexual wealth of niggers, the broad good heart of the Germans, the spiritual sympatheticness of Scandinavians, the thoroness of the French, the humanity of the old Greeks, the brutality of Romans, the Passionateness of Christians, & the pluckiness of these American mind-cults.

And then a word about my clothes & things: I cant say how they comfort me & bouy me up, all the fine things you choose for me. I feel I go to my battles shielded by an invunerable halo of gentlemanliness, good taste, (your taste) unanfechtbarkeit [German: incontestability; indisputability]. The things you choose, bright & pretty & happy & pukka, seem to me to express all I would wish [to] have expressed about me (this is like little Mrs K at her worst!) & present me in what is for me *the ideal aspect*. Every time I put the things on, "my furs", my browns, or grasp my music case, or recognise my bumbrello by its silver chee-an, the ever present warantee of mother & her good will & her brave support is like the snort of a battlesteed to me, & I feel an army behind me & myself a proper person, loved & bolstered up, & shot forth like a torpedo with expensive care ("your servants") & *bound to hit the mark*.

I wouldnt advise you to arrive before 29, or 30. You must let me know *at earliest* when, as rooms have to be ordered long in advance.

Later

My darling, that's **delicious** that you arrive Friday.

Augustin has already ordered a room for you *Friday evening next* (as you probably come by day boat) & for me *Saturday morn next*.

Of course dont come if the weather is very bad, but otherwise come by dayboat Friday arriving A'dam Friday evening, or by night boat by Flushing or night boat by Hoek. The day boat is only via Flushing.

I arrive Saturday morn late from Middelburg.

From A'dam take a cab (een rijteng pronounced like German "reihtench") to *American Hotel*.

35 The programme of Grainger's Amsterdam recital on 18 December 1911 included the first performance of a new series (the third) of Julius Röntgen's *Oud-Hollandsche Boerenliedjes* [Old Dutch Peasant Songs] Op. 51.

Augustin's telephone number is *Zuid 1372*.

Röntgens want us to dine with them Saturday at 7 o'clock. They are quite near at hand, & leave A'dam the next day.

You must try & come Friday night (weather allowing) if poss as rooms are ordered. Over rejoiced that you come Friday.

425   TO KAREN HOLTEN   American Hotel
[Original: Danish]   Amsterdam.
25.12.1911.

Little Karen.

There are so many things that I forgot to say in my last letter. For example that I am **so very** glad that you are working with Stockmarr, that I would be glad to get her address in Cope, etc. Is it sufficient for you to congratulate your brother very warmly from me, or should I write to him myself?

Will you do something for me? Will you buy H.C. Andersen's Stories (in Danish) in a cheap edition (complete or a part thereof — I don't want it to cost more than 2–3 Kr) and get it sent, with the enclosed card, to

    Miss Kapteijn
    Ossenmarkt
    Groningen   Holland.

You can just get the money from me later, can't you?

Yes, Chopin's B minor sonata is *quite enchanting*, but I think it is too difficult for me to play publicly. I am glad you are working on it.

I have already given 10 concerts here in this country, with almost more than my usual good luck. I earned very well in The Hague the day before yesterday, although not quite as much as the first year, but more than last year. One can't say it's going downhill here yet.

I have felt unusually fresh and un-nervous. The concerts have not been any misery for me, and I have not felt nearly as tired as I would have expected.

I like Holland very much this time. It leaves me cold, but I do not feel anything positively repugnant about the country and the people.

Just think, today I have no concert! But tomorrow it is on again. Augustin's address will find me.

I have gone through a remarkable quantity of different programmes, a Piano-evening programme Sunday, a quite different ditto on Monday, St Saëns Concerto Tuesday, Grieg Concerto Wednesday, etc. But it passed without real suffering. I am too proud for the moment to admit that anything could worry me or even let it worry me, and nothing has occurred recently to break down my courage or principles. I have no whips or curious books with me this time, and I don't intend to buy any, and haven't been naughty often, but was the day before yesterday and yesterday and for that reason I feel miserable today, but now the concerts are coming again and I shall see and stop.

I haven't heard anything from the lady in the Scotch train, although I sent her a photograph she wanted to have.

Why do you think that such things should be different for women than for men? I think that is unfair. I think there should not be the *slightest* difference. "Lechery" without what you call "enthusiasm" can possibly be "out of place", but why shouldn't a woman enjoy being tickled by a stranger if he tickles well? She hasn't got to feel more than just that, I think? Hasn't got to feel more worked up or any deeper feelings at all. One can still kiss and tickle in a comforting and dreamy-making way, and arouse sleepy but happy sensations, which are far different from wild sensuality or deep love. And these milder sensations can very well be connected with certain sexual feelings. It is for example more amusing to be tickled by the opposite than by one's own sex, isn't it? Therefore I can very well understand that the lady enjoyed passing the night in that way, and it seems to me that it was downright *beautiful and good* of her not to have scruples that forbad her to use such feelings as she had. What I don't understand so well is that she didn't have or didn't show *more sensuality*. I don't believe she had really *wild feelings*, and that I always think is so remarkable. But perhaps she just didn't want to show them.

I don't think the world *can* become better before women come to *force* men to *respect* and *satisfy* their (the women's) sensuality just as men now expect of women that they (the women) will satisfy and respect the men's. And therefore I am so full of admiration for every woman who comes out with what she really *wants* and is not afraid to tackle things.

When you are together with me you must always be kind enough to cast everything to the winds and *really* get *done what* **you** *want*. Let me feel that I, as far as my abilities go, really satisfy you bodily in the highest possible degree. Leave no "unchaste" movement unmade that can lead to greater sensual experiences for you. Do not feel I am a man, to whom you owe any modesty whatever, regard me as a kind of well wishing eunuch who is suitable for this or that.

Mother and I read a splendid book of Olive Schreiner: "Woman & Labor" It is excellent.[36]

Mother arrived 3 days ago and we are very well here in a very clean and comfortable Hotel.

A thousand thanks about writing the music. At the moment I don't have anything. I am inexpressibly grateful for the help you gave me at a time when I needed to get a lot copied. But I don't want to use you again for such a tedious and longwinded job which moreover doesn't teach you anything that you could ever have any use for later.

I often lie in bed a long time and think of the coming Svinkløv. If only it can become reality this summer.

36 Olive Emilie Albertina Schreiner (1855–1920), South African novelist and short-story writer. Her *Woman and Labour* was published in 1911.

1912

*The New Year of 1912 found Grainger midway through his Dutch tour. It
was basically a recital tour, though he also performed the Grieg and Saint-
Saëns piano concerti and the Franck Symphonic Variations. Two chamber-
music performances were given. He travelled to Siegen for a concert on 14
January, returning to Germany again for a visit to Frankfurt on 18 February, after completing his Dutch tour. His final performance was the
Grieg Piano Concerto in Heidelberg on 22 January.*

*Rose had returned to London on 4 January. Percy was home on the
24th.*

*Over the next two months he had a heavy travelling schedule. He was
in Belfast for a concert on 16 February, returned to London then left again
on the 18th for two concerts in Holland. He was back in London by 24
February, then left again on the 26th for a joint recital with Gervase Elwes
in Antwerp on the 27th. By 29 February he was back in London. On 3
March he left for a concert in Elberfeld on the 4th, returning the next day.
On 14 March he left for a series of concerts in Switzerland, returning via
Amsterdam where he played the Saint-Saëns concerto with the
Concertgebouw on the 24th. On 25 March he was in London.*

*Between-times — and this was perhaps part of his reason for continually
returning to London — he was busy with rehearsals for the Balfour
Gardiner choral and orchestral concerts, the first of which took place on
13 March and the second on 27 March. There were other performances of
some importance, particularly the first public performance of his* English
Dance, *which Thomas Beecham conducted at the National Sunday League
concert at the Palladium on 18 February.*

*By 28 March, Grainger reported to Karen Holten that the worst was over
of a busy period which had begun in September of 1911. On 29 March
Grainger's father, accompanied by his "niece" Winifred Falconer, arrived
in London on the* Orsova.

426   TO ROSE GRAINGER   Hotel Zeiler
5.1.1912   Baarn

It's so annoying, but none of my crits seem to be good this year. Young
cub Engelbert told me with to-be-looked-for glee the other day in Haarlem
that my last A'dam concert had been unsympatheticly noticed, & today's
Utrecht notice is more critical than admiring, to say the least.

Really this year I consider I've been well received only in London &
Cope, in Norway there was a quite critical note & here also. But I feel

London has never been better. No doubt it's largely a matter of programs. I must see gründlich [German: thoroughly] to programs before appearing abroad again, & stick to *big heavy* pieces; that's what I succeed best in.

Curiously, I often seem to have less success when I'm un-nervous; though I must say, success or not, I'm *frightfully* thankful to be *not nervous* this year. Luckily one cannot make oneself nervous even if one wanted to, so I don't feel any special duty in that line.

Of course, they've found me out, that's what it is — without having *wholly* found me out. And I'm full of will to get back all the cudos I possibly can, by work & cunning, & studying my "customers"; keen to get more out of them all, without feeling in the least hurt or lowerhearted because of their now attitude: Since I've "given up" Europeans they've no more power to wound me deeply, for me they are but fish in the sea, to be fished, corn to be mown. (if one mowes corn?) "But they (the Greeks according to O. Wilde) saw that the sands were to run upon & the sea to swim in": with like optimism must one be-Viking all "the plentiful little mannikins skipping about"

"They are positively not bugs or specks" (or some such?) on the contrary they hold the baglets from which one must, under false artistic pretences, pilfer the gold to eventually throw in their faces. My grown-big hatred of Europeans (my hatred of the coercion they force upon us all) has made it so much easier for me to carry on my trade, makes me able to do my job without any waste of sentiment or needless pain, my really genuine indifference to them all & my thorough lack of ambition in small matters makes it possible for me to lightly love & enjoy all the friendly foolish faces that look kindly at me from audiences & very nearly succeed in forgetting & overlooking all the unpleasant & unkind looking capable & clever faces.

From now on address c/o Augustin, my loved one, my little comrade, my guiding angel, & my solid instinct-lit business adviser.

I can tell you, I haven't lost my publics yet. Cram-jam tonight here, & my fee — 250.

Goodnight my darling.

427 TO ROSE GRAINGER   [PM Amsterdam]
[Postcard. PM 7 January 1912]
Sunday.

Just had my Xylophon lesson. Charming instr; all my passages easy playable. The nice man (Pennoerts[?]) also plays Mandolin Mandola guitar, lute. etc.

He thinks my guitar tunings & ways of playing stunning.

Am so happy.

Yr loving one

428 TO ROSE GRAINGER   Rotterdam Station
[Postcard]
10.1.12.

Now comes my crowded patch; Franck fiddle Sonata, Tartini fiddle Sonata, Fauré 4tet, Siegen, Franck Vars with orchestra, & other changes of Recital program, all with[in] a week.

I very much hope I will get a letter from you in Dord[rech]t thro Augustin, darling.

I'm happy & fit.

429 TO KAREN HOLTEN   Hotel "De Liggende Os"
[Original: Danish]   Utrecht.
18.1.1912.

Little Karentje.

Now nearly everything is accomplished, for the moment. It is such a *wonderful sensation*, after having kept so hard at it as I have since the beginning of September. Now I am travelling to Frankfurt, to make some visits there, which will possibly be useful for next winter, and from there to Heidelberg, where I am playing 22nd Jan. Thence direct to London, thank God, because I have scratched the Berlin concert, because the 27th turns out to be the Kaiser's birthday and thus an impossible date. Next winter then. Just write then to 31a Kings [Road], where I will be staying until the last 10 days of February. How I am looking forward to the time now coming in London, with rehearsals and time for myself.

Yesterday it was a French programme here in this town. C. Franck Symph.[onic] Var[iation]s. with orchestra, and Ravel, Fauré, & Debussy solos. The day before yesterday Fauré's 4tet (No 1) with Sevcik 4tet.[1] That was a happy evening for me; *how* I love that work! It is almost unbelievable to think that the winter's sufferings (which however have not been worth talking about, since I have been so well happy and un-nervous) are nearly over.

In Amsterdam recently I got an hour on Zylophone-playing; (it is what the Germans call "the wooden laughter" ["Das hölzerne gelächter"]) wooden blocks of different sizes which are hammered with two hammers, and for which instrument I have written a part in Strathspey and Reel.

In the train.

When one has a horse that in a given year has won a prize in a race, and on the whole is healthy and beautiful, then one is satisfied with him for that year, and happy. When one plants a tree, then one doesn't look for anything more from the tree than that it thrives and grows splendid, to be content with the tree.

I wonder why people expect more from love than they, with an eye to the nature of the matter, have any likelihood of obtaining?

Our European culture trains man for polygamy and woman for monandry. Our European polygamy costs man as good as nothing, our women's monandry costs them (the women) the loss of their life-happiness, disappointment.

That men are satisfied with the situation is not so surprising, since he wins all the time. But that the European woman upholds a thing that destroys everything for her is beyond my understanding. That idiots are satisfied I do understand, *but why do* **you** *do it?* Are you really not talented enough to comprehend the matter?

I gave you the chance to have my love *plus* polyandry as much as you liked, and I feel you would rather give up *everything* which is not in accordance with our European women's claims rather than accept something which is 10 times richer than these claims. You don't love me as much as bourgeois opinions which you owe to God knows who. You don't have faith in my opinions, you don't take notice of statements or opinions of sharp-thinking men and women of this and other countries. And why should you? I realise that everyone has the right not to worry about anyone else's opinions. But why worry about a whole heap of opinions and prejudices which *can*not be personal feelings but almost *must* be due to inherited *bourgeois stupidity*.

All of us inherit similar rubbish, but when we knock about with superior heads or think for ourselves for a time about the matter, then we take care to get rid of it as quickly as possible.

1 In Amsterdam on 16 January Grainger played the first Fauré Piano Quartet with three members of the Ševčik Quartet from Prague (Bohuslav Lhotský, violin; Karel Moravec, viola; L. Zelenka, cello. The second violin was Karel Procházka).

We have now been in a close mental association with each other for about 5 (?) 6 years and God help me if I can find anything you have learned from me or from the books I have referred you to.

If your own opinions were more revolutionary or more deeply instinctive than mine or the books', I would never offer you such food, but would hasten to learn *from you*.

But I certainly can't say that. I almost believe that your views would more or less agree with nearly every other good-hearted sweet girls' in ½-free lands.

Therefore it almost seems to me that I am *compelled* to regard you not only as mentally uneducated but also mentally *uneducatable*.

What is the use of your sexual bodily freedom (which I deeply admire) if your brain never loosens its bonds? Look how little this blasted love is good for when it comes to the point. I regard 1911 as the happiest and most fortunate year of my life. (up to now) Things that I have longed for for 15 years began in 1911 for the first time to be realised, in other words 1911 is for me a *turning-point* in my life's unbearable boredom.

You know all this, and nevertheless, when you look over the year, you speak of how much has changed in it, without giving the impression of being troubled with any particularly sharp awareness of happy changes.

Good, my life's happiness and my work's progress are unimportant to you. And why not? I have always insisted that selfishness is the only true basis (known to me) for actions and opinions. But where is then the giant-comradeship of great love? Quite ordinary friends reckon a year a fortunate one in which my deepest needs move with satisfaction, but a lover doesn't know any reason for rejoicing. On the contrary, the year seems to her almost sad. I can only think of these things with bitterness, for they are such a world away from everything desirable, from everything one could have hoped for.

One wouldn't expect that love should be so far behind quite ordinary friendship. Friends offer money for the use of art. Karen on the other hand accepts money. It is only nice that she accepts it, but why does it never occur to her to *give me* money? You have lived richer than I. Why are you the beggar and not me? Don't you see in all this the old dirty hated woman-and-man relationship? I do. That you use some few of my pennies for riding I don't speak of, for sport, at any rate, stands lifted high up above all other questions, just like art. But why has it never occurred to you to go out into the world to earn money for my art? You regard me as strangers do; you see my worldly ½-skill and think, he'll get through. You don't seem to see clearly enough, or be sensitive enough, or comrade enough to understand my life's hopelessness and misfortune. You don't seem to feel how sad it is that ½ my life has slipped past with almost nothing achieved, there are no pains for you that I am not nearly liberated yet. And you don't appreciate the courage with which I have struggled to make a weak and childish character into a skilful money-machine. On the contrary, it seems to you only tedious of me. You don't feel my life's sorrow, for you really only consider me as a tool. You don't regret that my gifts of composition go unused, either because you don't believe in them, or because you have that indifference for *creative work* which indeed is absolutely widespread and common everywhere in Germanic countries, but which we Englishmen find so hard to understand.

Just think how it would be if someone like me was married to or lived with someone like you. I who use everything for my art, you who use everything for life or love, or whatever it is called.

That my sufferings are unimportant to you or only opportunities for you to show your motherly-womanly (quite charming as it happens) comforting-gifts, and all my plans and artistic interests tedious and strange, that I don't say a word against. Each for himself I say as well; that I can well understand and appreciate. But that can't be said to be more than an

2 Karen replied, 22 January, ''I find your bitterness quite unfounded. Certainly at the moment that I wrote the remark that I was thinking about what result the year had given, I only thought of your and my personal relationship. But I have *so* often thought of and been glad about your success in various directions. I am really only *half* involved in the whole thing, if I were completely involved, I wonder whether you would then find anyone who could and would be more happy about each single happiness and success of yours, however small.

''I can so easily explain to you my love.

''*You* awoke love itself in me, it grew and grew, became so great and strong, filled me completely, and I gave you the whole of my soul. A year and a half ago, I think it was, I began to suspect that the relationship I wanted to stand in to you was already taken up by another, namely your Mother.

''About the same time, I also think, it became clear to her that she, in reality, despite certain remarks which could point in another direction, did not want any interference in the relationship between her and you.

''On your last visit you told me, in clear words, what the character of the relationship between your Mother and you was.

''Thereby you took the fight out of me.

''My relationship with you has **nothing** to do with middle-class considerations.

''I am sorry that you regard the fact that I do not have any desire or ability to separate eroticism from love, as such an idiotic failing in my character.

''Moreover you are completely wrong in [saying] that you haven't had any influence on me in all these years. You have had to a great extent. Among other things you have taught me, for example, to nourish a great wish to keep my appearance as beautiful as possible.

''If it should happen that a man turned up for whom I felt an attraction, I would not, as I certainly would have previously, regard it as out of the question to have anything to do with him.

extremely negative relationship between ''lovers''. Why don't you come forward with a believable explanation about the nature of your love? For one surely can't go and give oneself up to something for years at a time, without in the end being able to give some sort of explanation or description about it, can you?

Why don't you say ''straight out'' that my art is of no interest to you (I do know that you are interested in music generally, I am not as blind as that) and that my plans and struggles are only like stones in your road, but that my talent, beauty, and goodness are qualities that suit your objects (what are then your objects?) and that you taking all in all have use for me as a very good tool, but without entering into *my* purpose and *my* ideals.

Just say it, why not? What's the use of this everlasting unsatisfying silence? Explain everything you can, and let us see whether there isn't something good to be made out of all this. Because I personally haven't any interest in things which never lead to anything, neither to pleasure, nor experience, nor use, nor art, nor worldly profit. *I* can accurately explain everything I feel for you. I can in a few words say everything I desire from you and everything that I don't want. If you would do the same then we would have a mutual starting point.

What I desire, what I love about you:
> as often as possible;
> to see your beauty, to get to see into your enchanting personal soul, to use your lovely body for experiments, to talk seriously to you, and talk nonsense to you, to impress you and to attract you.

What I don't want:
> any unavoidable expenses at all, any disturbance at all of my life with my mother, no restrictions at all of my sexual life with other women, no belief at all that anything at all necessarily lasts longer than it happens to do of itself.

What I demand, what I expect:
> Nothing.

Will you let me hear properly from you sometime, you little greedy robber girl?[2]

Percy.

430 TO ROSE GRAINGER   On way to Heidelberg.
[Original: Danish]
[Postcard. 20.1.12]
Sat. eve.

I can't stand Fr[ankfurt] any longer. I cannot *understand* that we *could* live there for 6 years, and for you, sweetest little mother, it was 1000 times worse than for me of course.

431 TO KAREN HOLTEN   31A King's Road
[Original: Danish]   Sloane Square
31.1.12.   S W

My sweetest little meat-mate

I have waited so long for a moment when I could answer you properly for your last sweetest letter, but since I am still very busy I won't let time go further without sending you a few small heartfelt kisses and thanking you humbly for all your kindness.

There is truly something *about* you, and you have such a surprising and exceptional talent for expressing yourself in words that one knows *absolutely* accurately just what you want to say.

But the reply will come later.

I will only say that I am in the 7th heaven, quite taken up with composition-rehearsals and without many pupils, and quite without concerts until the 11th (Feb)

Have already tried the new Trio (you know I began in Norway) *excellent*,[3] and on Friday I have 8 string players and on Sunday 5 wind players and on Tuesday choir rehearsal with Royal Albert Hall Choral Society

Everything is going splendidly and I would kiss you from top to toe if I might

Fervent greetings from your happy lover and friend

Percy.

432   TO KAREN HOLTEN London.
[Original: Danish/English phrase]
7.2.12.

Last Friday the rehearsal with the 8 strings went *splendidly*. I am **very** satisfied with the strings (with which the guitars melt excellently together) in Strathspey and Reel, and "Willow willow" which I wrote last spring sounds splendid. The other things went quite satisfactorily.

Last Sunday the rehearsal with 5 wind players also went well, although not quite so nice. I had to alter a lot for the wind players in Strathspey etc.

Last night rehearsal with Fagge's choir.[4] "Irish" and "We have fed our sea" goes properly already, but "Faðir og dóttir" still requires much work.

Next Friday Beecham will presumably go through "English Dance" for the 1st time. One can't rely on the gifted charming little man, but he has 2–3 times said firmly that he will rehearse it on Friday.

Gardiner is, as you can imagine, splendid when he rehearses with the choir, or suchlike. Not at all nervous, *makes jokes* even, and enjoys himself so that ½ could be enough* the whole time. Afterwards he doesn't say "I think it will come to go well" or something like that, but just: "I **have** enjoyed myself this evening".

He is completely just and impartial towards the different composers, and from 1st to last *true* and unselfish (in a good sense) and noble. Englishmen mature late, but it doesn't fail to appear.

There is so much being done at the moment, that I could never finish telling you the ½ of it.

If only you were here and I could "kiss you as much as I wanted."

*A Danish expression, meaning: if something is so good, even half as good would still be excellent. *Transl.*

433   TO KAREN HOLTEN London.
[Original: Danish]
9.2.12. Frid.

Little meat-mate

Beecham is a *genius* and many things in E.D. sound stirring and great. Have never in my life heard a greater noise I believe I really will be able to write for the orchestra in time

"I have also learnt to control depression and that kind of thing pretty well.

"And there are certainly many more things, I don't think at all you should be dissatisfied with the result. That you have been quite unable to learn from me is only sad for *me*.

"Have you heard that Hjalmar Thuren is dead? You will indeed be sad for that. He died last Sunday. I would have written and told you at once, but had no address.

"You will always, my life through, be my really great only love, that I know, even if I am as stupid as you think. Karen."

3 The trio was probably *Handel in the Strand*, then called *Clog Dance*, which Grainger began while on tour in Norway in October 1911. Planned from the beginning to have "all parts double-able", it was performed in the version for piano and massed strings at Grainger's composition concert on 21 May 1912 and published by Schott & Co., London, in May and June of 1912. The change of title was suggested by William Gair Rathbone, to whom the work is dedicated, because he said the music "seemed to reflect both Handel and English musical comedy (the 'Strand' is the home of London musical comedy)". The work incorporates Grainger's variation on the theme of Handel's Air with variations "Harmonious Blacksmith", which piece Grainger played on the Scandinavian tour of September–October 1911. The choir was the London Choral Society (see letter 432 and note 4 below).

4 Arthur Fagge (1864–1943), English organist and conductor. He had founded the London Choral Society in 1903. At its zenith the choir had 400 voices.

The orchestra screamed and laughed and were extremely friendly and excited.

You can imagine it sounds wild enough. More difficult is to find one place that doesn't seem to be *fff* at least.

Beecham will perform it Sunday the 11th.[5] A pity I am in Ireland Friday and will probably not be able to hear any more rehearsals at all.

But he is a hero and so kind and *fine*.

5 Beecham conducted *English Dance* on 18 February. On Sunday 11 February, Grainger played the Franck *Symphonic Variations* under Beecham at the Palladium.

434 TO FREDERICK DELIUS   [London]
18.2.12.

My dear Delius

Beecham did your entr'acte music to "Romeo & J[uliet]" today just before my piece.[6] I never loved anything more in my life.

You are certainly the greatest living genius & one of the greatest & most adorably touching souls that ever lived.

I find that stuff of yours *perfect* in every deepest sense. Beecham did my thing like a *God*. Lots of it is imperfectly scored, but lots comes off well.

Your loving & thankful friend
Percy.

6 The programme of the concert on 18 February had included the entr'acte from Delius's opera *A Village Romeo and Juliet*. Grainger had not seen Delius's work when it was performed at Covent Garden in February 1910. Delius had sent Grainger's *English Dance* to Beecham in June 1911 to see if he would perform it.

435 TO KAREN HOLTEN   American Hotel
[Original: Danish]   Amsterdam.
20.2.1912.

Sweetest

English Dance was *splendidly* performed by Beecham on Sunday. He is a genius and *the sweetest person*.

But the piece does not have any effect.[7]

Nearly everything in it sounds more or less *good* but there are no contrasts and the whole thing is so *thick* that one goes to sleep of simply "porridge".

When I now come home on Saturday I must at once begin to re-write a good deal again. Balfour didn't think that the piece worked, but loves it and will give me 3 rehearsals of an hour each to give me every chance.

Cyril on the other hand thought the piece was *perfect* and shone like a little god of happiness and enthusiasm. Balfour is full of excellent technical advice.

I am so happy to have had the experience and to have Gard's 3 rehearsals and performance in addition, but I am sorry that I must waste time here with these swinish concerts.

Your score showed itself to be practical and satisfactory in every respect

It is a splendid piece of work, little meat-mate.

7 The critic of the *Daily Telegraph* wrote of the *English Dance* on 19 February, "The programme annotator states in his notes that the work 'is an excellent example of the composer's sympathy with the songs of the people.' But it did not strike us in the same light, for Mr Grainger's scoring and his 'polyphony' were in this case so complex that the thematic material was apt to be lost in the undergrowth, as it were", while the *Standard*'s critic observed, "As a clever piece of orchestral colouring Mr Grainger's 'English Dance' has many points of interest, but as 'an example of his sympathy with the songs of the people' the interest is not, perhaps, always so clear. Mr Beecham's reading of it was an extremely good one". Grainger's friend William Gair Rathbone disagreed, writing to Grainger that though the performance was an exciting one, it had not done "anything like justice" to what he described as the "finest orchestral piece going". He thought it was probably the orchestra's fault. Grainger himself wrote to Delius on 15 February: "He [Beecham] would do it *perfectly* if only the orchestral parts were not so badly copied" (by Karen Holten and Isabel Du Cane).

436 TO KAREN HOLTEN   On Board S.S. "Kon. Regentes"
[Original: Danish]
5.3.1912.

Today I am on the home trip from Elberfeld, where I played last night. I have travelled a lot in recent times. 10 days ago I was in Ireland, 12 days ago in Holland (2 cities), 8 days ago in Antwerp, and have been home for choral rehearsals and pupils between each trip.[8]

Fagge's choir is splendid and did my things in the most hopeful possible way at the last rehearsal. Fagge himself conducted the pieces so excellently during the preparation that I, with my usual "tact", have asked him to conduct 3 out of the 5 instead of me at the actual performance. I conduct Irish and "F[aðir] og D[óttir]" You can imagine Morning Song is not to be recognised with a large and good choir, so soft and flowing it sounds, and the climax is tremendous and ecstatic.

On Thursday choir rehearsal, Friday rehearsal of "E. Dance", Saturday the 2 final rehearsals for the 13th.

I broke a window in the train today and cut my hand, but only a little. I will send off the soap as soon as possible.

I am thinking almost quite-too-much about you and Svinkløv in these days. I have quite decided to come in the month of August, if you will have me. Will you, with all warmth and sweetness?[9]

But what a good expression it is in German; "sich ausleben" [to live one's life to the full] That we don't get to do that, we 2, that is the only thing that is wrong, but that is what so few people in Europe do, although that is no reason why we shouldn't.

You said recently something about women not being able to look so lightly on sexual things as men because it is the woman who bears the child. But that is not necessarily right. It is woman's economic dependence on the man that has made it inadvisable for her to behave with her person in a way which would violate [the] man's property-lust. One couldn't expect that a man would pay all expenses to a woman who was "equally nice" to men who didn't pay anything towards her "upkeep". As far as the seriousness of giving birth to a new being is concerned, that does not necessarily make woman less ready to act, less reckless, than all natural instincts are. It is, in my opinion, only a question of money, and man's hard hand and faulty precautionary measures that have made women so "niggardly" with love and so boring and narrow-minded in this matter.

When women all earn their bread just like men, or the state supports all women, or all children, then I believe that women (on the whole) will take their place in the world (free and spontaneous) as they do in Wagner's Operas, and that we will hear less nonsense about "faithfulness" and unselfishness and similar unpleasantness from the women's side.

The child should only make the woman more mature and free and self-contained than the reverse — if only it was not for lack of means! Moreover, we live in the century of the "condom", and it is quite meaningless, in our time, to talk of love and sexuality as if they (accidents excepted) need to have anything to do with child-birth and motherhood.

Unwillingness to grasp present day means in that field can only be put to the account of lack of interest in fleshly things, not anything necessarily bad, I admit, but still a lack not a virtue.

I have nothing against people being unenterprising, but I don't like it being made into a virtue.

I think it is so very easy to see that all these sexual questions are closely connected with *material conditions*, almost exclusively.

Love is a great human thing, but so is inventiveness and curiosity also.

I attack love only when it has an unfortunate influence on people, when it makes them heavy, melancholy, hopeless, ugly, and not disposed to grasp life as a whole and the need of the moment. I love everything, for itself, but everything should be happy and contribute to positive richness and multiplicity and not to negative asceticism or narrowness.

You sweet tempting charming little beloved
goodbye for now

Percy.

8 Grainger's engagements: On Friday 16 February, a joint recital with the singer Madame Kirkby Lunn at Ulster Hall, Belfast; on 21 February, the Saint-Saëns G minor Piano Concerto with the Concertgebouw orchestra under Mengelberg at Den Haag followed by a recital at Park Te Hoorn the next day; on 27 February a private "Invitation Evening" for Everard Feilding with Gervase Elwes in Antwerp; in Elberfeld, a joint recital with the singer Lula Mysz-Gmeiner of Berlin. At the Balfour Gardiner concert on 13 March, Arthur Fagge conducted a group of three of Grainger's settings of Kipling: *Morning Song in the Jungle, Tiger! Tiger!* and *We Have Fed Our Sea.*

9 Karen replied, 8 March, "If I want all 'the warmth and the sweetness' this summer in Svinkløv. That is indeed not easy to know. Certainly, in the bottom of my soul, my love for you lives; but besides [this] you give me only a little percentage of *your* love, and only have use for a small part of the great amount I had waiting for you; who knows how warmth and sweetness can then thrive".

437 TO H. BALFOUR GARDINER

London.
10.3.12.

My dear old Balfour

It was a lovely happy day yesterday, wasn't it, full of rich positive things & negatively enlivened by by the small squibs of the peppery ones.

I dont know what you were about when you wrote me about "Whydah" that it was *not* the sort of work I was longing for that time, for of course it *just is*, as rapecious as can be & quite as boisterous & ausgelassen [German: uninhibited] as I personally need anything, in that small hall, anyway.[10]

I wish you'd bring its full score to Tuesday's rehearsal, there are 1 or 2 suggestions I want to make & questions to put. It comes off absolutely, & the fine *stuff* & texture of it is *humanly* genuinely enriched & greatened in actual performance.

As for you yourself, I feel we know more really about you from seeing you these days in public activity than from years of mere personal friendship frousting. Curious how the cold problems of public activity call forth a man's inner warmth where the glow of friendly meetings chiefly entice his stubborn aloofness. Good job too, I loathe small pattings-on-the-back & joint bolstering-up clubs of small friends. This expensive mettlesome public game is far glossier.

Chorus & band & all of us love you at your public work, & all will get to love you who see you at it:— & "God is love"!

You are really giving us chaps *lovely chances* apart from musical honeymoon days; not the chances a rich man gives poorer, but the chances that only a thoroly pure sweet noble abstract lofty healthy animal can give others of his own ilk.

For the joy & good of all this is the human panorama it unrolls. If I didn't feel your human support behind me, encoraged by your absolute fairness, made momentarily happy (& therefor fit, & artistically digestive) by your friendship alongside me, & bold by the rare knowledge that your gentlemanliness will give you the corage to *force* things thro (where need be) for us chaps, I wouldn't be able to learn deeply from these experiences, & would merely feel bodily seasick & wash my inner hands of the whole bloody show. For I am aristocratic enough to "will have my (human) dues" first, & refuse to profit artistically in wrong human company.

As I said to mum (who has never had so happy a week in her life, she says) last summer, about this scheme: "With old Balfour it won't matter how rottenly the things go, it'll be a human feast all the same." The accident that the things all go toppingly *is* an accident, as far as I'm concerned.

Now, on the other hand, as to your being a bloody fool: I hear you dont propose giving away lots of free tickets.[11]

Let me begin by saying that I **personally** dont care *in the least* whether you give away none or 12 thousand.

But I ask you to lend me an ear re a point (concert managing & giving) in which my judgements have been successful in several countries, just as I (very thankfully by the way) profit by your advice in a province (orchestration) in which I'll never know as much as you can afford to forget.

You are giving these concerts precisely because other conductors & societies dont, & works ditto. The public, therefor, dont know these works, nor such schemes, & can't be expected to feel any interest in them in advance, since advertising conveys no tempting portrait of the actual dish, in such cases.

Your (& consequently our) only hope is that a stray listless outsiderish & thro-free-tickets-*enveigled* public will go away & caution its friends to

10 *News from Whydah*, a setting of the ballad by John Masefield for chorus and orchestra, composed by Balfour Gardiner in October 1911, was given its first performance, Gardiner conducting, at the first Balfour Gardiner concert on 13 March when it shared the evening's honours with Grainger's *Father and Daughter*.

11 That there is some substance in Grainger's advice is suggested by the remarks made by the Russian pianist Alexander Siloti and, coincidentally, reported in the *Daily Telegraph* on 19 March 1912: "He said 'In Leipzig the concert giver must send a free ticket to all his friends or they will not come to his concert. In Berlin, one must add a cab fare to the free ticket if one will not play to empty benches' ". In the event the concert was, so an enthusiastic press reported, an "exhilarating success".

12 Arnold Bax's *Enchanted Summer*, a setting of part of Shelley's *Prometheus Unbound* for two soprano voices, chorus and orchestra, was given its first performance, Balfour Gardiner conducting, at the first Balfour Gardiner concert on 13 March.

13 The critic of the *Daily Telegraph* wrote on 14 March 1912, "But not one of these musicians [Bantock, Elgar and 'no

turn up to the following concerts of this series, & to *next years series*, if there's to be 1.

Those *not* the friends of the free-ticket-enveigled public for Wednesday must be influenced by the *enthusiasm* of the press, which enthusiasm can *only* be born of the influence of the enveigled public upon the press. The press, like all the rest of us, lack Corage, in erste linie [German idiom: as a very first thing]. It takes corage to write coldly of works warmly welcomed by a large audience, just as it takes corage to write warmly of works performed before practically no audience (& therefor seemingly coldly received). Let us, for god's sake, appeal to the 1st cowardice.

If you can get Smith shake his feathers up a bit & send out *so many* free tickets *now at once* that any or some of the last minute *paying audience* are **turned away** you will make lifelong enthusiastic adherents of those turned away paying people *for life*.

This is not a joke, or Graingerism, this is *really life as she lives*.

Be a gentleman, & look the tyranny of comercial life in the face & realize that you can only stoop to conquer, & that you might as well try & do "Enchanted Summer" with an amateur band (why not?) as give the works you are so nobly bringing forward *their fair chance* without *sowing* London with free tickets.[12]

Goodbye, & a thousand thanks, & love & admiration from us both

Yr really loving friend
Percy.

Dont listen to what Smith (E.L.R.) says. "His is to do & die." *Wire Smith if you agree.*

438   TO KAREN HOLTEN   Hotel Univers
[Original: Danish]   Basel
15.3.1912

Dearest little Karen

God, it went well on Wednesday! I could never have thought it would act like that.

It was truly a victory, and "F[aðir] og D[óttir]" had to be repeated, and the papers splendid, and "Daily Telegraph" mad with praise![13]

You can imagine everything was fun and laughter; rehearsal and everything. Just imagine Gardiner at the rehearsals, not a bit nervous, but even and balanced and good-natured bis dorthinaus [*sic* German: to the last degree].

His sweetness, unselfishness and good-nature and depth of feeling move one to tears. The whole of this work has dug up everything that is big and human and tender in him. Cyril just the same; a sea of enthusiasm and fire.

When we meet you must hear by word of mouth some unforgettable funny things that happened during rehearsals, it is unbelievable that so much could happen in so short a time.

Now I am playing Tschaikowsky here 9 times in 6 days[14] and then Amsterdam (24th) St Saëns with Mengelberg and then Tschaikowsky with Gard (27th) and Broadwood Concert (28th) and then I am more or less finished for the moment.

It is wonderful to have success, I can't quite understand it. It is remarkable that I have the same power over the audience (perhaps more?) as conductor as I do as pianist

end of other' choral composers] has as yet come within measurable distance — for sheer beauty of polyphony and sense of climax — of Mr Percy Grainger. Yes — Mr Percy Grainger, the Australian pianist, who has now put all his cards upon the table, as it were, and proved himself to be not only a choral conductor of sheer genius but also a choral composer in a line by himself. His Faeroe Island ballad of the 'Father and Daughter,' for five men's solo voices, double mixed choir, strings, brass, and mandoline and guitar band, was in very truth the most stupendous crescendo from strength to strength that has come within our ken; its effect was literally terrific, and the piece had to be repeated. But this was a mere trifle by comparison with the wondrously beautiful setting for unaccompanied mixed choir, without words, of the glorious Londonderry air. Here Mr Grainger attained in his exquisite harmonisation, in heaven knows how many pure parts, to a height of choral beauty that frankly is unapproached by his contemporaries. Further, the splendid vigour and 'manliness' and freedom from ad captandum effects and sentimentality in his three Kipling settings, his sense of beauty in sound and of dignity, make it all the more remarkable that for so long he should have been content to allow the public to regard him as a pianist only. We are quite convinced, after last night's experience, that Mr Grainger will yet prove himself as great a composer and conductor as pianist, for that which he does in whatsoever the musical line is stamped with the true hall-mark of genius, and we have no hesitation in saying so". Following the performance Grainger received two messages: from John Singer Sargent, asking that *Father and Daughter* be dedicated to him (which it is), and from Roger Quilter, offering to pay all expenses for its publication.

14 Grainger's Swiss exploits were spectacular enough to warrant a mention in the *Daily Telegraph* of 26 March 1912. The nine performances included three rehearsals and six concerts.

On the 25th March "I'm 17" will be performed in London. I can just manage to hear it.[15]

You are absolutely right, little friend, that I can't expect "the whole warmth" and so on. I have no right to it. But would appreciate it all the same

You can imagine I am tired. Travelled here last night; and practised 5 hours today. I like Switzerland greatly.

If only Thuren was alive to hear what a success his songs had had![16] Can you give me his father's full name and address?

439   TO ROSE GRAINGER   Basel
[Postcard]
15.3.12.

I'm delighted with this place & people. It's such lovely dazzling sunny summer weather & the folk are so pleasant, tall, & fine looking & walk well, like Johanna.[17] They often recall Norwegians & look good & noble, tho' coarser & more material than Norwegians.

I feel happy here, & nearly all the living-pictures advertised are Danish.

Lovingly
Perks

440   TO ROSE GRAINGER   Hotel Univers
17.3.1912   Basel

My darling

Thanks for the letter to here.

I was well prepared, played well, & had great success yesterday. Delius' friend Suter, the conducter, is nice & enthusiastic, & a good conductor, without, perhaps, being what some folk consider me to be: "a conductor of sheer genius"!![18]

All the "bestyrelse" [Danish: management, committee, directors] seem nice & all the folk I meet here, anyway. Even the horses look free & openhearted, its curious the effect that polotics have upon horses; so much more than upon dogs, for instance. (of course, dogs are much more rarely used for money earning.)

It would be very nice if you'd send program & crits of March 13 to Mrs Grieg

· p. adr: Wilhelm Hansen's Musikforlag
Gothersgade 11. København.

soon. I've writ her from here & sent program of all Gard's concert[s], but not special one of 13.

I'm full of plans for my setting of "Lord Melbourne" for Men's chorus, baritone solo, brass, oboe solo & organ, which I began in Dunedin & hope to score very shortly. It would be a heroic & useful number.

Österreich joins me tomorrow in Victoria Hotel Zürich[19]

A friend of Herman (Sandby)'s from Frankfurt plays in the 1st fiddles & the 1st viola is a Dutchman, who thought *I* was Dutch & after a few moments conversation said. "But you must have lived long abroad, for you have quite a foreign accent"!

Goodbye adored mum.

---

15 Grainger's folksong setting *I'm Seventeen Come Sunday* was performed by the Edward Mason Choir, a choir specialising in the performance of new works by young British composers, at Queen's Hall on 25 March. The brass band accompaniment, arranged for orchestral brass by Cecil Forsyth, was played by the brass of the New Symphony Orchestra (see letter 443).

16 Hjalmar Thuren had died on 13 January 1912 at the age of thirty-eight.

17 Johanna Pressel, the Graingers' "lovely, athletic-limbed, robust Swiss maid".

18 On 16 and 17 March Grainger performed the Tchaikovsky B♭ minor Piano Concerto for the Allgemeine Musikgesellschaft Basel, under its conductor Hermann Suter. See also letter 347 and note 42, 1910. For "a conductor of sheer genius" see note 13 above.

19 Alfred von Österreich, a Russian born in Finland whom the Graingers had met on board the S.S. *Seidlitz* returning from Australia in 1909. He was, so Grainger told Karen on 22 June 1909, "nice" and "interesting".

441   TO ROSE GRAINGER

[PM Zürich]

[Original: Danish]
[Postcard]
18.3.12.

Andreae, the conductor here, is *excellent*.[20] He is really *1st class*. I have already some engagements here for next year. Andreae was *tremendously impressed* with me today in rehearsal.
Thanks for the letters here
I am *very well*

442   TO NINA GRIEG

London.

[Original: Danish/few words English]
[Postcard]
25.3.12

My dear Mrs Grieg

I will play the Grieg Concerto many places in Switzerland next winter and here in London the 23rd April (1912).[21] It was lovely in A'dam yesterday.
Very much love from your very fond friend

Percy.

For Grainger the spring and summer of 1912 were dominated by his composition exploits. The British Australasian *of 9 May 1912 noted this significant step forward in his career:*

> *The fact that Mr Percy Grainger, the Australian pianist, is a composer as well as an artist, had been known by his musical friends for some years, but until quite lately he has refused to let his works be performed. Now, however, they have been given to the public, and have aroused keen interest . . . The result of a performance of some of his works at the recent Balfour Gardiner concerts at the Queens Hall, was an extremely favourable crop of criticisms in the London papers . . .*

The Balfour Gardiner concerts had, however, also brought Grainger before the public as a conductor. His success in both roles was instantaneous. Rose's letters chart the response to his appearance in both roles at the Balfour Gardiner concert on 13 March. On 15 March she wrote, "It is quite extraordinary the way you have impressed everyone by yr conducting . . . Mrs Hunter telephoned this morning full of admiration for yr compositions & yr conducting". On 20 March, as the congratulatory messages continued to pour in, she concluded, "This compo come out is yr most instantaneous success so far in London". By 21 March she had collected "40 splendid critiques" and observed, ". . . these choruses of yours have been a real *success".*
Performances of Grainger's compositions continued throughout the spring and summer: Mock Morris *at the Balfour Gardiner concert of 17 April,* English Dance *at the Balfour Gardiner concert of 1 May, the orchestral version of* Green Bushes *at Aachen on 10 May,* Mock Morris *and* Molly on the Shore *in Birmingham on 19 June. Grainger also began to get "at home" engagements for his compositions. This year, his annual piano*

20 Volkmar Andreae (1879–1962), Swiss conductor and composer. From 1906 to 1949 he was the conductor of the Tonhalle Orchestra, Zurich. After the performance on 18 March, Grainger wrote to Rose, "I dont think I've *ever* had a more stupendous success than here (the most important Swiss town) last night". The concert was repeated on 19 March. In his autobiographical *Anecdotes* (1953) Grainger tells of this meeting with Andreae, "The first time I knew that Busoni had become viciously hostile to me was when I played with Volkmar Andrée [*sic*] (a composer as well as a conductor, & a delightful man) in Zürich, about 1911–1912. I had rehearsed the Grieg [*sic*] Concerto with Andrée & his orchestra & we were lunching together. I thought Andrée looked at me queerly. At last he said 'May I ask you something very personal? What can Busoni have meant when he said to me: "Sie machen sich lächerlich wenn Sie den Grainger engagieren. Er ist nur ein Charlatan". Denn Sie sind ja kein Charlatan [German: "You will make a laughing stock of yourself if you engage Grainger. He is nothing but a charlatan". But you are no charlatan.]'. I said, 'I suppose he meant just what he said' ". On 21 March Percy sent Rose a postcard with a photograph of Busoni on it, commenting, "That old Rascal Busoni's got a lovely romantic face on him, hasn't he?", a remark which perhaps echoes the anecdote, though without any particular reference to it and without its bitterness.

21 Grainger played the Grieg Piano Concerto once only in Switzerland in 1913, at his only Swiss concert, in Berne on 11 March. On 23 April 1912 he played it in Queen's Hall, London, with the Strolling Players Amateur Orchestral Society conducted by Joseph Ivimey.

recital in Aeolian Hall was replaced by a composition *concert on 21 May. This concert had been planned since November 1909. It represented, as the* Daily Telegraph *noted on 21 May, his "most important bid hitherto to be recognised as a composer". New publications continued to appear.*

Inevitably, however, he began to worry that one activity was affecting the other: that his prolonged absences from the London scene placed him in danger of being "forgotten", that his compositional activities had hindered him from writing the letters necessary to ensure the success of the following winter. By mid-June he was writing to Karen of his resolve not to continue with composing and conducting as public activities, "for the thing now is to get back to the horrible pianistic path again". These anxieties notwithstanding, it was a time of real artistic fulfilment for him as a composer; he enjoyed his success and the burgeoning plans for the future and relished the pleasure of being "a composer among composers".

---

443   TO KAREN HOLTEN   31A King's Road
[Original: Danish]   Sloane Square
10.4.12   SW

22 The effect of which, as the *Daily Telegraph* reported on 19 April 1912, "was immediate, and in a sense violent, for the audience cheered again and again until the composer, who conducted, was compelled to return and repeat his work". An image of Grainger the conductor is provided by Douglas Donaldson, writing in the *Musical Standard* of 8 June 1912: ". . . his exaggerated pantomime in conducting perfectly simple and straightforward little things may be regarded as a mild functional peculiarity of no great significance". The new pupil was Dagny Sørensen (later Mrs Dagny Petersen, d. 1982). She remained a lifelong friend.

I have been ½ sick for some few days but am now nearly well again. It was nothing other than sea-sick feeling in my stomach or such-like.

On Wednesday 17th (a week today) *I* (not Balfour) am conducting Mock Morris.[22] I am looking forward to it **terribly**. There's nothing to conducting. Either one does it badly or well, the effect is about the same (if it *isn't* a difficult piece like "E.D.") and it's really only a question of appearance and "personality" — in other words, something for me.

The 17th May I will *perhaps* conduct Green Bushes in Aachen.

For over a week I have worked about 7–10 hours a day on E.D. score and parts But now I am soon finished, with the alterations, in any case. Now there are only small corrections in the parts to come. Your poor E.D. score certainly doesn't look so beautiful and clean any more. It is repaired and pasted and inked-in everywhere. But I think the sound will be correspondingly better.

"I'm 17" had great success at Mason's concert. Had to be repeated etc, and was extremely emphasised and praised in the papers. Remarkable. If only I could keep on making *just* pieces that were so successful I would soon be secure as a composer. But that is something one cannot guess so surely with the pieces, I think. E.D. for example certainly won't be successful. But amuses me, all the same.

I have a very sweet pupil from Norway, ½ Danish ½ Norwegian, a Miss Sørensen. She is so pretty and good and fresh, she reminds me often of you.

Friday. The dentist has fixed something in my teeth that has to stay till next Thursday and it hurts. It is really annoying.

My composition concert is *almost* impossible to get fixed. Imagine having to fix up rehearsals for 20 people who are not used to coming together (as a 4tet or orchestra) and can't come at the same time of day, and everything.

But now the sun is coming again.

Shan't we exchange photographs, or don't you want to? I will in any case send some soon. Now I have almost finished with E.D.

Now comes the *most busy* time, for there are 2 pieces for 21 May that I have not written down yet Greetings to all at home

444 TO KAREN HOLTEN   London
[Original: Danish]
Saturday. 27.4.12.

Yes I certainly am a *very* lucky person, in nearly all respects, I concede that completely. But it is not at all true, that I now "have you where I want you", although I am very grateful that I am so fortunate as to have you (even where you are now) "without inconveniences".

Do you know, little Karen, that people like you and me one cannot see too much of, not think too long and too often about, nor grow too close together with. One would never become tired of our sort, and we would never become bored with each other. On the contrary, it is when people like us are separated that one runs the risk of becoming tired of each other. We are both fine and eager and have "much in" us, so presence and living-together can never disappoint.

I am not a complete idiot either. Therefore it would never occur to me to like a relationship between us that caused me to have you "not too close to myself".

The closer the better.

Therefore I will always regard those times (in the past) as quite the best (for us) when I *thought*, wrote, saw *most* of you, and experienced most with you.

For example a time (2–3 years ago) was ideal when I wrote small little scraps (of letters) to you between pupils, and looked at nude photos not a few times a day. You took up the whole of my mind almost without interruption and to a very great degree in a time like that. Such circumstances, such concentration cannot be other than the best conditions, between us.

Before the years when I was so strongly taken up with you I had never really known anything of that kind of splendid passion and love, and it was wonderful for me, a deep and lovely and rich experience. In that time I didn't experience *so* much in other directions either, which was also fortunate. I am extremely happy that we *had time* for our experiences.

Now I experience something else. Just as before our love-time I went and longed and hungered for passion and love, so during our love-time I went and hungered for composition experiences. These last have now fortunately been granted me with a similar completeness and wholeness and beauty as our love experiences were granted to me. You know how one must "dedicate oneself" entirely to something if one is to enjoy it to any degree. *Sufficient* time for anything, I have never had.

Our love experiences were often hurried, and my composition exploits are now also all only ½ done because of lack of time.

But I have been (in myself) "ganz dabei" [German: "quite with it"] both with you in love that time, and now as artist in my things.

And even lack of time doesn't matter so much. I have really been (up to now) a heavenly lucky lover and ditto composer.

But I have not got you where and how I would most want. On the contrary our relationship causes me many unhappy thoughts, for there is at the moment much that is "lukewarm" about our relationship and that cannot be other than hateful to us both, can it?

I would most like to have everything at once: Be a good and passionately devoted son to my mother, a complete and strongly involved artist, and a good and passionate friend-lover to you, and use all my best qualities and longings at one time.

But my abilities don't seem to be able to suffice. I am unfortunately compelled to give up a for b, b for c, c for a, etc. I don't see any way out.

But I could never be content about such a situation, and that I don't "have you close to my heart" at the moment would fill me with dread, if I had time for it. That people like us 2, that have loved each other as we have done and I hope *always will*, can be alive and compelled to *waste time* for each other as we do now, that is completely "atrocious" It is to squander the best things in life.

You can gladly think what you like of me, think that I am cold and stupid, and wrong, and ungrateful in *my actions* but you *must* not forget that no one can *think* and *remember* better than me. In my disposition I am very mature and grateful and just and warm, and I know how much I value what we mean to each other and with what longing I look forward to our coming happiness, if that is permitted to us.

I am *dreadfully* busy with E.D. parts. Working the whole day on it, day after day. When you get this (10–1 o'cl) on Monday I will have my last but one rehearsal. The last is Wednesday morning. I am looking forward to it indescribably.

Many tender kisses, sweetest meat-mate, from your happy and fortunate

Percy.

445 TO H. BALFOUR GARDINER   31A King's Road
2.5.12.   Sloane Square
                                                SW

Dear good old Balfour.

I want to thank you, with a real happiness, for all your motherly-kind & dangerously-socialistic goodness about my "English Dance".

Your unwordly moral support, & orchestrational hints for that work turned it from a rather boring failure into a deeply instructive almost respectable ¼-success. What I learnt & what I enjoyed by that piece was fat & I accept the whole boiling of it as a delightful gift from you, nobly & articly given, (without taint of generosity or much friendship) a free gift nowise called for by the "exergencies" of your concert scheme (which the work in *nowise* helped & certainly hampered; otherwise than my former practical & possibly useful groups) & to be laid at the door of only some not-needed-to-be-explained queer niceness & loftiness in you. I want you to know that your orchestration hints were one of the jolliest plums in an all-through sumptuous pie: I lapped up those knowledges with a sharp relish, there is nothing I like better than giving or taking a good lesson in something; & I should go to cremation at this moment knowing more through you in several ways than I would without.

As soon as hopes thoughts feelings take on form they take on sadness also, of course. So also your "1st Series, 1912" has its sadness for me. The successes, ½-failures, & ¼-successes that now people our consciousness of the various works instead of the vague affections approvals enthusiasms repulsions that colored all our views before the 1st note was sounded are a poor go-instead for these latter.

Then for instance, you, a successful composer, have, in a bundle of weeks, made me a ditto, or a probable ditto. Something to be happy of on your side if you like me & think me worthy; & yet the very successfulness that you yourself evidently smelt ahead & were cute & fine enough to make for me may one day, we can't know, soon or late, be a fog & a nuisance between us, clouding the old real good issue. The hope of success & the chance of it makes a thing a career for one, & in so far as you I or anyone gets drawn into a career so far is one banished from most of the maudlin human inspired· artistic gaiety of attitude that formed our past stock-in-untrade. As the rehearsals near the concert day we each & all get horrider, (given — like you & me — we've got guts enough to feel, do, & realize anything whatsomeever) more capable, higher strung, more momentary &

23 To the published score of his *Hill-Song No. 2* Grainger has added the dedication "for my great-hearted friend 'merkismaður' H. Balfour Gardiner".

24 On 21 April Karen had dislocated her ankle and broken two bones, necessitating an operation on 9 May. Her convalescence was protracted. It was while receiving treatment for her ankle at the clinic that she met her future husband. Karen asked Percy for 300 Kr. towards the cost of the operation; after some delay he sent it.

25 The *Morning Post* of 2 May 1912, for example, commented, "An 'English Dance' by Mr Percy Grainger, inspired by the thought: 'What a dance this England of ours is dancing to-day to be sure!' [failed by the lack of a thematic basis to throw light upon its text, but] gave further proof of Mr Grainger's resourcefulness in musical elaboration". When the critique was edited for publication in one of the regular pamphlets of press opinions, the passage in square brackets was omitted. The *Daily Telegraph*, having written of the piece in detail after the Beecham performance in

less immortal at every turn. Therefor the sweetness of the early amateurish rehearsals *could* not grow & the future may see them even dwindle, & why not?

But as for me, what I have loved & am thankful for is to have been witness & companion to all this swelling-out of heart within you that has driven you to these broad & worthy-of-you undertakings. I hope neither of us will forget the real genuine jollity of these times, nor forget each others inclusion in that jollity, not whether the future joins us nearer in jobs or whether it sunders us over jobs.

I want to dedicate some really decent work to you if you care for one.[23] Not in any way in connection with these concerts, though maybe in memory of the fun of them; but really only because I've always wanted to & never have, have forgot to ask you.

Till tomorrow at 6.30

fondly
Perks

446   TO KAREN HOLTEN   [London]
[Original: Danish]
Saturday. 4.5.12.

Sweetest. How awful for you.[24] It must have been a horrible business for you. I can scarcely think of anything that can hurt more than something with the ankles. I am so sorry for you. Does the doctor think it will leave any stiffness behind? For God's sake don't walk too soon on it, you know that doctors are never careful enough, and so often let people get up too soon in these cases.

Have they done anything with the broken tarsus bones, had they to be "set" or was that not necessary? It must be unpleasant to have massage after something like that.

Be very careful, little sweet Karen.

My "E.D." was **splendidly** played by the orchestra on Wednesday. I didn't hear *any mistakes*, I conducted by heart, and didn't forget a single "einsatz" [German: cue] as far as I know; on the contrary I was no doubt too vigorous, whereby the high points may have suffered, as "theatre" at any rate. I wasn't more than pleasantly nervous, although I think the piece is one of the most difficult there are for the conductor.

The piece was not really well received, which could never be expected either, at the end of a long programme, but it wasn't any fiasco either.[25] Many individuals, who were disappointed with Beecham's performance are now satisfied with the new orchestration, but most of them were indifferent. As far as my "career" is concerned, the piece has neither damaged it, nor been of value to it, but as experience it has been indescribably profitable. On the whole I am very happy and grateful about the outcome.

Cyril's 2 pieces went splendidly. He conducted one himself, quite splendidly, and madly amusing to look at, the dear little chap.

The human pleasures and experiences that Gardiner's concerts brought with them have truly been a rich feast.[26] I look forward to telling you by word of mouth about many things if you would like to hear about them in Svinklóv.

Tomorrow I must write about 18 pages of score — my "Robin is to the G-w. gone" which only exist in sketches, and must be written out (the parts) before the rehearsal on 13th May (2nd and last rehearsal is 19th May) On Friday I have rehearsal in Aachen (Tschaikowsky, soli, and conduct "G.B") Concert on Saturday.

February, did no more than note that it had been played. The *Musical Times* of 1 June 1912 described it as "a surprising example of fluent, striking music almost devoid of thematic interest". The programme had also included an *English Dance No. 1* by Cyril Scott, which he conducted himself, and his ballad for baritone and orchestra *Helen of Kirkconnel*.

26 The whole series of the Balfour Gardiner concerts had elicited feelings of warm enthusiasm and approbation, shared by and reflected in the press, and particularly in the *Daily Telegraph* which wrote, on 19 April, "No concerts in recent years have been one-half so enjoyable, or so valuable as showing the real trend of the best of our younger composers towards the light"; on 27 April: "Since Arthur Nikisch conducted Tschaikowsky's Fifth Symphony for the first time in England, some seventeen years ago, I have never witnessed such enthusiasm in a London concert-room as greeted Mr Balfour Gardiner after the performance of 'News from Whydah', or Mr Percy Grainger after his conducting of various compositions, and Dr Vaughan Williams after his 'Norfolk Rhapsodies'. Why this enthusiasm? It cannot be purely personal, for not one of these musicians is wont to appear as composer or conductor (or both) in London. There is no room for doubt, it seems to me, that it was called up by the fact that at last a British public had heard the kind of British music that it long sought, music that was not half folk-song and half German or French-workmanship" (Robin Legge); and on 2 May: "They are superb concerts . . . They have not been equalled in the past generation, either for the ability exhibited or for the genuine and spontaneous enthusiasm they have called forth". Gardiner's decision to give a second series in 1913 must surely have been influenced by the *Daily Telegraph*'s urgings that he should do so. On 20 July, the *Daily Telegraph* described them as "the cheeriest British concerts in an experience of thirty years".

Don't know how I will manage to learn the score by heart by that time. Can you read much in bed?

I should be in Copenhagen now. Never is being together sweeter, it seems to me, than when one of the two is lying in bed, less rather than more ill.

How does a pain like that feel? — similar to a toothache, or worse? Write soon.

It would amuse you to hear my piano playing in these days. My arms are just paralysed by the unusual violent movements. *When* I conduct I don't feel anything, but the piano playing muscles are still strongly affected. But it will disappear with time of course.

Best recovery and many tender thoughts
from your loving

Percy.

447   TO ROSE GRAINGER   [PM Aachen]
[Postcard]
9.5.12.

My darling.

I think one may call "G.B" quite satisfactory on the whole.[27] Nothing sounds really bad as it is & when a few small bits have been touched up I think it will be quite worth printing.

I'm feeling quite fit & nice. The band is very jolly & most agreeable, & their horns suit my stuff much better than ours. Augustin has come to hear it.

448   TO KAREN HOLTEN   [London]
[Original: Danish]
23.5.12.

Sweet meat-mate

The concert was a sensational success. Everything went well, but, strangely, I personally did not enjoy it much, except perhaps "Strathspey and R[eel]" The Hall was packed full, but expenses were also enormous, unfortunately. I will send the programme and 3 new printed things as soon as possible.[28]

Let me have a card about how you are.

I am very satisfied with the new blue which I got from a Norwegian book, and the paper of the cover is much better.

In great haste

your
Percy.

449   TO ERNEST THESIGER   31A King's Road
23.5.12.   Sloane Square
                                                              S W

Dearest Ernest.

You are a darling to like the concert so & write me such a lovely behappy-

27 The first version of Grainger's *Green Bushes*, for full orchestra, was given its first performance at the Philharmonic Concert at the Kurhaus an der Comphausbadstrasse, Bad Aachen, Grainger conducting, on 10 May 1912. Grainger played the Tchaikovsky B♭ minor Piano Concerto on the same programme, Fritz Dietrich conducting.

28 The "three new printed things" were *Died for Love, Willow, Willow* and *Clog Dance*, all of which were performed in the concert on 21 May.

ing letter. It would have been *too horrid* if you had not been there. In great joy at your sweet dear letter & very proud of your praise & sympathy

Yrs fondly
Perks

I enclose "Died for love". "Handel in the Strand" will be out soon.

450   TO KAREN HOLTEN   London.
[Original: Danish/some English]
1.6.12.

My little darling.

Now I am breathing a little more freely again.

Yesterday I had a rehearsal with Langley's string quartet for an "at home" on the 6th. I have worked up "My Robin is to the greenwood gone" for 2 strings and piano and Willow for ordinary quartet instead of for violin, viola, and 2 celli. It has taken a lot of time, but it was necessary, because it is not impossible that I, in the course of time, will get more engagements like this for my compositions, and then it is necessary to have more things for the same combination.

The critiques about the 21st have been of 2 kinds.

There has been one lot which have established the great external success of the evening, but have laid stress on the laughable side of my titles, and my whole method, and thus have taken an only ½ serious attitude to the matter. (which is my own fault.) But then there have been others who have found the serious behind the outwardly laughable, and treated the matter as a big event. In both cases the papers have given up their usual method of sliding over everything without really saying anything definite.

Almost the whole press has spoken *properly*, many very favourably, one *splendidly* clever (truly a critique of genius) and many frightfully amusing and witty. The public was enthusiastic, one could never say anything else, and I must have received nearly 100 lovely letters from all possible composers and innumerable "unexpected" personalities.

Nothing in my English career has up to now made me so well-known and so praised and talked of **on all sides** *as my compositions in the last 3 months*. That is clear.

But all the same I have made many mistakes.

"E.D." was a waste of time, it effected nothing for my outward career, and in my compositions concert there were too many "lively" energetic pieces, like "Shepherd's Hey" "Strathspey" "Molly" "Mock Morris" and too few serious ones, although there were several.

I stand at the moment at a turning point. Up to about 1904 I wrote almost exclusively serious, feeling-full, but unpractical things. Then I woke up, that time, and said to myself: "Now I will, for a number of years, see and write *only practical things*. The eye shall be turned to *tone* and *orchestration problems* above all, even if the actual content becomes thinner and more low-water-like".

This also happened, and the result is that I have really been able to learn something of "tone-problems" and to complete a whole pile of pieces which can only be said to be completely practical. On the other hand my "artistic ego" has starved somewhat during these undertakings.

And in the last few days, after experiences (both my personal ones and observations of the impressions of others) at my concert, it has become clear to me that the last 8 years have been a kind of "apprenticeship" in which the deeper voices have been as good as silent, that these 8 years have profited me considerably, but that this period now or soon should be over.

Now there must soon come something substantial again, something deeper and greater. I am indeed in part a "clown"-nature, but only in part. I have nothing against my clownery, but now it can almost be enough of it, for the moment.

It has been a very deep satisfaction to me to have had such a distinct success with my things. To know that one has the power to *get people's ears*, at a pinch. The success itself; to stand there and see people enthusiastic, has a slightly depressing effect on me, I don't know why. I hate everything to do with "public life" in whatever form, and I have more pleasure in correcting orchestral parts at home, than in conducting the same piece under the most favourable conditions.

But to know that *one's music touches people and means something for other people than oneself and one's circle of friends and lover*; that is something which makes me happy and calm and grateful in the highest possible degree.

Sir Henry Wood wants to perform Green Bushes at a Symphony Concert the 19th Oct in London; under my direction. That is a *very great honour*. It is not usual for new English works to be given at Symphony Concerts. Therefore I am scratching G.B. in Birmingham (so Wood can get 1st English performance) and will conduct "Molly" instead.[29]

Now I am very behind with piano practise, and since I cannot expect to get much time this summer to prepare compositions for next winter I almost think I will have to withdraw from Gardiner's concerts in 1912–13, and I don't propose to give another composition concert so soon again either. My "coming out with my compositions" is on account of mother so often saying "I am afraid I will die before I hear anything or get to know sometime whether the works are practical or not." Now I have shown that the works are practical and extremely successful, and that's enough, it seems to me.

Next time I appear with new compositions there had better be some really serious and personal (as for example "The Brides Tragedy") things among them and therefore it mustn't be too hurried.

Now I am going to print the score of "My Robin" "Willow" (?Walking Tune?) and perhaps "Green Bushes" after Wood's performance in Oct, and perhaps the score of Faðir og dóttir. In this way a large part of the things already performed will get their chance, and then one can see how they work out in the direction of sales.

The need I feel for expression of deeper feelings applies as well in other directions than composing. There can be years in which I seem to go round with only a ghost of myself:— and on account of money-shortage I will have to go on like this for many years yet.

But I can't say anything except that at the moment I definitely feel the *urge* for more.

I do wish we were together in Svinklóv now, and that I could touch all your body with kisses and caresses, and that your soul could express itself, and mine as well, in many different spheres, and that we could feel ourselves rejuvenated and deepened in that moving nature and in each other's rapturous company. I *remember* you well and often think of what I remember, but I need *new life*, and my memory new tasks.

We have consumed ourselves in these silent empty years. Such times as we have gone through are heavy and disgraceful; I would wish that the necessity for such things never had to exist. To really *waste time* (in the deepest sense), what can be a worse crime?

Whether there will be (in August, or later?) a better period for us I do not know, (this time it depends on *you*) but that I *long* truly for it, is so true.[30]

Be very careful now. Dont **walk** at all not even *as soon* as the *Doctor allows*

Doctor[s] are always *too soon* with things.

29 Grainger conducted his *Mock Morris* and *Molly on the Shore*, both in the versions for "string band", at the Theatre Royal, Birmingham, as part of the Eighth Annual Promenade Concert Season on 19 June 1912. The latter was the first performance in England of this version. At the same concert he played the Saint-Saëns G minor Piano Concerto, Landon Ronald conducting.

30 She replied, 5 June 1912, "How I love you Percy, how it is a sorrow to me, oh, so great and deep, that I am not allowed to give you all my strong love. Sometimes I feel a rankling grief not being able to live completely, I think I will grow to nothing at the end by living life like this. If possible I dismiss it all, but it exists in the bottom of my heart. It is terrible to feel that the part of myself which is most capable, is being neglected . . .", adding, on 31 July, "And you believe we will be even happier than before. I wonder if one can harvest without having sown?"

451 TO NINA GRIEG
4.7.12.

31A King's Road
Sloane Square
London. S.W.

My dear friend.

It has been a tremendous time since I last wrote. Apart from the 4 Balfour Gardiner concerts I have conducted things of mine in Aachen & Birmingham, & am going to conduct my "Green Bushes" (the piece I brought to Grieg to Troldhaugen, do you remember?) at the 1st Symphony concert of the Queen's Hall orchestra on Oct. 19. 1912. This is a very great honor, as they very seldom do English works at these important concerts. On May 21 (last) was my Composition concert in which mother & I played guitars, Roger Quilter the Xylophone, & Balfour Gardiner conducted 1 piece.

The concert was a *terrific* success. The hall was *crammed full*, & I have never imagined a chambermusic audience could be so wild & jolly. Schotts are publishing the critiques which I will send you later on. In the mean time I send critiques of the Balf. Gardiner concerts, of Mason's choir concert, & of Aachen. I have had several "at homes" with my things & have several more to come so altogether it has been a colosally busy summer, with hardly time to breathe.

Gardiner is going to give 4 more choral & orchestral concerts next year, & wants to do things of mine again, but I fear I cannot manage this. I have been spending a lot of time over my compositions of late & feel it is now time to come off the compositions & *concentrate again on the piano only*, for a year.

I do not wish to give up anything, only to add one thing to another.

Last night I practically fixed to play the Grieg concerto at the Birmingham Philharmonic in Feb. 1913. My Berlin concert is fixed for Oct 7, & Hamborg for Oct 11. (1912)

I wish you could have heard the 3rd of Gardiner's concerts (see program of April 17) in which the 2 adorable Grieg Psalms (op 74) were *beautifully* sung by *The Oriana Madrigal Society*.

Kennedy Scott (their conductor) is a religious enthusiastic nobleminded musician who takes *infinite* trouble over things, who *loved* and understood the Psalms & did the very best he could with them.[31]

I have shown Gardiner the score of the Grieg Folksongs for baritone & men's chorus, as I so long to hear a *really good* London performance of them.

How indescribably moving & wondrous is the part in "My Jesus sets me free" in the middle where the tune is in major (dur) & the accompaniment in minor (moll)? That is Grieg indeed.

I feel glad that all the fuss of my compositions is over. I am ever so thankful for the success of my things & the support & enthusiasm of my friends & of the public. But I am not really fond of the *public side* of performance of compositions. The nice part of compositions is the making of them *in quiet*. When that is done the best part of the feast is over, I feel.

In a way I am almost happiest over having such an unexpected success as a conductor. I do not conduct at all well yet, but I seem to have the power to make the players & the audience *friendly* & that is a great. [*sic*] That means that I may have a chance later on of being able to get some really good performances of the few works that lie nearest to my heart, & of perhaps being able to popularize them to some extent, such as: The Grieg Folksongs above mentioned, & particularly those beloved *Symfoniske Danse* which are far too seldom heard, & several Bach things, etc.

When shall we meet? I suppose there is no chance of your being in Berlin when I am there? It would be *glorious* if you were!

31 Charles Kennedy Scott (1876–1965), English choral conductor. He had founded the Oriana Madrigal Society, a choir of about sixty voices, in 1904.

I *may* come & give a Recital in København in October, or later, but I dont know yet. November I shall be in Holland. It is sad not to be coming to Norway this fall. That is always the sweetest & tenderest part of the year, & we both miss being able to look forward to it very much indeed. How is Troldhaugen?

The night before last I had 2 "at homes" first at Mr Rathbones where I played 4 Slåtter & Folkeviser op 66, & afterwards at a Mrs Gassiots, where I played 2 other Griegs.

Your card to mother has just arrived, to our great glee.

Mother joins me in much love to Miss Hagerup & yourself.

I do agree about dear Halvorsen. He is a *real man*, indeed, & such a Norwegian.

I shall write again soon.

Very fond love from
Percy.

On 15 August 1912 Grainger left London to join Karen Holten on holiday at Slettestrand, near Svinkløv, the place at which they had also spent their last summer holiday together, in 1909. It was to be, so he later wrote to his mother, his happiest holiday in that place. It was also his last.

Grainger's relationship with Karen had already begun to change. His decision not to come to Svinkløv in the summer of 1911 had been a bitter blow to her after their preceding long separation. One such disappointment she could, and did, accommodate. But when he cut short his Copenhagen visit of November 1911 in order to earn more money with extra engagements in Norway, it was as if she suddenly realised that there was no future in their relationship. From that time her letters began to change, to become more aloof, more distant and less frequent. The change is reflected in Percy's letters to her. Though the prose rattles on, the rhetoric has a hollow ring and elicits a fairly apathetic response. Compared with the ecstatic anticipation of the letters that preceded former reunions, those that precede the Slettestrand meeting seem quite "formal" in their politeness.

The affair was over. Doors were closing. Though they consolidated a loving friendship at Slettestrand that was to last for life, the excesses of Percy's erotic fancy were no longer possible. She had returned all his whips in November 1911.

This was also, of course, a turning point in his relationship with Rose, who was now, in his words, his "own life's-partner" and "the one and only really passionate relation of my life". In Rose's surviving letters to Percy from the Slettestrand holiday Karen is not mentioned.

Percy was back in London on 29 August. Rose had in the meantime taken a lodger, a young Norwegian girl from Bergen, Anna, the daughter of Pastor Høyer. She arrived on 21 September to live with Rose for a couple of months to learn English while Percy was away on tour.

452   TO ROSE GRAINGER   [PM London]
[Postcard. PM 15 August 1912]

Saw such a finelooking man in the underground. A working man with lovely eyes & Greek face
                    Fond love my sweetest mother

453   TO ROSE GRAINGER   [PM Fjerritslev]
Monday 19.8.12. 8 o'cl. forenoon.

Your 1st card reached me last night, tho' it was Sunday, for
Bjerregaard's son was in to Fjerritslev to take someone to the train. I was
so happy to get it. It is lovely & warm, though raining, the drops making
a delicious sound on the leaves of the creepers outside my window, &
earlier this morning there was lightning & the most lovely sounding thunder
(mellow & not harsh) near at hand. I got a message from the Schoŭ's last
night, & will go up to them, Larsens & Plantørens today, if it fines.

There is every reason to expect this to be my happiest little holiday in
these parts. I do not feel too eagerly urged by any duties or compositional
doubts.[32] Instead of the feverish everlasting wondering "will it come off?"
I have now more the thought to live as long & healthily as I can, & that
the rest seems to show signs of shaping itself, given time.

Please open Schott's account if it comes, darling.

Then all my other relations here seem to me truer & simpler & better
understood than ever before. It is better to have less glamor & more
clearheadedness in these matters. At least I am happiest so

I feel amazingly hungry here all the time & the more so just now before
breakfast. Yesterday there was Kylling & Rødgrød [Danish: chicken and
raspberry fool].

Karen is a good deal fatter from the enforced quiet, but looks much
better for it, happier & more herself. Her foot seems a splendid piece of
work & the doctor must have been a delightful doctor, careful about the
least detail.

This morn I'm going to do the band parts of "We have fed"
With the lovingest thoughts for my dearest comrade girl-mum

Percy.

32 Percy did, nonetheless, work
quite hard at his "composition
duties" during the 1912
Slettestrand holiday. As he
reported in his letters to Rose he:
finished the vocal scores of *Sir
Eglamore* and *The Inuit* for the
printer; did the band parts of *We
Have Fed Our Sea*; finished *Father
and Daughter*; wrote out "Music
Hall Tune" ("Gay but Wistful");
worked on *Colonial Song* and the
parts of *Green Bushes*. He was
also, though he does not mention
it to Rose, working on his setting
of "Silken Hair", later *The Merry
Wedding*.

454   TO ROSE GRAINGER   Slettestrand
Wednesday 20.8.12.

My own darling comrade-mum

When I walk the ways here & see the bumpy precipices we hauled the
bathchair over & see the scenes of that whole drama & recall thereby all
the smallness & idiocy & purposeless uncontrol & bad nature that I revealed
it is terrible to me that you, darling, must need go on through life without
being able to blot out the memory of that period, & perhaps ½ expecting
another or several similar occurances of such. For me, merely towards
myself, the affair hasnt that sting that the thought that it reacted on you
has. Partly because (I know not why) I have no ambitions towards being
any better than chance makes me, & partly because I was able to feel within
me my love for you burning as steadily & inevitably as on any day of my
best behavior towards you. If only you could now see into my heart of that
time, my own life's-partner, (into that Svinkløv time I mean) I feel sure you
would feel reassured & dismiss the details of my unforgivable behavior as
almost "unwesentlich" [German: insignificant], ungenuine & unaccountable, like wetting the bed.[33]

That my love for you was then the same as now & ever only makes my
guilt (then) the more. But with that I'm not concerned. I dont care how
guilty you know me to be, all I want you to know is that *never* ever has
anything for any moment threatened the one overwhelming sun of my life,
round which my good & ills twirl, my love & admiration for you & the
importance of you above all, the one & only really passionate relation of
my life.

33 Rose replied on 23 August,
"Now, my dearest, don't go
thinking you have so much to
blame yourself for, in regard to
the Svinkløv visit, when I look
back to it, I think *much* of it was
very happy, & my health being as
it is, is the only really miserable
event of my life". The incident in
1907 is unexplained, though
Grainger admits in his
autobiographical *Anecdotes* (1954)
that Karen and Rose had not got
on well. There is no doubt,
though, that Rose has in some
sense "won". When she discusses
Grainger's future now it is not in
terms of "marriage" but
"retirement" from concert life. It
is now seen as something they will
share together, with her giving
lessons, not as formerly to support
herself while he supports his wife,
but to supplement the income
from his invested concert earnings.

To think that I can have ever failed to shield that love, & that (among other places) these innocent scenes of sand & sea & heather have been the stage of wretched manifestations seems just too bad. And yet how like me? Of course I never guessed I would behave so silly. Because I always knew how I loved you, & never thought of small silly poisons festering like that.

If only you could once realize how unassailed our relation has always been, in fact that your life is simply my life you could then afford to remember my very worstnesses with no more tragedy than I do. If you *can* never doubt me ever, darling. Doubt my goodness reliability corage, suspect selfishness or anything like that, but let me feel you really accept the unbrokeness of our love as the first element of both our beings. I feel a ridiculous uncontrolled rage & fury if I think you are doubting what I feel for you. For I do feel it to be so unjust. It is my one point of utter integrity & I cannot bear to have to defend it.

So many glad thanks for your glorious & very mumsish letter of Aug. 17th. Yes, I feel glorious stretches of lovefilled healthy happy holiday activity [to] be before us. More & more we will come to our own & repay the joys of our life with good deeds & fine works to live long. I'm eating a lot, rearing (Dutch) "best" & generally enjoying a catholic digestion. Never have I been on this ground with such good nerves, & feel myself zugleich [German: at the same time] so healthy, guiltless, hopeful & appreciated. The last year has been kind to us. So will the long future be. Let us keep really wonderful health, my sweet mother, & never doubt our love.

It is really warm here.

Percy.

455   TO KAREN HOLTEN   31A King's Road
[Original: Danish]   Sloane Square
31.8.12. Saturday.   London. S W

My little Sister.

It was so infinitely sad to see you disappear that time, worse than ever before in Fredericia [?] it seems to me. I waited and saw the ferry sail right over to Strib and wept a little in that way you know I have acquired.

What a remarkable time it was we had together; so utterly different from what I had expected; much more beautiful, but at the same time much less entertaining than I could have imagined. There was, for me, a tinge of something tenderly weak and something distant about the whole of our being together, something lovely and loving and enchanting, I think. Perhaps your foot played its part.

I think I have more to thank you for than ever. You are so absolutely indescribably touchingly good and sisterlike to me. (I say that perhaps because I don't know what a sister is like) It is as if you understand me better than ever and have more sympathy with me than ever. You looked so beautiful in your national costume. Really you should preserve the costume as it is now, and not wear it out, but have a new one made. But the old one is so beautiful and should be preserved as pattern, it seems to me.

If only your little foot would be strong and firm as your sweet little mind. I remember that I didn't kiss your little foot at all as I should have, and will do so now. I am a little sore in my left eye. Possibly a little chill.

You are a sweet and good-tasting person, little Karen. It is enchanting to live close to you without interruption. You can be so good and so motherly, there streams a power of blessing from the whole of your beloved person both toward the small calves and toward your grateful deserted

Percy.[34]

34 Karen replied on 3 September, "Dear little friend, Thank you for your lovely little letter. Yes, we did have a wonderful time. I find there is such a safe feeling between us, knowing that we will remain good friends all life through . . . You were so nice this summer, gentle and good, the way I like you most of all . . . My heather looks so beautiful, it was a shame you forgot yours".

35 At the Promenade Concert in Queen's Hall. The reference here is to Christian Sandby's performance with the Women's Orchestra in Copenhagen on 23 October 1910. The "Proms" performance was such a success that the work was programmed

456 TO KAREN HOLTEN

[Original: Danish/private language]
5.9.12.

31A King's Road
Sloane Square
S W

My little meat-mate.

It was indeed a pure pleasure ("pure pleasures" the Schous understand no doubt!) to get your sweet little letter today. It is lovely to know that you, like I, also feel secure in our friendship. Often there can come more tremendous and more ecstatic feelings, but less than a good sweet secure friendship (also a lovely thing) it won't and must never be between us two good small souls.

No, how amusing it is to think how peculiarly embarrassing it was, the day when we were more or less ecstatic, and I dared to come with one of the small whips and you let your displeasure be known in unambiguous words!

I cannot remember a situation in which I have felt more foolish, without being unhappy in the least, only so really *outwardly foolish*!

But little Karen is damn well greedy for climaxes, that can't be denied; to have been a little annoyed would have been enough, but a climax would be much better, she thinks to herself.

The whole of this little event was funny and so typical of us both, actually.

One thing we didn't do enough this year; not enough for my satisfaction in any case: can you remember the very first year at the Planter's when I wrote "Gr. Bushes" score and you went to sleep with your hand on my penis? That was **so** lovely for me. It was as if the world was so far from being *empty*.

Last night Wood performed "Mock Morris"; good in tone, but in Sandby's tempo.[35] But it was a success all the same, and had to be repeated. I did not show myself. Today Fagge of "The London Choral Society" (which I did tell you Mrs Fagge just calls "The London") telephoned that he will perform *Irish Tune* and *Father and daughter* in the Queen's Hall, the 4th Dec. (1912)

Things are thus going well and steadily forward, and I can't think otherwise than that you will very easily have an opportunity later on to hear both "Brown is my silken hair" and many other things of mine performed, either here, or in Holland or Germany, or even in the "critical" little Copenhagen, who knows? It is something I long very much for, to stand sometime in front of you as a practical successful conductor in my own things. It would be something similar to standing in front of you with a large swollen phallus; something one would like to do but nevertheless is half shy about.

There is nothing in the world you can serve me better with than to be very patient and careful and at the same time eager so that you can gradually get your sweet little foot *quite quite* strong and fit again. It is so lovely when you can run and be fresh and young "and so quick of foot out in the grove". It would be a relief to me if you would wait a really long while (perhaps nearly a year?) before beginning riding again. I am **so** afraid of riding when there is *the slightest* thing wrong with one's legs or feet. Let me always have news about your foot, little girl-boy.

Arlaud shall have Sargent's when I send you the photograph.

Mother is better again. I have been afraid about her health recently, but I now think there is a real improvement again.

The day before yesterday we heard 5 orchestral pieces by *Arnold Schönberg* the Viennese composer. He is **excellent**, dear. Hear something of his if you in any way can. He is the greatest revolution I have witnessed. He opens great and rich freedoms for all of us composers.[36]

again by Wood on 10 September. This time the tempo was better (that is, faster), Percy reported to Karen, and the piece had still greater success and had to be repeated. "It is really remarkable (and pleasant) to have so much luck with such a little paltry piece", Percy wrote to Karen on 8 [9?] September, commenting further on 12 September, "It is almost idiotic". In the event *Mock Morris* was played on four occasions during the 1912 season of Promenade Concerts: 4 and 10 September, 5 and 26 October. Something of its impact may be traced through the pages of the *Daily Telegraph*, which wrote of the piece on 31 August, ". . . one of the most invigorating compositions that have come from our younger school of composers"; on 6 September: "It seems a foregone conclusion that this glorious little work will receive a permanent place in the Queen's Hall Orchestra repertoire"; and on 4 January 1913: "At Mr Gardiner's Concerts several works were heard for the first time that afterwards passed, as it were, into the language, such, for example, as Mr Percy Grainger's 'Mock Morris' ". The piece enjoyed continuing success throughout 1912, so much so that by 8 November Percy was reporting to Karen that there were now so many provincial performances of this piece and *Molly on the Shore* that he was unable to keep track of them all (see letter 464). The piece was, in the words of the *Daily Telegraph* of 22 October 1912, "by far the most popular piece of British music for a long time".

36 Grainger's opinion was not shared by the musical public at large, or at least that section of it which attended the Promenade Concert on 3 September. The *Daily Telegraph* of 4 September reported that the work had been hissed, commenting "Queen's Hall has probably never witnessed such a scene". The work was repeated at a Queen's Hall Orchestra Symphony Concert on 17 January 1914, this time with the composer himself conducting. The response was more favourable; the *Daily Telegraph*'s reviewer reported tittering, but no hissing.

457   TO HERMAN SANDBY   31A King's Road
[Original: Danish]   Sloane Square
17.9.12.   London. S W

Dear old Sæhrímnir

I am longing to hear further about the performance of "The Woman &
the bloody fiddler".[37] It was frightfully nice to get the programmes, and
it was not from lack of pleasure and interest that I didn't write sooner. But
the last ½ year was tremendously over-busy. What do you think of your
work, the sound and everything? Let me know as many details as you have
time and wish to do.

It is quite inexplicable the success I have had as a composer up to now,
and I am only deeply grateful for the audience, the critics, the choirs and
the orchestras for their help and warm good-will.

Up to now (of the performances I know anything about) there have been
performed.

Faðir og dóttur, Irish Tune (choir), 3 Kipling choruses, I'm 17 come
Sunday, English Dance, Green Bushes (in Aachen Germany in May), Mock
Morris many times (in London, Holland, Birmingham, Manchester,
Cardiff) and then a whole mass of lesser chamber-music things which I will
send you the programmes of. "Mock Morris" "Molly on the shore" and
the 3 piano pieces are already in 2nd edition.

Sir Henry Wood performed Mock Morris the other day in the "Proms"
and had to give it da capo, and has put it twice more on the "Proms"
programmes. He is performing "Molly on the shore" for string orchestra
in the "Proms" the 23rd Oct; on the same day there is a concert in
Amsterdam of chamber-music things of mine, with Ada Crossley and
Sevcik Quartet.

Other imminent things are:

Queen's Hall Orchestra Symphony Concert 19 Oct "Green Bushes"
   conduct myself.
London Choral Society 4th Dec. repeat performance of "Irish Tune"
   and "Faðir og dóttur" (with 40 guitars)
in Gardiner's concerts: (Feb and March 1913)
   "Colonial Song" (new) for sopr.[ano] solo, tenor solo, harp solo,
   and orchestra, possibly "Hillsong" for 29 wind players and
   percussion.
   "Sir Eglamore" double choir and orchestra, "Green Bushes" again
   and some smaller things.
Norwich Festival 1914 ⎰"The lads of Wamphray" choir and orchestra
                      ⎱"Brúnsveins vísa" (The merry wedding) (new)
                      on a Færoese text for solos (voices) choir,
                      organ and orchestra.

There is now coming out in print full score of "Faðir og dóttir" and a
quantity of chamber-music things "Walking Tune" "My Robin" 6tets
8tets etc, and in a ½ year perhaps "Green Bushes" score.

All these performances have meant a good deal of experience, as you will
understand, (and which I hope will show itself in the results) and a heap
of pleasure, for *all* have had a part in making everything as pleasant and
profitable for me as ever possible; the orchestral musicians for example
have been charming, *particularly the Germans in Aachen*! Think of it!

I have now a whole heap of programmes, and printed compositions etc,
that I would like to send you, but 1st I would like to know whether you
are still at Havhøj or have already [gone] to America. If this sort of thing
is difficult for you and only "fills suitcases" for nothing, just tell me and
I will send the above-mentioned things to you when you come back to
Denmark in the Spring.

37 *The Woman and the Fiddler*,
play in three acts by Arne
Norrevang, had been translated
from the Norwegian by Alfhild
Sandby and published by Brown
Brothers, Philadelphia, in 1911.
Herman Sandby wrote incidental
music for the play. The
performance is unidentified.

Here you have a letter full only of lists and titles, but I beg you let me have a similar one in return. Tell me as much as possible about your *things*!

With all warmest regards to Alfhild and yourself from mother and me, always your old

Percy.

Spent some lovely days in Slettestrand (near Svinkløv) recently. *Never* have I seen Jutland so enchanting as this year.

The greatest part of the winter I am away of course, in Germany, Switzerland, and Holland, etc. Russia next year!

On 30 September Percy and Rose, accompanied by Rose's friend Isabel Du Cane, left London for Berlin, where Percy was scheduled to give a recital, his first in that city, on 7 October, followed by a recital in Hamburg on 11 October. According to their plans, Rose was to stay on an extra day in Berlin after Percy left for Hamburg, then travel back to London with Miss Du Cane. Percy would arrive in London on 13 or 14 October.

In the event the recitals were cancelled and the three returned together around 6 October, going straight to the Du Canes' country house in Kent. Percy rested there until 12 October, when he returned to London to prepare for the performance of Green Bushes *he was to conduct on the 19th.*

What happened in Berlin? Percy's letter to Karen gives his immediate reasons for cancelling his concerts. But it is likely that these were merely catalysts and that in fact he experienced some kind of breakdown after the unrelenting pressures of the year. Rose had written to Percy at Slettestrand on 17 August, "Perhaps you have never had a harder year than this last one". His holiday with Karen, happy though it had been, had not been enough. On 8 September, after only ten days back in London, he wrote to Karen, "I am working tremendously at the moment, and am really a little nervy. I need a long holiday, half a year or something like that". On 25 September he wrote, "I am dreading these concerts this year more than ever before", and on 5 October, just two days before the projected Berlin recital, "If I wasn't so afraid and beaten-down I would be even more thirsty for you than is the case . . ." If the change in his relationship with Karen had anything to do with his breakdown, it is not mentioned in any of the extant letters.

Although Rose pronounced Percy "well again" after the rest in Kent and although his concert work continued as scheduled, it is clear that his health remained fragile through the remaining months of 1912.

On 21 October Grainger was off again, this time to Holland. He was accompanied by Rose, Miss Du Cane and Ada Crossley, who were with him for the concerts of his chamber music at Amsterdam and The Hague on 23 and 24 October. On 25 October Rose and the other ladies returned to London, while Percy continued with his Dutch tour.

458 TO KAREN HOLTEN   Ballards,
[Original: Danish]   Goudhurst,
Saturday. 12.10.12.   Kent.

My own little playmate.

Many thanks for your sweet letter to Berlin. It was good that you couldn't imagine me "having a concert in Berlin", since it didn't come to anything either.

Just think that you could walk a whole hour with your foot without a break. Can you "run" yet? But you would show me a *great* kindness if you wouldn't ride for the time being.

I was ruined in Berlin by the many ugly faces, the overheated rooms, the repulsive language, the bad food and smell of smoke and food everywhere. People were *everywhere* extremely kind to us, *everyone* one could say, I have not the slightest to complain about, but I just felt "rather die than play for these people", and felt weak and tearful and without memory.

So we went away, had a pleasant journey and said "yes" to Miss Du Cane's invitation to have us here in the country. Du Canes are 4 old maids, kind and pleasant; you probably know one of them. It is *charming* here, we have played tennis every day, and it is warm and moist and green and at the same time peaceful and full of life; everything that it wasn't in Berlin. Dogs bark in a friendly way, and cocks crow fresh and stridently in the air. We have had a very happy little holiday here but travel to London today.

To everyone you must be kind enough to say the same as I do: *only* that I was ill in Berlin and had to give up Berlin and Hamburg. People were too good to us to be able in decency to voice anything against Berlin.

I met 2 *sweet* important critics; and the Norwegian Consul and vice consul were kindness itself. And I *love* Fräulein Gerhardi; a talented friend of Delius.[38]

Now I am going to conduct Green Bushes today week, Saturday, and the 23rd, 24th, my chamber-music things are in A'dam and the Hague. After the 20th Oct my address is c/o: Herrn Hans Augustin Frans v. Mierisstr[aat] 101. A'dam. until further notice.

"M. Morris" was played again last Saturday and I see that Landon Ronald is performing it in February.

I received in Berlin a charming letter from the most important critic in A'dam about my printed things which I sent him.

I almost thought of asking you by telegram to come to Hamburg, but no doubt you couldn't have done it, and a thing like that it is best not to ask one to do.

If only I could feel your limbs about me, your white soft legs (mjöllhvit sá eri eg själv [flawed Icelandic: probably "snow-white as I am myself" or possibly "I myself (will) plough (the) snow-white sea"]) that are so indescribably lovely to touch between the body and the knees.

I feel well and happy, Believe me, I enjoyed the hours when I ought to have been concentrating but which were free.

I am your hot lecherous lover and your particularly good friend.

38 Ida Gerhardi (1867–1927), German-born, French-domiciled painter. Rose had met her in London in April 1911. The German and Dutch critics are not identified. Landon (later Sir Landon) Ronald (born Russell) (1873–1938), English conductor, pianist and composer. A person of some influence in London's musical life, he was at this time permanent conductor of the New Symphony Orchestra, with which he gave regular Sunday concerts at the Albert Hall and a series of symphony concerts at Queen's Hall. It was at one of the latter that he played *Mock Morris* on 6 February 1913. He was also principal of the Guildhall School of Music. In an article in the *Onlooker*, 4 March 1905, he had written, "After a somewhat extensive knowledge of Mr Grainger's prowess, I have come to the definite conclusion that he is quite one of the greatest pianists of the day". Evidence suggests that it was he who arranged Grainger's meeting with Kipling. Grainger first played under Ronald's baton at the Royal Albert Hall Sunday Concert, 23 June 1907.

459 TO KAREN HOLTEN
[Original: Danish]
Sunday. 20.10.12.

31A King's Road
Sloane Square
SW

Little Karen

The performance of "G. Bushes" yesterday was very gratifying. Already in the morning in rehearsal (only 40 minutes) it went excellently but in the afternoon considerably better. Wood was absolutely enthusiastic and the audience warm.

Particularly enthusiastic were Casals, Thibaud, and the Spaniard Rubio who were all there.[39]

I don't have the impression that the piece is *perfect* (in 10 years it will no doubt be rewritten) but it is the most characteristic and personal of all the things of mine that have been performed up to now, and since it appears to give pleasure and appeal to people I am going to let it be printed straight away, and have already packed up the whole affair for the printers.[40] Many things which I have altered since Aachen are obviously better now than then.

I conducted happily and without a trace of any kind of unpleasantness, and I conducted well without being brilliant. The piece is difficult to conduct, and I just managed to achieve the procurement of a *good* performance, but did not have the technical surplus enough as conductor to play with the matter and make it superb.

Mother unfortunately got a fishbone in her throat yesterday at lunch (which has now apparently disappeared) but all the same went to both the rehearsal and the concert and enjoyed it very much and was very satisfied.

As mother said at the concert, it was really a shame that *you* were not present to hear the piece for which you have written 2 scores and the parts. Don't you think that we must really arrange for you to hear a performance of something interesting of mine sometime soon?

My impression is then that "G.B." is really successful, and I anticipate profit from the piece, in my composing career; but without regarding the piece as being "final" in its present form.

I am now quite well again, and we travel to Holland tomorrow. Mother, Ada Crossley, and Miss Du Cane will be with me at the A'dam and Hague concerts 23–24 Oct, after which I will be alone again.

Now I want to hear more about your foot. Let me hear all the details, little comrade.

Goodbye for today, with many kisses from your lover

Percy.

The Svinkløv places in "G.B." sounded so warm and "affectionate". They are also the best parts, and really reproduce in part that time's honeymoon sentiment.

Receive herewith many sincere thanks for all your loving work and help with "Gr. B" over many years, which in the form of the "parts" ["stemmerne"] just as in the form of the "sentiment" ["stemming"] shared in yesterday's event.

Dare I ask you to let me have more nude photographs of yourself. It would be a delight to me.

39 Pablo Casals (1876–1973), Catalan cellist, conductor, pianist and composer; Jacques Thibaud (1880–1953), French violinist; Agustín Rubio (1856–1940), Spanish cellist. At the Queen's Hall Orchestra Symphony Concert on 19 October, Casals had had the first half of the programme to himself, playing Tartini's Concerto in D for cello, horns and strings and the Saint-Saëns Cello Concerto in A minor. He, Thibaud and pianist Harold Bauer had given two trio recitals in Queen's Hall on 9 and 16 October. Grainger had met Casals in Utrecht on 18 January 1911 when Grainger attended the rehearsal of Julius Röntgen's Cello Concerto, and again in Amsterdam a few days later.

40 Nine days later he had changed his mind, writing to Karen Holten on 29 October, "I have thought over the matter and will not publish 'Green Bushes' immediately. I am not so sure of the work and the press is a little divided (the majority almost against or cool) and I don't believe the piece deserves a more unanimous praise . . . If the conductors like the piece, then they can borrow the manuscript, and if many ask for it then one has a reason for printing it, but I have no desire to throw away about 1400 Kroner on a piece I am myself not convinced about". The instrumental version of *Green Bushes* was not, in fact, published until 1931, by which time it had been completely revised.

The next stage of Grainger's Dutch tour began with a solo recital at Leiden on 25 October. His last appearance was a chamber-music concert in Haarlem on 21 November. In total he made twenty appearances, one (the last) playing chamber music, two playing with orchestra, the rest being solo recitals. Two overlapping programmes, each with a slightly varied form, provided the basic solo repertoire for the tour. He had eleven free days.

With most concerts in smaller towns his nerves were not unduly stressed. But it was clear that his health was delicately balanced. Rose's letters reflect her concern, with their injunctions to eat raw eggs twice a day, drink much milk and eat heaps of butter and to play the big pieces with the music.

On 26 November, Grainger played the Tchaikovsky B♭ minor Piano Concerto at the Gürzenich-Concert in Cologne, Fritz Steinbach conducting. He was back in London by 28 November.

460 TO ROSE GRAINGER Gorcum.
[Original: Dutch/Danish/English — At the home of Dr. Dee.
a Dutch lesson for Rose]
Sunday, 27.Oct. 1912.

My own sweet little mother,

I am beginning to get my nerve-strength back again. The concert in Leiden was "suffering" ["lejden"] the whole time, but yesterday evening during the last half of the programme I felt quite happy.

I am the guest of a queer and pleasant little man, a Dr Dee, who is a teacher of Latin and Greek, and a painter as well.

I feel well and happy.

Gorcum is a very charming little town, with lovely canals, and age-old houses, and a large old wide church with a tower that is quite crooked.

A small Dutch town like this makes a perfect impression, everything holds together, the life, the people, and the old buildings and "articles".

In "Det Vaterland" (den Haag) was a horrid critique about *us all*, the Franck, our performances, & my compos, cheeky & wilfully nasty & Jewish-sounding.

I shall not take any further steps to have my compositions pushed in Holland. Piano things of mine I shall always play in my recitals (People *loved* "Mock Morris" here & Leiden) but other works I shall not bother about, neither in Concertgebouw or elsewhere.

I dont feel they fall on a fruitfull soil here. The glowing notices in "Niews v.d. dag" & "Nieuwe Courant" will be *very useful*, but in the future Holland, which treats me so satisfactorily pianistically, shall be merely pianisticly attacted & not exposed to any compositional bait that it likely will only fail to rise to, & merely create needless disappointment.[41]

And England that *has* treated me so magnificently compositionally shall be honored with the full blast of that battery.

What are we going to do about the 3 good Dutch compo crits? I shall send them to you Englished today or in a few days.

I am ready to pay for them to appear in "Daily Telegraph" 1st page & would like to include the few good words about Ada (if she is willing) at my expense of course.

Would Schotts like the matter to appear *under their Schott advs* on the 1st page, or sooner I did it seperately quite on my own. Or would they & you advise not to "D.T." these notices but rather just keep them for a booklet later on. I should think "D.T." them myself. I shall send you the translations & leave it wholly to you to decide in the matter.[42] I feel hopely that my concert nerves will be quite restored in a few days.

Your loving pet son
Perks.

461 TO ROSE GRAINGER Park Hotel
28. Oct. 1912 Hoorn.

My darling podgy little mumbly-chumbles.

I'm so happy & healthy here in Hoorn. Behind the Hotel the noise of the ZuiderZee & a high wind in the trees, in my belly a nice healthy wellcooked Weiner Schnitzel & in my buzum a high heart.

Got up at 6 this morn & got here early. I feel very at home in these Dutch towns. Yesterday was taken a 3 hour motor drive, along a high dyke, with fairy-like landscapes & delicious baby houses on either side, noble looking

41 The programme had hardly been revolutionary. In the first half, the Ševčik Quartet (with whom Grainger had performed previously in Amsterdam on 16 January 1912) played the Beethoven String Quartet Op. 18 No. 1, with Grainger then joining them for the César Franck Piano Quintet. After interval came a selection of Grainger's compositions: *Molly on the Shore* (string quartet); *My Robin is to the Greenwood Gone* (piano trio); *Handel in the Strand* (string trio and piano). Ada Crossley sang three songs: *Died for Love* (with three string instruments), *Six Dukes Went Afishin'* (with piano) and *Willow, Willow* (with string quartet and harp).

42 Rose advised for publication, commenting on 29 October, "Ada will love to have the bit about her in", referring probably to the complimentary remarks made by Herman Rutters in *De nieuwe Courant*, 25 October. Although the *Daily Telegraph* of 5 November noted the success of the Dutch concerts in its "Music of the Day" column, the notices were not published on page one of the paper. However, a booklet was made, "Percy Grainger. Dutch Criticisms of his Compositions", with extracts from reviews by Daniel de Lange in *Het nieuws van den Dag* (Amsterdam), 24 October, Herman Rutters in *De nieuwe Courant* (The Hague), 25 and 26 October and from the *Nieuwe Rotterdamsche Courant*, 24 October.

peasantry in queer get-ups, & through ducky little dorps, each with its crooked broad squat enthralling (generally ½ decayed) old church tower.

I like Dr Dee & his friends in Gorcum very much & the surroundings best of anything I've seen in Holland. I'd like to spend a holiday there with you.

Herewith the crits. I'd head it all:

Percy Grainger's chamber compositions in Holland.

or something like that.

I've Englished hurriedly, so maybe Roger or someone will clean it all up, & for "D.T." it'd need to be much shortened of course. But as enclosed it wouldn't be too long for the next Schotts compo booklet.

So sorry I've no more time to write, for I've so much to tell you, my own darling one.

So glad to get 2 cards here & hear of yr prizes.[43]

Yr loving
Percy.

Before printing these we'd better wait for Rutters detailed account of compos in his "Muziek-week"

462   TO ROSE GRAINGER
29.10.12.
1 o'clock

Hotel "De Zalm"
Gouda.

Darling.

Will you kindly post enclosed English letter & give the other to Mrs Grieg quick?[44]

Has Schott sent you printed *mandoline & guitar* "F & D" parts yet? If not I'd ring up Strecker.

I believe 31st is guitar rehearsal.[45] Wouldn't it be well to now ring up Fagge & fix a rehearsal after 28 Nov, when both he (to conduct) & I (to instruct) could hear a guitar rehearsal together?

Really all the smaller Dutch townlets are gems.

Hoorn is like being plumped down into the middleages & this town too is full of big & good old buildings.

Got up at 5.30 this morn, so as to get here early, & have already had a grand hot bath, shave, hairwash & lunch. Am feeling ever so well, & not a trace of nerves last night at Hoorn. In fact I believe that this winter's going to be the most nerveless one I've had. The whole secret is to get broken in in the smalls first, to have a Norwegian tour, or such, & then it bit by bit becomes just nothing at all. I was an idiot to *think* of starting off in Berlin!

Am longing to get more cards or letters from you. Perhaps here.

My publics seem bigger this year.

Leiden netto   160 gulden
Gorcum ”   90   ”
Hoorn   ”   150   ”

With much love, goodbye for today
Percy.

So glad to hear Miss Høyer thought "Molly" was so well received.[46]

43 Rose and her housekeeper/cook Mrs Kelford, had each won a fifteen shilling prize in a Meltonian competition: thirteen shillings in cash, and two shillings' worth of Meltonian products.

44 Nina Grieg was in London at this time. She played piano in a Grieg recital given jointly by Johanne Stockmarr and Ellen Beck at Aeolian Hall on 30 October, and accompanied three of Grieg's songs (plus a fourth as encore) included in a vocal duet recital by Saima Neovi and Ellen Beck at Steinway Hall on 9 November. Rose attended the concert on 30 October with Ada Crossley, Beryl Freeman and Anna Høyer, reporting to Percy next day that it had not been a good house and the audience had not been enthusiastic. Thereafter she met Mrs Grieg socially and entertained her. Mrs Grieg travelled on with her sister to Amsterdam on 10 November, staying several days there and meeting Percy at the Röntgens'.

45 Grainger was preparing his guitar players again for the performance of *Father and Daughter* by the London Choral Society on 4 December. Roger Quilter had taken the rehearsals in Grainger's absence, with Margot Harrison taking over when Roger could not attend.

46 Anna Høyer had attended the performance of Grainger's *Molly on the Shore* at the Queen's Hall Promenade Concert on 23 October. Rose wrote on the 27th, "Anna says 'Molly' was tremendously applauded . . . How wonderful to have written a piece that appeals so to an audience".

463   TO ROSE GRAINGER   [In the]
4.11.12. Monday.   Train Apeldoorn–Zwolle.

There is something sad about coming back to towns I often find; that such different things occur in the same places, & that one faces the same scenes in such varying spirits. I dont know why such things should be saddening, but I feel them so.

For instance, the last time I was in Apeldoorn I just arrived from A'dam, or somewhere far, in time for concert, (or from Deventer?) & found your wire in artists room saying we would meet in Dordrecht the next day. And it seemed so queer to finish up after the concert this time quietly in a lovely big airly bedroom, with a warm stove, & a nice light shining in from a streetlamp. The Moutons did not turn up from Deventer as usual, which I must say I was glad of, but 5 unknown backfische [German: half-grown schoolgirls (later, "flappers")] stormed into the artists room, one pretty. I told them they could hear me practise Sunday afternoon which they did.

They did not turn out flirtatious or amusing however, so yesterday (Sunday) evening I spent very quietly in my room at the Hotel. I saw my new guitar lying there done up in paper & couldn't resist it. I got it out & spent a regular honeymoon of an evening with it, & have begun such a funny piece for guitar & any number or fewness of other instruments & voices. The guitar plays the same bar over & over again thro'out, with some variation of technique & color, & all the other voices are so composed that they can begin whenever they like, & how they like (as to octave & expression), like an improvised Polynesian chorus.[47] Such an affair fascinates me; an artistic monotony soothes me & turns all my dark moods to bright ones.

Unhandy in omgang [Danish: dealings, associations] with people, backward & feeble & easily dissappointed & downhearted, a sure consolation lies for me in having a few hours alone with some instrument I dont know too much about. All the selfassertion & "plum" of my nature seems to ooze out like gum out of a tree, & I feel all my relations to the outer world vanish, & feel like some native, with only his music, his songs, his senses & his own near folk to console him.

I'm not fond of the outside world; tho' my heart loves humanity as a whole, seeing them, dealing with them only unnerves me & gives me no deep or truly personal pleasure in return. That is why, I suppose, I feel so much sadder this year than usual. I'm ever so thankful for the luck I've had, & I know it's all for the best, but the actual result to me is sadness. I feel as if life was ebbing from me, as if all my friends were dead & gone & the strings breaking that tie me to life. I've seldom felt so little hold on life. And this is not from any health matter. On the contrary, my small healthailments are more likely due to a sagging of my inner spirit than the other way round.

But I find I have been living on ideals all these years, & no actual events (be they better or worse than those ideals) seem actually to fill their place.

Balfour G, Mock M, English Dance, G. Bushes, Cyril's "Engl. Dance", "Fair Helen" my own compositional future, instead of being things of affection living their own emotional secret life within my heart & head, now possibly belong to the world, but to me no longer, or at least with no intimacy.

They are now the slaves of other's judgements, likes, plans.

Balfour is no longer an unknown quantaty, but a creature taking a certain place, acting thus & thus, known to me, known to others, forming a part, even if a good part, of this dreary general public affair "life."

To think that my works are actually published, for sale, performed anywhere, is for me prostitution, pure & simple, bringing with it that particular taste in the mouth that prostitution brings; tho' I see no *particular* **harm** in any sort of prostitution, only a dulness.

47 The genesis of *Random Round*, see letter 466.

Let us however not be downhearted on these accounts.

I am not really unhappy or pitiable because of the last year's events, I am only a *little* sadder, a *little* more lifeless than usual.

It all takes getting used to; & maybe in a few years time I'll be indifferent to the whole matter & will have learned to forget the whole matter & learn to ignore my compos once they are written & take my joys (composing, reading to the mum, guitaring with the mum & holding amateurish rehearsals, composing, translating, learning languages, swimming, sporting, sensualising, eating & drinking) quite privately as if I was just nobody at all.

I am feeling *absolutely well* today, all my diarrhoea gone, & a good appetite, my fingers all in gone [good] order, & everything as it should be.

Zwolle. later.

Delighted to get your letter here. Am sending dear little Miss Joseph a card.

Please send score of "F & D" to me p. adr. Augustin with *nicht nachsenden* on it. I will get it in A'dam in a few days.

I have booked Thursday 28. Nov.

2.30 Lois
3.30 Phillips
4.30 Harrison

that is all.

Dear mum. Will explain this joke when we meet.

464   TO KAREN HOLTEN   Hotel "De Liggende Os"
[Original: Danish]   Utrecht.
Saturday. 8.11.1912.

Did I forget to tell you that Russia is "off" for this year? Siloti and I couldn't find suitable dates, and it will be another time. It is lovely your foot is making steady progress. Poor Cai. It must be a frightful thing to undergo.

From London I am still hearing the nicest news. "Molly" and "M. Morris" are being performed so many places, all over the country, that I don't remember them all any more, and many good opinions and critiques have come in about "G.B.".

An American publisher would like to work with my things over there.[48] It wouldn't surprise me if I soon, or bit by bit, earned just as much from the compositions as from concerts. Prospects are indeed rosy, I must say.

I have received another guitar, as a gift, in Dordrecht recently, and have begun a new piece for guitars with all possible instruments.

48 Rose had been approached by Mr William Arms Fisher, publishing manager of the Oliver Ditson Company of Boston, wanting to publish Grainger's things in America. He had read an article on Grainger's music in the *New York Evening Post*, read Grainger's article "The Music of Cyril Scott" in the *Music Student* (London) of October 1912 and met Cyril Scott in Switzerland. Nothing came of the idea at this time, but Oliver Ditson was to publish *The Merry Wedding* in 1915.

The guitar plays about the same chord sequence right through the piece, and it doesn't matter how many other instruments play with it or *when they come in*, for everything is arranged in such a way, that the whole thing can be played as a kind of improvisation, each time differently. God knows how it will sound. It is certainly an idiotic idea, but the piece is soft and warm and could be called "Lullaby" although it is often forte. I don't think it will be "significant", but possibly amusing.

My concert nerves are like steel this year.

I forget the audience completely, and think about everything in the world, and most often play completely "preoccupied". I'd like to know if it sounds as uninteresting to the audience, as to me.

I don't make an effort to please, play as few encores as possible, and am in a word — really blasé.

But I can't be different this year. I would so like to, but can't. I have undergone so many frightful hours on the platform, and now that I by chance have a sleepy-peaceful period I can't avoid drawing pleasure from it.

I don't read the critiques: I am afraid of reading something unpleasant, for sometimes I play well sometimes badly. But the public is warm as usual and I do believe on the whole more *numerous than before*. Remarkable. I appear to be still on the rise here in this country; not in any visible decline at any rate.

But despite good platform nerves, I am in a nervous and bodily condition as if on the edge of an abyss. I am near a "nervous breakdown" the whole time, or imagine it, still have disorder with my bowels, my eyes are often bad, and I am not much like myself, or imagine so.

Recently I had four days with frightful diarrhoea, but that is over now.

You can imagine that I am feeling poorly when I assure you that I am scarcely ever naughty, and when I am, almost without excitement. Whether I have ruined my nerves by naughtiness, or excitement about my compositions must, as far as I am concerned, "dahingestellt bleiben" [German: be left undecided]; I will just as soon admit the one as the other. But what *is certain is*, that I will very soon have got over this rubbish. No question of me being "nervous", a weakling, one that one must "make allowances for".

If it is not better soon, I will give up concert life for a short time, and see and get quite healthy and strong again.

Isn't it fortunate that my concert nerves are so splendid at the moment? Otherwise it would be bad. But it so often appears to me that there is (at least with healthy and domineering people like me) a kind of compensation in things.

I have altered the date for Bournemouth which should have been 1st Febr. to another date, so I will hope to be able to have 1–2–3 (?) free days with you in Copenhagen after my God-forgotten piano-evening there. Are you glad?, I am.

Are you thinner now, you lustful fleshly little friend?

I was so glad for your little body in the summer, but it can't go on in that way, we all understand that, don't we?

It was alright this summer, but it was *right on the limit*, and we can't have that, can we?

I am profoundly proud about your little body, it is so young and well-kept. If you ruin it (by becoming fat) you will do me *great harm*. I have promised myself that one of the pleasures of my life will be to see your body keep its beauty and youth for many many years. Not because *it in any way* **belongs to me** but because *I admire* it abstractly and have fixed my pride on seeing your flesh (or not-flesh) conquer the years. Remember, once *over* the limit and it will never be the same again. It is important, sacred, little friend.

You are beautiful and fine, and must not lose a *spark* of your qualities yet. You mustn't become *coarse* in your body in any way. Will I get any photographs?

Your poor Ascetic.
Percy.

465   TO ROSE GRAINGER   Hotel "De Liggende Os"
Nov. 9. 1912.   Utrecht.
Saturday.

My darling.

All the letters (de Polignacs, etc) will be attended to tomorrow Sunday, when I have a free day in A'dam.

Yes, I too think it's time this endless exile was put a stop to.[49] It's not even the concerts I mind. My platform nerves get so easygoing once I get into swing that that part can easily be met,.but it seems so silly that we should be so long parted, when we both rejoice in being together, & there is *no compensation* in being apart. Then also I'm so tired of foreigners. I shall never get used to them, their smells, their food, their revolting points of view, particularly about art. Life on tour (except in Norway, or Australiasia or S. Africa) is not life for me at all, neither as an artist or as a man.

I hardly ever feel really well on tour, & all taken in all its not worth wasting ones life like that unless the reward is huge or the other chances miserable.

But now the pupil chance looms so luckily I think you are quite right to counsel not extending the touring needlessly.

2 or 3 months in Scandinavia on tour once a year or every 2 years & about a month in Holland a year, as long as they pay well will do no harm.

Let us now enjoy a little life together. Now's a chance. I can earn at home, I'm honored & encoraged at home, & I'm happy & well at home. Why flee it then? The advantage of keeping up a certain amount of touring is that it feeds me with pupils. Besides, one could always take it up again.

I have nothing against the Dutch. Year by year I find their good qualities hold good & many supposed unpleasant ones appear more distant. But they happen to have little to give me that I really like. I am, above all things, overmuch a poet, a rhythmic fever: the Dutch are above all prose all the time. And here am I, because of my health & *being able* to endure & put up with, wasting my life as surely as the delicate artist type that lives thoroughly but dies young, & so loses his future.

I must manage to live both much & long.

It's indeed a blessing that the pupils "open sesame" to our wishing for them, & we two will be able to manage them I feel sure, & even concentrating a lot on them wont be such a fiendish conclomoration of worries as pupils "foreign letters" & all combined & ever growing.

And all this "foreign intercourse" gives nought in return. If one met lovely folk, or passionate, or artistic, or immoral folk I would get some return, but nothing but Spiesbürger [German: narrow-minded or smug bourgeois] everywhere, ugly, hard to shake off, untempting & untemptable, it really is waste of life. And I shant do it. You & I are going to enjoy life occasionally, or bust.

Am reading Meridith's "Diana of the Xways."[50] Am ½ thro'. I find him a topping artist, occasionally full of rebellions & fiery flashes wholly sympathetic to me, but I find the *whole book* one of the most stinkingly revolting impure over-sexualized cruet-blends I've ever struck. I'm fond of sex, as a game, as an asset, as a recreation, but I really am too prudish to be able to swallow unabated phallicworship decked out in every rainbow color.

49 Rose had written on 5 November advising Grainger not to accept any second-rate engagements abroad. "Only accept engagements abroad as 'Star', by the time you go travelling about the money has gone, & you can do better at home." With new pupils coming every day Rose wrote that he could "make a go of it" with pupils.

50 George Meredith's *Diana of the Crossways* (1885).

Diana may be a nice woman. I cant judge. So may be many whores. But I regard the testing of the matter as too risky.

People who can never indulge sexual instincts without setting prices upon them, & who can also never refrain from their sexual instincts, I call whores, for want of better name. If I held the English views about natural animalism I should have to be a ascetic as well.

I couldnt brand a thing as filthy & then wallow in it.

Boring as I find foreign life, art, looks, food, on the other hand I would sooner die than **ever again** share *any* Englishman's (Meridith's, Kipling's, Roger's, Cyril's, Balfour's, Feilding's,) point of view on any subject under the sun.

I thank my stars for the good luck that has left England palatable to me, & yet un-anglicized me in every particular I am conscious of.

Sometimes worried or shy or tired I stand in an outwardly trying world.

But never impure, never pessimistic, never inwardly afraid or ashamed. I am ready at this & at all moments to deeply & conscientiously enjoy life, & do, & shall more & more. There is not one dark sad hopeless spot in my entire being. All is sun, lust, hunger, goodness, keenness, kindness, hope.

There's a grand time coming, my pet, my sister-mummy.

---

466   TO ROSE GRAINGER   (Steamer: Enkhuizen → Stavoren
[Postcard. (No. 3 of four)]   [Staveren] over the Zuider Zee)
14.11.12

May be one day our own mast will swell such a fleet as this? It would be jolly.

Yesterday morn (A'dam) Goemans came for a lesson & played thro a bit of the new silly piece, & it seems to sound quite hopeful when one hears the various parts joining in at random like that. I'll call it "Random round" or some like name. I also enjoy thinking of the "Arrival platform humlet" these days. My music seems to me so holiday-like, when I go to it suddenly from other music. I think I really am essentially a "weekend" composer, which includes the old famous "Messiah out of Cakewalk" in the Sat & Sunday contrasts.[51]

Longing to hear your piles are better.

51 See note 14, 1911.

467   TO ROSE GRAINGER   American Hotel
Sunday 17.11.1912.   Amsterdam.

Strecker's machinery is seemingly in action; for innocent provincial Dutch folk are the surprized getters of Sargented circulars!

I cannot manage to play the Beethoven "Choral Fantasia" for Fagge. It's the one I played in Frankfort & know well. If I lived several generations I could never learn to play it. I'm very sorry, as I'd have liked to please Fagge & to earn the fee. I'm returning music.

Many greetings to Anna, Johanna & Mrs Kelford, please.

Thanks for sending Fagge big MMS of "F & D" with piano version. Hasn't Strecker got out *Vocal & piano score* of "F & D" yet? The 5 singers (soli) will need it, or else please find bundle marked "F & D" parts & find the 5 narrators part there. Shame to bother you with so much "hunting" dearest.

Will explain re Isabel & "Green Bushes" when we meet.

Very many thanks re Köln piano address.

Re *B'mouth:* "Mock Morris" is no good together with either "Shepherd's Hey" or "Molly" as *all* are in G major, & in 2/2 time & have the same effect & go at same speed.

    Am willing to do "Mock Morris" *alone*

      or   (a) "My Robin"   (b) "M. Morris"

      or: (a) Mock M.   (b) "Green Bushes"

I dont wish longer solo than that, after a Concerto (the more so before conducting) never long solos

---

The M.M. mark in "Mock Morris" *always was* correct, thus it's purely the conducters fault, they simply ignore the M.M. marks!

I enjoyed the cake *intensely*. It was lovely. E. Smyth's article is great fun. Today have written Stanford, Roger, E. Smyth, Elwes (with letters enclosed) E. Röntgen, Cyril, Friedbergs wife, as well as 9 Dutch letters.

    I shall be staying p. adr: Professor Carl Friedberg
                         Stadtwaldgürtel 36
                         Cöln-Lindental
                         Germany.
at Cöln. Post to that address Friday evening, Saturday, & Sunday. Monday post again to Augustin.

    I pass thro here on my way back.

    Have read a delicious Dutch poem called "Beatrijs" by a new poet *P.C. Boutens.*[52] It is very simple & very fine I think, I should like Mrs Harrison to translate it, or else do it myself one day.

    Here's a sample verse:

        Zoo was haar doen éen zuivre vreugd
        Een orgel dat speelt zacht en ver
        Zijn hijmnen aan Maria's deugd:
        O Hemels deur, o Morgenster!

        Thus all she did was pure delight,
        like organ-playing sweet and far
        In Mary's praises sounding bright:
        O door of heav'n, O morning star!

    I'd hoped to write a proper letter today, but all my postal duties have stiffened my hand & emptied my head.

    All love from your adoring son.

[52] Petrus Cornelis Boutens (1870–1943), Dutch poet and classical scholar. Grainger's copy of his *Beatrijs* (Bussum, 1911) was a gift at Yule 1912 from his Dutch friends Bep van Rijsbergen and her mother.

---

468 TO ROSE GRAINGER   Hotel de la Couronne
Sunday evening 17.11.1912.   Breda.

    I came here by the Flushing train this evening, & it seemed very sad to have to leave it, when a few more sleepy hours would have landed me with you in London.

    Have been reading much of "Diana" over again & relishing & admiring it hugely. I naturally adore her 2 sudden acts, the going to the sick friend (Emma) & leaving the lover in the lurch, & her divulging of his secret to the editor later on.

    I love folk (including *women*) to be unreliable & to seemingly throw to the winds what years seem to have zealously gathered. That is "Nora" over again. If we refuse to trust instinct when it *acts dangerously* we cannot expect any fine freenzied flights of fancy, nobility, inventiveness, artisticness, brains, corage, tenderness, or anything else. Good form in art, such as Beethoven's, Bach's, Chopin's, W. Whitman's, my Rarotongan records, etc, is mainly a frantic corage (or so it would seem to the timid, to us artists it is natural & safe, of course) in throwing off "consequence" & plunging fleet-instinctively into the wildest, suddenest & wantonest contrast-demands, & turns of whim.

And now for my chewings-of-the-cud on sex-relationships. My ideas on these subjects seem to me deeper & of more human importance than my music. As a musician there is so much that is trite & lazy & versöhnend [German: conciliatory, placatory] about me, whereas if my real ideas on sex-relationships (so clear & final & unproblematical in my head) could ever reach & effect mankind anywhere I feel I might be reckoned among the fairly big chaps, in a way.

I start taking it that we all agree that sex can never be smothered, maybe occasionally in an individual, (a very abnormal one) *never* in a class. The person who escapes freest from its influence is probably the person who indulges freest in it, but then he doesnt *bodily* escape, only in soul, perhaps.

I feel sure it's largely the cramping & enslaving of the sex instinct that makes the middleclass so ugly, overbearing, troublesome & shudder-rousing. They have invented a soulful-restraint combined with bodily-gluttony which is more deforming than the harshest asceticism.

I personally take the view that all's right with the instincts of man, & that the general soul of the world is all for beauty health & improvement. The "general soul" of the world does not include its "ways & means", poverty [*sic*], work-madness, dirt, illness, decency, lies & all the other shabby results of biting off more than it can chew, which civilisation's done.

Of course I'm not concerned with this "general soul". It's like the "broad public" in musical matters. I trust it, own its got limitations, but am for it until a better thing crops up, & believe in clearing out of its way all the muddle & muck that slows its path. Nothing chocks [chokes?] humanity's ideal flow towards good more than sex-customs of every kind. Nearly all of us jog on nobly till we bundle up against sex, & then suffer a lowering, a muddy bath. Personally I take the view that *sex* in all its instincts (the birthing breeding instinct upwards — or downwards — to the most "abnormal" sideslips) is a thing worthy of being practised for its own sake, because it teaches & humanizes like art philos[o]phy science, & because (like all other big instincts) it is *always pure* if *genuinely instinctive*.

But let us shove this personal view aside & judge matters not from my personal sex-adoration point of view, but according to how it affects truth & ease of intercourse & growth of soul between men & women, men & men, women & women.

Humanity somehow or other has got hold of a view of "sex-purity", whence I know not. This view interferes with men & women being close friends almost to the extent of making it impossible (to the bulk of humanity anyhow) & is apt to brand close menfriends as buggers & women dittos as Lesbians. We have seen that hardly any of the finest of the world have escaped bother & hindrance from thes[e] tiresome ideas.

Even Cyril & I (seperately) have met the thing.

It is amazing how the impure "sex-purity" idea pervades ones actions & makes one either foul thoughted or sad almost every hour of the day. The shy-impure maidenly manners of almost any female who is in a railway carriage alone with men, or worse — gets left with one only; all simplicity gone, merely a nightmare of foul nonsense left. The son cannot travel in the mother's cabin.

Men & women are in clean earnest conversation, they reach either's bedroom & the simple intercourse is checked. A thousand times a day one is revoltingly & highly timewastingly reminded of the ridiculous fact that somewheres or others one goes about with another set of sexual machinery to the other ½ of the world: penalty for this still needful, or at any rate unalterable state of things; — constant unterbrechungen [German: interruptions] of conversations, constant befouling reversion of the mind to sexual matters (delightful at times but boring when out of place)

½ the charm of acting the lover to me is the momentary unfettering of these shackles, over against one person, at any rate. At last one may handle a female as innocently as one may a dog, at last even a bedroom may be a theatre of conversation, even the charmful hours of late night & early morn may witness rational & human behavior untainted & not suddenly insane.

Why, I wonder, does not an overwhelming overweight of enlightened mankind already see, clear as day, that our European sexual prejudices stand in the road of cleanliness, health, purity, comradeliness, truth, openness, & advance of every kind more than almost *any other* factor? We are agreed that woman must be no slave, therefor she must earn her way alongside man, (both sexes being gentlerly & more sensibly treated than at present) & both join economicly to give their joint offspring a good material chance in life.

Modern law & thought supports barreness in both sexes, so that "lust for lust's sake" is, thank god, already a working thing & no longer challenged.

Yet when all these heavy & volcanic changes are agreed upon the bulk of even the *clever* of men & woman still cannot see that to have *any notions of sex purity whatsoever* upsets the whole apple cart at one go. We have already given up purity notions with regard to doctors; an excellent thing; why not extend to the cause of truth, science, comradeship, freedom & innosence of intercourse those priveledges already claimed by health? Health is hardly more important than goodness, cleverness, success, truthfulness, & is oftenest the very same thing.

I'm found in a woman's room at 4 in morning. Who'd believe me if I said we were argueing. Isn't it ridiculous?

As long as women were only slaves, or supposed to be, it wasn't so ridiculous, because who'd want to argue with slaves?

Formerly to breed enough new folk was one of the problems. Better any old thing than nothing, when wars & bad drainage claimed a greedy pro cent. Now breeding's so profligate that noone's proud of it. Now we need *fine* folk, not merely folk. Intercourse is friendship & knowledge, experience & growth, therefor *nothing* innocent must stand in the way of intercourse. Without tons of intercourse we can expect no fine flowering mankind

Therefor it at all costs.

One might be asked: Why not intercourse without any taint of sex between man & woman, still less between the same sexes? It's no good, one cant suppress an instinct without increasing its all-importance. And the future of humanity demands that we dont make sex so important that it swallows up everything that comes into its path.

Let us have done with young women taking musiclessons to approach the musician, with concert halls as the addresses of absurd letters & all the rest of it.

Once women (enough of them) earn their living *unsexually*, in honest (I dont mean the term with any halo) work competitively with man (or *un*competitively with man under a possible socialism) woman's sexual acts will be of her own untrammelled choice as much as man's (witness "as long as there's a mill" etc in "Hindle Wakes")[53]

Then a clean intercourse (sexual or platonic) between the sexes may begin.

The economic rize (the wish to earn in women) is going along very hopefully.

53 *Hindle Wakes*, play by William Stanley Houghton (1881–1913). Rose had seen it in August 1912, in the production by Miss Horniman's Company at The Playhouse theatre.

Let us, the clever & thinking (& therefor the *thoughtaltering*) section of mankind not lag behind in either realising fathoming or spreading the knowledge of the *need of utter sexual freedom.*

"Free love" was tiresome (tho' better than nothing) it mostly meant "untidy unions." The term "love" should not enter at all into *public* opinions, views of conduct. The idea of "love" has already been so shockingly misused that one pauses chilled at its *public* appearance at all. Hence one's teeth on edge at arm in arm bethrotheds, wedding services, & all the rest of it.

Leaving "love" & "purity" chatter out altogether we'll be able to deal with sexual matters & even sexual crime quite firmly enough.

The matter with rape is the particular violence of it, not the character "etwa" [German: so to speak] the "locality" of the violence And so on all thro.

We need not worry about the breeding instinct going lost. The danger seems always to be the other way. Economic matters are what often already are, & surely always should be, its guides.

The life of the race is dear to us all nearly, & children are attractive enough in every way for there to be no danger of the yearning for them to fade away, under decent economic surroundings anyhow, & they are out of place elsewhere.

Not until spitting is thought more dishonorable than nakedness, dirt than lust, & freedom better than anything else will sex loosen its present ugly & filthy grip on us.

When men & women take their sexual pleasures & increase their sexual experiences as sanely & simply as they now take they [their] meals, & lessons in foreign tongues, then will sex take a sensible place, & refresh (even if it tires too) & improve us like sport & music & poetry & lots of other things that fanatics damned "i sin tid" [Danish: once, lit. in its time], & not be *indulged in so gluttonously either*, for it's far from being the only apple on the branch. Above all it will be *thought of* less, & when thought of, thought of *as itself* & not as a *manevolent* [sic] *spell* working dark disgusting oracles.

How awful would music be if we never listened to it for its own sake, but always only with regard to its mysterious influence on other matters!

I find very few folk *wholly sensible* about sex. I dont even know whether you've any really sun-clear *thoughts* on the matter, though you're certainly steeped with *comradelyness-versus-sex* which is the keynote of any possible modern morality in the matters.

I wouldnt trust any of my menfriends, except Cyril perhaps, but then he's possibly ascetic & therefor not clear-sailing. Women like Miss Du Cane are shy-in-thought I'd think & dont get far. Karen *behaves* perfectly sensibly when I'm with her, but I wouldnt like to trust her *thoughts* on the matter.

If I died tomorrow I dont know who I'd trust to proclaim my clean & thoroly jolly ideas on sex-relationships to the world.

That's not as it should be.

Therefor I write you this little ramble on the matter.

I may not be a very important person, but I feel inwardly very very sure there is nothing about which my personality bears richer fruit for humanity than on sex-matters. There I'm truly in my element, within my head, ecstatic & thankful for joys, yet painstakingly observant of all that health, goodness, freedom, cleanliness, & progress craves.

I'm "me mother's boy" with [in] other words.[54]

54 Rose replied on 19 November, "I am delighted with yr lovely long letter, & must carefully read it through several times, & think over it well. I love to have yr views on such subjects, & am *not at all sure* that mine are not very similar. We must speak together about the matter more closely, after I have digested yr letter, dearest".

469 TO KAREN HOLTEN   Hotel de la Couronne
[Original: Danish]   Breda.
19.11.1912.

Little Karen

How lovely it was to hear that you are just beginning to be able to run a little again. I have really (since we met in Slettestrand) never doubted that your foot would be *completely* as before. For you could make all the movements, it was only strength and speed that was lacking. I imagine that the thickness of the one muscle will disappear bit by bit, but something like that doesn't go from one day to the next. It is difficult for other people to put themselves into a thing like that, but I feel inside me that the whole thing must have been *infinitely* depressing for you. Your life is perhaps not so overful of diversions, and thus such a thing comes to act particularly strongly on your feelings. How awful it is when something bodily isn't quite normal any more, isn't it?

It is (so long [as] there is not the slightest thing wrong) difficult to understand in advance that one would have such a great and passionate love for *the usual*; but one has, to the highest degree.

But tell me, my "kind" Karen, are you not, leaving the foot business out of account, a little bit depressed? It appears to me as if you no longer revealed yourself completely to me.

Perhaps I haven't any right to wish it, but it is a great sorrow to me to think that you go round with a set of thoughts that you don't want, or don't have enough confidence in me, to talk of.

It appears to me a little as if we are drifting away from each other with time. Perhaps you answer that that is what I must desire. Only in a certain way. I would most like to loosen all bonds that hinder you from living life as freely and fully as possible, with or without me; but it is painful to me to feel that our friendship diminishes, and that it runs the risk of dying out on account of a kind of tediousness which you feel about the situation, which, moreover, I can very well understand, and even admit you are quite right about.

You know, I hope, that your inner mind, and all your views interest me above all, and you can never express yourself too extensively or too often about these things, as far as I am concerned. It is your remarkable sweet poor little soul that I thirst after above all, and always will thirst after, more or less, irrespective of whether my actions seem to deserve the longed-for enlightenment or not.

When you write, it is mostly concerning my activities and feelings. That is very sweet of you, and I am glad to hear from you whatever it may be; but it is not that that I am most interested in hearing from you. In my actions I am completely taken up with my own affairs, but not in the same way in my mental and spiritual interests. On the contrary. You are of course right with regard to photographs. I will bring my camera with me in January.

It was only in respect of Compositions that I heard from the Americans, not in regard to any tour, or such like.

It is extraordinary how lacking in sensuality I am.

I as good as never think about sensual things when I am sitting in the train, as I did before. And yet I am quite well again, and eager and capable in many ways.

How *dreadful* it must be for a woman to be married to a man and see him become old in that way!

Until 25 Nov my address is Augustin's. After that, London.

Goodbye, and many small cool kisses, my little treasure, and tell me everything you care to.

Your
Percy.

470 TO KAREN HOLTEN
[Original: Danish/English phrases]
23.11.12.

In the train
A'dam → Cöln

Have received your letter of 20 Nov. You are completely right in everything you say, except:

"To be so completely suited to you, it does
appear that I have not been able."

A thousand times *yes*; you *have* been able to in the highest degree. I admire your attitude towards me from the 1st moment until now, more than I can tell you. You have treated me with the greatest fineness, motherliness, and with an indescribable goodness.

When I in my last letter stated that I would so like to hear a little more of your inner feelings, it was simply something I felt at the moment; but I realise now that I don't any longer have a right to demand such a thing at all, and that you are perfectly right in not being able to comply with these desires of mine. The whole of your relationship to me, from the first, is for me a lovely uplifting human drama. I cannot think that there are many other beings in the world that I could have studied lovingly (as I have studied you) and found so much that is fine and upright, and so little that is violent, nasty and uncontrolled. You have a great culture in you, little Karen, and I cannot think of greater praise.

The splendid thing about you is your absolute freedom from "false pride". How one can talk to you about everything and be certain of getting an answer which truthfully contains your actual relation to *the matter* and not just your momentary reaction to the form of the question! In you there are great abstract depths, and I fancy I have learnt an enormous amount from having been together with you. Above all you are so tremendously literary-talented. Your last letter (20. Nov.) one could surely submit to men of letters as an example of a most uniquely *economical* way of expressing oneself in letter form. Irrespective of what you have to say in a letter, is contained nearly always in just that quantity of paper (2 or 4 pages) you chance to have at hand. That is a sign of an enormous literary technique.

Your letters are both German "knap" (concise) and Dutch "knap" (clever). The thing is you always appear to have a lightning-sharp picture of the true spiritual relation of things. Maeterlinck wrote about his wife that to live with her was "to observe the gestures of wisdom"; the same can be said about your letters. One gets the impression of seeing Psychological movements as something physical and tangible between the lines. I find your decisions and intuitions concerning our relationship in every way satisfactory and admirable, and I have found it and find it now a great "priviledge" to have had the opportunity of getting to know so closely such a "sublime creature" [German: "hehr ein wesen"] as you.

Your mental nature is formed with the same charm and delicacy as your external bodily features. A letter like your last calls up your knees, your hands, fingers, lines of your legs, and the smoothness of your skin for my eyes, and your beautiful hair. A joy to be able to study you internally and externally.

A little human being like you really deserves a finer and less vulgar comrade than I, but I am (in a faun-like rough way) very thankful for the innumerable sweet unforgettable undeserved insights I have had into your soul and body.

It is strange to see the years slip by and see things lie passive as though according to the law of least resistance, or something like that. This I see before me in life: a kind of autumn-like declining peaceful progress without special hope, but full of clear beauty and high goodness.

That time you first let me whip you, after my return from Australia, it was a very great experience for me, a kind of happiness prophetic of victory. It was as though victory and fortune *could* not be denied to someone who had had such a great thing "bestowed on him". Another great moment was a little over a year ago, when on my arrival in Copenhagen I found that my letter from Haugesund had not destroyed our friendship although it had played its part in killing a large part of your love. It was a great and lovely experience for me, something of the very best.

One more thing; you are *completely* right in everything you write, I admire and love you as you are, wish for nothing different, and only regret that I am such a poor partner to you and that I obviously satisfy you so little while you satisfy me so exceedingly.

Have you read d'Annunzio's "Gioconda"?[55] If not I think you would have much pleasure from it. It is brimming over with the sense of beauty; it strikes me as truly "Southern", but related in a way to Maeterlinck. I (personally) am not *particularly* interested in the **people** apart from "Sirenetta", but I find her excellent and her song touching and apt.

I am playing in Cologne on Monday and Tuesday.

Goodbye, and heartfelt thanks for everything. I am so happy with your letter.

Percy

55 Gabriele d'Annunzio (1863–1938), Italian poet, dramatist and novelist. Grainger was reading his drama in Dutch: *Gioconda:* Treurspel; Uit het italiaansch door J. Salomonson-Asser. (Almelo, 1900). Grainger's copy was a gift from the translator, 16 November 1912.

471   TO ROSE GRAINGER
23.11.12.

Amsterdam,
527. Heerengracht.

My darling

Yesterday & today my happiest days in Holland since you left.

Refinement & money are extremely real things to me. Only these lines to bear my love until I write from Cöln.

Yr *darling*.

472   TO ROSE GRAINGER
Tuesday. 26.11.12.

Cöln.

My own poppet.

How I throb to be back with you darling. I feel so strong & fit to enjoy our samvær [Danish: being together]. I want to read you some more [of] St's "In the Sth Seas" which I've been dipping into again.[56]

Last night was the Hauptprobe [German: final rehearsal], as important as tonight's concert, & much fuller always. All went very well, Steinbach very nice indeed & the audience very warm, quite 4–6 recalls after my soli, no encores allowed. But I suffered **cruelly** yesterday, felt like in Berlin. Tomorrow I dine with Labouchere's on my way thro A'dam, & will meet there the Griegs & the Röntgens. I like the Labies.

I enclose a letter from Karen I got ½ week ago, which I'd like you to read, if you dont mind. I think it's very satisfactory. I wrote in my last letter saying I thought she was not particularly communicative, & I hoped it was not because she imagined any lack of *interest* on my part, to which this is her reply.

56 Robert Louis Stevenson, *In the South Seas: being an account of experiences and observations in the Marquesas, Paumotus and Gilbert Islands in the course of two cruises, on the yacht* Casco *(1888) and the schooner* Equator *(1889).* Karen had brought Grainger the two-volume Tauchnitz edition (1901) when she visited London in July 1910.

It is only right that she should gradually feel less yearning to "ontboezem" (unbosom) as the years go on, since I can't give enough in return, but it's nice she feels genuine friendship for me all the same. The last page of her letter refers to my having said I am in a period of lack of sensualness.

I dont agree with her explaination. Sensualness is of the soul rather than the body as far as I'm concerned, & my present poverty of it is more due to my compositional joys & absorbedness than ought else, I think. I think Scandinavians have a wonderful gift of stating tersely in a short letter a whole situation of feeling, of placing their whole attitude before one by the very simplest means.

Such a letter as K's seems to me typical of a people who in their art produce Fru Fönss's letter.[57]

This is my last letter, dearest, before about 8 o'cl on Thursday morn.

57 "Fru Fønss", a short story by Jens Peter Jacobsen, published in his collection of short stories *Mogens og Andre Noveller* [Mogens and Other Romances] (Copenhagen, 1882).

The month of December saw several performances of Grainger's music in London: on 4 December, the London Choral Society did Father and Daughter *and* Irish Tune from County Derry *in Queen's Hall; on 5 December, Ada Crossley sang three folksong settings, Grainger accompanying, at the Thursday Twelve O'clocks at Aeolian Hall; on 11 December Grainger conducted* Mock Morris *at the Royal Amateur Orchestral Society's concert at Queen's Hall. Most notably, perhaps, when Thomas Beecham took an orchestra of seventy-five players and two concerts of British music to Berlin on 16 and 21 December,* Mock Morris *was included in both programmes. These performances were of some importance historically for the acceptance of English music and musicians abroad and the presence of Richard Strauss in the audience was to lead to a performance of* Mock Morris *in Berlin, Strauss conducting, on 27 February 1914.*

On 17 December Grainger left for a brief tour of Germany and Holland. The tour began in Coblenz where, on the same programme on 20 December, Grainger played the Tchaikovsky B♭ minor Piano Concerto and the César Franck Symphonic Variations, Willem Kes conducting. He then went to Holland where, in the six days from 22 to 27 December, he gave five recitals, using two of the same programmes as the October–November tour. The tour included matinee recitals in The Hague and Amsterdam. He reported to Karen Holten that he had somewhat overstrained himself in Coblenz, with the result that he had had to play half the programme in Holland with the music.

Rose left London on 20 December, travelling with Anna Høyer and meeting Percy at Arnhem on the 21st. She and Percy returned to London together on 28 December.

For Grainger the year ended triumphantly from a professional point of view. Its main event, indeed, one of the "sensations" of the season according to the Daily Telegraph *of 27 July, had been his coming forward as composer and conductor. This coming forward survived the pricks and arrows of incidental controversy to bring him to the point where* The Times*, never a paper to lend itself to wilful overstatement, pronounced on 31 December that Grainger "has proved in one sense the successful man of the year, for he has soothed the savage breast of the critic and charmed the stubborn one of the general public".*

From a personal point of view, however, the year ended on a more poignant note — of renunciation and loss.

473 TO ROSE GRAINGER   Palast Park-Hotel
Wed. eve. [18 December 1912]   Coblenz.

My darling.

Am not feeling unhappy yet, though I have seen a man tickle the inside
of his ear with a toothpick, repeatedly & determinedly
Have done a ferocious whack of practising today.
I'd advise you to be at Victoria *at least* ½ hour before train sails, or else
book train seats thro' Cooks. Otherwise it might be tiring & silly.
If any 10-stave MMS music paper comes from Augener (I ordered some)
please bring it for me to write "Twilight" on.
Should you be detained by bad weather, or else, wire to me here before
midnight Friday evening. If detained remember my concerts are
            Sunday: Winschoten
            Monday: Leeuwarden
            Tuesday: arrive Amsterdam.
Longing to see you Saturday early.

    Percy.

Am going to bed before 10 tonight after a few minutes at Hinemoa[58]

474   TO KAREN HOLTEN   Palast Park-Hotel
[Original: Danish]   Coblenz.
18.12.1912.
[Extract]

If only I could fold you in my arms, without explanations and corrections. We humans are forced to choose our way through life with regard
to so many many things. And so it must also be.
    But it would be so splendid just to give ourselves up to the quiet or
·stormy happiness (je nach dem [German idiom: whichever]) that I think is
always ours, when only we are together and have time for each other.
Neither Christmas nor New Year would be boring institutions if we could
be allowed to "kiss them in".
    Mother meets me in Arnhem (Holland) *on Saturday morning. Then we
travel home the 28th Dec.*

58 "The Story of Hine-moa (The
Maiden of Rotorua)" appears (in
English) as one of the chapters in
Sir George Grey's *Polynesian
Mythology*, which Grainger had
read early in 1909 (see note 1,
1909). While the exact meaning of
the reference here is uncertain, it is
most likely that Grainger was
reading the story in Maori as part
of his studies of the language. He
was probably reading *Hinemoa,
with notes & vocabulary* by the
Rev. H. J. Fletcher, published by
Whitcombe & Tombs Limited (in
New Zealand, Melbourne and
London, [18--]), a version of the
text for which he prepared his own
(undated) translation.

1913

After the heady euphoria of 1912, 1913 began quietly. More confident now in his compositions, Grainger looked forward with eager anticipation to the second series of the Balfour Gardiner Choral and Orchestral Concerts which began on 11 February and which included the first performance of his much valued Hill-Song.

Though the letters to Karen reflect the usual scramble and business of his London life, he had few public engagements: only fourteen over the first three months of the year. Perhaps this reflects Rose's concern that he should not jeopardise his health by accepting engagements indiscriminately. Those engagements which he did accept were nicely varied: five of the new type of "composition concert", at which he conducted his own works, sometimes appearing as soloist in the same programme; four concerto appearances; three solo recitals — two in which he contributed solos to a mixed programme. The decision that he should spend more time in Great Britain took him once again into the English provinces: Bournemouth, Birmingham, Nottingham. He had, in the previous couple of years, "given up bothering about the Provinces". He made two short journeys abroad: to Copenhagen between 24 and 28 January and to Switzerland for the concert in Berne on 11 March. He was also in Belfast on 7 February. His main source of income at this time was his pupils.

But the year quite soon began to bring its disappointments. First came Karen's announcement that she loved another man, with the result that although Grainger stayed at her home during his visit to Copenhagen, they were no longer lovers. Then came a cooling of critical enthusiasm for the Balfour Gardiner concerts in general and for Grainger's compositions in particular. By the end of February Rose was writing philosophically to Percy of the "failure" of his "soulful" works. Though his compositions were still popular in provincial concerts, such was his sensitivity to the nuances of criticism that he responded by announcing to Karen first that he would have to change his style, then that he was "retiring" from composition, then that he was not publishing anything for the time being.

At the beginning of April Grainger was in Holland for two performances of the César Franck Symphonic Variations *with Mengelberg and the Concertgebouw Orchestra, in The Hague on 5 April and Amsterdam on the 6th. The Dutch trip was not an unqualified success and Grainger wrote to his mother on 6 April that he felt it would be his last and to Karen on 13 April that he was giving up Holland for a while. The pendulum swung again with several quite successful appearances as composer/conductor and pianist in the English provinces during the months of April to June and with his London piano recital at Aeolian Hall on 29 April, which he de-*

scribed to Karen as a great success. The summer began well with many "at home" engagements and pupils.

Underneath the continuing talk of success and its occasional manifestations, there is, in the early part of 1913, an undercurrent of falling away, of sadness. It is against this uncertain background that ideas of extending his activities to America began to form again. There was a notion of a composer-tour put forward by Schott, an offer of a teaching position in New York from Frank Damrosch and news of the successful New York performances of some of Grainger's choruses. Then of course there was the constant model of Herman Sandby's lucrative American career. The Sandbys visited London in early May, on their way through to Denmark. Grainger had not seen Herman for five years. Nothing came of these American plans and intimations at this time. But they provide a backdrop for the events of 1914, if not for their timing.

475   TO KAREN HOLTEN
[Original: Danish]
6.1.13.

31A King's Road
Sloane Square
London. S.W

My dear little friend.

It was sweet of you to let me know as you did that you now love another man.[1]

"If you were my own daughter" (as it is called) I could not with greater truth wish you happiness, satisfaction and experience in this love.

Obviously it is best you do not tell me who it is, and obviously our relationship existing up to now must cease.

I am very grateful that you wrote; "not really for my sake". I could scarcely wish for anything sweeter.

You are a glorious creature, an unforgettable little comrade, with a delightful body and a good strong soul, and with a divine gift of being happy and *making* happy. That you may be it, and make it, that is my 1st wish.

To me you have been sweet, compassionate (*above all* compassionate) honest, true, brave. You are full of *life*, and where life is strongly, love (and happiness with it) cannot long be absent, I think.

Would that we could always remain dear close friends.

Above all we must see and avoid anything which might possibly cast any shadow at all over your relation with the other man.

I propose to come to Copenhagen about *the 24th*.

You surely do not mean me to come to Ceresvej despite this? Although you do not write to the contrary, I don't believe you can mean this.

For me to stay with you could possibly hurt the other man, or even lead to something or other unfortunate for you.

Don't you think, that if I stayed with you, that we would after all get into a fleshly situation with each other?

You cannot in any case expect any "moral support" from me. I am good, but selfish: "Lofty" in my thinking, but greedy in my actions, as you know.

In your presence I would most probably feel strong fleshly desires towards you. If you, above all things, didn't want to, then that would obviously be another matter.

But the danger would be there I think. Shouldn't we rather avoid it?

Do you want your letters to me back? I have them all. *Let me keep them if you in any way can do so.* You can rely on my "discretion" (as the Germans say).

What will you do with my letters to you? *Do not destroy them, if you can in any way refrain.*

1 Dr Asger Kellermann (1874–1954), her future husband. When Karen married him on 15 August 1916, after his divorce from his first wife, Grainger still did not know his name.

On the other hand, if anyone who loves you got to see them, it would certainly cause unnecessary pain or misunderstanding.

Could you not let me have the letters in my keeping? You could get them back at any time.

I have a lot of feeling for our letters to each other.

There is a lot of life in them, which was not allowed to live in any other way.

Shall I take our nude photographs, and the negatives of them, home with me from Copenhagen this time?

I only ask. Of course, everything must be as you advise. Further, there must be a whole pile of pictures of sculptures, etc which I took to Copenh. from Norway 2–3 years ago. They are not here, they *must* lie at your place.

Thanks about Birkerød, the programme is already rounded off.

Beecham performed "Mock Morris" in 2 Concerts in Berlin, *great* success each time. Many good critiques. R. Strauss was present, and Beecham says he (Strauss) will himself conduct "Mock M" at a concert in Berlin.[2]

Beecham will engage me (he says) to conduct 1 or 2 Operas in London in the month of May. This must be kept hidden, because Beecham is so unaccountable.

On Saturday aftern. I am playing S. Saëns, soli and conducting the 1st performance of "Colonial Song" in Bournemouth.

Everything is going well. I am *quite well* again. Good reports and critiques of my compositions from many different sides.

I am staying in London until I travel to Denmark.

Goodbye, my former little meat-mate, I am full of tenderness and hopeful thoughts about, and hope for you

Your loving
Percy.

476 TO KAREN HOLTEN   31A King's Road
[Original: Danish/some English]   Sloane Square
18.2.13.   SW

Dear little Karen.

I have surely not thanked you for the letter and the criticisms.

But when I tell you that on Sunday I had 4 different rehearsals, and in addition heard (in Palladium Concert) Beecham conduct "Mock M" again,[3] and wrote 26 pages (of 20-line music paper) score Sunday and Monday, and conducted 2 pieces at Lady Speyer's "at home" Monday evening, and today have gone through and made alterations in "Hillsong" and "Colonial Song" parts for the rehearsal on Friday, and since the 1st Balf Gard Concert altered a little in "Gr. Bs" again and made the score ready for the copyist, and in addition gone twice to "Rosenkavalier" and once to "Elektra" and am going this evening to "Salome", and have 2 or 5 pupils daily, then you will surely understand that I am well and happy but not particularly in letter writing mood.

"The Irish" for strings is a *complete success* and I will not be surprised if it is played just as much as "Mock M." I am completely satisfied with "The Irish" for strings.

"Inuit" sounded well and got da capo, but bad critiques on the other hand.

Gard's 1st Concert was "a-mile long" and **terribly** boring.[4]

"Gr Bs" is *much better* now, shorter and more "striking" in every way.

On Sunday I am playing in the *Albert Hall* on Wednesday week in *Birmingham* Grieg Concerto in both cases.[5]

2 See p.484. The highlights of the Berlin programmes, including *Mock Morris*, were performed at a kind of "Victory" concert at the Palladium on 12 January 1913. Nothing came of Beecham's operatic offer.

3 At a concert given by the Beecham Symphony Orchestra for the National Sunday League at the Palladium on 16 February 1913. Beecham's six-week winter season of grand opera and Russian ballet at Covent Garden had begun on 29 January with the first English performance of Strauss's opera *Der Rosenkavalier*. The season also included Strauss's *Elektra* (first given in London in February 1910) and his *Salome* (first given in London in December 1910) which was introduced on 18 February. Strauss was in London for *Der Rosenkavalier*. The season ended on 8 March.

4 In fact all the programmes were too long. The *Daily Telegraph*, reviewing the final concert on 19 March, expressed ". . . a pious hope that if these excellent and always decidedly interesting concerts are to be continued in another year a greater attention will be paid to the arrangement of the programme. In all cases during the season just closed the schemes were over-long . . ."

5 And in both cases under Landon Ronald: on 23 February with the New Symphony Orchestra for the Royal Albert Hall Sunday Concerts; on 26 February for the fourth concert of the third series of orchestral concerts of the Birmingham Philharmonic Society. The programme of the concert by the Edward Mason Choir on 27 February included Grainger's *Lord Maxwell's Goodnight* (with Ada Crossley) and his *Marching Tune*.

Rehearsals on Thursday, Friday, Monday, Tuesday and the following Thursday for Mason's Concert, same evening.

I am very captivated by Strauss's new things; never heard lovelier things of his than in "Rosenkavalier".

Many warm thanks, and grateful thoughts for the sweet Copenhagen hours from your *strong* (!) lucky happy

Percy.

477   TO KAREN HOLTEN   31A King's Road
[Original: Danish]   Sloane Square
Monday. 3.3.13.   S W

Little Karen.

Yesterday, for the first time in several weeks, I had 10 minutes quite free, without having to think of anything, or *prepare* my thoughts for anything, and I felt suddenly completely empty and I thought to myself: "What would I actually really like, is there anything?" And was quite surprised when the thought came; "most of all to write little Karen a little letter".

Tomorrow is the last B. Gard. Concert in which I am "engaged", and now I can think over everything, and gather hints for the future.

Hill-song was not a success. There are things in it that I am more satisfied with than almost anything else of mine, tender places, fine things, but the "wild" sections are not sharp or powerful enough. In a small hall it is better, but in the big Queen's Hall very slight. Instead of 28 instruments I must use about 40-60 for the piece, a military band, in other words, instead of *solo-wind-players*. But *one day* this piece will be one of my very best, I really believe.

"Colonial Song" sounds satisfactory. The tutti-section in the middle sounds crashing and grand, and the solo voices warm, vocal, and good. Col. Song will soon be printed for orchestra, 2 voices and orchestra, piano solo, and *Trio*.

My "At Twilight" will not be performed tomorrow. Fagge's choir can do so little of von Holst's work that Gard asked me to put *Irish* instead of it, so they could take time for v. Holst's work.[6]

"Eglamore" bores me, although I believe it is excellently orchestrated; but that I will know more about after the performance. The papers have not praised me this year, and the papers are right, and I am wrong. Once more I have produced the *same kind.* of small pieces as last year, and the papers, that wish me well, and have realised that there is "more in me" than has yet shown itself, are disappointed that I have not come forward with a larger work, or things with stronger *personal feelings* in them. It is only good that they make large demands on me.

"Inuit" makes *no* impression, many people find "Col. Song" unimportant and too sentimental (others like it) *surprisingly* many were *not unfavourably* disposed towards Hillsong, and I don't expect any profit from tomorrow. "G. Bs" has not received *any* bad critiques this time. The critics in other words have not found me *too wild*, but *too tamed*, and no one can complain at that. They want to see me go *"the whole hog"* and when I am man enough to "go the whole hog" it will after all be all right in time.

I am clever enough to realise my own faults, and learn from experience, without complaining or getting mad, or sulky. But of course it is not a very nice time for me all the same. After a brilliant year I now have my defeat, and although I can bear it, I don't exactly welcome it. [Lit.: I don't exactly have a sweet-tooth for it.] People regard me as someone who at the moment doesn't need support, Balfour supports me (and indeed quite rightly,

6 The programme of the third Balfour Gardiner Concert on 4 March included *The Cloud Messenger*, a forty-minute ode for chorus and orchestra by Gustav von Holst, founded on a Sanskrit poem of Kalidasa. Grainger's *At Twilight* was given its first performance by the London Choral Society, Arthur Fagge conducting, at its concert at the Queen's Hall on 3 December 1913. Of the performance of *Sir Eglamore* on 4 March the *Daily Telegraph* commented, "There is immense spirit and a healthy vitality in the work, though one could have wished, perhaps, for a little less 'vitality' — and a more agreeable tone — from the trombones to which Mr Grainger gives so much prominence".

490

I don't complain) less than last year, the other composers regard me as something inexplicably idiotic and unimportant (without unfriendliness) and on top of all that come cool critiques, and in addition my own dissatisfaction with my things, and my own awareness of how dull and unsatisfactory a great part of my things are.

And I haven't got sympathy and support from *your* side either. You have seen through me (and partly given me up) at the same time as the papers. And indeed just as rightly so as the papers. This sort of thing is always **just**. But not on that account necessarily pleasant.

I am not unhappy. Because I am clever and strong and untiring and will manage to learn from my own mistakes, and will yet triumph over many many "hindrances" before I have finished with things. But although I am not unhappy, I am nevertheless at the moment what is called a "little piano". I have had my "caning", from you, from the papers, from many other directions and am a little bit depressed although *enormously* hopeful. My whole mode of composing must be different. Won't you write to me?

7 On 11 March Grainger played the Grieg Concerto with the Bernischen Musikgesellschaft, Fritz Brun conducting. The engagement came through Engelbert Röntgen.

478   TO ROSE GRAINGER   Bern.⁷
[Postcard]
11.3.13. afternoon

It's not comfy playing with thoroughly bad musicians.
Otherwise the conductor is a nice enough chap. Weather gorgeous, alps a treat to see.
Be with you tomorrow midnight I hope. Ta for card. Percy.

479   TO ROSE GRAINGER   [PM 'sGravenhage]
[Postcard. PM 4 April 1913]

The worst Xing I've ever had, terrific bundling.
The poor man with me was volcanicly sick, but I wasn't.
Alas! Mengelberg takes *all* the tempi differently & it is appallingly hard to change so much at last mo. He has them from Pugno who had them from Franck.⁸
The speeds, etc, are delightful, but I wish I didnt have to do them all the same.
The Sixes are delightfully well & kind.
The poor Augustins are awfully affected.
You ought to buy "Everyman" of 4th April. I think it *absolutely* the best paper I've ever seen.

Fondest love
Percy.

8 Stéphane Raoul Pugno (1852–1914), French pianist and composer. On 7 April Grainger's Dutch friend Bertha Six wrote to Rose that the critics were not as enthusiastic about Grainger's performances as she would have been. The Augustins had lost their son Rudi in February 1913.

480   TO KAREN HOLTEN   31A King's Road
[Original: Danish/English phrases]   Sloane Square
25.4.13.   SW

Peculiar how composing-moods throw a particular colour and charm over periods which for non-composers might be remembered as ever so barren.
It will possibly appear to you a little unreasonable that your last visit to London is for mé a particularly rich and flourishing time. I know that I behaved miserably, and that this time was unpleasant and horrible and unjust seen from your side.

But I don't have any particularly sharp impression of all that, although I know that it *was* like that.

What *I* remember so lively is the blissful ecstatic moods which your presence set off in me this time, despite all my unpleasant behaviour and undeservedness. This time you acted quite unusually compositionally on me. I am not one of those who go and believe all that much in inspiration on the whole, least of all in a special *erotically compelling* inspiration, with regard to creative work. But that I *have* written certain things in which your personal influence (and the influence of the great joy that went out over me from you) stands out strongly, is (for me) undeniable.

Your presence filled me with such a raging happiness last time you were here, unlikely as it may sound, that this flowed over in the sketches for "When the world was young"

and another kind of tender and slightly melancholy trembling feeling which lay on me expressed itself in "Shallow Brown" which indeed came to life while you sat beside me in the music-room.

There are not many moments which I remember more clearly than that one when you sat there opposite me, with a curious devoted cat-contented kind of dreamy expression on you, and shook yourself a little and said (about "Shallow B") "that's sensual". That was a moving moment for me that I will never forget. Also a whole part (the story where the 2 voices begin with the 1st duet) in "Colonial Song" reflects that time's flourishing rich erotic-thankful blissful mood, although *these* sketches were written before you came to London.

I wonder whether, when you hear and play these pieces you will feel *my real* feelings in that time, and not only my unfortunate disturbing behaviour?

It would have a quite specially deep satisfaction for me to be able to convince you some time, by a good performance of a piece containing things from that time, of what I myself know: that this period was particularly full of sweet and tender feelings on my side, and it was really a kind of madness or weakness over me that it expressed itself so nastily and crookedly in actual deeds. The fortunate thing for a composer is that he has "the last word". For if these compositions are only from a musical point of view fortunate and good enough, then everyone will understand *my* feelings from that time, whereas if you don't express your impression of injustice and disappointment in an artistic or some other permanent way one will not know in the future how *you* felt. And I must say that I regret this. But I would be still more unhappy if one should never get to know what good sweet tender things went through me that time. It is indeed often the terribly unjust thing about artists, that what they *do* and how they *act* doesn't have any importance for themselves, while *the real life* consists for them in their thoughts, and artistic whims.

But the people that have to do with artists are not always witnesses to these thoughts and caprices, or these things do not have such a great importance to them, as they have for the artists themselves; especially when people are so little together, as we are, for example. I can so well understand that you think that I have been bad and tedious to you, and that "the game isn't worth the candle" as we say, but for me, on the contrary, it is impossible to believe other than that I have always been ideal towards you, for I live in my thoughts and imaginings about you, and I am convinced that no person has seen you more beautiful than I, and understood you with a warmer inward appreciation, or bathed deeper in your soul's purity and singularity. If you were to die now, I would be able to leave a description of the whole of your being, your appearance, and your mental and animal peculiarities as possibly no one else could.

You have never lived in what the folksongs call "the living life" cleaner higher more beautiful than you do in my memory and daily thoughts, and as you will come to do in the description I will one day make of you. And just because I do not idealise you a bit.

I have a really genuine notion of how you actually are in *your self*. Chance and circumstance cover up and fog the picture. But you have shown yourself to me in a pure light and in completeness, and I believe I have been able to "take advantage of my opportunities". That I have in addition disappointed you is a burden and a sorrow to me, but is after all a side-issue.

481   TO ROSE GRAINGER   Headinglea,
2.5.13.   Branksome Park,
                                                 Bournemouth.

Darling mum

My first impression of "Sh's Hey" is to be very delighted with it. It certainly *sparkles* very considerably & the hammerwood etc parts tell stunningly.[9]
Longing for you to hear & judge it tomorrow

Very lovingly
Percy.

9 On 3 May 1913 Grainger conducted the first performance of his *Shepherd's Hey* in the version for full orchestra. On the same programme he also conducted his *Irish Tune* in the version for strings and horn, and played the Tchaikovsky B♭ minor Piano Concerto and a group of two solos. Of the *Shepherd's Hey* performance Percy wrote to Karen on 4 May, "I am very satisfied with it myself and think it is by far the most 'sparkling' and 'brilliant' of my things for full orch. Much percussion is used, glockenspiel, piano, xylophone, triangle, harp etc, and the whole thing sounds very 'clattering' and 'sparkling' . . . Percussion has an enormous future, I am certain".

Now begins a strange interlude in Grainger's life: that of his courtship of Margot Harrison, daughter of Sargent's friend Peter Harrison and his wife Alma. Mrs Harrison, the translator Alma Strettel, had helped Grainger with his verses for At Twilight *and with the English version of the poem of* Father and Daughter. *The Graingers and the Harrisons had been acquainted since at least the beginning of 1906 and probably earlier.*

It was an interlude of high excitement and intensity leading to the announcement of Percy's engagement to Margot in early July, though truly culminating in the breaking of that engagement in early August.

It is easiest to attribute the breakdown of the marriage plans to the fact of Grainger's extraordinary closeness to his mother, and this is the explanation offered, without rancour, by Margot's father. It is indeed true that a regard for the impact that marriage would have on his daily life with his mother was one component in Grainger's hesitation.

But the documentation, incomplete though it is, suggests that there were deeper reasons. Most particularly, it suggests that beneath their genuine and strong affection and mutual regard, Percy and Margot discovered fundamental differences of opinion: overtly, to questions of the having and raising of children and notions of marital freedom; less overtly, perhaps, to the complexities of Percy's views on sexuality.

If, in his relationship with Margot, Grainger tried to rediscover or re-

create the liberality of his relationship with Karen, he did not succeed. And so they parted — with heartache and pain on her side and a lingering "malaise" on his, despite the unruffled appearance of his public life.

482   TO KAREN HOLTEN   London.
[Original: Danish]
11. June. 1913.

Dear lovely little Karen.

I am undergoing some strange feelings at the moment. In the last few days I feel the feeling of falling-in-love with someone here, and that is quite surprising, bitter and yet very sweet, although it is impossible for it to bring me or any other person anything except disappointment and sorrow in the long run, since I will never give way to my natural feelings, as long as I am capable of resisting them, and that I am able to do.

You have never seen or heard the name of the person involved, and it is also best in that way, although it hurts me very much that there must be the slightest caution and *secrecy* here in the world, above all from you. I have of course told her that I love someone already, without letting her know in what land you live, or anything more than that you filled my life in many sweet years (sweet for me) and do so now, only that I have behaved unsatisfactorily, to an impossible degree, and therefore can't mean so much for you now as formerly.

How impossible and hopeless feelings of love are, how disturbing also, yet they give a certain life, when they are new, that scarcely any other feeling is capable of.

I was so tired and finished in recent times, but this gives me new courage, I don't know why or to what end.

It amazes me beyond words that I, who felt myself so old and worn-out internally, can be whipped up to something after all, as little as it is, perhaps?

Little sweet meat-mate and comrade, how extraordinary it all is. To find again in another person the charming traits, sweetness, truth, courage, purity, humour, etc that you have taught me to know, and yet everything so different, and each with her personality, and each with her own separate sorrow and burden, derived from her nationality, class, circumstances, health or ill-health, so that no person in any way, *not for a moment*, can replace another, just as little as Strauss could replace Bach.

Dear darling and comrade, have sympathy with me and wish me, if you can without difficulty, all good things. From the feelings that I now feel at the moment, it is, as I have said, impossible for me to expect anything other than difficulty and disappointment, because of [a] 1000 things. Neither is it possible to see any possibility of the feelings finding any natural bodily expression or satisfaction.

But the chief point does not lie even there.

That there are people in the world who feel tenderly and warmly for me, and have sympathy for me, for that I can never be grateful enough. And it is an indescribable blessing to feel oneself destroyed by exaltation and hopeless hope.

A thing like that suits me. I feel ill, without appetite, and altogether out of joint, but I value that tremendously.

The first vague weak impressions one has in a new love's budding feelings, they are indeed divine, aren't they?

I have a *terrible* lot to do at the moment, am playing today in the Albert Hall on Friday at an "at home" on Monday play and conduct in Birmingham, on Wednesday play in Brighton with orchestra and after that a series of "at homes."

10 Thomas Beecham had given the first version of Strauss's opera *Ariadne auf Naxòs* for the first time in London at His Majesty's Theatre on 27 May 1913. In this version the opera is a pendant to Hoffmansthal's adaptation of Molière's play *Le Bourgeois Gentilhomme*. The play was given in an English adaptation by Somerset Maugham and in conjunction with Sir Herbert Beerbohm Tree, who also produced it and played Jourdain.

11 Grainger was staying at the country home of Lady Northcote (see note 25, 1911).

I am completely "taken" with Strauss's music at the moment. There are things in "Ariadne" and "Rosenkavalier" which have completely "captivated" me. "Ariadne" Vorspiel is for me Strauss's most moving work.[10] I am very bored with my own compositions at the moment. I am busy setting "Col. Song" as a Trio.

I am very glad both you and Cai are fond of that piece.

I would have written to you before about my "strange" feelings, if I had felt them before; but they are quite new, only a few days old.

Always your lover and tender friend
Percy.

483   TO ROSE GRAINGER   Eastwell Park,
[Original: Danish/English]   Ashford, Kent.[11]
21.6.13

My own pet

It will be more boring here than anything I have ever been to; but it is also *splendid* for the nerves and I feel now, after 2 hours indescribable tedium, just about new born.

The enclosed was found in the box just before I left home.

It must feel strange to feel so ardently yet impersonally well towards another being as a mother can, & particularly my old Battling Nelson.

Till Monday (11.30?), my own darling mum

Percy.

Have written Smyth & Polignac

484   TO KAREN HOLTEN   Eastwell Park,
[Original: Danish/English phrases/private language] Ashford, Kent.
Sunday. 22.6.13.

Little dear sweet Karen.

Just some few words to wish you a good journey to Norway, if you go there already the 26th.

You can imagine I am thinking a lot about you in this time. Just because other love-thoughts are now going on within me at the moment, I must remember with sweetness and bitterness the life we have lived together in many years, difficult, important years.

You will always be my first wife, whether there come more or not.

And if our love-life is wrecked, there still grew in it the same brave shoots, the same instinctive joy-bringing hope, and the same victory-anticipation that attend the paths of the most successful victorious love. Could there ever be anything sweeter, more moving, with stronger will to live in it than the evenings the first time in Svinklöv; when I wrote at Green Bushes and you slept at my side with your hand on my penis?

And when I came back from the Australian tour, and saw you in your red-yellow national costume in the distance (walking to and fro on the grass) on the drive from Fjerritslev.

And the small journeys we have made together from Fjerritslev to Aalborg, etc, and all that getting-up-early the last morning when we had to leave, and impressions of sunrise, etc. Sometimes it appears to me as if one can't have courage to live further, when one's heart is so full of gripping memories and the exact remembering of all the sweet things that wanted to come to life and thrive, and that one none-the-less didn't allow to come to anything, and that one is a kind of graveyard for. I shall of course go on living, and be well, and often be happy and often unhappy.

But when I think about what we have experienced, how hard I have acted and how tenderly I have felt (often) then I can so well understand that people can come to a point where they would rather be free of the whole thing.

On account of circumstances, on account of my nature, and of many other things it could not have been successful otherwise than it has been. There was no hope for us, but we felt hope all the same, oh so strongly, at least I. I felt such strong hope for things which I knew for all that could never become reality. Walt says: "Battles are lost in the same spirit in which they are won".

Our link was indeed not only an erotic or a love tie, although it was that as well. But we were really married people. Many generations' inherited marriage-feelings worked together and made us married and gave us marriage's particular feelings.

And although I always set myself particularly against just these marriage-feelings, they remain as something of the sweetest and most bitter.

I have perhaps ruined your life, have not been any support for you, but I believe that I have understood you. I have understood the courageous and the incredibly germinal in you, something wild and "hard-driven" in the midst of all your sweetness and tenderness.

And I have lived on my powers of imagination.

Inside me I have seen you old, seen you as mother, seen yours and my children, seen all possible things, more than you would believe perhaps. Not only you are disappointed, but I as well. Because I myself have operated the machinery of disappointment itself, the disappointment is not for that reason less, necessarily.

Never never will I hold the memories that I possess of you less dear. You fill now and always such a large place in my soul, where you live with an indescribable sweetness, freshness, life-force, tenderness, beauty, and *uniqueness*

My nature does not forget many things. My actions can be hard and stupid, but *I* am not, believe me.

It is peculiar with memories. Things don't get less when one has thought long about them. And they can often live stronger than the actual life one lives.

I don't regret anything. I am glad that you "have given me up as lover" as you wrote, for I have never believed that our love would succeed.

But I am full of inward sorrow all the same, and it would be so deeply good to talk long, long with you, little beloved merciful comrade.

Is it true that you believe we will always be good deep friends? Tell me whether you believe it.

I have just finished reading a book that I think extremely well of: *Mann av guds naade* [Man by the Grace of God] by Hulda Garborg.[12] Perhaps you would have pleasure in reading it. The language is charming in it.

Today the Trio-arrangement of "Col. Song" is ready for the printers.

On Tuesday I am playing once, on Thursday twice.

Goodbye, little friend, I hope you will have a nice time in Norway. I love Norway, more than I can say.

Your
Percy

12 Published by Aschehoug, Christiania, in 1908. The book had been a gift to Grainger from the author in September 1910.

485 TO KAREN HOLTEN   31A King's Road
[Original: Danish]   Sloane Square
4.7.13.   S W

My sweet little friend Karen

It is strange enough, but I am engaged; to Margot Harrison. I do not
think you have seen her, but perhaps her father, the painter, a close friend
of Sargent, who came and heard my compositions in Upper Cheyne Row,
possibly when you were there.

Mother is indescribably happy, for she has always been particularly fond
of her.

I long so dreadfully to be able to talk to you about so many things, you
who have always been so compassionate to me. If you can wish me everything good, from your heart, then that would do terribly much for me. But
if you feel *against me* then that would take a great strength and security
from me.

Be merciful and good to me for the 1000th time, little Karen, and do not
turn your heart from me, or be cold towards me, if you can do otherwise.

How marvellous it will be to see you and talk with you in Nov. if you
will let me.

Write soon to your loving

Percy.

486 TO KAREN HOLTEN   Hill
[Original: Danish/English phrases]   Theydon Mount
13.7.13.   Epping.

Little Karen

Many thanks for your letter of 9.7.13. It was however heavy to get, for
I have the impression that you don't after all feel what I call "compassion"
for me, and I know that the reason must be that you, when you review the
whole thing, must think that I have not been a good person, and that you
are disappointed at me or tired of me.

It is bad enough that you should nourish any cold feelings at all towards
me, because for many years there has been such a great confidence between
us, and absolute truth, that can be said without exaggeration.

Therefore I think that you must know me just *as I am* (it has always been
my object that you could do this, if you wanted to) and therefore it is sad
enough to know that you "cannot feel sympathy for my actions" and to
have the feeling that at bottom you think I am worth nothing. I know that
you are always kind and good, and it must be *my badness* which prevents
you feeling compassion about me now as before.

Nothing is so terrible as *deceit* and *lies* being mixed up with love. When
you think back now over everything with us and about things as they are
now, do you feel that you have encountered deceit and lies from me? Has
that after all occurred that I above all things would have prevented?

There is something in your next to last letter that I would like to touch
on. You write:

"This that you say there was every good thing in our love, but that
you knew it could not be successful, that I do not understand."

It seems to me this is not so obscure.

When we were first together in Oakley St I felt that we 2 had great
capabilities to be ideal lovers, friends, married people, or whatever it
should be, but very soon I also knew that it after all could never become
any satisfying reality, because, although inner feelings mean more to me

than to most people, still material circumstances do play a big part that it would be idiotic to ignore.

If you at that time had been rich, and 10 years younger, or I in possession of greater courage and capacity for work so that I could quickly have earned a lot of money, then everything could have been perfect between us. But your age was an insuperable thing, and I English enough to know that I would always have suffered under this. Our view of the appearance of the two sexes is once and for all very different, and the difference between a man of 40 and a woman of 42 or 44 could, *for me at any rate*, not be erased by love or comradeship, *unfortunately*. I knew that you wanted to have children, but I did not dare to bring penniless children into the world, and if I waited until I had collected enough money, then you would be perhaps 36 years old, and according to what I have heard and read it would be dangerous for you to get your 1st child at that age. And then it was a question whether I would *ever* be able to earn enough for my mother, for you, for myself, and a child or children. And this doubt was well founded, because I still haven't got by far sufficient means for this, and will possibly never have it. Therefore I knew from the first that you and I could never be married, and I tried to explain this in Upper Cheyne Row. Then you said: "If this is so, let me rather be happy now, and unhappy later on, than never to be happy with you." It was difficult for me to act firmly after that. All my natural feelings agreed with your "let us be happy now", and at the same time I thought: "What right have I to resist her demands of the moment (which are mine also) just because I know that it *in any case* must *end* unhappily with our love-instincts."

Later there came a time (after your father's death) when I was almost tempted to forget all my material considerations, and in my heart I would have been very happy, that time, if I could have managed to hold on to our love and let go of everything else. But my nature was not able to take such a great swing away from the sensible, and "at the back of my head" I didn't have any real hope anyhow, however much I wanted to.

If you and my mother had got on differently together and been united, again it might have been different, possibly.

And my greatest mistake lay here that I behaved so idiotically that you and mother "did not get a chance." It is bitter to think of; and if you knew *how differently* I would have liked to behave, that time!

It is clear that after a certain coolness between you and my mother, the hope for our love and for a marriage was almost certainly destroyed.

But our love was just as genuine great and sweet despite all external considerations. Our instinct was to be ideally happy together, to be life-comrades and our union when we were together, and our way of thinking when we were separate had that "stamp."

Then there came (about 1910 or 1911(?)) a quite peculiarly strong reaction in the direction of concentration on the practical side of my compositions, which affected us in so far as I thought less often about our love than in previous years, because thoughts of composition took up nearly the whole of my free time. I think this had a cooling effect on you. I thought just as tenderly and lovingly about you in that time (or at least it appears to me that I did) but you heard and saw less of it, and when after this I repeated the old doubts and hopelessnesses, then I do believe you saw things more clearly than before.

Then comes the day that you write that you love another, and later again, after we have seen each other in January, you write that you "have given me up as lover, but not as artist."

I cannot deny that after that I began to feel lonely. I cannot live without love and passion without suffering so much from it that all my other feelings and activities become infected by hopelessness and greyness.

About 3 months ago I began to feel feelings of love between Margot Harrison and myself. In the beginning quite weak and indefinite, but after the beginning of June a little more threatening and after 8th June quite clear, whereupon I immediately wrote to you about the matter.

In over a year I have certainly been very happy about Margot and found her more amusing than other pupils, but never imagined possibilities of love, and if you hadn't been in love with someone else and "given me up as lover" (to which you had an absolute right, of course) I would not have felt so free to love again as I now did.

Then you wrote that you wished me every good wish, but begged me not to make it as difficult for her as for you.

If the material conditions (money, age, etc) hadn't stood in our way, one of the objects of my life would have been to make you as happy as few women have been, and this you *must* have felt with your deep natural instinct, mustn't you?

Now I hope I will be able to make Margot very happy, and be so myself as well.

Now the material conditions are a little different anyway, and I see some hope.

Because your and my love was doomed to failure, I am no pessimist or ascetic and would like to enjoy as much happiness here in life as possible and contribute to others' happiness all I can. Do you think this is bad of me? Little Karen, won't you tell me more exactly which of my "actions you cannot with truth say you feel sympathy for"?

Everything you feel and think means so much to me, and I would so very much like to know what you think is bad in me. That I have made a terrible number of mistakes, that my manners were not good enough so that everything possible became more difficult than necessary, that is very true, but it is surely not this kind of weaknesses one cannot feel "sympathy" for. Rather it must be that you feel that I have behaved falsely, or with deceit or with coarseness. Do you really feel that? I can say with truth that I never for a single moment have wanted to betray you, or keep anything back from you, and if after all untruth and misunderstanding has crept in between us then I think it is a *real tragedy*, for this is indeed the worst that could ever happen between us. That I have not been able to give you everything you wished for, that *lay in the nature of the case from the first* and is therefore only sorrowful and sad, but not a tragedy, in my estimation. But deceit and misunderstanding and lies are indescribably bad, and almost unforgivable, it seems to me.

You are right when you say that one does not need compassion because one receives and gives great love. And it was not for that, that I wanted it.

When I ask for your compassion, I want to beg you to feel tender and good enough towards me to be able to really understand my feelings from first to last, and to forgive that part of my actions which have been against you, because you realise *that with my nature as it is*, I have not been able to *be otherwise*.

We would be able to forgive everything *everybody* did if we loved all people enough and knew all people sufficiently to *really understand* the reasons for their actions.

I think that you must know and love me enough to *get to the bottom* of all my feelings and motives. If not I think it is almost a tragedy. I have never seen anything about you that I couldn't understand and love, more or less, and it would be so glorious if you could feel the same about me. In any case it would be a great kindness towards me if you would say straight out what you understand and forgive and what not; if it doesn't bore you, of course.

Thank you for not having anything against meeting me later in life. With regard to November, it shall be as you wish, that we don't meet.

It is possible Margot and I will be married towards the end of November or beginning of Dec, but this is not decided yet.

A few days ago I got my first account from Schott. Very good, much better than I expected.

My "Royalties" (per cent on takings) up to now have made about £109. I have only paid about £71 of the costs of printing, since Schott's contributed to the expenses and takings have paid for the remaining expenses, which in total come to £300.

So that in less than 2 years I have earned over £18 on a capital of £71. Now I will have scarcely any more expenses (only relatively small expenses for reprinting) for several years, since I don't intend to publish anything for the time being, whereas I can expect an income of not less than £50 yearly, if all goes well.[13]

"*The merry wedding*" (Silkenhair) I would like to publish as soon as I can get time to complete it with as much care and perfection as possible.

As I have said, this piece is written entirely under your personal inspiration, and is a real portrait of you, not flattering perhaps, but as good as I was able to make it. I hope you will let me dedicate it to you, and also let me ask Schotts (when the piece comes out) to send all my "Royalties" of "*The merry wedding*" to you. We can't tell whether this piece will have a great success or not, but I think it could very well be successful, and it would be nice if you got material pleasure and profit from a little artistic work which is a portrait of yourself and was created so entirely under the charm and colour of your personality as this was.

Little little Karen, feel as forgiving and understanding towards me as you can. Do not believe that I have ever felt anything else than the finest feelings for you or ever could. I have only good feelings, and it is a waste of time to believe otherwise. And I regret my errors and weaknesses just as much as you or anyone can do.

I beg you once more, be as merciful as you can to me and don't feel any hardness toward your

Percy.

Many warm greetings to Miss Arlaud.

13 According to the contract of 9 July 1913 between Grainger and Schott, the cost.of publication was to be borne in equal parts by the composer and the publisher. The royalty payment was three pence in the shilling.

487   TO ROSE GRAINGER
Friday. Aug. 8. 1913

Hound House,
Shere,
Surrey.[14]

14 Grainger was staying at the country home of the Harrison family.

My own darling mum

Margot & I have broken off our engagement, & that fact will be announced publicly at the end of the month. She & I have talked carefully over everything & both feel that our purely personal & inconsiderate desires have led us into a situation that we can only make good by relinquishing altogether, & starting off cleanly from the beginning. I should never have *thought* of marriage with anyone without making every effort to know your feeling about it all accurately first, & also I should have adhered to my old resolve to finish the task of making you & me *quite* independant monetarily before thinking of taking on other ties. Also Margot feels that her readiness to put her desire through (her will to be married to me) at all costs, without considerately wondering how it would effect others was a thing unworthy of her very keen abstract principles, & her mother bears her out in that point, as she also does as regards the whole matter. Naturally, darling, she & I are more in love with each other now than ever before. Nothing binds one better to anyone than the feeling that they grasp the critical & controlled & finer side of one's nature & support it in actual action with corage & cheerfulness, does it?

All the same, this feeling of love is not intended to stand in the road of either she & I being free now to take any other love chances.

Since I am not offering her any definite result of her & my love I cannot wish to keep her from other life, though we both feel *now* that it would be a delightful thing if we always felt for each other as we do now. But time alone can show that.

In the meantime we part in complete harmony & Margot *has* been so sweet & kind to me, & so lifted above all her merely personal desires. Yesterday was an indescribably happy day for me.

I shall write later on today, dearie, telling you my arrival hour on Sunday, etc. This release from a false situation (the result of my weakness & selfishness) will make our winter still jollier, will it not?

Your adoring son
Percy.

488   TO ROSE GRAINGER   Sea Marge,
Thursday. Aug 14. '13.   Overstrand,
                                                          Norfolk.[15]

15 Grainger was staying at the country home of Sir Edgar and Lady Speyer. Gutrum Hyllested was a friend of Alfhild Sandby. The incident with "the Hyllested" is unexplained.

Darling Mum

It's lovely here. It's most amusing to compare a new rich style-less house like this with an older tasteful one like Hound House. Both have their points.

This place is more like a Hotel as to fittings, etc. Bathrooms, mirrors, etc, modern & delightful, those sort of things our age (to my mind) surpas[s]es past ages in easily. The new things are easier to keep clean, & that means so much. For instance, mirrors of glass only, with smooth round glass edges, cleaned with one flat wipe, no wooden frame for liquid to pour into, & fastened firmly to the wall with 2 screws thro' 2 holes in the glass. And of course really warm water. But where the modern types (or the taste-less types) fail is in profusion of useless things. My bedroom is full of 100s of useless small things, & books crowd the too small writing table, & such.

Now no really wellbroughtup thoroughly English country house makes those mistakes, economic the upper English are, though they have an amateurish streak that make[s] them put up with lukewarm hot water gear & the like.

I hope it will be jolly when Margot stays with us; but if it isn't it cant be helped, & it's no use looking the other way & pretending.

Let you & I darling, united as we are against any possibly hostile world, henceforward banish from the *mutual* part of our lives *all* **hensyn** [Danish: regard] *to other folk*. Kindly & loving & generous to others I hope we'll always [be] *when the mood takes us*, but less [let] us follow our feelings only, & *not even to each other take Hensyn*.

We will be ever so much the happier, I feel sure. Remember, darling, I loved you with the Hyllested & will always adore & support you (should you need or wish it) in any Icelandic outbursts of pure & regardless selfassertion. Politeness I love, too, but the 2 can go well together, & if one of the 2 has to go it has to be politeness, as far as I'm concerned.

From now on, sweet one, never feel you have to curb one iota of straight-out heedless selfexpression on my account. I will only love you the better for all your ownish ways & so will all other true friends.

I, too, on my hand, will always let you know just what I'm wanting, & will try to get it, too.

Lovingly & happily yr devoted one
Percy.

489   TO ROSE GRAINGER   Sea Marge,
Friday. 15.Aug 1913   Overstrand,
                                                          Norfolk.

My darling mum

Shall be with you tomorrow at about 12 or before.

I herewith enclose you a letter from Margot which I would very much like you to read & return to me when I get back. It is in reply to one of mine in which I mentioned the thrill & interest I felt in compositions & love matters until some definite *actuality* was reached, such as a rehearsal, performance, publishing, or the idea of engagement & marriage, & the disillusionment I felt at nearly all actualities of every kind, & therefore the advisability & [of] handling types like mine on a very free basis, if any good is to come of things. I also mentioned the disadvantage in love that accrues if either party **needs** the other, & to my mind the advantage if marriage thoughts & proposals were only entertained between such lovers as had freed themselves from actually standing *in need* of each other, so that the question of marriage or not could be entered into without the bias of too strong wilful desires or tyrant passions.

I think her reply puts us all on a still better basis than better [before], dont you? No thought of marriage is now *a need* to anybody concerned, yet there are no bitter feelings, & no real inner love relationship has been destroyed, so that *if* after I have earned a greater independance for you & me, & after you & I have had longer years to get to know Meg in & she us, she & I still feel really in love, & you think you could genuinely (without nasty effort) view her inclusion in our life *happily*, then there be no reason why even the idea of marriage should not be reopened again.

Before such a time came you & I (more experienced re Margot than at present) could confer carefully together, & any action should then be *real joint* action only, nothing less. If such could not be, the whole marriage idea could easily be put aside, then as now, nor would the real inner nature of Margot's & my love needfully suffer thereunder at all.

Now that all unfreedoms are removed, & no relationship remains but free uncalled-for undutiful intercourse between any of the 3 of us, I should think next week's meeting ought to be as comfortable as possible.

You, dearest darling one, need feel absolutely no other call on you towards her than towards any other friend I love & all light & truth on any point, however clear & sharp, will be welcomed thankfully by me.

Forgive my bothering you with all these sides of my affairs, but our lives are so everlastingly knit together, darling, that I **must** share all serious thoughts with you, *as long as you can stand them.*

Really everyone is very exceptionally good & kind to me

Till tomorrow

Yr fond one
Percy.

On 19 August Grainger made a highly successful appearance at the Queen's Hall Promenade Concert, conducting his winning 1913 combination of Shepherd's Hey *for orchestra and* Irish Tune *for strings and horn.*

On 30 August, having let their house at 31A Kings Road to Mrs George Young for eight months, Percy and Rose left London together on a tour which took them to Norway, Russia, Finland and Denmark.

The tour began with a recital at Christiania on 5 September. Between 5 September and 31 October, when the Norwegian segment of the tour ended, Grainger played his basic tour recital programme in thirty-two of the smaller towns. He also gave a second recital in Christiania and one in Bergen.

As in the previous years, his recital programmes included a bracket of his own compositions. But this year also marked a new departure. At each of the two orchestral concerts in Bergen and the two in Trondheim, in addition to his normal performance of a piano concerto and a group of solos, two of his orchestral works were played, one of which he conducted and in the other of which he played the piano part.

It seemed that the fortunes of his career were picking up again. His first Christiania recital was attended by royalty and was sold out, two sure ingredients of success in the Grainger canon. He told Karen that, to his surprise, the tour was more successful than ever before.

Rose stayed on in Christiania until 14 September, visiting friends, attending the theatre and concerts and earning a little money from teaching. She then travelled two days by boat to meet Percy at Stavanger. They travelled together until she arrived back in Christiania on 12 October. With the easier schedule of a provincial tour, its minimal stresses and the prolonged summer-like weather, they enjoyed many outdoor activities: walking, climbing and boating on the fjords. They also indulged their current passion for the "kino", visiting a cinematograph in nearly every town. Rose announced to her friends that she was in the best health for years.

Isabel Du Cane arrived in Christiania on 13 October, travelling with the Graingers at least until the end of October. Grainger was also back in Christiania for his second recital there on 17 October. By the end of October they were in Trondheim for Grainger's concerts there on the 29th and 31st.

Then, on 1 November they left for Russia. From 5 to 8 November they stayed in St Petersburg, where Grainger played the Grieg Concerto under Alexander Siloti on the 8th. They left immediately for Helsingfors for the recital on the 11th. By 13 November they were in Stockholm and later that same evening in Copenhagen. Next morning Percy met Karen briefly at Copenhagen railway station, on his way to Vejle for the last concert of the tour. This was to be their last meeting before the war. By 15 November the Graingers were on the boat for London, arriving on the 16th. By 17 November they had taken up temporary residence with Mrs Irvine at 24 Cheniston Gardens.

490   TO KAREN HOLTEN   Søstrene Larsens Hotel
[Original: Danish]   Christiania
6. Sept 1913

Dear little Karen.

I was so glad to hear from you again.

I would be *terribly happy* to spend some days with you at Ceresvej, but the thing is that I presumably will not come to Denmark in the Autumn, or if I do I will only be in Copenh in transit. I will explain this more fully, little friend, when I have more time in a few days.

I must now travel to Bergen, but would thank you first for your sweet letter.

The Concert here went splendidly. Entirely sold out and the King, Queen, and the English Princess Maud were present.

Until later.

Percy

I am *terribly well* at present

491 TO ROSE GRAINGER   pr. adr: *C. Rabe's Musikhandel*
8.8.1913. [*sic* 8.9.1913]   *Bergen*
12 oclock Midday.

My darling.

Just finished rehearsing Grieg Concerto & Mock Morris & Clog Dance, all of which go well.

From now on, please write to me to Rabe's above underlined address, darling, as I shall be leaving Troldh. in a day or so.[16] All are very nice & sweet to me & all is comfortable. Many greetings to you from the Rabe's. I gave them your message re Norwegian girls, etc.

I shall arrive in Stavanger early Tuesday Sept 16 & will go to the *Victoria Hotel.* So if you come to Stavanger, please arrive some time Sept 16, not *too* early. My concert there is Sept 17.

Or if you come to *Flekkefjord* arrive some time Sat (not too early in the day) Sept 20, & I will meet you. My concert there is Sept 21, so I could meet you Midnight after Sept 20, or any time you like. Only let me know which town you come to, dearie, & when I may expect you if possible.

I have such a funny feeling lately, as if we were all old old people, & everybody dying & all things passing away, not sadly or tragically, but as if we had all come to the end of everything quite pleasantly like at the end of life.

Particularly everything Scandinavian is giving me that feeling.

The result is that I feel very clingingly towards you, mummy darling, you seem to me the only reliable point, the only steadfast & lovingly-firm point amidst so much that is merely passing by. You & I seem to be lasting on united amongst a drift of floating other things.

Therefor I dont want you to even think in any way to separate us in the least degree. It isn't that I dont love little Margot, I do, & trust her, & would like to make her happy. But I'm not cut out to be beginning any "new life" now so late in the day as it feels to me, & what ever is to happen to me must simply grow naturally & fondly into your & my present mutual life. What cannot happen that way must just remain undone, I fear.

Your loving old partner & adoring son
Percy.

16 Grainger was staying with Mrs Grieg at Troldhaugen while giving his concerts in Bergen on 9 and 11 September. The programme for 9 September included *Mock Morris* in the version for strings, and *Handel in the Strand* in the version for piano and strings.

Theatret. Bergen

This is the theatre both the orchestral concerts are to be held in.

492   TO ROSE GRAINGER   Patersons Hotel Norge
9.8.1913. [*sic* 9.9.1913]   Bergen.
Tuesday 1.30 midday.

Am spending the day in town as we rehearsed this morn at 10 & the
concert's this eve, & I thought the traipsing back & forth to Troldh. too
much in the wet. Both the Beyers came to the rehearsal, (as he cannot be
out evenings now) & enjoyed themselves very much. I find him sweeter than
ever since his illness, & a relief after the "ladies", who, however are
pleasant enough. The Verlobung [German: engagement] subject has not
been mentioned by them, so I've just let it lie.

All the pieces went very well this morn.

I left some music on your table the night I left. You might bring with
you what of *my own* things were there, not the rest. Then we can send off
the pieces to Borgstrøm, if you will bring with you his address.

It seems to me as if we'd pretty soon be able to be using our winter
clothes. It's quite chilly here. I continue my belly exercises with very healthful feelings.

I hope you will come to Stavanger if you feel any lyst [Danish: desire]
to do so, I dont see why we should wait for Flekkefjord. There is no reason
or advantage.

I feel that you & I are closer together now than we have been for many
years; at least from my side. It is strange that in early youth or early
manhood there should be those shy doubting tendencies leading to small
misunderstandings. I always feared that my sensual & more "perverse"
tendencies would not be met sympatheticly by you, I could not foresee that
we could ever get really comfortable on such points. And perhaps there was
a little truth in it too, perhaps things would have surprized you more 12
years ago than they would now. It was the one shadow in my mind, that
I felt the need of holding back certain sides from you, because I feared you
might oppose them, or really dislike them, at any rate, & it had always a
curious painfulness for me that you, the being I loved best & who loved
me best, should perhaps be the one to uselessly stand between me & any
innocent pleasures; for that all my pleasures could never be anything but
innocent I always knew, for I have always known that there is no part of
my nature capable of anything un-innocent.

It was very stupid of me to have thought like that, or even imagined you
capable of wishing to oppose for a moment any really innocent pleasures.

I should have known that if you ever *did* oppose anything, it was no mere
opposition to real innocent pleasures, but because your critical capacity for
reading people made you smell a rat somewhere in whatever individual or
individuals happened to be connected with such pleasures. Time has shown
how right you have been in all the rats you have smelt. It has never been
that you have definitely set yourself against any particular person so much
as a feeling of *uncomfortableness* on your part, which, I knowing you so
well, could instantly note, but in my thickerskinnedness not always follow
or explain.

When Mrs Grieg stayed with us I certainly then could not understand
why you should have felt such a chaffing & surpressed uncomfortableness.
You may now have forgotten what you then felt, but I dont; & though you
were charming enough to her, I felt a keptback undercurrent strong
enough. Later events have shown how true & useful your instincts were in
her case.

To feel, as you "*intuitively*" do so absolutely who is our friend or foe
is a most **marvelous** asset, & I see how unjust & unwise I have been to that
instinct in the past. I was not able to foresee your instincts Cassandra-like
almost infallability & I must confess I sometimes felt it was rather a bore
to have such strong instinctive decisions going on around one about people
& things I myself saw no special danger or indeed import in. But I now not

only see that you have always been right, but also another thing: that if people & situations are not *quite right* for one they nearly always are *quite wrong instead*. As usual, there seems to be no "gyldne middelvej" [Danish: golden middle-way]

It was very unjust & suicidal of me that I should ever have brought the very least influence to bear on you in the direction of wishing you to *ever in the least* **suppress** any manifestations of your character reading instincts & rat-smellings. Suppression is **always wrong** in every case, anyhow. And in your case, of all! From now on I wish to follow your instincts blindly, & even *should* they make mistakes (which they are not likely to do, at any rate if you give them their head) I should like to make those mistakes with them.

And I hope you will allow this to soak into every question & branch of life. Even if I should tell you "I wish to get married" you must not let that be enough for you. It is essential that I should let you know my thoughts yearnings & wishes, but I do not want you to be guided by what I say. My expressions of feelings, hopes, desires are often (if not always) very partial & colored by momentary moods. I hardly think I know what I want, really, & I certainly dont know what's good for me.

Until you *yourself* feel; "he ought to marry, & just *that* person" I feel sure the time is not ripe, or the person not well-chosen. It is so easy for me to feel in love, so hard to judge of what any future life would be like. I cant judge people at all, or read them, nor can I at all foresee coming affairs or likelihoods. Therefor it will seldom be my place to decide anything in life.

But you **can** & I hope you will. I hope you will always help me through with all my affairs as you have heretofore, **only much more so,** & I hope I will always be still more trusting & much more obediant than I have always been.

Where I must show *my character* is in the control of all that pertains to my health, & in the keenness of my workmanship & untiringness of my efforts. We have each our own talents & must excercise them *to the full*.

I am being a good boy, no bad habits, & no useless nervousness before performing (for that is largely merely a bad habit too)

& ever your loving & yearning one

Percy.

---

493   TO KAREN HOLTEN   Grand Hotel
[Original: Danish/English phrase]   Egersund
19.8.1913.
[PG notes: "Should be Sept."]

Dear little Karen.

Forgive my long silence. But there was an awful lot to do in Bergen with the orchestral rehearsals and everything.

The tour is going much better than *ever before*; it surprises me, but it is so. My compositions for orchestra were a storming success in Bergen, Mock M. and Shepherd's Hey had to be given da capo and the whole atmosphere was screwed up to the highest. It was lovely in Troldhaugen. Mrs Grieg said you looked splendid, and that it was going well with your foot. Can you really *run* again, little friend?

It is so tedious that I won't have any time to be in Copenhagen this time. I have 3–4 engagements in the Danish provinces, play in St Petersburg the 9th Nov, and must conduct in Ipswich (England) already the 18th Nov. If I come to Copenhagen, we will no doubt arrive 11 o'cl in the evening and travel to Jutland early the next morning. But I can write in more detail about that later.

And now I am going and speculating about other things with respect to you and me. *For me* it will always be a pleasure to be together with you. I cannot believe anything else than that our friendship and love *through my whole life* will mean for me what it always has done, more or less. There are times when one concentrates more on one thing or on one person than at other times, but I see more and more in all things that I am a faithful person *in my own way*, and although I wander everywhere with my feelings, I always come back again to the same old dear things and people and interests.

But although the love and friendship between us can be ever so satisfying for me, I cannot avoid seeing that it may appear to you as ever so deficient from your side.

The feelings of love are composed of so many different things. The *quite abstract* spiritual feelings have blossomed very richly between us, it seems to me. You would, of course, rather have something more *real* and *active* in your love than just abstract and spiritual relationships, (I count sensual feelings under abstract in certain conditions) but you couldn't help being strongly endowed in these directions, so that when I could not offer practical relations rich in action, you couldn't avoid answering my abstract feelings with something similar from your side, although I well know that was not what you would have preferred.

It has perhaps been a great danger for you (or in any case the *practical* side of you) that you have such great abilities in abstract directions.

You are too fine, too critical, and too clear-seeing to be content with the more usual types who could better support your practical side, and therefore you are attracted to men who can be fine and kind and loving enough but let you down when it comes to *the real life*.

I would never be able to serve you in real life except as friend, and free comrade, and *wandering* lover. But that is not to say that you will never be able to find someone who will satisfy you in every way, both in the abstract spiritual and the practical acting directions.

At one time you believed it would be impossible for you to fall in love with another person, but thank heavens, your love for the other man has shown that I was right in this matter. You are so beautiful and fresh and young and lovable, it would surely be easy for you to find and attract *the right one* if only you **wanted to**. It was difficult for you to see that *I* was *not* the right one. Therefore I was so glad (not on the surface, on the surface I was sad at the moment, but deep within me I was glad and thankful) when you wrote: "I have given you up as lover, but not as artist."

Now comes the question: Wouldn't our sometimes coming together and being happy together perhaps hinder (or make difficult) your *looking* for **the right one** elsewhere? I would so hate to ruin your chances unnecessarily.

If you think that you could run the risk of *immersing* yourself in me again if we see each other more frequently, and in that way lose the chance of finding another who could bring more *satisfaction* into your life, *then I think unreservedly that we should give up coming together*, until such time as you have either found another, or are certain that *I won't hinder you* in seeking another. My feelings for you are *exclusively* good and kind feelings, and have always been so, but I realise (from what you have written to me yourself) that I have been *unfortunate* for you in the past, **and I don't want to be so any more.**

You have been in love with someone else (perhaps are still?) and I have been in love with someone else and still am — all this has after all made some difference in the relationship between us.

One's actions become different from changes of that kind, although I don't think that sort of thing makes so much difference to the *real inner* feelings

But anyhow things are a little different now than before, and I would so hate you and me to take up again or begin afresh any relationship at all that you think *could hinder you in finding your life's happiness*.

I say all this here without any selfish after-thoughts at all. The relationship between Margot and me is such that we won't see or write to each other (for some time at any rate) and we are both quite "free", so that I am so to speak not "reserved" at the moment.

But nevertheless I would rather be without the pleasures of love *my whole life* than cause hurt and waste of time to you or anyone else I love; rather miss you than be together with you in *any unequal relationship*. From my heart I would beg you never again to sacrifice yourself for me, and never go in to anything which *in the long run* cannot be satisfying for you.

On the other hand, if you in all truth can assure me that you still stand on the same footing with me as when you wrote: "I have given you up as lover", if you can assure me that I am only a dear and old friend and comrade, whom you can be happy with (with or without sensuality, which amounts to so little, in reality) when he *is there*, but whom you can well do without when he is away, and whom you never expect any marriage or any other *permanent relationship* with; if you, in other words, stand on about the same footing with me as I stand with you — then it seems to me there can't be any harm in us meeting again and being happy together, when it suits us both.

But let us not begin on any unequal relationship. You shouldn't *permit* me to cause you any harm or impracticality, when my feelings towards you are so sweet and pure as they are. And remember, that even as *comrade* you cannot be *certain* that I can be much for you *in the long run*. If for example I become married soon, one can't tell how that would react on external things in our comradely relations, although for me marriage could *never* influence my inner feelings, and preferably *ought* to make as little alteration as possible on external relationships. (But scandal must be avoided, for all concerned, I always think). And then it is not **impossible** that I will go and live in America for some years at a stretch. All these things are quite unknown, but they are not to be excluded, and ought to be taken into consideration.

My feelings for you are, as I have said, the old ones. They will indeed never change much. I found a great part of my life's happiness with you in a long time, and could do the same again under the same conditions, but "independent" of you I have always been and always will be, because it is the only kind of relationship which *suits me personally*, and seems natural to me. I cannot re-create myself. Any support, anything "for life" I can never be. But something like the girl in "The light that failed" meant when she said "I know I am only Miss Wrong, but you might as well have me till Miss Right comes along" I can well be.

Will you answer me about all this, little sweet Karen?

I am feeling *terribly well* at present. Have given up "naughtiness" and have the most lovely and most hopeful thoughts about my compositions and my future. Everything is beginning to "lighten" a little for me. The compositions are "going" excellently (have just heard that the 2 new things were played again "by request" at the "Promenade" Concerts)[17] my concert nerves have never been so good, mother is very well and happy, etc. Now comes a time (I hope) when I will be able to make all kinds of compositional experiments and experiences; with mechanical violins, and such like, for example.

One thing I will *earnestly ask of you*: To have yourself photographed (by a really good photographer) in your national costume (in the old loved one I know) in **many** different positions (whole figure mostly). Put the white sandshoes on, little friend! And everything as I know it. I will obviously pay for everything.

17 Grainger's *Irish Tune from County Derry* and *Shepherd's Hey* were "repeated by request" at the Queen's Hall Promenade Concert on 13 September.

Let us preferably get a proper number of the pictures of *each* and get the *negatives* if you can. If you don't get good ones from one photographer then go to another.

When we have got them good, then I would like to beg the *whole national costume* from you, which I would like to keep the whole of my life. It is connected with so many lovely unforgettable indescribably sweet times, so I feel I scarcely *can* do without it.[18]

I would like to have the skirt, bodice, the white under-bodice, and apron and a pair of white socks you used to have on with the rest.

I would like to have the *old* costume, which you wore in all these years. *Do not deny me* this, little sweet meat-mate. I will of course pay for a new one instead. All in all I would always be glad to be of assistance with *small* sums of money, like for the Norway journey, when I have the means for it. It will *always* be a profound pleasure. Furthermore I will soon begin on an English translation of "Silkenhair".

Goodbye.
Percy.

18 Karen finally gave Grainger her national costume in the summer of 1925. It is preserved to this day in the Grainger Museum at the University of Melbourne.

494 TO ROGER QUILTER
27. Sept 1913.

Hotel Norge.
Lillesand

Darling Roger.

Ever so Ta for your letter from Venice. I've got your tune in my head all the time lately.

It is a delightful bit of line, I think & so very harmonisable. I believe it forms part of your Overture, does it not? I should awfully like to see how you have treated it when I get back & we meet. I think it must lend itself to very charming things orchestrally.

I'm thinking of lots of reworkings; English Dance, Green Bushes, & others. Have just arranged "Molly" for Pianola & am now rechorising "The Bride's Tragedy" (a whole tone lower) & Englishing "The merry Wedding" prior to writing it out (chorising it)

I like the following verse, it's so silly:

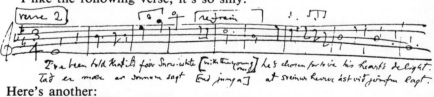

Here's another:
    She braided her hair with silken bands;
    she washed in water her milk-white hands.

We're having a delicious tour, bigger audiences than ever before, & jolly weather for the most part & everything pleasant & enjoyable

In this part of Norway (South Coast) the women are so attractive, with a slight Danish Anstrich [German fig.: element], smooth gentle & statuesque, with full & Grecian forms.

Longing to see my darling Roger soon, his fond & happy old

Percy.

Mum sends lots of love

495 TO GORDON BRYAN-SMITH[19]
Oct 1913.

Høyers Hotel.
Skien. Norway.

19 Gordon Bryan-Smith (a.k.a. Gordon Bryan) (b. 1895), English pianist and composer.

Dear Bryan-Smith.

Delighted to hear from you. **So** kind of you to send the cutting, which I was very happy to see. *So glad* my things were so liked in Brighton.

I should **much** like to hear you play some day. **Should** you ever wish to have lessons from me, I should be ever so pleased to give them to you, some time. I hope you'll have much success in Brighton when you play there.

Fancy, I *have* thought of scoring "Sussex Carol" for a similar combination to that you suggested, only I would like chorus along as well; the words are so jolly.

Am having a wildly successful tour here in Norway, also great fun — rowing in the sea & fjords very often. After here to Finland Russia & Denmark, returning London middle of November.

My address is now always:
   c/o Concert Direction E.L. Robinson
   7 Wigmore St. London. W.
Hearty thanks for your letter, & good luck till we meet

Yrs cordially
Percy Grainger

496 TO KAREN HOLTEN
[Original: Danish]
10.10.1913.

Hotel Kong Carl
Sandefjord,
Norway.

Sweet little Karen.

I was very glad to hear from you, and to hear that you think you can very well be good friends with me, and can well be together with me sometimes, without immersing yourself in our relationship as before, and therefore without feeling unhappy again. You also say: "But how really poor and remarkably unproductive it is that that shall be all that comes out of a relationship between 2 who have really loved each other." To tell the truth, I personally don't think it is so poor.

I think it is *very much*, that after a disappointment such as you have met in me, one can still be *real friends* and wish each other everything good, and have all possible good feelings for each other. Our love didn't get much soil or time to flourish in, and yet we will possibly end up being better friends than 1000 others who had 10 times better conditions, and who "sacrificed" all things possible for "love".

For it is true, I think, that neither *you* nor I would sacrifice more than a certain degree, and that, I think, was well done of both of us, for one doesn't get far with sacrifice, and sacrifice is not a suitable soil for love, it seems to me in any case.

Both you and I are people with a *goal*. It was so easy for us to fall in love with each other because we were both *lovable* in ourselves, good to look at, pleasant and kind in behaviour, true and good people, and people with much need of love in us, and — as G. Wied says — "blood in the small arteries." But have you noticed, that we never could really give up our original *goal*, however true and compelling our love was?

You expected *certain things* from life, and I expected certain other things from life, and neither you nor I *could* give up where these things were concerned. Love without children (at any rate in the beginning) and love without close *living together* you basically could not accept. And I, for my part, could not offer just that.

When you said in Upper Cheyne Row "I will always stay with you," I felt **at once** that it would never go, for I knew instinctively that what you demanded from love was almost the opposite of what I demanded, although the *love itself* was (in my opinion) equally genuine on both sides.

You knew straight away what you wanted, for when I suggested in Upper Cheyne Row that you should come and live in London so we could often be together, you immediately said No, definitely, that this couldn't make you happy; and in that you were certainly quite correct.

I do wish that you saw just as clearly as I see it (rightly, or wrongly, that I can't judge of course) that what *has always divided us* is neither my mother or my relationship to her, or my practical considerations, or anything outside us two, or any lack of love either from one side or the other, *but that we both moved towards entirely different* **ways of living**, *and therefore* couldn't accept what the other had to offer. It doesn't alter the case that you had *more to offer* than I. What you had to offer was not what I, with my instincts and viewpoints, *could* accept, not successfully in any case, *despite all love*. You acted in a similar manner when you refused to live in London, whereby you could have seen me much more often than has been the case; but of course you *had* to refuse it, since this was not anything you, with *your* instincts and viewpoints, could accept successfully.

Your conception of life appears to me, for a great part, to rest on your regarding sexual things (children, etc) erotic things and personal feelings in general as the most decisive things in life, and perhaps as the most decisive things in all great human questions.

You have of course many other things you are interested in, but everything you prefer in literature etc points to (if I understand you rightly) your regarding erotic feelings and actions as being almost *the most important things* that life holds.

I, on the other hand, regard these things as being almost completely *incidental and unimportant*, in any case for me, and also for mankind in general, according to my conception of "the demands of the present and the future."

You will perhaps answer: "You haven't always thought like that." But it seems to me I have, basically. This doesn't prevent erotic things being almost my greatest **pleasure** and *recreation*, but erotic things don't amount to a *mainspring* in me. And as soon as there is talk of my other more *serious* (mainspring-like) sides being sacrificed for the sake of erotic things, then I am always *compelled* instinctively to pull back; often unwillingly, but *compelled* by **inner** forces all the same. This is the way I see our types, taken by and large.

But the difficulty lies in this that neither you nor I are pure types. It is too easy for us to understand each other's need, we can too easily see the beauty in the other's goal and desires. Because of this we can easily appear "misleading". You certainly often believed that I would give in to your demands because I let you see I could sympathise with them. But I **could** not give way, and it was quite right (it seems to me) that neither you nor I really gave way, when it really came to the point.

We must not blind ourselves by emphasising that we were happy in our love *when* we were together. I believe we would *always* be happy together, for we both possess comradeship and love, and these things can't easily be worn out, *although they are not any foundation to build life on*, for they both (comradeship and love) stand outside the material practical decisive features of life. Love alone was not enough for you. You demanded being together, concentration, children, etc. Love wasn't enough for me either, I demanded freedom, independence, no expense, etc.

You write: "With regard to others, then, it is all right to change one's nature". Not at all, little Karen. My nature will always be the same. But it is not out of the question that I might find a woman that looked on these things about the same as I; whose life was independent of her erotic feelings, although quite able to use sexual, sensual possibilities as *amusement* and *recreation*, but without putting any serious demands on the feelings "connected with it", whose main interests lay in activities and work *quite outside* my life, whose happiness therefore did *not* rest in *my* hands, but in **her own**.

A woman like that I would not *necessarily* be afraid of marrying. It is not **marriage itself** that I am afraid of, but the demands and wishes which so often go together with marriage. Neither would I have anything against having children, but I would like to be able to expect in advance that they would grow up like the kind of woman-type I speak of, and like myself: with entirely immoral thoughts on all sexual questions, but on the other hand with strong moral convictions concentrated on art, science, truth, politics, etc. But if I was not absolutely certain that the woman belonged to the same development-type (I don't know at all whether my type is better or worse than others, but that doesn't matter to anyone) as I do, I could [not?] risk *breeding a regiment of opponents* against my own way of thinking and desires for the future. This would be a tragedy for me. It is not to say I will *ever* meet a woman of this type, but that's not necessary either, because I am *very happy* as I am. But *if* I meet one like that I don't think I would be afraid to marry her. But with you, despite all love, I knew (or believed) that marriage would mean unhappiness for us both, or in any case one of us, because our *goals* are "die entgegengesetzte" [German: the opposite ones, i.e. opposed].

Therefore I don't think that it is "poor" that we now stand with regard to each other where we do.

You are completely right to "give me up as lover", as it is not satisfying for you to have a love-relationship without concentration. I would only wish you could find another who could give you the things that you so rightly (as *you* are, and as things are) desire, and long for. *For me* the affair was of course ideal as it was (before 1913) but even so it could never be my wish that anything should continue which satisfied you as little as the relation between us 2 has done.

I don't think that the photographs in the national costume will be a disappointment. We can in any case try it. I don't believe it was the surroundings which made the beautiful impression. Because the costume suited you so absolutely, and you it, and both were so good in themselves, regarded from the most critical standpoint, that I don't think there was great need of surroundings. I will be *inexpressibly* grateful to get the photographs, and later on the costume. But don't send the dress before we have seen the photographs, for if they are not good at the 1st I would *very much* like to ask you to be so kind as to go to a 2nd photographer.

It would be an enormous pleasure to me to see you and talk to you. And I am very happy that you think this could occur without causing you new sorrow, and without binding you to me as before. It is unfortunate that I am not coming to Cope this time (perhaps not at all to Denmark?) in any case only passing through without staying. So I must hope for another time.

I have now translated "Silkehåret" [Silkenhair] completely into English and will fairly soon be able to begin the choral score. I have just heard that *Mengelberg* is going to conduct my Mock Morris at the 1st "Philharmonic" Concert in London in Nov.[20]

20 On Tuesday 5 November 1913.

Your old loving friend
Percy.

497 TO ROSE GRAINGER
19.10.1913.
Sunday morn. 11 oclock

Glatveds Hotel.
Hønefos.

21 In the spring of 1913 Grainger
had begun work on his *Tribute to
Foster*, a work freely based on
Stephen C. Foster's "Camptown
Races". Grainger had sketched the
"lullaby" section of this work, for
which he composed his own
(autobiographical) verses in the
style of Foster's, on 15–16 October
1913. The final scoring of the
work, for five single voices, mixed
chorus, musical glasses, solo piano
and orchestra, was completed in
1931. It was published by
G. Schirmer Inc., New York, in
1932.

A new little scraplet to the *Camptown Racecourse*[21]

It's a pity you're not here, darling, as this hotel lies so jolly, sourrounded by a river rushing downwards over stones on 3 sides. Quite a decent house last night. Was up at 5 o'clock this morn.

No further letter will reach you, so a loving goodbye till we meet, loved one.

Percy

498 TO ERNEST THESIGER
30.10.1913.

Britannia Hotel
Trondhjem

Darling Ernest.

We are just coming to an end of our *divine* tour here in Norway. 50 charming enjoyable concerts, ideal audiences, packed houses, dry warm weather, plenty of rowing & fun & gorgeous scenery. My compositions also have been a howling success here, encored every one.

Now we go to Russia, Finland & Denmark, getting home to conduct in Ipswich Nov. 18.[22]

Mother is very well & jolly, & of course I am.

22 His *Walking Tune* and *Mock
Morris*. On the same programme
he also played the Grieg Piano
Concerto, under Dr Sinclair, and a
group of piano solos.

Longing to see you again & hear your doings, hope you've been having a nice autumn.

I do so hope your father is better now.

Love to you all from us both

Ever fondly yrs
Perks

499 TO KAREN HOLTEN
[Original: Danish]
15.11.13.

Fredericia

Dear little Karen

It was so sweet to see you yesterday, but I didn't get said a single thing that I wanted to, the time was also so short.

Now I am looking forward to seeing the photograph today. If you still have the other "proofs" you could well send them to London. It could well be that *I* would think well of them even if others don't. I have a rather peculiar taste sometimes.

It was really a shame there wasn't more time this time. There were many things I would have liked to talk to you about, many amusing things I have experienced in recent times.

Here on the railway station there is a mass of Polish workers, they look so amusing, lovely dresses as well, and their language sounds to my ears like Russian. The population of the Slav countries has a very strong attraction for me.

Just think, E. Tang Kristensen was at the Concert last night, and I have spent the whole morning with him.[23] He is marvellous, *very* amusing to be with. Perhaps I will spend 3–4 days with him next summer or autumn with the phonograph so that together we can collect some remnants of Danish folksongs.

What have you in mind to do in the summer? Would you care to spend a few days with me (or longer) in Svinkløv or Slettestrand, or do you have other plans?

It was a shame I couldn't come out to you this time and that I had to ask you to come down to the station. We didn't arrive till 12.30 at night from Sweden, therefore I didn't telephone as it was so late.

I am sorry I didn't have more money with me yesterday. Perhaps I can soon send you a little more money for the piano from England.

There was great enthusiasm last night. It seems my luck is increasing in all countries. I get on so well everywhere, and people are so kind to me. I feel more and more that the good in me is understood and appreciated wherever I go, and that I am deeply grateful for. Now I have a nice time coming in England. A lot of performances of my things in different places which I am much looking forward to.

You looked so sweet yesterday, really well and young and lovable. Is your foot quite well? I didn't even hear about it!

Seeing dear people again always stirs me up, and then I forget everything and am only stupid and silent and embarrassed.

Many many kind regards to all at home from me.

Later.

Now I have seen the photograph-proofs and got your letter. I think the photographs are very good. May I have at least 2 of each, and then you would have some for yourself, wouldn't you? You can let me know what it costs later on can't you? I would like to have some photographs in national costume with the *whole* figure, perhaps Cai could take them or the photographer, just as you wish. Many thanks for the money back, but I don't understand it. Do you think it was too little I gave you. Then just say so, so I can send more. I had thought of sending 100 Kr if you thought it was suitable. You know I am so stupid about money, therefore I asked you. Just tell me whether you were offended, or what, and forgive me if I was hurtful. I am very happy about the photographs

23 See note 17, 1906.

500 TO ALFHILD SANDBY   [PM Kensington. W]
[Postcard]
2.12.13.

Awfully sorry to miss you this time. It has been an **appalling** rush since we got back from an adorable time in Russia Finland, etc.

Much love to you both, & good journey. Hope we meet in spring. Shall be writing Herman soon.

We are both so very sorry we shan't see you before you leave.

Am just off to Plymouth myself[24]

Percy

24 For his joint recital with singer Madame Amy Dewhurst for the Misses Lily and Florence Smith's Subscription Musical Matinées at the Assembly Rooms, Plymouth, on 3 December.

1914

The concert year began for Grainger with his appearance at the Albert Hall Ballad Concerts on 3 January 1914.

On 12 January he began a provincial tour in Holland with a recital at Hilversum. Twenty concerts took place in Holland, nineteen of them presentations of the tour-programme. One recital was given in Eupen, Belgium, on 4 February. There were no orchestral concerts included in this tour, and he did not appear in either Amsterdam or The Hague. Rose accompanied Percy on the tour, travelling with him for most of January then staying in The Hague. They returned to London after the final recital, at Rotterdam on 8 February, taking up temporary residence at 19 Cheniston Gardens.

Grainger was based in London until 22 February, when he left via an engagement in Sheffield for a short visit to Europe. He performed twice with orchestra in Saarbrücken, 27–28 February, gave his first recital in Plzeň, Bohemia, on 2 March, and returned via Holland where he gave two concerts on 5 and 9 March. He was back in London by 10 March. Rose remained in London during this trip. Projected concerts with the Concertgebouw later in March did not eventuate.

Grainger's compositions continued to attract considerable interest and attention. In March 1914 Grainger's publishers, Schott & Co., summarised for the press Grainger's international achievements as a composer, announcing that Mock Morris was performed more than five hundred times during 1913, and that this piece and his Molly on the Shore had been conducted in Holland and Germany by Mengelberg, Fritz Steinbach and Richard Strauss, in Norway by Halvorsen, in New York by Damrosch and in Chicago by Stock and Schindler. Schott also announced that Grainger's works were to be performed by leading orchestras at Wiesbaden, Frankfurt, Mannheim, Vienna and in Finland and Russia. As the Referee commented, on reprinting the Schott announcement on 29 March 1914, "It is doubtful if any living composer has achieved such widespread popularity with so few works as Mr Percy Grainger".

In April the Graingers moved again, into the last of their temporary residences, Balfour Gardiner's London house at 7 Pembroke Villas. In April Grainger also tried two new career developments. At the afternoon concert of the Torquay Festival on 16 April he gave his first performance of the Delius Piano Concerto, Thomas Beecham conducting. On 29 April

515

he gave a recital in the new hall at Horsmonden, a village in Kent. Largely organised by his friend Isabel Du Cane, it was modelled on his Norwegian experiences. Although highly successful and with a distinguished audience that included Rudyard Kipling, it was without follow-up.

501   TO KAREN HOLTEN   24. Cheniston Gardens.
[Original: Danish]   Kensington.
2.1.14.   London. W.

Sweet dear little Karen.

No present I received at Christmas gave me more pleasure than your photographs. They give just the impression I wanted. They don't flatter you, it is true, but the stance is good and typical, I think, and just the right one as far as the costume is concerned. Do I owe you anything for the photographs, little friend?

Yes, it is truly a long time since you heard from me. I have worked **so colossally** since I came home, and have written so much, begun a completely new piece "The Warriors" Ballet music (without ballet) *completely* different from all my previous things (harmonic sense is given up as much as possible, the chords and the voice-leading advance freely almost *without reference* to each other), have also arranged "Molly" for large orchestra, ditto "Mock Morris". These arrangements are requested so much at Schott's that I thought it was wise to do it. Have also rewritten "Bride's Tragedy" again, and heard it read from the page by a good little choir. It is not as difficult as I thought.

From America I have heard just in these days about several important performances of my things in New York, etc. Some will soon be performed in Finland and Russia by a *brilliant* conductor Georg Schnéevoigt. (Finnish)[1] I am looking forward **very much** to hearing from you that people liked "Col. Song" as Trio. To think, that Federspiels are married!

Tomorrow I am playing at a big Ballad Concert in the Albert Hall. After the 10th Jan my address is
      c/o: Herrn Hans Augustin
           Frans v. Mierisstr.[aat] 101. A'dam. Holland.
(From Holland I will send the money, **as soon as possible**)

You can imagine it is difficult to go back to piano practise after 2 weeks composition and scoring. I am now 31½ and have had to set aside composition more or less in the last 10–12 years, and must still put it aside for some years.

It is hard *how* long it takes to accumulate enough to live on, even when one is lucky as I have been, and saves as zealously as we do.

It is as if it gets harder every year to drive oneself to the boring work when the blessed happiness of work (of another kind) beckons just round the corner.

But it is splendid all the same that everything is going as well as it is, and that one will be able (if everything goes well) *sometime* soon to let go and throw oneself seriously into "the real thing".

All intentions of marriage are completely given up on both sides, now.

Sweetest Karen, I can't say how glad I am to have the pictures you were so kind as to pose for and send me.

A thousand thanks.

There is so much I would like to tell you about all possible things if we were together some time.

Many tender New Years wishes from

      your Percy.

1 Georg Lennart Schnéevoigt (1872–1947), Finnish conductor and cellist. Grainger was engaged to perform the Delius Piano Concerto under his direction in October 1914. The performance was cancelled.

516

2 Karen had given a chamber-music concert with her friend, violinist Elna Arlaud, Henry Bramsen assisting, in Odd Fellow-Palæets small hall on 11 February 1914. The programme included the first performance in Copenhagen of Grainger's *Colonial Song*, in the version for piano, violin and cello.

3 The response brought Grainger a new kind of fame, as reported in the *Daily Telegraph* on 9 December 1913, "Truly, Mr Percy Grainger is attaining greatness. His music, which over here we regard as refreshing, but otherwise 'harmless' has actually achieved in Berlin the dignity of being hissed! The other day Miss Isolde Menges, the clever young Brighton violinist, gave a couple of concerts in Berlin, under the direction of Mr Lyell-Taylor, and during one of Miss Menges's intervals of rest the orchestra played 'Shepherd's Hey'. Then began the hissing. (I wonder if any composer born under the British flag has ever before enjoyed the distinction.) But the curious thing is that, in spite of (or, perhaps, because of) the hissing, the piece had to be repeated owing to the exuberance of the applause of the non-hissing part of the audience".

4 In response to the interest shown in his compositions *Mock Morris* and *Molly on the Shore*, Grainger had prepared arrangements of both works for full orchestra early in 1914, introducing therewith a new instrument, the "resonophone" which, in addition to attracting significant attention in the newspapers, brought his mother into the orchestra as its performer. She and it made their first appearance in *Molly on the Shore* at the Winter Gardens, Bournemouth, on 21 February 1914. The programme also included the first performance of a new scoring of *Colonial Song*, with the full orchestra version of *Shepherd's Hey* being given as encore. In addition to conducting and playing piano in his own works, Grainger performed the Franck *Symphonic Variations* and the Liszt *Hungarian Fantasia*.

502   TO KAREN HOLTEN
[Original: Danish]
22.2.14.

19, Cheniston Gardens,
Kensington, W.

Sweetest little Karen.

A thousand thanks for your letter and the programme (a nice programme moreover).²

Of course I understand that you were very taken up, as I also have been to the highest degree; have worked night after night till 1 or 2 o'cl, in order to get the score and parts of a *completely* new orchestral arrangement of "Col. Song" ready for performance in Bournemouth yesterday.

The whole time I thought of sending you a telegram on the day of the concert, and every day I thought about it, but day after day went without getting to see from one of your letters what date it was. That's how it is when one is just too busy. So don't think I was quite so indifferent as it seemed.

I am very happy that your concert went so well, and that you are pleased with the new piano, but sorry that you felt so depressed of late. What a pity. It is so awful to feel unwell and "down".

I am now travelling to Sheffield, from there to Saarbrücken (Germany) and Pilsen (Bohemia) and Holland.
    Address from 2–8 March
      c/o: Freule Six
        42 Bankastr.[aat]
          Den Haag. Holland.
After 8 March I am **here** again.
Family Six is something like *Schous*.
Before the journey I will write again, probably.
Everything is going splendidly. Especially from America heartwarming letters, critiques, programmes etc. about my things.
"Sh's Hey" was performed for the 2nd time in Berlin recently and given da capo as usual.³
I have indeed already told you (haven't I?) that Mengelberg is giving 2–3 pieces of mine in Holland in March, and that Steinbach has already given some in Cologne.
Mother played yesterday (together with Miss Du Cane) a new instrument "Resonophone" (a kind of bass-glockenspiel) made by Hawkes & Sons for me. It sounded well in the orchestra.⁴
Many kisses and thoughts.

Percy.
When are you moving house?

503   TO ROSE GRAINGER
[Postcard]
28.2.14.

Saarbrücken.

Of course you are right, the Celesta must come out of "Col. Song" it does no good there, though it remains in "Molly" to replace your "Reson[ophone]."
Am going to lunch with the Conductor Cormann & his family.⁵ I shall make their hair stand on end with tales of your guitar and Resonophone exploits!

Fondest love, dearie.
Percy.
Send "Molly" proofs to Sixes.

504 TO ROSE GRAINGER   Hotel Waldek.
[Four postcards]   Plzen. [Bohemia]
2.3.1914. Monday midday.

My darling.

A new world of *enthralling* delights opened up to me.

I am *in love* with what I've seen of Austrian & Bohemian characteristics. How silly of me not to feel it in advance!

Nürnberg & the Bavarians made a very swinish impression on me yesterday, I must say, but when we came to the Austrian customs-town, & I saw really *Schneidig* [German: dashing] kjæk [Danish: cheerful] looking uniformed men walking about with refined dashing ways, bright keen gestures, their clothes well & curiously cut, their surroundings at once stick-in-the-mud & aristocratic, & their goings on full of pleasant civilities & proper childish bodily pride, reminding me most of Sweden, "ein licht ist mir aufgegangen" [German idiom: "it rang a bell"] suddenly, & I realized why Schubert is as he is, full of easy & neat almost niggery rhythms, easily pleased with happy little things, & with unstrained gushes of lightly teeming melody, yet without the deep soul-power of the more awful yet more stirring Germans.

Also Schönberg & Haydn I feel much more at home with than ever, & see clearer why they are as they are.

Bright *individual* piercing glances the Austrian officials had, with no officiousness, & one felt that they must be good cooks, somehow, I dont know why; as if things in their country would be sweet, wellseasoned, rich, luscious, & with a continual graceful eye to detail.

The Bohemians are utterly different again, but **most** fascinating to me. Things are dirty, unkept, furniture is wobbly as in Scandinavia, but the people look free, individual, undisciplined, gentle & jolly much as in Russia. They look weak, but full of a pleasant liveliness.

The children in the street (& other folk also) do more genuine dance-steps as they go along, or talk together, than any white people I've seen. They are very friendly, polite, kindly & helpful.

Often the clothing reminds of Finland.

When one looks at the folk one feels soon outside the town must be *real woods*, not merely small earth-scrapings by ½ town-like countryfolk as it mostly seems to be in Germany but more genuine backwoods life as in Finland for instance

Here I believe one would find a good deal of the charm of Russia without its terrors.

I should much like to know this country well & be liked here. The language seems to me surprizingly like Russian, I recognize heaps of words, & the sound is not unlike.

The secretary of the Music Soc. is a pleasant funny little creature with tiny tiny fish in glass bowls in his office (in Germany there isn't much interest in any tiny things, have you noticed?)

The whole hall will be crammed tonight, they say.

505 TO ROSE GRAINGER   Den Haag.
[Two postcards]
6.3.14.

My own dearest.

So very distressed you are not sleeping well & are feeling so bad. I too am not feeling well today, lowspirited & tired & irritable.

5 Victor Cormann (1871–1963), German conductor. He was musical director of the Gesellschaft der Musikfreunde Saarbrücken from 1904 to 1935, when the Society was dissolved.

6 For the performance by the Oriana Madrigal Society with the Queen's Hall Orchestra at the Society's concert in Queen's Hall on 10 March 1914.

7 Johannes Theodorus (or Theodoor) Toorop, known as Jan Toorop (1858–1928), Dutch artist. Grainger had visited an exhibition of his paintings and drawings at the Kunsthandel Theo Neuhuys in Den Haag. This is Grainger's last letter to Rose until March 1915.

8 Vincent Willem van Gogh (1853–90), Dutch painter.

9 The second annual musical festival at the Torquay Pavilion was held on 15–16 April 1914. The evening concert on 16 April also included Grainger's *Colonial Song* in the new scoring and the full orchestra version of *Molly on the Shore*. In a letter to Basil Cameron of 20 March 1952, Grainger recalls Thomas Beecham's response, "After the Torquay Festival (1914?), where Beecham heard my *Colonial Song*, he said to me: 'Grainger, you have achieved the almost impossible; you have written the worst orchestral piece of modern times' ".

10 Delius's Piano Concerto, composed in 1897, had been revised before 1904, in 1906–07 and 1909. Before its publication in 1907 by Verlag Harmonie, Berlin, the solo piano part had been rewritten by the Hungarian pianist Theodor Szántó, to whom the work is dedicated and who gave its first English performance, at a Queen's Hall Promenade Concert on 22 October 1907. Grainger's interest in the work had been stimulated by its performance by Evelyn Suart at the fourth concert of the second series of the Balfour Gardiner concerts, on 18 March 1913. After this performance Rose had written to Delius, "We enjoyed yr Concerto last night, but I think it required a man's power in the loud parts. Percy is practising it at this moment, & it suits him well, he has so much real strength; I long to hear him do it with orchestra". (The *Daily Telegraph*, taking perhaps a less partisan view of the occasion, complimented Miss Suart on her performance but spoke of the

Yesterday in *Helden* was magnificent. 150 gulden there, & Pilsen was 400 marks & S-brücken 500 marks Den Haag, 200 more in all than I expect.

I shall be back early Tuesday morn (8? ocl) so if you like you can tell K. Scott that I could go to rehearsal of "We have fed" any time Tuesday morning **if he likes**[6]

My pupils Tuesday are not before 2.30 Amer. Phillips 3.30 Muntz.

Do hope you will feel better.

Yr loving one

506   TO ROSE GRAINGER   Den Haag.
[Two postcards]
8.3.14.

We had great fun with the "R. Round" last night, 4 voices, 2 violins, 3 glasses (rubbed & hit) & piano.

Went to see Toorop exhibit. yesterday.[7] I find his work absolutely 1st class, especially the oil portraits. I saw the one you spoke about, with the bloodred ears & the brickred tie, & there was a still nicer one there. Have also seen a mass of reproductions of van Goch[8] pictures & drawings. v. G seems to me to have a greater *painters gift* than Gaugain, perhaps, but when I've seen about 50 of his stuff I feel a bit weighed down by the sombre hard-worked drabness of the emotional background. It's too Dutch for me, that *resigned* acceptance of, & even pleasure in, duties & difficulties, & my heart beats much higher at the joy-seeking, pleasure-insisting-upon lusciousness of Gaugain, though I feel deeply thankful for the genius of both of those 2 friends.

As soon as I get home I want to hunt up an Am. organ.

"Col. Song" parts, etc, all finished.

Yr adoring one
Percy.

507   TO FREDERICK DELIUS   7, Pembroke Villas,
26.4.14.   Kensington, W.

My dear Frederick

Torquay was *delicious*, & we wished you were there.[9] Beecham gave gorgeous performances of all your things & was ripping in the Concerto, which was a great success, & in which I felt very happy. It is a work one loves more & more as one knows it longer, & purely pianisticly speaking it is really effective and *rather easy*, thanks to its excellent Klaviersatz. I imagine Szanto's work on its Klaviersatz must have been jolly well done by him too.[10]

I enclose some notices you might like to see.

My agent has already written to Mengelberg of my wish to do your Concerto with him when next engaged there, & I am suggesting it here & abroad at every opportunity. When you see conductors abroad with whom you would like me to do the work I wish you would mention the matter to them, as I very much want to play it *everywhere* I can. You are now getting so universally loved & honored everywhere & the time seems to me just ripe for the lovely Concerto to come into its own.[11] It was greatly loved at Torquay.

I shall now write to Siloti about it re his St. Petersburg concerts.[12]

Above everything I am in love with your adorable "First Cuckoo", that goes to my very heart.[13] All the very particularly lovable vibrations of your tender lovable soul are so touchingly & compellingly voiced in that little gem. The mixture in it of a strange childlike wondering joy with a moaning grief-laden note also everpresent gets me entirely. The mood of it & lots of the Dance Rhapsody feel closer to me personally than my own work does, it utterly voices what I most inwardly long to hear expressed or to express. The Dance Rhap. is a *regular corker*. There is nothing I enjoy more.

Stimmungsbild No. 2 is delicious too. I heard them both (No. 1 for 2nd time) at Bristol (New Philharmonic Soc.) the other night (beautifully given by *Barter*, a charming musician) where I was playing and conducting.

We are both longing to see you both over here soon.[14]

We are both worked off our feet at present, a *terrible* rush. I tour in Norway, Russia, Finland & Denmark in the early autumn getting back here *early middle of November*, after which I am available for Great Britain & Continent.

With much love

Ever fondly
Percy.

Am sending critiques seperately tomorrow

508   TO KAREN HOLTEN   7, Pembroke Villas,
[Original: Danish/one sentence English]   Kensington, W.
Monday. 4.5.14   London.

Little old Comrade.

It is an awfully long time since I wrote, or heard from you.

I have read a splendid Russian book "Ssanin" by Artzibaschew (Artsibasjev) which I think could amuse you to read.[15] Apart from "Noa Noa" it is for me one of the most charming books I have come across. Ssanin is really an absolutely *clever* and *lucid* person, and it is certainly amusing. "Ssanin" is published (in German) by Georg Mueller, Munich.

You write that I have much good fortune in my career, etc. That is also quite right, but possibly the reality is not quite as it seems to be after all.

For my success I have to thank most of all the circumstance that I always looked at every step as far as possible from the viewpoint of other people. I follow as rarely as possible my own instinctive desires, otherwise things would look very different. It has always appeared to me that most people in our days are tied up with practical questions and difficulties. Not all gifted people have a tactful eye to other people's practical needs, not all gifted people take the trouble to, either. Nor have I always *felt like* it inwardly either, but I have realised that it was necessary if I was to get free in good time from money-slavery.

One mustn't therefore forget that my good fortune is very often more a "compromise" than anything else. If I were to begin now at this very time to do what I feel drawn to by my innermost artistic instincts, it would soon be the end of my "success", I think.

I have *never composed* one line from practical considerations, that I can say fortunately, but in the *choice* of the pieces to be published, I have allowed practical considerations to be the guide in most cases, so that one can well say that my works published up to date don't at all give a true picture of my composing activity or of the predominant colour or moods of my composing personality.

Some people are suited to compromise and self-effacement. But I am not. I am really a true and straightforward person (although a little complex)

"annihilating power of the orchestra".) In the event, Grainger did not fare so very much better at Torquay. As the *Daily Telegraph* reported on 17 April, "But although he produced, in the more strenuous passages, a powerful tone, he was not able always to cope with the excessive orchestral ardours allowed by Mr Beecham, who conducted the work. For this reason, and also because the performance failed to lay bare the more subtle beauties of the score, the Concerto went short of its full effect".

11 Rose had also noted, opportunely, the burgeoning of interest in Delius's music, commenting to Percy on 6 March, "Delius is being performed **all** over Germany, & a great deal here".

12 Grainger's letter to Siloti survives and is reprinted in *Alexander Il'yich Siloti 1863–1945 Reminiscences and Letters* (Leningrad 1963) p. 272. Dated 7 May 1914 it reads, "Dear Maestro! Heartfelt thanks for sending me the programmes of your last season. What *marvellous* programmes!

"I recall with great pleasure your splendid performance of the Tschaikowsky concerto, which I enjoyed so much and which taught me a great deal.

"I have been learning the excellent piano concerto of my dear friend Frederick Delius, and played it with great success recently at a big music festival in Torquay. I very much hope that I will have the opportunity some time of playing the Delius concerto under your direction. Delius himself selected this piece for me to play at the Music Festival, as well as in a grand concert of his works which is to take place at Bradford in the autumn.

"My two new scores also met with tremendous success at Torquay, where I conducted them.

"With a multitude of the friendliest thanks and greetings from my mother and myself, Your admirer, Percy Grainger". Published in Russian as a translation from the original German, it is here translated into English by Larry Bagg.

13 Willem Mengelberg had given the first English performance of Delius's *Two Pieces for Small Orchestra* (*On Hearing the First Cuckoo in Spring* and *Summer Night on the River*) at his concert for the Royal Philharmonic Society in London on 20 January 1914. Grainger was on tour in Holland at that time. In Bristol, where the two pieces were given on 22 April by the Bristol New Philharmonic Society conducted by Arnold Barter, Grainger conducted his *Irish Tune* and played in *Shepherd's Hey*, also playing the Grieg Piano Concerto.

14 Delius was in London for the special orchestral concert devoted to his works, given by the Beecham Symphony Orchestra, Beecham conducting, in the Royal Academy of Music on 8 July 1914. Grainger attended the concert. Delius attended Grainger's piano recital on 30 June, and met the Graingers for a weekend at Balfour Gardiner's country home on 4–5 July.

15 Grainger was reading *Ssanin* [Sanine]. Roman von M. Artzibaschew [Mikhail Petrovich Artsybashev]. Übertragen von André Villard und S. Bugow. Mit einer Einleitung von André Villard. München, G. Müller, 1909.

and my deepest instincts are all in the direction of openness and wholeness and — impracticality, if it can't be done without it.

Everything that comes under the heading "public life", everything to do with the public and newspapers is against me, not because the public itself is against me, (I love the public in themselves) but because (in a business society like ours) one can only approach the public by the help of lies, compromise, and externalities, and thereby destroying the whole relationship.

We all feel and know all this, of course, the difference between me and the other "true" and deep artists is almost only this: that most of them have not been clear-sighted enough in practical directions to realise the absolute necessity of the compromise and the lie. The majority of "true" artists choose to *fight* through, believing that "fighting" will change matters somewhat.

The fight becomes a drama (often a heroic and amusing one) in itself but never an alteration of the things themselves and most often a "side-issue". I can't have anything to do with that. Art for me is to create in peace and quiet, not to have skirmishes about the result.

Therefore two things tempt me: *Time* and *artistic experience*.

To get *time to work* I earn money (with as much compromise as matters require) to get *experience* with orchestra, choir, etc I have published my practically successful small pieces. But one mustn't go and think the practical return, nor the artistic experience either is greater than it really is.

Although my pieces are performed by the hundred the return at the moment is not terribly great; and can't be.

There is not very much to be earned on orchestral pieces alone. A "musical lending library" (like Goodwin & Tabb) buy a few copies and *lend* them out to the societies. The result is easily imagined. The choral societies have not *as yet* fallen over themselves particularly for my things.

What do earn money are *songs* and *piano-things* and these I can't be bothered to write, I don't know why, not many in any case. I don't deny that all my compositions sell *well* more or less, but it can't possibly resemble a "livelihood" for a long while, and then one must remember that printing costs are enormous, in my case up to now something like £400 or £500.

Then we come to earnings from piano-playing. Since I (on account of lack of courage, lack of easy memory, etc) am not suited to be one of the capital city pianists who play in Leipzig on Monday, Berlin Tuesday, Hamburg Wednesday, (which I could never stand) I must be content with smaller earnings in smaller towns. A travelling life like this has its amusing sides, and I have amused myself greatly often and often, but when one has a composer's nature, and would prefer to live and work peacefully and out-of-the-way in the country, it is not always the pleasantest thing to rush around year after year from place to place, without time, without possibilities to make the necessary experiments, without scientific study or investigation.

It would please me if I now had this whole pleasant life behind me and could now enter upon a richer more worthwhile life. I do not complain, but I don't rejoice either. I have spent my youth in compromise and slavish unsympathetic works (of course I only speak of my "public life", my private life has always been happy) while others have gone after their instincts, and to that extent have lived easier and with more satisfactions *for the moment*, and therefore I expect more of the future than many others. I have thrown away the greatest part of 15 years, and now I look for a great deal in return, not riches, but let us say £200 a year in interest, so we can both live in peace and have free time. It is not so easy to save much in London; one has to spend a lot, have a good house, etc otherwise one gets nothing back. But everything is going as it should, only a *little* too slowly, and one becomes impatient by degrees.

My fame as composer has also brought with it an enormous mass of extra work, *thousands of letters*, enquiries from Gramophone Cos, questions regarding the compositions, all very "nice" but far from being of any real value or real business value either. It seems to me that mother and I are writing *continuously*, hours every day, but we are never finished, and heaps of the great "unanswered" grow up more and more.

One *can* live through a whole lot of stuff and nonsense, but it is not fun, and it is not so amazingly "lucky" either, when a really talented person has to be incessantly taken up with such trifles. And if one were to give up these busy activities, everything would gradually come to a stop.

One gets on because in the end one *is able to* hold one's ground with all the practical questions, and because one is more accurate and untiring than most other talented artists.

Have achieved a number of "beautiful successes" recently. Delius piano concerto and the new score "Col. Song" and "Molly" (for full orchestra) had a great success at the Torquay Festival. The two last named are to be played at the "Proms" (Aug–Oct) The day before yesterday I played in the Albert Hall, yesterday in Queen's Hall (with Wood).

21.May.1914.

Today I am sending you "Mock M" arranged for violin and piano, just published. If you know someone who has a Pianola, or similar, try and hear my adaptation of "Molly on the Shore" (Orchestrelle Co., London TL 22081) just released and ditto of "Shepherds Hey" which is coming out from the same company in the month of July. I can scarcely imagine anything more successful. It is *charming* to write **specially** for the Pianola. Perhaps I am the 1st composer who has done so, at any rate in that degree, because I write things that can *only* be played on the mechanical piano, and have nothing to do with ordinary piano pieces. They are indeed brilliant and light-hearted. I don't have any "rolls" otherwise you would get them from me.

I will be conducting "Colonial Song" and "Molly" for large orchestra in the "Proms" in the middle of August,[16] then we are going on the Northern Countries tour about the 20th Aug. Then Finland (Riga?) late in Oct, Denmark *early* in Nov. Copenh. piano evening 7 Nov. After that Holland, then back to London 22nd Nov.

Would you like to ask Scheller whether Birkerød would like to engage me again, early in Nov.?

Possibly (?) I will go to Jutland in the last days of July or first days of Aug to make phonograph collections of some Jutland songs together with the dear Evald Tang Kristensen.

We have written about "Luck". I have often told you that the first strong feelings of Good Fortune I had was when you let me whip you, and altogether through the unbelievably harmonious way I experienced my sensual desires with you. The *essential* thing in composing is really the *work* **itself**, that **that** succeeds for one, at the moment. Whether the piece is successful, even whether it shows itself to be *good* or not, always seems to me to be something relatively unimportant. Thus in my "career" I have not really achieved a *feeling* of "Good Fortune". I am happy when people think well of my playing and still (many times) more when they think well of my compositions, but the whole thing moves me so little, all the same.

The work itself is really enough for me, to feel the happiness that the composing activity itself brings with it, that is enough for me, and I couldn't live happily without more or less continual enjoyment through creative activities, whether it is actually music or not.

One can indeed, also experience a large part of one's erotic ideals alone, both in reality and in thought. But in that way I don't in the long run get any feeling of "success" in that field. I never expected before to be able

16 On 18 August 1914.

to realise my partially abnormal desires, and thus I became as it were sprinkled over with feelings of good fortune when I experienced through you unexpected ideal joys and perfection. To be able to be absolutely *frank* and **open** all the time, that was so delightful, and is a rare possibility, perhaps. To be able to write to you as I did, and to be with you as I was, I will always regard that as a uniquely great benefit, the greatest *Good Fortune.* Most talented people have strong erotic desires, most of them have "difficult" desires, either on account of the nature of the desires, or on account of excessive refinement and tenderness of the whole soul. I believe very few get to be as fortunate as I. I can say as few can, that I have lived through something completely ideal and perfect and satisfying in that direction, and that I cannot think anything else than that I have had a quite unusually great luck, when I think back on everything we experienced.

The consciousness of this came terribly strongly over me last year when we journeyed to Norway. In the middle of the night I woke up when we lay in the harbour at Kristianssand (where the ships sail to Denmark from) in a thick fog. I went up on deck, saw it was Kr-sand, saw where the steamers to Frederikshavn must lie, and suddenly there came over me all the different thoughts that I previously had felt on arrival in Kr-sand. Always before there had been something magical and tenderly touching for me to see the ships that *could* take me to Jutland where I had experienced all the joys with you, the whole place always flooded for me with a sharp awareness of our lovely experiences.

Then I suddenly thought: Shall I be cut off from all this from now on; even from *the possibility*? **Never.** Even though I knew I had nothing more to hope for from you in that direction, it seemed an absolute crime to do anything which *in itself* prevented the possibility *in thought* at any rate.

I hope you don't think I write this from sentimentality. I think it is just as untrue to say too little as too much. And it happened as I write it. The arrival in Kr-sand was a chapter for me.

I will probably play again soon for the Gramophone, principally my own things.

Will you let me have the critiques back at your convenience, when you have read them?

Goodbye little sweet. Will you be in Copenhagen in the month of November?

Percy

The critiques will be sent in a few days, little friend.

The summer of 1914 began normally enough for the Graingers. They settled back into their house at 31A Kings Road on 1 June. Grainger busied himself with his usual summer activities, presenting his annual London piano recital at Aeolian Hall on 30 June. On 8 June he attended the performance of G. W. L. Marshall-Hall's opera Stella *at the Palladium. On 17 June, echoing times now gone by, he conducted three of his Kipling choruses at an "at home" for Lady Alice Bective.*

Grainger was engaged to conduct two of his compositions at the Queen's Hall Promenade Concert on 18 August and planned to leave London with Rose on 20 August on a three-month tour of Norway, Finland, Russia and Denmark. Before the start of this northern tour, Grainger intended to go to Jutland on 1 August, spend 3–5 August collecting folksongs with Evald Tang Kristensen, and visit Karen at Svinkløv between 6 and 10 August. The latter part of this plan was, however, abandoned when she asked him not to come. Later in the year various engagements in Great Britain were mooted, with a third series of the Balfour Gardiner concerts projected for December.

According to the British Australasian *of 6 August 1914, Grainger was ready to depart for Denmark on Saturday 1 August as arranged, with all preparations made, even his money changed into foreign currency. He was, it was reported, prevented from going by the illness of Rose. By the 6th, "All arrangements for concerts and tours are in abeyance, and it is even doubtful if his engagements in Great Britain can be fulfilled".*

War was declared on 4 August 1914. Ten days later Rose, who had earlier begun her usual preparations for packing and storing of their goods during the northern tour, sent out instructions for the clearing of household effects from the Kings Road house. On 19 August four containers of goods, including furniture and personal papers of various kinds, were stored in the Baker Street Bazaar Warehouse. They were to stay there until the middle of 1921.

The Graingers went to stay at Evergood Cottage in Kent, near the home of their friend Isabel Du Cane, where Percy made the most of the unexpected free time to work on his composing. On 2 September, after counselling his dearest composer friends to do likewise, Percy sailed with his mother on the R.M.S. Laconia *from Liverpool for the United States of America, leaving Isabel to find a place for the maid and the canary and to wind up their business affairs.*

509 TO KAREN HOLTEN   31A King's Road
[Original: Danish]   Sloane Square
25. June 1914.   S W

Sweet little Karen

It was lovely to hear from you, and what you wrote touches me much in many directions, but most of all to joy and hope on your account.

It will be awfully exciting if you will let me meet him next winter, and I am looking forward very much to that. A doctor can be something grand, and I can well think that it could suit you splendidly to be married to a lovable doctor. Something ideal and "aspiring" and gifted life must be, for it to suit you. What a pity that the law regarding marriage after separation is so impracticable in Denmark, can one think of anything more idiotic? It is to be hoped that it will be changed in time to be of some use to you. It is right and lovely that you get the opportunity to show the richness gifts sweetness goodness and liveliness of your nature.

It will be something grand and perfect to be married to you, little sweet comrade, for a good and lovely man, you who overflow with goodness charm abilities temptation and life's sweetness.

I can't tell you how it moves me to think the thought that one perhaps will be able to see children eventually who are little Karen's, what sweetness lies in that. It would be an awfully great joy to me if you got a child who resembled you.

A thousand thanks for the sweet little picture of you riding which pleased me much. If we meet in the summer I will take the camera with me, and I hope you will let me take some proper pictures of you, if I am able to. I am terribly glad that you think I will probably be able to meet you in Svinkløv if I go up there in the beginning of the month of August. So I will do that, and will soon write to the planter to book a room at his place. I am looking forward *indescribably* to seeing you and talking to you.

Could you take your national costume with you, if you are still so kind as to give it to me? But have you got yourself a new one in place of it? I hope you have, or will do so, for I think that everyone who will be fond of you would like to see you in that kind of costume because it suits you **so** splendidly, and you look unusually sweet in it.

How is your foot really, now? Is it **quite** like it was again? How funny that you got to know him out at the clinic! So "the riding" has also played its part, hasn't it? How tedious for him to have to work in the holidays, and how idiotic it is that men have to "support" their divorced wives. It is difficult to believe in order and convenience in love- and erotic-relationships before it is expected of all women that they earn their bread just like men, or that *all* women *always* are supported by the state, or something similar.

Very soon I will be able to send you the piano reduction of "The Brides Tragedy" which is to be performed late in November in Leytonstone and in London (B. Gard's concert) on 2nd Dec.

I hope that I will fairly soon be able to get your "The merry wedding" finished, perhaps in the winter next year. Now the whole contents will suit you better than it did before, won't it, little sweet comrade?

I am terribly busy with preparations for the enclosed programme on Tuesday.

Many warm greetings to all at home.

That you may live a full and lovely and happy life, you sweet little Karen, is my deepest wish

(It was sweet of you to allow me everything you did)

Your
Percy.

Will write soon again and let you know what date I will go to Svinkløv, and how long I propose to stay.

Have you got "Ondine" and "Le gibet" already? If not I would like to send them to you.[17]

17 From the suite *Gaspard de la Nuit* by Maurice Ravel. Grainger was playing these works in 1914 and included them in the programme of his recital on 30 June.

510   TO KAREN HOLTEN   31a Kings Rd
[Original: Danish]   Sloane Square
6. Aug. 1914.   London. S.W.

Dear little Karen.

Not improbably you find yourself in Copenhagen again, as I hear that there is mobilisation in Denmark. If only you and yours may be free from unpleasantnesses and danger. It is indeed an exciting time for the sweet little Denmark.

How do they take the whole thing? I can't imagine anything else than that the feeling is pretty anti-German. Small nations don't have particularly happy prospects if it goes well with Germany's plans.

I don't feel any patriotism for England as such. But I feel a strong hope that the victory may lie with some power or other which supports the small countries.

How are things in Copenhagen?

Here in London, there is nothing to show that the country is at war, or that anything at all abnormal is under way. One doesn't hear the war spoken of on the street. The barrel-organs are playing as usual, and the troops do not arouse any visible enthusiasm, no cheering or such like.

The bank across the street was opened again today, but was not visited more than usual.

Haven't the Belgians been grand? In any case it has been an apparently fortunate beginning for France and Belgium.

The whole of my life I have lived in fear of Germany, particularly with regard to the small countries like Denmark and Holland which I love so highly, and I still can't believe that the victory **can** go against this feared nation.

I live happy days, had to give up the journey to Jutland of course, but as against that am working all the day on the score of "Bride's Tragedy" which (since 1st Aug) is already ½ finished. I love to work in the war atmosphere. I did so also during the Boer War.

I would be enormously grateful to learn how you and yours are.

Percy. (Grainger.)

I would just wish the German soldiers will show themselves just as untalented as the German musicians always appear to me.

It is a terrible pity for the poor fine Frenchmen and I am very sorry for the Germans themselves. Such a war can't be fun to be in.

511   TO GORDON BRYAN-SMITH   31a Kings Rd
[week of 9 August 1914]   Sloane Square.
                                                        S.W.

My dear "Gordon Bryan".

A thousand thanks for your sweet letter, for all the nice things you say, & the friendly feelings you feel.

I am ever so delighted you fixed up with Torquay for Nov 5, & equally so about Harrogate.

Mother has written you re Blüthner's readiness to supply grand.

Of course have had to give up some 100 foreign concerts, & will now be able to devote some of that time to composition & the scoring of old works, etc. The war excitement is booming my pieces. I see Wood has suddenly included "Irish" & "Sh's Hey" in the program of the opening concert next Sat,[18] & as I shall conduct the other 2 as arranged on August 18, while from Margate I hear my things are being played almost daily down [there].

I shall be in England all the autumn & winter I hope, & if you want to do more work with me now's a fine opportunity.

Hoping your having a good time & with most cordial greetings to you & yours from mother & me

Ever warmly yrs
Percy.

18 On 15 August. They were repeated in the programme of 10 October.

512   TO WILHELM HANSEN   c/o Miss Isabel Du Cane
[Postcard. PM 30 August 1914]   "Ballards",
                                        Goudhurst, Kent
                                            England.

Owing to the war of course I shall have to put off my Piano Recital in Copenhagen this autumn, *until later*.

I am so relieved dear little Denmark is still out of the war.

Yrs heartily
Percy Grainger

513   TO ROGER QUILTER
Sunday Aug 31. 1914.

Permanent address until
further notice:
C/o Miss Isabel Du Cane
"Ballards", Goudhurst, Kent.

Darling Roger.

We are off to America on Tuesday ("Laconia" from L'pool to Boston, Cunard). Mother has been sleeping so badly, & I want to above all avert such troubles as she had in the Boer war.

It is too distressing & harrowing here in England & will not get better for sometime, & I feel a seatrip would do her good.

We arrive tomorrow (Monday) at Charing Cross (from Horsmonden) at 11.51 a.m, & leave St. Pancras for L'pool by midnight train.[19]

If you are in town tomorrow & could come & meet us at the train maybe we could lunch together, or we could meet some other time. If you are not at train we will ring up your house during the day & try & get on to you.

We'll have a lot to get through during the day of course.

I've done all B's Tragedy scoring & have ½ scored a March for Piano & Orchestra made up of material from "Prittling pratteling pretty Poll Parrot", "Widow's party March," etc. Jolly, I think.

Why dont you go to America too, dearest friend? You are too precious to art & the future for anything to happen to you & think [things] may be grim here soon, & we artists are no good, I feel, at this job, & way of feeling.

We **long** to see you before we go. Mum joins with tons of love. We are looking forward to our little trip.

If you could give me any letters to useful folk in U.S.A. I would be very grateful. I shall try to get all concert work, "at homes", & pupils I can, of course, though I hope we'll soon be back

Fondest love, darling Roger
from Percy

[written on sides]
Fondest love, do hope we see you tomorrow. If anything happens to us, think kindly of yr loving old friends. We have had many happy times together haven't we? Please give our love to yr Mother, & Mrs Koehler, whom I hope we meet again.
yrs affec ly Rose G.

514   TO FRANK ALDRIDGE   [R.M.S. *Laconia.*]
[Postcard. PM 1 September 1914]

Just off for a short trip to America, to give mother a change.
Fondest love from us both to darling Aunty Clara & to you from your fond nephew

Percy

515   TO ISABEL DU CANE
14 Sept 1914.

Commonwealth Hotel
Beacon Hill
Boston, Massachusetts

My dear Isabel

Isn't war news stunning? We hear on all hands such lovely things said of the English. We are **loving** things here so far.

19 The decision to leave for America was taken very suddenly. As Grainger wrote (in German) to his Dutch agent Hans Augustin on 12 September 1914, ". . . on Friday we had not even thought of it and already on Monday we were on the way".

Am sending you string parts of "B's Tragedy" to copy when you feel inclined. We'll need (beyond copies herewith sent):

7 1sts.
6 2nds.
5 violas
4 cellos
3 C-bs.

I have tried to keep to following rules, but maybe you will be able to stick to them better than I have been able.

Always:
Tempo marks above stave.
Bar numbers above stave.
Pizz & arco above stave mostly.
cresc, dim $<$ $>$, f, p, etc below stave usually.
on ⎫ with mutes.   con ⎫ sord   BELOW STAVE.
off ⎭   senza⎭
small marks $>$, sf, either above or below.

Please (in **my** copies too) put red-ink square around all bar numbers; [10] Cues either in small notes & rests (as in my copies) or in red ink, as you like.

You need not write yours so closely as I have mine; ten-stave paper would no doubt be better if you can get the turns-over to work well that way. If possible there should be about (at least) a bar's space either side of turn, or else a stop

When done please keep copies with you till further notice.
You must come & see this place some day.

In great haste with love
Percy.

Mother is sleeping so much better; its so jolly. It was a good move.

EPILOGUE

ROSE GRAINGER TO CECIL SHARP   The Southern
May 12. [1917]   680 Madison Avenue
                                                [New York]

Dear Mr Sharp.

Thank you very much for your letter. Percy & I are so glad your boy is improving in health, & that you have him home, & sincerely trust that he may in time be quite cured.

We expect to be in N. York June 26th & 27th unless some War Relief Recital is arranged for those dates — so far not. He is giving a Recital for Red X out of N.Y. June 23rd. If you could let us know in advance whether you could come to us on 26th or 27th to lunch, tea, or dinner, we wld be delighted to have you with us, & be immensely interested to hear all about your work, about which Percy is so keen an admirer. He is looking very thin, having had a terribly hard season, & is now preparing his 2 new works (for Rehearsals) for the coming Festivals, at Norfolk 1st week of June, & Worcester Festival in Sept.

Dear Mr Sharp, of course you should not contribute towards the Funds Percy is working for, you are more than doing your Share for England. Without Music & other Art what a world this would be?

Percy sends his love, & we both look forward to seeing you either 26th or 27th of June

Yrs sincerely
Rose Grainger.

I am happy to tell you that already the sale of tickets for the Recital Percy is giving for British-Am[erican] War Relief Fund next Tues., yesterday realised over 600 dollars.

Tel. when get N. York

ROSE GRAINGER TO CECIL SHARP   The Southern
June 26. [1917]   680 Madison Avenue
                                         [New York]

Dear Mr Sharp,

I have been very unwell, or I would have written to you earlier. Alas you cannot see Percy this trip, he enlisted in the U.S. American Regular Army, in the 15th Band (playing the Oboe) C.A.C. I thought when you telephoned to me, he might be here on leave to-day, but he cannot ask it, as he hopes to get permission next Saturday to give a Recital, for the benefit of the British & American Red Cross. He was allowed permission to give a Recital for the Red Cross last Sat & realised *2653 dollars* (after expenses) Should his Band not be sent abroad, he hopes to obtain permission to go on giving these War Relief Recitals, & thus help the suffering. The duties of the Band, if sent abroad will be, to play, & to bear Stretchers for the wounded.

Perhaps you & he may be able to meet on your next visit to N.Y. (if he be here, or near about) he wanted particularly to see you, as he feels so very grateful to you for all the lovely work you have done, with the folk songs, & cannot bear to think you may sometimes be feeling "hard up". Such a man as you ought to be splendidly paid for doing work for not only one nation, but many nations. When this terrible war be over, & Percy is able to earn again (if his life be spared) he wants to have a chat with you, if you will allow him.

I cannot get used to this new life, & miss my dear "boy" terribly. He loves his fellow Bandsmen, & the Leader whom he knew & admires greatly, & they seem to love him. Hoping your health is better now, & that all will go well with you

Yrs sincerely
Rose Grainger.

Grainger notes, "P.G.'s remarks on Rose Grainger's letters of May 12, 1917 & June 26, 1917 to Cecil J. Sharp"

Train, Kalamazoo–Wh.[ite] Pl[ain]s,
March 14, 1932

Note how every word tries to shield me from the disgrace I earned. Note how the mindslant is worded for that [which] will make one think
1.   that I am thin, having worked too hard,

2. that I am able to earn so much for British-American War Relief Fund,
3. that Sharp need not pay out towards the funds I am raising — he being soft-soaped into thinking his artwork out-of-the-way meaningfull & worthy, so that he may think the same of my artwork &, if may be, look upon me as a boon-bearer who should be "above the war" & its claims.
4. that I can leave my band only for some high duty, such as to play for Red X.
5. that I can "help the suffering" **if** my band does not go abroad (therefore — do not send it abroad!),
6. of the mankind-kindly nature of my war-front duties as a bandsman — setting me above a mere fighting soldier.
7. that C. Sharp's lifework is praised as booning "not only a nation, but many nations", thus leaning towards making Sharp see himself (&, if may be, me) as an international figure, "above the battle" & outside "this terrible war"
8. that if my life be spared (therefore — spare it) I will want to see Sharp, seemingly about something nice for Sharp.
9. that I had worthprized [Rocco] Resta aside from & before enlisting (which I didnt), that I loved my bandsmen (which I hardly did) & that they loved me (which they surely didnt).

Everything, in short to hide the fact that I was a selfish & unsocial cowardly renegade.

Am I ashamed of myself for being such a renegade? No. I am only afraid of being *punished* for it while I live. I know that my music will bring more honor to Australia than any soldier-work I could have done in British armies. The English-speaking world has already changed the way it looks upon the great war & its worth — but it has not changed the way it looks upon my music; in spite of my clearly being a renegade.

But I bitterly clear-see that my beloved mother had to die because of the shame my cowardly selfsavement brought upon us. The war claimed one of us, after all.

Index of Recipients

General Index

Bold figures indicate a major biographical reference.

Borgstrøm rigtig
annus 400?